Fodor's 2019

ESSENTIAL ITALY

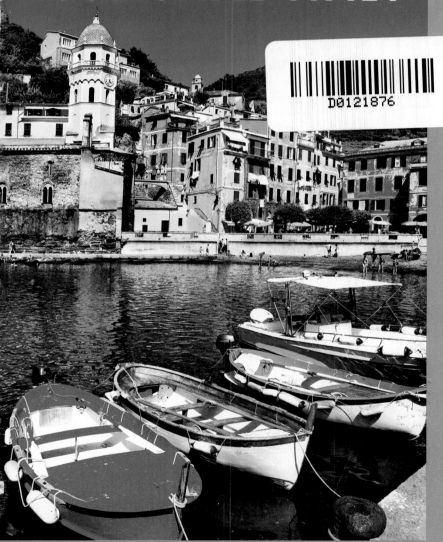

WELCOME TO ITALY

Italy is the kind of destination that travelers return to over and over. They come for awe-inspiring art and architecture that influenced Western civilization, and stunning historical ruins—as well as for some of the world's best food and wine. Also beckoning irresistibly are Italy's sun-kissed olive groves and vineyards, the sparkling waters of Lake Como and the Mediterranean, and atmospheric monasteries, castles, and farmhouses. And if you seek vibrant cities with renowned museums, restaurants, and shopping opportunities, Rome, Florence, and Milan await.

TOP REASONS TO GO

★ **Food:** Italy is a pasta lover's paradise; but don't forget the pizza and the gelato.

★ **Romance:** Whether you're strolling atmospheric Venice or sipping wine, Italy enchants.

★ **History:** The ruins of ancient Pompeii and the leaning tower of Pisa breathe antiquity.

★ **Art:** The big hitters—Botticelli, Michelangelo, Raphael, Caravaggio, and more

★ **Shopping:** Few things say quality or style like "made in Italy."

★ **Stunning landscapes:** Tuscany, the Amalfi Coast, the Cinque Terre, to name just a few

25 ULTIMATE EXPERIENCES

Italy offers terrific experiences that should be on every traveler's list. Here are Fodor's top picks for a memorable trip.

1 Hike Cinque Terre

Walk the scenic footpaths that connect the five former fishing villages that make up the Cinque Terre; each one appears to hang off the cliffs, allowing for absolutely stunning views of the vineyards above and blue waters below. *(Ch. 8)*

2 People-Watch in Venice

Venice's Piazza San Marco (St. Mark's Square), flanked by the gorgeous Basilica di San Marco, is certainly one of the world's loveliest squares for people-watching. *(Ch. 3)*

3 Shop in Milan

In Italy's fashion capital of Milan, you'll find the highest of high-end designers in the Quadrilatero della Moda district, north of the Duomo. *(Ch. 6)*

4 Enjoy Magical Views

Nowhere inspires as many oohs and aahs as the magnificent town of Positano, with its pastel-colored houses seemingly spilling off the mountainside. *(Ch. 13)*

5 Sail Away to Capri

This fabled island off the coast of Naples has long stood for glitz and glamour. It's a lovely place to escape to. *(Ch. 13)*

6 Discover Revello

Wander Amalfi Coast's refined mountaintop village and discover lush, hidden gardens, medieval fountains, and sweeping Mediterranean views. *(Ch. 13)*

7 See the Frescoes

The peaceful medieval town of Assisi is home to enormous Basilica di San Francesco, which includes 28 frescoes showing the life of St. Francis. *(Ch. 12)*

8 Visit the Vatican

The largest church in the world, the Basilica di San Pietro (St. Peter's Basilica) is completely breathtaking inside and out. *(Ch. 1)*

9 Rent a Villa in Tuscany

One of the supreme pleasures of a visit to the gorgeous countryside of Tuscany is the chance to stay in a villa—preferably one with a swimming pool and vineyard views. *(Ch. 11)*

10 Ponder the Last Supper

Restoration work has returned The Last Supper to its original glory, so the painting is amazingly clear and luminous. *(Ch. 6)*

11 Marvel at Mosaics

Some of the greatest Byzantine mosaics can be found in the unassuming city of Ravenna. You can view the most elaborate ones in the 5th-century Mausoleo di Galla Placidia. *(Ch 9)*

12 Go Wine Tasting

The Barolo region produces excellent wine and is filled with hill towns and vistas. Make an appointment for a tour and tasting at one of the many wineries. *(Ch. 7)*

13 Explore Lava Fields

The largest and highest volcano in Europe, Sicily's Mt. Etna, has moon-like dunes that you can walk across, or view from the comfort of a cable car (the Funivia dell'Etna). *(Ch. 15)*

14 Relax by the Sea

The lovely village of Portofino hugs the coast of the Italian Riviera, with the Santa Margherita cliffs on one side and the Ligurian Sea on the other. *(Ch. 8)*

15 Hit the Slopes

The gorgeous craggy peaks of the Dolomites make the perfect place for an unforgettable ski holiday in the winter or a rejuvenating hike in the spring and summer. *(Ch. 5)*

16 See Great Art

Florence's Galleria deglia Uffizi contains the collection of art from the Medicis, including Botticelli's Birth of Venus, Michelangelo's Doni Tondo, and Caravaggio's Bacchus. *(Ch. 10)*

17 Toss a Coin in Trevi

The can't-miss-Instagramming Trevi Fountain, in Rome, is a Baroque fantasy of sea beasts, seashells, and mermaids in front of a triumphal arch. *(Ch 1)*

18 Visit a Volcanic Island

Just a ferry away from Sicily's northeast coast sit the Aeolian Islands, seven volcanic islands offering dramatic scenery and wonderful snorkeling and scuba diving. *(Ch. 15)*

19 Feel Romantic

Set on the shores of beautiful Lake Como, Bellagio is often considered one of the loveliest towns in Italy. Its steep streets, lined with cobblestones, are supremely romantic. *(Ch. 6)*

20 Stand in Awe

Dominating Florence's skyline, the magnificent Duomo is an architectural marvel that took almost 600 years to complete. *(Ch. 10)*

21 Step Back in Time

The best-preserved excavated site in the world, the commercial center of Pompeii was frozen in time when Vesuvius erupted in AD 79. *(Ch. 13)*

22 Lounge on a Beach

The island of Sardinia is justly famed for its beautiful white sand beaches—in fact, beaches line more than 1,200 miles of the country's coastline. *(Ch. 16)*

23 Explore a Hill Town

Wander the narrow winding streets of the walled city of San Gimignano, which is filled with 14 soaring medieval towers (originally there were more than 70). *(Ch. 11)*

24 See a Medieval City

Perhaps Italy's best-preserved medieval city, Siena's narrow streets are fun to explore. The Piazza del Campo is one of the most beautiful squares in the country. *(Ch. 11)*

25 Enjoy the Coastline

In Italy's southern-most region of Puglia, around the heel of the boot, is a wonderfully dramatic coastline, with sandstone cliffs crashing into the ocean. *(Ch. 14)*

Fodor's ESSENTIAL ITALY 2019

Editorial: Douglas Stallings, *Editorial Director*; Margaret Kelly, Jacinta O'Halloran, *Senior Editors*; Kayla Becker, Alexis Kelly, Amanda Sadlowski, *Editors*; Teddy Minford, *Content Editor*; Rachael Roth, *Content Manager*

Design: Tina Malaney, *Design and Production Director;* Jessica Gonzalez, *Production Designer*

Photography: Jill Krueger, *Senior Photo Editor*

Maps: Rebecca Baer, *Senior Map Editor*; David Lindroth, Mark Stroud (Moon Street Carography), *Cartographers*

Production: Jennifer DePrima, *Editorial Production Manager*; Carrie Parker, *Senior Production Editor*; Elyse Rozelle, *Production Editor*

Business & Operations: Chuck Hoover, *Chief Marketing Officer*; Joy Lai, *Vice President and General Manager*; Stephen Horowitz, *Director of Business Development and Revenue Operations;* Tara McCrillis, *Director of Publishing Operations*

Public Relations and Marketing: Joe Ewaskiw, *Manager;* Esther Su, *Marketing Manager*

Writers: Robert Andrews, Nick Bruno, Agnes Crawford, Liz Humphreys, Fergal Kavanagh, Patricia Rucidlo, Liz Shermaria

Editor: Margaret Kelly

Production Editor: Elyse Rozelle

ISBN 978-1-64097-070-0

ISSN 2476-0692

Library of Congress Control Number 2018907409

All details in this book are based on information supplied to us at press time. Always confirm information when it matters, especially if you're making a detour to visit a specific place. Fodor's expressly disclaims any liability, loss, or risk, personal or otherwise, that is incurred as a consequence of the use of any of the contents of this book.

SPECIAL SALES

This book is available at special discounts for bulk purchases for sales promotions or premiums. For more information, e-mail SpecialMarkets@fodors.com.

PRINTED IN THE UNITED STATES OF AMERICA

10 9 8 7 6 5 4 3 2 1

CONTENTS

Fodor's Features

CONTENTS

MAPS

CONTENTS

ABOUT THIS GUIDE

Fodor's Recommendations

Everything in this guide is worth doing—we don't cover what isn't—but exceptional sights, hotels, and restaurants are recognized with additional accolades. Fodor'sChoice★ indicates our top recommendations. Care to nominate a new place? Visit Fodors.com/contact-us.

Trip Costs

We list prices wherever possible to help you budget well. Hotel and restaurant price categories from $ to $$$$ are noted alongside each recommendation. For hotels, we include the lowest cost of a standard double room in high season. For restaurants, we cite the average cost of a meal. The meal includes three courses: *primo* (usually pasta or an appetizer), *secondo* (meat or fish main course), and *dolce* (dessert). For attractions, we always list adult admission fees; discounts are usually available for children, students, and senior citizens.

Hotels

Our local writers vet every hotel to recommend the best overnights in each price category, from budget to expensive. Unless otherwise specified, you can expect private bath, phone, and TV in your room. For expanded hotel reviews, visit Fodors.com.

Top Picks		Hotels & Restaurants	
★ Fodor'sChoice		⊡	Hotel
		⤴	Number of rooms
Listings			
⊠	Address	⍾⃝	Meal plans
⊠	Branch address	✕	Restaurant
☎	Telephone	⬟	Reservations
🖷	Fax	🏛	Dress code
⊕	Website	▭	No credit cards
✎	E-mail	$	Price
⊠	Admission fee		
⊙	Open/closed times	**Other**	
Ⓜ	Subway	⇨	See also
⊹	Directions or Map coordinates	☞	Take note
		🏌	Golf facilities

Restaurants

Unless we state otherwise, restaurants are open for lunch and dinner daily. We mention dress code only when there's a specific requirement and reservations only when they're essential or not accepted. For expanded restaurant reviews, visit Fodors.com.

Credit Cards

The hotels and restaurants in this guide typically accept credit cards. If not, we'll say so.

EUGENE FODOR

Hungarian-born Eugene Fodor (1905–91) began his travel career as an interpreter on a French cruise ship. The experience inspired him to write *On the Continent* (1936), the first guidebook to receive annual updates and discuss a country's way of life as well as its sights. Fodor later joined the U.S. Army and worked for the OSS in World War II. After the war, he kept up his intelligence work while expanding his guidebook series. During the Cold War, many guides were written by fellow agents who understood the value of insider information. Today's guides continue Fodor's legacy by providing travelers with timely coverage, insider tips, and cultural context.

EXPERIENCE ITALY

ITALY TODAY

Enduring Cuisine

The old joke goes that three-quarters of the food and wine served in Italy is good—and the rest is amazing. In some sense, that's still true, and the "good" 75% has gotten even better. Those pundits would claim that ingredients that in the past were available only to the wealthy can now be found even in the remotest parts of the country at reasonable prices. Dishes originally conceived to make the most of inferior cuts of meat or the least flavorful part of vegetables are now made with the best.

But there's increasing evidence that many Italians would say that the food in Italy is getting worse. There's a proliferation of fast-food establishments, and increasing tourism has allowed many restaurants to lower their standards while raising their prices. This is true not only in Rome, but in most other tourist centers as well. The good news is Italy is home to one of the world's greatest cuisines, and its traditional favorites still put meat on bones and smiles on faces. Italian restaurateurs seem determined to make the most of the country's reputation for good food. Although quaint, family-run trattorias with checkered tablecloths, traditional dishes, and informal atmosphere are still common but on the decline, nearly every town has a newer eatery with matching flatware, a proper wine list, and an innovative menu.

The same is true of Italian wine. Today, through investment and experimentation, Italy's winemakers are figuring out how to get the most from their gorgeous vineyards. It's fair to say that Italy now produces more types of high-quality wine from more different grape varieties than any other country in the world.

Soccer Rules

Soccer (or, as the Italians say, *calcio*—which means "kick") stands without rival as the national sport of Italy, though some complain that big-money influence and loose financial regulations are polluting the beautiful game. That aside, Italy did win its fourth World Cup in 2006 (though another major success has since proved elusive), giving the country more world titles than any other this side of Brazil. Sadly, Italy did not qualify for 2018; the last time this happened was in the 1958 World Cup tournament. The game is still played at a high level and its teams do well in international tournaments (usually). More games in the schedule and a dwindling fan base mean fewer people are seen at the stadium. Still, fans can't stop watching the game on television.

An Aging Population

Italy's population was once the oldest in Europe (worldwide, only Germany and Japan are older)—the result of its low birth rate and one of the highest life-expectancy rates in the world. The median age of an Italian in 2015 was 45.9; projections for 2020 are 47.9.

The result is a remarkably stable population: the number of Italian residents barely rises most years, and, according to the most recent estimates, is projected to start contracting by 2020. But the situation is putting a strain on the country's pension system and on families, because elderly family members are likely to live with their children or grandchildren in a country where retirement homes are rare.

The trend also has an impact in other areas, including politics (where older politicians are eager to promote policies aimed at older voters), the popular culture (where everything from fashion to television programming takes older consumers into consideration), and a kind of far-reaching nostalgia. Thanks to a long collective memory, it's common to hear even younger Italians celebrate or rue something that happened 50 or 60 years earlier as if it had just taken place.

The Black-Market Economy

Nobody knows how big Italy's black-market economy is, though experts all agree it's massive. In October 2017, the Italian national statistics bureau, ISTAT, estimated that Italy's unreported economic activity amounted to 12.6% of its GNP. Put another way, if the highest estimates are correct, Italy's black market is about as large as the entire economy of Switzerland or Indonesia. If the estimated black-market figures were added to the official GDP, Italy would likely leapfrog France and the United Kingdom to become the world's fifth-largest economy.

The presence of the black market isn't obvious to the casual observer, but whenever a customer isn't given a printed receipt in a store or restaurant, tobacco without a tax seal is bought from a street seller, or a product or service is exchanged for another product or service, that means the transaction goes unrecorded, unreported, and untaxed. But that's all penny-ante stuff compared to what many professionals evade by neglecting to declare all they earn. Austerity measures imposed in 2012 have led to much disgruntlement among the population; now most shopkeepers insist that you take a receipt. If you don't, you could be fined, as could the shopkeeper. Austerity measures are still in place but the country still struggles to meet the 3% limit to its budget deficit as mandated by EU agreements.

It is pretty certain that Italy will struggle to meet this limit in coming years.

A Growing Parks System

Italy has 25 national parks covering a total of around 1½ million hectares (5,800 square miles), or about 6% of the entire surface area of the country—more than twice as much as 25 years ago.

Part of the reason for the expansion has been a growing environmental movement in Italy, which has lobbied the government to annex undeveloped land for parks, thus protecting against development. But the trend is a boon for visitors and nature lovers, who can enjoy huge expanses of unspoiled territory.

Staying Home in August

Italy used to be the best example of Europe's famous August exodus, when city dwellers would spend most of the month at the seaside or in the mountains, leaving the cities nearly deserted. Today the phenomenon continues, but is much less prevalent, as economic pressures have forced companies to keep operating through August. As a result, vacations are more staggered and vacationers' plans are often more modest.

The loss of shared vacation time for Italian workers means good things for visitors: in August there's more room (or a little more room, at any rate) at the seaside and in the mountains; in addition, cities have taken to promoting local events designed to appeal to nonvacationing natives. These days, summers in Italy offer a plethora of outdoor concerts and theatrical events, extended museum hours, and local festivals.

WHAT'S WHERE

1 **Rome.** Italy's capital is one of the greatest cities in Europe. It's a busy, modern metropolis where you'll encounter powerful evocations of its storied and spectacular past, from the Colosseum to St. Peter's.

2 **Side Trips from Rome.** The Eternal City is surrounded by intriguing towns and villages where you can explore without the crowds.

3 **Venice.** One of the world's most unusual—and beautiful—cities, Venice has canals instead of streets, along with an atmosphere of faded splendor.

4 **The Veneto and Friuli–Venezia Giulia.** The green plains stretching west of Venice hold three of northern Italy's most artistically significant midsize cities: Padua, Vicenza, and Verona. Farther north and east, Alpine foothills are dotted with welcoming villages and some of Italy's finest vineyards.

5 **The Dolomites.** Along Italy's northeast border, the Dolomites are the country's finest mountain playground, with gorgeous cliffs, curiously shaped peaks, lush meadows, and crystalline lakes. The skiing is good, and the scenery is different—and often more spectacular—than what you find in the Austrian, Swiss, or French Alps.

6 **Milan, Lombardy, and the Lakes.** The lakes of Lombardy have been attracting vacationers since the days of ancient Rome. At the center of Lombardy is Milan, Italy's second-largest city and its business capital. It holds Italy's most renowned opera house and is the hub of Italian fashion and design.

7 **Piedmont and Valle d'Aosta.** Here you'll find here great Alpine peaks, one of the most highly esteemed food-and-wine cultures in Italy, and an elegant regional capital in Turin.

8 **The Italian Riviera.** Northern Italy's most attractive coastline runs along the Italian Riviera in the region of Liguria. The best beaches and temperate winter climate are west of Genoa, but the main appeal lies to the east, where fishing villages dot the seaside cliffs and coves.

9 **Emilia-Romagna.** Many of Italy's signature foods come from the Emilia-Romagna region. Bologna is a significant cultural center, and the mosaics of Ravenna are glittering Byzantine treasures.

Elevation	
15,577	4,748
10,825	3,300
9,840	3,000
8,860	2,700
7,875	2,400
6,900	2,100
5,900	1,800
4,920	1,500
3,940	1,200
2,920	900
1,970	600
980	300
490	150
250	75
100	30
feet	meters

WHAT'S WHERE

10 Florence. The hub of the 15th century Renaissance, Florence is awash with artistic treasures, exceptional restaurants, and first-rate shopping, as well as a never-ending stream of tourists.

11 Tuscany. Nature outdid herself in Tuscany, the central Italian region has Florence as its principal city and many other interesting midsize towns. But the region's greatest appeal lies in the smaller towns, often perched on hilltops and not significantly altered since the Middle Ages.

12 Umbria and the Marches. A number of the smaller towns, particularly Assisi, Perugia, Spoleto, and Orvieto, are fun to explore and Umbria's Roman past is everywhere—expect to see Roman villas, aqueducts, and temples. Urbino's, Ducal Palace reveals more about the Renaissance than a shelf of art history books.

13 Naples and Campania. Campania is the gateway to southern Italy. Dream away two magical weeks on the pint-size islands of Capri and Ischia and the fabled resorts of the Amalfi Coast. Or explore the past at the archaeological ruins of Pompeii, Herculaneum, and Paestum. Naples is a fun, chaotic metropolis.

14 Puglia, Basilicata, and Calabria. The southernmost regions of the peninsula— Puglia, Basilicata, and Calabria—are known for their laid-back medieval villages, shimmering seas, and varied landscapes. The coastline of Puglia, along the heel of Italy's boot, is popular with beachgoers, but for the most part you're off the beaten path here.

15 Sicily. The breezes are sultry and everyday life is without pretense, as witnessed in the workaday stalls of the fish markets in ports all along the Tyrrhenian and Ionian coasts, bursting with tuna, swordfish, and sardines.

16 Sardinia. The beaches here rank among the Mediterranean's finest, and numerous ancient relics, ranging from the Carthaginian and Roman settlements of Nora and Tharros add to the island's distinctive character.

Elevation	
15,577	4,748
10,825	3,300
9,840	3,000
8,860	2,700
7,875	2,400
6,900	2,100
5,900	1,800
4,920	1,500
3,940	1,200
2,920	900
1,970	600
980	300
490	150
250	75
100	30
feet	meters

NEED TO KNOW

ITALY

Rome

SARDINIA

SICILY

Mediterranean Sea

AT A GLANCE

Capital: Rome

Population: 59,306,424

Currency: Euro

Money: ATMs are common; cash is more common than credit.

Language: Italian

Country Code: 39

Emergencies: 112

Driving: On the right

Electricity: 200v/50 cycles; electrical plugs have two round prongs.

Time: Six hours ahead of New York

Documents: Up to 90 days with valid passport; Schengen rules apply.

Mobile Phones: GSM (900 and 1800 bands)

Major Mobile Companies: Vodafone, TIM, Wind

WEBSITES

Italy: ⊕ *www.italia.it*

Farm stays: ⊕ *www. agriturismo.it*

Culture: ⊕ *www.beniculturali.it*

GETTING AROUND

✈ **Air Travel:** The major airports are Rome, Milan, and Venice.

🚌 **Bus Travel:** Good for smaller towns and the best way to travel the Amalfi Coast.

🚗 **Car Travel:** Rent a car to explore at your own pace, but never to use in the cities themselves (including Rome and Florence). Always rent a GPS along with the car, as Italy's roads can be confounding. Gas is very expensive.

🚆 **Train Travel:** Excellent and fast between major cities. Slower regional trains connect many smaller towns as well.

PLAN YOUR BUDGET

	HOTEL ROOM	MEAL	ATTRACTIONS
Low Budget	€140	€25	Visiting Florence's Duomo, free
Mid Budget	€290	€45	Ticket to the Vatican and the Sistine Chapel, €16
High Budget	€350	€60	Evening gondola ride in Venice, €150

WAYS TO SAVE

Stay at an *agriturismo*. Farm stays are Italy's best-kept secret. In beautiful settings, they sometimes include meals and are often half the price of a hotel.

Drink from the free fountains. No need to buy bottled water; fill up at the free public fountains, especially in Rome.

Book rail tickets in advance. Book online (⊕ *www.trenitalia.com*) at least a week in advance for half the price.

Enjoy an aperitivo. This Italian tradition entails a drink and a buffet (light or heavy) for about €8–€10.

PLAN YOUR TIME

Hassle Factor	Low. Flights to Rome, Milan, and Venice are frequent, and Italy has great transport elsewhere.
3 days	You can see some of the magic of Rome and perhaps take a day trip to Pompeii or Florence.
1 week	Spend time in Rome with a day trip to Pompeii, Umbria, or the Amalfi Coast, as well as an additional day or two in Florence. Alternatively, tour the main cities with three days in Rome, two in Florence, and one in Venice.
2 weeks	You have time to move around and for the highlights, including stops in Rome, Florence, and Venice, excursions to Pompeii, Naples, and the Amalfi Coast, and a trip to beautiful Tuscany or Umbria.

WHEN TO GO

High Season: June through September is expensive and busy. In August, most Italians take their own summer holidays; cities are less crowded, but many shops and restaurants close. July and August can be uncomfortably hot.

Low Season: Unless you are skiing, winter offers the least appealing weather, though it's the best time for airfare and hotel deals and to escape the crowds. Temperatures are still mild, especially in the south.

Value Season: By late September, temperate weather, saner airfares, and more cultural events can make for a happier trip. October is also great, but November is often rainy and (hence) quiet. From late April to early May, the masses have not yet arrived but cafés are already abuzz. March and early April can be changeable and wet.

BIG EVENTS

February: Carnival kicks off across Venice and around Italy. ⊕ www.carnevaleitaliano.it

April: Religious processions commemorate Easter. On Pasquetta (Easter Monday), most Italians picnic and almost everything is closed.

June: The Festa della Repubblica commemorates Italy's 1946 vote for the republic. ⊕ www.festadellarepubblica.it

October: Alba's Fiera del Tartufo is devoted to the area's white truffles. ⊕ www.fieradeltartufo.org

READ THIS

■ *Delizia! The Epic History of the Italians and Their Food,* John Dickie. A history of Italian flavors.

■ *Under the Tuscan Sun,* Frances Mayes. The memoir that launched a thousand Tuscan trips.

■ *Neapolitan Novels,* Elena Ferrante. A four-volume series focusing on two best friends growing up in Naples.

WATCH THIS

■ *Roman Holiday.* The 1953 classic starring Audrey Hepburn—and, of course, Rome.

■ *La Dolce Vita.* Fellini's famous study of glitzy 1950s Italy.

■ *Il Postino.* Romance in an Italian fishing village.

EAT THIS

■ *Mozzarella di bufala*: a specialty of Campania and the south.

■ *Prosciutto crudo*: tender, dry-cured ham, especially from Parma and San Daniele.

■ *Pasta carbonara*: a Roman dish of eggs, guanciale, cheese, and pepper.

■ *Wine*: from Barolo to Chianti to primitivo.

■ *Sfogliatelle*: a layered and filled southern Italian pastry.

MAKING THE MOST OF YOUR EUROS

Transportation

Italy's state-sponsored train system has been given a run for its money by a private company. Sadly, the competitor (Italo) only operates major, high-speed connections (such as Rome to Naples, Florence to Venice, Milan to Bologna) and not local routes. Because of the competition, Trenitalia and Italo engage in price wars, which only plays to the consumer's advantage; depending on time of day and how far in advance you purchase the tickets, great bargains can be had.

No such good news exists for the *regionali* trains. These are trains connecting cities, highly frequented by commuters, and used often by visitors who want to get to less-visible towns. These trains are habitually late and almost always crowded. Patience is a virtue, and much needed when taking them, particularly during high season.

Food and Drink

Always remember, when you enter a bar, that there is almost always a two-tier pricing system: one if you stand, and one if you sit. It's always cheaper to stand, but sometimes sitting is not only necessary, but fun: you can relax and watch the world go by. Italians love a good sandwich for lunch. Seek out popular sandwich shops (long lines signify that the place is worth visiting) or go to a *salumeria* (delicatessen) and have them make a sandwich for you. It will be simple—cheese and/or cold cuts with bread, no trimmings—but it will be made while you wait: fresh, delicious, and inexpensive.

Sights

There are plenty of free wonderful things to see. Visit the Musei Vaticani, the Uffizi, and the Accademia in Florence (book ahead whenever possible), but don't forget that many artistic gems are found in churches, most of which are free (some of Caravaggio's best work can be found in various churches in Rome). Also consider renting audio guides if you want direction to any specific place; if you find the idea of joining an organized tour daunting, most museums sell official guidebooks that can help you target what to see. Walking in *centri storici* (historic centers) is also a joy, and free. Seek out piazzas, climb towers, and look for views.

Lodging

High season in Italy runs from Easter to mid-October. If you want to have Florence practically to yourself, come in November or February (most Italian cities are very crowded during the Christmas holidays, which begin around Christmas and finish on January 6). Many hotels in cities offer bargain rates in July and August because most people are off to the beach or to the mountains. Remember to factor in great heat and massive crowds, along with the money you'll save. If you decide to travel then, ensure that you have access to a pool and/or air-conditioning.

A great budget-conscious way to travel is via Airbnb (⊕ *www.airbnb.com*). You can sleep on someone's couch, rent a private room in an apartment (sometimes with en suite bathroom), or rent an entire apartment or house. One of the best things about Airbnb is that many of these accommodations come with refrigerators and kitchens, which means you don't have to spend all your money eating out.

In general, book sooner rather than later. You'll often find better deals that way.

1

GREAT ITINERARIES

ROME IN 3 DAYS

Rome wasn't built in a day—and you shouldn't try to see it all in a day, either. But three days will give you a doable, if jam-packed, amount of time to visit the Ancient City's major attractions.

The first day focuses on Rome's renowned ancient sites—the monuments and ruins that make the city like nowhere else in the world. The second day takes you to the magnificent treasures found in Vatican City, including St. Peter's Basilica and Square and the Vatican Museums. The third day throws in a bit of everything for which Rome is known: Baroque sculptures, old master paintings, and grand palazzi, plus the unmissable Spanish Steps and Trevi Fountain, capped off with a stroll through one of Rome's most enchanting neighborhoods, Trastevere. You'll also have time built in to shop, eat, and drink (because what's a visit to Rome without wine?).

Note that much of the city shuts down on Sunday (including the Vatican Museums, though they are open the last Sunday of the month) and that many state museums and places to eat are closed on Monday, so be sure to plan your trip accordingly to avoid disappointment. To bypass some of the lines and enjoy your experience that much more, some reservations are also a good idea, particularly at the Colosseum and the Vatican Museums—and, in the case of the Galleria Borghese, which we've suggested for Day 3, reservations are always required.

Day 1: Monuments of Ancient Rome and Piazza Navona

Begin day one by fortifying yourself with one of Rome's renowned coffees and a pastry at a bar of your choosing before heading to the most can't-miss of all Rome's can't-miss attractions: the **Colosseum**. Try to start as early as possible to beat (some of) the crowds—or, better yet, book your tickets in advance online or by phone. Be sure to head next door to the spectacular **Arco di Costantino**, Rome's largest triumphal arch, before strolling up Via dei Fori Imperiali to the **Roman Forum**, the heart of ancient Rome. You'll want to spend time exploring the ruins, dating from about 500 BC to AD 400 (we recommend renting an audio guide to help make sense of it all) before heading over to **Palatine Hill**, where you'll need about two hours to stroll the gardens and the evocative ruins of the imperial palaces. Head back out onto Via dei Fori Imperiali and around the Vittorio Emanuele Monument (Il Vittoriano) to reach **Campidoglio**, also called **Capitoline Hill**. Climb the staircase ramp designed by Michelangelo for amazing views of Rome's ruins. To rest your legs and for a bite to eat, visit the café inside the **Musei Capitolini**. If you have time and inclination, the great Roman art treasures and Baroque paintings housed inside are well worth a stop. After your food and art break, it's just a short stroll or bus ride to the magnificent **Pantheon**, Rome's best-preserved ancient building and where painter Raphael is buried. Next it's a brief walk over to **Piazza Navona**, home to three fabulous fountains, including Bernini's famed Fontana dei Quattro Fiumi—with figures of four rivers representing the four corners of the world—Bernini sculptures, and prime people-watching. (If you're craving more caffeine, take another coffee break at Caffe Sant'Eustachio, thought to make Rome's best brew.) Consider seeing some of the world's preeminent ancient Roman statues at **Palazzo Altemps**, part of the Museo Nazionale Romano, or amazing works by Caravaggio in the Contarelli Chapel in **San Luigi dei Francesi**. Finally, relax at a wine bar or restaurant near Piazza Navona to cap off your history-filled day.

Day 2: The Vatican and Campo de' Fiori

You'll want to get up bright and early on your second day and, after a filling breakfast at or near your hotel, ride the metro or a bus from central Rome to beat the crowds at **Basilica di San Petro (St. Peter's Basilica)**, the largest church in the world and home to masterpieces by Bernini and Michelangelo. Take the elevator or stairs up to the roof for perfect views of the dome above you and piazza below you. Then head back down to wander around **Piazza di San Pietro (St. Peter's Square)**, one of the most spectacular squares in Italy, lined with 140 statues and an Egyptian obelisk at its center. If you're getting hungry at this point, you can choose from either casual fare or more sophisticated cuisine at one of the restaurants in the area. Once you're reenergized, head over to the **Vatican Museums** (save time by booking in advance online), which of course include the extraordinary **Sistine Chapel** with Michelangelo's magnificent ceiling fresco as well as the Belvedere Torso in the **Hall of the Muses**, the Apollo Belvedere in the **Octagonal Courtyard**, and the wonderful frescoes in the **Stanzi de Raffaello**. Then bus or walk over to **Castel Sant'Angelo**, a distinctive medieval castle completed around AD 140. End your day by taking a cab or train over to trendy **Campo de' Fiori** for a large choice of restaurants plus wine bars to relax in for a pre- or post-dinner drink.

Day 3: Villa Borghese, Spanish Steps, Trevi Fountain, and Trastevere

Hop on a bus over to the **Villa Borghese** park to visit the **Galleria Borghese**, which houses one of the world's best Baroque sculpture collections along with paintings by Rubens, Titian, Raphael, and other masters. (Note that visits to the museum are only by reservation, which you can make in advance through the museum's website.) Next, take a leisurely stroll through the park over to **Santa Maria del Popolo**, which contains a Raphael-designed chapel and two Caravaggio paintings, among other works of art. From there, it's just a short walk down to the lively and picture-perfect **Spanish Steps**, which inspired Keats, Byron, and countless other writers and artists. Stop for lunch at longtime favorite Tuscan trattoria Nino before spending some quality time browsing the high-end boutiques at the foot of the steps. From there, it's a short stroll down to the gorgeous **Trevi Fountain**; throw in a coin to ensure (so legend has it) your return to Rome. The magnificent Palazzo Colonna (Rome's grandest private palazzo with spectacular frescoes) and **Palazzo Doria Pamphilj** (an amazing 15th-century palace with a treasure-trove of old master paintings) are not far away. Next, hop on Tram No. 8 to reach the charming cobblestoned neighborhood of **Trastevere**. Start your visit in the lively Piazza di Santa Maria, where you can visit one of Rome's oldest and loveliest churches, **Santa Maria in Trastevere**. Then you'll want to wander the streets at your leisure—shopping, drinking, and dining at one of the many appealing restaurants as the sun goes down.

GREAT ITINERARIES

VENICE, FLORENCE, ROME, AND HIGHLIGHTS IN BETWEEN

This itinerary is designed for maximum impact. Think of it as a rough draft for you to revise according to your own interests and time constraints.

Day 1: Venice

Arrive in Venice's Marco Polo Airport (there are direct flights from the United States), hop on the bus to the main bus station in Venice, then check into your hotel, get out, and get lost in the back canals for a couple of hours before dinner. If you enjoy fish, you should indulge yourself at a traditional Venetian restaurant. There's no better place for sweet, delicate Adriatic seafood.

Logistics: At the airport, avoid the Alilaguna boat into Venice on arrival. It's expensive, slow, and singularly unromantic. The bus is quick and cheap—save the romance for later. When you get to the main station, transfer to the most delightful main-street "bus" in the world: the *vaporetto* ferry. Enjoy your first ride up the Grand Canal, and make sure you're paying attention to the *fermata* (or stop) where you need to get off. As for water taxis from the airport to the city, they're very expensive, although they'll take you directly to your hotel.

Day 2: Venice

Begin by skipping the coffee at your hotel and have a real Italian coffee at a real Italian coffee shop. Spend the day at Venice's top sights, including the Basilica di San Marco, Palazzo Ducale, and Galleria dell'Accademia; don't forget Piazza San Marco. The intense anticipation as you near the giant square through a maze of tiny shop-lined alleys and streets climaxes

TIPS

■ The itinerary can also be completed by car on the modern *autostrade* (four-lane highway system), although you'll run into dicey traffic in Florence and Rome. For obvious reasons, you're best off waiting to pick up your car until Day 3, when you leave Venice.

■ When it comes to trains, aim for the reservations-only Eurostar Italia or the relative newcomer to the scene, Italo.

■ The sights along this route are highly touristed; you'll have a better time if you make the trip outside the busy months of June, July, and August.

in the stunning view of the piazza (return at 7 am the next morning to see it *senza popolo* [without people], when it will look like a Canaletto painting come alive). Stop for lunch, perhaps sampling Venice's traditional specialty, *sarde in saor* (sardines in a mouthwatering sweet-and-sour preparation that includes onions and raisins), and be sure to check out the fish market at the foot of the Rialto Bridge; then sunset at the Zattere before dinner. Later, stop at one of the bars around the Campo San Luca or Campo Santa Margarita, where you can toast to being free of automobiles.

Logistics: Venice is best seen by wandering. The day's activities can be done on foot, with the occasional vaporetto ride if you feel the urge to be on the water. Never leave your lodgings without a city map: Venice is very easy to get totally lost in.

Day 3: Ferrara/Bologna

Get an early start and leave Venice on a Bologna-bound train. The ride to Ferrara, your first stop in Emilia-Romagna, is about an hour and a half. Visit the Castello Estense and Duomo before grabbing lunch. A panino and a glass of wine at one of Ferrara's cafés should fit the bill. Wander Ferrara's cobblestone streets, then hop on the train to Bologna (a ride of less than an hour). Once you've arrived, check into your hotel and walk around Piazza Maggiore before dinner. Later you can check out some of Italy's best nightlife.

Logistics: In Ferrara, the train station lies a bit outside the city center, so you may want to take a taxi or a less-expensive city bus into town (though the distance is easily walkable, too). Going out, there's a taxi stand near the back of the castle, toward Corso Ercole I d'Este. In Bologna the walk into town from the station is more manageable, particularly if you're staying along Via dell'Indipendenza. In any case, both walks are not scenic, nor are they short.

Day 4: Bologna/Florence

After breakfast, check out some of Bologna's churches and piazzas, including a climb up the leaning Torre degli Asinelli for a red-rooftop-studded panorama. After lunch, head back to the train station and take the short ride to Florence. You'll arrive in time for an afternoon siesta and an evening passeggiata.

Logistics: Florence's Santa Maria Novella train station is within easy access to some hotels, and farther from others. Taxis at the station are usually plentiful. (The taxi stand is just outside the station.)

Day 5: Florence

This is your day to see the sights of Florence. Start with the Uffizi Gallery (reserve your tickets in advance), where you'll see Botticelli's *Primavera* and *Birth of Venus*. Next, walk to Piazza del Duomo, the site of Brunelleschi's spectacular dome,

which you can climb for an equally spectacular view (reservations are necessary). By the time you descend, you'll be more than ready for a simple trattoria lunch. Depending on your preferences, either devote the afternoon to art or hike up to Piazzale Michelangelo, overlooking the city. Either way, finish the evening in style with a traditional *bistecca alla fiorentina* (grilled T-bone steak with olive oil).

Day 6: Lucca/Pisa

After breakfast, board a train for Lucca. It's an easy 1½-hour trip to see this walled medieval city. Don't miss the Romanesque Duomo, or a walk along the city's ramparts. Have lunch at a trattoria before continuing on to Pisa, where you'll spend an afternoon seeing—what else?—the Leaning Tower, along with the equally impressive Duomo and Battistero. Walk down to the banks of the Arno River, contemplate the majestic views at sunset, and have dinner at one of the many inexpensive local restaurants in the real city center—a bit removed from the most touristy spots.

Logistics: Lucca's train station lies just outside the walled city—it's a very easy walk. Pisa's train station isn't far from the city center, although it is on the other side of town from the Campo dei Miracoli (site of the Leaning Tower). Still, it's a pretty walk. Since Lucca and Pisa are only about a half hour apart by train, you may want to return from Pisa to spend the night in more-charming Lucca.

Day 7: Orvieto/Rome

Three hours south of Pisa is Orvieto, one of the prettiest and most characteristic towns of Umbria, conveniently situated right on the Florence–Rome train line. Check out the memorable cathedral before a light lunch accompanied by one

of Orvieto's famous white wines. Get back on a train bound for Rome, and in a little more than an hour you'll arrive in the Eternal City in time to make your way to your hotel and relax for a bit before you head out for the evening. When you do, check out Piazza Navona, Campo de' Fiori, and the Trevi Fountain—it's best in the evening—and have a stand-up *aperitivo* (Campari and soda is a classic) at an unpretentious local bar before dinner. It's finally pizza time; you can't go wrong at any of Rome's popular local pizzerias.

Logistics: To get from Pisa to Orvieto, you'll first catch a train to Florence and then get on a Rome-bound train from here. Be careful at Rome's Termini train station, a breeding ground for pickpockets. Keep your possessions close, and only get into a licensed taxi.

Day 8: Rome

Rome took millennia to build, but on this whirlwind trip you'll only have a day and a half to see it. In the morning, head to the Vatican Museums to see Michelangelo's glorious frescoes at the Sistine Chapel. See St. Peter's Basilica and Square before heading back into Rome proper for lunch around the Pantheon, followed by a coffee from one of Rome's famous coffee shops. Next, visit ancient Rome: first see

the magnificent Pantheon, and then head across to the Colosseum, stopping along the way along Via dei Fori Imperiali to check out the Roman Forum from above. From the Colosseum, walk or take a taxi to Piazza di Spagna, a good place to see the sunset and shop at stylish boutiques. Taxi to Piazza Trilussa at the entrance of Trastevere, a beautiful old working-class neighborhood where you'll have a relaxing dinner.

Day 9: Rome/Departure

Head by taxi to Termini station and catch the train to the Fiumicino airport.

Logistics: The train from Termini station to the airport is fast and easy—for most people, it's preferable to an exorbitantly priced taxi ride that, in bad traffic, can take twice as long and cost much, much more.

GREAT ITINERARIES

A GREAT NORTHERN ITALY ITINERARY

Northern Italy is a region with high fashion, big wines, and beautiful lakes.

Day 1: Milan

Start off in **Milan**, Italy's capital of art, fashion, and design. Explore the elegant shops around the **Duomo** and **Via Montenapoleone.** Some of Europe's great art treasures are housed in the **Brera Gallery.** Don't miss the two churches by Bramante, perhaps the most refined of the Italian High Renaissance architects. The elegant Basilica di Santa Maria presso San Satiro is about a 20-minute walk from Santa Maria delle Grazie, where Leonardo's stunning *Last Supper* is housed. Spend the evening taking in an opera at Italy's most illustrious opera house, **La Scala.**

Logistics: Central Milan is compact, with excellent public transportation. Milan does have its share of crime; keep an eye on your possessions, especially around the train station, and avoid hotels in that area.

Day 2: Bellagio

Lake Como combines some of Italy's most beautiful scenery with elegant historic villas and gardens. **Bellagio** is a pretty village with world-class restaurants and hotels, as well as more economical options. From Bellagio you can ferry to other points along the lake, take walking tours, hike, or just sit on a terrace watching the light play on the sapphire water and the snow-capped mountains.

Logistics: There are inexpensive bus-train combinations from Milan's Malpensa airport. A limousine service, Fly to Lake (☎ *0341/286887* ⊕ *www.flytolake.com*), leaves Malpensa four times per day (€27–€70 per person depending on the date and

the number of travelers; no service Sunday, late fall, or winter). The trip takes a little over two hours. In Bellagio you won't need a car, since most of your touring will be on foot, by ferry, or by bus.

Days 3 to 5: Verona/Mantua/Vicenza

Take an early express train to Verona (1½ hours from Milan) and settle into your hotel, where you'll stay for three nights; you'll be using this stately medieval city as your base to see three of the most important art cities in northern Italy.

Verona, with its ancient Roman arena, theater, and city gates, its brooding medieval palaces and castle, and its graceful bridge spanning the Adige, is probably the most immediately impressive of the three, and you'll want to spend the first day exploring its attractions. But the real artistic treasures are in the two smaller cities you'll see on day trips out of Verona.

The next day, take a short train trip to **Mantua** (30–45 minutes). Be sure to arrive in time for lunch, because Mantua has one of the most interesting local cuisines in northern Italy. The great specialty is *tortelli di zucca* (pumpkin-, cheese-, and almond-paste-filled ravioli), served with sage butter and Parmesan cheese.

The top artistic attractions are the Mantegna frescoes in the **Palazzo Ducale,** and you should also pay a visit to Giulio Romano's **Palazzo Te,** a 16th-century pleasure palace, on the outskirts of town. Take the train back to Verona in time for dinner, and perhaps catch an opera performance in Verona's Roman amphitheater.

The day after, take a short train trip to **Vicenza** (30 minutes) to see the palaces, villas, and public buildings of the lion of late-16th-century architecture, Andrea Palladio. Don't miss his **Teatro Olimpico** and his most famous villa, **La Rotonda,**

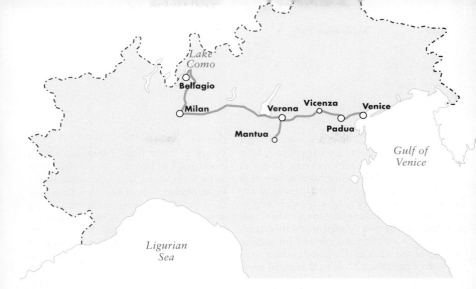

slightly out of town. For lunch, try the *baccalà alla vicentina,* the local version of salt cod, which is surprisingly good and not at all salty.

Also be sure to see the frescoes by Gianbattista and Giandomenico Tiepolo in the **Villa Valmarana ai Nani,** near the Rotonda. In spring and summer there are concerts in the **Teatro Olimpico;** if you want to attend, you'll have to book a hotel in Vicenza, since you'll miss the last train back to Verona.

Day 6: Padua

Most people visit this important art and university center on a day trip out of Venice, but then they miss one of Padua's main attractions: the nightlife that goes on in the city's wine bars and cafés from evening until quite late.

Most cities in northern Italy, even Venice and Milan, have surprisingly little to offer after dinner or the theater, but in Padua going out for a nightcap or coffee with friends is a tradition, not only for students but also for older folks, too.

Arrive early enough to see at least the Giotto frescoes in the **Cappella degli Scrovegni** and the **Basilica di San Antonio** before lunch, then spend a relaxing afternoon at the **Villa Pisani,** enjoying its gardens and important Tiepolo fresco.

Logistics: Trains are frequent to Padua from Verona (1 hour) and Vicenza (30 minutes); you don't really have to schedule ahead.

Day 7: Venice

The first things you'll probably want to do in Venice are to take a vaporetto ride down the **Grand Canal** and see **Piazza San Marco.** These are best done in the morning. If you go before 8:30, you'll avoid rush hour on the vaporetto, and although there's likely to be a line at San Marco when it opens, it'll be shorter than later in the day. After that, move on to the adjacent **Palazzo Ducale** and Sansovino's **Biblioteca Marciana,** facing it in the piazzetta.

For lunch, take vaporetto No. 1 to the Ca' Rezzonico stop and have a sandwich (and a *spritz* in **Campo Santa Margherita,** where you can mingle with university students in one of Venice's most lively squares. From there, make your way to the **Galleria dell'Accademia** and spend a few hours taking in its wonderful collection of Venetian paintings.

In the evening, take a walk up the Zattere and have a drink at one of the cafés overlooking the **Canale della Giudecca.**

Logistics: Be careful selecting your early train from Padua to Venice; some can be very slow. The 7:51 am (weekdays) is one of the fastest (27 minutes), and will get you into Venice in time to beat rush hour on the Grand Canal vaporetto. To get an early start, unless your hotel is very near San Marco, deposit your luggage at the station, and pick it up later, after you've seen the piazza. Seeing the Grand Canal and Piazza San Marco in relative tranquillity will be your reward for getting up at the crack of dawn and doing a little extra planning. There's no need to book in advance to see the Accademia; despite its marvelous collection, unlike museums in Florence and Rome, it is surprisingly free of tourists,

Day 8: Venice

If the Accademia has just whetted your appetite for Venetian painting, start the day by visiting churches and institutions where you can see more.

For Titian, go to **Santa Maria Gloriosa dei Frari** and **Santa Maria della Salute**; for Tintoretto, **Scuola Grande di San Rocco** and **Madonna dell'Orto**; for Bellini, the **Frari** and **San Giovanni e Paolo**; for Tiepolo, **Ca' Rezzonico, Scuola Grande dei Carmini,** and the **Gesuati**; for Carpaccio, **Scuola di San Giorgio**; and for Veronese, **San Sebastiano.**

If your taste runs to modern art, there are the Guggenheim Collection and, down the street, the Pinault Collection in the refashioned **Punta della Dogana.**

In the afternoon, head for the Fondamenta Nuova station to catch a vaporetto to the outer islands: **Murano,** where you can shop for Venetian glass and visit a glass museum and workshops; **Burano,** known for lace making and colorful houses; and **Torcello,** Venice's first inhabited island and home to a beautiful cathedral.

Day 9: Venice

Venice is more than a museum—it's a lively city. The best way to see that aspect of La Serenissima is to pay a visit to the **Rialto Market,** where the Venetians buy their fruits and vegetables and, most important, their fish, at one of Europe's largest and most varied fish markets. Note that the Rialto Market is closed on Sunday and Monday; since there is no fishing on Sunday, there can be no fresh fish available on Monday. In Venice, it is unthinkable to buy fish that is more than a day out of the sea.

Have lunch in one of the excellent restaurants in the market area. Then, on your last afternoon in Venice, allow time to sit and enjoy a coffee or spritz in one of the city's lively squares or in a café along the **Fondamenta della Misericordia** in Cannaregio, simply watching the Venetians go about their daily lives.

There's certainly a good deal more art and architecture to see in the city, and if you can't resist squeezing in a few more churches, you may want to see Palladio's masterpiece, the Redentore church on the **Giudecca,** or Tullio Lombardo's lyrical **Miracoli,** a short walk from the San Marco end of the Rialto Bridge.

Day 10: Venice/Departure

Take one last vaporetto trip up the Grand Canal to **Piazzale Roma** and, after saying good-bye to Venice, catch Bus No. 5 or an ATVO (private line) bus to the airport.

GREAT ITINERARIES

GREAT ITINERARIES IN CENTRAL ITALY

Visit central Italy for the great art, sumptuous countryside, and outstanding food and wine.

Day 1: Florence

If you're coming in on an international flight, you'll probably settle in Florence in time for an afternoon stroll or siesta (depending on your jet-lag strategy) before dinner.

Logistics: On your flight in, read through the restaurant listings in this guide and begin anticipating the first dinner of your trip. Look for a place near your hotel, and when you arrive, reserve a table (or have your concierge do it for you). Making a meal the focus of your first day is a great way to ease into Italian life.

Day 2: Florence

Begin your morning at the **Uffizi Gallery** (reserve your ticket in advance). The extensive collection will occupy much of your morning. Next, take in the neighboring **Piazza della Signoria**, one of Florence's impressive squares, then head a few blocks north to the **Duomo.** There, check out Ghiberti's famous bronze doors on the **Battistero** (they're high-quality copies; the originals are in the Museo dell'Opera del Duomo). Work up an appetite by climbing the 463 steps to the cupola of Brunelleschi's splendid cathedral dome, from which you'll experience a memorable view. Spend the afternoon relaxing, shopping, and wandering Florence's medieval streets; or, if you're up for a more involved journey, head out to **Fiesole** to experience the ancient amphitheater and beautiful views of the Tuscan countryside.

Day 3: Florence

Keep the energy level up for your second full day in Florence, sticking with art and architecture for the morning, trying to see most of the following: Michelangelo's *David* at the **Galleria dell'Accademia,** the **Medici Chapels,** the **Palazzo Pitti** and **Boboli Gardens,** and the churches of **Santa Maria Novella** and **Santa Croce.** If it's a clear day, spend the afternoon on a trip to **Piazzale Michelangelo,** high on a hill, for sweeping views of idyllic Florentine countryside. Given all the walking you've been doing, tonight would be a good night to recharge by trying the famed *bistecca alla fiorentina* (a grilled, very rare T-bone steak).

Logistics: You can get up to the Piazzale Michelangelo by taxi or by taking Bus No. 12 or 13 from the Lungarno. Otherwise, do your best to get around on foot; Florence is a brilliant city for walking.

Day 4: San Gimignano

Now that you've been appropriately introduced to the splendor of Renaissance Italy, it's time for a change of pace—and for a rental car, which will enable you to see the back roads of Tuscany and Umbria. After breakfast, pick up your car, fasten your seat belt and keep your lights on (even during the day), and take great care to attend to ZTLs (Zona Traffico Limitato—cross into one unwittingly, and you can expect huge fines to arrive at your doorstep many moons after your return), and head on out. On a good day the lazy drive from Florence to **San Gimignano,** past vineyards and typical Tuscan landscapes, is truly spectacular. The first thing that will hit you when you arrive at the hill town of San Gimignano will be its multiple towers. The medieval skyscrapers of Italy were public displays of wealth and family power. And they provided sanctuary and security during times of civic strife, which was often. After finding your way to a hotel in the old town, set out on foot and check out the city's turrets and alleyways, doing your best to get away from the trinket shops, and later enjoying a leisurely dinner with the light but delicious local white wine, Vernaccia di San Gimignano.

Logistics: Once you navigate your way out of Florence (no easy task), San Gimignano is only 57 km (35 miles) to the southwest, so it's an easy drive; you could even take a detour on the SS222 (Strada Chiantigiana), stop at one of the Chianti wine towns, and visit a winery along the way.

Day 5: Siena

In the morning, set out for nearby **Siena**, which is known worldwide for its Palio, a horse-race competition among the 17 *contrade* (medieval neighborhoods) of the city. Siena is one of Tuscany's most impressive sights; however many tourists you have to bump elbows with, it's hard not to be blown away by the city's precious medieval streets and memorable fan-shape **Piazza del Campo**. Not to be missed while in town are the spectacular **Duomo**, the **Battistero**, and the **Spedale di Santa Maria della Scala**, an old hospital and hostel that now contains an underground archaeological museum.

Logistics: It's a short and pretty drive from San Gimignano to Siena, but once there, parking can be a challenge. Look for the *stadio* (soccer stadium), where there's a parking lot that often has space.

Day 6: Arezzo/Cortona

Get an early start, because there's a lot to see today. From Siena you'll first head to **Arezzo**, home to the **Basilica di San Francesco**, which contains important frescoes by Piero della Francesca. Check out the

Piazza Grande along with its beautiful Romanesque church of **Pieve di Santa Maria**. Try to do all of this before lunch, after which you'll head straight to **Cortona**. If Arezzo didn't capture your imagination, Cortona, whose origins date to the 5th century BC, will. Olive trees and vineyards give way to a medieval hill town with views over idyllic Tuscan countryside and Lake Trasimeno. Cortona is a town for walking and relaxing, not sightseeing, so enjoy yourself, wandering through the **Piazza della Repubblica** and **Piazza Signorelli**, perhaps doing a bit of shopping.

Logistics: Siena to Arezzo is 63 km (39 miles) on the E78. From Arezzo to Cortona, it's just 30 km (18 miles)—take S71.

Day 7: Assisi

Today you'll cross over into Umbria, a region just as beautiful as Tuscany but still much less visited. Yet another impossibly beautiful hill town, **Assisi**, is the home of St. Francis and host to the many religious pilgrims who come to celebrate his legacy. Be prepared for the crowds. Upon arriving and checking into your lodging, head straight for the **Basilica di San Francesco**, which displays the tomb of St. Francis and unbelievable frescoes. From here take Via San Francesco to **Piazza del Commune** and see the **Tempio di Minerva** before a break for lunch. After lunch, see **San Rufino**, the town cathedral, and then go back through the piazza to Corso Mazzini and see **Santa Chiara**. If you're a true fan of the Franciscans, you could instead devote the afternoon to heading out 16 km (10 miles) to **Cannara**, where St. Francis delivered his sermon to the birds.

Logistics: From Cortona, take the S71 to the A1 autostrada toward Perugia. After about 40 km (24 miles), take the Assisi exit (E45), and it's another 14 km (8 miles) to Assisi.

Ligurian
Sea

Adriatic Sea

Florence

San Gimignano   **Arezzo**

Cortona

Siena   **Assisi**

Elba

Spoleto

CORSICA
(FRANCE)

Rome ✪

Day 8: Spoleto

This morning will take you from a small Umbrian hill town to a slightly bigger one: **Spoleto**, a walled city that's home to a world-renowned arts festival each summer. But Spoleto needs no festival to be celebrated. Its **Duomo** is wonderful. Its fortress, **La Rocca,** is impressive. And the **Ponte delle Torri,** a 14th-century bridge that separates Spoleto from Monteluco, is a marvelous sight, traversing a gorge 260 feet below and built upon the foundations of a Roman aqueduct. See all these during the day, stopping for a light lunch of a *panino* (sandwich) or salad, saving your appetite for a serious last dinner in Italy: Umbrian cuisine is excellent everywhere, but Spoleto is a memorable culinary destination. Do your best to sample black truffles, a proud product of the region; they're delicious on pasta or meat.

Logistics: One school of thought would be to time your visit to Spoleto's world-renowned arts festival that runs from mid-June through mid-July. Another would be to do anything you can to avoid it. It all depends on your taste for big festivals and big crowds. The trip from Assisi to Spoleto is a pretty 47-km (29-mile) drive (S75 to S3) that should take you less than an hour.

AN ITINERARY TIP

Because of spotty train service to Tuscan hill towns, this itinerary is extremely difficult to complete without a car. Driving is easy and often (but not always) relaxing in the region, whose roads can be winding but are generally wide, well kept, well marked, and not too crowded. If you absolutely don't want to drive, buses are the best way to go, but you'll often have to change buses in hubs like Florence, and it would be best to cut out some of the smaller Tuscan hill towns and spend extra time in Siena and Spoleto.

Day 9: Spoleto/Departure

It's a fair distance from Spoleto to the Florence airport, your point of departure. Depending on your comfort level with Italian driving, allow at least 2½ hours to reach Florence's airport.

Logistics: An alternative possibility would be to try to get a flight out of Perugia's tiny airport, which is a lot closer to Spoleto than Florence. It offers connections to Milan and Rome (Ciampino)—but not many. Otherwise, just get an early start and drive to Florence along the A1 autostrada.

GREAT ITINERARIES

A GREAT SOUTHERN ITALY ITINERARY

Come for the archaeological wonders, azure sea, and excellent Neapolitan fare.

Day 1: Naples

Fly into Naples's **Aeroporto Capodichino,** a scant 8 km (5 miles) from the city. Naples is rough around the edges and may be a bit jarring if you're a first-time visitor, but it's classic Italy, and most visitors end up falling in love with the city's alluring palazzi and spectacular pizza.

First things first, though: recharge with a nap and, after that, a good caffè—Naples has some of the world's best. Revive in time for an evening stroll down Naples's wonderful shopping street, Via Toledo, to Piazza Plebescito, before dinner and bed.

Logistics: Under no circumstances should you rent a car for Naples. Take a taxi from the airport—it's not far, or overly expensive—and you should face few logistical obstacles on your first day in Italy.

Day 2: Naples

Start the day at the **Museo Archaeologico Nazionale,** budgeting at least two hours for the collection. Then take **Via Santa Maria di Costantinopoli** and grab a caffè at one of the outdoor cafés in Piazza Bellini. From here, head down Via dei Tribunali for a pizza at **I Decumani** or **Di Matteo.** Continue along Tribunali, crossing Via Duomo (taking in a visit to the city's cathedral) to see Caravaggio's *The Seven Works of Mercy* at **Pio Monte della Misericordia.** Descend Via Duomo and turn right onto Spaccanapoli, turning off behind Piazza San Domenico for a brief stop at the **Cappella Sansevero** for a look at the pinnacle of Masonic sculpture. Continue along Spaccanapoli to Piazza del Gesù and the churches of **Il Gesù Nuovo**

and **Santa Chiara,** then walk downhill, and turn left to follow Via Monteoliveto and Via Medina to the port and the **Castel Nuovo,** and on past the **Teatro San Carlo** to the enormous **Palazzo Reale.** Walk 15 minutes south to the **Castel dell'Ovo** in the **Santa Lucia waterfront area,** one of Naples's most charming neighborhoods. Then it's back up to Via Caracciolo and the Villa Comunale, before heading back to your hotel for a short rest before dinner and perhaps a night out at one of Naples's lively bars or clubs.

Logistics: This entire day is easily done on foot.

Day 3: Pompeii/Sorrento

After breakfast, pack your luggage and head from Naples to **Pompeii,** one of the true archaeological gems of Europe. If it's summer, be prepared for an onslaught of sweltering heat as you make your way through the incredibly preserved ruins of a city that was devastated by the whims of **Mt. Vesuvius** nearly 2,000 years ago. You'll see the houses of noblemen and merchants, brothels, political graffiti, and more. From Pompeii, it's on to **Sorrento,** your first taste of the wonderful peninsula that marks the beginning of the fabled Amalfi Coast. Sorrento is touristy, but it may well be the Italian city of your imagination: cliffhanging, cobblestone-paved, and graced with an infinite variety of fishing ports and coastal views. There, have a relaxing dinner of fish and white wine before calling it a day.

Logistics: Naples to Pompeii by car is all about the A3: a short 24 km (15 miles) brings you to this archaeological gem. From Pompeii it's a short ride back on the A3 until the exit for Sorrento; from the exit, you'll take the SS145 to reach Sorrento. Most people choose the easier

option of the Circumvesuviana, a twice-hourly train to Sorrento, stopping at Pompeii's Villa dei Misteri.

Day 4: Positano/Ravello

Your stay in Sorrento will be short, as there's much of the **Amalfi Coast** still to see: **Positano,** your next stop, is a must. It's one of the most visited towns in Italy for good reason: its blue-green seas, stairs "as steep as ladders," and white Moorish-style houses make for a truly memorable setting. Walk, gaze, and eat (lunch), before heading on to the less traveled, even loftier town of **Ravello,** your Amalfi Coast dream come true, an aerie that's "closer to the sky than the sea." Don't miss the **Duomo, Villa Rufolo,** or **Villa Cimbrone** before settling in for a dinner in the sky.

Logistics: Sorrento to Positano is a 30-km (19-mile) jaunt, but the winding roads will draw it out for the better part of an hour—a scenic hour. From Positano, Ravello is another slow 18 km (11 miles) to the east, perched high above the rest of the world. The SITA bus is your best option; motorists should be prepared to use low gears if driving a stick shift (as they almost surely will be).

Day 5: Matera

Those with a car will have a bit of a drive to get to Basilicata from the Amalfi Coast; leaving Campania and entering Basilicata is generally a lonely experience. Little-traveled roads, wild hills, and distant farms are the hallmarks of this province, which produces deep, dark aglianico wines and has perfected the art of peasant food. You'll spend a while in your car to make it to **Matera,** a beautiful, ancient city full of Paleolithic **Sassi** (cave-like dwellings hewn out of rock)—but it's worth it. Spend the afternoon exploring the Sassi, then enjoy a relaxing dinner at one of Matera's excellent restaurants.

Logistics: It's a long haul from your starting point, Ravello, to Matera—if using public transportation you may find it easier to return first to Naples—but the effort is worth it, as Basilicata's landscape is so pretty. Once in Matera, if staying in the Sassi, motorists should get extra-detailed driving and parking instructions from the hotel beforehand—navigating thousand-year-old alleyways can be challenging.

Day 6: Lecce

This drive will take a good 2½ hours, so get an early start. Those without a car should return to Bari, then take the train south. The Baroque city of **Lecce** will mark your introduction to Puglia, the heel of Italy's boot. It's one of Italy's best-kept secrets, as you'll soon find out upon checking out the spectacular church of **Santa Croce,** the ornate Duomo, and the harmonious **Piazza Sant'Oronzo.** The shopping is great, the food is great, and the evening *passeggiata* (stroll) is great. Don't miss the opportunity, if you wind up at a bar or café in the evening, to chat with Lecce's friendly residents—unfazed by tourism, the welcoming Leccesi represent southern Italians at their best.

Logistics: It's not far from Matera to Lecce as the crow flies, but the trip is more involved than you might think; patience is required. The best route is via Taranto—don't make the mistake of going up through Bari.

Day 7: Bari

The trip from Lecce to **Bari** is a short one. Check into your hotel and spend the morning and afternoon wandering through Bari's *centro storico* (historic center). Don't miss Bari's castle and the walk around the ridge of the ancient city walls, with views of wide-open sea at every turn. Finish the day with a good fish dinner, and celebrate your last night in Italy by checking out one of the city's multitude of lively bars—Bari boasts some of southern Italy's most hopping nightlife.

Logistics: This is one of your most straightforward, if not quickest, connections: a direct train or the coastal S16 for 154 km (95 miles) until you hit Bari. The road is a two-lane highway, though, so don't be surprised if the trip takes two hours or more. If you get tired, beautiful Ostuni (dubbed the "città bianca," or "white city") is a perfect hilltop pit stop halfway there.

TIPS

EasyJet (⊕ *www.easyjet.com*) has inexpensive domestic air service and operates Milan (Malpensa and Linate)–Naples, London (Gatwick, Luton, and Stansted)–Naples, London Gatwick and Luton–Palermo, Catania–Naples, and Bari–Milan (Malpensa) routes. Volotea (⊕ *www.volotea.com*) operates a flight from Palermo to Naples, and Blu-Express (⊕ *www.blu-express.com*) flies from Rome (Fiumicino), and Milan (Linate) to Reggio Calabria. Also look at low-cost carriers such as Ryanair (⊕ *www.ryanair.com*) that shuttle passengers between London and southern Italy and Sardinia; however, beware of inconvenient connections in London (via Luton, for example).

Day 8: Bari/Departure

Bad news: this is your wake-up-and-leave day. Bari's Aeroporto Palese is small but quite serviceable. Exploit its absence of crowds and easy access and use it as a portal to your next destination. Connections through Rome or Milan are more frequent than you might think. Plan on leaving with southern Italy firmly established in your heart as the best place to see the Italy that once was—and be thankful that you were able to see it while it's still like this.

Logistics: Bari hotels offer easy airport transfers; take advantage of them. There are also regular public-transportation connections between the central train station and the airport. Return your rental car at the Bari airport; you won't have to arrive at the airport more than an hour or so before your flight.

ROME

WELCOME TO ROME

TOP REASONS TO GO

★ **The Vatican:** Although its population numbers only in the hundreds, the Vatican makes up for it with the millions who visit each year. Marvel at Michelangelo's Sistine Chapel and St. Peter's Basilica.

★ **The Colosseum:** The largest amphitheater of the Roman world was begun by Emperor Vespasian and inaugurated by his son Titus in AD 80.

★ **Piazza Navona:** You couldn't concoct a more Roman street scene: crowded caffè tables at street level, wrought-iron balconies above, and, at the center, Bernini's Fountain of the Four Rivers and Borromini's Sant'Agnese.

★ **Roman Forum:** This fabled labyrinth of ruins variously served as a political playground, a center of commerce, and a place where justice was dispensed during the Roman Republic and Empire.

★ **Trastevere:** Located across the Tiber River, this neighborhood is a maze of jumbled alleyways, traditional Roman trattorias, cobblestone streets, and medieval houses.

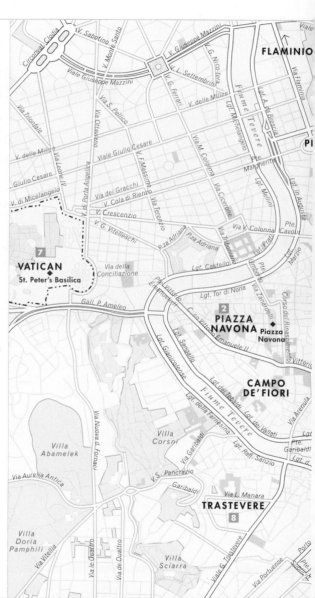

2

1 Ancient Rome. The Forum and Palatine Hill were once the hub of Western civilization.

2 Piazza Navona and Campo de' Fiori. This is the heart of the historic quarter.

3 The Jewish Ghetto. The Ghetto still preserves the flavor of Old Rome.

4 Piazza di Spagna. Travel back to the days of the Grand Tour in this area.

5 Repubblica and Quirinale. These areas house government offices, churches, and sights.

6 Villa Borghese and Piazza del Popolo. Rome's most famous park is home to the Galleria Borghese.

7 The Vatican. St. Peter's Basilica and the Sistine Chapel draw millions.

8 Trastevere. Rome's left bank has kept its authentic roots.

9 Via Appia Antica. Follow in the footsteps of St. Peter to this district.

10 Monti, Celio, Esquilino, and San Lorenzo. These neighborhoods have plenty of ancient sights and churches.

11 Aventino and Testaccio. Aventino is a posh residential area and Testaccio is more working class.

EAT LIKE A LOCAL IN ROME

In Rome, tradition is the dominant feature of the cuisine, with a focus on freshness and simplicity, so when Romans continue ordering the standbys, it's easy to understand why. That said, Rome is the capital of Italy, and the influx of residents from other regions of the country has yielded many variations on the staples.

ARTICHOKES

There are two well-known preparations of *carciofo*, or artichoke, in Rome. Carciofi *alla romana* are stuffed with wild mint, garlic, and pecorino, then braised in olive oil, white wine, and water. Carciofi *alla giudia* (Jewish-style) are whole artichokes, deep-fried twice, so that they open like a flower, the outer leaves crisp and golden brown, while the heart remains tender. When artichokes are in season—late winter through the spring—they're served everywhere.

BUCATINI ALL'AMATRICIANA

It might look like spaghetti with red sauce, but there's much more to *bucatini*

all'amatriciana. It's a spicy, rich, and complex dish that owes its flavor to *guanciale*, or cured pork jowl, as well as tomatoes and crushed red pepper flakes. It's often served over *bucatini*, a hollow, spaghetti-like pasta, and topped with grated pecorino Romano.

CODA ALLA VACCINARA

Rome's largest slaughterhouse in the 1800s was in the Testaccio neighborhood and that's where you'll find dishes like *coda alla vaccinara*, or "oxtail in the style of the cattle butcher." This dish is made from ox or veal tails stewed with tomatoes, carrots, celery, and wine, and it's usually seasoned with cinnamon. It's

2

simmered for hours and then finished with raisins and pine nuts or bittersweet chocolate.

GELATO

For many travelers, their first taste of gelato is revelatory. Its consistency is often said to be a cross between regular American ice cream and soft-serve. The best versions of gelato are extremely flavorful, and almost always made fresh daily. When choosing a *gelateria,* watch for signs that say *gelato artigianale* (artisan- or homemade): otherwise, keep an eye out for the real deal by avoiding gelato that looks too bright or fluffy.

PIZZA

There are two kinds of Roman pizza: *al taglio* (by the slice) and *tonda* (round pizza). The former has a thicker, focaccia-like crust and is cut into squares; these are sold by weight and generally available all day. The typical Roman pizza tonda has a very thin crust and is served almost charred—it's cooked in wood-burning ovens that reach extremely high temperatures. Because they're so hot, the ovens are usually fired up only in the evening, which is why Roman pizzerie tend to open for dinner only.

CACIO E PEPE

The name means "cheese and pepper" and it's a simple pasta dish from the *cucina povera,* or rustic cooking, tradition. It's a favorite Roman primo,

usually made with *tonnarelli* (fresh egg pasta a bit thicker than spaghetti), which is coated with a pecorino-cheese sauce and lots of freshly ground black pepper. Some restaurants serve the dish in an edible bowl of paper-thin baked cheese, for added delicious effect.

FRITTI

The classic Roman starter in a trattoria and especially at the pizzeria, is *fritti*: an assortment of fried treats, usually crumbed or in batter. Often, before ordering a pizza, locals will order their fritti: a *filetti di baccala* (salt cod in batter), *fiori di zucca* (zucchini flowers, usually stuffed with anchovy and mozzarella), *supplì* (rice balls stuffed with mozzarella and other ingredients), or *olive ascolane* (stuffed olives). Fritti can also be found at many pizza al taglio joints or at *tavole calde* (snack bars). They make a great quick snack.

LA GRICIA

This dish is often referred to as a "white amatriciana," because it's precisely that: pasta (usually spaghetti or rigatoni) served with pecorino cheese and guanciale—thus amatriciana without the tomato sauce. It's a lighter alternative to *carbonara* in that it doesn't contain egg, and its origins date back further than the amatriciana.

Updated
by Agnes
Crawford

The timeless city to which all roads lead, Mamma Roma, enthralls visitors today as she has since time immemorial. Here the ancient Romans made us heirs-in-law to what we call Western Civilization; where centuries later Michelangelo painted the Sistine Chapel; and where Gian Lorenzo Bernini's Baroque nymphs and naiads still dance in their marble fountains.

Today the city remains a veritable Grand Canyon of culture. Ancient Rome rubs shoulders with the medieval, the modern runs into the Renaissance, and the result is like nothing so much as an open-air museum.

But always remember: "*Quando a Roma vai, fai come vedrai*" (When in Rome, do as the Romans do). Don't feel intimidated by the press of art and culture. Instead, contemplate the grandeur from a table at a sun-drenched café on Piazza della Rotonda; let Rome's colorful life flow around you without feeling guilty because you haven't seen everything. It can't be done, anyway. There's just so much here that you'll have to come back, so be sure to throw a coin in the Trevi Fountain.

ROME PLANNER

WHEN TO GO

Spring and fall are the best times to visit, with mild temperatures and many sunny days. Summers are often sweltering so come in July and August if you like, but we advise doing as the Romans do—get up and out early, seek refuge from the afternoon heat, resume activities in early evening, and stay up late to enjoy the nighttime breeze.

Most attractions are closed on major holidays. Come August, many shops and restaurants close as locals head out for vacation. Remember that air-conditioning is still relatively rare in this city, so carrying a small paper fan in your bag can work wonders. Roman winters are relatively mild, with persistent rainy spells.

GETTING AROUND

Many of Rome's main attractions are concentrated in the centro storico and can be covered on foot. In addition, Rome has a good network of public transport, both above and below ground. The Metro Linea A will take you to Termini station, the Trevi Fountain (Barberini stop), the Spanish Steps (Spagna stop), St. Peter's (Ottaviano), and the Vatican Museums (Cipro), to name a few.

Single tickets (BIT) for the bus and Metro cost €1.50 and must be purchased before boarding. They are available at Termini station, from automatic ticket machines in Metro stations, and at most newsstands. These tickets can be used on all city buses and trams for 100 minutes or for a single Metro ride. A day pass (Roma 24h) covering all public transport costs €7, while a weekly ticket (CIS) is €24. Children under 10 travel free on all public transport when accompanied by an adult.

MAKING THE MOST OF YOUR TIME

There's so much to do in Rome that it's hard to fit it all in, no matter how much time you have. If you're a first-time visitor, the Vatican Museums and the remains of ancient Rome are must-sees, but both require at least half a day, so if you only have one day, you're best off picking one or the other. Save time and skip lines by purchasing tickets for the Vatican Museums and the Colosseum (with the Roman Forum and Palatine Hill) online beforehand. If you have more than one day, do one on one morning and the other on the next. If you're planning to visit the Galleria Borghese, tickets can sell out days (or weeks) in advance during high season, so make sure to book early.

ADDRESSES IN ROME

In the centro storico, most street names are posted on ceramic-like plaques on the side of buildings, which can make them hard to see. Addresses are fairly straightforward: the street name is followed by the street number, but it's worth noting that Roman street numbering, even in the newer outskirts of town, can be erratic. Usually numbers are even on one side of the street and odd on the other, but sometimes numbers are in ascending consecutive order on one side of the street and descending order on the other side.

ETIQUETTE

Although you may find Rome much more informal then many other European cities, Romans will nevertheless appreciate attempts to abide by local etiquette. When entering an establishment, the key words to know are: *buongiorno* (good morning), *buona sera* (good evening), and *buon pomeriggio* (good afternoon). These words can also double as a good-bye upon exit. Remember to avoid short hemlines and sleeveless or low-cut tops in churches. It is common practice (but not obligatory) to leave a tip in a restaurant: usually 5%–10% will be appreciated, or just round up. Taxi drivers don't expect tips, but if you round up the tab they will be grateful. Even in bars, leave a small coin for your cappuccino.

STREET SMARTS

As in most big cities, use common sense with your valuables. If you carry a purse, keep a firm grip on it, and don't leave it unattended or on the back of a chair, and be especially aware of pickpockets at major tourist sights and train stations. It's never a bad idea to look at menu prices before ordering and check your bill when leaving. Be careful when crossing streets, as Roman motorists have a rather carefree attitude toward traffic lights.

HOW TO SAVE MONEY

In addition to single- and multiday transit passes, a three-day Roma Pass (€36 ⊕ *www.romapass.it*) covers unlimited use of buses, trams, and the Metro, plus free admission to two museums or archaeological sites of your choice and discounted entrance to others. A two-day pass is €28 and includes one museum.

HOP-ON, HOP-OFF

Rome has multiple hop-on, hop-off sightseeing-bus tours, with competing operators aggressively trying to lure you with flyers, though City Sightseeing runs the ones you'll see most frequently. Note that Rome is actually not ideally served by bus tours, as most of the main sights are close together and on small streets not accessible by bus.

City Sightseeing. Hop-on, hop-off buses leave every 15–20 minutes daily, beginning at 9 am from Via Marsala (beside Termini station), on a 100-minute loop, which passes the Colosseum and St. Peter's, and makes stops close to the Trevi Fountain and Piazza Navona. ⊕ *www.city-sightseeing.com* ✉ *From €25.*

ROMAN HOURS

On Sunday, Rome virtually shuts down, and on Monday, most state museums and exhibition halls, plus many restaurants are closed. Daily food shop hours generally run 10 am–1 pm and 4 pm–7:30 pm or 8 pm, but other stores in the center usually observe continuous opening hours. Pharmacies tend to close for a lunch break and keep night hours (*ora rio notturno*) in rotation. As for churches, most open at 8 or 9 in the morning, close noon–3 or 4, then reopen until 6:30 or 7. St. Peter's, however, has continuous hours 7 am–7 pm (until 6 pm in the fall and winter); and the Vatican Museums are open Monday but closed Sunday (except for the last Sunday of the month).

VISITOR INFORMATION

The Department of Tourism in Rome, called Roma Capitale, staffs green information kiosks (with multilingual personnel) near important sights, as well as at Termini station and Leonardo da Vinci Airport.

EXPLORING ROME

Most visitors to Rome begin by discovering the grandeur that was Rome: the Colosseum, the Forum, and the Pantheon. Then many move on to the Vatican, the closest thing to heaven on Earth for some.

The historical pageant continues with the 1,001 splendors of the Baroque era: glittering palaces, jewel-studded churches, and Caravaggio

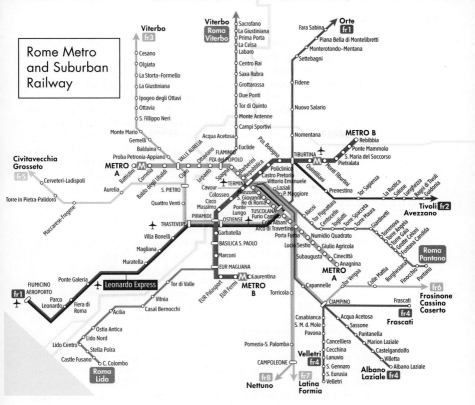

Rome Metro and Suburban Railway

masterpieces. Arrive refreshed—with the help of a shot of espresso—at the foot of the Spanish Steps, where the picturesque world of the classic Grand Tour (peopled by such spirits as John Keats and Tosca) awaits you.

Thankfully, Rome provides delightful ways to catch your historic breath along the way: a walk through the cobblestone valleys of Trastevere or an hour stolen alongside a splashing Bernini fountain. Keep in mind that an uncharted ramble through the heart of the old city can be just as satisfying as the contemplation of a chapel or a trek through marbled museum corridors. No matter which aspect of Rome you end up enjoying the most, a visit to the Eternal City will never be forgotten.

ANCIENT ROME

Time has reduced ancient Rome to fields of silent ruins, but the powerful impact of what happened here, of the genius and power that made Rome the center of the Western world, echoes across the millennia. In this one compact area of the city, you can step back into the Rome of Cicero, Julius Caesar, and Virgil. You can walk along the streets they knew, cool off in the shade of the Colosseum that loomed over the city, and see the sculptures poised over their piazzas. Today, this part of Rome, more than any other, is a perfect example of the layering of historic eras, the overlapping of ages, of religions, of a past that is very much a part of the present.

GETTING HERE AND AROUND

The Colosseo Metro station is right across from the Colosseum and a short walk from both the Roman and Imperial forums, as well as the Palatine Hill. Walking from the very heart of the historic center will take about 20 minutes, much of it along the wide Via dei Fori Imperiali. The little electric Bus No. 117 from the center or No. 175 from Termini will also deliver you to the Colosseum's doorstep. Any of the following buses will take you to or near the Roman Forum: Nos. 60, 75, 85, 95, and 175.

TOP ATTRACTIONS

Fodor's Choice ★ **The Campidoglio.** Spectacularly transformed by Michelangelo's late-Renaissance designs, the Campidoglio was once the epicenter of the Roman Empire, the place where the city's first shrines stood, including its most sacred, the Temple of Jupiter. In preparation for the impending visit of Charles V in 1536, his host, Pope Paul III Farnese, commanded Michelangelo to restore the site to glory; he added a third palace along with Renaissance-style facades and a grand paved piazza. Newly excavated ancient sculptures, designed to impress the visiting emperor, were installed in the palaces, and the piazza was ornamented with the giant stone figures of the Discouri and the ancient Roman equestrian statue of Emperor Marcus Aurelius (original now in Musei Capitolini)—the latter a visual reference to the corresponding glory of Charles V and the ancient emperor. The best view may be from the Tabularium, the arcade balcony below the Senatorio building and accessed with admission to the Musei Capitolini. ⊠ *Piazza dei Campidoglio, including the Palazzo Senatorio and the Musei Capitolini, the Palazzo Nuovo, and the Palazzo dei Conservatori, Piazza Venezia* Ⓜ *Colosseo.*

Fodor's Choice ★ **The Colosseum.** The most spectacular extant edifice of ancient Rome, the Colosseo has a history that is half gore, half glory—and still awes onlookers today with its power and might. Designed by order of the Flavian emperor Vespasian in AD 72, the arena has a circumference of 573 yards and was faced with travertine from nearby Tivoli. Its construction was a remarkable feat of engineering, for it stands on marshy terrain reclaimed by draining an artificial lake on the grounds of Nero's Domus Aurea. Once inside, take the steep stairs or elevator up to the second floor, where you can get a bird's-eye view of the hypogeum: the subterranean passageways that helped the slaughter above proceed like clockwork. In a scene prefiguring something from Dante's Inferno, hundreds of beasts would wait to be eventually launched via a series of slave-powered hoists and lifts into the bloodthirsty sand of the arena above. ⊠ *Piazza del Colosseo, Monti* ☎ *06/39967700* ⊕ *www.coopculture.it* 🎟️ *€12 (combined ticket with the Roman Forum and Palatine Hill, one entry for either site if used within 2 days)* Ⓜ *Colosseo; Bus 117, 75, 81, 673, 175, 204.*

Imperial Forums. A complex of five grandly conceived complexes flanked with colonnades, the Fori Imperiali contain monuments of triumph, law courts, and temples. The complexes were tacked on to the Roman

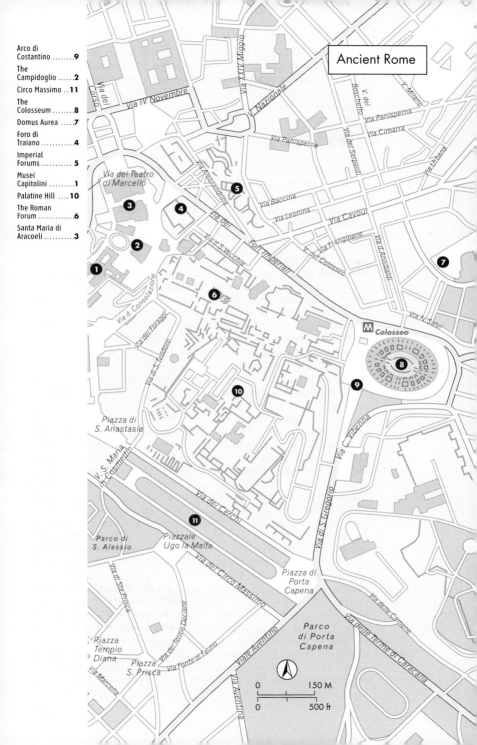

Ancient Rome

Via del Corso

Via IV Novembre

Via Nazionale

V. del Boschetto

V. Milano

V. Panisperna

Via Cimarra

Via Panisperna

Via dei Serpenti

Via Urbana

Via del Teatro
di Marcello

Via Alessandrina

Via Baccina

Via Leonina

Via Cavour

Via dei Fori Imperiali

Via di S. Vecchia

Via Frangipane

V. del Colosseo

V. d'Annibaldi

Via d. Consolazione

Via dei Fienili

Via di S. Teodoro

Via N. Salvi

Ⓜ Colosseo

Via C. Vibenna

Piazza di
S. Anastasia

V. S. Maria
in Cosmedin

Via dei Cerchi

Via di S. Gregorio

Parco di
S. Alessio

Piazzale
Ugo la Malfa

Piazza di
Porta
Capena

Via di Sta Prisca

Via del Circo Massimo

Piazza
Tempio
Diana

Piazza
S. Prisca

Via di Terme Deciane

Via di fonte del Fauno

Viale Aventino

Via Aventino

Parco
di Porta
Capena

Via delle Carmine

Via delle Terme di Caracalla

Via Marcella

0   150 M

0   500 ft

Forum, from the time of Julius Caesar in the 1st century BC until Trajan in the very early 2nd century AD, to accommodate the ever-growing need for buildings of administration and grand monuments.

From Piazza del Colosseo, head northwest on Via dei Fori Imperiali toward Piazza Venezia. Now that the road has been closed to private traffic, it's more pleasant for pedestrians (it's closed to all traffic on Sunday). On the walls to your left, maps in marble and bronze, put up by Benito Mussolini, show the extent of the Roman Republic and Empire (at the time of writing, these were partially obstructed by work on Rome's new subway line, Metro C). The dictator's own dreams of empire led him to construct this avenue, cutting brutally through the Fori Imperiali, and the medieval and Renaissance buildings that had grown upon the ruins, so that he would have a suitable venue for parades celebrating his expected military triumphs. Among the Fori Imperiali along the avenue, you can see the Foro di Cesare (Forum of Caesar) and the Foro di Augusto (Forum of Augustus). The grandest was the Foro di Traiano (Forum of Trajan), with its huge semicircular Mercati di Traiano and the Colonna Traiana (Trajan's Column). You can walk through part of Trajan's Markets on the Via Alessandrina and visit the Museo dei Fori Imperiali, which presents the Imperial Forums and shows how they would have been used through ancient fragments, artifacts, and modern multimedia. ⊠ *Via dei Fori Imperiali, Monti* 🕾 *06/0608* ⊕ *www.mercatiditraiano.it* 🖾 *Museum €15* Ⓜ *Colosseo.*

Fodor's Choice ★ **Musei Capitolini.** Surpassed in size and richness only by the Musei Vaticani, this immense collection was the first public museum in the world. A greatest-hits collection of Roman art through the ages, from the ancients to the Baroque, it is housed in the twin Museo Capitolino and Palazzo dei Conservatori that bookend Michelangelo's famous piazza. The collection was first assembled by Sixtus IV (1414–84), one of the earliest of the Renaissance popes; in it you'll find some of antiquity's most famous sculptures, such as the poignant *Dying Gaul,* the regal *Capitoline Venus,* the *Esquiline Venus* (identified as possibly another Mediterranean beauty, Cleopatra herself), and the *Lupa Capitolina,* the symbol of Rome. The heart of the museum is the Exedra of Marcus Aurelius (Sala Marco Aurelio), a large, airy room that showcases the spectacular original bronze statue of the Roman emperor, dating from the 2nd century AD, whose copy sits in the piazza below. ⊠ *Piazza del Campidoglio, Piazza Venezia* 🕾 *06/0608* ⊕ *www.museicapitolini.org* 🖾 *€13 (€15 with exhibitions); €16 with access to Centrale Montemartini; audio guide €6* Ⓜ *Colosseo; Bus Nos. 44, 63, 64, 81, 95, 85, and 492.*

Fodor's Choice ★ **Palatine Hill.** Just beyond the Arch of Titus, the Clivus Palatinus gently rises to the heights of the Colle Palatino (Palatine Hill)—the oldest inhabited site in Rome. Despite its location overlooking the Forum's traffic and attendant noise, the Palatine was the most coveted address for ancient Rome's rich and famous, including Hortensius, Cicero, Catiline, Crassus, and Agrippa. Augustus was born on the hill; the House of Livia, reserved for Augustus's wife, is today the hill's best-preserved structure. More than a few of the Twelve Caesars called the Palatine home, including Caligula, who was murdered in the still-standing and unnerving tunnel, the Cryptoporticus. The palace of Tiberius was the first to be built here; others followed, notably the gigantic extravaganza constructed for Emperor Domitian. But the most famous lodging goes back to Rome's very beginning; in 2007, archaeologists unearthed a sacred sanctuary dedicated to Romulus and Remus set beneath the House of Augustus near the Palatine Hill. ✉ *Entrances at Piazza del Colosseo and Via di San Gregorio 30, Monti* ☎ *06/39967700* ⊕ *www.coopculture.it* 🎟 *€12 combined ticket, includes single entry to Palatine Hill–Forum site and single entry to Colosseum (if used within 2 days)* Ⓜ *Colosseo.*

Fodor'sChoice **The Roman Forum.** From the entrance on Via dei Fori Imperiali, descend
★ into this extraordinary archaeological complex, once the very heart of the Roman world. The Forum began life as a marshy valley between the Capitoline and Palatine hills. Over the years a market center and some huts were established, and after the land was drained in the 6th century BC, the site eventually became a political, religious, and commercial center: the Forum. Though currently in a desolate state, this enormous area was once Rome's pulsating hub, filled with stately and extravagant temples, palaces, and shops, and crowded with people from all corners of the empire. The Forum developed over many centuries; what you see today are the ruins from a span of almost 900 years, from about 500 BC to AD 400. The enduring romance of the place makes for a quintessential Roman experience. ✉ *Entrance at Via dei Fori Imperiali, Monti* ☎ *06/39967700* ⊕ *www.coopculture.it* 🎟 *€12 (combined ticket with the Colosseum and Palatine Hill, if used within 2 days); audio guide €5* Ⓜ *Colosseo.*

WORTH NOTING

Arco di Costantino (*Arch of Constantine*). This majestic arch was erected in AD 315 to commemorate Constantine's victory over Maxentius at the Milvian Bridge. It was just before this battle, in AD 312, that Constantine—the emperor who converted Rome to Christianity—legendarily had a vision of a cross and heard the words, "In this sign thou shalt conquer." Many of the rich marble decorations for the arch were scavenged from earlier monuments, both saving money and placing Constantine in line with the great emperors of the past. It is easy to picture ranks of Roman centurions marching under the great barrel vault. ✉ *Piazza del Colosseo, Monti* Ⓜ *Colosseo.*

Circo Massimo (*Circus Maximus*). From the belvedere of the Domus Flavia on the Palatine Hill, you can see the Circus Maximus; there's also a great free view from Piazzale Ugo La Malfa on the Aventine Hill side. The giant arena where once 300,000 spectators watched chariot races while the emperor looked on is Ancient Rome's oldest and largest racetrack; it lies in a natural hollow between the two hills. The oval course stretches about 650 yards from end to end; on certain occasions, there were as many as 24 chariot races a day and competitions could last for 15 days. The charioteers could amass fortunes rather like the sports stars of today. (The Portuguese Diocles is said to have totted up winnings of 35 million sestertii.) The noise and the excitement of the crowd must have reached astonishing levels as the charioteers competed in teams, each with their own colors—the Reds, the Blues, etc. Betting also provided Rome's majority of unemployed with a potentially lucrative occupation. The central ridge was the site of two Egyptian obelisks (now in Piazza del Popolo and Piazza San Giovanni in Laterano). Picture the great chariot race scene from MGM's *Ben-Hur* and you have an inkling of what this all looked like. ⊠ *Between Palatine and Aventine hills, Aventino* Ⓜ *Circo Massimo.*

Domus Aurea (*Golden House of Nero*). Legend has it that Nero famously fiddled while Rome burned. Fancying himself a great actor and poet, he played, as it turns out, his harp to accompany his recital of "The Destruction of Troy" while gazing at the flames of Rome's catastrophic fire of AD 64. Anti-Neronian historians propagandized that Nero, in fact, had set the Great Fire to clear out a vast tract of the city center to build his new palace. Today's historians discount this as historical folderol (going so far as to point to the fact that there was a full moon on the evening of July 19, hardly the propitious occasion to commit arson). But legend or not, Nero did get to build his new palace, the extravagant Domus Aurea (Golden House)—a vast "suburban villa" that was inspired by the emperor's pleasure palace at Baia on the Bay of Naples. His new digs were huge and sumptuous, with a facade of pure gold, seawater piped into the baths, decorations of mother-of-pearl, fretted ivory, and other precious materials, and vast gardens. It was said that after completing this gigantic house, Nero exclaimed, "Now I can live like a human being!" Note that access to the site is currently only on weekends and exclusively via guided tours that use virtual reality headsets for part of the presentation. Booking ahead is essential. ⊠ *Via della Domus Aurea, Monti* ☏ *06/39967700 booking information* ⊕ *www.coopculture.it* ☐ *€16 including booking fee and guided visit* ⊘ *Closed weekdays* Ⓜ *Colosseo.*

Foro di Traiano (*Forum of Trajan*). Of all the Fori Imperiali, Trajan's was the grandest and most imposing, a veritable city unto itself. Designed by architect Apollodorus of Damascus, it comprised a vast basilica, two libraries, and a colonnade laid out around the square—all at one time covered with rich marble ornamentation. Adjoining the forum were the **Mercati di Traiano** (Trajan's Markets), a huge, multilevel brick complex of shops, taverns, walkways, and terraces, as well as administrative offices involved in the mammoth task of feeding the city. The **Museo dei Fori Imperiali** (Imperial Forums Museum) takes advantage of the Forum's soaring vaulted spaces to showcase archaeological fragments and sculptures while presenting a video re-creation of the original complex. In addition, the series of terraced rooms offers an impressive overview of the entire forum. A pedestrian-only walkway, the Via Alessandrina, also allows for an excellent (and free) view of Trajan's Forum.

To build a complex of this magnitude, Apollodorus and his patrons clearly had great confidence, not to mention almost unlimited means and cheap labor at their disposal (readily provided by slaves captured in Trajan's Dacian wars). The complex also contained two semicircular lecture halls, one at either end, which are thought to have been associated with the libraries in Trajan's Forum. The markets' architectural centerpiece is the enormous curved wall, or *exhedra*, that shores up the side of the Quirinal Hill excavated by Apollodorus's gangs of laborers. Covered galleries and streets were constructed at various levels, following the exhedra's curves and giving the complex a strikingly modern appearance.

As you enter the markets, a large, vaulted hall stands in front of you. Two stories of shops or offices rise up on either side. Head for the flight of steps at the far end that leads down to Via Biberatica. (*Bibere* is Latin for "to drink," and the shops that open onto the street are believed to have been taverns.) Then head back to the three tiers of shops and offices that line the upper levels of the great exhedra and look out over the remains of the Forum. Empty and bare today, the cubicles were once ancient Rome's busiest market stalls. Though it seems to be part of the market, the **Torre delle Milizie** (Tower of the Militia), the tall brick tower that is a prominent feature of Rome's skyline, was actually built in the early 1200s. ⊠ *Via IV Novembre 94, Monti* ☎ *06/0608* ⊕ *www.mercatiditraiano.it* ☎ *€15* Ⓜ *Cavour; Bus Nos. 85, 175, 186, 810, 850, H, 64, and 70.*

Santa Maria di Aracoeli. Sitting atop its 124 steps, Santa Maria di Aracoeli perches on the north slope of the Capitoline Hill. The church rests on the site of the temple of Juno Moneta (Admonishing Juno), which also housed the Roman mint (hence the origin of the word "money"). According to legend, it was here that the Sibyl, a prophetess, predicted to Augustus the coming of a Redeemer. He in turn responded by erecting an altar, the Ara Coeli (Altar of Heaven). This was eventually replaced by a Benedictine monastery, and then a church, which was passed in 1250 to the Franciscans, who restored and enlarged it in Romanesque-Gothic style. Today, the Aracoeli is best known for the **Santo Bambino,** a much-revered olivewood figure of the Christ Child (today a copy of the 15th-century original that was stolen in 1994). At Christmas, everyone pays homage to the "Bambinello" as children recite poems from a miniature pulpit. In true Roman style, the church interior is a historical hodgepodge, with classical columns and large marble fragments from pagan buildings, as well as a 13th-century Cosmatesque pavement. The richly gilded Renaissance ceiling commemorates the naval victory at Lepanto in 1571 over the Turks. The first chapel on the right is noteworthy for Pinturicchio's frescoes of San Bernardino of Siena (1486). ⊠ *Via del Teatro di Marcello, at top of long, steep stairway, Piazza Venezia* ☎ *06/69763838* Ⓜ *Colosseo; Bus Nos. 44, 160, 170, 175, and 186.*

PIAZZA NAVONA AND CAMPO DE' FIORI

Set between Via del Corso and the Tiber bend, these time-burnished districts are some of the city's most beautiful. They're filled with airy piazzas, half-hidden courtyards, and narrow streets bearing curious names. Some of Rome's most coveted residential addresses are nestled here. So, too, are the ancient Pantheon and the Renaissance square of Campo de' Fiori, but the spectacular, over-the-top Baroque monuments of the 16th and 17th centuries predominate.

The hub of the district is the queen of squares, Piazza Navona—a cityscape adorned with the most jaw-dropping fountain by Gian

Lorenzo Bernini, father of the Baroque. Streets running off the square lead to many historic must-sees, including noble churches by Borromini and Caravaggio's greatest paintings at San Luigi dei Francesi. This district has been an integral part of the city since ancient times, and its position between the Vatican and Lateran palaces, both seats of papal rule, put it in the mainstream of Rome's development from the Middle Ages onward. Craftsmen, shopkeepers, and famed artists toiled in the shadow of the huge palaces built to consolidate the power of leading figures in the papal court. Artisans and artists still live here, but their numbers are diminishing as the district becomes increasingly posh and—so critics say—"Disneyfied." But three of the liveliest piazzas in Rome—Piazza Navona, Piazza della Rotonda (home to the Pantheon), and Campo de' Fiori—are lodestars in a constellation of some of Rome's finest cafés, stores, and wine bars.

GETTING HERE AND AROUND

The Piazza Navona and Campo de' Fiori are an easy walk from the Vatican or Trastevere, or a half-hour stroll from the Spanish Steps. From Termini or the Vatican, take Bus No. 40 Express or No. 64 to Largo Torre Argentina; then walk 10 minutes to either piazza. Bus No. 116 winds from Via Veneto past the Spanish Steps to Campo de' Fiori.

TOP ATTRACTIONS

Campo de' Fiori. A bustling marketplace in the morning (Monday–Saturday 8–2) and a trendy meeting place the rest of the day and night, this piazza has plenty of earthy charm. Just after lunchtime, all the fruit and vegetable vendors disappear, and this so-called *piazza trasformista* takes on another identity, becoming a circus of bars particularly favored by study-abroads, tourists, and young expats. Brooding over the piazza is a hooded statue of the philosopher Giordano Bruno, who was burned at the stake here in 1600 for heresy, one of many victims of the Roman Inquisition. ✉ *Intersection of Via dei Baullari, Via Giubbonari, Via del Pellegrino, and Piazza della Cancelleria, Campo de' Fiori.*

Fodor's Choice ★ **Palazzo Altemps.** Containing some of the finest ancient Roman statues in the world, Palazzo Altemps is part of the Museo Nazionale Romano. The palace's sober exterior belies a magnificence that appears as soon as you walk into the majestic courtyard, studded with statues and covered in part by a retractable awning. The restored interior hints at the Roman lifestyle of the 16th–18th century while showcasing the most illustrious pieces from the Museo Nazionale, including the collection of the Ludovisi noble family. In the frescoed salons you can see the Galata Suicida, a poignant work portraying a barbarian warrior who chooses death for himself and his wife, rather than humiliation by the enemy. Another highlight is the large Ludovisi sarcophagus, magnificently carved from marble. In a place of honor is the Ludovisi Throne, which shows a goddess emerging from the sea and being helped by her acolytes. For centuries this was heralded as one of the most sublime Greek sculptures, but, today, at least one authoritative art historian considers it a colossally overrated fake. Look for the framed explanations of the exhibits that detail (in English) how and exactly where Renaissance sculptors, Bernini among them, added missing pieces to the classical works. In the lavishly frescoed Loggia stand busts of the

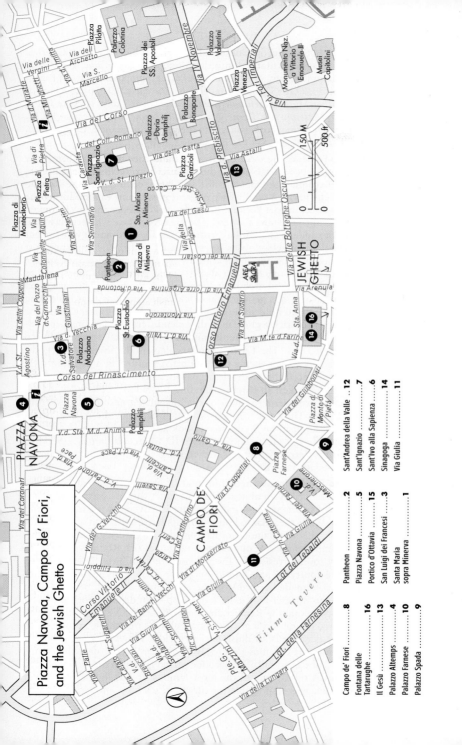

Piazza Navona, Campo de' Fiori, and the Jewish Ghetto

Caesars. In the wing once occupied by early-20th-century poet Gabriele d'Annunzio (who married into the Altemps family), three rooms host the museum's Egyptian collection. ✉ *Piazza Sant'Apollinare 46, Piazza Navona* ☎ *06/39967700* ⊕ *www.coopculture.it* ☜ *€10, or €12 including 3 other Museo Nazionale Romano sites over 7 days (Crypta Balbi, Palazzo Massimo alle Terme, Museo delle Terme di Diocleziano); €13, or €15 (including 3 other sites) if a special exhibit is on* ☽ *Closed Mon.* Ⓜ *Bus Nos. 70, 81, 87, 116T, 186, 492, and 628.*

Palazzo Farnese. The most beautiful Renaissance palace in Rome, the Palazzo Farnese is fabled for the Galleria Carracci, whose ceiling is to the Baroque age what the Sistine Chapel ceiling is to the Renaissance. The Farnese family rose to great power and wealth during the Renaissance, in part because of the favor Pope Alexander VI showed to the beautiful Giulia Farnese. The massive palace was begun when, with Alexander's aid, Giulia's brother became cardinal; it was further enlarged on his election as Pope Paul III in 1534. The uppermost frieze decorations and main window overlooking the piazza are the work of Michelangelo, who also designed part of the courtyard, as well as the graceful arch over Via Giulia at the back. The facade on Piazza Farnese has geometrical brick configurations that have long been thought to hold some occult meaning. When looking up at the palace, try to catch a glimpse of the splendid frescoed ceilings, including the **Galleria Carracci** vault painted by Annibale Carracci between 1597 and 1604. The Carracci gallery depicts the loves of the gods, a supremely pagan theme that the artist painted in a swirling style that announced the birth of the Baroque. Other opulent salons are among the largest in Rome, including the Salon of Hercules, which has an overpowering replica of the ancient *Farnese Hercules,* front and center. The French Embassy, which occupies the palace, offers tours (in English) on Wednesday; book at least eight days in advance through the website, and bring photo ID. ✉ *French Embassy, Servizio Culturale, Piazza Farnese 67, Campo de' Fiori* ☎ *06/686011* ⊕ *www.inventerrome.com* ☜ *€9* ☽ *Closed Thurs.–Tues.*

Palazzo Spada. In this neighborhood of huge, austere palaces, Palazzo Spada strikes an almost frivolous note, with its pretty ornament-encrusted courtyard and its upper stories covered with stuccoes and statues. While the palazzo houses an impressive collection of old master paintings, it's most famous for its trompe-l'oeil garden gallery, a delightful example of the sort of architectural games rich Romans of the 17th century found irresistible. Even if you don't go into the gallery, step into the courtyard and look through the glass window of the library to the colonnaded corridor in the adjacent courtyard. See—or seem to see—an 8-meter-long gallery quadrupled in depth, a sort of optical telescope taking the Renaissance's art of perspective to another level, as it stretches out for a great distance with a large statue at the end. In fact the distance is an illusion: the corridor grows progressively narrower and the columns progressively smaller as they near the statue, which is just 2 feet tall. The Baroque period is known for special effects, and this is rightly one of the most famous. It was long thought that Borromini was responsible for this ruse; it's now known that it was

2

designed by an Augustinian priest, Giovanni Maria da Bitonto. Upstairs is a seignorial picture gallery with the paintings shown as they would have been, piled on top of each other clear to the ceiling. Outstanding works include Brueghel's *Landscape with Windmills*, Titian's *Musician*, and Andrea del Sarto's *Visitation*. Look for the fact-sheets that have descriptive notes about the objects in each room. ⊠ *Piazza Capo di Ferro 13, Campo de' Fiori* ☎ *06/6861158* ⊕ *www.galleriaborghese. it* ⌨ *€5* ⊘ *Closed Tues.*

Fodor's Choice
★
Pantheon. One of the wonders of the ancient world, this onetime pagan temple, a marvel of architectural harmony and proportion, is the best-preserved ancient building in Rome—the result of its consecration as a church in AD 608. It was entirely rebuilt (and likely designed) by the emperor Hadrian around AD 120 on the site of an earlier pantheon erected in 27 BC. The most striking thing is not the Pantheon's size, immense though it is (until 1960 the dome was the largest ever built), nor even the phenomenal technical difficulties posed by so vast a construction; rather, it's the remarkable unity of the building: the diameter described by the dome is exactly equal to its height. It's why some call it the world's only architecturally perfect building. Today the Pantheon serves as one of the city's important burial places, with its most famous tomb that of Raphael. ⊠ *Piazza della Rotonda, Piazza Navona* ☎ *06/68300230* ⊕ *www.pantheonroma.com* ⌨ *Free; at the time of writing a €2 charge was scheduled to begin late 2018; audio guide €5* Ⓜ *Closest bus hub: Argentina (Bus Nos. 40, 85, 53, 46, 64, 87, and 571; Tram No. 8).*

Piazza Navona. Here, everything that makes Rome unique is compressed into one beautiful Baroque piazza. Always camera-ready, Piazza Navona has Bernini sculptures, three gorgeous fountains, a magnificently Baroque church (Sant'Agnese in Agone), and the excitement of so many people strolling, admiring the fountains, and enjoying the view. Although undoubtedly more touristy today, the square still has the carefree air of the days when it was the scene of medieval jousts and 17th-century carnivals. At center stage is the Fontana dei Quattro Fiumi, created for Innocent X by Bernini in 1651. Bernini's powerful figures of the four rivers represent the four corners of the world: the Nile; the Ganges; the Danube; and the Plata, with its hand raised. If you want a caffè with one of the most beautiful (if pricey) views in Rome, grab a seat; just be aware that the restaurants are geared toward tourists, so while lovely, you can find cheaper and more authentic meals elsewhere. ⊠ *Piazza Navona.*

Fodor's Choice
★
San Luigi dei Francesi. A pilgrimage spot for art lovers, San Luigi's Contarelli Chapel (the fifth and last chapel on the left, toward the main altar) is adorned with three stunningly dramatic works by Caravaggio (1571–1610), the Baroque master of the heightened approach to light and dark. They were commissioned for the tomb of Mattheiu Cointerel in one of Rome's French churches (San Luigi is St. Louis, patron saint of France). The inevitable coin machine will light up his *Calling of Saint Matthew, Saint Matthew and the Angel,* and *Martyrdom of Saint Matthew* (seen from left to right), and Caravaggio's mastery of light takes it from there. When painted, they caused considerable

consternation to the clergy of San Luigi, who thought the artist's dramatically realistic approach was scandalously disrespectful. A first version of the altarpiece was rejected; the priests were not particularly happy with the other two, either. Time has fully vindicated Caravaggio's patron, Cardinal Francesco del Monte, who secured the commission for these works and stoutly defended them. ⊠ *Piazza di San Luigi dei Francesi, Piazza Navona* ☎ *06/688271* ⊕ *www.saintlouis-rome.net* Ⓜ *Bus Nos. 40 and 87.*

Fodor's Choice
★
Santa Maria sopra Minerva. The name of the church reveals that it was built *sopra* (over) the ruins of a temple of Minerva, the ancient goddess of wisdom. Erected in 1280 by Dominicans along severe Italian Gothic lines, it has undergone a number of more or less happy restorations to the interior. Certainly, as the city's major Gothic church, it provides a refreshing contrast to Baroque flamboyance. Have a € 1 coin handy to illuminate the **Cappella Carafa** in the right transept, where Filippino Lippi's (1457–1504) glowing frescoes are well worth the small investment, opening up the deepest azure expanse of sky where musical angels hover around the Virgin. Under the main altar is the tomb of St. Catherine of Siena, one of Italy's patron saints. Left of the altar you'll find Michelangelo's *Risen Christ* and the tomb of the gentle artist Fra Angelico. Bernini's unusual and little-known monument to the Blessed Maria Raggi is on the fifth pier of the left-hand aisle. In front of the church, the little obelisk-bearing elephant carved by Bernini is perhaps the city's most charming sculpture. An inscription on the base of **Bernini's Elephant Obelisk** references the church's ancient patroness, reading something to the effect that it takes a strong mind to sustain solid wisdom. ⊠ *Piazza della Minerva, Piazza Navona* ☎ *06/6793926* ⊕ *www.santamariasopraminerva.it.*

Fodor's Choice
★
Sant'Ignazio. Rome's second Jesuit church, this 17th-century landmark harbors some of the most city's magnificent trompe-l'oeil. To get the full effect of the marvelous illusionistic ceiling by priest-artist Andrea Pozzo, stand on the small disk set into the floor of the nave. The heavenly vision above you, seemingly extending upward almost indefinitely, represents the *Allegory of the Missionary Work of the Jesuits* and is part of Pozzo's cycle of works in this church exalting the early history of the Jesuit Order, whose founder was the reformer Ignatius of Loyola. The saint soars heavenward, supported by a cast of thousands; not far behind is Saint Francis Xavier, apostle of the Indies, leading a crowd of Eastern converts; a bare-breasted, spear-wielding America in American Indian headdress rides a jaguar; Europe with crown and scepter sits serene on a heftily rumped horse; while a splendid Africa with gold tiara perches on a lucky crocodile. The artist repeated this illusionist technique, so popular in the late 17th century, in the false dome, which is actually a flat canvas—a trompe-l'oeil trick used when the budget drained dry. The overall effect of the frescoes is dazzling (be sure to have coins handy for the machine that switches on the lights) and was fully intended to rival that produced by Baciccia in the nearby mother church of Il Gesù. Scattered around the nave are several awe-inspiring altars; their soaring columns, gold-on-gold decoration, and gilded statues make these the last word in splendor. The church is often host to concerts of

sacred music performed by choirs from all over the world. Look for posters at the church doors or check the website for more information. ✉ *Piazza Sant'Ignazio, Piazza Navona* ☎ *06/6794406* ⊕ *www. chiesasantignazio.it.*

Fodor'sChoice **Via Giulia.** Still a Renaissance-era diorama and one of Rome's most
★ exclusive addresses, Via Giulia was the first street in Rome since ancient times to be deliberately planned. Straight as a die, it was named for Pope Julius II (of Sistine Chapel fame), who commissioned it in the early 1500s as part of a scheme to open up a grandiose approach to St. Peter's Basilica, and it is flanked with elegant churches and palaces. Although the pope's plans to change the face of the city were only partially completed, Via Giulia became an important thoroughfare in Renaissance Rome. Today, after more than four centuries, it remains the "salon of Rome," address of choice for Roman aristocrats, although controversy has arisen about a recent change—the decision to add a large parking lot along one side of the street—that meant steamrolling through ancient and medieval ruins underneath. A stroll will reveal elegant palaces and churches (one, **San Eligio,** on the little side street Via di Sant'Eligio, was designed by Raphael himself). The area around Via Giulia is wonderful to wander through and get the feel of daily life as carried on in a centuries-old setting. Among the buildings that merit your attention are **Palazzo Sacchetti** (Via Giulia 66), with an imposing stone portal (inside are some of Rome's grandest staterooms, still, after 300 years, the private quarters of the Marchesi Sacchetti), and the forbidding brick building that housed the **Carceri Nuove** (New Prison; Via Giulia 52), Rome's prison for more than two centuries and now the offices of Direzione Nazionale Antimafia. Near the bridge that arches over the southern end of Via Giulia is the church of **Santa Maria dell'Orazione e Morte** (Holy Mary of Prayer and Death), with stone skulls on its door. These are a symbol of a confraternity that was charged with burying the bodies of the unidentified dead found in the city streets. Home since 1927 to the Hungarian Academy, the **Palazzo Falconieri** (Via Giulia 1 ☎ *06/6889671*) was designed by Borromini—note the architect's rooftop belvedere adorned with statues of the family "falcons," best viewed from around the block along the Tiber embankment. (The Borromini-designed salons and loggia are sporadically open as part of a guided tour; call the Hungarian Academy for information.) Remnant of a master plan by Michelangelo, the arch over the street was meant to link massive Palazzo Farnese, on the east side of Via Giulia, with the building across the street and a bridge to the Villa Farnesina, directly across the river. Finally, on the right and rather green with age, dribbles that star of many a postcard, the Fontana del Mascherone. ✉ *Via Giulia, between Piazza dell'Oro and Piazza San Vincenzo Palloti, Campo de' Fiori.*

WORTH NOTING

Fodor'sChoice **Il Gesù.** The mother church of the Jesuits in Rome is the prototype of
★ all Counter-Reformation churches, and its spectacular interior tells a great deal about an era of religious triumph and turmoil. Its architecture influenced ecclesiastical buildings in Rome for more than a century (the overall design was by Vignola, the facade by della Porta) and was

exported by the Jesuits throughout the rest of Europe. Though consecrated in 1584, the interior of the church wasn't fully decorated for another 100 years. It was originally intended that the interior be left plain to the point of austerity—but, when it was finally embellished, the mood had changed and no expense was spared. Its interior drips with gold and lapis lazuli, gold and precious marbles, gold and more gold, all covered by a fantastically painted ceiling by Baciccia. Unfortunately, the church is also one of Rome's most crepuscular, so its visual magnificence is considerably dulled by lack of light.

The architectural significance of Il Gesù extends far beyond the splendid interior. As the first of the great Counter-Reformation churches, it was put up after the Council of Trent (1545–63) had signaled the determination of the Roman Catholic Church to fight back against the Reformed Protestant heretics of northern Europe. The church decided to do so through the use of overwhelming pomp and majesty, in an effort to woo believers. As a harbinger of ecclesiastical spectacle, Il Gesù spawned imitations throughout Italy and the other Catholic countries of Europe as well as the Americas.

The most striking element is the ceiling, which is covered with frescoes that swirl down from on high to merge with painted stucco figures at the base, the illusion of space in the two-dimensional painting becoming the reality of three dimensions in the sculpted figures. Baciccia, their painter, achieved extraordinary effects in these frescoes, especially in the *Triumph of the Holy Name of Jesus,* over the nave. Here, the figures representing evil cast out of heaven and seem to be hurtling down onto the observer. To appreciate in detail, the spectacle is best viewed through a specially tilted mirror in the nave.

The founder of the Jesuit order himself is buried in the Chapel of St. Ignatius, in the left-hand transept. This is surely the most sumptuous Baroque altar in Rome; as is typical, the enormous globe of lapis lazuli that crowns it is really only a shell of lapis over a stucco base—after all, Baroque decoration prides itself on achieving stunning effects and illusions. The heavy, bronze altar rail by architect Carlo Fontana is in keeping with the surrounding opulence. ⊠ *Piazza del Gesù, Campo de' Fiori* ☎ *06/697001* ⊕ *www.chiesadelgesu.org.*

Sant'Andrea della Valle. Topped by the highest dome in Rome after St. Peter's (designed by Maderno), this huge and imposing 17th-century church is remarkably balanced in design. Fortunately, its facade, which had turned a sooty gray from pollution, has been cleaned to a near-sparkling white. Use one of the handy mirrors to examine the early-17th-century frescoes by Domenichino in the choir vault and those by Lanfranco in the dome. One of the earliest ceilings done in full Baroque style, its upward vortex was influenced by Correggio's dome in Parma, of which Lanfranco was also a citizen. (Bring a few coins to light the paintings, which can be very dim.) The three massive paintings of Saint Andrew's martyrdom are by Maria Preti (1650–51). Richly marbled and decorated chapels flank the nave, and in such a space, Puccini set the first act of *Tosca.* ⊠ *Piazza Vidoni 6, Corso Vittorio Emanuele II, Campo de' Fiori* ☎ *06/6861339.*

Sant'Ivo alla Sapienza. The main facade of this eccentric Baroque church, probably Borromini's best, is on the stately courtyard of an austere building that once housed Rome's university. Sant'Ivo has what must surely be one of the most delightful "domes" in all of Rome—a dizzying spiral said to have been inspired by a bee's stinger. The apian symbol is a reminder that Borromini built the church on commission from the Barberini pope Urban VIII (a swarm of bees figure on the Barberini family crest), although it was completed by Alexander VII. The interior, open only for three hours on Sunday, is worth a look, especially if you share Borromini's taste for complex mathematical architectural idiosyncrasies. "I didn't take up architecture solely to be a copyist," he once said. Sant'Ivo is certainly the proof. ⊠ *Corso del Rinascimento 40, Piazza Navona* ☎ *06/6864987* ⊕ *www.060608.it* ☉ *Closed July and Aug., and Mon.–Sat.* Ⓜ *Bus Nos. 130, 116, 186, 492, 30, 70, 81, and 87.*

THE JEWISH GHETTO

Although today most of Rome's Jews live outside the Ghetto, the area remains the spiritual and cultural home of Jewish Rome, and that heritage permeates its small commercial area of Judaica shops, kosher bakeries, and restaurants. The Jewish Ghetto was established by papal decree in the 16th century. It was by definition a closed community, where Roman Jews lived under lock and key until Italian unification in 1870. In 1943–44, the already small Jewish population there was decimated by deportations. Today there are a few Judaica shops and kosher groceries, bakeries, and restaurants (especially on Via di Portico d'Ottavia), but the neighborhood mansions are now being renovated and much coveted by rich and stylish expats.

GETTING HERE AND AROUND
From the Vatican or the Spanish Steps, it's a 30-minute walk to the Jewish Ghetto, or take the No. 40 Express or the No. 64 bus from Termini station to Largo Torre Argentina.

TOP ATTRACTIONS

Fodor's Choice ★

Portico d'Ottavia. Looming over the Jewish Ghetto, this huge portico enclosure, with a few surviving columns, is one of the area's most picturesque set pieces, with the time-stained church of Sant'Angelo in Pescheria (seemingly under perpetual restoration) built right into its ruins. Named by Augustus in honor of his sister Octavia, it was originally 390 feet wide and 433 feet long, encompassed two temples, a meeting hall, and a library, and served as a kind of grandiose entrance foyer for the adjacent Teatro di Marcello. The ruins of the portico became Rome's *pescheria* (fish market) during the Middle Ages. A stone plaque on a pillar (a copy; the original is in the Musei Capitolini) states in Latin that the head of any fish surpassing the length of the plaque was to be cut off "up to the first fin" and given to the city fathers, or else the vendor was to pay a fine of 10 gold florins. The heads were used to make fish soup and were considered a great delicacy. ⊠ *Via Tribuna di Campitelli 6, Jewish Ghetto.*

Sinagoga. This synagogue has been the city's largest Jewish temple, and a Roman landmark with its aluminum dome, since its construction in

1904. The building also houses the Jewish Museum, with its precious ritual objects and other exhibits, which document the uninterrupted presence of a Jewish community in the city for nearly 22 centuries. Until the 16th century, Jews were esteemed citizens of Rome. Among them were bankers and physicians to the popes, who had themselves given permission for the construction of synagogues. But in 1555, during the Counter-Reformation, Pope Paul IV decreed the building of the walls of the Ghetto, confining the Jews to this small area and imposing a series of restrictions, some of which continued to be enforced until 1870. For security reasons, guided visits are mandatory, and tours in English start every hour at about 10 minutes past the hour; entrance to the synagogue is through the museum located in Via Catalana (*Largo 16 Ottobre 1943*). ⊠ *Lungotevere Cenci 15, Jewish Ghetto* ☎ *06/68400661* ⊕ *www.museoebraico.roma.it* ⊠ *€11* ⊙ *Museum closed Sat. and Jewish holidays* Ⓜ *Bus Nos. 46, 64, and 87; Tram No. 8.*

WORTH NOTING

Fontana delle Tartarughe. Designed by Giacomo della Porta in 1581 and sculpted by Taddeo Landini, this 16th-century fountain, set in venerable Piazza Mattei, is one of Rome's most charming. The focus of the fountain is four bronze boys, each grasping a dolphin spouting water into a marble shell. Bronze turtles held in the boys' hands drink from the upper basin. The turtles are thought to have been added in the 17th century by Bernini. ⊠ *Piazza Mattei, Jewish Ghetto.*

PIAZZA DI SPAGNA

In spirit (and in fact) this section of the city is its most grandiose. The overblown Vittoriano monument, the labyrinthine treasure-chest palaces of Rome's surviving aristocracy, even the diamond-draped denizens of Via Condotti's shops—all embody the exuberant ego of a city at the center of its own universe. Here's where you'll see ladies in furs gobbling pastries at café tables, and walk through a thousand snapshots as you climb the famous Spanish Steps, admired by generations from Byron to Versace. Cultural treasures abound around here: gilded 17th-century churches, glittering palaces, and the greatest example of portraiture in Rome, Velázquez's incomparable *Innocent X* at the Galleria Doria Pamphilj. Have your camera ready—along with a coin or two—for that most beloved of Rome's landmarks, the Trevi Fountain.

GETTING HERE AND AROUND

The Piazza di Spagna is a short walk from Piazza del Popolo, the Pantheon, and the Trevi Fountain. One of Rome's handiest subway stations, Spagna, is tucked just left of the steps. Bus Nos. 117 (from the Colosseum) and 119 (from Piazza del Popolo) hum through the area; the latter tootles up Via del Babuino, famed for its shopping.

TOP ATTRACTIONS

Fodor's Choice ★ **Ara Pacis Augustae** (*Altar of Augustan Peace*). This vibrant monument of the Imperial age is housed in one of Rome's newer architectural landmarks: a gleaming, rectangular glass-and-travertine structure designed by American architect Richard Meier. Overlooking the Tiber on one side and the ruins of the marble-clad **Mausoleo di Augusto** (Mausoleum of Augustus) on the other, the result is a serene, luminous oasis right in the center of Rome. The altar itself dates back to 13 BC; it was commissioned to celebrate the Pax Romana, the era of peace ushered in by Augustus's military victories. Like all ancient Roman monuments of this kind, you have to imagine its spectacular and moving relief sculptures painted in vibrant colors, now long gone. The reliefs on the short sides portray myths associated with Rome's founding and glory; the long sides display a procession of the imperial family. It's fun to try to play "who's who"—although half of his body is missing, Augustus is identifiable as the first full figure at the procession's head on the south-side frieze—but academics still argue over exact identifications of other figures. The small museum has a model and useful information about the Ara Pacis's original location and the surrounding Augustan monuments. ✉ *Lungotevere in Augusta, Piazza di Spagna* ☎ *06/0608* ⊕ *www.arapacis.it* 🎫 *€11, €17 when an exhibition is on* Ⓜ *Flaminio.*

Monumento a Vittorio Emanuele II, or Altare della Patria (*Victor Emmanuel II Monument, or Altar of the Nation*). The huge white mass of the "Vittoriano" is an inescapable landmark—Romans say you can avoid its image only if you're actually standing on it. Some have likened it to a huge wedding cake; others, to an immense typewriter. To create this elaborate marble monster and the vast piazza on which it stands, architects blithely destroyed many ancient and medieval buildings and altered the slope of the Campidoglio (Capitoline Hill), which abuts it. Built to honor the unification of Italy and the nation's first king, Victor Emmanuel II, it also shelters the eternal flame at the tomb of Italy's Unknown Soldier killed during World War I. The flame is guarded day and night by sentinels, while inside the building there is the (rather dry) Institute of the History of the Risorgimento. Take the elevator (entrance located several flights of stairs up on the right as you face the monument) up to the top to see some of Rome's most panoramic views. ✉ *Entrances on Piazza Venezia, Piazza del Campidoglio, and Via di San Pietro in Carcere, Piazza di Spagna* ☎ *06/0608* ⊕ *www.060608. it* 🎫 *Free, elevator €7* Ⓜ *Colosseo.*

FodorśChoice
★
Palazzo Colonna. Rome's grandest family built themselves Rome's grandest private palazzo, a fusion of 17th- and 18th-century buildings, on a spot they have occupied for a millennium. It's so immense that it faces Piazza dei Santi Apostoli on one side and the Quirinale (Quirinal Hill) on the other (a little bridge over Via della Pilotta links the palace with the gardens on the hill). While still home to some Colonna patricians, the palace also holds the family picture gallery, which is open to the public on Saturday mornings. The gallery is itself a setting of aristocratic grandeur; you might recognize the **Sala Grande** as the site where Audrey Hepburn meets the press in *Roman Holiday.* At one end looms the ancient red marble column (*colonna* in Italian), which is the family's emblem; above the vast room is the spectacular ceiling fresco of the Battle of Lepanto painted by Giovanni Coli and Filippo Gherardi in 1675—the center scene almost puts the computer-generated special effects of Hollywood to shame. Adding redundant luster to the opulently stuccoed and frescoed salons are works by Poussin, Tintoretto, and Veronese, and a number of portraits of illustrious members of the

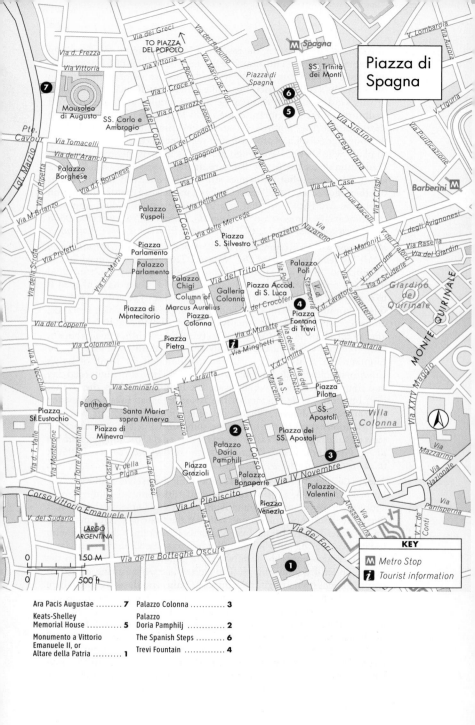

Piazza di Spagna

KEY

Ⓜ *Metro Stop*

🛈 *Tourist information*

family such as Vittoria Colonna, Michelangelo's muse and longtime friend, and Marcantonio Colonna, who led the papal forces in the great naval victory at Lepanto in 1577. Lost in the array of madonnas, saints, goddesses, popes, and cardinals is Annibale Carracci's lonely *Beaneater,* spoon at the ready and front teeth missing. (As W. H. Auden put it, "Grub first, art later.") At noon, there's a guided tour in English, included in your entrance fee. The gallery also boasts a café with a pleasant terrace. ⊠ *Via della Pilotta 17, Piazza di Spagna* ☎ *06/6784350* ⊕ *www.galleriacolonna.it* 🎫 *€12* ⊘ *Closed Sun.–Fri.* Ⓜ *Barberini.*

Fodor'sChoice ★ **Palazzo Doria Pamphilj.** Along with the Palazzo Colonna and the Galleria Borghese, this spectacular 15th-century family palace provides the best glimpse of aristocratic Rome. The main attractions are the legendary old master paintings, including treasures by Velázquez and Caravaggio, the splendor of the main galleries, and a unique suite of private family apartments. It passed through several hands before becoming the property of the famous seafaring Doria family of Genoa, who had married into the Roman Pamphilj (also spelled Pamphili) clan. The picture gallery contains 550 paintings, including three by Caravaggio—a young St. John the Baptist, Mary Magdalene, and the breathtaking *Rest on the Flight to Egypt.* Off the eye-popping Galleria degli Specchi (Gallery of Mirrors)—a smaller version of the one at Versailles—are the famous Velázquez *Pope Innocent X,* considered by some historians as the greatest portrait ever painted, and the Bernini bust of the same. ⊠ *Via del Corso 305, Piazza di Spagna* ☎ *06/6797323* ⊕ *www.doriap-amphilj.it* 🎫 *€12* Ⓜ *Barberini.*

FAMILY
Fodor'sChoice ★ **The Spanish Steps.** That icon of postcard Rome, the Spanish Steps (often called simply *la scalinata,* or "the staircase," by Italians) and the Piazza di Spagna from which they ascend both get their names from the Spanish Embassy to the Vatican on the piazza—even though the staircase was built with French funds in 1723. In honor of a diplomatic visit by the king of Spain, the hillside was transformed by architect Francesco de Sanctis to link the church of Trinità dei Monti at the top with the Via dei Condotti below. In an allusion to the church, the staircase is divided by three landings (beautifully banked with azaleas from mid-April to mid-May). For centuries, the scalinata has welcomed tourists, dukes, and writers in search of inspiration—among them Stendhal, Honoré de Balzac, William Makepeace Thackeray, and Byron. Bookending the bottom of the steps are the 18th-century Keats-Shelley House and Babington's Tea Rooms, both beautifully redolent of the Grand Tour era. ⊠ *Piazza di Spagna* Ⓜ *Spagna.*

Fodor'sChoice ★ **Trevi Fountain.** An aquatic marvel in a city filled with them, the unique drama of the Fontana di Trevi is largely due to the site: its vast basin is squeezed into the tight meeting of three little streets (the *tre vie,* which may give the fountain its name) with cascades emerging as if from the wall of Palazzo Poli. The dazzling Baroque pyrotechnics—the sculpted seashells, the roaring sea beasts, the divalike mermaids—have been slyly incorporated in a stately triumphal arch. To ensure a return trip to the Eternal City, the famous legend has it that you should throw a coin into the fountain; the right way involves tossing it with your right hand over your left shoulder, with your back to the fountain.

One coin means you'll return to Rome; two, you'll return and fall in love; three, you'll return, find love, and marry. ⊠ *Piazza di Trevi, Piazza di Spagna* Ⓜ *Barberini.*

WORTH NOTING

Keats-Shelley Memorial House. Sent to Rome in a last-ditch attempt to treat his consumptive condition, English Romantic poet John Keats lived—and died—in this house at the foot of the Spanish Steps. At that point, this was the heart of the colorful bohemian quarter of Rome that was especially favored by the English. Keats had become celebrated through such poems as "Ode to a Nightingale" and "Endymion," but his trip to Rome was fruitless. He took his last breath here on February 23, 1821, at only 25, forevermore the epitome of the doomed poet. In this "Casina di Keats," you can visit his rooms, though all his furnishings were burned after his death, as a sanitary measure by the local authorities. You'll also find a rather quaint collection of memorabilia of English literary figures of the period—Lord Byron, Percy Bysshe Shelley, Joseph Severn, and Leigh Hunt, as well as Keats—and an exhaustive library of works on the Romantics. ⊠ *Piazza di Spagna 26, Piazza di Spagna* ☎ *06/6784235* ⊕ *www.keats-shelley-house.org* ✉ *€5* ⊘ *Closed Sun.* Ⓜ *Spagna.*

REPUBBLICA AND THE QUIRINALE

This sector of Rome stretches down from the 19th-century district built up around the Piazza della Repubblica—originally laid out to serve as a monumental foyer between the Termini train station and the rest of the city—and over the rest of the Quirinale. The highest of ancient Rome's famed seven hills, it's crowned by the massive Palazzo Quirinale, home to the popes until 1870 and now Italy's presidential palace. Along the way, you can see ancient Roman sculptures, early Christian churches, and highlights from the 16th and 17th centuries, when Rome was conquered by the Baroque—and by Bernini.

Although Bernini's work feels omnipresent in much of the city center, the Renaissance-man range of his work is particularly notable here. The artist as architect considered the church of Sant'Andrea al Quirinale one of his best; Bernini the urban designer and water worker is responsible for the muscle-bound sea god who blows his conch so provocatively in the fountain at the center of whirling Piazza Barberini. And Bernini the master gives religious passion a joltingly corporeal treatment in what is perhaps his greatest work, the *Ecstasy of St. Teresa,* in the church of Santa Maria della Vittoria.

GETTING HERE AND AROUND

Located between Termini station and the Spanish Steps, this area is about a 15-minute walk from either. Bus No. 40 will get you from Termini to the Quirinale in two stops; from the Vatican take Bus No. 64. The very busy and convenient Repubblica Metro stop is on the piazza of the same name.

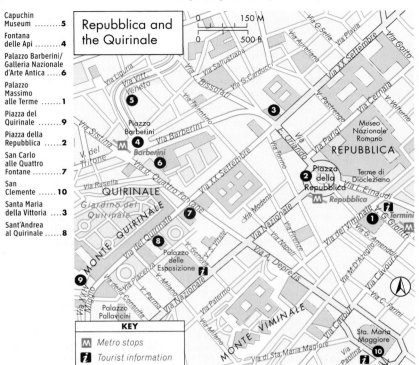

Repubblica and
the Quirinale

KEY

Ⓜ Metro stops

ℹ Tourist information

TOP ATTRACTIONS

Capuchin Museum. Devoted to teaching visitors about the Capuchin order, this museum is notable for a crypt visitable at the end of the museum circuit: not for the easily spooked, the crypt under the church of Santa Maria della Concezione holds the bones of some 4,000 dead Capuchin monks. With bones arranged in odd decorative designs around the shriveled and decayed skeletons of their kinsmen, a macabre reminder of the impermanence of earthly life, the crypt is strangely touching and beautiful. As one sign proclaims: "What you are, we once were. What we are, you someday will be." Upstairs in the church, the first chapel on the right contains Guido Reni's mid-17th-century *St. Michael Trampling the Devil*. The painting caused great scandal after an astute contemporary observer remarked that the face of the devil bore a surprising resemblance to the Pamphilj Pope Innocent X, archenemy of Reni's Barberini patrons. Compare the devil with the bust of the pope that you saw in the Palazzo Doria Pamphilj and judge for yourself. ⊠ *Via Veneto 27, Quirinale* ☎ *06/88803695* ⊕ *www.cappucciniviaveneto.it* 🎟 *€8.50* Ⓜ *Barberini.*

Fodor'sChoice
★

Palazzo Barberini/Galleria Nazionale d'Arte Antica. One of Rome's most splendid 17th-century palaces, the Palazzo Barberini is a landmark of the Roman Baroque style. Pope Urban VIII had acquired the property and given it to a nephew, who was determined to build an edifice worthy of his generous uncle and the ever-more-powerful Barberini clan. The result was, architecturally, a precedent-shattering affair: a "villa suburbana" set on what was then the edge of the city. The grand facade was designed by Carlo Maderno (aided by his nephew, Francesco Borromini), but when Maderno died, Borromini was passed over in favor of his great rival, Gianlorenzo Bernini.

Now home to the Galleria Nazionale d'Arte Antica, the palazzo holds a splendid collection that includes Raphael's *La Fornarina*, a luminous portrait of the artist's lover (a resident of Trastevere, she was reputedly a baker's daughter): study the bracelet on her upper arm bearing the artist's name. Also noteworthy are Guido Reni's portrait of the doomed *Beatrice Cenci* (beheaded in Rome for patricide in 1599)—Hawthorne called it "the saddest picture ever painted" in his Rome-based novel, *The Marble Faun*—and Caravaggio's dramatic *Judith and Holofernes*.

The showstopper here is the palace's Gran Salone, a vast ballroom with a ceiling painted in 1630 by the third (and too-often-neglected) master of the Roman Baroque, Pietro da Cortona. It depicts the *Glorification of Urban VIII's Reign* and has the spectacular conceit of glorifying Urban VIII as the agent of Divine Providence, escorted by a "bomber squadron" (to quote art historian Sir Michael Levey) of huge Barberini bees, the heraldic symbol of the family.

Palazzo Barberini is part of the family of museums that make up the Galleria Nazionale d'Arte, and the ticket is also valid for a visit to Palazzo Corsini in Trastevere during a 10-day period. Note that some rooms may be closed on Sundays. ⊠ *Via Barberini 18, Quirinale* ☎ *06/32810* ⊕ *www.galleriaborghese.it* 🎟 *€12, includes Palazzo Corsini* ⊘ *Closed Mon.* Ⓜ *Barberini; Bus Nos. 52, 56, 60, 95, 116, 175, and 492.*

Fodor'sChoice **Palazzo Massimo alle Terme.** Come here to get a real feel for ancient
★   Roman art—the collection rivals even the Vatican's. The Museo Nazionale Romano, with a collection ranging from striking classical Roman paintings to marble bric-a-brac, has four locations: Palazzo Altemps, Crypta Balbi, the Museo delle Terme di Diocleziano, and this, the Palazzo Massimo alle Terme. This vast structure holds the great ancient treasures of the archaeological collection and also the coin collection. Highlights include the Dying Niobid, the famous bronze Boxer, and the Discobolus Lancellotti. Pride of place goes, however, to the great ancient frescoes on view on the top floor, stunningly set up to "re-create" the look of the homes they once decorated. These include stuccoes and wall paintings found in the area of the Villa della Farnesina (in Trastevere) and the legendary frescoes from Empress Livia's villa at Prima Porta, delightful depictions of a garden in bloom and an orchard alive with birds. Their colors are remarkably well preserved. These delicate decorations covered the walls of cool, sunken rooms in Livia's summer house outside the city. ⊠ *Largo Villa Peretti 1, Repubblica* ☎ *06/39967700* ⊕ *www.coopculture.it* 🎟 *€10, or €13 for a combined ticket including access to Crypta Balbi, Museo delle Terme di Diocleziano, and Palazzo Altemps (valid for 3 days)* ⊘ *Closed Mon.* Ⓜ *Repubblica.*

2

Piazza del Quirinale. This strategic location atop the Quirinale has long been of great importance. It served as home of the Sabines in the 7th century BC—at that time, deadly enemies of the Romans, who lived on the Campidoglio and Palatino (all of 1 km [½ mile] away). Today, it's the foreground for the presidential residence, **Palazzo del Quirinale,** and home to the **Palazzo della Consulta,** where Italy's Constitutional Court sits. The open side of the piazza has an impressive vista over the rooftops and domes of central Rome and St. Peter's. The **Fontana di Montecavallo,** or Fontana dei Dioscuri, comprises a huge Roman statuary group and an obelisk from the tomb of the emperor Augustus. The group of the Dioscuri trying to tame two massive marble steeds was found in the Baths of Constantine, which occupied part of the summit of the Quirinale. Unlike just about every other ancient statue in Rome, this group survived the Dark Ages intact and accordingly became one of the city's great sights, especially during the Middle Ages. Next to the figures, the ancient obelisk from the Mausoleo di Augusto (Tomb of Augustus) was put here by Pope Pius VI at the end of the 18th century. ⊠ *Quirinale* Ⓜ *Barberini.*

Fodor'sChoice ★ **San Carlo alle Quattro Fontane.** Sometimes known as San Carlino because of its tiny size, this is one of Borromini's masterpieces. In a space no larger than the base of one of the piers of St. Peter's Basilica, he created a church that is an intricate exercise in geometric perfection, with a coffered dome that seems to float above the curves of the walls. Borromini's work is often bizarre, definitely intellectual, and intensely concerned with pure form. In San Carlo, he invented an original treatment of space that creates an effect of rippling movement, especially evident in the double-S curves of the facade. Characteristically, the interior decoration is subdued, in white stucco with no more than a few touches of gilding, so as not to distract from the form. Don't miss the cloister: a tiny, understated Baroque jewel, with a graceful portico and loggia above, echoing the lines of the church. ⊠ *Via del Quirinale 23, Quirinale* ☎ *06/4883109* ⊕ *www.sancarlino.eu* Ⓜ *Barberini.*

Fodor'sChoice ★ **San Clemente.** One of the most impressive archaeological sites in Rome, San Clemente is a historical triple-decker. A 12th-century church was built on top of a 4th-century church, which had been built over a 2nd-century pagan temple to the god Mithras and 1st-century Roman apartments. The layers were uncovered in 1857, when a curious prior, Friar Joseph Mullooly, started excavations beneath the present basilica. Today, you can descend to explore all three.

The **upper church** (at street level) is a gem in its own right. In the apse, a glittering 12th-century mosaic shows Jesus on a cross that turns into a living tree. Green acanthus leaves swirl and teem with small scenes of everyday life. Early Christian symbols, including doves, vines, and fish, decorate the 4th-century marble choir screens. In the left nave, the Castiglioni chapel holds frescoes painted around 1400 by the Florentine artist Masolino da Panicale (1383–1440), a key figure in the introduction of realism and one-point perspective into Renaissance painting. Note the large Crucifixion and scenes from the lives of Saints Catherine, Ambrose, and Christopher, plus the Annunciation (over the entrance).

To the right of the sacristy (and bookshop), descend the stairs to the **4th-century church,** used until 1084, when it was damaged beyond repair during a siege of the area by the Norman prince Robert Guiscard. Still intact are some vibrant 11th-century frescoes depicting stories from the life of St. Clement. Don't miss the last fresco on the left, in what used to be the central nave. It includes a particularly colorful quote—including "Go on, you sons of harlots, pull!"—that's not only unusual for a religious painting, but one of the earliest examples of written vernacular Italian.

Descend an additional set of stairs to the **mithraeum,** a shrine dedicated to the god Mithras. His cult spread from Persia and gained a foothold in Rome during the 2nd and 3rd centuries AD. Mithras was believed to have been born in a cave and was thus worshipped in cavernous, underground chambers, where initiates into the all-male cult would share a meal while reclining on stone couches, some visible here along with the altar block. Most such pagan shrines in Rome were destroyed by Christians, who often built churches over their remains, as happened here. ✉ *Via San Giovanni in Laterano 108, Celio* ☎ *06/7740021* ⊕ *www. basilicasanclemente.com* ⌨ *Archaeological area €10* Ⓜ *Colosseo.*

FodorśChoice
★
Santa Maria della Vittoria. Like the church of Santa Susanna across Piazza San Bernardo, this church was designed by Carlo Maderno, but this one is best known for Bernini's sumptuous Baroque decoration of the **Cappella Cornaro** (Cornaro Chapel, the last on the left as you face the altar), which houses his interpretation of divine love, the *Ecstasy of St. Teresa.* Your eye is drawn effortlessly from the frescoes on the ceiling down to the marble figures of the angel and the swooning saint to the earthly figures of the Cornaro family (some living, some dead at the time), who observe the scene from the opera boxes on either side, to the two inlays of marble skeletons in the pavement, representing the hope and despair of souls in purgatory.

As evinced in other works of the period, the theatricality of the chapel is the result of Bernini's masterly fusion of sculpture, light, architecture, painting, and relief; it's a multimedia extravaganza, and one of the key examples of the Roman High Baroque. Bernini's audacious conceit was to model the chapel as a theater. The members of the Cornaro family meditate on the communal vision of the great moment of divine love before them: the swooning saint's robes appear to be on fire, quivering with life, and the white marble group seems suspended in the heavens as golden rays illuminate the scene. An angel assists at the mystical moment of Teresa's vision as the saint abandons herself to the joys of heavenly love. Bernini represented this mystical experience in what, to modern eyes, may seem very earthly terms. Or, as the visiting French dignitary President de Brosses put it in the 18th century, "If this is divine love, I know all about it." No matter what your reaction, you'll have to admit it's great theater. ✉ *Via XX Settembre 17, Largo Santa Susanna, Repubblica* ☎ *06/42740571* ⊕ *www.chiesasantamariavittoriaroma.it* Ⓜ *Repubblica.*

FodorśChoice
★
Sant'Andrea al Quirinale. Designed by Bernini, this small church is one of the triumphs of the Roman Baroque period. His son wrote that Bernini considered it his best work and that he used to come here

occasionally, just to sit and contemplate. Bernini's simple oval plan, a classic form in Baroque architecture, is given drama and movement by the church's decoration, which carries the story of St. Andrew's martyrdom and ascension into heaven, starting with the painting over the high altar, up past the figure of the saint above, to the angels at the base of the lantern and the dove of the Holy Spirit that awaits on high. ⊠ *Via del Quirinale 29, Quirinale* ☎ *06/4740807* ⊕ *santandrea. gesuiti.it* ⊘ *Closed Mon.* Ⓜ *Barberini.*

WORTH NOTING

Fontana delle Api (*Fountain of the Bees*). Decorated with the famous heraldic bees of the Barberini family, the upper shell and the inscription are from a fountain that Bernini designed for Pope Urban VIII; the rest was lost when the fountain was moved to make way for a new street. The inscription was the cause of a considerable scandal when the fountain was first built in 1644. It said that the fountain had been erected in the 22nd year of the pontiff's reign, although in fact the 21st anniversary of Urban's election to the papacy was still some weeks away. The last numeral was hurriedly erased, but to no avail—Urban died eight days before the beginning of his 22nd year as pope. The superstitious Romans, who had immediately recognized the inscription as a foolhardy tempting of fate, were vindicated. ⊠ *Via Veneto, at Piazza Barberini, Quirinale* Ⓜ *Barberini.*

Piazza della Repubblica. Often the first view that spells "Rome" to weary travelers walking from Termini station, this round piazza was laid out in the late 1800s and follows the line of the caldarium of the vast ancient Terme di Diocleziano. At its center, the exuberant **Fontana delle Naiadi** (Fountain of the Naiads) teems with voluptuous bronze ladies happily wrestling with marine monsters. The nudes weren't there when the pope unveiled the fountain in 1870—sparing him any embarrassment—but when the figures were added in 1901, they caused a scandal. It's said that the sculptor, Mario Rutelli (grandfather of Francesco Rutelli, former mayor of Rome), modeled them on the ample figures of two musical-comedy stars of the day. The colonnades now house the luxe hotel Boscolo Exedra Roma, and a branch of foodie superstore Eataly. ⊠ *Repubblica* Ⓜ *Repubblica.*

VILLA BORGHESE AND PIAZZA DEL POPOLO

Touring Rome's artistic masterpieces while staying clear of its hustle and bustle can be, quite literally, a walk in the park. Some of the city's finest sights are tucked away in or next to green lawns and pedestrian piazzas, offering a breath of fresh air for weary sightseers, especially in the Villa Borghese park. One of Rome's largest, this park can alleviate gallery gout by offering an oasis in which to cool off under the ilex, oak, and umbrella pine trees. If you feel like a picnic, have an *alimentari* (food shop) make you some panini before you go; food carts within the park are overpriced.

GETTING HERE AND AROUND

The Metro stop for Piazza del Popolo is Flaminio on Line A. The Villa Giulia, the Galleria Nazionale d'Arte Moderna e Contemporanea, and the Bioparco in Villa Borghese are accessible from Via Flaminia, 1 km (½ mile) from Piazza del Popolo. Tram No. 19 and Bus No. 3 stop at each. Bus No. 119 connects Piazza del Popolo to Piazza Venezia. From the Colosseum, take No. 117 to Piazza del Popolo. Bus No. 116, starting near the Galleria Borghese, is the only bus that goes through the park.

TOP ATTRACTIONS

Fodor'sChoice ★ **Galleria Borghese.** The villa built for Cardinal Scipione Borghese in 1612 houses one of the finest collections of Baroque sculpture anywhere in the world. One of the most famous works in the collection is Canova's Neoclassical sculpture of Pauline Borghese as *Venus Victrix*. The next three rooms hold three key early Baroque sculptures: Bernini's *David*, *Apollo and Daphne*, and *Rape of Proserpina*. The Caravaggio Room houses works by this hotheaded genius; upstairs, the Pinacoteca (Picture Gallery) boasts paintings by Raphael (including his moving *Deposition*), Pinturicchio, Perugino, Bellini, and Rubens. Probably the gallery's most famous painting is Titian's allegorical *Sacred and Profane Love*, a mysterious and yet-unsolved image with two female figures, one nude, one clothed. ■ TIP→ Admission to the Galleria is by reservation only. Visitors are admitted in two-hour shifts 9–5. Prime-time slots can sell out days in advance, so in high season reserve directly through the Borghese's website. ⊠ *Piazza Scipione Borghese 5, off Via Pinciana, Villa Borghese* ☎ *06/32810 reservations, 06/8413979 info* ⊕ *www.galleriaborghese.it* ☜ *€15, including €2 reservation fee; increased fee during temporary exhibitions; audio guide €5* ⊗ *Closed Mon.; admission by reservation only* Ⓜ *Bus No. 910 from Piazza della Repubblica; Tram No. 19 or Bus No. 3 from Policlinico.*

MAXXI—Museo Nazionale delle Arti del XXI Secolo (*National Museum of 21st-Century Arts*). Designed by the late Anglo-Iraqi starchitect Zaha Hadid, this modern building plays with lots of natural light, curving and angular lines, and big open spaces, all meant to question the division between "within" and "without" (think glass ceilings and steel staircases that twist through the air). The MAXXI hosts temporary exhibitions of art, architecture, film, and more. The permanent collection, exhibited on a rotating basis, boasts more than 350 works from artists including Andy Warhol, Francesco Clemente, and Gerhard Richter. The pleasant café in the entrance courtyard is a favorite spot with local families. ⊠ *Via Guido Reni 4, Flaminio* ☎ *06/32810* ⊕ *www.maxxi.art* ☜ *€12* ⊗ *Closed Mon.* Ⓜ *Flaminio, then Tram No. 2 to Apollodoro; Bus Nos. 53, 217, 280, and 910.*

Fodor'sChoice ★ **Santa Maria del Popolo.** Standing inconspicuously in a corner of the vast Piazza del Popolo, this church often goes unnoticed, but the treasures inside make it a must for art lovers, as they include an entire chapel designed by Raphael and one adorned with two striking Caravaggio masterpieces. Bramante enlarged the apse of the church, which was rebuilt in the 15th century on the site of a much older place of worship. Inside, in the first chapel on the right, you'll see some frescoes by

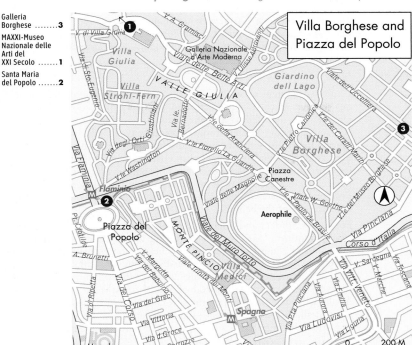

Pinturicchio from the mid-15th century; the adjacent **Cybo Chapel** is a 17th-century exercise in decorative marble. Raphael's famous **Chigi Chapel,** the second on the left, was built around 1513 and commissioned by the banker Agostino Chigi (who also had the artist decorate his home across the Tiber, the Villa Farnesina). Raphael provided the cartoons for the vault mosaic—showing God the Father in benediction—and the designs for the statues of Jonah and Elijah. More than a century later, Bernini added the oval medallions on the tombs and the statues of Daniel and Habakkuk, when, in the mid-17th century another Chigi, Pope Alexander VII, commissioned him to restore and decorate the building. The organ case by Bernini in the right transept bears the Della Rovere family oak tree, part of the Chigi family's coat of arms. Behind the main altar the **choir,** with vault frescoes by Pinturicchio, contains the handsome tombs of Ascanio Sforza and Girolamo della Rovere—both designed by Andrea Sansovino—and 16th-century stained glass, a rarity in central Italy. ■ **TIP→ To visit the choir ask at the information booth; entrance is free.** The best is for last: the **Cerasi Chapel,** to the left of the high altar, holds two Caravaggios: the *Crucifixion of St. Peter* and *Conversion of St. Paul.* Exuding drama and realism, both are key early Baroque works that show how "modern" 17th-century art can appear. Compare their style with the much more restrained and classically "pure" *Assumption of the Virgin* by Caravaggio's contemporary and rival, Annibale Carracci, which hangs over the altar of the chapel. ✉ *Piazza del Popolo 12, near Porta Pinciana, Piazza del Popolo* ☎ *06/3610836* ⊕ *www.santamariadelpopolo.it* Ⓜ *Flaminio.*

THE VATICAN

Climbing the steps to St. Peter's Basilica feels monumental, like a journey that has reached its climactic end. Suddenly, all is cool and dark… and you are dwarfed by the gargantuan nave and its magnificence. Above is a ceiling so high it must lead to heaven itself. Great, shining marble figures of saints frozen mid-whirl loom from niches and corners. And at the end, a throne for an unseen king whose greatness, it is implied, must mirror the greatness of his palace. For this basilica is a palace, the dazzling center of power for a king and a place of supplication for his subjects. Whether his kingdom is earthly or otherwise may lie in the eye of the beholder.

For good Catholics and sinners alike, the Vatican is an exercise in spirituality, requiring patience but delivering joy. Some come here for a transcendent glimpse of a heavenly Michelangelo fresco; others come in search of a direct connection with the divine. But what all visitors share, for a few hours, is an awe-inspiring landscape that offers a famous sight for every taste: rooms decorated by Raphael, antique sculptures like the Apollo Belvedere, famous paintings by Giotto and Bellini, and, perhaps most of all, the Sistine Chapel—for the lover of beauty, few places are as historically important as this epitome of faith and grandeur.

GETTING HERE AND AROUND

Metro stops Cipro or Ottaviano will get you within about a 10-minute walk of the entrance to the Musei Vaticani. Or, from Termini station, Bus No. 40 Express or the famously crowded No. 64 will take you to Piazza San Pietro. Both routes swing past Largo Argentina, where you can also get Bus No. 571 or 46.

A leisurely meander from the centro storico, across the exquisite Ponte Sant'Angelo, will take about a half hour.

TOP ATTRACTIONS

Fodor's Choice ★ **Basilica di San Pietro.** The world's largest church, built over the tomb of St. Peter, is the most imposing and breathtaking architectural achievement of the Renaissance (although much of the lavish interior dates to the Baroque). No fewer than five of Italy's greatest artists—Bramante, Raphael, Peruzzi, Antonio Sangallo the Younger, and Michelangelo—died while striving to erect this new St. Peter's. Highlights include the **Loggia delle Benedizioni** (Benediction Loggia), the balcony where newly elected popes are proclaimed; **Michelangelo's Pietà;** and Bernini's great bronze **Baldacchino,** a huge, spiral-columned canopy—at 100,000 pounds, perhaps the largest bronze object in the world—as well as many other Bernini masterpieces. There's also the collection of Vatican treasures in the **Museo Storico-Artistico e Tesoro,** and the **Grotte Vaticane** crypt. For views of both the dome above and the piazza below, take the elevator or stairs to the roof; those with more stamina (and without claustrophobia) can then head up more stairs to the apex of the dome. ■ TIP→ The Basilica is free to visit but a security check at the

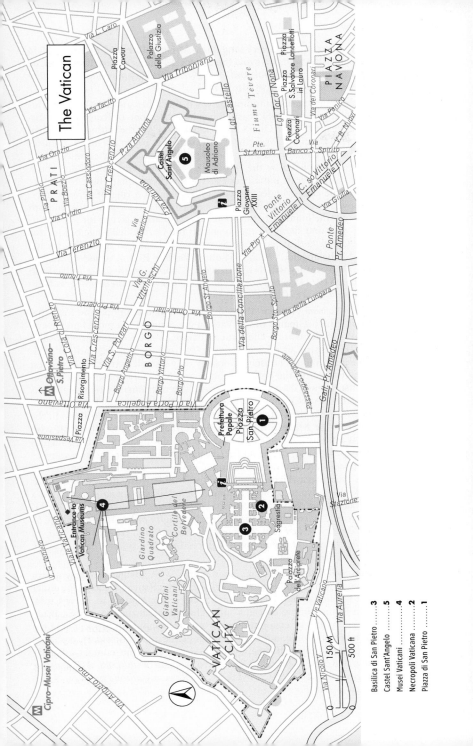

The Vatican

entrance can create very long lines. Arrive before 8:30 or after 5:30 to minimize the wait and avoid the crowds. ✉ *Piazza di San Pietro, Vatican* ⊘ *Closed during Papal Audience (Wed. until 1 pm) and during other ceremonies in piazza* Ⓜ *Ottaviano.*

FAMILY **Castel Sant'Angelo.** Standing between the Tiber and the Vatican, this circular and medieval "castle" has long been one of Rome's most distinctive landmarks. Opera lovers know it well as the setting for the final scene of Puccini's *Tosca*. In fact, the structure began life many centuries before as a mausoleum for the emperor Hadrian. Started in AD 135, it was completed by the emperor's successor, Antoninus Pius, about five years later. It initially consisted of a great square base topped by a marble-clad cylinder on which was planted a ring of cypress trees. Above them towered a gigantic statue of Hadrian. From the mid-6th century the building became a fortress, a place of refuge for popes during wars and sieges. In the rooms off the Cortile dell'Angelo, look for the Cappella di Papa Leone X (Chapel of Pope Leo X), with a facade by Michelangelo. The Sala Paolina (Pauline Room) was decorated in the 16th century with lavish frescoes. ✉ *Lungotevere Castello 50, Prati* ☎ *06/6819111 central line, 06/6896003 tickets* ⊕ *castelsantangelo.beniculturali.it* 🎟 *€10* Ⓜ *Lepanto.*

Fodor's Choice **Musei Vaticani** (*Vatican Museums*). Other than the pope and his papal
★ court, the occupants of the Vatican are some of the most famous artworks in the world. The **Vatican Palace**, residence of the popes since 1377, consists of an estimated 1,400 rooms, chapels, and galleries. The pope and his household occupy only a small part; most of the rest is given over to the Vatican Library and Museums. Beyond the glories of the Sistine Chapel, the collection is extraordinarily rich; highlights include the great antique sculptures (including the celebrated Apollo Belvedere in the **Octagonal Courtyard** and the Belvedere Torso in the **Hall of the Muses**); the **Stanzi de Raffaello** (Raphael Rooms), with their famous gorgeous frescoes; and the old master paintings, such as Leonardo da Vinci's beautiful (though unfinished) St. Jerome, some of Raphael's greatest creations, and Caravaggio's gigantic *Deposition* in the **Pinacoteca** (Picture Gallery). To avoid lengthy queues, book your ticket in advance online (⊕ *www.biglietteriamusei.vatican.va*) for a €4 surcharge. ✉ *Viale Vaticano, near intersection with Via Leone IV, Vatican* ⊕ *www.museivaticani.va* 🎟 *€21 with online reservations, €17 without; free last Sun. of month* ⊘ *Closed Sun. (except last Sun. of month) and church holidays* Ⓜ *Cipro–Musei Vaticani or Ottaviano–San Pietro. Bus No. 64 or 40.*

Necropoli Vaticana (*Vatican Necropolis*). With advance notice you can take a 1¼-hour guided tour in English of the Vatican Necropolis, under the Basilica di San Pietro, which gives a rare glimpse of Early Christian Roman burial customs and a closer look at the tomb of St. Peter. Apply by fax or email at least two months in advance, specifying the number of people in the group (all must be age 15 or older), preferred language, preferred time, available dates, and your contact information in Rome. ✉ *Piazza di San Pietro, Vatican* ☎ *06/69885318* ⊕ *www. vatican.va* 🎟 *€13* ⊘ *Closed Sun. and Roman Catholic holidays* Ⓜ *Ottaviano–San Pietro.*

Fodor's Choice **Piazza di San Pietro.** Mostly enclosed within high walls that recall the
★ papacy's stormy history, the Vatican opens the spectacular arms of Bernini's colonnade to embrace the world only at St. Peter's Square, scene
of the pope's public appearances. One of Bernini's most spectacular
masterpieces, the elliptical Piazza di San Pietro was completed in 1667
after only 11 years' work and holds about 100,000 people. Surrounded
by a pair of quadruple colonnades, it is gloriously studded with 140
statues of saints and martyrs. At the piazza's center, the 85-foot-high
Egyptian obelisk was brought to Rome by Caligula in AD 37 and moved
here in 1586 by Pope Sixtus V. The famous Vatican post offices (known
for fast handling of outgoing mail) can be found on both sides of St.
Peter's Square and inside the Vatican Museums complex. ■ TIP→ **The
main Information Office is just left of the basilica as you face it.** ✉ *West
end of Via della Conciliazione, Vatican* ☎ *06/69881662* Ⓜ *Cipro–Musei
Vaticani or Ottaviano–San Pietro.*

TRASTEVERE

Across the Tiber from the Jewish Ghetto is Trastevere (literally "across
the Tiber"), long cherished as Rome's Greenwich Village and now subject to rampant gentrification. In spite of this, Trastevere remains about
the most tightly knit community in the city, the Trasteverini proudly
proclaiming their descent from the ancient Romans. Ancient bridges—
the Ponte Fabricio and the Ponte Cestio—link Trastevere and the Ghetto
to the Isola Tiberina (Tiber Island), a diminutive sandbar and one of
Rome's most picturesque sights.

GETTING HERE AND AROUND
It's easy to get to Trastevere from Piazza Venezia: just take Tram No. 8
to the first stop on the other side of the river. You'll probably want to
head right to the Piazza di Santa Maria in Trastevere, the heart of this
lively area. Heading to the opposite side of Viale di Trastevere, though,
is a treat many tourists miss. The cobblestone streets around Piazza in
Piscinula and Via della Luce—locals peering down from balconies and
the smell of fresh-baked bread floating from bakeries—are much more
reminiscent of how Trastevere used to be than the touristic area to the
north. Either way, remember that many of Trastevere's lovely small
churches close, like others in Rome, in the afternoons. In the evenings,
the neighborhood heats up with locals and visitors alike, drinking, eating, and going for *passeggiate* (strolls)—a not-to-be-missed atmosphere,
especially for those with energy to burn.

TOP ATTRACTIONS
Isola Tiberina. It's easy to overlook this tiny island in the Tiber. Don't.
In terms of history and sheer loveliness, the charming Isola Tiberina—
shaped like a boat about to set sail—gets high marks.

Cross onto the island via Ponte Fabricio, constructed in 62 BC, Rome's
oldest remaining bridge; on the north side of the island crumbles the
romantic ruin of the Ponte Rotto (Broken Bridge), which dates back
to 179 BC. Descend the steps to the lovely river embankment to see
the island's claim to fame: a Roman relief of the intertwined-snakes
symbol of Aesculapius, the great god of healing. In 291 BC, a temple

Continued on page 92

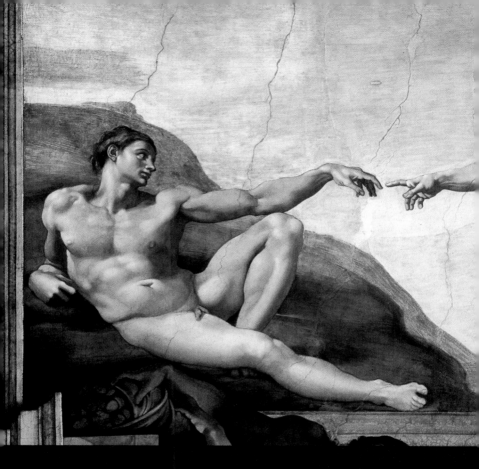

HEAVEN'S ABOVE:
THE SISTINE CEILING

Forming lines that are probably longer than those waiting to pass through the Pearly Gates, hordes of visitors arrive at the Sistine Chapel daily to view what may be the world's most sublime example of artistry:

Michelangelo: *The Creation of Adam*, Sistine Chapel, The Vatican, circa 1511.

Michelangelo's Sistine Ceiling. To paint this 12,000-square-foot barrel vault, it took four years, 343 frescoed figures, and a titanic battle of wits between the artist and Pope Julius II. While in its typical fashion, Hollywood focused on the element of agony, not ecstasy, involved in the saga of creation, a recently completed restoration of the ceiling has revolutionized our appreciation of the masterpiece of masterpieces.

By Martin Bennett

MICHELANGELO'S
MISSION IMPOSSIBLE

Designed to match the proportions of Solomon's Temple described in the Old Testament, the Sistine Chapel is named after Pope Sixtus VI, who commissioned it as a place of worship for himself and as the venue where new popes could be elected. Before Michelangelo, the barrel-vaulted ceiling was an expanse of azure fretted with golden stars. Then, in 1504, an ugly crack appeared. Bramante, the architect, managed do some patchwork using iron rods, but when signs of a fissure remained, the new Pope Julius II summoned Michelangelo to cover it with a fresco 135 feet long and 44 feet wide.

Taking in the entire span of the ceiling, the theme connecting the various participants in this painted universe could be said to be mankind's anguished waiting. The majestic panel depicting the Creation of Adam leads, through the stages of the Fall and the expulsion from Eden, to the tragedy of Noah found naked and mocked by his own sons; throughout all runs the underlying need for man's redemption. Witnessing all from the side and end walls, a chorus of ancient Prophets and Sibyls peer anxiously forward, awaiting the Redeemer who will come to save both the Jews and the Gentiles.

APOCALYPSE NOW

The sweetness and pathos of his Pietà, carved by Michelangelo only ten years earlier, have been left behind. The new work foretells an apocalypse, its congregation of doomed sinners facing the wrath of heaven through hanging, beheading, crucifixion, flood, and plague. Michelangelo, by nature a misanthrope, was already filled with visions of doom thanks to the fiery orations of Savonarola, whose thunderous preachments he had heard before leaving his hometown of Florence. Vasari, the 16th-century art historian, coined the word "terrabilità" to describe Michelangelo's tension-ridden style, a rare case of a single word being worth a thousand pictures.

Michelangelo wound up using a *Reader's Digest* condensed version of the stories from Genesis, with the dramatis personae overseen by a punitive and terrifying God. In real life, poor Michelangelo answered to a flesh-and-blood taskmaster who was almost as vengeful: Pope Julius II. Less vicar of Christ than latter-day Caesar, he was intent on uniting Italy under the power of the Vatican, and was eager to do so by any means, including riding into pitched battle. Yet this "warrior pope" considered his most formidable adversary to be Michelangelo. Applying a form of blackmail, Julius threatened to wage war on Michelangelo's Florence, to which the artist had fled after Julius canceled a commission for a grand papal tomb unless Michelangelo agreed to return to Rome and take up the task of painting the Sistine Chapel ceiling.

MICHELANGELO, SCULPTOR

A sculptor first and foremost, however, Michelangelo considered painting an inferior genre—"for rascals and sissies" as he put it. Second, there was the sheer scope of the task, leading Michelangelo to suspect he'd been set up by a rival, Bramante, chief architect of the new St. Peter's Basilica. As Michelangelo was also a master architect, he regarded this fresco commission as a Renaissance mission-impossible. Pope Julius's powerful will prevailed—and six years later the work of the Sistine Ceiling was complete. Irving Stone's famous novel *The Agony and the Ecstasy*—and the granitic 1965 film that followed—chart this epic battle between artist and pope.

THINGS ARE LOOKING UP

To enhance your viewing of the ceiling, bring along opera-glasses, binoculars, or just a mirror (to prevent your neck from becoming bent like Michelangelo's). Note that no photos are permitted. Insiders know the only time to get the chapel to yourself is during the papal blessings and public audiences held in St. Peter's Square. Failing that, get there during lunch hour. Admission and entry to the Sistine Chapel is only through the Musei Vaticani (Vatican Museums).

SCHEMATIC OF THE SISTINE CEILING

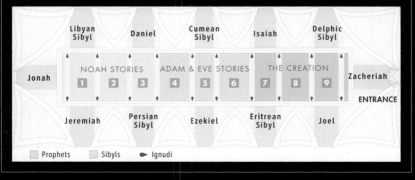

PAINTING THE BIBLE

The ceiling's biblical symbols were ideated by three Vatican theologians, Cardinal Alidosi, Egidio da Viterbo, and Giovanni Rafanelli, along with Mi-

chelangelo. As for the ceiling's painted "framework," this *quadratura* alludes to Roman triumphal arches because Pope Julius II was fond of mounting "triumphal entries" into his conquered cities (in imitation of Christ's

procession into Jerusalem on Palm Sunday).

THE CENTER PANELS

Prophet turned art-critic or, perhaps doubling as ourselves, the ideal viewer, Jonah the prophet (painted at the altar end) gazes up at the

Creation, or Michelangelo's version of it.

1 The first of three scenes taken from the Book of Genesis: God separates Light from Darkness.

2 God creates the sun and a craterless pre-Galilean moon

while the panel's other half offers an unprecedented rear view of the Almighty creating the vegetable world.

3 In the panel showing God separating the Waters from the Heavens, the Creator

tumbles towards us as in a self-made whirlwind.

4 Pausing for breath, next admire probably Western Art's most famous image—God giving life to Adam.

5 The Creation of Eve from Adam's rib leads to the sixth panel.

6 In a sort of diptych divided by the trunk of the Tree of Knowledge of Good and Evil, Michelangelo retells the Temptation and the Fall.

7 Illustrating Man's fallen nature, the last three panels narrate, in un-chronological order, the Flood. In the first Noah offers a pre-Flood sacrifice of thanks.

8 Damaged by an explosion in 1794, next comes Michel-

angelo's version of Flood itself.

9 Finally, above the monumental Jonah, you can just make out the small, wretched figure of Noah, lying drunk—in pose, the shrunken anti-type of the majestic Adam five panels down the wall.

THE CREATION OF ADAM

Michelangelo's Adam was partly inspired by the Creation scenes Michelangelo had studied in the sculpted doors of Jacopo della Quercia in Bologna and Lorenzo Ghiberti's Doors of Paradise in Florence. Yet in Michelangelo's version Adam's hand hangs limp, waiting God's touch to impart the spark of life. Facing his Creation, the Creator—looking a bit like the pagan god Jupiter—is for the first time ever depicted as horizontal, mirroring the Biblical "in his own likeness." Decades after its completion, a crack began to appear, amputating Adam's fingertips. Believe it or not, the most famous fingers in Western art are the handiwork, at least in part, of one Domenico Carnevale.

to Aesculapius was erected on the island. A ship had been sent to Epidaurus in Greece, heart of the cult of Aesculapius, to obtain a statue of the god. As the ship sailed back up the Tiber, a great serpent was seen escaping from it and swimming to the island—a sign that a temple to Aesculapius should be built here. In Imperial times, Romans sheathed the entire island with marble to make it look like Aesculapius's ship, replete with a towering obelisk as a mast. Amazingly, a fragment of the ancient sculpted ship's prow still exists. You can marvel at it on the downstream end of the embankment.

Today, medicine still reigns here. The island is home to the hospital of Fatebenefratelli (literally, "Do good, brothers"). Nearby is San Bartolomeo, built at the end of the 10th century by the Holy Roman Emperor Otto III and restored in the 18th century. Sometimes called the world's most beautiful movie theater, the open-air Cinema d'Isola di Tiberina operates from mid-June to early September as part of Rome's big summer festival, Estate Romana (⊕ *www.estateromana.comune.roma.it*). The 450-seat Arena unfolds its silver screen against the backdrop of the ancient Ponte Fabricio, while the 50-seat CineLab is set against Ponte Garibaldi facing Trastevere. Screenings usually start at 9:30 pm; admission is €6 for the Arena, €5 CineLab. Call ☎ 06/58333113 or go to ⊕ *isoladelcinema.com* for more information. Line up at the kiosk of La Grattachecca del 1915 (near the Ponte Cestio) for the most yum-ptious frozen ices in Rome. ⊠ *Trastevere ✛ Isola Tiberina can be accessed by Ponte Fabricio or Ponte Cestio.*

Fodor's Choice
★

Santa Cecilia in Trastevere. This basilica commemorates the aristocratic St. Cecilia, patron saint of musicians. One of ancient Rome's most celebrated Early Christian martyrs, she was most likely put to a supernaturally long death by the Emperor Diocletian just before the year AD 300. After an abortive attempt to suffocate her in the baths of her own house (a favorite means of quietly disposing of aristocrats in Roman days), she was brought before the executioner. But not even three blows of the executioner's sword could dispatch the young girl. She lingered for several days, converting others to the Christian cause, before finally dying. In 1595, her body was exhumed—it was said to look as fresh as if she still breathed—and the heart-wrenching sculpture by eyewitness Stefano Maderno that lies below the main altar was, the sculptor insisted, exactly how she looked. Time your visit to enter the cloistered convent to see what remains of Pietro Cavallini's *Last Judgment,* dating to 1293. It's the only major fresco in existence known to have been painted by Cavallini, a contemporary of Giotto. To visit the frescoes, ring the bell of the convent to the left of the church entrance. ⊠ *Piazza di Santa Cecilia in Trastevere 22, Trastevere* ☎ *06/5899289* ⊠ *Frescoes €2.50, underground €2.50* ⊗ *Access to frescoes closed in the afternoon.*

Fodor's Choice
★

Santa Maria in Trastevere. Originally built during the 4th century and rebuilt in the 12th century, this is one of Rome's oldest and grandest churches. It is also the earliest foundation of any Roman church to be dedicated to the Virgin Mary. With a nave framed by a processional of two rows of gigantic columns (22 in total) taken from the ancient Baths of Caracalla, and an apse studded with gilded mosaics, the interior conjures the splendor of ancient Rome better than any other in the

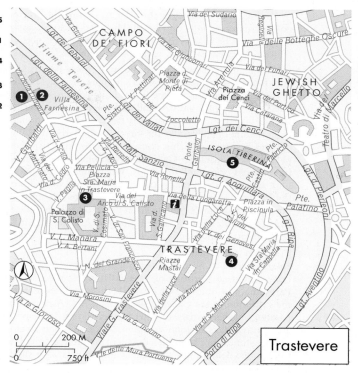

Trastevere

city. Overhead is Domenichino's gilded ceiling (1617). The 18th-century portico draws attention to the facade's 800-year-old mosaics, which represent the parable of the Wise and Foolish Virgins. They enhance the whole piazza, especially at night, when the church front and bell tower are illuminated. The church's most important mosaics, Pietro Cavallini's six panels of the *Life of the Virgin*, cover the semicircular apse. Note the building labeled "Taberna Meritoria" just under the figure of the Virgin in the Nativity scene, with a stream of oil flowing from it; it recalls the legend that a fountain of oil appeared on this spot, prophesying the birth of Christ. Off the piazza's northern side is a street called Via delle Fonte dell'Olio in honor of this miracle. ⊠ *Piazza Santa Maria in Trastevere, Trastevere* ☎ *06/5814802.*

Fodor'sChoice
★

Villa Farnesina. Money was no object to the extravagant Agostino Chigi, a banker from Siena who financed many papal projects. His munificence is evident in this elegant villa, built for him about 1511. He was especially proud of the decorative frescoes in the airy loggias, now glassed in to protect them. When Raphael could steal a little time from his work on the Vatican Stanze, he came over to execute some of the frescoes himself, notably a luminous *Triumph of Galatea*. In his villa, Agostino entertained the popes and princes of 16th-century Rome. He delighted in impressing his guests at alfresco suppers held in riverside pavilions by having his servants clear the table by casting the precious silver and gold dinnerware into the Tiber. (His extravagance was not quite so boundless as he wished to make it appear, however: nets were unfurled a foot or two beneath the water's surface to catch the valuable ware.)

In the magnificent **Loggia of Psyche** on the ground floor, Giulio Romano and others worked from Raphael's designs. Raphael's lovely *Galatea* is in the adjacent room. On the floor above you can see the trompe-l'oeil effects in the aptly named **Hall of Perspectives** by Peruzzi. Agostino Chigi's bedroom, next door, was frescoed by Il Sodoma with scenes from the life of Alexander the Great, notably the *Wedding of Alexander and Roxanne,* which is considered to be the artist's best work. The palace also houses the **Gabinetto Nazionale delle Stampe,** a treasure trove of old prints and drawings. When the Tiber embankments were built in 1879, the remains of a classical villa were discovered under the Farnesina gardens, and their decorations are now in the Museo Nazionale Romano's collections in Palazzo Massimo alle Terme. ⊠ *Via della Lungara 230, Trastevere* ☎ *06/68027268 info, 06/68027397 tour reservations* ⊕ *www.villafarnesina.it* ✉ *€6.*

WORTH NOTING

Palazzo Corsini. A brooding example of Baroque style, the palace (once home to Queen Christina of Sweden) is across the road from the Villa Farnesina and houses part of the 16th- and 17th-century sections of the collection of the Galleria Nazionale d'Arte Antica. Among the star paintings in this manageably sized collection are Rubens's *St. Sebastian* and Caravaggio's *St. John the Baptist.* Stop in if only to climb the 17th-century stone staircase, itself a drama of architectural shadows and sculptural voids. Behind, but separate from, the palazzo is the University of Rome's **Orto Botanico,** home to 3,500 species of plants, with various greenhouses around a stairway/fountain with 11 jets. ⊠ *Via della Lungara 10, Trastevere* ☎ *06/68802323 Galleria Corsini, 06/32810 Galleria Corsini tickets, 06/49912436 Orto Botanico* ⊕ *galleriacorsini.benicul-turali.it* ✉ *€12, including entrance to Palazzo Barberini* ⊘ *Closed Tues.*

VIA APPIA ANTICA

Far south of the Celio lies catacomb country—the haunts of the fabled underground graves of Rome's earliest Christians, arrayed to either side of the Queen of Roads, the Via Appia Antica (Appian Way). Strewn with classical ruins and dotted with grazing sheep, the road stirs images of chariots and legionnaires returning from imperial conquests. It was completed in 312 BC by Appius Claudius, who laid it out to connect Rome with settlements in the south, in the direction of Naples. Though time and vandals have taken their toll on the ancient relics along the road, the catacombs remain to cast their spirit-warm spell. Although Jews and pagans also used the catacombs, the Christians expanded the idea of underground burials to a massive scale. Persecution of Christians under pagan emperors made martyrs of many, whose bones, once interred underground, became objects of veneration. Today, the dark, gloomy catacombs contrast strongly with the Appia Antica's fresh air, verdant meadows, and evocative classical ruins.

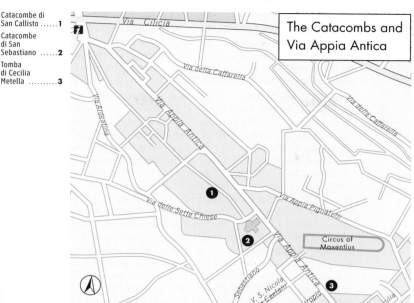

The Catacombs and
Via Appia Antica

Via Cilicia

Via della Caffarella

Via Ardeatina

Via Appia Antica

Via della Caffarella

Via delle Sette Chiese

Via Appia Pignatelli

Circus of
Maxentius

Via di Sebastiano

V. S. Nicola
de Caetani

V. Appia Antica

V. di Cecilia Metella

V. del Pagottropio

V. Capo di Bove

0   1/4 mile

0   400 meters

GETTING HERE AND AROUND

The initial stretch of the Via Appia Antica is not pedestrian-friendly—
there is fast, heavy traffic and no sidewalk all the way from Porta San
Sebastiano to the Catacombe di San Callisto. To reach the catacombs,
take Bus No. 218 from San Giovanni in Laterano. Alternatively, take
Metro Line A to Colli Albani and then Bus No. 660 to the Tomba di
Cecilia Metella. A more expensive option is the big, green Archeo-
bus from Piazza Venezia (Friday–Sunday, early June–early November
only); with an open-top deck, these buses allow you to hop on and off
as you please (€20 for 24 hours). Another attractive alternative is to
rent a bike—for example, at the Appia Antica Caffè near the Cecilia
Metella bus stop.

TOP ATTRACTIONS

Fodor'sChoice **Catacombe di San Sebastiano** (*Catacombs of St. Sebastian*). The 4th-cen-
★ tury church was named after the saint who was buried in the catacomb,
which burrows underground on four different levels. This was the only
early Christian cemetery to remain accessible during the Middle Ages,
and it was from here that the term *catacomb* is derived—it's in a spot
where the road dips into a hollow, known to the Romans as *catacumba*
(Greek for "near the hollow"). The Romans used the name to refer to
the cemetery that had existed here since the 2nd century BC, and it came

to be applied to all the underground cemeteries discovered in Rome in later centuries. As well as Christian burial areas, some very well preserved pagan mausolea were found here in the early 20th century, making this one of the more varied catacomb complexes in the area. ✉ *Via Appia Antica 136, Via Appia Antica* ☎ *06/7850350* ⊕ *www. catacombe.org* 🎫 *€8* ⊘ *Closed Sun.* Ⓜ *Bus No. 118, 218, or 660.*

Tomba di Cecilia Metella. For centuries, sightseers have flocked to this famous landmark, one of the most complete surviving tombs of ancient Rome. One of the many round mausoleums that once lined the Appian Way, this tomb is a smaller version of the Mausoleum of Augustus, but impressive nonetheless. It was the burial place of a Roman noblewoman: the wife of the son of Crassus, who was one of Julius Caesar's rivals and known as the richest man in the Roman Empire (infamously entering the English language as "crass"). The original decoration includes a frieze of bulls' skulls near the top. The travertine stone walls were made higher and the medieval-style crenellations were added when the tomb was transformed into a fortress by the Caetani family in the 14th century. An adjacent chamber houses a small museum of the area's geological phases. Entrance to this site also includes access to the splendid Villa dei Quintili, but you can get a super view without going in. ✉ *Via Appia Antica 162, Via Appia Antica* ☎ *06/39967700* ⊕ *www.archeoroma.beniculturali.it* 🎫 *€5, includes Villa dei Quintili (valid for 2 days)* ⊘ *Closed Mon.*

WORTH NOTING

Catacombe di San Callisto (*Catacombs of St. Calixtus*). Burial place of several very early popes, this is Rome's oldest and best-preserved underground cemetery. One of the (English-speaking) friars who act as custodians of the catacomb will guide you through its crypts and galleries, some adorned with early Christian frescoes. Watch out for wrong turns: this catacomb is five stories deep! ■ TIP→ **The large parking area means this is favored by large groups; it can get busy.** ✉ *Via Appia Antica 110/126, Via Appia Antica* ☎ *06/5310151* ⊕ *www.catacombe.roma.it* 🎫 *€8* ⊘ *Closed Wed., and mid-Jan.–Feb.* Ⓜ *Bus Nos. 118, 218.*

MONTI, CELIO, ESQUILINO, AND SAN LORENZO

Monti is the oldest *rione* (district) in Rome. Gladiators, prostitutes, and even Caesar made their homes in this area that stretches from Santa Maria Maggiore down to the Forum. Today, Monti is one of the best-loved neighborhoods in Rome, known for its appealing mix of medieval streets, old-school trattorias, and hip boutiques. Bordering it is **Celio**—named after the hill across from the Palatine and from the Colosseum—which has residential cobblestone streets, ancient churches, and some good authentic restaurants and wine bars. **Esquilino,** covering Rome's most sprawling hill—the Esquiline—lies at the edge of the tourist maps, near the Termini station. Today, culturally diverse inhabitants of different nationalities live and work in the area. It's not the cobblestone-street atmosphere that most think of when they think of Rome.

AVENTINO AND TESTACCIO

The **Aventino** district is somewhat rarefied, where some houses still have their own bell towers and private gardens are called "parks," without exaggeration. Like the emperors of old on the Palatine, the fortunate residents here look out over the Circus Maximus and the river, winding its way far below. **Testaccio** is perhaps the world's only district built on broken pots: the hill of the same name was born from discarded pottery used to store oil, wine, and other goods loaded from the nearby Ripa, when Rome had a port and the Tiber was once a mighty river to an empire. It's quiet during the day, but on Saturday buzzes with the loud music from rows of discos and clubs.

WHERE TO EAT

In Rome, the Eternal(ly culinarily conservative) City, simple yet traditional cuisine reigns supreme. Most chefs prefer to follow the mantra of freshness over fuss, and simplicity of flavor and preparation over complex cooking techniques.

Rome has been known since antiquity for its grand feasts and banquets, and dining out has always been a favorite Roman pastime. Until recently, the city's *buongustai* (gourmands) would have been the first to tell you that Rome is distinguished more by its enthusiasm for eating out than for a multitude of world-class restaurants—but this is changing. There is an ever-growing promotion of Slow Food practices, a focus on sustainably and locally sourced produce. The economic crisis has forced the food industry in Rome to adopt innovative ways to maintain a clientele who are increasingly looking to dine out but want to spend less. The result has been the rise of "street food" restaurants, selling everything from inexpensive and novel takes on classic *supplì* (Roman fried-rice balls) to sandwich shops that use a variety of organic ingredients.

Generally speaking, Romans like Roman food, and that's what you'll find in many of the city's trattorias and wine bars. For the most part, today's chefs cling to the traditional and excel at what has taken hundreds, sometimes thousands, of years to perfect. This is why the basic trattoria menu is more or less the same wherever you go. And it's why even the top Roman chefs feature their versions of simple trattoria classics like carbonara, and why those who attempt to offer it in a "deconstructed" or slightly varied will often come under criticism. To a great extent, Rome is still a town where the Italian equivalent of "What are you in the mood for?" still gets the answer, "Pizza or pasta."

	WHAT IT COSTS			
	$	$$	$$$	$$$$
At dinner	under €15	€15–€24	€25–€35	Over €35

Restaurant prices are the average cost of a main course at dinner or, if dinner is not served, at lunch.

Use the coordinate (✥ B2) at the end of each listing to locate a site on the Where to Eat in Rome map.

PIAZZA NAVONA AND THE CAMPO DE' FIORI

PIAZZA NAVONA

$$ ROMAN 🍴 **Armando al Pantheon.** In the shadow of the Pantheon, this small family-run trattoria, open since 1961, delights tourists and locals alike. There's an air of authenticity to the Roman staples here, and the quality of the ingredients and the cooking mean booking ahead is a must. **Known for:** traditional Roman cooking beautifully executed; spaghetti cacio e pepe; good wine list. [$] *Average main: €15* ✉ *Salita dei Crescenzi 31, Piazza Navona* ☎ *06/68803034* 🌐 *www.armandoalpantheon.it* 🕒 *Closed Sun., and Dec.–Jan. 6. No dinner Sat.* ✥ *1:E4.*

$ ITALIAN FAMILY 🍴 **Bar del Fico.** Everyone in Rome knows Bar del Fico, located right behind Piazza Navona, so if you're looking to hang out with the locals, this is the place to come for a drink or something to eat at any time of day or night. Just about every evening of the year, it's packed with people sipping cocktails in the square. **Known for:** outside tables in a pretty square; Italian-style brunch; buzzy atmosphere. [$] *Average main: €12* ✉ *Piazza de Fico 26, Piazza Navona* ☎ *06/68891373* 🌐 *www.bardelfico.com* ✥ *1:D4.*

$ CAFÉ 🍴 **Caffè Sant'Eustachio.** Frequented by tourists and government officials from the nearby Senate alike, this is considered by many to make Rome's best coffee. Take it at the counter Roman-style: servers are hidden behind a huge espresso machine, where they vigorously mix the sugar and coffee to protect their "secret method" for the perfectly prepared cup (if you want your caffè without sugar here, ask for it *amaro*). **Known for:** gran caffè (large sugared espresso); old-school Roman coffee bar vibe; '50s interior. [$] *Average main: €2* ✉ *Piazza Sant'Eustachio 82, Piazza Navona* ☎ *06/68802048* 🌐 *www.santeustachioilcaffe.it* ✥ *1:E4.*

$ WINE BAR Fodor's Choice ★ 🍴 **Cul de Sac.** This popular wine bar near Piazza Navona is among the city's oldest and offers a book-length selection of wines from Italy, France, the Americas, and elsewhere. Offering great value and pleasant service a stone's throw from Piazza Navona, it's open until 4 and from 6, making it a great spot for a late lunch or an early dinner when most restaurants aren't open. **Known for:** great wine list (and wine bottle–lined interior); eclectic Italian and Mediterranean fare; relaxed atmosphere and outside tables. [$] *Average main: €14* ✉ *Piazza Pasquino 73, Piazza Navona* ☎ *06/68801094* 🌐 *www.enotecaculdesacroma.it* ✥ *1:D4.*

$ ✕ **Etablì.** On a narrow *vicolo* (alley) off lovely cobblestone Piazza del
MEDITERRANEAN Fico, this multifunctional restaurant and lounge space is decorated
Fodor'sChoice according to what could be called a modern Italian farmhouse-chic aes-
★ thetic, with vaulted wood-beam ceilings, wrought-iron touches, plush
leather sofas, and chandeliers. The food is Mediterranean, with touches
of Asia in the raw-fish appetizers. **Known for:** popular after-dinner spot
for sipping; casually romantic boho-chic atmosphere; great location by
Piazza Navona. $ *Average main: €12* ⊠ *Vicolo delle Vacche 9/a, Piazza
Navona* ☎ *06/97616694* ⊕ *www.etabli.it* ✛ *1:D4.*

$$$$ ✕ **Il Convivio.** In a tiny, nondescript alley north of Piazza Navona, the
MODERN ITALIAN three Troiani brothers—Angelo in the kitchen, and brothers Giuseppe
Fodor'sChoice and Massimo presiding over the dining room and wine cellar—have
★ quietly been redefining the experience of Italian *alta cucina* (haute
cuisine) since 1990 at this well-regarded establishment. Service is
attentive without being overbearing, and the wine list is exceptional.
Known for: fine dining in elegant surroundings; inventive modern Italian cooking with exotic touches; amazing wine cellar and a great sommelier. $ *Average main: €40* ⊠ *Vicolo dei Soldati 31, Piazza Navona*
☎ *06/6869432* ⊕ *www.ilconviviotroiani.it* ☾ *Closed Sun., and 1 wk
in Aug. No lunch* ✛ *1:D3.*

$$ ✕ **La Ciambella.** The sprawling space is styled after American restau-
ITALIAN rants, with a lively bar in front, but the structure itself is all Roman,
with brick archways, high ceilings, and a skylight in one of the din-
ing rooms that allows guests to gaze at the fantastic Roman sky. The
emphasis here is on high-quality ingredients and classic Italian culi-
nary traditions. **Known for:** superb Pugliese burrata; thin-crust pizza;
grilled meats. $ *Average main: €17* ⊠ *Via dell'Arco della Ciambella 20,
Piazza Navona* ☎ *06/6832930* ⊕ *www.la-ciambella.it/en/la-ciambella*
☾ *Closed Sun. No lunch in Aug.* ✛ *1:E4.*

CAMPO DE' FIORI

$$ ✕ **Ditirambo.** Don't let the country-kitchen ambience fool you: at this
ITALIAN little spot off Campo de' Fiori, the constantly changing selection of
offbeat takes on Italian classics makes this a step beyond the ordinary. There are several good options for vegetarians. **Known for:** cozy
and casual atmosphere; hearty meat and pasta dishes; good vegetarian
options. $ *Average main: €16* ⊠ *Piazza della Cancelleria 74, Campo
de' Fiori* ☎ *06/6871626* ⊕ *www.ristoranteditirambo.it* ☾ *Closed Aug.
No lunch Mon.* ✛ *1:D4.*

$$ ✕ **Emma.** Opened by Rome's renowned family of bakers, the Rosciolis,
ROMAN this large, sleek, modern pizzeria is smack in the middle of the city,
FAMILY with the freshest produce right outside the door. The wine list features
Fodor'sChoice many local Lazio options. **Known for:** light and airy, casual atmosphere;
★ pancetta and chicory pizza; supplì (fried rice balls). $ *Average main:
€15* ⊠ *Via Monte della Farina 28–29, Campo de' Fiori* ☎ *06/64760475*
⊕ *www.emmapizzeria.com* ✛ *1:E4.*

$ ✕ **Filetti di Baccalà.** The window reads "Filetti di Baccalà," but the official
ITALIAN name of this small restaurant that specializes in one thing—deliciously
battered and deep-fried fillets of salt cod—is Dar Filettaro a Santa Bar-
bara. The location, down the street from Campo de' Fiori in a little
piazza in front of the beautiful Santa Barbara church, practically begs

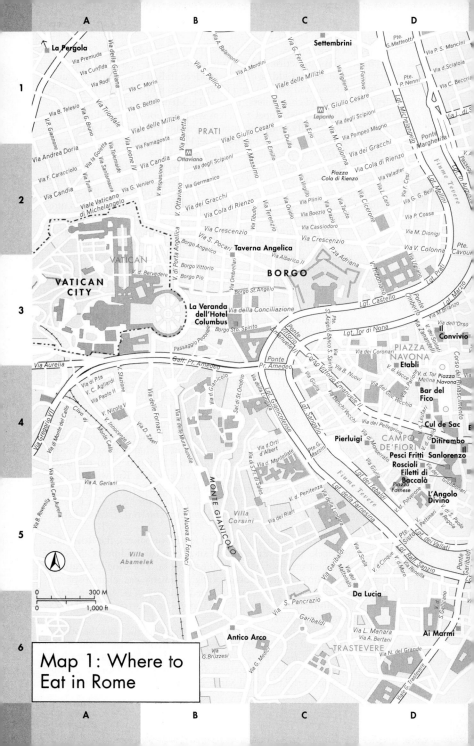

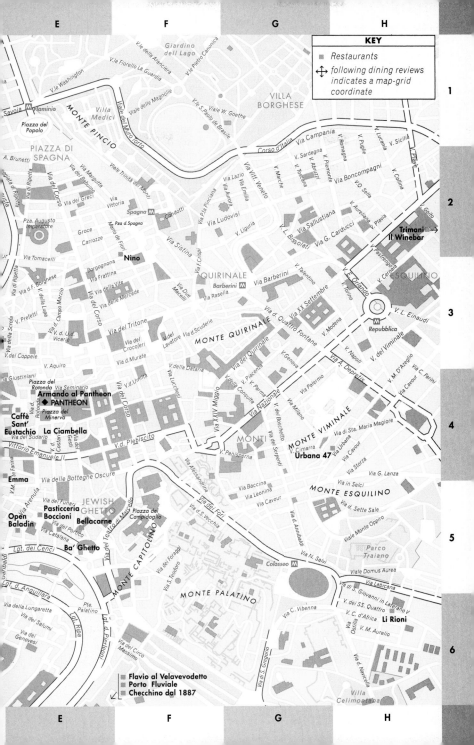

you to eat at one of the outdoor tables, where service is brusque. **Known for:** filetti di baccalà; functional "hole in the wall" interior; tables outside on the pretty square. $ *Average main: €12* ⊠ *Largo dei Librari 88, Campo de' Fiori* ☎ *06/6864018* ▤ *No credit cards* ⊘ *Closed Sun. and Aug. No lunch* ✛ *1:D5.*

$$$$
SEAFOOD
Fodor'sChoice
★

✕ **Il Sanlorenzo.** This gorgeous space, with its chandeliers and soaring original brickwork ceilings, houses one of the best seafood restaurants in the Eternal City. Order à la carte, or if you're hungry the eight-course tasting menu is extremely tempting—it might include the likes of cuttlefish-ink tagliatelle with mint, artichokes, and roe, or shrimp from the island of Ponza with rosemary, bitter herbs, and porcini mushrooms—and, given the quality of the fish, a relative bargain at €90. **Known for:** raw fish appetizer; spaghetti con ricci (sea urchins); elegant surroundings. $ *Average main: €36* ⊠ *Via dei Chiavari 4/5, Campo de' Fiori* ☎ *06/6865097* ⊕ *www.ilsanlorenzo.it* ⊘ *Closed 2 wks in Aug. No lunch Sat.–Mon.* ✛ *1:D4.*

$$
WINE BAR

✕ **L'Angolo Divino.** There's something about this cozy wine bar that feels as if it's in a small university town instead of a bustling metropolis. Serene blue-green walls lined with wooden shelves of wines from around the Italian peninsula add to the warm atmosphere, and the kitchen stays open until the wee hours on weekends. **Known for:** excellent wine selection and advice; cozy atmosphere; late-night snacks. $ *Average main: €15* ⊠ *Via dei Balestrari 12, Campo de' Fiori* ☎ *06/6864413* ⊕ *www. angolodivino.it* ⊘ *Closed 2 wks in Aug.* ✛ *1:D5.*

$
BURGER

✕ **Open Baladin.** The craft beer movement has taken hold in Italy, and this gorgeous, sprawling space down the road from Campo de' Fiori is headed up by the Baladin beer company. Staff members take their jobs—and brews—seriously, and they're helpful with recommendations from the more than 40 options on tap and the more than 100 bottles to choose from. **Known for:** great craft beer; hand-cut potato chips; plenty of burger and sandwich options. $ *Average main: €14* ⊠ *Via Degli Specchi 5–6, Campo de' Fiori* ☎ *06/6838989* ⊕ *www.baladin.it* ✛ *1:E5.*

$$
SOUTHERN
ITALIAN

✕ **Pesci Fritti.** This cute jewel box of a restaurant sits on the seating of the ancient Theatre of Pompey just behind Campo de' Fiori (note the curve of the street). Step inside, and the whitewashed walls with touches of pale sea blue will make you feel like you've escaped to the Mediterranean for seafood favorites. **Known for:** fried fish and seafood choices; spaghetti with clams; salted, cured fish roe. $ *Average main: €18* ⊠ *Via della Grottapinta 8, Campo de' Fiori* ☎ *06/68806170* ⊘ *Closed Mon. and Aug. No lunch* ✛ *1:D5.*

$$$
ITALIAN

✕ **Pierluigi.** This popular seafood restaurant is a fun spot on balmy summer evenings with tables out on the pretty Piazza de'Ricci. As at most Italian restaurants, fresh fish is sold per hg (100 grams, or about 3.5 ounces), so you may want to double-check the cost after it's been weighed. **Known for:** antipasto di pesce crudo (raw fish appetizer); spaghetti alle vongole (with clams); elegant atmosphere with great service. $ *Average main: €28* ⊠ *Piazza de Ricci 144, Campo de' Fiori* ☎ *06/6861302* ⊕ *www.pierluigi.it* ⊘ *Closed Mon.* ✛ *1:D4.*

$$ 🍴 **Roscioli.** The shop in front of this wine bar will beckon you in with top-quality comestibles like hand-sliced cured ham from Italy and Spain, more than 300 cheeses, and a dizzying array of wines—but venture further inside to try an extensive selection of unusual dishes and interesting takes on the classics. There are tables in the cozy wine cellar downstairs, but try and bag a table at the back on the ground floor (reserve well ahead; Roscioli is very popular). **Known for:** extensive wine list; arguably Rome's best spaghetti alla carbonara; best prosciutto in town. [$] *Average main: €22* ✉ *Via dei Giubbonari 21/22, Campo de' Fiori* ☎ *06/6875287* 🌐 *www.salumeriaroscioli.com/restaurant* 🕒 *Closed Sun., and 1 wk in Aug.* ✥ *1:D4.*

WINE BAR
Fodor's Choice ★

2

THE JEWISH GHETTO

$$ 🍴 **Ba' Ghetto.** This hot spot on the main promenade in the Jewish Ghetto has been going strong for years, with pleasant indoor and outdoor seating. The kitchen is kosher (many places featuring Roman Jewish fare are not) and serves meat dishes (so no dairy) both from the Roman tradition as well as from elsewhere in the Mediterranean; down the street is **Ba'Ghetto Milky** (*Via del Portico d'Ottavia 2/a*), the kosher dairy version of the original. **Known for:** carciofi alla giudia (deep-fried artichokes); dishes with couscous; salt cod with raisins and pine nuts. [$] *Average main: €22* ✉ *Via del Portico d'Ottavia 57, Jewish Ghetto* ☎ *06/68892868* 🌐 *www.kosherinrome.com* 🕒 *No dinner Fri. No lunch Sat.* ✥ *1:E5.*

ISRAELI
Fodor's Choice ★

$$ 🍴 **Bellacarne.** *Bellacarne* means "beautiful meat," and that's the focus of the menu here, though the double entendre is that it's also what a Jewish Italian grandmother might say while pinching her grandchild's cheek. The kosher kitchen makes its own pastrami, though the setting is definitely more fine-dining than deli. **Known for:** house-made pastrami; deep-fried artichokes; shawarma with hummus. [$] *Average main: €17* ✉ *Via Portico d'Ottavia 51, Jewish Ghetto* ☎ *06/6833104* 🌐 *www.bellacarne.it* 🕒 *No dinner Fri. No lunch Sat.* ✥ *1:E5.*

ROMAN

$ 🍴 **Pasticceria Boccione.** This tiny, old-school bakery is an institution in the Ghetto area and is famed for its Roman Jewish sweet specialties. Service is brusque, choices are few, what's available depends on the season, and when it's sold out, it's sold out. **Known for:** ricotta and cherry tarts; pizza ebraica ("Jewish pizza," a dense baked sweet rich in nuts and raisins); old-school bakery, so no frills and no seats. [$] *Average main: €4* ✉ *Via del Portico d'Ottavia 1, Jewish Ghetto* ☎ *06/6878637* 🕒 *Closed Sat.* ✥ *1:E5.*

BAKERY

PIAZZA DI SPAGNA

$$$ 🍴 **Nino.** A favorite among international journalists and the rich and famous for decades, Nino is Rome's best-loved dressed-up trattoria. The interior is country rustic *alla toscana,* and the menu accordingly sticks to the classics, featuring Roman and Tuscan staples. **Known for:** warm crostini spread with pâté; upscale old-school Italian; ribollita (Tuscan bean soup). [$] *Average main: €28* ✉ *Via Borgognona 11, Piazza di Spagna* ☎ *06/6786752* 🌐 *www.ristorantenino.it* 🕒 *Closed Sun. and Aug.* [M] *Spagna* ✥ *1:F2.*

ITALIAN
Fodor's Choice ★

REPUBBLICA

$$ ✕**Trimani Il Winebar.** This wine bar is run by the Trimani family of wine
WINE BAR merchants, whose shop next door has been in business for nearly two
centuries. Hot food is served at lunch and dinner in the minimalist inte-
rior, and it is also perfect for an aperitif or an early supper (it opens for
evening service at 5:30). **Known for:** candlelit second floor for sipping;
torte salate (savory tarts); historical wineshop around corner. $ *Aver-
age main: €15* ✉ *Via Cernaia 37/b, Repubblica* ☏ *06/4469630* ⊕ *www.
trimani.com* ⊘ *Closed Sun. and Aug.* Ⓜ *Castro Pretorio* ✣ *1:H2.*

AROUND THE VATICAN

$$$ ✕**La Veranda dell'Hotel Columbus.** Deciding where to sit at La Veranda
ROMAN isn't easy, because both the shady courtyard (torchlit at night), and
Fodor's Choice the elegant frescoed dining room are among Rome's most spectacular
★ settings. While La Veranda is known for classic Roman cuisine, many
of the seasonal dishes are served with refreshing twists on the familiar, and the cold cuts and bread come from the famed Roscioli store.
Known for: notable frescoed interior; spaghetti alla carbonara; beef
tartare. $ *Average main: €25* ✉ *Hotel Columbus, Borgo Santo Spirito
73, Borgo* ☏ *06/6872973* ⊘ *Closed Mon. No lunch* ✣ *1:B3.*

$$ ✕**Settembrini.** The modern, intimate dining room here hints at what
MODERN ITALIAN to expect from the kitchen and staff: elegant and restrained cooking,
Fodor's Choice friendly yet unobtrusive service, and an interesting and well-curated
★ wine list. There's also a sister café just round the corner at Piazza Mar-
tiri del Belfiore 12; between them something is always open from 7
am until 1 am, perfect for lunch or dinner, or simply a coffee break,
afternoon tea, or a snack after a visit to the Vatican. **Known for:** creative
twists on classic Italian ingredients; neighborhood gem; handy sister
café nearby. $ *Average main: €20* ✉ *Via Luigi Settembrini 21, Prati*
☏ *06/3232617* ⊕ *www.viasettembrini.com* ⊘ *Closed 2 wks in Aug.*
Ⓜ *Lepanto* ✣ *1:C1.*

$$ ✕**Taverna Angelica.** The Borgo area near St. Peter's Basilica hasn't been
MODERN ITALIAN known for culinary excellence, but this is starting to change, and Tav-
erna Angelica was one of the first refined restaurants in this part of
town. The dining room is small, which allows the chef to create a
menu that's inventive without being pretentious. **Known for:** eclectic
Italian dishes; elegant surroundings; tiramisù with amaretti biscuits.
$ *Average main: €22* ✉ *Piazza A. Capponi 6, Borgo* ☏ *06/6874514*
⊕ *www.tavernaangelica.it* ⊘ *Closed 2 wks in Aug. No lunch Mon.–Sat.*
Ⓜ *Ottaviano* ✣ *1:B3.*

TRASTEVERE

$ ✕**Ai Marmi** (*Panattoni*). The official name of this popular pizzeria is Pan-
PIZZA attoni, but everyone calls it "Ai Marmi" or "L'Obitorio" (the morgue)
FAMILY for its marble-slab tables. Contrary to what that might imply, this place
is actually about as lively as it gets—indeed, it's packed pretty much
every night, with diners munching on crisp pizzas that come out of the
wood-burning ovens at top speed. **Known for:** excellent wood-oven

pizzas; fried starts such as supplì (breaded fried rice balls); open until midnight for a late-night bite. [$] *Average main: €12* ⊠ *Viale Trastevere 53–57, Trastevere* ☎ *06/5800919* ⊘ *Closed Wed., and 3 wks in Aug. No lunch* ✛ *1:D6.*

$$$
MODERN ITALIAN
Fodor'sChoice
★

✕ **Antico Arco.** Founded by three friends with a passion for wine and fine food, Antico Arco attracts foodies from Rome and beyond with its refined culinary inventiveness. The location on top of the Janiculum Hill makes for a charming setting, and inside, the dining rooms are plush, modern spaces, with whitewashed brick walls, dark floors, and black velvet chairs. **Known for:** changing seasonal menu; inventive cooking (and a great molten chocolate cake); open noon until midnight daily. [$] *Average main: €28* ⊠ *Piazzale Aurelio 7, Trastevere* ☎ *06/5815274* ⊕ *www.anticoarco.it* ✛ *1:B6.*

$
ROMAN

✕ **Da Lucia.** There's no shortage of old-school trattorias in Trastevere, but Da Lucia has a strong following among them. Both locals and expats enjoy the brusque but "authentic" service and the hearty Roman fare; snag a table outside in warm weather for the true Roman experience of cobblestone-terrace dining. **Known for:** bombolotti (a tubular pasta) all'amatriciana; spaghetti cacio e pepe; beef rolls (involtini). [$] *Average main: €14* ⊠ *Vicolo del Mattonato 2b, Trastevere* ☎ *06/5803601* ⊘ *Closed Mon. and Aug.* ✛ *1:C5.*

MONTI, CELIO, AND ESQUILINO

MONTI

$$
MODERN ITALIAN
Fodor'sChoice
★

✕ **Urbana 47.** This restaurant serving breakfast through dinner embodies the *kilometro zero* concept, highlighting hyper-local food from the surrounding Lazio region. The local boho crowd comes in the morning for a continental or "American" breakfast (with free Wi-Fi); lunch means tasty "fast slow-food" options like grain salads and healthy panini as well as a few more substantial dishes, with a more extensive menu for dinner. **Known for:** healthy lunch options; aperitivo and tapas; hyper-local produce. [$] *Average main: €15* ⊠ *Via Urbana 47, Monti* ☎ *06/47884006* ⊕ *www.urbana47.it* Ⓜ *Cavour* ✛ *1:G4.*

ESQUILINO

$
PIZZA
FAMILY

✕ **Li Rioni.** This busy pizzeria conveniently close to the Colosseum has been serving real-deal Roman-style pizza—super thin and cooked to a crisp—since the mid-1980s. The magic might be due to the fact that they let their pizza dough rise 24–48 hours before baking to guarantee an extra-light pizza, said to be more easily digested than others. **Known for:** olive ascolane (fried, breaded olives stuffed with sausage); pizza Napoli; pizza Margherita. [$] *Average main: €12* ⊠ *Via dei Santi Quattro 24, Esquilino* ☎ *06/70450605* ⊕ *www.lirioni.it* ⊘ *Closed 2 wks in Aug. No lunch* Ⓜ *Colosseo* ✛ *1:H6.*

TESTACCIO

$$
ROMAN

✕ **Checchino dal 1887.** Literally carved out of a hill of ancient shards of amphorae, Checchino is an example of a classic, upscale, family-run Roman restaurant, with one of the best wine cellars in the region.

Although the slaughterhouses of Testaccio are long gone, their echo carries on in the restaurant's classic offal dishes (though there other options). **Known for:** old-school Roman cooking; old-school Roman waiters; coda alla vaccinara (Roman-style oxtail). $ *Average main: €23* ⊠ *Via di Monte Testaccio 30, Testaccio* 🕾 *06/5746318* ⊕ *www. checchino-dal-1887.com* ⊘ *Closed Mon., Aug., and 1 wk at Christmas. No dinner Sun.* Ⓜ *Piramide* ✛ *1:F6*.

$$
ROMAN
Fodor'sChoice
★

✕ **Flavio al Velavevodetto.** It's everything you're looking for in a true Roman eating experience: authentic, in a historic setting, and filled with Italians eating good food at good prices. In this very *romani di Roma* working-class neighborhood, surrounded by discos and bars sharing Monte Testaccio, you can enjoy a meal of classic Roman dishes from vegetable antipasto through cacio e pepe and lamb chops. **Known for:** authentic Roman atmosphere and food; outdoor covered terrace in summer; polpette di bollito (fried breaded meatballs). $ *Average main: €16* ⊠ *Via di Monte Testaccio 97, Testaccio* 🕾 *06/5744194* ⊕ *www. ristorantevelavevodetto.it* Ⓜ *Piramide* ✛ *1:F6*.

$
ITALIAN

✕ **Porto Fluviale.** This massive structure is on a stretch of street that's gone from gritty clubland to popular nightspot, thanks largely to Porto Fluviale, which has come to mean all things to all people: bar, café, pizzeria, lunch buffet, and lively evening restaurant. The food, too, is all-encompassing, featuring cuisine from all over Italy. **Known for:** good cocktails; pizza from wood-burning oven; cicchetti (Venetian-style tapas). $ *Average main: €14* ⊠ *Via del Porto Fluviale 22, Testaccio* 🕾 *06/5743199* ⊕ *www.portofluviale.com* Ⓜ *Piramide* ✛ *1:F6*.

MONTE MARIO

$$$$
MODERN ITALIAN
Fodor'sChoice
★

✕ **La Pergola.** Dinner here is a truly spectacular and romantic event, with incomparable views across the city matched by a stellar dining experience that includes top-notch service as well as sublimely inventive fare. The difficulty comes in choosing from among Chef Heinz Beck's alta cucina specialties. **Known for:** excitingly inventive Italian cuisine; extraordinary city views from rooftop windows; fagotelli carbonara. $ *Average main: €65* ⊠ *Rome Cavalieri, A Waldorf Astoria Resort, Via Alberto Cadlolo 101, Monte Mario* 🕾 *06/35092152* ⊕ *www.romecava-lieri.com/lapergola.php* ⊘ *Closed Sun. and Mon., 3 wks in Aug., and most of Jan. No lunch* 🏛 *Jacket and tie* ✛ *1:A1*.

WHERE TO STAY

It's the click of your heels on inlaid marble, the whisper of 600-thread-count Frette sheets, the murmured *buongiorno* of a coat-tailed porter bowing low as you pass. It's a rustic attic room with a wood-beam ceiling, a white umbrella on a roof terrace, a 400-year-old palazzo. Maybe it's birdsong pouring into your room as you swing open French windows to a sun-kissed view of the Colosseum, a timeworn piazza, or a flower-filled marketplace.

When it comes to accommodations, Rome offers a wide selection of high-end hotels, bed-and-breakfasts, designer boutique hotels—options that run the gamut from whimsical to luxurious. Whether you want a simple place to rest your head or a complete cache of exclusive amenities, you have plenty to choose from. *Hotel reviews have been shortened. For full information, visit Fodors.com.*

2

WHAT IT COSTS				
	$	$$	$$$	$$$$
For two people	under €125	€125–€200	€201–€300	over €300

Prices are for a standard double room in high season.

Use the coordinate (✣ B2) at the end of each listing to locate a site on the Where to Stay in Rome map.

PIAZZA NAVONA AND THE CAMPO DE' FIORI

PIAZZA NAVONA

$$$ HOTEL Fodor's Choice ★ 🏨 **Albergo Santa Chiara.** If you're looking for a good location and top-notch service at great rates—not to mention comfortable beds and a quiet stay—look no further than this historic hotel, run by the same family for some 200 years. **Pros:** great location near the Pantheon; free Wi-Fi; lovely terrace/sitting area in front, overlooking the piazza. **Cons:** some rooms are on the small side and need updating; breakfast selection isn't always the best; Wi-Fi can be slow. [$] *Rooms from: €270* ✉ *Via Santa Chiara 21, Piazza Navona* ☎ *06/6872979* 🌐 *www.albergosantachiara.com* 🛏 *102 rooms* 🍴 *Free Breakfast* [M] *Spagna* ✣ *2:E4.*

$$ HOTEL 🏨 **Hotel Genio.** Just outside one of Rome's most beautiful piazzas—Piazza Navona—this pleasant hotel has a lovely rooftop terrace perfect for enjoying a cappuccino or a glass of wine while taking in the view. **Pros:** friendly staff; breakfast buffet is abundant; free Wi-Fi; spacious, elegant bathrooms. **Cons:** rooms facing the street can be noisy; spotty Internet; beds can be too firm for some. [$] *Rooms from: €160* ✉ *Via Giuseppe Zanardelli 28, Piazza Navona* ☎ *06/6833781* 🌐 *www.hotelgenioroma.it* 🛏 *60 rooms* 🍴 *Free Breakfast* [M] *Spagna* ✣ *2:D3.*

$$$ HOTEL 🏨 **Relais Palazzo Taverna.** This little hidden gem on a side street behind the lovely Via dei Coronari is a good compromise for those looking for boutique-style accommodations on a budget. **Pros:** centrally located; spacious boutique-style accommodations at moderate prices; free Wi-Fi; friendly, responsive staff. **Cons:** staff on duty until 11 pm (can be contacted after-hours in an emergency); some rooms are starting to show wear and tear. [$] *Rooms from: €210* ✉ *Via dei Gabrielli 92, Piazza Navona* ☎ *06/20398064* 🌐 *www.relaispalazzotaverna.com* 🛏 *11 rooms* 🍴 *Free Breakfast* [M] *Spagna* ✣ *2:D3.*

CAMPO DE' FIORI

$$ HOTEL 🏨 **Albergo del Sole al Biscione.** This affordable and comfortable hotel, centrally located just off Campo de' Fiori and built atop the ruins of the ancient Theatre of Pompey, has warm, cozy decor and a rooftop terrace with a stunning view of Sant'Andrea delle Valle. **Pros:** parking garage in the hotel; reasonable rates for the location; nice rooftop terrace. **Cons:** some rooms are small and lack a/c; no elevator at the entrance of hotel;

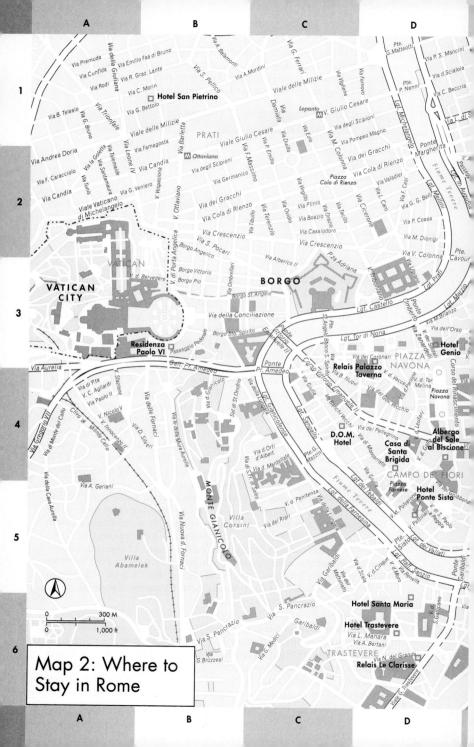

Map 2: Where to Stay in Rome

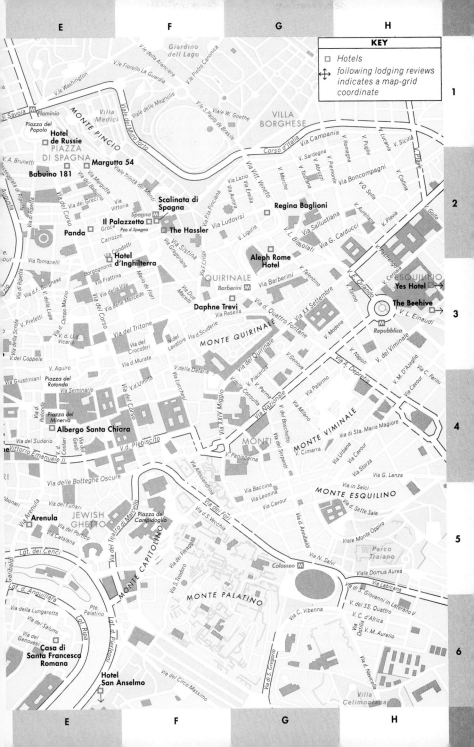

area can be a bit noisy. $\boxed{S}$ *Rooms from: €180* ⊠ *Via del Biscione 76, Campo de' Fiori* ☎ *06/68806873* ⊕ *www.soalbiscione.it* ↘ *59 rooms* ❍❘ *No meals* Ⓜ *Barberini* ✛ *2:D4.*

$$$ **Casa di Santa Brigida.** The friendly sisters of Santa Brigida oversee
B&B/INN simple, straightforward, and centrally located accommodations in
Fodor'sChoice one of Rome's loveliest convents, with a rooftop terrace overlooking
★ Palazzo Farnese. **Pros:** no curfew in this historic convent; insider papal tickets; large library and sunroof; free Wi-Fi. **Cons:** weak a/c; no TVs in the rooms (though there is a common TV room); not equipped for guests with disabilities; far from a Metro stop. $\boxed{S}$ *Rooms from: €210* ⊠ *Piazza Farnese 96, entrance around the corner at Via Monserrato 54, Campo de' Fiori* ☎ *06/68892596* ⊕ *www.brigidine.org* ↘ *20 rooms* ❍❘ *Free Breakfast* ✛ *2:D4.*

$$$$ **D.O.M. Hotel.** In an old convent on Via Giulia, one of Rome's romantic
HOTEL ivy-covered streets, the D.O.M. (Deo Optimo Maximo) is an ultrachic luxury hotel that resembles an aristocratic *casa nobile.* **Pros:** complimentary Aqua di Parma toiletries; heated towel racks; hip decor. **Cons:** an armed guard at the anti-terrorism headquarters opposite the hotel may be off-putting to some; delicious but expensive cocktails; standard rooms are small for a five-star hotel. $\boxed{S}$ *Rooms from: €380* ⊠ *Via Giulia 131, Campo de' Fiori* ☎ *06/6832144* ⊕ *www.domhotelroma.com* ↘ *18 rooms* ❍❘ *Free Breakfast* ✛ *2:C4.*

$$$ **Hotel Ponte Sisto.** Situated in a restored Renaissance palazzo with one
HOTEL of the prettiest patio-courtyards in Rome, this hotel is a relaxing retreat
Fodor'sChoice close to Trastevere and Campo de' Fiori. **Pros:** friendly staff; rooms
★ with views (and some with balconies and terraces); luxury bathrooms; beautiful courtyard garden. **Cons:** street-side rooms can be a bit noisy; some upgraded rooms are small and not worth the price difference; carpets starting to show signs of wear; aside from breakfast, restaurant caters only to groups and must be booked in advance. $\boxed{S}$ *Rooms from: €260* ⊠ *Via dei Pettinari 64, Campo de' Fiori* ☎ *06/6863100* ⊕ *www.hotelpontesisto.it* ↘ *107 rooms* ❍❘ *Free Breakfast* ✛ *2:D5.*

JEWISH GHETTO

$$ **Arenula.** This hotel is known for no-frills bargain accommodations
HOTEL in the center of Rome with especially good deals off season, when a double room can be as little as €70. **Pros:** a real bargain; conveniently located, near Campo de' Fiori and Trastevere; spotless. **Cons:** totally no-frills accommodations; no elevator; breakfast is nothing to write home about. $\boxed{S}$ *Rooms from: €200* ⊠ *Via Santa Maria dei Calderari 47, off Via Arenula, Jewish Ghetto* ☎ *06/6879454* ⊕ *www.hotelarenula.secure-booking-online.com* ↘ *50 rooms* ❍❘ *Free Breakfast* ✛ *2:E5.*

PIAZZA DI SPAGNA AND PIAZZA DEL POPOLO

$$$$ **Aleph Rome Hotel.** If you're wondering where to find the beautiful
HOTEL people, look no further than the Aleph, the most unfalteringly fash-
Fodor'sChoice ionable of Rome's luxury hotels. **Pros:** free access to the spa for hotel
★ guests; award-winning design; free Wi-Fi. **Cons:** rooms are too petite for the price; although the terrace is huge, the views aren't of Rome's

most flattering side; buffet breakfast not included. $ *Rooms from: €380* ✉ *Via San Basilio 15, Piazza di Spagna* ☎ *06/422901* ⊕ *alephrome.com* 🛏 *96 rooms* ⦿ *No meals* Ⓜ *Barberini* ✛ *2:G2*.

$$$$ 🏨 **Babuino 181.** On chic via del Babuino, known for its high-end bou-
HOTEL tiques and antiques shops, this discreet and stylish hotel is an ideal Roman pied à terre that has spacious rooms spread over two historic buildings. **Pros:** spacious suites; luxury Frette linens; iPhone docks and other handy in-room amenities. **Cons:** rooms can be a bit noisy; break-fast is nothing special. $ *Rooms from: €350* ✉ *Via Babuino 181, Piazza di Spagna* ☎ *06/32295295* ⊕ *www.romeluxurysuites.com/babuino* 🛏 *24 rooms* ⦿ *No meals* Ⓜ *Flaminio, Spagna* ✛ *2:E2*.

$$ 🏨 **Daphne Trevi.** This urban B&B is run by people who love Rome and
B&B/INN want to make sure you do, too—the staff will happily act as your personal travel planners, helping you map out destinations, plan day trips, choose restaurants, and organize transportation. **Pros:** kosher, gluten-free, and vegetarian breakfast options; friendly, helpful staff; beds have Simmons mattresses and fluffy comforters; free Wi-Fi. **Cons:** no TVs; two rooms share a bathroom. $ *Rooms from: €170* ✉ *Via degli Avignonesi 20, Piazza di Spagna* ☎ *06/89345781* ⊕ *www.daphne-rome. com* 🛏 *10 rooms* ⦿ *Free Breakfast* Ⓜ *Barberini* ✛ *2:G3*.

$$$$ 🏨 **The Hassler.** When it comes to million-dollar views, the best place
HOTEL to stay in the whole city is the Hassler. **Pros:** exclusive toiletries from
Fodor's Choice the hotel spa, Amorvero; prime location and panoramic views; stun-
★ ning rooms. **Cons:** VIP rates (10% V.A.T. not included); breakfast not included (continental option is €29 plus 10% V.A.T. per person). $ *Rooms from: €600* ✉ *Piazza Trinità dei Monti 6, Piazza di Spagna* ☎ *06/699340, 800/223–6800 from U.S.* ⊕ *www.hotelhasslerroma.com* 🛏 *96 rooms* ⦿ *No meals* Ⓜ *Spagna* ✛ *2:F2*.

$$$$ 🏨 **Hotel d'Inghilterra.** Situated in a 17th-century guesthouse and founded
HOTEL in 1845, Hotel D'Inghilterra has a long, storied history: it has been used as an aristocratic residence for visitors in Rome, and has been the home away from home to various monarchs, movie stars, and some of the greatest writers of all time—Lord Byron, John Keats, Mark Twain, Ernest Hemingway, and Elizabeth Taylor among them. **Pros:** distinct character and opulence; turndown service (with chocolates); genuinely friendly and attentive staff; excellent in-house restaurant. **Cons:** elevator is small and slow; the location, despite soundproofing, is still noisy; bathrooms are surprisingly petite; some rooms badly in need of renovations and maintenance. $ *Rooms from: €400* ✉ *Via Bocca di Leone 14, Piazza di Spagna* ☎ *06/699811* ⊕ *www.starhotel-scollezione.com/en/our-hotels/hotel-d-inghilterra-rome* 🛏 *88 rooms* ⦿ *Free Breakfast* Ⓜ *Spagna* ✛ *2:E2*.

$$$$ 🏨 **Hotel de Russie.** A ritzy retreat for government bigwigs and Hollywood
HOTEL high rollers, the Hotel de Russie is just steps from the famed Piazza
FAMILY del Popolo on chic Via del Babuino and occupies a 19th-century hotel
Fodor's Choice that once hosted royalty, Picasso, and Cocteau. **Pros:** big potential for
★ celebrity sightings; extensive gardens (including a butterfly reserve); first-rate luxury spa; Wi-Fi included. **Cons:** some rooms need updat-ing; breakfast not included; expensive. $ *Rooms from: €700* ✉ *Via del*

2

Babuino 9, Piazza del Popolo ☎ *06/328881* 🌐 *www.roccofortehotels.com* 🛏 *122 rooms* 🍴 *No meals* [M] *Flaminio* ✣ *2:E1.*

$$$$ B&B/INN Fodor's Choice ★ 🏨 **Il Palazzetto.** Once a retreat for one of Rome's richest noble families, this 15th-century house is one of the most intimate and luxurious hotels in Rome, with gorgeous terraces where you can watch the never-ending theater of the Scalinatella. **Pros:** location and view; free Wi-Fi; guests have full access to the Hassler's services; continental breakfast included (served at the Hassler). **Cons:** restaurant often rented out for crowded special events; bedrooms do not access communal terraces; often books up far in advance, particularly in high season; only three rooms have a view of Piazza di Spagna. [$] *Rooms from: €350* ✉ *Vicolo del Bottino 8, Piazza di Spagna* ☎ *06/699341000* 🌐 *www.ilpalazzettoroma.com* 🛏 *4 rooms* 🍴 *No meals* [M] *Spagna* ✣ *2:F2.*

$$$$ B&B/INN Fodor's Choice ★ 🏨 **Margutta 54.** Tucked away on a quiet, leafy street known for its art galleries, this four-suite property is like your very own hip, New York–style loft in the center of old-world Rome, with top-drawer amenities, contemporary design, and an ivy-draped courtyard. **Pros:** studio-loft feel in center of town; complete privacy; deluxe furnishings. **Cons:** breakfast not included (€20 per person), served at sister hotel Babuino 181; no staff available on-site after 8 pm. [$] *Rooms from: €380* ✉ *Via Margutta 54, Piazza di Spagna* ☎ *06/69921907* 🌐 *www.romeluxurysuites.com/margutta* 🛏 *4 suites* 🍴 *No meals* [M] *Spagna* ✣ *2:E2.*

$ HOTEL 🏨 **Panda.** Located near the Spanish Steps, this little gem of a hotel has excellent service that gives you more bang for your buck. **Pros:** free Wi-Fi; very high ceilings; on a quiet street, but still close to the Spanish Steps; some rooms share a bathroom. **Cons:** dim lighting; no elevator directly to floor; breakfast not included. [$] *Rooms from: €120* ✉ *Via della Croce 35, Piazza di Spagna* ☎ *06/6780179* 🌐 *www.hotelpanda.it* 🛏 *28 rooms* 🍴 *No meals* [M] *Spagna* ✣ *2:E2.*

$$$$ HOTEL 🏨 **Regina Baglioni.** The former playground of kings and poets, the Regina Baglioni, which enjoys a prime spot on the Via Veneto, is a favorite among today's international jet-setters. **Pros:** nice decor; luxury on-site spa; excellent on-site restaurant and bar. **Cons:** some rooms are noisy; service is hit-or-miss; spotty Internet. [$] *Rooms from: €380* ✉ *Via Veneto 72, Piazza di Spagna* ☎ *06/421111* 🌐 *www.reginabaglioni.com* 🛏 *143 rooms* 🍴 *Free Breakfast* [M] *Barberini* ✣ *2:G2.*

$$ B&B/INN Fodor's Choice ★ 🏨 **Scalinata di Spagna.** Perched atop the Spanish Steps, this charming boutique hotel makes guests fall in love over and over again—so popular, in fact, it's often booked far in advance. **Pros:** friendly and helpful concierge; fresh fruit in guest rooms; free Wi-Fi throughout. **Cons:** it's a hike up the hill to the hotel; small rooms; no porter and no elevator. [$] *Rooms from: €190* ✉ *Piazza Trinità dei Monti 17, Piazza di Spagna* ☎ *06/45686150* 🌐 *www.hotelscalinata.com* 🛏 *16 rooms* 🍴 *Free Breakfast* [M] *Spagna* ✣ *2:F2.*

REPUBBLICA

$ B&B/INN Fodor's Choice ★ 🏨 **The Beehive.** Living the American dream *dolce vita*–style is exactly what one Los Angeles couple started to do in 1999, when they opened the Beehive, a hip, alternative budget hotel near Termini station that feels somewhere between a hostel and a holistic center. **Pros:** massage and other therapies offered on-site; convenient to Termini station; very good prices (especially for beds in dorms) for variety of rooms, even in high season. **Cons:** some rooms do not have private baths; standard rooms lack TV and a/c; breakfast not included. [$] *Rooms from: €90* ✉ *Via Marghera 8, Repubblica* ☎ *06/44704553* 🌐 *www.the-beehive.com* 🛏 *8 rooms, 2 dormitories* 🍴 *No meals* [M] *Termini* ✥ *2:H3.*

$$ HOTEL Fodor's Choice ★ 🏨 **Yes Hotel.** This chic hotel may fool you into thinking the digs are expensive, but the contemporary coolness of Yes Hotel, located around the corner from Termini station, actually comes at a bargain. **Pros:** around the corner from Termini station; discount if you pay in cash; a great value without the budget feel. **Cons:** small rooms; fee for in-room Wi-Fi; not near many top sights. [$] *Rooms from: €140* ✉ *Via Magenta 15, Repubblica* ☎ *06/44363836* 🌐 *www.yeshotelrome.com* 🛏 *40 rooms* 🍴 *Free Breakfast* [M] *Termini, Castro Pretorio* ✥ *2:H3.*

AROUND THE VATICAN

$ HOTEL Fodor's Choice ★ 🏨 **Hotel San Pietrino.** This simple budget hotel on the third floor of a 19th-century palazzo offers rock-bottom rates at a five-minute walk from the Vatican. **Pros:** heavenly rates near the Vatican; free Wi-Fi; close to Rome's famous farmers' market, Mercato Trionfale. **Cons:** a couple of Metro stops from the centro storico; no breakfast (coffee/tea machine for guest use); no bar. [$] *Rooms from: €100* ✉ *Via Giovanni Bettolo 43, Prati* ☎ *06/3700132* 🌐 *www.sanpietrino.it* 🛏 *12 rooms* 🍴 *No meals* [M] *Ottaviano* ✥ *2:B1.*

$$$ HOTEL Fodor's Choice ★ 🏨 **Residenza Paolo VI.** Set in a former monastery—still an extraterritorial part of the Vatican—magnificently abutting Bernini's colonnade of St. Peter's Square, the Paolo VI (pronounced "Sesto," a reference to Pope Paul VI) is unbeatably close to St. Peter's, with guest rooms that are comfortable and amazingly quiet. **Pros:** unparalleled views of St. Peter's from the rooftop terrace; quiet rooms; huge breakfast spread. **Cons:** small rooms are really small; bathrooms are small; atmosphere at night is a little too quiet. [$] *Rooms from: €250* ✉ *Via Paolo VI 29, Borgo* ☎ *06/684870* 🌐 *www.residenzapaolovi.com* 🛏 *35 rooms* 🍴 *Free Breakfast* [M] *Ottaviano* ✥ *2:B3.*

TRASTEVERE

$$ HOTEL Fodor's Choice ★ 🏨 **Casa di Santa Francesca Romana.** In the heart of Trastevere but tucked away from the hustle and bustle of the medieval quarter, this cheap, clean, comfortable hotel in a former monastery is centered on a lovely green courtyard. **Pros:** rates can't be beat; excellent restaurants nearby; away from rowdy tourist side of Trastevere. **Cons:** thin walls; interior is a bit bland; spotty Wi-Fi. [$] *Rooms from: €130* ✉ *Via dei Vasceillari 61, Trastevere* ☎ *06/5812125* 🌐 *www.sfromana.it* 🛏 *37 rooms* 🍴 *Free Breakfast* [M] *Piramide, Circo Massimo* ✥ *2:E6.*

$$$ HOTEL Fodor's Choice ★ 🏨 **Hotel Santa Maria.** A Trastevere treasure with a pedigree going back four centuries, this ivy-covered, mansard-roof, rosy-brick-red, erstwhile Renaissance-era convent—just steps away from the glorious Santa Maria in Trastevere church and a few blocks from the Tiber—has sweet and simple guest rooms: a mix of brick walls, "cotto" tile floors,

modern oak furniture, and matching bedspreads and curtains. **Pros:** a quaint and pretty oasis in a central location; relaxing courtyard; fully stocked wine bar; free bicycles to use during your stay; kettle for tea and coffee in room. **Cons:** tricky to find; some of the showers drain slowly; finding a cab is not always easy in Trastevere. $\boxed{\$}$ *Rooms from: €230* ✉ *Vicolo del Piede 2, Trastevere* ☎ *06/5894626* ⊕ *www.hotelsantamariatrastevere.it* ⤳ *20 rooms* ⁑ *Free Breakfast* ✛ *2:D5.*

$ ⚎ **Hotel Trastevere.** This tiny hotel captures the villagelike charm of the
HOTEL Trastevere district and offers basic, clean, comfortable rooms in a great location. **Pros:** good rates for location; convenient to tram and bus; free Wi-Fi; friendly staff. **Cons:** rooms are a little worn on the edges; few amenities. $\boxed{\$}$ *Rooms from: €110* ✉ *Via Luciano Manara 24/a–25, Trastevere* ☎ *06/5814713* ⊕ *www.hoteltrastevere.net* ⤳ *18 rooms* ⁑ *Free Breakfast* Ⓜ *Trastevere, Mastai* ✛ *2:D6.*

$$ ⚎ **Relais Le Clarisse.** Set within the former cloister grounds of the Santa
B&B/INN Chiara order, with beautiful gardens, Le Clarisse makes you feel like a
Fodor's Choice personal guest at a friend's villa, thanks to the comfortable size of the
★ guest rooms and personalized service. **Pros:** spacious rooms with comfy beds; high-tech showers/tubs with good water pressure; complimentary Wi-Fi. **Cons:** this part of Trastevere can be noisy at night; rooms fill up quickly; reception unavailable after 10:30 pm. $\boxed{\$}$ *Rooms from: €180* ✉ *Via Cardinale Merry del Val 20, Trastevere* ☎ *06/58334437* ⊕ *www. leclarissetrastevere.com* ⤳ *17 rooms* ⁑ *Free Breakfast* ✛ *2:D6.*

AVENTINO

$$ ⚎ **Hotel San Anselmo.** This refurbished 19th-century villa is a romantic
HOTEL retreat from the city, set in a *molto* charming garden atop the Aventine Hill. **Pros:** free Wi-Fi; historic building with artful interior; great showers with jets; a garden where you can enjoy breakfast. **Cons:** a bit of a hike to sights; limited public transportation. $\boxed{\$}$ *Rooms from: €160* ✉ *Piazza San Anselmo 2, Aventino* ☎ *06/570057* ⊕ *www.aventinohotels.com* ⤳ *35 rooms* ⁑ *Free Breakfast* Ⓜ *Circo Massimo* ✛ *2:E6.*

NIGHTLIFE AND PERFORMING ARTS

NIGHTLIFE

"E mo' che fammo?" ("And now what do we do?" in local dialect)… For a great night out in Rome, all you need to do is to wander, because ready entertainment is sure to find you on every corner. It's important to follow Rome's rule of thumb: if you see an enoteca, stop in. Although most enoteche are tiny and offer a limited antipasti menu, they cover more ground in their wine lists and often have a charming gang of regulars. For the linguistically timid, there are also several stereotypical English and Irish pubs peppered around the city, complete with a steady stream of Guinness, darts, and rugby on their satellite televisions. Those oversize flat-screen TVs also show American football, baseball, and basketball—ideal for those who don't want to miss a playoff game.

Most visitors head out in the centro storico to find some fun; Piazza Navona, Pantheon, Campo de' Fiori, and even Trastevere may be filled with tourists, but more recently, several niche and boutique bars have opened. (In contrast, the Spanish Steps area is a ghost town by 9 pm.) If you want to get out of the comfort zone, head to the Testaccio and San Lorenzo areas. When it comes to clubs, discos, and DJs in Rome, Testaccio is considered a mecca—Via Galvani is Rome's Sunset Strip, where hybrid restaurant-clubs, largely identical in music and crowd, jockey for top ranking. And wherever you go, remember: Romans love an after-party, so plenty of nightlife doesn't start until midnight.

PIAZZA NAVONA AND CAMPO DE' FIORI

Fodor's Choice ★ **Etablì.** If you set up a wine bar in your living room, it'd feel a lot like Etablì. This is the perfect spot for meeting friends before a night out on the town. ⊠ *Vicolo delle Vacche 9, Piazza Navona* ☏ *06/97616694* ⊕ *www.etabli.it.*

La Cabala. Atop the medieval Hostaria dell'Orso, La Cabala is an after-dinner club and late-night dance party whose VIP room hosts wan-nabe models. Depending on the evening, the vibe can be chic, hipster, or clubby. Rome's version of a supper club, La Cabala is part of the Hostaria dell'Orso trio of restaurant, disco, and piano bar. Dress code is "stylish." ⊠ *Hostaria dell'Orso, Via dei Soldati 23, Piazza Navona* ☏ *06/68301192* ⊕ *www.hdo.it.*

L'Angolo Divino. Nestled on a quiet side street around the corner from the ever vivacious Campo de' Fiori, this wood-paneled enoteca is a hidden treasure of wines. Its extensive selection lists more than 1,000 labels to go along quite nicely with its quaint menu of delicious homemade pastas and local antipasti. And because it's open every night until 1:30 am, it's the ideal place for a late-night tipple. ⊠ *Via dei Balestrari 12, Campo de' Fiori* ☏ *06/6864413* ⊕ *www.angolodivino.it.*

Fodor's Choice ★ **Roof Garden Bar at Grand Hotel della Minerve.** During warm months, this lofty perch offers perhaps the most inspiring view in Rome—directly over the Pantheon's dome. The Roof Garden has an equally impressive cocktail menu. Take advantage of summer sunsets and park yourself in a front-row seat as the dome glows. ⊠ *Grand Hotel della Minerve, Piazza della Minerve 69, Piazza Navona* ☏ *06/695201* ⊕ *www.grand-hoteldelaminerve.com.*

Vinoteca Novecento. A lovely, tiny enoteca with a very old-fashioned vibe, Vinoteca Novecento has a seemingly unlimited selection of wines, proseccos, vini santi, and grappe, along with salami-and-cheese tasting menus. Inside is standing-room only; in good weather, sit outside on one of the oak barriques. ⊠ *Piazza delle Coppelle 47, Piazza Navona* ☏ *06/6833078.*

PIAZZA DI SPAGNA

Fodor's Choice ★ **Antica Birreria Peroni.** For beer lovers, the Art Nouveau–style halls of Antica Birreria Peroni will enchant you with their turn-of-the-20th-century atmosphere, not to mention the always-flowing taps. Expect filling canteen-style meals and big steins, with several taps featuring Peroni favorites. It's also the best place for hot dogs in Rome, however tasteless their presentation. ⊠ *Via di San Marcello 19, Piazza di Spagna* ☎ *06/6795310* ⊕ *www.anticabirreriaperoni.net.*

Wine Bar at the Palazzetto. The prize for perfect aperitivo spot goes to the Palazzetto, with excellent drinks and appetizers, as well as a breathtaking view of Rome's domes and rooftops—all from its fifth-floor rooftop overlooking Piazza di Spagna. Keep an eye on the sky, as any chance for a rainy day will close the terrace (as do special events). ⊠ *Vicolo del Bottino 8, Piazza di Spagna* ☎ *06/69934711* ⊕ *www.ilpalazzettoroma. com* Ⓜ *Spagna.*

PIAZZA DEL POPOLO

Stravinskij Bar at the Hotel de Russie. The Stravinskij Bar, in the Hotel de Russie's gorgeous garden, is the best place to catch a glimpse of la dolce vita. Celebrities, blue bloods, and VIPs hang out in the private courtyard garden where mixed drinks and cocktails are well above par. ⊠ *Hotel de Russie, Via del Babuino 9, Piazza del Popolo* ☎ *06/328881* ⊕ *www. roccofortehotels.com/hotels-and-resorts/hotel-de-russie/restaurant-and-bar/stravinskij-bar* Ⓜ *Flaminio.*

TRASTEVERE

Fodor'sChoice ★ **Freni e Frizioni.** This hipster hangout has a cute artist vibe, and is great for an afternoon coffee, tea, or aperitivo, or for late-night socializing. In warmer weather, the crowd overflows the large terrazzo overlooking the Tiber and the side streets of Trastevere. ⊠ *Via del Politeama 4, Trastevere* ☎ *06/45497499* ⊕ *www.freniefrizioni.com.*

MONTI

Fodor'sChoice ★ **Ai Tre Scalini.** An ivy-covered wine bar in the center of Monti, Rome's trendiest 'hood, Ai Tre Scalini has a warm and cozy menu of delicious antipasti and light entrées to go along with its enticing wine list. After about 8 pm, if you haven't booked, be prepared to wait—this is one extremely popular spot with locals. ⊠ *Via Panisperna 251, Monti* ☎ *06/48907495* ⊕ *www.aitrescalini.org* Ⓜ *Cavour.*

TESTACCIO

Ketum Bar. One of Rome's few "organic" happy hours, the price of a drink will buy you a spread of healthy and organic vegetarian appetizers. It also serves up a great weekend brunch. Aperitivo starts at 6:30 pm. ⊠ *Via Galvani 24, Testaccio* ☎ *06/57305338* ⊕ *www.ketumbar.it.*

PERFORMING ARTS

One of the pleasures of Rome is seeing a performance in one of the city's stunning venues, ancient or modern. This is the city where you might experience classical opera performed in a 3rd-century-AD theater, or enjoy an experimental dance show in a postindustrial space, or see a contemporary performance at the Renzo Piano–designed Auditorium Parco della Musica.

In summertime, most of the performing arts events move outdoors—any public space is fair game. Keep an eye on the Estate Romana website (⊕ *www.estateromana.comune.roma.it*) to find out what's happening in Rome on any night of the week. There is enough entertainment in Rome to take your breath away, in any season and in any location.

TICKETS

Orbis. An in-person, cash-only ticket vendor, Orbis stocks a wide array of tickets for music, cultural, and performance events. ✉ *Piazza dell'Esquilino 37, Repubblica* ☎ *06/4827403* ⊕ *www.boxofficelazio.it.*

VivaTicket. One of Italy's largest ticket vendors (both online and at ticket offices), VivaTicket covers major musical performances and cultural events in Rome and throughout Italy. ⊕ *www.vivaticket.it.*

DANCE

Teatro Olimpico. Part of Rome's theater circuit, the 1930s-era Teatro Olimpico is one of the main venues for cabaret, contemporary dance companies, visiting international ballet companies, touring Broadway shows, and TEDxRoma. ✉ *Piazza Gentile da Fabriano 17, Flaminio* ☎ *06/3265991* ⊕ *www.teatroolimpico.it.*

MAJOR VENUES

Fodor'sChoice ★ **Auditorium Parco della Musica.** Rome became a world-class arts contender when world-renowned architect Renzo Piano conceived and constructed the Parco della Musica, fondly known as "the Auditorium." The futuristic music complex is made up of three enormous, pod-shape concert halls, which have heard the live melodies of Luciano Pavarotti, Philip Glass, Tracy Chapman, Peter Gabriel, Burt Bacharach, Woody Allen, and many more. Likened to anything from beetles to computer "mice," the musical pods are consistently jammed with people: the Sala Santa Cecilia is a massive hall for grand orchestra and choral concerts; the Sala Sinopoli is more intimately scaled for smaller troupes; and the Sala Petrassi was designed for alternative events. All three are arrayed around the Cavea, a vast Greco-Roman-style theater.

The auditorium is more than just music. The music park also hosts seasonal festivals—including the Rome Film Fest, a Christmas Village, and a springtime science, math, and philosophy festival. The grounds also have restaurants, a charming café, a bookstore, an outdoor amphitheater, an archaeological site, and an outstanding children's playground. If you're here in summer, there will be outdoor concerts and festivals.

Located in the Flaminio neighborhood, the Auditorium is just 10 minutes from the city center, reachable by local tram transport. To book guided tours, email *visiteguidate@musicaperroma.it.* ✉ *Viale Pietro de Coubertin 30, Flaminio* ☎ *06/80241281* ⊕ *www.auditorium.com.*

OPERA

Fodor'sChoice ★ **Teatro dell'Opera.** Long considered a far younger sibling of La Scala in Milan and La Fenice in Venice, the company commands an audience during its mid-November–May season. In the hot summer months, the company moves to the Terme di Caracalla for its outdoor opera series. As can be expected, the oft-preferred performance is *Aida,* for its spectacle, which once included real elephants. The company has lately taken a new direction, using projections atop the ancient ruins to create cutting-edge sets. ✉ *Piazza Beniamino Gigli 8, Repubblica* ☎ *06/481601, 06/48160255 tickets* ⊕ *www.operaroma.it* Ⓜ *Repubblica.*

THEATER

Fodor's Choice ★ **Teatro Argentina.** A gorgeous 18th-century theater, the Teatro Argentina evokes glamour and sophistication with its velvet upholstery, large crystal chandeliers, and beautifully dressed theatergoers, who come to see international productions of stage and dance performances. ⊠ *Largo di Torre Argentina 52, Campo de' Fiori* 🕾 *06/684000311* ⊕ *www.teatrodiroma.net.*

SHOPPING

In Rome, shopping is an art form. Perhaps it's the fashionably bespectacled commuter wearing Giorgio Armani as he deftly zips through traffic on his Vespa, or all those Anita Ekberg, Audrey Hepburn, and Julia Roberts films that make us long to be Roman for a day. But with limited time and no Hollywood studio backing you, the trick is to find what you're looking for and still not miss out on the city's museums and monuments—and, of course, leave yourself plenty of euros to enjoy the rest of your trip.

SHOPPING DISTRICTS

The city's most famous shopping district, **Piazza di Spagna,** is conveniently compact, fanning out at the foot of the Spanish Steps in a galaxy of boutiques selling gorgeous wares with glamorous labels. Here you can prance back and forth from Gucci to Prada to Valentino to Versace with less effort than it takes to pull out your credit card. If your budget is designed for lower altitudes, you also can find great clothes and accessories at less extravagant prices. But here, buying is not necessarily the point—window displays can be works of art in themselves, and dreaming may be satisfaction enough. Via dei Condotti is the neighborhood's central axis, but there are shops on every street in the area bordered by Piazza di Spagna on the east, Via del Corso on the west, between Piazza San Silvestro and Via della Croce, and extending along Via del Babuino to Piazza del Popolo. Via Margutta, a few blocks north of the Spanish Steps, is a haven for contemporary art galleries.

Running from Piazza Venezia to Piazza del Popolo, the **Via del Corso** has more than a mile of shops. Unfortunately, these days most of it is taken up by the same chain stores you find worldwide (including Gap, H&M, and even an Athlete's Foot), rendering it little more interesting than a trip to one's local shopping mall. Running west from Piazza Navona, Via del Governo Vecchio has numerous women's boutiques and secondhand-clothing stores.

The Termini train station has become a good one-stop place for many shopping needs, although again, most stores are the same you see worldwide. Its 60-plus shops are open until 10 pm and include a Nike store, the Body Shop, Sephora, Mango (women's clothes), a UPIM department store, a grocery store, and a three-story bookstore with selections in English. For local designers and independent boutiques, don't miss the trendy shopping districts of **Monti** near the Forum and **Trastevere** across the Tiber from the centro storico.

PIAZZA NAVONA

CLOTHING

Arsenale. Roman designer Patrizia Pieroni's sleek, unique, high-end fashion items stand out no matter the season. Her store, Arsenale, features everything from cleverly cut, stylish overcoats and seductive bustiers to sexy, flowing dresses perfect for the summer. ⊠ *Via del Pellegrino 172, Piazza Navona* ☎ *06/68802424* ⊕ *www.patriziapieroni.it.*

Le Tartarughe. A familiar face on the catwalk of Rome's fashion shows, designer Susanna Liso, a Rome native, adds suggestive elements of playful experimentation to her haute couture and ready-to-wear lines, which are much loved by Rome's aristocracy and intelligentsia. With intense, enveloping designs, she mixes raw silks or cashmere and fine merino wool together to form captivating garments that mix seduction and linear form. ⊠ *Via Piè di Marmo 17, Piazza Navona* ☎ *06/6792240* ⊕ *www.letartarughe.eu.*

Vestiti Usati Cinzia. Vintage clothes hunters, costume designers, and stylists alike love browsing through the racks at Vestiti Usati Cinzia. The shop is fun and very inviting and stocked with wall-to-wall funky 1960s and '70s apparel and loads of goofy sunglasses. There's definitely no shortage of flower power bell bottoms and hippie shirts, embroidered tops, trippy and psychedelic boots, and other awesome accessories that will take you back to the days of peace and love. ⊠ *Via del Governo Vecchio 45, Piazza Navona* ☎ *06/6832945.*

FOOD AND WINE

Enoteca al Parlamento Achilli. The proximity of this traditional enoteca to Montecitorio, the Italian Parliament building, makes it a favorite with journalists and politicos, who often stop in for a glass of wine after work. But it's the tantalizing smell of truffles from the snack counter, where a sommelier waits to organize your tasting, that will probably lure you into Enoteca al Parlamento Achilli. There's also a lovely little restaurant where you can book a table and munch on a tempting array of cheese, salumi, and other cured meats. Don't forget to check out their wineshop to take home a bottle of your favorite wine. ⊠ *Via dei Prefetti 15, Piazza Navona* ☎ *06/6873446* ⊕ *www.enotecaalparlamento.it.*

Moriondo e Gariglio. Not exactly Willy Wonka (but in the same vein), Moriondo e Gariglio is a chocolate lover's paradise, churning out some of the finest chocolate delicacies in town. The shop dates back to 1850 and adheres strictly to family recipes passed on from generation to generation. Whether you favor marrons glacés or dark-chocolate truffles, you'll delight in choosing from more than 80 delicacies. ⊠ *Via Piè di Marmo 21, Piazza Navona* ☎ *06/6990856.*

JEWELRY

MMM—Massimo Maria Melis. Drawing heavily on ancient Roman and Etruscan designs, Massimo Maria Melis jewelry will carry you back in time. Working with 21-carat gold, he often incorporates antique coins in many of his exquisite bracelets and necklaces. Some of his pieces are done with an ancient technique, much-loved by the Etruscans, in which tiny gold droplets are fused together to create intricately patterned designs. ⊠ *Via dell'Orso 57, Piazza Navona* ☎ *06/6869188* ⊕ *www.massimomariamelis.com.*

Quattrocolo. This historic shop dating to 1938 showcases exquisite antique micro-mosaic jewelry painstakingly crafted in the style perfected by the masters at the Vatican mosaic studio. You'll also find 18th- and 19th-century cameos and beautiful engraved stones. Their small works were beloved by cosmopolitan clientele of the Grand Tour age and offer modern-day shoppers a taste of yesteryear's grandeur. ⊠ *Via della Scrofa 48, Piazza Navona* ☎ *06/68801367* ⊕ *www.quattrocolo.com.*

SHOES AND ACCESSORIES

Spazio IF. In a tiny piazza alongside Rome's historic Via dei Coronari, designers Irene and Carla Ferrara have created a tantalizing hybrid between fashion paradise and art gallery. Working with unconventional designers and artists who emphasize Sicilian design, the shop has more to say about the style of Sicily and the creativity of the island's inhabitants than flat caps, puppets, and rich pastries. Perennial favorites include handbags cut by hand in a shop in Palermo, swimsuits, designer textiles, jewelry, and sportswear. ⊠ *Via dei Coronari 44a, Piazza Navona* ☎ *06/64760639* ⊕ *www.spazioif.it.*

TOYS

FAMILY **Al Sogno.** If you're looking for quality toys that encourage imaginative play and learning, look no further than Al Sogno. With an emphasis on the artistic as well as the multisensory, the shop has a selection of toys that are both discerning and individual, making them perfect for children of all ages. Carrying an exquisite collection of fanciful puppets, collectible dolls, masks, stuffed animals, and illustrated books, this Navona jewel, around since 1945, is crammed top-to-bottom with beautiful, well-crafted playthings. If you believe that children's toys don't have to be high-tech, you will adore reliving some of your best childhood memories here. ⊠ *Piazza Navona 53, corner of Via Agonale, Piazza Navona* ☎ *06/6864198* ⊕ *www.alsogno.net.*

FAMILY **Bartolucci.** For more than 60 years and three generations, the Bartolucci
Fodor'sChoice family has been making whimsical, handmade curiosities out of pine,
★ including cuckoo clocks, bookends, bedside lamps, and wall hangings. You can even buy a child-size vintage car entirely made of wood (wheels, too). Don't miss the life-size Pinocchio pedaling furiously on a wooden bike. ⊠ *Via dei Pastini 98, Piazza Navona* ☎ *06/69190894* ⊕ *www.bartolucci.com.*

CAMPO DE' FIORI

SHOES, HANDBAGS, AND LEATHER GOODS

Ibiz–Artigianato in Cuoio. In business since 1970, this father-and-daughter team creates colorful, stylish leather handbags, belts, and sandals near Piazza Campo de' Fiori. Choose from the premade collection or order something made to measure; their workshop is right next door to the boutique. ⊠ *Via dei Chiavari 39, Campo de' Fiori* ☎ *06/68307297.*

PIAZZA DI SPAGNA

ACCESSORIES

Furla. Furla sells high-end quality handbags and purses at affordable prices. There are multiple locations throughout the Eternal City (including one at Fiumicino Airport), but its flagship store can be found in the heart of Piazza di Spagna. Be prepared to fight your way through crowds of passionate handbag lovers, all anxious to possess one of the delectable bags, wallets, or watch straps in ice-cream colors. ⊠ *Piazza di Spagna 22, Piazza di Spagna* ☎ *06/69200363* ⊕ *www.furla. com* Ⓜ *Spagna.*

CLOTHING

Dolce & Gabbana. Dolce and Gabbana met in 1980 when both were assistants at a Milan fashion atelier, and they opened their first store in 1982. With a modern aesthetic that screams sex appeal, the brand has always thrived on excess. The Rome store can be more than a little overwhelming, with its glossy decor and blaring music, but at least there's plenty of eye candy—masculine and feminine alike. There is a second location on Via dei Condotti. ⊠ *Piazza di Spagna 94–95, Piazza di Spagna* ☎ *06/6991592* ⊕ *www.dolcegabbana.it* Ⓜ *Spagna.*

Elena Mirò. Elena Mirò is a high-end brand that specializes in sophisticated, beautifully sexy clothes for curvy, European-styled women size 46 (U.S. size 12, U.K. size 14) and up. There are several locations in Rome, including one on Via Nazionale. ⊠ *Via Frattina 11–12, Piazza di Spagna* ☎ *06/6784367* ⊕ *www.elenamiro.it* Ⓜ *Spagna.*

Fodor's Choice ★ **Fendi.** Fendi has been a fixture of the Roman fashion landscape since "Mamma" Fendi first opened shop with her husband in 1925. With an eye for crazy genius, she hired Karl Lagerfeld, who began working with the group at the start of his career. His furs and runway antics have made him one of the most influential designers of the 20th century and brought international acclaim to Fendi along the way. The atelier, now owned by the Louis Vuitton group, continues to symbolize Italian glamour at its finest, though the difference in ownership is noticeable. It's also gotten new life in the Italian press for its "Fendi for Fountains" campaign, which included funding the restoration of Rome's Trevi Fountain. ⊠ *Largo Carlo Goldoni 419–421, Piazza di Spagna* ☎ *06/3344501* ⊕ *www.fendi.com* Ⓜ *Spagna.*

Giorgio Armani. One of the most influential designers of Italian haute couture, Giorgio Armani creates fluid silhouettes and dazzling evening gowns with décolletage so deep they'd make a grown man blush; his signature cuts are made with the clever-handedness and flawless technique achievable only by working with tracing paper and Italy's finest fabrics over the course of a lifetime. His menswear collection uses traditional textiles like wide-ribbed corduroy and stretch jersey in nontraditional ways while staying true to a clean, masculine aesthetic. It's true that exotic runway ideas and glamorous celebrities give Armani strong selling points, but his staying power is casual Italian elegance with just the right touch of whimsy and sexiness. ⊠ *Via dei Condotti 77–79, Piazza di Spagna* ☎ *06/6991460* ⊕ *www.giorgioarmani.com* Ⓜ *Spagna.*

Fodor's Choice   **Gucci.** As the glamorous fashion label approaches its centennial, the suc-
★   cess of the double-G trademark is unquestionable. The fashion house
is still seeking to maintain the label's trendiness while bringing in a
breath of fresh air, though old-school favorites like today's reinterpreted
horsebit styles and Jackie Kennedy scarves keep the design house on
top. And while Gucci remains a fashion must for virtually every A-list
celebrity, their designs have moved from heart-stopping sexy rock star
to something classically subdued and retrospectively feminine. There's
another store on Via Borgognona. ⊠ *Via dei Condotti 8, Piazza di
Spagna* ☎ *06/6790405* ⊕ *www.gucci.com* Ⓜ *Spagna.*

Fodor's Choice   **Laura Biagiotti.** For 40 years Laura Biagiotti has been a worldwide
★   ambassador of Italian fashion. Considered the Queen of Cashmere,
her soft-as-velvet pullovers have been worn by Sophia Loren, and her
snow-white cardigans were said to be a favorite of the late pope John
Paul II. Princess Diana even sported one of Biagiotti's cashmere mater-
nity dresses. Be sure to indulge in sampling her line of his-and-her
perfumes. ⊠ *Via Mario de' Fiori 26, Piazza di Spagna* ☎ *06/6791205*
⊕ *www.laurabiagiotti.it* Ⓜ *Spagna.*

Fodor's Choice   **Patrizia Pepe.** One of Florence's best-kept secrets for up-and-coming
★   fashions, Patrizia Pepe first emerged on the scene in 1993 with designs
both minimalist and bold, combining classic styles with low-slung
jeans and jackets with oversize lapels that are bound to draw attention. Her line of shoes is hot-hot-hot for those who can walk on stilts.
It's still not huge on the fashion scene as a stand-alone brand, but
take a look at this shop before the line becomes the next fast-tracked
craze. ⊠ *Via Frattina 44, Piazza di Spagna* ☎ *06/6781851* ⊕ *www.
patriziapepe.com* Ⓜ *Spagna.*

Fodor's Choice   **Prada.** Besides the devil, plenty of serious shoppers wear Prada season
★   after season, especially those willing to sell their souls for one of their
ubiquitous handbags. If you are looking for that blend of old-world
luxury with a touch of fashion-forward finesse, you'll hit pay dirt here.
You'll find the Rome store more service-oriented than the New York
City branches—a roomy elevator delivers you to a series of thickly
carpeted rooms where a flock of discreet assistants will help you pick
out dresses, shoes, lingerie, and fashion accessories. The men's store is
located at Via dei Condotti 88/90, women's down the street at 92/95.
⊠ *Via dei Condotti 88/90 and 92/95, Piazza di Spagna* ☎ *06/6790897*
⊕ *www.prada.com* Ⓜ *Spagna.*

Schostal. A Piazza di Spagna fixture since 1870, the shop was once the
go-to place for women looking to stock up on corsets, bonnets, stock-
ings and petticoats. Today, it's the place to stop for fine-quality shirts,
underwear, and handkerchiefs made of wool and pure cashmere at
affordable prices. There's a second location at Piazza Euclide. ⊠ *Via
della Fontanella Borghese 29, Piazza di Spagna* ☎ *06/6791240* ⊕ *www.
schostalroma.com* Ⓜ *Spagna.*

Fodor's Choice   **Valentino.** Since taking the Valentino reins, creative director Pierpaolo
★   Piccioli has faced numerous challenges, the most basic of which is keep-
ing Valentino true to Valentino after the designer's retirement in 2008.
He served as accessories designers under Valentino for more than a

decade and understands exactly how to make the next generation of Hollywood stars swoon. Valentino has taken over most of Piazza di Spagna, where multiple boutiques showcase designs with a romantic edginess; think kitten heels or a show-stopping prêt-à-porter evening gown worthy of the Oscars. ⊠ *Via dei Condotti 15, Piazza di Spagna* ☎ *06/6739420* ⊕ *www.valentino.com* Ⓜ *Spagna.*

Versace. Versace's Rome flagship is a gem of architecture and design, with Byzantine-inspired mosaic floors and futuristic interiors, not to mention, of course, fashion: here shoppers will find apparel, jewelry, watches, fragrances, cosmetics, and home furnishings in designs every bit as flamboyant as Donatella and Allegra (Gianni's niece), drawing heavily on the sexy rocker gothic underground vibe. There's also a smaller boutique on the Via Veneto with prêt-à-porter and jewelry. ⊠ *Piazza di Spagna 12, Piazza di Spagna* ☎ *06/6691773* ⊕ *www.versace.com* Ⓜ *Spagna.*

DEPARTMENT STORES

La Rinascente. Italy's best-known department store reopened in 2017 in a splendid new store. Here, one can find oodles of cosmetics on the ground floor, as well as a phalanx of ready-to-wear designer sportswear and blockbuster handbags and accessories, and kitchen and home ware in the basement. Even if you're not planning on buying anything, the basement excavations of a Roman aqueduct and the roof terrace with its splendid view are well worth a visit. ⊠ *Via del Tritone 61, Piazza di Spagna* ☎ *06/879161* ⊕ *www.rinascente.it* Ⓜ *Spagna.*

JEWELRY

Bulgari. Every capital city has its famous jeweler, and Bulgari is to Rome what Tiffany is to New York and Cartier to Paris. The jewelry giant has developed a reputation for meticulous craftsmanship melding noble metals with precious gems. In the middle of the 19th century, the great-grandfather of the current Bulgari brothers began working as a silver jeweler in his native Greece and is said to have moved to Rome with less than 1,000 lire in his pocket. Today the megabrand emphasizes colorful and playful jewelry as the principal cornerstone of its aesthetic. Popular collections include Parentesi, Bulgari-Bulgari, and B.zero1. ⊠ *Via dei Condotti 10, Piazza di Spagna* ☎ *06/696261* ⊕ *www.bulgari.com* Ⓜ *Spagna.*

MEN'S CLOTHING

Fodor'sChoice ★ **Brioni.** Founded in 1945 and hailed for its impeccable craftsmanship and flawless execution, the Brioni label is known for attracting and keeping the best men's tailors in Italy, where the exacting standards require that custom-made suits are designed from scratch and measured to the millimeter. For this personalized line, the menswear icon has 5,000 spectacular fabrics to select from. As thoughtful as it is expensive, one bespoke suit made from wool will take a minimum of 32 hours to create. Their prêt-à-porter line is also praised for peerless cutting and stitching. Past and present clients include Clark Gable, Barack Obama and, of course, James Bond. There is also a branch at Via dei Condotti 21a. ⊠ *Via del Babuino 38/40, Piazza di Spagna* ☎ *06/484517* ⊕ *www.brioni.com* Ⓜ *Spagna.*

SHOES

A. Testoni. Amedeo Testoni, the brand's founder and original designer, was born in 1905 in Bologna, the heart of Italy's shoemaking territory. In 1929, he opened his first shop and began producing shoes as artistic as the Cubist and Art Deco artwork of the period. His shoes have adorned the feet of Fred Astaire, proving that lightweight shoes can be comfortable and luxurious and still turn heads. Today the Testoni brand includes an extraordinary women's collection and a sports line that is relaxed without losing its artistic heritage. The soft, calfskin sneakers are a dream, as are the matching messenger bags. ⊠ *Via del Babuino 152, Piazza di Spagna* ☎ *06/6788944* ⊕ *www.testoni.com* Ⓜ *Spagna.*

Fodor's Choice
★

Braccialini. Founded in 1954 by Florentine stylist Carla Braccialini and her husband, Braccialini—currently managed by their sons—makes bags that are authentic works of art in delightful shapes, such as little gold taxis or Santa Fe stagecoaches. The delightfully quirky beach bags have picture-postcard scenes of Italian resorts made of brightly colored appliquéd leather: be sure to check out their eccentric Temi (Theme) creature bags; the opossum-shape handbag made out of crocodile skin makes a richly whimsical fashion statement. ⊠ *Galleria Alberto Sordi 20/21, Piazza Colonna, Piazza di Spagna* ☎ *06/6784339* ⊕ *www.braccialini.it* Ⓜ *Spagna.*

Fausto Santini. Shoe lovers with a passion for minimalist design flock to Fausto Santini to get their hands on his preppy-hipster/nerdy-chic shoes. Santini has been in business since 1970 and caters to a sophisticated, avant-garde clientele looking for elegant, classic shoes with a kick. An outlet at Via Cavour 106, named for Fausto's father, Giacomo, sells last season's shoes at a big discount. ⊠ *Via Frattina 120, Piazza di Spagna* ☎ *06/6784114* ⊕ *www.faustosantini.it* Ⓜ *Spagna.*

Fodor's Choice
★

Saddlers Union. Reborn on the mythical artisans' street, Via Margutta, across the street from Federico Fellini's old house, Saddlers Union first launched in 1957 and quickly gained a cult following among those who valued Italian artistry and a traditional aesthetic. If you're searching for a sinfully fabulous handbag in a graceful, classic shape or that "I have arrived" attorney's briefcase, you will find something guaranteed to inspire envy. Items are made on-site with true artistry and under the watchful eye of Angelo Zaza, one of Saddlers Union's original master artisans. Prices are a bit steep, but the quality is definitely worth it. ⊠ *Via Margutta 11, Piazza di Spagna* ☎ *06/32120237* ⊕ *www.saddlersunion.com* Ⓜ *Flaminio, Spagna.*

Fodor's Choice
★

Tod's. With just 30 years under its belt, Tod's has grown from a small family brand into a global powerhouse so wealthy that its owner, Diego Della Valle, donated €20 million to the Colosseum restoration project. The shoe baron's trademark is his simple, classic, understated designs. Sure to please are his light and flexible slip-on Gommini driving shoes with rubber-bottomed soles for extra driving-pedal grip—now you just need a Ferrari. There are also locations on Via dei Condotti and Via Borgogona. ⊠ *Via della Fontanella di Borghese 56a–57, Piazza di Spagna* ☎ *06/68210066* ⊕ *www.tods.com* Ⓜ *Spagna.*

THE VATICAN

RELIGIOUS SOUVENIRS

Savelli Arte e Tradizione. Here you'll find a fully stocked selection of holier-than-thou gifts and sacred trinkets to take home. This family business has been around for more than 100 years and specializes in everything from rosaries, crosses, religious artwork, and statues to Pope Francis memorabilia. The family name, Savelli, dates back to an old Roman family that boasts four popes in its bloodline: Benedict II, Gregory II, Honorius III, and Honorius IV. The store has three other locations: Galleria Savelli in St. Peter's Square; Savelli Gift in Via della Concilliazione; and Art Studio Cafè in Via dei Gracchi. ⊠ *Via Paolo VI 27, Borgo* ☏ *06/68307017* ⊕ *www.savellireligious.com* Ⓜ *Ottaviano.*

MONTI AND SAN LORENZO

CLOTHING

L'Anatra all'Arancia. Repetto ballerinas, chunky handbags, and funky dresses make L'Anatra all'Arancia one of the best local secrets of boho San Lorenzo. The shop showcases innovative designer clothes from Marina Spadafora, Antik Batik, See by Chloé, and Donatella Baroni (the store's owner). Leaning toward the alternative with an eclectic selection of handpicked Italian and French labels, Donatella also carries luxurious perfumes and beautiful jewelry. ⊠ *Via Tiburtina 105, San Lorenzo* ☏ *06/4456293* Ⓜ *Termini, Castro Pretorio.*

Fodor's Choice
★ **Le Gallinelle.** This tiny boutique may live in a former butcher's shop, but it houses some of the most sophisticated retro-inspired fashion garments around Rome. Its owner, Wilma Silvestri, cleverly combines ethnic and contemporary fabrics, evolving them into stylish clothing with a modern edge made for everyday wear. ⊠ *Via Panisperna 61, Monti* ☏ *06/4881017* ⊕ *www.legallinelle.com* Ⓜ *Cavour.*

TRASTEVERE

BOOKSTORES

Almost Corner Bookshop. Bursting at the seams, with not an ounce of space left on its shelves, this tiny little bookshop is a favorite meeting point for English speakers in Trastevere. Irish owner Dermot O'Connell goes out of his way to find what you're looking for, and if he doesn't have it in stock he'll make a special order for you. The shop carries everything from popular best sellers to translated Italian classics, as well as lots of good books about Rome. ⊠ *Via del Moro 45, Trastevere* ☏ *06/5836942.*

FLEA MARKETS

Porta Portese. One of the biggest flea markets in Italy—even in Europe, perhaps—Porta Portese welcomes visitors in droves every Sunday 7 am–2 pm. One can literally find anything and everything, including the kitchen sink. Treasure seekers and bargain hunters love scrounging around tents for new and used clothing, antique furniture, used books, accessories, and other odds 'n' ends—all at rock-bottom prices. Bring your haggling skills, and cash (preferably small bills—it'll work in your favor when driving a bargain); stallholders don't accept credit cards, and the nearest ATM is a hike. Keep your valuables close; pickpockets lurk nearby. Tram No. 8 is the best way to reach the market. ⊠ *Via Portuense and adjacent streets between Porta Portese and Via Ettore Rolli, Trastevere.*

SHOES

Fodor's Choice
★
Joseph DeBach. The best-kept shoe secret in Rome and open only in the evenings (or by appointment), Joseph DeBach has eccentric creations that are more art than footwear. Entirely handmade from wood, metal, and leather in his small and chaotic studio, his abacus wedge is worthy of a museum. Sometimes-outrageous styles earn a "wow" and are sometimes finished with hand-painted strings, odd bits of comic books, newspapers, or other unexpected baubles. ⊠ *Piazza de' Renzi 21, Trastevere* ☎ *3460255265* ⊕ *www.josephdebach.it.*

3

SIDE TRIPS
FROM ROME

WELCOME TO SIDE TRIPS FROM ROME

TOP REASONS TO GO

★ **Ostia Antica:** Perhaps even more than Pompeii, the excavated port city of ancient Rome conveys a picture of everyday life in the days of the empire.

★ **Tivoli's Villa d'Este:** Hundreds of fountains cascading and shooting skyward (one even plays music on organ pipes) will delight you at this spectacular garden.

★ **Castelli Romani:** Be a Roman for a day and enjoy an escape to the ancient hilltop wine towns on the city's doorstep.

★ **Viterbo:** This town may be modern, but it has a Gothic papal palace, a Romanesque cathedral, and the magical medieval quarter of San Pellegrino.

★ **Gardens bizarre and beautiful:** The 16th-century proto-Disneyland Parco dei Mostri (Monster Park) is famed for its fantastic sculptures; the Villa Lante, a few miles away, remains the stateliest Renaissance garden of them all.

All roads may lead to Rome, but for thousands of years emperors, popes, and princes have been heading *fuori porta* (beyond the gates). To the west is ancient Ostia Antica; north is Tuscia, with its gardens. Eastward is Tivoli, famed for chic retreats. To the south lie the enchanting towns of the Castelli Romani.

1 Tuscia. Viterbo is a 13th-century time capsule; at the gardens and palaces of nearby Bagnaia, Caprarola, and Bomarzo you can time-travel back to the Renaissance.

2 Ostia Antica. This ancient Roman port is now a parklike archaeological site.

3 Tivoli and Palestrina. Cool, green Tivoli is a fitting setting for the regal Villa Adriana and the unforgettable Villa d'Este, a park filled with gorgeous fountains.

4 The Castelli Romani. Clustered amid the Alban Hills, Frascati is home to the majestic Villa Aldobrandini, Castelgandolfo is the pope's summer retreat, Ariccia has its grand Palazzo Chigi, and Nemi enjoys an eagle's-nest perch.

Updated
by Agnes
Crawford

Lazio, the region that encompasses Rome, the capital, is often bypassed by foreign visitors. This is a pity, since the area, which stretches from the Apennine mountain range to the Mediterranean coast, holds dozens of fascinating towns and villages, as well as scenic lakes, national parks, and forests. A trip outside Rome introduces you to a more intimate aspect of Italy, where local customs and feast days are still enthusiastically observed, and local gastronomic specialties take pride of place on restaurant menus.

Despite these small towns' proximity to the capital and the increased commuter traffic congestion of today, they still each manage to preserve their individual character. Ostia Antica, ancient Rome's seaport, is one of the region's top attractions—it rivals Pompeii in the quality of its preservation, and for evocativeness and natural beauty, it easily outshines the Roman Forum. Emperors, cardinals, and popes have long escaped to green and verdant retreats in nearby Tivoli, Viterbo, and the Alban Hills, and their amazing villas, palaces, and gardens add to nature's allure. So if the screeching traffic and long lines at the Colosseum start to wear on you, do as the Romans do: get out of town. There's plenty to see and do.

PLANNING

MAKING THE MOST OF YOUR TIME
Ostia Antica is in many ways an ideal day trip from Rome: it's fascinating, it's not far from the city, it's reachable by public transit, and it takes about half a day to do. Villa d'Este and Villa Adriana in Tivoli also make for a manageable, though fuller, day trip. There's so much to see at these two sights alone, but also be sure to visit Tivoli's picturesque gorge, which is strikingly crowned by an ancient Roman temple to Vesta

Side Trips
from Rome

(now it's part of the famed Sibilla restaurant). Other destinations can be visited in a day, but you'll get more out of them if you stay the night.

One classic five-day itinerary that takes in the area's grand villas, ancient ruins, and pretty villages begins with Ostia Antica, the excavated port town of ancient Rome. Then head north to explore Viterbo's medieval streets on Day 2. On Day 3, take in the hot springs or the gardens of Bomarzo, Bagnaia, and Caprarola. For Day 4, head to Tivoli's delights. Then on Day 5 take a relaxing trip to the Castelli Romani, where Frascati wine is produced. Admire the monumental gardens of the aristocrats of yore and explore the narrow streets of these small hill towns—what more could any vacationer want?

GETTING HERE AND AROUND

There's reliable public transit from Rome to Ostia Antica, Tivoli, and Viterbo. COTRAL is the regional bus company. For other destinations, having a car is a big advantage—going by bus or Trenitalia can add hours to your trip, and the routes and schedules are often puzzling.

Contacts COTRAL. ⊠ *Via Bernardino Alimena 105* ☎ *800/174471* ⊕ *www. cotralspa.it.* **Trenitalia** (*Italian National Railway System*). ☎ *199/892021, 06/68475475* ⊕ *www.trenitalia.com.*

RESTAURANTS

You certainly won't go hungry when you're exploring the Roman countryside. Whether you choose a five-star establishment or a simple eatery, you can be sure of a fresh, clean tablecloth and friendly, attentive service. Odds are that the owner will be in the kitchen, personally preparing the time-honored dishes that have made Italian cuisine so famous.

HOTELS

Former aristocratic houses with frescoed ceilings, *agriturismi* farmhouses, luxury spas, and cozy bed-and-breakfasts are just a few of the lodging options here. You won't find much in the way of big chain hotels, though. *Hotel reviews have been shortened. For full information, visit Fodors.com.*

WHAT IT COSTS			
$	**$$**	**$$$**	**$$$$**
Restaurants	under €15	€15–€24	€25–€35	over €35
Hotels	under €125	€125–€200	€201–€300	over €300

Prices in the dining reviews are the average cost of a main course at dinner, or, if dinner is not served, at lunch. Prices in the reviews are the lowest cost of a standard double room in high season.

VISITOR INFORMATION

Tourist information kiosks, which are scattered around Rome's main squares and tourist sights, can give you information about the Castelli Romani, Ostia Antica, and Tivoli. The Tuscia area is served by the central tourist office in Viterbo.

Contact Visit Lazio. ⊕ *www.visitlazio.com.*

TUSCIA

Tuscia (the modern name for the Etruscan domain of Etruria) is a region of dramatic beauty punctuated by deep, rocky gorges and thickly forested hills, with dappled light falling on wooded paths. This has long been a preferred locale for the retreats of wealthy Romans, a place where they could build grand villas and indulge their sometimes-eccentric gardening tastes. The provincial capital, Viterbo, which overshadowed Rome as a center of papal power for a time during the Middle Ages, lies in the heart of Tuscia. The farmland east of Viterbo conceals small quarries of the dark, volcanic *peperino* stone, which shows up in the walls of many buildings here. Lake Bolsena lies in an extinct volcano, and the sulfur springs still bubbling up in the spas were used by the ancient Romans. Bagnaia and Caprarola are home to palaces and gardens; the garden statuary at Bomarzo is in a league of its own—somewhere between the beautiful and the bizarre.

The ideal way to explore this region is by car. From Rome you can reach Viterbo by train and then get to Bagnaia by local bus. If you're traveling by train or bus, check schedules carefully; you may have to allow for an overnight if you want to do a round of the region's sights.

VITERBO

104 km (64 miles) northwest of Rome.

Viterbo's moment of glory was in the 13th century, when it became the seat of the papal court. The medieval core of the city still sits within 12th-century walls. Its old buildings, with windows bright with geraniums, are made of dark peperino, the local stone that colors the medieval part of Viterbo a dark gray, contrasted here and there with the golden tufa rock of walls and towers. Peperino is also used in the characteristic and typically medieval exterior staircases that you see throughout the old town.

Viterbo has blossomed into a regional commercial center, and much of the modern city is loud and industrial. However, in Viterbo's San Pellegrino district you'll get the feel of the Middle Ages—daily life is carried on here in a setting that has remained practically unchanged over the centuries. The Palazzo Papale and the cathedral enhance the effect. The city has remained a renowned spa center for its natural hot springs just outside town, which have been frequented by popes and mere mortals alike since medieval times.

GETTING HERE AND AROUND

Viterbo is well served by public transport from Rome. Direct train service takes 1 hour 40 minutes. Try to avoid peak hours, as many commuters live in towns along the line. By road, take either the old Roman consular road, the Via Cassia, which passes near Caprarola, or, if you are in a hurry, the A1 toll highway to the Orte exit and then the 204 highway, with a detour to Bomarzo. The trip can take a couple of hours or even more, depending on traffic.

VISITOR INFORMATION
Contact **Viterbo Tourism Office.** ✉ *Piazza Martiri D'Ungheria* ☎ *0761/325992* ⊕ *www.promotuscia.it.*

EXPLORING

Cattedrale di San Lorenzo. Viterbo's Romanesque cathedral was built over the ruins of the ancient Roman Temple of Hercules. During World War II the roof and the vault of the central nave were destroyed by a bomb. Subsequently, the church was rebuilt to its original medieval design. Three popes are buried here, including Pope Alexander IV (1254–61), whose body was hidden so well by the canons, out of fear that it would be desecrated, that it has never been found. The small adjoining **Museo del Colle del Duomo** has a collection of 18th-century reliquaries, Etruscan sarcophagi, and a painting of the Crucifixion that has been attributed to Michelangelo. ✉ *Piazza San Lorenzo* ☎ *320/7911328* ⊕ *www.museocoll-edelduomo.com* 🏛 *Museum €3* ⊙ *Closed Mon., and 1st 2 wks in Jan.*

Palazzo Papale (*Papal Palace*). This Gothic palace was built in the 13th century as a residence for popes looking to get away from the city. At the time, Rome was notoriously unhealthful, ridden with malaria and plague, not to mention rampaging factions of rival barons. In 1271 the palace was the scene of a novel type of rebellion. A conclave held that year to elect a new pope dragged on for months. The people of Viterbo were exasperated by the delay, especially as custom decreed that they had to provide for the cardinals' board and lodging for the duration of the conclave. To speed up the deliberations the townspeople tore the roof off the great hall where the cardinals were meeting, and put them on bread and water. A new pope—Gregory X—was elected in short order. ■ TIP→ **Guided tours last 40 minutes and start from Museo del Colle del Duomo.** ✉ *Piazza San Lorenzo* ☎ *3207911328* ⊕ *www.museo-colledelduomo.com* 🏛 *€9, includes tour of Cattedrale di San Lorenzo, Palazzo Papale, and Museo del Colle del Duomo* ⊙ *Closed Mon.*

San Pellegrino. One of the best preserved medieval districts in Italy, San Pellegrino has charming vistas of arches, vaults, towers, exterior staircases, worn wooden doors on great iron hinges, and tiny hanging gardens. You pass many antiques shops and craft workshops as you explore the little squares and byways. The **Fontana Grande** in the piazza of the same name is the largest and most extravagant of Viterbo's Gothic fountains. ✉ *Via San Pellegrino, near Palazzo Papale and Cattedrale di San Lorenzo* ⊕ *www.promotuscia.it.*

Fodor'sChoice
★ **Terme dei Papi.** Viterbo has been a spa town for centuries, and this excellent spa continues the tradition, providing the usual health and beauty treatments with an Etruscan twist: try a facial with local volcanic mud, or a steam bath in an ancient cave, where scalding hot mineral water direct from the spring splashes down a waterfall to a pool beneath your feet. The Terme dei Papi's main draw, however, comes from the *terme* (baths) themselves: a 21,000-square-foot outdoor limestone pool, into the shallow end of which Viterbo's famous hot water pours at 59°C (138°F)—and gives a jolt with its sulfurous odor. Floats and deck chairs are for rent, but bring your own bathrobe and towel unless you're staying at the hotel. There are moonlight swims on Saturday nights, when

the pool is open (9 pm–1 am). ■ **TIP→ Shuttle buses operate between Rome and the Terme. Round-trip tickets cost €8; call or check website for travel times.** ✉ *Strada Bagni 12, 5 km (3 miles) west of town center* ☎ *0761/3501* 🌐 *www.termedeipapi.it* 🎟 *Pool €12 weekdays, €18 weekends* 🕒 *Closed Tues.*

WHERE TO EAT

$ ITALIAN Fodor's Choice ★ 🍴 **Osteria del Vecchio Orologio.** Tucked away in a side street off the medieval Piazza delle Erbe, the Osteria del Vecchio Orologio offers top-quality Tuscia specialties in a warm and informal atmosphere. They're a member of the Slow Food movement with a menu that changes according to the season. **Known for:** cute, cupboard-lined walls; free-range Maremma beef; preserves, olive oils, and wine for sale. [$] *Average main: €14* ✉ *Via Orologio Vecchio 25* ☎ *335/337754* 🌐 *osteria-del-vecchio-orologio.business.site* 🕒 *No lunch Mon. and Tues.*

$ ITALIAN 🍴 **Tre Re.** Viterbo's oldest restaurant—and one of the most ancient in Italy—has been operating in the *centro storico* (historic center) since 1622. The small, wood-paneled dining room, chummily packed with tables, was a favorite haunt of movie director Federico Fellini and, before that, of British and American soldiers during World War II. **Known for:** traditional local dishes; roasted suckling pig; locals touch the Tre Re (Three Kings) sign outside for luck. [$] *Average main: €14* ✉ *Via Macel Gattesco 3* ☎ *0761/304619* 🌐 *www.ristorantetrere.com* 🕒 *Closed Thurs.*

WHERE TO STAY

$$$ HOTEL 🏨 **Hotel Niccolò V.** The relaxed country-house elegance and comfortable rooms at this spa hotel are a sharp contrast to the brisk and clinical atmosphere of the Terme dei Papi spa itself, which bustles with doctors, bathers in bathrobes, and uniformed staff. **Pros:** friendly staff; comfortable rooms; relaxing. **Cons:** guests lounging in the lobby in bathrobes; several miles out of town; pervading sulfur smell from pool outside. [$] *Rooms from: €250* ✉ *Strada Bagni 12, 5 km (3 miles) west of town center* ☎ *0761/350555* 🌐 *www.termedeipapi.it* 🛏 *23 rooms* 🍽 *Free Breakfast.*

$ B&B/INN 🏨 **La Terrazza Medioevale.** The historic Palazzo Perotti in the center of old Viterbo's San Pellegrino district is the setting for three stylish double rooms. **Pros:** comfortable accommodation in the heart of the historic quarter at bargain price. **Cons:** no credit cards accepted; accessible only by flight of stairs. [$] *Rooms from: €80* ✉ *Via S. Pellegrino 1, near Cattedrale di San Lorenzo* ☎ *0761/307034* 🌐 *www.laterrazzamedioevale.it* 💳 *No credit cards* 🕒 *Closed Aug.* 🛏 *3 rooms* 🍽 *Free Breakfast.*

BAGNAIA

5 km (3 miles) east of Viterbo.

The village of Bagnaia is the site of the 16th-century cardinal Alessandro Montalto's summer retreat, which is quite an extravaganza.

GETTING HERE AND AROUND

Local buses from Viterbo are one way to get here. By local train, it's 10 minutes beyond the Viterbo stop—few local trains actually do stop, though, so be sure to check.

EXPLORING

Villa Lante. The main draw here is the hillside garden and park that surround the two small, identical residences of the 16th-century cardinal Alessandro Montalto. The garden and the park were designed by the virtuoso architect Giacomo Barozzi (circa 1507–73), known as Vignola, who later worked with Michelangelo on St. Peter's. On the lowest terrace a delightful Italian garden has a centerpiece fountain fed by water channeled down the hillside. On another terrace, a stream of water runs through a groove carved in a long stone table where the cardinal entertained his friends alfresco, chilling wine in the running water. That's only one of the most evident of the whimsical water games that were devised for the cardinal. The symmetry of the formal gardens contrasts with the wild, untamed park adjacent to it, reflecting the paradoxes of nature and artifice that are the theme of this pleasure garden. ⊠ *Via G. Baroni 71* ☎ *06/69994251* ⊕ *www.polomusealelazio.beniculturali.it/ index.php?it/243/villa-lante* ⬚*€5* ⊙ *Closed Mon.*

CAPRAROLA

21 km (13 miles) southeast of Bagnaia, 19 km (12 miles) southeast of Viterbo.

The wealthy and powerful Farnese family took over this sleepy village in the 1500s and had the architect Vignola design a huge palace and gardens to rival the great residences of Rome. He also rearranged the little town of Caprarola to enhance the palazzo's setting.

GETTING HERE AND AROUND

Caprarola is served by COTRAL bus, leaving from Rome's Saxa Rubra station on the Roma Nord suburban railway line.

EXPLORING

Fodor'sChoice   **Palazzo Farnese.** When Cardinal Alessandro Farnese, Pope Paul III's
★   grandson, retired to Caprarola, he intended to build a residence that would reflect the family's grandeur. In 1559, he entrusted the task to the leading architect Jacopo Barozzi da Vignola, who came up with some innovative ideas. A magnificent spiral staircase, lavishly decorated with allegorical figures, mythical landscapes, and grotesques by Antonio Tempesta, connected the main entrance with the cardinal's apartments on the main floor. The staircase was gently inclined, with very deep but low steps, so that the cardinal could ride his horse right up to his bedchamber. A tour includes the Hall of Farnese Triumphs, the Hercules Room, and the Antechamber of the Council of Trent, all painted by the Zuccari brothers. Of special interest is the Hall of the Maps, with the ceiling depicting the zodiac and the walls frescoed with maps of the world as known to 16th-century cartographers. The palace is surrounded by a formal Renaissance garden. ⊠ *Piazza Farnese 1* ☎ *0761/646052* ⊕ *www.caprarola.com* ⬚*€5, includes garden* ⊙ *Closed Mon.*

WHERE TO EAT

$$ × **Antica Trattoria del Borgo**. Visitors to Caprarola's landmark Palazzo
ROMAN   Farnese often round out the experience with a hearty meal at this
FAMILY   celebrated trattoria. There's a cozy atmosphere inside, and when the
weather permits, a pleasant seating area outside. **Known for:** grilled,
wild game; expansive wine cellar; some gluten-free pastas. $ *Average
main: €20* ✉ *Via Borgo Vecchio 107* ☎ *0761/645252* ⊕ *www.antica-
trattoriadelborgo.it* ⊘ *Closed all day Mon., and Tues. and Wed. eves.*

BOMARZO

15 km (9 miles) northeast of Viterbo.

Once a fief of the powerful Orsini family, Bomarzo is home to the Parco
dei Mostri, the town's main attraction, which was created to amuse and
astound the Orsini's guests. The 16th-century Palazzo Orsini is now
the seat of the town council. Inside, there is a princely hall, frescoed
by Pietro da Cortona, the famous Italian Baroque fresco painter and
architect.

GETTING HERE AND AROUND

Bomarzo is easily reached by car from the A1 autostrada. If you want
to go there directly, carry on to the Attigliano exit. Parco dei Monstri
is some 6 km (4 miles) from that point. Alternatively, come out at Orte
and branch off at Casalone on the Viterbo road. A public bus also goes
here, from Viterbo.

EXPLORING

FAMILY   **Parco dei Mostri** (*Monster Park*). This eerie fantasy, originally known as
the Village of Marvels, or the Sacred Wood, was created in 1552 by
Prince Vicino Orsini, with the aid of the famous artist Pirro Ligorio.
It's populated with weird and fantastic sculptures of mythical crea-
tures intended to astonish illustrious guests. The sculptures, carved in
outcroppings of mossy stone in shady groves and woodland, include
giant tortoises and griffins and an ogre's head with an enormous gap-
ing mouth. Children love it, and there are photo ops galore. The park
has a self-service café (open Sunday only, in winter) and a gift shop.
✉ *Localita Giardino, 1½ km (1 mile) west of Bomarzo* ☎ *0761/924029*
⊕ *www.parcodeimostri.com* ✉ *€10.*

OSTIA ANTICA

30 km (19 miles) southwest of Rome.

Founded around the 4th century BC, Ostia served as Rome's port city
for several centuries until the Tiber changed course, leaving the town
high and dry. What has been excavated here is a remarkably intact
Roman town. To get the most out of a visit, fair weather and good
walking shoes are essential. To avoid the worst extremes of hot days,
be here when the gates open or go late in the afternoon. A visit to the
excavations takes two to three hours, including 20 minutes for the
museum. Inside the site, there's a snack bar and a bookshop.

GETTING HERE AND AROUND

The best way to get to Ostia Antica is by train. The Ostia Lido train leaves every half hour from the station adjacent to Rome's Piramide Line B Metro station, stopping off at Ostia Antica en route; the trip takes 35 minutes. By car, take the Via del Mare that leads off from Rome's EUR district. Be prepared for heavy traffic, especially at peak hours, on weekends, and in summer.

EXPLORING

Fodor'sChoice
★

Scavi di Ostia Antica (*Ostia Antica excavations*). Tidal mud and wind-blown sand covered the ancient port town, which lay buried until the 19th century, when it was extensively excavated. A cosmopolitan population of rich businessmen, wily merchants, sailors, slaves, and their respective families once populated the city. The great warehouses were built in the 2nd century AD to handle goods which passed through the town, notably huge shipments of grain from Africa; the *insulae* (apartment buildings) provided housing for the city's growing population. The increasing importance of nearby Portus, and the inexorable decline of the Roman Empire eventually led to the port's abandonment. Over the last two millennia the coastline has retreated, and a 16th-century flood diverted the course of the Tiber so only a glimpse of the river (near the café) is to be seen today. The on-site **Museo Ostiense** displays sculptures, mosaics, and objects of daily use found here. There's a cafeteria on-site. ■TIP➜ **The recently excavated ports of Tiberius and Claudius are nearby and also well worth visiting.** ✉ *Viale dei Romagnoli 717* ☎ *06/56350215* ⊕ *www.ostiaantica.beniculturali.it* 🎟 *€10, includes Museo Ostiense (small increase if there is an exhibition); free 1st Sun. of month* ☉ *Closed Mon.*

WHERE TO EAT

$$
ROMAN
FAMILY

✕ **Sora Margherita al Borghetto.** This cozy trattoria is tucked away in the charming walled medieval *borgo* (old town) of Ostia Antica next to the Castello di Giulio II. A short walk from the excavations, it's an ideal spot to restore your energy with some seasonal produce, and there is pretty outside seating. **Known for:** traditional Roman food; helpful staff, no menu required; homemade pastas. Ⓢ *Average main: €15* ✉ *Via del Forno 11* ✛ *Go through stone archway leading into the medieval village* ☎ *06/56352956* ⊕ *www.soramargherita.com* ☉ *Closed Mon. No dinner Sun.*

TIVOLI AND PALESTRINA

Tivoli is a five-star draw, its main attractions being its two villas. There's an ancient one in which Hadrian reproduced the most beautiful monuments in the then-known world, and a Renaissance one, in which Cardinal Ippolito d'Este put a river to work for his delight. Unfortunately, the Via Tiburtina from Rome to Tivoli passes through miles of industrial areas with chaotic traffic, so whether you are driving or taking the bus take the A24 motorway to avoid it. Or take the train. Grit your teeth

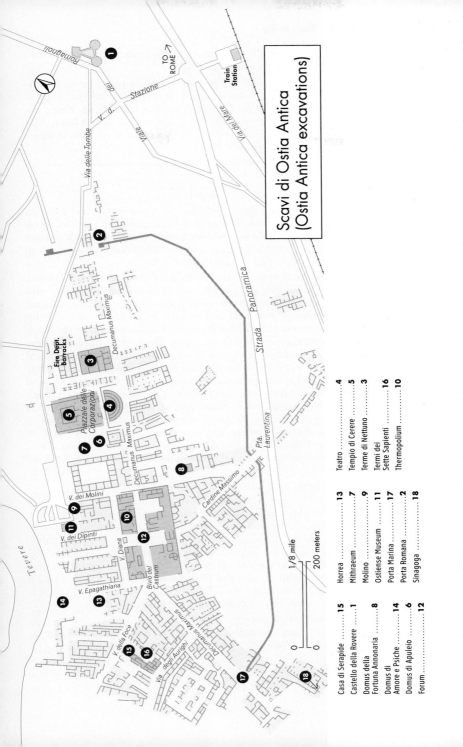

Scavi di Ostia Antica
(Ostia Antica excavations)

Tevere

Fire Dept.
Barracks

Piazzale delle
Corporazioni

Decumanus Maximus

Decumanus Maximus

V. dei Molini

V. dei Dipinti

V. Epagathiana

V. Diana

Bivio del
Castrum

Cardine Massimo

Decumanus Maximus

V. degli Aurighi

V. della foce

Pta. Laurentina

Strada Panoramica

Romagnoli

V. d. Stazione

Via delle Tombe

Viale

TO ROME

Via del Mare

Train Station

0   1/8 mile

0   200 meters

and persevere, and it'll be worth it: at the heart of this shell lie two pearls that are rightly world-famous.

You'll know you're close to Tivoli when you see vast quarries of travertine marble and smell the sulfurous vapors of the little spa, Bagni di Tivoli. Both sites in Tivoli are outdoors and entail walking. With a car, you can continue your loop through the mountains east of Rome, taking in the ancient pagan sanctuary at Palestrina, spectacularly set on the slopes of Mt. Ginestro.

TIVOLI

36 km (22 miles) northeast of Rome.

In ancient times, just about anybody who was anybody had a villa in Tivoli, including Crassus, Trajan, Hadrian, Horace, and Catullus. Tivoli fell into obscurity in the medieval era until the Renaissance, when popes and cardinals came back to the town and built villas showy enough to rival those of their extravagant predecessors.

Nowadays Tivoli is small but vibrant, with winding streets and views over the surrounding countryside. The deep Aniene River gorge runs through the center of town and comes replete with a romantically sited bridge, cascading waterfalls, and two jewels of ancient Roman architecture that crown its cliffs—the round Temple of Vesta (or the Sybil, the prophetess credited with predicting the birth of Christ) and the ruins of the rectangular Temple of the hero-god Tibur, the mythical founder of the city. These can be picturesquely viewed across the gorge from the Villa Gregoriana park, named for Pope Gregory XVI, who saved Tivoli from chronic river damage by diverting the river through a tunnel, weakening its flow. An unexpected side effect was the creation of the Grande Cascata (Grand Cascade), which shoots a huge jet of water into the valley below. You may also want to set your sights on the Antico Ristorante Sibilla, set right by the Temple of Vesta. From its dining terrace you can take in one of the most memorably romantic landscape views in Italy.

GETTING HERE AND AROUND

Unless you have nerves of steel, it's best not to drive to Tivoli. Hundreds of businesses line the Via Tiburtina from Rome and bottleneck traffic is nearly constant. You can avoid some, but not all, of the congestion by taking the Roma–L'Aquila toll road. Luckily, there's abundant public transport. Buses leave every 15 minutes from the Ponte Mammolo stop on Metro Line A; the ride takes an hour. Regional Trenitalia trains connect from both Termini and Tiburtina stations and will have you in Tivoli in under an hour. Villa d'Este is in the town center, and there is bus service from Tivoli's main square to Hadrian's Villa.

VISITOR INFORMATION

Contact PIT (Punto Informativo Turistico) *(Tivoli tourist office).* ⊠ *Piazzale Nazioni Unite* ☎ *0774/313536* ⊕ *www.comune.tivoli.rm.it/pit.*

EXPLORING

Fodor's Choice ★ **Villa Adriana** (*Hadrian's Villa*). An emperor's theme park, this astonishingly grand 2nd-century villa was an exclusive retreat below the ancient settlement of Tibur where the marvels of the classical world were reproduced for a ruler's pleasure. Hadrian, who succeeded Trajan as emperor in AD 117, was a man of genius and intellectual curiosity, fascinated by the accomplishments of the Hellenistic world. From AD 125 to 134, architects, laborers, and artists worked on the vast villa, re-creating some of the monuments and sights that the emperor had seen on his travels in Egypt, Asia Minor, and Greece.

During the Middle Ages, the site was sacked by barbarians and Romans alike, and many of the statues and architectural features ended up in the Vatican Museums. Nonetheless, the colossal remains are impressive: the ruins rise in a garden setting of green lawns framed with oleanders, pines, and cypresses. Not surprisingly, Villa Adriana is a UNESCO World Heritage Site, and it's one that has not yielded up all of its secrets. Archaeologists recently discovered the site of the Temple of Isis, complete with several sculptures, including one of the falcon-headed god Horus. ■ TIP→ **A visit to the villa takes at least two hours (carry water on hot days); maps dispensed at the ticket office will help you get your bearings.** ⊠ *Largo Margherite Yourcenar 1, 6 km (4 miles) southwest of Tivoli* ☎ *0774/530203* ⊕ *www.villaadriana.beniculturali.it* ▨€8 *(free 1st Sun. of month).*

Fodor's Choice ★ **Villa d'Este.** One of Italy's UNESCO World Heritage sites, Villa d'Este was created by Cardinal Ippolito d'Este in the 16th century. This villa in the center of Tivoli was the most amazing pleasure garden of its day, and it still stuns visitors with its beauty. Cardinal d'Este (1509–72), a devotee of the Renaissance celebration of human ingenuity over nature, was inspired by the excavation of Villa Adriana. He paid architect Pirro Ligorrio an astronomical sum to create a mythical garden with water as its artistic centerpiece and diverted the Aniene River to water the garden and feed the several hundred fountains that cascade, shoot skyward, imitate birdsong, and simulate rain. The musical **Fontana dell'Organo** has been restored to working order: the organ plays a watery tune every two hours (check times at the ticket office). Romantics will love the night tour of the gardens and floodlit fountains that takes place on Friday and Saturday in summer. ■ TIP→ **Allow at least an hour for a visit, which involves many stairs. There are vending machines for refreshments by the bookshop.** ⊠ *Piazza Trento 1* ☎ *0774/312070* ⊕ *www.villadestetivoli.info* ▨€8, *night tour €11; free 1st Sun. of month* ⊙ *Closed Mon.*

WHERE TO EAT AND STAY

$$$
ITALIAN
Fodor's Choice ★ **Antico Ristorante Sibilla.** Founded as a hotel and restaurant in 1730 beside the circular Roman Temple of Vesta and the Sanctuary of the Sybil, the idyllic wisteria-draped terrace has a spectacular view over the deep gorge of the Aniene River, with the thundering waters of the waterfall in the background. Standards are high, and seasonal produce and local dishes are a major part of the menu. **Known for:** among the most beautiful sights of Tivoli; homemade pasta and antipastas;

beautiful terrace with a super view. $ *Average main: €25* ✉ *Via della Sibilla 50* ☎ *0774/335281* ⊕ *www.ristorantesibilla.com* ☉ *Closed Mon.*

$
B&B/INN **Adriano.** The Cinelli family has run this hotel and restaurant beside the entrance to Hadrian's Villa for three generations. **Pros:** wonderful location; peaceful garden; attentive service. **Cons:** busloads of tourists disembark under the windows; some rooms are small. $ *Rooms from: €80* ✉ *Largo Yourcenar 2* ☎ *0774/030982* ⊕ *www.hoteladriano.com/en* ⤳ *13 rooms* ⦿| *Free Breakfast.*

$$
HOTEL **Hotel Torre Sant'Angelo.** A former monastery and residence of the Massimo princes now contains comfortable guest rooms equipped with modern amenities; best of all, it overlooks the old town, the Aniene Falls, and the Temple of the Sybil. **Pros:** 21st-century comfort in a historic mansion; pool; competitive rates. **Cons:** a mile out of town. $ *Rooms from: €140* ✉ *Via Quintilio Varo* ☎ *0774/332533* ⊕ *www.hoteltorresangelo.it* ⤳ *35 rooms* ⦿| *Free Breakfast.*

PALESTRINA

27 km (17 miles) southeast of Tivoli, 37 km (23 miles) east of Rome.

Except to students of ancient history and music lovers, Palestrina is little known outside Italy. Its most famous native son, Giovanni Pierluigi da Palestrina, born here in 1525, is considered the master of counterpoint and polyphony. He composed 105 masses, as well as madrigals, Magnificats, and motets. There is a small museum dedicated to his life and work in the town center.

Ancient Praeneste (modern Palestrina) flourished much earlier than Rome. It was the site of the Temple of Fortuna Primigenia, which dates from the 2nd century BC. This was one of the largest, richest, most frequented temple complexes in all antiquity—people came from far and wide to consult its famous oracle. In modern times no one had any idea of the extent of the complex until World War II bombings exposed ancient foundations occupying huge artificial terraces, which stretch from the upper part of the town as far downhill as its central Duomo.

GETTING HERE AND AROUND
COTRAL buses leave from the Anagnina terminal on Rome's Metro Line A and from the Tiburtina railway station. Alternatively, you can take a train to Zagarolo, where a COTRAL bus takes you on to Palestrina. The total trip takes 40 minutes. By car, take the A1 (Autostrada del Sole) to the San Cesareo exit and follow the signs to Palestrina. Expect it to take about an hour.

EXPLORING
Palazzo Barberini. A bomb blast during World War II uncovered the remains of the immense Temple of Fortune that covered the entire hillside under the present town. Large arches and terraces are now visible and you can walk or take a local bus up to the imposing Palazzo Barberini, which crowns the highest point. The palace was built in the 17th century along the semicircular lines of the original temple. It now contains the **Museo Nazionale Archeologico di Palestrina,** with material found on the site that dates from throughout the classical period.

A well-labeled collection of Etruscan bronzes, pottery, and terra-cotta statuary as well as Roman artifacts take second place to the main event, a 1st-century BC mosaic showing ancient Egyptian pleasure craft and African animals. This highly colorful and detailed work is worth the trip to Palestrina by itself. But there's more: a model of the temple as it was in ancient times helps you appreciate the immensity of the original construction. ⊠ *Piazza della Cortina 1* ☎ *06/9538100* 💷 *€5.*

WHERE TO EAT

$$ ⨉ **Il Piscarello.** Tucked away at the bottom of a steep side road, this
ITALIAN elegant dining room immersed in a garden comes as a bit of a surprise.
FAMILY Food is great and the service make this a favorite choice for wedding parties and anniversaries, which are usually in one of the private rooms. **Known for:** dishes made with white and black truffles; call 24 hrs ahead for gluten-free options; outdoor seating in summer. $ *Average main:* *€20* ⊠ *Via del Piscarello 2* ☎ *06/9574326* ⊕ *www.ristoranteilpiscarello.* *it* ⊗ *Closed Mon. No lunch Tues.–Thurs. No dinner Sun.*

THE CASTELLI ROMANI

These *castelli* aren't really castles, as their name would seem to imply. Rather, they're little towns that are scattered on the slopes of the Alban Hills near Rome. And the Alban Hills aren't really hills, but extinct volcanoes. There were castles here in the Middle Ages, however, when each of these towns, fiefs of rival Roman lords, had its own fortress to defend it. Some centuries later, the area was given over to villas and retreats, notably the pope's summer residence at Castel Gandolfo, and the 17th- and 18th-century villas that transformed Frascati into the Beverly Hills of Rome. Arrayed around the rim of an extinct volcano that encloses two crater lakes, the string of picturesque towns of the Castelli Romani are today surrounded by vineyards, olive groves, and chestnut woods—no wonder overheated Romans have always loved to escape here.

Ever since Roman times the Castelli have been renowned for their wine. In the narrow, medieval alleyways of the oldest parts you can still find old-fashioned taverns where the locals sit on wooden benches, quaffing the golden nectar straight from the barrel. Traveling around the countryside, you can also pop into some of the local vineyards, where they will be happy to give you a tasting of their wines. Exclusive local gastronomic specialties include the bread of Genzano, baked in traditional wood-fire ovens, the *porchetta* (roast suckling pig) of Ariccia, and the *pupi* biscuits of Frascati, shaped like women or mermaids with three or more breasts (an allusion to ancient fertility goddesses). Each town has its own feasts and saints' days, celebrated with costumed processions and colorful events. Some are quite spectacular, like Marino's annual Wine Festival in October, where the town's fountains flow with wine; or the Flower Festival of Genzano in June, when an entire street is carpeted with millions of flower petals, arranged in elaborate patterns.

FRASCATI

20 km (12 miles) south of Rome.

It's worth taking a stroll through Frascati's lively old center. Via Battisti, leading from the Belvedere, takes you into Piazza San Pietro with its imposing gray-and-white cathedral. Inside is the cenotaph of Prince Charles Edward, last of the Scottish Stuart dynasty, who tried unsuccessfully to regain the British Crown, and died an exile in Rome in 1788. A little arcade beside the monumental fountain at the back of the piazza leads into Market Square, where the smell of fresh baking will entice you into the Purificato family bakery to see the traditional pupi biscuits, modeled on old pagan fertility symbols.

Take your pick from the cafés and trattorias fronting the central Piazzale Marconi, or do as the locals do: buy fruit from the market gallery at Piazza del Mercato, then get a huge slice of porchetta from one of the stalls, a hunk of *casareccio* bread, and a few *ciambelline frascatane* (ring-shape cookies made with wine), and take your picnic to any one of the nearby *cantine* (homey wine bars), and settle in for some sips of tasty, inexpensive vino.

GETTING HERE AND AROUND

An hourly train service along a single-track line through vineyards and olive groves takes you to Frascati from Termini station. The trip takes 45 minutes. By car, take the Via Tuscolano, which branches off the Appia Nuova road just after St. John Lateran in Rome, and drive straight up.

VISITOR INFORMATION

Contact Frascati Point (tourism office). ⊠ *Piazza G. Marconi 5* ☎ *06/94184406* ⊕ *www.comune.frascati.rm.it.*

EXPLORING

Abbey of San Nilo Grottaferrata. In Grottaferrata, a busy village a couple of miles from Frascati, the main attraction is a walled citadel founded by St. Nilo, who brought his group of Basilian monks here in 1004, when he was 90. The order is unique in that it's Roman Catholic but observes Greek Orthodox rites.

The fortified abbey, considered a masterpiece of martial architecture, was restructured in the 15th century by Antonio da Sangallo for the future Pope Julius II. The abbey church, inside the second courtyard, is a jewel of Oriental opulence, with glittering Byzantine mosaics and a revered icon set into a marble tabernacle designed by Bernini. The Farnese chapel, leading from the right nave, contains a series of frescoes by Domenichino.

If you make arrangements in advance you can visit the library, which is one of the oldest in Italy. The abbey also has a famous laboratory for the restoration of antique books and manuscripts, where Leonardo's *Codex Atlanticus* was restored in 1962 and more than a thousand precious volumes were saved after the disastrous Florence flood in 1966. ⊠ *Corso del Popolo 128, Grottaferrata* ☎ *06/9459309* ⊕ *www.abbaziagreca.it* ☑ *Free.*

Villa Aldobrandini. Frascati was a retreat of prelates and princes who built magnificent villas, the most spectacular being the 16th-century Villa Aldobrandini, which dominates the town's main square from atop its steeply sloped park. The villa isn't open for touring, but the garden is a public park where you can stroll sweeping pathways lined with stone balustrades, box hedges, and the Baroque Teatro d'Acqua—the sort of showy sculpture group with water features that was a must-have garden adornment for every 16th-century millionaire, in this case Cardinal Pietro Aldobrandini, Pope Clement VIII's favorite nephew. The half circle of sculptures of mythical figures that adorn the "theater" reflect the grandeur and wealth of a prince of the church who thought nothing of diverting the entire water supply of the surrounding area to make his fountains perform. These days the fountains only play on special occasions. The villa is often rented out for private receptions; the gardens may be closed at these times. ⊠ *Via Cardinale Massaia 18, off Via del Tuscolo* ☎ *06/94184406* ⊕ *www.aldobrandini.it* ☒ *Free* ⊗ *Closed weekends.*

WHERE TO EAT AND STAY

$$
ROMAN

✕ **Antica Fontana Grottaferrata.** Across the road from the Abbey of San Nilo, this is one of Grottaferrata's most esteemed restaurants. Run by the Consoli family since 1989, the decor is rustic but stylish, with plants hanging from the ceiling and rows of polished antique copper pans and molds decorating the walls. **Known for:** mixed antipasti; fettuccine with porcini; pleasant outdoor terrace. $ *Average main: €24* ⊠ *Via Domenichino 24–26, Grottaferrata* ☎ *06/9413687* ⊗ *Closed Mon.*

$$
ITALIAN
Fodor'sChoice
★

✕ **Cacciani.** The Cacciani family has been running this stylish restaurant in the heart of Frascati old town since 1922 when it was a popular hangout for the likes of Clark Gable and Gina Lollobrigida. Perched high on a rise overlooking the town and the Roman plain, there are spectacular views from the Cacciani terrace. **Known for:** tonnarelli cacio e pepe; great view; friendly and family run. $ *Average main: €17* ⊠ *Via Armando Diaz 13/15* ☎ *06/9420378* ⊕ *www.cacciani.it* ⊗ *Closed Mon. No dinner Sun.*

$$
ITALIAN

✕ **Il Grottino Frascati.** This former wine cellar just beyond Frascati's market square is now an old-fashioned and cheerful trattoria serving traditional Roman dishes. In summer you can sit under an awning outside and can enjoy the sweeping view over the plain towards Rome. **Known for:** homemade pastas and gnocchi; casual atmosphere; stewed beans with pork skin. $ *Average main: €15* ⊠ *Viale Regina Margherita 41–43* ☎ *06/94289772* ⊕ *www.trattoriailgrottino.it* ⊗ *No lunch Thurs.*

$$
ITALIAN
Fodor'sChoice
★

✕ **Osteria Del Fico Vecchio.** Only a couple of miles outside Frascati, this 16-century coaching inn has a tastefully renovated dining room and an old fig tree (its namesake) that shades the restaurant's charming garden. The chef prepares typical Roman dishes, among them spaghetti *cacio e pepe* (with sheep's cheese and pepper), *pollo al diavolo* (spicy braised chicken), and *abbacchio allo scottadito* (spicy grilled lamb). **Known for:** pretty garden for outdoor dining; classic cacio e pepe; typical Roman dishes. $ *Average main: €20* ⊠ *Via Anagnini 257, Grottaferrata* ☎ *06/9459261* ⊕ *www.alfico.it.*

$ HOTEL Fodor's Choice ★ **Park Hotel Villa Grazioli.** One of the region's most famous residences, this patrician villa halfway between Frascati and Grottaferrata is now a first-class hotel, though the standard-issue guest rooms are a bit of a letdown amid the frescoed salons. **Pros:** wonderful views of the countryside; elegant atmosphere; friendly and professional staff. **Cons:** situated at the end of a long, narrow lane; not all rooms are in the main building. [$] *Rooms from: €120* ✉ *Via Umberto Pavoni 19, Grottaferrata* ✣ *Narrow turn-off from the SP216 road going from Grottaferrata roundabout to Frascati* ☎ *06/9454001* 🌐 *www.villagrazioli.com* 🛏 *62 rooms* 🍴 *All meals.*

CASTEL GANDOLFO

8 km (5 miles) southwest of Frascati, 25 km (15 miles) south of Rome.

This little town is the pope's summer retreat. It was the Barberini Pope Urban VIII who first headed here, eager to escape the malarial miasmas that afflicted summertime Rome; before long, the city's princely families also set up country estates around here.

The 17th-century **Villa Pontificia** has a superb position overlooking Lake Albano and is set in one of the most gorgeous gardens in Italy. Fortunately, these treasures are now open to the public as papal audiences are no longer held at Castel Gandolfo. On the little square in front of the palace there's a fountain by Bernini, who also designed the nearby Church of San Tommaso da Villanova, which has works by Pietro da Cortona.

The village has a number of interesting craft workshops and food purveyors, in addition to the souvenir shops on the square. On the horizon, the silver astronomical dome belonging to the Specola Vaticana observatory—one of the first in Europe—where the scientific Pope Gregory XIII indulged his interest in stargazing, is visible for miles around.

GETTING HERE AND AROUND

There's an hourly train service for Castel Gandolfo from Termini station (Rome–Albano line). Otherwise, buses leave frequently from the Anagnina terminal of Metro Line A. The trip takes about 30 minutes. By car, take the Appian Way from San Giovanni in Rome and follow it straight to Albano, where you branch off for Castel Gandolfo (about an hour, depending on traffic).

VISITOR INFORMATION

Contact PIT Tourist Office Castel Gandolfo. ✉ *Via Massimo D'Azeglio, Castel Gandolfo* ✣ *A green kiosk on your right as you walk up the road, just outside the town walls.*

EXPLORING

FAMILY **Lakeside Lido.** Lined with restaurants, ice-cream parlors, and cafés, this is a favorite spot for Roman families to relax. No motorized craft are allowed on the lake, but you can rent paddleboats and kayaks. In summer, you can also take a short guided boat trip to learn about the geology and history of the lake, which lies at the bottom of an extinct volcanic crater. The waters are full of swans, herons, and other birds, and there is a nature trail along the wooded end of the shore for those who want to get away from the throng. Deck chairs are available for rent; you might also want to stop for a plate of freshly prepared pasta or a gigantic Roman sandwich at one of the little snack bars under the oak and alder trees. There's also a small permanent fairground for children. ⊠ *Lake Albano, Castel Gandolfo* 🖾 *Free.*

Palazzo Apostolico di Castelgandolfo. For centuries the Apostolic Palace of Castelgandolfo was the summer retreat of popes. However, Pope Francis decided that he was too busy to use it and had it opened to the public. Inside you can view the Gallery of Pontifici Portraits, ceremonial garments, and the imposing papal throne in the Sala degli Svizzeri. The private area of the palace with the pope's bedchamber, his library, study, and offices—all strictly off-limits before 2016—are also open to visitors. ⊠ *Piazza della Libertà, Castel Gandolfo* ⊕ *www.museivaticani. va* 🖾 *€11* ⊘ *Closed on Catholic holidays.*

Fodor's Choice **Pontifical Gardens Villa Barberini.** In 2016, Pope Francis opened the
★ 136-acre Pontificial estate and its glorious gardens to the public. Once rarely accessible, the Pontificial gardens of Villa Barberini can now be visited in a 60-minute tour by an ecologically friendly electric vehicle. The tour takes in the landscaped gardens as well as the archaeological remains of the palace of the Roman Emperor Domitian and the home farm, which supplies the Vatican with fresh dairy products and eggs. Multilingual audio guides are included in the price. ■TIP→ **The tour can be combined with a visit to the Apostolic Palace (above) as part of a day trip by train from the Vatican City in Rome at a cost of €38.** ⊠ *Via Massimo D'Azeglio (entrance gate), Castel Gandolfo* ⊕ *www.museivati-cani.va/content/museivaticani/en.html* 🖾 *Villa Barberini gardens €20; train from Vatican, with Apostolic Palace and gardens €38* ⊘ *Closed on Catholic holidays.*

WHERE TO EAT AND STAY

$$$ ✕ **Antico Ristorante Pagnanelli.** One of most refined restaurants in the
ITALIAN Castelli Romani has been in the same family since 1882. Its dining-room windows open onto a breathtaking view across Lake Albano to the conical peak of Monte Cavo. **Known for:** homemade gnocchetti with clams and black truffles; elegant and cozy interior with an open fire in winter; a few outdoor tables with a spectacular view. Ⓢ *Average main: €25* ⊠ *Via Gramsci 4, Castel Gandolfo* ☎ *06/9361740* ⊕ *www.pagnanelli.it.*

$$ ✕ **Bucci.** Situated in the heart of the village of Castel Gandolfo, Bucci
ITALIAN occupies a splendid position overlooking Lake Albano far below with an outdoor terrace shaded by a grape pergola. Food is traditional and prepared with care. **Known for:** traditional menu; friendly vibe; cognac and fontina meatballs. Ⓢ *Average main: €15* ⊠ *Via De' Zecchini 31, Castel Gandolfo* ☎ *06/9323334* ⊕ *ristorantebucci.it* ⊘ *Closed Wed.*

$ 🖽 **Hotel Castelgandolfo.** Overlooking the volcanic crater of Lake Albano
HOTEL and a minute's walk from the Apostolic Palace, this intimate hotel in the heart of Castel Gandolfo makes an ideal retreat for romantics. **Pros:** convenient location; intimate; ideal for romantics. **Cons:** some rooms have street views; balconies are small and narrow. Ⓢ *Rooms from: €120* ⊠ *Via de Zecchini 27, Castel Gandolfo* ☎ *06/9360521* ⊕ *www.hotel-castelgandolfo.com* 🛏 *18 rooms* 🍴 *Free Breakfast.*

ARICCIA

8 km (5 miles) southwest of Castel Gandolfo, 26 km (17 miles) south of Rome.

Ariccia is a gem of Baroque town planning. When Fabio Chigi, scion of the superwealthy banking family, became Pope Alexander VII, he commissioned Gian Lorenzo Bernini to redesign his country estate to make it worthy of his new station. Bernini restructured not only the existing 16th-century palace, but also the town gates, the main square, with its loggias and graceful twin fountains, and the round church of Santa Maria dell'Assunzione (the dome is said to be modeled on the Pantheon). The rest of the village was coiled around the apse of the church down into the valley below.

Ariccia's splendid heritage was largely forgotten in the 20th century, and yet it was once one of the highlights of every artist's and writer's Grand Tour. Corot, Ibsen, Turner, Longfellow, and Hans Christian Andersen all came to stay here.

GETTING HERE AND AROUND

For Ariccia, take the COTRAL bus from the Anagnina terminal of Metro Line A. Buses on the Albano–Genzano–Velletri line stop under the monumental bridge that spans the Ariccia Valley, where an elevator whisks you up to the main town square. If you take a train to Albano, you can proceed by bus to Ariccia or go on foot (it's just under 3 km [2 miles]). If you're driving, follow the Via Appia Nuova to Albano and carry on to Ariccia.

EXPLORING

Fodor'sChoice
★

Palazzo Chigi. This is a true rarity: a Baroque residence whose original furniture, paintings, drapes, and decorations are largely intact. The Italian film director Luchino Visconti used the villa for most of the interior scenes in his 1963 film *The Leopard*. The rooms of the **piano nobile** (main floor)—which, like the rest of the palazzo's sections open to the public, can only be viewed on guided tours—contain intricately carved pieces of 17th-century furniture, as well as textiles and costumes from the 16th to the 20th century. The Room of Beauties is lined with paintings of the loveliest ladies of the day, and the Nuns' Room with portraits of 10 Chigi sisters, all of whom took the veil.

Open for touring only on weekends are **Le stanze del Cardinale** (Cardinal's Rooms), which were the suites occupied by the pleasure-loving Cardinal Flavio Chigi. The upper floors contain the **Museo del Barocco** (Baroque Museum), with an important collection of 17th-century paintings. The park stretching behind the palace is the last remnant of the ancient Latium forest, where herds of deer still graze under the trees. Tours in English are possible if you book ahead. ✉ *Piazza di Corte 14* ☎ *06/9330053* ⊕ *www.palazzochigiariccia.it* 🎫 *€14 full villa tour (when possible), €8 piano nobile, €6 Cardinal's Rooms, €6 Baroque Museum, €4 park* ☉ *Palazzo closed Mon. Park closed weekdays (except for prebooked groups), and Oct–Mar.*

WHERE TO EAT

A visit to Ariccia isn't complete without tasting the local gastronomic specialty: porchetta, a delicious roast whole pig stuffed with herbs. The shops on the Piazza di Corte will make up a sandwich for you, or you can do what the Romans do: head for one of the *fraschette* wine cellars, which also serve cheese, cold cuts, pickles, olives, and sometimes a plate of pasta. You sit on a wooden bench at a trestle table covered with simple white paper, but there's no better place to make friends and maybe join in a sing-along.

$ 🍴 **L'Ariccciarola.** This place near Palazzo Chigi is great for people-watching, which you can do while enjoying a platter of cold cuts and mixed cheeses, washed down with a carafe of local Castelli wine. At informal L'Aricciarola you'll be sitting on wooden benches with a paper tablecloth, surrounded by Roman families who come to Ariccia for its famous porchetta. **Known for:** porchetta; local cold cuts; very casual and friendly atmosphere. [$] *Average main: €10* ✉ *Via Borgo S. Rocco 9* ☎ *06/9334103* 🕓 *Closed Mon.*

ITALIAN
FAMILY

NEMI

8 km (5 miles) west of Ariccia, 34 km (21 miles) south of Rome.

A bronze statue of Diana the Huntress greets you at the entrance to Nemi, the smallest and prettiest village of the Castelli Romani. It's perched on a spur of rock 600 feet above the little oval-shape lake of the same name, which is formed from a volcanic crater. Nemi has an eagle's-nest view over the rolling Roman countryside as far as the coast, some 18 km (11 miles) away. The one main street, Corso Vittorio Emanuele, takes you to the baronial Castello Ruspoli (not open to the public), where there's an 11th-century watchtower, and the quaint Piazza Umberto I, lined with outdoor cafés serving the tiny wood strawberries harvested from the crater bowl.

If you continue on through the arch that joins the castle to the former stables, you come to the entrance of the dramatically landscaped public gardens, which curve steeply down to the panoramic Belvedere terrace, with a café that's open in summer. A pedestrian-only road runs down the crater side to the Roman Ships Museum. Otherwise, car access is from the town of Genzano on the opposite side of the lake.

GETTING HERE AND AROUND

Nemi is difficult to get to unless you come by car. Buses from the Anagnina station on Metro Line A go to the town of Genzano, where a local bus travels to Nemi every two hours. If the times aren't convenient, you can take a taxi or walk the 5 km (3 miles) around Lake Nemi. By car, take the panoramic route known as the Via dei Laghi (Road of the Lakes). Follow the Appia Nuova from St. John Lateran and branch off on the well-signposted route after Ciampino airport. Follow the Via dei Laghi toward Velletri until you see signs for Nemi.

EXPLORING

Museo delle Navi Romani (*Roman Ship Museum*). Nemi may be small, but it has a long and fascinating history. In Roman times it was an important sanctuary dedicated to the goddess Diana: it drew thousands of pilgrims from all over the Roman Empire. In the 1930s the Italian government drained the lake to recover two magnificent ceremonial ships, loaded with sculptures, bronzes, and art treasures, that were submerged for 2,000 years.

The Museo delle Navi Romani, on the lakeshore, was built to house the ships, but they were burned during World War II. Inside are scale models and finds from the sanctuary and the area nearby. There's also a colossal statue of the infamous Roman emperor Caligula, who had the ships built. Italian police snatched it just in time from tomb robbers as they were about to smuggle it out of the country. ✉ *Via del Tempio di Diana 9* ☎ *06/9398040* 🌐 *www.museonaviromane.it* 🎟 *€3.*

WHERE TO EAT

$$ ITALIAN Fodor's Choice ★ 🍴 **La Fiocina.** With its privileged position on the tranquil shores of Lake Nemi next to the Museum of Roman Ships, La Fiocina makes for a relaxing lunchtime stopover. The dining room is elegant and welcoming, and there's a terrace on which you can dine alfresco overlooking the small lakeside garden. **Known for:** coregone, a lake fish; pretty garden; tiny woodland Nemi strawberries. [$] *Average main: €15* ✉ *Via delle Navi Di Tiberio 9* ☎ *06/9391120* 🕒 *Closed Tues.*

$ ITALIAN 🍴 **Specchio di Diana.** Halfway down the main street is the town's most historic inn, where Byron stayed when visiting the area. Today it is a wine bar and café on street level, and a restaurant proper on the second floor with marvelous views over the lake. **Known for:** fettucine al sugo di lepre (hare sauce); spectacular lake view; local Nemi strawberries when in season. [$] *Average main: €14* ✉ *Corso Vittorio Emanuele 13* ☎ *06/9368805* 🌐 *specchiodidiana.it.*

VENICE

WELCOME TO VENICE

TOP REASONS TO GO

★ **Cruising the Grand Canal:** The beauty of its palaces, enhanced by light playing on the water, make a trip down Venice's "main street" unforgettable.

★ **Basilica di San Marco:** Don't miss the gorgeous mosaics inside—they're worth standing in line for.

★ **Santa Maria Gloriosa dei Frari:** Its austere, cavernous interior houses Titian's Assunta—one of the world's most beautiful altarpieces—plus several other spectacular art treasures.

★ **Gallerie dell'Accademia:** Legendary masterpieces of Venetian painting will overwhelm you in this fabled museum.

★ **Sipping wine and snacking at a bacaro:** For a sample of tasty local snacks and excellent Veneto wines in a uniquely Venetian setting, head for one of the city's many wine bars.

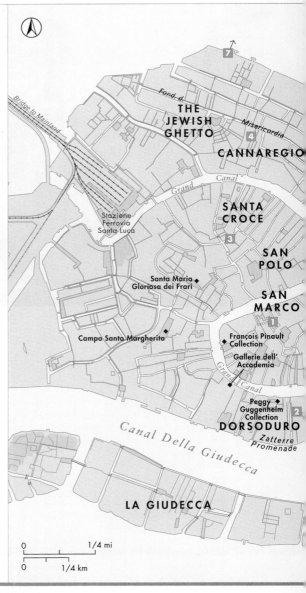

Ca' d'Oro

Basilica di
San Marco

Piazza
San Marco

CASTELLO 5

San Giorgio
Maggiore

6 **SAN
GIORGIO
MAGGIORE**

4

1 San Marco. The neighborhood at the center of Venice is filled with fashion boutiques, art galleries, and grand hotels.

2 Dorsoduro. This graceful residential area is home to the renowned art galleries and the Campo Santa Margherita is a lively student hangout.

3 San Polo and Santa Croce. These bustling sestieri have all sorts of shops, several major churches, and the Rialto fish and produce markets.

4 Cannaregio. This sestiere has some of the sunniest open-air canal-side walks in town and the Jewish Ghetto has a fascinating history.

5 Castello. With its gardens, park, and narrow, winding walkways, it's the sestiere least influenced by Venice's tourist culture.

6 San Giorgio Maggiore and the Giudecca. San Giorgio is graced with the magnificent church, San Giorgio Maggiore. Giudecca main attractions are the wonderful views of Venice.

7 Islands of the Lagoon. The islands of Venice's northern lagoon each has its own allure.

EATING AND DRINKING WELL IN VENICE

The catchword in Venetian restaurants is "fish." How do you learn about the catch of the day? A visit to the Rialto's *pescheria* (fish market) is more instructive than any book, and when you're dining at a well-regarded restaurant, ask for a recommendation.

Traditionally, fish is served with a bit of salt, maybe some chopped parsley, and a drizzle of olive oil—no lemon; lemon masks the flavor. Ask for an entire sea-caught fish; it's much more expensive than its farmed cousin, but certainly worth it. Antipasto may be *prosciutto di San Daniele* (cured ham of the Veneto region) or *sarde in saor* (fresh panfried sardines marinated with onions, raisins, and pine nuts). Risotto, cooked with shellfish or veggies, is a great first course. Pasta? Enjoy it with seafood sauce: this is *not* the place to order spaghetti with tomato sauce. Other pillars of regional cooking include *pasta e fagioli* (thick bean soup with pasta), polenta, often with *fegato alla veneziana* (liver with onion), and that dessert invented in the Veneto: *tiramisù*.

GOING BACARO

You can sample regional wines and scrumptious *cicheti* (small snacks) in *bacari* (wine bars), a great Venetian tradition. *Crostini* (toast with toppings) and *polpette* (meat, fish, or vegetable croquettes) are popular cicheti, as are small sandwiches, seafood salads, *baccalà mantecato* (creamy, whipped salt cod), and toothpick-speared items such as roasted peppers, marinated artichokes, and mozzarella balls.

SEAFOOD

Granseola (crab), *moeche* (tiny, locally caught soft-shell crabs), sweet *canoce* (mantis shrimp), *capelunghe* (razor clams), calamari, and *seppie* or *seppioline* (cuttlefish) are all prominently featured, as well as *rombo* (turbot), *branzino* (sea bass), *San Pietro* (John Dory), *sogliola* (sole), *orate* (gilthead bream), and *triglia* (mullet). Trademark dishes include sarde in saor, *la frittura mista* (tempura-like fried fish and vegetables), and baccalà mantecato.

RISOTTO, PASTA, POLENTA

Although legend has it that Venetian traveler Marco Polo brought pasta back from China, it isn't a traditional staple of Venetian cuisine. As a first course, Venetians favor the creamy rice dish risotto *all'onda* ("undulating," as opposed to firm), prepared with vegetables or shellfish. When pasta is served, it's generally accompanied by seafood sauces, too: *pasticcio di pesce* is lasagna-type pasta baked with fish, and *bigoli* is a strictly local whole wheat pasta shaped like thick spaghetti, usually served *in salsa* (an anchovy-onion sauce with a dash of cinnamon), or with *nero di seppia* (cuttlefish-ink sauce). Pasta e fagioli is a classic first course. *Polenta* (cornmeal gruel) is another staple that's served creamy or fried in wedges, generally as an accompaniment to stews or *seppie in nero* (cuttlefish in black ink).

VEGETABLES

The larger islands of the lagoon are legendary for fine vegetables, such as the Sant'Erasmo *castraure,* sinfully expensive but heavenly tiny white artichokes that appear for a few days in spring. Other regions produce baby artichokes, but only Sant'Erasmo has true castraure. Spring treats are fat white asparagus from neighboring Bassano or Verona, and artichoke bottoms (*fondi*), usually sautéed with olive oil, parsley, and garlic. From December to March the prized *radicchio di Treviso,* a local red endive, is grilled and served frequently with a bit of melted *taleggio* cheese from Lombardy. Fall brings small wild mushrooms called *chiodini,* and *zucca di Mantova,* a yellow squash with a gray-green rind used in soups, puddings, and to stuff ravioli.

SWEETS

Tiramisù lovers will have ample opportunity to sample this creamy delight made from ladyfingers soaked in espresso and rum or brandy and covered with mascarpone cream and cinnamon—a dessert invented in the Veneto. Gelati, *sgropini* (prosecco, vodka, and lemon sorbet), and *semifreddi* (soft, homemade ice cream) are other sweets frequently seen on Venetian menu, as are almond cakes and dry cookies served with dessert wine. Try *focaccia veneziana,* a sweet raised cake made in the late fall and winter.

4

Updated by
Liz Humphreys

Venice is often called La Serenissima, or "the most serene," a reference to the majesty, wisdom, and power of this city that was for centuries a leader in trade between Europe and Asia, and a major center of European culture. Built on water by people who saw the sea as a defense and ally, and who constantly invested in its splendor with magnificent architectural projects, Venice is a city unlike any other.

No matter how often you've seen it in photos and films, the real thing is more dreamlike than you could ever imagine. Its most notable landmarks, the Basilica di San Marco and the Palazzo Ducale, are exotic mixes of Byzantine, Romanesque, Gothic, and Renaissance styles, reflecting Venice's ties with the rest of Italy and with Constantinople in the east. Shimmering sunlight and silvery mist soften every perspective here; it's easy to understand how the city became renowned in the Renaissance for its artists' use of color. It's full of secrets, inexpressibly romantic, and frequently given over to pure, sensuous enjoyment.

You'll see Venetians going about their daily affairs in *vaporetti* (water buses), in the *campi* (squares), and along the *calli* (narrow streets). They are proud of their city and its history, and are still quite helpful to tourists, as long as the tourist shows proper respect for the city and its way of life.

VENICE PLANNER

MAKING THE MOST OF YOUR TIME

The hordes of tourists visiting Venice are legendary, especially in spring and fall, but during other seasons, too—there's really no "off-season" in Venice. Unfortunately, tales of impassable, tourist-packed streets and endless queues to get into the Basilica di San Marco are not exaggerated. A little bit of planning, however, will help you avoid the worst of the crowds.

The majority of tourists do little more than take the vaporetto down the Grand Canal to Piazza San Marco, see the piazza and the basilica, and walk up to the Rialto and back to the station. You'll want to visit these areas, too, but do so in the early morning, before most tourists have finished their breakfast cappuccinos. Because many of the tourists are other Italians who come for a weekend outing, you can further decrease your competition for Venice's pleasures by choosing weekdays to visit the city.

Away from San Marco and the Rialto, the streets and quays of Venice's beautiful medieval and Renaissance residential districts receive only a moderate amount of traffic. Besides the Grand Canal and the Piazza San Marco, and perhaps Torcello, the other historically and artistically important sites are seldom overcrowded. Even on weekends you probably won't have to queue up to get into the Gallerie dell'Accademia.

Venice proper is quite compact, and you should be able to walk across it in a couple of hours, counting even a few minutes for getting lost. The water buses will save wear and tear on tired feet, but won't always save you much time.

PASSES AND DISCOUNTS

Avoid lines and save money by booking services and venue entry online with **Venezia Unica City Pass** (⊕ *www.veneziaunica.it*). The seven-day pass costs €39.90 (with discounts for those under 30) and gives you free entry to the Palazzo Ducale, 10 of Venice's Civic Museums, the Quirini-Stampalia Museum, and the Jewish Museum. Note that the Gallerie dell'Accademia, the Guggenheim, the Ca' d'Oro, the Scuola di San Rocco and the Scuola di San Giorgio, and the Pinault collection at the Punta della Dogana are not Civic Museums, and therefore not included. It also gives you access to 16 of the most important churches in Venice. A reduced version of this pass gives you access to the Palazzo Ducale, three museums in Piazza San Marco, three churches of your choice, and the Quirini-Stampalia Museum for €28.90. You can also include public transportation in the pass for an additional cost.

Eighteen of Venice's most significant churches covered by the Venezia Unica City Pass are part of the **Chorus Foundation** umbrella group (☎ *041/2750462* ⊕ *www.chorusvenezia.org*), which coordinates their administration, hours, and admission fees. Churches in this group are open to visitors all day except Sunday morning. Single church entry costs €3; you have a year to visit all 15 with the €12 **Chorus Pass**, which you can get at any participating church or online.

The **Museum Pass** (€24) from **Musei Civici** (☎ *041/2405211*) includes single entry to 12 Venice city museums for six months.

GETTING HERE AND AROUND

AIR TRAVEL

Aeroporto Marco Polo. Venice's Aeroporto Marco Polo is on the mainland, 10 km (6 miles) north of the city. It's served by domestic and international flights, including connections from 21 European cities, plus direct flights from New York's JFK and other U.S. cities. It is reachable from Venice either by bus or by special vaporetto (Alilaguna). ☎ *041/2609260* ⊕ *www.veniceairport.it*.

LAND TRANSFERS

ATVO. Buses run by ATVO make a quick (20-minute) and cheap (€8) trip from the airport to Piazzale Roma, from where you can get a vaporetto to the stop nearest your hotel. Tickets are sold from machines and at the airport ground transportation booth (daily 9–7:30), and on the bus when tickets are otherwise unavailable. The public ACTV Bus No. 5 also runs to the Piazzale Roma in about the same time; tickets (€8) are available at the airport ground transportation booth. ☎ *0421/383672* ⊕ *www.atvo.it.*

WATER TRANSFERS

From Marco Polo terminal, it's a mostly covered seven-minute walk to the dock where boats depart for Venice's historic center. The ride is in a closed boat so you won't get much of a view; plus, it's more expensive and generally slower than the bus to Piazzale Roma (unless your hotel is near a boat station).

Alilaguna. This company has regular, scheduled ferry service from pre-dawn until nearly midnight. During most of the day there are two departures from the airport to Venice every hour, at 15 and 45 minutes after. Early-morning and evening departures are less frequent, but there is at least one per hour. The charge is €15, including bags, and it takes about 1½ hours to reach the landing near Piazza San Marco; some ferries also stop at Fondamente Nove, Murano, Lido, the Cannaregio Canal, and the Rialto. Slight reductions are possible if you book a round trip online. ☎ *041/2401701* ⊕ *www.alilaguna.it.*

CAR TRAVEL

Venice is at the end of SR11, just off the east–west A4 autostrada. There are no cars in Venice; if possible, return your rental when you arrive.

A warning: don't be waylaid by illegal touts, often wearing fake uniforms, who try to flag you down and offer to arrange parking and hotels. Use one of the established garages and consider reserving a space in advance. The **Autorimessa Comunale** (☎ *041/2727301* ⊕ *www.asmvenezia.it*) costs €26–€29 for 24 hours (slight discounts if you book online). The **Garage San Marco** (☎ *041/5232213* ⊕ *www.garagesanmarco.it*) costs €32 for 24 hours, slight discounts for prepaid online reservations. On its own island, **Tronchetto** (☎ *041/5207555*) charges €21 for 5–24 hours. Watch for signs coming over the bridge—you turn right just before Piazzale Roma. Many hotels and the casino have guest discounts with San Marco or Tronchetto garages. A cheaper alternative is to park in Mestre, on the mainland, and take a train (10 minutes, €1) or bus into Venice. The garage across from the station and the Bus No. 2 stop costs €8–€10 for 24 hours.

PUBLIC TRANSPORTATION

WATER BUSES

ACTV. The ACTV operates the land and water bus service in Venice. A single tourist ticket valid for 60 minutes costs €7.50, but there are also one-, two-, and three-day tickets plus a one-week ticket available, which represent considerable savings if you plan to move frequently around the city by public transportation. Water buses run 24 hours in Venice, because there are parts of the city that are accessible only by water. Service is quite frequent during the day. Routes and schedules are available on the ACTV website, or at individual vaporetto stations. Tickets are available at main vaporetto stops, at tobacconists, and at some newspaper kiosks. The tickets are valid on both the vaporetti in Venice and on the bus lines to Mestre and on the Lido. Controls are frequent and fines for traveling without a valid ticket are steep. If you plan an extended stay in Venice, or plan to make several trips, and have a local address (not a hotel or B&B), you can apply for a Venezia Unica City Pass (€50) valid for several years, which will give you substantially reduced rates on public transportation. ☎ *041/2424* ⊕ *www.actv.it.*

WATER TAXIS A *motoscafo* isn't cheap: you'll spend about €60 for a short trip in town, €80 to the Lido, and €90 or more per hour to visit the outer islands. It is strongly suggested to book through the Consorzio Motoscafi Venezia (☎ *041/5222303* ⊕ *www.motoscafivenezia.it*) to avoid having to argue with the driver over prices. A water taxi can carry up to 10 passengers, with an additional charge of €10 per person for more than 5 people, so if you're traveling in a group, it may not be that much more expensive than a vaporetto.

TRAIN TRAVEL

Venice has rail connections with many major cities in Italy and Europe. Note that Venice's train station is **Venezia Santa Lucia,** not to be confused with Venezia Mestre, which is the mainland stop prior to arriving in the historic center. Some trains don't continue beyond the Mestre station; in such cases you can catch the next Venice-bound train. Get a ticket from the newsstand on the platform and validate it (in the yellow time-stamp machine) to avoid a fine.

TOURS

If you want some expert guidance around Venice, you may opt for private, semiprivate, or large group tours. Any may include a boat tour as a portion of a longer walking tour. For private tours, make sure to choose an authorized guide.

LARGE-GROUP TOURS

Venice Tourism Office. Visit any Venice tourism office to book walking tours of the San Marco area (no Sunday tour in winter). There's also an afternoon walking tour that ends with a gondola ride, and a daily serenaded gondola ride. Check the main branch of the city's tourist office or their website for additional scheduled offerings, meeting places, prices, and times. ⊠ *San Marco 2637* ☎ *041/5298711* ⊕ *www.turismovenezia.it.*

PRIVATE TOURS

A Guide in Venice. This popular company offers a wide variety of innovative, entertaining, and informative themed tours for groups of up to eight people. Individual tours are also available and generally last two to three hours. The guide fee is €75 per hour, and does not include admissions or transportation fees. Small group tours are also available at €62.50 per person. ☎ *39/348-592-7974 Sabrina Scaglianti* ⊕ *www. aguideinvenice.com.*

Walks Inside Venice. For a host of particularly creative group and private tours, from historic to artistic to gastronomic, opt for one run by Walks Inside Venice. Tours are for groups up to six people and guides include people with advanced university degrees and published authors. ⊕ *www.walksinsidevenice.com.*

VISITOR INFORMATION
The multilingual staff of the **Venice tourism office** (☎ *041/5298711* ⊕ *www.turismovenezia.it*) can provide directions and up-to-the-minute information. Tourist office branches are at Marco Polo Airport; the Venezia Santa Lucia train station; Garage Comunale, on Piazzale Roma; and at Piazza San Marco near Museo Correr at the southwest corner. The train-station branch is open daily 7–9; other branches have similar hours.

EXPLORING VENICE

Venice proper is divided into six sestieri: Cannaregio, Castello, Dorsoduro, San Marco, San Polo, and Santa Croce. More sedate outer islands float around them—San Giorgio Maggiore and the Giudecca just to the south, beyond them the Lido, the barrier island; to the north, Murano, Burano, and Torcello.

SAN MARCO

Extending from the Piazza San Marco to the Rialto Bridge, San Marco comprises the historical and commercial heart of Venice. Aside from the Piazza itself—San Marco is the only square in Venice given full stature as a "piazza" and accordingly is often known simply as "the Piazza"—this sestiere is graced with some of Venice's finest churches and best-endowed museums. San Marco is also the shopping district of Venice, and its mazes of streets are lined with Venetian glass, fine clothing, and elegantly wrought jewelry. Most of the famous Venetian glass producers from Murano have boutiques in San Marco, as do most Italian designers.

TIMING
You can easily spend several days seeing the historical and artistic monuments in and around the Piazza San Marco alone, but at a bare minimum, plan on at least an hour for the basilica, with its wonderful mosaics. Add on another half hour if you want to see its Pala d'Oro, Galleria, and Museo di San Marco. You'll want at least an hour to appreciate the Palazzo Ducale. Leave another hour for the Museo Correr, through which you also enter the archaeological museum and the Libreria Sansoviniana. If you choose to take in the piazza itself from a café table with an orchestra, keep in mind there will be an additional charge for the music.

TOP ATTRACTIONS
Fodor'sChoice **Basilica di San Marco.** The basilica is not only Venice's religious center, but
★ also an expression of the political, intellectual, and economic aspiration and accomplishments of a city that for centuries was at the forefront of European culture. It was the doge's personal chapel, endowed with all the riches the Republic's admirals and merchants could carry off from the Orient (as the Byzantine Empire was known). When the present church was begun in the 11th century, rare colored marbles and gold leaf mosaics were used in its decoration. The 12th and 13th centuries were a period of intense military expansion, and by the early 13th

Continued on page 168

CRUISING THE GRAND CANAL

THE BEST INTRODUCTION TO VENICE IS A TRIP DOWN MAIN STREET

Venice's Grand Canal is one of the world's great thoroughfares. It winds its way from Piazzale Roma to Piazza San Marco, passing 200 palazzi built from the 13th to the 18th centuries by Venice's richest and most powerful families. There's a theatrical quality to a boat ride on the canal: it's as if each pink- or gold-tinted façade is trying to steal your attention from its rival across the way.

In medieval and Renaissance cities, wars and sieges required defense to be an element of design; but in rich, impregnable Venice, you could safely show off what you had. But more than being simply an item of conspicu-

ous consumption, a Venetian's palazzo was an embodiment of his person— not only his wealth, but also his erudition and taste.

The easiest and cheapest way to see the Grand Canal is to take the Line 1 vaporetto (water bus) from Piazalle Roma to San Marco. The ride takes about 35 minutes. Invest in a day ticket and you can spend the better part of a day hopping on and off at the vaporetto's many stops, visiting the sights along the banks. Keep your eyes open for the highlights listed here; some have fuller descriptions later in this chapter.

FROM PIAZZALE ROMA TO RIALTO

Palazzo Labia
Tiepolo's masterpiece, the cycle of Antony and Cleopatra, graces the grand ballroom in this palazzo. The Labia family, infamous for their ostentation, commissioned the frescos to celebrate a marriage and had Tiepolo use the face of the family matriarch, Maria Labia, for that of Cleopatra. Luckily, Maria Labia was known not only for her money, but also for her intelligence and her beauty.

Santa Maria di Nazareth

Ponte di Scalzi

R. Di BIASIO

Stazione Ferrovia Santa Lucia

FERROVIA

SANTA CROCE

Ponte di Calatrava

After you pass the Ferrovia, the baroque church immediately to your left is the baroque **Santa Maria di Nazareth**, called the Chiesa degli Scalzi (Church of the Barefoot).

After passing beneath the Ponte di Scalzi, ahead to the left, where the Canale di Cannaregio meets the Grand Canal, you'll spy **Palazzo Labia**, an elaborate 18th-century palace built for

the social-climbing Labia family. Known for their ostentation even in this city where modesty was seldom a virtue, the Labias chose a location that required three façades instead of the usual one.

A bit farther down, across the canal, is the 13th-century **Fondaco dei Turchi**, an elegant residence that served as a combination commercial center and ghetto for the Turkish com-

munity. Try not to see the side towers and the crenellations; they were added during a 19th-century restoration.

Beyond it is the obelisk-topped **Ca' Belloni-Battagia**, designed for the Belloni family by star architect Longhena. Look for the family crest he added prominently on the façade.

On the opposite bank is architect Mauro Codussi's magnificent **Palazzo Vendramin-Calergi**, designed just before 1500. Codussi ingeniously married the fortress-like Renaissance style of the Florentine Alberti's Palazzo Rucellai to the lacy delicacy of the Venetian Gothic, creating the prototype of

Palazzo Vendramin-Calergi

Venice's first Renaissance palazzo. Immediately recognized as a masterpiece, it was so highly regarded that later, when its subsequent owners, the Calergi, were convicted of murder and their palace was to be torn down as punishment, the main building was spared.

Ca' d'Oro

Inspired by stories of Nero's Domus Aurea (Golden House) in Rome, the first owner had parts of the façade gilded with 20,000 sheets of gold leaf. The gold has long worn away, but the Ca' D'Oro is still Venice's most beautiful Gothic palazzo.

Ca' Belloni-Battagia

Ca' Pesaro

Ca' da Mosto

Venice's oldest surviving palazzo gives you an idea of Marco Polo's Venice. More than any other Byzantine palazzo in town, it maintains its original 13th-century appearance.

GHETTO

S. MARCUOLA

S. STAE

Fondaco dei Turchi

Depositi del Megio

San Stae Church

SAN POLO

Ca' Corner della Regina

CA' D'ORO

Pescheria

Stop by in the morning to see the incredible variety of fish for sale. Produce stalls fill the adjacent fondamenta. Butchers and cheesemongers occupy the surrounding shops.

Rialto Mercato

Fondaco dei Tedeschi

Ca' dei Camerlenghi

RIALTO

SAN MARCO

the Venetian Renaissance palazzo. The palazzo is now Venice's casino.

The whimsically baroque church of **San Stae** on the right bank is distinguished by a host of marble saints on its façade.

Farther along the bank is one of Longhena's Baroque masterpieces, **Ca' Pesaro**. It is now the Museum of Modern Art.

Next up on the left is **Ca' d'Oro** (1421-1438), the canal's most spendid example of Venetian Gothic domestic design. Across from this palazzo is the loggia of the neo-Gothic **pescheria**, Venice's fish market.

Slightly farther down, on the bank opposite from the vegetable market, is the early 13th-century **Ca' da Mosto**, the oldest building on the Grand Canal. The upper two floors are later additions, but the ground floor and piano nobile give you a good idea of a rich merchant's house during the time of Marco Polo.

As you approach the Rialto Bridge, to the left, just before

the bridge, is the **Fondaco dei Tedeschi**. German merchants kept warehouses, offices, and residences here; its façade was originally frescoed by Titian and Giorgione.

FROM RIALTO TO THE PONTE DELL' ACCADEMIA

SAN POLO

Ponte di Rialto

▲ **RIALTO**

Palazzo Barzizza

Ca' Loredan

▲ *S. SILVESTRO*

Ca' Farsetti

Ca' Foscari
The canal's most imposing Gothic masterpiece, Ca' Foscari was built to blot out the memory of a traitor to the Republic.

Ca' Grimani

Palazzo Pisani Moretta

▲ *S. ANGELO*

TOMA ▲

Ca' Garzoni

Ca' Balbi

Palazzo Grassi

Ca' Rezzonico

SAN MARCO

REZZONICO ▲

ACCADEMIA ▲

Gallerie dell'Accademia

DORSODURO

The shop-lined **Ponte di Rialto** was built in stone after former wooden bridges had burned or collapsed. As you pass under the bridge, on your left stands star architect Sansovino's Palazzo Dolfin Manin. The white stone–clad Renaissance palace was built at huge expense and over the objections of its conservative neighbors.

A bit farther down stand **Ca' Loredan** and **Ca' Farsetti**, 13th-century Byzantine palaces that today make up Venice's city hall.

Along the same side is the **Ca' Grimani**, by the Veronese architect Sanmichele. Legend has it that the palazzo's oversized windows were demanded by the young Grimani's fiancée, who insisted that he build her a palazzo on the Canale Grande with windows larger than the portal of her own house.

At the Sant'Angelo landing, the vaporetto passes close to Codussi's **Ca' Corner-Spinelli**. Back on the right bank, in a lovely salmon color, is the graceful **Palazzo Pisani Moretta**, built in the mid-15th century and typical of the Venetian Gothic palazzo of the generation after the Ca' D'Oro.

A bit farther down the right bank, crowned by obelisks, is **Ca' Balbi**. Niccolò Balbi built this elegant palazzo in order to upstage his former landlord, who had insulted him in public.

Farther down the right bank, where the Canale makes a sharp turn, is the imposing **Ca' Foscari**. Doge Francesco Foscari tore down an earlier palazzo on this spot and built this splendid palazzo to erase memory of the traitorous former owner. It is now the seat of the University of Venice.

Continuing down the right bank you'll find Longhena's **Ca' Rezzonico**, a magnificent baroque palace. Opposite stands the Grand Canal's youngest palace, Giorgio Massari's **Palazzo Grassi**, commissioned in 1749. It houses part of the François Pinot contemporary art collection.

Near the canal's fourth bridge, is the former church and monastery complex that houses the world-renowned **Gallerie dell'Accademia**, the world's largest and most distinguished collection of Venetian art.

ARCHITECTURAL STYLES ALONG THE GRAND CANAL

BYZANTINE: 13th century
Distinguishing characteristics: high, rounded arches, relief panels, multicolored marble.
Examples: Fondaco dei Turchi, Ca' Loredan, Ca' Farsetti, Ca' da Mosto

GOTHIC: 14th and 15th centuries
Distinguishing characteristics: pointed arches, high ceilings, and many windows.
Examples: Ca' d'Oro, Ca' Foscari, Palazzo Pisani Moretta, Ca' Barbaro (and, off the canal, Palazzo Ducale)

RENAISSANCE: 16th century
Distinguishing characteristics: classically influenced emphasis on harmony and motifs taken from classical antiquity.

Examples: Palazzo Vendramin-Calergi, Ca' Grimani, Ca' Corner-Spinelli, Ca' dei Camerlenghi, Ca' Balbi, Palazzo Corner della Ca' Granda, Palazzo Dolfin Manin, and, off the canal, Libreria, Sansoviniana on Piazza San Marco

BAROQUE: 17th century
Distinguishing characteristics: Renaissance order wedded with a more dynamic style, achieved through curving lines and complex decoration.

Examples: churches of Santa Maria di Nazareth, San Stae, and Santa Maris della Salute; Ca' Belloni Battaglia, Ca' Pesaro, Ca' Rezzonico

FROM THE PONTE DELL'ACCADEMIA TO SAN ZACCARIA

Ca' Barbaro
John Singer Sargent, Henry James, and Cole Porter are among the guests who have stayed at Ca' Barbaro. It was a center for elegant British and American society during the turn of the 20th century.

Santa Maria Della Salute
Baldessare Longhena was only 26 when he designed this church, which was to become one of Venice's major landmarks. Its rotunda form and dynamic Baroque decoration predate iconic Baroque churches in other Italian cities.

SAN MARCO

Ponte dell' Accademia

Ca' Pisani-Gritti

Palazzo Corner della Ca' Granda

ACCADEMIA

DORSODURO

Casetta Rossa

S. M. DEL GIGLIO

Ca' Barbarigo

SALUTE

Palazzo Salviati

Palazzo Venier dei Leoni
Eccentric art dealer Peggy Guggenheim's personal collection of modern art is here. At the Grand Canal entrance to the palazzo stands Marino Marini's sexually explicit equestrian sculpture, the Angel of the Citadel. Numerous entertaining stories have been spun around the statue and Ms. Guggenheim's overtly libertine ways.

S. Maria della Salute

Ca' Dario
Graceful and elegant Ca' Dario is reputed to carry a curse. Almost all its owners since the 15th century have met violent deaths or committed suicide. It was, nevertheless, a center for elegant French society at the turn of the 20th century.

Down from the Accademia bridge, on the left bank next door to the fake Gothic Ca' Franchetti, is the beautiful **Ca' Barbaro**, designed by Giovanni Bon, who was also at work about that time on the Ca' D'Oro.

Farther along on the left bank Sansovino's first work in Venice, the **Palazzo Corner della Ca' Granda**, begun in 1533, still shows the influence of his Roman Renaissance contemporaries, Bramante and Giulio Romano. It faces the uncompleted **Palazzo Venier dei Leoni**, which holds the Peggy Guggenheim Collection, a good cross-section of the visual arts from 1940 to 1960.

Ca' Dario a bit farther down, was originally a Gothic palazzo, but in 1487 it was given an early Renaissance multicolored marble façade.

At this point on the canal the cupola of **Santa Maria della Salute** dominates the scene. The commission for the design of the church to celebrate the Virgin's rescuing Venice from the disastrous plague of 1630, was given to the 26-year-old

Longhena. The young architect stressed the new and inventive aspects of his design, likening the rotunda shape to a crown for the Virgin.

Across from the Salute, enjoying the magnificent view across the canal, are a string of luxury hotels whose historic

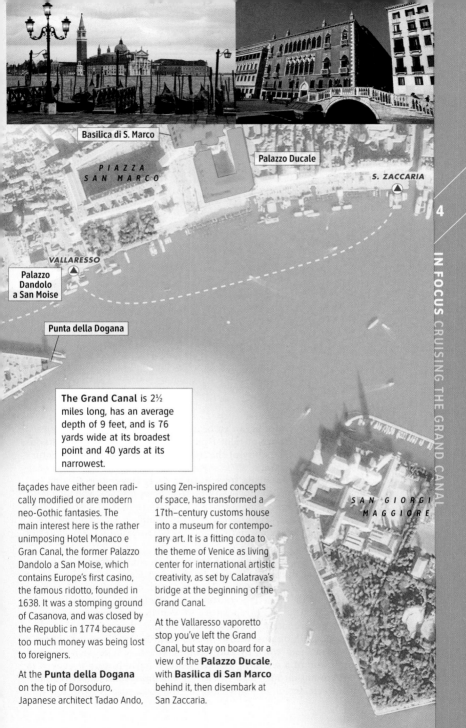

Basilica di S. Marco

Palazzo Ducale

S. ZACCARIA

PIAZZA SAN MARCO

VALLARESSO

Palazzo Dandolo a San Moise

Punta della Dogana

The Grand Canal is 2½ miles long, has an average depth of 9 feet, and is 76 yards wide at its broadest point and 40 yards at its narrowest.

SAN GIORGIO MAGGIORE

façades have either been radically modified or are modern neo-Gothic fantasies. The main interest here is the rather unimposing Hotel Monaco e Gran Canal, the former Palazzo Dandolo a San Moise, which contains Europe's first casino, the famous ridotto, founded in 1638. It was a stomping ground of Casanova, and was closed by the Republic in 1774 because too much money was being lost to foreigners.

At the **Punta della Dogana** on the tip of Dorsoduro, Japanese architect Tadao Ando,

using Zen-inspired concepts of space, has transformed a 17th–century customs house into a museum for contemporary art. It is a fitting coda to the theme of Venice as living center for international artistic creativity, as set by Calatrava's bridge at the beginning of the Grand Canal.

At the Vallaresso vaporetto stop you've left the Grand Canal, but stay on board for a view of the **Palazzo Ducale**, with **Basilica di San Marco** behind it, then disembark at San Zaccaria.

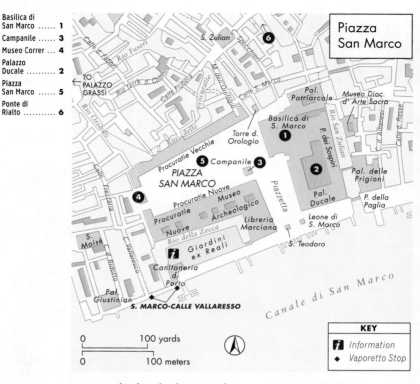

century, the facades began to bear testimony to Venice's conquests, including gilt-bronze ancient Roman horses taken from Constantinople in 1204. The glory of the basilica is its 12th- and 13th-century medieval mosaic work. ■TIP→ **Make a reservation, at no extra cost, on the website for visits from April to early November. Guards will deny admission to people in shorts, sleeveless dresses, and tank tops.** ⊠ *Piazza San Marco, San Marco 328, San Marco* 🕾 *041/2413817 tour info (weekdays 10–noon)* ⊕ *www.basilicasanmarco.it* ⊠ *Basilica free, Treasury €3, sanctuary and Pala d'Oro €2, museum €5* Ⓜ *Vallaresso/ San Zaccaria.*

Fodor's Choice   **Museo Correr.** This museum of Venetian art and history contains an
★   important sculpture collection by Antonio Canova and important paintings by Giovanni Bellini, Vittore Carpaccio (Carpaccio's famous painting of the Venetian courtesans is here), and other major local painters. It's the main repository of Venetian drawings and prints, which, unfortunately, can be seen only by special arrangement, or during special exhibitions. It also houses curiosities such as the absurdly high-soled shoes worn by 16th-century Venetian ladies (who walked with the aid of a servant). The city's proud naval history is evoked in several rooms through highly descriptive paintings and numerous maritime objects, including ships' cannons and some surprisingly large iron

mast-top navigation lights. The museum also has a significant collection of antique gems. The Correr exhibition rooms lead directly into the **Museo Archeologico,** which houses the Grimani collection—an important 16th- and 17th-century collection of Greek and Roman art, still impressive even after the transfer of many objects to Paris and Vienna during the Napoleonic and Austrian occupations—and the Stanza del Sansovino, the only part of the **Biblioteca Nazionale Marciana** open to visitors. ⊠ *Piazza San Marco, Ala Napoleonica, opposite basilica, Piazza San Marco* ☎ *041/2405211* ⊕ *correr.visitmuve.it* ⊠ *Museums of San Marco Pass €20, includes Museo Archeologico, Biblioteca Nazionale Marciana, and Palazzo Ducale. Free with Museum Pass* Ⓜ *Vaporetto: Vallaresso, San Zaccaria.*

4

Fodor's Choice
★

Palazzo Ducale (*Doge's Palace*). Rising majestically above the Piazzetta San Marco, this Gothic fantasia of pink-and-white marble—the doges' residence from the 10th century and the central administrative center of the Venetian Republic—is a majestic expression of Venetian prosperity and power. Upon entering, you'll find yourself in an immense courtyard with some of the first evidence of Venice's Renaissance architecture, including Antonio Rizzo's 15th-century *Scala dei Giganti* (Stairway of the Giants). The palace's sumptuous chambers have walls and ceilings covered with works by Venice's greatest artists. In the Anticollegio you'll find the *Rape of Europa* by Veronese and Tintoretto's *Bacchus and Ariadne Crowned by Venus*. The ceiling of the Sala del Senato (Senate Chamber), featuring *The Triumph of Venice* by Tintoretto, is magnificent, but it's dwarfed by his masterpiece *Paradise* in the Sala del Maggiore Consiglio (Great Council Hall), the world's largest oil painting. The popular Secret Itineraries tour lets you visit the doge's private apartments and hidden passageways. ⊠ *Piazzetta San Marco, Piazza San Marco* ☎ *041/42730892 tickets, outside Italy, 848/082000 tickets, within Italy* ⊕ *palazzoducale.visitmuve.it* ⊠ *Museums of San Marco Pass €20, includes Museo Correr, Museo Archeologico, and Biblioteca Nazionale Marciana; free with Museum Pass. Secret Itineraries tour €20* Ⓜ *Vaporetto: San Zaccaria, Vallaresso.*

Fodor's Choice
★

Piazza San Marco. One of the world's most beautiful squares, Piazza San Marco (St. Mark's Square) is the spiritual and artistic heart of Venice, a vast open space bordered by an orderly procession of arcades marching toward the fairy-tale cupolas and marble lacework of the Basilica di San Marco. From mid=morning on, it is generally packed with tourists. (If Venetians have business in the piazza, they try to conduct it in the early morning, before the crowds swell.) At night the piazza can be magical, especially in winter, when mists swirl around the lampposts and the campanile.

Facing the basilica, on your left, the long, arcaded building is the **Procuratie Vecchie,** renovated to its present form in 1514 as offices and residences for the powerful procurators (magistrates).

On your right is the **Procuratie Nuove,** built half a century later in a more imposing, classical style. It was originally planned by Venice's great Renaissance architect Jacopo Sansovino (1486–1570), to carry on the look of his Libreria Sansoviniana (Sansovinian Library), but he died before construction on the Nuove had begun. Vincenzo Scamozzi (circa 1552–1616), a pupil of Andrea Palladio (1508–80), completed the design and construction. Still later, the Procuratie Nuove was modified by architect Baldassare Longhena (1598–1682), one of Venice's Baroque masters.

When Napoléon (1769–1821) entered Venice with his troops in 1797, he expressed his admiration for the piazza and promptly gave orders to alter it. His architects demolished a church with a Sansovino facade in order to build the Ala Napoleonica (Napoleonic Wing), or Fabbrica Nuova (New Building), which linked the two 16th-century *procuratie* (procurators' offices) and effectively enclosed the piazza.

Piazzetta San Marco is the "little square" leading from Piazza San Marco to the waters of Bacino San Marco (St. Mark's Basin); its *molo* (landing) once served as the grand entrance to the Republic. Two imposing columns tower above the waterfront. One is topped by the winged lion, a traditional emblem of St. Mark that became the symbol of Venice itself; the other supports St. Theodore, the city's first patron, along with his dragon. (A third column fell off its barge and ended up in the bacino before it could be placed alongside the others.) Although the columns are a glorious vision today, the Republic traditionally executed convicts between them. Even today, some superstitious Venetians avoid walking between the two. ⊠ *San Marco* 🕾 Ⓜ *Vaporetto Calle Valaresso or San Zaccaria.*

Fodor's Choice ★ **Ponte di Rialto** (*Rialto Bridge*). The competition to design a stone bridge across the Grand Canal attracted the best architects of the late 16th century, including Michelangelo, Palladio, and Sansovino, but the job went to the less famous (but appropriately named) Antonio da Ponte (1512–95). His pragmatic design, completed in 1591, featured shop space and was high enough for galleys to pass beneath. Putting practicality and economy over aesthetic considerations—and unlike the classical plans proposed by his more famous contemporaries—Da Ponte's bridge essentially followed the design of its wooden predecessor; it kept decoration and cost to a minimum at a time when the Republic's coffers were low, due to continual wars against the Turks and the competition brought about by the Spanish and Portuguese opening of oceanic trade routes. Along the railing you'll enjoy one of the city's most famous views: the Grand Canal vibrant with boat traffic. ⊠ *San Marco* Ⓜ *Vaporetto: Rialto.*

WORTH NOTING

Campanile. Construction of Venice's famous brick bell tower (325 feet tall, plus the angel) began in the 9th century; it took on its present form in 1514. During the 15th century, the tower was used as a place of punishment: immoral clerics were suspended in wooden cages from the tower, some forced to subsist on bread and water for as long as a year; others were left to starve. In 1902, the tower unexpectedly collapsed, taking with it Jacopo Sansovino's marble loggia (1537–49) at its base. The largest original bell, called the *marangona,* survived. The crushed loggia was promptly reconstructed, and the new tower, rebuilt to the old plan, reopened in 1912. Today, on a clear day the stunning view includes the Lido, the lagoon, and the mainland as far as the Alps, but, strangely enough, none of the myriad canals that snake through the city. ⊠ *Piazza San Marco* ☎ *041/2708311* 🖃 *€8* Ⓜ *Vaporetto: Vallaresso, San Zaccaria.*

Palazzo Grassi. Built between 1748 and 1772 by Giorgio Massari for a Bolognese family, this palace is one of the last of the great noble residences on the Grand Canal. Once owned by auto magnate Giovanni Agnelli, it was bought by French businessman François Pinaut in 2005 to showcase his highly important collection of modern and contemporary art (which has now grown so large that Pinaut rented the Punta della Dogana, at the entryway to the Grand Canal, for his newest acquisitions). Pinaut brought in Japanese architect Tadao Ando to remodel the Grassi's interior. Check online for a schedule of temporary art exhibitions. ⊠ *Campo San Samuele, San Marco* ☎ *041/5231680* ⊕ *www.palazzograssi.it* 🖃 *€18 with Punta della Dogana* ☉ *Closed Tues.* Ⓜ *Vaporetto: San Samuele.*

DORSODURO

The sestiere Dorsoduro (named for its "hard back" solid clay foundation) is across the Grand Canal to the south of San Marco. It is a place of meandering canals, the city's finest art museums, monumental churches, and *scuole* (Renaissance civic institutions) filled with works by Titian, Veronese, and Tiepolo, and a promenade called the Zattere, where on sunny days you'll swear half the city is out for a passeggiata, or stroll. The eastern tip of the peninsula, the Punta della Dogana, is capped by the dome of Santa Maria della Salute and was once the city's customs point; the old customs house is now a museum of contemporary art.

Dorsoduro is home to the Gallerie dell'Accademia, with an unparalleled collection of Venetian painting, and the gloriously restored Ca' Rezzonico, which houses the Museo del Settecento Veneziano. Another of its landmark sites, the Peggy Guggenheim Collection, has a fine selection of 20th-century art.

TIMING

You can easily spend a full day in the neighborhood. Devote at least a half hour to admiring the Titians in the imposing and monumental Santa Maria della Salute, and another half hour for the wonderful Veroneses in the peaceful, serene church of San Sebastiano. The Gallerie dell'Accademia demands a few hours, but if time is short an audio guide can help you cover the highlights in about an hour. Ca' Rezzonico deserves at least an hour, as does the Peggy Guggenheim collection.

TOP ATTRACTIONS

Fodor'sChoice
★

Ca' Rezzonico. Designed by Baldassare Longhena in the 17th century, this gigantic palace was completed nearly 100 years later by Giorgio Massari and became the last home of English poet Robert Browning (1812–89). Stand on the bridge by the Grand Canal entrance to spot the plaque with Browning's poetic excerpt, "Open my heart and you will see graved inside of it, Italy…" on the palace's left side. The eye-popping Grand Ballroom has hosted some of the grandest parties in the city's history, from its 18th-century heyday to the 1969 Bal Fantastica (a Save Venice charity event that attracted notables from Elizabeth Taylor to Aristotle Onassis) to balls re-created for Heath Ledger's 2005 film *Casanova*. Today the upper floors of the Ca' Rezzonico are home to the especially delightful Museo del Settecento (Museum of Venice in the 1700s), decorated with period furniture and tapestries in gilded salons, as well as Tiepolo ceiling frescoes and oil paintings. ⊠ *Fondamenta Rezzonico, Dorsoduro 3136, Dorsoduro* ☎ *041/2410100* ⊕ *carezzonico.visitmuve.it* ✉ *€10 (free with Museum Pass)* ⊗ *Closed Tues.* Ⓜ *Vaporetto: Ca' Rezzonico.*

Fodor'sChoice ★ **Gallerie dell'Accademia.** The greatest collection of Venetian paintings in the world hangs in these galleries founded by Napoléon in 1807 on the site of a religious complex he had suppressed. They were carefully and subtly restructured between 1945 and 1959 by the renowned architect Carlo Scarpa. Highlights include works by Jacopo Bellini, the father of the Venetian Renaissance, as well as the richly colored paintings of his more accomplished son Giovanni; *Tempest* by Giorgione, a revolutionary work that has intrigued viewers and critics for centuries; *Feast in the House of Levi,* which got Veronese summoned to the Inquisition; and several of Tintoretto's finest works. Don't miss the views of 15th- and 16th-century Venice by Carpaccio and Gentile Bellini, Giovanni's brother—you'll see how little the city has changed. Booking tickets in advance isn't essential but costs only an additional €1.50. ⊠ *Dorsoduro 1050, Campo della Carità just off Accademia Bridge, Dorsoduro* ☎ *041/5222247, 041/5200345 reservations* ⊕ *www.gallerieaccademia.it/en* ✉ *€15, subject to increases for special exhibitions. Free 1st Sun. of month* Ⓜ *Vaporetto: Accademia.*

FAMILY **Peggy Guggenheim Collection.** Housed in the incomplete but nevertheless charming Palazzo Venier dei Leoni, this choice selection of 20th-century painting and sculpture represents the taste and extraordinary style of the late heiress Peggy Guggenheim. Through wealth, social connections, and a sharp eye for artistic trends, Guggenheim (1898–1979) became an important art dealer and collector from the 1930s through the 1950s, and her personal collection here includes works by Picasso, Kandinsky, Pollock, Motherwell, and Ernst (her onetime husband). The museum serves beverages, snacks, and light meals in its refreshingly shady and artistically sophisticated garden. On Sundays at 3 pm (except in August) the museum offers a free tour and art workshop for children (ages 4–10); it's conducted in Italian, but anglophone interns are generally on hand to help those who don't *parla italiano.* ⊠ *Fondamenta Venier dei Leoni, Dorsoduro 701, Dorsoduro* ☎ *041/2405411* ⊕ *www. guggenheim-venice.it* ✉ *€15* ⊗ *Closed Tues.* Ⓜ *Vaporetto: Accademia.*

Fodor'sChoice ★ **Punta della Dogana.** Funded by the billionaire who owns a major share in Christie's Auction House, the François Pinault Foundation had Japanese architect Tadao Ando redesign this fabled customs house—sitting at the *punta,* or very head, of the Grand Canal—and now home to a changing roster of works from Pinault's collection of contemporary art. The streaming light, polished surfaces, and clean lines of Ando's design contrast beautifully with the brick, massive columns, and sturdy beams of the original Dogana. Even if you aren't into contemporary art, a visit is

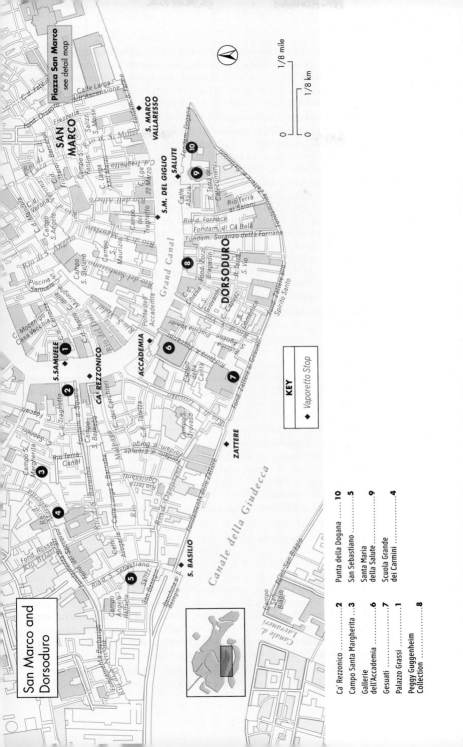

San Marco and Dorsoduro

KEY

♦ *Vaporetto Stop*

worthwhile just to see Ando's amazing architectural transformation. Be sure to walk down to the punta for a magnificent view of the Venetian basin. Check online for a schedule of temporary exhibitions. ⊠ *Punta della Dogana, Dorsoduro* 🕾 *041/2001057* ⊕ *www.palazzograssi.it* 🎫 *€18 with Palazzo Grassi* ⊘ *Closed Tues.* Ⓜ *Vaporetto: Salute.*

Fodor'sChoice   **San Sebastiano.** Paolo Veronese (1528–88), although still in his twenties,
★   was already the official painter of the Republic when he began the oil panels and frescoes at San Sebastiano, his parish church, in 1555. For decades he continued to embellish the church with very beautiful illusionistic scenes. The cycles of panels in San Sebastiano are considered to be his supreme accomplishment. Veronese is buried beneath his bust near the organ. The church itself, remodeled by Antonio Scarpagnino and finished in 1548, offers a rare opportunity to see a monument in Venice where both the architecture and the pictorial decoration all date from the same period. Be sure to check out the portal of the ex-convent, now part of the University of Venice, to the left of the church; it was designed in 1976–78 by Carlo Scarpa, one of the most important Italian architects of the 20th century. ⊠ *Campo San Sebastiano, Dorsoduro* 🕾 *041/2750462* ⊕ *www.chorusvenezia.org* 🎫 *€3 (free with Chorus Pass)* ⊘ *Closed Sun.* Ⓜ *Vaporetto: San Basilio.*

Fodor'sChoice   **Santa Maria della Salute.** The most iconic landmark of the Grand Canal,
★   La Salute (as this church is commonly called) is best viewed from the Riva degli Schiavoni at sunset or from the Accademia Bridge by moonlight. Baldassare Longhena (later Venice's most important Baroque architect) won a competition in 1631 to design a shrine honoring the Virgin Mary for saving Venice from a plague that over two years (1629–30) killed 47,000 residents, or one-third of the city's population. Outside, this ornate, white Istrian stone octagon is topped by a colossal cupola with snail-like ornamental buttresses. Inside, a white-and-gray color scheme is echoed in the polychrome marble floor and six chapels. An icon of Madonna della Salute (Madonna of Health) sits above the main altar; above is a sculpture showing Venice on her knees before the Madonna as she drives the plague from the city. Do not leave without visiting the Sacrestia Maggiore, which contains a dozen works by Titian. ⊠ *Punta della Dogana, Dorsoduro* 🕾 *041/2743928* ⊕ *basilicasalutevenezia.it* 🎫 *Church free, sacristy €4* Ⓜ *Vaporetto: Salute.*

WORTH NOTING

Campo Santa Margherita. Lined with cafés and restaurants generally filled with students from the nearby university, Campo Santa Margherita also has produce vendors and benches where you can sit and take in the bustling local life of the campo. Also close to the Ca' Rezzonico and the Scuola dei Carmini, and only a 10-minute walk from the Gallerie dell'Accademia, the square is the center of Dorsoduro social life. It takes its name from the church to one side, closed since the early 19th century and now used as an auditorium. On weekend evenings it sometimes attracts hordes of high school students from the mainland. ⊠ *Campo Santa Margherita, Dorsoduro.*

Gesuati (*Church of Santa Maria del Rosario*). When the Dominicans took over the church of Santa Maria della Visitazione from the suppressed order of Gesuati laymen in 1668, Giorgio Massari, the last of the great Venetian Baroque architects, was commissioned to build this structure between 1726 and 1735. It has an important Giovanni Battista Tiepolo (1696–1770) illusionistic ceiling and several other of his works, plus those of his contemporaries, Giambattista Piazzetta (1683–1754) and Sebastiano Ricci (1659–1734). ⊠ *Zattere, Dorsoduro* ☎ *041/2750462* ⊕ *www.chorusvenezia.org* 🎫 *€3 (free with Chorus Pass)* ⊙ *Closed Sun.* Ⓜ *Vaporetto: Zattere.*

Scuola Grande dei Carmini. When the order of Santa Maria del Carmelo commissioned Baldassare Longhena to finish the work on the Scuola Grande dei Carmini in the 1670s, their brotherhood of 75,000 members was the largest in Venice and one of the wealthiest. Little expense was spared in the decorating of stuccoed ceilings and carved ebony paneling, and the artwork is remarkable, even before 1739, when Giovanni Battista Tiepolo began painting the **Sala Capitolare.** In what many consider his best work, Tiepolo's nine great canvases vividly transform some rather conventional religious themes into dynamic displays of color and movement. ⊠ *Campo dei Carmini, Dorsoduro 2617, Dorsoduro* ☎ *041/5289420* ⊕ *www.scuolagrandecarmini.it* 🎫 *€5* Ⓜ *Vaporetto: Ca' Rezzonico.*

SAN POLO AND SANTA CROCE

The two smallest of Venice's six sestieri, San Polo and Santa Croce, were named after their main churches, though the Chiesa di Santa Croce was demolished in 1810. The city's most famous bridge, the Ponte di Rialto, unites San Marco (east) with San Polo (west). The Rialto takes its name from Rivoaltus, the high ground on which it was built. Shops abound in the area surrounding the Ponte di Rialto. On the San Marco side you'll find fashion, on the San Polo side, food.

TIMING

To do the area justice requires at least half a day. If you want to take part in the food shopping, come early to beat the crowds. Campo San Giacomo dell'Orio, west of the main thoroughfare that takes you from the Ponte di Rialto to Santa Maria Gloriosa dei Frari, is a peaceful place for a drink and a rest. The museums of Ca' Pesaro are a time commitment—you'll want at least two hours to see them both.

TOP ATTRACTIONS

Fodor's Choice
★

Santa Maria Gloriosa dei Frari. Completed in 1442, this immense Gothic church of russet-color brick—known locally as I Frari—is famous worldwide for its array of spectacular Venetian paintings. In the sacristy, see Giovanni Bellini's 1488 triptych *Madonna and Child with Saints,* painted for precisely this spot. The Corner Chapel is graced by Bartolomeo Vivarini's altarpiece *St. Mark Enthroned* and *Saints John the Baptist, Jerome, Peter, and Nicholas.* In the first south chapel of the chorus, there is a fine sculpture of St. John the Baptist by Donatello, dated 1438, with a psychological intensity rare for early Renaissance sculpture. You can see the rapid development of Venetian Renaissance painting by contrasting Bellini with the heroic energy of Titian's *Assumption,* over the main altar, painted only 30 years later.

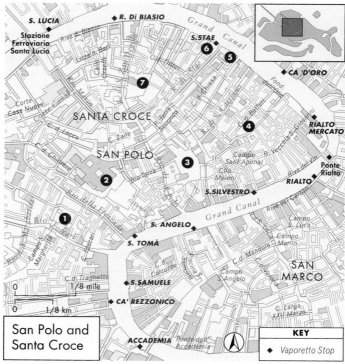

San Polo and
Santa Croce

KEY

♦ *Vaporetto Stop*

Titian's beautiful *Madonna di Ca' Pesaro* is in the left aisle; Titian disregarded the conventions of his time by moving the Virgin out of center and making the saints active participants. ⊠ *Campo dei Frari, San Polo* ☎ *041/2728618, 041/2750462 Chorus Foundation* ⊕ *www. basilicadeifrari.it* ⊠ *€3 (free with Chorus Pass)* Ⓜ *Vaporetto: San Tomà.*

Fodor'sChoice ★ **Scuola Grande di San Rocco.** This elegant example of Venetian Renaissance architecture, built between 1517 and 1560, was built for the essentially secular charitable confraternity bearing the saint's name. The Venetian "scuole" were organizations that sometimes had loose religious affiliations, through which the artisan class could exercise some influence upon civic life. Although San Rocco is bold and dramatic outside, its contents are even more stunning—a series of more than 60 paintings by Tintoretto. In 1564 Tintoretto edged out competition for a commission to decorate a ceiling by submitting not a sketch, but a finished work, which he moreover offered free of charge. *Moses Striking Water from the Rock, The Brazen Serpent,* and *The Fall of Manna* represent three afflictions—thirst, disease, and hunger—that San Rocco and later his brotherhood sought to relieve. ⊠ *Campo San Rocco, San Polo 3052, San Polo* ☎ *041/5234864* ⊕ *www.scuolagrandesanrocco.it* ⊠ *€10, includes audio guide* Ⓜ *Vaporetto: San Tomà.*

WORTH NOTING

Ca' Pesaro. Baldassare Longhena's grand Baroque palace, begun in 1676, is the beautifully restored home of two impressive collections. The **Galleria Internazionale d'Arte Moderna** has works by 19th- and 20th-century artists such as Klimt, Kandinsky, Matisse, and Miró. It also has a collection of representative works from Venice's Biennale art show that amounts to a panorama of 20th-century art. The pride of the **Museo Orientale** is its collection of Japanese art, and especially armor and weapons, of the Edo period (1603–1868). It also has a small but striking collection of Chinese and Indonesian porcelains and musical instruments. ⊠ *San Stae, Santa Croce 2076, Santa Croce* ☎ *041/721127 Galleria, 041/5241173 Museo Orientale* ⊕ *capesaro. visitmuve.it* 🎫 *€10, includes both museums (free with Museum Pass)* ⊙ *Closed Mon.* Ⓜ *Vaporetto: San Stae.*

Campo San Polo. Only Piazza San Marco is larger than this square, and the echo of children's voices bouncing off the surrounding palaces makes the space seem even bigger. Campo San Polo once hosted bull races, fairs, military parades, and packed markets, and now comes especially alive on summer nights, when it's home to the city's outdoor cinema. The **Chiesa di San Polo** has been restored so many times that little remains of the original 9th-century church, and sadly, 19th-century alterations were so costly that the friars sold off many great paintings to pay bills. Although Giambattista Tiepolo is represented here, his work is outdone by 16 paintings by his son Giandomenico (1727–1804), including the *Stations of the Cross* in the oratory to the left of the entrance. The younger Tiepolo also created a series of expressive and theatrical renderings of the saints. Look for altarpieces by Tintoretto and Veronese that managed to escape auction. San Polo's bell tower (begun 1362) remained unchanged through the centuries—don't miss the two lions playing with a disembodied human head and a serpent that guard it. Tradition has it that the head refers to that of Marino Faliero, the doge executed for treason in 1355. ⊠ *Campo San Polo, San Polo* ☎ *041/2750462 Chorus Foundation* ⊕ *www.chorusvenezia. org* 🎫 *Chiesa di San Polo: €3 (free with Chorus Pass)* ⊙ *Closed Sun.* Ⓜ *Vaporetto: San Silvestro, San Tomà.*

San Giacomo dell'Orio. This lovely square was named after a laurel tree (*orio*), and today trees lend it shade and character. Add benches and a fountain (with a drinking bowl for dogs), and the pleasant, oddly shaped campo becomes a place for friendly conversation and neighborhood kids at play. Legend has it the **Chiesa di San Giacomo dell'Orio** was founded in the 9th century on an island still populated by wolves. The current church dates from 1225; its short, unmatched Byzantine columns survived renovation during the Renaissance, and the church never lost the feel of an ancient temple sheltering beneath its 14th-century ship's-keel roof. In the sanctuary, large marble crosses are surrounded by a group of small medieval Madonnas. The altarpiece is *Madonna with Child and Saints* (1546) by Lorenzo Lotto (1480–1556), and the sacristies contain 12 works by Palma il Giovane (circa 1544–1628). ⊠ *Campo San Giacomo dell'Orio, Santa Croce* ☎ *041/2750462*

Chorus Foundation ⊕ *www.chorusvenezia.org* ✉ *Church €3 (free with Chorus Pass)* ⊘ *Church closed Sun.* Ⓜ *Vaporetto: San Stae.*

San Giovanni Elemosinario. Storefronts make up the facade, and the altars were built by market guilds—poulterers, messengers, and fodder merchants—at this church intimately bound to the Rialto Market. The original church was completely destroyed by a fire in 1514 and rebuilt in 1531 by Antonio Abbondi, who had also worked on the Scuola di San Rocco. During a recent restoration, workers stumbled upon a frescoed cupola by Pordenone (1484–1539) that had been painted over centuries earlier. Don't miss Titian's *St. John the Almsgiver* and Pordenone's *Sts. Catherine, Sebastian, and Roch.* ✉ *Rialto Ruga Vecchia San Giovanni, Santa Croce* ☎ *041/2750462 Chorus Foundation* ⊕ *www.chorusvenezia.org* ✉ *€3 (free with Chorus Pass)* ⊘ *Closed Mon.–Sat. after 1:15 and Sun.* Ⓜ *Vaporetto: San Silvestro, Rialto.*

San Stae. The church of San Stae—the Venetian name for San Eustacchio (Eustace)—was reconstructed in 1687 by Giovanni Grassi and given a new facade in 1707 by Domenico Rossi. Renowned Venetian painters and sculptors of the early 18th century decorated this church around 1717 with the legacy left by Doge Alvise Mocenigo II, who's buried in the center aisle. San Stae affords a good opportunity to see the early works of Gianbattista Tiepolo, Sebastiano Ricci, and Piazzetta, as well as those of the previous generation of Venetian painters, with whom they had studied. ✉ *Campo San Stae, Santa Croce* ☎ *041/2750462 Chorus Foundation* ⊕ *www.chorusvenezia.org* ✉ *€3 (free with Chorus Pass)* ⊘ *Closed Sun.* Ⓜ *Vaporetto: San Stae.*

CANNAREGIO

Seen from above, this part of town seems like a wide field plowed by several long, straight canals that are linked by intersecting straight streets—not typical of Venice, where the shape of the islands usually defines the shape of the canals. Cannaregio's main thoroughfare, the Strada Nova (literally, "New Street," as it was converted from a canal in 1871), is the longest street in Venice; it runs parallel to the Grand Canal. Today the Strada Nova serves as a pedestrian walkway from the train station almost to the Rialto. Cannaregio, first settled in the 14th century, is one of the more "modern" of Venice's neighborhoods, with walkways, or *fondamente*, along its major canals north of the Strada Nova, making it ideal for canal-side strolls where you can view some spectacular Gothic and Baroque facades.

TOP ATTRACTIONS

Fodor'sChoice ★ **Ca' d'Oro.** One of the postcard sights of Venice, this exquisite Venetian Gothic palace was once literally a "Golden House," when its marble traceries and ornaments were embellished with gold. It was created by Giovanni and Bartolomeo Bon between 1428 and 1430 for the patrician Marino Contarini, who had read about the Roman emperor Nero's golden house in Rome, and wished to imitate it as a present to his wife. Her family owned the land and the Byzantine *fondaco* (palace-trading house) previously standing on it; you can still see the round Byzantine arches on the entry porch incorporated into the Gothic building. The

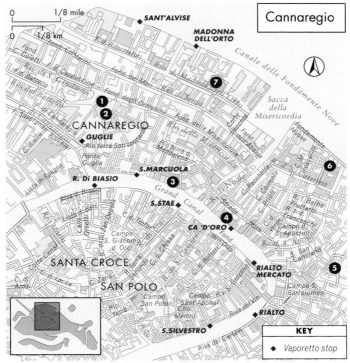

4

last proprietor, Baron Giorgio Franchetti, left Ca' d'Oro to the city, after having had it carefully restored and furnished with antiquities, sculptures, and paintings that today make up the Galleria Franchetti. It also contains the type of fresco that once adorned the exteriors of Venetian buildings (commissioned by those who could not afford a marble facade). ⊠ *Calle Ca' d'Oro, Cannaregio 3933, Cannaregio* ☎ *041/5200345* ⊕ *www.cadoro.org* 🎫 *€11 (free 1st Sun. of month)* Ⓜ *Vaporetto: Ca' d'Oro.*

Fodor'sChoice **Jewish Ghetto.** The neighborhood that gave the world the word *ghetto* is
★ today a quiet place surrounding a large campo. The area has Europe's highest density of Renaissance-era synagogues, and visiting them is interesting not only culturally but also aesthetically. In 1516 relentless local opposition forced the Senate to confine Jews to an island in Cannaregio, named for its *geto* (foundry). The term "ghetto" also may come from the Hebrew "ghet," meaning separation or divorce. Gates at the entrance were locked at night, and boats patrolled the surrounding canals. In the 16th century the community grew with refugees from the Inquisition. Although the gates were pulled down after Napoleon's 1797 arrival, the ghetto was reinstated during the Austrian occupation. Full freedom wasn't realized until 1866 with the founding of the Italian state. Many Jews fled Italy as a result of Mussolini's 1938 racial laws.

During World War II, the remaining 247 were deported by the Nazis; only eight returned. ⊠ *Campo del Ghetto Nuovo, Cannaregio* ⊕ *www. museoebraico.it* ⌦ *Museum Ebraico di Venezia (Jewish Museum of Venice)* €8; *synagogue tour + museum* €12 ⊘ *No tours Sat.*

Fodor's Choice

★

Madonna dell'Orto. Though built toward the middle of the 14th century, this church takes its character from its beautiful late-Gothic facade, added between 1460 and 1464; it's one of the most beautiful Gothic churches in Venice. Tintoretto lived nearby, and this, his parish church, contains some of his most powerful work. Lining the chancel are two huge (45 feet by 20 feet) canvases, *Adoration of the Golden Calf* and *Last Judgment.* In glowing contrast to this awesome spectacle is Tintoretto's *Presentation of the Virgin at the Temple* and the simple chapel where he and his children, Marietta and Domenico, are buried. Paintings by Domenico, Cima da Conegliano, Palma il Giovane, Palma il Vecchio, and Titian also hang in the church. A chapel displays a photographic reproduction of a precious *Madonna with Child* by Giovanni Bellini. The original was stolen one night in 1993. Don't miss the beautifully austere, late-Gothic cloister (1460), which you enter through the small door to the right of the church; it is frequently used for exhibitions but may be open at other times as well. ⊠ *Campo della Madonna dell'Orto, Cannaregio* ☎ *041/719933* ⊕ *www.madonnadellorto.org* ⌦€3 Ⓜ *Vaporetto: Orto.*

Museo Ebraico (*Jewish Museum*). The small but well-arranged museum highlights centuries of Venetian Jewish culture with splendid silver Hanukkah lamps and Torahs, and handwritten, beautifully decorated wedding contracts in Hebrew. Hourly tours in Italian and English (on the half hour) of the ghetto and its five synagogues leave from the museum. ⊠ *Campo del Ghetto Nuovo, Cannaregio 2902/B, Cannaregio* ☎ *041/715359* ⊕ *www.museoebraico.it* ⌦€8, €12 with synagogue guided tour ⊘ *Closed Sat.* Ⓜ *Vaporetto: San Marcuola, Guglie.*

Fodor's Choice

★

Santa Maria dei Miracoli. Tiny yet harmoniously proportioned, this Renaissance gem, built between 1481 and 1489, is sheathed in marble and decorated inside with exquisite marble reliefs. Architect Pietro Lombardo (circa 1435–1515) miraculously compressed the building into its confined space, then created the illusion of greater size by varying the color of the exterior, adding extra pilasters on the building's canal side and offsetting the arcade windows to make the arches appear deeper. The church was built to house *I Miracoli,* an image of the Virgin Mary by Niccolò di Pietro (1394–1440) that is said to have performed miracles—look for it on the high altar. ⊠ *Campo Santa Maria Nova, Cannaregio* ☎ *041/2750462 Chorus Foundation* ⊕ *www.chorusvenezia. org* ⌦€3 (free with Chorus Pass) ⊘ *Closed Sun.* Ⓜ *Vaporetto: Rialto.*

WORTH NOTING

Gesuiti (*Chiesa di Santa Maria Assunta*). The interior walls of this early-18th-century church (1715–30) resemble brocade drapery, and only touching them will convince skeptics that rather than embroidered cloth, the green-and-white walls are inlaid marble. This trompe-l'oeil decor is typical of the late Baroque's fascination with optical illusion. Toward the end of his life, Titian tended to paint scenes of suffering and sorrow in a nocturnal ambience. A dramatic example of this is on display above the first altar to the left: Titian's daring *Martyrdom of St. Lawrence* (1578), taken from an earlier church that stood on this site. To the left of the church is the Oratory of the Crociferi, which features some of Palma Giovane's best work, painted between 1583 and 1591. ⊠ *Campo dei Gesuiti, Cannaregio* ☎ *041/5286579* 🎟 *€1* 🕐 *Oratory closed Nov.–Mar. and Sun.–Thurs.* Ⓜ *Vaporetto: Fondamente Nove.*

Palazzo Vendramin-Calergi. Hallowed as the place of Richard Wagner's death and today's Venice's most glamorous casino, this magnficent edifice found its fame centuries before: Venetian star architect Mauro Codussi (1440–1504) essentially invented Venetian Renaissance architecture with this design. Built for the Loredan family around 1500, Codussi's palace married the fortresslike design of the Florentine Alberti's Palazzo Ruccelai with the lightness and delicacy of Venetian Gothic. Note how Codussi beautifully exploits the flickering light of Venetian waterways to play across the building's facade and to pour in through the generous windows.

Venice has always prized the beauty of this palace. In 1652 its owners were convicted of a rather gruesome murder, and the punishment would have involved, as was customary, the demolition of their palace. The murderers were banned from the Republic, but the palace, in view of its beauty and historical importance, was spared. Only the newly added wing was torn down. ⊠ *Cannaregio 2040, Cannaregio* ☎ *041/5297111* ⊕ *www.casinovenezia.it* 🎟 *Casinò €5–€10* Ⓜ *Vaporetto: San Marcuola.*

CASTELLO

Castello, Venice's largest sestiere, includes all of the land from east of Piazza San Marco to the city's easternmost tip. Its name probably comes from a fortress that once stood on one of the eastern islands. Not every well-off Venetian family could find a spot or afford to build a palazzo on the Grand Canal. Many who couldn't instead settled in western Castello, taking advantage of its proximity to the Rialto and San Marco, and built the noble palazzi that today distinguish this area from the fishermen's enclave in the more easterly streets of the sestiere. During the days of the Republic, eastern Castello was the primary neighborhood for workers in the shipbuilding Arsenale, which is located in its midst.

TOP ATTRACTIONS

Arsenale. Visible from the street, the impressive Renaissance gateway, the **Porta Magna** (1460), designed by Antonio Gambello, was the first classical structure to be built in Venice. It is guarded by four lions—war booty of Francesco Morosini, who took the Peloponnese from the Turks in 1687. The 10-foot-tall lion on the left stood sentinel more than 2,000 years ago near Athens, and experts say its mysterious inscription is runic "graffiti" left by Viking mercenaries hired to suppress 11th-century revolts in Piraeus. If you look at the winged lion above the doorway, you'll notice that the Gospel at his paws is open, but lacks the customary *Pax* inscription; praying for peace perhaps seemed inappropriate above a factory that manufactured weapons. The interior is not regularly open to the public, since it belongs to the Italian Navy, but it opens for the Biennale di Arte and for Venice's festival of traditional boats, **Mare Maggio**, held every May. If you're here during those times, don't miss the chance for a look inside; you can enter from the back via a northern-side walkway leading from the Ospedale vaporetto stop.

The Arsenale is said to have been founded in 1104 on twin islands. The immense facility that evolved—it was the largest industrial complex in Europe built prior to the Industrial Revolution—was given the old Venetian dialect name *arzanà,* borrowed from the Arabic *darsina'a,* meaning "workshop." At the height of its activity, in the early 16th century, it employed as many as 16,000 *arsenalotti,* workers who were among the most respected shipbuilders in the world. The Arsenale developed a type of pre–Industrial Revolution assembly line, which allowed it to build ships with astounding speed and efficiency. (This innovation existed even in Dante's time, and he immortalized these toiling workers armed with boiling tar in his *Inferno,* canto 21.) The Arsenale's efficiency was confirmed time and again—whether building 100 ships in 60 days to battle the Turks in Cyprus (1597) or completing one perfectly armed warship, start to finish, while King Henry III of France attended a banquet. ⊠ *Campo dell'Arsenale, Castello* Ⓜ *Vaporetto: Arsenale.*

Fodor'sChoice **San Francesco della Vigna.** Although this church contains some interesting
★ and beautiful paintings and sculptures, it's the architecture that makes it worth the hike through a lively, middle-class, residential neighborhood. The Franciscan church was enlarged and rebuilt by Jacopo Sansovino in 1534, giving it the first Renaissance interior in Venice; its proportions are said to reflect the mystic significance of the numbers three and seven dictated by Renaissance neo-Platonic numerology. The soaring but harmonious facade was added in 1562 by Palladio. The church represents a unique combination of the work of the two great stars of Veneto 16th-century architecture. As you enter, a late Giovanni Bellini *Madonna with Saints* is down some steps to the left, inside the Cappella Santa. In the Giustinian chapel to the left is Veronese's first work in Venice, an altarpiece depicting the Virgin and child with saints. In another, larger chapel, on the left, are bas-reliefs by Pietro and his son Tullio Lombardo. Be sure to ask to see the attached cloisters, which are usually open to visitors and quite lovely. ⊠ *Campo di San Francesco della Vigna, Castello* ☎ *041/5206102* 🎟 *Free* ☉ *Closed weekends* Ⓜ *Vaporetto: Celestia.*

Fodor'sChoice **Santi Giovanni e Paolo.** This gorgeous Italian Gothic church of the
★ Dominican order, consecrated in 1430, looms over one of the most picturesque squares in Venice: the Campo Giovanni e Paolo, centered around the magnificent 15th-century equestrian statue of Bartolomeo Colleoni by the Florentine Andrea Verrocchio. Bartolomeo Bon's portal, combining Gothic and classical elements, was added between 1458 and 1462, using columns salvaged from Torcello. The 15th-century Murano stained-glass window near the side entrance is breathtaking for its beautiful colors and figures. The second official church of the Republic after San Marco, San Zanipolo is the Venetian equivalent of London's Westminster Abbey, with a great number of important people, including 25 doges, buried here. Artistic highlights include an early polyptych by Giovanni Bellini, Alvise Vivarini's *Christ Carrying*

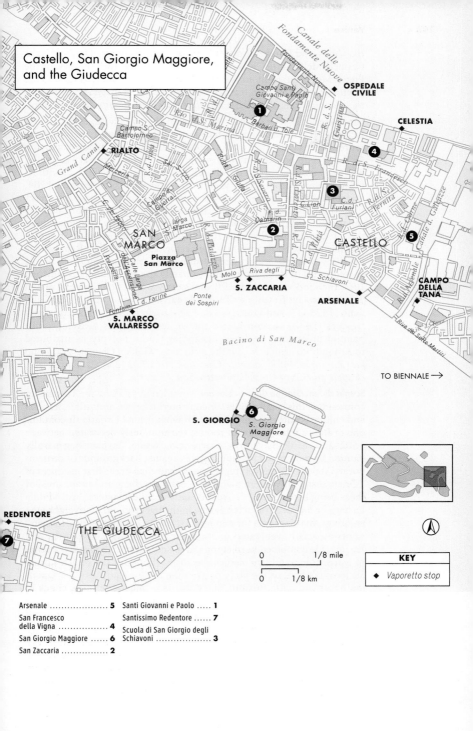

Castello, San Giorgio Maggiore, and the Giudecca

Canale delle Fondamente Nuove

Canale delle Fondamente Nuove

Campo Santi Giovanni e Paolo

Barbari d. Tole

OSPEDALE CIVILE

● 1

Campo S. Bartolomeo

CELESTIA

◆ RIALTO

Grand Canal

Merceria

Campo S. Lio

● 4

R. d. S. Francesco

● 3

C. d. Lion

Furlani

C. Larga Marco

SAN MARCO

Piazza San Marco

● 2

CASTELLO

● 5

Calle Larga dell'Ascensione

Frezzeria

S. MARCO VALLARESSO

Fontam d. Farine

Molo

Riva degli

Schiavoni

Ponte dei Sospiri

S. ZACCARIA

ARSENALE

CAMPO DELLA TANA

Riva dei Sette Martiri

Bacino di San Marco

TO BIENNALE →

S. GIORGIO

● 6

S. Giorgio Maggiore

REDENTORE

◆ 7

THE GIUDECCA

0   1/8 mile

0   1/8 km

KEY

◆ *Vaporetto stop*

the Cross, and Lorenzo Lotto's *Charity of St. Antonino.* Don't miss the Cappella del Rosario (Rosary Chapel), built in the 16th century, or the Pietro Mocenigo tomb to the right of the main entrance. ✉ *Campo dei Santi Giovanni e Paolo, Castello* ☎ *041/5235913* ⊕ *www.basilicasan-tigiovanniepaolo.it* ✆ *€3.50* Ⓜ *Vaporetto: Fondamente Nove, Rialto.*

Fodor'sChoice
★

San Zaccaria. Practically more a museum than a church, San Zaccaria bears a striking Renaissance facade, with central and upper portions representing some of Mauro Codussi's best work. The lower portion of the facade and the interior were designed by Antonio Gambello. The original structure of the church was 14th-century Gothic, with its facade completed in 1515, some years after Codussi's death in 1504, and it retains the proportions of the rest of the essentially Gothic structure. Inside is one of the great treasures of Venice, Giovanni Bellini's celebrated altarpiece, *La Sacra Conversazione,* easily recognizable in the left nave. Completed in 1505, when the artist was 75, it shows Bellini's ability to incorporate the aesthetics of the High Renaissance into his work. It bears a closer resemblance to the contemporary works of Leonardo (it dates from approximately the same time as the *Mona Lisa*) than it does to much of Bellini's early work. The **Cappella di San Tarasio** displays frescoes by Tuscan Renaissance artists Andrea del Castagno (1423–57) and Francesco da Faenza (circa 1400–51). Castagno's frescoes (1442) are considered the earliest examples of Renaissance painting in Venice. The three outstanding Gothic polyptychs attributed to Antonio Vivarini earned it the nickname "Golden Chapel." ✉ *Campo San Zaccaria, 4693 Castello, Castello* ☎ *041/5221257* ✆ *Church free, chapels and crypt €1* Ⓜ *Vaporetto: San Zaccaria.*

Fodor'sChoice
★

Scuola di San Giorgio degli Schiavoni. Founded in 1451 by the Dalmatian community, this small scuola, or confraternity, was, and still is, a social and cultural center for migrants from what is now Croatia. It contains one of Italy's most beautiful rooms, harmoniously decorated between 1502 and 1507 by Vittore Carpaccio. While Carpaccio generally painted legendary and religious figures against backgrounds of contemporary Venetian architecture, here is perhaps one of the first instances of "Orientalism" in Western painting. Note the turbans and exotic dress of those being baptized and converted, and even the imagined, arid Middle Eastern or North African landscape in the background of several of the paintings. In this scuola for immigrants, Carpaccio focuses on "foreign" saints especially venerated in Dalmatia: Sts. George, Tryphone, and Jerome. He combined keen empirical observation with fantasy, a sense of warm color, and late medieval realism. (Look for the priests fleeing St. Jerome's lion, or the body parts in the dragon's lair.) ■TIP→ **Opening hours are quite flexible. Since this is a "must-see" site, check in advance so you won't be disappointed.** ✉ *Calle dei Furlani, Castello 3259/A, Castello* ☎ *041/5228828* ✆ *€5* ⊘ *Closed Sun. afternoon and Mon. morning* Ⓜ *Vaporetto: Arsenale, San Zaccaria.*

SAN GIORGIO MAGGIORE AND THE GIUDECCA

Beckoning travelers across St. Mark's Basin is the island of San Giorgio Maggiore, separated by a small channel from the Giudecca. A tall brick campanile on that distant bank nicely complements the Campanile of San Marco. Beneath it looms the stately dome of one of Venice's greatest churches, San Giorgio Maggiore, the creation of Andrea Palladio. To the west, on the Giudecca, is Palladio's other masterpiece, the Church of the Santissimo Redentore.

You can reach San Giorgio Maggiore via Vaporetto Line 2 from San Zaccaria. The next three stops on the line take you to the Giudecca. The island's past may be shrouded in mystery, but despite recent gentrification by artists and well-to-do bohemians, it's still down-to-earth and one of the city's few remaining primarily working-class neighborhoods. Interestingly, you find that most Venetians don't even consider the Giudecchini Venetians at all.

TIMING

A half day should be plenty of time to visit the area. Allow about a half hour to see each of the churches and an hour or two to look around the Giudecca.

TOP ATTRACTIONS

Fodor's Choice
★

San Giorgio Maggiore. There's been a church on this island since the 8th century, with a Benedictine monastery added in the 10th century. Today's refreshingly airy and simply decorated church of brick and white marble was begun in 1566 by Palladio and displays his architectural hallmarks of mathematical harmony and classical influence. *The Last Supper* and the *Gathering of Manna*, two of Tintoretto's later works, line the chancel. To the right of the entrance hangs *The Adoration of the Shepherds* by Jacopo Bassano (1517–92); his affection for his home in the foothills, Bassano del Grappa, is evident in the bucolic subjects and terra-firma colors he chooses. The monks are happy to show Carpaccio's *St. George and the Dragon,* hanging in a private room, if they have time. The campanile dates from 1791, the previous structures having collapsed twice.

Adjacent to the church is the complex now housing the **Cini Foundation,** containing a very beautiful cloister designed by Palladio in 1560, his refectory, and a library designed by Longhena. Guided tours are given daily 10–5, April through September; reservations are not required. ⊠ *Isola di San Giorgio Maggiore, San Giorgio Maggiore* ☎ *041/5227827* ⊕ *www.abbaziasangiorgio.it* ⊠ *Church free, campanile €6* Ⓜ *Vaporetto: San Giorgio.*

Santissimo Redentore. After a plague in 1576 claimed some 50,000 people—nearly one-third of the city's population (including Titian)—Andrea Palladio was asked to design a commemorative church. Giudecca's Capuchin friars offered land and their services, provided the building was in keeping with the simplicity of their hermitage. Consecrated in 1592, after Palladio's death, the Redentore (considered Palladio's supreme achievement in ecclesiastical design) is dominated by a dome and a pair of slim, almost minaretlike bell towers. Its deceptively simple, stately facade leads to a bright, airy interior. There aren't any paintings or sculptures of note, but the harmony and elegance of the interior makes a visit worthwhile.

For hundreds of years, on the third weekend in July the doge would make a pilgrimage here to give thanks to the Redeemer for ending the 16th-century plague. The event has become the Festa del Redentore, a favorite Venetian festival featuring boats, fireworks, and outdoor feasting. It's the one time of year you can walk to Giudecca—across a temporary pontoon bridge connecting Redentore with the Zattere. ⊠ *Fondamenta San Giacomo, Giudecca* ☎ *041/5231415, 041/2750462 Chorus Foundation* 💶 *€3 (free with Chorus Pass)* ⊗ *Closed Sun.* Ⓜ *Vaporetto: Redentore.*

ISLANDS OF THE LAGOON

The perfect vacation from your Venetian vacation is an escape to Murano, Burano, and sleepy Torcello, the islands of the northern lagoon. Torcello is legendary for its beauty and offers ancient mosaics, greenery, breathing space, and picnic opportunities (remember to pack a lunch). Burano is an island of fishing traditions and houses painted in a riot of colors—blue, yellow, pink, ocher, and dark red. Visitors still love to shop here for "Venetian" lace, even though the vast majority of it is machine-made in Asia; visit the island's Museo del Merletto (Lace Museum) to discover the undeniable difference between the two.

Murano is renowned for its glass, plenty of which you can find in Venice itself. It's also notorious for high-pressure sales on factory tours, even those organized by top hotels. Vaporetto connections to Murano aren't difficult, and for the price of a boat ticket (included in any vaporetto pass) you'll buy your freedom and more time to explore. The Murano "guides" herding new arrivals follow a rotation so that factories take turns giving tours, but you can avoid the hustle by just walking away. ■TIP→ Don't take a "free" taxi to Murano; it only means that should you choose to buy (and you'll be strongly encouraged), your taxi fare and commission will be included in the price you pay.

The Lido is Venice's barrier island, forming the southern border of the Venetian Lagoon and protecting Venice from the waters of the Adriatic. It forms the beach of Venice, and is home to a series of bathing establishments both public and private—some luxurious and elegant, some quite simple and catering to Venetian families and their children. Buses run the length of the island.

■TIP→ San Michele, a vaporetto stop on the way to Murano, is the cemetery island of Venice, the resting place of many international artists who have chosen to spend eternity in this beautiful city. It also hosts Venice's first church to exhibit features of Renaissance architecture.

TIMING
Hitting all the sights on all the islands takes a busy, full day. If you limit yourself to Murano and San Michele, you can easily explore for an ample half day; the same goes for Burano and Torcello. In summer the express Vaporetto Line 7 will take you to Murano from San Zaccaria

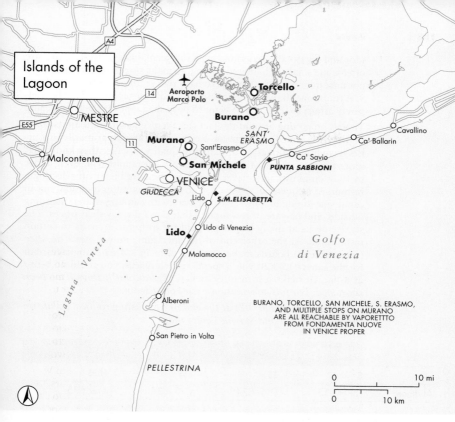

MESTRE

Aeroporto
Marco Polo

Torcello

Burano

Murano

SANT'
ERASMO

Sant'Erasmo

Ca' Ballarin

Cavallino

Malcontenta

San Michele

Ca' Savio

PUNTA SABBIONI

VENICE

GIUDECCA

Lido   **S.M.ELISABETTA**

Lido   Lido di Venezia

*Golfo
di Venezia*

Laguna   Veneta

Malamocco

BURANO, TORCELLO, SAN MICHELE, S. ERASMO,
AND MULTIPLE STOPS ON MURANO
ARE ALL REACHABLE BY VAPORETTO
FROM FONDAMENTA NUOVE
IN VENICE PROPER

Alberoni

San Pietro in Volta

PELLESTRINA

0   10 mi

0   10 km

(the Jolanda landing) in 25 minutes; Line 3 will take you from Piazzale Roma to Murano via the Canale di Cannaregio in 21 minutes; otherwise, local Line 4.1 makes a 45-minute trip from San Zaccaria every 20 minutes, circling the east end of Venice, stopping at Fondamente Nove and San Michele island cemetery on the way. To see glassblowing, get off at Colonna; the Museo stop will put you near the Museo del Vetro.

Line 12 goes from Fondamente Nove direct to Murano and Burano every 30 minutes (Torcello is a 5-minute ferry ride—Line 9—from there); the full trip takes 45 minutes each way. To get to Burano and Torcello from Murano, pick up Line 12 at the Faro stop (Murano's lighthouse).

WHERE TO EAT

Dining options in Venice range from the ultra–high end, where jackets are required and shorts are a no-go, to the very casual. Once staunchly traditional, many restaurants have revamped their menus along with their dining rooms, creating dishes that blend classic Venetian elements with ingredients and methods less common to the region.

Mid- and upper-range restaurants are often more willing to make the break, offering innovative options while keeping dishes like sarde in saor and fegato alla veneziana available as mainstays. Restaurants are often quite small with limited seating, so make sure to reserve ahead. It's not uncommon for restaurants to have two seatings per night, at 7 and 9. A traditional Italian meal includes several courses and should be a leisurely affair; so if you don't want to be rushed, opt for the later sitting.

There's no getting around the fact that Venice has more than its share of overpriced, mediocre eateries. Restaurants catering primarily to tourists have little motivation to maintain quality, because they know that most tourists are one-time, short-term visitors and will, even under the best circumstances, never return. So, you are better off selecting a restaurant frequented by locals, who are interested in the food, not in canal-side dining or views. Avoid places with cajoling waiters standing outside, and beware of restaurants that don't display their prices. The service desks at many hotels are paid off to funnel tourists to certain restaurants. At the other end of the spectrum, showy *menu turistico* (tourist menu) boards make offerings clear in a dozen languages, but for the same €15–€20 you'd spend at such places, you could do better at a bacaro making a meal of cicheti. *Restaurant listings have been shortened. For full information, visit Fodors.com.*

Use the coordinate (✛ B2) at the end of each listing to locate a site on the Where to Eat and Stay in Venice map.

WHAT IT COSTS				
	$	$$	$$$	$$$$
At dinner	under €15	€15–€24	€25–€35	over €35

Prices in the dining reviews are the average cost of a main course at dinner, or, if dinner is not served, at lunch.

SAN MARCO

$
CAFÉ

✕ **Bar all'Angolo.** This corner of Campo Santo Stefano is one of the most pleasing locations to sit and watch the Venetian world go by. The constant motion of the café staff assures you'll receive your coffee, spritz, panino, or *tramezzino* (sandwich on untoasted white bread, usually with a mayonnaise-based filling) in short order; consume it at your leisure either at one of the outdoor tables, at the bar, or take refuge at the tables in the back. **Known for:** simple yet satisfying fare, like tramezzini and panini; tasty desserts, including tiramisù and cakes; good people-watching in a lovely square. $ *Average main: €10* ✉ *Campo Santo Stefano, San Marco 3464, just in front of Santo Stefano church, San Marco* ☎ *041/5220710* ◷ *Closed Sun., and Jan.* Ⓜ *Vaporetto: Sant'Angelo* ✛ *C4.*

$$
CAFÉ
Fodor's Choice
★

✕ **Caffè Florian.** Founded in 1720, Florian is not only Italy's first café, but with its glittering neo-baroque decor and attractive 19th-century wall panels (depicting Venetian heroes), it's indisputably the most beautiful. The coffee, drinks, and snacks are quite good (think chocolate, hot or otherwise), but you really come here for the atmosphere and to be part of Venetian history: it was the only café to serve women during the 18th century (hence Casanova's patronage), and it was the café of choice for artistic notables such as Wagner, Goethe, Goldoni, Lord Byron, Marcel Proust, and Charles Dickens. **Known for:** prime location on St. Mark's Square; beautiful historic setting inside; hot chocolate, coffee, and quick nibbles. [$] *Average main: €22* ✉ *Piazza San Marco, San Marco 56, San Marco* ☎ *041/5205641* 🌐 *www.caffeflorian.com* 🕒 *Closed early Jan.* ✥ *E4.*

$$ VENETIAN

🍴 **Enoteca al Volto.** A short walk from the Rialto Bridge, this bar has been around since 1936; the satisfying cicheti and primi have a lot to do with its staying power. Grab one of the tables out front, or take refuge in two small, dark rooms with a ceiling plastered with wine labels that provide a classic backdrop for simple fare, including a delicious risotto that is served daily at noon, plus a solid wine list of both Italian and foreign vintages. **Known for:** great local and international wine selection; tasty and inexpensive cicheti; fantastic main courses, including risotto and pasta with seafood. [$] *Average main: €15* ✉ *Calle Cavalli, San Marco 4081, San Marco* ☎ *041/5228945* 🌐 *enotecaalvolto.com* [M] *Vaporetto: Rialto* ✥ *E3.*

$$$$ VENETIAN
Fodor's Choice ★

🍴 **Harry's Bar.** For those who can afford it, lunch or dinner at Harry's Bar is as much a part of a visit to Venice as a walk across the Piazza San Marco or a vaporetto ride down the Grand Canal. Inside, the suave, subdued beige-on-white decor is unchanged from the 1930s, and the classic Venetian fare is carefully and excellently prepared. **Known for:** being the birthplace of the Bellini cocktail; see-and-be-seen atmosphere; signature crepes flambées and famous Cipriani chocolate cake. [$] *Average main: €38* ✉ *Calle Vallaresso, San Marco 1323, San Marco* ☎ *041/5285777* 🌐 *www.cipriani.com/restaurant* 👔 *Jacket required* [M] *Vaporetto: San Marco (Calle Vallaresso)* ✥ *E4.*

$$$$ VENETIAN

🍴 **Ristorante Quadri.** Quadri, located above the famed café of the same name, is steeped in history (as a café, it was the first to introduce Turkish coffee to an already overcaffeinated city in the 1700s) and overstated Venetian ambience. Since the Alajmo family (of the celebrated Le Calandre restaurant near Padua) have taken over the restaurant and put their accomplished sous-chef from Padua in charge of the kitchen, the menu has developed increasing complexity, best sampled by choosing a tasting menu. **Known for:** sophisticated and modern Italian cuisine; tasting menus with seasonal ingredients; jaw-droppingly expensive prices. [$] *Average main: €65* ✉ *Piazza San Marco 121, San Marco* ☎ *041/5222105* 🌐 *www.alajmo.it/en/sezione/ristorante-quadri/ristorante-quadri* 🕒 *Closed Mon.* ✥ *E4.*

DORSODURO

$ CAFÉ

🍴 **Caffè Bar Ai Artisti.** Sitting on a campo made famous in films with Katharine Hepburn and Indiana Jones, Caffè Ai Artisti gives locals, students, and travelers alike good reason to pause and refuel. The location is central, pleasant, and sunny—perfect for people-watching and taking a break before the next destination—and the hours are long: you can come here for a morning cappuccino, or drop by late for an after-dinner spritz. **Known for:** relaxing with a coffee; evening Aperol spritz or wine; chilling with the locals. [$] *Average main: €8* ✉ *Campo San*

Barnaba, Dorsoduro 2771, Dorsoduro ☎ 041/5238994 ☐ No credit cards Ⓜ Vaporetto: Ca' Rezzonico ✛ C5.

§
WINE BAR
Fodor's Choice
★

✕ **Cantinone già Schiavi.** A mainstay for anyone living or working in the area, this beautiful, family-run, 19th-century bacaro across from the *squero* (gondola repair shop) of San Trovaso has original furnishings and one of the best wine cellars in town—the walls are covered floor to ceiling by bottles for purchase. The cicheti here are some of the most inventive—and freshest—in Venice (feel free to compliment the Signora, who makes them up to twice a day). **Known for:** excellent quality cicheti; plenty of wine choices; boisterous local atmosphere. Ⓢ *Average main: €8* ✉ *Fondamenta Nani, Dorsoduro 992, Dorsoduro* ☎ *041/5230034* ⊕ *www.cantinaschiavi.com* ☐ *No credit cards* ☾ *Closed Sun., and 3 wks in Aug.* Ⓜ *Vaporetto: Zattere, Accademia* ✛ C5.

§
ITALIAN

✕ **Imagina Caffè.** This friendly café and art gallery, located between Campo Santa Margherita and Campo San Barnaba, is a great place to stop for a spritz, or even for a light lunch or dinner. The highlights are the freshly made salads, but their panini and tramezzini are also among the best in the area. **Known for:** tasty sandwiches and salads; good wines and cocktails; pleasant outdoor seating. Ⓢ *Average main: €10* ✉ *Rio Terà Canal, Dorsoduro 3126, Dorsoduro* ☎ *041/2410625* ⊕ *www.imaginacafe.it/english.html* Ⓜ *Vaporetto Ca' Rezonnico* ✛ B4.

§
VENETIAN
Fodor's Choice
★

✕ **Impronta Cafe.** This sleek café is a favorite lunchtime haunt for professors from the nearby university and local businesspeople; unlike in more traditional places, it's quite acceptable to order only pasta or a secondo, without an antipasto or dessert. Although the restaurant is also open for dinner—and you can dine well and economically in the evening—the real bargain is lunch, where you can easily have a beautifully prepared primo or secondo, plus a glass of wine, for a reasonable price. **Known for:** well-prepared pasta and other classic dishes; gentle prices; friendly hours, from breakfast until late evening. Ⓢ *Average main: €12* ✉ *Crosera - San Pantalon, Dorsoduro 3815–3817, Dorsoduro* ☎ *041/2750386* ⊕ *www.improntacafevenice.com* ☾ *Closed Sun., and 2 wks in Aug.* ✛ B3.

§§
NORTHERN
ITALIAN
Fodor's Choice
★

✕ **La Bitta.** The decor is more discreet, the dining hours longer, and the service friendlier and more efficient here than in many small restaurants in Venice—and the nonfish menu (inspired by the cuisine of the Venetian terra firma) is a temptation at every course. Market availability keeps the menu changing almost every day. **Known for:** meat dishes (no seafood); seasonally changing menus; lovely homemade desserts. Ⓢ *Average main: €20* ✉ *Calle Lunga San Barnaba, Dorsoduro 2753/A, Dorsoduro* ☎ *041/5230531* ☐ *No credit cards* ☾ *Closed Sun. No lunch* Ⓜ *Vaporetto: Ca' Rezzonico* ✛ B5.

§
WINE BAR

✕ **Osteria al Squero.** It wasn't long after this lovely little locale appeared across from the Squero San Trovaso that it became a neighborhood—and citywide—favorite. The Venetian owner of this wine bar (not, as its name implies, a restaurant) has created a personal vision of what a good one should offer: a variety of sumptuous cicheti, panini, and cheeses to be accompanied by just the right regional wines (ask for his recommendation). **Known for:** authentic and satisfying Venetian cicheti; lots of wines to choose from; pleasant outdoor seating, across from a gondola boatyard. Ⓢ *Average main: €12* ✉ *Fondamenta Nani, Dorsoduro 943/944, Dorsoduro* ☎ *335/6007513* ⊕ *osteriaalsquero. wordpress.com* ☾ *Closed Mon.* Ⓜ *Vaporetto: Accademia, Zattere* ⊹ *C5.*

$$
VENETIAN
Fodor'sChoice
★

✕**Osteria alla Bifora.** A beautiful and atmospheric bacaro, Alla Bifora has such ample and satisfying food and wine selections that most Venetians consider it a full-fledged restaurant. Most of the offerings consist of overflowing trays of cold, sliced meats and cheeses, various preparations of baccalà, or Venetian classics such as polpette, sarde in saor, or marinated anchovies; there's a good selection of regional wines by the glass as well. **Known for:** platters of meats and cheeses; quality classic Venetian dishes; seppie nere con polenta (black ink cuttlefish with polenta). Ⓢ *Average main: €18* ✉ *Campo Santa Margherita, Dorsoduro 2930, Dorsoduro* ☎ *041/5236119* ▭ *No credit cards* ☾ *Closed Jan. and Aug.* ⊹ *B4.*

SAN POLO

$$$
MODERN ITALIAN
Fodor'sChoice
★

✕**Al Paradiso.** In a small dining room made warm and cozy by its pleasing and unpretentious decor, proprietor Giordano makes all diners feel like honored guests. Unlike many elegant restaurants, Al Paradiso serves generous portions, and many of the delicious antipasti and primi are quite satisfying; you may want to follow the traditional Italian way of ordering and wait until you've finished your antipasto or your primo before you order your secondo. **Known for:** large-sized appetizers and pasta courses; tasty meat and fish mains; central location near the Rialto Bridge. Ⓢ *Average main: €26* ✉ *Calle del Paradiso, San Polo 767, San Polo* ☎ *041/5234910* ☾ *Closed 3 wks in Jan. and Feb.* Ⓜ *Vaporetto: San Silvestro* ⊹ *D3.*

$$$
VENETIAN

✕**Alla Madonna.** "The Madonna" used to be world-famous as "the" classic Venetian trattoria but in the past decades has settled down into middle age. Owned and run by the Rado family since 1954, this Venetian institution looks like one, with its wood beams, stained-glass windows, and panoply of paintings on white walls; folks still head here to savor the classic Venetian repertoire as most dishes are properly prepared, albeit for stiff prices and without much variation or imagination. **Known for:** freshly prepared seafood; traditional Venetian cuisine; old-time atmosphere. Ⓢ *Average main: €30* ✉ *Calle della Madonna, San Polo 594, San Polo* ☎ *041/5223824* ⊕ *www.ristoranteallamadonna. com* ☾ *Closed Wed. and Jan.* Ⓜ *Vaporetto: San Silvestro* ⊹ *D3.*

$
CAFÉ

✕**All'Arco.** Just because it's noon and you only have time between sights for a sandwich doesn't mean that it can't be a satisfying, even awe-inspiring one. There's no menu at All'Arco, but a scan of what's behind the glass counter is all you need; order what entices you, or have Roberto or Matteo (father and son) suggest a cicheto or panino. **Known for:** top-notch cicheti; platters of meats and cheeses; friendly and helpful service. Ⓢ *Average main: €8* ✉ *Calle Arco, San Polo 436, San Polo* ☎ *041/5205666* ☾ *Closed weekends, 2 wks in Feb., and Aug. No dinner* Ⓜ *Vaporetto: San Silvestro* ⊹ *D3.*

$$$
VENETIAN

✕**Antiche Carampane.** Judging from its rather modest and unremarkable appearance, you wouldn't guess that Piera Bortoluzzi Librai's trattoria is among the finest fish restaurants in the city both because of the quality

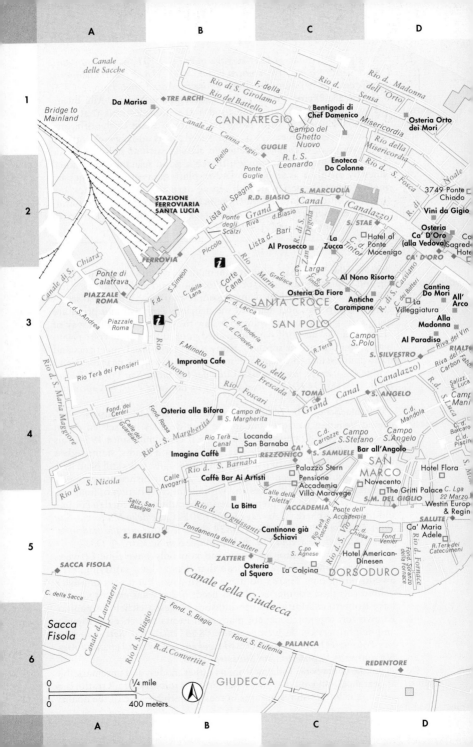

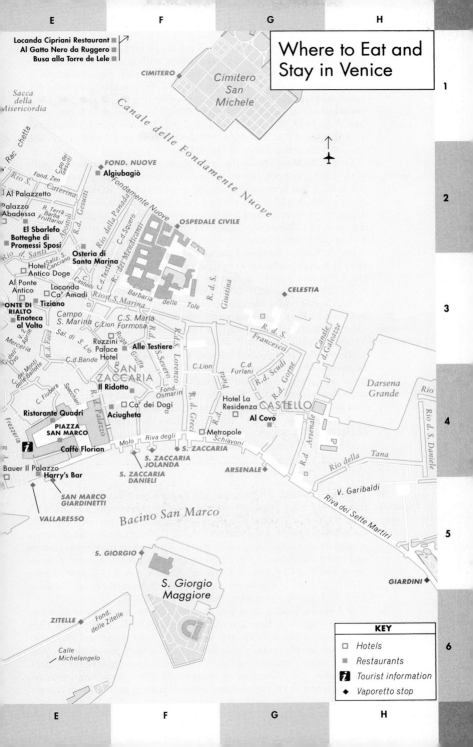

Where to Eat and Stay in Venice

Locanda Cipriani Restaurant
Al Gatto Nero da Ruggero
Busa alla Torre de Lele

CIMITERO

Cimitero
San
Michele

Sacca
della
Misericordia

Canale delle Fondamente Nuove

Rac chetta

Rio del Gesuiti

Fond. Zen

Al Palazzetto

Palazzo
Abadessa

R. Terrà
Barba
Fruttariol

FOND. NUOVE
Algiubagiò

R. d. Apostoli

Fondamente Nuove

Rio della Panada

R. d. Squero

OSPEDALE CIVILE

El Sbarlefo
Botteghe di
Promessi Sposi

Saliz. S.
Canciano

**Osteria di
Santa Marina**

Hotel
Antico Doge

C.
Castelli

R. d. Testa

R. dei Mendicanti

Al Ponte
Antico

Locanda
Ca' Amadi

Barbaria

CELESTIA

ONTE DI
RIALTO

Tiziano

Rio d. Santi

Saliz. S. Canciano

Rio S. Marina

delle

Tole

R. d. S.

R. d. S.

Canale
d. Galeazze

Enoteca
al Volto

Campo
S. Marina

C.Lion

C.S. Maria
Formosa

R. d. S.
Francesca

Mercería

V. 2
Aprile

Sal. di
S. Lio

Ruga
Giuffa

R. d. S. Severo

R. d. S.
Lorenzo

C.del
l'Ovo

C. del Monti
delle Balotte

C.d.Bande

Ruzzini
Palace
Hotel

Alle Testiere

C.Lion

R. d. S.

C.d.
Furlani

R.d. Scudi

Darsena
Grande

Rio

C. Fiubera

SAN
ZACCARIA

Il Ridotto

Fond.
Osmarin

C.Lion

C.d.
Greci

R. d. Gorne

R. d. S. Daniele

Specchieri

R. d. Palazzo

Ca' dei Dogi

R. d. S.

R. d.
Pietà

Hotel La
Residenza

CASTELLO

R. d.
Arsenale

Ristorante Quadri

PIAZZA
SAN MARCO

Aciugheta

Al Covo

Frezzeria

Caffè Florian

Molo

Riva degli

Metropole
Schiavoni

Riva della

Tana

Bauer Il Palazzo

Harry's Bar

S. ZACCARIA
JOLANDA

S. ZACCARIA

ARSENALE

V. Garibaldi

SAN MARCO
GIARDINETTI

S. ZACCARIA
DANIELI

Riva dei Sette Martiri

VALLARESSO

Bacino San Marco

S. GIORGIO

GIARDINI

ZITELLE

S. Giorgio
Maggiore

Fond. delle Zitelle

Calle
Michelangelo

KEY	
□	Hotels
■	Restaurants
🛈	Tourist information
◆	Vaporetto stop

of the ingredients and because of the chef's creative magic. You can choose from a selection of classic dishes with a modern and creative touch; the perfectly grilled fish is always freshly caught, and in spring, try the local, fried soft-shell crabs. **Known for:** superlative fish and seafood; modernized Venetian dishes; popularity with visitors and locals (so book ahead). [$] *Average main: €26* ✉ *Rio Terà della Carampane, San Polo 1911, San Polo* ☎ *041/5240165* 🌐 *www.antichecarampane.com* ⏲ *Closed Sun. and Mon., 10 days in Jan., and 3 wks in July and Aug.* [M] *Vaporetto: San Silvestro* ✥ *D3.*

$ WINE BAR

🍴 **Cantina Do Mori.** This is the original bacaro—in business continually since 1462; cramped but warm and cozy under hanging antique copper pots, it has been catering to the workers of the Rialto Market for generations. In addition to young local whites and reds, the well-stocked cellar offers more refined labels, many available by the glass; between sips you can choose to munch the myriad cicheti on offer, or a few well-stuffed, tiny tramezzini, appropriately called *francobolli* (postage stamps). **Known for:** good choice of wines by the glass; fine selection of cicheti and sandwiches; delicious baccalà mantecato, with or without garlic and parsley. [$] *Average main: €8* ✉ *Calle dei Do Mori, San Polo 429, San Polo* ☎ *041/5225401* 💳 *No credit cards* ⏲ *Closed Sun.* [M] *Vaporetto: Rialto Mercato* ✥ *D3.*

$$$$ VENETIAN
Fodor's Choice ★

🍴 **Osteria Da Fiore.** The understated atmosphere, simple decor, and quiet elegance featured alongside Da Fiore's modern take on traditional Venetian cuisine certainly merit its international reputation. With such beautifully prepared cuisine, you would expect the kitchen to be manned by a chef with a household name; however, the kitchen is headed by owner Maurizio Martin's wife, Mara, who learned to cook from her grandmother. **Known for:** sophisticated traditional Venetian dishes; delicious tasting menus; reservations required in advance. [$] *Average main: €40* ✉ *Calle del Scaleter, San Polo 2002, San Polo* ☎ *041/721308* 🌐 *www.dafiore.net* ⏲ *Closed Sun. and Mon., and 3 wks in Jan.* [M] *Vaporetto San Tomà* ✥ *C3.*

SANTA CROCE

$$ VENETIAN
FAMILY

🍴 **Al Nono Risorto.** Although in the Santa Croce neighborhood, this friendly trattoria popular with the locals is really only a short walk from the Rialto Market. The pizza—not a Venetian specialty, generally speaking—is pretty good here, but the star attractions are the generous appetizers and excellent shellfish pastas. **Known for:** traditional starters and pastas; quite tasty pizzas; pretty outdoor garden seating. [$] *Average main: €15* ✉ *Ramo de l'Arsenal, Santa Croce 2337, Santa Croce* ☎ *041/5241169* 🌐 *nonorisortovenezia.com* 💳 *No credit cards* ⏲ *Closed Wed. and Jan.* [M] *Vaporetto: Rialto Mercato* ✥ *D3.*

$$ WINE BAR

🍴 **Al Prosecco.** Locals drop into this friendly bacaro to explore wines from this region, or from any other in the country for that matter. They accompany a carefully chosen selection of meats, cheeses, and other food from small, artisanal producers, used in tasty panini like the *porchetta romane verdure* (roast pork with greens), or elegant cold platters. **Known for:** great selection of biodynamic wines, including prosecco; lovely meat and cheese platters; outdoor seating on the lively campo.

[$] *Average main: €20* ✉ *Campo San Giacomo dell'Orio, Santa Croce 1503, Santa Croce* ☎ *041/5240222* 🌐 *www.alprosecco.com* 💳 *No credit cards* 🕓 *Closed Sun.* [M] *Vaporetto: San Stae* ✥ *C2.*

$$ NORTHERN ITALIAN 🍴 **La Zucca.** The simple place settings, lattice-wood walls, and mélange of languages make La Zucca (the pumpkin) feel much like a typical, somewhat sophisticated vegetarian restaurant that you could find in any European city. What makes La Zucca special is the use of fresh, local ingredients (many of which, like the particularly sweet *zucca* itself, aren't normally found outside northern Italy), and simply great cooking. **Known for:** seasonal vegetarian-focused dishes; home-style Italian cooking; flan di zucca, a luscious pumpkin pudding topped with aged ricotta cheese. [$] *Average main: €21* ✉ *Calle del Tintor, at Ponte de Megio, Santa Croce 1762, Santa Croce* ☎ *041/5241570* 🌐 *www.lazucca.it* 🕓 *Closed Sun.* [M] *Vaporetto: San Stae* ✥ *C2.*

4

CANNAREGIO

$$$ ITALIAN 🍴 **Algiubagiò.** Algiubagiò has a dual personality: big salads at lunch (a better bet than the pizza); at dinner, creative primi like ravioli stuffed with *pecorino di fossa* (a hard sheep's-milk cheese) followed by elegant secondi such as Angus fillets with vodka and Gorgonzola. The young, friendly staff also serve ice cream, drinks, and sandwiches all day. **Known for:** salads and simpler cuisine for lunch; creative pasta and meat dishes for dinner; lovely waterfront seating with views of the Dolomites. [$] *Average main: €30* ✉ *Fondamente Nove, Cannaregio 5039, Cannaregio* ☎ *041/5236084* 🌐 *www.algiubagio.net* [M] *Vaporetto: Fondamente Nove* ✥ *E2.*

$$ VENETIAN 🍴 **Bentigodi di Chef Domenico.** Many claim that owner Domenico Iacuzio is one of Venice's best chefs, even though he hails from Italy's deep south. The chef marries delicious Venetian culinary traditions with southern accents; try sarde in saor, which perfectly balances sweet and savory, and the diced raw tuna *cipolata,* enlivened by sautéed onions and oranges, as well as seafood risottos, freshly caught fish, and—for the Venetian traditionalist—a first-class *fritto misto* (deep-fried seafood). **Known for:** satisfying Venetian food with a southern Italian twist; classic Italian desserts like cannoli and cassata (candied Sicilian cake); romantic, art-filled setting. [$] *Average main: €22* ✉ *Calesele, Cannargio 1423, Cannaregio* ☎ *041/8223714* 🌐 *www.bentigodi.com* 🕓 *Closed Tues.* [M] *Vaporetto San Marcuola* ✥ *C1.*

$$ VENETIAN 🍴 **Botteghe di Promessi Sposi.** Join locals at the *banco* (counter) premeal for an *ombra* (small glass of wine) and cicheti like polpette croquettes or violet eggplant rounds, or reserve a sit-down meal in the dining room or the intimate courtyard. A varied, seasonal menu includes local standards like calf's liver or grilled *canestrelli* (tiny Venetian scallops), along with creative, regional fusion variations incorporating classic Venetian fare, like homemade ravioli stuffed with *radicchio di Treviso* (red chicory leaves) or *orecchiette* ("small ear"–shape pasta) with a scrumptious sauce of minced duck. **Known for:** creative cicheti and wine; regularly changing menu with both traditional and modern choices; friendly, helpful service. [$] *Average main: €18* ✉ *Calle de l'Oca, just off Campo*

Santi Apostoli, Cannaregio 4367, Cannaregio ☎ *041/2412747* ⊘ *No lunch Mon.* Ⓜ *Vaporetto: Ca' d'Oro* ✛ *E3.*

$$
VENETIAN
Fodor's Choice
★

✕ **Da Marisa.** This is the most famous workingman's restaurant in Venice; if you can get a table for lunch, you'll eat, without any choice, what Marisa prepares for her workmen clientele—generally enormous portions of excellently prepared pasta, followed by a hearty roast meat course, frequently game, more infrequently fish, for an unbelievably inexpensive fixed price. Dinner is a bit more expensive, and you may have a bit of a choice, but not much; for the authentic "Marisa" experience, go for lunch. **Known for:** authentic, well-prepared Venetian food; limited menu choices; very reasonable prices. Ⓢ *Average main: €15* ⊠ *Cannaregio 625b, Fondamenta di San Giobbe, Cannaregio* ☎ *041/720211* ▭ *No credit cards* ⊘ *No dinner Sun., Mon., and Wed. Closed 1 wk. in Aug.* ✛ *B1.*

$
WINE BAR

✕ **El Sbarlefo.** This odd name is Venetian for "smirk," although you'd be hard-pressed to find one of those around this cheery, familiar wine bar with a wine selection as ample as the cicheti on offer. Making the most of their limited space, owners Alessandro and Andrea have installed counters and stools inside, tables outside, and external banco access for ordering a second round—and order you will, selecting from a spread of delectable cicheti from classic polpette of meat and tuna to tomino cheese rounds to speck and robiolo rolls, and more. **Known for:** classic cicheti such as sardines in saor and marinated anchovies; tasty meat and cheese platters; an impressive selection of wines by the glass. Ⓢ *Average main: €8* ⊠ *Salizzada del Pistor, off Campo Santi Apostoli, Cannaregio 4556/C, Cannaregio* ☎ *041/5233084* ⊕ *www.elsbarlefo.it* Ⓜ *Vaporetto: Ca d'Oro* ✛ *E2.*

$
WINE BAR

✕ **Enoteca Do Colonne.** Venetians from this working-class neighborhood frequent this friendly bacaro, not just for a glass of very drinkable wine, but also because of its excellent selection of traditional Venetian cicheti for lunch. There's not only a large selection of sandwiches and panini, but also luscious tidbits like grilled vegetables, breaded and fried sardines and shrimp, and a superb version of baccalà mantecato, along with Venetian working-class specialties such as *musetto* (a sausage made from pigs' snouts served warm with polenta) and *nervetti* (veal tendons with lemon and parsley). **Known for:** a cozy place for locals to hang out; classic cicheti and sandwiches; the best musetto (sausage with polenta) in town. Ⓢ *Average main: €8* ⊠ *Rio Terà Cristo, Cannaregio 1814, Cannaregio* ☎ *041/5240453* ⊕ *www.docolonne.it* Ⓜ *Vaporetto: San Marcuola* ✛ *C2.*

$
VENETIAN

✕ **Osteria Ca' D'Oro (alla Vedova).** "The best polpette in town," you'll hear fans of the venerable Vedova say, and that explains why it's an obligatory stop on any *giro d'ombra* (bacaro tour); the polpette are always hot and crunchy—and also gluten-free, as they're made with polenta. Ca' d'Oro is a full-fledged trattoria as well, but make sure to reserve ahead: it's no secret to those seeking traditional Venetian fare at a reasonable cost, locals and travelers alike. **Known for:** famous polpette (meatballs); classic Venetian cuisine; house wine served in tiny traditional glasses. Ⓢ *Average main: €12* ⊠ *Calle del Pistor, Cannaregio 3912, off Strada Nova, Cannaregio* ☎ *041/5285324* ⊘ *Closed Thurs. and Aug. No lunch Sun.* Ⓜ *Vaporetto: Ca d'Oro* ✛ *D2.*

$$$ ITALIAN 🍴 **Osteria Orto dei Mori.** This small and popular Cannaregio neighborhood restaurant specializes in creative versions of classic Italian (but not necessarily Venetian) dishes, and co-owner Micael has artfully created a regional wine list. The osteria is located canal-side, just under the nose of the campo's famous corner statue. **Known for:** traditional Italian dishes with modern accents; choice local wine selection; buzzing atmosphere with locals and tourists alike. [$] *Average main: €27* ✉ *Campo dei Mori, Fondamenta dei Mori, Cannaregio 3386, Cannaregio* ☎ *041/5235544* 🌐 *www.osteriaortodeimori.com* 🕒 *Closed Tues.* [M] *Vaporetto: Orto, Ca d'Oro, or San Marcuola* ✣ *D1.*

$ ITALIAN 🍴 **Tiziano.** A fine variety of excellent tramezzini lines the display cases at this *tavola calda* (roughly the Italian equivalent of a cafeteria) on the main thoroughfare from the Rialto to Santi Apostoli; inexpensive salad plates and daily pasta specials are also served. This is a great place for a light meal or snack before a performance at the nearby Teatro Malebran. **Known for:** quick meals or snacks, especially tramezzini; modest prices; efficient (if occasionally grumpy) service. [$] *Average main: €8* ✉ *Salizzada San Giovanni Crisostomo, Cannaregio 5747, Cannaregio* ☎ *041/5235544* 💳 *No credit cards* [M] *Vaporetto: Rialto* ✣ *E3.*

$$$ VENETIAN Fodor's Choice ★ 🍴 **Vini da Gigio.** Paolo and Laura, a brother-sister team, run this refined trattoria as if they've invited you to dinner in their home, while keeping the service professional; it's deservedly popular with Venetians and visitors alike. Indulge in pastas such as rigatoni with duck sauce and arugula-stuffed ravioli; the seafood risotto, made to order; or the fish—try the sesame-encrusted tuna—but the meat dishes steal the show. **Known for:** superb meat dishes, especially the fegato alla veneziana (Venetian-style liver with onions); one of the best wine cellars in the city; helpful and professional service. [$] *Average main: €25* ✉ *Fondamenta San Felice, Cannaregio 3628/A, Cannaregio* ☎ *041/5285140* 🕒 *Closed Mon. and Tues., and 2 wks in Aug.* [M] *Vaporetto: Ca' d'Oro* ✣ *D2.*

CASTELLO

$ WINE BAR 🍴 **Aciugheta.** Almost an institution, the "Tiny Anchovy" (as the name translates) doubles as a pizzeria-trattoria, but the real reason for coming is the tasty cicheti offered at the bar, like the eponymous anchovy minipizzas, the *arancioni* rice balls, and the polpette. The selection of wines by the glass changes daily, but there is always a good selection of local wines on hand, as well as some Tuscan and Piedmontese choices thrown in for good measure. **Known for:** pizzetta con l'acciuga (minipizza with anchovy); mix of traditional and more modern cicheti; good selection of Italian wines by the glass. [$] *Average main: €12* ✉ *Campo SS. Filippo e Giacomo, Castello 4357, Castello* ☎ *041/5224292* [M] *Vaporetto: San Zaccaria* ✣ *F4.*

$$$ VENETIAN 🍴 **Al Covo.** For years, Diane and Cesare Binelli's Al Covo has set the standard of excellence for traditional, refined Venetian cuisine; the Binellis are dedicated to providing their guests with the freshest, highest-quality fish from the Adriatic, and vegetables, when at all possible, from the islands of the Venetian lagoon and the fields of the adjacent Veneto region. Although their cuisine could be correctly termed "classic Venetian," it always offers surprises like the juicy crispness of their legendary

fritto misto—reliant upon a secret, nonconventional ingredient in the batter—or the heady aroma of their fresh anchovies marinated in wild fennel, an herb somewhat foreign to Veneto. **Known for:** sophisticated Venetian flavors; top-notch local ingredients; Diane's chocolate cake for dessert. [$] *Average main: €27* ✉ *Campiello Pescaria, Castello 3968, Castello* ☎ *041/5223812* 🌐 *www.ristorantealcovo.com* 🕓 *Closed Wed. and Thurs., 3 wks. in Jan., and 10 days in Aug.* [M] *Vaporetto: Arsenale* ✥ *G4.*

$$$ VENETIAN Fodor's Choice ★

🍴 **Alle Testiere.** The name is a reference to the old headboards that adorn the walls of this tiny, informal restaurant, but the food (not the decor) is undoubtedly the focus. Local foodies consider this one of the most refined eateries in the city thanks to chef Bruno Cavagni's gently creative take on classic Venetian fish dishes; the chef's artistry seldom draws attention to itself, but simply reveals new dimensions to familiar fare, creating dishes that stand out for their lightness and balance. **Known for:** daily changing fish, based on what's fresh at the market; excellent pasta with seafood; wonderful wine selection. [$] *Average main: €28* ✉ *Calle del Mondo Novo, Castello 5801, Castello* ☎ *041/5227220* 🌐 *www.osterialletestiere.it* 🕓 *Closed Sun. and Mon., 3 wks in Jan. and Feb., and 4 wks in July and Aug.* ✥ *F3.*

$$$ MODERN ITALIAN Fodor's Choice ★

🍴 **Il Ridotto.** Longtime restaurateur Gianni Bonaccorsi (proprietor of the popular Aciugheta nearby) has established an eatery where he can pamper a limited number of lucky patrons with his imaginative cuisine and impeccable taste in wine. *Ridotto* means a small, private place, which this very much is, evoking an atmosphere of secrecy and intimacy; the innovative menu employing traditional elements is revised daily, with the offerings tending toward lighter, but wonderfully tasty versions of classic dishes. The tasting menus—one meat, one fish—where Gianni "surprises" you with a selection of his own creations, never fail to satisfy. **Known for:** some of the most creative cuisine in Venice; excellent fish and meat/fish tasting menus; extensive wine recommendations. [$] *Average main: €35* ✉ *Campo SS Filippo e Giacomo, Castello 4509, Castello* ☎ *041/5208280* 🌐 *www.ilridotto.com* 🕓 *Closed Wed. No lunch Thurs.* [M] *Vaporetto: San Zaccaria* ✥ *F4.*

$$$ VENETIAN Fodor's Choice ★

🍴 **Osteria di Santa Marina.** The candlelit tables on this romantic campo are inviting enough, but it's this intimate restaurant's imaginative kitchen creations that are likely to win you over; you can order à la carte or opt for one of the rewarding tasting menus. The wine list is ample and well thought out, and service is gracious and cordial—just don't be in a terrible rush, or expect the server to be your new best friend. **Known for:** innovative and artfully presented modern Venetian food; charming and romantic setting; wonderful wine pairings. [$] *Average main: €30* ✉ *Campo Santa Marina, Castello 5911, Castello* ☎ *041/5285239* 🌐 *www.osteriadisantamarina.com* 🕓 *Closed Sun. and 2 wks. in Aug. No lunch Mon.* [M] *Vaporetto: Rialto* ✥ *E2.*

ISLANDS OF THE LAGOON

$$ SEAFOOD

🍴 **Al Gatto Nero da Ruggero.** Around since 1965, Al Gatto Nero da Ruggero offers the best fish on Burano; no matter what you order, though, you'll savor the pride the owner and his family have in their lagoon, their island, and the quality of their cucina (maybe even more so when enjoying it on the picturesque fondamenta). The fish is top quality and couldn't get any fresher; all pastas and desserts are made in-house; the fritto misto is outstanding for its lightness and variety of fish; *risotto de Gò (ghiozzo)* is a Burano *cucina povera* standard that had almost disappeared from local menus until Anthony Bourdain introduced it to travelers. **Known for:** the freshest fish and seafood around; risotto Burano style, using local ghiozzi fish; tagliolini with spider crab. Ⓢ *Average main: €22* ✉ *Fondamenta della Giudecca 88, Burano* ☎ *041/730120* ⊕ *www.gattonero.com* ⊗ *Closed Mon., 1 wk. in July, and 3 wks in Nov. No dinner Sun.* Ⓜ *Vaporetto: Burano* ⊹ *F1.*

$$ ✕ **Busa alla Torre da Lele.** If you're shopping for glass on Murano and
VENETIAN want to sample some first-rate home cooking for lunch, you can't do better than stopping in this unpretentious trattoria in the island's central square. The friendly waiters will bring you ample portions of pasta with freshly made seafood-based sauces, and there's also a substantial variety of carefully grilled or baked fish. **Known for:** tasty local fish and seafood; reliable lunch stop in Murano; outdoor dining on a square. Ⓢ *Average main: €20* ✉ *Campo Santo Stefano 3, Murano* ☎ *041/739662* ⊗ *Closed Mon. No dinner* Ⓜ *Vaporetto Murano Colonna* ⊹ *F1.*

$$$ ✕ **Locanda Cipriani Restaurant.** A nearly legendary restaurant—Heming-
VENETIAN way came here often to eat, drink, and brood under the green veranda—established by a nephew of Giuseppe Cipriani (the founder of Harry's Bar), this inn profits from its idyllic location on the island of Torcello. The food is not exceptional, especially considering the high-end prices, but dining here is more about getting lost in Venetian magic. **Known for:** wonderful historic atmosphere; traditional Venetian cuisine, with a focus on seafood; a peaceful lunch choice when you want to get away from Venice. Ⓢ *Average main: €34* ✉ *Piazza Santa Fosca 29, Locanda Cipriani, Torcello* ☎ *041/730150* ⊕ *www.locandacipriani. com* ⊗ *Closed Tues., and early Jan.–early Feb. No dinner Mon., Wed., Thurs., and Sun.* Ⓜ *Vaporetto: Torcello* ⊹ *F1.*

WHERE TO STAY

Venetian magic lingers when you retire for the night, whether you're staying in a grand hotel or budget *locanda* (inn). Some of the finest Venetian hotel rooms are lighted with Murano chandeliers and swathed in famed fabrics of Rubelli and Bevilacqua, with gilded mirrors and furnishing styles from Baroque to Biedermeier and Art Deco.

Even if well renovated, most hotels occupy very old buildings. Preservation laws prohibit elevators in some, so if climbing stairs is an issue, check before you book. In the lower price categories, hotels may not have lounge areas, and rooms may be cramped, and the same is true of standard rooms in more expensive hotels. Space is at a premium in Venice, and even exclusive hotels have carved out small, dowdy, Cinderella-type rooms in the "standard" category. It's not at all unusual for each room to be different even on the same floor: windows overlooking charming canals and bleak alleyways are both common. En suite bathrooms have become the norm; they're usually well equipped but sizes range from compact to more than ample; tubs are considered a luxury but are not unheard-of, even in less expensive lodging. Air-conditioning is rarely a necessity until mid-June. A few of the budget hotels make do with fans.

WHAT NEIGHBORHOOD SHOULD I STAY IN?

"Only a stone's throw from St. Mark's Square" is the standard hotel claim. Whether that's the case, it's not necessarily an advantage. In Venice, you can't go terribly wrong in terms of "good" areas in which to stay, and once you get your bearings, you'll find you're never far from anything.

You may, however, want to consider how close your hotel is to a vaporetto stop, and how many bridges there are to cross between your hotel and the vaporetto station. If you have lots of heavy baggage, carrying them over the bridges to and from your hotel can be quite a chore.

The area in and around San Marco will always be the most crowded and touristy and almost always more expensive: even two- and three-star hotels cost more here than they do in other parts of town. If you want to stay in less-trafficked surroundings, consider still convenient but more tranquil locations in Dorsoduro, Santa Croce, and Cannaregio (though hotels near the train station in Cannaregio can have their own crowd issues), or even Castello in the area beyond the Pietà church. A stay on the Lido in shoulder season offers serenity and beaches for the kids, but it also includes about a half-hour boat ride to the centro storico, and in summer it's crowded with beachgoers.

Substantial savings can be had by staying in a hotel in Mestre or Marghera, or near the airport, but you must count on at least an hour each way until you get into the centro storico. Touring in Venice can be physically taxing, involving a lot of walking on stone pavement, climbing stairs and foot bridges, and a paucity of places to sit down unless you've ordered a drink or a snack at a café. You may want to return to your hotel for a brief rest, or for a shower on a hot, humid summer day. Booking a hotel in the historic center will make a brief rest possible; a hotel on the mainland simply won't.

Venice is saturated with lodging options, but it is also one of the most popular destinations on Earth—so book your lodging as far in advance as possible.

FINDING YOUR HOTEL

It is essential to have detailed arrival directions along with the address, including the sestiere and preferably a nearby landmark; conveniently, most hotels include maps on their websites. Even if you choose a pricey water taxi, you may still have a walk, depending on where the boat leaves you. Nothing is obvious on Venice's streets (even if you have GPS); turn-by-turn directions can help you avoid wandering back and forth along side streets and across bridges, luggage in tow. *Use the coordinate (⊕ B2) at the end of each listing to locate a site on the Where to Eat and Stay in Venice map.*

PRICES

Hotel rates are about 20% higher than in Rome and Milan but can be reduced by as much as half off-season, from November to March (excluding Christmas, New Year's, and Carnevale), and likely in August as well. *Hotel reviews have been shortened. For full information, visit Fodors.com.*

WHAT IT COSTS				
	$	$$	$$$	$$$$
For two people	under €125	€125–€200	€201–€300	over €300

Prices in the reviews are the lowest cost of a standard double room in high season.

4

SAN MARCO

$$$$ HOTEL **Bauer Il Palazzo.** This palazzo with an ornate, 1930s neo-Gothic facade facing the Grand Canal has lavishly decorated guest rooms (large by Venetian standards) featuring high ceilings, tufted walls of Bevilacqua and Rubelli fabrics, Murano glass, marble bathrooms, damask drapes, and imitation antique furniture. **Pros:** pampering service; high-end luxury; Venice's highest rooftop terrace. **Cons:** decor could be a bit dark and old-fashioned for some; furnishings are, as is the facade, an imitation; no spa on-site. [$] *Rooms from: €562* ✉ *Campo San Moisè, San Marco 1413/D, San Marco* ☎ *041/5207022* 🌐 *www.bauervenezia.com* 🛏 *72 rooms* 🍴 *Free Breakfast* [M] *Vaporetto: Vallaresso* ✥ *E4.*

$$$$ HOTEL Fodor's Choice ★ **The Gritti Palace.** This hotel represents aristocratic Venetian living at its best, complete with handblown chandeliers, sumptuous textiles, and sweeping canal views. **Pros:** historic setting; Grand Canal location; classic Venetian experience. **Cons:** major splurge; food served at the hotel gets mixed reviews; few spa amenities. [$] *Rooms from: €850* ✉ *Campo Santa Maria del Giglio, San Marco 2467, San Marco* ☎ *041/794611* 🌐 *www.thegrittipalace.com* 🛏 *82 rooms* 🍴 *No meals* [M] *Vaporetto Santa Maria del Giglio* ✥ *D5.*

$$ HOTEL **Hotel Flora.** The elegant and refined facade announces a charming, and reasonably priced, place to stay; the hospitable staff, the tastefully decorated rooms, and the lovely garden, where guests can breakfast or drink, do not disappoint. **Pros:** central location; peaceful hidden garden; excellent breakfast. **Cons:** some rooms can be on the small side; no water views; old-fashioned lobby doesn't invite hanging out. [$] *Rooms from: €170* ✉ *Calle Bergamaschi, San Marco 2283/A, just off Calle Larga XXII Marzo, San Marco* ☎ *041/5205844* 🌐 *www.hotelflora.it* 🛏 *40 rooms* 🍴 *Free Breakfast* [M] *Vaporetto: San Marco (Vallaresso)* ✥ *D4.*

$$$ HOTEL Fodor's Choice ★ **Novecento.** A stylish yet intimate retreat tucked away on a quiet calle midway between Piazza San Marco and the Accademia Bridge offers exquisite rooms tastefully decorated with original furnishings and tapestries from the Mediterranean and Far East. **Pros:** intimate, romantic atmosphere; unique design sensibility; complimentary afternoon tea. **Cons:** most rooms only have showers, not tubs; no elevator; some rooms can be noisy. [$] *Rooms from: €202* ✉ *Calle del Dose, San Marco 2683/84, off*

Campo San Maurizio, San Marco ☎ *041/2413765* 🌐 *www.novecento.biz* 🛏 *9 rooms* 🍴 *Free Breakfast* [M] *Vaporetto: Santa Maria del Giglio* ✣ *C5.*

$$$$ HOTEL **Westin Europa & Regina.** Spread across five historic palazzi in the lee of San Marco, this contemporary hotel with a Venetian look boasts wonderful Grand Canal views and a location dangerously close to Venice's prime shopping streets. **Pros:** ideal location, with the über-boutiques of Via XXII Marzo and the Piazza San Marco a stone's throw away; the most terraces of any hotel in Venice; prime Grand Canal views. **Cons:** can feel more like a Westin chain hotel than a boutique property; some showers are claustrophobically small; service can be hit-or-miss. [$] *Rooms from: €410* ✉ *Corte Barozzi, San Marco 2159, San Marco* ☎ *041/2400001* 🌐 *www.westineuropareginavenice.com* 🛏 *180 rooms* 🍴 *No meals* ✣ *D5.*

DORSODURO

$$$$ HOTEL Fodor's Choice ★ **Ca' Maria Adele.** One of the city's most intimate and elegant getaways immerses guests in a mix of classic style (terrazzo floors, dramatic Murano chandeliers, antique-style furnishings) and touches of the contemporary, found in the African-wood reception area and breakfast room. **Pros:** quiet and romantic; imaginative contemporary decor; tranquil yet convenient spot near Santa Maria della Salute. **Cons:** no elevator and lots of stairs; bathrooms can be on the small side; no restaurant (just breakfast room). [$] *Rooms from: €410* ✉ *Campo Santa Maria della Salute, Dorsoduro 111, Dorsoduro* ☎ *041/5203078* 🌐 *www.camariaadele.it* ⏲ *Closed 3 wks. in Jan.* 🛏 *14 rooms* 🍴 *Free Breakfast* [M] *Vaporetto: Salute* ✣ *D5.*

$$ HOTEL **Hotel American–Dinesen.** If you're in Venice to see art, you can't beat the location, and you'll feel right at home in spacious guest rooms furnished in Venetian brocade fabrics with lacquered Venetian-style furniture; some front rooms have terraces with canal views. **Pros:** wonderfully located near Gallerie dell'Accademia, the Peggy Guggenheim Collection, and Punta della Dogana; on a bright, quiet, exceptionally picturesque canal; some rooms have balconies with San Vio Canal views. **Cons:** canal-view rooms are more expensive; style could be too understated for those expecting Venetian opulence; bathrooms can feel cramped. [$] *Rooms from: €200* ✉ *San Vio, Dorsoduro 628, Dorsoduro* ☎ *041/5204733* 🌐 *www.hotelamerican.it* 🛏 *34 rooms* 🍴 *Free Breakfast* [M] *Vaporetto: Accademia, Salute, and Zattere* ✣ *C5.*

$$ HOTEL **La Calcina.** Casual, comfy rooms with parquet floors, original 19th-century furniture, and firm beds enjoy an enviable position along the sunny Zattere, with front rooms offering vistas across the wide Giudecca Canal; a few have private terraces. **Pros:** panoramic views from some rooms; quiet, peaceful atmosphere; well-regarded restaurant with terrace over the Giudecca Canal. **Cons:** not for travelers who prefer ultramodern surroundings; no elevator; rooms with views are more expensive. [$] *Rooms from: €180* ✉ *Zattere, Dorsoduro 780, Dorsoduro* ☎ *041/5206466* 🌐 *www.lacalcina.com* 🛏 *25 rooms* 🍴 *Free Breakfast* [M] *Vaporetto: Zattere* ✣ *C5.*

$$ HOTEL **Locanda San Barnaba.** This charming family-run, value-for-money establishment is housed in a 16th-century palazzo and, if you're lucky, you'll bag one of the superior rooms or junior suites that have original

18th-century wall paintings; two of the rooms even have two small balconies with Rio Malpaga canal views. **Pros:** traditional furnishings make spacious rooms attractive and welcoming; lovely salon and garden to relax in; reasonable prices for Venice. **Cons:** no elevator; buffet breakfast gets mixed reviews; lacks the amenities of larger hotels (no restaurant or spa). $ *Rooms from: €175* ⊠ *Calle del Traghetto, Dorsoduro 2785–2786, Dorsoduro* ☎ *041/2411233* ⊕ *www.locanda-sanbarnaba. com* ⇆ *13 rooms* ❍❘ *Free Breakfast* Ⓜ *Vaporetto: Ca' Rezzonico* ✛ *B4.*

$$$$ ⊡ **Palazzo Stern.** This opulently refurbished neo-Gothic palazzo features
HOTEL   marble-columned arches, terrazzo floors, frescoed ceilings, mosaics, and
Fodor's Choice   a majestic carved staircase, and some rooms have tufted walls and parquet flooring, but the gracious terrace that overlooks the Grand Canal
★   is almost reason alone to stay here. **Pros:** excellent hotel service; lovely views from many rooms; modern renovation retains historic ambience. **Cons:** standard rooms don't have views; Grand Canal–facing rooms can be a bit noisy; no restaurant, gym, or spa. $ *Rooms from: €320* ⊠ *Calle del Traghetto, Dorsoduro 2792, Dorsoduro* ☎ *041/2770869* ⊕ *www.palazzostern.com* ⇆ *24 rooms* ❍❘ *Free Breakfast* Ⓜ *Vaporetto: Ca' Rezzonico* ✛ *C4.*

$$ ⊡ **Pensione Accademia Villa Maravege.** Behind iron gates in one of the
HOTEL   most densely packed parts of the city, you'll find yourself in front of a large and elegant garden and Gothic-style villa where accommodations are charmingly decorated with Venetian-style antique reproductions and fine tapestry. **Pros:** a unique villa in the heart of Venice; two gardens where guests can breakfast, drink, and relax; complimentary drinks and snacks at the bar. **Cons:** no guest rooms have Grand Canal views; bathrooms can be on the small side; no restaurant. $ *Rooms from: €187* ⊠ *Fondamenta Bollani, Dorsoduro 1058, Dorsoduro* ☎ *041/5210188* ⊕ *www.pensioneaccademia.it* ⇆ *27 rooms* ❍❘ *Free Breakfast* Ⓜ *Vaporetto: Accademia* ✛ *C4.*

SAN POLO

$$ ⊡ **La Villeggiatura.** If eclectic Venetian charm is what you seek, this
HOTEL   luminous residence near the Rialto offers six individually decorated rooms, each with its own original, theatrically themed wall painting by a local artist, and friendly, personalized service. **Pros:** relaxed atmosphere; meticulously maintained; well located near markets, artistic monuments, and restaurants. **Cons:** no elevator and lots of stairs; no view to speak of, despite the climb; no restaurant (though breakfast is served). $ *Rooms from: €144* ⊠ *Calle dei Botteri, San Polo 1569, San Polo* ☎ *041/5244673* ⊕ *www.lavilleggiatura.it* ⇆ *6 rooms* ❍❘ *Free Breakfast* Ⓜ *Vaporetto: Rialto Mercato* ✛ *D3.*

$$$ ⊡ **Oltre il Giardino.** It can be a challenge to find this secluded palazzo with
HOTEL   the feel of a country house, sheltered as it is behind a brick wall just over
Fodor's Choice   the bridge from the Frari church, but the search is well worth it: airy,
★   individually decorated guest rooms face a large garden, an oasis of peace (especially in high season). **Pros:** a peaceful, gracious, and convenient setting; glorious walled garden; friendly owners happy to share their Venice tips. **Cons:** a beautiful, but not particularly Venetian, ambience; rooms book up quickly; no in-house restaurant (though breakfast served).

[$] *Rooms from: €250* ✉ *Fondamenta Contarini, San Polo 2542, San Polo* ☎ *041/2750015* 🌐 *www.oltreilgiardino-venezia.com* 🕒 *Closed Jan.* 🛏 *6 rooms* 🍴 *Free Breakfast* [M] *Vaporetto: San Tomà* ✥ *C3.*

SANTA CROCE

$$ HOTEL Fodor's Choice ★ **Hotel al Ponte Mocenigo.** A columned courtyard welcomes you to this elegant, charming palazzo, former home of the Santa Croce branch of the Mocenigo family (which has a few doges in its past), and the canopied beds, striped damask fabrics, lustrous terrazzo flooring, and gilt-accented furnishings keep the sense of Venice's past strong in the guest rooms. **Pros:** enchanting courtyard; friendly and helpful staff; fantastic value. **Cons:** beds are on the hard side; standard rooms are small; rooms in the annex can be noisy. [$] *Rooms from: €160* ✉ *Fondamento de Rimpeto a Ca' Mocenigo, Santa Croce 2063, Santa Croce* ☎ *041/5244797* 🌐 *www.alpontemocenigo.com* 🛏 *11 rooms* 🍴 *Free Breakfast* [M] *Vaporetto: San Stae* ✥ *C2.*

CANNAREGIO

$ B&B/INN FAMILY **Al Palazzetto.** Understated Venetian decor, original open-beam ceilings and terrazzo flooring, and large rooms suitable for families or small groups are hallmarks of this intimate, family-owned guesthouse. **Pros:** authentic 18th-century palace; clean and quiet; good value for money. **Cons:** old-fashioned decor; not many amenities; a bit rough-around-the-edges. [$] *Rooms from: €110* ✉ *Calle delle Vele, Cannaregio 4057, Cannaregio* ☎ *041/2750897* 🌐 *www.guesthouse.it* 🛏 *5 rooms* 🍴 *Free Breakfast* [M] *Vaporetto: Ca' d'Oro* ✥ *E2.*

$$$$ HOTEL Fodor's Choice ★ **Al Ponte Antico.** This 16th-century palace inn has lined its Gothic windows with tiny white lights, creating an inviting glow that's emblematic of the hospitality and sumptuous surroundings that await you inside: rich brocade-tufted walls, period-style furniture, and hand-decorated beamed ceilings. **Pros:** upper-level terrace overlooks Grand Canal; family run; superior service. **Cons:** in one of the busiest areas of the city, although not particularly noisy; beds a little hard for some; hotel books up quickly. [$] *Rooms from: €330* ✉ *Calle dell'Aseo, Cannaregio 5768, Cannaregio* ☎ *041/2411944* 🌐 *www.alponteantico.com* 🛏 *9 rooms* 🍴 *Free Breakfast* [M] *Vaporetto: Rialto* ✥ *E3.*

$$$$ HOTEL Fodor's Choice ★ **Ca' Sagredo Hotel.** A study in Venetian opulence, this expansive palace has been the Sagredo family residence since the mid-1600s and has the decor to prove it: the massive staircase has Longhi wall panels soaring above it; the large common areas are adorned with original art by Tiepolo, Longhi, and Ricci; and guest rooms are traditional Venetian style, some retaining original art and architectural elements, many with full or partial canal and rooftop views. **Pros:** excellent location; some of the best preserved interiors in Venice; rooftop terrace and indoor bar. **Cons:** more opulent than intimate; views of the canal aren't as great as other hotels; restaurant gets mixed reviews. [$] *Rooms from: €445* ✉ *Campo Santa Sofia, Cannaregio 4198/99, Cannaregio* ☎ *041/2413111* 🌐 *www.casagredohotel.com* 🛏 *42 rooms* 🍴 *Free Breakfast* [M] *Vaporetto: Ca' d'Oro* ✥ *D3.*

$$ **Hotel Antico Doge.** Once the home of Doge Marino Faliero, the
HOTEL 14th-century doge who was executed for treason, this palazzo has
been attentively modernized in elegant 18th-century Venetian style:
all rooms are adorned with brocades, damask-tufted walls, gilt
mirrors, and parquet floors, and even the breakfast room comes
fitted out with a stuccoed ceiling and Murano chandelier. **Pros:**
romantic, atmospheric decor; convenient to the Rialto and beyond;
some rooms have Jacuzzi tubs. **Cons:** no outdoor garden or ter-
race; no elevator; area outside hotel can get very busy. **$** *Rooms
from: €144* ⊠ *Campo Santi Apostoli, Cannaregio 5643, Cannaregio*
☎ *041/2411570* ⊕ *www.anticodoge.com* ↝ *20 rooms* ᵀᴼᴵ *Free Break-
fast* Ⓜ *Vaporetto: Ca' d'Oro or Rialto* ✦ *E3.*

$$$ **Locanda Ca' Amadi.** A historic 13th-century palazzo near the Rialto
HOTEL Market is a welcome retreat on a tranquil *corte,* and individually deco-
rated rooms have tufted walls and views of a lively canal or a quiet
courtyard. **Pros:** classic Venetian style; some canal-view rooms; handy
for sightseeing. **Cons:** rooms vary a lot in size and quality; no restaurant (simple Continental breakfast served, though); canal-view rooms
can be noisy at night. **$** *Rooms from: €202* ⊠ *Corte Amadi, Cannare-
gio 5815, Cannaregio* ☎ *041/5285210* ⊕ *www.caamadi.it* ↝ *6 rooms*
ᵀᴼᴵ *Free Breakfast* Ⓜ *Vaporetto: Rialto* ✦ *E3.*

$$ **Palazzo Abadessa.** At this late-16th-century palazzo, you can experi-
HOTEL ence gracious hospitality, a luxurious atmosphere, a lush private garden,
Fodor's Choice and unusually spacious guest rooms well appointed with antique-style
★ furniture, frescoed or stuccoed ceilings, and silk fabrics. **Pros:** enormous
walled garden, a rare and delightful treat in crowded Venice; unique
and richly decorated guest rooms; superb guest service. **Cons:** some
bathrooms are small and plain; no restaurant (but buffet breakfast
served); hard beds not to everyone's taste. **$** *Rooms from: €195* ⊠ *Calle
Priuli, Cannaregio 4011, off Strada Nova, Cannaregio* ☎ *041/2413784*
⊕ *www.abadessa.com* ☾ *Closed last 2 wks in Jan.* ↝ *15 rooms* ᵀᴼᴵ *Free
Breakfast* Ⓜ *Vaporetto: Ca' d'Oro* ✦ *E2.*

$$ **3749 Ponte Chiodo.** Spending time at this charming guesthouse is
B&B/INN like staying with a friend; service is attentive and friendly, with lots
of suggestions for dining and sightseeing, and attractively appointed
guest rooms handy to the Ca' d'Oro vaporetto stop look past canals
or the spacious enclosed garden. **Pros:** highly attentive service; warm,
relaxed atmosphere; pretty private garden. **Cons:** some bathrooms
are smallish; no restaurant, though breakfast is served in the garden; not for those looking for large hotel amenities (no spa or gym).
$ *Rooms from: €180* ⊠ *Calle Racchetta, Cannaregio 3749, Can-
naregio* ☎ *041/2413935* ⊕ *www.pontechiodo.it* ↝ *6 rooms* ᵀᴼᴵ *Free
Breakfast* Ⓜ *Vaporetto: Ca' d'Oro* ✦ *D2.*

CASTELLO

$$ **Ca' dei Dogi.** A quiet courtyard secluded from the San Marco melee
HOTEL offers an island of calm in six individually decorated guest rooms
Fodor's Choice and two apartments (some with private terraces overlooking the
★ Doge's Palace, and one with a Jacuzzi) that feature contemporary
furnishings and accessories. **Pros:** amazing location close to Doge's

Palace and Piazza San Marco; balconies with wonderful views; in-house traditional Italian restaurant. **Cons:** rooms are on the small side; no elevator and lots of stairs; bathrooms can feel cramped. [$] *Rooms from: €145* ✉ *Corte Santa Scolastica, Castello 4242, Castello* ☎ *041/2413751* 🌐 *www.cadeidogi.it* ⏲ *Closed Dec.* 🛏 *6 rooms* 🍴 *Free Breakfast* [M] *Vaporetto: San Zaccaria* ✣ *F4.*

$ HOTEL **Hotel La Residenza.** Most rooms at this affordable renovated 15th-century Gothic-Byzantine palazzo set in a quiet campo are simple but spacious, while the lovely public spaces are filled with imitation period furnishings, 18th-century paintings, and chandeliers. **Pros:** lavish salon and breakfast room; quiet, residential area; affordable prices. **Cons:** no elevator; basic guest rooms; sparse breakfast. [$] *Rooms from: €115* ✉ *Campo Bandiera e Moro (or Bragora), Castello 3608, Castello* ☎ *041/5285315* 🌐 *www.venicelaresidenza.com* 🛏 *15 rooms* 🍴 *Free Breakfast* [M] *Vaporetto: Arsenale* ✣ *G4.*

$$$ HOTEL Fodor's Choice ★ **Metropole.** Atmosphere prevails in this labyrinth of intimate, opulent spaces featuring classic Venetian decor combined with exotic Eastern influences: the owner—a lifelong collector of unusual objects—fills common areas and the sumptuously appointed guest rooms with an assortment of antiques and curiosities. **Pros:** hotel harkens back to a gracious Venice of times past; suites have private roof terraces with water views; great restaurant and bar. **Cons:** one of the most densely touristed locations in the city; rooms with views are considerably more expensive; quirky, eccentric collections on display not for everyone. [$] *Rooms from: €240* ✉ *Riva degli Schiavoni, Castello 4149, Castello* ☎ *041/5205044* 🌐 *www.hotelmetropole.com* 🛏 *67 rooms* 🍴 *No meals* [M] *Vaporetto: San Zaccaria* ✣ *F4.*

$$ HOTEL **Ruzzini Palace Hotel.** Public rooms are Renaissance- and Baroque-style, with soaring spaces, Venetian terrazzo flooring, frescoed and exposed-beam ceilings, and Murano chandeliers, while guest rooms are essays in historic style but come integrated with contemporary furnishings and appointments. **Pros:** a luminous, aristocratic ambience; located on a lively Venetian campo not frequented by tourists; great buffet breakfast (not included in all rates). **Cons:** plain bathrooms; relatively far from a vaporetto stop; no restaurant. [$] *Rooms from: €188* ✉ *Campo Santa Maria Formosa, Castello 5866, Castello* ☎ *041/2410447* 🌐 *www.ruzzinipalace.com* 🛏 *28 rooms* 🍴 *No meals* [M] *Vaporetto: San Zaccaria or Rialto* ✣ *F3.*

NIGHTLIFE AND PERFORMING ARTS

NIGHTLIFE

Venice's offerings for nightlife are, even by rather sedate standards, fairly tame. Most bars must close by midnight, especially those that offer outdoor seating. Piazza San Marco is a popular meeting place in nice weather, when the cafés stay open relatively late and all seem to compete to offer the best live music. The younger crowd, Venetians and visitors alike, tend to gravitate toward the area around Rialto Bridge, with Campi San Bartolomeo and San Luca on one side and Campo

Rialto Nuovo on the other. Especially popular with university students and young people from the mainland are the bars around Campo Santa Margherita. Pick up a booklet of *2Night* or visit ⊕ *venezia.2night.it* for nightlife listings and reviews.

SAN MARCO AND DORSODURO

Al Chioschetto. While this popular place consists only of a kiosk set up to serve some outdoor tables, it is located on the Zattere, and thus provides panoramic views. It's a handy meet-up for locals and a stop-off for tourists in nice weather for a spritz, a panino, or a sunny read as the Venetian world eases by. But go for the view and the sunshine; the food and drink, while acceptable, are not exceptional. ⊠ *Near Ponte Lungo, Dorsoduro 1406/A, Dorsoduro* ☎ *348/3968466* Ⓜ *Vaporetto: Zattere.*

Fodor's Choice
★
Il Caffè (*Bar Rosso*). Commonly called "Bar Rosso" for its bright-red exterior, Il Caffè has far more tables outside than inside. A favorite with students and faculty from the nearby university, it's a good place to enjoy a spritz—the preferred Venetian aperitif of white wine, Campari or Aperol, soda water, an olive, and a slice of orange. It has excellent tramezzini (among the best in town) and panini, and a hip, helpful staff. It's been recently frequented by high-school students from the mainland on weekend nights, so it can be more enjoyable around lunchtime, or in the early evening. ⊠ *Campo Santa Margherita, Dorsoduro 2963, Dorsoduro* ☎ *041/5287998* ⊕ *www.cafferosso.it.*

Orange. Modern, hip, and complemented by an internal garden, this welcoming bar anchors the south end of Campo Santa Margherita, the liveliest campo in Venice. You can have *piadine* sandwiches, salads, and drinks while watching soccer games on a massive screen inside, or sit at the tables in the campo. Despite being close to the university, Orange is frequented primarily by young working people from the mainland and tourists. ⊠ *Campo Santa Margherita, Dorsoduro 3054/A, Dorsoduro* ☎ *041/5234740* ⊕ *www.orangebar.it.*

SAN POLO

Naranzaria. At the friendliest of the several bar-restaurants that line the Erbaria, near the Rialto Market, enjoy a cocktail outside along the Canal Grande or at a cozy table inside of the renovated 16th-century warehouse. Although the food is acceptable, the ambience is really the main attraction. After the kitchen closes at 10:30, light snacks are served until midnight, and live music (usually jazz, Latin, or rock) occasionally plays on Sunday evening. ⊠ *L'Erbaria, San Polo 130, along Canal Grande, San Polo* ☎ *041/7241035* ⊕ *www.naranzaria.it* Ⓜ *Vaporetto: Rialto Mercato.*

CASTELLO

Zanzibar. This kiosk bar is very popular on warm summer evenings with upper-class Venetians and tourists. It offers food, but that is mostly limited to conventional Venetian sandwiches and commercial ice cream. The most interesting thing about the place is its location with a view of the church of Santa Maria Formosa, which makes it a pleasant place for a drink and a good place for people-watching. ⊠ *Campo Santa Maria Formosa, Castello 5840, Castello* ☎ *345/9423998* Ⓜ *Vaporetto: San Zaccaria.*

PERFORMING ARTS

Visit ⊕ *www.aguestinvenice.com* for a preview of musical, artistic, and sporting events. *Venezia News* (*VENews*), available at newsstands, has similar information but also includes in-depth articles about noteworthy events. The tourist office publishes a handy, free quarterly *Calendar* in Italian and English, listing daily events and current museum and venue hours. *Venezia da Vivere* (⊕ *www.veneziadavivere.com*) is a seasonal guide listing nightspots and live music. For a Venice website that allows you to scan the cultural horizon before you arrive, try ⊕ *www.turismovenezia.it*. And don't ignore the posters you see plastered on the walls as you walk—they're often the most up-to-date information you can find.

CARNEVALE

Although Carnevale has traditionally been associated with the time leading up to the Roman Catholic period of Lent, it originally started out as a principally secular annual period of partying and feasting to celebrate Venice's victory over the patriarch of Ulrich Aquileia in 1162. To commemorate the annual tribute Ulrich was forced to pay, a bull and 12 pigs were slaughtered each year on the day before Lent in Piazza San Marco. The use of masks for Carnevale was first mentioned in 1268, and its direct association with Lent was not made until the end of the 13th century. Since then, for centuries the city marked the days preceding *quaresima* (Lent) with abundant feasting and wild celebrations. The word *carnevale* is derived from the words *carne* (meat) and *levare* (to remove), as eating meat was restricted during Lent.

Venice earned its international reputation as the "city of Carnevale" in the 18th century, when partying would begin several months before Lent and the city seemed to be one continuous masquerade. During this time, income from tourists became a major source of funds in La Serenissima's coffers. With the Republic's fall in 1797, Carnevale was prohibited by the French and the Austrians. From Italian reunification in 1866 until the fall of fascism in the 1940s, the event was alternately resumed and banned, depending on the government's stance.

It was revived for good in the 1970s, when residents began taking to the calli and campi in their own impromptu celebrations. It didn't take long for the tourist industry to embrace the revival as a means to stimulate business during low season. The efforts were successful. Each year over the 10- to 12-day Carnevale period (ending on the Tuesday before Ash Wednesday), more than a half-million people attend concerts, theater and street performances, masquerade balls, historical processions, fashion shows, and contests. Since 2008 Carnevale has been organized by **Venezia Marketing & Eventi** (⊕ *www.carnevale.venezia.it*). *A Guest in Venice* is also a complete guide to public and private Carnevale festivities. Stop by the **tourist office** (✆ *041/5298711* ⊕ *www.turismovenezia.it*) or Venice Pavilion for information, but be aware they can be mobbed. If you're not planning on joining in the revelry, you'd be wise to choose another time to visit Venice. Crowds throng the streets (which become one-way, with police directing foot traffic), bridges are designated "no-stopping" zones to avoid gridlock, and prices skyrocket.

FESTIVALS

The **Biennale** (⊕ *www.labiennale.org*) cultural institution organizes events year-round, including the **Venice Film Festival,** which begins the last week of August. **La Biennale di Venezia,** an international exhibition of contemporary art, is held in odd-numbered years, usually from mid-June to early November, at the Giardini della Biennale, and in the impressive Arsenale, while the international architecture exhibition is held at the same time in even-numbered years.

Festa del Redentore. On the third Sunday in July, crowds cross the Canale della Giudecca by means of a pontoon bridge, built every year to commemorate the doge's annual visit to Palladio's Chiesa del Redentore, to offer thanks for the end of a 16th-century plague. The evening before, Venetians, accompanied each year with an increasing number of tourists, set up tables and chairs along the canals. As evening falls, practically the whole city takes to the streets and tables, and thousands more take to the water. Boats decorated with colored lanterns (and well provisioned with traditional Redentore meals) jockey for position to watch the grand event. Half an hour before midnight, Venice kicks off a fireworks display over the Bacino, with the fireworks reflecting in its waters. Anywhere along the Riva degli Schiavoni you'll find good viewing; or try Zattere, as close to Punta Dogana as you can get, or on the Zitelle end of the Giudecca. After the fireworks you can join the young folks in staying out all night and greeting sunrise on the Lido beach, or rest up and make the procession to mass on Sunday morning. If you're on a boat, allow for a couple of hours to dislodge yourself from the nautical traffic jam when the festivities break up.

SHOPPING

Globalization has made most goods available in Venice and items like Venetian glass widely available in major cities throughout the world. While the selection of Italian and Venetian made goods may be a bit better in Venice than at home, the prices may actually be lower in the United States, especially considering that U.S. retailers discount sale goods quite radically. Venetian antiques, especially antique Venetian glass, is almost invariably cheaper in other places, because Venetians are ready to pay high prices for their own heritage. So, before your trip, check the prices at home on what you may wish to buy abroad before you leave.

Alluring shops abound in Venice. You'll find countless vendors of trademark Venetian wares such as glass and lace. The authenticity of some goods can be suspect, but they're often pleasing to the eye regardless of their place of origin. There are also some interesting craft and art studios, where you can find high-quality, one-of-a-kind articles, but Venice is a design center only for glass, lace, and high-end textiles. You will probably find a better choice of leather, clothing, and furnishings in other Italian cities.

Regular store hours are usually 9 to 12:30 and 3:30 or 4 to 7:30; some stores close Saturday afternoon or Monday morning. Food shops are open 8 to 1 and 5 to 7:30, and may close Wednesday afternoon and

Venetian Art Glass

The glass of Murano is Venice's number-one product, and you'll be confronted by mind-boggling displays of traditional and contemporary glassware—much of it kitsch and not made in Venice. Traditional Venetian glass is hot, blown glass, not lead crystal; it comes in myriad forms that range from the classic ornate goblets and chandeliers, to beads, vases, sculpture, and more. Beware of paying "Venetian" prices for glass made elsewhere. A piece claiming to be made in Murano may guarantee its origin, but not its value or quality; the prestigious Venetian glassmakers—like Venini, Seguso, Salviati, and others—sign their pieces, but never use the "made in Murano" label. To make a

smart purchase, take your time and be selective. You can learn a great deal without sales pressure at the Museo del Vetro ⊕ *museovetro.visitmuve.it* on Murano; unfortunately, you'll likely find the least-attractive glass where public demonstrations are offered. Although prices in Venice and on Murano are comparable, shops in Venice with wares from various glassworks may charge slightly less. ■TIP→ **A "free" taxi to Murano always comes with sales pressure. Take the vaporetto that's included in your transit pass, and, if you prefer, a private guide who specializes in the subject but has no affinity to any specific furnace.**

all day Sunday. Supermarkets are generally open every day, including Sunday, and have longer opening hours than independent stores. Many tourist-oriented shops are open all day, every day. Some shops close for both a summer and a winter vacation.

The **San Marco** area is full of shops and couture boutiques such as Armani, Missoni, Valentino, Fendi, and Versace. Le Mercerie, the Frezzeria, Calle dei Fabbri, and Calle Larga XXII Marzo, all leading from Piazza San Marco, are some of Venice's busiest shopping streets. Other good shopping areas surround Calle del Teatro and Campi San Salvador, Manin, San Fantin, and San Bartolomeo. You can find somewhat less expensive, more varied and imaginative shops between the Rialto Bridge and San Polo and in Santa Croce, and art galleries in Dorsoduro from the Salute to the Accademia.

SAN MARCO AND DORSODURO

GIFTS

Giuliana Longo. A hat shop that's been around since 1901 offers an assortment of Venetian and gondolier straw hats, Panama hats from Ecuador, caps and berets, and some select scarves of silk and fine wool; there's even a special corner dedicated to accessories for antique cars. ⊠ *Calle del Lovo, San Marco 4813, San Marco* ☏ *041/5226454* ⊕ *www. giulianalongo.com* ⊘ *Closed Sun.* Ⓜ *Vaporetto: San Marco.*

4

GLASS

Marina and Susanna Sent. The beautiful and elegant glass jewelry of Marina and Susanna Sent has been featured in *Vogue*. Look also for vases and other exceptional design pieces. Other locations are near San Moise in San Marco, on Murano on the Fondamenta Serenella, and in San Polo in the Sottoportico dei Oresi. ⊠ *Campo San Vio, Dorsoduro 669, Dorsoduro* ☎ *041/5208136 for Dorsoduro, 041/5204014 for San Marco, 041/5274665 for Murano* ⊕ *www.marinaesusannasent.com* Ⓜ *Vaporetto: Accademia/Zattere, Giglio, Murano Serenella.*

Venini. When connoisseurs of Venetian glass think of the firms who have restored Venice to its place as the epicenter of artistic glass production, Venini is, without any major discussion, the firm that immediately comes to mind. Since the beginning of the 20th century, Venini has found craftsmen and designers that have made their trademark synonymous with the highest quality both in traditional and in creative glass design. A piece of Venini glass, even one of modest price and proportions, will be considered not only a charming decorative object, but also a work of art that will maintain its value for years to come. While Venini's more exciting and innovative pieces may cost thousands of dollars, the Venini showrooms in the Piazza San Marco and on Fondamenta Vetrai in Murano also have small, more conventional designs for prices as low as €100. ⊠ *314 Piazzetta Leoncini, San Marco* ☎ *041/5224045 San Marco, 041/2737204 Murano* ⊕ *www.venini.com.*

LEATHER

Il Grifone. Very few artisan leather shops remain in Venice, and Il Grifone is the standout with respect to quality, tradition, and a guarantee for an exquisite product. For more than 30 years, Antonio Peressin has been making bags, purses, belts, and smaller leather items that have a wide following because of his precision and attention to detail. His prices remain reasonable and accessible. ⊠ *Fondamenta del Gaffaro, Dorsoduro 3516, Dorsoduro* ☎ *041/5229452* ⊕ *www.ilgrifonevenezia. it* ⊗ *Closed Sun. and Mon.* Ⓜ *Vaporetto: Piazzale Roma.*

SHOPPING CENTERS

Fondaco dei Tedeschi. This 15th-century Renaissance commercial center served as Venice's main post office for many years, but has now been remodeled and returned to its historical roots as a luxury department store. Here you can find a large assortment of high-end jewelry, clothing, and other luxury items. ⊠ *Calle Fondaco dei Tedeschi, near San Marco end of Rialto Bridge, San Marco* ☎ *041/3142000* ⊕ *www.dfs. com/en/venice/stores/t-fondaco-dei-tedeschi-by-dfs* Ⓜ *Rialto.*

TEXTILES

Fodor'sChoice ★ **Bevilacqua.** This renowned studio has kept the weaving tradition alive in Venice since 1875, using 18th-century hand looms for its most precious creations. Its repertoire of 3,500 different patterns and designs yields a ready-to-sell selection of hundreds of brocades, Gobelins, damasks, velvets, taffetas, and satins. You'll also find tapestry, cushions, and braiding. Fabrics made by this prestigious firm have been used to decorate the Vatican, the Royal Palace of Stockholm, and the White House. This listing is for the main retail outlet of the Bevilacqua establishment; there's another behind the San Marco Basilica. If you're interested in seeing the actual 18th-century looms in action making the most precious fabrics, request an appointment at the Luigi Bevilacqua production center in Santa Croce. ⊠ *Campo di Santa Maria del Giglio, San Marco 2520, San Marco* ☎ *041/2410662 main retail outlet, 041/5287581 retail outlet behind Basilica, 041/721566 Santa Croce production center* ⊕ *www.bevilacquatessuti.com* Ⓜ *Vaporetto: Giglio.*

Fodor'sChoice   **Jesurum.** A great deal of so-called Burano-Venetian lace is now
   ★   machine made in China—and there really is a difference. Unless you have some experience, you're best off going to a trusted place. Jesurum has been the major producer of handmade Venetian lace since 1870. Its lace is, of course, all modern production, but if you want an antique piece, the people at Jesurum can point you in the right direction. ⊠ *Calle Larga XII Marzo, San Marco 2401, San Marco* ☎ *041/5238969* ⊕ *www.jesurum.it.*

THE VENETO AND
FRIULI–VENEZIA GIULIA

WELCOME TO
THE VENETO AND
FRIULI–VENEZIA GIULIA

TOP REASONS TO GO

★ **Giotto's frescoes in the Cappella degli Scrovegni:** In this Padua chapel, Giotto's expressive and innovative frescoes foreshadowed the Renaissance.

★ **Villa Barbaro in Maser:** Master architect Palladio's graceful creation meets Veronese's splendid frescoes in a one-time-only collaboration.

★ **Opera in Verona's ancient arena:** The performances may not be top-notch, but even serious opera fans can't resist the spectacle of these shows.

★ **Roman and early-Christian ruins at Aquileia:** Aquileia's beautiful ruins offer an image of the transition from pagan to Christian Rome, and are almost entirely free of tourists.

★ **The wine roads north of Treviso:** A series of routes takes you through beautiful hillsides to some of Italy's finest wines.

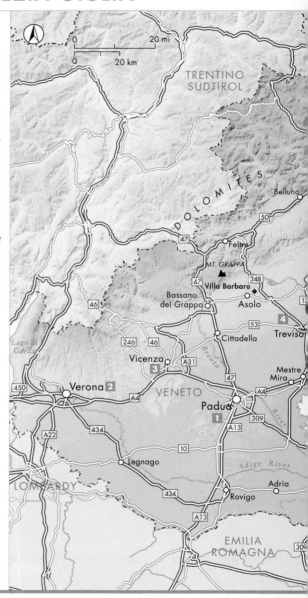

1 Padua. A city of both high-rises and history, Padua is most noted for Giotto's frescoes in the Cappella degli Scrovegni, where Dante's contemporary painted with a human focus that foreshadowed the Renaissance.

2 Verona. Shakespeare placed Romeo, Juliet, and a couple of gentlemen in Verona, one of the best-preserved and most beautiful cities in Italy. Try to catch *Aida* at the gigantic Roman arena.

3 Vicenza. This elegant art city, on the green plain reaching inland from Venice's lagoon, bears the signature of the great 16th-century architect Andrea Palladio, including several palazzi and other important buildings.

4 Treviso and the Hillside Towns. Treviso is a prosperous, busy town with more than a touch of Venetian style. Asolo, the "City of a Hundred Horizons," is the most popular destination in a series of towns that dot the wine-producing hills north of Treviso.

5 Friuli–Venezia Giulia. The port city of Trieste has a mixed Venetian-Austrian heritage and an important literary history. It contains several Belle Époque cafés and palaces built for Habsburg nobility.

EATING AND DRINKING WELL IN THE VENETO AND FRIULI–VENEZIA GIULIA

With the decisive seasonal changes of the Venetian Arc, it's little wonder that many restaurants shun printed menus. Elements from field and forest define much of the region's cuisine, including white asparagus, herbs, chestnuts, radicchio, and wild mushrooms.

Restaurants of the Venetian Arc tend to cling to tradition, not only in the food they serve, but also when they serve it. From 2:30 in the afternoon until about 7:30 in the evening most places are closed (though you can pick up a snack at a bar during these hours), and on Sunday afternoon restaurants are packed with Italian families and friends indulging in the weekly ritual of lunching out.

Meals are still sacred for most Italians, so don't be surprised if you get disapproving looks when you gobble down a sandwich or a slice of pizza while seated on the church steps or a park bench. In many places it's actually illegal to do so. If you want to fit in with the locals, snack while standing at the bar or seated in a café, and they may not even notice that you're a tourist.

THE BEST IN BEANS

Pasta e fagioli, a thick bean soup with pasta, served slightly warm or at room temperature, is made all over Italy. Folks in the Veneto, though, take special pride in their version, made from particularly fine beans grown around the village of Lamon, near Belluno.

Even when they're bought in the Veneto, the beans from Lamon cost more than double the next-most-expensive variety, but their rich and delicate taste is considered well worth the added expense. You never knew that bean soup could taste so good.

FISH

The catch of the day is always a good bet, whether it's sweet and succulent Adriatic shellfish, sea bream, bass, or John Dory, or freshwater fish from Lake Garda, near Verona. A staple in the Veneto is *baccalà,*: this is dried salt cod, which alongside *stoccafisso*, air-dried cod, were introduced to Italy during the Renaissance by northern European traders. Dried cod is soaked in water or milk and then prepared in a different way in each city. Confusingly in Vicenza, baccalà *alla vicentina* uses *stoccafisso* cooked with onions, milk, and cheese, and is generally served with polenta.

MEAT

In the Veneto traditional dishes foreground offal as much as the prime cuts. Beef (including veal), pork, rabbit, horse, and donkey meat are standards, while goose, duck, and guinea fowl are common poultry options. In Friuli–Venezia Giulia, menus show the influences of Austria–Hungary: you may find deer and hare on the menu, as well as Eastern European–style goulash. Throughout the Veneto an unusual treat is *nervetti*—cubes of gelatin from a calf's knee prepared with onions, parsley, olive oil, and lemon.

PASTA, RISOTTO, POLENTA

For *primi* (first courses), the Veneto dines on *bigoli* (thick whole-wheat pasta), generally served with an

anchovy-onion sauce delicately flavored with cinnamon, or risotto, creamy rice generally flavored with vegetables or shellfish. *Polenta* (cornmeal gruel) is everywhere, whether it's a stiff porridge topped with Gorgonzola, or a stew, or a patty grilled alongside meat or fish. Spaghetti and other types of pasta are widely available, but they are considered practically foreign. The same holds true for pizza.

RADICCHIO DI TREVISO

In fall and winter be sure to try the radicchio di Treviso, *pictured above,* a red endive grown near that town but popular all over the region. Cultivation is very labor-intensive, so it can be expensive. It's best in a stew with chicken or veal, in a risotto, or just grilled or baked with a drizzle of olive oil and perhaps a little taleggio cheese from neighboring Lombardy.

WINE

The Veneto produces more D.O.C. (Denominazione di Origine Controllata) wines than any other region in Italy. Amarone, the region's crowning achievement, is a robust, full-bodied red. The best of the whites are Soave, prosecco, and *pinot bianco* (pinot blanc). In Friuli–Venezia Giulia the local wines include *friulano,* a dry, lively white made from the sauvignon vert grape, and *picolit,* a dessert wine.

5

Updated by
Nick Bruno

The arc around Venice—stretching from Verona to Trieste, encompassing the Veneto and Friuli–Venezia Giulia regions—is indisputably one of most culturally rich areas in Italy, an intellectual and spiritual feast of architecture, painting, and sculpture. Since the 16th century, the art, architecture, and way of life here have all reflected Venetian splendor. Whether coastal or inland, the emblem of Venice, St. Mark's winged lion, is emblazoned on palazzi and poised on pedestals.

It wasn't always this way. Back in the Middle Ages, Padua and Verona were independent cities that developed substantial cultural traditions of their own, leaving behind many artistic treasures. And even while it was under Venice's political domination, 16th-century Vicenza contributed more to the cultural heritage of La Serenissima than it took from her, in large part because of its master architect, Andrea Palladio.

The area is primarily flat, green farmland. As you move inland, though, you encounter low hills, which swell and rise in a succession of plateaus and high meadows, culminating in the snowcapped Dolomite Alps. Much of the pleasure of exploring here comes from discovering the variations on the Venetian theme that give a unique character to each of the towns. Some, such as Verona, Treviso, and Udine, have a solid medieval look. Padua, with its narrow arcaded streets, is romantic; Vicenza, ennobled by the architecture of Palladio, is more elegant. Udine, in Friuli–Venezia Giulia, is a genteel, intricately sculpted city that's home to the first important frescoes by Gianbattista Tiepolo. In Trieste, once the main port of the Austro-Hungarian Empire, you can find survivors of those days in its Viennese-inspired coffeehouses and *buffets*—hole-in-the-wall eateries serving sausages and other pork dishes.

Unlike the western regions of northern Italy, the Veneto and Friuli–Venezia Giulia were slow to move from an agricultural to an industrial economy, and even now depend upon small and medium-size businesses, many of which are still family run. The area, therefore, attracted far fewer migrants from elsewhere in Italy, and it was able to maintain its local cultures to a substantial degree. Local dialects may have all but died out in places like Milan and Turin, but they still thrive in the Veneto and Friuli–Venezia Giulia, and even when the residents speak standard Italian, it is frequently laced with local words and usage.

THE VENETO AND FRIULI–VENEZIA PLANNER

PLANNING

Several of the most interesting and important sights in the Venetian Arc require reservations or are open only at limited times. If you want to make the most of your visit, it's important to plan ahead. For instance, reservations are required to see the Giotto frescoes in Padua's Cappella degli Scrovegni—though if there's space, you can "reserve" on the spot.

On the outskirts of Vicenza, the Villa della Rotonda, one of Palladio's masterpieces, is open to the public only from mid-March through mid-November, and only on Wednesday and Saturday. (Hours for visiting the grounds are less restrictive.) Another important Palladian villa, Villa Barbaro near Maser, is open weekends and several days during the week, from March to October; from November to February, it's open only on weekends.

MAKING THE MOST OF YOUR TIME

Lined up in a row west of Venice are Padua, Vicenza, and Verona—three prosperous small cities that are each worth at least a day on a northern Italy itinerary. Verona has the most charm and the widest selection of hotels and restaurants, so it's probably the best choice for a base in the area, even though it also draws the most tourists. The hills north of Venice make for good drives, with appealing villages set amid a visitor-friendly wine country.

East of the Veneto, the region of Friuli–Venezia Giulia is off the main tourist circuit. You probably won't go here on a first trip to Italy, but by your second or third visit you may be drawn by its caves and castles, its battle-worn hills, and its mix of Italian and Central European culture. The port city of Trieste, famous for its elegant cafés, has a quiet character that some people find dull but others find alluring.

GETTING HERE AND AROUND

BUS TRAVEL

There are interurban and interregional connections throughout the Veneto and Friuli, handled by nearly a dozen private bus lines. To figure out which line will get you where, the best strategy is to get assistance from local tourist offices.

CAR TRAVEL

Padua, Vicenza, and Verona are on the highway (and train line) between Venice and Milan. Seeing them without a car isn't a problem; in fact, having a car can complicate matters. The cities sometimes limit access, permitting cars only with plates ending in an even number on even days, odd on odd, or prohibiting cars altogether on weekends. There's no central source for information about these sporadic traffic restrictions; the best strategy is to check with your hotel before arrival for an update. You'll need a car to get the most out of the hill country that makes up much of the Venetian Arc, and it will be particularly useful for visiting Aquileia, since public transportation to that quite interesting site is limited.

The two main access roads to the Venetian Arc from southern Italy are both linked to the A1 (Autostrada del Sole), which connects Bologna, Florence, and Rome. They are the A13, which ends in Padua, and the A22, which passes through Verona running north–south. Linking the region from east to west is the A4, the primary route from Milan to Trieste, skirting Verona, Padua, and Venice along the way. The distance from Verona to Trieste via the A4 is 263 km (163 miles; 2½ hours), with one break in the autostrada near Venice/Mestre. Branches link the A4 with Treviso (A27), Pordenone (A28), and Udine (A23).

TRAIN TRAVEL

Trains on the main routes from the south stop almost hourly in Verona, Padua, and Venice. From northern Italy and the rest of Europe, trains usually enter via Milan or through Porta Nuova station in Verona. Treviso and Udine both lie on the main line from Venice to Tarvisio. Unfortunately, there are no daytime express trains between Venice and Tarvisio, only the slower inter-regional and regional service. There is also no through train service between this region and neighboring Slovenia, only an inconvenient and uncomfortable minibus. To the west of Venice, the main line running across the north of Italy stops at Padua (30 minutes from Venice), Vicenza (1 hour), and Verona (1½ hours); to the east is Trieste (2 hours). Local trains link Vicenza to Treviso (1 hour) and Udine to Trieste (1 hour).

Be sure to take Regionale Veloce (fast regional) trains whenever possible—a local "milk run" or Regionale that stops in every village along the way can take considerably longer. The fastest trains are the Frecce, but reservations are mandatory and fares are much higher than on regional services.

Contact Trenitalia. ☏ 892021 ⊕ www.trenitalia.com.

RESTAURANTS

Although the Veneto is not considered one of Italy's major cuisine areas, the region offers many opportunities for exciting gastronomic adventures. The fish offerings are among the most varied and freshest in Italy, and possibly Europe, and the vegetables from the islands in the Venetian lagoon are considered a national treasure. Take a break from pasta and try the area's wonderful, creamy risottos and hearty polenta. *Restaurant reviews have been shortened. For full information, visit Fodors.com.*

HOTELS

Rates tend to be higher in Padua and Verona; in Verona especially, seasonal rates vary widely and soar during trade fairs and the opera season. There are fewer good lodging choices in Vicenza, perhaps because more overnighters are drawn to the better restaurant scenes in Verona and Padua. *Agriturismo* (farm stay) information is available at tourist offices and sometimes on their websites. Ask about weekend discounts, often available at hotels catering to business clients.

Substantial savings can sometimes be had by booking through reservation services on the Internet. *Hotel reviews have been shortened. For full information, visit Fodors.com.*

WHAT IT COSTS				
	$	$$	$$$	$$$$
Restaurants	under €15	€15–€24	€25–€35	over €35
Hotels	under €125	€125–€200	€201–€300	over €300

Prices in the dining reviews are the average cost of a main course at dinner, or, if dinner is not served, at lunch. Prices in the reviews are the lowest cost of a standard double room in high season.

PADUA

A romantic warren of arcaded streets, Padua is a major cultural center in northern Italy. It has first-rate artistic monuments and, along with Bologna, is one of the few cities in the country where you can catch a glimpse of student life.

Its university, founded in 1222 and Italy's second oldest, attracted such cultural icons as Dante (1265–1321), Petrarch (1304–74), and Galileo (1564–1642), thus earning the city the sobriquet "La Dotta" (the Learned). Padua's Basilica di Sant'Antonio, begun around 1238, attracts droves of pilgrims, especially on his feast day, June 13. Three great artists—Giotto (1266–1337), Donatello (circa 1386–1466), and Mantegna (1431–1506)—left significant works in Padua. Giotto's Capella degli Scrovegni here is one of the best-known and most meticulously preserved works of art in the country. Today, a bicycle-happy student body—some 60,000 strong—flavors every aspect of local culture. Don't be surprised if you spot a *laurea* (graduation) ceremony marked by laurel leaves, mocking lullabies, and X-rated caricatures.

GETTING HERE AND AROUND

Many people visit Padua from Venice: the train trip between the cities is short, and regular bus service originates from Venice's Piazzale Roma. By car from Milan or Venice, Padua is on the Autostrada Torino–Trieste (A4/E70). Take the San Carlo exit and follow Via Guido Reni to Via Tiziano Aspetti into town. From the south, take the Autostrada Bologna–Padova (A13) to its Padua terminus at Via Ballaglia. Regular bus service connects Venice's Marco Polo airport with downtown Padua.

Padua is a walker's city—parking is difficult, and cars are prohibited in much of the city center. If you arrive by car, leave your vehicle in one of the parking lots on the outskirts, or at your hotel. Unlimited bus service is included with the PadovaCard (€16 or €21, valid for 48 or 72 hours), which allows entry to all the city's principal sights (€1 extra for a Capella degli Scrovegni reservation). It's available at tourist information offices and at some museums.

VISITOR INFORMATION

PadovaCard. ✉ *Padua* ⊕ *www.cappelladegliscrovegni.it.*

Padua Tourism Office. ✉ *Padova Railway Station* ☎ *049/2010080* ⊕ *www.turismopadova.it.*

EXPLORING

TOP ATTRACTIONS

Fodor's Choice
★

Basilica di Sant'Antonio (*Basilica del Santo*). Thousands of faithful make the pilgrimage here each year to pray at the tomb of St. Anthony, while others come to admire works by the 15th-century Florentine master Donatello. His equestrian statue (1453) of the *condottiere* (mercenary general) Erasmo da Narni, known as Gattamelata, in front of the church is one of the great masterpieces of Italian Renaissance sculpture. It was inspired by the ancient statue of Marcus Aurelius in Rome's Campidoglio. Donatello also sculpted the beautiful series of bronze reliefs in the imposing interior illustrating the miracles of St. Anthony, as well as the bronze statues of the Madonna and saints, on the high altar.

The huge church, which combines elements of Byzantine, Romanesque, and Gothic styles, was probably begun around 1238, seven years after the death of the Portuguese-born saint. It was completed in 1310, with structural modifications added from the end of the 14th century into the mid-15th century. Because of the site's popularity with pilgrims, masses are held in the basilica almost constantly, which makes it difficult to see these works. More accessible is the restored **Cappella del Santo** (housing the tomb of the saint), which dates from the 16th century. Its walls are covered with impressive reliefs by various important Renaissance sculptors, including Jacopo Sansovino (1486–1570), the architect of the library in Venice's Piazza San Marco, and Tullio Lombardo (1455–1532), the greatest in a family of sculptors who decorated many churches in the area, among them Venice's Santa Maria dei Miracoli. The **Museo Antoniano** (€2.50; closed Monday), part of the basilica complex, contains a Mantegna fresco and works by Tiepolo, Carpaccio, and Piazzetta. ✉ *Piazza del Santo* ☎ *049/8603236* ⊕ *www.basilicadelsanto.it.*

Fodor's Choice
★

Cappella degli Scrovegni (*The Arena Chapel*). The spatial depth, emotional intensity, and naturalism of the frescoes illustrating the lives of Mary and Jesus in this world-famous chapel—note the use of blue sky instead of the conventional, depth-destroying gold background of medieval painting—broke new ground in Western art. Enrico Scrovegno commissioned these frescoes to atone for the sins of his deceased father, Reginaldo, the usurer condemned to the Seventh Circle of the Inferno in Dante's *Divine Comedy*. Giotto and his assistants worked on the frescoes from 1303 to 1305, arranging them in tiers to be read from left to right. Opposite the altar is a *Last Judgment*, most likely designed and painted by Giotto's assistants, where Enrico offers his chapel to the Virgin, celebrating her role in human salvation—particularly appropriate, given the penitential purpose of the chapel.

■TIP➜ Mandatory reservations, nonrefundable and for a specific time, can be made in advance at the ticket office, online, or by phone.

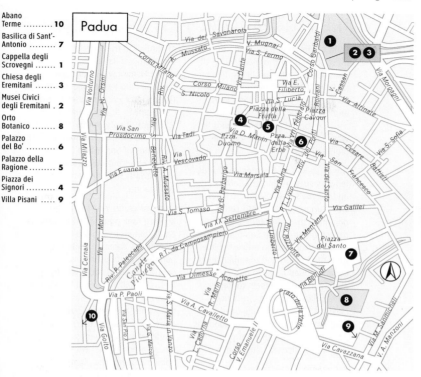

Payments online or by phone by credit card must be made one day in advance. Reservations are necessary even if you have a PadovaCard. In order to preserve the artwork, doors are opened only every 15 minutes. A maximum of 25 visitors at a time must spend 15 minutes in an acclimatization room before making a 15-minute (20 minutes in January, February, late June, July, November, and late December) chapel visit. Punctuality is essential; tickets should be picked up at least one hour before your reservation time. If you don't have a reservation, it's sometimes possible to buy your chapel admission on the spot—but you might have to wait a while until there's a group with an opening. You can see fresco details as part of a virtual tour at the Musei Civici degli Eremitani. A good place to get some background before visiting the chapel is the multimedia room, where there are films and interactive computer presentations. Between Christmas and Epiphany (January 6), the chapel sometimes has special late hours. ⊠ *Piazza Eremitani 8* ☎ *049/2010020 reservations* ⊕ *www.cappelladegliscrovegni.it* ⚲*€13, includes Musei Civici (€1 with PadovaCard).*

Palazzo della Ragione. Also known as Il Salone, the spectacular arcaded reception hall in Padua's original law courts is as notable for its grandeur—it's 85 feet high—as for its colorful setting, surrounded by shops, cafés, and open-air fruit and vegetable markets. Niccolò Miretto and

THE VENETIAN ARC, PAST AND PRESENT

Long before Venetians made their presence felt on the mainland in the 15th century, Ezzelino III da Romano (1194–1259) laid claim to Verona, Padua, and the surrounding lands and towns. He was the first of a series of brutal and aggressive rulers who dominated the cities of the region until the rise of Venetian rule.

After Ezzelino was ousted, powerful families such as Padua's Carrara and Verona's della Scala (Scaligeri) vied throughout the 14th century to dominate these territories. With the rise of Venetian rule came a time of relative peace, when noble families from the lagoon and the mainland commissioned Palladio and other accomplished architects to design their palazzi and villas. This rich classical legacy, superimposed upon medieval castles and fortifications, is central to the identities of present-day Padua, Vicenza, and Verona.

The region remained under Venetian control until the Napoleonic invasion and the fall of the Venetian Republic in 1797. The Council of Vienna ceded it, along with Lombardy, to Austria in 1815. The region revolted against Austrian rule and joined the Italian Republic in 1866.

Friuli–Venezia Giulia's complicated history is reflected in its architecture, language, and cuisine. It's been marched through, fought over, hymned by patriots, and romanticized by writers that include James Joyce, Rainer Maria Rilke, Ernest Hemingway, Pier Paolo Pasolini, Italo Svevo, and Jan Morris. The region has seen Fascists and Communists, Romans, Habsburgs, and Huns. It survived by forging sheltering alliances—Udine beneath the wings of San Marco (1420), Trieste choosing Duke Leopold of Austria (1382) over Venetian domination.

Some of World War I's fiercest fighting took place in Friuli–Venezia Giulia, where memorials and cemeteries commemorate the hundreds of thousands who died before the arrival of Italian troops in 1918 finally liberated Trieste from Austrian rule. Trieste, along with the whole of Venezia Giulia, was annexed to Italy in 1920. During World War II, Germany occupied the area and placed Trieste in an administrative zone along with parts of Slovenia. The only Nazi extermination camp on Italian soil, the Risiera di San Sabba, was in a suburb of Trieste. After the war, during a period of Cold War dispute, Trieste was governed by an allied military administration; it was officially re-annexed to Italy in 1954, when Italy ceded the Istrian peninsula to the south to Yugoslavia. These arrangements were not finally ratified by Italy and Yugoslavia until 1975.

Stefano di Ferrara, working from 1425 to 1440, painted the frescoes, following the plan of frescoes by Giotto destroyed by a fire in 1420. The stunning space hosts art shows, and an enormous wooden horse, crafted for a public tournament in 1466, commands pride of place. It is patterned after the famous equestrian statue by Donatello in front of the Basilica di San Antonio, and may, in fact, have been designed by Donatello himself in the last year of his life. ⌧ *Piazza della Ragione* ☎ *049/8205006* 🎫 *Salone €4 or €6 during exhibitions (free with PadovaCard)* ☾ *Closed Mon.*

Piazza dei Signori. Some fine examples of 15th- and 16th-century build-ings line this square. On the west side, the **Palazzo del Capitanio** (facade constructed 1598–1605) has an impressive **Torre dell'Orologio,** with an astronomical clock dating from 1344 and a portal made by Falconetto in 1532 in the form of a Roman triumphal arch. The 12th-century **Battistero del Duomo** (Cathedral Baptistry), with frescoes by Giusto de Menabuoi (1374–78), is a few steps away. ✉ *Piazza dei Signori* ☎ *049/656914* 🎫 *Battistero €3 (free with PadovaCard).*

FAMILY **Villa Pisani.** Extensive grounds with rare trees, ornamental fountains, and garden follies surround this extraordinary palace in Stra, 13 km (8 miles) southeast of Padua. Built in 1721 for the Venetian doge Alvise Pisani, it recalls Versailles more than a Veneto villa. This was one of the last and grandest of many stately residences constructed along the Brenta River from the 16th to 18th century by wealthy Venetians for their *villeggiatura*—vacation and escape from the midsummer humidity. Gianbattista Tiepolo's (1696–1770) spectacular fresco on the ballroom ceiling, *The Apotheosis of the Pisani Family* (1761), alone is worth the visit. For a relaxing afternoon, explore the gorgeous park and maze. To get here from Venice, take Bus No. 53 from Piazzale Roma. The villa is a five-minute walk from the bus stop in Stra. ■TIP➔ **Musso-lini invited Hitler here for their first meeting, but they stayed only one night because of the mosquitoes, which remain. If visiting on a late afternoon in summer, carry bug repellent.** ✉ *Via Doge Pisani 7, Stra* ☎ *049/502074* ⊕ *www.villapisani.beniculturali.it* 🎫 *€7.50, €4.50 park only* ☉ *Closed Mon.*

WORTH NOTING

Abano Terme. A very popular hot-spring spa town about 12 km (7 miles) southwest of Padua, Abano Terme lies at the foot of the Euga-nean Hills among hand-tilled vineyards. If a bit of pampering sounds better than traipsing through yet another church or castle, indulge yourself with a soak, a massage, stone therapy, a skin peel, or a series of mud treatments, which are especially recommended for joint aches. The nearest railway stop, on the Bologna–Padua line, is Terme Euganee–Montegrotto. Alternatively, you can board a train on the Milan–Venice line, disembark at Padua, and board an Abano-bound bus in front of the train station. The trip takes about half an hour. ✉ *Abano Terme* ⊹ *Take the Padua West exit off A4, or the Terme Euganee exit off A13* ⊕ *www.abano.it.*

Chiesa degli Eremitani. This 13th-century church houses substantial frag-ments of Andrea Mantegna's frescoes (1448–50), which were damaged by Allied bombing in World War II. Despite their fragmentary condi-tion, Mantegna's still beautiful and historically important depictions of the martyrdom of St. James and St. Christopher show the young artist's mastery of extremely complex problems of perspective. ✉ *Piazza degli Eremitani* ☎ *049/8756410.*

Musei Civici degli Eremitani (*Civic Museum*). This former monastery now houses works of Venetian masters, as well as fine collections of archaeological finds and ancient coins. Notable are the Giotto Cruci-fix, which once hung in the Scrovegni Chapel, and the *Portrait of a*

Young Senator, by Giovanni Bellini (1430–1516). ⊠ *Piazza Eremitani 8* ☎ *049/8204551* 🖾 *€10, €13 with Scrovegni Chapel (free with PadovaCard)* ⊘ *Closed Mon.*

Fodor'sChoice
★ **Orto Botanico** (*Botanical Garden*). The Venetian Republic ordered the creation of Padua's botanical garden in 1545 to supply the university with medicinal plants, and it retains its original layout. You can stroll the arboretum—still part of the university—and wander through hothouses and beds of plants that were introduced to Italy in this late-Renaissance garden. A St. Peter's palm, planted in 1585, inspired Goethe to write his 1790 essay, "The Metamorphosis of Plants." ⊠ *Via Orto Botanico 15* ☎ *049/8273939* ⊕ *www.ortobotanico.unipd.it* 🖾 *€10 (€5 with PadovaCard)* ⊘ *Closed Mon. (except Apr. and May).*

COCKTAIL HOUR ON PADUA'S PIAZZAS

A great Padua tradition is the outdoor consumption of aperitifs—a *spritz* (a mix of Aperol or Campari, soda water, and wine), prosecco, or wine—in the Piazza delle Erbe and Piazza delle Frutta. Several bars there provide drinks in plastic cups, so you can take them outside and mingle among the crowds. The ritual, practiced primarily by students, begins at 6 or so, at which hour you can also pick up a snack from an outdoor vendor. In recent years police have begun enforcing the mandated closing time for outside consumption, so bars generally close shortly after midnight.

Palazzo del Bo'. The University of Padua, founded in 1222, centers around this predominantly16th-century palazzo with an 18th-century facade. It's named after the Osteria del Bo' (*bo'* means "ox"), an inn that once stood on the site. It's worth a visit to see the perfectly proportioned anatomy theater (1594), the beautiful "Old Courtyard," and a hall with a lectern used by Galileo. You can enter only as part of a guided tour; most guides speak English, but it is worth checking ahead by phone. ⊠ *Via 8 Febbraio* ☎ *049/8275111 university switchboard* ⊕ *www.unipd.it* 🖾 *€7* ⊘ *Closed Sun. and public holidays.*

WHERE TO EAT

$$
ITALIAN ✕**Enoteca dei Tadi.** In this cozy and atmospheric cross between a wine bar and a restaurant you can put together an inexpensive dinner from the various classic dishes from all over Italy on offer. Portions are small, but prices are reasonable—just follow the local custom and order a selection. **Known for:** compact but interesting menu; intimate and rustic; bountiful wine and grappa list. 💲 *Average main: €18* ⊠ *Via dei Tadi 16* ☎ *049/8364099, 388/4083434 mobile* ⊕ *www.enotecadeitadi.it* ⊘ *Closed Mon., and 2 wks late June–July. No lunch.*

$$
WINE BAR ✕**L'Anfora.** This mix between a traditional *bacaro* (wine bar) and an *osteria* (tavernlike restaurant) is a local institution, opened in 1922. Stand at the bar with a cross section of Padovano society, from construction workers to professors, and let the knowledgeable proprietors help you choose a wine. **Known for:** atmospheric aged

wood and art-filled osteria; no-nonsense traditional Veneto food; cozy in winter, lively in summer. $ *Average main: €19* ⊠ *Via Soncin 13* ☎ *049/656629* ☽ *Closed Sun. (except in Dec.), 1 wk in Jan., and 1 wk in Aug.*

$$$
MODERN ITALIAN
✕ **Le Calandre.** If you're willing to shell out around €600 for a dinner for two and are gastronomically adventurous but not very hungry, then consider this elegant restaurant that critics often rave about. Traditional Veneto recipes are given a highly sophisticated and creative treatment, and the whole experience can be revelatory or uncomfortably overblown. **Known for:** theatrical, sensory dining experience; playful (or to some pretentious) touches; reservations essential. $ *Average main: €245* ⊠ *Via Liguria 1, Sarmeola* ✛ *7 km (4 miles) west of Padua* ☎ *049/630303* ⊕ *www.calandre.com* ☽ *Closed Sun. and Mon., mid-Aug.–Sept., and Jan. 1–17.*

$$
VENETIAN
✕ **Osteria Dal Capo.** A friendly trattoria in the heart of what used to be Padua's Jewish ghetto serves almost exclusively traditional Veneto dishes, and it does so with refinement and care. Everything from the well-crafted dishes to the unfussy ship's dining cabin–like decor and elegant plates reflect decades of Padovano hospitality. **Known for:** intimate and understated dining; elegant Veneto food at decent prices; limited tables mean reservations essential. $ *Average main: €21* ⊠ *Via degli Oblizzi 2* ☎ *049/663105* ☽ *Closed Sun. No lunch Mon.*

WHERE TO STAY

$
HOTEL
⛫ **Al Fagiano.** The delightfully funky surroundings in this boutique hotel include sponge-painted walls, brush-painted chandeliers, and some views of the spires and cupolas of the Basilica di Sant'Antonio. **Pros:** large rooms; relaxed atmosphere; convenient location; free Wi-Fi. **Cons:** no room service or help with baggage; some find the eccentric decoration a bit much. $ *Rooms from: €82* ⊠ *Via Locatelli 45* ☎ *049/8750073* ⊕ *www.alfagiano.com* ⇆ *40 rooms* ⦿ *No meals.*

$
HOTEL
⛫ **Albergo Verdi.** One of the best-situated hotels in the city provides tastefully renovated rooms and public areas that tend toward the minimalist without being severe; they also have the rare virtue of being absolutely quiet. **Pros:** excellent location close to the Piazza dei Signori; attentive staff; discounts available depending on time of year. **Cons:** hefty parking fee; few views; charge for Wi-Fi. $ *Rooms from: €110* ⊠ *Via Dondi dell'Orologio 7* ☎ *049/8364163* ⊕ *www.albergoverdipadova.it* ⇆ *14 rooms* ⦿ *Free Breakfast.*

$$
HOTEL
⛫ **Methis.** Four floors of sleekly designed guest rooms reflect the elements: gentle earth tones, fiery red, watery cool blue, and airy white in the top-floor suites. **Pros:** better breakfast than usual for Italy; helpful and attentive staff; pleasant extras such as umbrellas. **Cons:** a 15-minute walk from major sights and restaurants; uninviting public spaces. $ *Rooms from: €134* ⊠ *Riviera Paleocapa 70* ☎ *049/8725555* ⊕ *www.methishotel.com* ⇆ *59 rooms* ⦿ *Free Breakfast.*

NIGHTLIFE

Fodor'sChoice   **Caffè Pedrocchi.** No visit to Padua is complete without taking time to sit
★   in this massive café, as the French novelist Stendhal did shortly after
it was established, in 1831. Nearly 200 years later, it remains central to the city's social life. The café was built in the Egyptian Revival
style, which became popular after Napoléon's expeditions in Egypt.
The accomplished restaurant serves only lunch regularly, and dinner
on special occasions, and is proud of its innovative menu. ✉ *Piazzetta
Pedrocchi* ☎ *049/8781231* ⊕ *www.caffepedrocchi.it.*

VERONA

On the banks of the fast-flowing River Adige, enchanting Verona, 60
km (37 miles) west of Vicenza, has timeless monuments, a picturesque
town center, fascinating museums, and a romantic reputation as the
setting of Shakespeare's *Romeo and Juliet.* Verona grew to power and
prosperity within the Roman Empire as a result of its key commercial
and military position in northern Italy. With its Roman arena, theater,
and city gates, it has the most significant monuments of Roman antiquity north of Rome. After the fall of the empire, the city continued
to flourish under the guidance of barbarian kings such as Theodoric,
Alboin, Pepin, and Berenger I. It reached its cultural and artistic peak
in the 13th and 14th centuries under the della Scala (Scaligeri) dynasty.
(Look for the *scala,* or ladder, emblem all over town.) In 1404 Verona
traded its independence for security and placed itself under the control
of Venice. (The other recurring architectural motif is the lion of St.
Mark, a symbol of Venetian rule.)

With its lively Venetian air and proximity to Lake Garda, Verona attracts
many tourists, especially Germans and Austrians. Tourism peaks during
summer's renowned season of open-air opera in the arena and during
spring's Vinitaly, one of the world's most important wine and spirits expos.

If you're going to visit more than one or two sights, it's worth purchasing a VeronaCard, available at museums, churches, and tobacconists
for €18 (for 24 hours) or €22 (72 hours). It buys a single admission
to most of the city's significant museums and churches, plus you can
ride for free on city buses. If you're mostly interested in churches, a €6
Chiese Vive Card is sold at Verona's major houses of worship and gains
you entry to the Duomo, San Fermo Maggiore, San Zeno Maggiore,
and Sant'Anastasia (all also covered also by the VeronaCard). Verona's
churches enforce a dress code: no sleeveless shirts, shorts, or short skirts.

GETTING HERE AND AROUND

Verona is midway between Venice and Milan. Its small Aeroporto Valerio Catullo accommodates domestic and European flights, though many
travelers fly into Venice or Milan and drive or take the train to Verona.
Several trains per hour depart from any point on the Milan–Venice
line. By car, from the east or west, take the Autostrada Trieste–Torino
(A4/E70) to the SS12 and follow it north into town. From the north or
south, take the Autostrada del Brennero (A22/E45) to the SR11 East
(initially, called the Strada Bresciana) directly into town.

FESTIVALS

Vinitaly. This widely attended international wine and spirits event takes place for five days in April. Recent editions have attracted more than 4,000 exhibitors from two dozen countries. The festivities kick off with **Opera Wine** (⊕ *www.operawine.it*), a showcase for the top 100 Italian wines, as chosen by *Wine Spectator* magazine, that takes place in the Palazzo della Gran Guardia, in Piazza Bra. ⊠ *Fiera di Verona, Viale del Lavoro 8* ☎ *045/8101447* ⊕ *www.vinitaly.com.*

VISITOR INFORMATION

Contacts Verona Tourism Office (IAT Verona). ⊠ *Via degli Alpini 9, Piazza Bra* ⊕ *www.tourism.verona.it.* **VeronaCard.** ⊕ *www.turismoverona.eu.*

EXPLORING

In addition to ancient Verona's famous arena and Roman theater, two of its city gates and a beautiful triumphal arch—Porta dei Leoni, Porta dei Borsari, and Arco dei Gavi—have survived. These graceful and elegant portals provide an idea of the high aesthetic standards of the time.

5

TOP ATTRACTIONS

Fodor'sChoice ★ **Arco dei Gavi.** This stunning structure is simpler and less imposing, but also more graceful, than the triumphal arches in Rome. Built in the 1st century AD by the architect Lucius Vitruvius Cerdo to celebrate the accomplishments of the patrician Gavia family, it was highly esteemed by several Renaissance architects, including Palladio. ⊠ *Corso Cavour.*

FAMILY **Arena di Verona.** Only Rome's Colosseum and Capua's arena would dwarf this amphitheater, built for gymnastic competitions, choreographed sacrificial rites, and games involving hunts, fights, battles, and wild animals. Although four arches are all that remain of the arena's outer arcade, the main structure is complete and dates from AD 30. In summer, you can join up to 16,000 people packing the stands for spectacular opera productions. Even those not crazy about opera can sit in the stands and enjoy Italians enjoying themselves—including, at times, singing along with their favorite hits. ■TIP→ **The opera's the main thing here: when there is no opera performance, you can still enter the interior, but the arena is less impressive inside than the Colosseum or other Roman amphitheaters.** ⊠ *Piazza Bra 5* ☎ *045/8003204* ⊕ *www.arena.it* ☑ *€10 (free with VeronaCard)* ۞ *Closed Mon. in Oct.–May.*

Fodor'sChoice ★ **Castelvecchio.** This crenellated, russet brick building with massive walls, towers, turrets, and a vast courtyard was built for Cangrande II della Scala in 1354 and presides over a street lined with attractive old buildings and palaces of the nobility. Only by going inside the **Museo di Castelvecchio** can you really appreciate this massive castle complex with its vaulted halls. You also get a look at a significant collection of Venetian and Veneto art, medieval weapons, and jewelry. The interior of the castle was restored and redesigned as a museum between 1958 and 1975 by Carlo Scarpa, one of Italy's most accomplished architects. Behind the castle is the Ponte Scaligero (1355), which spans the River Adige. ⊠ *Corso Castelvecchio 2* ☎ *045/8062611* ☑ *€6 (free with VeronaCard).*

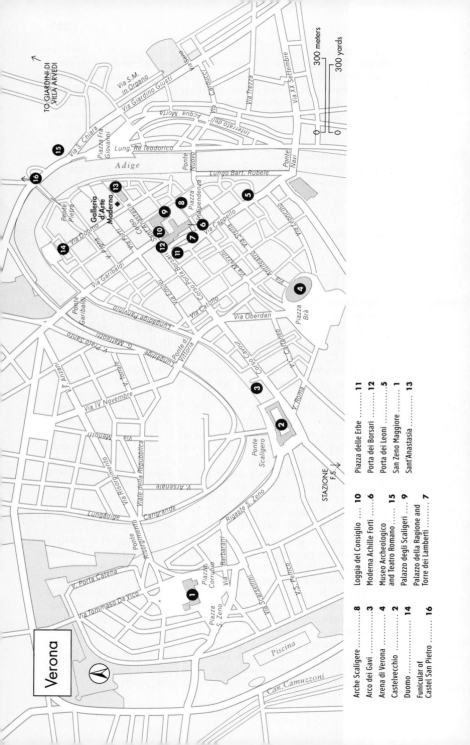

Verona

Arche Scaligere **8**
Arco dei Gavi **3**
Arena di Verona **4**
Castelvecchio **2**
Duomo **14**
Funicular of
Castel San Pietro **16**

Loggia del Consiglio **10**
Moderna Achille Forti **6**
Museo Archeologico
and Teatro Romano **15**
Palazzo degli Scaligeri **9**
Palazzo della Ragione and
Torre dei Lamberti **7**

Piazza delle Erbe **11**
Porta dei Borsari **12**
Porta dei Leoni **5**
San Zeno Maggiore **1**
Sant'Anastasia **13**

300 meters
300 yards

STAZIONE
F.S.

TO GIARDINI DI
VILLA ARVEDI

Duomo. The present church was begun in the 12th century in the Romanesque style; its later additions are mostly Gothic. On pilasters guarding the main entrance are 12th-century carvings thought to represent Oliver and Roland, two of Charlemagne's knights and heroes of several medieval epic poems. Inside, Titian's *Assumption* (1532) graces the first chapel on the left. ⊠ *Via Duomo* ☎ *045/592813* ⊕ *www.chieseverona. it* ⌨ *€3 (free with Chiese Vive or VeronaCard).*

FAMILY
Fodor's Choice
★

Funicular of Castel San Pietro. Opened in 2017, this funicular ride ascends 500 feet from near Teatro Romano up to a panoramic terrace, affording fabulous Veronese views and access to walks around the city walls. ⊠ *Via Fontanelle S. Stefano* ⊕ *www.agec.it* ⌨ *€2 return trip.*

Piazza delle Erbe. Frescoed buildings surround this medieval square, where a busy Roman forum once stood. During the week it's still bustling, as vendors sell produce and trinkets, much as they have been doing for generations. Relax at one of the cafés and take in the lively scene. ⊠ *Verona.*

Fodor's Choice
★

Porta dei Borsari. As its elegant decoration suggests, this is the main entrance to ancient Verona, and, in its present state, dates from the 1st century AD. It's at the beginning of Corso Porta Borsari, near Piazza della Erbe. ⊠ *Corso Porta Borsari.*

Porta dei Leoni. The oldest of Verona's elegant and graceful Roman portals, the Porta dei Leoni (on Via Leoni, just a few steps from Piazza delle Erbe), dates from the 1st century BC, but its original earth-and-brick structure was sheathed in local marble during early Imperial times. Like the city's other Roman structures, the gate gives us an idea of the high aesthetic standards of the time. ⊠ *Via Leoni.*

Fodor's Choice
★

San Zeno Maggiore. One of Italy's finest Romanesque churches is filled with treasures. A rose window by the 13th-century sculptor Brioloto represents a wheel of fortune, with six of the spokes formed by statues depicting the rising and falling fortunes of mankind. The 12th-century porch is the work of Maestro Niccolò; it's flanked by marble reliefs by Niccolò and Maestro Guglielmo depicting scenes from the Old and New Testaments and from the legend of Theodoric. The bronze doors date from the 11th and 12th centuries; some were probably imported from Saxony and some are from Veronese workshops. They combine allegorical representations with scenes from the lives of saints. Inside, look for the 12th-century statue of San Zeno to the left of the main altar. In modern times it has been dubbed the "Laughing San Zeno" because of a misinterpretation of its conventional Romanesque grin. A justly famous *Madonna and Saints* triptych by Andrea Mantegna (1431–1506) hangs over the main altar, and a peaceful cloister (1120–38) lies to the left of the nave. The detached bell tower was begun in 1045, before the construction of much of the present church, and finished in 1173. ⊠ *Piazza San Zeno* ☎ *045/592813* ⊕ *www.chieseverona.it* ⌨ *€3 (free with Chiese Vive or VeronaCard).*

Sant'Anastasia. Verona's largest church, begun in 1290 but only consecrated in 1471, is a fine example of Gothic brickwork and has a grand doorway with elaborately carved biblical scenes. The main reason for visiting this church, however, is *St. George and the Princess* (dated

5

1434, but perhaps earlier) by Pisanello (1377–1455). It's above the Pellegrini Chapel off the main altar. As you come in, look also for the *gobbi* (hunchbacks) supporting the holy-water basins. ✉ *Vicolo Sotto Riva 4* ☎ *045/592813* 🎟 *€3 (free with Chiese Vive or VeronaCard).*

WORTH NOTING

Arche Scaligere. On a little square off the Piazza dei Signori are the fantastically sculpted Gothic tombs of the della Scalas, who ruled Verona during the late Middle Ages. The 19th-century English traveler and critic John Ruskin described the tombs as graceful places where people who have fallen asleep live. The tomb of Cangrande I (1291–1329) hangs over the portal of the adjacent church and is the work of the Maestro di Sant'Anastasia. The tomb of Mastino II, begun in 1345, has an elaborate baldachin, originally painted and gilded, and is surrounded by an iron grillwork fence and topped by an equestrian statue. The latest and most elaborate tomb is that of Cansignorio (1375), the work principally of Bonino di Campione. The major tombs are all visible from the street. ✉ *Via Arche Scaligere.*

Loggia del Consiglio. This graceful structure on the north flank of the Piazza dei Signori was finished in 1492 and built to house city council meetings. Although the city was already under Venetian rule, Verona still had a certain degree of autonomy, which was expressed by the splendor of the loggia. Very strangely for a Renaissance building of this quality, its architect remains unknown, but it's the finest surviving example of late-15th-century architecture in Verona. The building is not open to the public, but the exterior is worth a visit. ✉ *Piazza dei Signori.*

Museo Archeologico and Teatro Romano. The archaeological holdings of this museum in a 15th-century former monastery consist largely of the donated collections of Veronese citizens proud of their city's classical past. You'll find few blockbusters here, but there are some noteworthy pieces (especially among the bronzes), and it is interesting to see what cultured Veronese collected between the 17th and 19th century. The museum complex includes the Teatro Romano, Verona's 1st-century-AD theater, which is open to visitors. ✉ *Rigaste del Redentore 2* ☎ *045/8000360* ⊕ *museoarcheologico.comune.verona.it* 🎟 *€4.50 (free with VeronaCard).*

Palazzo degli Scaligeri (*Palazzo di Cangrande*). The della Scalas ruled Verona from this stronghold, built at the end of the 13th century by Cangrande I. At that time Verona controlled the mainland Veneto from Treviso and Lombardy to Mantua and Brescia. The portal facing the Piazza dei Signori was added in 1533 by the accomplished Renaissance architect Michele Sanmicheli. You have to admire the palazzo from the outside, as it's not open to the public. ✉ *Piazza dei Signori.*

Palazzo della Ragione and Torre dei Lamberti. An elegant 15th-century pink marble staircase leads up from the *mercato vecchio* (old market) courtyard to the magistrates' chambers in this 12th-century palace, built at the intersection of the main streets of the ancient Roman city. The interior now houses exhibitions of art from the **Galleria dell'Arte Moderna Achille Forti** . You can get the highest view in town from atop the attached 270-foot-high, Romanesque Torre dei Lamberti. About 50 years after a lightning strike in 1403 knocked its top off, it was rebuilt and extended to its current height. ✉ *Piazza dei Signori* ☎ *045/9273027* 🎫 *Gallery and tower €8 (free with VeronaCard).*

WHERE TO EAT

$$ NORTHERN ITALIAN Fodor's Choice ★ 🍴 **Antica Osteria al Duomo.** This side-street eatery, lined with old wood paneling and decked out with musical instruments, serves traditional Veronese classics; mainstays include *bigoli* (thick whole-wheat spaghetti) with donkey ragù and *pastissada con polenta* (horse meat stew with polenta). Don't be deterred by the unconventional meats—they're tender and delicious, and this is probably the best place in town to sample them. **Known for:** blackboard menu, osteria bar, and wooden interiors; occasional live music; various nutritious horse meat dishes. [$] *Average main: €19* ✉ *Via Duomo 7/A* ☎ *045/8004505* 🕒 *Closed Sun. (except in Dec. and during wine fair).*

$$$$ MODERN ITALIAN Fodor's Choice ★ 🍴 **Il Desco.** *Cucina dell'anima*—food of the soul—is how chef Elia Rizzo describes his cuisine. True to Italian culinary traditions, he preserves natural flavors through quick cooking and selective ingredients, but tradition gives way to invention, even daring, in the combination of ingredients in dishes such as dumplings with cod tripe and black olives. **Known for:** inventive, colorful plates of food; elegant, arty surroundings fit for a modern opera; warm welcome from the Rizzos and team. [$] *Average main: €50* ✉ *Via Dietro San Sebastiano 7* ☎ *045/595358* 🌐 *www.ristoranteildesco.it* 🕒 *Closed Sun. and Mon. (but open for dinner Mon. in July, Aug., and Dec.).*

$$$ NORTHERN ITALIAN 🍴 **Ristorante 12 Apostoli.** In a city where many high-end restaurants tend toward nouvelle cuisine, this is an exceptional place to enjoy classic dishes made with elegant variations on traditional recipes. Near Piazza delle Erbe, it stands on the foundations of a Roman temple. **Known for:** elegant, atmospheric rooms and cantina; slow and sumptuous dining. [$] *Average main: €30* ✉ *Vicolo Corticella San Marco 3* ☎ *045/596999* 🌐 *www.12apostoli.com* 🕒 *Closed Mon., 2 wks in Jan., and 2 wks in June. No dinner Sun.*

WHERE TO STAY

Book hotels far in advance if you'll be in town during spring's Vinitaly, usually held in mid-April, and for opera season. Verona hotels are also very busy during the January, May, and September gold fairs in neighboring Vicenza. Hotels jack up prices considerably at all these times.

$$$ HOTEL 🏨 **Hotel Accademia.** The exterior columns and arches of this hotel in old Verona hint at what guests discover inside: elegance, gracious service, and comfortable, traditional furnishings. **Pros:** central location; old-world charm; up-to-date. **Cons:** expensive parking; prices increase greatly during summer opera season and trade fairs. [$] *Rooms from: €235* ✉ *Via Scala 12* ☎ *045/596222* 🌐 *www.accademiavr.it* 🛏 *95 rooms* 🍽 *Free Breakfast.*

5

$$$ HOTEL **Palazzo Victoria.** Business types and tourists experience tasteful luxury at the Victoria, whose rooms blend traditional and contemporary style. **Pros:** quiet and tasteful rooms; central location near the Piazza delle Erbe; good business center. **Cons:** no views; expensive parking (and rates); staff not particularly helpful. [$] *Rooms from: €300* ✉ *Via Adua 8* ☎ *045/5905664* 🌐 *www.palazzovictoria.com* 🛏 *74 rooms* 🍴 *Free Breakfast.*

$$ HOTEL **Torcolo.** In addition to a central location close to the arena and Piazza Bra, you can count on this budget choice for a warm welcome, helpful service, and pleasant rooms with late-19th-century furniture. **Pros:** nice rooms; staff give reliable advice. **Cons:** some street noise; showers but no tubs; pricey parking. [$] *Rooms from: €136* ✉ *Vicolo Listone 3* ☎ *045/8007512* 🌐 *www.hoteltorcolo.it* ⏲ *Closed 2 wks in Jan. and Feb.* 🛏 *19 rooms* 🍴 *No meals.*

PERFORMING ARTS

Fodor's Choice ★ **Arena di Verona.** Milan's La Scala and Parma's Teatro Regio offer performances more likely to attract serious opera fans, but neither offers a greater spectacle than the Arena di Verona. Many Italian opera lovers claim their enthusiasm began when they were taken as children to a production at the arena. During the venue's summer season (July to September) as many as 16,000 attendees sit on the original stone terraces or in modern cushioned stalls. Most of the operas presented are the big, splashy ones, like *Aida* or *Turandot,* which demand huge choruses, lots of color and movement, and, if possible, camels, horses, or elephants. Order tickets by phone or through the Arena website: if you book a spot on the cheaper terraces, be sure to take or rent a cushion—four hours on a 2,000-year-old stone bench can be an ordeal. ✉ *Box office, Via Dietro Anfiteatro 6/b* ☎ *045/8005151* 🌐 *www.arena.it* 🎟 *From €24 (for unnumbered, open seating).*

VICENZA

A visit to Vicenza is a must for any student or fan of architecture. This elegant, prosperous city bears the distinctive signature of the architect Andrea Palladio (1508–80), whose name has been given to the "Palladian" style of architecture.

Palladio emphasized the principles of order and harmony using the classical style of architecture established by Renaissance architects such as Brunelleschi, Alberti, and Sansovino. He used these principles and classical motifs not only for public buildings but also for private dwellings. His elegant villas and palaces were influential in propagating classical architecture in Europe, especially Britain, and later in America—most notably at Thomas Jefferson's Monticello.

In the mid-16th century Palladio was commissioned to rebuild much of Vicenza, which had been greatly damaged during wars waged against Venice by the League of Cambrai (1505), an alliance of the papacy, France, the Holy Roman Empire, and several neighboring city-states. He made his name with the renovation of Palazzo della Ragione, begun in 1549 in the heart of Vicenza, and then embarked on a series of noble buildings, all of which adhere to the same principles of classicism and harmony.

GETTING HERE AND AROUND

Vicenza is midway between Padua and Verona, and several trains leave from both cities every hour. By car, take the Autostrada Brescia–Padova/Torino–Trieste (A4/E70) to SP247 North directly into Vicenza.

VISITOR INFORMATION

Contact **Vicenza Tourism Office.** ⊠ *Piazza Giacomo Matteotti 12* ☎ *0444/320854* ⊕ *www.vicenzae.org.*

EXPLORING

TOP ATTRACTIONS

Palazzo Barbaran da Porto (Palladio Museum). Palladio executed this beautiful city palace for the Vicentine noble Montano Barbarano between 1570 and 1575. The noble patron, however, did not make things easy for Palladio; the plan had to incorporate at least two preexisting medieval houses, with irregularly shaped rooms, into his classical, harmonious plan, and to support the great hall of the *piano nobile* above the fragile walls of the original medieval structure. The wonder of it is that this palazzo is one of Palladio's most harmonious constructions; the viewer has little indication that this is actually a transformation of a medieval structure. The palazzo also contains a museum dedicated to Palladio and is the seat of a center for Palladian studies. ⊠ *Contra' Porti 11* ☎ *0444/323014* ⊕ *www.palladiomuseum.org* ⌨*€8; €15 Museum Card includes Palazzo Chiericati and Teatro Olimpico, plus other museums in Musei Civici group* ⊗ *Closed Mon.*

Fodor's Choice ★ **Teatro Olimpico.** Palladio's last, and perhaps most spectacular work, was begun in 1580 and completed in 1585, after his death, by Vincenzo Scamozzi (1552–1616). Based closely on the model of ancient Roman theaters, it represents an important development in theater and stage design and is noteworthy for its acoustics and the cunning use of perspective in Scamozzi's permanent backdrop. The anterooms are frescoed with images of important figures in Venetian history. One of the few Renaissance theaters still standing, it is used for concerts, operas, and other performances. ⊠ *Ticket office, Piazza Matteotti 12* ☎ *0444/222800* ⊕ *www.teatrolimpico.it* ⌨*€11; €15, includes Palazzo Chiericati and Palazzo Barbaran da Porto, plus other museums in Musei Civici group* ⊗ *Closed Mon.*

Fodor's Choice ★ **Villa della Rotonda** (*Villa Almerico Capra*). This beautiful Palladian villa, commissioned in 1556 as a suburban residence for Paolo Almerico, is the purest expression of Palladio's architectural theory and aesthetic. More a villa-temple than a residence, it contradicts the rational utilitarianism of Renaissance architecture and demonstrates the priority Palladio gave to the architectural symbolism of celestial harmony over practical considerations. A visit to view the interior can be difficult to schedule (mid March–early November: Wednesday and Saturday only)—the villa remains privately owned—but this is a worthwhile stop, if only to see how Palladio's harmonious arrangement of smallish, interconnected rooms around a central domed space paid little attention to the practicalities of living. The interior decoration, mainly later Baroque stuccowork, contains some allegorical frescoes in the cupola by Palladio's contemporary, Alessando Maganza. Even without a peek inside, experiencing the exterior and the grounds is a must for any visit to Vicenza, although the interiors are only open March 10–November 10 on Wednesday and Saturday. The villa is a 20-minute walk from town or a short ride on Bus No. 8 from Vicenza's Piazza Roma. Private tours by appointment only, see website for details. ⊠ *Via della Rotonda* ☎ *0444/321793* ⊕ *www.villalarotonda.it* ⊠ *€10 villa and grounds, €5 grounds only* ⊘ *Closed Mon.*

Fodor's Choice
★

Villa Valmarana ai Nani. Inside this 17th- to 18th-century country house, named for the statues of dwarfs adorning the garden, is a series of frescoes executed in 1757 by Gianbattista Tiepolo depicting scenes from classical mythology, *The Iliad,* Tasso's *Gerusalemme Liberata,* and Ariosto's *Orlando Furioso.* They include his *Sacrifice of Iphigenia,* a major masterpiece of 18th-century painting. The neighboring *foresteria* (guesthouse) is also part of the museum; it contains frescoes showing 18th-century life at its most charming, and scenes of chinoiserie popular in the 18th century, by Tiepolo's son Giandomenico (1727–1804). The garden dwarfs are probably taken from designs by Giandomenico. You can reach the villa on foot by following the same path that leads to Palladio's Villa della Rotonda. ⊠ *Via dei Nani 2/8* ☎ *0444/321803* ⊕ *www.villavalmarana.com* ⊠ *€10.*

WORTH NOTING

Palazzo Chiericati. This imposing Palladian palazzo (1550) would be worthy of a visit even if it didn't house Vicenza's **Museo Civico.** Because of the ample space surrounding the building, Palladio combined elements of an urban palazzo with those he used in his country villas. The museum's important Venetian holdings include significant paintings by Cima, Tiepolo, Piazzetta, and Tintoretto, but its main attraction is an extensive collection of rarely found works by painters from the Vicenza area, among them Jacopo Bassano (1515–92) and the eccentric and innovative Francesco Maffei (1605–60), whose work foreshadowed important currents of Venetian painting of subsequent generations. ⊠ *Piazza Matteotti* ☎ *0444/325071* ⊠ *€7; €15, includes Palazzo Barbaran da Porto and Teatro Olimpico, plus other museums in Musei Civici group.*

Piazza dei Signori. At the heart of Vicenza, this square contains the **Palazzo della Ragione** (1549), the project with which Palladio made his name by successfully modernizing a medieval building, grafting a graceful two-story exterior loggia onto the existing Gothic structure. Commonly known as Palladio's basilica, the palazzo served as a courthouse and public meeting hall (the original Roman meaning of the term *basilica*) and is now open only when it houses exhibits. The main point of interest, though, the loggia, is visible from the piazza. Take a look also at the **Loggia del Capitaniato,** opposite, which Palladio designed but never completed. ⊠ *Vicenza.*

Palazzo Barbaran da Porto (Palladio Museum) **7**
Palazzo Chiericati **3**
Piazza dei Signori **1**
Santa Corona **6**
Teatro Olimpico **2**
Villa della Rotonda **4**
Villa Valmarana ai Nani **5**

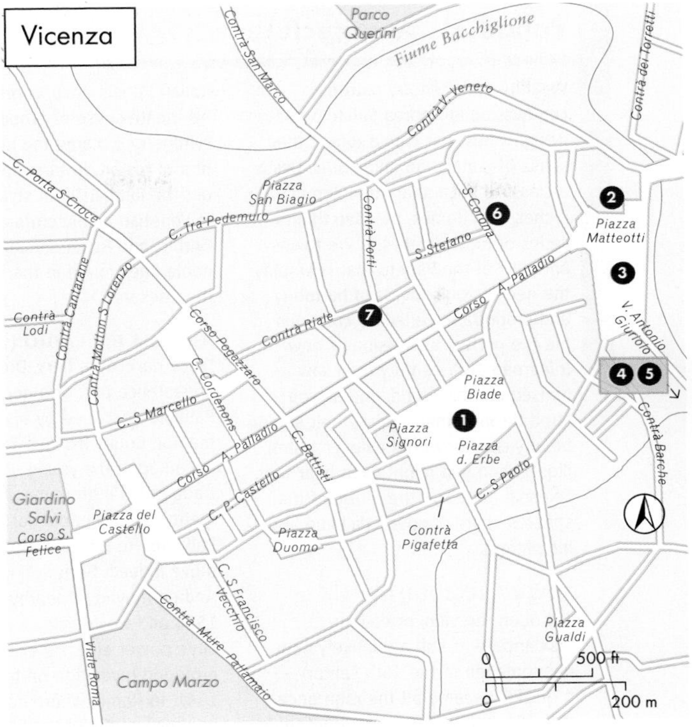

Santa Corona. An exceptionally fine *Baptism of Christ* (1502), a work of Giovanni Bellini's maturity, hangs over the altar on the left, just in front of the transept. The church also houses the elegantly simple Valmarana chapel, designed by Palladio. ✉ *Contrà S. Corona* ☎ *0444/222811* 🎫 *€3 (free with Musei Civici pass)* ⏲ *Closed Mon.*

WHERE TO EAT

$ PIZZA

🍴 **Da Vittorio.** You'll find little in the way of atmosphere or style at this tiny, casual place, but Vicentini flock here for what may be the best pizza north of Naples. There's an incredible array of toppings, from the traditional to the exotic (mango), but the pizzas taste so authentic you may feel transported to the Bay of Naples. **Known for:** authentic wood-fired Neapolitan pizza; cheery naive artworks; tables packed tightly makes for a warm atmosphere. [$] *Average main: €12* ✉ *Borgo Berga 52* ☎ *0444/525059* 💳 *No credit cards* ⏲ *Closed Tues., and 2 wks in July. No dinner Sun.*

$$ NORTHERN ITALIAN

🍴 **Ponte delle Bele.** Many of Vicenza's wealthier residents spend at least part of the summer in the Alps to escape the heat, and the dishes of this popular and friendly trattoria reflect the Alpine influences on local cuisine. The house specialty, *stinco di maiale al forno* (roast pork shank), is wonderfully fragrant, with herbs and aromatic vegetables. **Known**

Palladio's Architecture

Wealthy 16th-century patrons commissioned Andrea Palladio to design villas that would reflect their sense of cultivation and status. Using a classical vocabulary of columns, arches, and domes, he gave them a series of masterpieces in the towns and hills of the Veneto that exemplify the neo-Platonic ideals of harmony and proportion. Palladio's creations are the perfect expression of how a learned 16th-century man saw himself and his world, and as you stroll through them today, their serene beauty is as powerful as ever. Listen closely and you might even hear that celestial harmony, the music of the spheres, that so moved Palladio and his patrons.

TOWN AND COUNTRY

Although the *villa*, or country residence, was still a relatively new phenomenon in the 16th century, it quickly became all the rage once the great lords of Venice turned their eyes from the sea toward the fertile plains of the Veneto. They were forced to do this once their trade routes had faltered when Ottoman Turks conquered Constantinople in 1456 and Columbus opened a path for Spain to the riches of America in 1492. In no time, canals were built, farms were laid out, and the fashion for *villeggiatura*—the attraction of idyllic country retreats for the nobility—became a favored lifestyle. As a means of escaping an overheated Rome, villas had been the original brainchild of the ancient emperors and it was no accident that the Venetian lords wished to emulate this palatial style of country residence. Palladio's method of evaluating the standards, and standbys, of ancient Roman life through the eye of the

Italian Renaissance, combined with his innate sense of proportion and symmetry, became the lasting foundation of his art. In turn, Palladio threw out the jambalaya of styles prevalent in Venetian architecture—Byzantine, Gothic, and Renaissance—for the pure, noble lines found in the buildings of the Caesars.

ANDREA PALLADIO (1508–80)

"Face dark, eyes fiery. Dress rich. His appearance that of a genius." So was Palladio described by his wealthy mentor, Count Trissino. Trissino encouraged the young student to trade in his birth name, Andrea di Pietro della Gondola, for the elegant Palladio. He did, and it proved a wise move indeed. Born in Padua in 1508, Andrea moved to nearby Vicenza in 1524 and was quickly taken up by the city's power elite. He experienced a profound revelation on his first trip, in 1541, to Rome, where he sensed the harmony of the ancient ruins and saw the elements of classicism that were working their way into contemporary architecture. This experience led to his spectacular conversion of the Vicenza's Palazzo della Ragione into a Roman basilica, recalling the great meeting halls of antiquity. In years to come, after relocating to Venice, he created some memorable churches, such as S. Giorgio Maggiore (1564). Despite these varied projects, Palladio's unassailable position as one of the world's greatest architects is tied to the countryside villas, which he spread across the Veneto plains like a firmament of stars. Nothing else in the Veneto illuminates more clearly the idyllic beauty of the region than these elegant residences, their stonework now nicely mellowed and suntanned after five centuries.

VICENZIA

To see Palladio's pageant of palaces, head for Vicenza. His Palazzo della Ragione marks the city's heart, the Piazza dei Signori. This building rocketed young Palladio from an unknown to an architectural star. Across the way is his redbrick Loggia dei Capitaniato. One block past the Loggia is Vicenza's main street, appropriately named Corso Andrea Palladio. Just off this street is the Contrà Porti, where you'll find the Palazzo Barbaran da Porto (1570) at No. 11, with its fabulously rich facade erupting with Ionic and Corinthian pillars. Today, this is the Centro Internazionale di Studi di Architettura Andrea Palladio (⊕ *www. cisapalladio.org*), a study center which mounts impressive temporary exhibitions. A few steps away, on the Contrà San Gaetano Thiene, is the Palazzo Thiene (1542–58), designed by Giulio Romano and completed by Palladio. Doubling back to Contrà Porti 21, you find the Palazzo Iseppo da Porto (1544), the first palazzo where you can see the neoclassical effects of young Palladio's trip to Rome. Following the Contrà Reale, you come to Corso Fogazzaro 16 and the Palazzo Valmarana Braga (1565). Its gigantic pilasters were a first for domestic architecture. Returning to the Corso Palladio, head left to the opposite end of the Corso, about five blocks, to the Piazza Matteotti and Palazzo Chiericati (1550). This was practically a suburban area in the 16th century, and for the palazzo Palladio combined elements of urban and rural design. The pedestal raising the building and the steps leading to the entrance—unknown in urban palaces—were to protect from floods and to keep cows from wandering in the front door.

Across the Corso Palladio is Palladio's last and one of his most spectacular works, the Teatro Olimpico (1580). By careful study of ancient ruins and architectural texts, he reconstructed a Roman theater with archaeological precision. Palladio died before it was completed, but he left clear plans for the project. Although it's on the outskirts of town, the Villa Almerico Capra, better known as La Rotonda (1566), is an indispensable part of any visit to Vicenza. It's the iconic Palladian building, the purest expression of his aesthetic.

PALLADIO COUNTRY

At the Villa Barbaro (1554) near the town of Maser in the province of Treviso, 48 km (30 miles) northeast of Vicenza, you can see the results of a onetime collaboration between two of the greatest artists of their age. Palladio was the architect, and Paolo Veronese decorated the interior with an amazing cycle of trompe-l'oeil frescoes—walls dissolve into landscapes, and illusions of courtiers and servants enter rooms and smile down from balustrades. Legend has it a feud developed between Palladio and Veronese, with Palladio feeling the illusionistic frescoes detracted from his architecture; but there is practically nothing to support the idea of such a rift. It's also noteworthy that Palladio for the first time connected the two lateral granaries to the main villa. This was a working farm, and Palladio thus created an architectural unity by connecting with graceful arcades the working parts of the estate to the living quarters, bringing together the Renaissance dichotomy of the active and the contemplative life.

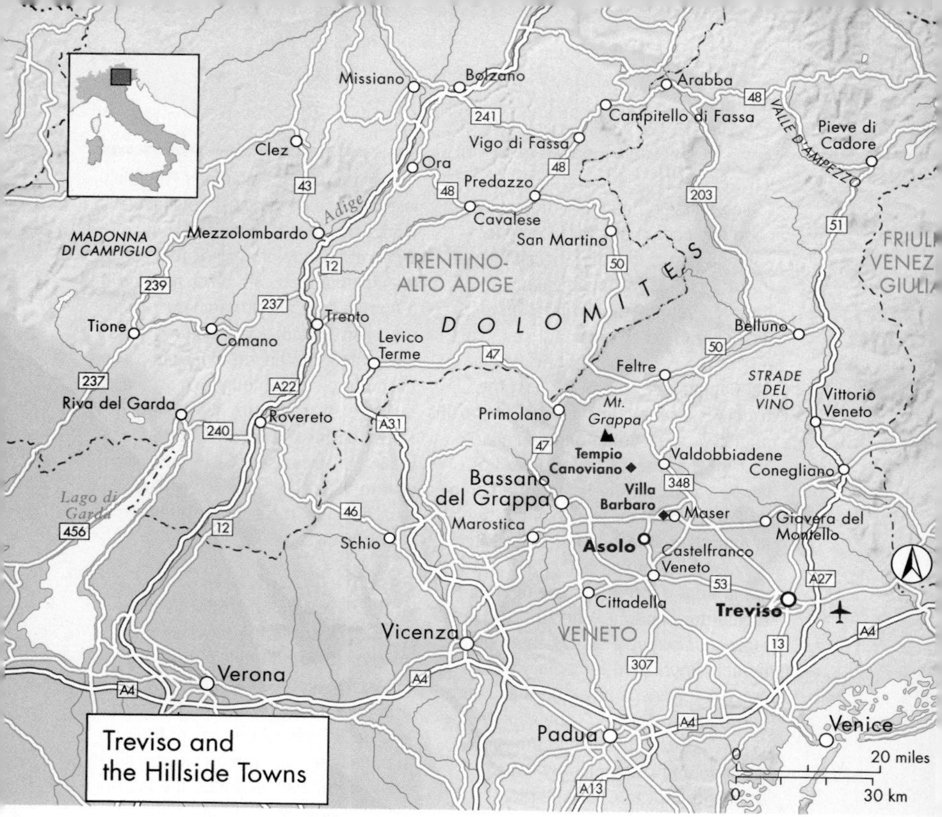
Treviso and
the Hillside Towns
Missiano
Bolzano
Arabba
Campitello di Fassa
Vigo di Fassa
Pieve di Cadore
VALLE D'AMPEZZO
Clez
Ora
Predazzo
Cavalese
San Martino
MADONNA DI CAMPIGLIO
Mezzolombardo
Adige
TRENTINO-ALTO ADIGE
DOLOMITES
FRIULI VENEZ GIULIA
Tione
Comano
Trento
Levico Terme
Belluno
Feltre
STRADE DEL VINO
Vittorio Veneto
Riva del Garda
Rovereto
Primolano
Mt. Grappa
Tempio Canoviano
Valdobbiadene
Conegliano
Bassano del Grappa
Villa Barbaro
Maser
Giavera del Montello
Lago di Garda
Marostica
Schio
Asolo
Castelfranco Veneto
Cittadella
Treviso
Vicenza
VENETO
Verona
Padua
Venice
0
20 miles
0
30 km
241
48
43
203
51
12
50
239
237
47
A22
A31
240
348
46
456
53
A27
A4
13
307
A13

for: hearty Vicentina classics including baccalà; unfussy, relaxed atmosphere; mountain cheeses and cold cuts. [$] *Average main: €17* ✉ *Contrà Ponte delle Bele 5* ☎ *0444/320647* 🌐 *www.pontedellebele.it* 🕓 *Closed Sun. and 2 wks in Aug.*

$ ITALIAN 🍴 **Righetti.** For a city of its size, Vicenza has few outstanding restaurants. That's why many people gravitate to this popular cafeteria, which serves well-prepared classic dishes without putting a dent in your wallet. **Known for:** self-service explained by the locals; very popular especially lunch; entertaining local atmosphere. [$] *Average main: €12* ✉ *Piazza Duomo 3* ☎ *0444/543135* 💳 *No credit cards* 🕓 *Closed weekends, and 1 wk in Jan. and Aug.*

WHERE TO STAY

During annual gold fairs in January, May, and September, it may be quite difficult to find lodging. If you're coming then, be sure to reserve well in advance and expect to pay higher rates.

$$ HOTEL 🏨 **Campo Marzio.** Rooms at this comfortable, full-service hotel, a five-minute walk from the train station and right in front of the city walls, are ample with a mix of contemporary and traditional accents; a 2017 face-lift added some swagger to some public areas, suites and bathrooms. **Pros:** free Wi-Fi in rooms; more amenities than its competitors;

set back from the street, so it's quiet and bright. **Cons:** breakfast room a tad uninspiring; expensive during fairs. $ *Rooms from: €125* ✉ *Viale Roma 21* ☎*0444/5457000* ⊕ *www.hotelcampomarzio.com* ⤳*36 rooms* ◎| *Free Breakfast.*

$ 📺 **Due Mori.** Rooms at one of the oldest (1883) hotels in the city, just off
HOTEL the Piazza dei Signori, are filled with turn-of-the-20th-century antiques,
Fodor'sChoice and regulars favor the place because the high ceilings in the main build-
★ ing make it feel light and airy. **Pros:** comfortable, tastefully furnished rooms; friendly staff; central location; rate same year-round; free Wi-Fi. **Cons:** no a/c (although ceiling fans minimize the need for it); no help with baggage; no TVs. $ *Rooms from: €90* ✉ *Contrà Do Rode 24* ☎*0444/321886* ⊕ *www.hotelduemori.com* ☽ *Closed 1st 2 wks in Aug., 2 wks in late Dec.* ⤳ *53 rooms* ◎| *No meals.*

TREVISO AND THE HILLSIDE TOWNS

5

North of Venice, rivers and streams flow down from the Dolomites through market towns dotting the foothills. Villa Barbaro, one of Palladio's most imposing country villas, is nearby, as are the arcaded streets and romantic canals of undiscovered Treviso and the graceful Venetian Gothic structures of smaller hill towns.

ASOLO

33 km (20½ miles) northwest of Treviso.

Once considered the most romantic and charming of Veneto towns, the hamlet of Asolo has unfortunately lost much of its appeal, now that it's given over completely to tourism and vacation houses, with almost no local population. It does still make a nice stop for lunch after a visit to the Palladian villa at Maser, but try to avoid it on weekends and holidays, when the crowds pour in.

Through the centuries, Veneto aristocrats built elegant villas on the hillside, and in the 19th century Asolo became the idyllic haunt of musicians, poets, and painters. Back then it was one of Italy's most perfectly situated villages, with views across miles of hilly countryside; now it bears some of the scars of modern development.

Asolo hosts a modest antiques market on the second Sunday of every month.

GETTING HERE AND AROUND

There's no train station in Asolo; the closest one is in Montebelluna, 12 km (7½ miles) away. Bus connections are infrequent, and buses are not coordinated with trains, making it about a 2½-hour trip from Venice via public transportation. The best option is to drive.

By car from Treviso take Via Feltrina and continue onto Via Padre Agostino Gemelli (SR348). Follow SR348 about 16 km (10 miles), then turn left on SP667, which you follow for almost 4 km (2½ miles). At the roundabout, take the first exit, Via Monte Grappa (SP284), and follow it for 6½ km (4 miles) to Via Loredan, where you turn right and then left onto Via Bordo Vecchio. Asolo is less than 7 km (4½ miles) away from the Palladian Villa Barbaro at Maser.

VISITOR INFORMATION

Contact Asolo Tourism Office. ⊠ *Piazza Maggiore (aka Piazza Garibaldi)* ☎ *0423/529046* ⊕ *www.asolo.it.*

EXPLORING

Brion Family Tomb. One of the major monuments of contemporary Italian architecture, the Brion family tomb was designed and built by the architect Carlo Scarpa (1906–78) between 1970 and 1972. Combining Western rationalism with Eastern spirituality, Scarpa avoids the gloom and bombast of conventional commemorative monuments, creating, in his words, a secluded Eden. ⊠ *SP6, Via Castellan, about 7 km (4½ miles) south of Asolo, near village of San Vito* ☜ *Free.*

Fodor's Choice ★ **Museo Canova** (*Gypsoteca*). The most significant cultural monument in the Asolo area is this museum dedicated to the work of the Italian Neoclassical sculptor Antonio Canova (1757–1822), whose sculptures are featured in many major European and North American cultural institutions. Set up shortly after the sculptor's death in his hometown, the village of Possagno, the museum houses most of the original plaster casts, models, and drawings made by the artist in preparation for his marble sculptures. In 1957 the Museo Canova was extended by the Italian architect Carlo Scarpa. ⊠ *Via Canova 74, 13½ km (8¼ miles) northwest of Asolo, Possagno* ☎ *0423/544323* ⊕ *www.museocanova. it* ☜ *€10* ☾ *Closed Mon.*

Museo Civico. In the Piazza Maggiore, the frescoed 15th-century Loggia del Capitano contains the Museo Civico, which displays a collection of eccentric memorabilia—the Italian actress Eleonora Duse's correspondence, the poet Robert Browning's spinet, and portraits of the noble Caterina Cornaro (1454–1510). ⊠ *Piazza Maggiore* ☎ *0423/952313* ☜ *€5, €7 with fortress ruins* ☾ *Closed weekdays, and weekends 12:30–3.*

Piazza Maggiore. Renaissance palaces and long-established cafés grace this piazza in Asolo's town center. ⊠ *Asolo.*

Fodor's Choice ★ **Tempio Canoviano.** One of the most impressive and historically significant Neoclassical buildings in Italy, the Tempio Canoviano was designed by Canova in 1819 and finished in 1830, incorporating motifs from the rotunda of the Roman Pantheon and the *pronaos* (inner portico) of the Parthenon. The church contains several works by Canova, including his tomb, along with paintings by Luca Giordano, Palma il Giovane, and Il Pordenone. ⊠ *Piazza Canova, 16 km (10 miles) north of Asolo, Possagno* ☎ *0423/544323* ☜ *Free.*

WHERE TO EAT

$$
NORTHERN
ITALIAN

✕ **Al Bacaro.** At this family-style restaurant, you may want take a leap and try a dish with stewed game, tripe, or snails. Less adventurous diners can go for other homey options, such as goulash, polenta with cheese and mushrooms, or one of Bacaro's open-face sandwiches, generously topped with fresh salami, speck, or other cold cuts. **Known for:** robust and meaty country fare; intimate and relaxed osteria atmosphere; seasonal vegetables. $ *Average main: €22* ⊠ *Via Browning 165* ☎ *0423/55150* ⊗ *Closed Wed.*

$$$

NORTHERN

ITALIAN

Fodor'sChoice

★

✕ **Locanda Baggio.** Even if the swarms of tourists and commercialization of Asolo put you off, a lunch or dinner at this family-run restaurant makes a trip to the hillside village worthwhile. This is the best restaurant in Asolo, and the prix-fixe menu is one of the best values in the region. **Known for:** inventive, tasty seasonal food; gorgeous garden; warm hospitality. $ *Average main: €26* ⊠ *Via Bassane 1* ☎ *0423/529648* ⊕ *www.locandabaggio.it* ⊗ *Closed Mon., and 2 wks in Aug.*

WHERE TO STAY

$$$

HOTEL

🏨 **Al Sole.** This elegant pink-washed hotel in a 16th-century building overlooks the main square and has wide views over picturesque Asolo or its leafy hinterland. **Pros:** central location; beautiful views; free shuttle service to the surrounding area. **Cons:** rates increase in the high season; standard rooms have less interesting views than more expensive ones. $ *Rooms from: €210* ⊠ *Via Collegio 33* ☎ *0423/951332* ⊕ *www.albergoalsole.com* ⊗ *Generally closed early Jan.–mid-Feb.* ⇆ *23 rooms* ◉❙ *Free Breakfast.*

$

HOTEL

🏨 **Hotel Duse.** A spiral staircase winds its way up this narrow, centrally located building to rooms with a view of the main square. **Pros:** simple but tasteful rooms; central location. **Cons:** some street noise; not as much of a bargain when you add the cost of breakfast and parking. $ *Rooms from: €120* ⊠ *Via Browning 190* ☎ *0423/55241* ⊕ *www.hotelduse.com* ⊗ *Closed 3 wks in Jan. and Feb.* ⇆ *14 rooms* ◉❙ *No meals.*

$$$

HOTEL

🏨 **Villa Cipriani.** From its 19th-century furnishings to a 21st-century spa and a romantic garden, this luxurious 16th-century villa turned hotel strives for opulence. **Pros:** incomparable views; truly elegant grounds; good spa services. **Cons:** small bathrooms; furnishings are old but not always tasteful; rooms in the annex are very small. $ *Rooms from: €285* ⊠ *Via Canova 298* ☎ *0423/523411* ⊕ *www.villaciprianiasolo.com* ⇆ *31 rooms* ◉❙ *Free Breakfast.*

TREVISO

35 km (22 miles) southeast of Maser, 30 km (19 miles) north of Venice.

Treviso has been dubbed "Little Venice" because of its meandering, moss-bank canals. They can't really compare with Venice's spectacular waterways, but on the whole, Treviso's historic center, with its medieval arcaded streets, has a great deal of charm. Treviso is a fine place to stop for a few hours on the way from Venice to the wine country in the north or to the Palladian villas in the hinterland.

Allied bombing on Good Friday in 1944 destroyed half the city—it was bombed by mistake after a report that Hitler would be in Tarvisio, on the Austrian border, was misread. Despite this, Treviso managed to preserve what remained of its old town's narrow streets while introducing modernity far more gently than in many other parts of Italy. These days it's one of the wealthiest small cities in the country, with fashionable shops and boutiques at every turn in the busy city center.

Traveling the Wine Roads

You'd be hard-pressed to find a more stimulating and varied wine region than northeastern Italy. From the Valpolicella, Bardolino, and Soave produced near Verona to the superlative whites of the Collio region, wines from the Veneto and Friuli–Venezia Giulia earn more Denominazione di Origine Controllata seals for uniqueness and quality than those of any other area of Italy.

You can travel on foot, by car, or by bicycle over hillsides covered with vineyards, each field nurturing subtly different grape varieties. On a casual trip through the countryside you're likely to come across wineries that will welcome you for a visit; for a more organized tour, check local tourist information offices, which have maps of roads, wineries, and vendors. Be advised that Italy has become more stringent about its driving regulations; designated drivers can help avoid the risk of fines, embarrassment, or worse.

One of the most hospitable areas in the Veneto for wine enthusiasts is the stretch of country north of Treviso, where you can follow designated wine roads—tours that blend a beautiful rural setting with the delights of the grape. Authorized wineshops, where you can stop and sample, are marked with a sign showing a triangular arrangement of red and yellow grapes. There are three routes to choose from, and they're manageable enough that you can do them all comfortably over the course of a day or two.

MONTELLO AND ASOLO HILLS
This route provides a good balance of vineyards and nonwine sights. It winds from Nervesa della Battaglia, 18 km (10 miles) north of Treviso, past two prime destinations in the area, the village of Asolo and the Villa Barbaro at Maser. Asolo produces good prosecco, while Montello, a hill near Nervesa, favors merlot and cabernet. Both areas also yield pinot noir and chardonnay.

PIAVE RIVER
The circular route follows the Piave River and runs through orchards, woods, and hills. Among the area's gems are the dessert wines Torchiato di Fregona and Refrontolo Passito, both made according to traditional methods.

Raboso del Piave, renowned since Roman times, ages well and complements local dishes such as beans and pasta or goose stuffed with chestnuts. Other reds include merlot and cabernet sauvignon. As an accompaniment to fish, try a Verduzzo del Piave or, for an aperitivo, the warm-yellow Pinot Grigio del Piave.

PROSECCO
This route runs for 47 km (29 miles) between Valdobbiadene and Conegliano, home of Italy's first wine institute, winding between knobby hills covered in grapevines. These hang in festoons on row after row of pergolas to create a thick mantle of green.

Turn off the main route to explore the narrower country lanes, most of which eventually join up. They meander through tiny hamlets and past numerous family wineries where you can taste and buy the wines. Spring is an excellent time to visit, with no fewer than 15 local wine festivals held between March and early June.

GETTING HERE AND AROUND

Treviso is 30 minutes by train from Venice; there are frequent daily departures. By car from Venice, pick up the SS13 (Via Terraglio) in Mestre and follow it all the way to Treviso; the trip takes about 45 minutes.

VISITOR INFORMATION

Contact **Treviso Tourism Office (IAT Treviso).** ✉ *Palazzo Scotti, Via Fumicelli 30* ☎ *0422/547632* ⊕ *turismo.provincia.treviso.it.*

EXPLORING

Duomo. Inside Treviso's Duomo, which was modified during the 19th century, is the Malchiostro Chapel. There you'll find an *Annunciation* by Titian (1520) and frescoes by Pordenone (1484–1539), including an *Adoration of the Magi.* The crypt has 12th-century columns. Bring a handful of coins for the coin-operated lights that illuminate the artwork. To the left of the Duomo is the Romanesque Battistero di San Giovanni (from the 11th to 12th century), which is probably quite similar in style to the medieval Duomo; it's open only for special exhibitions. ✉ *Piazza del Duomo* ☎ *0422/545720* ☾ *Closed Mon.*

Piazza dei Signori. The center of medieval Treviso, this piazza remains the town's social hub, with outdoor cafés and some impressive public buildings. The most important of these, the Palazzo dei Trecento (1185–1268), was the seat of the city government, composed of the Council of 300, during the Middle Ages. Behind it is a small alley that leads to the *pescheria* (fish market), on an island in one of the small canals that flow through town. ✉ *Treviso.*

Quartiere Latino. While strolling the city, take in this restored district between Riviera Garibaldi and Piazza Santa Maria Battuti. It's the site of university buildings, upscale apartments, and bustling restaurants and shops. If you walk along the northern part of the historic city wall, you'll look down on the island home of ducks, geese, and goats. Their little farm occupies some of the city's prettiest real estate. ✉ *Treviso.*

San Nicolò. The most important church in Treviso, this huge Venetian Gothic structure from the early 14th century has an ornate vaulted ceiling and frescoes (circa 1350) of saints by Tommaso da Modena (circa 1325–79) on the columns. The depiction of St. Agnes on the north side is particularly interesting, combining the naturalism initiated a few decades previous by Giotto with the grace and elegance of Gothic abstraction. Also worth examining are Tommaso's realistic portraits of 40 Dominican friars, found in the Sala del Capitolo of the seminary next door. They include the earliest-known painting of a subject wearing eyeglasses, an Italian invention (circa 1280–1300). ✉ *Seminario Vescovile, Via San Nicolò* ☎ *0422/548626* ☾ *Closed Mon.*

Fodor's Choice ★ **Villa Barbaro** (*Villa Maser*). At the Villa Barbaro (1554) near the town of Maser, a short drive from Asolo, you can see the results of a onetime collaboration between two of the greatest artists of their age. Palladio was the architect, and Paolo Veronese decorated the interior with an amazing cycle of trompe-l'oeil frescoes—walls dissolve into landscapes, and illusions of courtiers and servants enter rooms and smile down from balustrades. Legend has it a feud developed between Palladio and

Veronese, with Palladio feeling the illusionistic frescoes detracted from his architecture, but there's not much to support this idea.

It's also noteworthy that Palladio for the first time connected the two lateral granaries to the main villa. This was a working farm, and Palladio thus created an architectural unity by connecting with graceful arcades the working parts of the estate to the living quarters, bringing together the Renaissance dichotomy of the active and the contemplative life. Hours are variable; check the website. ✉ *Via Cornuda 7, Maser* ✣ *Most easily accessible by private car; closest train station is Montebelluna. Buses leave for Maser from the bus station at Treviso, Montebelluna, or Bassano di Grappa. The bus will leave you at a stop about 1½ km (1 mile) from Maser* ☎ *0432/923004* 🌐 *www.villadimaser.it* 🎫 *€9* 🕓 *Closed mid Dec.–Mar., except for Easter and rare events; closed Mon. Apr.–Oct.*

WHERE TO EAT

$$ VENETIAN 🍴 **All'Antico Portico.** This little old brick trattoria on a quiet square in Treviso's historic center is a favorite among locals and tourists. The menu changes daily but always features well-executed versions of simple local dishes. **Known for:** under the 15th-century porticoes; homemade pasta; mamma's baccalà alla veneziana recipe. [$] *Average main: €19* ✉ *Piazza Santa Maria Maggiore 18* ☎ *0422/545259* 🌐 *www.anticoportico.it* 🕓 *Closed Tues. No dinner Mon.*

$$$ VENETIAN 🍴 **Beccherie.** The name means "butcher shop," and this area behind Treviso's Palazzo Trecento is where people bought and sold meat for centuries. It is only fitting that Beccherie should specialize in *bollito,* a celebrated dish of assorted boiled meats and sauces, which originated in Piedmont but is now so much a part of Veneto cooking that most Veneti regard it as their own. **Known for:** inventive food and special tiramisù; stylish contemporary design above the canal; reservations are recommended for dinner. [$] *Average main: €27* ✉ *Piazza Ancilotto 10* ☎ *0422/540871* 🌐 *www.lebeccherie.it* 🕓 *No lunch Tues.*

$$ VENETIAN 🍴 **Il Basilisco.** Gastronomically adventurous diners who visit this simple restaurant will find Veneto cuisine in the *cucina povera* (poor people's food) tradition and discover that, with talent and imagination, tasty dishes can be created from the most humble and unusual ingredients. Start with a savory dish of pasta with rabbit tripe, or *nervetti,* gelatinous veal tendons in a sauce of celery root. **Known for:** inventive use of quinto quarto (offal); vibrant contemporary decor and design; homemade pasta, cured meats, and antipasti. [$] *Average main: €18* ✉ *Via Bison 34* ☎ *0422/541822* 🌐 *www.ristorantebasilisco.com* 🕓 *Closed Sun. No lunch Mon.*

$$ VENETIAN 🍴 **Toni del Spin.** Wood-paneled and with a 1930s-style interior, this bustling trattoria oozes old-fashioned character. The wholesome menu, chalked on a hanging wooden board, is based on local Veneto cooking. **Known for:** Veneto specialties and great enoteca wine choice; idiosyncratic/brusque service; can get very busy. [$] *Average main: €18* ✉ *Via Inferiore 7* ☎ *0422/543829* 🌐 *www.ristorantetonidelspin.com* 🕓 *Closed 3 wks in July and Aug. No lunch Mon.*

FRIULI–VENEZIA GIULIA

Friuli–Venezia Giulia is perhaps Italy's best-kept secret. It's home to impressive and beautiful medieval artistic monuments—some of which actually predate those in Venice—as well as important frescoes by the Venetian master painter Tiepolo. The atmospheric old Austrian port of Trieste was a major center of literature in the late 19th and early 20th century.

The peripheral location of the Friuli–Venezia Giulia region in Italy's northeastern corner makes it easy to overlook, but in addition to its artistic treasures, its mix of Italian, Slavic, and Central European cultures, evident in places like the medieval city of Udine, make it a fascinating area to explore. It's also got a strong wine tradition: Cividale del Friuli and the Collio wine regions are a short hop away from Udine.

UDINE

94 km (58 miles) northeast of Treviso, 127 km (79 miles) northeast of Venice.

The main reason for devoting some time to Udine is to see works by the last of the great Italian painters, Gianbattista Tiepolo (1696–1770). Distributed in several palaces and churches around town, this is the greatest assembly of his art outside Venice. In fact, Udine calls itself "la città di Tiepolo."

The largest city on the Friuli side of the region, Udine has a provincial, genteel atmosphere and lots of charm. The city sometimes seems completely unaffected by tourism, and things are still done the way they were decades ago. In the medieval and Renaissance historical center of town, you'll find unevenly spaced streets with appealing wine bars and open-air cafés. Friulani are proud of their culture, with many restaurants featuring local cuisine, and street signs and announcements written in both Italian and Friulano (Furlan). Although Friulano is sometimes classified as a dialect, it's really a separate language from Italian.

Commanding a view from the Alpine foothills to the Adriatic Sea, Udine stands on a mound that, according to legend, was erected so Attila the Hun could watch the burning of Aquileia, an important Roman center to the south. Although the legend is unlikely (Attila burned Aquileia about 500 years before the first historical mention of Udine), the view from Udine's castle across the alluvial plane down to the sea is impressive. In the Middle Ages Udine flourished, thanks to its favorable trade location and the right granted by the local patriarch to hold regular markets.

GETTING HERE AND AROUND

There's frequent train service from both Venice and Trieste; the trip takes about two hours from Venice, and a little over an hour from Trieste. By car from Venice, take the SR11 to the E55 and head east. Take the E55 (it eventually becomes the Autostrada Alpe Adria) to SS13 (Viale Venezia) east into Udine. Driving from Trieste, take the SS202 to the E70, which becomes the A4. Turn onto the E55 north, which is

the same road you would take coming from Venice. Driving times are 1½ hours from Venice and one hour from Trieste.

VISITOR INFORMATION

The tourist office sells the FVG (Friuli Venezia Giulia) Card, which includes admission to most museums in Udine and other important sites in the region. Its price ranges from €15 (for 48 hours) up to €29 (for one week).

Contact Udine Tourism Office. ⊠ *Piazza I Maggio 7* ☎ *0432/295972* ⊕ *www. turismofvg.it.*

EXPLORING

FodorśChoice ★ **Castello and Musei Civici.** From its hilltop site, the castle (construction began 1517) has panoramic views extending to Monte Nero (7,360 feet) in neighboring Slovenia. Here Udine's civic museums of art and archaeology are centralized under one roof. Particularly worthwhile is the national and regional art collection in the **Galleria d'Arte Antica,** which has canvases by Venetians Vittore Carpaccio (circa 1460–1525) and Gianbattista Tiepolo, an excellent Caravaggio, and carefully selected works by lesser known but still interesting Veneto and Friuli artists. ■ **TIP** → The museum's small collection of drawings includes several by Tiepolo; some find his drawings even more moving than his paintings.

✉ *Via Lionello 1* ☎ *0432/1272591* ⊕ *www.civicimuseiudine.it* 🎫 *€8 (free with FVG Card)* ⊗ *Closed Mon.*

Duomo. A few steps from the Piazza della Libertà is Udine's 1335 Duomo. Its Cappella del Santissimo has important early frescoes by Tiepolo, and the Cappella della Trinità has a Tiepolo altarpiece. There is also a beautiful late Tiepolo *Resurrection* (1751) in an altar by the sculptor Giuseppi Toretti. Ask the Duomo's attendant to let you into the adjacent **Chiesa della Puritá** to see more important late paintings by Tiepolo. ✉ *Piazza del Duomo 1* ☎ *0432/505302* ⊕ *www.cattedral-eudine.it* 🎫 *Free.*

Fodor's Choice ★ **Palazzo Arcivescovile.** The Palazzo Arcivescovile (also known as Palazzo Patriarcale) contains several rooms of frescoes by the young Gianbattista Tiepolo, painted from 1726 to 1732, which comprise the most important collection of early works by Italy's most brilliant 18th-century painter. The Galleria del Tiepolo (1727) contains superlative Tiepolo frescoes depicting the stories of Abraham, Isaac, and Jacob. The *Judgment of Solomon* (1729) graces the Pink Room. There are also beautiful and important Tiepolo frescoes in the staircase, throne room, and palatine chapel of this palazzo. Even in these early works we can see the Venetian master's skill in creating an illusion of depth, not only through linear perspective, but also through subtle gradations in the intensity of the colors, with the stronger colors coming forward and the paler ones receding into space. Tiepolo was one of the first artists to use this method of representing space and depth, which reflected the scientific discoveries of perception and optics in the 17th century. In the same building, the **Museo Diocesano** features a collection of sculptures from Friuli churches from the 13th through 18th century. ✉ *Piazza Patriarcato 1* ☎ *0432/25003* ⊕ *www.musdioc-tiepolo.it* 🎫 *€7, includes Museo Diocesano (Free with FVG Card)* ⊗ *Closed Tues.*

Piazza della Libertà. Udine was conquered by the Venetians in 1420, so there is a distinctly Venetian stamp on the architecture of the historic center, most noticeably here, in the large main square. The Loggia del Leonello, begun in 1428, dominates the square and houses the municipal government. Its similarity to the facade of Venice's Palazzo Ducale (finished in 1424) is clear, but there is no evidence that it is an imitation of that palace. It's more likely a product of the same architectural fashion. Opposite stands the Renaissance Porticato di San Giovanni (1533–35) and the Torre dell'Orologio, a 1527 clock tower with naked *mori* (Moors), who strike the hours on the top. ✉ *Udine.*

WHERE TO EAT

$$ FRIULIAN
Fodor's Choice ★ ✕**Hostaria alla Tavernetta.** One of Udine's most trusted restaurants is steps from the Piazza Duomo. The Hostaria alla Tavernetta, open since 1954, has rustic fireside dining downstairs and smaller, more elegantly decorated rooms upstairs, where there's also a small terrace. **Known for:** rustic, warm yet elegant rooms; Friulian ingredients and traditions; superb local Collio wine, grappa and regional selection. 🜉 *Average main: €23* ✉ *Via di Prampero 2* ☎ *0432/501066* ⊗ *Closed Sun. and Mon. No lunch Sat.*

$$$ ITALIAN Fodor's Choice ★ 🍴 **Vitello d'Oro.** Udine's very elegant, landmark restaurant is the one reserved by most local people for special occasions. The big terrace in front is popular for alfresco dining in summer. **Known for:** freshest seafood served raw and cooked; homemade pasta; professional service. [$] *Average main: €32* ✉ *Via Valvason 4* ☎ *0432/508982* 🌐 *www.vitellodoro.com* 🕒 *Closed Wed. in winter and Sun. in summer. No lunch Mon.*

WHERE TO STAY

$$ HOTEL 🏨 **Hostaria Hotel Allegria.** The 2006 renovation of this 15th-century building created contemporary minimalism throughout: the breakfast room, lounges, and guest rooms have plenty of light wood, sleek design, and mood lighting. **Pros:** well-appointed rooms; discounted weekend rates; within easy walking distance to the center. **Cons:** rooms may be too minimalist for some; fee for parking. [$] *Rooms from: €150* ✉ *Via Grazzano 18* ☎ *0432/201116* 🌐 *www.hotelallegria.it* 🛏 *21 rooms* 🍽 *Free Breakfast.*

$$ HOTEL 🏨 **Hotel Clocchiatti.** You have two choices here: in the 19th-century villa, where there are canopy beds and Alpine-style wood ceilings and paneling, and in the "Next Wing," with rich colors and spare furnishings in starkly angular rooms. **Pros:** individually decorated rooms; excellent breakfast; Wi-Fi. **Cons:** 10-minute drive from town center; small bathrooms; no restaurant. [$] *Rooms from: €130* ✉ *Via Cividale 29* ☎ *0432/505047* 🌐 *www.hotelclocchiatti.it* 🛏 *27 rooms* 🍽 *Free Breakfast.*

CIVIDALE DEL FRIULI

17 km (11 miles) east of Udine, 144 km (89 miles) northeast of Venice.

Cividale is the most important place for taking in the impressive and beautiful art of the Lombards, a Germanic people who entered Italy in 568 and who ruled parts of Italy until the late 8th century. The city was founded in AD 53 by Julius Caesar, then commander of Roman legions in the area. Here you can also find Celtic, Roman, and medieval Jewish ruins alongside Venetian Gothic buildings, including the Palazzo Comunale. Strolling through the part of the city that now occupies the former Gastaldia, the Lombard ducal palace, gives you spectacular views of the medieval city and the river.

GETTING HERE AND AROUND

There's hourly train service from Udine. Since the Udine–Cividale train line isn't part of the Italian national rail system, you have to buy the tickets from the tobacconist or other retailers within the Udine station. You can't buy a ticket through to Cividale from another city.

By car from Udine, take Via Cividale, which turns into SS54; follow SS54 into Cividale.

EXPLORING

Duomo. Cividale's Renaissance Duomo is largely the work of Pietro Lombardo, principal architect of Venice's famous Santa Maria dei Miracoli. The interior was restructured in the 18th century by another prominent Venetian architect, Giogio Massari. The church contains a magnificent 12th-century silver gilt altarpiece. ✉ *Piazza Duomo* ☎ *0432/731144.*

Museo Archeologico. Trace the area's history here and learn about the importance of Cividale and Udine in the period following the collapse of the Roman Empire. The collection includes weapons and jewelry from 6th-century Lombard warriors, who swept through much of what is now Italy. ✉ *Piazza Duomo 13* ☎ *0432/700700* 🌐 *www.museoarcheologicocividale.beniculturali.it* 🎫 *€4.*

Museo Cristiano e Tesoro del Duomo. Entered via a courtyard to the right of the Duomo, this museum contains two interesting, important, and surprisingly beautiful monuments of Lombard art: the Altar of Duke Ratchis (737–744) and the Baptistry of Patriarch Callisto (731–776). Both were found under the floor of the present Duomo in the early 20th century. The museum also has two fine paintings by Veronese, one by Pordenone, and a small collection of medieval and Renaissance vestments. ✉ *Via Candotti 1* ☎ *0432/730403* 🎫 *€4* ⏲ *Closed Mon. and Tues.*

Fodor's Choice ★ **Tempietto Longobardo** (*Lombard Church*). Seeing the beautiful and historically important Tempietto Longobardo from the 8th century is more than enough reason to visit Cividale. Now inside the 16th-century Monastery of Santa Maria in Valle, the Tempietto was originally the chapel of the ducal palace, known as the Gastaldia. The west wall is the best-preserved example of the art and architecture of the Lombards, a Germanic people who entered Italy in 568. It has an archway with an exquisitely rendered vine motif, guarded by an 8th-century procession of female figures, showing the Lombard interpretation of classical forms that resembles the style of the much earlier Byzantine mosaics in Ravenna, which had passed briefly to Lombard rule in 737. This procession of female figures had originally extended to the side walls of the Tempietto, but was destroyed by an earthquake in 1222. The post-Lombard frescoes decorating the vaults and the east wall date from the 13th and 14th centuries, and the fine carved wooden stalls also date from the 14th century. ✉ *Via Monastero Maggiore* ☎ *0432/700867* 🌐 *www.tempiettolongobardo.it* 🎫 *€4, combined ticket with Museo del Duomo and Museo Archiologico €9; free with FVG Card.*

WHERE TO STAY

$ B&B/INN 🏨 **La Cjase dai Toscans.** In a central location, this 15th-century palazzo, once home to the dukes of Tuscany, is now a charming and romantic bed-and-breakfast, with large rooms furnished in antique style. **Pros:** large, well-appointed rooms; high-speed Wi-Fi; nearby parking is free or at moderate cost. **Cons:** some noise from the street and the cathedral bells. [$] *Rooms from: €75* ✉ *Corso Mazzini 15/1* ☎ *3490/765288 (mobile)* 🛏 *4 rooms* 🍴 *Free Breakfast.*

AQUILEIA

77 km (48 miles) northwest of Trieste, 163 km (101 miles) east of Venice.

This sleepy little town is refreshingly free of the tourists that you might expect at such a culturally historic place. In the time of Emperor Augustus, it was Italy's fourth-most-important city (after Rome, Milan, and Capua), as well as the principal northern Adriatic port of Italy and the beginning of Roman routes north. Aquileia's Roman and early-Christian remains convey an image of the transition from pagan to Christian Rome.

GETTING HERE AND AROUND

Getting to Aquileia by public transportation is difficult but not impossible. There's frequent train service from Venice and Trieste to Cervignano di Friuli, which is 8 km (5 miles) from Aquileia by taxi (about €20), and infrequent bus service. (Ask the newsstand attendant or the railroad ticket agent for assistance.) By car from Venice or Trieste, take the A4 (Venezia–Trieste) to the Palmanova exit and continue 17 km (11 miles) to Aquileia. From Udine, take the A23 to the Palmanova exit.

VISITOR INFORMATION

Contact **Aquileia Infopoint.** ⊠ *Bus Terminal, Via Iulia Augusta* ☎ *0431/919491.*

EXPLORING

Archaeological Site. Roman remains of the forum, houses, cemetery, and port are surrounded by cypresses here. The little stream was once an important waterway extending to Grado. Unfortunately, many of the excavations of Roman Aquileia could not be left exposed because of the extremely high water table under the site and had to be reburied after archaeological studies had been conducted; nevertheless, what remains above ground, along with the monuments in the archaeological museum, gives an idea of the grandeur of this ancient city. The area is well signposted. ⊠ *Near basilica* ⌨ *Free.*

Fodor'sChoice ★

Basilica. The highlight here is the spectacular 3rd- to 4th-century mosaic covering the entire floor of the basilica and the adjacent crypt, making up one of the most beautiful and important of early-Christian monuments. Theodore, the basilica's first bishop, built two parallel basilicas, now the north and the south halls, on the site of a Gnostic chapel in the 4th century. These were joined by a third hall, forming a "U," with the baptismal font in the middle. The complex was rebuilt between 1021 and 1031, and later accumulated the Romanesque portico and the Gothic bell tower, producing the church you see today. The mosaic floor of the present-day basilica is essentially the remains of the floor of Theodore's south hall, while those of the Cripta degli Scavi are those of his north hall, along with the remains of the mosaic floor of a pre-Christian Roman house and warehouse.

The mosaics of the basilica are important not only because of their beauty, but also because they provide a window into Gnostic symbolism and the conflict between Gnosticism and the early-Christian church. In his north hall, Theodore retained much of the floor of the earlier Gnostic chapel, whose mosaics, done largely in the 3rd century, represent the ascent of the soul, through the realm of the planets and constellations, to God, who is represented as a ram. (The ram, at the head of the zodiac, is the Gnostic generative force.) Libra is not the scales, but rather a battle between good (the rooster) and evil (the tortoise); the constellation Cancer is represented as a shrimp on a tree. The basis for the representation in Aquileia is the Pistis Sophia, a 2nd-century Gnostic tract written in Alexandria.

This integration of Gnosticism into a Christian church is particularly interesting, since Gnosticism had already been branded a heresy by influential early Church fathers. In retaining these mosaics, Theodore may have been publicly expressing a leaning toward Gnosticism. Alternatively, the area of the north hall may have been Theodore's private residence, where the retention of Gnostic symbolism may have been more acceptable.

The 4th-century mosaics of the south hall (the present-day nave of the basilica) are somewhat more doctrinally conventional, and represent the story of Jonah as prefiguring the salvation offered by the Church.

Down a flight of steps, the **Cripta degli Affreschi** contains beautiful 12th-century frescoes, among them St. Peter sending St. Mark to Aquileia and the beheading of Sts. Hermagoras and Fortunatus, to whom the basilica is dedicated. ⊠ *Aquileia* ☎ *0431/91067* ⊕ *www.basilicadiaquileia.it* 🖾 *Basilica and crypt Affreschi €3, with Cripta degli Scavi €5, whole complex €10, campanile €2; all sites free with FGV Card* ⊙ *Campanile closed Oct.–Mar.*

Museo Archeologico. A wealth of material from the Roman era includes portrait busts from Republican times, semiprecious gems, amber—including preserved flies—and gold work, and a fine glass collection. Beautiful pre-Christian mosaics are from the floors of Roman houses and palaces. ⊠ *Via Roma 1* ☎ *0431/91096* ⊕ *www.museoarcheologicoaquileia.beniculturali.it* 🖾 *€2, free with FGV* ⊙ *Closed Mon.*

TRIESTE

71 km (44 miles) southeast of Cividale del Friuli, 163 km (101 miles) east of Venice.

Trieste is Italy's only truly cosmopolitan city. In a country, perhaps even in a continent, where the amalgamation of cultures has frequently proved difficult, Trieste stands out as one of the few authentic melting pots. Not only do Italian, Slavic, and Central European cultures meet here, they actually merge together to create a unique Triestino culture. To discover this culture, visiting Trieste's coffeehouses, local eateries, and piazzas is probably more important than visiting its churches and museums, interesting though they are.

Trieste is built along a fringe of coastline where a rugged karst plateau tumbles abruptly into the beautiful Adriatic. It was the only port of the Austro-Hungarian Empire and, therefore, a major industrial and financial center. In the early years of the 20th century, Trieste and its surroundings also became famous by their association with some of the most important names of Italian literature, such as Italo Svevo, and Irish and German writers. James Joyce drew inspiration from the city's multiethnic population, and Rainer Maria Rilke was inspired by the coast to the west.

The city has lost its importance as a port and a center of finance, but perhaps because of its multicultural nature, at the juncture of Latin, Slavic, and Germanic Europe, it's never fully lost its role as an intellectual center. In recent years the city has become a center for science and technology. The streets hold a mix of monumental Neoclassical and Art Nouveau architecture, built by the Austrians during Trieste's days of glory, granting an air of melancholy stateliness to a city that lives as much in the past as the present.

GETTING HERE AND AROUND

Trains to Trieste depart regularly from Venice, Udine, and other major Italian cities. By car, it's the eastern terminus of the Autostrada Torino–Trieste (E70). The city is served by Trieste–Friuli Venezia Giulia Airport, which receives flights from major Italian airports and some European cities. The airport is 33 km (20½ miles) from the city; transportation into Trieste is by taxi or Bus No. 51.

VISITOR INFORMATION

Contact Trieste Tourism Office. ⊠ *Via dell'Orologio 1, at Piazza dell'Unità d'Italia* ☎ *040/3478312* ⊕ *www.turismofvg.it.*

EXPLORING

TOP ATTRACTIONS

Castello di San Giusto. This hilltop castle, built between 1470 and 1630, was constructed on the ruins of the Roman town of Tergeste. Given the excellent view, it's no surprise that 15th-century Venetians turned the castle into a shipping observation point; the structure was further enlarged by Trieste's subsequent rulers, the Habsburgs. The castle also contains the Civic Museum, which has a small collection of furnishings, tapestries, and weaponry. ⊠ *Piazza della Cattedrale 3* ☎ *040/309362* ⊕ *www.castellodisangiustotrieste.it* 🎟 *Castle €3; €6 also includes all complex museums* ⊗ *Closed Mon.*

Piazza dell'Unità d'Italia. The imposing square, ringed by grandiose facades, was set out as a plaza open to the sea, like Venice's Piazza San Marco, in the late Middle Ages. It underwent countless changes through the centuries, and its present size and architecture are essentially products of late-19th- and early-20th-century Austria. It was given its current name in 1955, when Trieste was finally given to Italy. On the inland side of the piazza note the facade of the **Palazzo Comunale** (Town Hall), designed by the Triestino architect Giuseppi Bruni in 1875. It was from this building's balcony in 1938 that Mussolini proclaimed the infamous racial laws, depriving Italian Jews of most of their rights. The sidewalk cafés on this vast seaside piazza are popular meeting places in the summer months. ⊠ *Trieste.*

WORTH NOTING

OFF THE BEATEN PATH

Castello Di Duino. This 14th-century castle, the property of the Princes of Thurn and Taxis, contains a collection of antique furnishings and an amazing Palladian circular staircase, but the main attractions are the surrounding gardens and the spectacular views. In 1912 Rainer Maria Rilke wrote his masterpiece, the *Duino Elegies,* here. The easy path along the seacoast from the castle toward Trieste has gorgeous views that rival the Amalfi Coast and the Cinque Terre. ⊠ *Frazione Duino 32, 12 km (7½ miles) from Trieste, Duino* ✛ *Take Bus No. 44 or 51 from the Trieste train station* ☎ *040/208120* ⊕ *www.castellodiduino. it* 🎟 *€8* ⊗ *Closed Tues.*

Cattedrale di San Giusto. Dating from the 14th century and occupying the site of an ancient Roman forum, the cathedral contains remnants of at least three previous buildings, the earliest a hall dating from the 5th century. A section of the original floor mosaic still remains, incorporated into the floor of the present church. In the 9th and 11th centuries two adjacent churches were built—the Church of the Assumption and the Church of San Giusto. The beautiful apse mosaics of these churches, done in the 12th and 13th centuries by a Venetian artist, still remain in the apses of the side aisles of the present church. The mosaics in the main apse date from 1932. In the 14th century the two churches were joined and a Romanesque-Gothic facade was attached, ornamented with fragments of Roman monuments taken from the forum. The jambs of the main doorway are the most conspicuous Roman element. ✉ *Piazza della Cattedrale 2* ☎ *040/3224575.*

Piazza della Borsa. A statue of Habsburg emperor Leopold I looks out over this square, which contains Trieste's original stock exchange, the **Borsa Vecchia** (1805), an attractive Neoclassical building now serving as the chamber of commerce. It sits at the end of the Canal Grande, dug in the 18th century by the Austrian empress Maria Theresa as a first step in the expansion of what was then a small fishing village of 7,000 into the port of her empire. ✉ *Trieste.*

Risiera di San Sabba. In September 1943 the Nazi occupation established Italy's only concentration camp in this rice-processing factory outside of Trieste. In April 1944 a crematorium was put into operation. The Nazis destroyed much of the evidence of their atrocities before their retreat, but a good deal of the horror of the place is still perceivable in the reconstructed museum (1975). The site, an Italian national monument since 1965, receives more than 100,000 visitors per year. ✉ *Via Giovanni Palatucci 5* ✥ *Take municipal Bus No. 8 or 10; off the Autostrada A4, take exit Valmaura/Stadio/Cimitero* ☎ *040/826202* 🌐 *www.risierasansabba.it* 🎫 *Free, guided tour €3.*

San Silvestro. This small Romanesque gem, dating from the 9th to the 12th century, is the oldest church in Trieste that's still in use and in approximately its original form. Its interior walls still have some fragmentary remains of Romanesque frescoes. The church was deconsecrated under the secularizing reforms of the Austrian emperor Josef II in 1785 and was later sold to the Swiss Evangelical community; it then became, and is still, the Reformed Evangelical and Waldesian Church of Trieste. ✉ *Piazza San Silvestro 1* ☎ *040/632770* 🌐 *triestevangelica.org.*

WHERE TO EAT

$$$ SEAFOOD 🍴 **Al Bagatto.** At this warm little seafood place near the Piazza Unità, the chef-owner Roberto Marussi personally shepherds your meal from start to finish. The menu includes traditional dishes, among them *baccalà mantecato* (creamed cod with olive oil), as well as more inventive creations, such as sea-bass tartare with fresh ricotta. **Known for:** freshest seafood beautifully prepared; more than 300 wine labels to choose from; decades of family experience. [$] *Average main: €28* ✉ *Via L. Cadorna 7* ☎ *040/301771* 🌐 *www.albagatto.it* 🕓 *Closed Sun. No lunch.*

$$ **✗Buffet da Siora Rosa.** Serving delicious and generous portions of tra-
NORTHERN ditional Triestino buffet fare, such as boiled pork and sausages with
ITALIAN savory sauerkraut, Siora Rosa is a bit more comfortable than many
FAMILY buffets. In addition to ample seating in the simple dining room, there
are tables outside for when the weather is good. **Known for:** well-loved
Trieste institution—opened in 1921; big on atmosphere; meat dishes
galore. Ⓢ *Average main: €16* ✉ *Piazza Hortis 3* ☎ *040/301460* ▬ *No
credit cards* ⊘ *Closed Sun. and Mon.*

$ **✗Da Pepi.** A Triestino institution, this is the oldest and most esteemed
NORTHERN of the many "buffet" restaurants serving pork and sausages around
ITALIAN town. It and similar holes-in-the-wall (few tables, simple interior) are
Fodor'sChoice as much a part of the Triestino scene as the cafés. **Known for:** porky
★ platter La Caldaia Da Pepi; panino porzina with mustard and kren;
good for a snack on the hoof. Ⓢ *Average main: €12* ✉ *Via Cassa di
Risparmio 3* ☎ *040/366858* ⊕ *www.buffetdapepi.it* ⊘ *Closed Sun., and
last 2 wks in July.*

$ **✗Mare alla Voliga.** Hidden halfway up the hill to the Castello di San
SEAFOOD Giusto, in what the Triestini call the old city, this informal little res-
taurant specializes in traditional preparations from the cucina povera.
Inexpensive fish—bluefish, sardines, mackerel, mussels, and squid—are
accompanied by salad, potatoes, polenta, and house wine. **Known for:**
simply prepared tasty fish; locals packed in like sarde; relaxed beach-
hut decor and atmosphere. Ⓢ *Average main: €13* ✉ *Via della Fornace
1* ☎ *3336892093 (mobile)* ▬ *No credit cards* ⊘ *Closed Mon. and Tues.*

$$ **✗Suban.** An easy trip just outside town, this landmark trattoria has
NORTHERN been in business since 1865. Sit by the dining room fire or relax on a
ITALIAN huge terrace and watch the sunset. **Known for:** wonderful terrace with
pergola; jota carsolina (a rich soup of cabbage, potatoes, and beans);
warm hospitality. Ⓢ *Average main: €24* ✉ *Via Comici 2* ⊹ *By public
transit, take Bus No. 35 from Piazza Oberdan* ☎ *040/54368* ⊕ *www.
suban.it* ⊘ *Closed Tues., and 2 wks in early Jan.*

WHERE TO STAY

$$ **▦Duchi d'Aosta.** Each of these rooms on the spacious Piazza Unità
HOTEL d'Italia is beautifully furnished in Venetian-Renaissance style, with
Fodor'sChoice dark-wood antiques, rich carpets, and plush fabrics. **Pros:** lots of charm
★ paired with modern convenience; great location; sumptuous breakfast.
Cons: rooms overlooking the piazza can be very expensive; restaurant
overpriced; expensive parking. Ⓢ *Rooms from: €189* ✉ *Piazza Unità
d'Italia 2/1* ☎ *040/7600011* ⊕ *www.grandhotelduchidaosta.com* ⤳ *55
rooms* ⦿ *Free Breakfast.*

$ **▦L'Albero Nascosto Hotel Residence.** Rooms on a busy, narrow street
B&B/INN in the historic center contain paintings by local artists and antique
furniture, and most have kitchenettes. **Pros:** very central; spacious and
simple but tasteful rooms. **Cons:** no elevator; street noise can be a
problem (if noise sensitive, ask for a room in the back). Ⓢ *Rooms from:
€120* ✉ *Via Felice Venezian 18* ☎ *040/300188* ⊕ *www.alberonascosto.
it* ⤳ *10 rooms* ⦿ *Free Breakfast.*

$$$ **▦Riviera & Maximilian's.** Guest rooms come in different styles and sizes,
HOTEL but they all share the glorious vista across the Golfo di Trieste, and an
elevator whisks guests down to a private bathing quay and children's

play area. **Pros:** great views; gorgeous grounds. **Cons:** far from town; some rooms are cramped; some areas need renewal. $ *Rooms from: €225* ✉ *Strada Costiera 22, 7 km (4½ miles) north of Trieste* ☎ *040/224551* ⊕ *www.hotelrivieraemaximilian.com* ⇆ *58 rooms, 9 apartments* ⦿ *Free Breakfast.*

$$ ⌂ **Victoria Hotel Letterario.** A modern full-service hotel with updated
HOTEL
Fodor'sChoice
★
traditional decor, the Victoria is centrally located, helpful for those on business in Trieste, but it's also within easy reach of city's historic sites. **Pros:** large, pleasant rooms; in-room Wi-Fi; in-room hydromassage tubs; sauna; pleasant, helpful staff; reasonable prices. **Cons:** parking fee (€15). $ *Rooms from: €125* ✉ *Alfredo Oriani 2* ☎ *040/362415* ⊕ *www.hotelvictoriatrieste.com* ⇆ *44 rooms* ⦿ *No meals.*

NIGHTLIFE AND PERFORMING ARTS

Trieste is justly famous for its coffeehouses. The elegant civility of Trieste plays out in a café culture combining the refinement of Vienna with the passion of Italy. In Trieste, as elsewhere in Italy, ask for a caffè and you'll get a thimbleful of high-octane espresso. Your cappuccino here will come in the Viennese fashion, with a dollop of whipped cream. Many cafés are part of a *torrefazione* (roasting shop), so you can sample a cup and then buy beans to take with you.

Antico Caffè San Marco. Few cafés in Italy can rival Antico Caffè San Marco for its historic and cultured atmosphere. Founded in 1914, it was largely destroyed in World War I and rebuilt in the 1920s, then restored several more times, but some of the original Art Nouveau interior remains. It became a meeting place for local intellectuals and was the haunt of the Triestino writers Italo Svevo and Umberto Saba. It remains open until midnight on Friday and Saturday, and light meals are available. ✉ *Via Battisti 18* ☎ *040/0641724* ⊕ *www.caffesanmarco. com* ⊗ *Closed Mon.*

Caffè Degli Specchi. For a great view of the great piazza, you can't do better than this café, whose many mirrors make for engaging people-watching. Originally opened in 1839, it was taken over by the British Navy after World War II, and Triestini were not allowed in unless accompanied by an Englishman. Because of its location, the café, open until 9, is heavily frequented by tourists. It's now owned by the Segafredo Zanetti coffee company, and some feel it has lost its local character. ✉ *Piazza dell'Unità d'Italia 7* ☎ *040/365777.*

Caffè Tommaseo. Founded in 1830, this classic café is a comfortable place to linger, especially on weekend evenings and at lunchtime (11–1:30) on Sunday, when there's live music. Although you can still have just a coffee, Tommaseo has evolved into a restaurant, with an extensive menu. It's open nightly until 10 and Friday and Saturday until midnight. ✉ *Piazza Tommaseo 4/C* ☎ *040/362666* ⊕ *www.caffetommaseo.it.*

Teatro Verdi. Trieste's main opera house, built under Austrian rule in 1801, is of interest to aficionados of fine architecture as well as music lovers. Gian Antonio Selva, the architect of Venice's Teatro La Fenice, designed the interior, and Matteo Pertsch, responsible for Milan's Teatro alla Scala, designed the facade. You'll have to attend a performance to view Teatro Verdi's interior; guided tours aren't conducted

5

for individuals. ■TIP→ Opera season runs from October through May, with a brief operetta festival in July and August. ⊠ *Piazza Verdi 1* ☎ *040/6722111* ⊕ *www.teatroverdi-trieste.com.*

SHOPPING

Trieste has some 60 local dealers in jewelry, antiques, and antique wannabes; the city's old center hosts a street market on the third Sunday of each month and a large antiques fair at the end of October. Trieste's busy shopping street, **Corso Italia,** is off the Piazza della Borsa.

CASTELLO DI MIRAMARE

7 km (4½ miles) northwest of Trieste.

The 19th-century castle on the Gulf of Trieste is nothing less than a major expression of the culture of the decaying Austrian Habsburg monarchy. Nowhere else—not even in Vienna—can you savor the decadent opulence of the last years of the Empire.

GETTING HERE AND AROUND

Bus No. 36 from Piazza Oberdan in Trieste runs here every half hour.

EXPLORING

FAMILY

Fodor's Choice

★

Miramar. Maximilian of Habsburg, brother of Emperor Franz Josef and the retired commander of the Austrian Navy, built this seafront extravaganza between 1856 and 1860, complete with a throne room under wooden ceiling in the shape of a ship's keel. In keeping with late-19th-century taste, the rooms are generally furnished with elaborate, somewhat ponderous copies of medieval, Renaissance, and French period furniture, and the walls are covered in red damask. Maximilian's retirement was interrupted in 1864, when he became emperor of Mexico at the initiative of Napoléon III. He was executed three years later by a Mexican firing squad. His wife, Charlotte of Belgium, went mad and returned to Miramar, and later to her native country. During the last years of the Habsburg reign, Miramar became one of the favorite residences of Franz Josef's wife, the Empress Elizabeth (Sissi). The castle was later owned by Duke Amadeo of Aosta, who renovated some rooms in the rationalist style and installed modern plumbing in his Art Deco bathroom. Tours in English are available by reservation. Surrounding the castle is a 54-acre park, partly wooded and partly sculpted into attractive gardens. ⊠ *Viale Miramare, off SS14, Trieste* ☎ *040/224143* ⊕ *www.castello-miramare.it* ▣ *Castle €10, park free.*

6

THE DOLOMITES

WELCOME TO THE DOLOMITES

TOP REASONS TO GO

★ **Driving in the Dolomites:** Your rental Fiat will think it's a Ferrari on a gorgeous drive through the heart of the Dolomites.

★ **Hiking:** No matter your fitness level, there's an unforgettable walk in store for you here.

★ **Skiing:** The Dolomites are renowned as one of Europe's top locations for winter sports.

★ **Museo Archeologico dell'Alto Adige, Bolzano:** The impossibly well-preserved body of the iceman Ötzi, the star attraction at this museum, provokes countless questions about what life was like 5,000 years ago.

★ **Trento:** A graceful fusion of Austrian and Italian styles, this breezy, frescoed town is famed for its imposing castle.

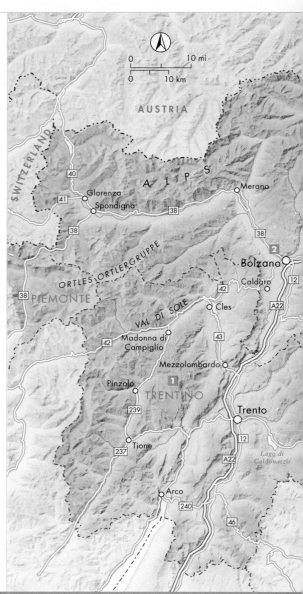

1 Trentino. This butterfly-shape province is Italy with a German accent. Its principal city, history-rich Trento, is at the center.

2 Bolzano (Bozen). Alto Adige's capital is the Dolomites' liveliest city. Look for high-gabled houses, wrought-iron signs, and centuries-old wine cellars.

3 Alto Adige. This region was a part of Austria until the end of World War I, and Austrian sensibilities still predominate over Italian. At the spa town of Merano you can soak in hot springs, take the "grape cure." Caldaro has an appealing wine region.

4 The Heart of the Dolomites. The spectacular Sella mountain range and the surrounding Val di Fassa and Val Gardena make up this region. It's distinguished by great views and great mountain sports, in both summer and winter.

5 Cortina d'Ampezzo. Once a trendy hangout, Cortina has aged gracefully into the grande dame of Italian ski resorts. Summer's are great, with countless options for hiking and mountain activities.

6

EATING AND DRINKING WELL IN THE DOLOMITES

Everything in Alto Adige (and, to a lesser extent, Trentino) has more than a tinge of the Teutonic—and food is no exception. The rich and creamy cuisine here, including fondues, polentas, and barley soups, reflects the Alpine climate and Austrian and Swiss influences.

The quintessential restaurant here is the wood-panel Tirolean *Stube* (pub) serving hearty meat-and-dumpling fare, and there's also a profusion of pastry shops and lively beer halls.

Although the early dining schedule you'll find in Germany or Austria is often somewhat tempered here, your options for late-night meals are more limited than they are in places farther south, where *la dolce vita* has a firmer grip.

Thankfully, the coffee is every bit as good as in parts south—just expect to hear "*danke, grazie*" when paying for your cappuccino.

BEST OF THE WURST

Not to be missed are the outdoor wurst carts, even (or perhaps especially) in colder weather. After placing your order you'll get a sheet of wax paper, followed by a dollop of mustard, a kaiser roll, and your chosen sausage.

You can sometimes make your selection by pointing to whatever picture is most appealing; if not, pass on the familiar-sounding *Frankfurter* and try the local *Meraner*. Carts can reliably be found in Bolzano (try Piazza delle Erbe, or in front of the archaeological museum) and Merano (Piazza del Grano, or along the river).

POLENTA AND DUMPLINGS

Polenta is a staple in the region, in both its creamy and firm varieties, often topped with cheese or mushrooms (or both). Dumplings also appear on many menus; the most distinctive to the region are *canederli* (also known as *Knödel*), *pictured at right,* made from seasoned bread in many variations, and served either in broth or with a sauce.

Other dumplings to look for are the dense *strangolapreti* (literally, "priest-chokers") and *gnocchi di ricotta alla zucca* (ricotta and pumpkin dumplings).

CHEESE

Every isolated mountain valley in the Trentino–Alto Adige seems to make its own variety of cheese, and the local specialty is often simply called *nostrano* (ours).

The best known of the cheeses are the mild Asiago and *fontal* and the more pungent *puzzone di Moena* (literally, "stinkpot"). Try the *schiz*: fresh cheese that's sliced and fried in butter, sometimes with cream added.

PASTRIES AND BAKED GOODS

Bakeries turn out a wide selection of crusty dark rolls and caraway-studded rye breads—maybe not typical Italian bread, but full of flavor. Pastries are reminiscent of what you'd expect to find in Vienna. Apple strudel is everywhere, and for good reason: the best apples in Italy are grown here. There are other

exceptional fruits as well, including pears, plums, and grapes that make their way into baked goods.

ALIMENTARI

If you're planning a picnic or getting provisions for a hike, you'll be well served by the fine *alimentari* (food shops) of Trentino and Alto Adige. They stock a bounty of regional specialties, including cheeses, pickles, salami, and smoked meats. These are good places to pick up a sample of *speck tirolese,* the salt-cured, cold-smoked, deboned ham hock usually cut in paper-thin slices, like prosciutto (though proud speck producers often bristle at the comparison). Don't discard the fat—it's considered the best part.

WINE

Although Trentino and Alto Adige aren't as esteemed for their wines as many other Italian regions, they produce a wide variety of crisp, dry, and aromatic whites—*Kerner, Müller-Thurgau,* and *Traminer,* to name a few—not surprisingly, more like what you'd expect from German vineyards than Italian. Among the reds, look for *lagrein* and the native *teroldego,* a fruity, spicy variety produced only in the tiny valley north of Trento. The Trento D.O.C. appellation yields a marvelous sparkling wine in a class with Champagne.

Updated
by Fergal
Kavanagh

The Dolomites, the inimitable craggy peaks Le Corbusier called "the most beautiful work of architecture ever seen," are never so arresting as at dusk, when the last rays of sun create a pink hue that languishes into purple—locals call this magnificent transformation the *enrosadira*. You can certainly enjoy this glow from a distance, but the Dolomites are such an appealing year-round destination precisely because of the many ways to get into the mountains themselves. In short order, your perspective—like the peaks around you—will become a rosier hue.

The Dolomites are strange, rocky pinnacles that jut straight up like chimneys; they are, in fact, the otherworldly pinnacles that Leonardo depicted in the background of his *Mona Lisa*. In spite of this incredible beauty, the vast, mountainous domain of northeastern Italy has remained relatively undeveloped. Below the peaks, rivers meander through valleys dotted with peaceful villages, while pristine lakes are protected by picture-book castles. In the most secluded Dolomite vales, unique cultures have flourished: the Ladin language, an offshoot of Latin still spoken in the Val Gardena and Val di Fassa, owes its unlikely survival to centuries of topographic isolation.

The more accessible parts of Trentino–Alto Adige, on the other hand, have a history of near-constant intermingling of cultures. The region's Adige and Isarco valleys make up the main access route between Italy and Central Europe, and as a result, the language, cuisine, and architecture are a blend of north and south. The province of Trentino is largely Italian-speaking, but Alto Adige is predominantly Germanic: until World War I the area was Austria's Südtirol. As you move north toward the famed Brenner Pass—through the prosperous valley towns of Rovereto, Trento, and Bolzano—the Teutonic influence is increasingly dominant; by the time you reach Bressanone, it's hard to believe you're in Italy at all.

THE DOLOMITES PLANNER

MAKING THE MOST OF YOUR TIME

For a brief stay, your best choice for a base is vibrant Bolzano, where you can get a sense of the region's contrasts—Italian and German, medieval and modern. After a day or two in town, venture an hour south to history-laden Trento, north to the lovely spa town of Merano, or southwest to Caldaro and its Strada di Vino; all are viable day trips from Bolzano, and Trento and Merano make good places to spend the night as well.

If you have more time, you'll want to get up into the mountains, which are the region's main attraction. The trip on the Grande Strada delle Dolomiti (Great Dolomites Road) through the Heart of the Dolomites from Bolzano to Cortina d'Ampezzo is one of Italy's most spectacular drives. Summer or winter, this is a great destination for mountain sports, with scores of trails for world-class hiking and skiing.

Be sure to look into the Südtirol Museumobil Card when planning your visit. Besides entry to more than 90 museums, the card allows you free use of the regional train system from Brennero to Trento, and the use of all public buses in Südtirol. The card is available for three days (€30) or seven days (€34). The Museumobil Card can be purchased at train stations, tourist offices, some museums, and hotels (⊕ *www.mobilcard. info*). The Brixen Card (free with paid lodging in Bressanone) offers free transportation throughout Südtirol (South Tyrol) and Trentino, and entrance to more than 80 museums, plus free guided tours and discounts at partner venues. See ⊕ *www.brixencard.info* for a list of participating hotels and bed-and-breakfasts. Detailed information about Vie Ferrate in the eastern Dolomites can be found at ⊕ *www.dolomiti.org.* Capable tour organizers include the **Scuola di Alpinismo** (Mountaineering School) in Madonna di Campiglio (☎ *0465/442634* ⊕ *www.guidealpinecampiglio.it*) and Cortina d'Ampezzo (☎ *0436/868505* ⊕ *www. guidecortina.com*).

GETTING HERE AND AROUND

BUS TRAVEL

Regular bus service connects larger cities to the south (Verona, Venice, and Milan) with valley towns in Trentino–Alto Adige (Rovereto, Trento, Bolzano, and Merano). You'll need to change to less-frequent local buses to reach resorts and smaller villages in the mountains beyond.

If you're equipped with current schedules and don't mind adapting your schedules to theirs, it's possible to visit even the remotest villages by bus. ATVO provides year-round service to Cortina from Venice's Piazzale Roma bus park (daily in high season, weekends only in low season), while CortinaExpress has a fast winter bus connection to Venice airport and the nearby Mestre train station. DolomitiBus covers the eastern Dolomites, including a number of small towns. SAD provides service from Bolzano and Bressanone, as does the seasonal Val Gardena Ski Express. SIT provides further information on local services.

Contacts ATVO. ☎ *0421/5944* ⊕ *www.atvo.it.* **CortinaExpress.** ☎ *0436/867350* ⊕ *www.cortinaexpress.it.* **DolomitiBus.** ☎ *0437/217111*

6

⊕ *www.dolomitibus.it.* **SAD.** ☎ *0471/450111* ⊕ *www.sad.it.* **SIT** (*Servizio Integrato di Trasporto).* ☎ *0471/551155, 840/000471 toll-free* ⊕ *www.sii.bz.it.* **Trentino Trasporti.** ☎ *0461/821000* ⊕ *www.ttesercizio.it.*

CAR TRAVEL

Driving is easily the most convenient way to travel in the Dolomites; it can be difficult to reach the ski areas (or any town outside of Rovereto, Trento, Bolzano, and Merano) without a car. Driving is also the most exhilarating way to get around, as you rise from broad valleys into mountains with narrow, winding roads straight out of a sports-car ad. The most important route in the region is the A22, the main north–south highway linking Italy with Central Europe by way of the Brenner Pass. It connects Innsbruck with Bressanone, Bolzano, Trento, and Rovereto, and near Verona joins the A4 autostrada (which runs east–west across northern Italy, from Trieste to Turin). By car, Trento is 3 hours from Milan and 2½ hours from Venice. Bolzano is another 45-minute drive to the north, with Munich four hours farther on.

Caution is essential (tap your horn in advance of hairpin turns), as are chains in winter, when roads are often covered in snow. Sudden closures are common, especially on high mountain passes, and can occur as early as September and as late as May. Even under the best conditions, expect to negotiate mountain roads at speeds no greater than 50 kph (30 mph).

TRAIN TRAVEL

The rail line following the course of the Isarco and Adige valleys—from Munich and Innsbruck, through the Brenner Pass, and southward past Bressanone, Bolzano, Trento, and Rovereto en route to Verona—is well trafficked, making trains a viable option for travel between these towns. Eurocity trains on the Dortmund–Venice and Munich–Innsbruck–Rome routes stop at these stations, and you can connect with other Italian lines at Verona. Although branch lines from Trento and Bolzano do extend into some of the smaller valleys (including hourly service between Bolzano and Merano), most of the mountain attractions are beyond the reach of trains.

Contacts Trenitalia. ☎ *892021 within Italy* ⊕ *www.trenitalia.com.*

RESTAURANTS

When dining out in the Dolomites, it's evident you are in a part of Italy that was once part of the Austrian Empire. While you can still find traditional Italian pasta and pizza, in this region the tastes blend with Austro-Germanic flare. Sausages, *spätzle* (like pasta but with a different consistency), meats, cheeses, and polenta can be found on nearly every menu—foods that will sustain the body through a long day of skiing or hiking. Many restaurants either raise their own crops and livestock, or have a direct relationship with their farmers and providers. *Restaurant reviews have been shortened. For full information, visit Fodors.com.*

HOTELS

Classic Dolomite lodging options include restored castles, chalets, and stately 19th-century hotels. The small villages that pepper the Dolomites often have scores of flower-bedecked inns, many of them inexpensive. Hotel information offices at train stations and tourist offices can help if you've arrived without reservations. The Bolzano train station has a 24-hour hotel service, and tourist offices will give you a list of all the hotels in the area, arranged by location, stars, and price. Hotels at ski resorts cater to longer stays at full or half board. Many Italians come to the Dolomites every winter for their Settimana Bianca (White Week), and if you care to join them you should book ski vacations as packages well in advance. Most rural accommodations close from early November to mid- or late December, as well as for a month or two after Easter. The majority of *rifugi* (mountain huts) on hiking trails are operated by the **Club Alpino Italiano** (⊕ *www.cai.it*). Contact information for both CAI-run and private rifugi is available from local tourist offices; most useful are those in Madonna di Campiglio (⊕ *www.campiglio.com*), Cortina d'Ampezzo (⊕ *www.dolomiti.org*), Val di Fassa (⊕ *www.fassa.com*), and Val Gardena (⊕ *www.val-gardena.com*). *Hotel reviews have been shortened. For full information, visit Fodors.com.*

WHAT IT COSTS			
$	**$$**	**$$$**	**$$$$**
Restaurants	under €15	€15–€24	€25–€35	over €35
Hotels	under €125	€125–€200	€201–€300	over €300

Prices in the dining reviews are the average cost of a main course at dinner, or, if dinner is not served, at lunch. Prices in the reviews are the lowest cost of a standard double room in high season.

TRENTINO

Until the end of World War I, Trentino was Italy's frontier with the Austro-Hungarian Empire, and although this province remains unmistakably Italian, Germanic influences are tangible in all aspects of life here, including architecture, cuisine, culture, and language. Visitors are drawn by historical sites reflecting a strategic position at the intersection of southern and Central Europe: Trento was the headquarters of the Catholic Counter-Reformation. Numerous year-round mountain resorts, including fashionable Madonna di Campiglio, are in the wings of the butterfly-shape region.

TRENTO

58 km (36 miles) south of Bolzano.

Trento is a prosperous, cosmopolitan university town that retains an architectural charm befitting its historical importance. It was here, from 1545 to 1563, that the structure of the Catholic Church was redefined at the Council of Trent. This was the starting point of the Counter-Reformation, which brought half of Europe back to Catholicism. The word *consiglio* (council) appears everywhere in Trento—in hotel, restaurant, and street names, and even on wine labels.

Today the Piazza del Duomo remains splendid, and its enormous medieval palazzo dominates the city landscape in virtually its original form. The 24-hour Trentino Card (⊕ *www.visittrentino.it*) is given free to hotel guests, and grants admission to one museum as well as all public transportation. Non–hotel guests can make use of the 48-hour Museum Pass (€22), which allows unlimited access to all sights in Trento and Rovereto as well as free public transportation in Trentino (⊕ *www. museumpass.it*). It can be bought at tourist offices or participating museums, and can even be converted into a three-month card for no extra charge.

GETTING HERE AND AROUND

The A22 is the main highway to Trento. From the north, take the Trento Nord exit; from the south, take the Trento Sud exit. There are signs directing you to the city center. Trento is easily accessible from Venice (2½ hours) and Verona (just over an hour), and is only 4½ hours from Munich. The city center is pedestrian-friendly, or you can use the transit options in conjunction with the Trento Card for discounts on the city buses.

TOURS

Guided Tours of Trento. Guided tours of Trento begin from the tourism office on Saturdays at 3 pm. Private tours can be arranged for any time; tours of less than 25 people for three hours cost €147, while tours for 25–50 people are €155. ■ TIP➔ Tours are not always offered in English; to guarantee an English-speaking guide, call for reservations. ⊠ *Piazza Dante 24* ☎ *0461/216000* ⊕ *www.discovertrento.it/en/citta-di-trento/ visite-guidate* 🎫 *€6.*

VISITOR INFORMATION

Contact Trento Tourism Office. ⊠ *Piazza Dante 24* ☎ *0461/216000* ⊕ *www. discovertrento.it.*

EXPLORING

TOP ATTRACTIONS

Fodor's Choice ★ **Castello del Buonconsiglio** (*Castle of Good Counsel*). The position and size of this stronghold of the prince-bishops made it easier to defend than the Palazzo Pretorio. Look for the evolution of architectural styles: the medieval fortifications of the Castelvecchio section (on the far left) were built in the 13th century; the fancier Renaissance Magno Palazzo section (on the far right) wasn't completed until 300 years later. The 13th-century **Torre dell'Aquila** (Eagle's Tower) is home to the castle's artistic highlight, a 15th-century *ciclo dei mesi* (cycle of the months). The four-wall fresco is full of charming and detailed scenes of medieval life in both court and countryside. ⊠ *Via Bernardo Clesio 5* ☎ *0461/233770* ⊕ *www.buonconsiglio.it* 🎫 *€10; Torre dell'Aquila €2* ⊗ *Closed Mon.*

Museo Diocesano Tridentino. Located inside the **Palazzo Pretorio,** the Museo Diocesano Tridentino is where you can see paintings and other objects that come from the treasury of the adjoining Cathedral of San Vigilio. This includes the seating plan of the prelates during the Council of Trent; early-16th-century tapestries by Pieter van Aelst (1502–56), the Belgian artist who carried out Raphael's 15th-century designs for the Vatican tapestries; many carved wood altars and statues; and an

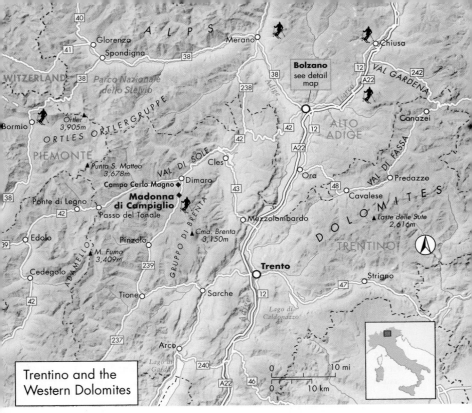

Trentino and the
Western Dolomites

11th-century sacramentary, or book of services. The palazzo itself was built in the 13th century and designed to seem like a wing of the Duomo; it became the fortified residence of the prince-bishops, who enjoyed considerable power and autonomy within the medieval hierarchy. The remarkable palazzo has lost none of its original splendor. Accessible through the museum, although currently closed, a subterranean archaeological area reveals the 1st-century Roman Porta Veronensis, which marked the road to Verona. ⊠ *Piazza del Duomo 18* ☎ *0461/234419* ⊕ *www.museodiocesanotridentino.it* ⊠ *€7; free 1st Sun. of month* ⊗ *Closed Tues.*

Tridentum. The ancient Roman city of Tridentum lies beneath much of Trento's city center. Centuries of Adige River flooding buried ruins that only recently have been unearthed on public and private land. Beneath this piazza lies the largest of the archaeological sites, revealing some marvels of Roman technology, such as under-floor home heating and under-street sewers complete with manhole covers. The Romans also used lead pipes for four centuries before recognizing it was hazardous to health. ⊠ *Piazza Cesare Battisti* ☎ *0461/230171* ⊠ *€2.50* ⊗ *Closed Mon.*

WORTH NOTING

Belvedere di Sardagna. Take the Funivia Trento–Sardagna cable car up to the Belvedere di Sardagna, a lookout point 1,200 feet above medieval Trento. ■ TIP→ **This is open year-round, but can close due to inclement weather.** ✉ *Via Monte Grappa 1* ☎ *0461/232154* 🎫 *€5 round-trip.*

Santa Maria Maggiore. Many sessions of the Council of Trent met in this Renaissance church. Limited light enters through the simple rose window over the main door, so you have to strain to see the magnificent ceiling, an intricate combination of stucco and frescoes. The church is off the northwest side of the Piazza del Duomo, about 200 yards down Via Cavour. ✉ *Vicolo Orsoline 1* ☎ *0461/891111.*

Via Belenzani. Locals refer to this street as Trento's outdoor gallery because of the frescoed facades of the hallmark Renaissance palazzi. It's an easy 50-yard walk up the lane behind the church of Santa Maria Maggiore. ✉ *Trento.*

WHERE TO EAT

$ NORTHERN ITALIAN 🍴 **Al Vò.** Trento's oldest trattoria (it's the descendant of a 14th-century tavern) remains one of its most popular lunch spots. Locals crowd into a simple, modern dining room to enjoy regional specialtes such as gnocchi with vegetables, and *baccalà* (salt cod). **Known for:** Trento's oldest eatery; knowledgeable welcoming staff; its fine selection of wines. [$] *Average main: €11* ✉ *Vicolo del Vò 11* ☎ *0461/985374* 🌐 *www.ristorantealvo.it* 🕒 *Closed Sun. No dinner Mon.–Wed. and Sat.*

$ NORTHERN ITALIAN 🍴 **Antica Birreria Pedavena.** Come here for the beer—five different varieties are brewed in-house and served in the charismatic beer hall. Meals include wursts, meat and cheese platters, pizzas, and huge salads. **Known for:** the fine selection of brewed in-house beers; the typical Bavarian meats; its enormous beer hall. [$] *Average main: €10* ✉ *Via Santa Croce 15* ☎ *0461/986255* 🌐 *www.birreriapedavena.com.*

$$ NORTHERN ITALIAN 🍴 **Le Due Spade.** An intimate dining room that started out as a Tirolean tavern around the time of the Council of Trent, this is known for superb cuisine, both traditional and more innovative, adeptly served amid the coziness of wood paneling and an antique stove. The menu, which is updated throughout the year, is divided into mountain and seafood specialties. **Known for:** fine dining; knowledgeable, welcoming personnel; cozy wood paneling interior. [$] *Average main: €20* ✉ *Via Rizzi 11* ☎ *0461/234343* 🌐 *www.leduespade.com* 🕒 *Closed Sun. No lunch Mon.*

$ NORTHERN ITALIAN 🍴 **Scrigno del Duomo.** More than 30 wines by the glass, accompanied by an excellent selection of local cheeses, are served in this chic eatery, with outside seating in the piazza. Salads and regional specialties are prepared in the open kitchen by gourmet chefs; they also bake their own bread daily. **Known for:** traditional food and local wine; fine views of the cathedral; local art and history. [$] *Average main: €13* ✉ *Piazza del Duomo 29* ☎ *0461/220030* 🌐 *www.scrignodelduomo.com.*

$$ NORTHERN ITALIAN 🍴 **Trattoria Orso Grigio.** The family-run trattoria is located down a nondescript side street and serves tasty fare in a congenial atmosphere. Choose from typical regional dishes—look for *rufioi* (homemade ravioli stuffed with savoy cabbage)—served in a bright garden courtyard when the weather is nice. **Known for:** friendly congenial atmosphere; generations of culinary expertise; the shady vine-covered courtyard.

$ *Average main: €17* ✉ *Via degli Orti 19* ☎ *0461/984400* 🌐 *www.orsogrigiotrento.com* ⏲ *Closed Sun.*

WHERE TO STAY

$ HOTEL 🏨 **Accademia.** Stylish, contemporary bedrooms with comfortable beds and handsome lithographs occupy an ancient, character-filled house close to the railway station and Piazza del Duomo. **Pros:** central location; beautiful courtyard; gluten-free breakfast. **Cons:** some rooms are small; guests have complained about flies. $ *Rooms from: €107* ✉ *Vicolo Colico 4* ☎ *0461/233600* 🌐 *www.accademiahotel.it* ⏲ *Closed 1 wk at Christmas* 🛏 *40 rooms* 🍴 *Free Breakfast.*

$ B&B/INN Fodor's Choice ★ 🏨 **Castel Pergine.** Tucked into a 13th-century castle's labyrinth of stone and brick chambers, prisons, and chapels are sparse, rustic rooms with carved-wood trim, lace curtains, and heavy wooden beds, some canopied. **Pros:** romantic setting; great restaurant. **Cons:** simple accommodations; need a car to get around. $ *Rooms from: €124* ✉ *Via al Castello 10, 11 km (7 miles) east of Trento, Pergine Valsugana* ☎ *0461/531158* 🌐 *www.castelpergine.it* ⏲ *Closed Nov.–Mar.* 🛏 *20 rooms* 🍴 *Free Breakfast.*

$$ HOTEL 🏨 **Grand Hotel Trento.** A contemporary rounded facade stands out among the ancient palaces nearby; inside you'll find a handsome marble-paved lobby, rich draperies in the restaurant, and ample rooms with clubby wood-trim furniture. **Pros:** near train station; professional service; wellness center. **Cons:** busy neighborhood. $ *Rooms from: €125* ✉ *Piazza Dante 20* ☎ *0461/271000* 🌐 *www.grandhoteltrento.com* 🛏 *136 rooms* 🍴 *No meals.*

$$ HOTEL 🏨 **Hotel Garni Aquila d'Oro.** Each room has its own contemporary design, some have saunas with hot tubs and stunning views, and all enjoy a prime location near Piazza del Duomo. **Pros:** excellent location; friendly service. **Cons:** common areas rather cramped. $ *Rooms from: €160* ✉ *Via Belenzani 76* ☎ *0461/986282* 🌐 *www.aquiladoro.it* 🛏 *16 rooms* 🍴 *Free Breakfast.*

$ B&B/INN 🏨 **Hotel Garni Venezia.** For reasonably priced accommodations, it's hard to beat this *garni* (bed-and-breakfast) right on Piazza Duomo, where six of the simple rooms have wonderful views. **Pros:** great location; friendly environs. **Cons:** piazza can be noisy; not all rooms have private baths. $ *Rooms from: €83* ✉ *Via Belenzani 70, Piazza Duomo 45* ☎ *0461/234559* 🌐 *www.hotelveneziatn.it* 🛏 *43 rooms* 🍴 *Free Breakfast.*

$ RESORT 🏨 **Imperial Grand Hotel Terme.** If you're in the mood for some pampering, choose a grand room with a frescoed ceiling in the graciously restored, golden-yellow palace in the nearby spa town of Levico Terme. **Pros:** beautiful park setting; pleasant indoor pool. **Cons:** standard rooms are small; use of thermal baths costs extra. $ *Rooms from: €79* ✉ *Via Silva Domini 1, 20 km (12 miles) east of Trento, Levico Terme* ☎ *0461/700512* 🌐 *www.hotel-imperial-levico.com* 🛏 *81 rooms* 🍴 *No meals.*

NIGHTLIFE AND PERFORMING ARTS

I Suoni delle Dolomiti (*The Sounds of the Dolomites*). This annual series of free concerts is held high in the hills of Trentino in July and August, offering the wonderful experience of enjoying chamber music played in grassy meadows. ⊠ *Trento* ☎ *0461/219300* ⊕ *www.isuonidelledolomiti.it.*

SHOPPING

Enoteca di Corso. This atmospheric shop, a bit outside the town center, is laden with local products, including wine and sweets. ⊠ *Corso 3 Novembre 64* ☎ *0461/916424* ⊕ *www.enotecadelcorsotrento.it.*

La Salumeria Lunelli. This specialty food shop boasts an impressive array of sauces, as well as wines, grappas, and liqueurs. A picnic can be handily assembled from a huge assortment of local salamis and cheeses. ⊠ *Via Mazzini 46* ☎ *0461/238053* ⊕ *www.lunelli.it.*

Panificio Pulin. Whole-grain breads and delicate pastries are on offer in this fragrant bakery. ⊠ *Via Cavour 23* ☎ *0461/234544.*

Piazza Alessandro Vittoria. You can pick up meats, cheeses, produce, local truffles, and porcini mushrooms at the small morning market in the square. ⊠ *Trento.*

MADONNA DI CAMPIGLIO

80 km (50 miles) northwest of Trento, 100 km (62 miles) southwest of Bolzano.

The winter resort of Madonna di Campiglio vies with Cortina d'Ampezzo as the most fashionable place for Italians to ski and be seen in the Dolomites. Madonna's popularity is well deserved, with 62 lifts connecting more than 150 km (93 miles) of well-groomed ski runs and equally good lodging and trekking facilities. The resort itself is a modest 5,000 feet above sea level, but the downhill runs, summer hiking paths, and mountain-biking trails venture high up into the surrounding peaks (including Pietra Grande at 9,700 feet).

GETTING HERE AND AROUND

By car from Trento, take the SS45 toward Vezzano. After Vezzano, continue to the SS237 until Ragoli, and turn onto the SP34. Follow the SP34 for 6 km (4 miles), and turn onto the SS239 for another 23 km (15 miles) until you arrive at Madonna di Campiglio. The more convenient railway station is at Trento; then you can ride the Trentino Trasporti bus for two and a half hours from Trento for €5.10.

VISITOR INFORMATION

Contact Madonna di Campiglio Tourism Office. ⊠ *Via Pradalago 4* ☎ *0465/447501* ⊕ *www.campigliodolomiti.it.*

EXPLORING

Campo Carlo Magno. The stunning pass at Campo Carlo Magno (5,500 feet) is 3 km (2 miles) north of Madonna di Campiglio. This is where Charlemagne is said to have stopped in AD 800 on his way to Rome to be crowned emperor. Stop here to glance over the whole of northern Italy. If you continue north, take the descent with caution—in the space of a mile or so, hairpin turns and switchbacks deliver you down more than 2,000 feet. ⊠ *Madonna di Campiglio.*

WHERE TO EAT

$$

NORTHERN ITALIAN

✕**Cascina Zeledria.** Although the majority of meals in Madonna are taken in resort hotels, Italians consider an on-mountain dinner like one in this remote, rustic refuge to be an indispensable part of a proper ski week. In winter, you'll be collected on a Sno-Cat and ferried up the slopes (you'll hike up in warmer months). **Known for:** rural mountain setting; transport by Sno-Cat; local food and wine. $ *Average main:* €18 ⊠ *Località Zeledria* ☎ *0465/440303* ⊕ *www.zeledria.it* ⊗ *Closed May, June, Oct., and Nov.*

$$$

WINE BAR

✕**Ferrari Spazio Bollicine Nabucco.** This intimate venue has the feel of a rustic-yet-stylish chalet and is done in a black-and-white color scheme. Guests settle into these pleasant surroundings for an après-ski aperitif or a light meal based on local ingredients and paired with sparkling wines from Ferrari, a well-known Trentino vintner. **Known for:** predinner cocktails; intimate atmosphere; central location. $ *Average main:* €30 ⊠ *Piazza Righi B3* ☎ *0465/440756* ⊕ *www.ferrarispaziobollicine. it* ⊗ *Closed May–Nov.*

WHERE TO STAY

$$

HOTEL

Golf Hotel. You need to make your way north to the Campo Carlo Magno Pass to reach this grand hotel, the former summer residence of Habsburg emperor Franz Josef, replete with verandas, Persian rugs, and bay windows. **Pros:** attractive indoor pool; elegant rooms. **Cons:** long walk into town; popular with business groups. $ *Rooms from:* €140 ⊠ *Via Cima Tosa 3* ☎ *0465/441003, 049 /2956411 bookings* ⊕ *www.th-resorts.com/golf-hotel-campiglio* ⊗ *Closed late Apr.–June and Sept.–early Dec.* ⟲ *109 rooms* ⊙| *Free Breakfast.*

$$$

HOTEL

Fodor's Choice

★

Grifone. At this comfortable lodge with a distinctive wood facade, flower-bedecked balconies catch the sun and contemporary guest rooms and suites have views of the forested slopes. **Pros:** convenient location; charming decor. **Cons:** lacks air-conditioning; a bit out of town (but the Spinale cable car is nearby). $ *Rooms from:* €250 ⊠ *Via Vallesinella 7* ☎ *0465/442002* ⊕ *www.stylehotelgrifone.it* ⊗ *Closed mid-Apr.–June and Sept.–Nov.* ⟲ *40 rooms* ⊙| *No meals.*

$$

HOTEL

Hotel Casa del Campo. This charming Tirolean-style hotel is just yards from the ski slopes and paths for "ski-fondo" (cross-country skiing). **Pros:** fantastic service; great location for outdoor activities. **Cons:** seven-day minimum stay, or 20% service fee for shorter stays in high season. $ *Rooms from:* €200 ⊠ *Passo Campo Carlo Magno* ☎ *0465/443130* ⊕ *www.casadelcampo.it* ⌂ *Reservations essential* ⟲ *15 rooms* ⊙| *No meals.*

$$$

HOTEL

Savoia Palace. At Madonna's most traditional lodging, guest rooms and lounges are full of carved-wood and mountain-style furnishings and two fireplaces blaze away in the bar, where you can relax as you recall the day's exploits on the ski slopes. **Pros:** central location in town; warm atmosphere; nice spa. **Cons:** a minimum seven-day stay with half board is mandatory; faces a busy street. $ *Rooms from:* €250 ⊠ *Viale Dolomiti di Brenta 18* ☎ *0465/441004* ⊕ *www.savoiapalace.it* ⊗ *Closed mid-Apr.–June and Sept.–Dec.* ⟲ *55 rooms* ⊙| *Some meals.*

6

SPORTS AND THE OUTDOORS

HIKING AND CLIMBING

The Madonna di Campiglio tourism office has maps of a dozen trails leading to waterfalls, lakes, and stupefying views.

Monte Spinale (*Spinale Peak*). The cable car to 6,900-foot-high Monte Spinale offers skiers magnificent views of the Brenta Dolomites in winter. It also runs during peak summer season. ⊠ *Off Via Monte Spinale* 📞 *0465/447744* ⊕ *www.funiviecampiglio.it/it/meteo-campiglio/41-estate/85-cabinoviaspinale* 💷 *€10 round-trip.*

SKIING

Funivie Madonna di Campiglio. Miles of interconnecting ski runs—some of the best in the Dolomites—are linked by the cable cars and lifts of Funivie Madonna di Campiglio. Advanced skiers will like the extremely difficult terrain found on certain mountain faces, but there are also many intermediate and beginner runs, all accessible from town. There are also plenty of off-piste opportunities. Passes can be purchased at the main *funivia* (cable car) in town, and multiday passes are available. ⊠ *Via Presanella 12* 📞 *0465/447744* ⊕ *www.funiviecampiglio.it* 💷 *Passes €46–€51 per day.*

BOLZANO (BOZEN)

32 km (19 miles) south of Merano, 50 km (31 miles) north of Trento.

Bolzano (Bozen), capital of the autonomous province of Alto Adige, is tucked among craggy peaks in a Dolomite valley 77 km (48 miles) from the Brenner Pass and Austria. Tirolean culture dominates Bolzano's language, food, architecture, and people. It may be hard to remember that you're in Italy when walking the city's colorful cobblestone streets and visiting its lantern-lighted cafés, where you may enjoy sauerkraut and a beer among a lively crowd of blue-eyed German speakers. However, the fine Italian espresso and the boutiques will help remind you where you are. The long, narrow arcades of its Via dei Portici house shops that specialize in Tirolean crafts and clothing, as well as many Italian designers. With castles and steeples topping the landscape, this quiet city at the confluence of the Isarco (Eisack) and Talvera rivers has retained its provincial appeal. Proximity to fabulous skiing and mountain climbing—not to mention the world's oldest preserved human body—make it a worthwhile tourist destination. And its streets are immaculate: after Milan, residents here have the highest per capita earnings of any city in Italy.

The Bolzano-Bozen Card (€38), on sale at the tourist office, gives free entry to 90 museums in Bolzano and Alto Adige, as well as free transport throughout the region, guided tours, and bike rental.

GETTING HERE AND AROUND

By car from Trento, take the A22 for 60 km (37 miles) to Bolzano Sud. The train station is just steps away from Piazza Walther, and has regular service from Italy and Munich (four hours). The SASA bus can help you connect between Bolzano and other parts of the region. There is

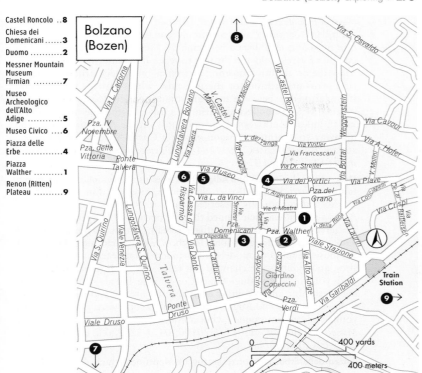

an airport in Bolzano, but its connections are not as convenient as the larger airports at Venice, Verona, and Munich.

VISITOR INFORMATION

Contact **Bolzano Tourism Office.** ✉ *Via Alto Adige 60, Bolzano* ☎ *0471/307000* ⊕ *www.bolzano-bozen.it.*

EXPLORING

TOP ATTRACTIONS

Chiesa dei Domenicani. The 13th-century Dominican Church is renowned for its **Cappella di San Giovanni,** where you can see frescoes from the Giotto school that show the birth of a pre-Renaissance sense of depth and individuality. ✉ *Piazza Domenicani, Bolzano* ☎ *0471/973133.*

Duomo. A lacy spire looks down on the mosaiclike roof tiles of the city's Gothic cathedral, built between the 12th and 14th century. Inside are 14th- and 15th-century frescoes and an intricately carved stone pulpit dating from 1514. Outside, don't miss the **Porta del Vino** (Wine Gate) on the northeast side; decorative carvings of grapes and harvest workers attest to the long-standing importance of wine to this region. ✉ *Piazza della Parrocchia 27, Bolzano* ☎ *0471/978676.*

Fodor'sChoice   **Messner Mountain Museum Firmian.** Perched on a peak overlooking Bol-
★   zano, 10th-century Castle Sigmundskron is home to one of six mountain museums established by Reinhold Messner—the first climber to
conquer Everest solo and the first to reach its summit without oxygen.
The Tibetan tradition of *kora,* a circular pilgrimage around a sacred
site, is an inspiration for the museum, where visitors contemplate
the relationship between man and mountain, guided by images and
objects Messner collected during his adventures. The museum is 3
km (2 miles) southwest of Bolzano, just off the Appiano exit on the
highway to Merano. ⊠ *Sigmundskron Castle 53, Sigmundskroner-
strasse, Bolzano* ☎ *0471/631264* ⊕ *www.messner-mountain-museum.
it* ⊠ *€12* ⊘ *Closed Thurs.*

Fodor'sChoice   **Museo Archeologico dell'Alto Adige.** This museum has gained international
★   fame for Ötzi, its 5,300-year-old iceman, discovered in 1991 and the
world's oldest naturally preserved body. In 1998 Italy acquired it from
Austria after it was determined that the body lay 100 yards inside Italian territory. The iceman's leathery remains are displayed in a freezer
vault, preserved along with his longbow, ax, and clothing. The rest of
the museum relies on models and artifacts from nearby archaeological
sites, and exhibits are changed out regularly. An English audio guide
leads you not only through Ötzi's Copper Age, but also into the preceding Mesolithic and Neolithic eras, and the Bronze and Iron Ages that
followed. In July and August, the museum's supervised play area keeps
young children entertained while adults experience the museum. ⊠ *Via
Museo 43, Bolzano* ☎ *0471/320100, 0471/320120* ⊕ *www.iceman.it*
⊠ *€9* ⊘ *Closed Mon.*

Piazza delle Erbe. A bronze statue of Neptune, which dates to 1745,
presides over a bountiful fruit-and-vegetable market in this square. The
stalls spill over with colorful displays of local produce; bakeries and
grocery stores showcase hot breads, pastries, cheeses, and delicatessen
meats—a complete picnic. Try the *speck tirolese* (a thinly sliced smoked
ham) and the apple strudel. ⊠ *Bolzano.*

Piazza Walther. This pedestrians-only square is Bolzano's heart; in
warmer weather it serves as an open-air living room where locals and
tourists can be found at all hours sipping a drink (such as a glass of
chilled Riesling). In the center stands Heinrich Natter's white-marble,
neo-Romanesque **Monument to Walther,** built in 1889. The piazza's
namesake was the 12th-century German wandering minstrel Walther
von der Vogelweide, whose songs lampooned the papacy and praised
the Holy Roman Emperor. ⊠ *Piazza Walther, Bolzano.*

WORTH NOTING

Castel Roncolo (*Schloss Runkelstein*). Green hills and farmhouses north
of town surround this meticulously kept castle with a tiled roof. It was
built in 1237, destroyed half a century later, and then rebuilt soon
thereafter. The world's largest cycle of secular medieval frescoes, beautifully preserved, is inside. A tavern in the courtyard serves excellent
local food and wines. To get here from Piazza Walther, take the free
shuttle (Tuesday through Sunday every half hour 10–5), or Bus No. 12
or 14. It's a 45-minute walk from Piazza delle Erbe: head north along

Via Francescani, continue through Piazza Madonna, connecting to Via Castel Roncolo. ⊠ *Via San Antonio 15, Bolzano* ☎ *0471/329808 castle, 0471/324073 tavern* ⊕ *www.roncolo.info* ☁ *€8* ⊙ *Closed Mon.*

Museo Civico. Bolzano's municipal museum has a rich collection of traditional costumes, wood carvings, and archaeological exhibits. Not all floors are currently open, but entrance is free while renovations are ongoing. Climb to the fourth floor for a full view of the city and the surrounding mountains. ⊠ *Via Cassa di Risparmio 14, Bolzano* ☎ *0471/997960* ⊕ *www.comune.bolzano.it/museo_civico* ☁ *Free* ⊙ *Closed Mon.*

Renon (Ritten) Plateau. The earth pyramids of Renon Plateau are a bizarre geological formation where erosion has left a forest of tall, thin, needle-like spires of rock, each topped with a boulder. To get here, take the Soprabolzano cable car from Via Renon, about 300 yards left of the Bolzano train station. At the top, switch to the electric train that takes you to the plateau, which is in Collalbo, just above Bolzano. The two rides cost €15 round-trip and take about 12 minutes total. The final 30-minute hike along gentle Trail No. 24 is free. ⊠ *Via Renon, Collalbo* ☎ *0471/356100* ⊕ *www.ritten.com* ☁ *€15 round-trip.*

6

WHERE TO EAT

$
WINE BAR

✕**Batzen Brau.** Locals hold animated conversations over glasses of regional wine in a modern take on a traditional Stube. Tasty south Tirolean specialties include speck tirolese and *mezzelune casarecce ripiene* (house-made stuffed half-moons of pasta). **Known for:** convivial atmosphere; large portions; late dining. $ *Average main: €14* ⊠ *Via Andreas Hofer 30, Bolzano* ☎ *0471/050950* ⊕ *www.batzen.it.*

$$
NORTHERN
ITALIAN

✕**Cavallino Bianco Weisses Rossl.** A spacious, comfortable dining room near Via dei Portici is a dependable favorite with residents as well as visitors. A wide selection of Italian and German dishes are served to large tables of families enjoying their meals together. **Known for:** generations of cooking; crowded, friendly atmosphere; local dishes. $ *Average main: €16* ⊠ *Via Bottai 6, Bolzano* ☎ *0471/973267* ⊕ *www.weissesroessl.org* ⊙ *Closed Sun. No dinner Sat.*

$
NORTHERN
ITALIAN

✕**Hopfen & Co.** Fried white *Würstel* (sausage), sauerkraut, and grilled ribs complement the excellent home-brewed Austrian-style pilsner and wheat beer at this bustling pub-restaurant, which attracts Bolzano's students and young professionals. **Known for:** home-brewed beer; bustling atmosphere; traditional pub environment. $ *Average main: €10* ⊠ *Piazza delle Erbe, Obstplatz 17, Bolzano* ☎ *0471/300788.*

$$
NORTHERN
ITALIAN

✕**Wirthaus Vögele.** Ask residents of Bolzano where they like to dine out, and odds are good they'll tell you Vögele, one of the area's oldest inns. The classic wood-paneled dining room on the ground level is often packed, but don't despair, as the restaurant has two additional floors. **Known for:** friendly vibe; late dining; local dishes. $ *Average main: €20* ⊠ *Goethestr 3, Bolzano* ☎ *0471/973938* ⊕ *www.voegele.it* ⊙ *Closed Sun.*

$$$ NORTHERN ITALIAN
🍴 **Zür Kaiserkron.** Traditional Tirolean opulence and attentive service set the stage for some of the best food in town. Appetizers might include potato blini with salmon caviar, and marinated artichokes with butter (not to be missed if available). **Known for:** fine dining; sophisticated atmosphere; central location. [$] *Average main: €26* ✉ *Piazza della Mostra 1, Bolzano* ☎ *0471/980214* 🌐 *www.zurkaiserkron.com* ⏲ *Closed Sun. and holidays.*

WHERE TO STAY

$$$ HOTEL Fodor's Choice ★
🏨 **Hotel Greif.** Individually designed guest rooms in a centuries-old Bolzano landmark feature clean-line modern furnishings and contemporary art paired with 19th-century paintings and sketches. **Pros:** elegant decor; helpful staff; central location. **Cons:** rooms vary in size. [$] *Rooms from: €206* ✉ *Piazza Walther 1, Bolzano* ☎ *0471/318000* 🌐 *www.greif.it* 🛏 *33 rooms* 🍽 *Free Breakfast.*

$$ HOTEL
🏨 **Luna-Mondschein.** Comfortable, wood-paneled rooms, some with balconies, overlook a garden or the mountains, and all are swathed in the charming ambience of this inn from 1798. **Pros:** central location; great buffet breakfast. **Cons:** some rooms are small; rooms facing garage can be noisy. [$] *Rooms from: €150* ✉ *Via Piave 15, Bolzano* ☎ *0471/975642* 🌐 *www.hotel-luna.it* 🛏 *80 rooms* 🍽 *Free Breakfast.*

$$ HOTEL
🏨 **Parkhotel Laurin.** An exercise in Art Nouveau opulence, presiding over a large park in the middle of town, is one of the best hotels in all of Alto Adige, with art-filled modern guest rooms and handsome public spaces. **Pros:** convenient location; excellent restaurant. **Cons:** rooms facing park can be noisy; can be packed with business groups. [$] *Rooms from: €188* ✉ *Via Laurin 4, Bolzano* ☎ *0471/311000* 🌐 *www.laurin.it* 🛏 *100 rooms* 🍽 *Free Breakfast.*

$ B&B/INN
🏨 **Schloss Korb.** This romantic 13th-century castle with crenellations and a massive tower is perched in a park amid vine-covered hills, viewed from some of the cozy rooms through Romanesque arched windows. **Pros:** romantic setting; charming traditional furnishings. **Cons:** not all rooms are in the castle; need a car to get around. [$] *Rooms from: €114* ✉ *Via Castel d'Appiano 5, Missiano* ☎ *0471/636000* 🌐 *www.schloss-hotel-korb.com* ⏲ *Closed Nov.–Mar.* 🛏 *49 rooms* 🍽 *Free Breakfast.*

SPORTS AND THE OUTDOORS

BIKING

Alp Bike. If you're in decent shape, a great way to see some of the surrounding castles, lakes, and forested valleys of the Dolomites is by bike. Alp Bike leads different guided excursions almost every day, at all levels, but you must reserve a week or more ahead for the more ambitious trips. It is suggested that you email (*info@alpbike.it*), as they are often away from the office. They can help with bike rentals as well. ✉ *Via Castel Flavon 101, Bolzano* ☎ *338/1126584* 🌐 *www.alpbike.it.*

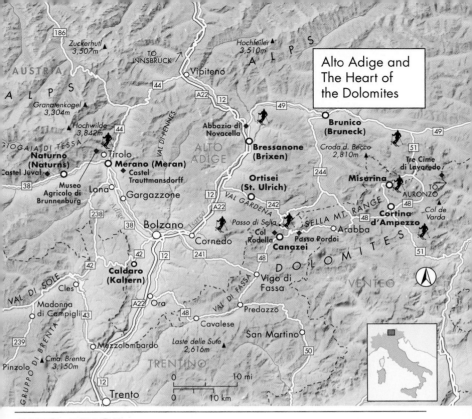

ALTO ADIGE

Prosperous valley towns (such as the famed spa center of Merano) and mountain resorts entice those seeking both relaxation and adventure. Alto Adige (Südtirol) was for centuries part of the Austro-Hungarian Empire, only ceded to Italy at the end of World War I. Ethnic differences led to inevitable tensions in the 1960s and again in the '80s, though a large measure of provincial autonomy has, for the most part, kept the lid on nationalist ambitions. Today Germanic and Italian balance harmoniously, as do medieval and modern influences, with ancient castles regularly playing host to contemporary art exhibitions.

MERANO (MERAN)

29 km (18 miles) north of Bolzano, 16 km (10 miles) east of Naturno.

The second-largest town in Alto Adige, Merano (Meran) was once the capital of the Austrian region of Tirol. When the town and surrounding area were ceded to Italy as part of the 1919 Treaty of Versailles, Innsbruck became Tirol's capital. Merano continued to be known as a spa town, attracting European nobility for its therapeutic waters and its "grape cure," which consists simply of eating the grapes grown on the surrounding hillsides. Sheltered by mountains, Merano has an unusually mild climate, with summer temperatures rarely exceeding 80°F (27°C) and winters that usually stay above freezing, despite the skiing that's within easy reach. Along the narrow streets of Merano's old town, houses have little towers and huge wooden doors, and the pointed arches of the Gothic cathedral sit next to Neoclassical and Art Nouveau buildings. Merano serves as a good respite from mountain adventures, or from the bustle of nearby Trento and Bolzano.

GETTING HERE AND AROUND

By car from Bolzano, take the SP165 to the SP117 toward Merano (29 km [18 miles]). There is regular service by Trenitalia to the train station in Merano from all points in Italy.

VISITOR INFORMATION

Contact Merano Tourism Office. ⊠ *Corso Libertà 45, Merano* ☎ *0473/272000* ⊕ *www.meran.eu.*

EXPLORING

TOP ATTRACTIONS

Castel Trauttmansdorff. This Gothic castle was restored in the 19th century and now serves as a museum, celebrating 200 years of tourism in south Tirol. Outside, a sprawling garden has an extensive display of exotic flora organized by country of origin. The castle is about 2 km (1 mile) southeast of town on the Sentiero di Sissi; you can also take Bus No. 4 or 1B from the station. ⊠ *Via Valentino 51a, Merano* ☎ *0473/235730* ⊕ *www.trauttmansdorff.it* ⌑ *€13* ⊘ *Closed mid-Nov.–Mar.*

Museo Agricolo di Brunnenburg. Overlooking the town atop Mt. Tappeinerweg is Castel Fontana, which was the home of poet Ezra Pound from 1958 to 1964. Still in the Pound family, the castle now houses the Museo Agricolo di Brunnenburg, devoted to Tirolean country life. Among its exhibits are a blacksmith's shop and a room with Pound memorabilia. ⊠ *Via Castello 17, Tirolo* ⊹ *Take Bus No. 3, which departs every hr on the hr from Merano to Dorf Tirol (20 mins)* ☎ *0473/923533* ⊕ *www. brunnenburg.net* ⌑ *€6* ⊘ *Closed Fri. and Sat.*

Fodor'sChoice ★ **Promenades.** A stroll along one of Merano's well-marked, impossibly pleasant promenades may yield even better relaxation than time in its famous spa. **Passeggiata Tappeiner** (Tappeiner's Promenade) is a 3-km (2-mile) path with panoramic views from the hills north of the Duomo and diverse botanical pleasures along the way. **Passeggiata d'Estate** (Summer Promenade) runs along the shaded south bank of the Passirio River, and the **Passeggiata d'Inverno** (Winter Promenade), on the exposed north bank, provides more warmth and the Wandelhalle—a sunny area decorated with idyllic paintings of surrounding villages. The popular Austrian empress Sissi (Elisabeth of Wittelsbach, 1837–98) put Merano on the map as a spa destination; a trail named in her honor, the **Sentiero di Sissi** (Sissi's Walk), follows a path from Castel Trauttmansdorff to the heart of Merano. ⊠ *Merano.*

QUICK BITES

Cafe Saxifraga. An extensive selection of teas and other beverages can be enjoyed on the patio; the café has an enviable position overlooking Merano and the peaks enveloping the town. ⊠ *Via Monte San Zeno 33, Tappeiner Promenade, Merano* ☎ *366 /7002240* ⊕ *www.saxifraga.it* ۩ *Closed Tues., and Nov.–Mar.*

WORTH NOTING

Duomo. The 14th-century Gothic cathedral, with a crenellated facade and an ornate campanile, sits in the heart of the old town. The Capella di Santa Barbara, just behind the Duomo, is an octagonal church containing a 15th-century pietà. ■ TIP→ **Mass is held in German only.** ⊠ *Piazza del Duomo, Merano* ☎ *0473/230174.*

FAMILY **Terme di Merano.** This sprawling spa complex has 25 pools (including a brine pool with underwater music) and five saunas (with an indoor "snow room" available for cooling down). Along with the family-friendly options for bathing, personalized services for grown-ups include traditional cures using local products, such as grape-based applications and whey baths. An admission charge of €13 gets you two hours in thermal baths; €25 is for a full day's use of all baths and saunas. ⊠ *Piazza Terme 9, Merano* ☎ *0473/252000* ⊕ *www.termemerano.it.*

6

WHERE TO EAT

$$ ✕ **Sieben.** Young Meraners crowd the bar on the ground floor of
ITALIAN this modern bistro, in the town's central arcade. Upstairs, an older crowd enjoys the contemporary cooking and attentive service in the stylish dining room. **Known for:** welcoming atmosphere; fine wines; central location. $ *Average main: €21* ⊠ *Via dei Portici 234, Merano* ☎ *0473/210636* ⊕ *www.bistrosieben.it* ۩ *Closed Sun., and Nov.–Apr.*

$$$ ✕ **Sissi.** In relaxed, light-filled surroundings a short walk from Via
NORTHERN dei Portici, rustic regional dishes are prepared with precision at this
ITALIAN Michelin-starred eatery. Menu choices may include gnocchi *di formag-*
Fodor'sChoice *gio con salsa all' erba cipollina* (with cheese and chives) and *vitello alle*
★ *castagne e tartufo nero* (veal with chestnuts and black truffles). **Known for:** has Michelin star; varied tasting menu; bright surroundings. $ *Average main: €32* ⊠ *Via Galilei 44, Merano* ☎ *0473/231062* ۩ *Closed Mon., and 3 wks in Feb. and Mar. No lunch Tues.*

WHERE TO STAY

$ ⌂ **Conte di Merano.** Steps away from Via dei Portici and open year-
HOTEL round, these simple, comfortable rooms done in pleasing traditional style are an efficient base for exploring the town. **Pros:** central; reasonable rates. **Cons:** basic decor. $ *Rooms from: €110* ⊠ *Via delle Corse 78, Merano* ☎ *0473/490260* ⊕ *www.grafvonmeran.com* ₪ *18 rooms* ⦿ *Free Breakfast.*

$$$$ ⌂ **Meister's Hotel Irma.** This goal of this hotel and spa, opened in 1924, is
RESORT to relax the body and the spirit. **Pros:** great service; spectacular gardens and spa. **Cons:** expensive restaurant and bar. $ *Rooms from: €360* ⊠ *Via Belvedere 17, Merano* ☎ *0437/212000* ⊕ *www.hotel-irma.com* ۩ *Closed mid-Nov.–mid-Mar.* ₪ *69 rooms* ⦿ *Free Breakfast.*

STUMBLING ON ÖTZI

It was at the Similaun rifugio in September 1991 that a German couple arrived talking of a dead body they'd discovered near a "curious pickax." The couple, underestimating the age of the corpse by about 5,300 years, thought it was a matter for the police. This was to be the world's introduction to Ötzi, the oldest mummy ever found. World-famous mountaineers Reinhold Messner and Hans Kammerlander happened to be passing through the same rifugio during a climbing tour, and a few days later they were on the scene, freeing the iceman from the ice.

Ötzi's remarkable story was under way. You can see him on display, along with his longbow, ax, and clothes, at Bolzano's Museo Archeologico dell'Alto Adige, where he continues to be preserved at freezing temperatures.

NATURNO (NATURNS)

44 km (27 miles) northwest of Bolzano, 61 km (38 miles) east of Passo dello Stelvio.

As the name suggests, Naturno is a great location for a nature-based vacation; you can access a number of hiking trails to explore the area by foot. City planners have redesigned the town, reducing traffic and making the town more pedestrian-friendly. The locals take great pride in their produce; the fresh fruit, wine, and cheeses of this area are alone worth the drive.

GETTING HERE AND AROUND

By car from Bolzano, take the SS42 to the SS38 toward Merano. Naturno is 15 km (9 miles) past Merano. The town is very pedestrian-friendly, so talk to your hotel about where to leave your car, or head straight to a parking garage. Naturno is easily accessible by train from Bolzano or Merano.

VISITOR INFORMATION

Contact Naturno Tourism Office. ⊠ *Piazza Municipio 1, Naturno* ☎ *0473/666077* ⊕ *www.naturns.it.*

EXPLORING

Castel Juval. Since 1983 this 13th-century castle in the hills above the hamlet of Stava has been the summer home of the south Tirolese climber and polar adventurer Reinhold Messner—the first climber to conquer Everest solo. Part of the castle has been turned into one of six in Messner's chain of mountain museums, where guided tours are required to view his collection of Tibetan art and masks from around the world. It's a 10-minute shuttle ride from the car park below or an hour hike on many local trails. ⊠ *Juval 3, Castelbello* ☎ *0348/4433871, 0471/631264* ⊕ *www.messner-mountain-museum.it* ⊠ *€10* ⊙ *Closed Wed., and Nov.–Mar., July, and Aug.*

San Procolo (*Prokolus*). Frescoes here are some of the oldest in the German-speaking world, dating from the 8th century. A small, modern museum offers multimedia installations (in Italian or German only) presenting four epochs in the region's history: ancient, medieval, Gothic, and the era of the Great Plague of 1636 (which claimed a quarter of Naturno's population, some of whom are buried in the church's cemetery). There are leaflets and other information in English on request. ⌧ *Via San Procolo, Naturno* ☎ *0473/667312 church, 0473/673139 museum* ⊕ *www.procolo.org* ⬚ *Church €2 (suggested donation), museum €4.50* ⊘ *Closed Mon., and Nov.–mid-Mar.*

WHERE TO EAT

$$

NORTHERN
ITALIAN

Fodor's Choice
★

✕ **Schlosswirt Juval.** Reinhold Messner's restored farmhouse, which is below Castel Juval, holds an old-style restaurant serving traditional local dishes. Not to be missed are the smoked hams and flavorful cheeses provided by the farm outside; they are well paired with the estate's Castel Juval wine. **Known for:** mountaintop dining; farm-to-table fare; local wine. ⓢ *Average main: €22* ⌧ *Juval 2, Castelbello* ☎ *0473/668056* ⊕ *www.schlosswirtjuval.it* ⊘ *Closed Wed., and Nov.–Mar.*

EN
ROUTE

FORST Brewery. The source of the full-flavor beer served throughout the region is the striking FORST Brewery, on the road connecting Naturno and Merano. Tours can be arranged if you call ahead, but you can turn up any time of year to sample the product line. In high season, cross a covered, flower-lined wooden bridge to reach the delightful beer garden. ⌧ *Via Venosta 8, Lagundo* ☎ *0473/260111* ⊕ *www.forst.it.*

CALDARO (KALTERN)

15 km (9 miles) south of Bolzano.

A vineyard village with clear views of castles high up on the surrounding mountains represents the centuries of division that forged the unique character of the area. Caldaro architecture is famous for the way it blends Italian Renaissance elements of balance and harmony with the soaring windows and peaked arches of the Germanic Gothic tradition. The church of Santa Caterina, on the main square, is a good example. The warmest bathing lake in the Alps is just 4 km (2½ miles) away.

GETTING HERE AND AROUND

By car from Bolzano, follow the SS42 south toward Caldaro. This road is famously known as the "Strada del Vino," or "Wine Road"—you will pass several vineyards along the way. If you head straight to the Wine Museum in Caldaro, you can pick up maps and plan a route through the vineyards based on specific tastes.

BRESSANONE (BRIXEN)

42 km (25 miles) northeast of Bolzano.

Bressanone is an important artistic center and was the seat of prince-bishops for centuries. Like their counterparts in Trento, these medieval administrators had the delicate task of serving two masters—the pope (the ultimate spiritual authority) and the Holy Roman Emperor (the civil and military power), who were virtually at war throughout the Middle Ages. Bressanone's prince-bishops became experts at tact and diplomacy.

The Brixen Card offers free transportation throughout Südtirol (South Tyrol) and entrance to more than 80 museums, plus free guided tours and discounts at partner venues; it's free to guests of local hotels (🌐 *www.brixencard.info*).

GETTING HERE AND AROUND

Driving from Bolzano, follow the SS12 northeast 42 km (26 miles) to Bressanone. Trains run from Bolzano, as does SAD Bus No. 350.

VISITOR INFORMATION

Contact Bressanone Tourism Office. ✉ *Viale Ratisbona 9, Bressanone* ☎ *0472/836401* 🌐 *www.brixen.org.*

EXPLORING

Abbazia di Novacella. This Augustinian abbey founded in 1142 has been producing wine for at least nine centuries and is most famous for the delicate stone-fruit character of its dry white Sylvaner. You can wander the delightful grounds; note the progression of Romanesque, Gothic, and Baroque building styles. Guided tours of the abbey (in Italian and German) depart daily at 10, 11, 2, 3, and 4, as well as at noon and 1 in summer; from January through March, tours are by reservation only. Guided tours of the gardens and vineyard are also available in season. ✉ *Via Abbazia 1, 3 km (2 miles) north of Bressanone, Varna* ☎ *0472/836189* 🌐 *www.abbazianovacella.it* 🎫 *Guided tours €9, wine tastings €9* ⏲ *Closed Sun., and Mon. in winter.*

Duomo. The imposing town cathedral was built in the 13th century but acquired a Baroque facade 500 years later; its 14th-century cloister is decorated with medieval frescoes. Guided tours are available Easter–November 1, Monday–Saturday at 10:30 am. ✉ *Piazza Duomo 1, Bressanone.*

Museo Diocesano (*Diocesan Museum*). The Bishop's Palace houses an abundance of local medieval art, particularly Gothic wood carvings. The wooden statues and liturgical objects were all collected from the cathedral treasury. During the Christmas season, curators arrange the museum's large collection of antique Nativity scenes; look for the shepherds wearing Tirolean hats. ✉ *Palazzo Vescovile 2, Bressanone* ☎ *0472/830505* 🌐 *www.hofburg.it* 🎫 *€8; Nativity scenes €5* ⏲ *Closed Mon., and Nov. and Jan.–mid-Mar.*

WHERE TO EAT AND STAY

$ NORTHERN ITALIAN

🍴 **Fink.** This warm, wood-paneled, upstairs dining room is under the arcades of the pedestrians-only town center. Among the house specialties are *carré di maiale gratinato* (pork chops roasted with cheese and served with cabbage and potatoes) and *castrato alla paesana*, a substantial lamb stew. **Known for:** local specialties; bustling atmosphere; central location. [$] *Average main: €12* ✉ *Via Portici Minori 4, Bressanone* ☎ *0472/834883* 🌐 *www.restaurant-fink.it* ⏲ *Closed Wed. No dinner Tues.*

$$ HOTEL Fodor's Choice ★

🏨 **Elephant.** At this cozy inn, over 450 years old and still one of the region's best, each room is unique and many are filled with antiques and paintings. **Pros:** lovely ambience; good restaurant; lavish breakfast. **Cons:** rooms vary in size; guests have complained about flies. [$] *Rooms from: €192* ✉ *Via Rio Bianco 4, Bressanone* ☎ *0472/832750* 🌐 *www.hotelelephant.com* 🛏 *44 rooms* 🍽 *Free Breakfast.*

BRUNICO (BRUNECK)

33 km (20 miles) east of Bressanone, 65 km (40 miles) northwest of Cortina d'Ampezzo.

Brunico's medieval quarter nestles below a 13th-century bishop's castle. In the heart of the Val Pusteria, this quiet and quaint town is divided by the Rienza River, with the old quarter on one side and the modern town on the other.

GETTING HERE AND AROUND

From Bressanone follow the E66 east for 30 km (19 miles) to Brunico. If driving from Cortina d'Ampezzo, take the SR48 over the Passo Falzarego and continue to the SP244 toward Brunico. There are bus (SAD) and train (Trenitalia) connections available at Bolzano.

VISITOR INFORMATION

Contact Brunico Tourism Office. ✉ *Piazza Municipio 7, Brunico* ☎ *0474/555722* ⊕ *www.bruneck.com.*

EXPLORING

FAMILY **South Tyrolean Folklore Museum.** A re-creation of a Middle Ages rural village is built around a 300-year-old mansion. The wood-carving displays are especially interesting. ✉ *Herzog-Diet-Strasse 24, Brunico* ☎ *0474/552087* ⊕ *www.volkskundemuseum.it* 🎟 *€7* ⊙ *Closed Mon. (except Aug.).*

WHERE TO STAY

$$$$ 🏨 **Alpine Wellness Resort Majestic.** Right in front of the Plan de Corones,
HOTEL this is a great base for a skiing or hiking vacation, with bus service to the ski slopes and a spa and pools on-site to unwind after a big day out. **Pros:** convenient for skiers and hikers. **Cons:** meal portions are a little small. 🟅 *Rooms from: €358* ✉ *Via Im Gelande 20, Brunico* ☎ *0474/410993* ⊕ *www.hotel-majestic.it* ⊙ *Closed Easter–May* 🛏 *60 rooms* ⧓ *Some meals.*

SPORTS AND THE OUTDOORS

SKIING

Alta Badia. The Alta Badia ski area, which includes 53 ski lifts and 130 km (80 miles) of slopes, can be reached by heading 30 km (19 miles) south on SS244 from Brunico. It's cheaper and more Austrian in character than the more famous ski destinations in this region. Groomed trails for cross-country skiing (usually loops marked off by the kilometer) accommodate differing degrees of ability. Inquire at the local tourist office. ✉ *Brunico* ☎ *0471/836176 Corvara tourism office* ⊕ *www.altabadia.org.*

THE HEART OF THE DOLOMITES

The area between Bolzano and the mountain resort Cortina d'Ampezzo is dominated by two major valleys, Val di Fassa and Val Gardena. Both share the spectacular panorama of the Sella mountain range, known as the Heart of the Dolomites. Val di Fassa cradles the beginning of the Grande Strada delle Dolomiti (Great Dolomites Road; SS48 and SS241), which runs from Bolzano as far as Cortina. This route, opened in 1909, comprises 110 km (68 miles) of relatively easy grades and smooth driving between the two towns—a slower, more scenic alternative to traveling by way of Brunico and Dobbiaco along SS49. And scenic it is: the road passes into a stark, high-altitude landscape punctuated with needlelike mountain peaks, climbing to 7,346 feet.

In both Val di Fassa and Val Gardena, recreational options are less expensive, though less comprehensive, than in better-known resorts like Cortina. The culture here is firmly Germanic. Val Gardena is freckled with well-equipped, photo-friendly towns with great views overlooked by the oblong Sasso Lungo (Long Rock), which is more than 10,000 feet above sea level. It's also home to the Ladins, descendants of soldiers sent by the Roman emperor Tiberius to conquer the Celtic population of the area in the 1st century AD. Forgotten in the narrow cul-de-sacs of isolated mountain valleys, the Ladins have developed their own folk traditions and speak an ancient dialect that is derived from Latin and similar to the Romansch spoken in some high valleys in Switzerland.

MISURINA

115 km (71 miles) east of Bolzano.

Nestled on the shores of Lake Misurina, among the Dolomites, Misurina's high altitude, low air humidity, and total absence of dust mites and air pollution, has some saying the "Pearl of the Dolomites" has some of the purest air in the world.

The town itself is rather small, but it's a perfect base to explore Lake Misurina and the Tre Cime of Lavaredo. The mountains surrounding are rich in history and artifacts from WWI, as well as earlier wars. Along some of the hikes and *vie ferrate* (mountain paths with steel cables and fixed anchors and ladders), you can explore caves and trenches complete with informational placards giving details about troop positions and fighting.

GETTING HERE AND AROUND

From Brunico, drive southeast on the SS49/E66 to Dobbiaco. Turn right onto SS51 and drive for 13 km (8 miles). Turn left onto 48bis in the direction of Auronzo. Arrive at Lago di Misurina in 6 km (4 miles).

VISITOR INFORMATION

Contact Misurina Tourism Office. ⊠ *Via Monte Piana 2* ☎ *0435/39016, 0435/99603* ⊕ *www.auronzomisurina.it.*

EXPLORING

Tre Cime of Lavaredo. Without a doubt, the Three Peaks—Cima Piccola (9,373 feet), Cima Grande (9,839 feet), and Cima Ovest (9,753 feet)—are the symbol for the Dolomite UNESCO World Heritage Site. From the town of Misurina, only two of the Tre Cime are visible. In order to get up close and personal, drive or take a bus along the dedicated toll road from May through October (car parking is €25). Once at the top, follow Footpath 101 from Rifugio Auronzo to Forcella Laveredo (easy) for about an hour. There are many other footpaths and vie ferrate which allow you to climb the cime and access the base. The rifugios (mountain huts) offer hot meals without a reservation, and dorm-style lodging, which is best reserved in advance. ⊠ *Parco Naturale Tre Cime, Auronzo di Cadore* ☎ *0435/39002.*

WHERE TO EAT AND STAY

$$
NORTHERN
ITALIAN
FAMILY

✕ **Malga Rin Bianco.** When in the mood for fresh, properly cooked regional food, this *malga* (Alpine hut) with great mountain views can't be beat. The salamis and cheeses are made on-site, and the bar boasts a variety of homemade and commercial grappas, many of which are brewed with local herbs and plants. **Known for:** mountain location; local food; great views. $ *Average main: €20* ⊠ *Via Monte Piana 35, Strada Tre Cime* ☎ *0435/39048* ⊕ *www.villasoranzo.com/malgarin* ⊙ *Closed Wed. and Nov.*

$$
B&B/INN
FAMILY

⌕ **Chalet Lago Antorno.** Located in a quiet, panoramic spot, the chalet is an ideal place for anyone looking to explore the mountains or those wanting to relax and unwind in the most beautiful scenery of the Alps. **Pros:** family-run; typical decor and regional flavor. **Cons:** away from town center; not suitable for large groups. $ *Rooms from: €130* ⊠ *Loc. Lago Misurina* ☎ *0435/39148* ⊕ *www.lagoantorno.it* ⊙ *Closed Mar.– May and Nov.* ↩ *10 rooms* ℃ *No meals.*

$
HOTEL
FAMILY

⌕ **The Grand Hotel Misurina.** On the shores of beautiful Lake Misurina, this grand hotel is but a few kilometers from the renowned winter resort, Cortina d'Ampezzo. **Pros:** located in town center; perfect for large groups; shuttle to ski areas. **Cons:** rooms have simple furnishings. $ *Rooms from: €110* ⊠ *Via Monte Piana 21* ☎ *0435/39191* ⊕ *www.grandhotelmisurina.com* ⊙ *Closed Nov. and Apr.* ↩ *125 rooms* ℃ *All-inclusive.*

SPORTS AND THE OUTDOORS

BIKING

Cycling enthusiasts flock to the Dolomites to take part in the challenges the mountains have to offer. Much of the region is used by Olympic athletes to train, and several important bike races (such as the Giro di Italia) take place in the area. Some of the descents along gravely roads are high adrenaline rushes, while others follow paved roads and bike paths. The Auronzo-Misurina Cycle Track provides about 32 km (20 miles) of bicycle path between the two towns.

SKIING

Two major ski lifts service the area from Misurina and Auronzo. From Misurina take the Col de Varda lift. Auronzo di Cadore is about a 30-minute drive from Misurina, where the Monte Agudo lift goes from Taiarezze (2,952 feet) to Rifugio Monte Agudo (5,160 feet). There are restaurants and maps available at the top. Views from Auronzo differ from Misurina in that all three cime are visible from here.

FAMILY
Col de Varda. The major ski lift servicing the area from Misurina climbs to Col de Varda, with a summit of 6,909 feet. Rifugio Col de Varda, at the top, has a bar and restaurant, as well as rooms to rent. In the summer, the area is an excellent starting point for great hiking and biking excursions. At any time of the year, the views of Lake Misurina, Mt. Cristallo, the Sesto Dolomites, and the Cadini, Sorapiss, and Tofane

6

massifs are breathtaking. ⊠ *Misurina* ☏ *0435/99603* ⊕ *www.rifugio-coldevarda.it* ⌦ *€11.50 round-trip.*

Monte Cristallo. Some of the most impressive views (and steepest slopes) are on Monte Cristallo. ⊠ *Misurina.*

CANAZEI

45 km (28 miles) southwest of Misurina.

Of the year-round resort towns in the Val di Fassa, Canazei is the most popular. The mountains around this small town are threaded with hiking trails and ski slopes, surrounded by large clutches of conifers.

GETTING HERE AND AROUND

There is bus service from Bolzano and Bressanone (the nearest train stations), but the service is infrequent, and often has interruptions and cancellations. By car from the A22, take the Bolzano Nord exit onto the SS241. Cross the Passo Costalunga into the Val di Fassa. From the town of Vigo, follow signs for Canazei.

VISITOR INFORMATION

Contact **Canazei Tourism Office.** ⊠ *Piazza Marconi 5* ☏ *0462/609600* ⊕ *www. fassa.com.*

EXPLORING

Fodor'sChoice
★

Col Rodella. An excursion from Campitello di Fassa, about 4 km (2½ miles) west of Canazei, to the vantage point at Col Rodella has unmissable views. A cable car rises some 3,000 feet to a full-circle vista of the Heart of the Dolomites, including the Sasso Lungo and the rest of the Sella range. ⊠ *Localita' Ischia 1* ☏ *0462/608811* ⌦ *Cable car €17 round-trip.*

Passo Pordoi. At 7,346 feet, Passo Pordoi is the highest surface road pass in the Dolomites. The pass connects Arabba, in Val Cordevole (Province of Belluno), with Canazei, in Val di Fossa (Province of Trento). Views from the top include the Sassolungo and Sella group of mountains, and even the Marmolada Glacier. There are several hotels and a ski school located at the pass, as well as some souvenir shops, restaurants, and snack carts. While the hotels are not glamorous, some do offer half-board packages at reasonable rates.

The cable car (May through October) takes you to the Sass Pordoi, often called the "Terrace of the Dolomites." At more than 9,100 feet, it offers myriad hiking trails and vie ferrate with varying degrees of difficulty (none of which are easy), leading to rifugi and the region's other peaks and passes.

Skiing is available year-round. The most popular winter skiing areas are Belvedere and Sella Ronda, and much of the area is part of the Dolomiti Superski package. Even if the road for the pass is closed, many of the cable cars in neighboring valley towns will be running to various summits.

From Passo Pordoi to Canazei there are 28 hairpin turns. There are a few scenic and picnic pull-offs along the way. ⊠ *Strada del Pordoi* ⊕ *www.passo-pordoi.com* ⌦ *Cable car €17 round-trip.*

WHERE TO STAY

$$ ☼ **Alla Rosa.** The view of the imposing Dolomites is the real attraction in
HOTEL rooms that pleasantly blend rustic and contemporary furnishings, so ask
for a balcony. **Pros:** in the center of town; great views. **Cons:** half board
mandatory in winter high season; busy neighborhood. $ *Rooms from:*
€200 ☒ *Strada del Faure 18* ☎ *0462/601107* ⊕ *www.hotelallarosa.com*
↩ *49 rooms* ⦿ *Free Breakfast.*

ORTISEI (ST. ULRICH)

28 km (17 miles) northwest of Canazei.

Ortisei (St. Ulrich), the jewel in the crown of Val Gardena's resorts, is a
hub of activity in both summer and winter; there are hundreds of miles
of hiking trails and accessible ski slopes.

For centuries Ortisei has also been famous for the expertise of its wood-
carvers, and there are still numerous workshops. Apart from making
religious sculptures—particularly the wayside calvaries you come upon
everywhere in the Dolomites—Ortisei's carvers were long known for
producing wooden dolls, horses, and other toys. As itinerant peddlers,
they traveled every spring on foot with their loaded packs as far as
Paris, London, and St. Petersburg. Shops in town still sell woodcrafts.

Ortisei has been a family-friendly mountain-vacation destination since
the 1930s. The most famous cable car in the area, the Alpe di Siusi,
operates in summer and winter. The largest village in the Val Gardena,
Ortisei makes a picturesque and practical base for exploring much of
the heart of the Dolomites.

GETTING HERE AND AROUND

By car from Bolzano, take the SS12 to the SS242 in the direction of
Ortisei. From Canazei, follow the SS242 north to Ortisei. Bus service
is available on the Val Gardena network from Bolzano and Bressanone.

VISITOR INFORMATION

Contact Ortisei Tourist Office. ☒ *Via Rezia 1, Ortisei* ☎ *0471/777600,*
0471/777777 Val Gardena ⊕ *www.valgardena.it.*

EXPLORING

Alpe di Siusi cable car. First opened in 1935, the cable car from Ortisei
to Alpe di Siusi climbs more than 6,100 feet to the widest plateau in
Europe. There are more than 57 square km (22 square miles) of Alpine
pastures lined with summertime hiking trails. In the winter, 20 ski lifts
and cross-country ski paths keep active visitors happy. There is a res-
taurant at the top of the Mt. Seuc ski lift, or you can pick up a map at
the tourist office in Ortisei listing the mountain huts and restaurants
that can be reached by foot. Opening days and times depend on the
season and daily weather conditions. Check the website or call ahead
to avoid disappointment. ☒ *Setil Str. 9, Ortisei* ☎ *0471/797897* ⊕ *www.*
alpedisiusi-seiseralm.com ⦿ *€18.30 round-trip.*

Museo della Val Gardena. Fine historic and contemporary examples of
local woodworking are on display here, as well as a retrospective on
the life of local film director Luis Trenker. ☒ *Via Rezia 83, Ortisei*
☎ *0471/797554* ⊕ *www.museumgherdeina.it* ⦿ *€7.*

WHERE TO STAY

$$$$ RESORT FAMILY **Cavallino Bianco Family Spa Grand Hotel.** With delicate wooden balconies and an eye-catching wooden gable, the pink Cavallino Bianco (Little White Horse) looks like a gigantic dollhouse, and it is in fact marketed especially toward families with children. **Pros:** family-friendly; cheerful rooms. **Cons:** in the busy town center; a bit impersonal. [$] *Rooms from: €500* ✉ *Via Rezia 22, Ortisei* ☎ *0471/783333* 🌐 *www.cavallino-bianco.com* 🕒 *Closed mid-Apr.–mid-May* 🛏 *104 rooms* 🍴 *All-inclusive.*

$$$ HOTEL **Hotel Grones.** The attention to detail at this family-run hotel, located just a few minutes' walk from the ski slopes or downtown, makes it a great base for a mountain vacation. **Pros:** friendly staff; quiet location; gluten-free options. **Cons:** it's an uphill walk from town; half-board mandatory. [$] *Rooms from: €235* ✉ *110 Stufan St., Ortisei* ☎ *0471/797040* 🌐 *www.grones.info/en* 🕒 *Closed Apr., May, and mid-Oct.–early Dec.* 🛏 *25 rooms* 🍴 *Some meals.*

SPORTS AND THE OUTDOORS

SKIING

With almost 600 km (370 miles) of accessible downhill slopes and more than 90 km (56 miles) of cross-country skiing trails, Ortisei is one of the most popular ski resorts in the Dolomites. Prices are good, and facilities are among the most modern in the region. In warmer weather, the slopes surrounding Ortisei are a popular hiking destination, as well as a playground for vehicular mountain adventures like biking, rafting, and paragliding.

Sella Ronda. An immensely popular ski route, the Sella Ronda relies on well-placed chairlifts to connect 26 km (16 miles) of downhill skiing around the colossal Sella massif, passing through several towns along the way. You can ski the loop, which requires intermediate ability and a full day's effort, either clockwise or counterclockwise. Going with a guide is recommended. ✉ *Ortisei* 🌐 *www.sella-ronda.info.*

CORTINA D'AMPEZZO

60 km (37 miles) east of Ortisei (St. Ulrich).

The archetypal Dolomite resort, Cortina d'Ampezzo entices those seeking both relaxation and adventure. The town is the western gateway to the Strade Grande delle Dolomiti, and actually crowns the northern Veneto region and an area known as Cadore in the northernmost part of the province of Belluno. Like Alto Adige to the west, Cadore (birthplace of the Venetian Renaissance painter Titian) was on the Alpine front during WWI, and was the scene of many battles that have been commemorated in refuges and museums.

Although its appeal to younger Italians has been eclipsed by the steeper, sleeker Madonna di Campiglio, Cortina remains, for many, Italy's most idyllic incarnation of an Alpine ski town.

GETTING HERE AND AROUND

To drive to Cortina d'Ampezzo from Trento or Bolzano, take the A22 north to Bressanone/Pustertal. Turn right on the SS49/E66, then right on to the SS51 and follow it into Cortina. The Dolomiti Bus provides service to and from Cortina, but it's not very convenient or reliable. The town itself is pedestrian friendly and has local bus service to area ski slopes. Beware of taxis, as the rates are very high, and the fare may begin from the taxi's point of origin, not necessarily where you get in the vehicle.

VISITOR INFORMATION

Contact Cortina d'Ampezzo Tourism Office. ✉ *Piazza Roma 1* ☎ *0436/869086* 🌐 *www.cortinadolomiti.eu.*

EXPLORING

Surrounded by mountains and dense forests, the "Queen of the Dolomites" is in a lush meadow 4,000 feet above sea level. The town hugs the slopes beside a fast-moving stream, and a public park extends along one bank. Higher in the valley, luxury hotels and the villas of the rich are identifiable by their attempts to hide behind stands of firs and spruces. The bustling center of Cortina d'Ampezzo has little nostalgia, despite its Alpine appearance with its tone set by shops and cafés as chic as their well-dressed patrons. Unlike neighboring resorts that have a strong Germanic flavor, Cortina d'Ampezzo is unapologetically Italian and distinctly fashionable.

WHERE TO EAT

$$$ NORTHERN ITALIAN

🍴 **Ristorante Lago Pianozes.** This small, endearing establishment is just outside Cortina, beside the picturesque Lago Pianozes. Massimo, the owner, is friendly and knowledgeable, not only about his food and wine, but also about the surrounding region. **Known for:** delightful location; local dishes; friendly staff. [$] *Average main: €28* ✉ *Campo di Sotto Pianozes 1* ☎ *0436/5601* ⏲ *Closed May.–mid-June and mid-Sept.–Oct.*

WHERE TO STAY

$$ HOTEL

🏨 **Corona.** Noted ski instructor Luciano Rimoldi, who has coached such luminaries as Alberto Tomba, runs an inviting Alpine lodge where modern art adorns small but comfortable pine-paneled rooms. **Pros:** quiet location; friendly staff; ski shuttle stops out front. **Cons:** small rooms; outside the town center. [$] *Rooms from: €200* ✉ *Via Val di Sotto 12* ☎ *0436/3251* 🌐 *www.hotelcoronacortina.it* ⏲ *Closed Apr., May, and mid-Sept.–Nov.* 🛏 *44 rooms* 🍽 *Free Breakfast.*

$$$$ RESORT Fodor's Choice ★

🏨 **Cristallo.** This luxury grande dame is lauded for its service, spa, and more; the architecture was immortalized in 1963's *The Pink Panther.* **Pros:** stellar food and service; great spa; wonderful atmosphere. **Cons:** not in town; not accessible for all budgets. [$] *Rooms from: €525* ✉ *Via R. Menardi 42* ☎ *0436/881111* 🌐 *www.cristallo.it* ⏲ *Closed Nov. and Apr.–June* 🛏 *74 rooms* 🍽 *Free Breakfast.*

$$$ HOTEL

🏨 **De la Poste.** Loyal skiers return year after year to this old-school mountain retreat, where each unique room has antiques in characteristic Dolomite style (almost all have wooden balconies) and the main terrace bar is one of Cortina's social centers. **Pros:** professional service; romantic. **Cons:** a bit stuffy; expensive. [$] *Rooms from: €249* ✉ *Piazza*

Roma 14 ☎ *0436/4271* ⊕ *www.delaposte.it* ⊘ *Closed Apr.–mid-June and Oct.–mid-Dec.* ↩ *68 rooms* ¶○¶ *Free Breakfast.*

SPORTS AND THE OUTDOORS

HIKING AND CLIMBING

Hiking information is available from the excellent local tourism office.

Gruppo Guide Alpine Cortina Scuola di Alpinismo (*Mountaineering School*). This group organizes climbing trips and trekking adventures. ⊠ *Corso Italia 69/a* ☎ *0436/868505* ⊕ *www.guidecortina.com.*

SKIING

Cortina's long and picturesque ski runs will delight intermediates, but advanced skiers may pine for steeper terrain, which can be found only off-piste. Efficient ski-bus service connects the town with the high-speed chairlifts and gondolas that ascend in all directions from the valley.

Dolomiti Superski pass. The Dolomiti Superski pass provides access to the surrounding Dolomites, with 450 lifts and gondolas serving 1,200 km (750 miles) of trails. Buy one at the ticket office next to the bus station and at other outlets in the Dolomites. ⊠ *Via Marconi 15* ☎ *0471/795397* ⊕ *www.dolomitisuperski.com* 🎟 *€47–€59 per day.*

Faloria gondola. The Faloria gondola runs from the center of town. From its top you can get up to most of the central mountains. ⊠ *Via Ria de Zeta 10* ☎ *0436/2517* ⊕ *www.cortinacube.it* 🎟 *€19 round-trip.*

Passo Falzarego. The topography of the Passo Falzarego ski area, 16 km (10 miles) east of town, is dramatic. The cable car takes you to one of the highest points in the Dolomites (Rifugio Lagazuoi)—on a clear day, you'll experience some of the best views from here. It's also easy to see why this was such a deadly area for soldiers in WWI. Hiking is uneven in places, and there are vie ferrate that require the use of helmets and flashlights; there are other paths that lead to tunnels that don't require helmets. ⊠ *Cortina d'Ampezzo* ⊕ *www.rifugiolagazuoi.com* 🎟 *€14.80 round-trip.*

MILAN, LOMBARDY, AND THE LAKES

WELCOME TO
MILAN, LOMBARDY, AND THE LAKES

TOP REASONS TO GO

★ **Lake Como, one of the most beautiful lakes in the world:** Ferries crisscross the waters, taking you from picture-book villages to stately villas to Edenic gardens, all backdropped in the distance by the snowcapped Alps.

★ **Leonardo's Last Supper:** Behold one of the world's most famous works of art for yourself.

★ **The sky's no limit:** A funicular ride in Bergamo whisks you up to the magnificent medieval city.

★ **Milan alla Moda:** As you window-shop the afternoon away in Milan's Quadrilatero shopping district, catch a glimpse of fashion's latest trends.

★ **A night at La Scala:** What the Louvre is to art, Milan's La Scala is to the world of opera.

1 **Milan.** Home of the Italian stock exchange, it's also one of the world's fashion capitals and has cultural and artistic treasures that rival those of Florence and Rome.

2 **Bergamo, Pavia, Cremona, and Mantua.** South of Milan are the walled cities where Renaissance dukes built towering palaces and ornate churches.

3 **Lake Iseo and Franciacorta.** Sleepy Lake Iseo has only recently started to gain popularity thanks to its temporary art exhibits and the nearby wine region.

4 **Lake Garda.** Italy's largest lake is more laid-back than the other lakes and popular with active types.

5 **Lake Como.** This relatively narrow lake is probably the country's best-known and most charmingly populated body of water.

6 **Lake Maggiore.** Lake Maggiore is impressively picturesque, with the Alps as a backdrop. One of the greatest pleasures here is exploring the lake's islands.

7

EATING WELL IN MILAN, LOMBARDY, AND THE LAKES

Lombardy may well offer Italy's most varied, rich, and refined cuisine. Local cooking is influenced by the neighboring regions of the north; foreign conquerors have left their mark; and today, well-traveled Milanese, business visitors, and industrious immigrants are likely to find more authentic ethnic cuisine in Milan than in any other Italian city.

Milan runs counter to many of the established Italian dining customs. A "real" traditional Milanese meal is a rarity; instead, Milan offers a variety of tastes, prices, and times of day, from expense-account elegance in fancy restaurants to abundant *aperitivo*-time nibbles. The city's cosmopolitan nature means trends arrive here first, and things move fast. Meals are not the drawn-out pastime they tend to be elsewhere in Italy. But the food is still consistently good: competition among restaurants is fierce and the local clientele is demanding, which means you can be reasonably certain that if a place looks promising, it won't disappoint.

THE COTOLETTA QUESTION

Everyone has an opinion on *cotoletta (photo lower right)*, the breaded veal cutlet known across Italy as *una Milanese*.

It's clearly related to Austria's Wiener schnitzel, but did the Austrians introduce it when they dominated Milan or did they take it home when they left? Should it be with bone or without? Some think it's best with fresh tomato and arugula on top; others find this sacrilege.

Two things unite all camps: the meat must be well beaten until it's thin, and it must never leave a grease spot after it's fried.

REGIONAL SPECIALTIES

Ask an Italian what Lombards eat, and you're likely to hear *cotoletta, càsoeûla,* and *risotto giallo*—all dishes that reinforce Lombardy's status as the crossroads of Italy. *Cotoletta alla Milanese* may very well have Austrian roots. *Càsoeûla* is a cabbage-and-pork stew that resembles French cassoulet, though some say it has Spanish origins. *Risotto giallo* (also known as *risotto Milanese*) is colorful and perfumed with exotic saffron. With no tomatoes, olive oil, or pasta, these dishes hardly sound Italian.

BUTTER AND CHEESE

Agricultural traditions and geography mean that animal products are more common here than in southern Italy—and that means butter and cream take olive oil's place. A rare point of agreement about cotoletta is that it's cooked in butter. The first and last steps of risotto making—toasting the rice and letting it "repose" before serving—use ample amounts of butter. And the second-most-famous name in Italian cheese (after Parmesan) is likely Gorgonzola, named for a town near Milan; the best now comes from Novara.

RISOTTO

Rice is Lombardy's answer to pasta, and the region is the center of Italian (and European) rice production. From Milan's risotto giallo, with its costly saffron tint, to Mantua's risotto with

pumpkin or sausage, there's no end to the variety of rice dishes. Canonical risotto should be *all'onda,* or flow off the spoon like a wave. Keeping with the Italian tradition of nothing wasted, yesterday's risotto is flattened in a pan and fried in butter to produce *riso al salto,* which at its best has a crispy crust and a tender middle.

PANETTONE

Panettone, a tall, fluffy, sweet, yeast bread, is flavored with sweet candied fruit, *pictured above*. Invented in Milan, it graces nearly every table during the Christmas holiday. Consumption begins on December 7, Milan's patron saint's day, and goes until supplies run out at January's end.

WINE

Lombardy isn't one of Italy's most heralded wine regions, but the Franciacorta region around Brescia makes highly regarded sparkling wines, often called the "Champagne of Italy" since they're produced using the same labor-intensive method. The Valtellina area to the northeast of Milan produces two notable reds from the *nebbiolo* grape: Valtellina Superiore and the intense dessert wine Sforzato di Valtellina. Lake breezes bring crisp, smooth whites from the shores around Lake Garda.

7

Updated by
Liz Humphreys

Lombardy is one of Italy's most dynamic regions—offering everything from world-class ski slopes to luxurious summer lake resorts. Milan is the pulse of the nation—commercial, fashionable, and forward-looking. The great Renaissance cities of the Po Plain—Pavia, Cremona, and Mantua—offer the romantic Italian characteristics visitors dream about, embracing their past by preserving national treasures while ever keeping an eye on the present. Topping any list of the region's attractions are the glacial lakes. Above them stand the Alps, which have been praised as the closest thing to paradise by writers throughout the ages, from Virgil to Hemingway.

Millions of travelers have concurred: for sheer beauty, the lakes of northern Italy—Como, Maggiore, Garda, Iseo, and Orta—have few equals. Along their shores are 18th- and 19th-century villas, exotic formal gardens, sleepy villages, and dozens of Belle Époque–era resorts that were once Europe's most fashionable, and that still retain a powerful allure.

Milan can be disappointingly modern and congested—a little too much like the place you've come to Italy to escape—but its historic buildings and art collections in many ways rival those of Florence and Rome. And if you love to shop, Milan is one of the world's great fashion centers, and offers experiences and goods for every taste, from Corso Buenos Aires, which has a higher ratio of stores per square foot than anywhere else in Europe, to the edgy street style of Corso di Porta Ticinese and upscale Via Montenapoleone, where there's no limit on what you can spend. Milan is home to global fashion giants such as Armani, Prada, Versace, Salvatore Ferragamo, and Ermenegildo Zegna; behind them stands a host of less famous designers who help fill all those fabulous shops.

MILAN, LOMBARDY, AND THE LAKES PLANNER

MAKING THE MOST OF YOUR TIME

Italy's commercial hub isn't usually at the top of the list for visiting tourists, but Milan is the nation's most modern city, with its own sophisticated appeal: its fashionable shops rival those of New York and Paris, its soccer teams are Italy's answer to the Yankees and the Mets, its opera performances set the standard for the world, and its art treasures are well worth the visit.

The biggest draw in the region, though, is the Lake District. Throughout history, the magnificently beautiful lakes of Como, Garda, Maggiore, Iseo, and Orta have attracted their fair share of well-known faces—from Winston Churchill and Russian royalty to George Clooney and Madonna. Each lake town has its own history and distinct character. If you have limited time, visit the lake you think best suits your style, but if you have time to spare, make the rounds to two or three to get a sense of their contrasts.

GETTING HERE AND AROUND

AIR TRAVEL

The region's main international gateway airport is Aeroporto Malpensa (☎ 02/232323 ⊕ www.milanomalpensa-airport.com), 48 km (30 miles) northwest of Milan. Some international and domestic flights also fly into more central Aeroporto Linate (☎ 02/232323 ⊕ www.milano-linate-airport.com), 7 km (4 miles) east of Milan, while European low-cost carriers like Ryanair use Aeroporto Milano Bergamo Orio al Serio (☎ 035/326323 ⊕ www.orioaeroporto.it), 55 km (34 miles) northeast of Milan and 5 km (3 miles) south of Bergamo.

BOAT TRAVEL

Frequent daily ferry and hydrofoil services link the lakeside towns and villages. Residents take them to get to work and school, while visitors use them for exploring the area. There are also special round-trip excursions, some with (optional) dining service on board.

Boat Contacts Navigazione Laghi. ☎ 800/551801 within Italy ⊕ www. navigazionelaghi.it.

BUS TRAVEL

Bus service isn't the best way to travel between cities here, because trains are faster, cheaper, and more convenient. There's regular bus service for reaching and traveling between the small towns on the lakes. It's less convenient than going by boat or by car, and it's used primarily by locals (particularly schoolchildren), but sightseers can use it as well. The bus service around Lake Garda serves mostly towns on the western shore.

Bus Contacts Arriva Italia. ☎ 02/34534110 ⊕ www.arriva.it. **Autostradale.** ☎ 02/30089000 ⊕ www.autostradale.it.

CAR TRAVEL

Getting almost anywhere by car is a snap, as several major highways intersect at Milan, all connected by the *tangenziale*, the city's ring road. The A4 autostrade runs west to Turin and east to Venice; the A1 leads south to Bologna, Florence, and Rome; the A7 angles southwest down to Genoa. The A8 goes northwest toward Lake Maggiore, and the A9 north runs past Lake Como and into Switzerland's southernmost tip.

To get around the lakes themselves by car, you have to follow secondary roads. The SP572 follows the southern and western shores of Lake Garda, the SS45bis edges the northernmost section of the western shore, and the SR249 runs along the eastern shore. Around Lake Como, follow the SS340 along the western shore, the SS36 on the eastern shore, and the SP583 on the lower arms. The SS33 and SS34 trace the western shore of Lake Maggiore. The SP469 runs on the western side of Lake Iseo, while the SP510 borders the east. Although the roads around the lakes can be beautiful, they're full of harrowing twists and turns, making for a slow, challenging drive—often with an Italian speed racer on your tail.

Contacts ACI. ☎ 803/116 ⊕ www.aci.it.

TRAIN TRAVEL

Milan's majestic Central Station (Milano Centrale), 3 km (2 miles) northwest of the Duomo, has frequent service within the region to Como, Bergamo, Brescia, Sirmione, Pavia, Cremona, and Mantua. There are plenty of signs to help you get around, but its sheer size requires considerable walking and patience, so allow for some extra time here.

Tickets bought without a reservation need to be validated by stamping them in yellow machines on the train platforms. Tickets with reservations don't require validation. When in doubt, validate—it can't hurt.

For general information on trains and schedules, as well as online ticket purchases, visit the website of the Italian national railway, **Ferrovie dello Stato (FS)** (⊕ www.trenitalia.com).

RESTAURANTS

You'll find lots of traditional northern Italian restaurants in this region, and can pretty much count on menus divided into pasta, fish, and meat options. As in the rest of Italy, it's common for dishes to feature seasonal and local ingredients. Meal prices in Milan tend to be higher than in the rest of the region (and quite high for European cities in general), though this is also where you'll see examples of the latest food trends and more adventurous choices on the menus. *Restaurant reviews have been shortened. For full information, visit Fodors.com.*

HOTELS

Given that this is the wealthiest part of Italy, most hotels here cater to a clientele willing to pay for extra comfort. Outside Milan, many are converted villas with well-landscaped grounds. Most of the famous lake resorts are expensive; many smaller lakeside hotels are more reasonably priced. Local tourism offices throughout the region are an excellent source of information about affordable lodging.

Please note that the time for "high season" can vary here—in the lakes it's at the height of summer, not surprisingly, but in Milan it depends on what fairs and exhibitions are being staged. Prices in almost all hotels can go up dramatically during the Furniture Fair in early April. Fashion, travel, and tech fairs also draw big crowds throughout the year, raising prices. In contrast to other cities in Italy, however, you can often find discounts on weekends. The four lakes—Maggiore, Garda, Como, and Iseo—have little to offer except quiet from November to March, when most gardens, hotels, and restaurants are closed. *Hotel reviews have been shortened. For full information, visit Fodors.com.*

WHAT IT COSTS				
	$	$$	$$$	$$$$
Restaurants	under €15	€15–€24	€25–€35	over €35
Hotels	under €125	€125–€200	€201–€300	over €300

Prices in the dining reviews are the average cost of a main course at dinner, or, if dinner is not served, at lunch. Prices in the lodging reviews are the lowest cost of a standard double room in high season.

MILAN

Milan is Italy's business hub and crucible of chic. Between the Po's rich farms and the industrious mountain valleys, it's long been the country's capital of commerce, finance, fashion, and media. Rome may be bigger and have the political power, but Milan and the affluent north are what really make the country go. It's also Italy's transport hub, with the biggest international airport, the most rail connections, and the best subway system. Leonardo da Vinci's *Last Supper* and other great works of art are here, as well as a spectacular Gothic Duomo, the finest of its kind. Milan even reigns supreme where it really counts (in the minds of many Italians), routinely trouncing the rest of the nation with its two premier soccer teams.

And yet, Milan hasn't won the battle for hearts and minds when it comes to tourism. Most visitors prefer Tuscany's hills and Venice's canals to Milan's hectic efficiency and wealthy indifference, and it's no surprise that in a country of medieval hilltop villages and skilled artisans, a city of grand boulevards and global corporations leaves visitors asking the real Italy to please stand up. They're right, of course: Milan is more European than Italian, a new buckle on an old boot, and although its old city can stand cobblestone for cobblestone against the best of them, seekers of Roman ruins and fairy-tale towns may pass. But Milan's secrets reveal themselves slowly to those who look. A side street conceals a garden complete with flamingos (Giardini Invernizzi, on Via dei Cappuccini, just off Corso Venezia; closed to the public, but you can still catch a glimpse), and a renowned 20th-century art collection hides modestly behind an unspectacular facade a block from Corso Buenos Aires (the Casa-Museo Boschi di Stefano). Visitors lured by the world-class shopping will appreciate Milan's European sophistication while discovering unexpected facets of a country they may have only thought they knew.

Virtually every invader in European history—Gaul, Roman, Goth, Lombard, and Frank—as well as a long series of rulers from France, Spain, and Austria, took a turn at ruling the city. After being completely sacked by the Goths in AD 539 and by the Holy Roman Empire under Frederick Barbarossa in 1157, Milan became one of the first independent city-states of the Renaissance. Its heyday of self-rule proved comparatively brief. From 1277 until 1500 it was ruled first by the Visconti and then the Sforza dynasties. These families were known, justly or not, for a peculiarly aristocratic mixture of refinement, classical learning, and cruelty; much of the surviving grandeur of Gothic and Renaissance art and architecture is their doing. Be on the lookout in your wanderings for the Visconti family emblem—a viper, its jaws straining wide, devouring a child.

GETTING HERE AND AROUND

The city center is compact and walkable; trolleys and trams make it even more accessible, and the efficient Metropolitana (subway) and buses provide access to locations farther afield. Driving in Milan is difficult and parking a real pain, so a car is a liability. In addition, drivers within the second ring of streets (the *bastioni*) must pay a daily congestion charge on weekdays between 7:30 am and 7:30 pm (till 6 pm on Thursday). You can pay the charge at news vendors, tobacconists, Banca Intesa Sanpaolo ATMs, or online at ⊕ *www.atm-mi.it/en*; parking meters and parking garages in the area also include it in the cost.

BICYCLE TRAVEL

Bicycle Contacts BikeMI. ☎ *02/48607607* ⊕ *www.bikemi.com.*

PUBLIC TRANSPORTATION

A standard public transit ticket costs €1.50 and is valid for a 90-minute trip on a subway, bus, or tram. An all-inclusive subway, bus, and tram pass costs €4.50 for 24 hours or €8.25 for 48 hours. Individual tickets and passes can be purchased from news vendors, tobacconists, at ticket machines at all subway stops, at ticket offices at the Duomo and other subway stops, and on your phone via the ATM Milano app. Another option is a *carnet* (€13.80), good for 10 tram or subway rides; a B14 4-journey integrated ticket (€6), good for four rides; or a *ricaricaMI* top-up card (€2.50), which you can "top up" with tickets as you need them. Once you have your ticket or pass, either stamp it or insert it into the slots in station turnstiles or on poles inside trolleys and buses. (The electronic tickets won't function if they become bent or demagnetized. If you have a problem, contact a station manager, who can usually issue a new ticket.) Trains run from 6 am to 12:30 am.

Contacts ATM (*Azienda Trasporti Milanesi*). ☎ *02/48607607* ⊕ *www.atm-mi.it/ en.* **Radiobus.** ☎ *02/48034803* ⊕ *www.atm-mi.it/en.*

TAXI TRAVEL

Taxi fares in Milan are higher than in American cities; a short ride can run about €15 during rush hour or during fashion week. You can get a taxi at a stand with an orange "Taxi" sign, or by calling one of the taxi companies. Most also have apps you can download to order taxis from your phone; some let you text or use WhatsApp to hail a cab.

Dispatchers may speak some English; they'll ask for the phone number you're calling from, and they'll tell you the number of your taxi and how long it'll take to arrive. If you're in a restaurant or bar, ask the staff to call a cab for you.

Taxi Contacts 026969. ☎ *02/6969* ⊕ *www.026969.it.* **Autoradiotaxi.** ☎ *02/8585* ⊕ *www.028585.it.* **Radio Taxi Freccia.** ☎ *02/4000* ⊕ *www.024000.it.* **Taxiblu.** ☎ *02/4040* ⊕ *www.taxiblu.it.*

TOURS

Tour Companies City Sightseeing Milano. ☎ *02/867131* ⊕ *www.city-sightseeing.it/en/milan.*

VISITOR INFORMATION

Contacts Milan Tourism Office. ⊠ *Galleria Vittorio Emanuele II, Piazza del Duomo, corner of Piazza della Scala, Duomo* ☎ *02/88455555* ⊕ *www.turismo. milano.it.*

EXPLORING

DUOMO

Milan's main streets radiate out from the massive Duomo, a late-Gothic cathedral begun in 1386. Heading north is the handsome Galleria Vittorio Emanuele, an enclosed shopping arcade that opens at one end to the world-famous opera house known as La Scala. Heading northeast from La Scala is Via Manzoni, which leads to the Quadrilatero della Moda, or fashion district.

Heading northeast from the Duomo is the pedestrians-only street Corso Vittorio Emanuele. Northwest of the Duomo is Via Dante, at the top of which is the imposing outline of the Castello Sforzesco.

TOP ATTRACTIONS

Fodor's Choice ★ **Duomo.** There is no denying that for sheer size and complexity, the Duomo is unrivaled in Italy. It is the second-largest church in the country—the largest being St. Peter's in Rome—and the fifth largest in the world. This intricate Gothic structure has been fascinating and exasperating visitors and conquerors alike since it was begun by Galeazzo Visconti III (1351–1402), first duke of Milan, in 1386. Consecrated in the 15th or 16th century, it was not completed until just before the coronation of Napoléon as king of Italy in 1809. Although the capacity is estimated to be 40,000, it is usually empty, a sanctuary from the frenetic pace of life outside and the perfect place for solitary contemplation.

The building is adorned with 135 marble spires and 2,245 marble statues. The oldest part is the apse. Its three colossal bays of curving and counter-curved tracery, especially the bay adorning the exterior of the stained-glass windows, should not be missed. At the end of the southern transept down the right aisle lies the **tomb of Gian Giacomo Medici.** The tomb owes some of its design to Michelangelo but was executed by Leone Leoni (1509–90) and is generally considered to be his masterpiece; it dates from the 1560s. Directly ahead is the Duomo's most famous sculpture, the gruesome but anatomically instructive figure of San Bartolomeo (St. Bartholomew), who was flayed alive. As you enter the apse to admire those splendid windows, glance at the sacristy doors to the right and left of the altar. The lunette on the right dates from 1393 and was decorated by Hans von Fernach. The one on the left also dates from the 14th century and is ascribed jointly to Giacomo da Campione and Giovanni dei Grassi.

The roof is worth a look: walk out the left (north) transept to the stairs and elevator. As you stand among the forest of marble pinnacles, remember that virtually every inch of this gargantuan edifice, including the roof itself, is decorated with precious white marble dragged from quarries near Lake Maggiore by Duke Visconti's team along road laid fresh for the purpose and through the newly dredged canals. Exhibits at the **Museo del Duomo** shed light on the cathedral's history and include some of the treasures removed from the exterior for preservation purposes, while the early Christian **Baptistry of St. John** can be seen in the **archaeological area** underneath the cathedral. ⊠ *Piazza del Duomo, Duomo* ☎ *02/72022656* ⊕ *www.duomomilano.it* ☑ *Cathedral and museum €3 (€7 with archaeological area), stairs to roof €9, elevator €13* Ⓜ *Duomo.*

Fodor'sChoice ★
Galleria Vittorio Emanuele II. This spectacular, late-19th-century, Belle Époque tunnel is essentially one of the planet's earliest and most select shopping malls, with upscale tenants that include Gucci, Prada, Versace, and Louis Vuitton. This is the city's heart, midway between the Duomo and La Scala. It teems with life, inviting people-watching from the tables that spill from the bars and restaurants, where you can enjoy an overpriced coffee. Books, clothing, food, hats, and jewelry are all for sale. Known as Milan's "parlor," the Galleria is often viewed as a barometer of the city's well-being. The historic, if somewhat overpriced and inconsistent, Savini restaurant hosts the beautiful and powerful of the city, just across from McDonald's. Even in poor weather the great glass dome above the octagonal center is a splendid sight. The paintings at the base of the dome represent Europe, Asia, Africa, and America. Those at the entrance arch are devoted to science, industry, art, and agriculture. And the floor mosaics are a vastly underrated source of pleasure, even if they are not to be taken too seriously. Be sure to follow tradition and spin your heels once or twice on the more "delicate" parts of the bull beneath your feet in the northern apse; the Milanese believe it brings good luck. ⊠ *Piazza del Duomo, Duomo* Ⓜ *Duomo.*

Fodor'sChoice ★
Palazzo Reale. Elaborately decorated, this former royal palace close to the Duomo with painted ceilings and grand staircases is almost worth a visit in itself, but it also functions as one of Milan's major art exhibition spaces, with a focus on modern artists. Recent exhibits have highlighted works by Chagall, Escher, Warhol, Pollock, and Kandinsky. Check the website before you visit to see what's on; purchase tickets online in advance to save time in the queues, which are often long and chaotic. ⊠ *Piazza Duomo 12, Duomo* ☎ *02/8929711* ⊕ *www.palazzorealemilano.it* ☑ *Price varies for exhibitions* Ⓜ *Duomo.*

Pinacoteca Ambrosiana. Cardinal Federico Borromeo, one of Milan's native saints, founded this picture gallery in 1618 with the addition of his personal art collection to a bequest of books to Italy's first public library. The core works of the collection include such treasures as Caravaggio's *Basket of Fruit,* Raphael's monumental preparatory drawing (known as a "cartoon") for *The School of Athens,* which hangs in the Vatican, and Leonardo da Vinci's *Portrait of a Musician.* The highlight for many is Leonardo's *Codex Atlanticus,* which features thousands of his sketches and drawings. In addition to works by Lombard artists are paintings by Botticelli, Luini, Titian, and Jan Brueghel. A wealth of charmingly idiosyncratic items on display include 18th-century scientific instruments and gloves worn by Napoléon at Waterloo. Access to the library, the Biblioteca Ambrosiana, is limited to researchers who apply for entrance tickets. ⊠ *Piazza Pio XI 2, Duomo* ☎ *02/806921* ⊕ *www. leonardo-ambrosiana.it* 🎟 *€15* ⊘ *Closed Mon.* Ⓜ *Duomo.*

Santa Maria Presso San Satiro. Just a few steps from the Duomo, this architectural gem was first built in 876 and later perfected by Bramante (1444–1514), demonstrating his command of proportion and perspective, hallmarks of Renaissance architecture. Bramante tricks the eye with a famous optical illusion that makes a small interior seem extraordinarily spacious and airy, while accommodating a beloved 13th-century fresco. ⊠ *Via Torino 17–19, Duomo* ☎ *02/874683* Ⓜ *Duomo; Tram No. 2, 3, 4, 12, 14, 19, 20, 24, or 27.*

WORTH NOTING

Battistero Paleocristiano/Baptistry of San Giovanni alle Fonti. More specifically known as the Baptistry of San Giovanni alle Fonti, this 4th-century baptistry is one of two that lie beneath the Duomo. Although opinion remains divided, it is widely believed to be where Ambrose, Milan's first bishop and patron saint, baptized Augustine. Tickets also include a visit to the Duomo and its museum. ⊠ *Piazza del Duomo, enter through Duomo, Duomo* ☎ *02/72022656* ⊕ *www.duomomilano. it* 🎟 *€7, includes admission to Duomo* Ⓜ *Duomo.*

Museo del Novecento. Ascend a Guggenheim-esque spiral walkway to reach the modern art collection at this petite yet jam-packed collection of Italian contemporary art adjacent to the Duomo. The museum highlights 20th-century Italian artists, including a strong showing of Futurist artists such as Boccioni and Severini and sculptures from Marini, along with a smattering of works by other European artists including Picasso, Braque, and Matisse. ⊠ *Via Marconi 1, Duomo* ☎ *02/88444061* ⊕ *www.museodelnovecento.org* 🎟 *€5; free 2 hrs before closing and on Tues. after 2* Ⓜ *Duomo.*

CASTELLO

Castello Sforzesco. Wandering the grounds of this tranquil castle and park near the center of Milan is a great respite from the often-hectic city, and the interesting museums inside are an added bonus. The castle's crypts and battlements, including a tunnel that emerges well into the Parco Sempione behind, can be visited with privately reserved guides from **Ad Artem** or **Opera d'Arte.**

For the serious student of Renaissance military engineering, the Castello must be something of a travesty, so often has it been remodeled or rebuilt since it was begun in 1450 by the *condottiere* (hired mercenary) who founded the city's second dynastic family, Francesco Sforza, fourth duke of Milan. Although today "mercenary" has a pejorative ring, during the Renaissance all Italy's great soldier-heroes were professionals hired by the cities and principalities they served. Of them—and there were thousands—Francesco Sforza (1401–66) is considered one of the greatest, most honest, and most organized. It is said he could remember the names not only of all his men but of their horses as well. His rule signaled the enlightened age of the Renaissance but preceded the next foreign rule by a scant 50 years.

Since the turn of the 20th century, the Castello has been the depository of several city-owned collections of Egyptian and other antiquities, musical instruments, arms and armor, decorative arts and textiles, prints and photographs (on consultation), paintings, and sculpture. Highlights include the **Sala delle Asse,** a frescoed room still sometimes attributed to Leonardo da Vinci (1452–1519), which is currently undergoing restoration, though it's still open to the public. Michelangelo's unfinished *Rondanini Pietà,* believed to be his last work—an astounding achievement for a man nearly 90, and a moving coda to his life—is housed in the **Museo Pieta Rondanini.** The *pinacoteca* (picture gallery) features 230 paintings from medieval times to the 18th century, including works by Antonello da Messina, Canaletto, Andrea Mantegna, and Bernardo Bellotto. The **Museo dei Mobili** (furniture museum), which illustrates the development of Italian furniture from the Middle Ages to current design, includes a delightful collection of Renaissance treasure chests of exotic woods with tiny drawers and miniature architectural details. A single ticket purchased in the office in an inner courtyard admits visitors to these separate installations, which are dispersed around the castle's two immense courtyards. ⊠ *Piazza Castello, Castello* ☏ *02/88463700* ⊕ *www.milanocastello.it* ✉ *Castle free, museums €5 (free Tues. 2–5:30, Wed.–Fri. and weekends 4:30–5:30, and 1st Sun. of month)* ☉ *Museums closed Mon.* Ⓜ *Cadorna, Lanza, or Cairoli; Tram No. 1, 2, 4, 12, 14, or 19; Bus No. 18, 37, 50, 58, 61, or 94.*

SEMPIONE

Parco Sempione. Originally the gardens and parade grounds of the Castello Sforzesco, this open space was reorganized during the Napoleonic era, when the arena on its northeast side was constructed, and then turned into a park during the building boom at the end of the 19th century. It is still the lungs of the city's fashionable western neighborhoods, and the **Aquarium** still attracts Milan's schoolchildren. The park became a bit of a design showcase in 1933 with the construction of the Triennale. ⊠ *Sempione* ☉ *Aquarium closed Mon.* Ⓜ *Cairoli, Lanza or Cadorna; Tram No. 1, 2, 4, 12, 14, 19, or 27; Bus No. 43, 57, 61, 70, or 94.*

Torre Branca. It is worth visiting Parco Sempione just to see the Torre Branca. Designed by the architect Gio Ponti (1891–1979), who was behind so many of the projects that made Milan the design capital that it is, this steel tower rises 330 feet over the Triennale. Take the elevator to get a nice view of the city, then have a drink at the glitzy Just Cavalli Restaurant and Club at its base. ⊠ *Parco Sempione, Sempione* ☏ *02/3314120* ⊕ *www.turismo.milano.it* ✉ *€5* ☉ *Closed Mon. year-round and Tues., Thurs., and Fri. mid-Sept.–mid-May* Ⓜ *Cadorna; Tram No. 1; Bus No. 61.*

BRERA

To the north of the Duomo lie the winding streets of this elegant neighborhood, once the city's bohemian quarter.

Fodor'sChoice ★ **Pinacoteca di Brera** (*Brera Gallery*). The collection here is star-studded even by Italian standards. The museum has nearly 40 rooms, arranged in chronological order—so pace yourself. One highlight is the somber, moving *Cristo Morto* (Dead Christ) by Mantegna, which dominates Room VI with its sparse palette of umber and its foreshortened perspective. Mantegna's shocking, almost surgical precision tells of an all-too-human agony. It's one of Renaissance painting's most quietly wondrous achievements, finding an unsuspected middle ground between the excesses of conventional gore and beauty in representing the Passion's saddest moment.

Room XXIV offers two additional highlights of the gallery. Raphael's (1483–1520) *Sposalizio della Vergine* (Marriage of the Virgin) with its mathematical composition and precise, alternating colors, portrays the betrothal of Mary and Joseph. *La Vergine con il Bambino e Santi* (Madonna with Child and Saints), by Piero della Francesca (1420–92), is an altarpiece commissioned by Federico da Montefeltro (shown kneeling, in full armor, before the Virgin); it was intended for a church to house the duke's tomb. Room XXXVII houses one of the most romantic paintings in Italian history: *Il Bacio,* by Francesco Hayez (1791–1882), depicts a couple from the Middle Ages engaged in a passionate kiss. The painting was meant to portray the patriotic spirit of Italy's Unification and freedom from the Austro-Hungarian empire. ✉ *Via Brera 28, Brera* ☎ *02/722631* ⊕ *www.pinacotecabrera. org* ✑ *€10 (free 1st Sun. of month)* ⊗ *Closed Mon.* Ⓜ *Montenapoleone or Lanza; Tram No. 1, 4, 12, 14, or 27; Bus No. 61.*

Triennale Design Museum. In addition to honoring Italy's design talent, the Triennale also offers a regular series of exhibitions on design from around the world. A spectacular bridge entrance leads to a permanent collection, an exhibition space, and a stylish café and rooftop restaurant with expansive views. The Triennale also manages the fascinating museum-studio of designer Achille Castiglioni, in nearby Piazza Castello (hour-long guided tours Tuesday–Friday at 10, 11, and noon; €10. Call or email in advance to book: ☎ *02/805–3606* or ✐ *info@ achillecastiglioni.it*). ✉ *Via Alemagna 6, Brera* ☎ *02/724341* ⊕ *www. triennale.org* ✑ *€12* ⊗ *Closed Mon.* Ⓜ *Cadorna; Bus No. 61.*

QUADRILATERO

Via Manzoni, which lies northeast of La Scala, leads to Milan's Quadrilatero della Moda, or fashion district.

Museo Bagatti Valsecchi. Glimpse the lives of 19th-century Milanese aristocrats with a visit to this lovely historic house museum, once the home of two brothers, Barons Fausto and Giuseppe Bagatti. Family members inhabited the house until 1974; it opened to the public as a museum in 1984. The house is decorated with the brothers' fascinating collection of 15th- and 16th-century Renaissance art, furnishings, and objects, including armor, musical instruments, and textiles. The detailed audio guide included with admission provides a thorough insight into the

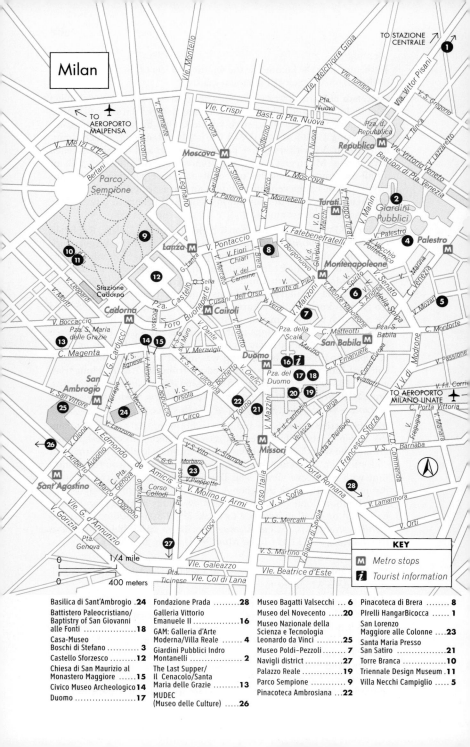

Milan

TO STAZIONE
CENTRALE

TO
AEROPORTO
MALPENSA

TO AEROPORTO
MILANO LINATE

Parco
Sempione

Stazione
Cadorna

Pta.
Nuova

Pza. d.
Repubblica

Moscova

Lanza

Cairoli

Duomo

Pza. del
Duomo

Missori

Sant'Agostino

San
Ambrogio

Pta.
Genova

Pta.
Ticinese

Republica

Turati

Giardini
Pubblici

Palestro

Montenapoleone

San Babila

San
Lorenzo

San Satiro

history of the artworks and intriguing stories of the family itself. ⊠ *Via Gesu 5, Quadrilatero* ☎ *02/76006132* ⊕ *museobagattivalsecchi.org* 🎫 *€9 (€6 on Wed.)* ⊙ *Closed Mon.* Ⓜ *Montenapoleone; Tram No. 1.*

Museo Poldi-Pezzoli. This exceptional museum, opened in 1881, was once a private residence and collection, and contains not only pedigreed paintings but also porcelain, textiles, and a cabinet with scenes from Dante's life. The gem is undoubtedly the *Portrait of a Lady* by Antonio Pollaiuolo (1431–98), one of the city's most prized treasures and the source of the museum's logo. The collection also includes masterpieces by Botticelli (1445–1510), Andrea Mantegna (1431–1506), Giovanni Bellini (1430–1516), and Fra Filippo Lippi (1406–69). ⊠ *Via Manzoni 12, Quadrilatero* ☎ *02/794889* ⊕ *www.museopoldipezzoli.it* 🎫 *€10* ⊙ *Closed Tues.* Ⓜ *Montenapoleone or Duomo; Tram No. 1.*

BUENOS AIRES

Casa-Museo Boschi di Stefano (*Boschi di Stefano House and Museum*). To most people, Italian art means Renaissance art, but the 20th century in Italy was also a time of artistic achievement. An apartment on the second floor of a stunning Art Deco building designed by Milan architect Portaluppi houses this collection, which was donated to the city of Milan in 2003 and is a tribute to the enlightened private collectors who replaced popes and nobles as Italian patrons. The walls are lined with the works of postwar greats, such as Fontana, De Chirico, and Morandi. Along with the art, the museum holds distinctive postwar furniture and stunning Murano glass chandeliers. ⊠ *Via Jan 15, Buenos Aires* ☎ *02/20240568* ⊕ *www.fondazioneboschidistefano.it* 🎫 *Free* ⊙ *Closed Mon.* Ⓜ *Lima; Tram No. 33; Bus No. 60.*

PALESTRO

GAM: Galleria d'Arte Moderna/Villa Reale. One of the city's most beautiful buildings is an outstanding example of Neoclassical architecture, built between 1790 and 1796 as a residence for a member of the Belgioioso family. It later became known as the Villa Reale when it was donated to Napoléon, who lived here briefly with Empress Josephine. Its origins as a residence are reflected in the elegance of its proportions and its private garden behind. The museum provides a unique glimpse of the splendors hiding behind Milan's discreet and often stern facades.

The collection comes from private donations from prominent Milanese art collectors and their families. It focuses mainly on 18th- and 19th-century Italian works, with a smattering of 20th-century pieces from Italian artists as well as international works from Van Gogh and Picasso, among others. ⊠ *Via Palestro 16, Palestro* ☎ *02/88445947* ⊕ *www.gam-milano.com* 🎫 *€5; free Wed.–Sun. after 4:30 and Tues. after 2* ⊙ *Closed Mon.* Ⓜ *Palestro or Turati; Tram No. 1 or 2; Bus No. 94 or 61.*

Villa Necchi Campiglio. In 1932, architect Piero Portaluppi designed this sprawling estate in an Art Deco style, with inspiration coming from the decadent cruise ships of the 1920s. Once owned by the Necchi Campiglio industrial family, the tasteful and elegant home—which sits on Via Mozart, one of Milan's most exclusive streets—is a reminder of the refined, modern culture of the nouveaux riches who accrued financial power in Milan during that era. Visits are by guided tour

only and can be reserved over the phone or by emailing fainecchi@
fondoambiente.it. There is also a well-regarded café on the grounds
that is open for lunch. ■ TIP→ **Tours of the estate last about one hour
and include English-speaking guides if needed.** ✉ *Via Mozart 14, Palestro* ☎ *02/76340121* ⊕ *www.fondoambiente.it/luoghi/villa-necchi-
campiglio* ⌖ *€12* ⊘ *Closed Mon. and Tues.* Ⓜ *Palestro, San Babila, or
Montenapoleone; Bus No. 54, 61, or 94.*

SANT'AMBROGIO

If the part of the city to the north of the Duomo is dominated by its
shops, Sant'Ambrogio and other parts to the south are known for their
works of art. The most famous is *Il Cenacolo*—known in English as
The Last Supper. If you have time for nothing else, make sure you see
this masterpiece. You will need reservations to see this fresco, which
is housed in the refectory of Santa Maria delle Grazie. Make these at
least three weeks before you depart for Italy, so you can plan the rest
of your time in Milan.

TOP ATTRACTIONS

Basilica di Sant'Ambrogio (*Basilica of St. Ambrose*). Milan's bishop, St.
Ambrose (one of the original Doctors of the Catholic Church), consecrated this church in AD 387. St. Ambroeus, as he is known in Milanese
dialect, is the city's patron saint, and his remains—dressed in elegant
religious robes, a miter, and gloves—can be viewed inside a glass case in
the crypt below the altar. Until the construction of the more imposing
Duomo, this was Milan's most important church. Much restored and
reworked over the centuries (the gold-and-gem-encrusted altar dates
from the 9th century), Sant'Ambrogio still preserves its Romanesque
characteristics, including 5th-century mosaics. The church is often closed
for weddings on Saturday. ✉ *Piazza Sant'Ambrogio 15, Sant'Ambrogio*
☎ *02/86450895* ⊕ *www.basilicasantambrogio.it* Ⓜ *Sant'Ambrogio; Bus
No. 50, 58, or 94.*

Fodor'sChoice **The Last Supper/Il Cenacolo/Santa Maria delle Grazie.** Leonardo da Vin-
★ ci's *The Last Supper,* housed in this church and former Dominican
monastery, has had an almost unbelievable history of bad luck and
neglect—its near destruction in an American bombing raid in August
1943 was only the latest chapter in a series of misadventures, including,
if one 19th-century source is to be believed, being whitewashed over by
monks. Well-meant but disastrous attempts at restoration have done
little to rectify the problem of the work's placement: it was executed
on a wall unusually vulnerable to climatic dampness. Yet Leonardo
chose to work slowly and patiently in oil pigments—which demand dry
plaster—instead of proceeding hastily on wet plaster according to the
conventional fresco technique. After years of restorers patiently shifting
from one square centimeter to another, Leonardo's masterpiece is now
free of centuries of retouching, grime, and dust. Astonishing clarity and
luminosity have been regained.

Despite Leonardo's carefully preserved preparatory sketches, in
which the apostles are clearly labeled by name, there still remains
some small debate about a few identities in the final arrangement.
But there can be no mistaking Judas, small and dark, his hand calmly

reaching forward to the bread, isolated from the terrible confusion that has taken the hearts of the others. One critic, Frederick Hartt, offers an elegantly terse explanation for why the composition works: it combines "dramatic confusion" with "mathematical order." Certainly, the amazingly skillful and unobtrusive repetition of threes—in the windows, in the grouping of the figures, and in their placement—adds a mystical aspect to what at first seems simply the perfect observation of spontaneous human gesture.

Reservations are required to view the work. Viewings are in 15-minute, timed-entry slots, and visitors must arrive 15 minutes before their assigned time in order not to lose their place. Reservations can be made by phone or online; it is worthwhile to call, as a number of tickets are set aside for phone reservations. Call at least three weeks ahead if you want a Saturday slot, two weeks for a weekday slot. The telephone reservation office is open Monday–Saturday 8–6:30. Operators do speak English, though not fluently, and to reach one you must wait for the Italian introduction to finish and then press "2." However, you can sometimes get tickets from one day to the next. Some city bus tours include a visit in their regular circuit, which may be a good option.

The painting was executed in what was the order's refectory, which is now referred to as the **Cenacolo Vinciano.** Take a moment to visit Santa Maria delle Grazie itself. It's a handsome, completely restored church, with a fine dome, which Bramante added along with a cloister about the time that Leonardo was commissioned to paint *The Last Supper.* ✉ *Piazza Santa Maria delle Grazie 2, off Corso Magenta, Sant'Ambrogio* ☎ *02/92800360 reservations, 02/4676111 church* ⊕ *www.cenacolovinciano.net, legraziemilano.it* ✎ *Last Supper €10 plus €2 reservation fee; free 1st Sun. of month* ☉ *Closed Mon.* Ⓜ *Cadorna or Conciliazione; Tram No. 18.*

WORTH NOTING

Chiesa di San Maurizio al Monastero Maggiore. Next to the Museo Civico Archeologico, you'll find this little gem of a church, constructed starting in 1503 and decorated almost completely with magnificent 16th-century frescoes. The modest exterior belies the treasures inside, including a concealed back room once used by nuns that includes a fascinating fresco of Noah loading the ark with animals, including two unicorns. ✉ *Corso Magenta 15, Sant'Ambrogio* ☎ *02/20404175* ☉ *Closed Mon.* Ⓜ *Cadorna or Cairoli; Tram No. 16 or 27; Bus No. 50, 58, or 94.*

Museo Civico Archeologico (*Municipal Archaeological Museum*). Appropriately situated in the heart of Roman Milan, this museum housed in a former monastery displays everyday utensils, jewelry, silver plate, and several fine examples of mosaic pavement from Mediolanum, the ancient Roman name for Milan. The museum opens into a garden that is flanked by the square tower of the Roman circus and the polygonal Ansperto tower, adorned with frescoes dating to the end of the 13th and 14th centuries that portray St. Francis and other saints receiving the stigmata. ✉ *Corso Magenta 15, Sant'Ambrogio* ☎ *02/88445208* ⊕ *www.museoarcheologicomilano.it* ✎ *€5; free Tues. after 2 and Wed.–Sun. after 4:30* ☉ *Closed Mon.* Ⓜ *Cadorna or Cairoli; Tram No. 16 or 27; Bus No. 50, 58, or 94.*

FAMILY   **Museo Nazionale della Scienza e Tecnologia Leonardo da Vinci** (*National Museum of Science and Technology*). This converted cloister is best known for the collection of models based on Leonardo da Vinci's sketches. One of the most visited rooms features interactive, moving models of the famous *vita aerea* (aerial screw) and *ala battente* (beating wing), thought to be forerunners of the modern helicopter and airplane, respectively. The museum also houses a varied collection of industrial artifacts including trains and several reconstructed workshops including a watchmaker's, a lute maker's, and an antique pharmacy. Reserve tickets for the celebrated Italian-built submarine and helicopter simulator in advance online or by phone to avoid disappointment. Displays also illustrate papermaking and metal founding, which were fundamental to Milan's—and the world's—economic growth. There's a bookshop and a bar. ■ TIP→ **Avoid this museum on weekends. It's a popular spot for families, and there are long lines on those days.** ⊠ *Via San Vittore 21, Sant'Ambrogio* ☎ *02/48555558* ⊕ *www.museoscienza.org* 🎟 *€10* ⊘ *Closed Mon.* Ⓜ *Sant'Ambrogio; Bus No. 50, 58, or 94.*

PORTA VENEZIA

FAMILY   **Giardini Pubblici Indro Montanelli** (*Public Gardens Indro Montanelli*). Giuseppe Piermarini, architect of La Scala, laid out these gardens across Via Palestro from the Villa Reale in 1770. Designed as public pleasure gardens, today they still are popular with families who live in the city center. Generations of Milanese have taken pony rides and gone on the miniature train and merry-go-round. The park also contains a small planetarium and the **Museo Civico di Storia Naturale** (Municipal Natural History Museum). ⊠ *Corso Venezia 55, Porta Venezia* ☎ *02/88463337* ⊕ *www.assodidatticamuseale.it* 🎟 *Gardens free; museum €5, free on Tues. after 2, Wed.–Sun. after 4:30, and 1st Sun. of month* ⊘ *Museum closed Mon.* Ⓜ *Palestro; Tram No. 9, 29, or 30.*

BICOCCA

Pirelli HangarBicocca. Anselm Kiefer's *The Seven Heavenly Palaces*—seven cement towers extending 43–52 feet high, along with five of Kiefer's large-scale paintings—is the must-see permanent installation at this impressive gallery in a former train factory. There are also temporary exhibitions of contemporary art throughout the year; check the website for the latest showings. ⊠ *Via Chiese 2* ☎ *02/66111573* ⊕ *www.hangarbicocca.org* 🎟 *Free* ⊘ *Closed Mon.–Wed.* Ⓜ *Via Chiese; Bus No. 87 or 51.*

NAVIGLI

Navigli District. In medieval times, a network of *navigli*, or canals, crisscrossed the city. Almost all have been covered over, but two—Naviglio Grande and Naviglio Pavese—are still navigable. The area's chock-full of boutiques, art galleries, cafés, bars, and restaurants, and at night the Navigli serves up a scene about as close as you will get to southern-style Italian street life in Milan. On weekend nights, it is difficult to walk among the youthful crowds thronging the narrow streets along the canals. Check out the antiques fair on the last Sunday of the month from 9 am to 6 pm. ■ TIP→ **During the summer months, be sure to put on some mosquito repellent.** ⊠ *South of Corso Porta Ticinese, Navigli* Ⓜ *Porta Genova; Tram No. 2, 3, 9, 14, 15, 29, or 30.*

TICINESE

MUDEC (Museo delle Culture). Home to a permanent collection of ethnographic displays as well as temporary exhibitions of big-name artists such as Basquiat and Miró, MUDEC is in the vibrant and developing Zona Tortona area of the city. British architect David Chipperfield designed the soaring space in a former factory. The permanent collection includes art, objects, and documents from Africa, Asia, and the Americas. Book in advance for the most popular temporary exhibits. There's also a highly rated restaurant, Enrico Bartolini Mudec, as well as a more casual bistro. ✉ *Via Tortona 56, Ticinese* ☎ *02/54917* ⊕ *www. mudec.it* ✉ *€5 for permanent collection, €15 for exhibitions* ⊗ *Closed Mon. until 2:30 pm* Ⓜ *Sant'Agostino or Porta Genova; Tram No. 2 or 14; Bus No. 68 or 90/91.*

San Lorenzo Maggiore alle Colonne. Sixteen ancient Roman columns line the front of this sanctuary; 4th-century paleo-Christian mosaics survive in the Cappella di Sant'Aquilino (Chapel of St. Aquilinus). ✉ *Corso di Porta Ticinese 39, Ticinese* ☎ *02/89404129* ⊕ *www.sanlorenzomaggiore.com* ✉ *Mosaics €2* Ⓜ *Missori.*

LARGO ISARCO

Fodor's Choice ★ **Fondazione Prada.** Housed in former distillery buildings from the 1910s and revamped alongside new structures of metal and glass, this collection of modern art in about 205,000 square feet of exhibition space is not for the faint of heart. Permanent pieces, such as Louise Bourgeois's *Haunted House,* are avant-garde and challenging, while temporary exhibitions highlight cutting-edge Italian and international artists. Although navigating the expansive grounds can be confusing, the knowledgeable staff will help guide lost visitors. Don't miss the Wes Anderson–designed café, Luce Bar, for a drink or snack before you leave. The Fondazione is a hike from the city center; expect a 10-minute walk from the metro station to the galleries. ✉ *Largo Isarco 2* ☎ *02/56662611* ⊕ *www.fondazioneprada.org* ✉ *€10* ⊗ *Closed Tues.* Ⓜ *Lodi TIBB; Tram No. 24; Bus No. 65.*

WHERE TO EAT

DUOMO

$$$
ITALIAN
✕ **Don Carlos.** One of the few restaurants open after La Scala lets out, Don Carlos, in the Grand Hotel et de Milan, is nothing like its indecisive operatic namesake (whose betrothed was stolen by his father). Flavors are bold, presentation is precise and full of flair, and the service is attentive. **Known for:** veal Milanese; house-made pasta; late-night hours. Ⓢ *Average main: €34* ✉ *Grand Hotel et de Milan, Via Manzoni 29, Duomo* ☎ *02/72314640* ⊕ *www.ristorantedoncarlos.it* ⊗ *No lunch* Ⓜ *Montenapoleone; Tram No. 1 or 2.*

$$$
ITALIAN
✕ **Giacomo Arengario.** Join businesspeople, ladies who lunch, and in-the-know tourists at this elegant restaurant with a glorious view of the Duomo atop the Museo del Novecento. To complement the vistas, renowned Milanese restaurateur Giacomo Bulleri offers up a mix of well-prepared seafood, pasta, and meat courses for lunch and dinner. **Known for:** amazing Duomo views from tables by the

windows; contemporary Milanese dishes; extensive wine list. [$] *Average main: €30* ✉ *Via Marconi 1, Duomo* ☎ *02/72093814* 🌐 *giacomoarengario.com* [M] *Duomo.*

$ VEGETARIAN 🍴 **La Vecchia Latteria.** With only two small dining rooms, this family-owned lunch spot dishes out an impressive amount of vegetarian cuisine. Nestled on a small street just steps away from the Duomo, it offers an array of freshly prepared, in-season selections with a daily-changing menu; try the mixed plate (*misto forno*), which offers a taste of several different small dishes. **Known for:** Italian-focused vegetarian cuisine; daily-changing combination platters; retro '50s atmosphere. [$] *Average main: €9* ✉ *6 Via dell'Unione, Duomo* ☎ *02/874401* 🕒 *Closed Sun. No dinner Mon., Wed., Fri., or Sat.* [M] *Duomo or Missori.*

$ PIZZA FAMILY 🍴 **Piz.** Fun, lively, and full of locals, this casual and inexpensive pizzeria on a side street near the Duomo has just three kinds of thin-crust pizza on the menu—luckily, all are excellent. Choose from margherita, bianca (white, with no tomato), and marinara (with no mozzarella); although you'll inevitably need to wait, you'll get a free glass of prosecco and a slice of pizza with cheese while you do. **Known for:** delicious thin-crust pizzas; free before- and after-dinner drinks; bustling vibe. [$] *Average main: €9* ✉ *Via Torino 34, Duomo* ☎ *02/86453482* [M] *Duomo; Tram No. 2, 3, or 14.*

$ ECLECTIC 🍴 **Rinascente Food & Restaurants.** The seventh floor of this famous Italian department store is a gourmet food market surrounded by several small restaurants that can be a good option for lunch, an aperitivo overlooking the Duomo, or dinner after a long day of shopping. There are several places to eat, including the popular mozzarella bar Obica, My Sushi, De Santis for "slow food" sandwiches, and the sophisticated Maio restaurant. **Known for:** good selection of foods; inexpensive meals and snacks; terrace overlooking the Duomo. [$] *Average main: €10* ✉ *Piazza Duomo, Duomo* ☎ *02/8852471* 🌐 *www.rinascente.it* [M] *Duomo.*

BRERA

$$$ MODERN ITALIAN 🍴 **Fioraio Bianchi Caffe.** A French-style bistro in the heart of Milan, Fioraio Bianchi Caffe was opened more than 40 years ago by Raimondo Bianchi, a great lover of flowers; in fact, eating at this restaurant is like dining in the middle of a boutique Parisian flower shop. Despite the French atmosphere, the many pasta and meat dishes have Italian flair and ensure a classy, inventive meal. **Known for:** flowers everywhere; charming shabby-chic look; creative Italian-style bistro food. [$] *Average main: €28* ✉ *Via Montebello 7, Brera* ☎ *02/29014390* 🌐 *www.fioraiobianchicaffe.it* 🕒 *Closed Sun., and 3 wks in Aug.* [M] *Turati.*

QUADRILATERO

$ MODERN ITALIAN 🍴 **Chic & Go Milano.** Step into these chic and trendy surroundings for a quick sandwich as exquisite as the fashion found in the nearby shops. Though the lobster panini will run you a pretty penny, other top-notch ingredients like angus tartare, crab, salmon, prosciutto, and mozzarella di bufala are not bad value considering the designer labels that abound in the neighborhood. **Known for:** gourmet sandwiches; gentle prices; convenient location near shopping. [$] *Average main: €8* ✉ *Via Montenapoleone 25, Quadrilatero* ☎ *02/782648, 02/43986187* 🌐 *www.chic-and-go.com* [M] *Montenapoleone; Tram No. 1.*

$$$$ MODERN ITALIAN Fodor's Choice ★ 🍴 **Seta.** Modern Italian dishes with interesting ingredients are the draw at this sophisticated restaurant located within Milan's Mandarin Oriental Hotel. The best way to get a sense of the intricate dishes is through the five-course tasting menu; for a less expensive option, opt for the two- or three-course "business lunch." In a masculine setting with brown and green decor, sample such signature dishes as *cavolfiore* (cauliflower with almond-milk sauce, yuzu juice, and seafood) and *riso* (risotto with vegetables, Maccagno cheese, and raspberry powder). **Known for:** ultracreative dishes; extensive wine list focused on Italian producers; top-notch service. [$] *Average main: €45* ✉ *Via Andegari 9, Quadrilatero* ☎ *02/87318897* 🌐 *www.mandarinoriental.com/milan/fine-dining/seta* ⏲ *Closed Sun., and 1st wk of Jan. No lunch Sat.* [M] *Montenapoleone; Tram No. 1.*

CINQUE GIORNATE

$$$ ITALIAN 🍴 **Da Giacomo.** The fashion and publishing crowd, as well as international bankers and businesspeople, favor this Tuscan-Ligurian restaurant. The emphasis is on fish; with its tile floor and bank of fresh seafood, the place has a refined neighborhood-bistro style. **Known for:** sophisticated dining; Italian-slanted fish and seafood dishes; good wine selection. [$] *Average main: €32* ✉ *Via P. Sottocorno 6, entrance in Via Cellini, Cinque Giornate* ☎ *02/76023313* 🌐 *www.giacomoristorante.com* [M] *Tram No. 9, 12, 23, or 27; Bus No. 60 or 73.*

GARIBALDI

$$$ CONTEMPORARY Fodor's Choice ★ 🍴 **Ceresio 7 Pools & Restaurant.** Book well in advance for one of Milan's most fashionable eateries, where the tables are lacquered red and modern artwork crowds the walls—exactly what you'd expect from the twin brothers Dean and Dan Caten behind the fashion label Dsquared2. The food cred matches the scene, with sophisticated dishes using luxe ingredients like lobster, king crab, and truffles. **Known for:** place for seeing and being seen; upscale Italian cuisine; fabulous outdoor seating. [$] *Average main: €32* ✉ *Via Ceresio 7, Garibaldi* ☎ *02/31039221* 🌐 *www.ceresio7.com* [M] *Garibaldi; Tram No. 2, 4, 12, or 14; Bus No. 37 or 190.*

$ PIZZA FAMILY 🍴 **Pizzeria Fabbrica.** This lively pizzeria has two wood-burning ovens going full-steam every day of the week. Skip the appetizers and go straight to the pizzas, which vary from traditional (*quattro stagioni*) to vegetable based (with zucchini, spinach, rucola, and more) to in-house specialties like the *tartufona* (with truffle oil). **Known for:** well-regarded pizzas; family-friendly atmosphere; outdoor seating. [$] *Average main: €9* ✉ *Viale Pasubio 2, Garibaldi* ☎ *02/6552771* 🌐 *www.lafabbricapizzeria.it* [M] *Garibaldi.*

LORETO

$ ITALIAN 🍴 **Da Abele.** If you love risotto, then make a beeline for this neighborhood trattoria. The superb risotto dishes change with the season, and every day there are three on the menu—one meat, one fish, and one vegetarian—and it's tempting to try them all. **Known for:** delicious risotto in several flavors; cozy atmosphere; gentle prices. [$] *Average main: €12* ✉ *Via Temperanza 5, Loreto* ☎ *02/2613855* 🌐 *www.trattoriadaabele.it* ⏲ *Closed Mon., Aug., and Dec. 24–Jan. 3. No lunch* [M] *Pasteur.*

PORTA ROMANA

$$ NORTHERN ITALIAN 🍴 **U Barba.** Simple, fresh, authentic Ligurian specialties (in Ligurian dialect the name means "the uncle") will take you back to lazy summer days on the Italian Riviera—even during Milan's wet winter weather. Such classic coastal specialties as *trofie al pesto* (an egg-free pasta served with pesto) and *cozze ripieni* (stuffed mussels), coupled with a basket of warm focaccia, reign supreme in this favorite of Milan's fashion crowd. **Known for:** authentic Italian Riviera cuisine; charming setting with vintage furniture; cool dining scene. [$] *Average main: €20* ✉ *Via Pier Candido Decembrio 33, Porta Romana* ☎ *02/45487032* 🌐 *www.ubarba.it* 🕒 *Closed Mon., and 2 wks in Aug. No lunch Tues.–Fri.* [M] *Lodi TIBB; Tram No. 16; Bus No. 90.*

PORTA VENEZIA

$$$ VEGETARIAN 🍴 **Joia.** At this haute-cuisine vegetarian haven near Piazza della Repubblica, delicious dishes—all without eggs and many without flour—are artistically prepared by chef Pietro Leemann. Vegetarians, who often get short shrift in Italy, will marvel at the variety of culinary offerings and artistry here. **Known for:** imaginative vegetarian cuisine; elaborate tasting menus; well-thought-out wine selection. [$] *Average main: €35* ✉ *Via Panfilo Castaldi 18, Porta Venezia* ☎ *02/29522124* 🌐 *www.joia.it* 🕒 *Closed Sun., 1 wk in Aug., and Dec. 24–Jan. 7* [M] *Repubblica or Porta Venezia; Tram No. 1, 5, 9, or 33.*

$ PIZZA FAMILY 🍴 **Pizza OK.** The thin-crust pizza wins raves from locals at this family-run pizzeria with four locations, the oldest near Corso Buenos Aires in the Porta Venezia area. The pizza is extra thin and large, and possibilities for toppings seem endless. **Known for:** thin-crust pizza; family-friendly dining; inexpensive eats. [$] *Average main: €8* ✉ *Via Lambro 15, Porta Venezia* ☎ *02/29401272* 🕒 *Closed Aug. 7–20 and Dec. 24–Dec. 26* [M] *Porta Venezia; Tram No. 5, 23, or 33.*

CAIROLI

$$$$ MILANESE 🍴 **ATMosfera.** Take a ride on Milan's 1930s-era trams, enjoy a tour of the city, and have a romantic dinner at the same time. Diners can choose between a meat, fish, and vegetarian four-course set menu, which varies throughout the year, and prices also include a bottle of wine, mineral water, and coffee. **Known for:** dining on tram is unique way to experience Milan; sophisticated romance; solid set menus; mandatory online reservations. [$] *Average main: €70* ✉ *Piazza Castello, Cairoli* ☎ *02/48607607* 🌐 *atmosfera.atm.it* 🕒 *Closed Jan. 1–16* [M] *Cairoli Castello; Tram No. 1 or 4; Bus No. 61.*

WHERE TO STAY

DUOMO

$$$$ HOTEL 🏨 **Grand Hotel et de Milan.** Only blocks from La Scala you'll find everything you hope for in a traditionally elegant European hotel, with ancient tapestries and persimmon velvet enlivening the 19th-century look without sacrificing dignity and luxury. **Pros:** traditional and elegant; great location off Milan's main shopping streets; staff goes above and beyond to meet guests' needs. **Cons:** gilt decor may not suit those who like more modern design; no spa; some small rooms. [$] *Rooms*

from: €374 ✉ Via Manzoni 29, Duomo ☎ 02/723141 ⊕ www.grandhoteletdemilan.it ⇨ 95 rooms ¶ No meals Ⓜ Montenapoleone.

$$ HOTEL **Hotel Gran Duca di York.** These spare but classically elegant and efficient rooms are arranged around a courtyard—four have private terraces—and are very good value for pricey Milan. **Pros:** central location; friendly staff; good breakfast. **Cons:** rooms are simple, with many on the small side; dated decor. *$ Rooms from: €182 ✉ Via Moneta 1/a, Duomo ☎ 02/874863 ⊕ www.ducadiyork.com ⇨ 33 rooms ¶ Free Breakfast Ⓜ Cordusio or Duomo; Tram No. 2, 12, 14, 16, or 27.*

$$$ HOTEL **Hotel Spadari al Duomo.** The fact that this chic city center inn is owned by an architect's family shows in the details, including custom-designed furniture and paintings by young Milanese artists on rotating display in the stylish guest rooms. **Pros:** good breakfast; central location; attentive staff. **Cons:** some rooms on the small side; street noise can be a problem. *$ Rooms from: €280 ✉ Via Spadari 11, Duomo ☎ 02/72002371 ⊕ www.spadarihotel.com ⇨ 40 rooms ¶ Free Breakfast Ⓜ Duomo; Tram No. 2, 3, 12, 14, 16, 24, or 27.*

$$ HOTEL **Hotel Star.** The price is extremely reasonable, the staff are helpful, and the rooms are well equipped and comfortable, some with touches like Jacuzzi tubs and balconies. **Pros:** centrally located near key attractions; reasonably priced; breakfast is included. **Cons:** Wi-Fi can be iffy; street noise in some rooms. *$ Rooms from: €155 ✉ Via dei Bossi 5, Duomo ☎ 02/801501 ⊕ www.hotelstar.it ⇨ 30 rooms ¶ Free Breakfast.*

$$$$ HOTEL Fodor's Choice ★ **Park Hyatt Milan.** Extensive use of warm travertine stone and modern art creates a sophisticated yet inviting and tranquil backdrop in these spacious and opulent guest rooms. **Pros:** central location; contemporary decor and amenities; refined atmosphere. **Cons:** not particularly intimate; very expensive; some rooms showing a little wear. *$ Rooms from: €590 ✉ Via Tommaso Grossi 1, Duomo ☎ 02/88211234 ⊕ milan.park.hyatt.com ⇨ 106 rooms ¶ No meals Ⓜ Duomo; Tram No. 1.*

$$$ HOTEL Fodor's Choice ★ **Room Mate Giulia.** For a hip and affordable design-focused place to stay with a friendly feel and prime location right next to the Galleria and around the corner from the Duomo, Milan visitors can't do much better than the city's first outpost from Spanish hotel chain Room Mate. **Pros:** amazing central location; fresh, appealing design; affordable rates for Milan. **Cons:** breakfast room a bit cramped; gym on the small side; busy location means some noise in rooms. *$ Rooms from: €269 ✉ Via Silvio Pellico 4, Duomo ☎ 02/80888900 ⊕ www.room-matehotels.com/en/giulia ⇨ 85 rooms ¶ No meals Ⓜ Duomo; Tram No. 1.*

$$$ HOTEL **UNA Maison Milano.** Inside this faithfully restored palazzo dating from the early 1900s, spaciousness is accentuated with soft white interiors, muted fabrics and marble, and clean, contemporary lines. **Pros:** the warmth of a residence and the luxury of a design hotel; lovely bathrooms; modern amenities. **Cons:** breakfast not included; not much of a lobby. *$ Rooms from: €260 ✉ Via Mazzini 4, Duomo ☎ 02/85605 ⊕ www.unamaisonmilano.it ⇨ 27 rooms ¶ No meals Ⓜ Duomo; Tram No. 2, 3, 12, 14, 16, 24, or 27.*

QUADRILATERO

$$$$ HOTEL Fodor's Choice ★ **Armani Hotel Milano.** Located in Milan's fashion district, this minimalist boutique hotel looks like it has been plucked from the pages of a sleek shelter magazine, and it should: it was designed by fashion icon Giorgio Armani to evoke the same sculptural, streamlined aesthetic—and tailored comfort—as his signature clothing. **Pros:** complimentary minibar (minus alcohol); lovely spa area and 24-hour gym; great location near major shopping streets. **Cons:** exclusive vibe not for everyone; some noise issues from neighboring rooms; a few signs of wear and tear. [$] *Rooms from: €540* ✉ *Via Manzoni 31, Quadrilatero* ☎ *02/88838888* 🌐 *www.armanihotelmilano.com* 🛏 *95 rooms* 🍴 *No meals* [M] *Montenapoleone.*

$$$$ HOTEL **Four Seasons.** Built in the 15th century as a convent and surrounding a colonnaded cloister, this sophisticated retreat in the heart of Milan's upscale shopping district certainly exudes a feeling that is anything but urban. **Pros:** quiet, elegant setting that feels removed from noisy central Milan; friendly and helpful staff; large rooms. **Cons:** rooms feel a little bland and old-fashioned; breakfast isn't included in the rate; extremely expensive. [$] *Rooms from: €850* ✉ *Via Gesù 6–8, Quadrilatero* ☎ *02/77088* 🌐 *www.fourseasons.com/milan* 🛏 *118 rooms* 🍴 *No meals* [M] *Montenapoleone; Tram No. 1.*

$$$$ HOTEL FAMILY Fodor's Choice ★ **Mandarin Oriental, Milan.** A sense of refined luxury pervades the guest rooms and public spaces of the first Mandarin Oriental in Italy, located just off the main Via Montenapoleone shopping street. **Pros:** wonderful and attentive service; tranquil spa and 24-hour fitness center; top restaurant on-site. **Cons:** very expensive; only some rooms have views; can be difficult to find. [$] *Rooms from: €750* ✉ *Via Andegari 9, Quadrilatero* ☎ *02/87318888* 🌐 *www.mandarinoriental.com/milan* 🛏 *104 rooms* 🍴 *No meals* [M] *Montenapoleone; Tram No. 1.*

SANT'AMBROGIO

$$ HOTEL **Antica Locanda Leonardo.** A relaxed feeling prevails in this 19th-century building, and the neighborhood (the church that houses *The Last Supper* is a block away) is one of Milan's most desired and historic. **Pros:** very quiet and homey; breakfast is ample; hotel has relationship with car service. **Cons:** more like a bed-and-breakfast than a hotel; old-fashioned decor; breakfast not included. [$] *Rooms from: €159* ✉ *Corso Magenta 78, Sant'Ambrogio* ☎ *02/48014197* 🌐 *www.anticalocandaleonardo.com* ⏲ *Closed 1st wk in Jan. and 3 wks in Aug.* 🛏 *16 rooms* 🍴 *No meals* [M] *Conciliazione, Sant'Ambrogio, or Cadorna; Tram No. 1, 16, 19, or 27.*

REPUBBLICA

$$$ HOTEL **Hotel Principe di Savoia Milano.** Milan's grande dame has all the trappings of an exquisite traditional luxury hotel: lavish mirrors, drapes, and carpets, limousine services, and the city's largest guest rooms, outfitted with eclectic fin-de-siècle furnishings. **Pros:** substantial spa–health club; close to Central Station. **Cons:** located in a not-very-central or attractive neighborhood; breakfast and other meals overly expensive. [$] *Rooms from: €265* ✉ *Piazza della Repubblica 17, Repubblica* ☎ *02/62301* 🛏 *301 rooms* 🍴 *No meals* [M] *Repubblica; Tram No. 1, 9, or 33.*

$$$ HOTEL ME Milan Il Duca. The first Italian hotel from the Spanish ME by Melia brand has a lively party atmosphere, with rousing music playing in the lobby, a design-conscious vibe, and a happening rooftop bar with panoramic city views. **Pros:** great rooftop bar; spacious rooms; young, vibrant atmosphere. **Cons:** no spa; may feel overdesigned to some; can be noisy. [$] *Rooms from: €299* ✉ *Piazza della Repubblica 13, Repubblica* ☎ *02/84220107* 🌐 *www.melia.com/en/hotels/italy/milan/home.htm* 🛏 *132 rooms* 🍴 *No meals* [M] *Repubblica; Tram No. 1, 5, 9, 10, or 33.*

"LET'S GO TO THE COLUMNS"

"Andiamo al Le Colonne" in Milanese youthspeak means to meet up at the sober Roman columns in front of the Basilica San Lorenzo Maggiore. Attracted to the Corso di Porta Ticinese by its bars and shops, hipsters spill out on the street to chat and drink. Neighbors may complain about the noise and confusion, but students and nighthawks find it indispensable for socializing at all hours. It's a street—no closing time.

$$$$ HOTEL **Westin Palace.** Don't be fooled by the functional 1950s-era exterior of one of Milan's premier business addresses: inside, many rooms have been renovated into a contemporary look with soothing gray walls and brown marble bathrooms, while other rooms are furnished with Empire-style antiques. **Pros:** full-service hotel with extensive amenities; renovated rooms in both modern and more traditional styles. **Cons:** lacking in local character; not in the most central or attractive location. [$] *Rooms from: €312* ✉ *Piazza della Repubblica 20, Repubblica* ☎ *02/63361* 🌐 *www.westinpalacemilan.it* 🛏 *227 rooms* 🍴 *No meals* [M] *Repubblica; Tram No. 1, 5, 9, or 33.*

TICINESE

$$$ HOTEL **Hotel Magna Pars Suites Milano.** Next to the trendy Navigli canals area, this ultrastylish all-suites boutique hotel in a former perfume factory boasts Italian-designed furniture and paintings from local Brera Academy artists; all rooms overlook one of two tranquil central courtyards, ensuring a quiet night's sleep. **Pros:** modern, design-y feel; attentive service; wonderful food at the attached restaurant. **Cons:** spa on the small side; a bit of a trek to central Milan attractions; fragranced rooms not for everyone. [$] *Rooms from: €261* ✉ *Via Forcella 6, Porta Ticinese* ☎ *02/8338371* 🌐 *www.magnapars-suitesmilano.it* 🛏 *39 suites* 🍴 *Free Breakfast* [M] *Porta Genova; Tram No. 2, 9, or 19.*

$$$ HOTEL Fodor's Choice ★ **The Yard.** Knickknacks and memorabilia from sports including golf, horseback riding, and boxing inspire the room decor in this eclectic and extremely hip hotel at the foot of the lively Corso di Porta Ticinese by the Navigli canals—but even if you're not a sports fan, you'll appreciate this friendly boutique hotel's contemporary flair. **Pros:** extremely attractive and comfortable; interesting location near many restaurants and bars; ultrafriendly staff. **Cons:** lacking some of the amenities of large hotels; about a half-hour hike from the Duomo and central Milan attractions. [$] *Rooms from: €249* ✉ *Piazza XXIV Maggio 8, Porta Ticinese* ☎ *02/89415901* 🌐 *www.theyardmilano.com* 🛏 *14 rooms* 🍴 *Free Breakfast* [M] *Tram 3 or 9.*

NIGHTLIFE AND PERFORMING ARTS

NIGHTLIFE

The aperitivo, or prelunch or predinner drink, is available everywhere in Italy, but in Milan it is a big part of life and a must-try. Milan bar owners have enriched the usual nibbles of olives, nuts, and chips with full finger (and often fork) buffets serving cubes of pizza and cheese, fried vegetables, rice salad, sushi, and even pasta, and they've baptized it "Appy Hour," with the first "h" dropped and the second one pronounced. For the price of a drink (around €8), you can make a meal of hors d'oeuvres—but don't be greedy.

DUOMO

Bar STRAF. This architecturally stimulating but dimly lit place has such artistic features as recycled fiberglass panels and vintage 1970s furnishings. The music is an eclectic mix of chilling tunes during the daytime, with more upbeat and vibrant tracks pepping it up at night. Located on a quiet side street near the Duomo, STRAF draws a young and lively, if tourist-heavy, crowd. ⊠ *Via San Raffaele 3, Duomo* ☎ *02/805081* ⊕ *www.straf.it/bar* Ⓜ *Duomo.*

Café Trussardi. Open throughout the day, this is a great place for coffee and bumping into Milan's elite. ⊠ *Piazza della Scala 5, Duomo* ☎ *02/80688295* ⊕ *www.trussardiallascala.com* Ⓜ *Tram No. 1.*

Fodor's Choice **Peck Italian Bar.** This foodie paradise near the Duomo with an enormous
★   deli featuring Italian specialty foods also has a bar and restaurant that serves up traditional—and excellent—pastas, pizza slices, olives, toasted nuts, and a good selection of wines by the glass in a refined setting. ⊠ *Via Cesare Cantù 3, Duomo* ☎ *02/8693017* ⊕ *www.peck.it* ۞ *Closed Sun.* Ⓜ *Duomo; Tram No. 2, 12, 14, 16, or 27.*

BRERA

Bulgari Hotel Bar. Having drinks or a light lunch at the Bulgari Hotel Bar lets you step off the asphalt and into one of the city's most impressive, private urban gardens—even indoors you seem to be outside, separated from the elements by a spectacular wall of glass. This is a great place to run into international hotel guests and jet-setting Milanese, and the bar staff mixes up a wide range of traditional and novel drinks—including the Bulgari Cocktail with gin, aperol, and orange, pineapple, and lime juices. ⊠ *Via Privata Fratelli Gabba 7/b, Brera* ☎ *02/8058051* ⊕ *www.bulgarihotels.com* Ⓜ *Montenapoleone; Tram No. 1.*

Jamaica Bar. A traditional hangout for students from the nearby Brera art school, this bar pulses with life on summer nights and is great for people-watching if you can snag an outdoor table. ⊠ *Via Brera 32, Brera* ☎ *02/876723* ⊕ *www.jamaicabar.it* Ⓜ *Lanza or Montenapoleone; Tram No. 1, 2, 4, 12, or 14.*

'N Ombra de Vin. This highly rated enoteca serves wine by the glass and, in addition to the plates of sausage and cheese nibbles, has light food and not-so-light desserts. It's a great place for people-watching on Via San Marco, while indoors offers a more dimly lit, romantic setting. Check out the impressive vaulted basement, where bottled wine and spirits are sold. ⊠ *Via S. Marco 2, Brera* ☎ *02/6599650*

⊕ *www.nombradevin.it* Ⓜ *Lanza, Turati, or Montenapoleone; Tram No. 1, 2, 4, 12, or 14.*

QUADRILATERO

Armani/Bamboo Bar. The Bamboo Bar at the Armani Hotel Milano has kept Milan abuzz since its opening in 2011. This modern architectural marvel has high ceilings, louvered windows, and expansive views of the city's rooftops. It's great for a relaxing after-work tea with friends or a predinner aperitivo. ⊠ *Via Manzoni 31, Quadrilatero* 🕾 *02/88838888* ⊕ *www.armanihotelmilano.com* Ⓜ *Montenapoleone; Tram No. 1.*

REPUBBLICA

Radio Rooftop Bar. Milan's most beautiful people congregate for aperol spritz and a selection of international tapas on this terrace with panoramic views of the city. Located at the top of the ME Milan Il Duca, the bar has heat lamps to keep visitors here even in cooler weather. There's also lunch Monday through Saturday and brunch on Sunday. ⊠ *Piazza della Repubblica 13, Repubblica* 🕾 *02/84220109* ⊕ *radiorooftop.com/milan* Ⓜ *Repubblica; Tram No. 1, 5, 9, 10, or 33.*

GARIBALDI

Blue Note. The first European branch of the famous New York nightclub features regular performances by some of the most famous names in jazz, as well as blues and rock concerts. Dinner is available, and there's a popular jazz brunch on Sunday. It's closed Monday. ⊠ *Via Borsieri 37, Garibaldi* 🕾 *02/69016888* ⊕ *www.bluenotemilano.com* Ⓜ *Isola; Tram No. 7, 31, or 33.*

Dry Cocktails & Pizza. A hot spot for both classic and creative cocktails, this trendy industrial space packed with hip locals has a pizza joint in the back if you get hungry. There's a second location at Viale Vittorio Veneto 28. ⊠ *Via Solferino 33, Garibaldi* 🕾 *02/63793414* ⊕ *www.drymilano.it* Ⓜ *Moscova, Turati, or Repubblica; Tram No. 1, 9, or 33; Bus No. 37.*

PORTA VIGENTINA

Magazzini Generali. What was once an abandoned warehouse is now a fun, futuristic venue for dancing. It also is a popular spot for fashion shows, and its concert schedule attracts well-known international acts. It's usually standing room only for concerts. ⊠ *Via Pietrasanta 16, Porta Vigentina* 🕾 *02/5393948* ⊕ *www.magazzinigenerali.org* Ⓜ *Tram No. 24; Bus No. 79, 90, or 91.*

CORSO COMO

Tocqueville 13. Regular nightclub fare from Thursday through Sunday is embellished with occasional live music, featuring young and emerging talent. ⊠ *Via Alexis de Tocqueville 13, Corso Como* 🕾 *3939527044* ⊕ *www.tocqueville13.club* ⊘ *Closed Mon.–Wed.* Ⓜ *Porta Garibaldi.*

BEYOND CITY CENTER

Plastic. Its venerable age notwithstanding (it opened in 1980), this is still one of Milan's most avant-garde and fun clubs, complete with drag-queen shows. The action starts late, even by Italian standards—don't bother going before midnight. They don't take reservations, and there aren't any tables. Entrance on Sunday is free. ⊠ *Via Gargano 15* 🕾 *02/733996* ⊘ *Closed Mon.–Thurs.* Ⓜ *Tram No. 27; Bus No. 60, 62, 66, 73, or K511.*

PERFORMING ARTS

For events likely to be of interest to non–Italian speakers, see *Hello Milano* (⊕ *www.hellomilano.it*), a monthly magazine available online and in print at the tourist office in Piazza Duomo; *Where Milan* (⊕ *www.wheremilan.com*); or the *American* (⊕ *www.theamericanmag.com*), which has a thorough cultural calendar.

MUSIC

Auditorium di Milano. This modern hall, known for its excellent acoustics, is home to the **Orchestra Verdi** and **Choir of Milano.** The season, which runs from September to June, includes many top international performers and rotating guest conductors. ⊠ *Largo Gustav Mahler Corso, San Gottardo 39, at Via Torricelli, Conchetta, Castello* ☎ *02/83389401* ⊕ *www.laverdi.org* Ⓜ *Tram No. 3 or 15; Bus No. 59 or 91.*

Conservatorio. The two halls belonging to the Conservatorio host some of the leading names in classical music. Series are organized by several organizations, including the venerable chamber music society the **Società del Quartetto.** ⊠ *Via del Conservatorio 12, Duomo* ☎ *02/762110, 02/76005500 Società del Quartetto* ⊕ *www.consmilano.it* Ⓜ *San Babila; Tram No. 9, 12, 23, or 27; Bus No. 60 or 73.*

Teatro Dal Verme. Frequent classical music concerts are staged here from October to May. ⊠ *Via San Giovanni sul Muro 2, Castello* ☎ *02/87905* ⊕ *www.dalverme.org* Ⓜ *Cairoli; Tram No. 1 or 4.*

OPERA

Fodor's Choice ★ **Teatro alla Scala.** You need know nothing of opera to sense that La Scala is closer to a cathedral than an auditorium. Hearing opera sung in the magical setting of La Scala is an unparalleled experience. Here, Verdi established his reputation and Maria Callas sang her way into opera lore. It looms as a symbol—both for the performer who dreams of singing here and for the opera buff. Audiences are notoriously demanding and are apt to jeer performers who do not measure up.

If you are lucky enough to be here during the opera season, do whatever is necessary to attend. Tickets go on sale two months before the first performance and are usually sold out the same day. The season runs from December 7, the feast day of Milan patron St. Ambrose, through June. For tickets, visit the **Biglietteria Centrale** (*Galleria del Sagrato, Piazza Del Duomo; daily noon–6*), which is in the Duomo subway station. Tickets are also available online or via La Scala's automated booking system. To pick up tickets for performances—from two hours prior to 15 minutes after the start of a performance—go to the box office at the theater, which is around the corner at Via Filodrammatici 2. Although you might not get seats for the more popular operas with big-name stars, it is worth trying; ballets are easier. There are also 140 tickets available on a first-come, first-served basis starting 2½ hours before the start of each performance at the theater box office. The theater is closed from the end of July through August and on national and local holidays.

At the **Museo Teatrale alla Scala** you can admire an extensive collection of librettos, paintings of the famous names of Italian opera, posters, costumes, antique instruments, and design sketches for the theater. It is also possible to take a look at the theater itself. Special exhibitions reflect current productions. ✉ *Piazza della Scala, Largo Ghiringhelli 1, Duomo* ☎ *02/72003744 theater, 02/88797473 museum, 02/860775 automated booking system* ⊕ *www.teatroallascala.org* 🎫 *Museum €9* Ⓜ *Duomo or Cordusio; Tram No. 1.*

SHOPPING

Milan is the birthplace of many of the world's most celebrated brands and high-ticket retail establishments: Prada, Versace, and Armani all call Milan home. The city has produced some of the industry's biggest talents, and reigns as one of the most important fashion capitals in the world. "Fashion tourists" come from cities like Shanghai, Moscow, and Tokyo to shop here.

Weekly open markets selling fruits and vegetables—and a great deal more—are still a regular sight in Milan. Many also sell clothing and shoes.

DUOMO

Borsalino. The kingpin of milliners, Borsalino has managed to stay trendy since it opened in 1857. ✉ *Galleria Vittorio Emanuele II 92, Duomo* ☎ *02/89015436* ⊕ *www.borsalino.com* Ⓜ *Duomo; Tram No. 1.*

Gucci. This Florence-born brand attracts lots of fashion-forward tourists in hot pursuit of its monogrammed bags, shoes, and accessories. ✉ *Galleria Vittorio Emanuele II, Duomo* ☎ *02/8597991* ⊕ *www.gucci. com* Ⓜ *Duomo; Tram No. 1.*

La Rinascente. The flagship location of this always-bustling and very central department store—adjacent to both the Duomo and the Galleria Vittorio Emanuele II—carries a wide range of Italian and international brands, both high-end and casual, for men, women, and children. There's also a fine selection of beauty and home products. ✉ *Piazza Duomo, Duomo* ☎ *02/88521* ⊕ *www.rinascente.it* Ⓜ *Duomo; Tram No. 1, 2, 12, 14, 16, or 27.*

Trussardi. This family-run label offers sleek, fashion-forward accessories, leather goods, and clothes at its flagship store. ✉ *Piazza della Scala 5, Duomo* ☎ *02/80688242* ⊕ *www.trussardi.com* Ⓜ *Duomo; Tram No. 1.*

Versace. Run by flamboyant Donatella Versace and known for its rock-and-roll styling, Versace's first store opened on Via della Spiga in 1978, and its latest flagship is inside the Galleria Vittorio Emanuele II. ✉ *Galleria Vittorio Emanuele II 33/35, Duomo* ☎ *02/89011479* ⊕ *www.versace.com* Ⓜ *Duomo; Tram No. 1.*

BRERA

With its narrow streets and outdoor cafés, Brera is one of Milan's most charming neighborhoods. Wander through it to find smaller shops with some appealing offerings from lesser-known names that cater to the well-schooled taste of this upscale area. The densest concentration is along Via Brera, Via Solferino, and Corso Garibaldi.

Mercato di Via S. Marco. The Monday- and Thursday-morning markets here cater to the wealthy residents of the central Brera neighborhood. In addition to food stands where you can get cheese, roast chicken, and dried beans and fruits, there are several clothing and shoe stalls that are important stops for some of Milan's most elegant women. ⊠ *Via San Marco, near Via Castelfidardo, Brera* Ⓜ *Lanza; Tram No. 2, 4, 12, or 14.*

QUADRILATERO

The heart of Milan's shopping reputation is the Quadrilatero della Moda district north of the Duomo. Here the world's leading designers compete for shoppers' attention, showing off their ultrastylish clothes in stores that are works of high style themselves. It's difficult to find any bargains, but regardless of whether you're making a purchase, the area is a great place for window-shopping and people-watching.

Armani Megastore. Armani Casa (furniture), Armani Junior, Emporio Armani, Armani Fiori (flowers), Armani Dolci (chocolate), Armani Jeans, and Armani Libri (books) are all under this monumental store's roof. ⊠ *Via Manzoni 31, Quadrilatero* ☎ *02/72318600* ⊕ *www.armani. com* Ⓜ *Montenapoleone; Tram No. 1.*

Fodor'sChoice
★
DMagazine Outlet. This store boasts some of the best prices in the area for luxury items such as Prada, Gucci, Lanvin, and Cavalli. DMagazine has two other locations, at Via Forcella 13 and Via Bigli 4. ⊠ *Via Manzoni 44, Quadrilatero* ☎ *02/36514365* ⊕ *www.dmagazine.it* Ⓜ *Montenapoleone; Tram No. 1.*

Fodor'sChoice
★
Dolce & Gabbana. This fabulous duo has created an empire based on sultry designs for men and women. The gorgeous flagship store, in a 19th-century palazzo, features two floors of women's wear and accessories, and one floor of menswear. ⊠ *Via Montenapoleone 4, Quadrilatero* ☎ *02/77123711* ⊕ *www.dolcegabbana.it* Ⓜ *Montenapoleone; Tram No. 1.*

Giorgio Armani. Find Armani's women's, men's, and ready-to-wear collections inside a historic palazzo. ⊠ *Via Montenapoleone 2, Quadrilatero* ☎ *02/76003234* ⊕ *www.armani.com* Ⓜ *San Babilo.*

Missoni. Famous for their kaleidoscope-patterned knits, this family-run brand sells whimsical designs for men and women. ⊠ *Via Montenapoleone 8, Quadrilatero* ☎ *02/76003555* ⊕ *www.missoni.com* Ⓜ *Montenapoleone or San Babila; Tram No. 1.*

Miu Miu. Prada's more upbeat, youthful brand has a wide offering of boldly printed women's fashions and accessories. ⊠ *Via Sant'Andrea 21, Quadrilatero* ☎ *02/76001799* ⊕ *www.miumiu.com* Ⓜ *Montenapoleone, San Babila, or Palestro; Tram No. 1.*

Moschino. Known for its bold prints, colors, and appliqués, Moschino is a brand for daring fashionistas. ⊠ *Via Sant'Andrea 25, Quadrilatero* ☎ *02/76022639* ⊕ *www.moschino.com* Ⓜ *Montenapoleone, San Babila, or Palestro; Tram No. 1.*

Prada. Founded in Milan, Prada has several locations throughout the city. Its Via della Spiga location carries upscale accessories and bags coveted by women worldwide, while its stores on Via Montenapoleone showcase its women's (Via Montenapoleone 8) and men's fashions (Via Montenapoleone 6). ⊠ *Via della Spiga 18, Quadrilatero* ☎ *02/780465* ⊕ *www. prada.com* Ⓜ *Montenapoleone, San Babila, or Palestro; Tram No. 1.*

Roberto Cavalli. Famous for his wild-animal prints, Roberto Cavalli creates sexy designs for men and women. ⊠ *Via Montenapoleone 6, Quadrilatero* ☎ 02/7630771 ⊕ *www.robertocavalli.com* Ⓜ *San Babila.*

Salvatore Ferragamo Donna. This Florence-based brand is a leader in leather goods and accessories, and carries designs for women in this store. ⊠ *Via Montenapoleone 3, Quadrilatero* ☎ 02/76000054 ⊕ *www. ferragamo.com* Ⓜ *San Babila.*

Salvatore Ferragamo Uomo. Ferragamo's men's accessories, leather goods, and ties are a staple for Milan's male fashion set. ⊠ *Via Montenapoleone 20/4, Quadrilatero* ☎ 02/76006660 ⊕ *www.ferragamo.com* Ⓜ *Montenapoleone; Tram No. 1.*

Tod's. This leather-goods leader sells luxury handbags as well as a variety of shoes for men and women. It also sells a complete line of men's and women's clothing. ⊠ *Via della Spiga 22, Quadrilatero* ☎ 02/76002423 ⊕ *www.tods.com* Ⓜ *Montenapoleone, San Babila, or Palestro; Tram No. 1.*

Valentino. Even after the departure of its founding father, Valentino Garavani, this Roman-based fashion brand still flourishes. ⊠ *Via Montenapoleone 20, Quadrilatero* ☎ 02/76006182 ⊕ *www.valentino.com* Ⓜ *Montenapoleone; Tram No. 1.*

CENTRO DIREZIONALE

Antonioli. Antonioli raises the bar for Milan's top trendsetters. Uniting the most cutting-edge looks of each season, it is perhaps the most fashion-forward concept store in the city. Aside from Italian brands like Valentino, it also stocks a competitive international array of designers like Ann Demeulemeester, Rick Owens, Givenchy, Gareth Pugh, Haider Ackermann, Maison Martin Margiela, and Christopher Kane. ⊠ *Via Pasquale Paoli 1, Centro Direzionale* ☎ 02/36561860 ⊕ *www.antonioli.eu* Ⓜ *Porta Genova; Tram No. 2; Bus No. 47 or 74.*

PORTA VENEZIA

Milan has several shopping streets that serve nearby residential concentrations. **Corso Buenos Aires** begins in the Porta Venezia area, and runs northeast from the Giardini Pubblici. The wide and busy street is lined with affordable shops. It has the highest concentration of clothing stores in Europe, so be prepared to give up halfway. Avoid Saturday after 3, when it seems the entire city is here looking for bargains.

VIA TORINO

For inexpensive and trendy clothes—for the under-25 set—stroll **Via Torino,** which begins in Piazza Duomo. Stay away on Saturday afternoon if you don't like crowds.

CORSO COMO

Fodor's Choice
★
10 Corso Como. A shrine to Milan's creative fashion sense, 10 Corso Como was founded by the former fashion editor and publisher Carla Sozzani. The clothing and design establishment also includes a restaurant-café, gallery, and small hotel. ⊠ *Corso Como 10, Corso Como* ☎ 02/29002674 ⊕ *www.10corsocomo.com* Ⓜ *Porta Garibaldi.*

BERGAMO, PAVIA, CREMONA, AND MANTUA

Once proud medieval towns rivaling Milan in power, these centers of industry and commerce still play a key role in Italy's wealthiest, most populous region. Pavia is celebrated for its extraordinarily detailed Carthusian monastery, and Cremona for its incomparable violin-making tradition. Mantua—the most picturesque of the towns—was the home of the fantastically wealthy Gonzaga dynasty for almost 300 years. While Pavia, Cremona, and Mantua are on the low-lying Po Plain, Bergamo is nestled against the foothills of the Alps.

BERGAMO

52 km (32 miles) northeast of Milan.

If you're driving from Milan to Lake Garda, the perfect deviation from your autostrada journey is the lovely medieval town of Bergamo, which is also a wonderful side trip by train from Milan. With direct service from Milan, you'll be whisked from the restless pace of city life to the medieval grandeur of Bergamo Alta in less than an hour.

From behind a set of battered Venetian walls high on an Alpine hilltop, Bergamo majestically surveys the countryside. Behind are the snowcapped Bergamese Alps, and two funiculars connect the modern **Bergamo Bassa** (Lower Bergamo) to the ancient **Bergamo Alta** (Upper Bergamo). Bergamo Bassa's long arteries and ornate piazze speak to its centuries of prosperity, but it's nonetheless overshadowed by Bergamo Alta, whose magnificent architecture has a fairy-tale allure.

GETTING HERE AND AROUND

Bergamo is along the A4 autostrada. By car from Milan, take the A51 out of the city to pick up the A4; the drive is 52 km (32 miles) and takes about 45 minutes. By train, Bergamo is about one hour from Milan and 1½ hours from Sirmione.

VISITOR INFORMATION

Contacts Bergamo Tourism Office. ⊠ *Torre del Gombito, Via Gombito 13, Bergamo Alta* ☎ *035/242226* ⊕ *www.visitbergamo.net* ⊠ *Piazzale Guglielmo Marconi* ☎ *035/210204* ⊕ *www.visitbergamo.net.*

EXPLORING

Accademia Carrara. Bergamo is home to an art collection that's surprisingly rewarding given its size and remote location. Many of the Venetian masters are represented—Mantegna, Bellini, Carpaccio (circa 1460–1525/26), Tiepolo (1727–1804), Francesco Guardi (1712–93), Canaletto (1697–1768)—as well as Botticelli (1445–1510). ⊠ *Piazza Carrara 82, Bergamo Bassa* ☎ *035/234396* ⊕ *www.lacarrara.it* ⊠ *€10* ⊘ *Closed Tues.*

Cappella Colleoni. Bergamo's **Duomo** and **Battistero** are the most substantial buildings in Piazza Duomo. But the most impressive structure is the Cappella Colleoni, which boasts a kaleidoscope of marble decoration and golden accents. ⊠ *Piazza Duomo, Bergamo Alta* ☎ *035/210061 Duomo, 035/210061 Cappella* ⊘ *Closed Mon.*

Torre Civica. The massive 13th-century Torre Civica offers a great view of the two cities. Climb the stairs or take an elevator to the top of the tower, where the bells ring every half hour. ✉ *Piazza Vecchia, Bergamo Alta* ☎ *035/247116* 🎟 *€5* ⏲ *Closed Mon.*

WHERE TO EAT

$$ NORTHERN ITALIAN Fodor's Choice ★ 🍴 **Al Donizetti.** Find a table in the back of this central, cheerful restaurant before choosing local cured meats and cheeses to accompany your wine (more than 900 bottles are available, many by the glass). Heartier meals are also available, such as polenta with Asiago cheese and smoked ham, but save room for the desserts, which go well with the dessert wines. **Known for:** seasonal and local ingredients; fantastic wine selection; extensive dessert options. [$] *Average main: €18* ✉ *Via Gombito 17/a, Bergamo Alta* ☎ *035/242661* 🌐 *www.donizetti.it* ⏲ *Closed Tues.*

$ NORTHERN ITALIAN 🍴 **Da Ornella.** The vaulted ceilings of this popular trattoria on the main street in the upper town are marked with ancient graffiti, created by (patiently) holding candles to the stone overhead. The house specialties are simple but tasty: polenta taragna cooked with butter and cheese, and served with rabbit, chicken, or sliced mushrooms with oil, garlic, and parsley. **Known for:** polenta specialties; traditional dishes; good choice of wines. [$] *Average main: €14* ✉ *Via Gombito 15, Bergamo Alta* ☎ *035/232736* ⏲ *Closed Thurs.*

$$$ INTERNATIONAL 🍴 **Taverna Colleoni dell'Angelo.** Pierangelo Cornaro is the name behind the Taverna Colleoni, on the Piazza Vecchia right behind the Duomo. He serves imaginative fish, mushroom, and meat dishes, both regional and international, all expertly prepared. **Known for:** sophisticated gourmet dishes; picturesque setting; outdoor seating on the piazza. [$] *Average main: €28* ✉ *Piazza Vecchia 7, Bergamo Alta* ☎ *035/232596* 🌐 *www.colleonidellangelo.com* ⏲ *Closed Mon.*

$$ WINE BAR 🍴 **Vineria Cozzi.** The wine list at this romantic but informal *vineria* (wine bar) is exceptional, whether you order by the glass or the bottle. There's also an array of flavorful foods, from snacks to sumptuous full-course meals typical of the region. **Known for:** quirky, historic decorations; large selection of Italian wines; interesting and fresh food combinations. [$] *Average main: €16* ✉ *Via B. Colleoni 22, Bergamo Alta* ☎ *035/238836* 🌐 *www.vineriacozzi.it.*

WHERE TO STAY

$ HOTEL 🏨 **Excelsior San Marco.** This extremely well-located hotel in Bergamo Bassa is a short walk from the funicular to reach the upper town, and some of the comfortable-if-generic rooms have balconies with amazing Bergamo Alta views. **Pros:** convenient location; modern, businesslike surroundings; lots of rooms, so a good chance of availability. **Cons:** hotel decor is nothing special; rooms a little dated. [$] *Rooms from: €120* ✉ *Piazza della Repubblica 6, Bergamo Bassa* ☎ *035/366111* 🌐 *www.hotelsanmarco.com* 🛏 *154 rooms* 🍽 *Free Breakfast.*

$$$ HOTEL Fodor's Choice ★ 🏨 **Relais San Lorenzo.** Ideally positioned on the edge of Bergamo Alta, a stone's throw from the old town's delightful shops and restaurants, this ultramodern luxury hotel nods to its historic location by incorporating Roman ruins found during construction into the restaurant and bar. **Pros:** wonderful old town location; top-notch restaurant; quiet and peaceful atmosphere; spa. **Cons:** rooms on the pricey side; parking

in the underground garage isn't free. $ *Rooms from: €285* ⊠ *Piazza Mascheroni 9, Bergamo Alta* ☎ *035/237383* ⊕ *www.relaisanlorenzo. com* ⊘ *Closed 2 wks in Jan.* ⇝ *30 rooms* ⦿| *Free Breakfast.*

PAVIA

40 km (25 miles) south of Milan.

Pavia was once Milan's chief regional rival. The city dates from at least the Roman era and was the capital of the Lombard kings for two centuries (572–774). It was at one time known as "the city of a hundred towers," but only a few have survived the passing of time. Its prestigious university was founded in 1361 on the site of a 10th-century law school, but it has roots that can be traced to antiquity.

GETTING HERE AND AROUND

By car from Milan, start out on the A7 autostrada and exit onto the A53 as you near Pavia; the drive is 40 km (25 miles) and takes about 45 minutes. Pavia is 30–40 minutes by train from Milan and 1½ hours (by slower regional service) from Cremona. The Certosa is 30 minutes by train from several Milan stations.

VISITOR INFORMATION

Contact Pavia Tourism Office. ⊠ *Palazzo del Broletto, Via del Comune 18* ☎ *0382/079943* ⊕ *www.vivipavia.it.*

EXPLORING

Castello Visconteo. The town's 14th-century fortress-castle now houses the local **Museo Civico** (Municipal Museum), with a Romanesque and Renaissance sculpture gallery, an archaeological collection, and a large picture gallery displaying works by Correggio, Bellini, Tiepolo, Hayez, Pelizza da Volpedo, and La Foppa, among others. ⊠ *Viale XI Febbraio 35, near Piazza Castello* ☎ *0382/399770* ⊕ *www.museicivici.pavia.it* 🖅 *€8* ⊘ *Closed Mon.*

Certosa (*Carthusian monastery*). The main draw in Pavia is the Certosa, 9 km (5½ miles) north of the city center. Its elaborate facade shows the same relish for ornamentation as Milan's Duomo. The Certosa's extravagant grandeur was due in part to the plan to have it house the tombs of the family of the first duke of Milan, Galeazzo Visconti III (who died during a plague, at age 49, in 1402). The best marble was used, taken undoubtedly by barge from the quarries of Carrara, roughly 240 km (150 miles) away. Although the floor plan is Gothic—a cross shape divided into a series of squares—the gorgeous fabric that rises above it is triumphantly Renaissance. On the facade, in the lower frieze, are medallions of Roman emperors and Eastern monarchs; above them are low reliefs of scenes from the life of Christ and from the career of Galeazzo Visconti III.

The first duke was the only Visconti to be interred here, and not until some 75 years after his death, in a tomb designed by Gian Cristoforo Romano. Look for it in the right transept. In the left transept is a more appealing tomb—that of a rather stern middle-aged man and a beautiful young woman. The man is Ludovico il Moro Sforza, seventh duke of Milan, who commissioned Leonardo to paint *The Last*

Supper. The woman is Ludovico's wife, Beatrice d'Este (1475–97), one of the most celebrated women of her day, the embodiment of brains, culture, birth, and beauty. Married when he was 40 and she was 16, they had enjoyed six years together when she died while delivering a stillborn child. Ludovico commissioned the sculptor Cristoforo Solari to design a joint tomb for the high altar of Santa Maria delle Grazie in Milan. Originally much larger, the tomb for some years occupied the honored place as planned. Then, for reasons that are still mysterious, the Dominican monks sold the tomb to their Carthusian brothers in Pavia and part of it and its remains are lost. ⊠ *Certosa, Località Monumento 4, 9 km (5½ miles) north of Pavia* ☎ *0382/925613* ⊕ *www. certosatourism.it* ⌨ *Free* ⊘ *Closed Mon.*

San Pietro in Ciel d'Oro. This basilica, a Romanesque masterpiece, houses the tomb of Christianity's most celebrated convert, St. Augustine (354–430), who rests in an intricately carved, Gothic, white-marble ark on the high altar. ⊠ *San Pietro in Ciel d'Oro 2* ☎ *0382/303036* ⊕ *santagostinopavia.wordpress.com* ⊘ *Closed daily noon–3.*

WHERE TO EAT

$$$
NORTHERN
ITALIAN

✕ **Locanda Vecchia Pavia al Mulino.** In sophisticated Art Nouveau surroundings, you can find creative versions of traditional Lombard cuisine. All seafood dishes are done with verve, as are *lasagnette di pasta fresca alla robiola spinaci* (lasagna with fresh soft cheese and spinach), *nocette d'agnello* (noisette of lamb), and veal-shank stew. **Known for:** classic Lombard dishes; excellent wine menu; house-made risotto and pasta. Ⓢ *Average main: €31* ⊠ *Via al Monumento 5, Certosa di Pavia* ☎ *0382/925894* ⊕ *www.vecchiapaviaalmulino.it* ⊘ *Closed Aug. and Jan. No lunch Mon. and Tues. Apr.–Oct.; no lunch Sun. and Mon. Nov.–Mar.*

CREMONA

85 km (53 miles) east of Pavia, 100 km (62 miles) southeast of Milan.

Cremona is a classical-music lover's dream. With violin shops on every block along its crooked old streets, it is where the world's best violins are crafted. Andrea Amati (1510–80) invented the modern instrument here in the 16th century. Though cognoscenti continue to revere the Amati name, it was an apprentice of Amati's nephew for whom the fates had reserved wide and lasting fame. In a career that spanned an incredible 68 years, Antonio Stradivari (1644–1737) made more than 1,200 instruments—including violas, cellos, harps, guitars, and mandolins, in addition to his fabled violins. They remain the most coveted, most expensive stringed instruments in the world.

Strolling about this quiet, medium-size city, you can't help noting that violin making continues to flourish. There are, in fact, more than 140 *liutai* (violin makers), many of them graduates of the Scuola Internazionale di Liuteria (International School of Violin Making). You're usually welcome in these ateliers, where traditional craftsmanship reigns supreme, especially if you're contemplating the acquisition of your own instrument; the tourist office can provide addresses.

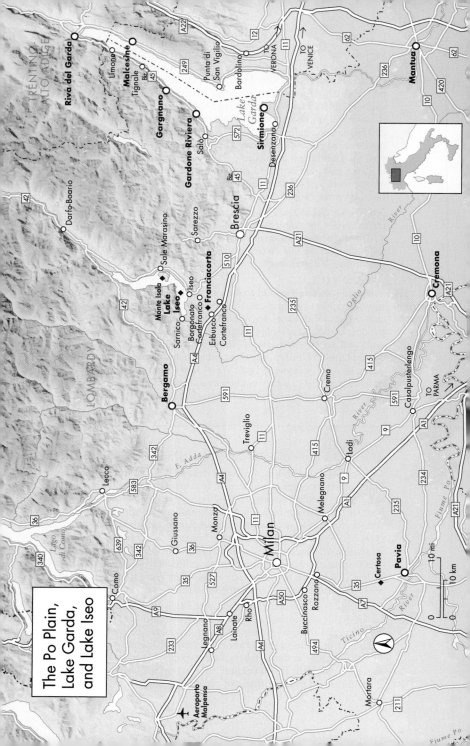

The Po Plain,
Lake Garda,
and Lake Iseo

Cremona's other claim to fame is *torrone* (nougat), which is said to have been created here in honor of the marriage of Bianca Maria Visconti and Francesco Sforza, which took place in October 1441. The new confection, originally prepared by heating almonds, egg whites, and honey over low heat, and shaped and named after the city's tower, was created in symbolic celebration. The annual Festa del Torrone is held in the main piazza over the third or fourth week of November.

GETTING HERE AND AROUND

By car from Milan, start out on the A1 autostrada and switch to the A21 at Piacenza; the drive is about 100 km (62 miles) and takes about 1½ hours. From Pavia, take the SP617 to the A21; the trip is 85 km (53 miles) and takes about an hour. By train, Cremona is about an hour from Milan and 1½ hours from Desenzano, near Sirmione on Lake Garda.

VISITOR INFORMATION

Contact **Cremona Tourism Office.** ⊠ *Piazza del Comune 5* ☎ *0372/406391* ⊕ *www.turismocremona.it.*

EXPLORING

TOP ATTRACTIONS

Duomo. Cremona's Romanesque Duomo was consecrated in 1190. It's an impressive structure in a breathtaking piazza, and certainly one of the most beautiful churches in Italy. Here you can find the *Story of the Virgin Mary and the Passion of Christ,* the central fresco of an extraordinary cycle commissioned in 1514 and featuring the work of local artists, including Boccaccio Boccanccino, Giovanni Francesco Bembo, and Altobello Melone. ⊠ *Piazza del Comune* ☎ *0372/495011* ⊕ *www. cattedraledicremona.it.*

Fodor's Choice
★
Museo del Violino. At this lovely and informative museum dedicated to all things violin, even those not already enamored by the instrument will find something to appreciate. Historic violins made in Cremona by masters including Stradivari are presented as works of art; be sure to get the audio guide included with admission to listen to recordings as you stroll. An audio chamber lets you hear more beautiful violin concerts performed by famed artists—and if you're lucky, there will be a live concert going on at the innovative on-site auditorium, where the seats wrap around the stage and musicians for an immersive experience. ⊠ *Palazzo dell'Arte, Piazza Marconi 5* ☎ *0372/801801, 0372/080809 tickets* ⊕ *www.museodelviolino.org* ☎ *€10* ⊗ *Closed Mon.*

Piazza del Comune. The Duomo, tower, baptistery, and Palazzo Communale (city hall) surround this distinctive and harmonious square: the combination of old brick, rose- and cream-color marble, terra-cotta, and old copper roofs brings Romanesque, Gothic, and Renaissance together with unusual success. ⊠ *Piazza del Comune 8.*

WORTH NOTING

No. 1 Piazza Roma. Legendary violin maker Antonio Stradivari lived, worked, and died near the verdant square at Piazza Roma 1 (not open to the public). According to local lore, Stradivari kept each instrument in his bedroom for a month before varnishing it, imparting part of his soul before sealing and sending it out into the world. In the center of the park is **Stradivari's grave**, marked by a simple tombstone. ✉ *Cremona.*

Torrazzo (*Big Tower*). Dominating Piazza del Comune is perhaps the tallest campanile in Italy, visible for a considerable distance across the Po Plain. It's open to visitors, but in winter, hours fluctuate depending on the weather. The tower's astronomical clock is the 1583 original. ✉ *Piazza del Comune* ☎ *0372/495029* 🎟 *€5 (€6 with baptistery)* 🕒 *Closed daily 12:30–2:30.*

WHERE TO EAT AND STAY

$$ NORTHERN ITALIAN

🍴 **La Sosta.** This traditional osteria, which prides itself on being part of the international Slow Food movement, looks to the 16th century for culinary inspiration, following a time-tested recipe for a favored first course, gnocchi *Vecchia Cremona* (stuffed with sausage and baked with poppy seeds, sesame, and Parmesan). The homemade salami is also excellent. **Known for:** traditional seafood and meat dishes; extensive wine cellar; cheese plate with homemade mustards. [$] *Average main: €22* ✉ *Via Sicardo 9* ☎ *0372/456656* 🌐 *www.osterialasosta.it* 🕒 *Closed Mon., and 3 wks in Aug. No dinner Sun.*

$ CAFÉ

🍴 **Pasticceria Duomo.** This portal to the past opened in 1883 and still serves up such handmade local delights as *pan torrone* (a loaf cake made with chunks of nougat) and *torta cremona* (a cake made with almond flour and filled with amarena cherries). A relaxing stop between visiting museums, it's the perfect place to have a cappuccino and relax by the fireplace. **Known for:** Cremona torrone (nougat), with almonds, honey, and egg whites; delicious local cakes and cookies; good place for a break. [$] *Average main: €10* ✉ *Via Boccaccino 6* ☎ *0372/22273* 🌐 *www.pasticceriaduomo.it.*

$$ HOTEL

🏨 **Delle Arti Design Hotel.** The name suits the elegant modern interiors and eclectic designer furniture, all geared to solid comfort. **Pros:** affordable modern design; friendly staff. **Cons:** small bathrooms; some rooms can be a little dark. [$] *Rooms from: €125* ✉ *Via Bonomelli 8* ☎ *0372/23131* 🌐 *www.dellearti.com* 🕒 *Closed Aug. 5–29 and late Dec.* 🛏 *33 rooms* 🍽 *Free Breakfast.*

$ HOTEL

🏨 **Hotel Impero.** This comfortable hotel is well equipped to satisfy both leisure and business travelers, offering pleasant and functional rooms, the best of which overlook the piazza. **Pros:** central location; highly professional staff. **Cons:** rooms are a little bland and out of style; can be noisy. [$] *Rooms from: €90* ✉ *Piazza della Pace 21* ☎ *0372/413013* 🌐 *www.hotelimpero.cr.it* 🛏 *53 rooms* 🍽 *Free Breakfast.*

SHOPPING

Sperlari. Head to this famed shop for a taste of Cremona's famous nougat. Cremona's best *mostarda* (a mustardy condiment made from preserved fruit and served with meat and cheese) has also been sold from this handsome shop since 1836; Sperlari and parent company Fieschi have grown into a confectionary empire. Look for the historical product display in the back. The store also sells teas, marmalades, and other Italian delights. ✉ *Via Solferino 25* ☎ *0372/22346* 🌐 *www.sperlari1836.com* 🕒 *Closed Mon.*

MANTUA

192 km (119 miles) southeast of Milan.

Mantua (Mantova in Italian) stands tallest among the ancient walled cities of the Po Plain; it may not be flashy or dramatic, but its beauty is subtle and deep, hiding a rich trove of artistic, architectural, and cultural gems beneath its slightly somber facade. Its fortifications are circled on three sides by the passing Mincio River, which long provided Mantua with protection, fish, and a steady stream of river tolls as it meandered from Lake Garda to join the Po. Although Mantua first came to prominence in Roman times as the home of Virgil, its grand monuments date to the glory years of the Gonzaga dynasty. From 1328 until the Austrian Habsburgs sacked the city in 1708, the dukes and marquesses of the Gonzaga clan reigned over a wealthy independent commune, and the arts thrived in the relative peace of that period. Raphael's star pupil, Andrea Mantegna, who served as court painter for 50 years, was the best known of a succession of artists and architects who served Mantua through the years, and some of his finest work, including his only surviving fresco cycle, can be seen here. Giulio Romano (circa 1499–1546), Mantegna's apprentice, built his masterpiece, Palazzo Te, on an island in the river. Leon Battista Alberti (1404–72), who designed two impressive churches in Mantua, was widely emulated later in the Renaissance.

GETTING HERE AND AROUND

Mantua is 5 km (3 miles) west of the A22 autostrada. The drive from Milan, following the A4 to the A22, takes a little more than two hours. The drive from Cremona, along the SP10, is 1¼ hours. Most trains arrive in just under 2 hours from Milan, depending on the type of service, and in about 1½ hours from Desenzano, near Sirmione on Lake Garda, via Verona.

VISITOR INFORMATION

Contact Mantua Tourism Office. ☒ *Piazza A. Mantegna 6* ☏ *0376/432432* ⊕ *www.turismo.mantova.it.*

EXPLORING

You can pick up a Mantova Card at the tourism office, which entitles you to visit 11 museums for one price (⊕ *www.mantovacard.it*).

Casa di Andrea Mantegna. Serious Mantegna aficionados will want to visit the house the artist designed and built around an intriguing circular courtyard, which is usually open to view. The exterior is interesting for its unusual design, and the interior, with its hidden frescoes, can be seen by appointment or during occasional art exhibitions. Hours and prices vary depending on the exhibition. ☒ *Via Acerbi 47* ☏ *0376/360506* ⊕ *www.casadelmantegna.it* ☚ *Price varies by exhibition* ☺ *Closed Mon.*

Palazzo Ducale. The 500-room palace that dominates the Mantua skyline was built for the Gonzaga family, though much of the art within the castle was sold or stolen as the dynasty waned in power and prestige. A glimpse of past grandeur can still be spotted in the Camera Degli Sposi (literally, the "Chamber of the Wedded Couple") where Duke Ludovico and his wife held court. Mantegna painted the hall over a nine-year period at the height of his power, finishing at age 44. He made a startling advance in painting by organizing the picture plane in a way that systematically mimics the experience of human vision. The circular trompe-l'oeil around the vaulted ceiling is famous for the many details that attest to Mantegna's greatness: the three-dimensional quality of the seven Caesars (the Gonzagas saw themselves as successors to the Roman emperors and paid homage to classical culture throughout the palazzo); the self-portrait of Mantegna (in purple, on the right side of the western fresco); and the dwarf peering out from behind the dress of Ludovico's wife (on the northern fresco). Only 20 people at a time are allowed in the Camera degli Sposi, and for only 10 minutes at a time. Reservations are recommended for Camera degli Sposi, either by phone or online (🌐 *www.ducalemantova.org*). ✉ *Piazza Sordello 40* ☎ *041/2411897* 🌐 *www.mantovaducale.beniculturali.it* 🎫 *€12; €1 reservation fee for Camera Degli Sposi and Castello di San Giorgio. Free 1st Sun. of month* 🕒 *Closed Mon.*

Palazzo Te. One of the greatest of all Renaissance palaces, built between 1525 and 1535 by Federigo II Gonzaga, is the Mannerist masterpiece of artist-architect Giulio Romano, who created a pavilion where the strict rules of courtly behavior could be relaxed for libertine pastimes. Romano's purposeful breaks with classical tradition are lighthearted and unprecedented. For example, note the "slipping" triglyphs along the upper edge of the inside courtyard. Two highlights are the Camera di Amore e Psiche (Room of Cupid and Psyche) that depicts a wedding set among lounging nymphs, frolicking satyrs, and even a camel and an elephant; and the gasp-producing Camera dei Giganti (Room of the Giants) that shows Jupiter expelling the Titans from Mount Olympus. The scale of the work is overwhelming; the floor-to-ceiling work completely envelops the viewer. The room's rounded corners, and the river rock covering the original floor, were meant to make it seem cavelike. It is a "whisper chamber" in which words softly uttered in one corner can be heard in the opposite one. Note the graffiti from as far back as the 17th century. ✉ *Viale Te 13* ☎ *0376/323266* 🌐 *www.palazzote.it* 🎫 *€12.*

Sant'Andrea. Mantegna's tomb is in the first chapel to the left in the basilica of Sant'Andrea, most of which was built in 1472. The current structure, a masterwork by the architect Alberti, is the third built on this spot to house the relic of the Precious Blood: the crypt holds two reliquaries containing earth believed to be soaked in the blood of Christ, brought to Mantua by Longinus, the soldier who pierced his side. They are displayed only on Good Friday. ✉ *Piazza di Mantegna* ☎ *0376/328504* 🌐 *www.parrocchiasantanselmomantova.it.*

WHERE TO EAT AND STAY

$$$$ NORTHERN ITALIAN

🍴 **Ambasciata.** Heralded as one of Italy's classic gourmet restaurants, Ambasciata (Italian for "embassy") emphasizes elegance and service in tiny Quistello, 20 km (12 miles) southeast of Mantua. Chef Romano Tamani, who is co-owner with his brother Francesco, offers those willing to make the trek (and pay the bill) an ever-changing array of superlative creations. **Known for:** intricate and a bit old-fashioned cuisine; high prices; attentive service. [$] *Average main: €55* ✉ *Via Martiri di*

Belfiore 33, Quistello ☎ *0376/619169* ⏲ *Closed Mon., Jan. 1–15, and 2 wks in Aug. No dinner Sun.*

$$ HOTEL 🏨 **Casa Poli.** Refreshing, minimalist influences, creative touches (like the room number projected onto the hall floor), and attention to detail create a welcoming ambience with contemporary flair. **Pros:** attentive staff; tasteful and modern; families welcome. **Cons:** although convenient, not in the absolute center of the city; some traffic noise in front-facing rooms; no on-site restaurant. [$] *Rooms from: €170* ✉ *Corso Garibaldi 32* ☎ *0376/288170* 🌐 *www.hotelcasapoli.it* 🛏 *27 rooms* 🍴 *Free Breakfast.*

LAKE ISEO AND FRANCIACORTA

104 km (65 miles) east of Milan.

If you tire of the crowds on Lake Como or Garda, sleepy Lake Iseo is one of the Italian lake region's lesser-known lakes, yet it's only about an hour's drive from Milan. Lake Iseo gained much more interest—and many more tourists—in June and July 2016, when renowned installation artist Christo opened his temporary Floating Piers project connecting Monte Isola Island, the largest island within a European lake, to the mainland. The island is still worth visiting by ferry for lovely views and charming restaurants. The two main lakeside towns, Iseo and Sarnico, also merit a stop for waterfront eateries and gelaterias surrounded by postcard-pretty settings.

Lake Iseo is also on the northern edge of the Franciacorta wine region, home to production of Italy's up-and-coming sparkling wine, also known as "Italy's Champagne" since it uses the same labor-intensive process. There are more than 110 wineries in the region, and though many welcome visitors for a tour and taste, nearly all require advance appointments. Find more information and a list of all the wineries at 🌐 *www.franciacorta.net/en.*

GETTING HERE AND AROUND

Frequent trains run from Milan to Brescia; the trip takes about 55 minutes from the Central Station. From there, trains run to the town of Iseo—the trip takes about half an hour—and then up Lake Iseo's eastern shore about once an hour. You'll need a car to reach the western side. To drive from Milan or Bergamo, take A4/E64; exit at Rovato on SP51 in the direction of Iseo. The trip takes about 1 hour 20 minutes from Milan and a half hour from Bergamo. Ferries run from Sulzano, Sale Marasino, Iseo, and Tavernola Bergamasca to Monte Isola.

VISITOR INFORMATION

Lake Iseo and Franciacorta Tourism Office. ✉ *Lungolago Marconi 2/c* ☎ *030/3748733* 🌐 *www.visitlakeiseo.info.*

EXPLORING

Ca' del Bosco. Within the grounds filled with modern art sculptures, this respected producer of Franciacorta wines (one of the largest wineries in the region) offers enjoyable hour-long cellar tours with a tasting at the end. Tour availability can be requested online. ✉ *Via Albano Zanella 13, Erbusco* ☎ *030/7766111* 🌐 *www.cadelbosco.com* 🎫 *From €20* 🕒 *Closed weekdays 12:30–2.*

Fodor's Choice ★ **Monte Isola.** The largest island within any European lake, Monte Isola allows no cars, except for authorized vehicles, making it the perfect place for leisurely walks and bike rides. The main towns are Siviano, with medieval mansions; Peschiero Maraglio, an old fishing village with 16th-century homes and the Church of St. Michele; and Carzano, with the 18th-century San Giovanni Battista church. Walk around the water and stop at the many restaurants and gelaterias or, for more exercise, take a trek uphill to admire the views back to the shore. Frequent ferries from Sulzano stop at Peschiera Maraglio, and ferries from Sale Marasino arrive at Carzano. There are less frequent ferries from Iseo and Tavernola Bergamasca. ✉ *Monte Isola* 🌐 *www.navigazionelagoiseo.it.*

WHERE TO EAT AND STAY

$$$ NORTHERN ITALIAN Fodor's Choice ★ 🍴 **Due Colombe Ristorante Al Borgo Antico.** Visitors to Lake Iseo would do well to follow the locals' lead to sample chef Stefano Cerveni's delightful cooking at his cozy restaurant just south of the lake. The elegant dining area with beamed ceilings and stone walls juxtaposes with the thoroughly modern menu offering a choice of "classic" and "creative" dishes, though all use local ingredients in unexpected ways. **Known for:** tasting menus with unusual combinations; seasonal cuisine; charming setting. [$] *Average main: €30* ✉ *Via Foresti 13, Borgonato* ☎ *030/9828227* 🌐 *www.duecolombe.com* 🕒 *Closed Mon. No dinner Sun.*

$$$$ HOTEL Fodor's Choice ★ 🏨 **L'Albereta.** Perched in the vineyard-covered hills of Franciacorta, this charming Relais & Chateaux property features an enormous 21,000-square-foot spa, the perfect antidote to the city's chaos. **Pros:** cozy, calm, and luxurious atmosphere in a villa set in lovely grounds; excellent on-site restaurants; second-to-none spa facilities. **Cons:** rooms quite varied in terms of size and level of renovation; not all rooms have Lake Iseo views; no outdoor pool. [$] *Rooms from: €315* ✉ *Via Vittorio Emanuele 23, Erbusco* ☎ *030/7760550* 🌐 *www.albereta.it* 🛏 *57 rooms* 🍽 *Free Breakfast.*

LAKE GARDA

Lake Garda has had a perennial attraction for travelers and writers alike; even the essayist Michel de Montaigne (1533–92), whose 15 months of travel journals contain not a single other reference to nature, paused to admire the view down the lake from Torbole, which he called "boundless."

Lake Garda is 50 km (31 miles) long, ranges roughly 1–16 km (½–10 miles) wide, and is as much as 1,135 feet deep. The terrain is flat at the lake's southern base and mountainous at its northern tip. As a consequence, its character varies from stormy inland sea to crystalline Nordic-style fjord. It's the biggest lake in the region and by most accounts the cleanest. If you're driving, take care on the hazardous hairpin turns on the lake road.

GETTING HERE AND AROUND

The town of Sirmione, at the south end of the lake, is 10 km (6 miles) from Desenzano, which has regular train service; it's about an hour and 20 minutes by train from Milan and 25 minutes from Verona. The A4 autostrada passes to the south of the lake, and the A22 runs north–south about 10 km (6 miles) from the eastern shore.

SIRMIONE

138 km (86 miles) east of Milan.

Dramatically rising out of Lake Garda is the enchanting town of Sirmione. "*Paene insularum, Sirmio, insularumque ocelle,*" wrote Catullus in a homecoming poem: "It is the jewel of both peninsulas and islands." The forbidding Castello Scaligero stands guard behind the small bridge connecting Sirmione to the mainland; beyond, cobbled streets wind their way through medieval arches past lush gardens, stunning lake views, and gawking crowds. Originally a Roman resort town, Sirmione served under the dukes of Verona and later Venice as Garda's main point of defense. It has now reclaimed its original function, bustling with visitors in summer. Cars aren't allowed into town; parking is available by the tourist office at the entrance.

VISITOR INFORMATION

Contact Sirmione Tourism Office. ✉ *Viale Marconi 6* ☎ *030/3748721, 030/3748722* ⊕ *www.sirmionebs.it.*

EXPLORING

Bardolino. This small town, one of the most popular summer resorts on the lake, is 32 km (20 miles) north of Sirmione along Lake Garda's eastern shore, at the wider end. It's most famous for its red wine, which is light, dry, and often slightly sparkling; the Festa dell'Uva e del Vino (Grape and Wine Festival), held here in late September–early October, is a great excuse to indulge in the local product. Bardolino has two handsome Romanesque churches, both near the center: **San Severo,** from the 11th century, and **San Zeno,** from the 9th. ✉ *Bardolino* ⊕ *www. bardolinoweb.com.*

Castello Scaligero. As hereditary rulers of Verona for more than a century before they lost control of the city in 1402, the Della Scala counted Garda among their possessions. It was they who built this lakeside redoubt, along with almost all the other castles on the lake. You can go inside to take in the nice view of the lake from the tower, or you can swim at the nearby beach. ✉ *Piazza Castello* ☎ *030/916468* 🎫*€5* ⊙ *Closed Mon.*

Grotte di Catullo (*Grottoes of Catullus*). Locals will almost certainly tell you that these romantic lakeside ruins were once the site of the villa of Catullus (87–54 BC), one of the greatest pleasure-seeking poets of all time. Present archaeological wisdom, however, does not concur, and there is some consensus that this was the site of two villas of slightly different periods, dating from about the 1st century AD. But never mind—the view through the cypresses and olive trees is lovely, and even if Catullus didn't have a villa here, he is closely associated with the area and undoubtedly did have a villa nearby. The ruins are at the top of the isthmus and are poorly signposted: walk through the historic center and past the various villas to the top of the spit; the entrance is on the right. Alternately, take one of the frequent tourist trains from town for a small fee. A small **museum** offers a brief overview of the ruins (on the far wall). ✉ *Piazzale Orti Manara* ☎ *030/916157* ⊕ *www.grottedicatullo.beniculturali.it* 🎫 *€6; free 1st Sun. of month* ⊗ *Closed Mon.*

WHERE TO EAT AND STAY

$$

ITALIAN

✕ **La Rucola 2.0.** Next to Sirmione's castle, this elegant, intimate restaurant is often referred to as Sirmione's finest. Tucked into three charming rooms, it has a creative menu focused on fish and accompanied by a good choice of wines. **Known for:** innovative and modern fish and seafood dishes; local ingredients; fantastic wine list. $ *Average main: €20* ✉ *Via Strentelle 3* ☎ *030/916326* ⊕ *www.ristorantelarucola.it* ⊗ *Closed Wed. in Jan. and Feb.*

$$

SEAFOOD

✕ **Ristorante Al Pescatore.** Lake fish is the specialty at this simple, popular restaurant in Sirmione's historical center. For a reasonably priced meal, try grilled trout with a bottle of local white wine and settle your meal with a walk in the nearby park. **Known for:** local fish from the lake; pasta with seafood; inexpensive meals. $ *Average main: €15* ✉ *Via Piana 20* ☎ *030/916216* ⊕ *www.ristorantealpescatore.com.*

$$$

HOTEL

🛏 **Hotel Sirmione e Promessi Sposi.** Scandinavian slat beds, matching floral draperies and wall coverings, and built-in white furniture impart a homey feel that, along with the luxurious thermal spa, keeps many guests returning year after year. **Pros:** next to the lake and near Castello; beautiful grounds; nice spa area. **Cons:** not all rooms have lake views; hotel could use a refresh; service can be indifferent. $ *Rooms from: €248* ✉ *Piazza Castello 19* ☎ *030/916331, 030/9904922 booking* ⊕ *www.termedisirmione.com* 🛏 *100 rooms* ❢⊙❢ *Free Breakfast.*

$$$$

HOTEL

Fodor'sChoice

★

🛏 **Palace Hotel Villa Cortine.** This former private villa in a secluded park risks being just plain ostentatious, but it's saved by the sheer luxury of the lakeside setting, the charming decor of the older rooms, and the high professionalism of its staff. **Pros:** an opulent experience; lovely pool area; beautiful grounds. **Cons:** very expensive; no spa at hotel but thermal baths a short walk away; no gym. $ *Rooms from: €494* ✉ *Viale C. Gennari 2* ☎ *030/9905890* ⊕ *www.palacehotelvillacortine. com* ⊗ *Closed mid-Oct.–late Mar.* 🛏 *54 rooms* ❢⊙❢ *Free Breakfast.*

MALCESINE

63 km (39 miles) northeast of Sirmione, 180 km (112 miles) northeast of Milan.

Malcesine is one of the loveliest areas along the upper eastern shore of Lake Garda. It's principally known as a summer resort, with sailing and windsurfing schools. It tends to be crowded in season, but there are nice walks from the town toward the mountains. Six lifts and more than 11 km (7 miles) of runs of varying degrees of difficulty serve skiers.

VISITOR INFORMATION
Contact **Malcesine Tourism Office.** ✉ *Via Gardesana 238* ☎ *045/7400044* ⊕ *www.visitmalcesine.com.*

EXPLORING
Castello Scaligero. Dominating the town is a 12th-century castle built by Verona's dynastic Della Scala family. ✉ *Via Castello 39* ☎ *045/6570333* ☞ *€6* ⊙ *Closed early Nov.–mid-Mar.*

Monte Baldo. The futuristic *funivia* (cable car), zipping visitors to the top of Monte Baldo (5,791 feet), is unique because it rotates. After a 10-minute ride, you're high in the Veneto where you can take a stroll and enjoy spectacular views of the lake. You can ride the cable car down or bring along a mountain bike (or even a hang glider) for the descent. In the winter, there's skiing, snowboarding, and snowshoeing. ✉ *Via Navene Vecchia 12* ☎ *045/7400206* ⊕ *www.funiviedelbaldo.it* ☞ *Apr.–Oct.: €20 round-trip; mid-Dec.–Mar.: €22 round-trip weekends and holidays, €15 round-trip weekdays* ⊙ *Closed early Nov.–mid-Dec. and early Mar.–early Apr.*

RIVA DEL GARDA

18 km (11 miles) north of Malcesine, 180 km (112 miles) northeast of Milan.

Riva del Garda is set on the northern tip of Lake Garda, against a dramatic backdrop of jagged cliffs and miles of beaches. The old city, surrounding a pretty harbor, was built up during the 15th century, when it was a strategic outpost of the Venetian Republic.

VISITOR INFORMATION
Contact **Riva del Garda Tourism Office.** ✉ *Largo Medaglie d'Oro al Valor Militare 5* ☎ *0464/554444* ⊕ *www.gardatrentino.it.*

EXPLORING
Piazza 3 Novembre. This lakeside plaza, the heart of Riva del Garda, is surrounded by medieval palazzi. Standing in the piazza and looking out onto the lake you can understand why Riva del Garda has become a windsurfing destination: air currents ensure good breezes on even the most sultry midsummer days. ✉ *Riva del Garda.*

Torre Apponale. Predating the Venetian period by three centuries, this sturdy tower looms above the medieval residences of the main square; its crenellations recall its defensive purpose. You can climb the 165 steps to see the view from the top. ✉ *Piazza III Novembre* ☎ *0464/573869*

🌐 *www.gardatrentino.it* 🎟 *€2* ⏲ *Closed early Nov.–mid-Mar., and Mon. mid-Mar.–May and Oct.–early Nov.*

WHERE TO EAT

$$$ NORTHERN ITALIAN 🍴 **Ristorante Castel Toblino.** A lovely stop for a lakeside drink or a romantic dinner, this 16th-century castle is right on a lake in Sarche, about 20 km (12 miles) north of Riva toward Trento. Dishes highlight seasonal, local ingredients including mountain cheeses, salmon trout (a type of trout), duck, and deer. **Known for:** using local ingredients in innovative ways; lovely location inside a castle on the lake; wonderful wine menu featuring many local varieties. [$] *Average main: €26* ✉ *Via Caffaro 1, Sarche* ☎ *0461/864036* 🌐 *www.casteltoblino.com* ⏲ *Closed Mon., Tues., and mid-Oct.–late Mar.*

$$ ITALIAN FAMILY 🍴 **Spiaggia degli Olivi.** This casual bistro occupies an iconic building and former man-made beach on the shores of Lake Garda, commissioned by Italian poet Gabriele D'Annunzio and designed by Giancarlo Maroni in 1934. Today diners can sit inside the charmingly renovated beach house, or outside on an expansive terrace, with superb lake and mountain views, and savor simple but tasty dishes with a tempting selection of pasta, fish, and salads and a good choice of wines by the glass. **Known for:** historic setting; wonderful views; well-prepared light meals. [$] *Average main: €17* ✉ *Giardini di Porta Orientale 5* ☎ *0464/755353* 🌐 *www.spiaggiadegliolivi.it.*

WHERE TO STAY

$$$ RESORT FAMILY 🏨 **Du Lac et du Parc Grand Resort.** Riva's largest resort has elegance befitting its cosmopolitan name, with comfortable, well-appointed rooms, including bungalows perfect for families and personalized service rarely found on Lake Garda since its aristocratic heyday. **Pros:** expansive and lush surroundings; pampering and indulgent staff; lovely spa area. **Cons:** not that cozy; no beach of its own. [$] *Rooms from: €281* ✉ *Viale Rovereto 44* ☎ *0464/566600* 🌐 *www.dulacetduparc.com* ⏲ *Closed mid-Nov.–late-Mar.* 🛏 *254 rooms* 🍽 *Free Breakfast.*

$$ HOTEL 🏨 **Hotel Sole.** Comfortable and relatively affordable rooms occupy this classic lakeside 15th-century palazzo in the center of town, and those in front have terraces that open to breathtaking views of the lake. **Pros:** prime location on the lake; modern hotel conveniences; comfortable beds. **Cons:** sometimes taken over by tour groups; not for those looking for ultracontemporary design; food gets mixed reviews. [$] *Rooms from: €200* ✉ *Piazza 3 Novembre 35* ☎ *0464/552686, 0464/557809 booking office* 🌐 *www.hotelsoleriva.it* ⏲ *Closed Nov.–Dec. 22 and mid-Jan.–Mar.* 🛏 *80 rooms* 🍽 *Free Breakfast.*

$$$$ HOTEL Fodor's Choice ★ 🏨 **Lido Palace.** The chicest option in Riva, with ultramodern rooms inside a 19th-century palace, this beautiful hotel right on the lake also includes a high-end spa and the best restaurant in town. **Pros:** friendly service; gorgeous spa and pools; top-notch food. **Cons:** not all rooms have lake views or balconies; pricey. [$] *Rooms from: €442* ✉ *Viale Carducci 10* ☎ *0464/021899* 🌐 *www.lido-palace.it* ⏲ *Closed mid-Jan.–late Mar.* 🛏 *41 rooms* 🍽 *Free Breakfast.*

$$ **Luise.** This modern hotel with spacious rooms and comfy beds boasts
HOTEL a big garden, a large swimming pool, and the use of free bikes to explore
FAMILY the paths around the lake. **Pros:** pleasant service; reasonably priced;
Fodor's Choice great for kids. **Cons:** some rooms can be noisy; 10-minute walk to cen-
★ ter of Riva. $ *Rooms from: €184* ⊠ *Viale Rovereto 9* ☎ *0464/550858*
⊕ *www.hotelluise.com* ⊗ *Closed mid-Nov.–late Mar.* ⤳ *68 rooms*
Free Breakfast.

EN
ROUTE After passing the town of Limone—where it's said the first lemon trees
in Europe were planted—take the fork to the right about 5 km (3 miles)
north of Gargnano and head to Tignale. The view from the Madonna
di Montecastello church, some 2,000 feet above the lake, is spectacular.
Adventurous travelers will want to follow this pretty inland moun-
tain road to Tremosine. Be warned that the road winds its way up the
mountain through hairpin turns and blind corners that can test even
the most experienced drivers.

GARGNANO

*30 km (19 miles) southwest of Riva del Garda, 144 km (89 miles)
northeast of Milan.*

This small port town was an important Franciscan center in the 13th
century, and now comes alive in the summer months when German
tourists, many of whom have villas here, crowd the small pebble beach.
An Austrian flotilla bombarded the town in 1866, and some of the
houses still bear marks of cannon fire. Mussolini owned two houses in
Gargnano: one is now a language school and the other, Villa Feltrinelli,
has been restored and reopened as a luxury hotel.

VISITOR INFORMATION
Contact Gargnano Tourism Office. ⊠ *Piazza Boldini 2* ☎ *0365/791243*
⊕ *www.gargnanosulgarda.it.*

WHERE TO EAT AND STAY

$$$ ╳ **La Tortuga.** This rustic trattoria is more sophisticated than it first
NORTHERN appears, with an extensive wine cellar and nouvelle-style twists on local
ITALIAN dishes. Specialties include *persico con rosmarino* (perch with rosemary)
and the *palette di piccoli campioni di lago e di mare* (mixed lake and
sea fish), a worthy introduction to regional delights. **Known for:** seasonal cuisine of excellent quality; great wine selection; delightful service.
$ *Average main: €30* ⊠ *Via XXIV Maggio 5* ☎ *0365/71251* ⊕ *www.ris-
torantelatortuga.it* ⊗ *Closed Tues., and Nov.–Feb. No lunch Mon.–Sat.*

$ **Garni Bartabel.** At this cozy inn on the main street of town, rooms are
HOTEL small but attractive, with Venetian-style furnishings and pastel decor,
and reasonable prices. **Pros:** very attractive lake views; a bargain for this
area. **Cons:** few luxuries; modest furnishings. $ *Rooms from: €80* ⊠ *Via
Roma 39* ☎ *0365/71300* ⊕ *www.hotelbartabel.it* ⊗ *Closed Nov.–Mar.*
⤳ *11 rooms* *Free Breakfast.*

$$$$ **Lefay Resort & Spa Lago di Garda.** The first thing you'll notice about
RESORT this elegant resort in the hills above Gargnano are the stupendous views
of the lake and mountains; the second thing will be the 32,000-square-
foot spa, where you may just want to stay all day—and some guests

do. **Pros:** fabulously relaxing spa; lovely location; delicious breakfast buffet. **Cons:** village of Gargnano is down a steep and twisty road; dining at the property is quite expensive. $ *Rooms from: €525* ⊠ *Via Angelo Feltrinelli 136* ☎ *0365/241899* ⊕ *lagodigarda.lefayresorts.com* ⊘ *Closed Jan.–early Feb.* 🛏 *90 rooms* ⦿ *Free Breakfast.*

$$$$ 🏛 **Villa Feltrinelli.** This 1892 Art Nouveau villa hotel, named for the
HOTEL   Italian publishing family that used to vacation here, has attracted the likes of Winston Churchill, D.H. Lawrence, and Benito Mussolini. **Pros:** first-class luxury hotel; like stepping into a bygone era; amazing service. **Cons:** one of the most expensive hotels on the lake (or elsewhere); no spa or gym; some find the attitude a bit arrogant. $ *Rooms from: €1500* ⊠ *Via Rimembranza 38/40* ☎ *0365/798000* ⊕ *www.villafeltrinelli.com* ⊘ *Closed mid-Oct.–mid-Apr.* 🛏 *20 suites* ⦿ *Free Breakfast.*

GARDONE RIVIERA

12 km (7 miles) southwest of Gargnano, 139 km (86 miles) northeast of Milan.

Now pleasantly faded, this once-fashionable 19th-century resort is best known these days for the hilltop estate of the poet Gabriele d'Annunzio, made as an elaborate memorial to himself. The middle-European appearance of its towers and palaces helps set this lakeside town apart from the rest of Italy. With the Italian Alps in the backdrop and crystalline lake views in the summer, it's a gorgeous, albeit under-appreciated, destination.

EXPLORING

Heller Garden. More than 2,000 Alpine, subtropical, and Mediterranean species thrive at the Giardino Botanico Heller. ⊠ *Via Roma 2* ☎ *0366/410877* ⊕ *www.hellergarden.com* 💲*€12* ⊘ *Closed Nov.–Feb.*

Il Vittoriale. The estate of the larger-than-life Gabriele d'Annunzio (1863–1938), one of Italy's major modern poets, and later war hero and supporter of Mussolini, is filled with the trappings of conquests in art, love, and war. His eccentric house crammed with quirky memorabilia can only be seen during a 30-minute guided tour, also given in English, and the extensive gardens are definitely worth a stroll, particularly to see the curious full-size warship's prow. There's also an imposing mausoleum, made of white marble, along with two museums showcasing personal items from d'Annunzio's exploits. ⊠ *Via Vittoriale 12* ☎ *0365/296511* ⊕ *www.vittoriale.it* 💲*€16 for park, d'Annunzio Eroe and d'Annunzio Segreto museums, and guided tour of house; €13 for park and both museums; €8 for park* ⊘ *House and museum closed Mon. late Oct.–late Mar.*

WHERE TO EAT AND STAY

$$$ ✕ **Ristorante Lido 84.** Dining in this bright, airy space feels like dining
MODERN ITALIAN   in a fabulous friend's modern lake cottage—if the friend had floor-
Fodor's Choice   to-ceiling windows overlooking Lake Garda and a top-notch chef on
★   hand. Choose from two tasting menus—one a "surprise" menu with dishes chosen by the chef—for an adventure in tastes from all over Italy. **Known for:** seasonal ingredients from all across Italy; sophisticated cooking techniques; exquisite setting in a cottage on the lake.

$ *Average main: €25* ⊠ *Corso Zandarelli 196* ☎ *0365/20019* ⊕ *www. ristorantelido84.com* ⊗ *Closed Tues., Wed., and early Jan–mid-Feb.*

$$$
HOTEL
Fodor's Choice
★
🏨 **Grand Hotel Fasano.** Used as a hunting lodge in the 19th century, the Fasano has matured into a seasonal hotel of a high standard, with opulent, old-fashioned-style rooms and many amenities, including a well-regarded gourmet restaurant, Il Fagiano, plus three other more casual eateries. **Pros:** exquisitely stylish rooms; relaxing surroundings; gorgeous spa. **Cons:** not all rooms have lake views; staff can be indifferent. $ *Rooms from: €230* ⊠ *Corso Zanardelli 190* ☎ *0365/290220* ⊕ *www.ghf.it* ⊗ *Closed Nov.–Mar.* ⇆ *75 rooms* ❄ *Free Breakfast.*

$$$
HOTEL
🏨 **Grand Hotel Gardone.** At this majestic 1800s palace surrounded by attractive landscaped gardens, many of the rooms have balconies that look out over the water, and the service is top-notch. **Pros:** well-appointed; expansive gardens; lakeside pool. **Cons:** not much to do in the immediate area; Wi-Fi in guest rooms can be iffy. $ *Rooms from: €282* ⊠ *Via Zanardelli 84* ☎ *0365/20261* ⊕ *www.grandhotelgardone. it* ⊗ *Closed mid-Oct.–Mar.* ⇆ *168 rooms* ❄ *Free Breakfast.*

$$$$
HOTEL
🏨 **Villa Fiordaliso.** This pink-and-white lakeside villa is now a fine restaurant, but it also has five tastefully furnished rooms, some overlooking the lake. **Pros:** combines a movie set–worthy charm with the intimacy of a B&B; amazing setting on the lake; elaborate breakfast spread served at any time you want. **Cons:** short on amenities (no spa or pool); staff can be less than friendly; may be too small for some people. $ *Rooms from: €350* ⊠ *Corso Zanardelli 150* ☎ *0365/20158* ⊕ *www.villafiordaliso.it* ⊗ *Closed Nov.–mid-Mar.* ⇆ *5 rooms* ❄ *Free Breakfast.*

LAKE COMO

If you're after palatial villas, rose-laden belvederes, hanging wisteria and bougainvillea, lanterns casting a glow over lakeshore restaurants, and majestic Alpine vistas, then Lake Como is for you. Although summer crowds threaten to diminish the lake's dreamy mystery and slightly faded old-money gentility, the allure of this spectacular place endures. Como remains a consummate pairing of natural and man-made beauty. The villa gardens, like so many in Italy, are a union of two landscape traditions: that of Renaissance Italy, which values order, and that of Victorian England, which strives to create the illusion of natural wildness. Such gardens are often framed by vast areas of picturesque farmland—fruit trees, olive groves, and vineyards.

Lake Como is some 47 km (30 miles) long north to south and is Europe's deepest lake (almost 1,350 feet). Car ferries and *vaporetti* (water buses) traverse the lake in season, making it easy to get to the other main towns, Cernobbio, Tremezzo, and Varenna. Many travelers head directly to boats waiting to take them to Bellagio and the *centro di lago,* the center region of the lake's three branches, and its most beautiful section. You should not pass by the 2,000-year-old walled city of Como, however, a leading textile center famous for its silks—even if you only linger long enough to see the medieval town center and pretty lakefront. Remember that Lake Como is extremely seasonal: if you go

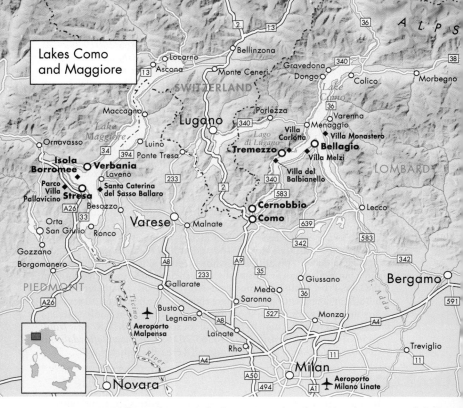

to Bellagio, for example, from November through February, you'll find nothing open—not a bar, restaurant, or shop.

GETTING HERE AND AROUND

Trains run regularly from Milan to the town of Como; the trip takes half an hour from the Central Station and an hour from the Cardorna Station. There's also service to the tiny town of Varenna, just across the lake from Bellagio; the trip from Milan takes 1¼ hours. Como is off the A9 autostrada. To get to the town from Milan, take the A8 to the A9; the drive takes about an hour. Ferries (mainly pedestrian) run regularly from Como and Varenna to different spots around the lake. For schedules, visit ⊕ *www.navigazionelaghi.it.*

BELLAGIO

30 km (19 miles) northeast of Como, 56 km (35 miles) northwest of Bergamo.

Sometimes called the prettiest town in Europe, Bellagio always seems perfectly adorned, with geraniums ablaze in every window and bougainvillea veiling its staircases, or *montées*. At dusk Bellagio's nightspots—including the wharf, where an orchestra may be serenading dancers under the stars—beckon you to come and make merry. It's an impossibly enchanting location, one that inspired the French composer Gabriel Fauré to call Bellagio "a diamond contrasting brilliantly with the sapphires of the three lakes in which it is set."

GETTING HERE AND AROUND

Boats can take you from here to Tremezzo, where Napoléon's worst Italian enemy, Count Sommariva, resided at Villa Carlotta; and a bit farther south of Tremezzo, to Villa Balbianello. Check with the tourist office for the hours of the launch to Tremezzo.

VISITOR INFORMATION

Contact Bellagio Tourism Office. ⊠ *Piazza Mazzini* ☎ *031/950204* ⊕ *www. bellagiolakecomo.com.*

EXPLORING

Villa Melzi. The famous gardens of the Villa Melzi were once a favorite picnic spot for Franz Lizst, who advised author Louis de Ronchaud in 1837, "When you write the story of two happy lovers, place them on the shores of Lake Como. I do not know of any land so conspicuously blessed by heaven." The gardens are open to the public, and though you can't get into the 19th-century villa, don't miss the lavish Empire-style family chapel. The Melzi were Napoléon's greatest allies in Italy (the family has passed down the name "Josephine" to the present day). Guided tours are available with advance booking. ⊠ *Via Melzi d'Eril 8* ☎ *339/4573838* ⊕ *www.giardinidivillamelzi.it* ⊠ *€6.50* ☉ *Closed Nov.–late Mar.*

Villa Monastero. By ferry from Bellagio it's a quick trip across the lake to Varenna. The principal sight here is the spellbinding garden of the Villa Monastero, which, as its name suggests, was originally a monastery. There's also a house museum where you can admire 18th-century furnishings, as well as an international science and convention center. ⊠ *Viale Giovanni Polvani 4, Varenna* ☎ *0341/295450* ⊕ *www.villa-monastero.eu* ⊠ *Garden €5, house and garden €8* ☉ *Garden and house closed Mon.–Sat. in Jan. (except for 1st wk of Jan.), Feb., Nov., and Dec. (except Dec. 26–31). House also closed Mon.–Thurs. Mar.–May, Oct., and Nov., and Mon. in June, July, and Sept.*

Villa Serbelloni Garden. This property of the Rockefeller Foundation has celebrated gardens on the site of Pliny the Elder's villa, overlooking Bellagio. There are only two 1½-hour-long guided visits per day at 11 am and 3:30 pm, restricted to 30 people each, and in May these tend to be commandeered by group bookings. It's wise to arrive early to sign up. The garden also closes due to bad weather, so call in advance. ⊠ *Near Palazza della Chiesa* ☎ *031/951555* ⊕ *www.bellagiolakecomo. com* ⊠ *€9* ☉ *Closed Mon., and early Nov.–mid-Mar.*

WHERE TO EAT AND STAY

$$

ITALIAN

Fodor'sChoice

★

✕ **Ristorante La Punta.** When tourist-heavy Bellagio starts to wear you down, take respite at this charming restaurant located literally on the town's northern point, with amazing lake views both of Varenna to the north and Tremezzo to the west; it's about a 10-minute scenic walk from the center of town. As you might expect, the menu is heavy on lake fish, so you'll want to start with the *antipasto di lago* (mixed fish platter) or the *patè di pesce* (fish pâté); for the mains, the baked lasagna and gnocchi with cream and Gorgonzola sauce get rave reviews. **Known for:** super-fresh lake fish; superlative Lake Como views; friendly service. $ *Average main: €20* ⊠ *Via Eugenio Vitali 19* ☎ *031/951888* ⊕ *www.ristorantelapunta.it* ⊗ *Closed Oct.–Mar.*

$$
HOTEL

Du Lac. Most rooms at this comfortable old hotel owned by an Anglo-Italian family have views of the lake and mountains, while the rooftop terrace garden is a perfect spot for drinks or dozing. **Pros:** pleasant in-house restaurant; comfortable; friendly service. **Cons:** some decor a little worn around the edges; not all rooms have lake views. $ *Rooms from: €190* ⊠ *Piazza Mazzini 32* ☎ *031/950320* ⊕ *www.bellagiohoteldulac.com* ⊗ *Closed Nov.–Mar.* ⌁ *41 rooms* ⏦ *Free Breakfast.*

$$$$
HOTEL
Fodor's Choice
★

Grand Hotel Villa Serbelloni. This grand lakeside hotel, designed to cradle nobility in high style, remains a refined haven for the discreetly wealthy. **Pros:** historic lake hotel; great pool and health club; beautiful public spaces. **Cons:** could use some sprucing up; showers on the small side; expensive food and drink. $ *Rooms from: €555* ⊠ *Via Roma 1* ☎ *031/950216* ⊕ *www.villaserbelloni.com* ⊗ *Closed Nov.–early Apr.* ⌁ *95 rooms* ⏦ *Free Breakfast.*

$$$$
HOTEL

Hotel Belvedere. In Italian, belvedere means "beautiful view," and it's an apt name for this enchanting spot where antique furniture and eye-catching rugs complement the modern rooms, many of which have balconies and views of the lake. **Pros:** attention to detail; great views; lovely pool. **Cons:** a climb from the waterfront; need to request a lake-view room in advance. $ *Rooms from: €360* ⊠ *Via Valassina 31* ☎ *031/950410* ⊕ *www.belvederebellagio.com* ⊗ *Closed Nov.–Mar.* ⌁ *63 rooms* ⏦ *Free Breakfast.*

$$
HOTEL

Hotel Florence. Most of the large and comfortable rooms in this villa dating from the 1880s are furnished with interesting antiques and have splendid views of the lake. **Pros:** central location; appealing public spaces. **Cons:** location may feel too central if you're looking to get away from it all; some bathrooms only have handheld showers and iffy water pressure. $ *Rooms from: €165* ⊠ *Piazza Mazzini 46* ☎ *031/950342* ⊕ *www.hotelflorencebellagio.it* ⊗ *Closed mid-Oct.–mid-Apr.* ⌁ *30 rooms* ⏦ *Free Breakfast.*

TREMEZZO

34 km (21 miles) north of Cernobbio, 78 km (48 miles) north of Milan.

The dreamy lakeside town of Tremezzo is close to two outstanding and magical villas, as well as sprawling gardens and one of the lake's grandest hotels.

EXPLORING

Villa Carlotta. If you're lucky enough to visit Tremezzo in late spring or early summer, you will find the magnificent Villa Carlotta a riot of color, with more than 14 acres of azaleas and dozens of varieties of rhododendrons in full bloom. The height of the blossoms is late April to early May. The villa was built between 1690 and 1743 for the luxury-loving marquis Giorgio Clerici. The garden's collection is remarkable, particularly considering the difficulties of transporting delicate plants before the age of aircraft. Palms, banana trees, cacti, eucalyptus, a sequoia, orchids, and camellias are among the more than 500 species.

The villa's interior is worth a visit, particularly if you have a taste for the romantic sculptures of Antonio Canova (1757–1822). The best known is his *Cupid and Psyche,* which depicts the lovers locked in an odd but graceful embrace, with the young god above and behind, his wings extended, while Psyche awaits a kiss that will never come. The villa can be reached by boat from Bellagio and Como. ⊠ *Via Regina 2* ☎ *0344/40405* ⊕ *www.villacarlotta.it* 🎟 *€10* ⊗ *Closed early Nov.–mid-Mar.*

Villa del Balbianello. The relentlessly picturesque Balbianello may be the most magical house in all of Italy; you probably know it from cameos in the movies *Casino Royale* and *Star Wars Episode II: Attack of the Clones.* It sits on its own little promontory, Il Dosso d'Avedo, around the bend from the tiny fishing village of Ossuccio. The villa is composed of loggias, terraces, and *palazzini* (tiny palaces), all spilling down verdant slopes to the lakeshore, where you'll find an old Franciscan church, a magnificent stone staircase, and a statue of San Carlo Borromeo blessing the waters.

The villa is usually reached from Como and Bellagio by boat, which leaves you at the village of Lenno. From there, marked signs lead you to the villa—it's either accessible by foot via a 20-minute walk or a more challenging 45-minute hike, or there is often private boat service for €7 round-trip, €5 one-way. ⊠ *Il Dosso d'Avedo, ferry stop Lenno, Lenno* ✛ *5 km (3 miles) southwest of Tremezzo* ☎ *0344/56110* ⊕ *www. fondoambiente.it/luoghi/villa-del-balbianello* 🎟 *€20 villa and gardens, includes 1-hr guided tour; €10 gardens only* ⊗ *Closed Mon. and Wed., and mid-Nov.–mid-Mar.*

WHERE TO EAT AND STAY

$$$$
ITALIAN
Fodor'sChoice
★

✕ **La Locanda dell'Isola.** For a dining experience you won't soon forget, make your way to Sala Comacina (about a 10-minute drive south of Tremezzo) and take a five-minute speedboat to Lake Como's only island, Isola Comacina. There you'll be treated to the same rustic set menu served at La Locanda since 1947: veggie antipasti; thinly sliced prosciutto and *bresaola* (air-dried beef); grilled salmon trout; fried chicken with salad; parmigiano cheese sliced from an enormous wheel; and oranges or peaches with ice cream for dessert. **Known for:** historic charm; tasty set menus; wonderful scenery; credit cards not accepted. Ⓢ *Average main: €77* ⊠ *Isola Comacina* ☎ *0344/55083, 0344/56755* ⊕ *comacina.it* ▭ *No credit cards* ⊗ *Closed Tues. (except in summer), and Nov.–Feb.*

$$$$
RESORT
Fodor'sChoice
★

🏨 **Grand Hotel Tremezzo.** Creature comforts in this turn-of-the-20th-century building—one of the top grand hotels on the lake—include a lush park, three heated swimming pools (one of them floats on pontoons on the lake), a small private beach, and sumptuous guest rooms where old-world style is accented with modern amenities. **Pros:** lakeside location with beautiful views; attractive spa; gracious service. **Cons:** not well situated if you're looking for shopping or nightlife; very expensive; somewhat busy road between hotel and lake. Ⓢ *Rooms from:*

€770 ✉ Via Regina 8 ☎ 0344/42491 🌐 www.grandhoteltremezzo.com ⏲ Closed mid-Nov.–Feb. 🛏 90 rooms 🍴 Free Breakfast.

$$ B&B/INN 🏨 **Hotel Rusall.** On the hillside above Tremezzo in the middle of a large garden, this hotel has small, comfortably simple rooms that offer quiet, privacy, and the chance to lie by the pool and enjoy a nice view. **Pros:** lovely walks into town and in the countryside; more intimate than grander lake hotels; good on-site restaurant. **Cons:** takes some effort to reach the hillside location; not all rooms have air-conditioning. *[$] Rooms from: €125 ✉ Via San Martino 2 ☎ 0344/40408 🌐 www.rusallhotel.com ⏲ Closed weekdays. Nov. and Dec., and Jan.–Mar. 🛏 23 rooms 🍴 Free Breakfast.*

CERNOBBIO

5 km (3 miles) north of Como, 53 km (34 miles) north of Milan.

The legendary resort of Villa d'Este is reason enough to visit this jewel on the lake, but the town itself is worth a stroll. The place still has a neighborhood feel to it, especially on summer evenings and weekends when the piazza is full of families and couples strolling.

VISITOR INFORMATION

Contact Cernobbio Tourism Office. ✉ *Via Regina 6* ☎ *031/4446483* 🌐 *www.comune.cernobbio.co.it.*

WHERE TO EAT AND STAY

$$$ NORTHERN ITALIAN 🍴 **Il Gatto Nero.** A vantage point in the hills above Cernobbio provides a splendid view of the lake at this longtime favorite. Specialties include house-made pastas and a good variety of meat dishes with an international flair. **Known for:** sophisticated Italian cuisine; good high-end wine selection; lovely terrace in the summer. *[$] Average main: €28 ✉ Via Monte Santo 69 ☎ 031/512042 🌐 www.ristorantegattonero.it.*

$$ ITALIAN 🍴 **Lido di Cernobbio.** Right next to the Cernobbio ferry stop, this pretty restaurant specializes in traditional Italian fare enjoyed next to fabulous lake views. The chefs strive to use local ingredients when possible in their pizza, pasta, fish, and meat dishes, and offer a nice selection of local wines. **Known for:** lovely lake scenery; solid Italian dishes; family-friendly atmosphere. *[$] Average main: €20 ✉ Piazza Risorgimento 5 ☎ 031/4446437 🌐 www.lidodicernobbio.com ⏲ Closed Mon., and Nov.–Mar.*

$$$$ HOTEL Fodor's Choice ★ 🏨 **Villa d'Este.** One of the grandest hotels in Italy has long welcomed Europe's rich and famous, housing them in guest rooms still furnished in the Empire style. **Pros:** fine service; amazing grounds; excellent restaurant. **Cons:** may seem too formal to some; not all rooms feature lake views; all this grandness comes with a hefty price tag. *[$] Rooms from: €870 ✉ Via Regina 40 ☎ 031/3481 🌐 www.villadeste.it ⏲ Closed mid-Nov.–mid-Mar. 🛏 152 rooms 🍴 Free Breakfast.*

COMO

5 km (3 miles) south of Cernobbio, 30 km (19 miles) southwest of Bellagio, 49 km (30 miles) north of Milan.

Como commands the south shore of the lake. In its center, elegant cobblestone pedestrian streets wind their way past parks and bustling cafés. However, it's only partly a resort: the city also has an industrial heritage, deeply rooted in the production of textiles, particularly silk and the silk trade. If you're traveling by car, leave it at the edge of the town center in the well-lighted underground parking facility right on the lake.

VISITOR INFORMATION

Contact Como Tourism Office. ⊠ *Broletto Tower, Piazza Duomo* ☎ *031/304137* ⊕ *www.visitcomo.eu/en.*

EXPLORING

Duomo. The splendid 15th-century Renaissance-Gothic Duomo was begun in 1396. The facade was added in 1455, and the transepts were completed in the mid-18th century. The dome was designed by Filippo Juvara (1678–1736), chief architect of many of the sumptuous palaces of the royal house of Savoy. The facade has statues of two of Como's most famous sons, Pliny the Elder and Pliny the Younger, whose writings are among the most important documents from antiquity. Inside, the works of art include Luini's *Holy Conversation,* a fresco cycle by Morazzone, and the *Marriage of the Virgin Mary* by Ferrari. ⊠ *Piazza del Duomo* ☎ *031/3312275* ⊕ *www.cattedraledicomo.it.*

Museo Didattico della Seta (*Silk Museum*). From silkworm litters to textile finishing machinery, this small but complete collection preserves the history of a manufacturing region that continues to supply almost three-fourths of Europe's silk. The friendly staffers will give you an overview of the museum; they are also happy to provide brochures and information about local retail shops. The location isn't well marked: follow the textile school's driveway around to the low-rise concrete building on the left, and take the shallow ramp down to the entrance. ⊠ *Via Castelnuovo 9* ☎ *031/303180* ⊕ *www.museosetacomo.com* 🎫 *€10* ⊘ *Closed Sun. and Mon., and Sat. after 1.*

San Fedele. At the heart of Como's medieval quarter, the city's first cathedral is well worth a peek. The apse walls and ceiling are completely frescoed, as are the ceilings above the altar. ⊠ *Piazza San Fedele* ☎ *031/267295* ⊕ *www.parrocchiasanfedelecomo.it.*

Sant'Abbondio. If you head into Como's industrial quarter, you will come upon this beautiful church, a gem of Romanesque architecture begun by Benedictine monks in 1013 and consecrated by Pope Urban II in 1095. Inside, the five aisles converge on a presbytery with a semicircular apse decorated with a cycle of 14th-century frescoes by Lombard artists heavily influenced by the Sienese school. To see them, turn right as you enter and put €0.50 in the mechanical box for a few minutes of lighting. In the nave, the cubical capitals are the earliest example of this style in Italy. ⊠ *Via Sant'Abbondio* ☎ *031/304518* ⊕ *www.santabbondio.eu.*

WHERE TO EAT AND STAY

$$$ MODERN ITALIAN 🍴 **The Market Place.** This intimate restaurant just outside Como's historic center serves up full-flavored modern Italian food in interesting combinations—and its five- or six-course tasting menus, with wine pairings if you'd like, are simply delicious. Although the decor is on the sparse side, you'll be spending your time focusing on the well-presented dishes; the young, helpful servers take time to describe each course. **Known for:** seasonal ingredients; innovative flavor combinations; friendly and helpful staff. [$] *Average main: €26* ✉ *Via Borsieri 21/a* ☎ *031/270712* 🌐 *www.themarketplace.it* 🕒 *Closed Sun., and 2 wks in Aug. No lunch Mon.*

$$$ HOTEL 🏨 **Albergo Terminus.** This early-20th-century Art Nouveau landmark commands a panoramic view over Lake Como; inside, the marbled public spaces and old-fashioned guest rooms are done up in floral patterns and furnished with large walnut wardrobes and silk-covered sofas. **Pros:** old-world charm; right on the lake; sauna and gym. **Cons:** limited number of rooms with lake views; decor in some rooms seems dated. [$] *Rooms from: €222* ✉ *Lungo Lario Trieste 14* ☎ *031/329111* 🌐 *www.albergoterminus.it* 🛏 *50 rooms* 🍽 *No meals.*

$$$$ HOTEL 🏨 **CastaDiva Resort & Spa.** If you're looking for an extravagant hotel with a modern feel away from the hustle and bustle, this collection of seven 19th-century villas, named for opera singer and former resident Guiditta Pasta, has been brought thoroughly into the 21st century. **Pros:** lovely, secluded lakeside location; fabulous, extensive spa area; knowledgeable staff. **Cons:** a 10- to 15-minute drive to the town of Como; lack of dining options nearby; some may find the decor more over-the-top than refined. [$] *Rooms from: €900* ✉ *Via Caronti 69, Blevio* ☎ *031/32511* 🌐 *www.castadivaresort.com* 🕒 *Closed Nov.–mid-Mar.* 🛏 *75 rooms* 🍽 *Free Breakfast.*

$$$$ HOTEL 🏨 **Il Sereno Lago di Como.** The first European outpost of the luxe Il Sereno Hotel in St. Barths, this Lake Como gem boasts rooms with floor-to-ceiling windows overlooking the water and an understated retro-mod design. **Pros:** cool modern design; hushed elegance throughout; fabulous views. **Cons:** extremely expensive; service a bit spotty; restaurant food not worthy of the setting. [$] *Rooms from: €960* ✉ *Via Torrazza 10* ☎ *031/5477800* 🌐 *www.ilsereno.com* 🕒 *Closed Nov.–mid-Mar.* 🛏 *30 rooms* 🍽 *Free Breakfast.*

$$ HOTEL 🏨 **Posta Design Hotel.** This boutique hotel on pedestrian-only Piazza Volta in downtown Como, just a block from the lake, infuses minimalist modern design into a sleek 1931 building designed by Rationalist architect Giuseppe Terragni. **Pros:** central location; comfortable rooms; friendly service. **Cons:** rooms on lower floors can be noisy; sparse amenities (no minibars in rooms, no breakfast, no gym); reception only staffed after 2 pm. [$] *Rooms from: €126* ✉ *Via Garibaldi 2* ☎ *031/2769011* 🌐 *www.postadesignhotel.com* 🛏 *14 rooms* 🍽 *No meals.*

SPORTS AND THE OUTDOORS

Lake Como has lots of ways to stay active and outdoors, from windsurfing at the lake's northern end, to boating, sailing, and Jet Skiing at Como and Cernobbio. The lake is also quite swimmable in summer. For hikers there are lovely paths all around the lake. For an easy trek, take the funicular up to Brunate, and walk along the mountain to the lighthouse for a stunning view of the lake.

LAKE MAGGIORE

Magnificently scenic, Lake Maggiore has a unique geographical position: its mountainous western shore is in Piedmont, its lower eastern shore is in Lombardy, and its northern tip is in Switzerland. The lake stretches nearly 50 km (30 miles) and is up to 5 km (3 miles) wide. The better-known resorts are on the western shore.

GETTING HERE AND AROUND

Trains run regularly from Milan to the town of Stresa on Lake Maggiore; the trip takes 1–1½ hours, depending on the type of train. By car from Milan to Stresa, take the A8 autostrada to the A8dir, and from the A8dir take the A26; the drive is about 1¼ hours.

STRESA AND THE ISOLE BORROMEE

80 km (50 miles) northwest of Milan.

One of the better-known resorts on the western shore, Stresa is a tourist town that provided one of the settings for Hemingway's *A Farewell to Arms*. It has capitalized on its central lakeside position, though the luxurious elegance that distinguished its heyday has faded; the grand hotels are still grand, but traffic now encroaches on their parks and gardens.

The best way to escape to yesteryear is to head for the Isole Borromee (Borromean Islands) in Lake Maggiore. Boats to the three islands depart every 15–30 minutes from the dock at Stresa's Piazza Marconi, as well as from Piazzale Lido at the northern end of the promenade. There's also a boat from Verbania; check locally for the seasonal schedule. Although you can hire a private boat, it's cheaper and just as convenient to use the regular service. Make sure you buy a ticket allowing you to visit all the islands—Bella, Dei Pescatori, and Madre. The islands take their name from the Borromeo family, which has owned them since the 12th century.

VISITOR INFORMATION

Contacts Isole Borromee Information. ☎ *0323/933478* ⊕ *www.isoleborromee.it.* **Stresa Tourism Office.** ⊠ *Piazza Marconi, Stresa* ☎ *0323/31308* ⊕ *www.stresaturismo.it.*

EXPLORING

Funivia. For amazing views, take the funivia—a cable car that takes you to heights from which you can see seven lakes: Maggiore, Orta, Mergozzo, Varese, Camabbio, Monate, and Biandronno. Situated between Lakes Maggiore and Orta, it offers tourists 360-degree views of the Po Valley right across to the distant Alpine peaks. At the top, nature- and adventure-lovers can rent mountain bikes and ride on properly marked paths, while others can just relax at a local restaurant. ⊠ *Piazzale Lido 8, Stresa* ☎ *0323/30295* ⊕ *www.stresa-mottarone.it* ⧠ *€19 round-trip.*

7

Isola Bella (*Beautiful Island*). The most famous of the three Isole Borromee (Borromean Islands), and the first that you'll visit, is named after Isabella, whose husband, Carlo III Borromeo (1538–84), built the palace and terraced gardens here for her as a wedding present. Before Count Carlo began his project, the island was rocky and almost devoid of vegetation; the soil for the garden had to be transported from the mainland. Wander up the 10 terraces of the gardens, where peacocks roam among the scented shrubs, statues, and fountains, for a splendid view of the lake. Visit the palazzo to see the rooms where famous guests—including Napoléon and Mussolini—stayed in 18th-century splendor. Those three interlocked rings on walls and even streets represent the powerful Borromeo, Visconti, and Sforza families. ⊠ *Isola Bella* ☎ *0323/933478* ⊕ *www.isoleborromee.it* ⊠ *Garden, palazzo, and painting gallery €16* ⊗ *Closed late Oct.–late Mar.*

Isola dei Pescatori (*Island of the Fishermen, also known as Isola Superiore*). Stop for a while at the smallest Borromean Island, less than 100 yards wide and only about ½ km (¼ mile) long. It's the perfect place for a seafood lunch before, after, or in between your visit to the other two islands. Of the 10 or so restaurants on this tiny island, the 2 worth visiting are **Ristorante Verbano** (☎ *0323/30408*) and **Ristorante Belvedere** (☎ *0323/32292*). The island's little lanes strung with fishing nets and dotted with shrines to the Madonna are the definition of picturesque; little wonder that in high season the village is crowded with postcard stands. ⊠ *Isola dei Pescatori.*

Isola Madre (*Mother Island*). All of this Borromean Island is a botanical garden, with a season that stretches from late March to late October due to the climatic protection of the mighty Alps and the tepid waters of Lago Maggiore. The cacti and palm trees here, so far north and so near the border with Switzerland, are a beautiful surprise. Take time to see the profusion of exotic trees and shrubs running down to the shore in every direction. Two special times to visit are April (for the camellias) and May (for azaleas and rhododendrons). Also on the island is a 16th-century palazzo, where the Borromeo family still lives for part of the year. The palazzo has an antique puppet theater on display, complete with string puppets, prompt books, and elaborate scenery designed by Alessandro Sanquirico, who was a scenographer at La Scala in Milan. ⊠ *Isola Madre* ☎ *0323/933478* ⊕ *www.isoleborromee. it* ⊠ *€13* ⊗ *Closed late Oct.–late Mar.*

Parco Villa Pallavicino. As you wander around the palms and semitropical shrubs, don't be surprised if you're followed by a peacock or even an ostrich: they're part of the zoological garden and are allowed to roam almost at will. From the top of the hill on which the villa stands you can see the gentle hills of the Lombardy shore of Lake Maggiore and, nearer and to the left, the jewel-like Isole Borromee. In addition to a bar and restaurant, the grounds also have picnic spots. ⊠ *Via Sempione 8, Stresa* ☎ *0323/31533* ⊕ *www.parcopallavicino.it* ⊠ *€9.50* ⊗ *Closed early Nov.–mid-Mar.*

WHERE TO EAT AND STAY

$$ NORTHERN ITALIAN Fodor's Choice ★

🍴 **Ristorante LaStresa.** This modern, buzzy eatery and local favorite on one of Stresa's main streets highlights seasonal ingredients and interesting wines from the region and across Italy; ask for recommendations from the friendly and knowledgeable waitstaff. Though it looks nondescript from the outside, inside the decor is stylish and chic. **Known for:** seasonally changing dishes; fish fresh from the lake; wonderful wine list. [$] *Average main: €19* ✉ *Via Principessa Margherita 22, Stresa* ☎ *0323/33240* 🌐 *www.ristorantelastresa.it* ⏲ *Closed Tues. Sept.–June.*

$$ MODERN ITALIAN

🍴 **Trattoria due Piccioni.** In a town with an overabundance of touristy pizza and pasta places, this unassumingly modern family-run bistro raises the bar. While the shabby-chic decor and friendly service entice, the real draw is the short but smart menu, chock-full of thoughtful and inventive twists on Italian cuisine. **Known for:** inventive local cuisine; intriguing desserts including "birramisù"; attentive service. [$] *Average main: €16* ✉ *Via P. Tomaso 61, Stresa* ☎ *0323/934556* 🌐 *www.duepiccioni.it* ⏲ *Closed Wed.*

$$$ HOTEL Fodor's Choice ★

🏨 **Grand Hotel des Iles Borromees.** This palatial, Liberty-style hotel has catered to a demanding European clientele since 1863, and spacious salons and guest rooms still have the lavish furnishings of the turn of the 20th century. **Pros:** the grace and style of a bygone era, with modern amenities; sumptuously decorated rooms, particularly the fabulous Hemingway Suite; nice pool and spa selection. **Cons:** very expensive; decor may be over the top for some. [$] *Rooms from: €246* ✉ *Corso Umberto I 67, Stresa* ☎ *0323/938938* 🌐 *www.borromees.com* ⏲ *Closed Dec. and Jan.* 🛏 *179 rooms* 🍽 *Free Breakfast.*

$ HOTEL

🏨 **Primavera.** These compact, simply furnished rooms in a 1950s building hung with flower boxes are a few blocks up from the lake. **Pros:** good value; convenient location. **Cons:** limited lake views; small, plainly furnished rooms. [$] *Rooms from: €95* ✉ *Via Cavour 39, Stresa* ☎ *0323/31286* 🌐 *www.hotelprimaverastresa.it* ⏲ *Closed Jan.* 🛏 *34 rooms* 🍽 *Free Breakfast.*

VERBANIA

16 km (10 miles) north of Stresa, 95 km (59 miles) northwest of Milan.

The quaint town of Verbania is across the Gulf of Pallanza from its more touristy neighbor, Stresa. It is known for the Villa Taranto, which has magnificent botanical gardens. With its majestic gardens and greenery, Verbania is often called the Garden of Lake Maggiore.

EXPLORING

Villa Taranto. The Villa Taranto was acquired in 1931 by Scottish captain Neil McEachern, who helped make the magnificent gardens here what they are today, adding terraces, waterfalls, more than 3,000 plant species from all over the world—including 300 varieties of dahlias—and broad meadows sloping gently to the lake. While the gardens can be visited, the villa itself is not open to the public. ✉ *Via Vittorio Veneto 111* ☎ *0323/556667* 🌐 *www.villataranto.it* 🎟 *€10* ⏲ *Closed early Nov.–mid-Mar.*

Santa Caterina del Sasso Ballaro. Near the town of Laveno, this beautiful lakeside hermitage was constructed in the 12th century by a local merchant to express his gratitude for having been saved from the wrath of a storm. Seemingly carved out of its supporting cliff, it's particularly striking as you approach it by boat or ferry. ⊕ *www.santacaterinadelsasso.com* ⊙ *Closed weekends Nov.–Feb.*

WHERE TO STAY

$
HOTEL
⊡ **Il Chiostro.** Using space formed from a 17th-century monastery merged with an adjoining 19th-century textile factory, this hotel offers plain, functional rooms, some overlooking a lovely garden. **Pros:** friendly and efficient staff; quiet atmosphere; affordable for the area. **Cons:** rooms are fairly plain; limited amenities. Ⓢ *Rooms from: €94* ⊠ *Via Fratelli Cervi 14* 🕾 *0323/404077* ⊕ *www.chiostrovb.it* 🛏 *104 rooms* ⦿| *Free Breakfast.*

$$
HOTEL
⊡ **Il Sole di Ranco.** For more than 150 years the same family has run this elegant lakeside inn about an hour's drive from Verbania, where guest rooms and suites are in two late-19th-century villas surrounded by a garden perched high on the banks of the lake opposite Stresa. **Pros:** classic lake setting; tranquil grounds; lovely pool area. **Cons:** a bit distant from lake's tourist center (although the hotel offers tours with private drivers); decor on the old-fashioned side. Ⓢ *Rooms from: €190* ⊠ *Piazza Venezia 5, Ranco* 🕾 *0331/976507* ⊕ *www.ilsolediranco.it* ⊙ *Closed Jan.–early Feb.* 🛏 *14 rooms* ⦿| *Free Breakfast.*

8

PIEDMONT AND
VALLE D'AOSTA

WELCOME TO PIEDMONT AND VALLE D'AOSTA

TOP REASONS TO GO

★ **Sacra di San Michele:** Explore one of the country's most spectacularly situated religious monuments.

★ **Castello Fénis:** This castle transports you back in time to the Middle Ages.

★ **Monte Bianco:** A cable car ride over the snow-capped mountain will take your breath away.

★ **Turin's Museo Egizio:** A surprising treasure—one of the world's richest collections of Egyptian art outside Cairo.

★ **Regal wines:** Some of Italy's most revered reds—led by Barolo, "the king of wines"—come from the hills of southern Piedmont.

★ **Turin's Galleria Sabauda:** Witness to the regal splendor of the reigning House of Savoy, this museum is famed for its spectacular old master collection.

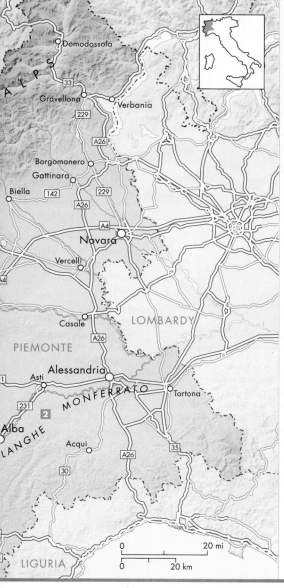

1 Turin. The region's main city isn't just the car capital of Italy and home to the Holy Shroud. Neoclassical piazzas, shops filled with chocolates and chic fashions, and elegant Baroque palazzi have been restored in grand style.

2 The Monferrato and the Langhe. These hills are famous among food and wine connoisseurs. Asti gave the world Asti Spumante, Alba is known for its truffles and mushrooms, and the Langhe hills produce some of Italy's finest wines.

3 Valle d'Aosta. The mountains and valleys of this region cry out to be strolled, climbed, and skied. Here, the highest Alpine peaks—including Monte Bianco (Mont Blanc) and the Matterhorn—shelter resorts such as Breuil-Cervinia and Courmayeur and the great nature preserve known as the Gran Paradiso.

4 The Colline and Savoy Palaces. West of Turin, this is a region of medieval castles and fortifications, the highlight of which is the storybook town of Rivoli.

8

EATING AND DRINKING WELL IN PIEDMONT AND VALLE D'AOSTA

In Piedmont and Valle d'Aosta you can find rustic specialties from farmhouse hearths, fine cuisine with a French accent, and everything in between. The Piedmontese take their food and wine very seriously.

There's a significant concentration of upscale restaurants in Piedmont, with refined cuisine designed to showcase the region's fine wines. Wine-oriented menus are prevalent both in cities and in the country, where even simply named trattorias may offer a *menu di degustazione* (a multicourse tasting menu that highlights the chef's specialties) accompanied by wines paired with each dish.

In Turin the ritual of the *aperitivo* (aperitif) has been finely tuned, and most cafés from the early evening onward provide lavish buffets that are included in the price of a cocktail—a respectable substitute for dinner if you're traveling on a limited budget. As a result, restaurants in Turin tend to fill only after 9 pm.

GREAT GRISSINI

Throughout the region—especially in Turin—you'll find that most meals are accompanied by *grissini* (bread sticks).

When they are freshly made and hand-rolled, these renditions are a far cry from the thin and dry, plastic-wrapped versions available elsewhere.

Grissini were invented in Turin in the 17th century to ease the digestive problems of little Prince Vittorio Amedeo II (1675–1730). Napoléon called them *petits batons* and was supposedly addicted to them.

TRUFFLES

The *tartufo* (truffle) is a peculiar delicacy—a gnarly clump of fungus that grows wild in forests a few inches underground. It's hunted down using truffle-sniffing dogs. The payoff is a powerful, perfume flavor that makes gourmets swoon, and that they are willing to pay a small fortune for. Although truffles are more abundant farther south in Umbria, the most coveted ones are the *tartufi bianchi* (white truffles) from Alba in Piedmont. A thin shaving of truffle often tops pasta dishes; they're also used to flavor soups and other dishes.

POLENTA AND PASTA

The area's best-known dish is probably polenta, creamy cornmeal served with *carbonada* (a meat stew), melted cheese, or wild mushrooms. *Agnolotti*—crescent-shape pasta stuffed with meat filling—is another specialty, often served with the pan juices of roast veal. Agnolotti *del plin* is a smaller version topped with melted butter and shaved truffles.

CHEESE

In keeping with their northern character, Piedmont and Valle d'Aosta are both known for *fonduta*, a version of fondue made with melted cheese, eggs, and sometimes grated truffles. Fontina and ham also often deck out the ubiquitous French-style crepes *alla valdostana*, served casserole-style.

MEAT

The locally raised beef of Piedmont is some of Italy's most highly prized; it's often braised or stewed with the region's hearty red wine. In winter, *bollito misto* (various meats, boiled and served with a rich sauce) shows up on many menus, and *fritto misto*, a combination of fried meats and vegetables, is another specialty.

DESSERTS AND SWEETS

Though desserts here are less sweet than in some other Italian regions, treats like *panna cotta* (a cooked milk custard), *torta di nocciole* (hazelnut torte), and *bonet* (a pudding made with hazelnuts, cocoa, milk, and macaroons) are delights. Turin is renowned for its delicate pastries and fine chocolates, especially for *gianduiotti*, made with hazelnuts.

WINE

Piedmont is one of Italy's most important wine regions, producing full-bodied reds, such as Barolo, Barbaresco, freisa, barbera, and the lighter dolcetto. Asti Spumante, a sweet sparkling wine, comes from the region, while Valle d'Aosta is famous for brandies made from fruits or herbs.

8

Updated by
Liz Shemaria

Northwest Italy's Piedmont and Valle d'Aosta regions come with a large dose of mountain splendor, bourgeois refinement, culinary achievement, and scenic beauty. Two of Europe's most famous peaks, Monte Bianco (Mont Blanc) and Monte Cervino (the Matterhorn), straddle Valle d'Aosta's borders with France and Switzerland, and the region draws skiers and hikers from all over. You can ascend the mountains by cable car, or, if you're an experienced climber, make a go of it with professional guides. For the less actively inclined, a visit to the mountain museum in Bard might well do the trick.

To the south, the mist-shrouded lowlands skirting the Po River are home to Turin, a city that may not have the artistic treasures of Rome or the cutting-edge style of Milan, but has developed a sense of urban sophistication that makes it a pleasure to visit. The first capital of unified Italy and the fourth-largest city in the country, it was once often overlooked on tourist itineraries as a mere industrial center (FIAT is based here). It was the Winter Olympic Games of 2006 that put Turin on many tourists' map. Still, despite its higher profile, and its many excellent museums, cafés, and restaurants, Turin never feels overrun.

Farther south, vineyards carpet the rolling hills of the Langhe and Monferrato areas, where Barolo, Barbaresco, and Asti Spumante wines, some of Italy's finest, are produced. It's here, as well, that the prized white truffle of Alba is found and celebrated during an autumn fair.

Piedmont has the longest border with France of any other region, and the fact of its having been ruled by the French Savoy for centuries is revealed in a Gallic influence in all walks of life—especially in the food and architecture. Turin's mansard roofs and porticoed avenues can make a walk through its streets feel like a stroll down a Parisian boulevard. Food is richer, creamier, and perhaps more refined than many other parts of Italy, and the standard of service, even in simple restaurants, is often very high.

PIEDMONT AND VALLE D'AOSTA PLANNER

MAKING THE MOST OF YOUR TIME

Turin needs at least two or three days to visit properly. If you have extra time, visit one of the magnificent palaces and hunting lodges built by the Savoy family. They surround Turin in the so-called *corona di delizie* (crown of delights) and make for an easy day trip.

Plan on several days to visit the Langhe and Monferrato areas. The towns of Alba and Asti should not be missed, but neither should the smaller wine towns that dot the rolling hills of both regions. You'll need your own car here, but will be rewarded with great views, great food, and great wine. If you're coming here in September and October, when there are festivals in both Alba and Asti, make sure to book your trip well in advance.

Unless you are planning on a skiing or hiking holiday, the Valle d'Aosta requires less time to visit. The emphasis here is on the natural beauty of the mountains, but if you are driving between France and Italy, the region certainly merits a one- or two-night stopover, in either Courmayeur or Aosta; be sure not to miss the Castello di Fénis and the Forte di Bard on your way.

GETTING HERE AND AROUND

BUS TRAVEL

Turin's main bus station is on the corner of Corso Inghilterra and Corso Vittorio Emanuele. There's also a major bus station at Aosta, across the street from the train station.

GTT. Urban buses, trams, and the subway are all operated by this company. ⊠ *Turin* ☎ *800/019152 toll-free in Italy* ⊕ *www.comune.torino. it/gtt.*

SADEM. This Turin-based bus line provides service throughout Piedmont and Valle d'Aosta, as well as a regular shuttle service to Caselle, the Turin airport, and to the Malpensa airport outside Milan. Tickets for the airport shuttle can be purchased online. ⊠ *Turin* ☎ *800/801600 toll-free in Italy* ⊕ *www.sadem.it.*

SAVDA. This Aosta-based company specializes in mountain service, providing frequent links between Aosta, Turin, and Courmayeur as well as Milan. ⊠ *Aosta* ☎ *0165/367011* ⊕ *www.savda.it.*

CAR TRAVEL

Like any mountainous region, the Italian Alps can be tricky to navigate by car. Roads that look like highways on the map can be narrow and twisting, with steep slopes and cliff-side drops. Generally, roads are well maintained, but the distance covered by all of those curves tends to take longer than you might expect, so it's best to figure in extra time for getting around. This is especially true in winter, when weather conditions can slow traffic and close roads. Check with local tourist offices or, in a pinch, with the police to make sure roads are passable and safe, and to find out whether you need tire chains for snowy and icy roads.

For travel across the French, Swiss, and Italian borders in Piedmont and Valle d'Aosta, only a few routes are usable year-round: the 12-km (7-mile) Mont Blanc tunnel connecting Chamonix with Courmayeur; the Colle del Gran San Bernardo/Col du Grand St. Bernard (connecting Martigny to Aosta on Swiss highway E27 and Italian highway SS27, with 6 km [4 miles] of tunnel); and the Traforo del Fréjus (between Modane and Susa, with 13 km [8 miles] of tunnel). Other passes become increasingly unreliable between November and April.

TRAIN TRAVEL

Turin is on the main Paris–Rome TGV express line and is also connected with Milan, 90 minutes away on the fast train. The fastest (Frecciarossa) trains cover the 667-km (414-mile) trip to Rome in just over four hours; other trains take between five and seven hours.

Services to the larger cities east of Turin are part of the extensive and reliable train network of the Lombard Plain. West of the region's capital, however, the train services soon peter out in the mountains. Continuing connections by bus serve these valleys; information about train-bus mountain services can be obtained from train stations and tourist information offices, or by contacting FS–Trenitalia, the Italian national train service.

Italo. Italian state-run railway's only competition, Italo operates fast, dependable, and often less expensive train service between many (but not all) of Italy's major cities. ☎ 06/0708 ⊕ www.italotreno.it.

Trenitalia. Italy's national train service. ☎ 06/68475475 toll-free in Italy ⊕ www.trenitalia.com.

RESTAURANTS

In the region's restaurants you'll taste a mountain-city contrast: the hearty peasant cooking served in tiny stone villages and the French-accented delicacies found in the plain are both eminently satisfying. *Restaurant reviews have been shortened. For full information, visit Fodors.com.*

HOTELS

High standards and opulence are characteristic of Turin's better hotels, and the same is true at the top mountain resorts. Hotels in Turin and other major towns are generally geared to business travelers; make sure to ask whether lower weekend rates or special deals for two- or three-night stays are available.

Summer vacationers and winter skiers keep occupancy rates and prices high at resorts during peak seasons. Many mountain hotels require guests to pay for either half or full board and insist on a stay of several nights; some have off-season rates that can reduce the cost by a full price category. If you're planning to ski, ask about package deals that give you a discount on lift tickets. *Hotel reviews have been shortened. For full information, visit Fodors.com.*

WHAT IT COSTS				
	$	$$	$$$	$$$$
Restaurants	under €15	€15–€24	€25–€35	over €35
Hotels	under €125	€125–€200	€201–€300	over €300

Prices in the dining reviews are the average cost of a main course at dinner, or, if dinner is not served, at lunch. Prices in the reviews are the lowest cost of a standard double room in high season.

TURIN

Turin—Torino, in Italian—is roughly in the center of Piedmont–Valle d'Aosta and 128 km (80 miles) west of Milan; it's on the Po River, on the edge of the Po Plain, which stretches east all the way to the Adriatic. Turin's flatness and wide, angular, tree-lined boulevards are a far cry from Italian *metropoli* to the south; the region's decidedly northern European bent is quite evident in its nerve center. Apart from its role as northwest Italy's major industrial, cultural, intellectual, and administrative hub, Turin also has a reputation as Italy's capital of black magic and the supernatural. This distinction is enhanced by the presence of Turin's most famous and controversial relic, the Sacra Sindone (Shroud of Turin), still believed by many Catholics to be Christ's burial shroud. (For its part, the Vatican has not taken an official position on its authenticity.)

8

GETTING HERE AND AROUND

Turin is well served by the Italian *autostrade* (highway) system and can be reached easily by car from all directions: from Milan on the A4 autostrada (2 hours); from Bologna (4 hours) and Florence (5 hours) on the A1 and A21; from Genoa on the A6 (2 hours).

Bus service to and from other major Italian cities is also plentiful, and Turin can be reached by fast train service from Paris in less than six hours. Fast train service also connects the city with Milan, Genoa, Bologna, Florence, and Rome.

Public boats, operated by Turin's public transport system (☎ *800/019152* or ☎ *011/5764733* ⊕ *www.comune.torino.it/gtt*), make for a pleasant way to reach the Borgo Medioevale from the Murazzi dock at the northern end of the Parco del Valentino.

VISITOR INFORMATION

Turin's group and personally guided tours are organized by the city's tourist office. It also provides maps and details about a wide range of thematic self-guided walks through town. The Torino+Piemonte Card, which provides discounts on transportation and museum entrances for two-, three-, five-, or seven-day visits, can be purchased here.

Contact Turin Tourist Information Center. ⊠ *Piazza Castello, at Via Garibaldi* ☎ *011/535181* ⊕ *www.turismotorino.org.*

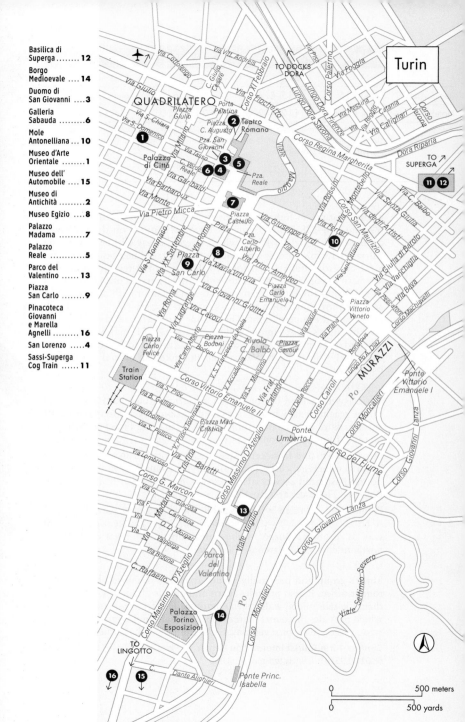

Turin

EXPLORING

DOWNTOWN TURIN

Many of Turin's major sights are clustered around Piazza Castello, and others are on or just off the portico-lined Via Roma, one of the city's main thoroughfares, which leads 1 km (½ mile) from Piazza Castello south to Piazza Carlo Felice, a landscaped park in front of the train station. First opened in 1615, Via Roma was largely rebuilt in the 1930s, during the Mussolini era.

TOP ATTRACTIONS

Duomo di San Giovanni. The most impressive part of Turin's 15th-century cathedral is the shadowy, black-marble-walled **Cappella della Sacra Sindone** (Chapel of the Holy Shroud), where the famous relic was housed before a fire in 1997. The chapel was designed by the priest and architect Guarino Guarini (1604–83), a genius of the Baroque style who was official engineer and mathematician to the court of Duke Carlo Emanuele II of Savoy. The fire caused severe structural damage, and the chapel is closed indefinitely while restoration work proceeds.

The Sacra Sindone is a 4-yard-long sheet of linen, thought by millions to be the burial shroud of Christ, bearing the light imprint of his crucified body. The shroud first made an appearance around the middle of the 15th century, when it was presented to Ludovico of Savoy in Chambéry. In 1578 it was brought to Turin by another member of the Savoy royal family, Duke Emanuele Filiberto. It was only in the 1990s that the Catholic Church began allowing rigorous scientific study of the shroud. Not surprisingly, the results have been hazy, bolstering both sides of the argument. On one hand, three separate university teams—in Switzerland, Britain, and the United States—have concluded, as a result of carbon-14 dating, that the cloth dates from between 1260 and 1390. On the other hand, they are unable to explain how medieval forgers could have created the shroud's image, which resembles a photographic negative, and how they could have had the knowledge or means to incorporate traces of Roman coins covering the eyelids and endemic Middle Eastern pollen woven into the cloth. Either way, the shroud continues to be revered as a holy relic, exhibited to the public on very rare occasions. At other times, it is preserved in a sealed casket in the left aisle of the cathedral. In lieu of the real thing, a photocopy is on permanent display nearby. ⊠ *Via XX Settembre 87, Centro* ☎ *011/4361540* ⊕ *www.duomoditorino.it.*

Galleria Sabauda. Housed in the restored *Manica Nuova* (new wing) of the **Palazzo Reale,** the gallery displays some of the most important paintings from the vast collections of the house of Savoy. The collection is particularly rich in Dutch and Flemish paintings: note the *Stigmate di San Francesco* (*St. Francis Receiving the Stigmata*) by Jan Van Eyck (1395–1441), in which the saint receives the marks of Christ's wounds while a companion cringes beside him. Other Dutch masterpieces include paintings by Anthony Van Dyck (1599–1641) and Rembrandt (1606–69). L'arcangelo Raffaele e Tobiolo (*Tobias and the Angel*) by Piero del Pollaiuolo (circa 1443–96) is showcased, and other featured Italian artists include Fra Angelico (circa 1400–55), Andrea Mantegna

(1431–1506), and Paolo Veronese (1528–88). ⊠ *Piazetta Reale 1, Centro* ☎ *011/5641729* ⊕ *www.museireali.beniculturali.it* 🖃 *€12, includes Palazzo Reale, Armeria Reale, and Museo Archeologico* ⊘ *Closed Mon.*

Mole Antonelliana. You can't miss the unusual square dome and thin, elaborate spire of this Turin landmark above the city's rooftops. This odd structure, built between 1863 and 1889, was intended to be a synagogue, but costs escalated and eventually it was bought by the city of Turin. In its time it was the tallest brick structure in the world, and it is still the tallest building in Italy. You can take the crystal elevator to reach the terrace at the top of the dome for an excellent view of the city, the plain, and the Alps beyond. Also worth a visit is the Mole Antonelliana's **Museo Nazionale del Cinema** (National Cinema Museum), which covers more than 34,000 square feet and houses many items of film memorabilia as well as a film library with some 7,000 titles. ⊠ *Via Montebello 20, Centro* ☎ *011/8138563 museum* ⊕ *www.museocinema. it* 🖃 *Museum €10, elevator €7; combination ticket €14* ⊘ *Closed Tues.*

Museo d'Arte Orientale. Housed in the magnificently renovated 17th-century Palazzo Mazzonis, this is a beautifully displayed collection of Southeast Asian, Chinese, Japanese, Himalayan, and Islamic art, including sculptures, paintings, and ceramics. Highlights include a towering 13th-century wooden statue of the Japanese temple guardian Kongo Rikishi and a sumptuous assortment of Islamic manuscripts. ⊠ *Via San Domenico 11, Centro* ☎ *011/4436932* ⊕ *www.maotorino.it* 🖃 *€10* ⊘ *Closed Mon.*

Fodor'sChoice
★

Museo Egizio. The Egyptian Museum's superb collection includes statues of pharaohs and mummies and entire frescoes taken from royal tombs—it's one of the world's finest and largest museums of its kind. The striking sculpture gallery, designed by the Oscar-winning production designer Dante Ferretti, is a veritable who's who of ancient Egypt. Look for the magnificent 13th-century-BC statue of Ramses II and the fascinating Tomb of Kha. The latter was found intact with furniture, supplies of food and clothing, writing instruments, and a complete set of personal cosmetics and toiletries. The museum is housed in the **Palazzo dell'Accademia delle Scienze,** a Baroque tour de force designed by the priest and architect Guarino Guarini. ⊠ *Via Accademia delle Scienze 6, Centro* ☎ *011/4406903* ⊕ *www.museoegizio.it* 🖃 *€13 (plus €2 presale fee if purchased online).*

Palazzo Madama. In the center of Piazza Castello, this castle was named for the Savoy queen Madama Maria Cristina, who made it her home in the 17th century. The building incorporates the remains of a Roman gate with later-medieval and Renaissance additions, and the monumental Baroque facade and grand entrance staircase were added by Filippo Juvarra (1678–1736). The palace now houses the **Museo Civico d'Arte Antica,** whose collections comprise more than 30,000 items dating from the Middle Ages to the Baroque era. The paintings, sculptures, illuminated manuscripts, and various decorative objects on display illustrate almost 10 centuries of Italian and European artistic production. Works by Jan Van Eyck, Antonella da Messina (circa 1430–79), and Orazio Gentileschi (1563–1639) highlight the collection. ⊠ *Piazza Castello 10,*

Centro ☎ *011/4433501* ⊕ *www.palazzomadamatorino.it* 🎫 *Staircase and courtyard free, museum €12* 🕐 *Closed Tues.*

Palazzo Reale. This 17th-century palace, a former Savoy royal residence, is an imposing work of brick, stone, and marble that stands on the site of one of Turin's ancient Roman city gates. In contrast to its sober exterior, the two main floors of the palace's interior are swathed in luxurious rococo trappings, including tapestries, gilt ceilings, and sumptuous 17th- to 19th-century furniture. You also can head down to the basement and the old kitchens to see where food for the last kings of Italy was once dished up. The **Armeria Reale** (Royal Armory) wing holds one of Europe's most extensive collections of arms and armor. Note that certain parts of the palace are closed on varying days. ✉ *Piazzetta Reale 1, Centro* ☎ *011/4361455* ⊕ *www.ilpalazzorealeditorino.it* 🎫 *€12, includes Armeria Reale, Galleria Sabauda, and Museo Archeologico* 🕐 *Closed Mon.*

Piazza San Carlo. Surrounded by shops, arcades, fashionable cafés, and elegant Baroque palaces, this is one of the most beautiful squares in Turin. In the center stands a statue of Duke Emanuele Filiberto of Savoy, the victor at the battle of San Quintino, in 1557. The melee heralded the peaceful resurgence of Turin under the Savoy after years of bloody dynastic fighting. The fine bronze statue erected in the 19th century is one of Turin's symbols. At the southern end of the square, framing the continuation of Via Roma, are the twin Baroque churches of San Carlo and Santa Cristina. ✉ *Piazza San Carlo, Centro.*

San Lorenzo. Architect, priest, and mathematician Guarino Guarini was in his mid-sixties when he began this church in 1668. The masterful use of geometric forms and the theatrical control of light and shadow show him working at his mature and confident best. ■TIP→ **Stand in the center of the church and look up into the cupola to appreciate the full effect.** ✉ *Via Palazzo di Città 4, Centro* ☎ *011/4361527* ⊕ *www.sanlorenzo.torino.it.*

ALONG THE PO

The Po River is narrow and unprepossessing here in Turin, only a hint of the broad waterway that it becomes as it flows eastward toward the Adriatic. It's flanked, however, by formidable edifices, a park, and a lovely pedestrian path.

TOP ATTRACTIONS

FAMILY **Borgo Medioevale.** Along the banks of the Po, this complex, built for a General Exhibition in 1884, is a faithful reproduction of a typical Piedmont village in the Middle Ages. Crafts shops, houses, a church, and stores are clustered in the narrow lanes, and in the center of the village is the **Rocca Medioevale**, a medieval castle that's its main attraction. ✉ *Viale Virgilio 107, San Salvario* ☎ *011/4431701* ⊕ *www.borgomedioevaletorino.it* 🎫 *Village free, Rocca Medioevale €6, Garden €3.*

FAMILY
Fodor'sChoice
★

Museo dell'Automobile. No visit to this motor city would be complete without a pilgrimage to see the perfectly preserved Bugattis, Ferraris, and Isotta Fraschinis at this museum. Here you can get an idea of the importance of FIAT—and cars in general—to Turin's economy. There's a collection of antique cars from as early as 1896, and displays show

how the city has changed over the years as a result of the auto industry. ✉ *Corso Unità d'Italia 40, Millefonti* ☎ *011/677666* ⊕ *www.museoauto.it* ✉ *€12.*

Parco del Valentino. This pleasant riverside park is a great place to stroll, bike, or jog. Originally the grounds of a relatively simple hunting lodge, the park owes its present arrangement to Madama Maria Cristina of France, who received the land and lodge as a wedding present after her marriage to Vittorio Amedeo I of Savoy. With memories of 16th-century French châteaux in mind, she began work in 1620 and converted the lodge into a magnificent palace, the **Castello del Valentino.** The building, now home to the University of Turin's Faculty of Architecture, is not open to the public. Next to the palace are the university's **botanical gardens,** established in 1729, where local and exotic flora can be seen in a hothouse, herbarium, and arboretum. ✉ *Parco del Valentino, San Salvario* ☎ *011/6705970 botanical gardens* ⊕ *www.ortobotanico.unito. it* ✉ *Botanical gardens €5* ⊘ *Botanical gardens closed Nov.–mid-Apr.*

Fodor's Choice ★ **Pinacoteca Giovanni e Marella Agnelli.** This gallery was opened by Gianni Agnelli (1921–2003), the head of FIAT and patriarch of one of Italy's most powerful families, just four months before his death. The emphasis here is on quality rather than quantity: 25 works of art from the Agnelli private collection are on permanent display, along with temporary exhibitions. There are four magnificent scenes of Venice by Canaletto (1697–1768); two splendid views of Dresden by Canaletto's nephew, Bernardo Bellotto (1720–80); several works by Manet (1832–83), Renoir (1841–1919), Matisse (1869–1954), and Picasso (1881–1973); and fine examples of the work of Italian futurist painters Balla (1871–1958) and Severini (1883–1966). The gallery is on the top floor of the **Lingotto,** a former FIAT factory that was completely transformed between 1982 and 2002 by architect Renzo Piano. The multilevel complex now holds a shopping mall, several movie theaters, restaurants, two hotels, and an auditorium. ■**TIP➔ Don't miss the beautifully preserved spiral ramps that once took cars up and down the original building.** ✉ *Via Nizza 230, Lingotto* ☎ *011/0062713* ⊕ *www.pinacoteca-agnelli. it* ✉ *€10, €8 without temporary exhibitions* ⊘ *Closed Mon.*

WORTH NOTING

Basilica di Superga. Visible from miles around, this thoroughly Baroque church was designed by Juvarra in the early 18th century and, since 1731, has been the burial place of kings: no fewer than 58 members of the Savoy family are memorialized in the crypt. ✉ *Strada Basilica di Superga 75, Sassi* ☎ *011/8997456* ⊕ *www.basilicadisuperga.com* ✉ *Basilica free, crypt €5* ⊘ *Closed Wed.*

FAMILY **Sassi-Superga Cog Train.** The 18-minute ride from Sassi up the Superga hill is a real treat on a clear day. The view of the Alps is magnificent at the hilltop **Parco Naturale Collina Torinese,** a tranquil retreat from the bustle of the city. If you feel like a little exercise, you can walk back down to Sassi (about two hours) on one of the well-marked wooded trails that start from the upper station. Other circular trails lead through the park and back to Superga. Note that a bus replaces the train on Tuesdays, although the ride up the hill is still just as lovely. ✉ *Piazza*

G. Modena, Sassi ☎ *800/019152 toll-free in Italy* 🌐 *www.gtt.to.it/cms/turismo/sassisup* 🎟 *€4 one-way on weekdays, €6 one-way on weekends* 🕓 *Closed Wed.*

WHERE TO EAT

$$$ PIEDMONTESE Fodor's Choice ★

🍴 **Al Garamond.** The well-spaced tables and the ancient brick vaulting in this small, bright space set the stage for traditional meat and seafood dishes served with creative flair. Try the tantalizing *rombo in crosta di patate al barbera* (turbot wrapped in sliced potatoes and baked with barbera wine) or the equally delicious *brasatura della guancetta di vitella su vellutata di cavolfiori* (braised veal cheek with creamed cauliflower). **Known for:** attentive staff; traditional dishes with a twist; tasting menus. [$] *Average main: €25* ✉ *Via G. Pomba 14, Centro* ☎ *011/8122781* 🌐 *www.algaramond.it* 🕓 *Closed Aug. No lunch weekends.*

$$$ PIEDMONTESE Fodor's Choice ★

🍴 **Casa Vicina.** Hidden away in the basement of the Lingotto food emporium, this is one of Turin's top destinations for fine dining. The decor is starkly modern and, without windows, it might seem claustrophobic to some, but the food makes up for everything. **Known for:** modern decor; encyclopedic wine list; inventive northern Piedmont dishes like Russian salad and pasta with veal. [$] *Average main: €30* ✉ *Via Nizza 224, Lingotto* ☎ *011/19506840* 🌐 *www.casavicina.com* 🕓 *Closed Mon. No dinner Sun.*

$$ PIEDMONTESE

🍴 **Consorzio.** Extremely popular for lunch during the week, this lively and informal osteria is in Turin's business district. The service is relaxed, the decor low-key, and the menu highlights organic meats and vegetables from the region. **Known for:** organic meats and produce; Piedmont wines; popular lunch spot. [$] *Average main: €16* ✉ *Via Monte di Pietà 23, Centro* ☎ *011/2767661* 🌐 *www.ristoranteconsorzio.it* 🕓 *Closed Sun. No lunch Sat.*

$$ TUSCAN

🍴 **Da Mauro.** This bustling spot in the center of Turin's business district teems with locals at both lunch and dinner. After a flux of Tuscan migrants moved to Turin in the '60s, Da Mauro was one of the first restaurants to cater to their tastes. **Known for:** Tuscan dishes; well-prepared meats and seafood; efficient service. [$] *Average main: €15* ✉ *Via Maria Vittoria 21, Centro* ☎ *011/8170604* 💳 *No credit cards* 🕓 *Closed Mon.*

$$$$ PIEDMONTESE

🍴 **Del Cambio.** Set in a palace dating from 1757, this is one of Europe's most beautiful and historic restaurants, with decorative moldings, mirrors, and hanging lamps that look just as they did when Italian national hero Cavour dined here more than a century ago. The cuisine draws heavily on Piedmontese tradition and is paired with fine wines of the region. **Known for:** regional wine pairings; historical, lavish setting; inventive meat dishes. [$] *Average main: €38* ✉ *Piazza Carignano 2, Centro* ☎ *011/546690* 🌐 *www.delcambio.it* 🕓 *Closed Mon. No dinner Sun.; no lunch Tues.*

$ PIEDMONTESE

🍴 **Pastificio Defilippis.** Famous for freshly made pasta since 1872, this shop also serves pasta creations to a packed lunch crowd all week long. Depending on the season, some of the favorites include *rigatoni all'arrabbiata* (with a spicy tomato and meat sauce) and *agnolotti di* *prosciutto e zucchine al burro* (with ham, zucchini, and melted butter). **Known for:** classic fresh pasta; indoor and outdoor dining ; seasonal sauces. [$] *Average main: €13* ✉ *Via Lagrange 39, Centro* ☎ *011/542137* 🌐 *www.pastificiodefilippis.it* 💳 *No credit cards.*

$$$ SEAFOOD 🍴 **Trattoria Anna.** If you are hankering for something different from the usual meat-based Piedmontese cuisine, give this simple, extremely popular, family-run spot a try. They serve only seafood, and they do it well. **Known for:** seafood-focused menu; popular with locals; family-run. [$] *Average main: €25* ✉ *Via Bellezia 20, Centro* ☎ *011/4362134* ⏲ *Closed Mon., and 2 wks in Aug. No lunch.*

$$$ NORTHERN ITALIAN 🍴 **Vintage 1997.** The first floor of an elegant town house in the center of Turin makes a fitting location for this sophisticated restaurant. You might try such specialties as *vitello tonnato alla vecchia maniera* (roast veal with a light tuna sauce made without mayonnaise) or *merluzzo in crosta di erbette con patate e scalogno caramellato* (cod fillet in a crust of herbs served with potatoes and caramelized scallions). **Known for:** extensive wine list; sophisticated crowd; multi-course set menu. [$] *Average main: €25* ✉ *Piazza Solferino 16/h, Centro* ☎ *011/535948* 🌐 *www.vintage1997.com* ⏲ *Closed Sun. No lunch Sat.*

WHERE TO STAY

The Turin Tourist Information Center provides a booking service for accommodations in the city and throughout the region. Book hotels through them at least 48 hours in advance, B&Bs at least seven days in advance.

$$ HOTEL 🏨 **Genio.** Although they're just steps away from the main train station, these spacious and tastefully decorated rooms are a quiet haven from the bustle of the city. **Pros:** close to the central train station; very friendly service. **Cons:** 15-minute walk to the center of town; area around the hotel is a little seedy. [$] *Rooms from: €170* ✉ *Corso Vittorio Emanuele II 47, Centro* ☎ *011/6505771* 🌐 *www.hotelgenio.it* 🛏 *115 rooms* 🍽 *Free Breakfast.*

$$ HOTEL 🏨 **Grand Hotel Sitea.** One of the city's finest hotels, the Sitea is in the historic center and decorated in a warmly classical style; the public areas and guest rooms are elegant, spacious, and comfortable. **Pros:** central location; well-appointed rooms; large bathrooms. **Cons:** air-conditioning can be noisy; carpets are a little worn. [$] *Rooms from: €139* ✉ *Via Carlo Alberto 35, Centro* ☎ *011/5170171* 🌐 *www.grandhotelsitea.it* 🛏 *120 rooms* 🍽 *Free Breakfast.*

$$ HOTEL 🏨 **LingottoTech.** Designed by architect Renzo Piano, this luxury hotel is part of the former Lingotto FIAT factory. **Pros:** interesting design and location; good weekend rates sometimes available. **Cons:** outside the city center; many signs of wear and tear. [$] *Rooms from: €150* ✉ *Via Nizza 262, Lingotto* ☎ *011/6642000* 🌐 *www.nh-hotels.it/hotel/nh-torino-lingotto-tech* 🛏 *240 rooms* 🍽 *Free Breakfast.*

$$ HOTEL Fodor's Choice ★ 🏨 **Victoria.** Rare style, attention to detail, and comfort are the hallmarks of this in-town retreat that's furnished and managed along the lines of a refined English town house. **Pros:** tranquil location in the center of town; excellent spa facilities; wonderful breakfast. **Cons:** standard

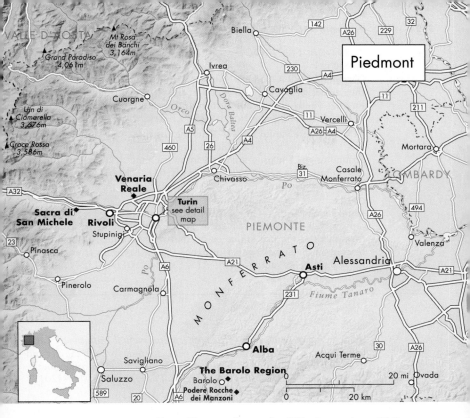

rooms are small; parking nearby can be difficult; no views. $ *Rooms from: €150* ⊠ *Via Nino Costa 4, Centro* ☎ *011/5611909* ⊕ *www.hotel-victoria-torino.com* ⇔ *106 rooms* ⦵ *Free Breakfast.*

NIGHTLIFE AND PERFORMING ARTS

NIGHTLIFE

Two areas of Turin are enormously popular nightlife destinations: the Quadrilatero, to the north of the city center, and the Murazzi embankment, near the Ponte Vittorio Emanuele I. The center of town is also popular, especially earlier in the evening.

Caffè Elena. This wine bar is a trendy place for an aperitif or for a drink before going clubbing. It's in the large piazza at the end of Via Po. ⊠ *Piazza Vittorio Veneto 5, Centro* ☎ *011/3295767414.*

Pastis. The Quadrilatero Romano, which roughly corresponds to the grid pattern of Roman Turin near Piazza della Reppublica, is a hopping area filled with nightclubs and ethnic restaurants. Places open and close with startling frequency here, but Pastis has shown considerable staying power—several local cultural groups hold their meetings in the bar. ⊠ *Piazza Emanuele Filiberto 9b, Centro* ☎ *011/5211085.*

PERFORMING ARTS

MUSIC

Giovanni Agnelli Auditorium. Classical music concerts are held at the theater designed by Renzo Piano in the renovated Lingotto building; internationally famous conductors and orchestras are frequent guests. ⊠ *Via Nizza 280, Lingotto* ☎ *011/6313721* ⊕ *www.lingottomusica.it.*

MITO Settembre Musica Festival. Running for three weeks in September, this popular festival of classical music is held in a variety of venues around town. The program of performances and tickets become available in June each year. ⊠ *Via Meucci 4* ☎ *011/01124777* ⊕ *www.mito-settembremusica.it.*

OPERA

Teatro Regio. Premieres at the Teatro Regio, one of Italy's leading opera houses, sell out well in advance. You can buy tickets for most performances at the box office or on the website, where discounts are offered on the day of the performance. The season runs from October through July. ⊠ *Piazza Castello 215, Centro* ☎ *011/8815241* ⊕ *www.teatroregio.torino.it.*

SPORTS AND THE OUTDOORS

BICYCLING

Ufficio Iniziative Ambientali (*Office for Environmental Initiatives*). Turin has about 160 km (100 miles) of bike paths running through the city and its parks. Bicycles are available for daily rental at stands throughout the city all year. ⊠ *Via Padova 29, Madonna di Campagna* ☎ *011/4420177* ⊕ *www.comune.torino.it/bici.*

SHOPPING

Many people know that Turin produces more than 75% of Italy's cars, but they're often unaware that it's also a hub for clothing manufacturing. Top-quality boutiques stocking local, national, and international lines are clustered along Via Roma and Via Garibaldi. Piazza San Carlo, Via Po, and Via Maria Vittoria are lined with antiques shops, some of which specialize in 18th-century furniture and domestic items.

CHOCOLATE

The Italian tradition of making chocolate began in Turin during the early 17th century. Chocolate at that time was an aristocratic drink, but in the 19th century a Piedmontese invention made it possible to further refine cocoa to create solid bars and candies.

Peyrano. The most famous of all Turin chocolates is the wedge-shape gianduiotto, flavored with hazelnuts and first concocted in 1867. The tradition has been continued at this family-run shop, where more than 80 types of chocolates are made. ⊠ *Corso Moncalieri 47, Centro* ☎ *011/6602202* ⊕ *www.peyrano.com/en.*

Stratta. In business since 1836, this famed shop sells confectionery of all kinds—not just the chocolates in the lavish window displays but also fancy cookies, rum-laced fudges, and magnificent cakes. ⊠ *Piazza San Carlo 191, Centro* ☏ *011/547920* ⊕ *www.stratta1836.it.*

MARKETS

Balon Flea Market. Go to this famous market on Saturday morning for bargains on secondhand books, antiques, and clothing. There is good browsing to be had among the stalls, which spill out of Borgo Dora into the surrounding side streets. During the second weekend of every month, the market extends its hours into Sunday, becoming the so-called Gran Balon. (Be aware, however, that the market is also famous for its pickpockets.) ⊠ *Borgo Dora, Centro* ⊕ *www.balon.it.*

Fodor'sChoice
★
Mercato di Porta Palazzo. For food lovers, people-watchers, or anyone interested in the lively local scene, the immensely popular market in this huge square to the north of town is not to be missed. Outdoors, the keepers of hundreds of vegetable stalls vie with one another to create the most appetizing displays. Indoors, the meat vendors provide an equally tantalizing array of local products, while the fishmongers proudly display the fresh catch of the day. ⊠ *Piazza della Repubblica, Centro* ⊕ *www.scopriportapalazzo.com.*

SPECIALTY FOOD AND DELIS

Borgiattino. Specialty food stores and delicatessens abound in central Turin, but for a truly spectacular array of cheeses and other delicacies this should be your first stop. ⊠ *Corso Vinzaglio 29, Centro* ☏ *011/5629075* ⊕ *www.borgiattino.com.*

Eataly. Now with branches in Milan, Bologna, New York, and Tokyo, this is probably Turin's most famous food emporium. In addition to a food market, food-related bookstore, kitchen equipment, and a wine bar, there are several different food counters and restaurants serving hamburgers, haute cuisine, and lots more in between. ⊠ *Via Nizza 230, Lingotto* ☏ *011/19506801* ⊕ *www.eatalytorino.it.*

THE MONFERRATO AND THE LANGHE

Southeast of Turin, in the hilly, wooded area around Asti known as the Monferrato, and farther south in a similar area around Alba known as the Langhe, the landscape is a patchwork of vineyards and dark woods, dotted with hill towns and castles. This is wine country, producing some of Italy's most famous reds and sparkling whites. And hidden away in the woods are the secret places where hunters and their dogs unearth the precious, aromatic truffles worth their weight in gold at Alba's truffle fair.

ASTI

60 km (37 miles) southeast of Turin.

Asti is best known outside Italy for its wines—excellent reds as well as the famous sparkling white *spumante*. The town itself has some impressive reminders of the days when its strategic position on trade routes between Turin, Milan, and Genoa gave it broad economic power. In the 12th century Asti began to develop as a republic, at a time when other

Italian cities were also flexing their economic and military muscles. It flourished in the following century, when the inhabitants began erecting lofty towers (west end of Corso Vittorio Alfieri) for its defense. As in Pavia, near Milan, this gave rise to the medieval nickname "city of a hundred towers." In the center of Asti some of these remain, among them the 13th-century **Torre Comentina** and the well-preserved **Torre Troyana**, a tall, slender tower attached to the **Palazzo Troya**. The 18th-century church of **Santa Caterina** has incorporated one of Asti's medieval towers, the **Torre Romana** (itself built on an ancient Roman base), as its bell tower. Corso Vittorio Alfieri is Asti's main thoroughfare, running west–east across the city. This road, known in medieval times as Contrada Maestra, was built by the Romans.

GETTING HERE AND AROUND
Asti is less than an hour away from Turin by car on the A21. GTT bus service connects the two towns, but isn't direct. Train service to Asti, on the other hand, is frequent and fast.

FESTIVALS
Douja d'Or National Wine Festival. For 10 days in mid-September, Asti is host to a popular wine festival—an opportunity to see Asti and celebrate the product that made it famous. During the course of the festival a competition is held to award "Oscars" to the best wine producers, and stands for wine tastings allow visitors to judge the winners for themselves. Musical events and other activities accompany the festival. Check the festival's website for the schedule of events. ☒ *Asti* ☎ *0141/530357 tourist office* ⊕ *www.doujador.it.*

Palio di Asti. September is a month of fairs and celebrations in Asti, and this horse race that runs through the streets of town is the highlight. First mentioned in 1275, this annual event has been going strong ever since. After an elaborate procession in period costumes, nine horses and jockeys representing different sections of town vie for the honor of claiming the *palio,* a symbolic flag of victory. The race happens on a Sunday at the beginning of September each year. ☒ *Asti* ⊕ *www. comune.asti.it/pagina875_il-palio-di-asti.html.*

VISITOR INFORMATION
Contact Asti Tourism Office. ☒ *Piazza Alfieri 34* ☎ *0141/530357* ⊕ *www. astiturismo.it.*

EXPLORING
Duomo. Dedicated to the Assumption of the Virgin, the Duomo is an object lesson in Italian Gothic architecture. Built in the early 14th century, it is decorated so as to emphasize geometry and verticality: pointed arches and narrow vaults are completely covered with frescoes that help the eye to soar upward. The porch on the south side of the cathedral facing the square was built in 1470; it represents the Gothic style at its most florid and excessive. ☒ *Piazza Cattedrale 1* ☎ *0141/592924.*

San Secondo. This Gothic church is dedicated to Asti's patron saint, believed by some to have been decapitated by the Emperor Hadrian on this very spot. San Secondo is also the patron of the city's favorite folklore and sporting event, the annual Palio di Asti, a colorful medieval-style horse race that's similar to Siena's. It's held each year on a Sunday in early September in the vast Campo del Palio to the south of the church. ✉ *Piazza San Secondo, south of Corso Vittorio Alfieri* ☎ *0141/530066.*

WHERE TO EAT AND STAY

$$$ PIEDMONTESE 🍴 **Gener Neuv.** Run by the same family for three generations, this restaurant, one of Italy's finest, is known for its superb food. Regional specialties may include agnolotti *ai tre stufati* (with fillings of ground rabbit, veal, and pork) or the equally delicious ravioli *ripieni di baccalà su passato di finocchi* (filled with salt cold with fennel sauce). **Known for:** first-rate wine list; regionally focused house specialties; fixed-price menus. [$] *Average main: €27* ✉ *Via Carlo Leone Grande 3* ☎ *0141/557270* 🌐 *www.generneuv.it* 🕒 *Closed Mon., and Aug. No dinner Sun.*

$$ PIEDMONTESE 🍴 **L'Angolo del Beato.** Regional specialties such as *bagna cauda* (literally "hot bath," a dip for vegetables made with anchovies, garlic, butter, and olive oil) and *tagliolini al ragu di anatra* (pasta with a duck sauce) are the main attractions at this Asti institution, housed in a building that dates to the 12th century. There's also an extensive list of several hundred Piedmont wines. **Known for:** extensive Piedmont wine list; regional dishes; 12th-century building. [$] *Average main: €15* ✉ *Vicolo Cavalleri 2* ☎ *0141/531668* 🌐 *www.angolodelbeato.it* 🕒 *Closed Sun., 1st wk of Jan., and 3 wks in Aug.*

$ B&B/INN 🏨 **Reale.** Spacious rooms in a 19th-century building on Asti's main square are eclectically decorated, with a mix of contemporary and period furniture. **Pros:** spacious rooms; central location. **Cons:** lobby area is a little worn; rooms facing the main square can be noisy. [$] *Rooms from: €110* ✉ *Piazza Alfieri 5* ☎ *0141/530240* 🌐 *www.hotelristorantereale.it* 🛏 *26 rooms* 🍽 *Free Breakfast.*

$ HOTEL 🏨 **Relais Sant'Uffizio.** It's surprising to know that this now delightfully peaceful and elegant retreat, with a luxurious spa and swimming pool, surrounded by vineyards and rolling hills, was home to the Inquisition in the 16th century. **Pros:** tranquil and beautiful location; excellent spa and exercise facilities; very good value. **Cons:** 20 km (12 miles) north of Asti and isolated; private transportation required. [$] *Rooms from: €119* ✉ *Strada Sant Uffizio 1, Cioccaro di Penango* ☎ *0141/916292* 🌐 *www.relaissantuffizio.com* 🛏 *41 rooms* 🍽 *Free Breakfast.*

SHOPPING

Tuit. This shop and café on a quiet street just off Piazza Alfieri is a branch of Turin's Eataly food emporium. It's a great place to shop for local and regional food specialties or to enjoy a light meal. Both the *tortino di melanzane di pomodori pachino* (eggplant flan with Sicilian cherry tomatoes) and the risotto *mantecato alla zucca e amaretti* (with butter, pumpkin, and amaretti cookies) are delicious. ✉ *Via Carlo Grandi 3* ☎ *0141/095813* 🌐 *www.generneuv.it.*

ALBA

30 km (18 miles) southwest of Asti.

This small town has a gracious atmosphere and a compact core, studded with medieval towers and Gothic buildings. In addition to being a wine center of the region, Alba is known as the "City of the White Truffle" for dirty little tubers that cost as much as €2,200 a pound. For picking out your truffle and having a few wisps shaved on top of your food, expect to shell out an extra €16 or so—which may be worth it, at least once.

GETTING HERE AND AROUND

By car from Turin follow the A6 south to Marene and then take the A33 east. The A33 autostrada connects Asti and Alba. GTT offers frequent bus service between Alba and Turin—the journey takes approximately 1½ hours. There's no direct train service, but you can get to Alba from Turin by making one transfer in Asti, Bra, or Cavallermaggiore; the entire trip takes about 1½ hours.

FESTIVALS

Fodor's Choice ★ **Fiera Internazionale del Tartufo Bianco** (*International White Truffle Fair*). From early October to mid- to late November, Alba hosts an internationally famous truffle fair, held on weekends. Merchants, chefs, and other aficionados of this pungent, yet delicious, fungus come from all over the world to buy and to taste white truffles at the height of their season. Although the affair is very commercialized, it still makes Alba a great place to visit in the fall. ■ TIP→ **Hotel and restaurant reservations for October and November should be made well in advance.** ✉ *Piazza Medford 2* ☎ *0173/361051* 🌐 *www.fieradeltartufo.org.*

VISITOR INFORMATION

Contact Alba Tourism Office. ✉ *Piazza Risorgimento 2* ☎ *0173/35833* 🌐 *www.langheroero.it.*

WHERE TO EAT

$$ PIEDMONTESE 🍴 **La Libera.** Modern and subdued, this small spot on a quiet backstreet is conducive to slow, relaxed dining. The antipasti include a splendid *piatto della tradizione* (an array of typical Piedmont starters). **Known for:** Barolo wines; superb meat dishes and cheese selection; slow, relaxed atmosphere. [$] *Average main: €20* ✉ *Via Elvio Pertinace 24a* ☎ *0173/293155* 🌐 *www.lalibera.com* ⏲ *Closed Sun., 3 wks in Aug. and late Dec.–mid.-Jan.*

$$$ PIEDMONTESE Fodor's Choice ★ 🍴 **Locanda del Pilone.** The elegant, formal dining room of the Locanda del Pilone hotel is one of the best restaurants in the region (with a Michelin star to prove it) and serves refined variations of traditional dishes. The *scamone di fassone* (rump of Fassone veal which can be served with Jewish artichoke and cheese) is as delicious as it is unusual. **Known for:** refined traditional dishes; vast, more than 1,400-label wine list; formal dining setting. [$] *Average main: €25* ✉ *Località Madonna di Como 34* ☎ *0173/366616* 🌐 *www.locandadelpilone.com* ⏲ *Closed Tues. and Wed.*

$$$ PIEDMONTESE Fodor's Choice ★ 🍴 **Massimo Camia.** Chef Massimo Camia's restaurant is in an elegant and modern space, with views of the Barolo vineyards that surround the Damilano winery; the service is impeccable and the food is divine. Try the well-prepared and inventive meat and seafood dishes. **Known for:** vineyard views; excellent service; amuse-bouche and wine pairings. [$] *Average main: €28* ✉ *Via Alba–Barolo 122, La Morra* ☎ *0173/56355* 🌐 *www.massimocamia.it* ⏲ *Closed Tues. No lunch Wed.*

$$ PIEDMONTESE 🍴 **Osteria dell'Arco.** Delicious, hearty dishes using local ingredients are served here in a lovely setting. Expect lots of game such as duck, rabbit, and deer, but you'll also find a nice selection of seafood dishes with a hint of nearby Liguria flavors. **Known for:** local ingredients; game and seafood dishes; Ligurian flavors. [$] *Average main: €16* ✉ *Piazza Savona 5* ☎ *0173/363974* 🌐 *www.osteriadellarco.it* ⏲ *Closed Sun.*

$$ PIEDMONTESE 🍴 **Osteria Italia.** A short drive from the center of Alba brings you to the hamlet of San Rocco Seno d'Elvio and this old-style trattoria. The decor is as simple as the menu, which makes a pleasant change from the more elaborate restaurants that you often find in the center of the city. **Known for:** black and white truffle dishes, depending on the season; rustic trattoria setting; traditional menu. [$] *Average main: €15* ✉ *Frazione San Rocco Seno d'Elvio 6, 5 km (3 miles) southeast of Alba* ☎ *0173/286942* 🌐 *www.osteriaitalia.it.*

$$ PIEDMONTESE 🍴 **L'indeito: Vigin Mudest.** Delicious regional specialties are served at this bustling, family-run restaurant in the center of Alba. There's a fixed-price tasting menu, and their version of *carne cruda albese* (beef carpaccio in the style of Alba) is a favorite with the locals who flock here. **Known for:** regional meat and pasta dishes; tasting menu; local crowd. [$] *Average main: €18* ✉ *Via Vernazza 11* ☎ *0173/441701* 🌐 *ineditoviginmudest.myadj.it/v/ineditoviginmudest* ⏲ *Closed Wed.*

8

$$ WINE BAR 🍴 **Vincafè.** This excellent *enoteca* specializes in tastes of Langhe wines, accompanied by *salumi* (cured meats), cheeses, and other regional products. On the menu, you'll find a whole range of Piedmont specialties including *tajarin al ragù di salsiccia di Bra* (egg pasta with Bra sausage sauce) which is particularly good. **Known for:** Langhe wine pairings; Piedmont specialties; late-night dining. [$] *Average main: €15* ✉ *Via Emanuele 12* ☎ *0173/364603* 🌐 *www.vincafe.com.*

WHERE TO STAY

$ B&B/INN 🏨 **La Meridiana.** This lovely manor house is on a hill overlooking the historic center, surrounded by dolcetto and nebbiolo grapevines. **Pros:** friendly, family atmosphere; in a secluded setting convenient for exploring the Langhe; nice views from the many terraces and balconies. **Cons:** long walk to nearest restaurants (though some units have kitchens); no a/c in some rooms. [$] *Rooms from: €100* ✉ *Località Altavilla 9* ☎ *0173/440112* 🌐 *www.villalameridianaalba.it* 💳 *No credit cards* 🛏 *9 rooms* 🍽 *Free Breakfast.*

$$ B&B/INN 🏨 **Locanda del Pilone.** It would be hard to imagine a more commanding position for these simply but tastefully decorated accommodations above Alba. **Pros:** spectacular location with 360-degree views; excellent restaurant. **Cons:** while not far from Alba, you do need a car to get around. [$] *Rooms from: €177* ✉ *Località Madonna di Como 34* ☎ *0173/366616* 🌐 *www.locandadelpilone.it* 🛏 *8 rooms* 🍽 *Free Breakfast.*

$$ B&B/INN [H] **Palazzo Finati.** This carefully restored 19th-century town house has charm and character that set it apart from the other, more business-oriented hotels in Alba. **Pros:** quiet location in the center of town; rooms facing the courtyard have terraces; changing exhibitions of contemporary art adorn the walls. **Cons:** staff coverage is limited at night; breakfast room is a bit gloomy. [$] *Rooms from: €170* ✉ *Via Vernazza 8* ☎ *0173/366324* 🌐 *www.palazzofinati.it* 🕓 *Closed 2 wks in Aug., and Christmas–mid-Jan.* 🛏 *9 rooms* 🍴 *Free Breakfast.*

$$$ HOTEL [H] **Villa Beccaris.** This beautiful property consists of an old villa and two newer buildings in the heart of one of the Langhe's most charming villages. **Pros:** lovely gardens and pool area; located in great village with lots of good restaurants. **Cons:** the classic rooms are on the small side. [$] *Rooms from: €220* ✉ *Via Bava Beccaris 1, Monforte d'Alba* ☎ *0173/78158* 🌐 *www.villabeccaris.com* 🕓 *Closed Jan. 8–Feb. 8* 🛏 *23 rooms* 🍴 *Free Breakfast.*

THE BAROLO REGION

17 km (11 miles) southwest of Alba, 72 km (45 miles) southeast of Turin.

The Langhe district may not get as much attention as other wine-producing regions in Italy, but the payoff for visiting can be just as satisfying. Try to schedule a day trip to one or several of the wine estates here.

GETTING HERE AND AROUND

The easiest way to reach Barolo and its wineries is to drive from Alba.

EXPLORING

Famiglia Anselma. Probably best for wine lovers who have at least reached an intermediate level of fandom, this winery is known for its steadfast commitment to produce only Barolo—nothing else—and for its policy of holding wines for several years before release. The winemaker here, Maurizio Anselma, is something of a prodigy in the Barolo world, and he's quite open to visitors. ✉ *Loc. Castello della Volta, Barolo* ☎ *0173/560511* 🌐 *www.anselma.it.*

Marchesi di Barolo. Right in the town of Barolo, this wine estate makes an easy, if touristy, option for getting to know the local wines. In the estate's user-friendly enoteca you can taste wine, buy thousands of different bottles from vintages going way back, and look at display bottles, including an 1859 Barolo. Marchesi di Barolo's *cantine* (wine cellars), at Via Roma 1, are open daily. ✉ *Via Alba 12, Barolo* ☎ *0173/564491* 🌐 *www.marchesibarolo.com.*

Podere Rocche dei Manzoni. A good, accessible example of the new school of local wine making is this wine estate, about 6 km (4 miles) south of Barolo. The facade of the cantina is like a Roman temple of brick, complete with imposing columns. Rocche dei Manzoni's reds include four Barolos, one dolcetto, two Langhe Rossos, two Langhe D.O.C.s, and two Barbera d'Albas. ✉ *3 Località Manzini Soprano, Monforte d'Alba* ☎ *0173/78421* 🌐 *www.barolobig.com.*

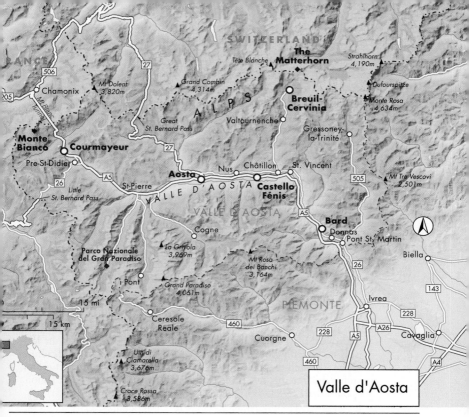

Valle d'Aosta

VALLE D'AOSTA

In Valle d'Aosta, a semiautonomous, bilingual region near the border with France and Switzerland, the unspoiled beauty of the highest peaks in the Alps, the Matterhorn and Monte Bianco, competes with the magnificent scenery of Italy's oldest national park, Gran Paradiso. Luckily, you don't have to choose—the region is small, so you can fit skiing, après-ski, and wild ibex into one memorable trip. The main Aosta Valley, largely on an east–west axis, is hemmed in by high mountains where glaciers have gouged out 14 tributary valleys, 6 to the north and 8 to the south. A car is helpful here, but take care: though distances are relatively short as the crow flies, steep slopes and winding roads add to your mileage and travel time.

Coming up from Turin, beyond Ivrea, the road takes you through steep ravines guarded by brooding, romantic castles. Pont St. Martin, about 18 km (11 miles) north of Ivrea, is the beginning of bilingual (Italian and French) territory.

BARD

65 km (40 miles) north of Turin.

This small medieval town clings to a rocky crag that almost completely blocks the entrance to the Valle d'Aosta from Piedmont. Recognized for its strategic importance since prehistoric times, the location was first fully fortified by the Romans, and then by the Ostrogoths in the 6th century. As befits its military heritage, the village is rather gray and somber, but the magnificent fortress that sits atop it makes a visit well worthwhile.

GETTING HERE AND AROUND

Bard is just off the A5 autostrada, which runs north from Turin into the Valle d'Aosta—by car the trip takes about an hour. Train service from Turin is infrequent, but there's regular service to and from Aosta. Traveling to Bard by bus is not a viable option.

EXPLORING

FAMILY
Fodor's Choice
★

Forte di Bard. A few minutes beyond the French-speaking village of Pont St. Martin, you pass through the narrow Gorge de Bard to reach the fortress that has stood guarding the valley entrance for more than eight centuries. In 1800 Napoléon entered Italy through this valley, using the cover of darkness to get his artillery units past the castle unnoticed. Ten years later he remembered this inconvenience and had the fortress destroyed. It was rebuilt in the 19th century and now houses the lavishly multimedia **Museo delle Alpi**, dedicated to the history and culture of the Alps and the Valle d'Aosta region. There's also a fun section for young children that's dedicated to the geology and history of the region. ⊠ *Bard* ☎ *0125/833811* ⊕ *www.fortedibard.it* ⊡ *€8.*

■ EN
ROUTE

Between Bard and the town of Donnas, 5 km (3 miles) south along the S26, you can walk on a short but fascinating section of a 1st-century Roman consular road that passed here on its way to France. Still showing the deeply worn tracks left by the passage of cart and chariot wheels, this section of road includes an archway carved through solid rock (used during the Middle Ages as the city gate of Donnas) and a milestone ("XXXVI," to indicate 36 Roman miles from Aosta).

BREUIL-CERVINIA/THE MATTERHORN

50 km (30 miles) north of Bard, 116 km (72 miles) north of Turin.

Sitting in a huge natural basin at the foot of the Matterhorn, this town, once a high Alpine pasture, grew to become one of Europe's most famous ski areas, when a road connecting it to the Valle d'Aosta was completed in 1934. It bustles in the winter and has become a popular spot for hikers in the summer, but it's sleepy for much of the rest of the year.

GETTING HERE AND AROUND

From Aosta take the A5 and then the SR46 (1 hour); from Turin take the A5 and then the SR46 (90 minutes). SADEM has regular bus service from Turin; SAVDA buses travel here from Milan. Breuil-Cervinia isn't on a train line.

VISITOR INFORMATION

Contact Breuil-Cervinia Tourism Office. ✉ *Piazzale Funivie, Breuil-Cervinia* ☎ *0166/944311* 🌐 *www.cervinia.it.*

EXPLORING

Matterhorn (*Monte Cervino in Italian; Mont Cervin in French*). The famous peak straddles the border between Italy and Switzerland, and all sightseeing and skiing facilities are operated jointly. Splendid views of the peak can be seen from **Plateau Rosa** and the **Cresta del Furggen,** both of which can be reached by cable car from the center of Breuil-Cervinia. Although many locals complain that the tourist facilities and condominiums have changed the face of their beloved village, the cable car does give access to climbing and off-trail skiing in ridges that were once inaccessible. ✉ *Breuil-Cervinia* 🌐 *www.lovevda.it.*

WHERE TO STAY

$ B&B/INN 🏨 **Cime Bianche.** This calm, quiet mountain lodge offers commanding views of the Matterhorn and surrounding peaks from the balconies of its simply furnished, wood-paneled guest rooms. **Pros:** next to the ski slopes; great restaurant; lovely views. **Cons:** lobby is showing wear; busy during the ski season; location is far from everything but slopes. [$] *Rooms from: €90* ✉ *Località La Vieille 44, near ski lift, Breuil-Cervinia* ☎ *0166/949046* 🌐 *www.hotelcimebianche.com* 🕒 *Closed May and June* 🛏 *13 rooms* 🍴 *No meals.*

$$$$ RESORT 🏨 **Hermitage.** The entryway's marble relief of St. Theodolus reminds you that this was the site of a hermitage, but asceticism has given way to comfort and elegance—a fire is always glowing in the enormous hearth, the dining room is candlelit, the bright bedrooms have balconies, and the suites have antique fireplaces and 18th-century furnishings. **Pros:** superlative staff; refined atmosphere; frequent shuttle service into town and to ski lifts. **Cons:** located 2 km (1 mile) from the town center; half board is mandatory during the winter season; very expensive. [$] *Rooms from: €350* ✉ *Via Piolet 1, Località Chapellette, Breuil-Cervinia* ☎ *0166/948998* 🌐 *www.hotelhermitage.com* 🕒 *Closed May, June, Sept., Oct., and Nov.* 🛏 *47 rooms* 🍴 *No meals.*

$$$ B&B/INN 🏨 **Les Neiges d'Antan.** In an evergreen forest at Perrères, just outside Cervinia, this family-run inn is quiet and cozy, with three big fireplaces and a nice view of the Matterhorn. **Pros:** secluded and beautiful setting; excellent restaurant; well-designed spa facilities. **Cons:** 5 km (3 miles) outside Breuil-Cervinia (a car is essential); entrance and lobby areas are showing some wear. [$] *Rooms from: €240* ✉ *Frazione Perrères 10, Breuil-Cervinia* ☎ *0166/948775* 🌐 *www.lesneigesdantan.com* 🕒 *Closed May and June* 🛏 *24 rooms* 🍴 *Free Breakfast.*

SPORTS AND THE OUTDOORS

CLIMBING

Serious climbers can make the ascent of the Matterhorn from Breuil-Cervinia after registering with the local mountaineering officials at the tourist office. This ascent is for experienced climbers only. Less demanding hikes follow the lower slopes of the valley of the River Marmore, to the south of town.

Società delle Guide Alpine. The Society's guides are available to accompany you on treks and also lead skiing, canyoning, and ice-climbing excursions. ⊠ *Strada Villair 2, Courmayeur* ☎ *0165/842064* ⊕ *www.guidecourmayeur.com.*

SKIING

Sixty lifts and a few hundred miles of ski runs ranging from beginner to expert make Breuil-Cervinia one of the best and most popular resort areas in Italy. Because the slopes border a glacier, there's skiing year-round.

CASTELLO FÉNIS

34 km (22 miles) northwest of Bard, 104 km (65 miles) north of Turin.

The tiny town of Fénis owes its origins to the presence of the medieval castle that once provided shelter for the local peasants that lived nearby. Today, the population of the town is less than 2,000, with most either farmers or part of the tourist industry.

GETTING HERE AND AROUND

To reach the castle by car, take the Nus exit from the main A5 autostrada. SAVDA buses provide infrequent service between Aosta and Fénis. The closest train station, in Nus, is a 5-km (3-mile) walk from the castle.

EXPLORING

FAMILY

Fodor'sChoice

★

Castello Fénis. The best-preserved medieval fortress in Valle d'Aosta, this many-turreted castle was built in the mid-14th century by Aimone di Challant, a member of a prolific family related to the Savoys. The castle, which used a double ring of walls for its defense, would make a perfect setting for a fairy tale, given its pointed towers, portcullises, and spiral staircases. The 15th-century courtyard surrounded by wooden balconies is elegantly decorated with well-preserved frescoes. Inside you can see the kitchen, with an enormous fireplace that provided central heat in winter; the armory; and the spacious, well-lighted rooms used by the lord and lady of the manor. If you have time to visit only one castle in Valle d'Aosta, this should be it. ⊠ *Località Chez-Sapin 1, Fénis* ☎ *0165/764263* ⊕ *www.lovevda.it* 🎫 *€7.*

AOSTA

12 km (7 miles) west of Castello Fénis, 113 km (70 miles) north of Turin.

Aosta stands at the junction of two of the important trade routes that connect France and Italy, the valleys of the Rhône and the Isère. Its significance as a trading post was recognized by the Romans, who built a garrison here in the 1st century BC, and the present-day layout of the streets is the clearest example you'll find of Roman urban planning in Italy. Well-preserved Roman walls form a perfect rectangle around the center, and the regular pattern of streets reflects its role as a military stronghold. Although its gray-stone buildings and slate roofing give the town a rather cold feeling, Aosta has recently begun to appear on several lists as one of the most livable towns in Italy.

GETTING HERE AND AROUND

Aosta can easily be reached by car or bus from Milan and Turin. The town is off the main A5 autostrada. SAVDA buses regularly travel to and from Milan, Turin, and Chamonix in France. Direct train service (2 hours) is also available from Turin, but a change of trains is required if traveling here from Milan (3 hours).

FESTIVALS

Sant'Orso Fair. On the last weekend of January, the streets of Aosta are brightened by an arts-and-crafts market that brings artisans from all over the Valle d'Aosta. All the traditional techniques are featured: wood carving and sculpture, soapstone work, wrought iron, leather, wool, lace, and household items of all kinds. Food and wine are sold at outdoor stands, and wandering minstrels enliven the whole event. ⊠ *Aosta* ☏ *0165/274597* ⊕ *www.fieradisantorso.it.*

VISITOR INFORMATION

Contact Aosta Tourism Office. ⊠ *Piazza Porta Praetoria 3* ☏ *0165/236627* ⊕ *www.lovevda.it.*

EXPLORING

TOP ATTRACTIONS

Arco di Augusto. At the eastern entrance to town, and commanding a fine view over Aosta and the mountains, stands the Arco di Augusto (Arch of Augustus), built in 25 BC to mark Rome's victory over the Celtic Salassi tribe. (The sloping roof was added in 1716 in an attempt to keep rain from seeping between the stones.) ⊠ *Piazza Arco d'Augusto.*

Collegiata di Sant'Orso. This church has layers of history literally visible in its architecture. Originally there was a 6th-century chapel on this site founded by the Archdeacon Orso, a local saint. Most of this structure was destroyed or hidden when an 11th-century church was erected over it. This church, in turn, was encrusted with Gothic, and later Baroque, features, resulting in a jigsaw puzzle of styles, that, surprisingly, manage to work together. The 11th-century features are almost untouched in the crypt, and if you go up the stairs on the left from the main church you can see the 11th-century frescoes (ask the sacristan, who'll let you in). These restored frescoes depict the life of Christ and the apostles. Although only the tops are visible, you can see the expressions on the faces of the disciples. Take the outside doorway to the right of the main entrance to see the church's crowning glory, its 12th-century cloister, enclosed by some 40 stone columns with masterfully carved capitals depicting scenes from the Old and New Testaments and the life of St. Orso. The turrets and spires of Aosta peek out above. ⊠ *Via Sant'Orso 14* ☏ *0165/236627* ⊕ *www.diocesiaosta.it.*

Duomo. Aosta's cathedral dates from the 10th century, but all that remains from that period are the bell towers. The decoration inside is primarily Gothic, but the main attraction of the cathedral predates that era by 1,000 years: among the many ornate objects housed in the treasury is a carved ivory diptych from AD 406 portraying the Roman emperor Honorius. ⊠ *Piazza Papa Giovanni XXIII* ☏ *0165/236627* ⊕ *www.cattedraleaosta.it* 🎟 *Duomo free, treasury €4, frescoes and museum €6.*

WHERE TO EAT

$ NORTHERN ITALIAN 🍴 **Praetoria.** Just outside the Porta Pretoria, this simple and unpretentious restaurant serves hearty local dishes such as *crespelle alla valdostana* (crepes with ham and cheese) and polenta with a variety of sauces and accompaniments. The pasta is made on the premises, and all of the menu offerings are prepared from traditional recipes. **Known for:** hearty traditional recipes; fresh pasta; savory crepes. [$] *Average main: €14* ✉ *Via Sant'Anselmo 9* ☎ *0165/35473* 🌐 *www.trattoriapraetoria.it* 🕓 *Closed Wed.*

$$$ NORTHERN ITALIAN 🍴 **Vecchio Ristoro.** The elegant, intimate spaces of this converted mill are furnished with antiques, and a traditional ceramic stove provides additional warmth in cool weather. The chef-proprietor takes pride in creative versions of regional recipes, including *gnocchi* and rabbit. **Known for:** cozy atmosphere; creative versions of regional recipes; indulgent desserts. [$] *Average main: €25* ✉ *Via Tourneuve 4* ☎ *0165/33238* 🌐 *www.ristorantevecchioristoro.it* 🕓 *Closed Mon. No dinner Sun.*

WHERE TO STAY

$$ B&B/INN 🏨 **Casa Ospitaliera del Gran San Bernardo.** Here's your chance to sleep in a 12th-century castle without emptying your wallet. **Pros:** good base for budget-conscious skiers and hikers; secluded atmosphere. **Cons:** isolated location (no towns or restaurants nearby); extremely simple accommodations. [$] *Rooms from: €129* ✉ *Rue de Flassin 3, Saint-Oyen* ☎ *277/871153* 🌐 *www.gsbernard.net* 🛏 *30 rooms* 🍽 *Free Breakfast.*

$$ B&B/INN 🏨 **Le Miramonti.** Built on the banks of a branch of the Dora Baltea River, this delightful, small, family-run establishment offers all the woody Alpine interiors, traditional regional furnishings, and other homey comforts needed for a relaxing evening after a strenuous day. **Pros:** friendly, efficient service; excellent location for outdoor sports. **Cons:** isolated location in a small village; the rooms near the river may seem noisy to some. [$] *Rooms from: €160* ✉ *Via Piccolo San Bernardo 3, La Thuile* ☎ *0165/883084* 🌐 *www.lemiramonti.it* 🕓 *Closed mid-Apr.–early July and mid-Sept.–early Dec.* 🛏 *40 rooms* 🍽 *Free Breakfast.*

$$ B&B/INN Fodor's Choice ★ 🏨 **Milleluci.** At this small and inviting family-run hotel overlooking Aosta, bedrooms, some with balconies, are bright and charmingly decorated; all have splendid views of the city and mountains. **Pros:** panoramic views; great spa facilities; cozy and traditionally decorated rooms. **Cons:** 1 km (½ mile) north of town—need a car to get around; no a/c. [$] *Rooms from: €200* ✉ *Località Porossan Roppoz 15* ☎ *0165/235278* 🌐 *www.hotelmilleluci.com* 🛏 *31 rooms* 🍽 *Free Breakfast.*

COURMAYEUR/MONTE BIANCO

35 km (21 miles) northwest of Aosta, 150 km (93 miles) northwest of Turin.

The main attraction of Courmayeur is a knock-'em-dead view of Europe's tallest peak, Monte Bianco. The celebrities and the wealthy who come here these days are following a tradition that dates back to the late 17th century, when Courmayeur's natural springs first began to attract visitors. The spectacle of the Alps gradually surpassed the springs as the biggest draw: the Alpine letters of the English poet Percy Bysshe Shelley were almost advertisements for the region. Since 1965, when the Mont Blanc tunnel opened, ever-increasing numbers of travelers have passed through the area, and it's now hugely popular with both skiers and hikers during the winter and summer months.

Planners have managed to keep some restrictions on wholesale development within the town, and its angled rooftops and immaculate cobblestone streets maintain a cozy feeling.

GETTING HERE AND AROUND

Courmayeur is on the main A5 autostrada and can easily be reached by car from both Turin and Milan via Aosta. SAVDA buses run regularly from both Turin and Milan. Train service isn't available.

VISITOR INFORMATION

Contact Courmayeur Tourism Office. ⊠ *Piazzale Monte Bianco 13, Courmayeur* ☎ *0165/842060* ⊕ *www.courmayeurmontblanc.it.*

EXPLORING

Monte Bianco (*Mont Blanc*). Monte Bianco's attraction is not so much its shape (much less distinctive than that of the Matterhorn) as its expanse and the awesome vistas from the top. You can reach the summit via a cable car that ascends from Entrèves, just below the Mont Blanc Tunnel. In summer, if you get the inclination, you can then switch cable cars and descend into Chamonix, in France. In winter you can ski parts of the route off-piste. The Funivie Entrèves whisks you up first to the Pavillon du Mont Fréty in just four minutes—a starting point for many beautiful hikes—and then in six minutes to the spectacular viewing platform at **Punta Helbronner** (more than 11,000 feet), which is also the border post with France.

The next stage up—only in summer—is on the **Télépherique de L'Aiguille du Midi,** as you pass into French territory. The trip is particularly impressive; you dangle over a huge glacial snowfield (more than 2,000 feet below) and make your way slowly to the viewing station above Chamonix. It's one of the most dramatic rides in Europe. From this point you're looking down into France, and if you change cable cars at the Aiguille du Midi station, you can make your way down into Chamonix itself. ⊠ *Strada Statale 26, Courmayeur* ☎ *0165/89925 in Courmayeur, 0450/532275 in Chamonix* ⊕ *www.montebianco. com* ⊠ *€28 round-trip to Pavillon du Mont Fréty, €49 round-trip to Helbronner; additional €89 round-trip from Helbronner to Chamonix* ⊘ *Closed Nov. and depending on weather conditions and demand.*

Parco Nazionale del Gran Paradiso. Cogne, 52 km (32 miles) southeast of Courmayeur, is the gateway to this huge park, which was once the domain of King Vittorio Emanuele II (1820–78). Bequeathed to the nation after World War I, it is one of Europe's most rugged and unspoiled wilderness areas, with wildlife and many plant species protected by law. The park is one of the few places in Europe where you can see the ibex (a mountain goat with horns up to 3 feet long) and the chamois (a small antelope). The park, which is 703 square km (271 square miles), is open free of charge throughout the year; there's an information office in Cogne. ■ TIP→ Try to visit in May, when spring flowers are in bloom and most of the meadows are clear of snow. ⌂ *Villaggio Cogne 81, Cogne* ☎ *0165/753011* ⊕ *www.pngp.it.*

WHERE TO EAT

$$
NORTHERN
ITALIAN

✕ **Cadran Solaire.** The Garin family made over the oldest tavern in Courmayeur to create a warm and inviting restaurant that has a 17th-century stone vault, old wooden floor, and huge stone fireplace. The menu offers seasonal specialties and innovative interpretations of regional dishes: when available, the ravioli *maison* (filled with ricotta cheese flavored with walnuts and bathed with butter and sage) are particularly delicious. **Known for:** stone fireplace; cozy bar; regional dishes. Ⓢ *Average main: €22* ⌂ *Via Roma 122, Courmayeur* ☎ *0165/844609* ⊙ *Closed Tues., and May and Oct.*

$$$
NORTHERN
ITALIAN
Fodor's Choice
★

✕ **Maison de Filippo.** Here you'll find country-style home cooking in a mountain house with lots of atmosphere that's furnished with antiques, farm tools, and bric-a-brac of all kinds. There's a set menu, which includes an abundance of antipasti, a tempting choice of local soups and pasta dishes, and an impressive array of traditional second courses, including cheese fondue, and an equally hearty *carbonada* (beef stew and polenta). **Known for:** abundant fixed-price menus; country-style home cooking; rustic setting. Ⓢ *Average main: €30* ⌂ *Via Passerin d'Entrèves 8, Courmayeur* ☎ *0165/869797* ⊙ *Closed Tues. and May, June, Oct., and Nov.*

WHERE TO STAY

$$$
HOTEL

🏠 **Auberge de la Maison.** Most rooms here have balconies with spectacular views of Monte Bianco, and Alpine prints on the walls, plush fabrics, and wood-burning stoves give the feeling of a cozy country inn. **Pros:** secluded location in the center of Entrèves; nice spa; charming decor. **Cons:** minimum night stay required in high seasons (summer and winter); not all standard rooms have views of Monte Bianco. Ⓢ *Rooms from: €210* ⌂ *Via Passerin d'Entrèves 16, Courmayeur* ☎ *0165/869811* ⊕ *www.aubergemaison.it* ⊙ *Closed for 15 days in May and 20 days in Nov.* ⤳ *33 rooms* ⦿❘ *Free Breakfast.*

$$
HOTEL

🏠 **Croux.** Half the rooms at this bright, comfortable hotel near the town center have balconies, and the other half have great views of the mountains. **Pros:** central location; great views. **Cons:** rooms are very simple and could use a revamp; on a busy road. Ⓢ *Rooms from: €148* ⌂ *Via Croux 8, Courmayeur* ☎ *0165/846735* ⊕ *www.hotelcroux.it* ⊙ *Closed mid-Apr.–mid-June, Oct., and Nov.* ⤳ *31 rooms* ⦿❘ *Free Breakfast.*

$$$$
HOTEL

🏠 **Royal e Golf.** With wide terraces and wood paneling, this longtime landmark in the center of Courmayeur is the most elegant spot in town, and the cheery rooms have plenty of amenities. **Pros:** central location on Courmayeur's main pedestrian street; panoramic views; heated outdoor pool. **Cons:** standard rooms can be small and outdated; meal plan required; expensive. Ⓢ *Rooms from: €304* ⌂ *Via Roma 87, Courmayeur* ☎ *0165/831611* ⊕ *www.hotelroyalegolf.com* ⊙ *Closed Easter–mid-June and mid-Sept.–Nov.* ⤳ *86 rooms* ⦿❘ *Free Breakfast.*

$$$
B&B/INN
Fodor's Choice
★

🏠 **Villa Novecento.** Run with friendly charm and efficiency, the Novecento is a peaceful haven with the style of a comfortable mountain lodge, complete with a log fire in winter, traditional fabrics, wooden furnishings, and early-19th-century prints. **Pros:** charming and cozy; good restaurant; close to town center but away from the hubbub. **Cons:**

parking is limited; no a/c. $ *Rooms from: €235* ✉ *Viale Monte Bianco 64, Courmayeur* ☎ *0165/843000* ⊕ *www.villanovecento.it* 🔖 *26 rooms* 🍴 *Free Breakfast.*

THE COLLINE AND SAVOY PALACES

As you head west from Turin into the Colline ("little hills"), castles and medieval fortifications begin to pepper the former dominion of the house of Savoy, and the Alps come into better and better view. In this region lie the storybook medieval town of Rivoli; 12th-century abbeys; and, farther west in the mountains, the ski resort of Sestriere, one of the venues used during the 2006 Winter Olympics.

VENARIA REALE

10 km (6 miles) northwest of Turin.

This immense palace was built in the 16th century as a hunting lodge.

GETTING HERE AND AROUND

Starting in Turin, from the north side of Piazza della Reppublica, take Bus No. 11 to reach Venaria; the trip takes approximately 40 minutes. By car, follow Corso Regina Margherita to the A55 autostrada. Head north and leave the highway at the Venaria exit, following signs for the Venaria Reale.

EXPLORING

Fodor's Choice ★ **Reggia di Venaria Reale.** Extensive Italianate gardens surround this 16th-century hunting lodge built for Carlo Emanuele II of Savoy. Inside, its Great Gallery is worthy of Versailles. The basements now house a historical exhibition that relates the story of the Savoy. The upper floors are given over to changing exhibitions. A sound-and-light show by the British film director Peter Greenaway enlivens rooms throughout the palace, and a permanent installation of works by the Arte Povera artist Giuseppe Penone can be seen in the gardens outside. ✉ *Piazza della Reppublica 4* ☎ *011/4992333* ⊕ *www.lavenaria.it* 🎫 *€16* ☾ *Closed Mon. and Feb. 12–Mar. 5.*

RIVOLI

16 km (10 miles) southwest of Venaria, 13 km (8 miles) west of Turin.

The Savoy court was based in Rivoli in the Middle Ages, and the town retains several remnants from that richly dramatic period.

GETTING HERE AND AROUND

GTT buses and trams regularly link central Turin with Rivoli. The journey takes just over one hour.

By car, follow Corso Francia from central Turin all the way to Rivoli. Unless there's a lot of traffic the trip should take a half hour.

EXPLORING

Casa del Conte Verde (*House of the Green Count*). The richly decorated House of the Green Count, in the oldest part of Rivoli, attests to the wealth and importance of its onetime owner, Amedeo VI of Savoy

(1334–83). Legend has it that the count attended tournaments dressed all in green, hence the name. Inside, a small gallery occasionally hosts temporary exhibitions, which may increase the entrance fee. ⊠ *Via Fratelli Piol 8* ☎ *011/9563020* 🎫 *€5 (varies with exhibits)* ⊘ *Closed Mon.*

SACRA DI SAN MICHELE

26 km (17 miles) west of Rivoli, 43 km (27 miles) west of Turin.

Perhaps best known as inspiration for the setting of Umberto Eco's novel *The Name of the Rose,* this abbey was built on Monte Pirchiriano in the 11th century so it would stand out: it occupies the most prominent location for miles around, hanging over a 3,280-foot bluff. When monks came to enlarge the abbey they had to build part of the structure on supports more than 90 feet high—an engineering feat that was famous in medieval Europe and is still impressive today. By the 12th century this important abbey controlled 176 churches in Italy, France, and Spain; one of the abbeys under its influence was Mont-Saint-Michel, in France. Because of its strategic position, the Abbey of St. Michael came under frequent attacks over the next five centuries and was eventually abandoned in 1622. It was restored, somewhat heavy-handedly, in the late 19th and early 20th centuries.

GETTING HERE AND AROUND

Unless you want to do a 14-km (9-mile) uphill hike from the town of Avigliana, a car is essential for an excursion here—take the Avigliana Est exit from the Torino–Bardonecchia autostrada (A32).

EXPLORING

Sacra di San Michele. To reach the church, you must climb 150 steps, past 12th-century sculptures, from the **Porta dello Zodiaco,** a splendid Romanesque doorway decorated with the signs of the zodiac. On the left side of the interior are 16th-century frescoes representing New Testament themes; on the right are depictions of the founding of the church. In the crypt are some of the oldest parts of the structure, three small 9th- to 12th-century chapels. Note that some sections of the abbey are open only on weekends and, when particularly crowded, visits may be limited to hour-long tours. ■ TIP→ **Weather permitting, the views from the walls and terraces surrounding the church are breathtaking.** ⊠ *Via Sacra di San Michele 14, Sant'Ambrogio di Torino* ☎ *011/939130* ⊕ *www.sacradisanmichele.com* 🎫 *€8* ⊘ *Closed Mon.*

THE ITALIAN RIVIERA

WELCOME TO THE ITALIAN RIVIERA

TOP REASONS TO GO

★ **The Cinque Terre:** Hike the famous Cinque Terre trails past gravity-defying vineyards, colorful, rock-perched villages, and the deep blue Mediterranean Sea.

★ **Portofino:** See the world through rose-tinted sunglasses at this glamorous little harbor village.

★ **Genoa's historical center and port:** From the palaces of Via Garibaldi to the labyrinthine backstreets of the old city to the world-class aquarium, the city is full of surprising delights.

★ **Giardini Botanici Hanbury:** A spectacular natural setting harbors one of Italy's largest, most exotic botanical gardens.

★ **Pesto:** The basil-rich sauce was invented in Liguria, and it's never been equaled elsewhere.

A thin crescent of rugged and verdant land surrounded by France, Piedmont, Tuscany, the Alps, and the Mediterranean Sea, Liguria is best known as the Italian Riviera. Genoa, the region's largest city and one of Italy's most important ports, lies directly in the middle, with the Riviera di Ponente to the northwest and the Riviera di Levante to the southeast. It's here that the Italians perfected *il dolce far niente*—the sweet art of idleness.

1 Cinque Terre. Five isolated seaside villages seem removed from the modern world—despite the many hikers who populate the trails between them.

2 Riviera di Levante. East of Genoa, the Riviera of the Rising Sun has tiny bays and inlets, set among dramatic cliffs and mountainsides, making for some of the most beautiful coastline in Italy. The pastel-hue town of Portofino has charmed generations of the rich and famous.

3 Genoa. Birthplace of Christopher Columbus, this city is an urban anomaly among Liguria's charming villages. At its heart is Italy's largest historic district, filled with beautiful architecture.

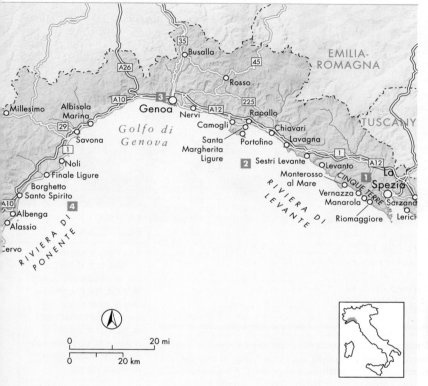

4 Riviera di Ponente. The Riviera of the Setting Sun, reaching from the French border to Genoa, has protected bays and sandy beaches. The seaside resorts of Bordighera and San Remo share some of the glitter of their French cousins to the west.

9

EATING AND DRINKING WELL IN THE ITALIAN RIVIERA

Ligurian cuisine might surprise you. As you'd expect given the long coastline, it employs all sorts of seafood, but its real claim to fame is the exemplary use of vegetables and herbs.

Basil is practically revered in Genoa (the word is derived from the Greek *basileus,* meaning "king"), and the city is considered the birthplace of pesto, the basil-rich pasta sauce. This and other herbs—laurel, fennel, and marjoram—are cultivated, but also grow wild on the sun-kissed hillsides. Naturally, seafood plays a prominent role on the menu, appearing in soups, salads, and pasta dishes. Especially bountiful are anchovies, sea bass, squid, and octopus. Vegetables—particularly artichokes, eggplant, and zucchini—are abundant, usually prepared with liberal amounts of olive oil and garlic.

Like much of Italy, Liguria has a wide range of eating establishments from cafeteria-like *tavole calde* to family-run trattorias to sophisticated *ristoranti.* Lunch is served between 12:30 and 2:30 and dinner between 7:30 and 11. Also popular, especially in Genoa, are *enoteche* (wine bars), which serve simply prepared light meals late into the night.

FABULOUS FOCACCIA

When you're hankering for a snack, turn to bakeries and small eateries serving focaccia. The flat bread here is more dense and flavorful than what's sold as focaccia in American restaurants; it's the region's answer to pizza, usually eaten on the go.

It comes simply salted and dribbled with olive oil; flavored with rosemary and olives; covered with cheese or anchovies; and even *ripiena* (filled), usually with cheese or vegetables and herbs. Another local delicacy is *farinata,* a chickpea pancake baked like a pizza.

ANTIPASTI

Seafood antipasti are served in abundance at most Ligurian restaurants. These usually include marinated anchovies from Monterosso, *cozze ripiene* (mussel shells stuffed with minced mussel meat, prosciutto, Parmesan, herbs, and bread crumbs), and *sopressato di polpo* (flattened octopus in olive oil and lemon sauce).

PASTA

Liguria's classic pasta sauce is pesto, made from basil, garlic, olive oil, pine nuts, and hard cheese. It's usually served with *trenette* (similar to spaghetti) or the slightly sweet *testaroli* (a flat pasta made from chestnut flour).

You can also find *pansotti* (triangular pockets of pasta filled with a cheese mixture), and *trofie* (short pasta twists) with *salsa di noci,* a rich sauce of garlic, walnuts, and cream that, as with pesto, is ideally pounded with a mortar and pestle.

Spaghetti *allo scoglio* has an olive oil, tomato, and white-wine-based sauce containing an assortment of local *frutti di mare* (seafood) including shrimp, clams, mussels, and cuttlefish.

FISH AND MEAT

Fish is the best bet for a second course: the classic preparation is a whole grilled or baked whitefish—*branzino* (sea bass) and *orata* (dorado) are good choices—served *alle Ligure,* with olives, potatoes,

tomatoes, Ligurian spices, and a drizzle of olive oil. A popular meat dish is *cima alla Genovese,* a veal roll stuffed with a mixture of eggs and vegetables, served as a cold cut.

PANIGACCI

One of the real treats of the region is *panigacci* from the Lunigiana area. Small, terra-cotta dishes known as *testine* are placed in a wood-burning oven or fire to heat at the highest of temperatures. Then balls of dough are laid in the dishes and stacked one on top of the other in order to flatten and cook the dough. What emerges is flat, firm, almost pitalike bread. Panigacci is usually served with *stracchino* cheese (similar to cream cheese), pesto or nut sauce, and cold cuts—a delicious, hearty meal.

WINE

Local vineyards produce mostly light and refreshing whites such as pigato from the Ponente and vermentino from the Levante, although both light reds and appealing *rosati* (Italy's form of rosé) are on the rise. Rossese di Dolceacqua, from near the French border, is considered the best red wine the region has to offer, but for a more robust accompaniment to meats, opt for the more full-bodied reds of the neighboring Piedmont region. For a postdinner or dessert wine, try the "hard to find the real thing" *sciacchetrà,* made exclusively in the Cinque Terre.

Updated by
Liz Shemaria

Nestled between the south of France and the Tuscan border lies the region of Liguria, with verdant and lush mountains to the north and east, and the sapphire-blue Mediterranean to the south and west. In between is a land of lush vegetation, medieval hilltop hamlets, panoramic vistas, colorful seaside villages, pristine beaches, and one of Italy's most underrated cities, Genoa.

There is plenty to do—from hiking and biking, to water sports and fishing, to eating (very) well—and plenty to see, including some of Italy's most aesthetically pleasing architecture, to just enjoying la dolce vita along its coast, better known as the Italian Riviera.

The Italian Riviera oozes charm and irresistible allure, with many seaside resort towns and colorful villages that stake intermittent claim to the rocky shores of the Ligurian Sea and seem like the long-lost cousins of newer seaside paradises found elsewhere. It has been a haven for artists, writers, celebrities, and royalty since the 1800s, and continues to fascinate visitors throughout the year due to its mild climate. Here the grandest palazzi share space with frescoed, angular *terratettos* (tall, skinny houses). The rustic and elegant, the provincial and chic, the small-town and cosmopolitan all collide here in a sun-drenched blend that defines the Italian side of the Riviera. There are chic resort towns such as San Remo and Portofino, the unique beauty and outdoor adventures of the Cinque Terre, numerous quaint seaside and hilltop villages to explore, plus the history and architectural charm of Genoa. Mellowed by the balmy breezes blowing off the sea, travelers bask in the sun, explore the picturesque fishing villages, and pamper themselves at the resorts that dot this ruggedly beautiful landscape.

THE ITALIAN RIVIERA PLANNER

MAKING THE MOST OF YOUR TIME

Your first decision, particularly given limited time, is between the two Rivieras. The Riviera di Levante, east of Genoa, is more rustic and has a more distinct personality, with the unique Cinque Terre, ritzy Portofino, and the panoramic Gulf of Poets. The Riviera di Ponente, west of Genoa, is a classic European resort experience with many white-sand beaches and more nightlife and accommodation choices—similar to, but not as glamorous as, the French Riviera across the border.

In either case, your second decision is whether to visit Genoa. Despite its rough exterior and (diminishing) reputation as a seamy port town, Genoa's artistic and cultural treasures are significant—you won't find anything remotely comparable elsewhere in the region. Unless your goal is to avoid urban life entirely, consider a night or two in the city.

The Italian Riviera is extremely seasonal. From April to October, the area's bustling with shops, cafés, clubs, and restaurants that stay open late. In high season (Easter and June–August), it can be very crowded and lively. Yet, the rest of the year, the majority of resorts close down, and you'll be hard-pressed to find accommodations or restaurants open.

GETTING HERE AND AROUND

BUS TRAVEL

Generally speaking, buses are a difficult way to come and go in Liguria. Although there are local buses that run between villages along the Riviera Ponente, it's not an extensive network and can be a challenge to navigate.

ATP. Things run somewhat easier along the Riviera Levante where ATP has regular, regional services. ☎ *0185/3731* ⊕ *www.atp-spa.it.*

Volpibus. This firm provides service from the airport in Milan, but there's no bus service between Genoa and other major Italian cities. ☎ *010/561661* ⊕ *www.volpibus.com and www.statturismo.com.*

CAR TRAVEL

With the freedom of a car, you could drive from one end of the Riviera to the other on the autostrada in about three hours. Two good roads run parallel to each other along the coast of Liguria. Closer to shore and passing through all the towns and villages is SS1, the Via Aurelia, which was laid out by the ancient Romans and has excellent views at almost every turn but gets crowded in July and August. More direct and higher up than SS1 are Autostrade A10, west of Genoa, and A12, to the south—engineering wonders with literally hundreds of long tunnels and towering viaducts. These routes save time on weekends, in summer, and on days when festivals slow traffic in some resorts to a standstill.

TRAIN TRAVEL

Train travel is by far the most convenient mode of transportation throughout the region. It takes 3½ hours for an express train to cover the entire Liguria coast. Local trains take upward of five hours or more to get from one end of the coast to the other, stopping in or near all the towns along the way.

For schedules, check the website of the national railway, **Ferrovie dello Stato** (FS ☎ *892021* ⊕ *www.trenitalia.com*).

HIKING

Walking Liguria's extensive network of trails, and taking in the gorgeous views, is a major outdoor activity and an attraction to the region. The mild climate and laid-back state of mind can lull you into underestimating just how strenuous such walks can be. Wear good shoes, use sunscreen, and carry plenty of water—you'll be glad you did. Trail maps are available from tourist information offices, or upon entry to the Cinque Terre National Park.

On the Portofino promontory, the relatively easy walk to the Abbazia di San Fruttuoso is popular, and there's a more challenging hike from Ruta to the top of Monte Portofino and back down to Camogli. From Genoa, you can take the Zecca–Righi funicular up to Righi and walk along the ring of fortresses that used to defend the city.

Walking tours can introduce you to lesser-known aspects of the region. For the Cinque Terre and the rest of the Province of La Spezia, the **Cooperativa Arte e Natura** (⊠ *Viale Amendola 172, La Spezia* ☎ *0187/739410*) is a good source for English-speaking guides as well as other languages. A full day costs around €150 for small groups of 10 or less, €240 for 10 to 35 people, and €280 for groups up to 35.

RESTAURANTS

While fine dining can be found in Liguria, you are more likely to enjoy a casual atmosphere, often with an amazing sea view. Expect both the decor and dishes to be simple but flavorful. *Restaurant reviews have been shortened. For full information, visit Fodors.com*

HOTELS

Liguria's lodging options may be a step behind such resort areas as Positano and Taormina, so reservations for its better accommodations (and for the more limited ones in the Cinque Terre) should be made far in advance. Lodging tends to be pricey in high season, particularly June to August. *Hotel reviews have been shortened. For full information, visit Fodors.com*

WHAT IT COSTS			
$	**$$**	**$$$**	**$$$$**
Restaurants	under €15	€15–€24	€25–€35	over €35
Hotels	under €125	€125–€200	€201–€300	over €300

Restaurant prices are the average cost of a main course at dinner or, if dinner is not served, at lunch. Hotel prices are the lowest cost of a standard double room in high season.

CINQUE TERRE

The photogenic and preposterously beautiful Cinque Terre is the heart of the Italian Riviera. In their rugged simplicity, the five old fishing towns of Monterosso, Vernazza, Corniglia, Manarola, and Riomaggiore seem to mock the caked-on artifice of glitzy neighboring resorts. With a clear blue sea in the foreground, spectacularly multicolor buildings emerge almost seamlessly from cliffs, and rocky mountains rise precipitously to gravity-defying vineyards and dusty olive groves. The five small villages (Cinque Terre literally means "Five Lands") cling to the cliffs along a gorgeous stretch of the Ligurian coast. The geography here prevents expansion or extensive technological advancement, which allows these small towns to retain most of their enchanting old-world charm.

The terrain is so steep that for centuries, footpaths were the only way to get from place to place. These footpaths provide beautiful views of the rocky coast tumbling into the sea, as well as access to secluded beaches and grottoes. Since its designation in 1997 as a UNESCO World Heritage Site, Cinque Terre has become one of Italy's most popular destinations. Despite summer crowds and some lingering damage from the 2011 flash floods, the villages remain alluringly characteristic and the views from the trails in between are as breathtaking as ever.

RIOMAGGIORE

17 km (11 miles) southwest of La Spezia, 101 km (60 miles) southeast of Genoa.

At the eastern end of the Cinque Terre, Riomaggiore is built into a river gorge (thus the name, which means "major river") and is easily accessible from La Spezia by train or car. The landscape is terraced and steep—be prepared for many stairs!—and leads down to a small harbor, protected by large slabs of alabaster and marble that serve as tanning beds for sunbathers. The harbor is also the site of several outdoor cafés with fine views. According to legend, the settlement of Riomaggiore dates as far back as the 8th century, when Greek religious refugees came here to escape persecution by the Byzantine emperor.

The village is divided into two parts. If you arrive by train, you will have to pass through a tunnel that flanks the train tracks to reach the historic side of town. To avoid the crowds and get a great view of the Cinque Terre coast, walk straight uphill as soon as you exit the station. This winding road takes you over the hill to the 14th-century **church of St. John the Baptist,** toward the medieval town center and the Genovese-style tower houses that dot the village. Follow Via Roma (the Old Town's main street) downhill, pass under the train tracks, and you'll arrive in the charming fishermen's port of the village. Lined with traditional fishing boats and small trattorias, this is a lovely spot for a romantic lunch or dinner. Unfortunately, Riomaggiore doesn't have as much old-world charm as its sister villages; its easy accessibility has brought traffic and more modern construction here than elsewhere in the Cinque Terre.

CLOSE UP

Accessing the Trails of the Cinque Terre

WHEN TO GO

The ideal times to visit the Cinque Terre are September and May, when the weather is mild and the summer tourist season isn't in full swing (between June and August it can be unbearably hot and crowded).

GETTING HERE AND AROUND

There is now a local train between La Spezia and Levanto that stops at each of the Cinque Terre villages, and runs approximately every 30 minutes throughout the day. Tickets for each leg of the journey (€1.90) are available at the five train stations. In Corniglia, the only one of the Cinque Terre that isn't at sea level, a shuttle service (€1.50) is provided for those who don't wish to climb (or descend) 300-plus steps that link the train station with the clifftop town.

Along the Cinque Terre coast two ferry lines operate. From June to September, Golfo Paradiso runs from Genoa and Camogli to Monterosso al Mare and Vernazza. The smaller but more frequent Golfo dei Poeti stops at each village from Lerici (east of Riomaggiore) to Monterosso, with the exception of Corniglia, four times a day. A one-day ticket costs €35.

ADMISSION

Entrance tickets for using the trails are available at ticket booths located at the start of each section of Trail No. 2, and at information offices in the Levanto, Monterosso, Vernazza, Corniglia, Manarola, Riomaggiore, and La Spezia train stations.

A one-day pass costs €7.50, which includes a trail map and an information leaflet; a two-day pass is €14.50. The Cinque Terre Card combines park entrance fees with unlimited daily use of the regional train between La Spezia, the five villages, and Levanto just north of Monterosso, and costs €19.50 for a one-day pass and €31.50 for a two-day pass.

FOR MORE INFORMATION

🌐 *www.cinqueterre.com*; 🌐 *www.lecinqueterre.org*; 🌐 *www.parconazionale-5terre.it*; 🌐 *www.rebuildmonterosso.com*; 🌐 *savevernazza.com*; 🌐 *www.littleparadiso.com* (blog).

GETTING HERE AND AROUND

The enormous parking problems presented by these cliff-dwelling villages have been mitigated somewhat by a large, covered parking structure at La Spezia Centrale station, which costs €1.50 per hour. It's clean and secure (you cannot enter without a ticket code to open the door), and it's open 24/7. This is a good backup solution for those with cars, although others may choose to take a day trip from Pisa or Lucca and rely on bus and train services. Arrive early as it can fill up by mid-morning, especially in the high season.

WHERE TO EAT

$$$ LIGURIAN 🍴 **Dau Cila.** There's wonderful seaside dining on Riomaggiore harbor, with a menu of local Ligurian dishes and an extensive wine list. **Known for:** sea views; extensive wine list; local flavors. [$] *Average main: €25* ✉ *Via San Giacomo 65* ☎ *0187/760032* 🕒 *Closed Nov.–Mar.*

Continued on page 402

HIKING THE CINQUE TERRE

FIVE REMOTE VILLAGES MAKE ONE MUST-SEE DESTINATION

"Charming" and "breathtaking" are adjectives that get a workout when you're traveling in Italy, but it's rare that both apply to a single location. The Cinque Terre is such a place, and this combination of characteristics goes a long way toward explaining its tremendous appeal.

The area is made up of five tiny villages (Cinque Terre literally means "Five Lands") clinging to the cliffs along a gorgeous stretch of the Ligurian coast. The terrain is so steep that for centuries footpaths were the only way to get from place to place. It just so happens that these paths provide beautiful views of the rocky coast tumbling into the sea, as well as access to secluded beaches and grottoes.

Backpackers "discovered" the Cinque Terre in the 1970s, and its popularity has been growing ever since. Despite summer crowds, much of the original appeal is intact. Each town has maintained its own distinct charm, and views from the trails in between are as breathtaking as ever.

Monterosso

Corniglia

Terracing around Cornigli[a]

HIKING THE CINQUE TERRE

Mount Malpertuso

Mount Castello

Monterosso—Vernazza Trail
The most demanding portion of the trail. Often narrow, with significant climbs and descents, particularly near Vernazza. Your labors are rewarded with the Trail No. 2's best views.

Le Stalle

Trail No 8a

Mount Gaginara

38

Drignana

(Red Trail)

Vernazza—Corniglia Trail
Ups and downs interspersed with olive groves and terraced vineyards.

370 **Madonna di Soviore**

Trail No 1

Santuario del Reggio

Santuario Bernardino

1hr 30min

51

1hr

1hr

Trail No 89

Trail No 8

S. Bernardo
Trail No 8

Trail No 7

3 km/2 mi–1 hr 30 min

Trail No 2 (Blue Trail)

3 km/2 mi–2 hrs

Vernazza

Guvano Beach

del Frate Island

Palma Pt

Molinara Pt

Monterosso al Mare

0 ———— 1 mi

0 ———— 1 km

Monterosso
The most resort-like of the villages, with the largest beach.

Vernazza
Pretty and visitor-friendly. The best spot for lingering in a café and watching waves crash against the shore.

FERRY TO LEVANTO

THE CLASSIC HIKE

Hiking is the most popular way to experience the Cinque Terre, and Trail No. 2, the Sentiero Azzurro (Blue Trail), is the most traveled path (€7.50 for a day ticket). To cover the entire trail is a full day: it's approximately 13 km (8 miles) in length, takes you to all five villages, and requires about five hours, not including stops, to complete. The best approach is to start at the eastern-most town of Riomaggiore and warm up your legs on the easiest segment of the trail. As you work your way west, the hike gets progressively more demanding. Between Corniglia and Manarola take the ferry (which provides its own beautiful views) or the inland train running between the towns instead. Note: At the time of this writing, sections of the trail are closed for restoration work.

Manarola

Along Lovers' Lane

Via dell'Amore

Corniglia—Manarola Trail
This section of the trail is currently closed. The trail is expected to re-open sometime in 2019.

Manarola—Riomaggiore Trail
Known as the Via dell'Amore (Lovers' Lane). A wide, paved, flat path with fine views. The main part of the trail is closed until 2021.

KEY

··················	*Major footpaths*
------------	*Sanctuary footpaths*
- - - - - - -	*Connecting footpaths*
45min	*Hiking times*
☖	*Sanctuaries*

Mount Capri

Mount Galera

Mount Grosso

1 (Red Trail)

Mount Cuna

Trail No 6

Trail No 7a

Trail No 6d

Trail No 2 (Blue Trail) (this section closed)

1hr 30min

Madonna della Salute ☖

1hr

Volastra

Trail No 02

Trail No 3

Madonna di Montenero ☖ 45min

3 km/2 mi—1 hr

51

370

370

Spiaggione di Corniglia

TO → LA SPEZIA

Corniglia

uogo Pt

Ligurian Sea

Manarola ☖

Buonfiglio Pt

Trail No 2 (Blue Trail)

30min

Via dell' Amore

Riomaggiore

Torre Guardiola

C di M Nero

Corniglia
Perched on a cliff 00 ft. above the ea, reached by a witchback path (or by huttle bus).

Manarola
The most photogenic of the villages, best seen from the cemetery a few minutes up the path toward Corniglia.

Riomaggiore
Cliff-clinging buildings are almost as striking as those in Manarola. Stairs to the left of the train station entrance cross over the tracks and lead to the trailhead.

BEYOND TRAIL NO.2

Trail No. 2 is just one of a network of trails crisscrossing the hills. If you're a dedicated hiker, spend a few nights and try some of the other routes. Trail No. 1, the Sentiero Rosso (Red Trail), climbs from Portovenere (east of Riomaggiore) and returns to the sea at Levanto (west of Monterosso al Mare). To hike its length takes from 9 to 12 hours; the ridge-top trail provides spectacular views from high above the villages, each of which can be reached via a steep path. Other shorter trails go from the villages up into the hills, some leading to religious sanctuaries. Trail No. 9, for example, starts from the old section of Monterosso and ends at the Madonna di Soviore Sanctuary.

CLOSE UP

Hiking the Cinque Terre

Although often described as relaxing and easy, the Cinque Terre also have several hiking options if you wish to exert yourself a little. Many people do not realize just how demanding parts of these trails can be—it's best to come prepared. We recommend bringing a Cinque Terre Card and cash (smaller shops, eateries, and the park entrances do not accept credit cards).

When all trails are completely open, a hike through the entire region takes about four to five hours; add time for exploring each village and taking a lunch break. It's an all-day, if not two-day trek. We recommend an early start, especially in summer when midday temperatures can rise to 90°F. Note that only Sentiero Azzuro (Trail No. 2) requires the Cinque Terre Card. The other 20-plus trails in the area are free. All trails are well marked with a red-and-white hiking-trail sign. The trails from village to village get progressively steeper as you move from south (Riomaggiore) to the north (Monterosso). If you're a day-tripper arriving by car, use the new underground lot at La Spezia Centrale train station (€2.30 per hour in summer) and take the train to Riomaggiore (6–8 minutes) to begin your hiking adventure.

OUR FAVORITES

Other trails to consider include: **Monterosso to Santuario Madonna di Soviore**, a fairly strenuous but rewarding 1½ hours up to a lovely 8th-century sanctuary. There is also a restaurant and a priceless view. **Riomaggiore to Montenero and**

Portovenere is one hour up to the sanctuary and another three hours on to Portovenere, passing through some gorgeous, less-traveled terrain. **Manarola to Volastra to Corniglia** runs high above the main trail and through vineyards and lesser-known villages. **Monterosso to Levanto** is a good 2½-hour hike, passing over Punta Mesco with glorious views of the Cinque Terre to the south, Corsica to the west, and the Alps to the north.

Each town has something that passes for a beach (usually with lots of pebbles or slabs of terraced rock), but there is only one option for both sand and decent swimming—in Monterosso, just across from the train station. It's equipped with chairs, umbrellas, and snack bars.

PRECAUTIONS

If you're hitting the trails, carry water with you, wear sturdy shoes (hiking boots are best), and have a hat and sunscreen handy. Note that the lesser-used trails aren't as well maintained as Trail No. 2. If you're undertaking the full Trail No. 1 hike, bring something to snack on as well as your water bottle. Note that currently the Via dell'Amore and the portion of Trail No. 2 between Manarola and Corniglia were closed indefinitely due to landslides. ■TIP→ **Check weather reports; especially in late fall and winter, thunderstorms can make shelterless trails slippery and dangerous. Rain in October and November can cause landslides and close the trails.**

MANAROLA

16 km (10 miles) southwest of La Spezia, 117 km (73 miles) southeast of Genoa.

Fodor's Choice ★ The enchanting pastel houses of Manarola spill down a steep hill overlooking a spectacular turquoise swimming cove and a bustling harbor. The whole town is built on black rock. Above the town, ancient terraces still protect abundant vineyards and olive trees. This village is the center of wine and olive-oil production in the region, and its streets are lined with shops selling local products.

Surrounded by steep terraced vineyards, Manarola's one road tumbles from the **Chiesa di San Lorenzo** (14th century) high above the village, down to the rocky port below. Since the Cinque Terre wine cooperative is located in **Groppo,** a hamlet overlooking the village (and reachable by foot or by the green Park bus; ask at Park offices for schedules), the vineyards are accessible. If you'd like to snap a shot of the most famous view of the town, you can walk from the port area to the cemetery above. Along the way you'll pass the town's play yard, uncrowded bathrooms, and a tap with clean drinking water.

WHERE TO STAY

$$$ HOTEL Fodor's Choice ★ **La Torretta.** One of the Cinque Terre's few "boutique" hotels is in a 17th-century tower that sits high on the hill above the rainbow-hue village of Manarola with truly lovely views of the terraced vineyards, colorful village homes, and the Mediterranean sea; inside, decor is chic, sleek, and antiques bedecked. **Pros:** well maintained; a cut above most lodging in the Cinque Terre. **Cons:** if the luggage shuttle is not running during its limited hours (7 am–7 pm), it is a steep walk up to the hotel. [$] *Rooms from: €250* ✉ *Vico Volto 20, Cinque Terre* ☎ *0187/920327* 🌐 *www.torrettas.com* 🕒 *Closed Nov.–mid-Mar.* 🛏 *11 rooms* 🍴 *Free Breakfast.*

9

CORNIGLIA

27 km (17 miles) northwest of La Spezia, 100 km (60 miles) southeast of Genoa.

Fodor's Choice ★ The buildings, narrow lanes, and stairways of Corniglia are strung together amid vineyards high on the cliffs. On a clear day, views of the entire coastal strip are excellent, from Elba in the south to the Italian Alps in the north. The high perch and lack of harbor make this farming community the most remote and therefore least crowded of the Cinque Terre. In fact, the 365 steps that lead from the train station to the town center dissuade many tourists from making the hike to the village. You can also take the green Park bus, but they run infrequently and are usually packed with tired hikers.

Corniglia is built along one road edged with small shops, bars, gelaterias, and restaurants. Midway along Via Fieschi is the **Largo Taragio,** the main square and heart of the village. Shaded by leafy trees and umbrellas, this is a lovely spot for a mid-hike gelato break. Here you'll find the 14th-century **Chiesa di San Pietro.** Its rose window of marble imported from Carrara is impressive, particularly considering the work required to get it here!

VERNAZZA

27 km (17 miles) west of La Spezia, 96 km (59 miles) southeast of Genoa.

Fodor's Choice ★ With its narrow streets and small squares, Vernazza is arguably the most charming of the five Cinque Terre towns, and usually the most crowded. Historically, it was the most important of them, since it was the only one fortunate enough to have a natural port and, therefore, became wealthier than its neighbors—as evinced by the elaborate arcades, loggias, and marble work lining Via Roma and Piazza Marconi.

The village's pink, slate-roof houses and colorful squares contrast with the remains of the medieval fort and castle, including two towers, in the Old Town. The Romans first inhabited this rocky spit of land in the 1st century.

Today, Vernazza has a fairly lively social scene. **Piazza Marconi** looks out across Vernazza's small sandy beach to the sea, towards Monterosso. The numerous restaurants and bars crowd their tables and umbrellas on the outskirts of the piazza, creating a patchwork of sights and sounds that form one of the most unique and beautiful places in the world.

EXPLORING

If mass is not going on (there will be a cord blocking the entrance if it is), take a peek into the **church of St. Margaret of Antioch.** Little changed since its enlargement in the 1600s, this 14th-century edifice has simple interiors but truly breathtaking views toward the sea: a stark contrast to the other, elaborate churches of the Cinque Terre.

On the other side of the piazza, stairs lead to a lookout **fortress and cylindrical watchtower,** built in the 11th century as protection against pirate attacks. For a small fee you can climb to the top of the tower for a spectacular view of the coastline.

WHERE TO EAT AND STAY

$$ LIGURIAN 🍴 **Gambero Rosso.** Relax on Vernazza's main square at this fine trattoria looking out at a church. Enjoy such delectable dishes as shrimp salad, vegetable torte, and squid-ink risotto. **Known for:** piazza view; fresh seafood; pesto dishes. [$] *Average main: €22* ✉ *Piazza Marconi 7* ☎ *0187/812265* 🌐 *www.ristorantegamberorosso.net* 🕒 *Closed Thurs., and Nov.–Mar.*

$$$ LIGURIAN Fodor's Choice ★ 🍴 **Ristorante Belforte.** High above the sea in one of Vernazza's remaining stone towers is this unique spot serving delicious Cinque Terre cuisine such as branzino *sotto sale* (sea bass cooked under salt), stuffed mussels, and *insalata di polpo* (octopus salad). The setting is magnificent, so try for an outdoor table. **Known for:** incredible views; octopus salad; lively atmosphere. [$] *Average main: €25* ✉ *Via Guidoni 42* ☎ *0187/812222* 🌐 *www.ristorantebelforte.it* 🕒 *Closed Tues., and Nov.–Easter.*

$$ B&B/INN 🏨 **La Malà.** A cut above other lodging options in the Cinque Terre, these small guest rooms are equipped with flat-screen TVs, air-conditioning, marble showers, comfortable bedding, and have views of the sea or the port, which can also be enjoyed at their most bewitching from the shared terrace literally suspended over the Mediterranean. **Pros:** clean, fresh-feeling rooms; oh, the views. **Cons:** there are some

stairs involved; for the price, one should not have to go to a bar for a small continental breakfast. [$] *Rooms from: €160* ✉ *Giovanni Battista 29* ☎ *334/2875718* 🌐 *www.lamala.it* ⏲ *Closed Jan. 8–Mar. 1* 🛏 *4 rooms* 🍴 *No meals.*

MONTEROSSO AL MARE

32 km (20 miles) northwest of La Spezia, 89 km (55 miles) southeast of Genoa.

Fodor's Choice ★

It's the combined draw of beautiful beaches, rugged cliffs, crystal clear turquoise waters, and plentiful small hotels and restaurants that make Monterosso al Mare into the largest of the Cinque Terre villages (population 1,800) and also the busiest in midsummer.

Monterosso has the most festivals of the five villages, starting with the Lemon Feast on the Saturday preceding Ascension Sunday, followed by the Flower Festival of Corpus Christi, celebrated yearly on the second Sunday after Pentecost. During the afternoon, the streets and alleyways of the historic center are decorated with thousands of colorful flower petals set in beautiful designs that the evening procession passes over. Finally, the Salted Anchovy and Olive Oil Festival takes place each year during the second weekend of September.

EXPLORING

From the train station, heading west, you pass through a tunnel and exit into the *centro storico* (historic center) of the village. Nestled into the wide valley that leads to the sea, Monterosso is built above numerous streams, which have been covered to make up the major streets of the village. Via Buranco, the oldest street in Monterosso, leads out to the most characteristic piazza of the village, Piazza Matteotti (locals pass through here daily to shop at the supermarket and butcher). This piazza also contains the oldest and most typical wineshop in the village, Enoteca da Eliseo—stop here between 6 pm and midnight to share tables with fellow tourists and locals over a bottle of Cinque Terre wine. There's also the **Chiesa di San Francesco,** built in the 12th century, which is an excellent example of the Ligurian Gothic style. Its distinctive black stripes and marble rose window make it one of the most photographed sites in the Cinque Terre.

Fegina, the newer side of the village (and site of the train station), has relatively modern homes ranging from Liberty style (Art Nouveau) to the early 1970s. At the far eastern end of town, you'll run into a private sailing club sheltered by a vast rock carved with an impressive statue of Neptune. From here, you can reach the challenging trail to Levanto (a great 2½-hour hike). This trail has the added bonus of a five-minute detour to the **ruins of a 14th-century monastery.** The expansive view from this vantage point allowed the monks who were housed here to easily scan the waters for enemy ships that might invade the villages and alert residents to coming danger. Have your camera ready for this Cinerama-like vista.

Although it has the most nightlife on the Cinque Terre (thanks to its numerous wine bars and pubs), Monterosso is also the most family-friendly. With its expanse of free and equipped beaches, extensive pedestrian areas, large children's play park, and summer activities, Monterosso is a top spot for kids.

The **local outdoor market** is held on Thursday and attracts crowds of tourists and villagers from along the coast to shop for everything from pots, pans, and underwear to fruits, vegetables, and fish. Often a few stands sell local art and crafts, as well as olive oil and wine.

WHERE TO EAT

$$ WINE BAR 🍴 **Enoteca Internazionale.** Located on the main street, this wine bar offers a large variety of vintages, both local and from farther afield, plus delicious light fare; its umbrella-covered patio is a welcoming spot to recuperate after a day of hiking. Susanna, the owner, is a certified sommelier who's always forthcoming with helpful suggestions on pairing local wines with their tasty bruschettas. **Known for:** extensive wine list; patio dining; helpful staff. [$] *Average main: €15* ✉ *Via Roma 62* ☎ *0187/817278* 🕓 *Closed Tues., and Jan.–Mar.*

$$$ SEAFOOD 🍴 **Miky.** This is arguably the best restaurant in Monterosso, specializing in tasty, fresh seafood dishes including grilled calamari and monkfish ravioli. The *catalana* (poached lobster and shrimp with sliced raw fennel and carrot) is a winner. **Known for:** sunny garden setting; fresh seafood; fine dining. [$] *Average main: €28* ✉ *Via Fegina 104* ☎ *0187/817608* 🌐 *www.ristorantemiky.it* 🕓 *Closed mid-Nov.–mid-Mar.*

WHERE TO STAY

$$ B&B/INN 🏨 **Bellambra B&B.** Modern rooms with charm and comfort in the heart of the old town make this a terrific base for exploring the Cinque Terre. **Pros:** relatively new; spacious rooms and bathrooms; location; helpful service. **Cons:** can be a bit noisy; no elevator with steep, narrow stairs. [$] *Rooms from: €170* ✉ *Via Roma 64* ☎ *39/3920121912* 🌐 *www.bellambra5terre.com* 🛏 *5 rooms* 🍽 *Free Breakfast.*

$$ B&B/INN 🏨 **Il Giardino Incantato.** With wood-beam ceilings and stone walls, the stylishly restored and updated rooms in this 16th-century house in the historic center of Monterosso ooze comfort and old-world charm. **Pros:** spacious rooms; gorgeous garden; excellent hosts. **Cons:** no views. [$] *Rooms from: €180* ✉ *Via Mazzini 18* ☎ *0185/818315* 🌐 *www.ilgiardinoincantato.net* 🕓 *Closed Nov.–early Apr.* 🛏 *4 rooms* 🍽 *Free Breakfast.*

$$$$ HOTEL 🏨 **Porto Roca.** Far from the madding crowds, one of Cinque Terre's only high-end hotel is perched on the famous terraced cliffs right over the main beach and magnificent sea with large balconies to savor all the panoramic views. **Pros:** unobstructed sea views; tranquil location; pool. **Cons:** some of the rooms could use a revamp; back-facing rooms can be a bit dark; expensive for level of comfort offered. [$] *Rooms from: €340* ✉ *Via Corone 1* ☎ *0187/817502* 🌐 *www.portoroca.it* 🕓 *Closed Nov.–Mar.* 🛏 *45 rooms* 🍽 *Free Breakfast.*

RIVIERA DI LEVANTE

Stretching east from Lerici to Genoa (and incorporating Cinque Terre) lies the Riviera di Levante (Riviera of the Rising Sun). It has a more raw, unpolished side to it than the Riviera di Ponente, east of Genoa, and its stretches of rugged coastline are dotted with colorful fishing villages. It's also home to one of Europe's well-known playgrounds for the rich and famous, the inlet of Portofino. Around every turn of this area's twisting roads the hills plummet sharply to the sea, forming deep, hidden bays and coves. Beaches on this coast tend to be rocky, backed by spectacular sheer cliffs, yet there are some rather lovely sandy beaches in Lerici, Monterosso, Levanto, and Paraggi near Portofino.

LERICI

106 km (66 miles) southeast of Genoa, 65 km (40 miles) west of Lucca.

Lerici is located in the spectacular Bay of La Spezia, otherwise known as the Gulf of Poets, and is famous for its natural beauty. Near Liguria's border with Tuscany, this picturesque village dates back to medieval times when, under the rule of Pisa, it fought cross-bay battles with Genovese Portovenere, as well as with local pirates. The town is set on a magnificent coastline of gray cliffs jutting down into a crystal clear sea and surrounded by a national park that is like an unframed painting of pine forests, olive trees, and tiny colorful hamlets. The waterfront piazza is filled with trompe-l'oeil frescoed buildings, and seaside cafés line a charming little harbor that holds sailboats and *gozzi,* the typical small fishing boats of the area.

There are several white-sand beaches and bathing establishments dotting the 2-km (1-mile) walk along the bay from the village center to nearby San Terenzo. From the village, you can also reach some beautiful hiking trails that head southeast to both seaside and hilltop villages like Fiascherino, Tellaro, and Montemarcello.

GETTING HERE AND AROUND
By car, Lerici is less than a 10-minute drive west from the A12 with plenty of blue signs indicating the way. There's a large pay-parking lot about a 10-minute walk along the seaside promenade from the center. By train, the closest station is either Sarzana (10-minute drive) or La Spezia Centrale (20-minute drive) on the main north–south line between Genoa and Pisa.

VISITOR INFORMATION
Contact Lerici Tourism Office. ⊠ *Via Biaggini 6* ☎ *0187/967164* ⊕ *www. comune.lerici.sp.it.*

EXPLORING
Castello di Lerici. The promontory is dominated by this 13th-century Pisan castle that now houses a museum of paleontology and art exhibits, and offers a superb position for weddings—it overlooks the entire Gulf of Poets. ⊠ *Piazza S. Giorgio 1* ☎ *0187/969042* ⊠ *€6.*

WHERE TO EAT
$$$$ ✕ **Bonta Nascoste.** In the local dialect, *bonta nascoste* means "hidden good-
ITALIAN ness," a reference to the back-alleyway location and consistently delicious dishes, including fresh pasta and local fish. This charming spot also serves a handful of delicious meat choices. **Known for:** fresh pasta; cozy atmosphere; local fish. $ *Average main: €40* ⊠ *Via Cavour 52* ☎ *0187/965500* ⊕ *www.bontanascoste.it* ☉ *Closed Mon. and Tues. Nov.–Mar.*

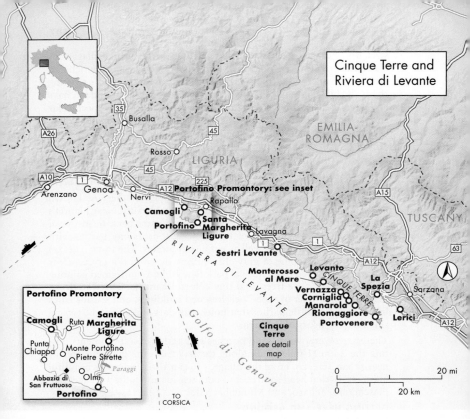

Portofino Promontory: see inset

Portofino Promontory

Cinque Terre see detail map

$$ ✕ **Il Frantoio.** Located in an old olive-oil mill (the enormous wood grinder
LIGURIAN still sits in the middle of the dining room), this is a no-frills but fine-
food restaurant serving excellent antipasti *al mare* and homemade pasta
dishes. You can eat very well for a bit less than at most of the touristy
spots in town. **Known for:** reasonable prices; rustic setting; homemade
pasta. $ *Average main: €18* ⊠ *Via Cavour 21* ☎ *0187/964174.*

$$ ✕ **La Caletta.** One of the few restaurants in Tellaro to remain open year-
LIGURIAN round (due to its popularity), this family-run trattoria serves delectable
Fodor'sChoice seafood dishes in a warm and friendly atmosphere. Do not miss the
★ seafood antipasto with fresh fish and seasonally available ingredients
including stuffed mussels, crab claws, swordfish, and grilled anchovies.
Known for: family-run friendly atmosphere; seafood antipasto; catch-
of-the-day specialties. $ *Average main: €16* ⊠ *Via Fiascherino 100,
Tellaro* ☎ *0187/964000* ⊕ *www.osterialacaletta.com* ☾ *Closed Tues.
(except in summer)* ⊟ *No credit cards.*

WHERE TO STAY

$$ ⌂ **Doria Park.** The junior suites have large terraces and Jacuzzi tubs, but
HOTEL any of the sea-view rooms are a real value, and the location, between
FAMILY olive-tree hills and the village center, is among the best in Lerici. **Pros:**
Fodor'sChoice sea views; comfortable beds; not far from the main piazza and harbor.
★ **Cons:** many stairs, including several sets that can be challenging for

people with weak knees or heavy bags. $ *Rooms from: €169* ✉ *Via Carpanini 9* ☎ *0187/967124* ⊕ *www.doriaparkhotel.it* 🛏 *54 rooms* ❁ *Free Breakfast.*

$$
HOTEL
FAMILY
⬚ **Florida.** Extras such as sea-view balconies make this seafront, family-run establishment well worth the euros. **Pros:** beachfront location; bay views; friendly staff. **Cons:** small rooms; beach across the street can be noisy, especially in summer. $ *Rooms from: €130* ✉ *Lungomare Biaggini 35* ☎ *0187/967332* ⊕ *www.hotelflorida.it* ♥ *Closed approximately Dec.–Feb.* 🛏 *40 rooms* ❁ *Free Breakfast.*

LA SPEZIA

11 km (7 miles) northwest of Lerici, 103 km (64 miles) southeast of Genoa.

La Spezia is sometimes thought of as nothing but a large, industrialized naval port en route to the Cinque Terre and Portovenere, but it does possess some charm, and it gives you a look at a less tourist-focused part of the Riviera. Its palm-lined promenade, fertile citrus parks, renovated Liberty-style palazzi, and colorful balcony-lined streets make parts of La Spezia surprisingly beautiful. Monday through Saturday mornings, you can stroll through the fresh fish, produce, and local-cheese stalls at the outdoor market on Piazza Cavour, and on Friday take part in the busy flea market on Via Garibaldi. There's also Porto Mirabello, a newly built tourist port with a pool club, shops, and several restaurants that overlook the fleet of superyachts.

GETTING HERE AND AROUND
By car, take La Spezia exit off the A12. La Spezia Centrale train station is on the main north–south railway line between Genoa and Pisa.

VISITOR INFORMATION
Contact La Spezia Tourism Office. ✉ *Via del Prione 22* ☎ *0187/026152* ⊕ *turismocultura.spezianet.it.*

EXPLORING

FAMILY **Castello di San Giorgio.** The remains of this massive 13th-century castle atop a small hill above the modern town now house a small museum dedicated to local archaeology. ✉ *Via XXVII Marzo* ☎ *0187/751142* ⊕ *museodelcastello.spezianet.it* 🎟 *€5.50.*

WHERE TO EAT

$$
PIZZA
✕ **La Pia.** Considered an institution, this *farinateria* and pizzeria dates back to 1887. During the lunch hour, you will probably find a line out the door, while inside—and on the patio in summer—locals munch on farinata, a chickpea pancake that's a Ligurian delicacy, and on thick-crust pizzas served hot out of the wood-burning oven. **Known for:** thick-crust pizzas; chickpea pancakes; traditional recipes. $ *Average main: €15* ✉ *Via Magenta 12* ☎ *0187/739999* ⊕ *www.lapia.it* ♥ *Closed Sun., and 2 wks in Aug. and Nov.*

PORTOVENERE

12 km (7 miles) south of La Spezia, 114 km (70 miles) southeast of Genoa.

The colorful facades and pedestrian-only *calata* (promenade) make Portovenere the quintessential Ligurian seaside village; it's often referred to as the sixth town of the Cinque Terre, but it has half the crowds. As a UNESCO World Heritage Site, its harbor is lined with tall, thin terratetto houses that date from as far back as the 11th century and are connected in a wall-like formation to protect against attacks by the Pisans and local pirates. Its tiny *carruggi* (alleylike passageways) lead to an array of charming shops, homes, and gardens, and eventually to the village's impressive **Castle Doria,** high on the olive-tree-covered hill. To the west, standing guard over the Mediterranean, is the picturesque medieval **Chiesa di San Pietro,** once the site of a temple to Venus (Venere in Italian), from which Portovenere gets its name. Nearby, in a rocky area leading to the sea, is Byron's Cave, one of the poet's favorite spots for swimming out into the sea.

GETTING HERE AND AROUND

By car from the port city of La Spezia, follow the blue signs for Portovenere. It's about a 20-minute winding drive along the sea through small fishing villages. From La Spezia train station you can hire a taxi for about €30. By bus from Via Garibaldi in La Spezia (a 10-minute walk from the train station) it takes 20 minutes.

VISITOR INFORMATION

Portovenere doesn't have a tourist office; you can get information at the Comune (Town Hall) or at the tourist office in La Spezia Centrale train station.

EXPLORING

Grotto Arpaia. Lord Byron (1788–1824) is said to have written *Childe Harold's Pilgrimage* in Portovenere. Near the entrance to the huge, strange Grotto Arpaia, at the base of the sea-swept cliff, is a plaque recounting the poet's strength and courage as he swam across the gulf to the village of San Terenzo, near Lerici, to visit his friend Shelley (1792–1822). ⊠ *Portovenere.*

San Pietro. This 13th-century Gothic church is built on the site of an ancient pagan shrine, on a formidable solid mass of rock above the Grotto Arpaia. With its black-and-white-striped exterior, it is a spectacular landmark recognizable from far out at sea and upon entering the village. There's a fantastic view of the Cinque Terre coastline from the front porch of the church. ⊠ *Waterfront promenade.*

WHERE TO EAT AND STAY

$$
LIGURIAN
FAMILY
Fodor's Choice
★

✕ **Il Timone.** Find some of the best food in Portovenere right as you disembark the ferry in this charming and affordable little port-side restaurant. Dishes are typical "Ligure," ranging from roasted rabbit to spaghetti with La Spezia mussels as well as farinata, focaccia, and pizza with different toppings. **Known for:** affordable prices; varied menu from pizza to meat dishes; port-side dining. Ⓢ *Average main: €15* ⊠ *Via Olivo 29* ☎ *347/2601008* ⊕ *www.pizzeriailtimone.it* ☾ *Closed Tues.*

$$$$ 🍴 **Locanda Lorena.** Across the small bay of Portovenere lies the rugged
LIGURIAN island of Palmaria. There are only a few restaurants on the island, and here Iseo (aka Giuseppe), an accomplished chef, does the cooking. **Known for:** fun atmosphere; views of Portovenere Bay; fresh pasta and local fish. [$] *Average main: €50* ✉ *Palmaria Island* ☎ *0187/792370* 🌐 *www.locandalorena.com* 🕓 *Closed Nov.*

$$$ 🏨 **Grand Hotel Portovenere.** This 13th-century Franciscan convent turned
HOTEL elegant hotel recently received a much needed face-lift while retaining the structure's impressive rose facade, arches, and frescoes. **Pros:** excellent location and views. **Cons:** updated rooms bring new hefty rates. [$] *Rooms from: €250* ✉ *Via Giuseppe Garibaldi 5* ☎ *0187/777751* 🌐 *www.portoveneregrand.it* 🕓 *Closed Nov.–mid-Mar.* 🛏 *52 rooms* 🍽 *Free Breakfast.*

$$ 🏨 **Hotel Belvedere.** True to the name, the best rooms in this sunny Lib-
HOTEL erty-style building face the bay of Portovenere, with lovely views of Palmaria Island and the Gulf of Poets. **Pros:** reasonably priced rooms with water views. **Cons:** parts of the hotel could use a makeover; limited parking. [$] *Rooms from: €130* ✉ *Via G. Garibaldi 26* ☎ *0187/790608* 🌐 *www.belvedereportovenere.it* 🕓 *Closed Nov.–mid-Mar.* 🛏 *17 rooms* 🍽 *Free Breakfast.*

LEVANTO

8 km (5 miles) northwest of Monterosso al Mare, 60 km (36 miles) southeast of Genoa.

Nestled at the end of a valley of pine forests, olive groves, vineyards, and medieval villages lies this sunny seaside town: an alternative and usually less expensive base to explore the Cinque Terre and the Riviera di Levante.

GETTING HERE AND AROUND

By car, take the Carodanno/Levanto exit off the A12 for 25 minutes to the town center. By train, Levanto is on the main north–south railway, one stop north of Monterosso.

VISITOR INFORMATION

Contact Levanto Tourism Office. ✉ *Piazza Cavour 1* ☎ *0187/808125* 🌐 *www.visitlevanto.it.*

EXPLORING

There's a long, sandy beach and a charming, colorful old quarter with plenty of shops, bars, and restaurants. Levanto has become a haven for not only sun worshippers but also divers, surfers, and hikers (and the path between Levanto and Monterosso, about a 2½-mile hike with free entrance, is breathtakingly beautiful in its own right). It's also an ideal starting point for day trips by train or boat to many interesting places along the Riviera such as Portovenere, Lerici, Tellaro, and Fiascherino heading toward La Spezia; and Portofino, Santa Margherita, Camogli, and Sestri Levante heading toward Genoa.

WHERE TO STAY

$$ HOTEL **La Giada del Mesco.** Tastefully decorated and bright guest rooms on the Punto Mesco headland have unobstructed vistas of the Mediterranean Sea and Riviera coastline. **Pros:** great position; nice pool. **Cons:** shuttle service is not always available; the 3½ km (1½ miles) into town is quite a walk, so you'll need a car. *Rooms from: €150 Via Mesco 16 0187/802674 www.lagiadadelmesco.com Closed mid-Nov.–Feb. 12 rooms Free Breakfast.*

SESTRI LEVANTE

37 km (22 miles) northwest of Levanto and 28 km (17 miles) southeast of Santa Margherita Ligure.

Halfway between the Cinque Terre and Portofino lies this lovely seaside resort. The old village is located on a peninsula with the beautiful Baia del Silenzio on one side and the Baia delle Favole and promenade on the other. These two bays were named in honor of the Danish author Hans Christian Andersen, who lived in Sestri for a short time.

GETTING HERE AND AROUND

By car, it is a five-minute drive off the A12. The Sestri Levante train station is located on the main north–south train line between Genoa and Pisa and is just a five-minute walk to the beach and old village.

VISITOR INFORMATION

Contact Sestri Levante Tourist Office. *Corso Colombo 50, Genoa 0185/478530 www.mediaterraneo.it.*

EXPLORING

Baia del Silenzio. The Bay of Silence is a sandy cove east of the pedestrian street in the old town, with pastel-colored buildings housing bars and restaurants edging the sand and bobbing boats dotting the horizon. It's a picture-postcard public beach and an idyllic setting for a dip in the Mediterranean, frequented mostly by locals and some visiting crowds in summer. You can also take a short walk up to the Convento dei Cappuccini, a church dedicated to the Virgin Mary. The monastery was built at the end of the 17th century and offers a spectacular panoramic view.

WHERE TO STAY

$$$ B&B/INN **Grand Hotel dei Castelli.** Originally built as a safeguard against pirates in the 11th century, this castle set on the edge of town, on a promontory overlooking the two bays, offers an ideal location with lots of character and beautiful grounds. **Pros:** grand setting with spectacular views; beautiful grounds; private inlet for guests only. **Cons:** some rooms and communal areas have a dated feel and could use updating; steep walk (or slow elevator) down to the beach. *Rooms from: €219 Via Penisola di Levante 26 0185/487020 www.hoteldeicastelli.it/en Closed Nov.–mid-Mar. 50 rooms Free Breakfast.*

SANTA MARGHERITA LIGURE

60 km (37 miles) northwest of Levanto, 31 km (19 miles) southeast of Genoa.

A beautiful old resort town favored by well-to-do Italians, Santa Margherita Ligure has everything a Riviera playground should have—including plenty of palm trees and attractive hotels, cafés, and a marina packed with yachts. Some of the older buildings here are still decorated on the outside with the trompe-l'oeil frescoes typical of this part of the Riviera. This is a pleasant, convenient base, which for many represents a perfect balance on the Italian Riviera: more spacious than the Cinque Terre; less glitzy than San Remo; more relaxing than Genoa and environs; and ideally situated for day trips, such as an excursion to Portofino.

GETTING HERE AND AROUND

By car, take the Rapallo exit off the A12 and follow the blue signs, about a 10-minute drive. The Santa Margherita Ligure train station is on the main north–south line between Genoa and Pisa.

VISITOR INFORMATION

Contact Santa Margherita Ligure Tourism Office. ⊠ *Piazza Vittorio Veneto* ☎ *0185/287485* ⊕ *www.smlturismo.it.*

WHERE TO EAT

$$ ╳ **La Paranza.** From the piles of tiny *bianchetti* (young sardines) in oil
LIGURIAN and lemon that are part of the antipasto di mare, to the simple, perfectly grilled sea bass, fresh seafood in every shape and form is the specialty in this unfussy spot just off Santa Margherita's port. Mussels, clams, octopus, or whatever else is fresh that day is what's on the menu. **Known for:** popular with locals; antipasto di mare; varied fresh seafood menu. Ⓢ *Average main: €15* ⊠ *Via Jacopo Ruffini 46* ☎ *0185/283686* ⊕ *www.laparanzasantamargherita.it* ☽ *Closed Mon.*

$$$ ╳ **La Stalla dei Frati.** The breathtaking hilltop views of Santa Margherita
LIGURIAN from this villa-turned-restaurant are worth the harrowing 3-km (2-mile)
Fodor'sChoice drive from the port. Cesare Frati, your congenial host, is likely to tempt
★ you with his homemade fettuccine ai frutti di mare followed by the *pescato del giorno alla moda ligure* (catch of the day baked Ligurian-style, with potatoes, olives, and pine nuts) and a delightfully fresh lemon sorbet to complete the feast. **Known for:** hilltop views; fresh catch of the day; homemade fettuccine. Ⓢ *Average main: €30* ⊠ *Via G. Pino 27, Nozarego* ☎ *0185/289447* ⊕ *www.ristorantelastalladeifrati.it* ☽ *Closed Mon. and Nov.*

$ ╳ **U' Giancu.** Owner Fausto Oneto is a man of many hats. Though
LIGURIAN original cartoons cover the walls of his restaurant and a playground is
Fodor'sChoice the main feature of the outdoor seating area, he is completely serious
★ about his cooking. **Known for:** cooking lessons; creative and playful setting; vegetables from the restaurant's garden. Ⓢ *Average main: €14* ⊠ *Via San Massimo 78, Località San Massimo* ☎ *0185/261212* ⊕ *www.ugiancu.it* ☽ *Closed Wed. and Nov.*

9

WHERE TO STAY

$$ **Continental.** A stately seaside mansion surrounded by a lush garden
HOTEL shaded by tall palms and pine trees offers stylish accommodations done
in a blend of classic furnishings, mostly inspired by the 19th century.
Pros: lovely location; private beach. **Cons:** rooms in the annex need to
be refurbished. $ *Rooms from: €140* ⊠ *Via Pagana 8* ☎ *0185/286512*
⊕ *www.hotel-continental.it* ☉ *Closed in winter until Mar. 16* ⇆*72
rooms* ⧖ *Free Breakfast.*

$$$ **Grand Hotel Miramare.** Classic Riviera elegance prevails at this palatial
RESORT hotel overlooking the bay, where antique furniture and crystal chande-
liers fill the high-ceiling rooms. **Pros:** top-notch service; private beach;
well-maintained rooms and marble bathrooms. **Cons:** traffic in summer
from the road in front of the hotel. $ *Rooms from: €206* ⊠ *Via Milite
Ignoto 30* ☎ *0185/287013* ⊕ *www.grandhotelmiramare.it* ☉ *Closed
Jan. 7–end of Mar.* ⇆ *82 rooms* ⧖ *Free Breakfast.*

$$$$ **Santa Margherita Palace.** Just a short walk from the old town, a well-
HOTEL kept and well-equipped hotel offers modern rooms with contemporary
furnishings, an abundant breakfast, and two spas. **Pros:** nice-size rooms
with plenty of storage; modern bathrooms; spas. **Cons:** the neighborhood is less charming than the old town and seaside. $ *Rooms from:
€339* ⊠ *Via Roma 9* ☎ *0185/287139* ⊕ *www.santamargheritapalace.
com* ⇆ *26 rooms* ⧖ *Free Breakfast.*

PORTOFINO

*5 km (3 miles) southeast of Santa Margherita Ligure, 36 km (22 miles)
east of Genoa.*

One of the most photographed villages along the coast, with a decidedly
romantic and affluent aura, Portofino has long been a popular destination for the rich and famous. Once an ancient Roman colony and taken
by the Republic of Genoa in 1229, it's also been ruled by the French,
English, Spanish, and Austrians, as well as by marauding bands of 16th-
century pirates. Elite British tourists first flocked to the lush harbor in
the mid-1800s. Some of Europe's wealthiest drop anchor in Portofino
in summer, but they stay out of sight by day, appearing in the evening
after buses and boats have carried off the day-trippers.

There's not actually much to *do* in Portofino other than stroll around
the wee harbor, see the castle, walk to Punta del Capo, browse at the
pricey boutiques, and sip a coffee while people-watching. However,
weaving through picture-perfect cliff-side gardens and gazing at yachts
framed by the sapphire Ligurian Sea and the cliffs of Santa Margherita
can make for quite a relaxing afternoon. There are also several tame,
photo-friendly hikes into the hills to nearby villages.

Unless you're traveling on a deluxe budget, you may want to stay in
Camogli or Santa Margherita Ligure rather than at one of Portofino's
few very expensive hotels. Restaurants and cafés are good but also
pricey (don't expect to have a beer here for much under €10).

GETTING HERE AND AROUND

By car, exit at Rapallo off the A12 and follow the blue signs (about a 20-minute drive mostly along the coast). The nearest train station is Santa Margherita Ligure.

Trying to reach Portofino by bus or car on the single narrow road can be a nightmare in summer and on holiday weekends. No trains go directly to Portofino: you must stop at Santa Margherita and take public Bus No. 82 from there (€3). An alternative is to take a boat from Santa Margherita.

Portofino can also be reached from Santa Margherita on foot: it's about a 40-minute (very pleasant) walk along the sea.

VISITOR INFORMATION

Contact **Portofino Tourism Office.** ⊠ *Via Roma 35* ☎ *0185/269024* ⊕ *www. turismoinliguria.it.*

EXPLORING

Abbazia di San Fruttuoso (*Abbey of San Fruttuoso*). A medieval stronghold built by the Benedictines of Monte Cassino protects a minuscule fishing village that can be reached only on foot or by water—a 20-minute boat ride from Portofino and also reachable from Camogli, Santa Margherita Ligure, and Rapallo. The restored abbey is now the property of a national conservation fund (FAI) and occasionally hosts temporary exhibitions and contains the tombs of some illustrious members of the Doria family. Plan on spending a few hours enjoying the abbey and grounds, and perhaps lunching at one of the modest beachfront trattorias nearby (open only in summer). Boatloads of visitors can make this place very crowded very fast; you might appreciate it most off-season. ⊠ *15-min boat ride or 2-hr walk northwest of Portofino* ☎ *0185/772703* 🎫 *€7 guided tours with a reservation in English or other foreign language for €170* ⏱ *Closed Mon. in Nov., Dec., and Jan.*

Castello Brown. From the harbor, follow the signs for the climb to Castello Brown—the most worthwhile sight in Portofino—with its medieval relics, impeccable gardens, and sweeping views. The castle was founded in the Middle Ages but restored in the 16th through 18th centuries. In true Portofino form, it was owned by Genoa's English consul from 1870 until it opened to the public in 1961. ⊠ *Above harbor, Via alla Penisola 13a* ☎ *335/8371156* ⊕ *www.castellobrown.com* 🎫 *€5.*

Paraggi. The only sand beach near Portofino is at Paraggi, a cove on the road between Santa Margherita and Portofino. The bus will stop here on request. ⊠ *Portofino.*

Punta Portofino. Pristine views can be had from the deteriorating *faro* (lighthouse) at Punta Portofino, a 15-minute walk along the point that begins at the southern end of the port. Along the seaside path you can see numerous impressive, sprawling private residences behind high iron gates. ⊠ *Portofino.*

San Giorgio. This small church, sitting on a ridge above Portofino, is said to contain the relics of its namesake, brought back from the Holy Land by the Crusaders. Portofino enthusiastically celebrates St. George's Day every April 23. ⊠ *Above harbor* ☎ *0185/269337.*

9

WHERE TO EAT

$
BAKERY

×**Canale.** If the staggering prices at virtually all of Portofino's cafés and restaurants are enough to ruin your appetite, join the long line outside this family-run bakery where you will find affordable and delicious eats worth waiting for. Here all the focaccia Genovese is baked on the spot and served fresh from the oven, along with all kinds of sandwiches, pastries, and other refreshments. **Known for:** fresh-baked focaccia; pastries and desserts; affordable prices. $ *Average main: €10* ⊠ *Via Roma 30* ☎ *0185/269248* ⊕ *www.panificiocanale.it* ⊟ *No credit cards* ⊙ *Closed Nov.–Feb.*

$$$$
LIGURIAN

×**Ristorante Puny.** If you want to be in the middle of everything, dine well, and don't mind spending a small fortune, then you'll want (and need) a reservation at this waterfront restaurant in Portofino. Quite simply, it's *the* place to be seen. **Known for:** waterfront dining; baked fish; fresh pappardelle. $ *Average main: €40* ⊠ *Piazza Martiri dell'Olivetta 4–5, on harbor* ☎ *0185/269037* ⊙ *Closed Thurs., and Jan. and Feb.*

WHERE TO STAY

$$$$
HOTEL

Belmond Hotel Splendido. This 1920s luxury hotel is where the rich and famous come to relax and play on the Italian Riviera and it appropriately oozes charm, taste, scenery and, of course, money. **Pros:** all rooms have garden or sea views; caring staff; lovely gardens. **Cons:** be prepared to spend upward of €100 for a simple lunch for two (it's not just the rooms that are pricey). $ *Rooms from: €980* ⊠ *Salita Baratta 16* ☎ *0185/267801* ⊕ *www.belmond.com/hotel-splendido-portofino* ⊙ *Closed Nov.–Mar.* ⬦ *108 rooms* ⦿ *Free Breakfast.*

$$$$
HOTEL

Eight Hotel Portofino. Immaculate, comfortable, and soothingly designed guest rooms some with canopy beds, and pastel walls, and ultramodern bathrooms spread across two small 19th-century town houses on a quiet backstreet. **Pros:** luxurious accommodations in the middle of the village; secluded garden at the back. **Cons:** some of the lower-level rooms don't receive much light; no sea views. $ *Rooms from: €463* ⊠ *Via Del Fondaco 11* ☎ *0185/26991* ⊕ *www.eighthotels.it* ⊙ *Closed Dec.–Mar.* ⬦ *18 rooms* ⦿ *Free Breakfast.*

SPORTS AND THE OUTDOORS

HIKING

If you have the stamina, you can hike to the Abbazia di San Fruttuoso from Portofino. It's a steep climb at first, and the walk takes about 2½ hours one way. If you're extremely ambitious and want to make a day of it, you can hike another 2½ hours all the way to Camogli. Much more modest hikes from Portofino include a one-hour uphill walk to Cappella delle Gave, a bit inland in the hills, from where you can continue downhill to Santa Margherita Ligure (another 1½ hours) and a gently undulating paved trail leading to the beach at Paraggi (½ hour). Finally, there's a 2½-hour hike from Portofino that heads farther inland to Ruta, through Olmi and Pietre Strette. The trails are well marked and maps are available at the tourist information offices in Rapallo, Santa Margherita Ligure, Portofino, and Camogli.

CAMOGLI

15 km (9 miles) northwest of Portofino, 20 km (12 miles) southeast of Genoa.

Camogli, at the edge of the large promontory and nature reserve known as the Portofino Peninsula, has always been a town of sailors. By the 19th century it was leasing its ships throughout the continent. Today multicolor houses, remarkably deceptive trompe-l'oeil frescoes, and a massive 17th-century seawall mark this appealing harbor community, which is perhaps as beautiful as Portofino but without the glamour. When exploring on foot, don't miss the second, more antiquated harbor, which is reached through a narrow archway at the northern end of the first one.

GETTING HERE AND AROUND

By car, exit the A12 at Recco and follow the blue signs. There are several pay-parking lots near the village center. Camogli is on the main north–south railway line between Genoa and La Spezia.

VISITOR INFORMATION

Contact Camogli Tourism Office. ✉ *Via XX Settembre 33/R* ☎ *0185/7771066* 🌐 *www.camogliturismo.it.*

EXPLORING

OFF THE BEATEN PATH

Ruta. The footpaths that leave from Ruta, 4 km (2½ miles) east of Camogli, thread through rugged terrain and contain a multitude of plant species. Weary hikers are sustained by stunning views of the Riviera di Levante from various vantage points along the way. ✉ *Camogli.*

WHERE TO EAT AND STAY

$$ SEAFOOD

🍴 **Vento Ariel.** This small, friendly restaurant serves some of the best seafood in town. Dine on the shaded terrace in summer and watch the bustling activity in the nearby port. **Known for:** shady terrace with port views; friendly atmosphere; mixed grilled fish dishes. [$] *Average main: €22* ✉ *Calata Porticciolo 1* ☎ *0185/771080* 🌐 *www.ventoariel.it.*

$$$ HOTEL

🏨 **Cenobio dei Dogi.** Perched majestically a step above Camogli, many of the rooms in the former summer palace of Genoa's doges have expansive balconies with commanding vistas of Camogli's cozy port. **Pros:** location and setting are wonderful; lovely pool and gardens; private beach. **Cons:** crowds make it seem overbooked in summer; decor is a bit old-fashioned. [$] *Rooms from: €220* ✉ *Via Nicolò Cuneo 34* ☎ *0185/7241* 🛏 *108 rooms* 🍽 *Free Breakfast.*

$$ B&B/INN Fodor's Choice ★

🏨 **Locanda I Tre Merli.** Located in a typical Ligurian terratetto on the old port, this charming locanda is reminiscent of old-world travel but with all the necessary amenities to make it a comfortable and relaxing stop for the modern traveler. **Pros:** great location and lovely views; breakfast on the patio overlooking the port. **Cons:** can be a bit noisy in the summer months; located right on port, so you have to park a distance away. [$] *Rooms from: €190* ✉ *Via Scalo 5* ☎ *0185/776752* 🌐 *locandaitremerli.com* 🛏 *5 rooms* 🍽 *Free Breakfast.*

$$ B&B/INN

🏨 **Villa Rosmarino.** A beautiful Ligurian villa in the beautiful hills just above Camogli offers chic, contemporary, and comfortable accommodations, along with well-manicured gardens and a welcoming pool.

Pros: large beds; well-equipped bathrooms; total sense of relaxation. **Cons:** some of the rooms are small and may not have enough amenities for everyone's taste; a 15-minute hike up from the village. $ *Rooms from: €170* ⊠ *Via Figari 38* ☎ *0185/771580* ⊕ *www.villarosmarino. com* ⟿ *6 rooms* ❍¶ *Free Breakfast.*

NIGHTLIFE AND THE PERFORMING ARTS

Sagra del Pesce. The highlight of the festival of San Fortunato is held on the second Sunday of May each year. It's a crowded, colorful, and free-to-the-public feast of freshly caught fish, cooked outside at the port in a frying pan 12 feet wide. ⊠ *Camogli* ⊕ *www.liguriaguide.com/ sagra-del-pesce.html.*

GENOA

Genoa (Genova in Italian) was the birthplace of Christopher Columbus, but the city's proud history predates that explorer by hundreds of years. Genoa was already an important trading station by the 3rd century BC, when the Romans conquered Liguria. The Middle Ages and the Renaissance saw it rise to become a jumping-off place for the Crusaders, a commercial center of tremendous wealth and prestige, and a strategic bone of international contention. A network of fortresses defending the city connected by a wall second only in length to the Great Wall of China was constructed in the hills above, and Genoa's bankers, merchants, and princes adorned the city with palaces, churches, and impressive art collections.

Crammed into a thin crescent of land between sea and mountains, Genoa expanded up rather than out, taking on the form of a multilayer wedding cake, with churches, streets, and entire residential neighborhoods built on others' rooftops. Public elevators and funiculars are as common as buses and trains.

But with its impressive palaces and museums, the largest medieval city center in Europe, and an elaborate network of ancient hilltop fortresses, Genoa may be just the dose of culture you're looking for. Europe's biggest boat show, the annual Salone Nautico Internazionale, is held here. Fine restaurants are abundant, and classical dance and music are richly represented. The Teatro Carlo Felice is the local opera venue, and it's where the internationally renowned annual Niccolò Paganini Violin Contest takes place.

GETTING HERE AND AROUND

By car, take the Genoa Ovest exit off the A12 and take the upper bridge (*sopralevata*) to the second exit, Genova Centro–Piazza Corvetto. But be forewarned: driving in Genoa is harrowing and best avoided whenever possible. If you want to see the city on a day trip, go by train; regular train service operates from Genoa's two stations. If you're staying in the city, park in a garage or by valet and go by foot and taxi throughout your stay.

The best way by far to get around Genoa is on foot, with the occasional assistance of public transportation. Many of the more interesting districts are either entirely closed to traffic, have roads so narrow that no car could fit, or are, even at the best of times, blocked by gridlock. Although it might seem a daunting task, exploring the city is made simple by its geography. The historical center of Genoa occupies a relatively narrow strip of land running between the mountains and the sea. You can easily visit the most important monuments in one or two days. The main bus station in Genoa is at Piazza Principe. Local buses operated by the municipal transport company, AMT, serve the steep valleys that run to some of the towns along the western coast. Tickets may be bought at local bus stations or at newsstands. (You must have a ticket before you board.) This company also operates the funicular railways and the elevators that service the steeper sections of the city.

Transportation Contacts AMT. ☒ *Piazza Acquaverde* ☎ *010/5582414* ⊕ *www.amt.genova.it.* **Stazione Brignole.** ☒ *Piazza Giuseppe Verdi, Foce* ☎ *010/892021.* **Stazione Principe.** ☒ *Piazza del Principe, San Teodoro.*

VISITOR INFORMATION

Contacts Genoa Tourism Offices. ☒ *Via Garibaldi, 12r, Maddalena* ☎ *010/5572903* ⊕ *www.genova-turismo.it* ☒ *Aeroporto Internazionale Cristoforo Colombo, Sestri Ponente* ☎ *010/6015247.*

EXPLORING

THE MEDIEVAL CORE AND POINTS ABOVE

The medieval center of Genoa, threaded with tiny streets flanked by 11th-century portals, is roughly the area between the port and Piazza de Ferrari. This mazelike pedestrian zone is officially called the Caruggi District, but the Genovese, in their matter-of-fact way, simply refer to the area as the place of the *vicoli* (alleys). In this warren of narrow, cobbled streets extending north from Piazza Caricamento, the city's oldest churches sit among tiny shops selling antique furniture, coffee, cheese, rifles, wine, gilt picture frames, camping gear, and even live fish. The 500-year-old apartment buildings lean so precariously that penthouse balconies nearly touch those across the street, blocking what little sunlight would have shone down onto the cobblestones. Wealthy Genovese built their homes in this quarter in the 16th century, and prosperous guilds, such as the goldsmiths for whom Vico degli Indoratori and Via degli Orefici were named, set up shop here.

TOP ATTRACTIONS

Cimitero Monumentale di Staglieno. One of the most famous of Genovese landmarks is this bizarrely beautiful cemetery; its fanciful marble and bronze sculptures sprawl haphazardly across a hillside on the outskirts of town. A pantheon holds indoor tombs and some remarkable works like an 1878 *Eve* by Villa. Don't miss Rovelli's 1896 **Tomba Raggio,** which shoots Gothic spires out of the hillside forest. The cemetery began operation in 1851 and has been lauded by such visitors as Mark Twain and Evelyn Waugh. It covers a good deal of ground (allow at least half a day to explore). Take Bus Nos. 12, 13, and 14 from the Stazione Genova Brignole, Bus Nos. 34 and 48 from Stazione Principe, or a taxi. ☒ *Piazzale Resasco 2, Piazza Manin* ☎ *010/5576400* ⊕ *www.asef.it/cimitero-di-staglieno* ☒ *Free.*

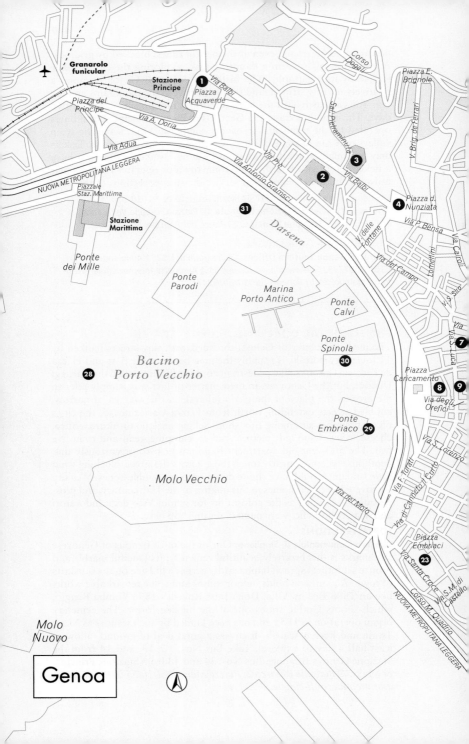

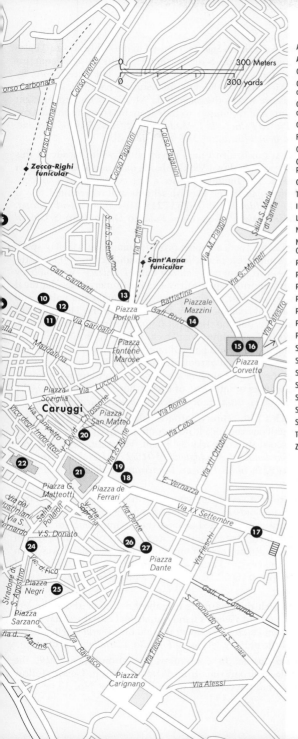

Galleria Nazionale di Palazzo Spinola. Housed in the richly adorned **Palazzo Spinola** north of Piazza Soziglia, this beautiful museum contains masterpieces by Luca Giordano and Guido Reni. The *Ecce Homo,* by Antonello da Messina, is a hauntingly beautiful painting, of historical interest because it was the Sicilian da Messina who first brought Flemish oil paints and techniques to Italy from his sojourns in the Low Countries. ✉ *Piazza Pellicceria 1, Maddalena* ☏ *010/2705300* ⊕ *www. palazzospinola.beniculturali.it* 🎫 *€6* ⊘ *Closed Mon.*

Palazzo Bianco. It's difficult to miss the splendid white facade of this town palace as you walk down Via Garibaldi, once one of Genoa's most important streets. The building houses a fine collection of 17th-century art, with the Spanish and Flemish schools well represented. ✉ *Via Garibaldi 11, Maddalena* ☏ *010/5572193* ⊕ *www.museidigenova. it* 🎫 *€9, includes Palazzo Rosso and Palazzo Doria Tursi* ⊘ *Closed Mon. and Dec. 25.*

Fodor'sChoice ⭐ **Palazzo Reale.** Lavish rococo rooms provide sumptuous display space for paintings, sculptures, tapestries, and Asian ceramics. The 17th-century palace—also known as Palazzo Balbi Durazzo—was built by the Balbi family, enormously wealthy Genovese merchants. Its regal pretensions were not lost on the Savoy, who bought the palace and turned it into a royal residence in the early 19th century. The gallery of mirrors and the ballroom on the upper floor are particularly decadent. Look for works by Sir Anthony Van Dyck, who lived in Genoa for six years, beginning in 1621, and painted many portraits of the Genovese nobility. ■TIP→ **The formal gardens (€1 entrance fee and free on the first Sunday of the month) provide a welcome respite from the bustle of the city, as well as great views of the harbor.** ✉ *Via Balbi 10, Pré* ☏ *010/2710286* ⊕ *www.palazzorealegenova.beniculturali.it* 🎫 *€6.*

Palazzo Rosso. This 17th-century Baroque palace was named for the red stone used in its construction. It now contains, apart from a number of lavishly frescoed suites, works by Titian, Veronese, Reni, and Van Dyck. ✉ *Via Garibaldi 18, Maddalena* ☏ *010/2759185* ⊕ *www.museidigenova.it* 🎫 *€9, includes Palazzo Bianco and Palazzo Doria Tursi* ⊘ *Closed Mon.*

Zecca-Righi funicular. A seven-stop commuter funicular begins at Piazza della Nunziata and ends at a high lookout on the fortified gates in the 17th-century city walls. Ringed around the circumference of the city are a number of huge fortresses; this gate was part of the city's system of defenses. From Righi you can undertake scenic all-day hikes from one fortress to the next. ✉ *Piazza della Nunziata, Pré* ☏ *010/5582414* ⊕ *www.amt.genova.it* 🎫 *€2.50, €4.50 for 24-hr Genovapass.*

WORTH NOTING

Castelletto. To reach this charming neighborhood high above the city center, you take one of Genoa's handy municipal elevators that whisk you skyward from Piazza Portello, at the end of Galleria Garibaldi, for a good view of the old city. ✉ *Piazza Portello, Castelletto* 🎫 *€0.90.*

FAMILY **Ferrovia Genova–Casella.** In continuous operation since 1929, the Genova–Casella Railroad runs from Piazza Manin in Genoa (follow Via Montaldo from the center of town, or take Bus No. 33 or 34 to

Piazza Manin) through the beautiful countryside above the city, finally arriving in the rural hill town of Casella. On the way, the tiny train traverses a series of precarious switchbacks that afford sweeping views of the forested Ligurian hills. In Casella Paese (the last stop) you can hike, eat lunch, or just check out the view and ride back. There are a few restaurants and pizzerias near the Casella station; try local cuisine at Trattoria Teresin on Via Avosso. **Canova** (two stops from the end of the line) is the start of two possible hikes through the hills: one a two-hour (one-way) trek to a small sanctuary, **Santuario della Vittoria,** and the other a more grueling four-hour hike to the hill town of **Creto.** Another worthwhile stop along the rail line is **Sant'Olcese Tullo,** where you can take a half-hour (one-way) walk along a river and through the **Sentiero Botanico di Ciaé,** a botanical garden and forest refuge with labeled specimens of Ligurian flora and a tiny medieval castle. For Canova and Sant'Olcese, inform your conductor that you want him to stop. The Genova–Casella Railroad is a good way to get a sense of the rugged landscape around Genoa, and you may have it to yourself. The train departs about every hour. ⊠ *Piazza Manin* 🕾 *010/5582414* ⊕ *www.ferroviagenovacasella.it* 🎫 *€4.50 round-trip.*

FAMILY **Granarolo Funicular.** Take a cog railway up the steeply rising terrain to another part of the city's fortified walls. It takes 15 minutes to hoist you from Stazione Principe, on Piazza Acquaverde, to **Porta Granarolo,** 1,000 feet above, where the sweeping view gives you a sense of Genoa's size. The funicular departs about every 40 minutes. ⊠ *Piazza del Principe, San Teodoro* 🕾 *010/5582414* ⊕ *www.amt.genova.it* 🎫 *€2.50.*

Loggia dei Mercanti. This merchants' row dating from the 16th century is lined with shops selling local foods and gifts, as well as raincoats, rubber boots, and fishing line. ⊠ *Piazza Banchi, Maddalena.*

Museo d'Arte Orientale Chiossone. One of Europe's most noteworthy collections of Japanese, Chinese, and Thai objects is housed in galleries in the Villetta di Negro park on the hillside above Piazza Portello. There's also a fine view of the city from the museum's terrace. ⊠ *Piazzale Mazzini 4, Maddalena* 🕾 *010/542285* ⊕ *www.museidigenova.it/it/content/museo-darte-orientale* 🎫 *€5* ☾ *Closed Mon.*

Palazzo dell'Università. Built in the 1630s as a Jesuit college, this has been Genoa's university since 1803. The exterior is unassuming, but climb the stairway flanked by lions to visit the handsome courtyard, with its portico of double Doric columns. ⊠ *Via Balbi 5, Pré* 🕾 *010/20991* ⊕ *www.unige.it.*

Palazzo Doria Tursi. In the 16th century, wealthy resident Nicolò Grimaldi had a palace built of pink stone quarried in the region. It's been reincarnated as Genoa's Palazzo Municipale (Municipal Building), and so most of the goings-on inside are the stuff of local politics and quickie weddings. You can visit the richly decorated **Sala Paganini,** where the famous Guarnerius violin that belonged to Niccolò Paganini (1782–1840) is displayed, along with the gardens that connect the palace with the neighboring Palazzo Bianco. ⊠ *Via Garibaldi 9, Maddalena* 🕾 *010/5572193* ⊕ *www.visitgenoa.it* 🎫 *€9, includes Palazzo Bianco and Palazzo Rosso* ☾ *Closed Mon.*

9

San Siro. Genoa's oldest church was the city's cathedral from the 4th to the 9th century. Rebuilt in the 16th and 17th centuries, it now feels a bit like a haunted house—imposing frescoes line dank hallways, and chandeliers hold crooked candles flickering in the darkness. ⊠ *Via San Siro 3, Maddalena* ☎ *010/2461674.*

Santissima Annunziata del Vastato. Exuberantly frescoed vaults decorate the 16th- to 17th-century church, which is an excellent example of Genovese Baroque architecture. ⊠ *Piazza della Nunziata, Pré* ☎ *010/2465525.*

SOUTHERN DISTRICTS AND THE AQUARIUM

Inhabited since the 6th century BC, the oldest section of Genoa lies on a hill to the southwest of the Caruggi District. Today, apart from a section of 9th-century wall near Porta Soprana, there's little to show that an imposing castle once stood here. Though the neighborhood is considerably run-down, some of Genoa's oldest churches make it a worthwhile excursion. No visit to Genoa is complete, however, without at least a stroll along the harbor front. Once a squalid and unsafe neighborhood, the port was given a complete overhaul during Genoa's preparations for the Columbus quincentennial celebrations of 1992, and additional restorations in 2003 and 2004 have done much to revitalize the waterfront. You can easily reach the port on foot by following Via San Lorenzo downhill from Genoa's cathedral, Via delle Fontane from Piazza della Nunziata, or any of the narrow vicoli that lead down from Via Balbi and Via Pré.

TOP ATTRACTIONS

FAMILY **Acquario di Genova.** Europe's biggest aquarium is the third-most-visited museum in Italy and a must for children. Fifty tanks of marine species, including sea turtles, dolphins, seals, eels, penguins, and sharks, share space with educational displays and re-creations of marine ecosystems, including a tank of coral from the Red Sea. An entire "Aquarium Village" has been created, which also includes a biosphere, hummingbird forest, and interactive submarine exhibit. If arriving by car, take the Genova Ovest exit from the autostrada. ⊠ *Ponte Spinola, Porto Vecchio* ☎ *0101/2345678* ⊕ *www.acquariodigenova.it* ⊠ *€26; Aquarium Village €54 (entrance to all attractions).*

Consorzio Liguria Viamare. Boat tours of the harbor, operated by the Consorzio Liguria Viamare, launch from the aquarium pier and last about an hour. The tours include a visit to the breakwater outside the harbor, the Bacino delle Grazie, and the Molo Vecchio (Old Port). There are also daily excursions down the coast as far as the Cinque Terre and Portovenere. ⊠ *Ponte dei Mille–Piano Calata, Porto Vecchio* ☎ *010/265712* ⊕ *www.liguriaviamare.it* ⊠ *Port tour €6, tours to Cinque Terre from €40 (summer only).*

Galata Museo del Mare. Devoted entirely to the city's seafaring history, this museum is probably the best way, at least on dry land, to get an idea of the changing shape of Genoa's busy port. Highlighting the displays is a full-size replica of a 17th-century Genovese galleon. ⊠ *Calata de Mari 1, Ponte dei Mille* ☎ *010/2345655* ⊕ *www.galatamuseodelmare.it* ⊠ *€12; €40 includes aquarium and submarine Nazario Sauro.*

The Harbor. A boat tour gives you a good perspective on the layout of the harbor, which dates to Roman times. The Genoa inlet, the largest along the Italian Riviera, was also used by the Phoenicians and Greeks as a harbor and a staging area from which they could penetrate inland to form settlements and to trade. The port is guarded by the Diga Foranea, a striking 5-km-long (3-mile-long) wall built into the ocean. The **Lanterna,** a lighthouse more than 360 feet tall, was built in 1544; it's one of Italy's oldest lighthouses and a traditional emblem of Genoa. ⊠ *Genoa.*

Palazzo Ducale. This palace was built in the 16th century over a medieval hall, and its facade was rebuilt in the late 18th century and later restored. It now houses temporary exhibitions and a restaurant-bar serving fusion cuisine. Reservations are necessary to visit the dungeons and tower. Guided tours (€5) of the palace, its prison tower, and its exhibitions are available. ⊠ *Piazza Matteotti 9, Portoria* ☎ *010/8171600* ⊕ *www.palazzoducale.genova.it* 🎫 *Free, specific exhibits vary.*

San Lorenzo. Contrasting black slate and white marble, so common in Liguria, embellishes the cathedral at the heart of medieval Genoa, inside and out. Consecrated in 1118, the church honors St. Lawrence, who passed through the city on his way to Rome in the 3rd century. For hundreds of years the building was used for religious and state purposes such as civic elections. Note the 13th-century Gothic portal, the fascinating twisted barbershop columns, and the 15th- to 17th-century frescoes inside. The last campanile dates from the early 16th century. The **Museo del Tesoro di San Lorenzo** (San Lorenzo Treasury Museum) housed inside has some stunning pieces from medieval goldsmiths and silversmiths, for which medieval Genoa was renowned. ⊠ *Piazza San Lorenzo, Molo* ☎ *010/2091863* 🎫 *Cathedral free, museum €6.*

Sant'Agostino. This 13th-century Gothic church was damaged during World War II, but still has a fine campanile and two well-preserved cloisters that house an excellent museum displaying pieces of medieval architecture and fresco paintings. Highlights of the collection are the enigmatic fragments of a tomb sculpture by Giovanni Pisano (circa 1250–1315). ⊠ *Piazza Sarzano 35/R, Molo* ☎ *010/2511263* ⊕ *www.museidigenova.it/it/content/museo-di-santagostino* 🎫 *€5* ☉ *Closed Mon.*

Santa Maria di Castello. One of Genoa's most significant religious buildings, an early-Christian church, was rebuilt in the 12th century and finally completed in 1513. You can visit the adjacent cloisters and see the fine artwork contained in the museum. Hours vary during religious services. ⊠ *Salita di Santa Maria di Castello 15, Molo* ☎ *347/9956740* ⊕ *www.santamariadicastello.it* 🎫 *Free.*

WORTH NOTING

Accademia delle Belle Arti. Founded in 1751, the city's famous art school houses a collection of paintings from the 16th to the 19th century. Genovese artists of the Baroque period are particularly well represented. ⊠ *Largo Pertini 4, Portoria* ☎ *010/506131* ⊕ *www.museo.accademialigustica.it* 🎫 *€5* ☉ *Closed weekends.*

Childhood Home of Christopher Columbus. The ivy-covered remains of this fabled medieval house stand in the gardens below the Porta Soprana.

CLOSE UP

The Art of the Pesto Pestle

You may have known Genoa primarily for its salami or its brash explorer, but the city's most direct effect on your life away from Italy may be through its cultivation of one of the world's best pasta sauces. The sublime blend of basil, extra-virgin olive oil, garlic, pine nuts, and grated pecorino and Parmigiano-Reggiano cheeses that forms *pesto alla Genovese* is one of Italy's crowning culinary achievements, a concoction that Italian food guru Marcella Hazan has called "the most seductive of all sauces for pasta." Ligurian pesto is served only over spaghetti, gnocchi, lasagna, or—most authentically—*trenette* (a flat, spaghetti-like pasta) or *trofie* (short, doughy pasta twists), and

then typically mixed with boiled potatoes and green beans. Pesto is also occasionally used to flavor minestrone.

The small-leaf basil grown in the region's sunny seaside hills is considered by many to be the best in the world, and pesto sauce was invented primarily as a showcase for that singular flavor. The simplicity and rawness of pesto is one of its virtues, as cooking (or even heating) basil ruins its delicate flavor. In fact, pesto aficionados refuse even to subject the basil leaves to an electric blender; Genovese (and other) foodies insist that true pesto can be made only with mortar and pestle.

A small collection of objects and reproductions relating to the life and travels of Columbus are on display inside. ⊠ *Piazza Dante, Molo* ☎ *010/2516714* ☜ *€5.*

FAMILY **Il Bigo.** This spiderlike white structure, designed by world-renowned architect Renzo Piano, was erected in 1992 to celebrate the Columbus quincentenary. You can take its **Ascensore Panoramico Bigo** (Bigo Panoramic Elevator) up 650 feet for a 360-degree view of the harbor, city, and sea. In winter there's an ice-skating rink next to the elevator, in an area covered by sail-like awnings. ⊠ *Ponte Spinola, Porto Vecchio* ☎ *010/2485711 skating rink* ☜ *Elevator €4.*

Mercato Orientale. In the old cloister of a church along Via XX Settembre, this bustling produce, fish, and meat market is a wonderful sensory overload. Get a glimpse of colorful everyday Genovese life watching the merchants and buyers banter over prices. ⊠ *Via XX Settembre, Portoria* ☉ *Closed Sun.*

Porta Soprana. A striking 12th-century twin-tower structure, this medieval gateway stands on the spot where a road from ancient Rome entered the city. It is just steps uphill from Columbus's boyhood home, and legend has it that the explorer's father was employed here as a gatekeeper. ⊠ *Piazza Dante, Molo.*

San Donato. Although somewhat marred by 19th- and 20th-century restorations, the 12th-century San Donato—with its original portal and octagonal campanile—is a fine example of Genovese Romanesque architecture. Inside, an altarpiece by the Flemish artist Joos Van Cleve (circa 1485–1540) depicts the Adoration of the Magi. ⊠ *Piazza San Donato, Portoria* ☎ *010/2468869* ⊕ *www.sandonato.org.*

San Matteo. This typically Genovese black-and-white-striped church dates from the 12th century; its crypt contains the tomb of Andrea Doria (1466–1560), the Genovese admiral who maintained the independence of his native city. The well-preserved Piazza San Matteo was, for 500 years, the seat of the Doria family, which ruled Genoa and much of Liguria from the 16th to the 18th century. The square is bounded by 13th- to 15th-century houses decorated with portals and loggias. ✉ *Piazza San Matteo, Maddalena* ☎ *010/2474361.*

Teatro Carlo Felice. The World War II–ravaged opera house in Genoa's modern center, Piazza de Ferrari, was rebuilt and reopened in 1991 to host the fine Genovese opera company; its massive tower has been the subject of much criticism. Lavish productions of old favorites and occasional world premieres are staged from October to May. ✉ *Piazza de Ferrari, Passo Eugenio Montale 4, Portoria* ☎ *010/53811* 🌐 *www.carlofelice.it.*

WHERE TO EAT

$$ LIGURIAN 🍴 **Da Gaia.** For a truly Genovese experience, this unassuming restaurant, located in the cantina of an old palazzo in the heart of the centro storico between Strada Nuova and the port, is just the place. From stuffed anchovies to sublime pesto, you'll find some of the best, most authentic food in the city. **Known for:** sublime pesto; stuffed anchovies; authentic local experience. [$] *Average main: €15* ✉ *Vico dell'Argento, Maddalena* ☎ *010/2461629.*

$$ LIGURIAN 🍴 **Enoteca Sola.** Menus are chosen specifically to complement wines at Pino Sola's airy, casually elegant enoteca in the heart of the modern town. The short menu emphasizes seafood and varies daily but might include stuffed artichokes or baked stockfish. **Known for:** extensive wine list; well-curated menu; elegant setting. [$] *Average main: €22* ✉ *Via C. Barabino 120/R, Foce* ☎ *010/594513* 🌐 *www.enotecaristorantesola.com* 🕒 *Closed Sun.*

$$$ LIGURIAN 🍴 **iCuochi.** This delicious bistro-style restaurant has taken over the space belonging to once-popular Bakari Trattoria and is proving to be a great alternative, popular with locals and visitors alike. The decor retains the same funky Art Nouveau theme, while the food is refined, almost elegant. **Known for:** Art Nouveau interior; refined dishes; local atmosphere. [$] *Average main: €25* ✉ *Vico del Fieno 18r, Maddalena* ☎ *010/2476170.*

$ LIGURIAN 🍴 **Il Genovese.** Roberto Panizza's cute trattoria has some of the city's best and least expensive Ligurian dishes. The setting is casual and comfortable, and the staff friendly and knowledgeable about the region's delicacies featured on the always interesting menu. **Known for:** reasonable prices; casual atmosphere; incredible pesto. [$] *Average main: €12* ✉ *Via Galata 35r, Brignole* ☎ *010/8692937* 🌐 *www.ilgenovese.com* 🕒 *Closed Sun.*

$ LIGURIAN 🍴 **Trattoria Ugo.** This unassuming trattoria is full of old-world Genovese charm and delicious dishes. Popular among locals for the homemade pastas and Ligurian cima, the menu changes daily and consists of only a few choices, all relatively inexpensive. **Known for:** small, inexpensive menu; old-world Genovese charm; local atmosphere. [$] *Average main: €12* ✉ *Via dei Gustiniani 86, Maddalena* ☎ *010/2469302* ⏲ *Closed Sun. and Mon.*

WHERE TO STAY

$ HOTEL FAMILY 🏨 **Best Western Metropoli.** Rooms and bathrooms are bright and spacious at this welcoming inn on the border of the historic district and Via Garibaldi. **Pros:** guest rooms and bathrooms are large; great rooms for families. **Cons:** parking lot is a bit of a hike; can be confusing to find if you are driving. [$] *Rooms from: €117* ✉ *Piazza Fontane Marose, Portoria* ☎ *010/2468888* 🌐 *www.hotelmetropoli.it* 🛏 *48 rooms* 🍴 *Free Breakfast.*

$$ HOTEL 🏨 **Bristol Palace.** One of Europe's gracious 19th-century grand hotels carefully guards its reputation for courtesy, service, and elegance, with spacious, handsomely furnished high-ceiling guest rooms and lovely public spaces. **Pros:** new outdoor dining terrace is lovely; in the heart of the shopping district. **Cons:** busy street outside can sometimes be noisy. [$] *Rooms from: €180* ✉ *Via XX Settembre 35, Portoria* ☎ *010/592541* 🌐 *www.hotelbristolpalace.com* 🛏 *133 rooms* 🍴 *Free Breakfast.*

$$ HOTEL FAMILY 🏨 **Grand Hotel Savoia.** Old-world glamour and service meets modern design and comfort in this flamboyant, pink-and-white 1897 building convenient to the port, train station (across the street), shopping, and the old town. **Pros:** nice-size rooms; rooftop restaurant and bar. **Cons:** its neighborhood near the Principe station is not as nice as other nearby neighborhoods. [$] *Rooms from: €162* ✉ *Via Arsenale di Terra 5* ☎ *010/27721* 🌐 *www.grandhotelsavoiagenova.it* 🛏 *117 rooms* 🍴 *Free Breakfast.*

SHOPPING

Liguria is famous for its fine laces, silver-and-gold filigree work, and ceramics. Also look for bargains in velvet, macramé, olivewood, and marble. Genoa is the best spot to find all these specialties. In the heart of the medieval quarter, Via Soziglia is lined with shops selling handicrafts and tempting foods. Via XX Settembre and Via Roma are famous for their exclusive shops. High-end shops line Via Luccoli. The best shopping area for trendy-but-inexpensive Italian clothing is near San Siro, on Via San Luca.

CLOTHING AND LEATHER GOODS

Pescetto. Look for designer clothes, perfumes, and fancy gifts at Pescetto. ✉ *Via Scurreria 8, Molo* ☎ *010/2473433.*

JEWELRY

Codevilla. The well-established Codevilla is one of the best jewelers in the city. They sell top-of-the-line watches and custom jewelry. ✉ *Via Roma 83/85r* ☎ *010/8938278* 🌐 *www.luigicodevilla.it/codevilla.*

WINES

Vinoteca Sola. You can purchase the best Ligurian wines and have them shipped home. You can even buy futures for vintages to come. ⊠ *Piazza Colombo 13–15/R, near Stazione Brignole, Foce* ☎ *010/561329* ⊕ *www.vinotecasola.it.*

NERVI: SIDE TRIP FROM GENOA

11 km (7 miles) east of Genoa.

The identity of this stately late-19th-century resort, famous for its 1½-km-long (1-mile-long) seaside **Passeggiata Anita Garibaldi,** its palm-lined roads, and its 300 acres of parks rich in orange trees, is given away only by the sign on the sleepy train station. Although Nervi is technically part of the city, its peace and quiet are as different from Genoa's hustle and bustle as its clear blue water is from Genoa's crowded port. From the centrally located train station, walk east along the seaside promenade to reach the beaches, a cliff-side restaurant, and the 2,000 varieties of rose in the public **Parco Villa Grimaldi,** all the while enjoying one of the most breathtaking views on the Riviera. Nervi and the road between it and Genoa are known for their nightlife in summer.

GETTING HERE

By car, exit the A12 at Genova Nervi and follow the "Centro" signs. The Nervi train station is on the main north–south line, and you can also take the commuter trains from Genova Principe and Brignole. It can also be reached on Bus No. 15 from Genoa's Piazza Cavour.

WHERE TO STAY

$$
HOTEL
Fodor's Choice
★

Romantik Hotel Villa Pagoda. A 19th-century merchant's mansion modeled after a Chinese temple has a private park, access to the famed cliff-top walk, and magnificent ocean views; request a tower room for the best vantage point. **Pros:** lovely guest and common rooms; everything has a touch of class. **Cons:** nearby train can be softly heard. $ *Rooms from: €125* ✉ *Via Capolungo 15* 📞 *010/323200* 🌐 *www.villapagoda.it* ⊙ *Typically closed Nov.–Mar.* ⇴ *17 rooms* ❑ *Free Breakfast.*

RIVIERA DI PONENTE

The Riviera di Ponente (Riviera of the Setting Sun) covers the narrow strip of northwest Liguria from Genoa to the French border. The sapphire Mediterranean Sea to one side and the verdant foothills of the Alps on the other allow for temperate weather and a long growing season—which it is why it's also called the "Riviera dei Fiori" (Riviera of the Flowers). Once filled with charming seaside villages, elegant homes, and sophisticated visitors, this area now struggles to maintain a balance between its natural beauty and development. Highly populated resort areas and some overly industrialized areas are jammed into the thin stretch of white-sand and pebble beaches. But, there are still several worthwhile villages along the sea and hinterland. While its sister, the Riviera di Levante, may retain more of its natural beauty, the Ponente remains a popular retreat for visitors looking for sunshine, nightlife, and relaxation.

FINALE LIGURE

72 km (44 miles) southwest of Genoa.

Lovely Finale Ligure is actually made up of three small villages: Finalmarina, Finalpia, and Finalborgo, and makes a wonderful base for exploring the Ponente. The former two have fine sandy beaches and a mix of traditional and modern resort amenities. Finalborgo, less than 1 km (½ mile) inland, is an attractive medieval walled village with nice shops and restaurants. Just above is a hauntingly preserved medieval settlement, planned to a rigid blueprint, with 15th-century walls. The surrounding countryside is pierced by deep, narrow valleys and caves; the limestone outcroppings provide the warm pinkish stone found in many buildings in Genoa. Rare reptiles lurk among the exotic flora.

GETTING HERE AND AROUND

By car, take the Finale Ligure exit off the A10 and follow the "Centro" signs. Finale Ligure is on the main train line between Genoa and France.

VISITOR INFORMATION

Contact Finale Ligure Tourism Office. ✉ *Via San Pietro 14* 📞 *019/681019* 🌐 *turismo.comunefinaleligure.it.*

EXPLORING

OFF THE BEATEN PATH

Noli. Just 9 km (5½ miles) northeast of Finale Ligure, the ruins of a castle loom benevolently over the tiny medieval gem of Noli. It's hard to imagine that this charming seaside village was—like Genoa, Venice, Pisa, and Amalfi—a prosperous maritime republic in the Middle Ages. Let yourself get lost among its labyrinth cobblestone streets filled with shops and cafés or enjoy a day in the sun on its lovely stretch of beach. If you don't have a car, get a bus for Noli at Spotorno, where local trains stop. ✉ *Finale Ligure* 🌐 *www.tpllinea.it.*

WHERE TO EAT AND STAY

$$$ LIGURIAN

🍴 **Ai Torchi.** You could easily become a homemade-pesto snob at this restored 5th-century olive-oil mill–turned–chic restaurant in the historical center of Finalborgo. The high prices are justified by excellent and inventive seafood and meat dishes as well as the lovely setting. **Known for:** excellent pesto; inventive seafood and meat dishes; chic atmosphere. [$] *Average main: €25* ✉ *Via dell'Annunziata 12* ☎ *019/690531* 🌐 *www.ristoranteaitorchi.com* 🕓 *Closed Jan. 10–Feb. 10.*

$$ B&B/INN

🏨 **Ca de' Tobia.** This lovely guesthouse consists of five rooms and a suite on the seafront promenade of Noli and is stylishly done with wood floors, splashes of bright colors, and modern decor. **Pros:** ultrachic; full of modern amenities. **Cons:** right on the main road through town, so there is some street noise. [$] *Rooms from: €150* ✉ *Via Aurelia 35, Noli* ☎ *0197/485845* 🌐 *www.cadetobia.it* 🛏 *6 rooms* 🍽 *Free Breakfast.*

$$ HOTEL Fodor's Choice ★

🏨 **Hotel San Pietro Palace.** Originally built in the 17th century, this palatial hotel—centrally located next to the main piazza, and facing the lovely, palm-tree-lined, seafront promenade—has been elegantly restored. **Pros:** decent on-site restaurant; very nice accommodations; great sea views. **Cons:** central location leads to some noise from the promenade as well as early-morning trash trucks; parking is off-site and expensive. [$] *Rooms from: €168* ✉ *Via San Pietro 9* ☎ *019/6049156* 🌐 *www.hotelsanpietropalace.it* 🕓 *Closed Nov. 5–Dec. 26 and Jan. 8–Mar.* 🛏 *31 rooms* 🍽 *Free Breakfast.*

$$ HOTEL FAMILY

🏨 **Punta Est.** An old villa with a newer wing is perched on a fragrant hillside just above the white-sand beaches, making this a wonderful retreat from the crowds down at the water's edge. **Pros:** nice pool and charming garden areas. **Cons:** some rooms are a bit outdated. [$] *Rooms from: €190* ✉ *Via Aurelia 1* ☎ *39/019600611* 🌐 *www.puntaest.com* 🕓 *Closed mid-Oct.–mid-Apr.* 🛏 *39 rooms* 🍽 *Free Breakfast.*

ALBENGA

20 km (12 miles) southwest of Finale Ligure, 90 km (55 miles) southwest of Genoa.

Albenga has a medieval core, with narrow streets laid out by the ancient Romans. A network of alleys is punctuated by centuries-old towers surrounding the 18th-century Romanesque cathedral, with a late-14th-century campanile and a baptistery dating to the 5th century. It's a nice place to take an afternoon stroll and explore its many quaint shops and cafés.

GETTING HERE AND AROUND

By car, take the Albenga exit off the A10 and follow the "Centro" signs. Albenga is on the main train line between Genoa and France.

VISITOR INFORMATION

Contact Albenga Tourism Office. ✉ *Piazza del Popolo* ☎ *0182/558444.*

EXPLORING

OFF THE BEATEN PATH

Bardineto. For a look at some of the Riviera's mountain scenery, make an excursion by car to this attractive village in the middle of an area rich in mushrooms, chestnuts, and raspberries, as well as local cheeses. A ruined castle stands above the village. From Borghetto Santo Spirito (between Albenga and Finale Ligure), drive inland 25 km (15 miles). ✉ *Via Roascio 5, Bardineto* 🌐 *www.comune.bardineto.sv.it.*

IMPERIA

12 km (7 miles) southwest of Cervo, 116 km (71 miles) southwest of Genoa.

Imperia actually consists of two towns: Porto Maurizio, a medieval town built on a promontory, and Oneglia, now an industrial center for oil refining and pharmaceuticals. Porto Maurizio has a virtually intact medieval center, an intricate spiral of narrow streets and stone portals, and some imposing 17th- and 18th-century palaces. There's little of interest in modern Oneglia, except for a visit to the olive-oil museum.

GETTING HERE AND AROUND

By car, take the Imperia Est exit off the A10 and follow the signs for "Centro" or "Porto Maurizio." Both Imperia and Porto Maurizio are on the main rail line between Genoa and France.

EXPLORING

Museo dell'Olivo. Imperia is king when it comes to olive oil, and the story of the olive is the theme of this small museum. Displays of the history of the olive tree, farm implements, presses, and utensils show how olive oil has been made in many countries throughout history. A multilanguage audio guide is available for €3. ✉ *Via Garessio 13* ☎ *0183/295762* 🌐 *www.museodellolivo.com* 🎫 *€5* 🕒 *Closed Sun.*

WHERE TO STAY

$$ B&B/INN

🏨 **Relais San Damian.** All the rooms are suites at this charming inn, set among the olive trees high above Porto Maurizio and the Mediterranean sea. **Pros:** large suites and plenty of outdoor space; gorgeous pool area. **Cons:** limited amenities (no TVs or phones). [$] *Rooms from: €140* ✉ *Strada Vasia 47* ☎ *0183/280309* 🌐 *www.san-damian.com* 🛏 *10 rooms* 🍴 *Free Breakfast.*

SAN REMO

50 km (31 miles) southwest of Cervo, 146 km (90 miles) southwest of Genoa.

Once the crown jewel of the Riviera di Ponente, San Remo is still the area's largest resort, lined with polished hotels, exotic gardens, and seaside promenades. Renowned for its VIPs, glittering casino, annual music festival, and romantic setting, San Remo maintains remnants of its glamorous past from the late 19th century to World War II, but it also suffers from the same epidemic of overbuilding that has changed so much of the Ponente for the worse. Still, it continues to be a lively town, even in the off-season.

The Mercato dei Fiori, Italy's most important wholesale flower market, is held here in a market hall between Piazza Colombo and Corso Garibaldi, though it's open to dealers only. More than 20,000 tons of carnations, roses, mimosa flowers, and innumerable other kinds of cut flowers are dispatched from here each year. As the center of northern Italy's flower-growing industry, the town is surrounded by hills where verdant terraces are now blanketed with plastic to form immense greenhouses.

GETTING HERE AND AROUND
By car, take the San Remo exit off the A10 and follow the "Centro" signs. San Remo is on the main train line between Genoa and France.

VISITOR INFORMATION
Contact **San Remo Tourism Office.** ⊠ *Corso Gardibaldi 1* ☎ *0184/580500* ⊕ *www.turismoinliguria.it.*

EXPLORING
Cristo Salvatore, Santa Caterina d'Alessandria, e San Serafino di Sarov. This onion-dome Russian Orthodox church testifies to a long Russian presence on the Italian Riviera. Russian empress Maria Alexandrovna, wife of Czar Alexander I, built a summerhouse here, and in winter San Remo was a popular destination for other royal Romanovs. The church was consecrated in 1913. ⊠ *Via Nuvoloni 2* ☎ *0184/531807* ☑ *€1 donation.*

La Pigna (*The Pinecone*). San Remo's "old city" climbs upward to Piazza Castello, which offers a splendid view of the town and sea below. Some lovely old palazzi and squares have been restored, and the neighborhood gives you a sense of what it was like to live in San Remo in centuries gone by. ⊠ *San Remo* ⊕ *www.turismoinliguria.it.*

San Remo Casinò. In addition to gaming, this lovely Art Nouveau landmark offers a restaurant, a nightclub, and a theater that hosts concerts and the annual San Remo Music Festival. There is free admission, but if you want to try your luck at the gaming tables, bets begin at around €10, depending on the time of day or night. ■TIP→ **Dress is elegant, with jacket and tie requested at the French gaming tables.** ⊠ *Corso Inglesi 18* ☎ *0184/5951* ⊕ *www.casinosanremo.it.*

OFF THE BEATEN PATH

Bussana Vecchia. In the hills where flowers are cultivated for export, this self-consciously picturesque former ghost town is a flourishing artists' colony. The town was largely destroyed by an earthquake in 1877, when the inhabitants packed up and left en masse. For almost a century the houses, church, and crumbling bell tower were empty shells, overgrown by weeds and wildflowers. Since the 1960s painters, sculptors, artisans, and bric-a-brac dealers have restored the dwellings as houses and studios. ⊠ *8 km (5 miles) east of San Remo* ⊕ *www. bussanavecchia.it.*

WHERE TO EAT AND STAY

$$
LIGURIAN

✕ **Nuovo Piccolo Mondo.** Old wooden chairs dating from the 1920s, when the place opened, evoke the homey charm of this small, family-run trattoria. A faithful clientele keeps the kitchen busy, so get here early to grab a table and order Ligurian specialties such as *sciancui* (a roughly cut flat pasta with a mixture of beans, tomatoes, zucchini, and pesto) and *polpo e patate* (stewed octopus with potatoes). **Known for:** homey charm; busy local atmosphere; stewed octopus with potatoes. Ⓢ *Average main: €17* ✉ *Via Piave 7* ☎ *0184/509012* ☾ *Closed Sun.*

$$
LIGURIAN

✕ **Taverna al 29.** At the entrance of the old town is this intimate and comfortable dining establishment run by a husband (host) and wife (chef). The tavern's cuisine is linked to the Ligurian territory with old recipes revisited with creativity yet authenticity. **Known for:** traditional Ligurian dishes; gluten-free options; cozy atmosphere. Ⓢ *Average main: €20* ✉ *Piazza Cassini 5* ☎ *0184/570034* ⊕ *tavernaal29.com.*

$$
HOTEL

▦ **Paradiso.** Bright, well-equipped rooms face a quiet palm-fringed garden and pool; some enjoy sea views from nice-size balconies. **Pros:** friendly service; nice pool; free loungers and umbrellas at nearby beach. **Cons:** a steep walk up some stairs and a hill from town. Ⓢ *Rooms from: €130* ✉ *Via Roccasterone 12* ☎ *0184/571211* ⊕ *www.paradisohotel.it* ⤳ *41 rooms* ⦿ *Free Breakfast.*

$$$$
HOTEL

▦ **Royal.** This is arguably Liguria's second-most-luxurious resort after the Splendido in Portofino: each room has a unique and beautiful design, all have modern amenities, and most have views of the sea. **Pros:** the glamour of yesteryear with all the expected high-end amenities; reasonable prices given the surroundings. **Cons:** on-site meals and beverages are expensive. Ⓢ *Rooms from: €314* ✉ *Corso Imperatrice 80* ☎ *0184/5391* ⊕ *www.royalhotelsanremo.com* ☾ *Closed mid-Nov.–Feb 1* ⤳ *127 rooms* ⦿ *Free Breakfast.*

BORDIGHERA

12 km (7 miles) southwest of San Remo, 155 km (96 miles) southwest of Genoa.

Bordighera sits as an attractive seaside resort with panoramas from Genoa (on a clear day) to Monte Carlo. A large English colony, attracted by the mild climate, settled here in the second half of the 19th century and is still very much in evidence today; you regularly find people taking afternoon tea in the cafés, and streets are named after Queen Victoria and Shakespeare. This was the first town in Europe to grow date palms, and its citizens still have the exclusive right to provide the Vatican with palm fronds for Easter celebrations.

Thanks partly to its many year-round English residents, Bordighera doesn't close down entirely in the off-season like some Riviera resorts, but rather serves as a quiet winter haven for all ages. With plenty of hotels and restaurants and a lovely seafront promenade, Bordighera makes a good base for exploring the region and is quieter and less commercial than San Remo.

GETTING HERE AND AROUND

By car, take the Bordighera exit off the A10 and follow the signs for "Centro," about a 10-minute drive. Bordighera is on the main railway line between Genoa and France.

VISITOR INFORMATION

Contact Bordighera Tourism Office. ✉ *Via Vittorio Emanuele 172* ☎ *0184/262882* 🌐 *www.bordighera.it.*

EXPLORING

Lungomare Argentina. Running parallel to the ocean, Lungomare Argentina is a pleasant promenade, 1½ km (1 mile) long, which begins at the western end of the town and provides good views westward to the French Côte d'Azur. ✉ *Bordighera.*

WHERE TO EAT AND STAY

$$ SEAFOOD 🍴 **Agua.** This beachfront dining establishment has changed name and owners several times, but it continues to have some of the best food in town with a fantastic setting. The brothers running it have some very inventive and delicious dishes on their menu, including calamari sautéed with strips of artichoke and seared tuna on a bed of radicchio. **Known for:** ocean views; well-curated wine list; inventive seafood dishes. [$] *Average main: €15* ✉ *Lungomare Aregntina 10* ☎ *0184/261393* 🕒 *Closed in Nov. No dinner Mon.*

$$ LIGURIAN Fodor's Choice ★ 🍴 **Magiargè.** A mix of great charm and great food make this small osteria in the historic center an absolute dining delight. Dishes are Ligurian with a creative twist, such as the *stoccafisso sopra panissa* (salt cod served over a chickpea polenta) and *fritteline di bianchetti* (small frittatas made with tiny white fish). **Known for:** salt cod dishes; local wines; cozy atmosphere. [$] *Average main: €18* ✉ *Via Dritta 2* ☎ *0184/262946* 🌐 *www.magiarge.it* 🕒 *Closed Mon.*

$$ HOTEL 🏨 **Hotel Piccolo Lido.** Sea-view rooms at this small hotel along the promenade have nice little balconies, and there's a terrace perfect for enjoying the sunset and vistas of France. **Pros:** a good value; nice views. **Cons:** some of the rooms on the lower floors are in need of a revamp. [$] *Rooms from: €132* ✉ *Lungomare Argentina 2* ☎ *0184/261297* 🌐 *www.hotelpiccololido.it* 🛏 *33 rooms* 🍽 *Free Breakfast.*

$ HOTEL 🏨 **Hotel Villa Elisa.** On a street filled with beautiful old villas, this Victorian-era former residence has a relaxed and friendly atmosphere, beautiful gardens, a spa, and well-equipped rooms at reasonable prices. **Pros:** helpful staff; a good value; pool and garden make this a good choice for children. **Cons:** only partial views in sea-view rooms; limited parking; covered parking costs extra. [$] *Rooms from: €120* ✉ *Via Romana 70* ☎ *0184/261313* 🌐 *www.villaelisa.com* 🕒 *Closed Nov.–Dec. 22 and Jan. 7–Feb. 10* 🛏 *35 rooms* 🍽 *Free Breakfast.*

GIARDINI BOTANICI HANBURY

10 km (6 miles) west of Bordighera.

GETTING HERE AND AROUND
Take the SS1 along the coast west from Bordighera, through the town of Ventimiglia, and toward the French border. The gardens are about 1 km (½ mile) beyond the tunnel.

EXPLORING

Fodor'sChoice
★

Giardini Botanici Hanbury. Mortola Inferiore, only 2 km (1 mile) from the French border, is the site of the world-famous Hanbury Botanical Gardens, one of the largest and most beautiful in Italy. Planned and planted in 1867 by a wealthy English merchant, Sir Thomas Hanbury, and his botanist brother, Daniel, the terraced gardens contain species from five continents, including many palms and succulents. There are panoramic views of the sea from the gardens. ⊠ *Corso Montecarlo 43, Località Mortola Inferiore, Ventimiglia* ☎ *0184/229507* ⊕ *www.giardinihanbury.com* ✆ *€7.50 July 1–Mar. 19; €9 Mar. 20–June 30* ☉ *Closed Mon. Nov. 1–end of Feb.*

OFF THE
BEATEN
PATH

Balzi Rossi. Prehistoric humans left traces of their lives and magic rites in the Balzi Rossi (Red Rocks), caves carved in the sheer rock. You can visit the caves and a small museum displaying some of the objects found there. ⊠ *Via Balzi Rosso 9, 2 km (1 mile) west of Giardini Botanici Hanbury* ☎ *0184/38113* ✆ *€4.*

EMILIA–ROMAGNA

WELCOME TO EMILIA-ROMAGNA

TOP REASONS TO GO

★ **The signature food of Emilia:** This region's food—prosciutto crudo, Parmigiano-Reggiano, balsamic vinegar, and above all, pasta—makes the trip to Italy worthwhile.

★ **Mosaics that take your breath away:** The intricate tiles in Ravenna's Mausoleo di Galla Placidia, in brilliantly well-preserved colors, depict vivid portraits and pastoral scenes.

★ **Arguably Europe's oldest wine bar:** Nicholas Copernicus tippled here while studying at Ferrara's university in the early 1500s—Osteria al Brindisi, in the centro storico, has been pouring wine since 1435.

★ **The nightlife of Bologna:** This red-roof city has had a lively student culture since the university—Europe's oldest—was founded in the late 11th century.

★ **The medieval castles of San Marino:** Its three castles dramatically perch on a rock more than 3,000 feet above the flat landscape of Romagna.

Emilia-Romagna owes its beginnings to the Romans, who built the Via Emilia in 187 BC. Today the road bisects the flat, foggy region, paralleling the Autostrada del Sole (A1), making it easy to drive straight through. Bologna is in the middle of everything, with Piacenza, Parma, and Modena to the northwest, and the Adriatic to the southeast. Ferrara and Ravenna are the only detours—both north of the Via Emilia.

1 Emilia. A landscape of medieval castles and crumbling farmhouses begins just east of Milan, in the western half of Emilia-Romagna. Here you'll find the delicious delights of **Parma,** with its buttery prosciutto, famous cheese, and dazzling palaces. Next along the road, continuing east, comes **Reggio Emilia,** of Parmigiano-Reggiano fame, then **Modena,** the city of balsamic vinegar.

2 Bologna. Emilia's principal cultural and intellectual center is famed for its arcaded sidewalks, grandiose medieval towers, and sublime restaurants.

3 Ferrara. This prosperous, tidy city north of Bologna has a rich medieval past and its own distinctive cuisine.

4 Romagna. The eastern half of Emilia-Romagna begins east of Bologna, where spa towns extend north and south of the Via Emilia and the A1 autostrada, and runs to the Adriatic. **San Marino,** south

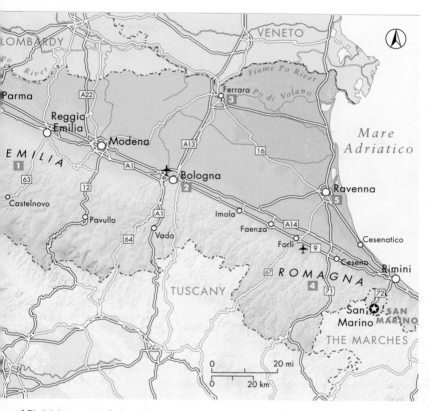

of Rimini, is an anomaly in every way. As its own tiny republic, it hangs implausibly on a cliff above the Romagna plain.

5 Ravenna. The main attractions of this well-preserved Romagna city are its memorable mosaics—glittering treasures left from Byzantine rule.

EATING AND DRINKING WELL IN EMILIA-ROMAGNA

Italians rarely agree about anything, but many concede that some of the country's finest foods originated in Emilia-Romagna. Tortellini, fettuccine, Parmesan cheese, prosciutto crudo, and balsamic vinegar are just a few of the Italian delicacies born here.

One of the beauties of Emilia-Romagna is that its exceptional food can be had without breaking the bank. Many trattorias serve up classic dishes, mastered over the centuries, at reasonable prices. Cutting-edge restaurants and wine bars are often more expensive; their inventive menus are full of *fantasia*—reinterpretations of the classics. For the budget-conscious, Bologna, a university town, has great places for cheap eats.

Between meals, you can sustain yourself with the region's famous sandwich, the *piadina*. It's made with pitalike thin bread, usually filled with prosciutto or mortadella, cheese, and vegetables, then put under the grill and served hot, with the cheese oozing at the sides. These addictive sandwiches can be savored at sit-down places or ordered to go.

THE REAL RAGÙ

Emilia-Romagna's signature dish is *tagliatelle al ragù* (flat noodles with meat sauce), known as "spaghetti Bolognese" most everywhere else. This *primo* (first course) is on every menu, and no two versions are the same. The sauce starts in a sauté pan with finely diced carrots, onions, and celery. Purists add nothing but minced beef, but some use *guanciale* (pork cheek), sausage, veal, or chicken. Regular ministrations of broth are added, and sometimes wine, milk, or cream. After a couple of hours of cooking, the ragù is ready to be joined with pasta and Parmigiano-Reggiano and brought to the table.

PORK PRODUCTS

It's not just mortadella and cured pork products like prosciutto crudo and *culatello* that Emilia-Romagnans go crazy for—they're wild about the whole hog.

You'll frequently find cotechino and zampone, both *secondi* (second courses), on menus. *Cotechino* is a savory, thick, fresh sausage served with lentils on New Year's Eve (the combination is said to augur well for the new year) and with mashed potatoes year-round. *Zampone*, a stuffed pig's foot, is redolent of garlic and deliciously fatty.

BOLLITO MISTO

The name means "mixed boil," and they do it exceptionally well in this part of Italy. According to Emilia-Romagnans, it was invented here, although other Italians—especially those from Milan and the Piedmont—might argue this point. Chicken, beef, tongue, and zampone are tossed into a stockpot and boiled; they're then removed from the broth and served with a fragrant *salsa verde* (green sauce), made green by parsley and spiced with anchovies, garlic, and capers. This simple yet rich dish is usually served with mashed potatoes on the side, and savvy diners will mix some of the piquant salsa verde into the potatoes as well.

STUFFED PASTA

Among the many Emilian variations on stuffed pasta, *tortellini* are the smallest. *Tortelli* and *cappellacci* are larger pasta "pillows," about the size of a brussels sprout, but with the same basic form as tortellini. They're often filled with pumpkin or spinach and cheese.

Tortelloni are, in theory, even bigger, although their sizes vary. Stuffed pastas are generally served simply, with melted butter, sage, and Parmigiano-Reggiano cheese or, in the case of tortellini, *in brodo* (in beef, chicken, or capon broth or a combination of any of them), which brings out the subtle richness of the filling.

WINES

Emilia-Romagna's wines accompany the region's fine food rather than vying with it for accolades. The best-known is *lambrusco*, a sparkling red produced on the Po Plain that has some admirers and many detractors. It's praised for its tartness and condemned for the same; it does, however, pair brilliantly with the local fare. The region's best wines include Sangiovese di Romagna (somewhat similar to Chianti), from the Romagnan hills, and barbera from the Colli Piacetini and Apennine foothills. Castelluccio, Bonzara, Zerbina, Leone Conti, and Tre Monti are among the region's top producers.

10

Updated by Patricia Rucidlo

Gourmets the world over claim that Emilia-Romagna's greatest contribution to humankind has been gastronomic. Birthplace of fettuccine, tortellini, lasagna, prosciutto, and Parmigiano-Reggiano cheese, the region has a spectacular culinary tradition. But there are many reasons to come here aside from the desire to be well fed: Parma's Correggio paintings, Giuseppe Verdi's villa at Sant'Agata, the medieval splendor of Bologna's palaces, Ferrara's medieval alley, the rolling hills of the Romagna countryside, and, perhaps foremost, the Byzantine beauty of mosaic-rich Ravenna—glittering as brightly today as it did 1,500 years ago.

As you travel through Emilia, the western half of the region, you'll encounter the sprawling plants of Italy's industrial food giants, like Barilla and Fini, standing side by side with the fading villas and farmhouses that have long punctuated the flat, fertile land of the Po Plain. Bologna, the principal city of Emilia, is a busy cultural and, increasingly, business center, less visited but in many ways just as engaging as the country's more famous tourist destinations—particularly given its acknowledged position as the leading city of Italian cuisine. The rest of the region follows suit: eating is an essential part of any Emilian experience.

The area's history is laden with culinary legends, such as how the original tortellino was modeled on the shape of Venus's navel and the original *tagliolini* (long, thin egg pasta) was served at the wedding banquet of Annibale Bentivoglio and Lucrezia d'Este—a marriage uniting two of the noblest families in the region. You'll need to stay focused just to make sure you try all the basics: Parma's famed prosciutto and Parmigiano-Reggiano cheese, Modena's balsamic vinegar, the ragù whose poor imitations are known worldwide as "Bolognese"—and, of course, the best pasta in the world.

The historic border between Emilia to the west and Romagna to the east lies near the fortified town of Dozza. Emilia is flat; but just east of the Romagnan border the landscape gets hillier and more sparsely settled, in places covered with evergreen forests and steaming natural springs. Finally, it flattens again into the low-lying marshland of the Po Delta, which meets the Adriatic Sea. Each fall, in both Romagna and Emilia, the trademark fog rolls in off the Adriatic to hang over the flatlands in winter, coloring the region with a spooky, gray glow.

EMILIA–ROMAGNA PLANNER

MAKING THE MOST OF YOUR TIME

Plan on spending at least two days in Bologna, the region's cultural and historical capital. You shouldn't miss Parma, with its stunning food and graceful public spaces. Also plan on visiting Ferrara, a misty, mysterious medieval city. If you have time, go to Ravenna for its memorable Byzantine mosaics and Modena for its harmonious architecture and famous balsamic vinegar.

If you have only a few days in the region, it's virtually impossible to do all five of those cities justice. If you're a dedicated gourmand (or *buona forchetta,* as Italians say), move from Bologna west along the Via Emilia (SS9) to Modena and Parma. If you're more interested in architecture, art, and history, choose the eastern route, heading north on the A13 to Ferrara and then southeast on the SS16 to Ravenna.

If you have more time, you won't have to make such tough choices. You can start in Milan, go east, and finish on the Adriatic—or vice versa.

GETTING HERE AND AROUND

CAR TRAVEL

Driving is the best way to get around Emilia-Romagna. Roads are wide, flat, and well marked; distances are short; and beautiful farmhouses and small villages offer undemanding detours.

A car is particularly useful for visiting the spa towns of Romagna, which aren't well connected by train. Historic centers are off-limits to cars, but they're also quite walkable, so you may just want to park your car and get around on foot once you arrive.

Entering Emilia-Romagna by car is as easy as it gets. Coming in from the northwest on the Autostrada del Sole (A1), you'll first hit Piacenza, a mere 45-minute drive southeast of Milan. On the other side of the region, Venice is about an hour from Ferrara by car on the A13.

Bologna is on the autostrada, so driving between cities is a breeze, though take special care if you're coming from Florence, as the road is winding and the drivers speed. The Via Emilia (SS9), one of the oldest roads in the world, runs through the heart of the region. Although less scenic, the A1 toll highway, which runs parallel to the Via Emilia from Bologna, can get you where you're going about twice as fast. From Bologna, the A13 runs north to Ferrara, and the A14 takes you east to Ravenna. Much of the historic center of Bologna is closed off to cars daily from 7 am to 8 pm.

10

TRAIN TRAVEL

When it comes to public transportation in the region, trains are better than buses—they're fairly efficient, quite frequent, and most stations aren't too far from the center of town. The railroad track follows the Via Emilia (SS9). In Emilia it generally takes 30–45 minutes to get from one major city to the next. To reach Ferrara or Ravenna, you typically have to change to a local train at Bologna. Ferrara is a half hour north of Bologna on the train, and Ravenna is just over an hour.

Bologna is an important rail hub for northern Italy and has frequent, fast service to Milan, Florence, Rome, and Venice. The routes from Bologna to the south usually go through Florence, about 40 minutes away on a high-speed train. The high-speed train service Alta Velocità cuts the time from Milan to Bologna to only one hour. On the northeastern edge of the region, Venice is 1½ hours east of Ferrara by train. Check the website of the state railway, the **Ferrovie dello Stato** (FS ⊕ *www.trenitalia.com*), for information, or stop in a travel agency, as many sell train tickets (without a markup) and agents often speak English. **Italo** (⊕ *www.italotreno.it*), a privately owned high-speed train line, competes with the state-sponsored service. Italo's Turin–Salerno line makes stops in Bologna, Florence, Rome, Naples, and Salerno; the Venice–Napoli line stops in Padova, Bologna, Florence, and Rome. Some of these also stop at secondary stations.

RESTAURANTS

Dining options range from mom-and-pop-style informal trattorias to three-star Michelin restaurants. Food in Emilia-Romagna is not for the faint of heart (or those on diets): it is rich, creamy, and cheesy. Local wines pair remarkably well with this sumptuous fare. You may want to rethink Lambrusco, as it marries well with just about everything on the menu. *Restaurant reviews have been shortened. For full information, visit Fodors.com.*

HOTELS

Emilia-Romagna has a reputation for demonstrating a level of efficiency uncommon in most of Italy. Even the smallest hotels are usually well run, with high standards of quality and service. Bologna is very much a businessperson's city, and many hotels here cater to the business traveler, but there are smaller, more intimate hotels as well. It's smart to book in advance—the region hosts many fairs and conventions that can fill up hotels even during low season. *Hotel reviews have been shortened. For full information, visit Fodors.com.*

WHAT IT COSTS			
$	**$$**	**$$$**	**$$$$**
Restaurants	under €15	€15–€24	€25–€35	over €35
Hotels	under €125	€125–€200	€201–€300	over €300

Restaurant prices are the average cost of a main course at dinner, or, if dinner is not served, at lunch. Hotel prices are the lowest cost of a standard double room in high season.

EMILIA

The Via Emilia runs through Emilia's heart in a straight shot from medieval Piacenza, 67 km (42 miles) southeast of Milan, through Bologna, and ultimately to Romagna and the Adriatic Coast. On the way you encounter many of Italy's cultural riches—from the culinary and artistic treasures of Parma to the birthplace and home of Giuseppe Verdi. Take time to veer into the countryside, with its ramshackle farmhouses and 800-year-old abbeys; to stop for a taste of prosciutto; and to detour north to the mist-shrouded tangle of streets that make up Ferrara's old Jewish ghetto.

PIACENZA

67 km (42 miles) southeast of Milan, 150 km (93 miles) northwest of Bologna.

Piacenza has always been associated with industry and commerce. Its position on the Po River has made it an important inland port since the earliest times; the Etruscans, and then the Romans, had thriving settlements here. As you approach the city today you could be forgiven for thinking that it holds little of interest. Piacenza is surrounded by ugly industrial suburbs (with particularly unlovely concrete factories and a power station), but if you forge ahead you'll discover a preserved medieval center and an unusually clean city. Its prosperity is evident in the great shopping to be had along Corso Vittorio Emanuele II.

GETTING HERE AND AROUND

Regional trains run often from Milan to Piacenza and take a little more than an hour; Eurostar service cuts the travel time in half, and Alta Velocità trains make it from Milan to Bologna in an hour. The Intercity from Bologna to Piacenza takes about 1½ hours and closer to 2 hours on regional trains. Both have frequent service. Piacenza is easily accessible by car via the A1, either from Milan or from Bologna. If you're coming from Milan, take the Piacenza Nord exit; from Bologna, the Piacenza Est exit.

VISITOR INFORMATION

Contact Piacenza Tourism Office. ⊠ *Piazza Cavalli 7* ☎ *0523/492111* ⊕ *www. comune.piacenza.it.*

EXPLORING

Duomo. Attached like a sinister balcony to the bell tower of Piacenza's 12th-century Duomo is a *gabbia* (iron cage), where miscreants were incarcerated naked and subjected to the scorn of the crowd in the marketplace below. Inside the cathedral, less evocative but equally impressive medieval stonework decorates the pillars and the crypt, and there are extravagant frescoes in the dome of the cupola begun by Morazzone (1573–1626). Guercino (1591–1666) completed them upon Morazzone's death. The Duomo can be reached by following Via XX Settembre from Piazza dei Cavalli. ⊠ *Piazza Duomo* ☎ *0523/335154.*

10

EMILIA-ROMAGNA THROUGH THE AGES

Ancient History. Emilia-Romagna owes its beginnings to a road. In 187 BC the Romans built the Via Aemilia—a long road running northwest from the Adriatic port of Rimini to the central garrison town of Piacenza—and it was along this central spine that the primary towns of the region developed.

Despite the unifying factor of what came to be known as the Via Emilia, this section of Italy has had a fragmented history. Its eastern part, roughly the area from Faenza to the coast (known as Romagna), looked first to the Byzantine east and then to Rome for art, political power, and, some say, national character. The western part, from Bologna to Piacenza (Emilia), looked more to the north with its practice of self-government and dissent.

Bologna was founded by the Etruscans and eventually came under the influence of the Roman Empire. The Romans established a garrison here, renaming the old Etruscan settlement Bononia. It was after the fall of Rome that the region began its fragmentation. Romagna, centered in Ravenna, was ruled from Constantinople. Ravenna eventually became the capital of the empire in the west in the 5th century, passing to papal control in the 8th century.

Even today, the city is still filled with reminders of two centuries of Byzantine rule.

Family Ties. The other cities of the region, from the Middle Ages on, became the fiefdoms of important noble families—the Este in Ferrara and Modena, the Pallavicini in Piacenza, and the Bentivoglio in Bologna. Today all these cities bear the marks of their noble patrons. When in the 16th century the papacy managed to exert its power over the entire area, some of these cities were divided among the papal families—hence the stamp of the Farnese family on Parma and Piacenza.

A Leftward Tilt. Bologna and Emilia-Romagna have established a robust tradition of rebellion and dissent. The Italian socialist movement was born in the region, as was Benito Mussolini. In keeping with the political climate of his home state, he was a firebrand socialist during the early part of his career. Despite having Mussolini as a native son, Emilia-Romagna didn't take to Fascism: it was here that the anti-Fascist resistance was born, and during World War II the region suffered terribly at the hands of the Fascists and the Nazis.

Musei di Palazzo Farnese. The city-owned museum of Piacenzan art and antiquities is housed in the vast **Palazzo Farnese.** The ruling family had commissioned a monumental palace, but construction, begun in 1558, was never completed as planned. The highlight of the museum's eclectic collection is the tiny 2nd-century BC Etruscan *Fegato di Piacenza*, a bronze tablet shaped like a *fegato* (liver), marked with the symbols of the gods of good and ill fortune. By comparing this master "liver" with one taken from the body of a freshly slaughtered sacrifice, priests predicted the future. The collection also contains Botticelli's beautiful *Madonna and Child with St. John the Baptist*. Because it's under glass, you have the rare opportunity of getting very close to the piece to

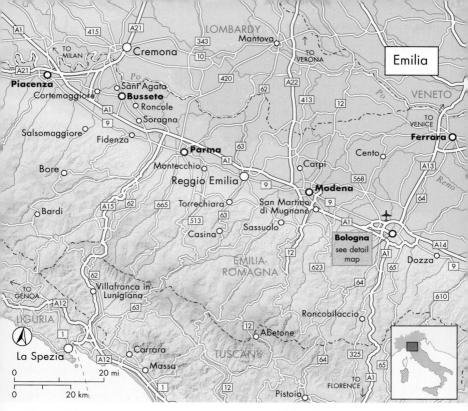

admire the artist's brushwork. Reserve ahead for free 1½-hour guided tours. ⊠ *Piazza Cittadella 29* ☎ *0523/492661* ⊕ *www.palazzofarnese. piacenza.it* 🎫 *€6* 🕙 *Closed Mon.*

Piazza dei Cavalli (*Square of the Horses*). The hub of the city is the Piazza dei Cavalli. The flamboyant equestrian statues from which the piazza takes its name are depictions of Ranuccio Farnese (1569–1622) and, on the left, his father, Alessandro (1545–92). The latter was a beloved ruler, enlightened and fair; Ranuccio, his successor, less so. Both statues are the work of Francesco Mochi, a master Baroque sculptor. Dominating the square is the massive 13th-century **Palazzo Pubblico,** also known as Il Gotico. This two-tone, marble-and-brick, turreted and crenellated building was the seat of town government before Piacenza fell under the iron fists of the ruling Pallavicini and Farnese families. ⊠ *Piacenza.*

BUSSETO

30 km (19 miles) southeast of Piacenza, 25 km (16 miles) south of Cremona in Lombardy.

Sleepy Busseto's greatest claim to fame is local son Giuseppe Verdi (1813–1901), who was not exactly born here—he was born in Le Roncole, a stone's throw away. However, he always considered this town his home. It's in the middle of cultivated countryside, and was known, since Carolingian times, as "Buxetum." It attracted the attention of Habsburg emperor Charles V in 1533, who became lord of the city. Now it attracts opera lovers who wish to walk in the grand maestro's footsteps—either by hearing one of his works at the local theater, or by touring either of his country estates.

GETTING HERE AND AROUND

If you're coming by car from Parma, drive along the A1/E35 and follow signs for the A15 in the direction of Milan/La Spezia. Choose the exit in the direction of Fidenza/Salsomaggiore Terme, following signs to the SP12, which connects to the SS9W. At Fidenza, take the SS588 heading north, which will take you into Busseto. If you're without a car, you'll have to take a bus from Parma, as there's no train service.

VISITOR INFORMATION

Contact Busseto Tourism Office. ⊠ *Piazza G. Verdi 10* ☎ *0524/92487* ⊕ *www. bussetolive.com.*

EXPLORING

Teatro Verdi. In the center of Busseto is the lovely Teatro Verdi, dedicated, as you might expect, to the works of the hamlet's famous son. Guided tours (in both English and Italian) of the well-preserved, ornate, 19th-century-style theater are offered every half hour. Check with the Busseto tourist office for the performance schedule. ⊠ *Piazza G. Verdi 10* ☎ *0524/92487* 🎫 *Tours €4* ⊗ *Closed Mon.*

Villa Pallavicino. Busseto's main claim to fame is its native son, master composer Giuseppe Verdi (1813–1901). The 15th-century Villa Pallavicino is where Verdi worked and lived with his mistress (and later wife) Giuseppina Strepponi. Recently renovated, it displays the maestro's piano, scores, composition books, and walking sticks. ⊠ *Via Provesi 35* ☎ *0524/931002* ⊕ *www.museogiuseppeverdi.it* 🎫 *€9* ⊗ *Closed Mon.*

Villa Sant'Agata. For Verdi lovers, Villa Sant'Agata (also known as Villa Verdi) is a veritable shrine. It's the grand country home Verdi built for himself in 1849—and the place where some of his greatest works were composed. Visits are by tour only, and you have to reserve a few days in advance by phone or online. ⊠ *Via Verdi 22, 4 km (2½ miles) north of Busseto on SS588, toward Cremona, Sant'Agata* ☎ *0523/830000* ⊕ *www.villaverdi.org* 🎫 *Tours €9* ⊗ *Closed weekdays Nov.–Feb., and Mon. Mar.–Oct.*

PARMA

40 km (25 miles) southeast of Busseto, 97 km (60 miles) northwest of Bologna.

Parma stands on the banks of a tributary of the Po River. Despite damage during World War II, much of the stately historic center seems untouched by modern times. This is a prosperous city, and it shows in its well-dressed residents, clean streets, and immaculate piazzas.

Bursting with gustatory delights, Parma draws crowds for its sublime cured pork product, *prosciutto crudo di Parma* (known locally simply as "prosciutto crudo"). The pale-yellow Parmigiano-Reggiano cheese produced here and in nearby Reggio Emilia is the original—and best— of a class known around the world as "Parmesan."

Almost every major European power has had a hand in ruling Parma at one time or another. The Romans founded the city—then little more than a garrison on the Via Emilia—after which a succession of feudal lords held sway. In the 16th century came the ever-conniving Farnese family, which died out in 1731 on the death of Antonio Farnese. It then went to the Spanish, and fell into French hands in 1796. In 1805 Marie-Louise (better known to the Parmigiani as Maria Luigia), the wife of Napoléon, took command of the city. She was a much-beloved figure in her adopted town until her death in 1847.

GETTING HERE AND AROUND

Train service, via Eurostar, Intercity, and Regionale trains, runs frequently from Milan and Bologna. It takes a little over an hour from Milan and slightly less than an hour from Bologna. By car, Parma is just off the A1 autostrada, halfway between Bologna and Piacenza.

VISITOR INFORMATION

Contact Parma Tourism Office. ⊠ *Piazza Garibaldi 1* ☎ *0521/218889* ⊕ *www. turismo.comune.parma.it.*

EXPLORING

TOP ATTRACTIONS

Battistero (*Baptistery*). Baptisms still happen (one Saturday and one Sunday a month) in this baptistery, which has a simple pink-stone Romanesque exterior and an uplifting Gothic interior. The doors are richly decorated with figures, animals, and flowers, and inside, the building is adorned with stucco figures (probably carved by Antelami) showing the months and seasons. Early-14th-century frescoes depicting scenes from the life of Christ grace the walls. ⊠ *Piazza del Duomo* ⊕ *www. piazzaduomoparma.it* 🖾 *€8.*

Fodor'sChoice
★

Camera di San Paolo. This was the reception room for the erudite abbess Giovanna da Piacenza. In 1519 she hired Correggio to provide its decoration. Mythological scenes are depicted in glorious frescoes of the *Triumphs of the Goddess Diana*, the *Three Graces,* and the *Three Fates.* ⊠ *Via Melloni 15, off Strada Garibaldi, near Piazza Pilotta* ☎ *0521/233309* 🖾 *€2* ☉ *Closed Sun.*

Duomo. The magnificent 12th-century cathedral has two vigilant stone lions standing guard beside the main door. The arch of the entrance is

10

decorated with a delicate frieze of figures representing the months of the year, a motif repeated inside the baptistery. Some of the church's original artwork still survives, notably the simple yet evocative *Descent from the Cross*, a carving in the right transept by Benedetto Antelami (active 1178–1230), whose masterwork is this cathedral's baptistery. It's an odd juxtaposition to turn from his austere work to the exuberant fresco in the dome, the *Assumption of the Virgin* by Antonio Allegri, better known to us as Correggio (1494–1534). The fresco was not well received when it was unveiled in 1530. "A mess of frogs' legs," the bishop of Parma is said to have called it. Today Correggio is acclaimed as one of the leading masters of Mannerist painting. The fresco is best viewed when the sun is strong, as this building is not particularly well lit. ⊠ *Piazza del Duomo.*

Museo del Parmigiano Reggiano. The trademark crumbly cheese is the focus of this museum, which is part of the collective known as Musei del Cibo whose goal is showcase the region's most famous foods. There's a video demonstrating the process of making Parmigiano-Reggiano and some 120 exhibits that explore the history of the cheese. Tastings are also offered, and cheese is available to purchase. Call before making the trek, though, as opening hours are limited, and reservations are often necessary (especially for a tour in English, which should be booked at least a month in advance). ⊠ *c/o Corte Castellazzi, Via Volta 5, Soragna, 28 km (17 miles) northwest of Parma, Soragna* ☎ *0524/931800* ⊕ *www.museidelcibo.it* ☜ *€5* ☉ *Closed weekends, and Dec.–Feb.*

Museo del Pomodoro. It's hard to imagine what Italian cuisine would be like without the New World tomato. This museum, which is part of the collective known as Musei del Cibo, explains all the mysteries. There's about a hundred exhibits explaining the history of the tomato, its farming, and its processing. If you want to book a guided tour, it's necessary to call in advance. ■ TIP→ Call before making the trek, though, as opening hours are limited, and reservations are often necessary. ⊠ *Corte di Giarola, Strada Giarola 11, 12 km (7 miles) from Parma, Collecchio* ☎ *0521/931800* ⊕ *www.museidelcibo.it* ☜ *€5* ☉ *Closed weekdays, and Dec. 9–Apr. 30.*

Museo del Prosciutto. Part of the collective known as Musei del Cibo, which works to showcase the region's most famous foods, this museum offers an in-depth look at Italy's most famous cured pork product. It offers tastings, a bit of history on prosciutto, and a tour through the process of making it. A gift shop ensures that you can take some of this marvelous product home. ■ TIP→ Call before planning your trip as opening hours are limited, and reservations are often necessary. ⊠ *c/o Ex Foro Boario 7, Via Bocchialini, Langhirano, 22 km (13 miles) from Parma* ☎ *0521/931800* ⊕ *www.museidelcibo.it* ☜ *€5* ☉ *Closed daily Dec.–Mar., weekdays Mar.–Dec.*

Museo del Salame di Felino. This museum, part of the collective know as Musei del Cibo which works to showcase the region's most famous food, is all about cured meats. There are tastings, a bit of history, and a tour through the process of making these specialties. Guided tours in English are available upon request. ■ TIP→ Call before you plan a trip as opening hours are limited, and reservations are often necessary. ⊠ *Strada al Castello 1, near Castello di Felino, 17 km (10 miles) southwest of Parma* 🕾 *0521/931800* ⊕ *www.museidelcibo.it* 🔖 *€5* ⊘ *Closed weekdays, and Jan. and Feb.*

Piazza del Duomo. This spacious cobblestone piazza contains the cathedral and the Battistero, plus the Palazzo del Vescovado (Bishop's Palace). Behind the Duomo is the Baroque church of San Giovanni Evangelista. ⊠ *Parma.*

Fodor's Choice ⋆ **Teatro Farnese/Galleria Nazionale.** To enter the gallery, you pass through the magnificent Baroque Teatro Farnese, built in 1617–18. Made entirely of wood, it was largely destroyed in a 1944 Allied bombing, but it's been flawlessly restored. Inside the gallery masterpieces by Correggio, Parmigianino, Leonardo da Vinci (1452–1519), El Greco (1541–1614), and Bronzino (1503–72) hang at the little-visited Galleria Nazionale. The museum is housed on the *piano nobile* (main floor) of the massive and somewhat forbidding **Palazzo della Pilotta,** which was constructed on the riverbank in 1618. The palazzo takes its name from the game *pilotta,* a sort of handball played within the palace precincts in the 17th century. The building also suffered much damage in a May 1944 Allied bombing, and has been greatly restored. ⊠ *Piazza della Pilotta* ⊕ *www.gallerianazionaleparma.it* 🔖 *€10* ⊘ *Closed Mon.*

WORTH NOTING

Piazza Garibaldi. This is the heart of Parma, where people gather to pass the time of day, start their *passeggiata* (evening stroll), or simply hang out. Strada Cavour, leading off the piazza, is Parma's prime shopping street: it's also crammed with wine bars teeming with locals. This square and nearby Piazza del Duomo make up one of the loveliest historic centers in Italy, so it's a perfect place to stop for a snack or light lunch. ⊠ *Parma.*

San Giovanni Evangelista. Beyond the elaborate Baroque facade of San Giovanni Evangelista, the Renaissance interior reveals several works by Correggio: *St. John the Evangelist* (in the lunette above the door in the left transept) is considered among his finest. Also in this church (in the second and fourth chapels on the left) are works by Parmigianino (1503–40), a contemporary of Correggio's. Once seen, Parmigianino's long-necked Madonnas are never forgotten. ⊠ *Piazzale San Giovanni 1, Piazza del Duomo* 🕾 .

Santa Maria della Steccata. Dating from the 16th century, this delightful church has one of Parma's most recognizable domes. In the dome's large arch there's a wonderful decorative fresco by Francesco Mazzola, better known as Parmigianino. He took so long to complete it that his patrons briefly imprisoned him for breach of contract. ⊠ *Piazza Steccata 9, off Via Dante near Piazza Garibaldi* 🕾 *0521/234937* ⊕ *www. diocesi.parma.it.*

WHERE TO EAT

$
WINE BAR ✕ **Enoteca Antica Osteria Fontana.** Low prices draw Parma's gregarious twentysomethings (and everyone else), with customers often spilling out of this old-school enoteca (wine bar) and onto the street, wine glasses in hand. Grab a table inside and feast on tartines (little bread

10

squares with creative toppings) or grilled panini—the seemingly endless options for the latter include *coppa* (a cured pork product), pancetta, and Gorgonzola. **Known for:** the famed culatello cured ham; enormous selection of wine bottles to go; teeming with happy locals. $ *Average main: €5* ⊠ *Strada Farini 24/a, near Piazza Garibaldi* ☎ *0521/286037* ⊗ *Closed Sun. and Mon.*

$$
EMILIAN
FAMILY

✕ **La Filoma.** The dining room here evokes the turn of the 19th century with its high ceilings and damask drapes, though an element of kitsch prevails. The food shines, from the classic *anolini in brodo di manzo e cappone* (a local variation on tortellini in brodo) to the exquisite guinea fowl stuffed with prosciutto and Parmesan. **Known for:** Parmesan specialties that don't break the bank; delicious vegetarian options; excellent wine list. $ *Average main: €16* ⊠ *Borgo XX Marzo 15* ☎ *0521/2061811* ⊕ *www.lafiloma.it* ⊗ *Closed Tues.; closed weekends in July and Aug. No lunch Wed.*

$$
ITALIAN

✕ **La Forchetta.** Sicilian-born Parma transplant Angelo Cammarata creates magic in his small eatery on the ground floor of a 16th-century palazzo. The menu teems with Parma classics, as well as modern takes on Sicilian dishes. **Known for:** minimalistic interior with exposed brick and muted gray walls; great fish dishes; best cannoli outside Sicily. $ *Average main: €20* ⊠ *Borgo San Biagio 6* ☎ *0521/208812* ⊕ *www.laforchettaparma.it.*

$$$$
EMILIAN
Fodor'sChoice
★

✕ **Parizzi Ristorante.** Chef-owner Marco Parizzi is the third-generation cook in this elegant restaurant, which evolved from his grandfather's *salumeria* (delicatessen) into a restaurant serving Parmesan classics and contemporary cuisine. The Piatti Tipici (list of typical dishes) include an *anolini in brodo di gallina e manzo* (stuffed pasta in meat broth), redolent with hints of nutmeg, that shouldn't be missed. **Known for:** local specialties; inventive terra (earth) and mare (sea) tasting menus; affordable, well-currated wine list. $ *Average main: €60* ⊠ *Strada Repubblica 71* ☎ *0521/285952* ⊕ *www.ristoranteparizzi.it* ⊗ *Closed Mon., and Aug. and Jan. 8–15.*

$
EMILIAN
Fodor'sChoice
★

✕ **Tabarro.** A favorite little wine bar on one of Parma's main drags has a couple of keg tables outside, a few stools on the ground floor, and a communal table upstairs. The simple food, based largely on pork products (equine as well: people in this part of the world like to eat horse), is delicious but is meant mainly to pair with, and accentuate, the fine wines on offer. **Known for:** its international wine list; delicious crostini; the ebullient host. $ *Average main: €12* ⊠ *Strada Farini 5/b* ☎ *0521/200223* ⊕ *www.tabarro.net* ⊗ *Closed Tues.*

$
EMILIAN
Fodor'sChoice
★

✕ **TCafe.** The beauty of TCafe is that it does just about everything: the festivities begin with breakfast and end with evening aperitivi. Locals flock to this place, which once housed the aristocratic Dalla Rosa Prati's art collection, to catch up on gossip, read the papers, and have lunch. **Known for:** the wide-ranging menu; its long opening hours; lunchtime local specialties, soup du jour, and tasty salads. $ *Average main: €12* ⊠ *Strada del Duomo 7* ☎ *0521/386429* ⊕ *www.temporarypalazzo.it.*

WHERE TO STAY

$
HOTEL
Fodor's Choice
★

◫ Palazzo dalla Rosa Prati. Marchese Vittorio dalla Rosa Prati has converted part of his family's 15th-century palace on Piazza del Duomo into luxurious, self-catering accommodations, and those with connecting rooms are ideal for families. **Pros:** spacious, well-appointed rooms; two-seater electric car to tool around town in; room service of Continental breakfast included in the price. **Cons:** staff leave at 10 pm; parking can sometimes be a problem. $ *Rooms from: €95* ✉ *Strada al Duomo 7* ☎ *0521/386429* ⊕ *www.palazzodallarosaprati.it* ⇆ *18 rooms* ⦿ *Free Breakfast.*

$
B&B/INN

◫ Parizzi Suites and Studio. A 17th-century palace has been refurbished with 21st-century amenities to provide a lovely place to rest one's head. **Pros:** central location; great staff; breakfast served in rooms. **Cons:** staff not always at desk; might be too chic for some. $ *Rooms from: €60* ✉ *Strada della Republica 71* ☎ *0521/207032* ⊕ *www.ristoranteparizzi. it* ⇆ *13 rooms* ⦿ *Free Breakfast.*

MODENA

56 km (35 miles) southeast of Parma, 38 km (24 miles) northwest of Bologna.

Modena is famous for local products: Maserati, Ferrari, and opera star Luciano Pavarotti, born near here and buried in his family plot in Montale Rangone in 2007. However, it's Modena's heavenly scented balsamic vinegar, aged up to 40 years, that's probably its greatest achievement. The town has become another Emilian food mecca, with terrific restaurants and *salumerie* (delicatessens) at every turn. Although extensive modern industrial sprawl surrounds the city, the small historic center is filled with narrow medieval streets, pleasant piazzas, and typical Emilian architecture.

GETTING HERE AND AROUND

Modena, on the Bologna–Milan line, is easily accessible by train, and it's an easy walk from the station to the centro storico. The Intercity connection from Florence takes about 90 minutes. By car, Modena is just off the A1 autostrada.

10

TOURS

Consorzio Produttori Aceto Balsamico Tradizionale di Modena. Connoisseurs of balsamic vinegar can arrange visits to local producers through the Consorzio. It's best to contact the organization via its website to set things up. ✉ *Strada Vaciglio Sud 1085/1* ☎ *059/395633* ⊕ *www.balsamico.it* ◫ *Free.*

VISITOR INFORMATION

Contact Modena Tourism Office. ✉ *Piazza Grande 14* ☎ *059/2032660* ⊕ *www.visitmodena.it.*

EXPLORING

Duomo. The 12th-century Romanesque cathedral was begun by the architect Lanfredo in 1099 and consecrated in 1184. Medieval sculptures depicting scenes from Genesis adorn the facade, but walk around to the Piazza Grande side as well to see the building's marvelous arcading. It's a rare example of a cathedral having more than one principal view. The interior, completely clad in brick, imparts a sober and beautiful feel. An elaborate gallery has scenes of the Passion of Christ carved by Anselmo da Campione and his assistants circa 1160–80. The tomb of San Geminiano is in the crypt. The white-marble bell tower is known as **La Torre Ghirlandina** (the Little Garland Tower) because of its distinctive weather vane. ⊠ *Piazza Grande* ☎ *059/216078* ⊕ *www. duomodimodena.it.*

Museo Ferrari. This museum has become a pilgrimage site for auto enthusiasts. It takes you through the illustrious history of Ferrari, from early 1951 models to the present—the legendary F50 and cars driven by Michael Schumacher in Formula One victories being highlights. You can also take a look at the glamorous life of founder Enzo Ferrari (a re-creation of his office is on-site), and a glance into the production process. ⊠ *Via Dino Ferrari, Maranello, 17 km (11 miles) south of Modena* ☎ *0536/949713* ⊕ *www.museiferrari.com* 💲 *€16.*

Palazzo dei Musei. Modena's principal museum is housed in the Palazzo dei Musei, a short walk from the Duomo. The collection was assembled in the mid-17th century by Francesco d'Este (1610–58), Duke of Modena, and the **Galleria Estense** is named in his honor. The gallery also houses the **Biblioteca Estense,** a huge collection of illuminated manuscripts, of which the best known is the beautifully illustrated *Bible of Borso d'Este* (1455–61). A map dated 1501 was one of the first in the world to show that Columbus had discovered America. To get here, follow the Via Emilia, which runs through the heart of the town, to Via di Sant'Agostino. ⊠ *Piazza Sant'Agostino 337* ☎ *059/4395711* 💲 *€6* ☉ *Museum closed Mon., gallery closed Sun. and Mon.*

WHERE TO EAT

$ ✕**Aldina.** On the second floor of a building across from the covered
EMILIAN   market, steps from the Piazza Grande, this simple, typical trattoria is in the very nerve center of the city. Here you'll find exemplary preparations of the region's crown jewels: tortellini in brodo, tagliatelle al ragù, and roast meats. **Known for:** inexpensive local food; modern take on old favorites; locals love it. 💲 *Average main: €12* ⊠ *Via Albinelli 40* ☎ *059/236106* 🚫 *No credit cards* ☉ *Closed Sun., and July and Aug. No dinner Mon.–Thurs.*

$ ✕**Archer.** Bibliophile proprietor (she named her charming establish-
ITALIAN   ment after a Henry James heroine) Marina Bersani presides over this sleek wine bar. High ceilings provide plenty of places to store her vast collection of unique wines and the short-but-sweet menu offers lots of traditional classics like *affettati misti* (sliced, cured pork products), as well as cheese plates and salads. **Known for:** good wine list; crostini for snacking; outdoor seating. 💲 *Average main: €12* ⊠ *Via Cesare Battisti 54* ☎ *059/237656.*

$$$ ✕**Hosteria Giusti.** In the back room of the Salumeria Giusti, established
EMILIAN   in 1605 and reportedly the world's oldest deli, you'll find just four tables
Fodor'sChoice   in a room tastefully done with antique furnishings. You'll also find
★   some of the best food in Emilia-Romagna—perfectly executed takes on traditional dishes. **Known for:** gnocco fritto (fried dough) with salumi (cured meats); outstanding pastas; diminutive size (just four tables).

Continued on page 460

EMILIA
ONE TASTE AT A TIME

4 towns, dozens of foods, and a mouthful of flavors you'll never forget

Imagine biting into the silkiest prosciutto in the world or the most delectable homemade tortellini you've ever tasted. In Emilia, Italy's most famous food region, you'll discover simple tastes that exceed all expectations. Beginning in Parma and moving eastward to Bologna, you'll find the epicenters of such world-renowned culinary treats as *prosciutto crudo*, Parmigiano-Reggiano, *aceto balsamico*, and tortellini. The secret to this region is not the discovery of new and exotic delicacies, but rather the rediscovery of foods you thought you already knew—in much better versions than you've ever tasted before.

TASTE 1 | PROSCIUTTO CRUDO

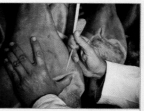
Quality testing

From Piacenza to the Adriatic, ham is the king of meats in Emilia-Romagna, but nowhere is this truer than in **Parma**.

Parma is the world's capital of *prosciutto crudo*, raw cured ham (*crudo* for short). Ask for *crudo di Parma* to signal its local provenance; many other regions also make their own crudo.

CRUDO LANGUAGE

It's easy to get confused with the terminology. Crudo is the product that Americans simply call "prosciutto" or the Brits might call "Parma ham." *Prosciutto* in Italian, however, is a more general term that means any kind of ham, including *prosciutto cotto*, or simply *cotto*, which means "cooked ham." Cotto is an excellent product and frequent pizza topping that's closer to (but much better than) what Americans would put in a deli sandwich.

Greasing the ham

Crudo is traditionally eaten in one of three ways: in a dry sandwich (*panino*); by itself as an appetizer, often with shaved butter on top; or as part of an appetizer or snack platter of assorted *salumi* (cured meats).

WHAT TO LOOK FOR

For the best crudo di Parma, look for slices, always cut to order, that are razor thin and have a light, rosy red color (not dark red). Don't be shy about going into a simple *salumeria* (a purveyor of cured meats) and ordering crudo by the pound. You can enjoy it straight out of the package on a park bench—and why not?

Fire branding

BEST SPOT FOR A SAMPLE

You can't go wrong with any of Parma's famed salumerie, but **Salumeria Garibaldi** is one of the town's oldest and most reliable. You'll find not only spectacular prosciutto crudo, but also delectable cheeses, wines, porcini mushrooms, and more.

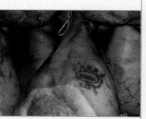
Quality trademark

LEARN MORE

For more information on crudo di Parma, contact the **Consorzio del Prosciutto di Parma** through the tourist office, or stop by the famous store, La Prosciutteria.

TASTE 2 | PARMIGIANO-REGGIANO

From Parma, it's only a half-hour trip east to **Reggio Emilia,** the birthplace of the crumbly and renowned Parmigiano-Reggiano cheese. Reggio (not to be confused with Reggio di Calabria in the south) is a charming little Emilian town that has been the center of production for this legendary cheese for more than 70 years.

Warming milk in copper cauldrons

SAY CHEESE
Grana is the generic Italian term for hard, aged, full-flavored cheese that can be grated. Certain varieties of Pecorino Romano, for example, or Grana Padano, also fall under this term, but Parmigiano-Reggiano, aged for as long as four years, is the foremost example.

Breaking up the curds

NOT JUST FOR GRATING
In Italy, Parmigiano-Reggiano is not only grated onto pasta, but also often served by itself in chunks, either as an appetizer—perhaps accompanied by local salumi (cured meats)—or even for dessert, when it might be drizzled with honey or Modena's balsamic vinegar.

MEET THE MAKERS
If you're a cheese enthusiast, you shouldn't miss the chance to take a free two-hour guided tour of a Parmigiano-Reggiano–producing farm. You'll witness the entire process and get to meet the cheesemakers. Tours can be arranged by contacting the farms directly. The **Consorzio del Formaggio Parmigiano-Reggiano** (www.parmigianoreggiano.com) has a list of dairies that allow visits; some offer tours in English.

Placing cheese in molds

BEST SPOT FOR A SAMPLE
The production of Parmigiano-Reggiano is heavily controlled by the Consorzio del Formaggio, so you can buy the cheese at any store or supermarket in the region and be virtually guaranteed equal quality and price. For a more distinctive shopping experience, however, try buying Parmigiano-Reggiano at the street market on Reggio's central square. The market takes place on Tuesday and Friday from 8 AM to 1 PM year-round. You can pick up a small piece to eat while you're in Italy, or have larger pieces shrink-wrapped to take home.

Aging cheese wheels

Parmigiano-Reggiano

TASTE 3 | ACETO BALSAMICO DI MODENA

Tasting tradizionale vinegar

Modena is home to *Aceto Balsamico Tradizionale di Modena*, a kind of balsamic vinegar unparalleled anywhere else on Earth. The balsamic vinegar you've probably tried—even the pricier versions sold at specialty stores—may be good on salads, but it bears only a fleeting resemblance to the real thing.

HOW IS IT MADE?

The *tradizionale* vinegar that passes strict government standards is made with Trebbiano grape must, which is cooked over an open fire, reduced, and fermented from 12 to 25 or more years in a series of specially made wooden casks. As the vinegar becomes more concentrated, so much liquid evaporates that it takes more than 6 gallons of must to produce one quart of vinegar 12 years later. The result is an intense and syrupy concoction best enjoyed sparingly on grilled meats, strawberries, or Parmigiano-Reggiano cheese. The vinegar has such a complexity of flavor that some even drink it as an after-dinner liqueur.

Wooden casks for fermenting

BEST SPOT FOR A SAMPLE

The **Consorzio Produttori Aceto Balsamico Tradizionale di Modena** offers tours and tastings by reservation only. The main objective of the consortium is to monitor the quality of the authentic balsamic vinegar, made by only a few licensed restaurants and small producers.

The consortium also limits production, keeping prices sky high. Expect to pay €60 for a 100-ml (3.4 oz) bottle of tradizionale, which is generally aged 12 to 15 years, or €90 and up for the older tradizionale extra vecchio variety, which is aged 25 years.

But perhaps the best place to sample this vinegar, in its various stages and permutations, is in situ—that is, in any one of Modena's remarkable restaurants. You can have a simple trattoria meal at Ermes, whose recipes rely heavily on that liquid gold. Or you can splurge at Osteria Francescana, where three-starred Michelin chef Massimo Bottura works miracles with local ingredients.

OTHER TASTES OF EMILIA

- **Cotechino**: a sausage made from pork and lard, a specialty of Modena

- **Culatello de Zibello**: raw cured ham produced along the banks of the Po River, and cured and aged for more than 11 months

- **Mortadella**: soft, smoked sausage made with beef, pork, cubes of pork fat, and seasonings, a specialty of Bologna

- **Ragù**: a sauce made from minced pork and beef, simmered in milk, onions, carrots, and tomatoes

- **Salama da sugo**: salty, oily sausage aged and then cooked, a specialty of Ferrara

- **Tortelli and cappellacci**: pasta pillows with the same basic form as tortellini, but stuffed with cheese and vegetables

TASTE 4 | TORTELLINI

The venerable city of **Bologna** is called "the Fat" for a reason: this is the birthplace of tortellini, not to mention other specialties such as mortadella and ragù. Despite the city's new reputation for chic nightclubs and flashy boutiques, much of the food remains as it ever was.

You'll find the many Emilian variations on stuffed pasta all over the region, but they're perhaps at their best in Bologna, especially the native tortellini.

INSPIRED BY THE GODS

According to one legend, tortellini was inspired by the navel of Venus, goddess of love. As the story goes, Venus and some other gods stopped at a local inn for the night. A nosy chef went to their room to catch a glimpse of Venus. Peering through the keyhole, he saw her lying only partially covered on the bed. He was so inspired after seeing her perfect navel that he created a stuffed pasta, tortellini, in its image.

ON THE MENU

Tortellini is usually filled with beef (sometimes cheese), and is served two ways: *asciutta* is "dry," meaning it is served with a sauce such as ragù, or perhaps just with butter and Parmigiano. *Tortellini in brodo* is immersed in a lovely, savory beef broth.

Tortellini alla panna contains a meat filling and is sauced with cream. Aficionados, however, argue frequently about what to stuff into these little bundles, and probably no two cooks do it the same. Some purists insist that only beef will do; others mix it up with sausages, mortadella, spices, and cheese (usually Parmigiano).

BEST SPOT TO BUY

Don't miss **Tamburini,** Bologna's best specialty food shop, where aromas of Emilia-Romagna's famous specialties waft out through the room and into the streets.

Stretching the dough

Adding the filling

Shaping each piece

Tortellini di Bologna

IN FOCUS EMILIA: ONE TASTE AT A TIME

10

$ *Average main: €26* ✉ *Vicolo Squallore 46* ☎ *059/222533* ⊕ *www. hosteriagiusti.it* ⊘ *Closed Sun. and Mon., and Dec.–Jan. 10. No dinner.*

$$
ECLECTIC
Fodor's Choice
★

✕**Mon Café.** Locals love this café because it does just about everything and does it well, beginning at 7 in the morning with tasty breakfast pastries and ending long after dark with nightcaps. In between, lunch is served, as is dinner. **Known for:** wide-ranging menu; tapas; opens early and closes late. $ *Average main: €16* ✉ *Corso, Canalchiaro 128* ☎ *059/223257* ⊕ *www.mon-cafe.it* ⊘ *Closed Mon.*

$$$
EMILIAN
Fodor's Choice
★

✕**Osteria Francescana.** Chef-proprietor Massimo Bottura has done stints with Adrià and Ducasse, takes inspiration from music and literature, and pours all these influences into creating some of the most memorable food in all of Italy while remaining true to his Modenese roots. The restaurant contains only 12 tables and although it's possible to order à la carte, most everyone opts for one of the two tasting menus—either Festina Lente (9 courses) or Tutto ("everything," 12 courses). **Known for:** a chef who makes food art; its tasting menus; reservation made months in advance. $ *Average main: €250* ✉ *Via Stella 22* ☎ *059/223912* ⊕ *www. osteriafrancescana.it* ⊘ *Closed Sun. No lunch Sat.*

WHERE TO STAY

$$
B&B/INN

🛏 **La Maison du Charme.** Gracious host Maria Luisa Valentini has turned part of her family's early-20th-century villa into a charming bed-and-breakfast complete with period-appropriate furniture and bright aqua walls. **Pros:** quiet location, yet close to the center; intimate experience. **Cons:** books up quickly. $ *Rooms from: €130* ✉ *Via Usiglio 12* ☎ *349/1984584* ⊕ *www.bblamaisonducharmemodena.it* ⇌ *2 rooms* ⚍ *Free Breakfast.*

$$
B&B/INN
Fodor's Choice
★

🛏 **Quarto Piano.** Proprietors Antonio di Resta and Alessandro Bertoni have combined their impeccable sense of style and love of things French to produce a lovely little bed-and-breakfast located just a few steps away from the Duomo. **Pros:** intimate (just two rooms); lovely bath products and fluffy towels. **Cons:** with only two rooms it books up quickly. $ *Rooms from: €140* ✉ *Via Bonacorsa 27* ☎ *059/8755487* ⊕ *www.bbquartopiano.it* ⊘ *Closed Aug.* ⇌ *2 rooms* ⚍ *Free Breakfast.*

BOLOGNA

Bologna, a city rich with cultural jewels, has long been one of the best-kept secrets in northern Italy. Tourists in the know can bask in the shadow of its leaning medieval towers and devour the city's wonderful food.

The charm of the centro storico, with its red-arcaded passageways and sidewalks, can be attributed to wise city counselors who, at the beginning of the 13th century, decreed that roads couldn't be built without *portici* (porticoes). Were these counselors to return to town eight centuries later, they'd marvel at how little has changed.

Bologna, with a population of about 373,000, has a university-town vibe—and it feels young and lively in a way that many other Italian cities don't. It also feels full of Italians in a way that many other towns, thronged with tourists, don't. Bolognesi come out at aperitivo time, and you might be struck by the fact that it's not just youngsters who are out doing the passeggiata, or having a glass of wine with affettati misti.

From as early as the Middle Ages the town was known as "Bologna the Fat" for the agricultural prosperity that resulted in a well-fed population. In the 21st century Bolognese food remains, arguably, the best in Italy. With its sublime cuisine, lively spirit, and largely undiscovered art, Bologna is a memorable destination.

GETTING HERE AND AROUND

Frequent train service from Florence to Bologna makes getting here easy. The Italo and Frecciarossa and Frecciaargento (high-speed trains) run several times an hour and take just under 40 minutes.

Otherwise, you're left with the *regionali* (regional) trains, which putter along and get you to Bologna in just over two hours. The historic center is an interesting and relatively effortless walk from the station—though it takes about 20 minutes.

If you're driving from Florence, take the A1, exiting onto the A14, and then get on the RA1 to Uscita 7–Bologna Centrale. The trip takes about an hour. From Milan, take the A1, exiting to the A14 as you near the city; from there, take the A13 and exit at Bologna; then follow the RA1 to Uscita 7–Bologna Centrale. The trip takes just under three hours.

VISITOR INFORMATION

Contacts Bologna Tourism Offices. ⊠ *Aeroporto di Bologna* ☏ *051/6472201* ⊕ *www.bolognawelcome.it* ⊠ *Piazza Maggiore 1* ☏ *051/231415* ⊕ *www. bolognawelcome.it.*

EXPLORING

Piazza Maggiore and the adjacent Piazza del Nettuno are the historic centers of the city. Arranged around these two squares are the imposing Basilica di San Petronio, the massive Palazzo Comunale, the Palazzo del Podestà, the Palazzo Re Enzo, and the Fontana del Nettuno—one of the most visually harmonious groupings of public buildings in the country. From here, sights that aren't on one of the piazzas are but a short walk away, along delightful narrow cobblestone streets or under the ubiquitous arcades that double as municipal umbrellas. Take at least a full day to explore Bologna; it's compact and lends itself to easy exploration, but there's plenty to see.

10

TOP ATTRACTIONS

Basilica di San Petronio. Construction on this vast cathedral began in 1390; and the work, as you can see, still isn't finished more than 600 years later. The wings of the transept are missing and the facade is only partially decorated, lacking most of the marble that was intended to adorn it. The main doorway was carved in 1425 by the great Sienese master Jacopo della Quercia. Above the center of the door is a Madonna and Child flanked by saints Ambrose and Petronius, the city's patrons. Michelangelo, Giulio Romano, and Andrea Palladio (among others), submitted designs for the facade, which were all eventually rejected.

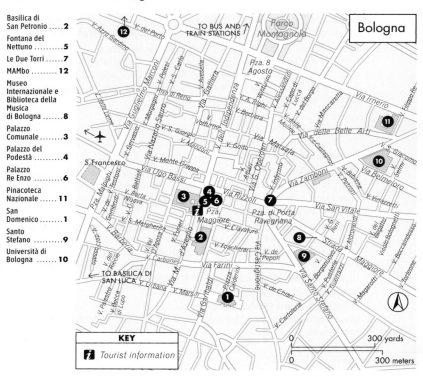

The interior of the basilica is huge. The Bolognesi had planned an even bigger church—you can see the columns erected to support the larger version outside the east end—but had to tone down construction when the university seat was established next door in 1561. The **Museo di San Petronio** contains models showing how it was originally supposed to look. The most important art in the church is in the fourth chapel on the left: these frescoes by Giovanni di Modena date to 1410–15. ⊠ *Piazza Maggiore* ☎ *051/231415* 🔊 *Free.*

Fontana del Nettuno. Sculptor Giambologna's elaborate 1563–66 Baroque fountain and monument to Neptune occupying Piazza Nettuno has been aptly nicknamed "Il Gigante" (The Giant). Its exuberantly sensual mermaids and undraped god of the sea drew fire when it was constructed, but not enough, apparently, to dissuade the populace from using the fountain as a public washing stall for centuries. Restoration efforts are planned for most of 2017. ⊠ *Piazza Nettuno, next to Palazzo Re Enzo, Piazza Maggiore.*

Le Due Torri. Two landmark towers, mentioned by Dante in *The Inferno,* stand side by side in the compact Piazza di Porta Ravegnana. Once every family of importance had a tower as a symbol of prestige and power—and as a potential fortress. Now only 60 remain out of more than 200 that once presided over the city. **Torre Garisenda** (late 11th century), which tilts 10 feet off perpendicular, was shortened to 165 feet in the 1300s and is now closed to visitors. **Torre degli Asinelli** (circa 1109) is 320 feet tall and leans 7½ feet. If you're up to a serious physical challenge—and not claustrophobic—you may want to climb its 500 narrow, wooden steps to get the view over Bologna. ✉ *Piazza di Porta Ravegnana, East of Piazza Maggiore* ⊕ *www.duetorribologna. com* ✉ *€5.*

FAMILY

Fodor's Choice

★

Santo Stefano. This splendid and unusual basilica contains between four and seven connected churches (authorities differ). A 4th-century temple dedicated to Isis originally occupied this site, but much of what you see was erected between the 10th and 12th centuries. The oldest existing building is **Santi Vitale e Agricola,** parts of which date from the 5th century. The exquisite beehive-shape San Sepolcro contains a Nativity scene much loved by Bologna's children, who come at Christmastime to pay their respects to the Christ child. Just outside the church, which probably dates from the 5th century (with later alterations), is the **Cortile di Pilato** (Pilate's Courtyard), named for the basin in the center. Despite the fact that the basin was probably crafted around the 8th century, legend has it that Pontius Pilate washed his hands in it after condemning Christ. Also in the building are a museum displaying various medieval religious works and its shop, which sells honey, shampoos, and jams made by the monks. ✉ *Piazza Santo Stefano, Via Santo Stefano 24, University area* ☎ *051/223256* ⊙ *Closed daily noon–3:30.*

Università di Bologna. Take a stroll through the streets of the university area: a jumble of buildings, some dating as far back as the 15th century and most to the 17th and 18th. The neighborhood, as befits a college town, is full of bookshops, coffee bars, and inexpensive restaurants. Though not particularly distinguished, they're characteristic of student life in the city. Try eating at the *mensa universitaria* (cafeteria) if you want to strike up a conversation with local students (most speak English). Political slogans and sentiments are scrawled on walls all around the university and tend to be ferociously leftist, sometimes juvenile, and often entertaining. Among the university museums, the most interesting is the **Museo di Palazzo Poggi,** which displays scientific instruments plus paleontological, botanical, and university-related artifacts. ✉ *Via Zamboni 33, University area* ☎ *051/2099610* ⊕ *www.museopalazzo-poggi.unibo.it* ✉ *€6.*

WORTH NOTING

MAMbo. The name of this museum stands for Museo d'Arte Moderna di Bologna, or Bologna's Museum of Modern Art. It houses a permanent collection of modern art (defined as post–World War II until five minutes ago) and stages a revolving series of temporary exhibitions by cutting-edge artists. All of this is set within a remarkable space: you might have a hard time telling that the sleek minimalist structure was built in 1915 as the Forno del Pane, a large bakery that made bread for city residents. A bookshop and a restaurant complete the complex, the latter offering Sunday brunch and delicious aperitivi. ✉ *Via Don Minzoni 14* ☎ *051/6496611* ⊕ *www.mambo-bologna.org* ✉ *€6* ⊙ *Closed Mon.*

10

Museo Internazionale e Biblioteca della Musica di Bologna. The music museum in the spectacular Palazzo Aldini Sanguinetti, with its 17th- and 18th-century frescoes, offers among its exhibits a 1606 harpsichord and a collection of beautiful music manuscripts dating from the 1500s. ⊠ *Strada Maggiore 34, University area* ☎ *051/2757720* ⊕ *www.musei- bologna.it* 🎫 *Free* ⊘ *Closed Sun. and Mon., and 2 wks in Aug.*

Palazzo Comunale. A mélange of building styles and constant modifica- tions characterize this huge palace dating from the 13th to 15th cen- tury. When Bologna was an independent city-state, this was the seat of government—a function it still serves today. Over the door is a statue of Bologna-born Pope Gregory XIII (reigned 1572–85), most famous for reorganizing the calendar. There are good views from the upper stories of the palace. The first-floor **Sala Rossa** (Red Room) is open on advance request and during some exhibitions, and the **Sala del Consiglio Comu- nale** (City Council Hall) is open to the public for a few hours in the late morning. The old stock exchange, part of the Palazzo Comunale, which you enter from Piazza Nettuno, has been turned into a library. Dubbed the **Sala Borsa** (⊕ *www.bibliotecasalaborsa.it*), it has an impressive inte- rior courtyard. Within the palazzo are two museums. The **Collezioni Comunali d'Arte** exhibits paintings from the Middle Ages as well as some Renaissance works by Luca Signorelli (circa 1445–1523) and Tintoretto (1518–94). Underground caves and the foundations of the old cathedral can be visited by appointment made through the tourist office. ⊠ *Piazza Maggiore 6, Piazza Maggiore* ☎ *051/2194400 Palazzo/ Sala Borsa,* 🎫 *€5, except during special art exhibitions* ⊘ *Closed Sun.*

Palazzo del Podestà. This classic Renaissance palace facing the Basilica di San Petronio was erected in 1484, and attached to it is the soaring **Torre dell'Arengo.** The bells in the tower have rung whenever the city has celebrated, mourned, or called its citizens to arms. ⊠ *Piazza Net- tuno, Piazza Maggiore.*

Palazzo Re Enzo. Built in 1244, this palace became home to King Enzo of Sardinia, who was imprisoned here in 1249 after he was captured during the fierce battle of Fossalta. He died here 23 years later. The palace has other macabre associations as well: common criminals received last rites in the tiny courtyard chapel before being executed in Piazza Maggiore. The courtyard is worth peeking into, but the palace merely houses government offices. ⊠ *Piazza Re Enzo, Piazza Maggiore* ☎ *051/6375111.*

Pinacoteca Nazionale. Bologna's principal art gallery contains many works by the immortals of Italian painting. Its prize possession is the *Ecstasy of St. Cecilia* by Raphael (1483–1520). There's also a beautiful polyptych by Giotto (1267–1337), as well as *Madonna and Child with Saints Margaret, Jerome, and Petronio* by Parmigianino (1503–40): note the rapt eye contact between St. Margaret and the Christ child. ⊠ *Via delle Belle Arti 56, University area* ☎ *051/4209411* ⊕ *www.pina- cotecabologna.beniculturali.it* 🎫 *€6* ⊘ *Closed Mon.*

San Domenico. The tomb of St. Dominic, who died here in 1221, is called the **Arca di San Domenico,** and is found in this church in the sixth chapel on the right. Many artists participated in its decoration, notably Niccolò di Bari, who was so proud of his 15th-century contribution that he changed his name to Niccolò dell'Arca to recall this famous work. The young Michelangelo (1475–1564) carved the angel on the right. In the right transept of the church is a tablet marking the last resting place of hapless King Enzo, the Sardinian ruler imprisoned in the Palazzo Re Enzo. The attached museum contains religious relics. ✉ *Piazza San Domenico 13, off Via Garibaldi, South of Piazza Maggiore* ☎ *051/6400411* 🌐 *www.conventosandomenico.org.*

WHERE TO EAT

$$ EMILIAN Fodor's Choice ★ 🍴 **Da Cesari.** Host Paolino Cesari has been presiding over his eatery since 1955, and he and his staff go out of their way to make you feel at home. The food's terrific—if you love pork products, try anything on the menu with *mora romagnola*. Paolino has direct contact with the people who raise this breed that nearly became extinct (he calls it "my pig"). **Known for:** pork dishes made from Mora Romagnola breed of pig; wine list with lots of local bottles; the genial host. [$] *Average main: €18* ✉ *Via de' Carbonesi 8, South of Piazza Maggiore* ☎ *051/237710* 🌐 *www.da-cesari.it* 🕒 *Closed Sun., Aug., and 1 wk in Jan.*

$ EMILIAN Fodor's Choice ★ 🍴 **Da Gianni a la Vecia Bulagna.** Though the interior is plain and unremarkable, it doesn't much matter—this place is all about food. The usual starters such as a tasty tortellini in brodo are on hand, as are daily specials such as gnocchi made with pumpkin, then sauced with melted cheese. **Known for:** tortellini in brodo; bollito misto; local favorite. [$] *Average main: €12* ✉ *Via Clavature 18, Piazza Maggiore* ☎ *051/229434* 🌐 *www.trattoria-gianni.it* 🕒 *Closed Mon. No dinner Sun.*

$ WINE BAR 🍴 **Tamburini.** Two small rooms inside plus kegs and bar stools outside make up this lively, packed little spot. The overwhelming plate of affettati misti is crammed with top-quality local ham products and succulent cheeses (including, sometimes, a goat Brie) and the adjacent salumeria offers many wonderful things to take away. **Known for:** cheese and salumi plates; excellent primi and secondi; lively atmosphere with a big selection of wine. [$] *Average main: €10* ✉ *Via Drapperie 1, Piazza Maggiore* ☎ *051/234726* 🌐 *www.tamburini.com.*

$ EMILIAN 🍴 **Trattoria del Rosso.** Although its interior—glaring yellow walls and the oddly placed ceramic plate—is nothing to write home about, this trattoria pulls in the locals. A mostly young crowd chows down on basic regional fare at rock-bottom prices. **Known for:** great food at rock-bottom prices; affordable wine list; party atmosphere. [$] *Average main: €9* ✉ *Via Augusto Righi 30, University area* ☎ *051/236730* 🌐 *www.trattoriadelrosso.com* 🕒 *Closed Thurs.*

$ EMILIAN 🍴 **Trattoria di Via Serra.** Much care has been taken with the decor: the rooms, overseen by host Flavio, are small and intimate, and the wooden walls painted a creamy whitish gray. Chef Tommaso gives equal care to the menu and deftly turns out Bolognese classics, as well as dishes with a modern twist: his *tosone fresco avvolta nella pancetta* is basically spun sugar, though his medium is Parmesan, with unsmoked bacon and greens. **Known for:** not in the centro storico but still close to train station; modern riffs on classic dishes; lively dining room. $ *Average main: €13* ⊠ *Via Serra 9B, Beyond the City Center* ☎ *051/3612330* ⊕ *www.trattoriadiviaserra.it* ⊘ *Closed Mon. and Tues. No lunch Wed. and Thurs.*

WHERE TO STAY

$ ⌂ **Albergo Centrale.** A stone's throw from Piazza Maggiore, this place
HOTEL that started out as a pensione in 1875 has been brought firmly into the 21st century and offers the winning combination of comfort, affordability, and some family-size rooms. **Pros:** very good value; excellent location. **Cons:** might be too plain for some tastes; street-facing rooms can get some noise; some rooms have a shared bath. $ *Rooms from: €90* ⊠ *Via della Zecca 2, Piazza Maggiore* ☎ *051/225114* ⊕ *www.albergocentralebologna.it* ⊅ *25 rooms* ⊗ *Free Breakfast.*

$$$ ⌂ **Art Hotel Novecento.** This swank place, inspired by the 1930s Vien-
HOTEL nese Secession movement, is in a little piazza just minutes from Piazza
Fodor's Choice Maggiore. **Pros:** spacious single rooms ideal for solo travelers; friendly,
★ capable concierge service; sumptuous buffet breakfast. **Cons:** some standard doubles are small; might be too trendy for some. $ *Rooms from: €201* ⊠ *Piazza Galileo 4/3, Piazza Maggiore* ☎ *051/7457311* ⊕ *www.bolognarthotels.it/novecento* ⊅ *25 rooms* ⊗ *Free Breakfast.*

$ ⌂ **Art Hotel Orologio.** The location of this stylish and welcoming family-
HOTEL run hotel can't be beat: it's right around the corner from Piazza Mag-
Fodor's Choice giore on a quiet piazza. **Pros:** central location; family-friendly rooms;
★ welcomes all animals. **Cons:** some steps to elevator; pet-friendly environment may not appeal to allergy sufferers. $ *Rooms from: €120* ⊠ *Via IV Novembre 10, Piazza Maggiore* ☎ *051/7457411* ⊕ *www.bolognarthotels.it/orologio* ⊅ *33 rooms* ⊗ *Free Breakfast.*

NIGHTLIFE AND PERFORMING ARTS

NIGHTLIFE

As a university town, Bologna has long been known for its busy nightlife. As early as 1300 it was said to have 150 taverns. Most of the city's current 200-plus pubs and bars are frequented by Italian students, young adults, and international students, with the university district forming the hub. In addition to the university area, the pedestrian zone on Via del Pratello, lined with plenty of bars, has a hopping nightlife scene; as does Via delle Moline, which promises cutting-edge cafés and bars. A more upscale, low-key evening experience can be had at one of Bologna's many wine bars, where the food is often substantial enough to constitute dinner.

BARS

Bar Calice. A year-round indoor-outdoor operation (with heat lamps), this bar is extremely popular with thirtysomethings, sometimes pushing baby carriages. Its large menu includes raw oysters. ⊠ *Via Clavature 13/a, at Via Marchesana, Piazza Maggiore* ☎ *051/236523* ⊕ *www.barilcalice.it.*

Fodor'sChoice ★ **Nu Bar Lounge.** This high-energy place draws a cocktail-loving crowd that enjoys fun drinks such as "I'm Too Sexy for This Place," a combination of vodka, triple sec, apple juice, and lemon. ⊠ *Via de' Musei 6, off Buca San Petronio, Piazza Maggiore* ☎ *051/222532* ⊕ *www.nulounge.com.*

Osteria del Sole. Although "osteria" in an establishment's name suggests that food will be served, such is not the case here. This place is all about drinking wine; the entrance door has warnings such as "He who doesn't drink will please stay outside" and "Dogs who don't drink are forbidden to come in." It's been around since 1465, and locals pack in, bearing food from outside to accompany the wine. ⊠ *Vicolo Ranocchi 1/d, Piazza Maggiore* ☎ ⊕ *www.osteriadelsole.it.*

CAFÉS

Fodor'sChoice ★ **Zanarini.** Chic Bolognesi congregate at this bar that serves coffee in the morning and swank aperitivi in the evening. Tasty sandwiches and pastries are also available. ⊠ *Piazza Galvani 1* ☎ *051/2750041.*

MUSIC VENUES

Cantina Bentivoglio. With live music staged every evening, Cantina Bentivoglio is one of Bologna's most appealing nightspots. You can enjoy light and more substantial meals here as well. ⊠ *Via Mascarella 4/b, University area* ☎ *051/265416* ⊕ *www.cantinabentivoglio.it.*

Osteria Buca delle Campane. In a 13th-century building, this underground tavern has good, inexpensive food and the after-dinner scene is popular with locals, including students, who come to listen to live music. The kitchen stays open until long past midnight. Reservations are strongly advised. ⊠ *Via Benedetto XIV 4/a, University area* ☎ *051/220918* ⊕ *www.bucadellecampane.it.*

PERFORMING ARTS

MUSIC AND OPERA

Teatro Comunale. This 18th-century theater presents concerts by Italian and international orchestras throughout the year, but the highly acclaimed opera performances from November through May are the main attraction. Reserve seats for those performances well in advance. ⊠ *Largo Respighi 1, University area* ☎ *051/529958* ⊕ *www.tcbo.it.*

10

SHOPPING

CLOTHING

Castel Guelfo Outlet City. If you don't feel like paying Galleria Cavour prices, this mall is about 20 minutes outside Bologna. It includes about 50 discounted stores, some from top designers such as Ferré. ⊠ *Via del Commercio 20/a, Loc. Poggio Piccolo, Castel Guelfo* ✛ *Take A14 toward Imola, Castel San Pietro Terme exit; 980 feet after tollbooth, turn right onto Via San Carlo* ☎ *0542/670765* ⊕ *www.thestyleoutlets. it* ☉ *Closed Mon. morning.*

Galleria Cavour. One of the most upscale malls in Italy, the Galleria houses many of the fashion giants, including Prada, Fendi, and jeweler-watchmaker Bulgari. ⊠ *Via Luigi Carlo Farini, South of Piazza Maggiore* ⊕ *www.galleriacavour.it.*

WINE AND FOOD

Bologna is a good place to buy wine. Several shops have a bewilderingly large selection—to go straight to the top, ask the managers which wines have won the prestigious Tre Bicchieri (Three Glasses) award from Gambero Rosso's wine bible, *Vini d'Italia.*

Eataly. At this lively shop—the original location in the now ubiquitous Italian cuisine empire—with an attached bookstore you can grab a bite to eat or have a glass of wine while stocking up on high-quality olive oil, vinegar, cured meats, and artisanal pasta. On the top floor, you can have a full-fledged trattoria meal, but what you can't have is anything decaffeinated: it's considered "chemical." ⊠ *Via degli Orafici 19, Piazza Maggiore* ☎ *051/0952820* ⊕ *www.eataly.it.*

Enoteca Italiana. Consistently recognized as one of the best wine stores in the country, Enoteca Italiana lives up to its reputation with shelves lined with excellent selections from all over Italy at reasonable prices. The delicious sandwiches, served with wines by the glass, make a great light lunch. ⊠ *Via Marsala 2/b, North of Piazza Maggiore* ☎ *051/235989* ⊕ *www.enotecaitaliana.it.*

La Baita. Fresh tagliolini, tortellini, and other Bolognese pasta delicacies are sold here, along with sublime food to take away. The cheese counter is laden with superlative local specimens. ⊠ *Via Pescherie Vecchia 3/a, Piazza Maggiore* ☎ *051/223940.*

Majani. Classy Majani has been producing chocolate since 1796. Its staying power may be attributed to high-quality confections that are as pretty to look at as they are to eat. ⊠ *Via de'Carbonesi 5, Piazza Maggiore* ☎ *051/234302* ⊕ *www.majani.it* ⊙ *Closed Sun.*

Mercato delle Erbe. This food market and food hall that's more than a century old bustles year-round. ⊠ *Via Ugo Bassi 25, Piazza Maggiore* ☎ *051/6592765* ⊕ *www.mercatodelleerbe.it* ⊙ *Closed Sun.*

Fodor'sChoice ★ **Mercato di Mezzo.** Formerly a fruit and vegetable market, the Mercato has morphed into a food hall. Various stalls offer the best that Bologna has to offer, and the Bolognesi are gobbling it up. Order from whatever place strikes your fancy, and sit anywhere there's room. ⊠ *Via Peschiere Vecchie, Piazza Maggiore.*

Paolo Atti & Figli. This place has been producing some of Bologna's finest pastas, cakes, and other delicacies for more than 130 years. ⊠ *Via Caprarie 7, Piazza Maggiore* ☎ *051/233349* ⊕ *www.paoloatti.com.*

Fodor'sChoice ★ **Roccati.** Sculptural works of chocolate, as well as basic bonbons and simpler sweets, have been crafted here since 1909. ⊠ *Via Clavature 17/a, Piazza Maggiore* ☎ *051/261964* ⊕ *www.roccaticioccolato.com.*

Scaramagli. Friendly owners run this midsize, down-to-earth wine store. ⊠ *Strada Maggiore 31/d, University area* ☎ *051/227132* ⊕ *www.scaramagli.it.*

FERRARA

47 km (29 miles) northeast of Bologna, 74 km (46 miles) northwest of Ravenna.

When the legendary Ferrarese filmmaker Michelangelo Antonioni called his beloved hometown "a city that you can see only partly, while the rest disappears to be imagined," perhaps he was referring to the low-lying mist that rolls in off the Adriatic each winter and shrouds Ferrara's winding knot of medieval alleyways, turreted palaces, and ancient wine bars—once inhabited by the likes of Copernicus—in a ghostly fog. But perhaps Antonioni was also suggesting that Ferrara's striking beauty often conceals a dark and tortured past.

Today you're likely to be charmed by Ferrara's prosperous air and meticulous cleanliness, its excellent restaurants and chic bars (for coffee and any other liquid refreshment), and its lively wine-bar scene. You'll find aficionados gathering outside any of the wine bars near the Duomo even on the foggiest of weeknights. Although Ferrara is a UNESCO World Heritage Site, the city draws amazingly few tourists—which only adds to its appeal.

■TIP→ **If you plan to explore the city fully, consider buying a Card Musei (Museum Card, also known as "My Ferrara Tourist Card"). Two days cost €12, three days €14, and six days €18. Purchase the card at the Palazzo dei Diamanti or any of Ferrara's museums; it grants admission to every museum, palace, and castle in town. The first Monday of the month is free at many museums.**

GETTING HERE AND AROUND

Train service is frequent from Bologna (usually three trains per hour) and takes either a half hour or 45 minutes, depending on which train type you take. It's 37 minutes from Florence to Bologna, and then about a half hour from Bologna to Ferrara. The walk from the station is easy, takes about 20 minutes, and is not particularly interesting. You can take either Bus No. 1 or No. 9 from the station to the center; buy your ticket at the newsagent inside the station and remember to stamp your ticket upon boarding the bus. If you're driving from Bologna, take the RA1 out of town, then the A13 in the direction of Padova, exiting at Ferrara Nord. Follow the SP19 directly into the center of town. The trip should take about 45 minutes.

10

VISITOR INFORMATION

Contact Ferrara Tourism Office. ⊠ *Castello Estense, Piazza Castello* ☎ *0532/299303* ⊕ *www.ferrarainfo.com.*

EXPLORING

TOP ATTRACTIONS

Fodor's Choice
★

Castello Estense. The former seat of Este power, this massive castle dominates the center of town. The building was a suitable symbol for the ruling family: cold and menacing on the outside, lavishly decorated within. The public rooms are grand, but deep in the bowels of the castle are chilling dungeons where enemies of the state were held in wretched conditions—a function these quarters served as recently as 1943, when anti-Fascist prisoners were detained there. In particular, the **Prisons of Don Giulio, Ugo,** and **Parisina** have some fascinating features, like 15th-century graffiti protesting the imprisonment of lovers Ugo and Parisina, who were beheaded in 1425 because Ugo's father, Niccolò III, didn't like the fact that his son was cavorting with Niccolò's wife.

The castle was established as a fortress in 1385, but work on its luxurious ducal quarters continued into the 16th century. Representative of Este grandeur are the **Sala dei Giochi,** extravagantly painted with athletic scenes, and the **Sala dell'Aurora,** decorated to show the times of the day. The terraces of the castle, and the hanging garden—once reserved for the private use of the duchesses—have fine views of the town and the surrounding countryside. You can cross the castle's moat, traverse its drawbridge, and wander through many of its arcaded passages at any time. ⊠ *Piazza Castello* 🕾 *0532/299233* ⊕ *www.castelloestense.it* 🖃 *€6.*

Duomo. The magnificent Gothic cathedral, a few steps from the Castello Estense, has a three-tier facade of slender arches and beautiful sculptures over the central door. Work began in 1135 and took more than 100 years to complete. The interior was completely remodeled in the 17th century. At this writing, the facade was scaffolded and undergoing a major restoration. ⊠ *Piazza delle Cattedrale* 🕾 *0532/207449.*

Museo Ebraico (*Jewish Museum*). The collection of ornate religious objects here bears witness to the long history of the city's Jewish community. This history had its high points—1492, for example, when Ercole I invited the Jews to come over from Spain—and its lows, notably 1627, when Jews were enclosed within the **ghetto,** where they were forced to live until the advent of a united Italy in 1860. The triangular warren of narrow cobbled streets that made up the ghetto originally extended as far as Corso Giovecca (originally Corso Giudecca, or Ghetto Street). When it was enclosed, the neighborhood was restricted to the area between Via Scienze, Via Contrari, and Via di San Romano. The museum, in the center of the ghetto, was once Ferrara's synagogue. All visits are led by a museum guide. ⊠ *Via Mazzini 95* 🕾 *0532/769137* ⊕ *www.coopculture.it* 🖃 *€4* ⊘ *Closed Mon.*

Palazzo dei Diamanti (*Palace of Diamonds*). Named for the 12,600 small, pink-and-white marble pyramids (or "diamonds") that stud its facade, this building was designed to be viewed in perspective—both faces at once—from diagonally across the street. Work began in the 1490s and finished around 1504. Today the palazzo contains the **Pinacoteca Nazionale,** an extensive art gallery that also hosts temporary exhibits. ⊠ *Corso Ercole I d'Este 19–21* 🕾 *0532/244949* ⊕ *www.palazzodiamanti.it* 🖃 *€13.*

Via delle Volte. One of the best-preserved medieval streets in Europe, the Via delle Volte clearly evokes Ferrara's past. The series of ancient *volte* (arches) along the narrow cobblestone alley once joined the merchants' houses on the south side of the street to their warehouses on the north side. The street ran parallel to the banks of the Po River, which was home to Ferrara's busy port. ⊠ *Ferrara.*

WORTH NOTING

Casa Romei. This ranks among Ferrara's loveliest Renaissance palaces. Built by the wealthy banker Giovanni Romei (1402–83), it's a vast structure with a graceful courtyard. Mid-15th-century frescoes decorate rooms on the ground floor; the piano nobile contains detached frescoes from local churches as well as lesser-known Renaissance sculptures. The Sala delle Sibelle has a very large 15th-century fireplace and beautiful wood-coffered ceilings. ⊠ *Via Savonarola 30* ☎ *0532/234130,* ⊕ *www. beniculturali.it* 🎟 *€3 (free 1st Sun. of month).*

Museo della Cattedrale. Some of the original decorations of the town's main church, the former church, and cloister of San Romano, reside in the Museo della Cattedrale, which is across the piazza from the Duomo. Inside you'll find 22 codices commissioned between 1477 and 1535; early-13th-century sculpture by the Maestro dei Mesi; a mammoth oil on canvas by Cosmé Tura from 1469; and an exquisite Jacopo della Quercia, the *Madonna della Melograno.* Although this last work dates from 1403 to 1408, the playful expression on the Christ child seems very 21st century. ⊠ *Via San Romano 1* ☎ *0532/761299* ⊕ *www.arte-cultura.fe.it* 🎟 *€6* ☽ *Closed Mon.*

WHERE TO EAT

$ ✕**Enoteca Enotria.** This little two-room enoteca opened in 1986 in the
EMILIAN old Jewish section of town and has been pouring noteworthy wines (French and other bottles) ever since. The first room has just a counter where the wine is poured, a couple of stools, and a table; two more tables in the other room, lined with wine bottles, complete the space. **Known for:** wines and bubbly by the glass; nice small plates; premeal wine and snack stop. 💲*Average main: €9* ⊠ *Via Saraceno 39/A–41* ☎ *0532/209166* ⊕ *www.enotecaenotria.it* ☽ *Closed Mon.*

$$ ✕**il Sorpasso.** Named after a 1962 cult movie, *Il Sorpasso* (*The Easy*
EMILIAN *Life*) serves terrific, honestly priced food. The interior's unassuming: white walls lined with movie posters, and white floors. **Known for:** excellent polpettine alici (anchovy fish balls) and pasta dishes; using local ingredients whenever possible; vegan and vegetarian options. 💲*Average main: €16* ⊠ *Via Saraceno 118* ☎ *0532/790289* ⊕ *www. trattoriailsorpasso.it* ☽ *Closed Tues. No dinner Mon.*

$$ ✕**L'Oca Giuliva.** Food, service, and ambience harmonize blissfully at
EMILIAN this casual but elegant restaurant inside a 12th-century building. The chef shows a deft hand with area specialties and shines with the fish dishes: his *scampo saltato su una crema di fave e cime di rape* (a sweet crustacean, quickly sautéed, with a fava-bean puree with cooked bitter greens) shifts the palate into gear. **Known for:** creative antipasti and seafood dishes; cappellacci di zucca (pumpkin-stuffed pasta); tasting menus. 💲*Average main: €18* ⊠ *Via Boccanale di Santo Stefano 38* ☎ *0532/207628* ⊕ *www.ristorantelocagiuliva.it* ☽ *Closed Tues.*

$ ✕**Osteria al Brindisi.** Ferrara is a city of wine bars, beginning with this
WINE BAR one (allegedly Europe's oldest) which opened in 1435—Copernicus
Fodor'sChoice drank here while a student in the late 1400s and the place still has
★ an undergraduate aura. The twentysomething staff pours well-selected

10

wines by the glass, and offers three different sauces (butter and sage, tomato, or ragù) with the *cappellacci di zucca* (pasta stuffed with butternut squash). **Known for:** set menus at great prices; marvelous salads; full of locals, students, and visitors. $\$$ *Average main: €10* ⊠ *Via degli Adelardi 11* ☎ *0532/209142* ⊕ *www.albrindisi.net.*

$\$\$$ ✕ **Quel Fantastico Giovedì.** Locals and other cognoscenti frequent this
EMILIAN   sleek eatery just minutes away from Piazza del Duomo. Chef Gabriele
Fodor'sChoice   Romagnoli uses prime local ingredients to create gustatory taste sen-
★   sations on a menu that changes daily. **Known for:** the seasonality of
the menu; salamina e Parmigiano; beloved by locals with great taste.
$\$$ *Average main: €17* ⊠ *Via Castelnuovo 9* ☎ *0532/760570* ⊕ *www. quelfantasticogiovedi.it* ☉ *Closed Wed. No lunch Tues.*

$\$\$$ ✕ **Ristorante Centrale.** Pasta constantly being produced from scratch is the
EMILIAN   big draw here. Order a plate of cappellaci di zucca *alla ferrarese* (pump-
kin-stuffed pasta with a hearty meat ragù), and depending on where you sit you might actually witness your pasta being rolled out, stuffed, and sauced. **Known for:** house-made pasta; salamina in sugo; gracious waitstaff. $\$$ *Average main: €15* ⊠ *Via Boccaleone 8* ☎ *0532/470940* ☉ *Closed Sun.*

WHERE TO STAY

$\$$ ⛫ **Hotel Annunziata.** Brightly colored fittings enliven the white-walled,
HOTEL   hardwood-floor guest rooms—think minimalism with a splash—at this
hotel on a quiet little piazza near the forbiddingly majestic Castello Estense. **Pros:** perfect location (you can't get much more central); stellar staff; terrific buffet breakfast. **Cons:** it books up quickly. $\$$ *Rooms from: €89* ⊠ *Piazza, Repubblica 5* ☎ *0532/201111* ⊕ *www.annunziata. it* ↗ *27 rooms* ⦿*| Free Breakfast.*

$\$\$$ ⛫ **Hotel Ripagrande.** The courtyards, vaulted brick lobby, and breakfast
HOTEL   room of this 15th-century noble's palazzo retain much of their lordly
Renaissance flair. **Pros:** beyond-helpful staff; good choice for families. **Cons:** staff goes home at midnight; parking can be a problem. $\$$ *Rooms from: €150* ⊠ *Via Ripagrande 21* ☎ *0532/765250* ⊕ *ripagrande.hotels-ferrara.com/en* ↗ *40 rooms* ⦿*| Free Breakfast.*

$\$$ ⛫ **Locanda Borgonuovo.** In the early 18th century this lodging began
B&B/INN   life as a convent (later suppressed by Napoléon) but now it's a delight-
Fodor'sChoice   ful city-center bed-and-breakfast, popular with performers at the city's
★   Teatro Comunale. **Pros:** phenomenal breakfast featuring local foods
and terrific cakes made in-house; bicycles can be borrowed for free. **Cons:** steep stairs to reception area and rooms; must reserve far in advance as this place books quickly. $\$$ *Rooms from: €100* ⊠ *Via Cairoli 29* ☎ *0532/211100* ⊕ *www.borgonuovo.com* ↗ *6 rooms* ⦿*| Free Breakfast.*

ROMAGNA

Anywhere in Emilia-Romagna, the story goes, a weary, lost traveler will be invited into a family's home and offered a drink. But the Romagnesi claim that he'll be served water in Emilia and wine in Romagna. The hilly, mostly rural, and largely undiscovered Romagna region has

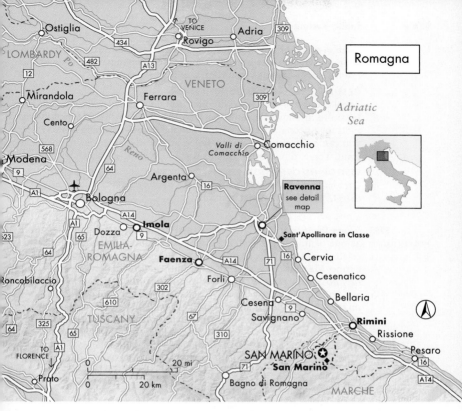

crumbling farmhouses dotting rolling hills, smoking chimneys, early-Christian churches, and rowdy local bars dishing out rounds and rounds of *piadine* (a pitalike thin bread filled with meat, cheese, vegetables, or any combination thereof, and then quickly grilled). Ravenna, the site of shimmering Byzantine mosaics, dominates the region.

Heading southeast from Bologna, Via Emilia (SS9) and the parallel A14 autostrada lead to the town of Faenza. From here, go north to the Adriatic Coast on the SS71 to reach Ravenna. Alternatively, the slower SS16 cuts a northwest–southeast swath through Romagna.

IMOLA

42 km (26 miles) southeast of Bologna.

Affluent Imola, with its wide and stately avenues, lies on the border between Emilia and Romagna. It was populated as early as the Bronze Age, came under Roman rule, and was eventually annexed to the Papal States in 1504. Imola is best known for its Formula One auto-racing tradition: the San Marino Grand Prix has been held here every spring since 1981. Auto racing as a serious sport in Imola dates to 1953, when, with the support of Enzo Ferrari, the racetrack just outside the city center was inaugurated. However, unless you happen to pop into town in mid-April for the race, you'll more likely find yourself in Imola shopping for its well-known ceramics or sampling the cuisine at the town's world-famous restaurant, San Domenico.

GETTING HERE AND AROUND

Local trains from Bologna run often and take a little under a half hour. If you're driving from Bologna, take the RA1 to the A14 (following signs for Ancona). Take the exit for Imola. If you're coming from Milan, you can catch the Eurostar to Bologna, and then transfer to the local train. Travel time from Milan to Bologna is a little over an hour.

VISITOR INFORMATION

Contact Imola Tourism Office. ✉ *Galleria del Centro Cittadino, Via Emilia 135* ☎ *0542/602207* 🌐 *www.visitareimola.it.*

WHERE TO EAT

$$$$ | MODERN ITALIAN | Fodor's Choice ★

🍴 **San Domenico.** Year after year this restaurant defends its position as one of Italy's most refined dining destinations, and heads of state, celebrities, and lovers of fine food venture here to savor the fare. Valentino Marcattili's wondrous creations, like his memorable *uovo in raviolo San Domenico,* in which a large raviolo is stuffed with a raw egg yolk—which miraculously cooks only a little, then spills out and mixes with Parmesan cheese, *burro di malga* (butter from an Alpine dairy farm), and sensational white truffles. **Known for:** uovo in raviolo San Domenico; epic wine list; impeccable service. [$] *Average main: €83* ✉ *Via G. Sacchi 1* ☎ *0542/29000* 🌐 *www.sandomenico.it* ⏲ *Closed Mon. year-round and Sun. June–Aug. No dinner Sun.; no lunch Sat. June–Aug.*

FAENZA

49 km (30 miles) southeast of Bologna.

In the Middle Ages Faenza was the crossroads between Emilia-Romagna and Tuscany, and the 15th century saw many Florentine artists working in town. In 1509, when the Papal States took control, Faenza became something of a backwater town. It did, however, continue its 12th-century tradition of making top-quality ceramics. In the 16th century local artists created a color called *bianchi di Faenza* (Faenza white), which was widely imitated and wildly desired all over Europe. The Frenchified *faience,* referring to the color and technique, soon entered the lexicon, where it remains to this day. In the central **Piazza del Popolo,** dozens of shops sell the native ceramic wares.

GETTING HERE AND AROUND

Trains run frequently from Bologna to Faenza, making the trip in about a half hour. There's also sporadic service from Florence, a beautiful two-hour ride. The walk to the centro storico, though easy, isn't especially interesting. By car it takes about an hour from Bologna. Follow the SP253 to the RA1, at which point pick up on the A14/E45 heading in the direction of Ancona. Exit and take the SP8 into Faenza.

VISITOR INFORMATION

Contact Faenza Tourism Office. ✉ *Voltore Molinella 2* ☎ *0546/25231* 🌐 *www.prolocofaenza.it.*

EXPLORING

Museo Internazionale delle Ceramiche. One of the largest ceramics museums in the world has a well-labeled, well-lit collection, with objects from the Renaissance among its highlights. Although the emphasis is clearly on local work, the rest of Italy is also represented. Don't miss the 20th- and 21st-century galleries, which prove that decorative arts often surpass their utile limitations and become genuinely sculptural. ✉ *Viale Baccarini 19* ☎ *0546/697311* 🌐 *www.micfaenza.org* 🎟 *€10* 🕒 *Closed Mon.*

WHERE TO EAT

$ EMILIAN 🍴 **Marianaza.** A large open-hearth fireplace dominates this simple trattoria, and wonderful aromas of grilled meats and garlic greet you as you walk in. Marianaza, like the town of Faenza itself, successfully blends the best of Emilia-Romagna and Tuscany: the extraordinary primi are mostly tortellini based, and the secondi rely heavily on the grill. **Known for:** grilled meats; a woman at the grill (rare in Italy); delicious Emilian and Tuscan specialties. [$] *Average main: €10* ✉ *Via Torricelli 21* ☎ *0546/681461* 🌐 *www.marianaza.com.*

RIMINI

52 km (32 miles) southeast of Ravenna, 121 km (75 miles) southeast of Bologna.

Rimini is one of the most popular summer resorts on the Adriatic Coast and one of the most popular in Italy. July and August are the most crowded, packed with people who don't mind crammed beaches and not-terribly-blue water. In the off-season (October through March), Rimini is a cold, windy fishing port with few places open. Any time of year, one of Rimini's least touristy areas is the port; rambling down the **Via Sinistra del Porto** or **Via Destra del Porto** past all the fishing boats, you're far from the crush of sunbathers.

The town stands at the junction of two great Roman consular roads, the Via Emilia and the Via Flaminia. In Roman times it was an important port, making it a strategic and commercial center. From the 13th century onward, Rimini was controlled by the Malatesta family, an unpredictable clan capable of grand gestures and savage deeds.

GETTING HERE AND AROUND

Trains run hourly from Ravenna to Rimini and take about an hour. By car from Ravenna, take the SS16/E55, then follow the SS3bis/E45/E55 in the direction of Roma/Ancona. Follow directions for Ancona Nord, then follow signs for Ancona. Take the A14/E55 to the Rimini Nord exit, then the SP136 to the SS16, and follow signs for the center of town. Alternatively, take the coastal road, SS16, which hugs the shoreline much of the way, passing through Cervia. Although its length of 52 km (32 miles) is not great, this scenic route is naturally slower (beware of fog in winter). The coast north of Rimini is lined with dozens of small resort towns, but only one really has any charm—the seaport of Cesenatico; the others are mini-Riminis, and in summer the narrow road is hopelessly clogged with traffic.

There's frequent train service (usually four trains per hour) from Bologna to Rimini. It takes 1–1½ hours, depending upon what type of train you choose. By car from Bologna, take the SP253 out of town, pick up the RA1, and then enter the A14 heading toward Ancona. Get off at the Rimini Nord exit, follow the SP136 to the SS16 to the center of town.

VISITOR INFORMATION

Contact Rimini Tourism Office. ⊠ *Piazzale Federico Fellini 3* ☎ *0541/704587* ⊕ *www.riminiturismo.it.*

EXPLORING

Arco d'Augusto. Rimini's oldest monument is the Arco d'Augusto, now stranded in the middle of a square just inside the city ramparts. It was erected in 27 BC, making it the oldest surviving ancient Roman arch. ⊠ *Largo Giulio Cesare at Corso d'Augusto.*

Tempio Malatestiano. The Malatesta family constructed the Tempio Malatestiano, also called the Basilica Cattedrale, with a masterful facade by Leon Battista Alberti (1404–72). Inside, the chapel to the right of the high altar contains a wonderful (if faded) fresco by Piero della Francesca (1420–92) depicting Sigismondo Maletesta kneeling before a saint. The two greyhounds in the right corner are significantly less faded than the rest. ⊠ *Via IV Novembre 35* ☎ ⊕ *www.diocesi.rimini.it* ☑ *Free.*

WHERE TO EAT AND STAY

$$
EMILIAN
✕ **La Marianna.** A welcoming spot that is all about fish, and aside from vegetable side dishes and dessert there's little on the menu that wasn't recently swimming (or lurking) in the sea. Locals flock here, and with good reason—the food is excellent, and the prices are reasonable. **Known for:** any dish with local mazzancolle in it; tagiolini with vongole, calamari, e broccoli; well-priced tasting menu. $ *Average main: €15* ⊠ *Via Tiberio 19* ☎ *0541/22530* ⊕ *www.trattorialamarianna.it.*

$$$$
HOTEL
FAMILY
⊞ **Grand Hotel.** This 1908 extravaganza, made famous by Federico Fellini in his film *Amarcord,* is grander than ever with ongoing restorations that keep the place completely current while maintaining its old-world charm. **Pros:** sumptuous buffet breakfast that starts early (7 am) and ends late (11 am); the American Bar; beach across the street; programs for children in summer. **Cons:** not in the center of town; some rooms more fabulous than others. $ *Rooms from: €425* ⊠ *Parco Federico Fellini* ☎ *0541/56000* ⊕ *www.grandhotelrimini.com* ↩ *167 rooms* ⊺❙ *Free Breakfast.*

SAN MARINO

90 km (56 miles) southeast of Faenza, 139 km (86 miles) southeast of Bologna.

The world's smallest and oldest republic, as San Marino dubs itself, is surrounded entirely by Italy. It consists of three ancient castles perched on sheer cliffs rising implausibly out of the flatlands of Romagna, and a tangled knot of cobblestone streets below that are lined with tourist boutiques, cheesy hotels and restaurants, and gun shops. The 1½-hour drive from Faenza is justified, however, by the sweeping views from the castle of the countryside. The 3,300-foot-plus precipices will make jaws drop and acrophobes quiver.

Visiting San Marino in winter (off-season) increases the appeal of the experience, as tourist establishments shut down and you more or less have the castles to yourself. In August every inch of walkway on the rock is mobbed with sightseers. Don't worry about changing money, showing passports, and the like (although the tourist office at Contrada del Collegio will stamp your passport for €2.50). San Marino is, for all practical purposes, Italy—except, that is, for its majestic perch, its lax gun laws, and its reported 99% national voter turnout rate.

GETTING HERE AND AROUND

To get to San Marino by car, take highway SS72 west from Rimini. From Borgo Maggiore, at the base of the rock, a cable car will whisk you up to the town. Alternatively, you can drive up the winding road; public parking is available. There is a regular bus service to and from Rimini, with service sometime every hour throughout the year (less frequent service on Sunday); a one-way ticket from Rimini to San Marino costs €4.50. The trip takes about 45 minutes.

VISITOR INFORMATION

Contact **State Board of Tourism.** ✉ *Contrada Omagnano 20* ☎ *0549/882914* ⊕ *www.visitsanmarino.com.*

EXPLORING

Piazza della Libertà. One must-see is the Piazza della Libertà, where the Palazzo Pubblico is guarded by soldiers in green uniforms. As you'll notice by peering into the shops along the old town's winding streets, the republic is famous for crossbows and other items (think fireworks or firearms) that are illegal almost everywhere else. ✉ *San Marino.*

Tre Castelli. San Marino's headline attractions are its Tre Castelli—medieval architectural wonders that appear on every coat of arms in the city. Starting in the center of town, walk a few hundred yards past the trinket shops, along a paved cliff-top ridge, from the 10th-century **Rocca della Guaita** to the 13th-century **Rocca della Cesta** (containing a museum of ancient weapons that's worthwhile mostly for the views from its terraces and turrets) and finally to the 14th-century **Rocca Montale** (closed to the public), the most remote of the castles. Every step of the way affords spectacular views of Romagna and the Adriatic—it's said that on a clear day you can see Croatia. The walk makes for a good day's exercise, but is by no means arduous. Even if you arrive after visiting hours, it's supremely rewarding. ✉ *San Marino* ☎ *0549/991369* 💲 *Il Torre Guaita and Il Torre Cesta €4.*

RAVENNA

76 km (47 miles) east of Bologna, 93 km (58 miles) southeast of Ferrara.

A small, quiet, well-heeled city, Ravenna has brick palaces, cobblestone streets, magnificent monuments, and spectacular Byzantine mosaics. The high point in its civic history occurred in the 5th century, when Pope Honorious moved his court here from Rome. Gothic kings

Odoacer and Theodoric ruled the city until it was conquered by the Byzantines in AD 540. Ravenna later fell under the sway of Venice, and then, inevitably, the Papal States.

Because Ravenna spent much of its past looking east, its greatest art treasures show that Byzantine influence. Churches and tombs with the most unassuming exteriors contain within them walls covered with sumptuous mosaics. These beautifully preserved Byzantine mosaics put great emphasis on nature, which you can see in the delicate rendering of sky, earth, and animals. Outside Ravenna, the town of Classe hides even more mosaic gems.

GETTING HERE AND AROUND

By car from Bologna, take the SP253 to the RA1, and then follow signs for the A14/E45 in the direction of Ancona. From here, follow signs for Ravenna, taking the A14dir Ancona–Milano–Ravenna exit. Follow signs for the SS16/E55 to the center of Ravenna. From Ferrara the drive is more convoluted, but also more interesting. Take the SS16 to the RA8 in the direction of Porto Garibaldi taking the Roma/Ravenna exit. Follow the SS309/E55 to the SS309dir/E55, taking the SS253 Bologna/Ancona exit. Follow the SS16/E55 into the center of Ravenna.

VISITOR INFORMATION

Contact **Ravenna Tourism Office.** ⊠ *Piazza San Francesco* ☎ *0544/35755* ⊕ *www.turismo.ra.it.*

EXPLORING

A combination ticket (available at ticket offices of all included sights) admits you to four of Ravenna's important monuments: the Mausoleo di Galla Placidia, the Basilica di San Vitale, the Battistero Neoniano, and Sant'Apollinare Nuovo. Start out early in the morning to avoid lines (reservations are necessary for the Mausoleo and Basilica in May and June). A half day should suffice to walk the town; allow a half hour for the Mausoleo and the Basilica.

TOP ATTRACTIONS

Fodor'sChoice
★
Basilica di San Vitale. The octagonal church of San Vitale was built in AD 547, after the Byzantines conquered the city, and its interior shows a strong Byzantine influence. The area behind the altar contains the most famous works, depicting Emperor Justinian and his retinue on one wall, and his wife, Empress Theodora, with her retinue, on the opposite one. Notice how the mosaics seamlessly wrap around the columns and curved arches on the upper sides of the altar area. ▮TIP→ **Reservations are recommended March–mid-June.** ⊠ *Via San Vitale, off Via Salara* ☎ *0544/541688 reservations* ⊕ *www.ravennamosaici.it* ⊠ *€9.50 (includes all diocesan monuments)* ⊘ *Closed Jan. 1 and Dec. 25.*

Fodor'sChoice
★
Battistero Neoniano. Next door to Ravenna's 18th-century cathedral, the baptistery has one of the town's most important mosaics. It dates from the beginning of the 5th century AD, with work continuing through the century. In keeping with the building's role, the great mosaic in the dome shows the baptism of Christ, and beneath are the Apostles. The lowest register of mosaics contains Christian symbols, the Throne of God, and

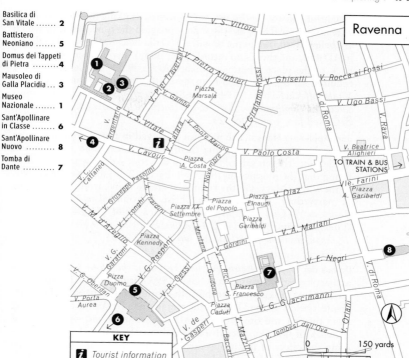

the Cross. Note the naked figure kneeling next to Christ—he is the personification of the River Jordan. ✉ *Via Battistero* ☎ *0544/541688 reservations, 800/303999 info (toll-free)* ⊕ *www.ravennamosaici.it* 🎟 *€9.50 (includes all diocesan monuments)* ⊘ *Closed Jan. 1 and Dec. 25.*

Fodor's Choice **Mausoleo di Galla Placidia.** The little tomb and the great church stand side
★ by side, but the tomb predates the Basilica di San Vitale by at least 100 years. These two adjacent sights are decorated with the best-known, most elaborate mosaics in Ravenna. Galla Placidia was the sister of the Roman emperor Honorius, who moved the imperial capital to Ravenna in AD 402. She is said to have been beautiful and strong-willed, and to have taken an active part in the governing of the crumbling empire. This mausoleum, constructed in the mid-5th century, is her memorial.

Viewed from the outside, it's a small, unassuming redbrick building: the exterior's seeming poverty of charm only serves to enhance by contrast the richness of the interior mosaics, in deep midnight blue and glittering gold. The tiny central dome is decorated with symbols of Christ, the evangelists, and striking gold stars. Over the door is a depiction of the Good Shepherd. Eight of the Apostles are represented in groups of two on the four inner walls of the dome; the other four appear singly on the walls of the two transepts. Notice the small doves at their feet, drinking from the water of faith. Also in the tiny transepts are some

10

delightful pairs of deer (representing souls), drinking from the fountain of resurrection. There are three sarcophagi in the tomb, none of which are believed to contain the remains of Galla Placidia. She died in Rome in AD 450, and there's no record of her body's having been transported back to the place where she wished to lie. ■ TIP→ **Reservations are required for the Mausoleo from March through mid-June.** ⊠ *Via San Vitale, off Via Salara* ☎ *0544/541688 reservations* ⊕ *www.ravennamosaici.it* ⊠ *Combination ticket €9.50 (includes all diocesan monuments)* ⊘ *Closed Jan. 1 and Dec. 25.*

Fodor's Choice
★

Sant'Apollinare Nuovo. The mosaics displayed in this church date from the early 6th century, making them slightly older than those in San Vitale. Since the left side of the church was reserved for women, it's only fitting that the mosaics on that wall depict 22 virgins offering crowns to the Virgin Mary. On the right wall are 26 men carrying the crowns of martyrdom. They approach Christ, surrounded by angels. ⊠ *Via Roma, at Via Guaccimanni* ☎ *0544/219518, 0544/541688 reservations* ⊕ *www.ravennamosaici.it* ⊠ *Combination ticket €9.50 (includes all diocesan monuments)* ⊘ *Closed Jan 1 and Dec. 25.*

WORTH NOTING

Domus dei Tappeti di Pietra (*Ancient Home of the Stone Carpets*). This archaeological site was uncovered in 1993 during digging for an underground parking garage near the 18th-century church of Santa Eufemia. Ten feet below ground level lie the remains of a Byzantine palace dating from the 5th and 6th centuries AD. Its beautiful and well-preserved network of floor mosaics displays elaborately designed patterns, creating the effect of luxurious carpets. ⊠ *Via Barbiani, enter through Sant'Eufemia* ☎ *0544/32512* ⊕ *www.domusdeitappetidipietra.it* ⊠ *€4.*

Museo Nazionale (*National Museum of Ravenna*). Next to the Church of San Vitale and housed in a former Benedictine monastery, the museum contains artifacts from ancient Rome, Byzantine fabrics and carvings, and pieces of early Christian art. The collection is well displayed and artfully lighted. In the first cloister are marvelous Roman tomb slabs from excavations nearby; upstairs, you can see a reconstructed 18th-century pharmacy. ⊠ *Via Fiandrini* ☎ *0544/543711* ⊠ *€6* ⊘ *Closed Mon.*

Sant'Apollinare in Classe. This church about 5 km (3 miles) southeast of Ravenna is landlocked now, but when it was built it stood in the center of the busy shipping port known to the ancient Romans as Classis. The arch above and the area around the high altar are rich with mosaics. Those on the arch, older than the ones behind it, are considered superior. They show Christ in Judgment and the 12 lambs of Christianity leaving the cities of Jerusalem and Bethlehem. In the apse is the figure of Sant'Apollinare himself, a bishop of Ravenna, and above him is a magnificent Transfiguration against blazing green grass, animals in odd perspective, and flowers. ⊠ *Via Romea Sud 224, off SS71, Classe* ☎ *0544/473569* ⊠ *€5.*

Tomba di Dante. The tomb of Dante is in a small Neoclassical building next door to the large church of St. Francis. Exiled from his native Florence, the author of *The Divine Comedy* died here in 1321. The

Florentines have been trying to reclaim their famous son for hundreds of years, but the Ravennans refuse to give him up, arguing that since Florence did not welcome Dante in life it does not deserve him in death. Perhaps as penance, every September the Florentine government sends olive oil that's used to fuel the light hanging in the chapel's center. ☒ *Via Dante Alighieri 4 and 9* 🎫 *Free.*

WHERE TO EAT

$$ ✕ **Bella Venezia.** Pale yellow walls, crisp white tablecloths, and warm
EMILIAN light provide the backdrop for some seriously good regional food. The menu offers local specialties, but also gives a major nod to Venice—Ravenna's conqueror of long ago. **Known for:** truffle and mushroom dishes; outdoor garden; family-owned and operated. [$] *Average main: €15* ☒ *Via IV Novembre 16* 🕾 *0544/212746* ⊕ *www.bellavenezia.it* ⊘ *Closed Sun., and 3 wks in Dec. and Jan.*

$$ ✕ **Ca' de' Ven.** These buildings, joined by a glass-ceilinged courtyard,
EMILIAN date from the 15th century, so the setting itself is reason enough to come; that the food is so good makes a visit here all the more satisfying. At lunchtime Ca' de' Ven teems with locals tucking in to piadine, stuffed or topped with various ingredients, and the grilled dishes—including *tagliata di pollo* (sliced chicken breast tossed with arugula and set atop exquisitely roasted potatoes)—are among the highlights. **Known for:** piadine; grilled meats; majestic space. [$] *Average main: €15* ☒ *Via Corrado Ricci 24* 🕾 *0544/30163* ⊕ *www.cadeven.it.*

$ ✕ **I Battibecchi.** Simple, honest food doesn't get any tastier than what's
EMILIAN served at this tiny venue (there are about 20 seats) with an even tinier kitchen. Nicoletta Molducci, chef and owner, takes pride in turning out terrific regional dishes. **Known for:** simple food; seasonal menu; gracious staff. [$] *Average main: €14* ☒ *Via della Tesoreria Vecchia 16* 🕾 *0544/219536* ⊕ *www.osteriadeibattibecchi.it.*

$$ ✕ **Osteria del Tempo Perso.** A couple of jazz-, rock-, and food-loving
EMILIAN friends joined forces to open this smart little restaurant in the cen-
Fodor's Choice ter. The interior's warm, terra-cotta-sponged walls give off an orange
★ glow, and wine bottles line the walls, interspersed with photographs of musical greats. **Known for:** terrific fish dishes; fine wine list; classic pastas. [$] *Average main: €18* ☒ *Via Gamba 12* 🕾 *0544/215393* ⊕ *www. osteriadeltempoperso.it* ⊘ *No lunch weekdays, and in July and Aug.*

WHERE TO STAY

$$ 🏨 **Albergo Cappello.** In operation since the late 19th century and restored
HOTEL a century later, this charming place reflects a Venetian influence, with many Murano chandeliers hanging in the high-ceiling, wood-coffered public rooms. **Pros:** good location; accommodating staff; good restaurant. **Cons:** only seven rooms. [$] *Rooms from: €189* ☒ *Via IV Novembre 41* 🕾 *0544/219876* ⊕ *www.albergocappello.it* 🛏 *7 rooms* ⦿*No meals.*

$ 🏨 **Sant'Andrea.** For a lovely little B&B on a residential street a stone's
B&B/INN throw from the Basilica of San Vitale, look no further—it even has a delightful garden. **Pros:** children under 12 stay free; discounts for stays

of three nights or more; cheery and helpful staff. **Cons:** can get a little noisy; staff goes home in the early evening. $ *Rooms from: €93* ✉ *Via Carlo Cattaneo 33* ☎ *0544/215564* ⊕ *www.santandreahotel.com* ↪ *12 rooms* ⦿| *Free Breakfast.*

NIGHTLIFE AND PERFORMING ARTS

Mosaics by Night. On Friday nights from June to August, the Byzantine mosaic masterpieces at the Basilica of San Vitale and the Mauseleo di Galla Placida are illuminated. The event is also held on certain Tuesdays. To check, call the tourist office, which offers guided tours. ✉ *Ravenna* ⊕ *www.ravennamosaici.it.*

Ravenna Festival. Orchestras from all over the world perform in city churches and theaters during this music festival that takes place in June and July, as well as a few days at the end of November and the beginning of December. ✉ *Ravenna* ⊕ *www.ravennafestival.org.*

Teatro di Tradizione Dante Alighieri. Operas and dance productions are staged here, usually on weekends, from November to March. If your Italian is up to it, you could also attend any of the theatrical productions. ✉ *Via Mariani 2* ☎ *0544/249244* ⊕ *www.teatroalighieri.org.*

FLORENCE

WELCOME TO FLORENCE

TOP REASONS TO GO

★ **Galleria degli Uffizi:**
Italian Renaissance art doesn't get much better than this vast collection bequeathed to the city by the last Medici, Anna Maria Luisa.

★ **Brunelleschi's Dome:**
His work of engineering genius is the city's undisputed centerpiece.

★ **Michelangelo's *David:***
One look and you'll know why this is one of the world's most famous sculptures.

★ **The view from Piazzale Michelangelo:** From this perch the city is laid out before you. The colors at sunset heighten the experience.

★ **Piazza Santa Croce:**
After you've had your fill of Renaissance masterpieces, hang out here and watch the world go by.

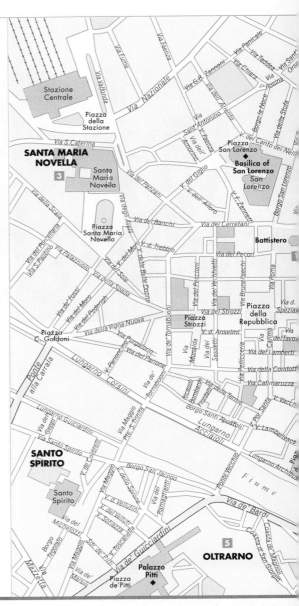

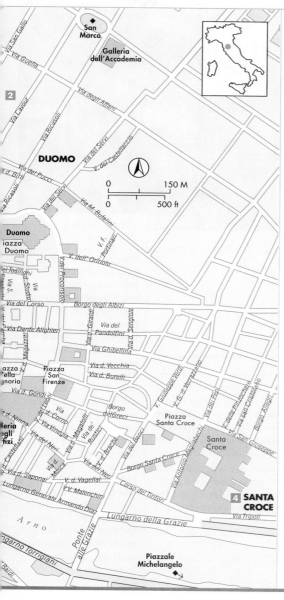

1 **Around the Duomo.**
You're in the heart of
Florence here. Among the
numerous highlights are the
city's greatest museum (the
Uffizi) and arguably its most
impressive square (Piazza
della Signoria).

2 **San Lorenzo.** The blocks
from the basilica of San
Lorenzo to the Galleria
dell'Accademia bear the
imprints of the Medici and
of Michelangelo, culminating
in the latter's masterful
David. The former convent
of San Marco is an oasis of
artistic treasures.

3 **Santa Maria Novella.**
This part of town includes
the train station,
16th-century palaces, and
the city's most swank
shopping street, Via
Tornabuoni.

4 **Santa Croce.** The district
centers on its namesake
basilica, which is filled with
the tombs of Renaissance
(and other) luminaries. The
area is also known for its
leather shops.

5 **The Oltrarno.** Across the
Arno you encounter the
massive Palazzo Pitti and
the narrow streets of the
Santo Spirito neighborhood,
filled with artisans'
workshops and antiques
stores.

EATING AND DRINKING WELL IN FLORENCE

In Florence simply prepared meats, grilled or roasted, are the culinary stars, usually paired with seasonal vegetables like artichokes or porcini. Bistecca's big here, but there's plenty more that tastes great on the grill, too.

Traditionalists go for their gustatory pleasures in trattorie and osterie, places where decor is unimportant and place mats are mere paper. Culinary innovation comes slowly in this town, though some cutting-edge restaurants have been appearing, usually with young chefs who've worked outside Italy. Some of these places lack charm, but their menus offer updated versions of Tuscan standards.

By American standards, Florentines eat late: 1:30 or 2 is typical for lunch and 9 for dinner is considered early. Consuming a primo, secondo, and dolce is largely a thing of the past. For lunch, many Florentines simply grab a panino and a glass of wine at a bar. Those opting for a simple trattoria lunch often order a plate of pasta and dessert.

STALE AND STELLAR

Florence lacks signature pasta and rice dishes, perhaps because it has raised frugality with bread to culinary craft. Stale bread is the basis for three classic Florentine primi: *pappa al pomodoro*, *ribollita*, and *panzanella*. Pappa is made with either fresh or canned tomatoes and that stale bread. Ribollita is a vegetable soup with *cavolo nero* (called Tuscan kale in the United States), cannellini beans, and thickened with bread. Panzanella, a summertime dish, is reconstituted Tuscan bread combined with tomatoes, cucumber, and basil. They all are enhanced with a generous application of fragrant Tuscan olive oil.

A CLASSIC ANTIPASTO: *CROSTINI DI FEGATINI*

This beloved dish consists of a chicken-liver spread, served warm or at room temperature, on toasted, garlic-rubbed bread. It can be served smooth, like a pâté, or in a chunkier, more rustic version. It's made by sautéing chicken livers with finely diced carrot and onion, enlivened with the addition of wine, broth, or Marsala reductions, and mashed anchovies and capers.

A CLASSIC SECONDO: *BISTECCA FIORENTINA*

The town's culinary pride and joy is a thick slab of beef, resembling a T-bone steak, from large white oxen called Chianina. The meat's slapped on the grill and served rare, sometimes with a pinch of salt.

It's always seared on both sides, and just barely cooked inside (experts say 5 minutes per side, and then 15 minutes with the bone sitting perpendicularly on the grill). To ask for it more well done is to incur disdain; if you can't eat it this way, do please order something else.

A CLASSIC CONTORNO: *CANNELLINI BEANS*

Simply boiled, they provide the perfect accompaniment to bistecca. The small white beans are best when they go straight from the garden into the pot. They should be anointed with a generous dose of Tuscan olive oil; the

combination is oddly felicitous, and it goes a long way toward explaining why Tuscans are referred to as *mangiafagioli* (bean eaters) by other Italians.

A CLASSIC DOLCE: *BISCOTTI DI PRATO*

These are sometimes the only dessert on offer (if you find yourself in such a restaurant, you'll know you're in a really, truly Tuscan eatery) and are more or less an afterthought to the glories that have preceded them. *Biscotti* means twice-cooked (or, in this case, twice baked). They are hard almond cookies that soften considerably when dipped languidly into *vin santo* ("holy wine"), a sweet dessert wine, or into a simple *caffè*.

A CLASSIC WINE: *CHIANTI CLASSICO*

This blend from the region just south of Florence relies mainly on the local, hardy *sangiovese* grape; it's aged for at least one year before hitting the market. (*Riserve*—reserves—are aged at least an additional six months.)

Chianti is usually the libation of choice for Florentines, and it pairs magnificently with grilled foods and seasonal vegetables. Traditionalists opt for the younger, fruitier (and usually less expensive) versions often served in straw flasks. You can sample Chianti Classico all over town, and buy it in local supermarkets.

Updated by Patricia Rucidlo

Why visit Florence, the city that shook up the Western world in the Middle Ages and gifted it with what would later be called the Renaissance? There are many reasons: its biggest draw is its unsurpassable art, from the sensuousness of Botticelli's nudes to the muscularity, masculinity, and virtual perfection of Michelangelo's *David*. Also to see firsthand Brunelleschi's engineering and architectural genius, from the powerful cupola crowning the cathedral to his Ospedale degli Innocenti (arguably the first Renaissance building in Italy).

Visitors have been captivated by this city along the Arno for centuries, and it has always been high on the list of places to visit on the Grand Tour. For centuries it has captured the imaginations of travelers in search of rooms with views and phenomenal art. Florence's is a subtle beauty—its staid palaces built in local stone are not showy, even though they are very large. A walk along the Arno offers views that don't quit and haven't much changed in 700 years. Navigating Piazza della Signoria and other major squares, always packed with tourists, requires patience. There's a reason why everyone wants to be here. Florence's *centro storico* (historic center) is little changed since Lorenzo de' Medici roamed its streets; outside the center, where most of the city's residents live, is less picturesque, but full of Florentines (they tend not to hang out in the historic center if they can help it).

When the sun sets over the Arno and, as Mark Twain described it, "overwhelms Florence with tides of color that make all the sharp lines dim and faint and turn the solid city to a city of dreams," it's hard not to fall under the city's spell.

FLORENCE PLANNER

MAKING THE MOST OF YOUR TIME

With some planning, you can see Florence's most famous sights in a couple of days. Start off at the city's most awe-inspiring architectural wonder, the **Duomo**, climbing to the top of the dome if you have the stamina (and are not claustrophobic: it gets a little tight going up and coming back down). On the same piazza, check out Ghiberti's bronze doors at the **Battistero**. (They're actually high-quality copies; the Museo dell'Opera del Duomo has the originals.) Set aside the afternoon for the **Galleria degli Uffizi**, making sure to reserve tickets in advance.

On Day 2, visit Michelangelo's *David* in the **Galleria dell'Accademia**— reserve tickets here, too. Linger in **Piazza della Signoria**, Florence's central square, where a copy of *David* stands in the spot the original occupied for centuries, then head east a couple of blocks to **Santa Croce**, the city's most artistically rich church. Double back and walk across Florence's landmark bridge, the **Ponte Vecchio**.

Do all that, and you'll have seen some great art, but you've just scratched the surface. If you have more time, put the **Bargello**, the **Museo di San Marco**, and the **Cappelle Medicee** at the top of your list. When you're ready for an art break, stroll through the **Boboli Gardens** or explore Florence's lively shopping scene, from the food stalls of the **Mercato Centrale** to the chic boutiques of the **Via Tornabuoni**.

HOURS

Florence's sights keep tricky hours. Some are closed Wednesday, some Monday, some every other Monday. Quite a few shut their doors each day (or on most days) by 2 in the afternoon. Things get even more confusing on weekends. Make it a general rule to check the hours closely for any place you're planning to visit; if it's someplace you have your heart set on seeing, it's worthwhile to call to confirm.

Here's a selection of major sights that might not be open when you'd expect *(consult the sight listings within this chapter for the full details)*. And be aware that, as always, hours can and do change. Also note that on the first Sunday of the month, all state museums are free. That means that the Accademia and the Uffizi, among others, do not accept reservations. Unless you are a glutton for punishment (i.e., large crowds), these museums are best avoided on that day.

The **Accademia** and the **Uffizi** are both closed Monday.

The **Battistero** is open Monday through Saturday 8:15–10:15 and 11:15–8; Sunday 8:30–2.

The **Bargello** closes at 1:50 pm, and is closed entirely on alternating Sundays and Mondays. However, it's often open much later during high season and when there's a special exhibition on.

The **Cappelle Medicee** are closed alternating Sundays and Mondays (those Sundays and Mondays when the Bargello is open).

The **Duomo** closes at 4:30 on Thursday, as opposed to 5 other weekdays, 4:45 Saturday, and Sunday it's open only 1:30–4:45. The dome of the Duomo is closed Sunday.

Museo di San Marco closes at 1:50 weekdays but stays open until 4:45 weekends—except for alternating Sundays and Mondays, when it's closed entirely.

Palazzo Medici-Riccardi is closed Wednesday.

RESERVATIONS

At most times of day you'll see a line of people snaking around the Uffizi. They're waiting to buy tickets, and you don't want to be one of them. Instead, call ahead for a reservation (☎ *055/294883*; reservationists speak English). You'll be given a reservation number and a time of admission—the sooner you call, the more time slots you'll have to choose from. Go to the museum's reservation door 10 minutes before the appointed hour, give the clerk your number, pick up your ticket, and go inside. (Know that often in high season, there's at least a half-hour wait to pick up the tickets and often an even longer wait to get into the museum.) You'll pay €4 for this privilege, but it's money well spent. You can also book tickets online through the website ⊕ *www.polomuseale. firenze.it*; the booking process takes some patience, but it works.

Use the same reservation service to book tickets for the Galleria dell'Accademia, where lines rival those of the Uffizi. (Reservations can also be made for the Palazzo Pitti, the Bargello, and several other sights, but they usually aren't needed—although, lately, in summer, lines can be long at Palazzo Pitti.) An alternative strategy is to check with your hotel—many will handle reservations.

GETTING HERE AND AROUND

AIR TRAVEL

Aeroporto A. Vespucci. Florence's small Aeroporto A. Vespucci, commonly called **Peretola**, is just outside of town and receives flights from Milan, Rome, London, and Paris. ✉ *10 km (6 miles) northwest of Florence* ☎ *055/30615* ⊕ *www.aeroporto.firenze.it.*

To get into the city center from the airport by car, take the autostrada A11. A SITA bus will take you directly from the airport to the center of town. Buy the tickets within the train station.

Aeroporto Galileo Galilei. Pisa's Aeroporto Galileo Galilei is the closest landing point with significant international service, including a few direct flights from New York each week on Delta. Sadly, the flight is seasonal and shuts down when it's cold outside. It's a straight shot down the SS67 to Florence. A train service, which used to connect Pisa's airport station with Santa Maria Novella, has as of press time been temporarily suspended. It's easy to take the shuttle bus to the train station at Pisa Centrale, and then go on to Florence Santa Maria Novella. ✉ *12 km (7 miles) south of Pisa and 80 km (50 miles) west of Florence* ☎ *050/849300* ⊕ *www.pisa-airport.com.*

BUS TRAVEL

Florence's flat, compact city center is made for walking, but when your feet get weary you can use the efficient bus system, which includes small electric buses making the rounds in the center. Buses also climb to Piazzale Michelangelo and San Miniato south of the Arno.

Maps and timetables for local bus service are available for a small fee at the ATAF (Azienda Trasporti Area Fiorentina) booth next to the train station, or for free at visitor information offices. Tickets must be bought in advance from tobacco shops, newsstands, automatic ticket machines near main stops, or ATAF booths. The ticket must be canceled in the small validation machine immediately upon boarding.

You have several ticket options, all valid for one or more rides on all lines. A €1.20 ticket is good for one hour from the time it is first canceled. A multiple ticket—four tickets, each valid for 70 minutes—costs €4.50. A 24-hour tourist ticket costs €5. Two-, three-, and seven-day passes are also available.

Long-distance buses provide inexpensive service between Florence and other cities in Italy and Europe. **SITA** (⊠ *Via Santa Caterina da Siena 17/r* ☎ *055/47821* ⊕ *www.sitabus.it*) is the major line.

CAR TRAVEL

Florence is connected to the north and south of Italy by the Autostrada del Sole (A1). It takes about 1½ hours of driving on scenic roads to get to Bologna (although heavy truck traffic over the Apennines often makes for slower going), about 3 hours to Rome, and 3–3½ hours to Milan. The Tyrrhenian Coast is an hour west on the A11.

An automobile in Florence is a major liability. If your itinerary includes parts of Italy where you'll want a car (such as Tuscany), pick the vehicle up on your way out of town.

TAXI TRAVEL

Taxis usually wait at stands throughout the city (in front of the train station and in Piazza della Repubblica, for example), or you can call for one (☎ *055/4390 or 055/4242*). The meter starts at €3.30 from any taxi stand; if you call Radio Dispatch (that means that a taxi comes to pick you up wherever it is you are), it starts at €5.30. Extra charges apply at night, on Sunday, for radio dispatch, and for luggage. Women out on the town after midnight seeking taxis are entitled to a 10% discount on the fare; you must, however, request it.

TRAIN TRAVEL

Florence is on the principal Italian train route between most European capitals and Rome, and within Italy it is served frequently from Milan, Venice, and Rome by Intercity (IC) and nonstop Eurostar trains. Avoid trains that stop only at the Campo di Marte or Rifredi station, which are not convenient to the city center.

Stazione Centrale di Santa Maria Novella. Florence's main train station is in the center of town. ⊠ *Florence* ☎ *892021* ⊕ *www.trenitalia.com.*

VISITOR INFORMATION

The Florence tourist office, known as the APT (☎ *055/290832* ⊕ *www. firenzeturismo.it*), has branches next to the Palazzo Medici-Riccardi, across the street from Stazione di Santa Maria Novella (the main train station), and at the Bigallo, in Piazza del Duomo. The offices are generally open from 9 in the morning until 7 in the evening. The multilingual staff will give you directions and the latest on happenings in the city. It's particularly worth a stop if you're interested in finding out about performing-arts events. The APT website provides information in both Italian and English.

EXPLORING

AROUND THE DUOMO

The heart of Florence, stretching from the Piazza del Duomo south to the Arno, is as dense with artistic treasures as any place in the world. Its churches, medieval towers, Renaissance palaces, and world-class museums and galleries contain some of the most outstanding achievements of Western art.

Much of the *centro storico* (historic center) is closed to automobile traffic, but you still must dodge mopeds, cyclists, and masses of fellow tourists as you walk the narrow streets, especially in the area bounded by the Duomo, Piazza della Signoria, Galleria degli Uffizi, and the Ponte Vecchio. Via dei Calzaiuoli, between Piazza del Duomo and Piazza della Signoria, is the city's favorite *passeggiata*.

TOP ATTRACTIONS

Bargello. This building started out as the headquarters for the Capitano del Popolo (captain of the people) during the Middle Ages, and was later used as a prison. The exterior served as a "most wanted" billboard: effigies of notorious criminals and Medici enemies were painted on its walls. Today it houses the Museo Nazionale, home to what is probably the finest collection of Renaissance sculpture in Italy. The concentration of masterworks by Michelangelo, Donatello, and Benvenuto Cellini is remarkable; the works are distributed among an eclectic collection of arms, ceramics, and miniature bronzes, among other things. For Renaissance art lovers, the Bargello is to sculpture what the Uffizi is to painting. In 1401 Filippo Brunelleschi and Lorenzo Ghiberti competed to earn the most prestigious commission of the day: the decoration of the north doors of the Baptistery in Piazza del Duomo. Though the judges chose Ghiberti, view both artists' bronze bas-relief panels to see if you agree. ⊠ *Via del Proconsolo 4, Bargello* ☎ *055/294883* ⊕ *www.polo-museale.firenze.it* ⬚*€9* ⊘ *Closed 1st, 3rd, 5th Sun. of month; closed 2nd and 4th Mon. of month.*

Battistero (*Baptistery*). The octagonal Baptistery is one of the supreme monuments of the Italian Romanesque style and one of Florence's oldest structures. Modern excavations suggest that its foundations date from the 1st century AD. The round Romanesque arches on the exterior date from the 11th century, and the interior dome mosaics from the beginning of the mid-13th century are justly renowned, but they could never outshine the building's famed bronze Renaissance doors decorated with panels crafted by Lorenzo Ghiberti. These doors—or at least copies of them—on which Ghiberti worked most of his adult life are on the north and east sides of the Baptistery (the original doors are now on display in the Museo dell'Opera del Duomo), and the Gothic panels on the south door were designed by Andrea Pisano in 1330. Michelangelo declared

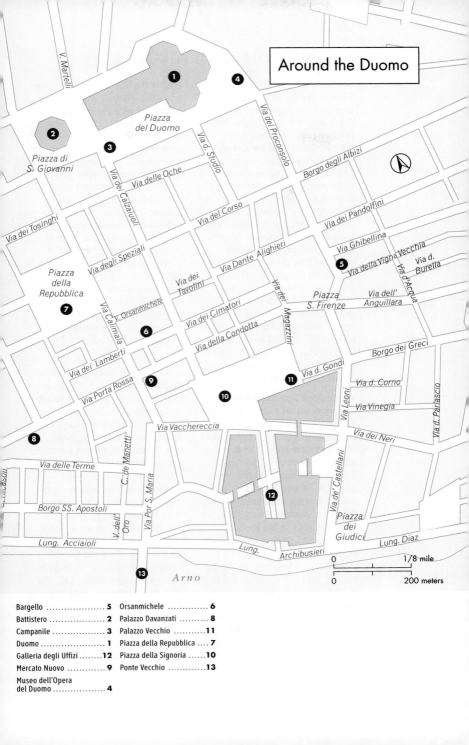

Around the Duomo

Piazza del Duomo

Piazza di S. Giovanni

V. Martelli

Via d. Studio

Via del Proconsolo

Borgo degli Albizi

Via dei Pandolfini

Via Ghibellina

Via delle Oche

Via dei Calzaiuoli

Via del Corso

Via dei Tosinghi

Via degli Speziali

Via Dante Alighieri

Via della Vigna Vecchia

Via d. Burella

Via d'Acqua

Piazza della Repubblica

Via dei Tavolini

V. Orsanmichele

Via dei Cimatori

Via della Condotta

Via dei Magazzini

Piazza S. Firenze

Via dell' Anguillara

Via Calimala

Via d. Lamberti

Borgo dei Greci

Via d. Gondi

Via d. Corno

Via Vinegia

Via dei Neri

Via Leoni

Via d. Parlascio

Via Porta Rossa

Via Vaccherreccia

Via delle Terme

C. de Manetti

Via Por S. Maria

V. dell' Oro

Borgo SS. Apostoli

Via de' Castellani

Piazza dei Giudici

Lung. Acciaioli

Lung. Archibusieri

Lung. Diaz

Arno

0   1/8 mile

0   200 meters

Bargello	5	Orsanmichele	6
Battistero	2	Palazzo Davanzati	8
Campanile	3	Palazzo Vecchio	11
Duomo	1	Piazza della Repubblica	7
Galleria degli Uffizi	12	Piazza della Signoria	10
Mercato Nuovo	9	Ponte Vecchio	13
Museo dell'Opera del Duomo	4		

FLORENCE THROUGH THE AGES

Guelph vs. Ghibelline. Although Florence can lay claim to a modest importance in the ancient world, it didn't come into its own until the Middle Ages. In the early 1200s the city, like most of the rest of Italy, was rent by civic unrest. Two factions, the Guelphs and the Ghibellines, competed for power. The Guelphs supported the papacy, and the Ghibellines supported the Holy Roman Empire. Bloody battles—most notably one at Montaperti in 1260—tore Florence and other Italian cities apart. By the end of the 13th century the Guelphs ruled securely, and the Ghibellines had been vanquished. This didn't end civic strife, however: the Guelphs split into the Whites and the Blacks for reasons still debated by historians. Dante, author of *The Divine Comedy*, was banished from Florence in 1301 because he was a White.

The Guilded Age. Local merchants had organized themselves into guilds by sometime beginning in the 12th century. In that year, they proclaimed themselves the *primo popolo* (literally, "first people"), making a landmark attempt at elective, republican rule. Though the episode lasted only 10 years, it constituted a breakthrough in Western history. Such a daring stance by the merchant class was a by-product of Florence's emergence as an economic powerhouse. Florentines were papal bankers; they instituted the system of international letters of credit; and the gold florin became the international standard of currency. With this economic strength came a building boom. Sculptors such as Donatello and Ghiberti decorated them; painters such as Giotto and Botticelli frescoed their walls.

Mighty Medici. Though ostensibly a republic, Florence was blessed (or cursed) with one very powerful family, the Medici, who came to prominence in the 1430s and were initially the de facto rulers and then the absolute rulers of Florence for several hundred years. It was under patriarch Cosimo il Vecchio (1389–1464) that the Medici's position in Florence was securely established. Florence's golden age occurred during the reign of his grandson Lorenzo de' Medici (1449–92). Lorenzo was not only an astute politician but also a highly educated man and a great patron of the arts. Called "Il Magnifico" (the Magnificent), he gathered around him poets, artists, philosophers, architects, and musicians.

Lorenzo's son Piero (1471–1503) proved inept at handling the city's affairs. He was run out of town in 1494, and Florence briefly enjoyed its status as a republic while dominated by the Dominican friar Girolamo Savonarola (1452–98). After a decade of internal unrest, the republic fell and the Medici returned to power, but Florence never regained its former prestige. By the 1530s most of the major artistic talent had left the city—Michelangelo, for one, had settled in Rome. The now-ineffectual Medici, eventually attaining the title of grand dukes, remained nominally in power until the line died out in 1737, after which time Florence passed from the Austrians to the French and back again until the unification of Italy (1865–70), when it briefly became the capital under King Vittorio Emanuele II.

them so beautiful that they could serve as the Gates of Paradise. ✉ *Piazza del Duomo* ☎ *055/2302885* ⊕ *www.operaduomo.firenze.it* 🎫*€15.*

Fodor's Choice **Duomo.** *(See the highlighted listing in this chapter.)* ✉ *Piazza del Duomo* ☎ *055/2302885* ⊕ *www.operaduomo.firenze.it* 🎫 *Church free; combination ticket €15, includes Baptistery, Crypt, Museo, Campanile, cupola.*

Fodor's Choice **Galleria degli Uffizi.** The Medici installed their art collections at Europe's
★ first modern museum, open to the public (at first only by request) since 1591. Among the highlights are Paolo Uccello's *Battle of San Romano*; the *Madonna and Child with Two Angels,* by Fra Filippo Lippi; the *Birth of Venus* and *Primavera* by Sandro Botticelli; the portraits of the Renaissance duke Federico da Montefeltro and his wife Battista Sforza, by Piero della Francesca; the *Madonna of the Goldfinch* by Raphael; Michelangelo's *Doni Tondo*; the *Venus of Urbino* by Titian; and the splendid *Bacchus* by Caravaggio. Don't forget to see the Caravaggios and the Raphaels, which you'll pass through during the exiting process. Late in the afternoon is the least crowded time to visit. ■TIP→ **For a €4 fee, advance tickets can be reserved by phone, online, or at the Uffizi reservation booth on the Piazza Pitti at least one day in advance of your visit. That's a very good idea.** ✉ *Piazzale degli Uffizi 6, Piazza della Signoria* ☎ *055/23885* ⊕ *www.uffizi.firenze.it; www.polomuseale. firenze.it for reservations* 🎫*€20; reservation fee €4* ⊗ *Closed Mon.*

Piazza della Signoria. This is by far the most striking square in Florence. It was here, in 1497, that the famous "bonfire of the vanities" took place, when the fanatical friar Savonarola induced his followers to hurl their worldly goods into the flames. The statues in the square and in the 14th-century Loggia dei Lanzi on the south side vary in quality. Cellini's famous bronze *Perseus* holding the severed head of Medusa is certainly the most important; other works include *The Rape of the Sabine* and *Hercules and the Centaur,* both late-16th-century works by Giambologna. In the square, the Neptune Fountain was created by Bartolomeo Ammannati between 1550 and 1575, who considered it a failure. Giambologna's equestrian statue, to the left of the fountain, portrays Grand Duke Cosimo I. Occupying the steps of the Palazzo Vecchio are copies of famous sculptures now housed in museums around the city, including Michelangelo's *David,* as well as Baccio Bandinelli's *Hercules.* ✉ *Florence.*

Ponte Vecchio (*Old Bridge*). This charmingly simple bridge was built in 1345 to replace an earlier bridge swept away by flood. Its shops first housed butchers, then grocers, blacksmiths, and other merchants. But in 1593 the Medici grand duke Ferdinand I, whose private corridor linking the Medici palace (Palazzo Pitti) with the Medici offices (the Uffizi) crossed the bridge atop the shops, decided that all this plebeian commerce under his feet was unseemly. So he threw out the butchers and blacksmiths and installed 41 goldsmiths and eight jewelers. The bridge has been devoted solely to these two trades ever since. The **Corridoio Vasariano** (✉ *Piazzale degli Uffizi 6, Piazza della Signoria,* ☎ *055/23885,* ☎ *055/294883*), the private Medici elevated passageway, was built by Vasari in 1565; it was most likely designed so that

Continued on page 501

THE DUOMO
FLORENCE'S BIGGEST MASTERPIECE

For all its monumental art and architecture, Florence has one undisputed centerpiece: the Cathedral of Santa Maria del Fiore, better known as the Duomo. Its cupola dominates the skyline, presiding over the city's rooftops like a red hen over her brood. Little wonder that when Florentines feel homesick, they say they have *"nostalgia del cupolone."*

The Duomo's construction began in 1296, following the design of Arnolfo da Cambio, Florence's greatest architect of the time. By modern standards, construction was slow and haphazard—it continued through the 14th and into the 15th century, with some dozen architects having a hand in the project.

In 1366 Neri di Fioravante created a model for the hugely ambitious cupola: it was to be the largest dome in the world, surpassing Rome's Pantheon. But when the time finally came to build the dome in 1418, no one was sure how—or even if—it could be done. Florence was faced with a 143-ft hole in the roof of its cathedral, and one of the greatest challenges in the history of architecture.

Fortunately, local genius Filippo Brunelleschi was just the man for the job. Brunelleschi won the 1418 competition to design the dome, and for the next 18 years he oversaw its construction. The enormity of his achievement can hardly be overstated. Working on such a large scale (the dome weighs 37,000 tons and uses 4 million bricks) required him to invent hoists and cranes that were engineering marvels. A "dome within a dome" design and a novel herringbone bricklaying pattern were just two of the innovations used to establish structural integrity. Perhaps most remarkably, he executed the construction without a supporting wooden framework, which had previously been thought indispensable.

Brunelleschi designed the lantern atop the dome, but he died soon after its first stone was laid in 1446; it wouldn't be completed until 1461. Another 400 years passed before the Duomo received its façade, a 19th-century neo-Gothic creation.

DUOMO TIMELINE

1296 Work begins, following design by Arnolfo di Cambio.

1302 Arnolfo dies; work continues, with sporadic interruptions.

1331 Management of construction taken over by the Wool Merchants guild.

1334 Giotto appointed project overseer, designs campanile.

1337 Giotto dies; Andrea Pisano takes leadership role.

1348 The Black Plague; all work ceases.

1366 Vaulting on nave completed; Neri di Fioravante makes model for dome.

1417 Drum for dome completed.

1418 Competition is held to design the dome.

1420 Brunelleschi begins work on the dome.

1436 Dome completed.

1446 Construction of lantern begins; Brunelleschi dies.

1461 Antonio Manetti, a student of Brunelleschi, completes lantern.

1469 Gilt copper ball and cross added by Verrocchio.

1587 Original façade is torn down by Medici court.

1871 Emilio de Fabris wins competition to design new façade.

1887 Façade completed.

WHAT TO LOOK FOR INSIDE THE DUOMO

The interior of the Duomo is a fine example of Florentine Gothic with a beautiful marble floor, but the space feels strangely barren—a result of its great size and the fact that some of the best art has been moved to the nearby **Museo dell'Opera del Duomo.**

Notable among the works that remain are two towering equestrian frescoes of famous mercenaries: *Niccolò da Tolentino* (1456), by Andrea del Castagno, and *Sir John Hawkwood* (1436), by Paolo Uccello. There's also fine terra-cotta work by Luca della Robbia. Ghiberti,

Brunelleschi's great rival, is responsible for much of the stained glass, as well as a reliquary urn with gorgeous reliefs. A vast fresco of the Last Judgment, painted by Vasari and Zuccari, covers the dome's interior. Brunelleschi had wanted mosaics to go there; it's a pity he didn't get his wish.

In the crypt beneath the cathedral, you can explore excavations of a Roman wall and mosaic fragments from the late sixth century; entry is near the first pier on the right. On the way down you pass Brunelleschi's modest tomb.

1. Entrance; stained glass by Ghiberti
2. Fresco of Niccolò da Tolentino by Andrea del Castagno
3. Fresco of John Hawkwood by Paolo Uccello
4. *Dante and the Divine Comedy* by Domenico di Michelino
5. Lunette: *Ascension* by Luca della Robbia
6. Above altar: two angels by Luca della Robbia. Below the altar: reliquary of St. Zenobius by Ghiberti.
7. Lunette: *Resurrection* by Luca della Robbia
8. Entrance to dome
9. Bust of Brunelleschi by Buggiano
10. Stairs to crypt
11. Campanile

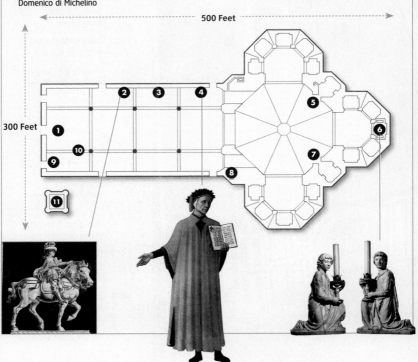

MAKING THE CLIMB

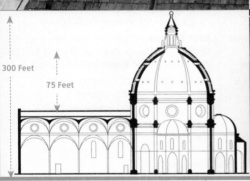

Climbing the 463 steps to the top of the dome is not for the faint of heart—or for the claustrophobic—but those who do it will be awarded a smashing view of Florence ❶. Keep in mind that the way up is also the way down, which means that while you're huffing and puffing in the ascent, people very close to you in a narrow staircase are making their way down ❷.

300 Feet

75 Feet

DUOMO BASICS

- Advance reservations are required to climb the dome. You can buy a ticket and book your time slot online.

- For an alternative to the dome, consider climbing the less trafficked campanile, which gives you a view from on high of the dome itself.

- Dress code essentials: covered shoulders, no short shorts, and hats off upon entering.

🌐 www.museumflorence.com

🎫 Free to visit cathedral, but a combined ticket for the dome, crypt, baptistry, bell tower, and museum costs €18

🕐 Crypt: Mon.–Wed., Fri.; Thurs. 10–4:30; Sat. 10–4:30.

🕐 Dome: Weekdays 8:30–7, Sat. 8:30–5, Sun. 1–4. Duomo: Mon.–Wed. and Fri. 10–5, Thurs. 10–4:30, Sat., 10–4:30, Sun 1:30–4:45.

BRUNELLESCHI vs. GHIBERTI
The Rivalry of Two Renaissance Geniuses

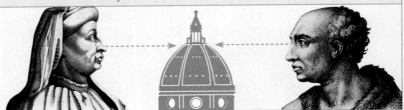

In Renaissance Florence, painters, sculptors, and architects competed for major commissions, with the winner earning the right to undertake a project that might occupy him (and keep him paid) for a decade or more. Stakes were high, and the resulting rivalries fierce—none more so than that between Filippo Brunelleschi and Lorenzo Ghiberti.

The two first clashed in 1401, for the commission to create the bronze doors of the Baptistery. When Ghiberti won, Brunelleschi took it hard, fleeing to Rome, where he would remain for 15 years. Their rematch came in 1418, over the design of the Duomo's cupola, with Brunelleschi triumphant. For the remainder of their lives, the two would miss no opportunity to belittle each other's work.

FILIPPO BRUNELLESCHI (1377–1446)

MASTERPIECE: The dome of Santa Maria del Fiore.

BEST FRIENDS: Donatello, whom he stayed with in Rome after losing the Baptistery doors competition; the Medici family, who rescued him from bankruptcy.

SIGNATURE TRAITS: Paranoid, secretive, bad tempered, practical joker, inept businessman.

SAVVIEST POLITICAL MOVE: Feigned sickness and left for Rome after his dome plans were publicly criticized by Ghiberti, who was second-in-command. The project proved too much for Ghiberti to manage on his own, and Brunelleschi returned triumphant.

MOST EMBARRASSING MOMENT: In 1434 he was imprisoned for two weeks for failure to pay a small guild fee. The humiliation might have been orchestrated by Ghiberti.

OTHER CAREER: Shipbuilder. He built a huge vessel, *Il Badalone*, to transport marble for the dome up the Arno. It sank on its first voyage.

INSPIRED: The dome of St. Peter's in Rome.

LORENZO GHIBERTI (1378–1455)

MASTERPIECE: *The Gates of Paradise*, the ten-paneled east doors of the Baptistery.

BEST FRIEND: Giovanni da Prato, an underling who wrote diatribes attacking the dome's design and Brunelleschi's character.

SIGNATURE TRAITS: Instigator, egoist, know-it-all, shrewd businessman.

SAVVIEST POLITICAL MOVE: During the Baptistery doors competition, he had an open studio and welcomed opinions on his work, while Brunelleschi labored behind closed doors.

OTHER CAREER: Collector of classical artifacts, historian.

INSPIRED: *The Gates of Hell* by Auguste Rodin.

The Gates of Paradise detail

the Medici family wouldn't have to walk amid the commoners. It can sometimes be visited by prior special arrangement. Call for the most up-to-date details. ⊠ *Florence*.

WORTH NOTING

Campanile. The Gothic bell tower designed by Giotto (circa 1266–1337) is a soaring structure of multicolor marble originally decorated with sculptures by Donatello and reliefs by Giotto, Andrea Pisano, and others (which are now in the Museo dell'Opera del Duomo). A climb of 414 steps rewards you with a close-up of Brunelleschi's cupola on the Duomo next door and a sweeping view of the city. ⊠ *Piazza del Duomo* ☎ *055/2302885* ⊕ *www.operaduomo.firenze.it* ⊠ *€15*.

FAMILY **Mercato Nuovo** (*New Market*). The open-air loggia, built in 1551, teems with souvenir stands, but the real attraction is a copy of Pietro Tacca's bronze *Porcellino* (which translates as "little pig" despite the fact the animal is, in fact, a wild boar). The *Porcellino* is Florence's equivalent of the Trevi Fountain: put a coin in his mouth, and if it falls through the grate below (according to one interpretation), it means you'll return to Florence someday. What you're seeing is a copy of a copy: Tacca's original version, in the Museo Bardini, is actually a copy of an ancient Greek work. ⊠ *Via Por Santa Maria at Via Porta Rossa, Piazza della Repubblica* ⊗ *Closed Sun*.

Museo dell'Opera del Duomo (*Cathedral Museum*). A seven-year restoration of this museum and its glorious reopening in October 2015 have given Florence one of its most modern, up-to-date museums. Exhibition space has doubled in size, and the old facade of the cathedral, torn down in the 1580s, has been re-created with a 1:1 relationship to the real thing. Both sets of Ghiberti's doors adorn the same room. Michelangelo's *Pietà* finally has the space it deserves, as does Donatello's *Mary Magdalene*. ⊠ *Piazza del Duomo 9, Duomo* ☎ *055/2302885* ⊕ *www. operaduomo.firenze.it* ⊠ *€15* ⊗ *Closed 1st Tues. of month*.

Orsanmichele. This multipurpose structure began as an 8th-century oratory and then in 1290 was turned into an open-air loggia for selling grain. Destroyed by fire in 1304, it was rebuilt as a loggia-market. Between 1367 and 1380 the arcades were closed and two stories were added above; finally, at century's end it was turned into a church. Inside is a beautifully detailed 14th-century Gothic tabernacle by Andrea Orcagna (1308–68). The exterior niches contain sculptures (all copies) dating from the early 1400s to the early 1600s by Donatello and Verrocchio (1435–88), among others, which were paid for by the guilds. Although it is a copy, Verrocchio's *Doubting Thomas* (circa 1470) is particularly deserving of attention. Here you see Christ, like the building's other figures, entirely framed within the niche, and St. Thomas standing on its bottom ledge, with his right foot outside the niche frame. This one detail, the positioning of a single foot, brings the whole composition to life. It's possible to see the original sculptures at the **Museo di Orsanmichele**, which is open Monday only. ⊠ *Via dei Calzaiuoli, Piazza della Repubblica* ☎ *055/284944* ⊕ *www.polomuseale.firenze.it* ⊠ *Free* ⊗ *Closed Tues.–Sun*.

Palazzo Davanzati. The prestigious Davizzi family owned this 14th-century palace in one of Florence's swankiest medieval neighborhoods (it was sold to the Davanzati in the 15th century). The place is a delight, as you can wander through the surprisingly light-filled courtyard, and climb the steep stairs to the piano nobile (there's also an elevator), where the family did most of its living. The beautiful *Sala dei Pappagalli* (Parrot Room) is adorned with trompe-l'oeil tapestries and gaily painted birds. ⊠ *Piazza Davanzati 13, Piazza della Repubblica* ☎ *055/2388610* ⊕ *www.polomuseale.firenze.it* 🎟 *€6* ⊘ *Closed 1st, 3rd, 5th Sun. of the month, and 2nd and 4th Mon. of month.*

FAMILY **Palazzo Vecchio** (*Old Palace*). Florence's forbidding, fortresslike city hall was begun in 1299, presumably designed by Arnolfo di Cambio, and its massive bulk and towering campanile dominate Piazza della Signoria. It was built as a meeting place for the guildsmen governing the city at the time; today it is still City Hall. The main attraction is on the second floor, the opulently vast **Sala dei Cinquecento** (Room of the Five Hundred), named for the 500-member Great Council that met here. Giorgio Vasari and others decorated the room, around 1563–65, with gargantuan frescoes celebrating Florentine history. In comparison, the little **Studiolo,** just off the Sala dei Cinquecento's entrance, was a private room meant for the duke and those whom he invited in. ⊠ *Piazza della Signoria* ☎ *055/27684224* ⊕ *museicivicifiorentini.comune.fi.it* 🎟 *Museo €10, Museo and Torre €14.*

Piazza della Repubblica. The square marks the site of the ancient forum that was the core of the original Roman settlement. While the street plan around the piazza still reflects the carefully plotted Roman military encampment, the Mercato Vecchio (Old Market), which had been here since the Middle Ages, was demolished and the current piazza was constructed between 1885 and 1895 as a Neoclassical showpiece. The piazza is lined with outdoor cafés, affording an excellent opportunity for people-watching. ⊠ *Florence.*

SAN LORENZO

A sculptor, painter, architect, and poet, Florentine native son Michelangelo was a consummate genius, and some of his finest creations remain in his hometown. The Biblioteca Medicea Laurenziana is perhaps his most fanciful work of architecture. A key to understanding Michelangelo's genius can be found in the magnificent Cappelle Medicee, where both his sculptural and architectural prowess can be clearly seen. Planned frescoes were never completed, sadly, for they would have shown in one space the artistic triple threat that he certainly was. The towering yet graceful *David,* perhaps his most famous work, resides in the Galleria dell'Accademia.

After visiting San Lorenzo, resist the temptation to explore the market that surrounds the church: the market is open until 7 pm, while the churches and museums you may want to visit are not. Come back to the market later, after other sites have closed. Note that the Museo di San Marco closes at 1:50 on weekdays.

TOP ATTRACTIONS

Cappelle Medicee (*Medici Chapels*). This magnificent complex includes the Cappella dei Principi, the Medici chapel and mausoleum begun in 1605 that kept marble workers busy for several hundred years, and the Sagrestia Nuova (New Sacristy), designed by Michelangelo and so called to distinguish it from Brunelleschi's Sagrestia Vecchia (Old Sacristy). Michelangelo received the commission for the New Sacristy in 1520 from Cardinal Giulio de' Medici, who later became Pope Clement VII. The cardinal wanted a new burial chapel for his cousins Giuliano, Duke of Nemours, and Lorenzo, Duke of Urbino, and he also wanted to honor his father, also named Giuliano, and his uncle, Lorenzo il Magnifico. The result was a tour de force of architecture and sculpture. Architecturally, Michelangelo was as original here as ever, but it is the powerfully sculpted tombs that dominate the room. The figures on the tomb on the right represent Day and Night; those on the tomb to the left represent Dawn and Dusk. ⊠ *Piazza di Madonna degli Aldobrandini, San Lorenzo* ☎ *055/294883 reservations* ⊕ *www.polomuseale.firenze.it* 🎫 *€8* ⊗ *Closed 1st, 3rd, and 5th Mon. and 2nd and 4th Sun. of month.*

FAMILY **Galleria dell'Accademia** (*Accademia Gallery*). The collection of Florentine paintings, dating from the 13th to the 18th century, is largely unremarkable, but the sculptures by Michelangelo are worth the price of admission. The unfinished *Slaves,* fighting their way out of their marble prisons, were meant for the tomb of Michelangelo's overly demanding patron Pope Julius II. But the focal point is the original *David,* commissioned in 1501 by the Opera del Duomo (Cathedral Works Committee), which gave the 26-year-old sculptor a leftover block of marble that had been ruined 40 years earlier by two other sculptors. Michelangelo didn't give the statue perfect proportions—the head is slightly too large for the body, the arms too large for the torso, and the hands dramatically large for the arms. But he did it to express and embody an entire biblical story. ■ TIP➔ **Today David is beset not by Goliath but by tourists; save yourself a long wait in line by reserving tickets in advance.** ⊠ *Via Ricasoli 60, San Marco* ☎ *055/294883 reservations, 055/2388609 gallery* ⊕ *www.accademia.org* 🎫 *€12.50; reservation fee €4* ⊗ *Closed Mon.*

Fodor's Choice ★ **Mercato Centrale.** Some of the food at this huge, two-story market hall is remarkably exotic. The ground floor contains meat and cheese stalls, as well as some very good bars that have panini. In 2014, a second-floor food hall opened, eerily reminiscent of food halls everywhere. The quality of the food served, however, more than makes up for this. ⊠ *Piazza del Mercato Centrale, San Lorenzo* ⊕ *www.mercatocentrale.it* ⊗ *Market: Closed Sun.*

Museo di San Marco. A Dominican convent adjacent to the church of San Marco now houses this museum, which contains many stunning works by Fra Angelico (circa 1400–55), the Dominican friar famous for his piety as well as for his painting. When the friars' cells were restructured between 1439 and 1444, he decorated many of them with frescoes meant to spur religious contemplation. His unostentatious and direct paintings exalt the simple beauties of the contemplative life. Fra Angelico's works are everywhere, from the friars' cells to the superb panel paintings on view in the museum. Don't miss the famous *Annunciation,*

CLOSE UP

Florence's Trial by Fire

One of the most striking figures of Renaissance Florence was Girolamo Savonarola, a Dominican friar who, for a moment, captured the spiritual conscience of the city. In 1491 he became prior of the convent of San Marco, where he adopted a life of austerity and delivered sermons condemning Florence's excesses and the immorality of his fellow clergy. Following the death of Lorenzo de' Medici in 1492, Savonarola was instrumental in the re-formation of the republic of Florence, ruled by a representative council with Christ enthroned as monarch. In one of his most memorable acts he urged Florentines to toss worldly possessions—from sumptuous dresses to Botticelli paintings—onto a "bonfire of the vanities" in Piazza della Signoria. Savonarola's antagonism toward church hierarchy led to his undoing: he was excommunicated in 1497, and the following year was hanged and burned on charges of heresy. Today, at the Museo di San Marco, you can visit Savonarola's cell.

on the upper floor, and the works in the gallery off the cloister as you enter. Here you can see his beautiful *Last Judgment*; as usual, the tortures of the damned are far more inventive and interesting than the pleasures of the redeemed. ⊠ *Piazza San Marco 1* ☏ *055/2388608* ⊕ *www.polomuseale.firenze.it* 🎫 *€4* ⊘ *Closed 1st, 3rd, and 5th Sun., and 2nd and 4th Mon. of month.*

San Lorenzo. Filippo Brunelleschi designed this basilica, as well as that of Santo Spirito in the Oltrarno, in the 15th century. He never lived to see either finished. The two interiors are similar in design and effect. San Lorenzo, however, has a grid of dark, inlaid marble lines on the floor, which considerably heightens the dramatic effect. The grid makes the rigorous geometry of the interior immediately visible, and is an illuminating lesson on the laws of perspective. If you stand in the middle of the nave at the church entrance, on the line that stretches to the high altar, every element in the church—the grid, the nave columns, the side aisles, the coffered nave ceiling—seems to march inexorably toward a hypothetical vanishing point beyond the high altar, exactly as in a single-point-perspective painting. Brunelleschi's **Sagrestia Vecchia** (Old Sacristy) has stucco decorations by Donatello; it's at the end of the left transept. ⊠ *Piazza San Lorenzo* 🎫 *€6* ⊘ *Closed Sun. Nov.–Feb.*

WORTH NOTING

Biblioteca Medicea Laurenziana (*Laurentian Library*). Michelangelo the architect was every bit as original as Michelangelo the sculptor. Unlike Brunelleschi (the architect of the Spedale degli Innocenti), however, he wasn't obsessed with proportion and perfect geometry. He was interested in experimentation and invention and in the expression of a personal vision that was at times highly idiosyncratic.

It was never more idiosyncratic than in the Laurentian Library, begun in 1524 and finished in 1568 by Bartolomeo Ammannati. Its famous **vestibolo,** a strangely shaped anteroom, has had scholars scratching their heads for centuries. In a space more than two stories high, why

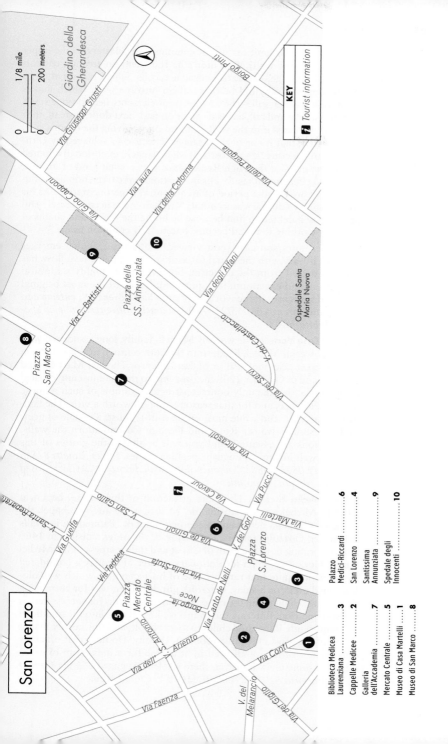

San Lorenzo

0 — 1/8 mile
0 — 200 meters

Giardino della
Gherardesca

KEY

ℹ️ Tourist information

Via Giuseppe Giusti
Via Gino Capponi
Via Laura
Via della Colonna
Via della Pergola
Borgo Pinti

Piazza San Marco

Piazza della
SS. Annunziata

Via C. Battisti
Via degli Alfani
V. del Castellaccio
Via dei Servi

Ospedale Santa
Maria Nuova

Via Ricasoli
Via S. San Gallo
Via Guelfa
V. Santa Reparata

Via Cavour
Via Puccí
Via de Ginori
V. del Gori
Via Martelli

Piazza
S. Lorenzo

Piazza
Mercato
Centrale

Borgo la
Noce
Via della Stufa
Via Taddea
Via dell' S. Antonio
Via Canto de Nelli
Via Faenza
V. del Melarancio
V. del Giglio
Via Conti

Biblioteca Medicea
Laurenziana **3**

Cappelle Medicee **2**

Galleria
dell'Accademia **7**

Mercato Centrale **5**

Museo di Casa Martelli **1**

Museo di San Marco **8**

Palazzo
Medici-Riccardi **6**

San Lorenzo **4**

Santissima
Annunziata **9**

Spedale degli
Innocenti **10**

did Michelangelo limit his use of columns and pilasters to the upper two-thirds of the wall? Why didn't he rest them on strong pedestals instead of on huge, decorative curlicue scrolls, which rob them of all visual support? Why did he recess them into the wall, which makes them look weaker still? The architectural elements here do not stand firm and strong and tall, as inside San Lorenzo, next door; instead, they seem to be pressed into the wall as if into putty, giving the room a soft, rubbery look that is one of the strangest effects ever achieved by 16th-century architecture. It's almost as if Michelangelo intentionally flouted the conventions of the High Renaissance to see what kind of bizarre, mannered effect might result. His innovations were tremendously influential, and produced a period of architectural experimentation. As his contemporary Giorgio Vasari put it, "Artisans have been infinitely and perpetually indebted to him because he broke the bonds and chains of a way of working that had become habitual by common usage."

The anteroom's staircase (best viewed straight on), which emerges from the library with the visual force of an unstoppable lava flow, has been exempted from the criticism, however. In its highly sculptural conception and execution, it is quite simply one of the most original and fluid staircases in the world. ⊠ *Piazza San Lorenzo 9, entrance to left of San Lorenzo* ☎ *055/210760* ⊕ *www.bml.firenze.sbn.it* ⌦ *Special exhibitions €3.*

Museo di Casa Martelli. The wealthy Martelli family, long associated with the all-powerful Medici, lived, from the 16th century, in this palace on a quiet street near the basilica of San Lorenzo. The last Martelli died in 1986, and in October 2009 the *casa-museo* (house-museum) opened to the public. It's the only nonreconstructed example of such a house in all of Florence, and for that reason alone it's worth a visit. The family collected art, and while most of the stuff is B-list, a couple of gems by Beccafumi, Salvatore Rosa, and Piero di Cosimo adorn the walls. Reservations are essential, and you will be shown the glories of this place by well-informed, English-speaking guides. ⊠ *Via Zanetti 8, San Lorenzo* ☎ *055/294883* ⊕ *www.polomuseale.firenze.it* ⌦ *€3* ⊙ *Closed 2nd and 4th Sun. of month.*

Palazzo Medici-Riccardi. The main attraction of this palace, begun in 1444 by Michelozzo for Cosimo de' Medici, is the interior chapel, the so-called **Cappella dei Magi** on the piano nobile. Painted on its walls is Benozzo Gozzoli's famous *Procession of the Magi,* finished in 1460 and celebrating both the birth of Christ and the greatness of the Medici family. Gozzoli wasn't a revolutionary painter, and today is considered by some not quite first-rate because of his technique, which was old-fashioned even for his day. Gozzoli's gift, however, was for entrancing the eye, not challenging the mind, and on those terms his success here is beyond question. Entering the chapel is like walking into the middle of a magnificently illustrated children's storybook, and this beauty makes it one of the most enjoyable rooms in the city. Do note that officially only eight visitors are allowed in at a time for a maximum of seven minutes; sometimes, however, there are lenient guards. ⊠ *Via Cavour 1, San Lorenzo* ☎ *055/2760340* ⌦ *€10* ⊙ *Closed Wed.*

11

Santissima Annunziata. Dating from the mid-13th century, this church was restructured in 1447 by Michelozzo, who gave it an uncommon (and lovely) entrance cloister with frescoes by Andrea del Sarto (1486–1530), Pontormo (1494–1556), and Rosso Fiorentino (1494–1540). The interior is a rarity for Florence: an overwhelming example of the Baroque. But it's not really a fair example, because it's merely 17th-century Baroque decoration applied willy-nilly to an earlier structure—exactly the sort of violent remodeling exercise that has given the Baroque a bad name. The **Cappella dell'Annunziata,** immediately inside the entrance to the left, illustrates the point. The lower half, with its stately Corinthian columns and carved frieze bearing the Medici arms, was commissioned by Piero de' Medici in 1447; the upper half, with its erupting curves and impish sculpted cherubs, was added 200 years later. Fifteenth-century-fresco enthusiasts should also note the very fine *Holy Trinity with St. Jerome* in the second chapel on the left. Done by Andrea del Castagno (circa 1421–57), it shows a wiry and emaciated St. Jerome with Paula and Eustochium, two of his closest followers. ⊠ *Piazza di Santissima Annunziata* ☏.

Spedale degli Innocenti. The building built by Brunelleschi in 1419 to serve as an orphanage takes the historical prize as the very first Renaissance building. Brunelleschi designed its portico with his usual rigor, constructing it from the two shapes he considered mathematically (and therefore philosophically and aesthetically) perfect: the square and the circle. Below the level of the arches, the portico encloses a row of perfect cubes; above the level of the arches, the portico encloses a row of intersecting hemispheres. The entire geometric scheme is articulated with Corinthian columns, capitals, and arches borrowed directly from antiquity. At the time he designed the portico, Brunelleschi was also designing the interior of San Lorenzo, using the same basic ideas. But because the portico was finished before San Lorenzo, the Spedale degli Innocenti can claim the honor of ushering in Renaissance architecture. The 10 ceramic medallions depicting swaddled infants that decorate the portico are by Andrea della Robbia (1435–1525/28), done in about 1487.

Within the Spedale degli Innocenti is a small museum, or **Pinacoteca** (€7; *Thurs.–Tues. 9–7*). Most of the objects are minor works by major artists, but well worth a look is Domenico Ghirlandaio's (1449–94) *Adorazione dei Magi* (*Adoration of the Magi*), executed in 1488. His use of color, and his eye for flora and fauna, shows that art from north of the Alps made a great impression on him. ⊠ *Piazza di Santissima Annunziata 12* ☏ *055/20371* ▭ *€7*.

SANTA MARIA NOVELLA

Piazza Santa Maria Novella is a gorgeous, pedestrian-only square, with grass (laced with roses) and plenty of places to sit and rest your feet. The streets in and around the piazza have their share of architectural treasures, including some of Florence's most tasteful palaces. Between Santa Maria Novella and the Arno is Via Tornabuoni, Florence's swankiest shopping street.

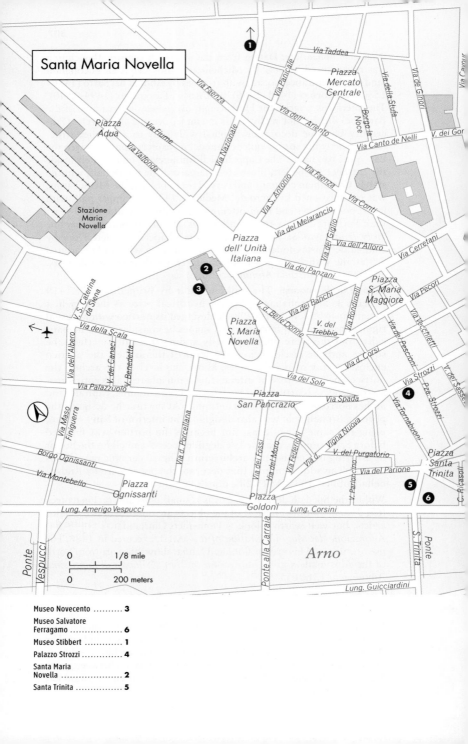

Santa Maria Novella

Piazza
Adua

Stazione
Maria
Novella

Piazza
dell' Unità
Italiana

Piazza
S. Maria
Novella

Piazza
San Pancrazio

Piazza
Ognissanti

Piazza
Goldoni

Via Taddea

Piazza
Mercato
Centrale

Via Canto de Nelli

V. dei Gor

Piazza
S. Maria
Maggiore

V. del
Trebbio

Piazza
Santa
Trinita

Arno

Ponte
Vespucci

Lung. Amerigo Vespucci

Lung. Corsini

Lung. Guicciardini

Ponte
Trinita

0   1/8 mile

0   200 meters

CLOSE UP

Meet the Medici

11

The Medici were the dominant family of Renaissance Florence, wielding political power and financing some of the world's greatest art. You'll see their names at every turn around the city. These are some of the clan's more notable members:

Cosimo il Vecchio (1389–1464), incredibly wealthy banker to the popes, was the first in the family line to act as de facto ruler of Florence. He was a great patron of the arts and architecture; he was the moving force behind the family palace and the Dominican complex of San Marco.

Lorenzo il Magnifico (1449–92), grandson of Cosimo il Vecchio, presided over a Florence largely at peace with her neighbors. A collector of cameos, a writer of sonnets, and lover of ancient texts, he was the preeminent Renaissance man.

Leo X (1475–1521), also known as Giovanni de' Medici, became the first Medici pope, helping extend the family power base to include Rome and the Papal States. His reign was characterized by a host of problems, the biggest one being a former friar named Martin Luther.

Catherine de' Medici (1519–89) was married by her great uncle Pope Clement VII to Henry of Valois, who later became Henry II of France. Wife of one king and mother of three, she was the first Medici to marry into European royalty. Lorenzo il Magnifico, her great-grandfather, would have been thrilled.

Cosimo I (1537–74), the first grand duke of Tuscany, should not be confused with his ancestor Cosimo il Vecchio.

TOP ATTRACTIONS

Santa Maria Novella. The facade of this church looks distinctly clumsy by later Renaissance standards, and with good reason: it is an architectural hybrid. The lower half was completed mostly in the 14th century; its pointed-arch niches and decorative marble patterns reflect the Gothic style of the day. About 100 years later (around 1456), architect Leon Battista Alberti was called in to complete the job, adding architectural motifs in an entirely different style. Don't miss the church's store of remarkable art treasures. Highlights include the 14th-century stained-glass rose window depicting the *Coronation of the Virgin*; the Cappella Filippo Strozzi, containing late-15th-century frescoes and stained glass by Filippino Lippi; the cappella maggiore, displaying frescoes by Ghirlandaio; and the Cappella Gondi, containing Filippo Brunelleschi's famous wood crucifix, carved around 1410. Of special interest for its great historical importance and beauty is Masaccio's *Trinity*; painted around 1426–27, it unequivocally announced the arrival of the Renaissance. ✉ *Piazza Santa Maria Novella 19* ☎ *055/219257 museo* ⊕ *www. smn.it/en* 🖾 *€7.50.*

Santa Trinita. Started in the 11th century by Vallombrosian monks and originally Romanesque in style, the church underwent a Gothic remodeling during the 14th century. (Remains of the Romanesque construction are visible on the interior front wall.) The major works are the fresco cycle and altarpiece in the Cappella Sassetti, the second to the high altar's right, painted by Ghirlandaio between 1480 and 1485. His work here possesses such graceful decorative appeal as well as a proud depiction of his native city (most of the cityscapes show 15th-century Florence in all her glory). The wall frescoes illustrate scenes from the life of St. Francis, and the altarpiece, depicting the *Adoration of the Shepherds,* veritably glows. ⊠ *Piazza Santa Trinita, Santa Maria Novella* ☎ *055/216912.*

WORTH NOTING

Museo Novecento. It began life as a 13th-century Franciscan hostel offering shelter to tired pilgrims. It later became a convalescent home, and in the late 18th century it was a school for poor girls. Now the former Ospedale di San Paolo houses a museum devoted to Italian art of the 20th century. Admittedly, most of these artists are not exactly household names, but the museum is so beautifully well done that it's worth a visit. The second floor contains works by artists from the second half of the century; start on the third floor, and go directly to the collection of Alberto della Ragione, a naval engineer determined to be on the cutting edge of art collecting. ⊠ *Piazza, Santa Maria Novella 10, Santa Maria Novella* ☎ *055/286132* ⊕ *www.museonovecento.it* 🎟 *€8.50* 🕙 *Closed Fri.–Wed. Oct.–Mar.; closed Sat.–Wed. Apr.–Sept.*

Museo Salvatore Ferragamo. If there's such a thing as a temple for footwear, this is it. The shoes in this dramatically displayed collection were designed by Salvatore Ferragamo (1898–1960) beginning in the early 20th century. Born in southern Italy, the late master jump-started his career in Hollywood by creating shoes for the likes of Mary Pickford and Rudolph Valentino. He then returned to Florence and set up shop in the 13th-century Palazzo Spini Ferroni. The collection includes about 16,000 shoes, and those on exhibition are frequently rotated. Special exhibitions are also mounted here and are well worth visiting—past shows have been devoted to Audrey Hepburn, Greta Garbo, and Marilyn Monroe. ⊠ *Via dei Tornabuoni 2, Santa Maria Novella* ☎ *055/3562846* ⊕ *www.ferragamo.com* 🎟 *€6.*

Museo Stibbert. Federico Stibbert (1838–1906), born in Florence to an Italian mother and an English father, liked to collect things. Over a lifetime of doing so, he amassed some 50,000 objects. This museum, which was also his home, displays many of them. He had a fascination with medieval armor and also collected costumes, particularly Uzbek costumes, which are exhibited in a room called the Moresque Hall. These are mingled with an extensive collection of swords, guns, and other devices whose sole function was to kill people. The paintings, most of which date from the 15th century, are largely second-rate. The house itself is an interesting amalgam of neo-Gothic, Renaissance, and English eccentric. To get here, take Bus No. 4 (across the street from the station at Santa Maria Novella) and get off at the stop marked "Fabbroni 4," then follow signs to the museum. ⊠ *Via Federico Stibbert 26* ☎ *055/475520* ⊕ *www.museostibbert.it* 🎟 *€8* 🕙 *Closed Thurs., Jan. 1, Easter, May 1, Aug. 15, and Dec. 25.*

Palazzo Strozzi. The Strozzi family built this imposing palazzo in an attempt to outshine the nearby Palazzo Medici. Based on a model by Giuliano da Sangallo (circa 1452–1516) dating from around 1489 and executed between 1489 and 1504 under il Cronaca (1457–1508) and Benedetto da Maiaino (1442–97), it was inspired by Michelozzo's earlier Palazzo Medici-Riccardi. The palazzo's exterior is simple, severe, and massive: it's a testament to the wealth of a patrician, 15th-century Florentine family. The interior courtyard, entered from the rear of the palazzo, is another matter altogether. It is here that the classical vocabulary—columns, capitals, pilasters, arches, and cornices—is given uninhibited and powerful expression. The palazzo frequently hosts blockbuster art shows. ⊠ *Via Tornabuoni, Piazza della Repubblica* ☎ *055/2645155* ⊕ *www.palazzostrozzi.org* ⊡ *Free.*

SANTA CROCE

The Santa Croce quarter, on the southeast fringe of the historic center, was built up in the Middle Ages outside the second set of medieval city walls. The centerpiece of the neighborhood was (and is) the basilica of Santa Croce, which could hold great numbers of worshippers; the vast piazza could accommodate any overflow and also served as a fairground and, allegedly since the middle of the 16th century, as a playing field for no-holds-barred soccer games. A center of leatherworking since the Middle Ages, the neighborhood is still packed with leatherworkers and leather shops.

TOP ATTRACTIONS

Piazza Santa Croce. Originally outside the city's 12th-century walls, this piazza grew with the Franciscans, who used the large square for public preaching. During the Renaissance it was used for *giostre* (jousts), including one sponsored by Lorenzo de' Medici. "Bonfires of the vanities" occurred here, as well as soccer matches in the 16th century. Lined with many palazzi dating from the 15th and 16th centuries, the square remains one of Florence's loveliest piazze and is a great place to people-watch. ⊠ *Florence.*

Fodor's Choice ★ **Santa Croce.** As a burial place, this Gothic church with a 19th-century facade probably contains more skeletons of Renaissance celebrities than any other in Italy. Besides Michelangelo, famous tombs include that of Galileo Galilei; Niccolò Machiavelli; Lorenzo Ghiberti, creator of the Baptistery doors; and composer Gioacchino Rossini. The collection of art within is by far the most important of any church in Florence. The most famous works are probably the Giotto frescoes in the two chapels immediately to the right of the high altar. They illustrate scenes from the lives of St. John the Evangelist and St. John the Baptist (in the right-hand chapel) and scenes from the life of St. Francis (in the left-hand chapel). Among the church's other highlights are Donatello's *Annunciation*; 14th-century frescoes by Taddeo Gaddi (circa 1300–66) illustrating scenes from the life of the Virgin Mary; and Donatello's Crucifix, criticized by Brunelleschi for making Christ look like a peasant. ⊠ *Piazza Santa Croce 16* ☎ *055/2466105* ⊕ *www.santacroceopera. it* ⊡ *Church and museum €8.*

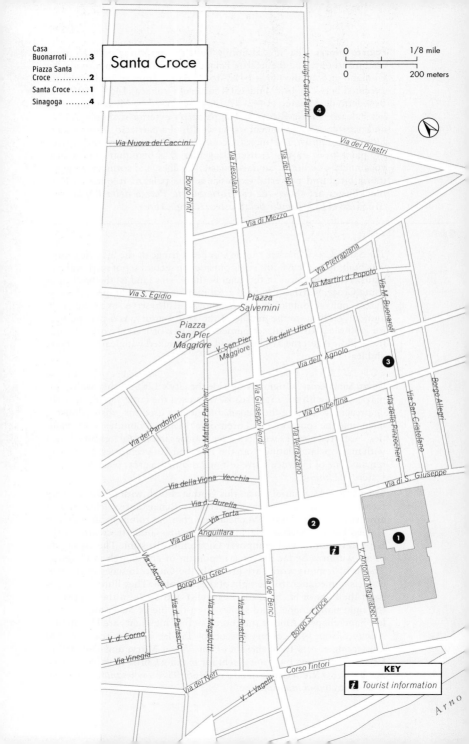

Santa Croce

0   1/8 mile

0   200 meters

V. Luigi Carlo Farini

Via Nuova dei Caccini

Via dei Pilastri

Via Fiesolana

Via dei Pepi

Via di Mezzo

Via Pietrapiana

Via Martiri d. Popolo

Via M. Buonarroti

Via S. Egidio

Piazza
Salvemini

Piazza
San Pier
Maggiore

V. San Pier
Maggiore

Via dell' Ulivo

Via dell' Agnolo

Via dei Pandolfini

Via Matteo Palmieri

Via Giuseppi Verdi

Via Ghibellina

Via delle Pinzochere

Via San Cristofano

Borgo Allegri

Via della Vigna Vecchia

Via Verrazzano

Via di S. Giuseppe

Via d. Buretta

Via Torta

Via dell' Anguillara

Via d'Acqua

Borgo dei Greci

Via de' Benci

Borgo S. Croce

V. Antonio Magliabechi

Via d. Parlascio

Via d. Magalotti

Via d. Rustici

V. d. Corno

Via Vinegia

Via dei Neri

Corso Tintori

V. d. Vageili

Arno

Borgo Pinti

KEY
i *Tourist information*

Sinagoga. Jews were well settled in Florence by the end of the 14th century, but by 1570 they were required to live within the large "ghetto," at the north side of today's Piazza della Repubblica, by decree of Cosimo I, who had cut a deal with Pope Pius V (1504–72): in exchange for ghettoizing the Jews, he would receive the title Grand Duke of Tuscany. Construction of the modern Moorish-style synagogue began in 1874 as a bequest of David Levi, who wished to endow a synagogue "worthy of the city." Falcini, Micheli, and Treves designed the building on a domed Greek cross plan with galleries in the transept and a roofline bearing three distinctive copper cupolas visible from all over Florence. The exterior has alternating bands of tan travertine and pink granite, reflecting an Islamic style repeated in Giovanni Panti's ornate interior. Of particular interest are the cast-iron gates by Pasquale Franci, the eternal light by Francesco Morini, and the Murano glass mosaics by Giacomo dal Medico. The gilded doors of the Moorish ark, which fronts the pulpit and is flanked by extravagant candelabra, are decorated with symbols of the ancient Temple of Jerusalem and bear bayonet marks from vandals. The synagogue was used as a garage by the Nazis, who failed to inflict much damage in spite of an attempt to blow up the place with dynamite. Only the columns on the left side were destroyed, and even then, the Women's Balcony above did not collapse. Note the Star of David in black and yellow marble inlay on the floor. The original capitals can be seen in the garden.

Some of the oldest and most beautiful Jewish ritual artifacts in all of Europe are displayed upstairs in the small **Museo Ebraico.** Exhibits document the Florentine Jewish community and the building of the synagogue. The donated objects all belonged to local families and date from as early as the late 16th century. Take special note of the exquisite needlework and silver pieces. A small but well-stocked gift shop is downstairs. ⊠ *Via Farini 4, Santa Croce* 🕾 *055/2346654* ⊕ *www. coopculture.it* ⌨ *Synagogue and museum €6.50* ☉ *Closed Sat. and Jewish holidays.*

WORTH NOTING

Casa Buonarroti. If you really enjoy walking in the footsteps of the great genius, you may want to complete the picture by visiting the Buonarroti family home. Michelangelo lived here from 1516 to 1525, and later gave it to his nephew, whose son, called Michelangelo il Giovane (Michelangelo the Younger) turned it into a gallery dedicated to his great-uncle. The artist's descendants filled it with art treasures, some by Michelangelo himself. Two early marble works—the *Madonna of the Steps* and the *Battle of the Centaurs*—show the boy genius at work. ⊠ *Via Ghibellina 70, Santa Croce* 🕾 *055/241752* ⊕ *www.casabuonarroti.it* ⌨ *€6.50* ☉ *Closed Tues.*

THE OLTRARNO

A walk through the Oltrarno (literally "the other side of the Arno") takes in two very different aspects of Florence: the splendor of the Medici, manifest in the riches of the mammoth Palazzo Pitti and the gracious Giardino di Boboli; and the charm of the Oltrarno, a slightly gentrified but still fiercely proud working-class neighborhood with artisans' and antiques shops.

Farther east across the Arno, a series of ramps and stairs climb to Piazzale Michelangelo, where the city lies before you in all its glory (skip this trip if it's a hazy day). More stairs (behind La Loggia restaurant) lead to the church of San Miniato al Monte. You can avoid the long walk by taking Bus No. 12 or 13 at the west end of Ponte alle Grazie and getting off at Piazzale Michelangelo; you still have to climb the monumental stairs to and from San Miniato, but you can then take the bus from Piazzale Michelangelo back to the center of town. If you decide to take a bus, remember to buy your ticket before you board.

TOP ATTRACTIONS

Fodor'sChoice **Giardino Bardini.** Garden lovers, those who crave a view, and those who
★ enjoy a nice hike should visit this lovely villa and garden, whose history spans centuries. The villa had a walled garden as early as the 14th century; the "Grand Stairs"—a zigzag ascent well worth scaling—have been around since the 16th. The garden is filled with irises, roses, and heirloom flowers, and includes a Japanese garden and statuary. A very pretty walk (all for the same admission ticket) takes you through the Giardino di Boboli and past the Forte Belvedere to the upper entrance to the giardino. ✉ *Via de'Bardini, San Niccolò* ☎ *055/294883* 🎟*€10 combined ticket, includes Galleria del Costume, Giardino di Boboli, Museo degli Argenti, Museo delle Porcellane* ✆ *Closed 1st and last Mon. of month.*

Giardino di Boboli (*Boboli Gardens*). The main entrance to these landscaped gardens is from the right side of the courtyard of **Palazzo Pitti**. The gardens began to take shape in 1549, when the Pitti family sold the palazzo to Eleanor of Toledo, wife of the Medici grand duke Cosimo I. Niccolò Tribolo (1500–50) laid out the first landscaping plans, and after his death, Ammannati, Giambologna, Bernardo Buontalenti (circa 1536–1608), and Giulio (1571–1635) and Alfonso Parigi (1606–56), among others, continued his work. Italian landscaping is less formal than French, but still full of sweeping drama. A copy of the famous *Morgante*, Cosimo I's favorite dwarf astride a particularly unhappy tortoise, is near the exit. Sculpted by Valerio Cioli (circa 1529–99), the work seems to illustrate the perils of culinary overindulgence. A visit here can be disappointing, because the gardens are somewhat underplanted and undercared for, but it's still a great walk with some terrific views. ✉ *Enter through Palazzo Pitti* ☎ *055/294883* ⊕ *www. polomuseale.firenze.it* 🎟 *€10 combined ticket, includes Museo degli Argenti, Museo delle Porcellane, Villa Bardini, and Giardino Bardini* ✆ *Closed 1st and last Mon. of month.*

Palazzo Pitti. This enormous palace is one of Florence's largest architectural set pieces. The original palazzo, built for the Pitti family around 1460, comprised only the main entrance and the three windows on either side. In 1549 the property was sold to the Medici, and Bartolomeo Ammannati was called in to make substantial additions. Today the palace houses several museums. The **Museo degli Argenti** displays a vast collection of Medici treasures, including exquisite antique vases

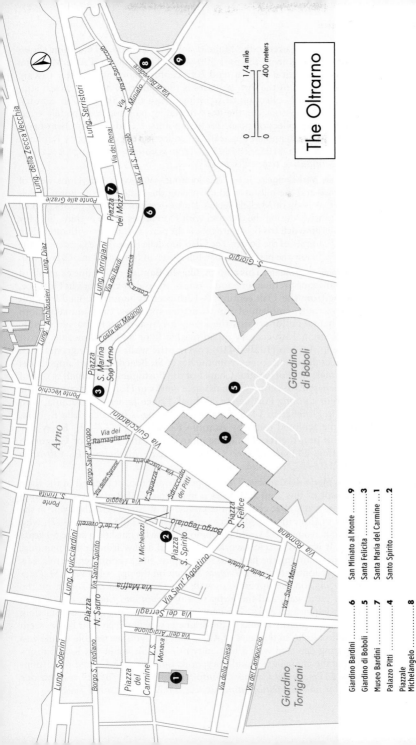

The Oltrarno

0 ⊢—⊣ 1/4 mile
0 ⊢—⊣ 400 meters

belonging to Lorenzo the Magnificent. The **Galleria del Costume** showcases fashions from the past 300 years. The **Galleria d'Arte Moderna** holds a collection of 19th- and 20th-century paintings, mostly Tuscan. Most famous of the Pitti galleries is the **Galleria Palatina**, which contains a broad collection of paintings from the 15th to 17th century. Though some consider the floor-to-ceiling paintings completely over-the-top, the collection possesses high points, including a number of portraits by Titian and an unparalleled collection of paintings by Raphael. ⊠ *Piazza Pitti* ☎ *055/294883* ⊕ *www.polomuseale.firenze.it* ⚏ *€16, €38 cumulative ticket* ⊘ *Closed Mon.*

FAMILY **Piazzale Michelangelo.** From this lookout you have a marvelous view of Florence and the hills around it, rivaling the vista from the Forte di Belvedere. A copy of Michelangelo's *David* overlooks outdoor cafés packed with tourists during the day and with Florentines in the evening. In May the **Giardino dell'Iris** (Iris Garden) off the piazza is abloom with more than 2,500 varieties of the flower. The **Giardino delle Rose** (Rose Garden) on the terraces below the piazza is also in full bloom in May and June. ⊠ *Florence.*

San Miniato al Monte. This church, like the Baptistery, is a fine example of Romanesque architecture and is one of the oldest churches in Florence, dating from the 11th century. A 12th-century mosaic topped by a gilt bronze eagle, emblem of San Miniato's sponsors, the Calimala (cloth merchants' guild) crowns the lovely green-and-white marble facade. Inside are a 13th-century inlaid-marble floor and apse mosaic. Artist Spinello Aretino (1350–1410) covered the walls of the **Sagrestia** with frescoes depicting scenes from the life of St. Benedict. The **Cappella del Cardinale del Portogallo** (Chapel of the Portuguese Cardinal) is one of the richest 15th-century Renaissance works in Florence. It contains the tomb of a young Portuguese cardinal, Prince James of Lusitania, who died in Florence in 1459. Its glorious ceiling is by Luca della Robbia, and the sculpted tomb by Antonio Rossellino (1427–79). Every day at 6:30 pm, the monks fill the church with the sounds of Gregorian chanting. ⊠ *Viale Galileo Galilei, Piazzale Michelangelo, Oltrarno* ☎ *055/2342731* ⊕ *www.sanminiatoalmonte.it.*

Santa Maria del Carmine. The **Cappella Brancacci,** at the end of the right transept of this church, houses a masterpiece of Renaissance painting: a fresco cycle that changed the course of Western art. The cycle is the work of three artists: Masaccio and Masolino (1383–circa 1447), who began it around 1424, and Filippino Lippi, who finished it some 50 years later. It was Masaccio's work that opened a new frontier for painting, as he was among the first artists to employ single-point perspective. His style predominates in the *Tribute Money,* on the upper-left wall; *St. Peter Baptizing,* on the upper altar wall; the *Distribution of Goods,* on the lower altar wall; and the *Expulsion of Adam and Eve,* on the chapel's upper-left entrance pier. The figures of Adam and Eve possess a startling presence primarily thanks to the dramatic way in which their bodies seem to reflect light. In the faces of Adam and Eve, you see terrible shame and suffering depicted with a humanity rarely achieved in art. Reservations to see the chapel are mandatory; your time inside is limited to 15 minutes. ⊠ *Piazza del Carmine, Santo Spirito* ☎ *055/2768224 reservations* ⊕ *www.museicivicifiorentini.comune.fi.it* ⚏ *€6* ⊘ *Closed Tues.*

Continued on page 523

WHO'S WHO IN RENAISSANCE ART

Michelangelo. Leonardo da Vinci. Raphael. This heady triumvirate of the Italian Renaissance is synonymous with artistic genius. Yet they are only three of the remarkable cast of characters whose work defines the Renaissance, that extraordinary flourishing of art and culture in Italy, especially in Florence, as the Middle Ages drew to a close. The artists were visionaries, who redefined painting, sculpture, architecture, and even what it means to be an artist.

THE PIONEER. In the mid-14th century, a few artists began to move away the flat, two-dimensional painting from the Middle Ages. **Giotto,** who painted seemingly three-dimensional figures who show emotion, had a major impact on the artists of the next century.

THE GROUNDBREAKERS. The generations of **Brunelleschi** and **Botticelli** took center stage in the 15th century. **Ghiberti, Masaccio, Donatello, Uccello, Fra Angelico,** and **Filippo Lippi** were other major players. Part of the Renaissance (or "re-birth") was a renewed interest in classical sources—the texts, monuments, and sculpture of Ancient Greece and Rome. Perspective and the illusion of three-dimensional space in painting was another discovery of this era, known as the Early Renaissance. Suddenly the art appearing on the walls looked real, or more realistic than it used to.

Roman ruins were not the only thing to inspire these artists. There was an incredible exchange of ideas going on. In Santa Maria del Carmine, Filippo Lippi was inspired by the work of Masaccio, who in turn was a friend of Brunelleschi. Young artists also learned from the masters via the apprentice system. Ghiberti's workshop (*bottega* in Italian) included, at one time or another, Donatello, Masaccio, and Uccello. Botticelli was apprenticed to Filippo Lippi.

THE BIG THREE. The mathematical rationality and precision of 15th-century art gave way to what is known as the High Renaissance. **Leonardo, Michelangelo,** and **Raphael** were much more concerned with portraying the body in all its glory and with achieving harmony and grandeur in their work. Oil paint, used infrequently up until this time, became more widely employed: as a result, Leonardo's colors are deeper, more sensual, more alive. For one brief period, all three were in Florence at the same time. Michelangelo and Leonardo surely knew one another, as they were simultaneously working on frescoes (never completed) inside Palazzo Vecchio.

When Michelangelo left Florence for Rome in 1508, he began the slow drain of artistic exodus from Florence, which never really recovered her previous glory.

A RENAISSANCE TIMELINE

IN THE WORLD

Black Death in Europe kills one third of the population, 1347-50.

Joan of Arc burned at the stake, 1431.

IN FLORENCE

Founding of the Medici bank, 1397.

Medici family made official papal bankers.

1434, Cosimo il Vecchio becomes de facto ruler of Florence. The Medici family will dominate the city until 1494.

Dante, a native of Florence, writes *The Divine Comedy*, 1302-21.

1300

1400

IN ART

EARLY RENAISSANCE

Masaccio and Masolino fresco San Maria del Carmine, 1424-28.

GIOTTO (ca. 1267-1337)

BRUNELLESCHI (1377-1446)

LORENZO GHIBERTI (ca. 1381-1455)

Giotto fresoes in Santa Croce,

1320-25.

DONATELLO (ca. 1386-1466)

PAOLO UCCELLO (1397-1475)

FRA ANGELICO (ca. 1400-1455)

MASACCIO (1401-1428)

FILIPPO LIPPI (ca. 1406-1469)

1334, 67-year-old Giotto is appointed chief architect of Santa Maria del Fiore, Florence's Duomo (below). He begins to work on the Campanile, which will be completed in 1359, after his death.

Donatello sculpts his bronze *David*, ca. 1440.

Fra Angelico frescoes friars' cells in San Marco, 1438-45.

Ghiberti wins the competition for the Baptistery doors (above) in Florence, 1401.

Uccello's *Sir John Hawkwood*, ca. 1436.

Brunelleschi wins the competition for the Duomo cupola (right), 1418.

▼ Gutenberg Bible is printed, 1455.

▼ Columbus discovers America, 1492.

▼ Martin Luther posts his 95 theses on the door at Wittenberg, kicking off the Protestant Reformation, 1517.

Constantinople falls to the Turks, 1453.

▼ Machiavelli's *Prince* appears, 1513.

▼ Copernicus proves that the earth is not the center of the universe, 1530-43.

Lorenzo "il Magnifico" (right), the Medici patron of the arts, rules in Florence, 1449-92.

Two Medici popes Leo X (1513-21) and Clement VII (1523-34) in Rome.

Catherine de'Medici becomes Queen of France, 1547.

1450

1500

1550

HIGH RENAISSANCE

MANNERISM

▼ Fra Filippo Lippi's *Madonna and Child*, ca. 1452.

▼ 1508, Raphael begins work on the chambers in the Vatican, Rome.

▼ Giorgio Vasari publishes his first edition of *Lives of the Artists*, 1550.

▼ 1504, Michelangelo's *David* is put on display in Piazza della Signoria, where it remains until 1873.

▼ Botticelli paints the *Birth of Venus*, ca. 1482.

▼ Michelangelo begins to fresco the Sistine Chapel ceiling, 1508.

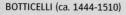
BOTTICELLI (ca. 1444-1510)

LEONARDO DA VINCI (1452-1519)

RAPHAEL (1483-1520)

MICHELANGELO (1475-1564)

▼▼ Leonardo paints *The Last Supper* in Milan, 1495-98.

Giotto's *Nativity*   Donatello's *St. John the Baptist*   Ghiberti's *Gates of Paradise*

GIOTTO (CA. 1267-1337)

Painter/architect from a small town north of Florence.

He unequivocally set Italian painting on the course that led to the triumphs of the Renaissance masters. Unlike the rather flat, two-dimensional forms found in then prevailing Byzantine art, Giotto's figures have a fresh, life-like quality. The people in his paintings have bulk, and they show emotion, which you can see on their faces and in their gestures. This was something new in the late Middle Ages. Without Giotto, there wouldn't have been a Raphael.

In Florence: **Santa Croce; Uffizi; Campanile; Santa Maria Novella**
Elsewhere in Italy: **Scrovegni Chapel, Padua; Vatican Museums, Rome**

FILIPPO BRUNELLESCHI (1377-1446)

Architect/engineer from Florence.

If Brunelleschi had beaten Ghiberti in the Baptistery doors competition in Florence, the city's Duomo most likely would not have the striking appearance and authority that it has today. After his loss, he sulked off to Rome, where he studied the ancient Roman structures first-hand. Brunelleschi figured out how to vault the Duomo's dome, a structure unprecedented in its colossal size and great height. His Ospedale degli Innocenti employs classical elements in the creation of a stunning, new architectural statement; it is the first truly Renaissance structure.

In Florence: **Duomo; Ospedale degli Innocenti; San Lorenzo; Santo Spirito; Baptistery Doors Competition Entry, Bargello; Santa Croce**

LORENZO GHIBERTI (CA. 1381-1455)

Sculptor from Florence.

Ghiberti won a competition—besting his chief rival, Brunelleschi—to cast the gilded bronze North Doors of the Baptistery in Florence. These doors, and the East Doors that he subsequently executed, took up the next 50 years of his life. He created intricately worked figures that are more true-to-life than any since antiquity, and he was one of the first Renaissance sculptors to work in bronze. Ghiberti taught the next generation of artists; Donatello, Uccello, and Masaccio all passed through his studio.

In Florence: **Door Copies, Baptistery; Original Doors, Museo dell'Opera del Duomo; Baptistry Door Competition Entry, Bargello; Orsanmichele**

DONATELLO (CA. 1386-1466)

Sculptor from Florence.

Donatello was an innovator who, like his good friend Brunelleschi, spent most of his long life in Florence. Consumed with the science of optics, he used light and shadow to create the effects of nearness and distance. He made an essentially flat slab look like a three-dimensional scene. His bronze is probably the first free-standing male nude since antiquity. Not only technically brilliant, his work is also emotionally resonant; few sculptors are as expressive.

In Florence: **David, Bargello; St. Mark, Orsanmichele; Palazzo Vecchio; Museo dell'Opera del Duomo; San Lorenzo; Santa Croce**
Elsewhere in Italy: **Padua; Prato; Venice**

Fra Angelico's *The Deposition*   Masaccio's *Trinity*   Filippo Lippi's *Madonna and Child*

PAOLO UCCELLO (1397-1475)
Painter from Florence.
Renaissance chronicler Vasari once observed that had Uccello not been so obsessed with the mathematical problems posed by perspective, he would have been a very good painter. The struggle to master single-point perspective and to render motion in two dimensions is nowhere more apparent than in his battle scenes. His first major commission in Florence was the gargantuan fresco of the English mercenary Sir John Hawkwood (the Italians called him Giovanni Acuto) in Florence's Duomo.

In Florence: *Sir John Hawkwood,* **Duomo;** *Battle of San Romano,* **Uffizi; Santa Maria Novella**
Elsewhere in Italy: **Urbino, Prato**

FRA ANGELICO (CA. 1400-1455)
Painter from a small town north of Florence.
A Dominican friar, who eventually made his way to the convent of San Marco, Fra Angelico and his assistants painted frescoes for aid in prayer and meditation. He was known for his piety; Vasari wrote that Fra Angelico could never paint a crucifix without a tear running down his face. Perhaps no other painter so successfully translated the mysteries of faith and the sacred into painting. And yet his figures emote, his command of perspective is superb, and his use of color startles even today.

In Florence: **Museo di San Marco; Uffizi**
Elsewhere in Italy: **Vatican Museums, Rome; Fiesole; Cortona; Perugia; Orvieto**

MASACCIO (1401-1428)
Painter from San Giovanni Valdarno, southeast of Florence.
Masaccio and Masolino, a frequent collaborator, worked most famously together at Santa Maria del Carmine. Their frescoes of the life of St. Peter use light to mold figures in the painting by imitating the way light falls on figures in real life. Masaccio also pioneered the use of single-point perspective, masterfully rendered in his Trinity. His friend Brunelleschi probably introduced him to the technique, yet another step forward in rendering things the way the eye sees them. Masaccio died young and under mysterious circumstances.

In Florence: **Santa Maria del Carmine;** *Trinity,* **Santa Maria Novella**

FILIPPO LIPPI (CA. 1406-1469)
Painter from Prato.
At a young age, Filippo Lippi entered the friary of Santa Maria del Carmine, where he was highly influenced by Masaccio and Masolino's frescoes. His religious vows appear to have made less of an impact; his affair with a young nun produced a son, Filippino (Little Philip, who later apprenticed with Botticelli), and a daughter. His religious paintings often have a playful, humorous note; some of his angels are downright impish and look directly out at the viewer. Lippi links the earlier painters of the 15th century with those who follow; Botticelli apprenticed with him.

In Florence: **Uffizi; Palazzo Medici Riccardi; San Lorenzo; Palazzo Pitti**
Elsewhere in Italy: **Prato**

Botticelli's *Primavera*

Leonardo's *Portrait of a Young Woman*

Raphael's *Madonna on the Meadow*

BOTTICELLI (CA. 1444-1510)

Painter from Florence.
Botticelli's work is characterized by stunning, elongated blondes, cherubic angels (something he undoubtedly learned from his time with Filippo Lippi), and tender Christs. Though he did many religious paintings, he also painted monumental, nonreligious panels—his *Birth of Venus* and *Primavera* being the two most famous of these. A brief sojourn took him to Rome, where he and a number of other artists frescoed the Sistine Chapel walls.

In Florence: ***Birth of Venus**, **Primavera**,* Uffizi; Palazzo Pitti
Elsewhere in Italy: Vatican Museums, Rome

LEONARDO DA VINCI (1452-1519)

Painter/sculptor/engineer from Anchiano, a small town outside Vinci.
Leonardo never lingered long in any place; his restless nature and his international reputation led to commissions throughout Italy, and took him to Milan, Vigevano, Pavia, Rome, and, ultimately, France. Though he is most famous for his mysterious *Mona Lisa* (at the Louvre in Paris), he painted other penetrating, psychological portraits in addition to his scientific experiments: his design for a flying machine (never built) predates Kitty Hawk by nearly 500 years. The greatest collection of Leonardo's work in Italy can be seen on one wall in the Uffizi.

In Florence: ***Adoration of the Magi**,* Uffizi
Elsewhere in Italy: ***Last Supper**,* Santa Maria delle Grazie, Milan

RAPHAEL (1483-1520)

Painter/architect from Urbino.
Raphael spent only four highly productive years of his short life in Florence, where he turned out made-to-order panel paintings of the Madonna and Child for a hungry public; he also executed a number of portraits of Florentine aristocrats. Perhaps no other artist had such a fine command of line and color, and could render it, seemingly effortlessly, in paint. His painting acquired new authority after he came up against Michelangelo toiling away on the Sistine ceiling. Raphael worked nearly next door in the Vatican, where his figures take on an epic, Michelangelesque scale.

In Florence: Uffizi; Palazzo Pitti
Elsewhere in Italy: Vatican Museums, Rome

MICHELANGELO (1475-1564)

Painter/sculptor/architect from Caprese.
Although Florentine and proud of it (he famously signed his St. Peter's *Pietà* to avoid confusion about where he was from), he spent most of his 89 years outside his native city. He painted and sculpted the male body on an epic scale and glorified it while doing so. Though he complained throughout the proceedings that he was really a sculptor, Michelangelo's Sistine Chapel ceiling is arguably the greatest fresco cycle ever painted (and the massive figures owe no small debt to Giotto).

In Florence: ***David**,* Galleria dell'Accademia; Uffizi; Casa Buonarroti; Bargello
Elsewhere in Italy: St. Peter's Basilica, Vatican Museums, and Piazza del Campidoglio in Rome

Santo Spirito. The interior of this church is one of a pair designed in Florence by Filippo Brunelleschi in the early decades of the 15th century (the other is San Lorenzo). It was here that Brunelleschi supplied definitive solutions to the two major problems of interior Renaissance church design: how to build a cross-shape interior using classical architectural elements borrowed from antiquity, and how to reflect in that interior the order and regularity that Renaissance scientists were at the time discovering in the natural world around them.

Brunelleschi's solution to the first problem was brilliantly simple: turn a Greek temple inside out. His solution to the second problem—making the entire interior orderly and regular—was mathematically precise: he designed the ground plan of the church so that all its parts were proportionally related. He believed that mathematical regularity and aesthetic beauty were flip sides of the same coin, that one was not possible without the other. ⊠ *Piazza Santo Spirito* ☎ *055/2382383* ⊕ *www.basilicasantospirito.it* ☜ *Church free* ☉ *Church closed Wed.*

WORTH NOTING

Museo Bardini. The 19th-century collector and antiquarian Stefano Bardini turned his palace into his own private museum. Upon his death, the collection was turned over to the state and includes an interesting assortment of Etruscan pieces, sculpture, paintings, and furniture that dates mostly from the Renaissance and the Baroque. ⊠ *Piazza de' Mozzi 1* ☎ *055/2342427* ⊕ *museicivicifiorentini.comune.fi.it* ☜ *€6* ☉ *Closed Tues. and Wed.*

Santa Felicita. This late Baroque church (its facade was remodeled between 1736 and 1739) contains the mannerist Jacopo Pontormo's *Deposition,* the centerpiece of the Cappella Capponi (executed 1525–28) and a masterpiece of 16th-century Florentine art. The remote figures, which transcend the realm of Renaissance classical form, are portrayed in tangled shapes and intense pastel colors (well preserved because of the low lights in the church), in a space and depth that defy reality. Note, too, the exquisitely frescoed *Annunciation,* also by Pontormo, at a right angle to the *Deposition.* The granite column in the piazza was erected in 1381 and marks a Christian cemetery. ⊠ *Piazza Santa Felicita, Via Guicciardini, Palazzo Pitti.*

WHERE TO EAT

Florence's popularity with tourists means that, unfortunately, there's a higher percentage of mediocre restaurants here than you'll find in most Italian towns (Venice, perhaps, might win that prize). Some restaurant owners cut corners and let standards slip, knowing that a customer today is unlikely to return tomorrow, regardless of the quality of the meal. So, if you're looking to eat well, it pays to do some research, starting with the recommendations here. Dining hours start at around 1 for lunch and 8 for dinner. Many of Florence's restaurants are small, so reservations are a must. You can sample such specialties as creamy *fegatini* (a chicken-liver spread) and *ribollita* (minestrone thickened with bread and beans and swirled with extra-virgin olive oil) in a bustling, convivial trattoria, where you share long wooden tables set with paper place mats, or in an upscale *ristorante* with linen tablecloths and napkins.

WHAT IT COSTS			
$	$$	$$$	$$$$
At dinner under €15	€15–€24	€25–€35	over €35

Restaurant prices are the average cost of a main course at dinner or, if dinner is not served, at lunch.

Use the coordinate (✚ B2) at the end of each listing to locate a site on the Where to Eat and Stay in Florence map. Restaurant reviews have been shortened. For full information, visit Fodors.com.

AROUND THE DUOMO

$$
ITALIAN
✕ **Coquinarius.** This rustically elegant space, which has served many purposes over the past 600 years, offers some of the tastiest food in town at great prices. It's the perfect place to come if you aren't sure what you're hungry for, as they offer a little bit of everything: salad-lovers will have a hard time choosing from among the lengthy list (the Scozzese, with poached chicken, avocado, and bacon, is a winner); those with a yen for pasta will face agonizing choices (the ravioli with pecorino and pears is particularly good). **Known for:** marvelous salads; gently priced wine list; service can be erratic. $ *Average main: €17* ✉ *Via delle Oche 15/r, Duomo* ☎ *055/2302153* ⊕ *www.coquinarius.it* ✚ *E3.*

$
ITALIAN
✕ **'ino.** Serving arguably the best panini in town, proprietor Alessandro sources only the very best ingredients. Located right behind the Uffizi, 'ino is a perfect place to grab a tasty sandwich and glass of wine before forging on to the next museum. **Known for:** the bread; interesting ingredient combinations; sourcing the best ingredients. $ *Average main: €8* ✉ *Via dei Georgofili 3/r–7/r, Piazza della Signoria* ☎ *055/219208* ⊕ *www.inofirenze.com* ✚ *E4.*

$$
ITALIAN
✕ **Pegna.** Looking for some cheddar cheese to pile in your panino? Pegna has been selling both Italian and non-Italian food since 1860. **Known for:** gourmet supermarket; international foodstuffs; food on the go. $ *Average main: €24* ✉ *Via dello Studio 8, Duomo* ☎ *055/282701* ⊕ *www.pegna.it* ⊙ *Closed Sun., Sat. afternoon in July and Aug., and Wed. afternoon Sept.–June* ✚ *F3.*

$$
ITALIAN
Fodor'sChoice
★
✕ **Rivoire.** One of the best spots in Florence for people-watching offers stellar service, light snacks, and terrific aperitivi. It's been around since the 1860s, and has been famous for its hot and cold chocolate (with or without cream) for more than a century. **Known for:** hot chocolate; friendly bartenders; the view on the piazza. $ *Average main: €15* ✉ *Via Vacchereccia 4/r, Piazza della Signoria* ☎ *055/214412* ⊕ *www. rivoire.it* ✚ *E4.*

SAN LORENZO

$ INTERNATIONAL Fodor's Choice ★ 🍴 **Baroni.** The cheese collection at Baroni may be the most comprehensive in Florence. They also have high-quality truffle products, vinegars, and other delicacies. **Known for:** expansive cheese selection; top-notch foodstuff; products packed for shipping. [$] *Average main: €10* ✉ *Mercato Central, enter at Via Signa, San Lorenzo* ☎ *055/289576* 🌐 *www.baronialimentari.it* ✥ *D1.*

$ TUSCAN Fodor's Choice ★ 🍴 **da Nerbone.** This *tavola calda* in the middle of the covered Mercato Centrale has been serving up food to Florentines who like their tripe since 1872. Tasty primi and secondi are available every day, but cognoscenti come for the *panino con il lampredotto* (tripe sandwich). **Known for:** tripe sandwich; frequented by local regulars; favorite dishes sell out. [$] *Average main: €10* ✉ *Mercato San Lorenzo* ☎ 💳 *No credit cards* ⏲ *Closed Sun. No dinner* ✥ *D1.*

$ TUSCAN Fodor's Choice ★ 🍴 **da Sergio.** Run by the Gozzi family for just over a hundred years, the food here is terrific, eminently affordable, and just across the way from the basilica of San Lorenzo, which means that you can imbibe well-prepared food while marveling at the Brunelleschi and Michelangelo you've just seen. The menu is short, and changes daily. **Known for:** local favorite; ever-changing menu; true Tuscan food. [$] *Average main: €9* ✉ *Piazza San Lorenzo 8/r, San Lorenzo* ⏲ *Closed Sun. No dinner* ✥ *E1.*

$ ITALIAN 🍴 **Gelateria Carabe.** Specializing in things Sicilian, this shop is known for its tart and flavorful *granità* (granular flavored ices), which are great thirst-quenchers. **Known for:** best gelato around; close to the Accademia; no-frills shop. [$] *Average main: €3* ✉ *Via Ricasoli 60/r, San Marco* ☎ *055/942478* 🌐 *www.parcocarabe.it* 💳 *No credit cards* ✥ *F1.*

$$ TUSCAN 🍴 **il Desco.** Owned by the Bargiacchi family, who are proprietors of the lovely hotel Guelfo Bianco just next door, their organic farm in the Tuscan countryside provides much of what is on the frequently changing menu. The menu plays to all tastes—Tuscan classics such as *peposo* (a hearty, black pepper–filled beef stew) can be found, as well as vegetarian dishes. **Known for:** fine vegetarian and vegan dishes; just a few tables; clever wine list. [$] *Average main: €16* ✉ *Via Cavour 55/r, San Lorenzo* ☎ *055/288330* 🌐 *www.ildescofirenze.it* ✥ *F1.*

$ TUSCAN Fodor's Choice ★ 🍴 **Mario.** Florentines flock to this narrow family-run trattoria near San Lorenzo to feast on Tuscan favorites served at simple tables under a wooden ceiling dating from 1536. A distinct cafeteria feel and genuine Florentine hospitality prevail: you'll be seated wherever there's room, which often means with strangers. **Known for:** grilled meats; roasted potatoes; festive atmosphere. [$] *Average main: €10* ✉ *Via Rosina 2/r, corner of Piazza del Mercato Centrale, San Lorenzo* ☎ *055/218550* 🌐 *www.trattoria-mario.com* ⏲ *Closed Sun. and Aug. No dinner* ✥ *E1.*

$$ ITALIAN Fodor's Choice ★ 🍴 **Perini.** It's possible to break the bank here, as this might be the best salumeria in Florence. Perini sells prosciutto, mixed meats, sauces for pasta, and a wide assortment of antipasti, and is closed Sunday. [$] *Average main: €20* ✉ *Mercato Centrale, enter at Via dell'Aretino, San Lorenzo* ☎ *055/2398306* ⏲ *Closed Sun.* ✥ *E1.*

$$ TUSCAN Fodor's Choice ★ 🍴 **Taverna del Bronzino.** Located in the former studio of Santi di Tito, a student of Bronzino's, Taverna has a simple, formal decor, with white tablecloths and place settings. The classic, elegantly presented Tuscan food is superb, and the solid, affordable wine list rounds out the menu—especially because Stefano, the sommelier, really knows his stuff. **Known for:** creative menu; lots of fish; wonderful sommelier. [$] *Average main: €24* ✉ *Via delle Ruote 25/r, San Marco* ☎ *055/495220* 🌐 *www.tavernadelbronzino.net* ⊗ *Closed Sun. and 3 wks in Aug.* ✥ *G1.*

SANTA MARIA NOVELLA

$$$ TUSCAN 🍴 **Buca Lapi.** The Antinori family started selling wine from their palace's basement in the 15th century and six hundred years later, this *buca* (hole) is a lively, subterranean restaurant filled with Florentine aristocrats chowing down on what might be the best (and most expensive) bistecca fiorentina in town. The classical Tuscan menu has the usual suspects: *crostino di cavolo nero* (black cabbage on toasted garlic bread), along with ribollita and pappa al pomodoro. **Known for:** its gargantuan bistecca fiorentina; adherence to Tuscan classics; superb service. [$] *Average main: €35* ✉ *Via del Trebbio 1, Santa Maria Novella* ☎ *055/213768* 🌐 *www.bucalapi.com* ⊗ *Closed Sun.* ✥ *D3.*

$$$ TUSCAN 🍴 **Cantinetta Antinori.** After a morning of shopping on Via Tornabuoni, stop for lunch in this 15th-century palazzo in the company of Florentine ladies (and men) who come to see and be seen over lunch. The panache of the food matches its clientele: expect treats such as *tramezzino con pane di campagna al tartufo* (country pâté with truffles served on bread) and the *insalata di gamberoni e gamberetti con carciofi freschi* (crayfish and prawn salad with shaved raw artichokes). **Known for:** chic clientele; most ingredients come from the family farm; high prices to match the excellent food and wine. [$] *Average main: €26* ✉ *Piazza Antinori 3, Santa Maria Novella* ☎ *055/292234* 🌐 *www.cantinetta-antinori.com* ⊗ *Closed weekends, 20 days in Aug., and Dec. 25–Jan. 6* ✥ *D3.*

$ TUSCAN Fodor's Choice ★ 🍴 **Mangiafoco.** It's got brightly colored purple and orange walls, and a warren of small rooms; it also has a large room along with a counter that sells terrific take-away options. Created by Francesco and Elisa in 2001, this little spot, nestled in the heart of the centro storico on a romantic medieval side street, serves Tuscan classics *con fantasia* (with fantasy) created by Luca, Elisa's brother. **Known for:** phenomenal wines by the glass (and by the bottle); creative, seasonal menu changes daily; lovely waitstaff. [$] *Average main: €12* ✉ *Borgo Santi Apostoli 26/r, Santa Maria Novella* ☎ *055/2658170* 🌐 *www.mangiafoco.com* ⊗ *Closed Sun.* ✥ *D4.*

$$ ITALIAN 🍴 **Obicà.** Mozzarella takes center stage at this sleek eatery on Florence's swankiest street. The cheese, along with its culinary cousin *burrata* (a fresh cheese filled with cream), arrives daily from southern Italy to become the centerpiece for various salads and pastas. **Known for:** mozzarella-laden menu; outstanding pizza and desserts; nightly happy hour and outdoor seating in nice weather. [$] *Average main: €18* ✉ *Via Tornabuoni 16, Santa Maria Novella* ☎ *055/2773526* 🌐 *www.obica.com* ✥ *D3.*

$$ ✕ **Procacci.** At this classy Florentine institution dating to 1885, try one of
ITALIAN the panini tartufati and swish it down with a glass of prosecco. **Known**
Fodor'sChoice **for:** pane tartufati; excellent wines by the glass; the calm and serenity
★ of the space. $ *Average main: €15* ✉ *Via Tornabuoni 64/r, Santa Maria
Novella* ☎ *055/211656* ⊕ *www.procacci1885.it* ⊙ *Closed Sun.* ✛ *D3.*

$ ✕ **Shake.** If you're on your way to the train station, or arriving from the
ITALIAN train station, this little juice bar at Piazza Santa Maria Novella provides
a perfect place for a rest stop. They serve tasty croissants and panini all
day, and make wraps, salads, and sandwiches at lunch (all of which are
neatly packed and available to go). **Known for:** juices and smoothies;
good food on the go; sandwiches. $ *Average main: €5* ✉ *Via degli Avelli
2/r, Santa Maria Novella* ☎ *055/295310* ⊕ *www.shakecafe.bio* ✛ *D2.*

$$ ✕ **Trattoria Sostanza (il Troia).** Since opening its doors in 1869, this trat-
TUSCAN toria has been serving top-notch, unpretentious food to Florentines who
Fodor'sChoice like their bistecca fiorentina very large and very rare. Along with fine
★ Tuscan classics, they have two signature dishes: the *tortino di carciofi*
(artichoke tart) and the *pollo al burro* (chicken with butter). **Known
for:** Tuscan classics; delicious desserts; no-frills decor. $ *Average main:
€15* ✉ *Via della Porcellana 25, Santa Maria Novella* ☎ *055/212691*
▭ *No credit cards* ✛ *B3.*

$ ✕ **vincanto.** It opens at 11 am and closes at midnight: this is a rarity
ITALIAN in Florentine dining. They do a little bit of everything here, including fine pastas, salads, pizzas, and even an American-style breakfast.
Known for: a wide-ranging menu; kitchen stays open; outside terrace
with views of a beautiful square. $ *Average main: €12* ✉ *Piazza Santa
Maria Novella 23/r, Santa Maria Novella* ☎ *055/2679300* ⊕ *www.ris-
torantevincanto.com* ✛ *C2.*

SANTA CROCE

$$ ✕ **Antico Noe.** The short menu at the one-room eatery relies heavily on
TUSCAN seasonal ingredients picked up daily at the market. Although the secondi
are good, the antipasti and primi really shine. **Known for:** attention to
seasonal vegetables; their artichoke dishes; their porcini dishes. $ *Aver-
age main: €15* ✉ *Volta di San Piero 6/r, Santa Croce* ☎ *055/2340838*
⊙ *Closed Sun. and 2 wks in Aug.* ✛ *G3.*

$$$$ ✕ **Cibrèo.** The food at this upscale trattoria is fantastic, from the creamy
TUSCAN crostini *di fegatini* (a savory chicken-liver spread) to the melt-in-your-
Fodor'sChoice mouth desserts. Many Florentines hail this as the city's best restaurant,
★ and justifiably so. **Known for:** authentic Tuscan food; no written menu;
multilingual waitstaff. $ *Average main: €40* ✉ *Via A. del Verrocchio
8/r, Santa Croce* ☎ *055/2341100* ⊙ *Closed Sun. and Mon., and July
25–Sept. 5* ✛ *H3.*

$$ ✕ **Cibrèo Trattoria.** This intimate little trattoria, known to locals as Cibre-
TUSCAN ino, shares its kitchen with the famed Florentine culinary institution
from which it gets its name. Start with *il gelatina di pomodoro* (tomato
gelatin) liberally laced with basil, garlic, and a pinch of hot pepper, and
then sample the justifiably renowned *passato in zucca gialla* (pureed
yellow-pepper soup) before moving on to any of the succulent secondi.
Known for: excellent meal at a moderate price; clever riffs on classic
dishes; go early to avoid a wait. $ *Average main: €15* ✉ *Via dei Macci*

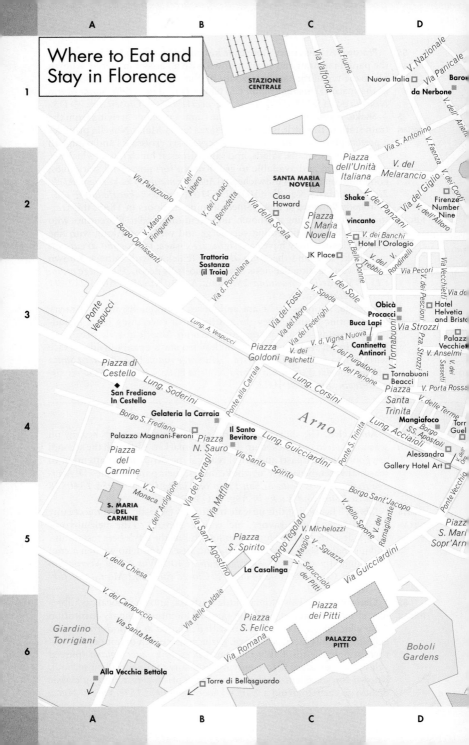

Where to Eat and Stay in Florence

A **B** **C** **D**

1

STAZIONE CENTRALE

Via Fiume

Via Valfonda

V. Nazionale

Nuova Italia

V. Panicale

Baron

da Nerbone

V. dell'Ariento

Piazza dell'Unità Italiana

Via S. Antonino

V. del Melarancio

V. Faenza

V. del Giglio

V. dei Conti

Firenze Number Nine

V. dell'Alloro

2

Via Palazzuolo

V. dell'Albero

V. dei Canaci

V. Benedetta

Via della Scala

SANTA MARIA NOVELLA

Casa Howard

Piazza S. Maria Novella

Shake

V. dei Panzani

vincanto

V. dei Banchi

Hotel l'Orologio

V. d. Belle Donne

V. del Trebbio

V. dei Rondinelli

Via Pecori

Via Vecchietti

Via de

V. Maso Finiguerra

Borgo Ognissanti

JK Place

V. del Sole

Obicà

Via Strozzi

Hotel Helvetia and Bristol

3

Ponte Vespucci

Lung. A. Vespucci

Trattoria Sostanza (il Troia)

Via d. Porcellana

Via dei Fossi

V. Spada

Via del Moro

Via dei Federighi

Procacci

Buca Lapi

V. dei Pesciani

Pza. Strozzi

Cantinetta Antinori

Palazzo Vecchie

V. Anselmi

V. dei Sasseti

Piazza Goldoni

V. dei Palchetti

V. di Vigna Nuova

V. del Purgatorio

V. del Parione

Via Tornabuoni

Tornabuoni Beacci

Piazza Santa Trinita

V. Porta Rossa

Borgo SS. Apostoli

Mangiafoco

Torr Guel

4

Piazza di Cestello

Lung. Soderini

♦

San Frediano In Cestello

Gelateria la Carraia

Borgo S. Frediano

Palazzo Magnani-Feroni

Il Santo Bevitore

Piazza N. Sauro

Ponte alla Carraia

Lung. Corsini

Arno

Lung. Guicciardini

Ponte S. Trinita

Lung. Acciaioli

V. delle Terme

Alessandra

Gallery Hotel Art

V. dell'Or

Ponte Vecchio

5

Piazza del Carmine

V. S. Monaca

V. dell'Ardiglione

Via dei Serragli

Via Sant'Agostino

Via Maffia

Via Santo Spirito

Piazza S. Spirito

Borgo Tegolaio

V. Michelozzi

V. Maggio

V. Sguazza

V. Sdrucciolo dei Pitti

V. dello Sprone

V. dei Ramaglianto

Borgo Sant'Jacopo

Via Guicciardini

Piazz S. Mari Sopr'Arn

6

Giardino Torrigiani

V. della Chiesa

V. del Campuccio

Via Santa Maria

Via delle Caldaie

La Casalinga

Piazza S. Felice

Via Romana

Piazza dei Pitti

PALAZZO PITTI

Boboli Gardens

Alla Vecchia Bettola

Torre di Bellosguardo

↓ ↓

A **B** **C** **D**

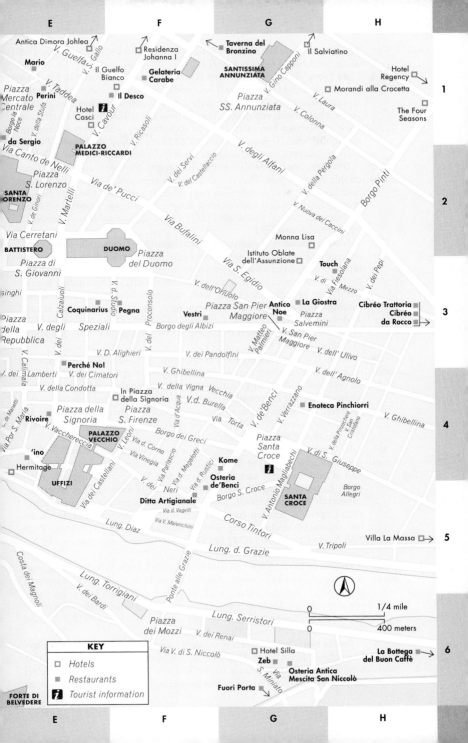

118, Santa Croce ☎ *055/2341100* 🖃 *No credit cards* ⊘ *Closed Sun. and Mon., and July 25–Sept. 5* ✛ *H3.*

$ ✕ **da Rocco.** At one of Florence's biggest markets you can grab lunch to
TUSCAN   go, or you could cram yourself into one of the booths and pour from the
straw-cloaked flask (wine here is *da consumo,* which means they charge
you for how much you drink). Food is abundant, Tuscan, and fast; locals
pack in. **Known for:** tasty food at rock-bottom prices; ever-changing
menu; take-out. $ *Average main: €7* ✉ *Mercato Sant'Ambrogio, Piazza
Ghiberti, Santa Croce* 🖃 *No credit cards* ⊘ *Closed Sun. No dinner* ✛ *H3.*

$ ✕ **Ditta Artigianale.** Seattle has finally come to Florence, and coffee fans
ITALIAN   couldn't be happier. This place is always crowded with mostly young
folk lingering over non-Italian cups of coffee. **Known for:** non-Italian
coffee; tasty food; long opening hours. $ *Average main: €8* ✉ *Via
de'Neri 32, Santa Croce* ☎ *055/2741541* ⊕ *www.dittaartigianale.it*
🖃 *No credit cards* ✛ *F5.*

$$$$ ✕ **Enoteca Pinchiorri.** A sumptuous Renaissance palace with high frescoed
ITALIAN   ceilings and bouquets in silver vases provides the backdrop for this restaurant, one of the most expensive in Italy. Some consider it one of the
best, and others consider it a non-Italian rip-off, as the kitchen is presided over by a Frenchwoman with sophisticated, yet internationalist,
leanings. **Known for:** creative food; wine cellar; exorbitantly high prices.
$ *Average main: €85* ✉ *Via Ghibellina 87, Santa Croce* ☎ *055/242777*
⊕ *www.enotecapinchiorri.it* ⊘ *Closed Sun., Mon., and Aug. No lunch*
🎩 *Jacket required* ✛ *G4.*

$$ ✕ **Kome.** If you're looking for a break from the ubiquitous ribollita, stop
JAPANESE   in at this eatery, which may be the only Japanese restaurant in the world
to be housed in a 15th-century Renaissance palazzo. High, vaulted
arches frame the Kaiten sushi conveyor belt. **Known for:** creative sushi;
Japanese barbecue prepared table-side; cocktail bar in the basement.
$ *Average main: €20* ✉ *Via de' Benci 41/r, Santa Croce* ☎ *055/2008009*
⊕ *www.komefirenze.it* ✛ *G4.*

$$$ ✕ **La Giostra.** This clubby spot, whose name means "carousel" in Ital-
ITALIAN   ian, was created by the late Prince Dimitri Kunz d'Asburgo Lorena,
Fodor'sChoice   and is now expertly run by Soldano and Dimitri, his friendly twin
★   sons. In perfect English they will describe favorite dishes from the
constantly changing menu, which regularly has terrific vegetarian and
vegan options. **Known for:** wonderful pasta; carefully curated wine
list; vegetarian and vegan options. $ *Average main: €30* ✉ *Borgo Pinti
12/r, Santa Croce* ☎ *055/241341* ⊕ *www.ristorantelagiostra.com* ⊘ *No
lunch weekends* ✛ *G3.*

$$ ✕ **Osteria de'Benci.** A few minutes from Santa Croce, this charming oste-
ITALIAN   ria serves some of the most eclectic food in Florence. Try the spaghetti
Fodor'sChoice   *degli eretici* (in tomato sauce with fresh herbs). **Known for:** weekly sea-
★   sonal specials; eclectic menu; Tuscan-heavy wine list. $ *Average main:
€15* ✉ *Borgo Santa Croce 31/r, Santa Croce* ☎ *055/2344923* ⊘ *Closed
2 wks in Aug. No lunch Mon.–Thurs.* ✛ *F5.*

$ ✕ **Perché No!** They've been making ice cream at this much-loved-by-
CAFÉ   Florentines place since 1939. Such continuity is the reason why this
Fodor'sChoice   might be the best gelateria in the historic center. **Known for:** gelati
★   made every day; one of the oldest gelaterias in the city; unusual flavors

and vegan options. $ *Average main: €3* ✉ *Santa Croce* ☎ *055/2398969* ⊕ *www.percheno.firenze.it* ▭ *No credit cards* ✛ *E3.*

$$ ✕**Touch.** Called "Touch" because it's the first restaurant in Florence
MODERN ITALIAN with the menu written on an iPad, owners Stefano, Matteo, and Max met at hotel school a few years ago and their imaginative food plays with the classics in a marvelous way. The classic bollito is redone with meats combined, encased with a raviolo covering, and graced with an egg sauce. **Known for:** creative menu that changes often; good wine list; ebullient hosts. $ *Average main: €17* ✉ *Via Fiesolana 18/r, Santa Croce* ☎ *055/2466150* ⊕ *www.touchflorence.com* ☾ *No lunch* ✛ *H3.*

$ ✕**Vestri.** This shop is devoted to chocolate in all its guises. The small
ITALIAN but sublime selection of chocolate-based gelati includes one with hot peppers. **Known for:** chocolate gelato; chocolates; hot chocolate with whipped cream. $ *Average main: €3* ✉ *Borgo Albizi 11/r, Santa Croce* ☎ *055/2340374* ⊕ *www.vestri.it* ▭ *No credit cards* ✛ *F3.*

THE OLTRARNO

$$ ✕**Alla Vecchia Bettola.** The name doesn't exactly mean "old dive," but it
TUSCAN comes pretty close. The recipes here come from "wise grandmothers" and celebrate Tuscan food in its glorious simplicity—prosciutto is sliced with a knife, portions of grilled meat are tender and ample, service is friendly, and the wine list is well priced and good. **Known for:** its grilled meats; firmly Tuscan menu; outside of centro storico but worth the taxi ride. $ *Average main: €16* ✉ *Viale Vasco Pratolini, Oltrarno* ☎ *055/224158* ☾ *Closed Sun. and Mon.* ✛ *A6.*

$ ✕**Fuori Porta.** One of the oldest and best wine bars in Florence, in busi-
WINE BAR ness since 1987, this place serves cured meats and cheeses, as well
Fodor'sChoice as daily specials such as the sublime spaghetti *al curry*. *Crostini* and
★ *crostoni*—grilled breads topped with a mélange of cheeses and meats— are the house specialty; the *verdure sott'olio* (vegetables with oil) are divine. **Known for:** the wine list; crostini and crostoni; changing daily specials. $ *Average main: €10* ✉ *Via Monte alle Croci 10/r, San Niccolò* ☎ *055/2342483* ⊕ *www.fuoriporta.it* ✛ *G6.*

$ ✕**Gelateria la Carraia.** Although it's a bit of a haul to get here (it's at
ITALIAN the foot of Ponte Carraia, two bridges down from the Ponte Vecchio), you'll be well rewarded for doing so. They do standard flavors, and then creative ones such as *limone con biscotti* (lemon sorbet with cookies), and they do both of these very well. **Known for:** super-creamy gelato; generous €1 tasting cones; every flavor is delicious. $ *Average main: €3* ✉ *Piazza Nazario Sauro 2, Santo Spirito* ☎ *055/280695* ⊕ *www. lacarraiagroup.eu* ▭ *No credit cards* ✛ *B4.*

$$ ✕**Il Santo Bevitore.** Florentines and other lovers of good food flock to
TUSCAN "The Holy Drinker" for tasty, well-priced dishes. Unpretentious white walls, dark wood furniture, and paper place mats provide the simple decor; start with the exceptional verdure sott'olio or the *terrina di fega-tini* (a creamy chicken-liver spread) before sampling any of the divine pastas, such as the fragrant spaghetti with shrimp sauce. **Known for:** pasta; verdure sott'olio; friendly waitstaff. $ *Average main: €16* ✉ *Via Santo Spirito 64/66r, Santo Spirito* ☎ *055/211264* ⊕ *www.ilsantobevi-tore.com* ☾ *No lunch Sun.* ✛ *B4.*

$$$$ MODERN ITALIAN 🍴 **La Bottega del Buon Caffè.** It translates to "The Shop of Good Coffee," which may be the biggest understatement in the Florentine dining scene. This recently relocated restaurant (it used to be outside the centro storico) is a symphony in gustatory pleasures in a room with exposed sandy brick walls and high, luminous windows. **Known for:** farm to table; cutting-edge fare; stupendous wine list. [$] *Average main: €45* ✉ *Lungarno, Cellini, 69/r, Oltrarno* ☎ *055/5535677* 🌐 *www.borgointhecity.com* ✥ *H6.*

$ TUSCAN Fodor's Choice ★ 🍴 **La Casalinga.** *Casalinga* means "housewife," and this place, which has been around since 1963, has the nostalgic charm of a mid-century kitchen with Tuscan comfort food to match. If you eat ribollita anywhere in Florence, eat it here—it couldn't be more authentic. **Known for:** ribollita; liver, Venetian style; great food at great prices. [$] *Average main: €13* ✉ *Via Michelozzi 9/r, Santo Spirito* ☎ *055/218624* 🌐 *www.trattorialacasalinga.it* ⏲ *Closed Sun., 1 wk at Christmas, and 3 wks in Aug.* ✥ *C5.*

$ TUSCAN 🍴 **Osteria Antica Mescita San Niccolò.** Always crowded, always good, and always inexpensive, the osteria is next to the church of San Niccolò and if you sit in the lower part you'll find yourself in what was once a chapel dating from the 11th century. The subtle but dramatic background is a nice complement to the food, which is simple Tuscan at its best. **Known for:** delicious soup; great, simple salads; outdoor seating in a small, lovely square. [$] *Average main: €12* ✉ *Via San Niccolò 60/r, San Niccolò* ☎ *055/2342836* 🌐 *www.osteriasanniccolo.it* ✥ *G6.*

$ TUSCAN 🍴 **Zeb.** Incredibly tasty and gently priced, Zeb stands for *zuppa e bollito* (soup and boiled things) and nothing at this small *alimentari* (delicatessen) disappoints. It's home-style Tuscan cuisine at its very best, served in unpretentious, intimate surroundings: there's room for only about 15 guests. **Known for:** fantastic soup; terrific pasta; lovely wine list. [$] *Average main: €14* ✉ *Via San Miniato 2, Oltrarno* ☎ *055/2342864* 🌐 *www.zebgastronomia.com* ⏲ *Closed Wed. No dinner Sun.–Tues.* ✥ *G6.*

WHERE TO STAY

Florence is equipped with hotels for all budgets; for instance, you can find both budget and luxury hotels in the centro storico and along the Arno. Florence has so many famous landmarks that it's not hard to find lodging with a panoramic view. The equivalent of the genteel *pensioni* of yesteryear can still be found, though they are now officially classified as "hotels." Generally small and intimate, they often have a quaint appeal that usually doesn't preclude modern plumbing. Florence's importance not only as a tourist city but also as a convention center and the site of the Pitti fashion collections guarantees a variety of accommodations.

The high demand also means that, except in winter, reservations are a must. If you find yourself in Florence with no reservations, go to **Consorzio ITA** (Stazione Centrale, Santa Maria Novella ☎ *055/282893*). You must go there in person to make a booking.

WHAT IT COSTS				
	$	**$$**	**$$$**	**$$$$**
For two people	under €125	€125–€200	€201–€300	over €300

Exact prices listed are for a standard double room in high season.

Use the coordinate (✛ B2) at the end of each listing to locate a site on the Where to Eat and Stay in Florence map. Hotel reviews have been shortened. For full information, visit Fodors.com.

AROUND THE DUOMO

$$$
HOTEL

Hermitage. All rooms here are decorated with lively wallpaper, and some have views of Palazzo Vecchio and others of the Arno. **Pros:** views; friendly, English-speaking staff; enviable position a stone's throw from the Ponte Vecchio. **Cons:** short flight of stairs to reach elevator. $ *Rooms from: €220* ✉ *Vicolo Marzio 1, Piazza della Signoria* ☎ *055/287216* ⊕ *www.hermitagehotel.com* 🛏 *28 rooms* ⦿ *Free Breakfast* ✛ *E4.*

$$$$
HOTEL

Hotel Helvetia and Bristol. From the cozy yet sophisticated lobby with its stone columns to the guest rooms decorated with prints, you might feel as if you're a guest in a sophisticated manor house. **Pros:** central location; superb staff; old-world charm. **Cons:** rooms facing the street get some noise. $ *Rooms from: €585* ✉ *Via dei Pescioni 2, Piazza della Repubblica* ☎ *055/26651* ⊕ *www.starhotelscollezione.com* 🛏 *67 rooms* ⦿ *No meals* ✛ *D3.*

$$$
B&B/INN
Fodor'sChoice
★

In Piazza della Signoria. A cozy feeling permeates these charming rooms, all of which are uniquely decorated and lovingly furnished; some have damask curtains, others fanciful frescoes in the bathroom. **Pros:** marvelous staff; tasty breakfast with a view of Piazza della Signoria; some rooms easily accommodate three. **Cons:** short flight of stairs to reach elevator. $ *Rooms from: €250* ✉ *Via dei Magazzini 2, Piazza della Signoria* ☎ *055/2399546* ⊕ *www.inpiazzadellasignoria.com* 🛏 *13 rooms* ⦿ *Free Breakfast* ✛ *F4.*

$$$$
HOTEL

Palazzo Vecchietti. If you're looking for a swank setting, and the possibility of staying in for a meal (each room has a tiny kitchenette), look no further than this hotel which, while thoroughly modern, dates to the 15th century. **Pros:** great service; central location; good-size rooms. **Cons:** no restaurant. $ *Rooms from: €473* ✉ *Via degli Strozzi 4, Duomo* ☎ *055/230–2802* ⊕ *www.palazzovecchietti.it* 🛏 *14 rooms* ⦿ *Free Breakfast* ✛ *D3.*

SAN LORENZO

$$
B&B/INN
Fodor'sChoice
★

Antica Dimora Johlea. Lively color runs rampant on the top floor of this 19th-century palazzo, with a charming flower-filled rooftop terrace where you can sip a glass of wine while taking in a view of Brunelleschi's cupola. **Pros:** great staff; cheerful rooms; honor bar. **Cons:** staff goes home at 7:30; narrow staircase to get to roof terrace; steps to breakfast room. $ *Rooms from: €143* ✉ *Via San Gallo 80, San Marco*

☎ *055/4633292* ⊕ *www.antichedimorefiorentine.it* ▭ *No credit cards* ⇱ *6 rooms* ⊙| *Free Breakfast* ✛ *E1.*

$$$
HOTEL
⊡ **Firenze Number Nine.** Those wanting an elegant hotel with a walk-in gym in the historic center should look no further. **Pros:** location; couldn't be more central; great staff; walk-in gym and spa; sumptuous breakfast. **Cons:** location; lots of street noise. Ⓢ *Rooms from: €224* ⊠ *del Conti 9/31r, San Lorenzo* ☎ *055/293777* ⊕ *www.firenzenumber-nine.com* ⇱ *45 rooms* ⊙| *No meals* ✛ *D2.*

$$
HOTEL
FAMILY
⊡ **Hotel Casci.** In this refurbished 14th-century palace, the home of Giacchino Rossini from 1851 to 1855, the friendly Lombardi family runs a hotel with spotless, functional rooms. **Pros:** helpful staff; good option for families; English-language DVD collection with good selections for kids. **Cons:** bit of a college-dorm atmosphere; small elevator. Ⓢ *Rooms from: €150* ⊠ *Via Cavour 13, San Marco* ☎ *055/211686* ⊕ *www.hotelcasci.com* ⇱ *24 rooms* ⊙| *Free Breakfast* ✛ *E1.*

$$
HOTEL
⊡ **Il Guelfo Bianco.** The 15th-century building has all modern conveniences, but Renaissance charm still shines in the high-ceiling rooms. **Pros:** stellar multilingual staff. **Cons:** rooms facing the street can be noisy. Ⓢ *Rooms from: €178* ⊠ *Via Cavour 29, San Marco* ☎ *055/288330* ⊕ *www.ilguelfobianco.it* ⇱ *40 rooms* ⊙| *Free Breakfast* ✛ *F1.*

$$
B&B/INN
⊡ **Residenza Johanna I.** Savvy travelers and those on a budget should look no further, as this *residenza* is a tremendous value for quality and location. **Pros:** great value. **Cons:** staff go home at 7; no credit cards. Ⓢ *Rooms from: €142* ⊠ *Via Bonifacio Lupi 14, San Marco* ☎ *055/481896* ⊕ *www.antichedimorefiorentine.it* ▭ *No credit cards* ⇱ *11 rooms* ⊙| *No meals* ✛ *F1.*

SANTA MARIA NOVELLA

$$
B&B/INN
⊡ **Alessandra.** An aura of grandeur pervades these clean, ample rooms a block from the Ponte Vecchio. **Pros:** several rooms have views of the Arno; the spacious suite is a bargain; tiny terrace allows for solitude while sipping a glass of wine. **Cons:** stairs to elevator; two rooms do not have en suite baths. Ⓢ *Rooms from: €150* ⊠ *Borgo Santi Apostoli 17, Santa Maria Novella* ☎ *055/283438* ⊕ *www.hotelalessandra.com* ⊙ *Closed Dec. 10–26* ⇱ *30 rooms* ⊙| *Free Breakfast* ✛ *D4.*

$$
HOTEL
⊡ **Casa Howard.** This unassuming little inn has no two rooms alike, and an aura of eclectic funk pervades: one room takes its inspiration from Japan; others are geared to families; others have access to a garden. **Pros:** great location near the basilica of Santa Maria Novella; good vibe; dogs allowed. **Cons:** limited concierge service; staff go home early in the evening; breakfast must be taken elsewhere. Ⓢ *Rooms from: €129* ⊠ *Via della Scala 18, Santa Maria Novella* ☎ *06/69924555* ⊕ *www.casahoward.com* ⇱ *13 rooms* ⊙| *No meals* ✛ *C2.*

$$$$
HOTEL
⊡ **Gallery Hotel Art.** High design resides at this art showcase near the Ponte Vecchio, where sleek, uncluttered rooms are dressed mostly in neutrals and luxe touches, such as leather headboards and kimono robes, abound. **Pros:** cool atmosphere; beautiful people; the in-house Fusion Bar, which pours delightful cocktails. **Cons:** too cool for some. Ⓢ *Rooms from: €326* ⊠ *Vicolo dell'Oro 5, Santa Maria Novella*

☎ *055/27263* 🌐 *www.lungarnocollection.com* 🛏 *74 rooms* 🍴 *Free Breakfast* ⊕ *D4.*

$$$ HOTEL 🏨 **Hotel L'Orologio.** The owner of this quietly understated, elegant hotel has a real passion for watches, which is why he chose to name his hotel after them (and why you will see them in many places). **Pros:** location; great staff; stunning breakfast room; fantastic in-house bar. **Cons:** some folks think it's too close to the train station. [$] *Rooms from: €240* ✉ *Piazza Santa Maria Novella 24, Santa Maria Novella* ☎ *055/277380* 🌐 *www.hotelorologioflorence.com* 🛏 *52 rooms* 🍴 *Free Breakfast* ⊕ *C2.*

$$$$ HOTEL Fodor's Choice ★ 🏨 **JK Place.** Hard to spot from the street, these sumptuous appointments provide all the comforts of a luxe home away from home—expect soothing earth tones in the guest rooms, free minibars, crisp linens, and a room service menu with organic dishes. **Pros:** private, intimate feel; stellar staff; free minibar; organic meal choices; small dogs allowed. **Cons:** breakfast at a shared table (which can be easily gotten around with room service); books up quickly. [$] *Rooms from: €550* ✉ *Piazza Santa Maria Novella 7* ☎ *055/2645181* 🌐 *www.jkplace.com* 🛏 *20 rooms* 🍴 *Free Breakfast* ⊕ *C3.*

$ HOTEL FAMILY 🏨 **Nuova Italia.** The genial English-speaking Viti family oversee these clean and simple rooms near the train station and well within walking distance of the sights. **Pros:** reasonable rates; close to everything. **Cons:** no elevator. [$] *Rooms from: €99* ✉ *Via Faenza 26, Santa Maria Novella* ☎ *055/268430* 🌐 *www.hotel-nuovaitalia.com* ⏲ *Closed Dec. 8–26* 🛏 *20 rooms* 🍴 *Free Breakfast* ⊕ *D1.*

$$ HOTEL 🏨 **Tornabuoni Beacci.** Florentine pensioni don't get any classier than this: old-fashioned style with enough modern comfort to keep you happy in a 14th-century palazzo. **Pros:** multilingual staff; flower-filled terrace. **Cons:** hall noise can sometimes be a problem. [$] *Rooms from: €187* ✉ *Via Tornabuoni 3, Santa Maria Novella* ☎ *055/212645* 🌐 *www.tornabuonihotels.com* 🛏 *60 rooms* 🍴 *Free Breakfast* ⊕ *D4.*

$$ B&B/INN 🏨 **Torre Guelfa.** If you want a taste of medieval Florence, try one of these character-filled guest rooms—some with canopied beds, some with balconies—housed within a 13th-century tower. **Pros:** rooftop terrace with tremendous views; wonderful staff; some family-friendly triple and quadruple rooms. **Cons:** 72 steps to get to the terrace. [$] *Rooms from: €161* ✉ *Borgo Santi Apostoli 8, Santa Maria Novella* ☎ *055/2396338* 🌐 *www.hoteltorreguelfa.com* 🛏 *31 rooms* 🍴 *Free Breakfast* ⊕ *D4.*

SANTA CROCE

$$$$ HOTEL 🏨 **The Four Seasons.** Seven years of restoration have turned this 15th-century palazzo in Florence's center into a luxury hotel where no two guest rooms are alike; many have original 17th-century frescoes, some face the garden, others quiet interior courtyards. **Pros:** a unique "city meets country" experience; the marvelous garden. **Cons:** for this price, breakfast really should be included; some feel it's a little too removed from the historic center. [$] *Rooms from: €1,100* ✉ *Borgo Pinti 99e, Santa Croce* ☎ *055/26261* 🌐 *www.fourseasons.com/florence* 🛏 *117 rooms* 🍴 *No meals* ⊕ *H1.*

$$$$ ⚏ **Hotel Regency.** Rooms dressed in richly colored fabrics and antique-
HOTEL   style furniture remain faithful to the premises' 19th-century origins as a
private mansion. **Pros:** faces one of the few green parks in the center of
Florence. **Cons:** a small flight of stairs takes you to reception. Ⓢ *Rooms*
from: €324 ⊠ *Piazza d'Azeglio 3, Santa Croce* ☎ *055/245247* ⊕ *www.*
regency-hotel.com ↝ *32 rooms* ⦿*Free Breakfast* ✛ *H1.*

$ ⚏ **Istituto Oblate dell'Assunzione.** Seven nuns run this convent, minutes
B&B/INN   from the Duomo, with spotlessly clean, simple rooms; some have views
of the cupola, and others look out onto a carefully tended garden where
you are welcome to relax. **Pros:** bargain price; great location; quiet
rooms; garden. **Cons:** curfew; no credit cards. Ⓢ *Rooms from: €40*
⊠ *Borgo Pinti 15, Santa Croce* ☎ *055/2480582* ⊕ *www.monasterystays.*
com ⊟ *No credit cards* ↝ *28 rooms* ⦿*No meals* ✛ *G3.*

$$$ ⚏ **Monna Lisa.** Although some rooms are small, they are tastefully deco-
HOTEL   rated, and best of all, housed in a 15th-century palazzo that retains some
Fodor's Choice   of its wood-coffered ceilings from the 1500s, as well as its original stair-
★   case. **Pros:** lavish buffet breakfast; cheerful staff; garden. **Cons:** rooms in
annex are less charming than those in palazzo; street noise in some rooms.
Ⓢ *Rooms from: €220* ⊠ *Borgo Pinti 27, Santa Croce* ☎ *055/2479751*
⊕ *www.monnalisa.it* ↝ *45 rooms* ⦿*Free Breakfast* ✛ *G2.*

$$ ⚏ **Morandi alla Crocetta.** You're made to feel like privileged friends of
B&B/INN   the family at this charming and distinguished residence, furnished
Fodor's Choice   comfortably in the classic style of a gracious Florentine home. **Pros:**
★   interesting, offbeat location near the sights; terrific staff; great value;
courtesy tea/coffee tray in each room. **Cons:** two flights of stairs to
reach reception and rooms. Ⓢ *Rooms from: €162* ⊠ *Via Laura 50,*
Santissima Annunziata ☎ *055/2344747* ⊕ *www.hotelmorandi.it* ↝ *10*
rooms ⦿*No meals* ✛ *H1.*

THE OLTRARNO

$$ ⚏ **Hotel Silla.** Rooms in this 15th-century palazzo, entered through a
HOTEL   courtyard lined with potted plants and sculpture-filled niches, are sim-
ply furnished and walls are papered; some have views of the Arno,
others have stuccoed ceilings. **Pros:** in the middle of everything except
the crowds. **Cons:** some readers complain of street noise and too-
small rooms. Ⓢ *Rooms from: €181* ⊠ *Via de' Renai 5, San Niccolò*
☎ *055/2342888* ⊕ *www.hotelsilla.it* ↝ *36 rooms* ⦿*Free Breakfast*
✛ *G6.*

$$$$ ⚏ **Palazzo Magnani-Feroni.** The perfect place to play the part of a Flo-
HOTEL   rentine aristocrat is here at this 16th-century palazzo, which, despite
its massive halls and sweeping staircase, could almost feel like home.
Pros: 24-hour room service; billiards room; generous buffet breakfast
including prosecco; terrific staff. **Cons:** a few steps up to the elevator;
many steps up to the rooftop terrace. Ⓢ *Rooms from: €330* ⊠ *Borgo*
San Frediano 5, Oltrarno ☎ *055/2399544* ⊕ *www.florencepalace.it*
↝ *12 rooms* ⦿*No meals* ✛ *B4.*

BEYOND THE CITY CENTER

11

$$$$
HOTEL
Fodor's Choice
★

Il Salviatino. The dramatic approach (via a curving private drive lined with cypresses) to this 14th-century villa sets the tone: it's all uphill from there, from the welcome glass of prosecco in the hall, to its remarkable rooms. **Pros:** great views; attentive staff; startlingly original breakfast; views; not in town. **Cons:** not in town; some hall noise. $ *Rooms from: €500* ✉ *Via del Salviatino 21* ☎ *055/904111* ⊕ *www.salviatino.com* ↗ *44 rooms* ○ *Free Breakfast* ✛ *G1.*

$$$
B&B/INN
FAMILY
Fodor's Choice
★

Torre di Bellosguardo. *Bellosguardo* means "beautiful view," and given the view of Florence you get here, the name is fitting. **Pros:** great for escaping heat of the city in summer; a villa experience with the city just minutes away; some rooms can accommodate three and four people. **Cons:** a car is a necessity; breakfast is not included during high season. $ *Rooms from: €300* ✉ *Via Roti Michelozzi 2* ☎ *055/2298145* ⊕ *www. torrebellosguardo.com* ↗ *16 rooms* ○ *No meals* ✛ *B6.*

$$$$
HOTEL
Fodor's Choice
★

Villa La Massa. In this tall and imposing villa, 15 minutes out of town, public rooms are outfitted in Renaissance style and guest rooms have high ceilings, plush carpeting, and deep bathtubs. **Pros:** pleasing mix of city and country life; sumptuous buffet breakfast; views of the Tuscan hills; the restaurant; phenomenal staff. **Cons:** not open year-round. $ *Rooms from: €530* ✉ *Via della Massa 24, Candeli* ☎ *055/62611* ⊕ *www.villalamassa.com* ⊙ *Closed Dec.–Mar.* ↗ *37 rooms* ○ *Free Breakfast* ✛ *H5.*

NIGHTLIFE AND PERFORMING ARTS

NIGHTLIFE

Florentines are rather proud of their nightlife options. Most bars now have some sort of happy hour, which usually lasts for many hours and often has snacks that can substitute for a light dinner. (Check, though, that the buffet is free or comes with the price of a drink.) Clubs typically don't open until very late in the evening, and don't get crowded until 1 or 2 in the morning.

AROUND THE DUOMO

Hard Rock Cafe. Hard Rock packs in young Florentines and travelers eager to sample the iconic chain's take on classic American grub. ✉ *Piazza della Repubblica, Piazza della Repubblica* ☎ *055/277841* ⊕ *www. hardrock.com.*

Fodor's Choice
★

il bar de l'O. This swanky, American-style bar is attached to the Hotel l'Orologio. It's a good spot for a well-executed cocktail with tasty snacks; when it's warm, you can sit outside and gaze at the beautiful facade of Santa Maria Novella. ✉ *Via delle Belle Donne 34/r, Duomo* ☎ *055/277380* ⊕ *www.ilbardelo.com.*

Yab. Yab never seems to go out of style, though it increasingly becomes the haunt of Florentine high schoolers and university students intent on dancing and doing vodka shots. ✉ *Via Sassetti 5/r, Piazza della Repubblica* ☎ *055/215160* ⊕ *www.yab.it.*

SAN LORENZO

Kitsch. Choose from indoor or outdoor seating and take advantage of the great list of wines by the glass. At aperitivo time €12 will buy you a truly tasty cocktail and give you access to the tremendous buffet; it's so good, you won't need dinner afterward—in fact, they called it "Apericena." That means, roughly, drink and dinner. ⊠ *Via San Gallo 22/r, San Marco* ☎ *055/3841358* ⊕ *www.kitschfirenze.com.*

SANTA CROCE

Jazz Club. Enjoy live music in this small basement club. ⊠ *Via Nuova de' Caccini 3, at Borgo Pinti, Santa Croce* ☎ *055/5271815.*

Sant'Ambrogio Caffè. Come here in the summer for outdoor seating with a view of an 11th-century church (Sant'Ambrogio) directly across the street. Come here when it's not for perfectly mixed drinks and a lively atmosphere filled with (mostly) locals. ⊠ *Piazza Sant'Ambrogio 7–8/r, Santa Croce* ☎ *055/2477277.*

THE OLTRARNO

Montecarla. People sip cocktails against a backdrop of exotic flowers, leopard-print chairs and chintz, and red walls on the two crowded floors at Montecarla. ⊠ *Via de' Bardi 2, San Niccolò* ☎ *055/2480918.*

Negroni. Well-dressed young Florentines flock to Negroni at happy hour. ⊠ *Via de' Renai 17/r, San Niccolò* ☎ *055/247883* ⊕ *www.negronifirenze.it.*

Zoe. Though it's called a *caffetteria,* and coffee is served (as well as terrific salads and burgers at lunchtime), Zoe's fine cocktails are the real draw for elegant, youngish Florentines who come here to see and be seen. Here's people-watching at its very best. ⊠ *Via de' Renai 13/r, San Niccolò* ☎ *055/243111* ⊕ *www.zoebar.it.*

PERFORMING ARTS

Florence has a lively classical music scene. The internationally famous annual Maggio Musicale lights up the musical calendar in early spring, and continues throughout most of the rest of the year. Fans of rock, pop, and hip-hop might be somewhat surprised by the absence of live acts that make it to town (for such offerings, travel to Rome or Milan is often a necessity). What it lacks in contemporary music, however, is more than made up for with its many theatrical offerings.

FESTIVALS AND SPECIAL EVENTS

Festa di San Giovanni (*Feast of St. John the Baptist*). On June 24 Florence grinds to a halt to celebrate the Festa di San Giovanni in honor of its patron saint. Many shops and bars close, and at night a fireworks display lights up the Arno and attracts thousands. ⊠ *Florence.*

Scoppio del Carro (*Explosion of the Cart*). On Easter Sunday Florentines and foreigners alike flock to the Piazza del Duomo to watch as the Scoppio del Carro, a monstrosity of a carriage, pulled by two huge oxen decorated for the occasion, makes its way through the city center and ends up in the piazza. Through an elaborate wiring system, an object representing a "dove" is sent from inside the cathedral to the Baptistery across the way. The dove sets off an explosion of fireworks that come streaming from the carriage. You have to see it to believe it. If you don't like crowds, don't worry: video replays figure prominently on the nightly newscasts afterward. ⊠ *Florence.*

MUSIC

Accademia Bartolomeo Cristofori. Also known as the Amici del Fortepiano (Friends of the Fortepiano), the Accademia Bartolomeo Cristofori sponsors fortepiano concerts throughout the year. ⊠ *Via di Camaldoli 7/r, Santo Spirito* ☎ *055/221646* ⊕ *www.accademiacristofori.it.*

Amici della Musica. This organization sponsors classical and contemporary concerts at the Teatro della Pergola (*Box office, Via Alamanni 39, Lungarno North* ☎ *055/210804* ⊕ *www.teatrodellapergola.com*). ⊠ *Via Pier Capponi 41* ⊕ *www.amicimusica.fi.it.*

Maggio Musicale Fiorentino. After some delay due to funding issues, a new music hall opened in 2014; the area is called the Parco della Musica (Music Park), and was designed by Paolo Desideri and associates. Three concert halls (two indoor, one outdoor) are planned, and only one has been completed. Maggio Musicale has taken up residence there, and continues to hold forth at the Teatro Comunale (*Corso Italia 16, Lungarno North* ☎ *055/287222* ⊕ *www.maggiofiorentino.com*). Within Italy you can purchase tickets from late April through July directly at the box office or by phone (☎ *055/2779309*). You can also buy them online. ⊠ *Via Alamanni 39* ☎ *055/2001278* ⊕ *www.operadifirenze.it/it.*

OBIHALL. This large exhibition space, formerly Teatro Saschall, hosts many events throughout the year, including a large Christmas bazaar run by the Red Cross, visiting rock stars, and trendy bands from all over Europe. ⊠ *Lungarno Aldo Moro 3, Santa Maria Novella* ☎ *055/6504112* ⊕ *www.obihall.it.*

Orchestra da Camera Fiorentina. This orchestra performs various concerts of classical music throughout the year at Orsanmichele, the grain market–turned–church. ⊠ *Via Monferrato 2, Piazza della Signoria* ☎ *055/783374* ⊕ *www.orchestrafiorentina.it.*

Orchestra della Toscana. The concert season of the Orchestra della Toscana runs from November to June. ⊠ *Via Ghibellina 101, Santa Croce* ☎ *055/2342722* ⊕ *www.orchestradellatoscana.it.*

SHOPPING

Window-shopping in Florence is like visiting an enormous contemporary-art gallery. Many of today's greatest Italian artists are fashion designers, and most keep shops in Florence. Discerning shoppers may find bargains in the street markets. ■**TIP**➜ **Do not buy any knockoff goods from any of the hawkers plying their fake Prada (or any other high-end designer) on the streets. It's illegal, and fines are astronomical if the police happen to catch you. (You pay the fine, not the vendor.)**

Shops are generally open 9–1 and 3:30–7:30, and are closed Sunday and Monday mornings most of the year. Summer (June to September) hours are usually 9–1 and 4–8, and some shops close Saturday afternoon instead of Monday morning. When looking for addresses, you'll see two color-coded numbering systems on each street. The red numbers are commercial addresses and are indicated, for example, as "31/r." The blue or black numbers are residential addresses. Most shops take major credit cards and ship purchases, but because of possible delays it's wise to take your purchases with you.

SHOPPING DISTRICTS

Florence's most fashionable shops are concentrated in the center of town. The fanciest designer shops are mainly on **Via Tornabuoni** and **Via della Vigna Nuova**. The city's largest concentrations of antiques shops are on **Borgo Ognissanti** and the Oltrarno's **Via Maggio**. The **Ponte Vecchio** houses reputable but very expensive jewelry shops, as it has since the 16th century. The area near **Santa Croce** is the heart of the leather merchants' district.

AROUND THE DUOMO

ART

Mandragora Art Store. This is one of the first attempts in Florence to cash in on the museum-store craze. It's a lovely store with reproductions of valued works of art and jewelry. ⊠ *Piazza del Duomo 50/r, Duomo* ☎ *055/2654384* ⊕ *www.mandragora.it.*

CLOTHING

Fodor's Choice ★ **Bernardo.** Come here for men's trousers, cashmere sweaters, and shirts with details like mother-of-pearl buttons. ⊠ *Via Porta Rossa 87/r, Piazza della Repubblica* ☎ *055/283333* ⊕ *www.bernardofirenze.it.*

Cabó. Missoni knitwear is the main draw at Cabó. ⊠ *Via Porta Rossa 77–79/r, Piazza della Repubblica* ☎ *055/215774.*

Diesel. Trendy Diesel started in Vicenza; its gear is on the "must have" list of many self-respecting Italian teens. ⊠ *Via dei Lamberti 13/r, Piazza della Signoria* ☎ *055/2399963* ⊕ *www.diesel.com* ☉ *Closed Sun.*

Patrizia Pepe. The Florentine designer has body-conscious clothes perfect for all ages, especially for women with a tiny streak of rebelliousness. Women who are not size zero—or close to it—need not apply. ⊠ *Via Strozzi 11/19r, Duomo* ☎ *055/2302518* ⊕ *www.patriziapepe.com.*

Spazio A. For cutting-edge fashion, these fun and funky window displays merit a stop. The shop carries such well-known designers as Alberta Ferretti and Moschino, as well as lesser-known Italian, English, and French designers. ⊠ *Via Porta Rossa 109–115/r, Piazza della Repubblica* ☎ *055/6582109* ⊕ *www.spazioafirenze.it.*

MARKETS

Mercato dei Fiori (*flower market*). Every Thursday morning from September through June the covered loggia in Piazza della Repubblica hosts a Mercato dei Fiori; it's awash in a lively riot of plants, flowers, and difficult-to-find herbs. ⊠ *Piazza della Repubblica.*

Mercato del Porcellino. If you're looking for cheery, inexpensive trinkets to take home, you might want to stop and roam through the stalls under the loggia of the Mercato del Porcellino. ✉ *Via Por Santa Maria at Via Porta Rossa, Piazza della Repubblica.*

SHOES AND LEATHER ACCESSORIES

Furla. Internationally renowned Furla makes beautiful leather bags, shoes, and wallets in up-to-the-minute designs. ✉ *Via Calzaiuoli 10/r, Piazza della Repubblica* ☎ *055/2382883* 🌐 *www.furla.com.*

SAN LORENZO

JEWELRY AND ACCESSORIES

Fodor's Choice ★ **Penko.** Renaissance goldsmiths provide the inspiration for this dazzling jewelry with a contemporary feel. ✉ *Via F. Zannetti 14/16r, Duomo* ☎ *055/211661* 🌐 *www.paolopenko.com.*

MARKETS

FAMILY Fodor's Choice ★ **Mercato Centrale.** This huge indoor food market offers a staggering selection of all things edible. Downstairs is full of vendors hawking their wares—meat, fish, fruit, vegetables; upstairs (daily 8 am–midnight) is full of food stalls offering up the best of what Italy has to offer. ✉ *Piazza del Mercato Centrale, San Lorenzo* 🌐 *www.mercatocentrale.it* ⏲ *Downstairs closed Sun., and after 2 Mon.–Sat.*

FAMILY **Mercato di San Lorenzo.** The clothing and leather-goods stalls of the Mercato di San Lorenzo in the streets next to the church of San Lorenzo have bargains for shoppers on a budget. Do please remember that you get what you pay for. ✉ *Florence.*

SANTA MARIA NOVELLA

BOOKS AND PAPER

Alberto Cozzi. You'll find an extensive line of Florentine papers and paper products here. The artisans in the shop rebind and restore books and works on paper. Their hours are tricky, so it's best to call first before stopping by. ✉ *Via del Parione 35/r, Santa Maria Novella* ☎ *055/294968.*

Fodor's Choice ★ **Pineider.** Although it has shops throughout the world, Pineider started out in Florence and still does all its printing here. Stationery and business cards are the mainstay, but the stores also sell fine leather desk accessories as well as a less stuffy, more lighthearted line of products. ✉ *Piazza Rucellai, Santa Maria Novella* ☎ *055/284656* 🌐 *www.pineider.com.*

CLOTHING

Emilio Pucci. The aristocratic Marchese di Barsento, Emilio Pucci, became an international name in the late 1950s when the stretch ski clothes he designed for himself caught on with the *dolce vita* crowd—his pseudo-psychedelic prints and "palazzo pajamas" became all the rage. ✉ *Via Tornabuoni 20–22/r, Santa Maria Novella* ☎ *055/2658082* 🌐 *www.emiliopucci.com.*

Principe. This Florentine institution sells casual clothes for men, women, and children at far-from-casual prices. It also has a great housewares department. ✉ *Via del Sole 2, Santa Maria Novella* ☎ *055/292764* ⊕ *www.principedifirenze.com.*

FRAGRANCES

Antica Officina del Farmacista Dr. Vranjes. Dr. Vranjes elevates aromatherapy to an art form, with scents for the body and for the house. ✉ *Via della Spada 9* ☎ *055/288796* ⊕ *www.drvranjes.it.*

Fodor's Choice ★ **Officina Profumo Farmaceutica di Santa Maria Novella.** The essence of a Florentine holiday is captured in the sachets of this Art Nouveau emporium of herbal cosmetics and soaps that are made following centuries-old recipes created by friars. It celebrated its 400th birthday in 2012. ✉ *Via della Scala 16, Santa Maria Novella* ☎ *055/216276* ⊕ *www.smnovella. it.*

JEWELRY

Fodor's Choice ★ **Angela Caputi.** Angela Caputi wows Florentine cognoscenti with her highly creative, often outsize plastic jewelry. A small, but equally creative, collection of women's clothing made of fine fabrics is also on offer. ✉ *Borgo Santi Apostoli 44/46* ☎ *055/216276* ⊕ *www.angelacaputi.com.*

Carlo Piccini. Still in operation after several generations, this Florentine institution sells antique jewelry and makes pieces to order; you can also get old jewelry reset here. ✉ *Ponte Vecchio 31/r, Piazza della Signoria* ☎ *055/210891* ⊕ *www.carlopiccini.com.*

Cassetti. This jeweler combines precious and semiprecious stones and metals in contemporary settings. ✉ *Ponte Vecchio 54/r, Piazza della Signoria* ☎ *055/2396028* ⊕ *www.cassetti.it.*

Gatto Bianco. This contemporary jeweler has breathtakingly beautiful pieces worked in semiprecious and precious stones. ✉ *Borgo Santi Apostoli 12/r, Santa Maria Novella* ☎ *055/282989* ⊕ *www.gattobiancogioielli.com.*

Oro Due. Gold jewelry and other beauteous objects are priced according to the level of craftsmanship and the price of gold bullion that day. ✉ *Via Lambertesca 12/r, Piazza della Signoria* ☎ *055/292143.*

Tiffany. One of Florence's oldest jewelers has supplied Italian (and other) royalty with finely crafted gems for centuries. Its selection of antique-looking classics has been updated with contemporary silver. ✉ *Via Tornabuoni 25/r, Santa Maria Novella* ☎ *055/215506* ⊕ *www.tiffany.it.*

LINENS AND FABRICS

Fodor's Choice ★ **Loretta Caponi.** Synonymous with Florentine embroidery, the luxury lace, linens, and lingerie have earned the eponymous signora worldwide renown. There's also beautiful (and expensive) clothing for children. ✉ *Piazza Antinori 4/r, Santa Maria Novella* ☎ *055/213668* ⊕ *www. lorettacaponi.com.*

SHOES AND LEATHER ACCESSORIES

Casadei. The ultimate fine leathers are crafted into classic shapes, winding up as women's shoes and bags. ✉ *Via Tornabuoni 74/r, Santa Maria Novella* ☎ *055/287240* ⊕ *www.casadei.com.*

Cellerini. In a city where it seems just about everybody wears an expensive leather jacket, Cellerini is an institution. ⊠ *Via del Sole 37/r, Santa Maria Novella* ☎ *055/282533* ⊕ *www.cellerini.it.*

Ferragamo. This classy institution, in a 13th-century palazzo, displays designer clothing and accessories, though elegant footwear still underlies the Ferragamo success. ⊠ *Via Tornabuoni 2/r, Santa Maria Novella* ☎ *055/292123* ⊕ *www.ferragamo.com.*

Giotti. You'll find a full line of leather goods, including clothing. ⊠ *Piazza Ognissanti 3–4/r, Lungarno North* ☎ *055/294265* ⊕ *www.giotti. com.*

SANTA CROCE

MARKETS

Mercato di Sant'Ambrogio. It's possible to strike gold at this lively market, where clothing stalls abut the fruits and vegetables. ⊠ *Piazza Ghiberti, off Via dei Macci, Santa Croce.*

SHOES AND LEATHER ACCESSORIES

Fodor'sChoice ★ **Scuola del Cuoio.** A consortium of leatherworkers ply their trade at Scuola del Cuoio (Leather School), in the former dormitory of the convent of Santa Croce; high-quality, fairly priced jackets, belts, and purses are sold here. ⊠ *Piazza Santa Croce 16* ☎ *055/244533* ⊕ *www. scuoladelcuoio.com.*

THE OLTRARNO

BOOKS AND PAPER

Fodor'sChoice ★ **Giulio Giannini e Figlio.** One of Florence's oldest paper-goods stores is *the* place to buy the marbleized stock, which comes in many shapes and sizes, from flat sheets to boxes and even pencils. ⊠ *Piazza Pitti 37/r, Oltrarno* ☎ *055/212621* ⊕ *www.giuliogiannini.it.*

Fodor'sChoice ★ **Il Torchio.** Photograph albums, frames, diaries, and other objects dressed in handmade paper are high-quality, and the prices lower than usual. ⊠ *Via dei Bardi 17, San Niccolò* ☎ *055/2342862* ⊕ *www.legatoriailtorchio.com.*

CLOTHING

Maçel. Browse collections by lesser-known Italian designers, many of whom use the same factories as the A-list, at this women's clothing shop. ⊠ *Via Guicciardini 128/r, Palazzo Pitti* ☎ *055/287355.*

Fodor'sChoice ★ **Madova.** Complete your winter wardrobe with a pair of high-quality leather gloves, available in a rainbow of colors and a choice of linings (silk, cashmere, and unlined), from Madova. ⊠ *Via Guicciardini 1/r, Palazzo Pitti* ☎ *055/2396526* ⊕ *www.madova.com.*

MARKETS

Santo Spirito flea market. The second Sunday of every month brings the Santo Spirito flea market. On the third Sunday of the month, vendors at the Fierucola organic fest sell such delectables as honeys, jams, spice mixes, and fresh vegetables. ⊠ *Florence.*

BEYOND THE CITY CENTER

For bargains on Italian designer clothing, you need to leave the city.

Barberino Designer Outlet. Hugo Boss, Michael Kors, Furla, and Dolce & Gabbana, among others, are all found at Barberino Designer Outlet. To get here, take the A1 to the Barberino di Mugello exit, and follow signs to the mall. ⊠ *Via Meucci snc* ☎ *055/842161* ⊕ *www.mcarthurglen.com.*

Mall. One-stop bargain shopping awaits at this collection of stores selling goods by such names as Bottega Veneta, Giorgio Armani, Loro Piana, Sergio Rossi, and Yves St. Laurent. ⊠ *Via Europa 8* ☎ *055/8657775* ⊕ *www.themall.it.*

Prada Outlet. Cognoscenti drive 45 minutes (or take the train to Montevarchi, and then a taxi) to find a bargain here. ⊠ *Levanella Spacceo, Estrada Statale 69, Montevarchi* ☎ *055/9196528* ⊕ *www.prada.com.*

FIESOLE: SIDE TRIP FROM FLORENCE

A half-day excursion to Fiesole, in the hills 8 km (5 miles) above Florence, gives you a pleasant respite from museums and a wonderful view of the city. From here the view of the Duomo gives you a new appreciation for what the Renaissance accomplished. Fiesole began life as an ancient Etruscan and later Roman village that held some power until it succumbed to barbarian invasions. Eventually it gave up its independence in exchange for Florence's protection. The medieval cathedral, ancient Roman amphitheater, and lovely old villas behind garden walls are clustered on a series of hilltops. A walk around Fiesole can take from one to two or three hours, depending on how far you stroll from the main piazza.

GETTING HERE AND AROUND

The trip from Florence by car takes 20–30 minutes. Drive to Piazza Liberta and cross the Ponte Rosso heading in the direction of the SS65/SR65. Turn right on to Via Salviati and continue on to Via Roccettini. Make a left turn to Via Vecchia Fiesolana, which will take you directly to the center of town. There are several possible routes for the two-hour walk from central Florence to Fiesole. One route begins in a residential area of Florence called Salviatino (Via Barbacane, near Piazza Edison, on the No. 7 bus route), and after a short time, offers peeks over garden walls of beautiful villas, as well as the view over your shoulder at the panorama of Florence in the valley.

VISITOR INFORMATION

Contact Fiesole Tourism Office. ⊠ *Via Portigiani 3* ☎ *055/5961311* ⊕ *www. fiesoleforyou.it.*

EXPLORING

Anfiteatro Romano (*Roman Amphitheater*). The beautifully preserved 2,000-seat Anfiteatro Romano, near the Duomo, dates from the 1st century BC and is still used for summer concerts. To the right of the amphitheater are the remains of the **Terme Romani** (Roman Baths), where you can see the gymnasium, hot and cold baths, and rectangular chamber where the water was heated. A beautifully designed **Museo Archeologico,** its facade evoking an ancient Roman temple, is built amid the ruins and contains objects dating from as early as 2000 BC. The nearby **Museo Bandini** is filled with the private collection of Canon Angelo Maria Bandini (1726–1803); he fancied 13th- to 15th-century Florentine paintings, terra-cotta pieces, and wood sculpture, which he later bequeathed to the Diocese of Fiesole. ✉ *Via Portigiani 1* ☎ *055/5961293* 🌐 *www.museidifiesole.it* 🎫 *€12, includes access to archaeological park and museums* 🕒 *Closed Tues. in Nov.–Feb.*

Badia Fiesolana. From the church of San Domenico it's a five-minute walk northwest to the Badia Fiesolana, which was Fiesole's original cathedral. Dating to the 11th century, it was first the home of the Camaldolese monks. Thanks to Cosimo il Vecchio, the complex was substantially restructured. The facade, never completed owing to Cosimo's death, contains elements of its original Romanesque decoration. The attached convent once housed Cosimo's valued manuscripts. Its mid-15th-century cloister is well worth a look. ✉ *Via della Badia dei Roccettini 11* ☎ *055/46851* 🌐 *www.eui.eu* 🕒 *Closed Sat. afternoon and Sun.*

Duomo. A stark medieval interior yields many masterpieces. In the raised presbytery, the **Cappella Salutati** was frescoed by 15th-century artist Cosimo Rosselli, but it was his contemporary, sculptor Mino da Fiesole (1430–84), who put the town on the artistic map. The Madonna on the altarpiece and the tomb of Bishop Salutati are fine examples of the artist's work. ✉ *Piazza Mino da Fiesole* ☎.

San Domenico. If you really want to stretch your legs, walk 4 km (2½ miles) toward the center of Florence along Via Vecchia Fiesolana, a narrow lane in use since Etruscan times, to the church of San Domenico. Sheltered in the church is the *Madonna and Child with Saints* by Fra Angelico, who was a Dominican friar here. ✉ *Piazza San Domenico, off Via Giuseppe Mantellini* ☎ 🕒 *Closed Sun.*

San Francesco. This lovely hilltop church has a good view of Florence and the plain below from its terrace and benches. Off the little cloister is a small, eclectic museum containing, among other things, two Egyptian mummies. Halfway up the hill you'll see sloping steps to the right; they lead to a fragrant wooded park with trails that loop out and back to the church. ✉ *Fiesole.*

WHERE TO EAT AND STAY

$$ ITALIAN

🍴 **La Reggia degli Etruschi.** Located on a steep hill on the way up to the church of San Francesco, this lovely little eatery is certainly worth the trek. Indulge in inventive reworkings of Tuscan classics, like the *mezzaluna di pera a pecorino* (little half moon pasta stuffed with pear and pecorino) sauced with Roquefort and poppy seeds. **Known for:** out-of-the-way location; good wine list and friendly service; small terrace with outdoor seating. [$] *Average main: €21* ✉ *Via San Francesco* ☎ *055/59385* 🌐 *www.lareggiadeglietruschi.com.*

$ HOTEL **Villa Aurora.** The attractive, simply furnished hotel on the main piazza takes advantage of its hilltop spot, with beautiful views in many of the rooms, some of which are on two levels with beamed ceilings and balconies. **Pros:** some rooms have pretty views; air quality better than in Florence. **Cons:** no elevator; steps to breakfast room. [$] *Rooms from: €109* ✉ *Piazza Mino da Fiesole 39* ☎ *055/59363* 🌐 *www.villaurorafiesole.com* 🛏 *23 rooms* 🍴 *Free Breakfast.*

$$$$ HOTEL **Villa San Michele.** The cypress-lined driveway provides an elegant preamble to this incredibly gorgeous (and very expensive) hotel nestled in the hills of Fiesole. **Pros:** exceptional convent conversion. **Cons:** money must be no object. [$] *Rooms from: €840* ✉ *Via Doccia 4* ☎ *055/5678200* 🌐 *www.villasanmichele.com* 🕓 *Closed Nov.–Easter* 🛏 *45 rooms* 🍴 *No meals.*

NIGHTLIFE AND PERFORMING ARTS

Estate Fiesolana. From June through August, Estate Fiesolana, a festival of theater, music, dance, and film, takes place in Fiesole's churches and in the Roman amphitheater—demonstrating that the ancient Romans knew a thing or two about acoustics. ✉ *Teatro Romano* ☎ *055/59611* 🌐 *www.comune.fiesole.fi.it.*

TUSCANY

WELCOME TO TUSCANY

TOP REASONS TO GO

★ **Piazza del Campo, Siena:** Sip a cappuccino or enjoy some gelato as you take in this spectacular shell-shape piazza.

★ **Piero della Francesca's True Cross frescoes, Arezzo:** If your Holy Grail is great Renaissance art, seek out these 12 enigmatic scenes in Arezzo's Basilica di San Francesco.

★ **San Gimignano:** Grab a spot at sunset on the steps of the Collegiata as flocks of swallows swoop in and out of the famous medieval towers.

★ **Wine tasting in Chianti:** Sample the fruits of the region's gorgeous vineyards, either at the wineries themselves or in the wine bars found in the towns.

★ **Leaning Tower of Pisa:** It may be touristy, but it's still a whole lot of fun to climb to the top and admire the view.

12

1 Lucca. This laid-back yet elegant town is surrounded by tree-bedecked 16th-century ramparts that are now a delightful promenade.

2 Pisa. Thanks to an engineering mistake, the name Pisa is recognized the world over.

3 Chianti. The heart of Italy's most famous wine region is dotted with towns. The largest, Greve, comes alive with a bustling local market every Saturday.

4 Hill Towns Southwest of Florence. The search for the best tiny hill town always leads to San Gimignano, known as the "medieval Manhattan" for its 13th-century stone towers.

5 Siena. This is one of Italy's most enchanting medieval towns

6 Arezzo and Cortona. Arezzo is best known for its sublime frescoes by Piero della Francesca. Cortona sits high above the perfectly flat Valdichiana.

7 Southern Tuscany. Among the highlights of Tuscany's southern reaches are the wine-producing centers of Montalcino and Montepulciano.

EATING AND DRINKING WELL IN TUSCANY

The influence of the ancient Etruscans—who favored the use of fresh herbs—is still felt in Tuscan cuisine three millennia later. Simple and earthy, Tuscan food celebrates the seasons with fresh vegetable dishes, wonderful bread-based soups, and meats perfumed with sage, rosemary, and thyme.

Throughout Tuscany there are excellent upscale restaurants that serve elaborate dishes, but to get a real taste of the flavors of the region, head for the family-run trattorias found in every town. The service and setting are often basic, but the food can be memorable.

Few places serve lighter fare at midday, so expect substantial meals at lunch and dinner, especially in out-of-the-way towns. Dining hours are fairly standard: lunch between 12:30 and 2, dinner between 7:30 and 10.

HOLD THE SALT

Tuscan bread is famous for what it's missing: salt. That's because it's intended to pick up seasoning from the food it accompanies; it's not meant to be eaten alone or dipped in a bowl of oil (which is a custom developed by American restaurants—it's not standard practice in Italy).

That doesn't mean Tuscans don't like to start a meal with bread, but usually it's prepared in some way. It can be grilled and drizzled with olive oil (*fettunta*), covered with chicken liver spread (*crostino nero*), or toasted, rubbed with garlic, and topped with tomatoes (*bruschetta*).

12

AFFETTATI MISTI

The name, roughly translated, means "mixed cold cuts," and it's something Tuscans do exceptionally well. A platter of cured meats, served as an antipasto, is sure to include *prosciutto crudo* (ham, cut paper-thin) and *salame* (dry sausage, prepared in dozens of ways— some spicy, some sweet). The most distinctly Tuscan affettati are made from *cinta senese* (a once nearly extinct pig found only in the heart of the region) and *cinghiale* (wild boar, which roam all over central Italy). You can eat these delicious slices unadorned or layered on a piece of bread.

PASTA

Restaurants throughout Tuscany serve dishes similar to those in Florence, but they also have their own local specialties. Many recipes are from the *nonna* (grandmother) of the restaurant's owner, handed down over time but never written down.

Look in particular for pasta creations made with *pici* (a long, thick, hand-rolled spaghetti). *Pappardelle* (a long, ribbonlike pasta noodle) is frequently paired with sauces made with game, such as *lepre* (hare) or cinghiale. In the northwest, a specialty of Lucca is *tordelli di carne al ragù* (meat-stuffed pasta with a meat sauce).

MEAT

Bistecca fiorentina (a thick T-bone steak, grilled rare) is the classic meat dish of Tuscany, but there are other specialties as well. Many menus will include *tagliata di manzo* (thinly sliced, roasted beef, drizzled with olive oil), *arista di maiale* (roast pork with sage and rosemary), and *salsiccia e fagioli* (pork sausage and beans). In the southern part of the region, don't be surprised to find *piccione* (pigeon), which can be roasted, stuffed, or baked.

WINE

Grape cultivation here also dates from Etruscan times, and vineyards are abundant, particularly in Chianti. The resulting medium-body red wine is a staple on most tables; however, you can select from a multitude of other varieties, including such reds as Brunello di Montalcino and Vino Nobile di Montepulciano and such whites as vermentino and vernaccia.

Super Tuscans (a fanciful name given to a group of wines by American journalists) now command attention as some of the best produced in Italy; they have great depth and complexity. The dessert wine *vin santo* is made throughout the region, and is often sipped with *biscotti* (twice-baked almond cookies), perfect for dunking.

Updated by Patricia Rucidlo

Midway down the Italian peninsula, Tuscany (Toscana in Italian) is distinguished by rolling hills, snowcapped mountains, dramatic cypress trees, and miles of coastline on the Tyrrhenian Sea—which all adds up to gorgeous views at practically every turn. The beauty of the landscape proves a perfect foil for the region's abundance of superlative art and architecture. It also produces some of Italy's finest wines and olive oils. The combination of unforgettable art, sumptuous landscapes, and eminently drinkable wines that pair beautifully with its simple food makes a trip to Tuscany something beyond special.

Many of Tuscany's cities and towns have retained the same fundamental character over the past 500 years. Civic rivalries that led to bloody battles centuries ago have given way to soccer rivalries. Renaissance pomp lives on in the celebration of local feast days and centuries-old traditions such as the Palio in Siena and the Giostra del Saracino (Joust of the Saracen) in Arezzo. Often, present-day Tuscans look as though they might have served as models for paintings produced hundreds of years ago. In many ways, the Renaissance lives on in Tuscany.

TUSCANY PLANNER

MAKING THE MOST OF YOUR TIME

Tuscany isn't the place for a jam-packed itinerary. One of the greatest pleasures here is indulging in rustic hedonism, marked by long lunches and showstopping sunsets. Whether by car, by bike, or on foot, you'll want to get out into the glorious landscape, but it's smart to keep your plans modest. Set a church or a hill town or an out-of-the-way restaurant as your destination, knowing that half the pleasure is in getting there—admiring as you go the stately palaces, the tidy geometry of row

12

upon row of grapevines, the fields vibrant with red poppies, sunflowers, and yellow broom.

You'll need to devise a strategy for seeing the sights. Take Siena: this beautiful, art-filled town simply can't be missed; it's compact enough that you can see the major sights on a day trip, and that's exactly what most people do. Spend the night, though, and you'll get to see the town breathe a sigh and relax on the day-trippers' departure. In Pisa, the famous tower and rest of the Camposanto are not only worth seeing but a must-see, a highlight of any trip to Italy. But nearby Lucca must not be overlooked either. In fact, this walled town has greater charms than Pisa does, making it a better choice for an overnight, so you should come up with a plan that takes in both places.

GETTING HERE AND AROUND

BUS TRAVEL

Buses are a reliable but time-consuming means of getting around the region because they tend to stop in every town. Trains are a better option in virtually every respect when you're headed to Pisa, Lucca, Arezzo, and other cities with good rail service. But for most smaller towns, buses are the only option. Be aware that making arrangements for bus travel, particularly for a non–Italian speaker, can be a test of patience.

Bus Contacts CPT. ☎ *050/884111* ⊕ *www.pisa.cttnord.it.* **SENA.** ☎ *0861/1991900* ⊕ *www.sena.it.* **SITA.** ✉ *Via Santa Caterina da Siena 17/r, Florence* ☎ *No phone* ⊕ *www.sitabus.it.* **Tra-In.** ☎ *0577/204111* ⊕ *www. trainspa.it.*

CAR TRAVEL

Driving is the only way (other than hiking or biking) to reach many of Tuscany's small towns and vineyards. The cities west of Florence are easily accessed by the A11, which leads to Lucca and then to the sea. The A1 takes you south from Florence to Arezzo and Chiusi (where you turn off for Montepulciano). Florence and Siena are connected by a *superstrada* and also the scenic Via Cassia (SR2) and even more panoramic Strada Chiantigiana (SR222), both of which thread through Chianti, skirting rolling hills and vineyards. The hill towns north and west of Siena lie along superstrade and winding local roads—all are well marked, but you should still arm yourself with a good map.

TRAIN TRAVEL

Trains on Italy's main north–south rail line stop in Florence as well as Prato, Arezzo, and Chiusi. Another major line connects Florence with Pisa, and the coastal line between Rome and Genoa passes through Pisa as well. There's regular, nearly hourly service from Florence to Lucca, and several trips a day between Florence and Siena. Siena's train station is 2 km (1 mile) north of the *centro storico* (historic center), but cabs and city buses are readily available, as is a very handy funicular.

For other parts of Tuscany—Chianti, Montalcino, and Montepulciano, for example—you're better off traveling by bus or by car. Train stations, when they exist, are far from the historic centers (usually in the valleys below hill towns), and service is infrequent.

Train Contacts Trenitalia. ☎ *892021 toll-free in Italy* ⊕ *www.trenitalia.com.*

RESTAURANTS

A meal in Tuscany traditionally consists of five courses, and every menu you encounter will be organized along this plan of antipasto, primo, secondo, contorno, and dolce. The crucial rule of restaurant dining is that you should order at least two courses. Otherwise, you'll likely end up with a lonely piece of meat and no sides. *Restaurant reviews have been shortened. For full information, visit Fodors.com.*

HOTELS

A visit to Tuscany is a trip into the country. There are plenty of good hotels in the larger towns, but the classic experience is to stay in one of the rural accommodations—often converted private homes, sometimes working farms or vineyards (known as *agriturismi*).

Although it's tempting to think you can stumble upon a little out-of-the-way hotel at the end of the day, you're better off not testing your luck. Make reservations before you go. If you don't have a reservation, you may be able to get help finding a room from the local tourist office. *Hotel reviews have been shortened. For full information, visit Fodors.com.*

WHAT IT COSTS				
	$	**$$**	**$$$**	**$$$$**
Restaurants	under €15	€15–€24	€25–€35	over €35
Hotels	under €125	€125–€200	€201–€300	over €300

Prices in the dining reviews are the average cost of a main course at dinner, or, if dinner is not served, at lunch. Prices in the reviews are the lowest cost of a standard double room in high season.

VISITOR INFORMATION

Many towns in Tuscany have tourist information offices, which can be useful resources for trip-planning advice (and sometimes maps). Such offices are typically open from 8:30 to 1 and 3:30 to 6 or 7; those in smaller towns are usually closed Saturday afternoon and Sunday, and often shut down entirely from early November through Easter.

The tourist information office in Greve is an excellent source for general information about the Chianti wine region and its hilltop towns. In Siena, the centrally located tourist office in Piazza del Campo has information about Siena and its province. Both offices book hotel rooms for a nominal fee. Offices in smaller towns can also be a good place to check if you need last-minute accommodations.

LUCCA

Ramparts built in the 16th and 17th centuries enclose a charming fortress town filled with churches (99 of them), terra-cotta–roofed buildings, and narrow cobblestone streets, along which locals maneuver bikes to do their daily shopping. Here Caesar, Pompey, and Crassus agreed to rule Rome as a triumvirate in 56 BC; Lucca was later the first Tuscan town to accept Christianity. The town still has a mind of its own, and when most of Tuscany was voting communist as a matter of course, Lucca's citizens rarely followed suit. The famous composer Giacomo Puccini (1858–1924) was born here; he is celebrated during the summer Opera Theater and Music Festival of Lucca. The ramparts circling the centro storico are the perfect place to stroll, bicycle, or just admire the view.

GETTING HERE AND AROUND

You can reach Lucca easily by train from Florence; the centro storico is a short walk from the station. If you're driving, take the A11/E76.

VISITOR INFORMATION

Contact Lucca Tourism Office. ⊠ *Piazzale Verdi* ☎ *0583/583150* ⊕ *luccaitinera.it.*

EXPLORING

Traffic (including motorbikes) is restricted in the walled historic center of Lucca. Walking is the best, most enjoyable way to get around. Or you can rent a bicycle; getting around on bike is easy, as the center is quite flat.

TOP ATTRACTIONS

Duomo. The blind arches on the cathedral's facade are a fine example of the rigorously ordered Pisan Romanesque style, in this case happily enlivened by an extremely varied collection of small, carved columns. Take a closer look at the decoration of the facade and that of the portico below; they make this one of the most entertaining church exteriors in Tuscany. The Gothic interior contains a moving Byzantine crucifix—called the Volto Santo, or Holy Face—brought here, according to legend, in the 8th century (though it probably dates from between the 11th and early 13th century). The masterpiece of the Sienese sculptor Jacopo della Quercia (circa 1371–1438) is the marble *Tomb of Ilaria del Carretto* (1407–08). ⊠ *Piazza San Martino* ☎ *0583/490530* ⊕ *www. museocattedralelucca.it* 🎫 *€3.*

FAMILY
Fodor's Choice
★

Passeggiata delle Mura. Any time of day when the weather is nice, you can find the citizens of Lucca cycling, jogging, strolling, or kicking a soccer ball in this green, beautiful, and very large linear park—neither inside nor outside the city but rather right atop and around the ring of ramparts that defines Lucca. Sunlight streams through two rows of tall plane trees to dapple the *passeggiata delle mura* (walk on the walls), which is 4.2 km (2½ miles) in length. Ten bulwarks are topped with lawns, many with picnic tables and some with play equipment for children. Be aware at all times of where the edge is—there are no railings, and the drop to the ground outside the city is a precipitous 40 feet. ⊠ *Lucca* ⊕ *www.lemuradilucca.it.*

QUICK BITES

Gelateria Veneta. This place makes outstanding gelato, sorbet, and ices (some sugar-free). They prepare their confections three times a day, using the same recipes with which the Brothers Arnoldo opened the place in 1927. Known for: longtime institution; stuffed frozen fruits; delicious ices. ✉ *Via V. Veneto 74* ☎ *0583/467037* 🌐 *www.gelateriaveneta.net* 🕓 *Closed Nov.–Mar.*

FAMILY **Piazza dell'Anfiteatro Romano.** Here's where the ancient Roman amphitheater once stood; some of the medieval buildings built over the amphitheater retain its original oval shape and brick arches. ✉ *Piazza Anfiteatro.*

San Frediano. A 14th-century mosaic decorates the facade of this church just steps from the Anfiteatro. Inside are works by Jacopo della Quercia (circa 1371–1438) and Matteo Civitali (1436–1501), as well as the lace-clad mummy of St. Zita (circa 1218–78), the patron saint of household servants. ✉ *Piazza San Frediano* ☎ *No phone.*

San Michele in Foro. The facade here is even more fanciful than that of the Duomo. Its upper levels have nothing but air behind them (after the front of the church was built, there were no funds to raise the nave), and the winged Archangel Michael, who stands at the very top, seems precariously poised for flight. The facade, heavily restored in the 19th century, displays busts of such 19th-century Italian patriots as Garibaldi and Cavour. Check out the superb Filippino Lippi (1457/58–1504) panel painting of Saints Jerome, Sebastian, Rocco, and Helen in the right transept. ✉ *Piazza San Michele.*

FAMILY **Torre Guinigi.** The tower of the medieval Palazzo Guinigi contains one of the city's most curious sights: a grove of ilex trees has grown at the top of the tower, and their roots have pushed their way into the room below. From the top you have a magnificent view of the city and the surrounding countryside. (Only the tower is open to the public, not the palazzo.) ✉ *Via Sant'Andrea* ☎ *0583/48090* 🎫 *€4.*

WORTH NOTING

Museo Nazionale di Villa Guinigi. On the eastern end of the historic center, this sadly overlooked museum has an extensive collection of local Etruscan, Roman, Romanesque, and Renaissance art. The museum represents an overview of Lucca's artistic traditions from Etruscan times until the 17th century, housed in the 15th-century former villa of the Guinigi family. ✉ *Via della Quarquonia 4* ☎ *0583/496033* 🌐 *www.luccamuseinazionali.it* 🎫 *€4* 🕓 *Closed Mon.*

WHERE TO EAT

$$ TUSCAN Fodor's Choice ★ 🍴 **Buca di Sant'Antonio.** The staying power of Buca di Sant'Antonio—it's been around since 1782—is the result of superlative Tuscan food brought to the table by waitstaff who don't miss a beat. The menu includes the simple but blissful *tortelli lucchesi al sugo* (meat-stuffed pasta with a tomato-and-meat sauce), and more daring dishes such as roast *capretto* (kid) with herbs. **Known for:** superlative pastas; excellent sommelier; classy, family-run ambience. [$] *Average main: €17* ✉ *Via*

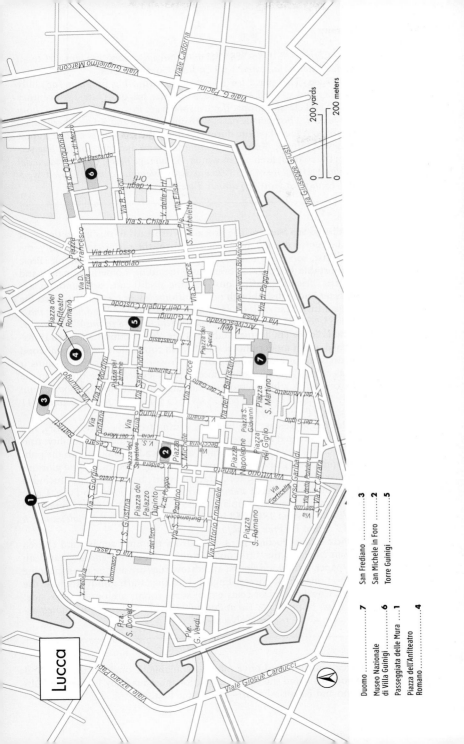

Lucca

200 yards
200 meters

Duomo **7**

Museo Nazionale
di Villa Guinigi ... **6**

Passeggiata delle Mura **1**

Piazza dell'Anfiteatro
Romano **4**

San Frediano **3**

San Michele in Foro **2**

Torre Guinigi **5**

della Cervia 3 ☎ 0583/55881 🌐 www.bucadisantantonio.com ⏲ Closed Mon., 1 wk in Jan., and 1 wk in July. No dinner Sun.

$$ TUSCAN 🍴 **Il Giglio.** This place for all seasons, with a big fireplace for chilly weather and an outdoor terrace in summer, has quiet late-19th-century charm and classic cuisine. If mushrooms are in season, try the *tacchoni con funghi,* a homemade pasta with mushrooms and a native herb called *nepitella.* A local favorite during winter is the *coniglio con olive* (rabbit stew with olives). **Known for:** creative menu and ingredients; fine service; the roaring fireplace in winter. [$] *Average main: €18 ✉ Piazza del Giglio 2 ☎ 0583/494508 🌐 www.ristorantegiglio.com ⏲ Closed Wed. and 15 days in Nov. No dinner Tues.*

WHERE TO STAY

$ B&B/INN FAMILY Fodor's Choice ★ 🏨 **Albergo San Martino.** The brocade bedspreads of this inn in the heart of the centro storico are fresh and crisp, the proprietor friendly, the breakfast, served in a cheerful apricot room, more than ample. **Pros:** comfortable beds; great breakfast, including homemade cakes and pastries; friendly staff. **Cons:** parking is difficult; surroundings are pleasant and stylish though not luxurious; a wee bit of noise when the Lucca Music Festival is on. [$] *Rooms from: €105 ✉ Via della Dogana 9 ☎ 0583/469181 🌐 www.albergosanmartino.it 🛏 8 rooms 🍽 No meals.*

$$ HOTEL 🏨 **Hotel Ilaria.** The former stables of the Villa Bottini have been transformed into a modern hotel with stylish rooms done in a warm wood veneer with blue-and-white fittings. **Pros:** one Fodor's reader sums it up as a "nice, modern small hotel"; free bicycles. **Cons:** though in the city center, it's a little removed from main attractions. [$] *Rooms from: €189 ✉ Via del Fosso 26 ☎ 0583/47615 🌐 www.hotelilaria.com 🛏 41 rooms 🍽 Free Breakfast.*

$$ HOTEL 🏨 **Palazzo Alexander.** The building, dating from the 12th century, has been restructured to create the ease common to Lucchesi nobility: timbered ceilings, warm yellow walls, and brocaded chairs adorn the public rooms, and guest rooms have high ceilings and that same glorious damask. **Pros:** intimate feel; gracious staff; bacon and eggs included in the buffet breakfast; a short walk from San Michele in Foro. **Cons:** some Fodor's readers complain of too-thin walls. [$] *Rooms from: €179 ✉ Via S. Giustina 48 ☎ 0583/583571 🌐 www.hotelpalazzoalexander.it 🛏 13 rooms 🍽 Free Breakfast.*

$ HOTEL 🏨 **Piccolo Hotel Puccini.** Steps away from the busy square and church of San Michele, this little hotel is quiet and calm—and a great deal: wallpaper, hardwood floors, and throw rugs are among the handsome decorations. **Pros:** cheery, English-speaking staff; good value for the price. **Cons:** breakfast costs extra; some rooms are on the dark side. [$] *Rooms from: €95 ✉ Via di Poggio 9 ☎ 0583/55421 🌐 www.hotelpuccini.com 🛏 14 rooms 🍽 No meals.*

SHOPPING

Lucca's justly famed olive oils are available throughout the city (and exported around the world). Look for those made by Fattoria di Fubbiano and Fattoria Fabbri—two of the best.

Antica Bottega di Prospero. Stop by this shop for top-quality local food products, including farro, dried porcini mushrooms, olive oil, and wine. ✉ *Via San Lucia 13.*

Fodor'sChoice ★ **Caniparoli.** Chocolate lovers will be pleased with the selection of artisanal chocolates. This artisanal shop is so serious about their sweets that they do not make any in August (so the shop closes) because of the heat. ✉ *Via San Paolino 96* ☎ *0583/53456* ⊕ *www.caniparolicioccolateria.it.*

Fodor'sChoice ★ **Enoteca Vanni.** A huge selection of wines, as well as an ancient cellar, make this place worth a stop. For the cost of the wine only, tastings can be organized through the shopkeepers and are held in the cellar or outside in a lovely little piazza. All of this can be paired with affettati misti and cheeses of the highest caliber. ✉ *Piazza San Salvatore 7* ☎ *0583/491902* ⊕ *www.enotecavanni.com.*

Fodor'sChoice ★ **Pasticceria Taddeucci.** A particularly delicious version of *buccellato*—the sweet, anise-flavored bread with raisins that is a Luccan specialty—is baked at Pasticceria Taddeucci. ✉ *Piazza San Michele 34* ☎ *0583/494933* ⊕ *www.buccellatotaddeucci.com.*

SPORTS AND THE OUTDOORS

A good way to spend the afternoon is to go biking around the large path atop the city's ramparts. There are two good spots right next to each other where you can rent bikes. The prices are about the same (about €15 per day and €3 per hour for city bikes) and they are centrally located, just beside the town wall.

Berutto Nedo. The vendors at Berutto Nedo, who sell bikes near the Piazza dell'Anfiteatro, are friendly and speak English. ✉ *Via dei Gaspari Alcide 83/a, Anfiteatro* ☎ *0583/517073* ⊕ *www.beruttonedo.com.*

Poli Antonio Biciclette. This is the best option for bicycle rental on the east side of town. ✉ *Piazza Santa Maria 42, Lucca East* ☎ *0583/493787* ⊕ *www.biciclettepoli.com.*

PISA

If you can get beyond the kitsch of the stalls hawking cheap souvenirs around the Leaning Tower, you'll find that Pisa has much to offer. Its treasures aren't as abundant as those of Florence, to which it is inevitably compared, but the cathedral-baptistery-tower complex of Piazza del Duomo, known collectively as the Campo dei Miracoli (Field of Miracles), is among the most dramatic settings in Italy.

Pisa may have been inhabited as early as the Bronze Age. It was certainly populated by the Etruscans and, in turn, became part of the Roman Empire. In the early Middle Ages this city on the Arno River flourished as an economic powerhouse—along with Amalfi, Genoa, and Venice, it was one of the four maritime republics. The city's economic and political power ebbed in the early 15th century as it fell under Florence's domination, though it enjoyed a brief resurgence under Cosimo I de' Medici in the mid-16th century. Pisa sustained heavy damage during

World War II, but the Duomo and the Leaning Tower were spared, along with some other grand Romanesque structures.

GETTING HERE AND AROUND

Pisa is an easy hour's train ride from Florence. By car it's a straight shot on the Firenze–Pisa–Livorno ("Fi-Pi-Li") autostrada. The Pisa–Lucca train runs frequently and takes about 30 minutes.

VISITOR INFORMATION

Contact Pisa Tourism Office. ⊠ *Piazza Vittorio Emanuele II 16* ☎ *050/550100* ⊕ *www.turismo.pisa.it.*

EXPLORING

Pisa, like many Italian cities, is best explored on foot, and most of what you'll want to see is within walking distance. The views along the Arno River are particularly grand and shouldn't be missed—there's a feeling of spaciousness that isn't found along the Arno in Florence.

As you set out, note that there are various combination-ticket options for sights on the Piazza del Duomo.

TOP ATTRACTIONS

Battistero. This lovely Gothic baptistery, which stands across from the Duomo's facade, is best known for the pulpit carved by Nicola Pisano (circa 1220–84; father of Giovanni Pisano) in 1260. Every half hour, an employee will dramatically close the doors, then intone, thereby demonstrating how remarkable the acoustics are in the place. ⊠ *Piazza del Duomo* ☎ *050/835011* ⊕ *www.opapisa.it* ☑ *€5, discounts available if bought in combination with tickets for other monuments.*

Duomo. Pisa's cathedral brilliantly utilizes the horizontal marble-stripe motif (borrowed from Moorish architecture) that became common to Tuscan cathedrals. It is famous for the Romanesque panels on the transept door facing the tower that depict scenes from the life of Christ. The beautifully carved 14th-century pulpit is by Giovanni Pisano. ⊠ *Piazza del Duomo* ☎ *050/835011* ⊕ *www.opapisa.it* ☑ *€5.*

Fodor's Choice ★ **Leaning Tower (Torre Pendente).** Legend holds that Galileo conducted an experiment on the nature of gravity by dropping metal balls from the top of the 187-foot-high Leaning Tower of Pisa (whether it's true is a matter of debate). Work on this tower, built as a campanile for the Duomo, started in 1173: the lopsided settling began when construction reached the third story. The tower's architects attempted to compensate by making the remaining floors slightly taller on the leaning side, but the extra weight made the problem worse. By the late 20th century, many feared the tower would simply topple over. The structure has since been firmly anchored to the earth, and by 2002, the tower was restored to its original tilt of 300 years ago. Reservations, which are essential, can be made online or by calling the Museo dell'Opera del Duomo; it's also possible to arrive at the ticket office and book for the same day. ⊠ *Piazza del Duomo* ☎ *050/835011* ⊕ *www.opapisa.it* ☑ *€18.*

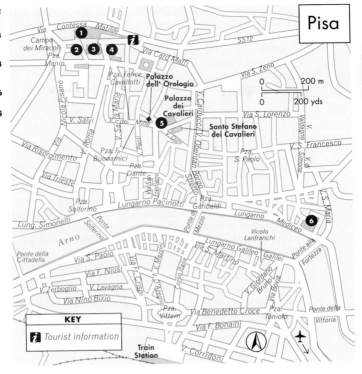

KEY

ℹ️ *Tourist information*

WORTH NOTING

Camposanto. According to legend, the cemetery—a walled structure on the western side of the Piazza dei Miracoli—is filled with earth that returning Crusaders brought back from the Holy Land. Contained within are numerous frescoes, notably *The Drunkenness of Noah*, by Renaissance artist Benozzo Gozzoli (1422–97), and the disturbing *Triumph of Death* (14th century; artist uncertain), whose subject matter shows what was on people's minds in a century that saw the ravages of the Black Death. ✉ *Piazza del Duomo* ☎ *050/835011* ⊕ *www.opapisa. it* ✒ *€5, discounts available if bought in combination with tickets for other monuments.*

Museo Nazionale di San Matteo. On the north bank of the Arno, this museum contains some beautiful examples of local Romanesque and Gothic art. ✉ *Piazza Matteo in Soarta 1* ☎ *050/541865* ✒ *€5.*

Piazza dei Cavalieri. The piazza, with its fine Renaissance **Palazzo dei Cavalieri, Palazzo dell'Orologio,** and Chiesa di **Santo Stefano dei Cavalieri,** was laid out by Giorgio Vasari in about 1560. The square was the seat of the Ordine dei Cavalieri di San Stefano (Order of the Knights of St. Stephen), a military and religious institution meant to defend the coast from possible invasion by the Turks. Also in this square is the prestigious **Scuola Normale Superiore,** founded by Napoléon in 1810 on the French model. Here graduate students pursue doctorates in literature, philosophy, mathematics, and science. In front of the school is a large statue of Ferdinando I de' Medici dating from 1596. On the extreme left is the tower where the hapless Ugolino della Gherardesca (died 1289) was imprisoned with his two sons and two grandsons—legend holds that he ate them. Dante immortalized him in Canto XXXIII of his *Inferno*. Duck into the **Church of Santo Stefano** (if you're lucky enough to find it open) and check out Bronzino's splendid *Nativity of Christ* (1564–65). ⊠ *Piazza dei Cavalieri.*

WHERE TO EAT

$$$
TUSCAN
Fodor's Choice
★

✕ **Beny.** Apricot walls hung with etchings of Pisa make this small, single-room restaurant warmly romantic. Husband and wife Damiano and Sandra Lazzerini have been running the place for two decades, and it shows in their obvious enthusiasm while talking about the menu (fish is a focus) and daily specials, which often astound. **Known for:** superb fish dishes; gracious service; wine list. $ *Average main: €27* ⊠ *Piazza Gambacorti 22* ☎ *050/25067* ◷ *Closed Sun. and 2 wks in mid-Aug. No lunch Sat.*

$
ITALIAN

✕ **Osteria dei Cavalieri.** This charming white-wall restaurant, a few steps from Piazza dei Cavalieri, is reason enough to come to Pisa. They can do it all here—serve up exquisitely grilled fish dishes, please vegetarians, and prepare tagliata for meat lovers. **Known for:** land tasting menu; sea tasting menu; vegetable tasting menu. $ *Average main: €14* ⊠ *Via San Frediano 16* ☎ *050/580858* ⊕ *www.osteriacavalieri.pisa.it* ◷ *Closed Sun., 2 wks in Aug., and Dec. 29–Jan. 7. No lunch Sat.*

$
ITALIAN

✕ **Trattoria la Faggiola.** It's only seconds away from the Leaning Tower, which probably explains the "No Pizza" sign written in big letters on the blackboard outside. Inside, another blackboard lists two or three primi and secondi: the problem is deciding, because everything's good, from the *pasta pasticciata con speck e carciofi* (oven-baked penne with cured ham and artichokes) to the finishing touch of *castagnaccio con crema di ricott*a (a chestnut flan topped with ricotta cream). **Known for:** great food at affordable prices; menu that changes daily; young, polite waitstaff. $ *Average main: €10* ⊠ *Via della Faggiola 1* ☎ *050/556179* ⊕ *www.trattoriadellafaggiola.it* ▭ *No credit cards* ◷ *Closed Tues.*

WHERE TO STAY

$
B&B/INN
FAMILY
Fodor's Choice
★

▦ **Fattoria di Migliarino.** Martino Salviati and his wife Giovanna have turned their working *fattoria* (farm)—on which they raise soybeans, corn, and sugar beets—into an inn with charming, spacious apartments that accommodate two to eight people and are rustically furnished, many of them with fireplaces. **Pros:** near Pisa airport, a good choice for a tranquil last night in Italy; quiet country living; the pool. **Cons:** mandatory one-week apartment stay during high season; pets not allowed. $ *Rooms from: €110* ⊠ *Via dei Pini 289, 10 km (6 miles) northwest of Pisa, Migliarino* ☎ *050/803046, 335/6608411 mobile* ⊕ *www.fattoriadimigliarino.it* ⤴ *23 rooms* ¡◎¡ *Free Breakfast.*

12

$$ 🛏 **Hotel Relais dell'Orologio.** What used to be a private family palace is
HOTEL now an intimate hideaway where 18th-century antiques fill the rooms
and public spaces and some rooms have stenciled walls and wood-
beam ceilings. **Pros:** location—in the center of town, but on a quiet side
street; its simple elegance; cheery guest rooms. **Cons:** breakfast costs
extra. $ *Rooms from: €140* ⊠ *Via della Faggiola 12/14, off Campo dei
Miracoli* ☎ *050/830361* ⊕ *www.hotelrelaisorologio.com* ⇥ *19 rooms*
¶○¶ *Free Breakfast.*

$ 🛏 **Royal Victoria.** In a pleasant palazzo facing the Arno, a 10-minute
HOTEL walk from the Campo dei Miracoli, the hotel has room styles that
range from the 1800s, complete with frescoes, to the 1920s; the most
charming are in the old tower. **Pros:** friendly staff; lovely views of the
Arno from many rooms. **Cons:** rooms vary significantly in size; all are a
little worn; eight rooms do not have private bath. $ *Rooms from: €85*
⊠ *Lungarno Pacinotti 12* ☎ *050/940111* ⊕ *www.royalvictoria.it* ⇥ *48
rooms* ¶○¶ *Free Breakfast.*

CHIANTI

This is the heartland: both sides of the Strada Chiantigiana (SR222) are
embraced by glorious panoramic views of vineyards, olive groves, and
castle towers. Traveling south from Florence, you first reach the aptly
named one-street town of Strada in Chianti. Farther south, the number
of vineyards on either side of the road dramatically increases—as do
the signs inviting you in for a free tasting of wine. Beyond Strada lies
Greve in Chianti, completely surrounded by wineries and filled with
wineshops. There's art to be had as well: Passignano, west of Greve,
has an abbey that shelters a 15th-century *Last Supper* by Domenico
and Davide Ghirlandaio. Farther still, along the Strada Chiantigiana,
are Panzano and Castellina in Chianti, both hill towns. It's from near
Panzano and Castellina that branch roads head to the other main towns
of eastern Chianti: Radda in Chianti, Gaiole in Chianti, and Castelnu-
ovo Berardenga.

The Strada Chiantigiana gets crowded during the high season, but no
one is in a hurry. The slow pace gives you time to soak up the beauti-
ful scenery.

GREVE IN CHIANTI

*27 km (17 miles) south of Florence, 40 km (25 miles) northeast of
Colle Val d'Elsa.*

If there is a capital of Chianti, it is Greve, a friendly market town with
no shortage of cafés, enoteche, and crafts shops lining its streets.

GETTING HERE AND AROUND
Driving from Florence or Siena, Greve is easily reached via the Strada
Chiantigiana (SR222). SITA buses travel frequently between Florence
and Greve. Tra-In and SITA buses connect Siena and Greve, but a direct
trip is virtually impossible. There is no train service.

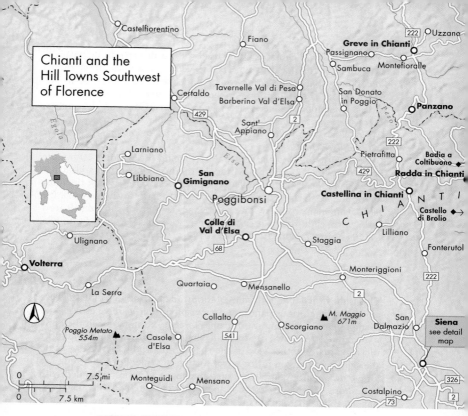

Map: Chianti and the Hill Towns Southwest of Florence

Castelfiorentino · Fiano · Uzzano · 222 · Greve in Chianti · Passignano · Sambuca · Montefioralle · San Donato in Poggio · Certaldo · Tavernelle Val di Pesa · Barberino Val d'Elsa · 429 · 2 · Panzano · Sant' Appiano · Esola · Elsa · 222 · Pietrafitta · Badia a Coltibuono · Larniano · 429 · Radda in Chianti · Libbiano · San Gimignano · Castellina in Chianti · C H I A N T I · Poggibonsi · Castello di Brolio · Colle di Val d'Elsa · Lilliano · Ulignano · 68 · Staggia · Fonterutol · Volterra · Monteriggioni · 222 · La Serra · Quartaia · Mensanello · 2 · Collalto · M. Maggio 671m · San Dalmazio · Siena see detail map · Poggio Metato 554m · Scorgiano · Casole d'Elsa · 541 · 0 7.5 mi · 0 7.5 km · Moneguidi · Mensano · Costalpino · 326 · 73 · 2

VISITOR INFORMATION

Contact Greve in Chianti tourism office. ⊠ *Piazza Matteotti 10* ☎ *055/8546299.*

EXPLORING

Montefioralle. A tiny hilltop hamlet, about 2 km (1 mile) west of Greve in Chianti, Montefioralle is the ancestral home of Amerigo Vespucci (1454–1512), the mapmaker, navigator, and explorer who named America. (His niece Simonetta may have been the inspiration for Sandro Botticelli's *Birth of Venus*, painted sometime in the 1480s.) ⊠ *Greve in Chianti.*

Piazza Matteotti. Greve's gently sloping and asymmetrical central piazza is surrounded by an attractive arcade with shops of all kinds. In the center stands a statue of the discoverer of New York harbor, Giovanni da Verrazzano (circa 1480–1527). Check out the lively market held here on Saturday morning. ⊠ *Greve in Chianti.*

WHERE TO EAT

$ × **Da Padellina.** Locals don't flock to this restaurant on the outskirts of
TUSCAN Strada in Chianti for the art on the walls, some of it questionable, most of it kitsch, but for the bistecca fiorentina. As big as a breadboard and served rare, one of these justly renowned steaks is enough to feed a family of four, with doggy bags willingly provided if required. **Known**

for: great grilled meats; unpretentious local choice; large, diverse wine list. $ *Average main: €11* ⊠ *Via Corso del Popolo 54, 10 km (6 miles) north of Greve* ☎ *055/858388* ⊘ *Closed Tues.*

$ ✕ **Enoteca Fuoripiazza.** Detour off Greve's flower-strewn main square
TUSCAN for food that relies heavily on local ingredients (like cheese and salami produced nearby). The lengthy wine list provides a bewildering array of choices to pair with affettati misti or one of their primi—the *pici* (a thick, short noodle) are deftly prepared here. **Known for:** alfresco dining; local cheese and salami; attentively prepared food. $ *Average main: €14* ⊠ *Via I Maggio 2* ☎ *055/8546313* ⊕ *www.enotecafuoripiazza.it* ⊘ *Closed Mon. Nov.–Apr.*

$$ ✕ **Ristoro di Lamole.** Although off the beaten path up a winding road lined
TUSCAN with olive trees and vineyards, this place is worth the effort to find. The view from the outdoor terrace is divine, as is the simple, exquisitely prepared Tuscan cuisine: start with the bruschetta drizzled with olive oil or the sublime *verdure sott'olio* (marinated vegetables) before moving on to any of the fine secondi. **Known for:** fantastic primi; sweeping view from the terrace; your hosts Paolo and Filippo. $ *Average main: €19* ⊠ *Via di Lamole 6, Località Lamole* ☎ *055/8547050* ⊕ *www.ristorodilamole.it* ⊘ *Closed Wed. and Nov.–Apr.*

WHERE TO STAY

$ 🛏 **Albergo del Chianti.** Simply but pleasantly decorated bedrooms with
B&B/INN plain modern cabinets and wardrobes and wrought-iron beds have views of the town square or out over the tile rooftops toward the surrounding hills. **Pros:** central location; best value in Greve; swimming pool. **Cons:** rooms facing the piazza can be noisy; small bathrooms. $ *Rooms from: €110* ⊠ *Piazza Matteotti 86* ☎ *055/853763* ⊕ *www.albergodelchianti.it* ⊘ *Closed Jan.* ⏎ *16 rooms* ⎮◯⎮ *Free Breakfast.*

$$$ 🛏 **Villa Bordoni.** David and Catherine Gardner, Scottish expats, have
B&B/INN transformed a ramshackle 16th-century villa into a stunning little
Fodor'sChoice retreat where no two rooms are alike—all have stenciled walls; some
★ have four-poster beds, others small mezzanines. **Pros:** splendidly isolated in the hills above Greve; beautiful decor; wonderful hosts. **Cons:** on a long and bumpy dirt road; need a car to get around; books up quickly. $ *Rooms from: €210* ⊠ *Via San Cresci 31/32* ☎ *055/8546230* ⊕ *www.villabordoni.com* ⊘ *Closed 3 wks in Jan. and Feb.* ⏎ *11 rooms* ⎮◯⎮ *Free Breakfast.*

$$ 🛏 **Villa Il Poggiale.** Renaissance gardens, beautiful rooms with high ceil-
B&B/INN ings and elegant furnishings, a panoramic pool, and expert staff are just
Fodor'sChoice a few of the things that make a stay at this 16th-century villa memo-
★ rable. **Pros:** beautiful gardens and panoramic setting; elegant historical building; exceptionally professional staff. **Cons:** a little isolated, making private transportation necessary; some rooms face a country road and may be noisy during the day. $ *Rooms from: €155* ⊠ *Via Empolese 69, 20 km (12 miles) northwest of Greve, San Casciano Val di Pesa* ☎ *055/828311* ⊕ *www.villailpoggiale.it* ⊘ *Closed Jan. and Feb.* ⏎ *22 rooms* ⎮◯⎮ *Free Breakfast.*

12

PANZANO

7 km (4½ miles) south of Greve, 36 km (22 miles) south of Florence.

The magnificent views of the valleys of the Pesa and Greve rivers easily make Panzano one of the prettiest stops in Chianti. The triangular Piazza Bucciarelli is the heart of the new town. A short stroll along Via Giovanni da Verrazzano brings you up to the old town, Panzano Alto, which is still partly surrounded by medieval walls. The town's 13th-century castle is now almost completely absorbed by later buildings (its central tower is now a private home).

GETTING HERE AND AROUND

From Florence or Siena, Panzano is easily reached by car along the Strada Chiantigiana (SR222). SITA buses travel frequently between Florence and Panzano. From Siena, the journey by bus is extremely difficult because SITA and Tra-In do not coordinate their schedules. Train service is not available.

EXPLORING

San Leolino. Ancient even by Chianti standards, this hilltop church probably dates from the 10th century, but was completely rebuilt in the Romanesque style sometime in the 13th century. It has a 14th-century cloister worth seeing. The 16th-century terra-cotta tabernacles are attributed to Giovanni della Robbia, and there's also a remarkable triptych (attributed to the Master of Panzano) that was executed sometime in the mid-14th century. Open days and hours are unpredictable; check with the tourist office in Greve in Chianti for the latest. ✉ *Località San Leolino, 3 km (2 miles) south of Panzano.*

WHERE TO EAT AND STAY

$$ INTERNATIONAL FAMILY Fodor's Choice ★

🍴 **Dario Doc.** Local butcher and restaurateur, Dario Cecchini, has extended his empire of meat to include this space located directly above his butcher's shop. Here, you'll find only four items on the menu: the Dario DOC, a half-pound burger, without bun, served with roasted potatoes and onions; the Super Dario, the former with salad and beans added; the Welcome, with four different dishes of beef and pork served with fresh garden vegetables; and a vegetarian dish. **Known for:** the best burger in Italy; performing waitstaff; lively atmosphere. [$] *Average main: €15* ✉ *Via XX Luglio 11* ☎ *055/852176* 🌐 *www.dariocecchini.com* 🕒 *Closed Sun.*

$$$ TUSCAN

🍴 **Solociccia.** "Abandon all hope, ye who enter here," announces the menu, "you're in the hands of a butcher." Indeed you are, for this restaurant is the creation of Dario Cecchini, Panzano's local merchant of meat. Served at communal tables, there are three set meals to choose from, all of which highlight meat dishes chosen at Dario's discretion. **Known for:** choice of three set menus with everything but steak; fun communal tables; Dario grew up on this food. [$] *Average main: €30* ✉ *Via Chiantigiana 5* ☎ *055/852727* 🌐 *www.dariocecchini.com* 🕒 *Closed Mon.–Wed. No dinner Sun.*

$$ B&B/INN Fodor's Choice ★

🏨 **Villa Le Barone.** Once the home of the Viviani della Robbia family, this 16th-century villa in a grove of ancient cypress trees retains many aspects of a private country dwelling, complete with homey guest quarters. **Pros:** beautiful location; wonderful restaurant; great base for exploring the region. **Cons:** some rooms are a bit small; 15-minute walk to nearest town. $ *Rooms from: €199* ⊠ *Via San Leolino 19* 🕾 *055/852621* ⊕ *www.villalebarone.com* ⊗ *Closed Nov.–Easter* ⤺ *28 rooms* ⦿ *Free Breakfast.*

12

RADDA IN CHIANTI

26 km (15 miles) southeast of Panzano, 55 km (34 miles) south of Florence.

Radda in Chianti sits on a ridge stretching between the Val di Pesa and Val d'Arbia. It is easily reached by following the SR429 from Castellina. It's another one of those tiny villages with steep streets for strolling; follow the signs that point you toward the *camminamento medioevale,* a covered 14th-century walkway that circles part of the city inside the walls.

GETTING HERE AND AROUND

Radda can be reached by car from either Siena or Florence along the SR222 (Strada Chiantigiana), and from the A1 autostrada. Three Tra-In buses make their way from Siena to Radda. One morning SITA bus travels from Florence to Radda. There is no train service convenient to Radda.

VISITOR INFORMATION

Contact Radda in Chianti Tourism Office. ⊠ *Piazza Castello 6* 🕾 *0577/738494.*

EXPLORING

Badia a Coltibuono (*Abbey of the Good Harvest*). North of Gaiole a turn-off leads to this Romanesque abbey that has been owned by Lorenza de' Medici's family for more than a century and a half (the family isn't closely related to the Renaissance-era Medici). Wine has been produced here since the abbey was founded by Vallombrosan monks in the 11th century. Today the family continues the tradition, making Chianti Classico and other wines, along with cold-pressed olive oil and various flavored vinegars and floral honeys. A small church with campanile is surrounded by 2,000 acres of oak, fir, and chestnut woods threaded with walking paths—open to all—that pass two small lakes. Although the abbey itself, built between the 11th and 18th century, serves as the family's home, parts are open for tours (in English, German, or Italian). Visit the jasmine-draped main courtyard, the inner cloister with its antique well, the musty old aging cellars, and the Renaissance-style garden redolent of lavender, lemons, and roses. The Badia is closed on public holidays. ⊠ *Località Badia a Coltibuono, 4 km (2½ miles) north of Gaiole, Gaiole in Chianti* 🕾 *0577/74481 tours* ⊕ *www.coltibuono. com* ◲ *Abbey €10* ⊗ *Tours by request Jan. and Feb.*

Fodor's Choice
★ **Castello di Brolio.** If you have time for only one castle in Tuscany, this is it. At the end of the 12th century, when Florence conquered southern Chianti, Brolio became Florence's southernmost outpost. Brolio was built about AD 1000 and owned by the monks of the Badia Fiorentina; the "new" owners, the Ricasoli family, have been in possession since 1141. Bettino Ricasoli (1809–80), the so-called Iron Baron, was one of

the founders of modern Italy, and is said to have invented the original formula for Chianti wine. Brolio, one of Chianti's best-known labels, is still justifiably famous. Its cellars may be toured by appointment. The grounds are worth visiting, even though the 19th-century manor house is not open to the public. A small museum, where the Ricasoli Collection is housed in a 12th-century tower, displays objects that relate the long history of the family and the origins of Chianti wine. ✉ *Località Madonna a Brolio, 2 km (1 mile) southeast of Gaiole, Gaiole in Chianti* ☎ *0577/730280* 🌐 *www.ricasoli.it* 🎟 *€5 gardens, €8 gardens and museum* 🕒 *Closed Nov.–mid-Mar.*

Palazzo del Podestà. Radda's town hall (aka Palazzo Comunale), in the middle of town, was built in the second half of the 14th century and has served the same function ever since. Fifty-one coats of arms (the largest is the Medici's) are imbedded in the facade, representing the past governors of the town, but unless you have official business, the building is closed to the public. ✉ *Piazza Ferrucci 1.*

WHERE TO EAT

$$ TUSCAN Fodor's Choice ★ 🍴 **Osteria Le Panzanelle.** Silvia Bonechi's experience in the kitchen—with the help of a few precious recipes handed down from her grandmother—is one of the reasons for the success of this small restaurant in the tiny hamlet of Lucarelli; the other is the front-room hospitality of Nada Michelassi. These two *panzanelle* (women from Panzano) serve a short menu of tasty and authentic dishes at what the locals refer to as *il prezzo giusto* (the right price). **Known for:** fine home cooking; good wine list; unpretentious atmosphere. [$] *Average main: €15* ✉ *Località Lucarelli 29, 8 km (5 miles) northwest of Radda on the road to Panzano* ☎ *0577/733511* 🌐 *www.lepanzanelle.it* 🕒 *Closed Mon., and Jan. and Feb.*

WHERE TO STAY

$ B&B/INN 🏨 **La Bottega di Giovannino.** This is a fantastic place for the budget-conscious traveler, as rooms are immaculate and most have a stunning view of the surrounding hills. **Pros:** great location in the center of town; close to restaurants and shops; super value. **Cons:** some rooms are small; some bathrooms are down the hall; basic decor. [$] *Rooms from: €90* ✉ *Via Roma 6–8* ☎ *0577/735601* 🌐 *www.labottegadigiovannino.it* 🛏 *10 rooms* 🍽 *Free Breakfast.*

$$$ B&B/INN Fodor's Choice ★ 🏨 **La Locanda.** At an altitude of more than 1,800 feet, this converted farmhouse is probably the loftiest luxury inn in Chianti. **Pros:** idyllic setting; panoramic views; wonderful host. **Cons:** on a very rough gravel access road; isolated location; need a car to get around. [$] *Rooms from: €220* ✉ *Località Montanino di Volpaia, off Via della Volpaia, 13 km (8 miles) northwest of Radda* ☎ *0577/738833* 🌐 *www.lalocanda.it* 🕒 *Closed mid-Oct.–mid-Apr.* 🛏 *7 rooms* 🍽 *Free Breakfast.*

$ HOTEL 🏨 **Palazzo San Niccolò.** The wood-beam ceilings, terra-cotta floors, and some of the original frescoes of a 19th-century town palace remain, but the marble bathrooms have all been updated, some with Jacuzzi tubs. **Pros:** central location; friendly service. **Cons:** some rooms face a main street; room sizes vary. [$] *Rooms from: €123* ✉ *Via Roma 16*

☎ *0577/735666* 🌐 *www.hotelsanniccolo.com* 🕒 *Closed Nov.–Mar.* 🛏 *18 rooms* 🍴 *Free Breakfast.*

$$ B&B/INN Fodor's Choice ★ 🏨 **Relais Fattoria Vignale.** A refined and comfortable country house offers numerous sitting rooms with terra-cotta floors and attractive stonework, as well as wood-beamed guest rooms filled with simple wooden furnishings and handwoven rugs. **Pros:** intimate public spaces; excellent restaurant; nice grounds and pool. **Cons:** single rooms are small; annex across a busy road. [$] *Rooms from: €134* ✉ *Via Pianigiani 9* ☎ *0577/738300 hotel, 0577/738094 restaurant* 🌐 *www.vignale.it* 🕒 *Closed Nov.–Mar. 15* 🛏 *42 rooms* 🍴 *Free Breakfast.*

CASTELLINA IN CHIANTI

14 km (8 miles) west of Radda, 59 km (35 miles) south of Florence.

Castellina in Chianti—or simply Castellina—is on a ridge above three valleys: the Val di Pesa, Val d'Arbia, and Val d'Elsa. No matter what direction you turn, the panorama is bucolic. The strong 15th-century medieval walls and fortified town gate give a hint of the history of this village, which was an outpost during the continuing wars between Florence and Siena. In the main square, the Piazza del Comune, there's a 15th-century palace and a 15th-century fort constructed around a 13th-century tower. It now serves as the town hall.

GETTING HERE AND AROUND

As with all the towns along the Strada Chiantigiana (SR222), Castellina is an easy drive from either Siena or Florence. From Siena, Castellina is well served by the local Tra-In bus company. However, only one bus a day travels here from Florence. The closest train station is at Castellina Scalo, some 15 km (9 miles) away.

VISITOR INFORMATION

Contact Castellina in Chianti Tourism Office. ✉ *Via Ferruccio 40* ☎ *0577/741392.*

WHERE TO EAT AND STAY

$$$ TUSCAN 🍴 **Albergaccio.** The fact that the dining room can seat only 35 guests makes a meal here an intimate experience, and the ever-changing menu mixes traditional and creative dishes. In late September and October *zuppa di funghi e castagne* (mushroom and chestnut soup) is a treat; grilled meats and seafood are on the list throughout the year. **Known for:** creative menu; superb wine list; marvelous waitstaff. [$] *Average main: €25* ✉ *Via Fiorentina 63* ☎ *0577/741042* 🌐 *www.albergacciocast.com* 🕒 *Closed Sun.*

$$ TUSCAN 🍴 **Ristorante Le Tre Porte.** Grilled meat dishes are the specialty at this popular restaurant, with a bistecca fiorentina (served very rare, as always) taking pride of place; paired with grilled fresh porcini mushrooms when in season (spring and fall), it's a heady dish. The panoramic terrace is a good choice for dining in summer. **Known for:** views from the terrace; their way with mushrooms; fine wine list with lots of local bottles. [$] *Average main: €16* ✉ *Via Trento e Trieste 4* ☎ *0577/741163* 🌐 *www.treporte.com.*

$$ TUSCAN 🍴 **Sotto Le Volte.** As the name suggests, you'll find this small restaurant under the arches of Castellina's medieval walkway, and the eatery's vaulted ceilings make for a particularly romantic setting. The menu is short and eminently Tuscan, with typical soups and pasta dishes. **Known for:** unique setting; flair for Tuscan classics; attentive waitstaff. [$] *Average main: €20* ✉ *Via delle Volte 14–16* ☎ *0577/741299* 🌐 *www.ristorantesottolevolte.it* ⏲ *Closed Jan.–Mar.*

$$ B&B/INN Fodor's Choice ★ 🏨 **Palazzo Squarcialupi.** In this lovely 15th-century palace, rooms are spacious, with high ceilings, tile floors, and 18th-century furnishings, and many have views of the valley below. **Pros:** great location in town center; elegant public spaces; nice spa, pool, and grounds. **Cons:** on a street with no car access; across from a busy restaurant. [$] *Rooms from: €135* ✉ *Via Ferruccio 22* ☎ *0577/741186* 🌐 *www.squarcialupirelaxinchianti.com* ⏲ *Closed Nov.–Mar.* 🛏 *15 rooms* 🍽 *Free Breakfast.*

HILL TOWNS SOUTHWEST OF FLORENCE

Submit to the draw of Tuscany's enchanting fortified cities that crown the hills west of Siena, many dating to the Etruscan period. San Gimignano, known as the "medieval Manhattan" because of its forest of stout medieval towers built by rival families, is the most heavily visited. This onetime Roman outpost, with its tilted cobbled streets and ancient buildings, can make the days of medieval Guelph-Ghibelline conflicts palpable. Rising from a series of bleak gullied hills and valleys, Volterra has always been popular for its minerals and stones, particularly alabaster, which was used by the Etruscans for many implements. Examples are now displayed in the exceptional (and exceptionally large) Museo Etrusco Guarnacci.

VOLTERRA

75 km (47 miles) southwest of Florence.

As you approach the town through bleak, rugged terrain, you can see that not all Tuscan hill towns rise above rolling green fields. Volterra stands mightily over Le Balze, a stunning series of gullied hills and valleys formed by erosion that has slowly eaten away at the foundation of the town—now considerably smaller than it was during its Etruscan glory days 25 centuries ago. The town began as the northernmost of the 12 cities that made up the Etruscan League, and excavations in the 18th century revealed a bounty of relics, which are on exhibit at the impressively overstocked Museo Etrusco Guarnacci. The Romans and later the Florentines laid siege to the town to secure its supply of minerals and stones, particularly alabaster, which is still worked into handicrafts on sale in many of the shops around town.

GETTING HERE AND AROUND

By car, the best route from San Gimignano follows the SP1 south to Castel San Gimignano and then the SS68 west to Volterra. Coming from the west, take the SS1, a coastal road to Cecina, then follow the SS68 east to Volterra. Either way, there's a long, winding climb at the end of your trip. Traveling to Volterra by bus or train is complicated; avoid it if possible, especially if you have lots of luggage. From Florence or Siena the journey by public transit is best made by bus and involves a change in Colle di Val d'Elsa. From Rome or Pisa, it is best to take the train to Cecina and then take a bus to Volterra or a train to the Volterra-Saline station. The latter is 10 km (6 miles) from town.

VISITOR INFORMATION

Contact **Volterra tourism office.** ✉ *Piazza dei Priori 10* ☎ *0588/86150* ⊕ *www.provolterra.it.*

EXPLORING

Duomo. Behind the textbook 13th-century Pisan–Romanesque facade is proof that Volterra counted for something during the Renaissance, when many important Tuscan artists came to decorate the church. Three-dimensional stucco portraits of local saints are on the gold, red, and blue ceiling (1580) designed by Francesco Capriani. The highlight of the Duomo is the brightly painted 13th-century wooden life-size *Deposition* in the chapel of the same name. The unusual Cappella dell'Addolorata (Chapel of the Grieved) has two terra-cotta Nativity scenes. The 16th-century pulpit in the middle of the nave is lined with fine 14th-century sculpted panels, attributed to a member of the Pisano family. Across from the Duomo in the center of the piazza is the **Battistero,** with stripes that match the Duomo. ✉ *Piazza San Giovanni* ☎.

Fodor's Choice

★

Museo Etrusco Guarnacci. An extraordinarily large and unique collection of Etruscan relics is made all the more interesting by clear explanations in English. The bulk of the collection is comprised of roughly 700 carved funerary urns: the oldest, dating from the 7th century BC, were made from tufa (volcanic rock); a handful are made of terra-cotta; and the vast majority—from the 3rd to 1st century BC—are from alabaster. The urns are grouped by subject and taken together form a fascinating testimony about Etruscan life and death. Some illustrate domestic scenes, others the funeral procession of the deceased. Greek gods and mythology, adopted by the Etruscans, also figure prominently. The sculpted figures on many of the covers may have been made in the image of the deceased, reclining and often holding the cup of life overturned. Particularly well known is *Gli Sposi (Husband and Wife)*, a haunting, elderly duo in terra-cotta. The *Ombra della Sera (Evening Shadow)*—an enigmatice bronze statue of an elongated, pencil-thin male nude—highlights the collection. Also on display are Attic vases, bucchero ceramics, jewelry, and household items. ✉ *Via Don Minzoni 15* ☎ *0588/86347* 🔖 *€16, includes Pinacoteca and Teatro Romano.*

Pinacoteca. One of Volterra's best-looking Renaissance buildings contains an impressive collection of Tuscan paintings arranged chronologically on two floors. Head straight for Room 12, with Luca Signorelli's (circa 1445–1523) *Madonna and Child with Saints* and Rosso Fiorentino's later *Deposition*. Though painted just 30 years apart, they serve to illustrate the shift in style from the early-16th-century Renaissance ideals to full-blown mannerism: the balance of Signorelli's composition becomes purposefully skewed in Fiorentino's painting, where the colors go from vivid but realistic to emotively bright. Other important paintings in the small museum include Ghirlandaio's *Apotheosis of*

Christ with Saints and a polyptych of the *Madonna and Saints* by Taddeo di Bartolo, which once hung in the Palazzo dei Priori. ✉ *Via dei Sarti 1* ☎ *0588/87580* 💶 *€16, includes Museo Etrusco Guarnacci and Teatro Romano.*

Porta all'Arco Etrusco. Even if a good portion of the arch was rebuilt by the Romans, three dark and weather-beaten 4th-century-BC heads (thought to represent Etruscan gods) still face outward to greet those who enter here. A plaque on the outer wall recalls the efforts of the locals who saved the arch from destruction by filling it with stones during the German withdrawal at the end of World War II. ✉ *Via Porta all'Arco.*

Teatro Romano. Just outside the walls past Porta Fiorentina are the ruins of the 1st-century-BC Roman theater, one of the best preserved in Italy, with adjacent remains of the Roman *terme* (baths). You can enjoy an excellent bird's-eye view of the theater from Via Lungo le Mura. ✉ *Viale Francesco Ferrucci* 💶 *€5; €16, includes Museo Etrusco Guarnacci and Pinacoteca.*

WHERE TO EAT AND STAY

$
TUSCAN
✕ **Da Badò.** This is the best place in town to eat traditional food elbow-to-elbow with the locals. Da Badò is family-run, with Lucia in the kitchen and her sons Giacomo and Michele waiting tables. **Known for:** excellent traditional dishes; small menu; local favorite. 💲 *Average main: €14* ✉ *Borgo San Lazzaro 9* ☎ *0588/86477* ⊕ *www.trattoriadabado.com* 𝕺 *Closed Wed.*

$$
TUSCAN
✕ **Il Sacco Fiorentino.** Start with the *antipasti del Sacco Fiorentino*—a medley of sautéed chicken liver, porcini mushrooms, and polenta drizzled with balsamic vinegar. The meal just gets better when you move on to the *tagliatelle del Sacco Fiorentino,* a riot of curried spaghetti with chicken and roasted red peppers. **Known for:** inventive food; tranquil setting; excellent wine list. 💲 *Average main: €17* ✉ *Via Giusto Turazza 13* ☎ *0588/88537* 𝕺 *Closed Wed.*

$
B&B/INN
🛏 **Etruria.** The rooms are modest and there's no elevator, but the central location, the ample buffet breakfast, and the modest rates make this a good choice for those on a budget. **Pros:** great central location; friendly staff; tranquil garden with rooftop views. **Cons:** some rooms can be noisy during the day; no a/c; no elevator. 💲 *Rooms from: €73* ✉ *Via Matteotti 32* ☎ *0588/87377* ⊕ *www.albergoetruria.it* 𝕺 *Closed Jan. and Feb.* 🛏 *18 rooms* 🍴 *Free Breakfast.*

SAN GIMIGNANO

27 km (17 miles) northeast of Volterra, 54 km (34 miles) southwest of Florence.

Fodor's Choice ★
When you're on a hilltop surrounded by soaring medieval towers silhouetted against the sky, it's difficult not to fall under the spell of San Gimignano. Its tall walls and narrow streets are typical of Tuscan hill towns, but it's the medieval "skyscrapers" that set the town apart from its neighbors. Today 14 towers remain, but at the height of the Guelph–Ghibelline conflict there was a forest of more than 70, and it was possible to cross the town by rooftop rather than by road. The towers were

built partly for defensive purposes—they were a safe refuge and useful for pouring boiling oil on attacking enemies—and partly for bolstering the egos of their owners, who competed with deadly seriousness to build the highest tower in town.

Today San Gimignano isn't much more than a gentrified walled city, touristy but still very much worth exploring because, despite the profusion of cheesy souvenir shops lining the main drag, there's some serious Renaissance art to be seen here. Tour groups arrive early and clog the wine-tasting rooms—San Gimignano is famous for its light, white vernaccia—and art galleries for much of the day, but most sights stay open through late afternoon, when all the tour groups have long since departed.

San Gimignano is particularly beautiful in the early morning. Take time to walk up to the *rocca* (castle), at the highest point of town. Here you can enjoy 360-degree views of the surrounding countryside. Apart from when it's used for summer outdoor film festivals, it's always open.

GETTING HERE AND AROUND

You can reach San Gimignano by car from the Florence–Siena Superstrada. Exit at Poggibonsi Nord and follow signs for San Gimignano. Although it involves changing buses in Poggibonsi, getting to San Gimignano by bus from Florence is a relatively straightforward affair. SITA operates the service between Siena or Florence and Poggibonsi. From Siena, Tra-In offers direct service to San Gimignano several times daily. You cannot reach San Gimignano by train.

VISITOR INFORMATION

Contact San Gimignano tourism office. ⊠ *Piazza Duomo 1* ☎ *0577/940008* ⊕ *www.sangimignano.com.*

EXPLORING

Fodor's Choice ★ **Collegiata.** The town's main church is not officially a *duomo* (cathedral), because San Gimignano has no bishop. But behind the simple facade of the Romanesque Collegiata lies a treasure trove of fine frescoes, covering nearly every part of the interior. Bartolo di Fredi's 14th-century fresco cycle of Old Testament scenes extends along one wall. Their distinctly medieval feel, with misshapen bodies, buckets of spurting blood, and lack of perspective, contrasts with the much more reserved scenes from the *Life of Christ* (attributed to 14th-century artist Lippo Memmi), painted on the opposite wall just 14 years later. Taddeo di Bartolo's otherworldly *Last Judgment* (late 14th century), with its distorted and suffering nudes, reveals the great influence of Dante's horrifying imagery in *Inferno* and was surely an inspiration for later painters. Proof that the town had more than one protector, Benozzo Gozzoli's arrow-riddled *St. Sebastian* was commissioned in gratitude after the locals prayed to the saint for relief from plague. The Renaissance **Cappella di Santa Fina** is decorated with a fresco cycle by Domenico Ghirlandaio illustrating the life of St. Fina. A small girl who suffered from a terminal disease, Fina repented her sins—among them having accepted an orange from a boy—and in penance lived out the rest of her short life on a wooden board, tormented by rats. The scenes depict the arrival of St. Gregory, who appeared to assure her that death was near; the flowers that miraculously grew from the wooden plank; and the miracles that accompanied her funeral, including the healing of her nurse's paralyzed hand and the restoration of a blind choirboy's vision. ⊠ *Piazza Pecori 1–2, entrance on left side of church* ☎ *0577/286300* ⊕ *www.duomosangimignano.it* ⬛ *€4; €6 includes Museo d'Arte Sacra* ⊙ *Closed Jan. 1, Jan. 15–31, Mar. 12, Nov. 15–30, and Dec. 25.*

Museo Civico. The impressive civic museum occupies what was the "new" Palazzo del Popolo; the Torre Grossa is adjacent. Dante visited San Gimignano for only one day as a Guelph ambassador from Florence to ask the locals to join the Florentines in supporting the pope—just long enough to get the main council chamber, which now holds a 14th-century *Maestà* by Lippo Memmi, named after him. Off the stairway is a small room containing the racy frescoes by Memmo di Filippuccio (active 1288–1324), depicting the courtship, shared bath, and wedding of a young, androgynous-looking couple. That the space could have been a private room for the commune's chief magistrate may have something to do with the work's highly charged eroticism.

Upstairs, paintings by famous Renaissance artists Pinturicchio (*Madonna Enthroned*) and Benozzo Gozzoli (*Madonna and Child*), and two large *tondi* (circular paintings) by Filippino Lippi (circa 1457–1504) attest to the importance and wealth of San Gimignano. Also worth seeing are Taddeo di Bartolo's *Life of San Gimignano,* with the saint holding a model of the town as it once appeared; Lorenzo di Niccolò's gruesome martyrdom scene in the *Life of St. Bartholomew* (1401); and scenes from the *Life of St. Fina* on a tabernacle that was designed to hold her head. Admission includes the steep climb to the top of the **Torre Grossa,** which on a clear day has spectacular views. ⊠ *Piazza Duomo 2* ☎ *0577/990312* ⊕ *www.sangimignanomusei.it* ⬛ *€9.*

Sant'Agostino. Make a beeline for Benozzo Gozzoli's superlative 15th-century fresco cycle depicting scenes from the life of St. Augustine. The saint's work was essential to the early development of church doctrine. As thoroughly discussed in his autobiographical *Confessions* (an acute dialogue with God), Augustine, like many saints, sinned considerably in his youth before finding God. But unlike the lives of other saints, where the story continues through a litany of deprivations, penitence, and often martyrdom, Augustine's life and work focused on philosophy and the reconciliation of faith and thought. Benozzo's 17 scenes on the choir wall depict Augustine as a man who traveled and taught extensively in the 4th and 5th centuries. The 15th-century altarpiece by Piero del Pollaiolo (1443–96) depicts *The Coronation of the Virgin* and the various protectors of the city. On your way out of Sant'Agostino, stop in at the **Cappella di San Bartolo,** with a sumptuously elaborate tomb by Benedetto da Maiano (1442–97). ⊠ *Piazza Sant'Agostino 10* ☎ *0577/907012* ⊕ *www.sangimignano.com* ⬛ *Free.*

WHERE TO EAT

$$ ✕ **Osteria del Carcere.** Although it calls itself an *osteria* (tavern), this place
ITALIAN   much more resembles a wine bar, with a bill of fare that includes several different types of pâtés and a short list of seasonal soups and salads. The sampler of goat cheeses, which can be paired with local wines, should

not be missed. **Known for:** its female proprietor/chef; inventive dishes; the fact that it's an ex-jail. [$] *Average main: €16* ✉ *Via del Castello 13* ☎ *0577/941905* ⏲ *Closed Wed., and early Jan.–Mar. No lunch Thurs.*

WHERE TO STAY

$$$ HOTEL **La Collegiata.** After serving as a Franciscan convent and then the residence of the noble Strozzi family, the Collegiata has been converted into a fine hotel, with no expense spared in the process. **Pros:** gorgeous views from terrace; elegant rooms in main building. **Cons:** long walk into town; service can be impersonal; some rooms are dimly lit. [$] *Rooms from: €220* ✉ *Località Strada 27, 1 km (½ mile) north of San Gimignano town center* ☎ *0577/943201* 🌐 *www.lacollegiata.it* ⏲ *Closed Nov.–Mar.* 🛏 *21 rooms* 🍴 *Free Breakfast.*

$$ B&B/INN FAMILY **Torraccia di Chiusi.** A perfect retreat for families, this tranquil hilltop *agriturismo* (farm stay) offers simple, comfortably decorated accommodations on extensive grounds 5 km (3 miles) from the hubbub of San Gimignano. **Pros:** tranquil haven close to San Gimignano; great walking possibilities; family-run hospitality; delightful countryside views. **Cons:** 30 minutes from the nearest town on a winding gravel road; need a car to get here. [$] *Rooms from: €150* ✉ *Località Montauto* ☎ *0577/941972* 🌐 *www.torracciadichiusi.it* 🛏 *11 rooms* 🍴 *Free Breakfast.*

COLLE DI VAL D'ELSA

15 km (9 miles) southeast of San Gimignano, 51 km (32 miles) south of Florence.

Most people pass through on their way to and from popular tourist destinations Volterra and San Gimignano—a shame, since Colle di Val d'Elsa has a lot to offer. It's another town on the Via Francigena that benefited from trade along the pilgrimage route to Rome. Colle got an extra boost in the late 16th century when it was given a bishopric, probably related to an increase in trade when nearby San Gimignano was cut off from the well-traveled road. The town is arranged on two levels, and from the 12th century onward the flat lower portion was given over to a flourishing papermaking industry; today the area is mostly modern, and efforts have shifted toward the production of fine glass and crystal.

GETTING HERE AND AROUND

You can reach Colle di Val d'Elsa by car on either the SR2 from Siena or the Florence–Siena superstrada. Bus service to and from Siena and Florence is frequent.

VISITOR INFORMATION

Contact **Colle di Val d'Elsa Tourism Office.** ✉ *Via del Castello 33/b* ☎ *0577/922791.*

EXPLORING

Make your way from the newer lower town (Colle Bassa) to the prettier, upper part of town (Colle Alta). The best views of the valley are to be had from Viale della Rimembranza, the road that loops around the western end of town, past the church of San Francesco. The early-16th-century Porta Nuova was inserted into the preexisting medieval walls, just as several handsome Renaissance palazzi were placed into the medieval neighborhood to create what is now called the Borgo. The Via Campana, the main road, passes through the facade of the surreal Palazzo Campana, an otherwise unfinished building that serves as a door connecting the two parts of the upper town. Via delle Volte, named for the vaulted arches that cover it, leads straight to Piazza del Duomo. There is a convenient parking lot off the SS68, with stairs leading up the hill. Buses arrive at Piazza Arnolfo, named after the town's favorite son, Arnolfo di Cambio (circa 1245–1302), the early-Renaissance architect who designed Florence's Duomo and Palazzo Vecchio (but sadly nothing here).

WHERE TO EAT AND STAY

$$$$
MODERN ITALIAN
Fodor's Choice
★

✕ **Ristorante Arnolfo.** Food lovers should not miss Arnolfo, one of Tuscany's most highly regarded restaurants, where Chef Gaetano Trovato sets high standards of creativity; his dishes daringly ride the line between innovation and tradition, almost always with spectacular results. The menu changes frequently but you are always sure to find fish and lots of fresh vegetables in the summer. **Known for:** its talented chef; imaginative dishes; superb wine list. $ *Average main: €120* ⊠ *Via XX Settembre 50* 🕾 *0577/920549* ⊕ *www.arnolfo.com* ☉ *Closed Tues. and Wed., and mid-Jan.–Feb.*

$$$
B&B/INN

🛏 **Palazzo San Lorenzo.** A 17th-century palace in the historic center of Colle boasts rooms that exude warmth and comfort, with light-color wooden floors, soothingly tinted fabrics, and large windows. **Pros:** central location; indoor pool; extremely well maintained. **Cons:** caters to business groups; some of the public spaces feel rather sterile. $ *Rooms from: €240* ⊠ *Via Gracco del Secco 113* 🕾 *0577/923675* ⊕ *www.palazzosanlorenzo.it* 🛏 *48 rooms* ⦁◯⦁ *Free Breakfast.*

SIENA

With its narrow streets and steep alleys, a Gothic Duomo, a bounty of early Renaissance art, and the glorious Palazzo Pubblico overlooking its magnificent Campo, Siena is often described as Italy's best-preserved medieval city. It is also remarkably modern: many shops sell clothes by up-and-coming designers. Make a point of catching the *passeggiata* (evening stroll), when locals throng the Via di Città, Banchi di Sopra, and Banchi di Sotto, the city's three main streets.

Victory over Florence in 1260 at Montaperti marked the beginning of Siena's golden age. Even though Florentines avenged the loss nine years later, Siena continued to prosper. During the following decades Siena erected its greatest buildings (including the Duomo); established a model city government presided over by the Council of Nine; and became a great art, textile, and trade center. All of these achievements came together in the decoration of the Sala della Pace in Palazzo Pubblico. It makes you wonder what greatness the city might have gone on to achieve had its fortunes been different, but in 1348 a plague decimated the population, brought an end to the Council of Nine, and left Siena economically vulnerable. Siena succumbed to Florentine rule in the mid-16th century, when a yearlong siege virtually eliminated the native population. Ironically, it was precisely this decline that, along

12

with Sienese pride, prevented further development, to which we owe the city's marvelous medieval condition today.

But although much looks as it did in the early 14th century, Siena is no museum. Walk through the streets and you can see that the medieval *contrade*—17 neighborhoods into which the city has been historically divided—are a vibrant part of modern life. You may see symbols of the *contrada* emblazoned on banners and engraved on building walls: Tartuca (turtle), Oca (goose), Istrice (porcupine), Torre (tower). The Sienese still strongly identify themselves by the contrada where they were born and raised; loyalty and rivalry run deep. At no time is this more visible than during the centuries-old Palio, a twice-yearly horse race held in the Piazza del Campo, but you need not visit then to come to know the rich culture of Siena, evident at every step.

GETTING HERE AND AROUND

From Florence, the quickest way to Siena is via the Florence–Siena superstrada. Otherwise, take the Via Cassia (SR2) for a scenic route. Coming from Rome, leave the A1 at Valdichiana, and follow the Siena–Bettole superstrada. SITA provides excellent bus service between Florence and Siena. Because buses are direct and speedy, they are preferable to the train, which sometimes involves a change in Empoli.

If you come by car, you're better off leaving it in one of the parking lots around the perimeter of town. Driving is difficult or impossible in most parts of the city center. Practically unchanged since medieval times, Siena is laid out in a "Y" over the slopes of several hills, dividing the city into *terzi* (thirds).

Bus Contacts Tra-In. ☎ *0577/204111* ⊕ *www.trainspa.it.*

TIMING

It's a joy to walk in Siena—hills notwithstanding—as it's a rare opportunity to stroll through a medieval city rather than just a town. (There is quite a lot to explore, in contrast to tiny hill towns that can be crossed in minutes.) The walk can be done in as little as a day, with minimal stops at the sights. But stay longer and take time to tour the churches and museums, and to enjoy the streetscapes themselves. Many of the sites have reduced hours Sunday afternoon and Monday.

VISITOR INFORMATION

Contact Siena tourism office. ✉ *Piazza del Duomo 2* ☎ *0577/280551* ⊕ *www. terresiena.it.*

EXPLORING

TOP ATTRACTIONS

Fodor's Choice ★ **Cripta.** After it had lain unseen for possibly 700 years, a crypt was rediscovered under the grand *pavimento* (floor) of the Duomo during routine excavation work and was opened to the public in 2003. An unknown master executed the breathtaking frescoes here sometime between 1270 and 1280; they retain their original colors and pack an emotional punch even with sporadic damage. The *Deposition/Lamentation* gives strong evidence that the Sienese school could paint emotion just as well as the

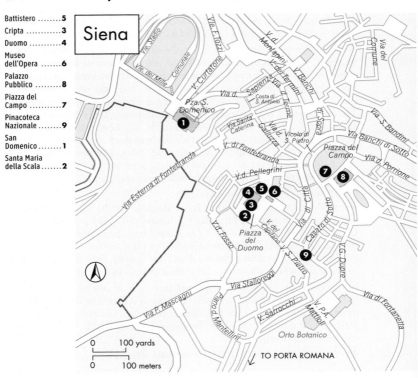

Florentine school—and did it some 20 years before Giotto. Guided tours in English take place more or less every half hour and are limited to no more than 35 persons. ⊠ *Scale di San Giovanni, Città ✣ Down steps to right side of cathedral* ☎ *0577/286300* ⊕ *www.operaduomo. siena.it* ⊠ *€7; €13 combined ticket includes the Duomo, Battistero, and Museo dell'Opera.*

Fodor's Choice **Duomo.** Siena's cathedral, completed in two brief phases at the end
★ of the 13th and 14th centuries, is beyond question one of the finest Gothic churches in Italy. The multicolored marbles and painted decoration are typical of the Italian approach to Gothic architecture, and the amazingly detailed facade has few rivals in the region. Highlights include the Duomo's striking interior, with its black-and-white striping and finely coffered and gilded dome; the oldest example of stained glass in Italy (from 1288) that fills the circular window; the carousel pulpit, carved around 1265; and the magnificent Renaissance frescoes in the Biblioteca Piccolomini. The Duomo is most famous for its unique and magnificent inlaid-marble floors, which took almost 200 years to complete; more than 40 artists contributed to the work, made up of 56 separate compositions depicting biblical scenes, allegories, religious symbols, and civic emblems. The floors are covered for most of the year, but are unveiled during September and October. ⊠ *Piazza*

del Duomo, Città ☎ 0577/286300 ⊕ www.operaduomo.siena.it ☑ €5 Nov.–Aug., €9 Sept. and Oct.; €13 combined ticket includes Cripta, Battistero, and Museo dell'Opera.

Fodor's Choice **Museo dell'Opera.** Part of the unfinished nave of what was to have been
★ a new cathedral, the museum contains the Duomo's treasury and some of the original decoration from its facade and interior. The first room on the ground floor displays weather-beaten 13th-century sculptures by Giovanni Pisano that were brought inside for protection and replaced by copies, as was a tondo of the *Madonna and Child* (now attributed to Donatello) that once hung on the door to the south transept. The masterpiece is unquestionably Duccio's *Maestà,* one side with 26 panels depicting episodes from the Passion, the other side with a *Madonna and Child Enthroned.* The second floor is divided between the treasury, with a crucifix by Giovanni Pisano, and La Sala della Madonna degli Occhi Grossi (the Room of the Madonna with the Big Eyes), named after the 13th-century painting. There is a fine view from the tower inside the museum. ⊠ *Piazza del Duomo 8, Città ☎ 0577/286300 ⊕ www. operaduomo.siena.it ☑ €7; €13 combined ticket includes the Duomo, Cripta, and Battistero.*

Palazzo Pubblico. The Gothic Palazzo Pubblico, the focal point of the Piazza del Campo, has served as Siena's town hall since the 1300s. It now also contains the Museo Civico, with walls covered in early Renaissance frescoes. The nine governors of Siena once met in the Sala della Pace, famous for Ambrogio Lorenzetti's frescoes called *Allegories of Good and Bad Government*, painted in the late 1330s to demonstrate the dangers of tyranny. The good government side depicts utopia, showing first the virtuous ruling council surrounded by angels and then scenes of a perfectly running city and countryside. Conversely, the bad government fresco tells a tale straight out of Dante. The evil ruler and his advisers have horns and fondle strange animals, and the town scene depicts the seven mortal sins in action. Interestingly, the bad government fresco is severely damaged, and the good government fresco is in terrific condition. The **Torre del Mangia,** the palazzo's famous bell tower, is named after one of its first bell ringers, Giovanni di Duccio (called Mangiaguadagni, or earnings eater). The climb up to the top is long and steep, but the view makes it worth every step. ⊠ *Piazza del Campo 1, Città ☎ 0577/292232 ⊕ www.comune.siena.it ☑ Museum €9, ticket sales end 30 mins before closing; tower €10, ticket sales end 45 mins before closing.*

Fodor's Choice **Piazza del Campo.** The fan-shape Piazza del Campo, known simply as
★ il Campo (The Field), is one of the finest squares in Italy. Constructed toward the end of the 12th century on a market area unclaimed by any contrada, it's still the heart of town. The bricks of the Campo are patterned in nine different sections—representing each member of the medieval Government of Nine. At the top of the Campo is a copy of the early 15th-century **Fonte Gaia** by Siena's greatest sculptor, Jacopo della Quercia. The 13 sculpted reliefs of biblical events and virtues that line the fountain are 19th-century copies; the originals are in the museum complex of Santa Maria della Scala. On Palio horse-race days (July 2 and August 16), the Campo and all its surrounding buildings are packed

with cheering, frenzied locals and tourists craning their necks to take it all in. ⊠ *Piazza del Campo, Città.*

Pinacoteca Nazionale. The superb collection of five centuries of local painting in Siena's national picture gallery can easily convince you that the Renaissance was by no means just a Florentine thing—Siena was arguably just as important a center of art and innovation as its rival to the north, especially in the mid-13th century. Accordingly, the most interesting section of the collection, chronologically arranged, has several important firsts. Room 1 contains a painting of the *Stories of the True Cross* (1215) by the so-called Master of Tressa, the earliest identified work by a painter of the Sienese school, and is followed in Room 2 by late-13th-century artist Guido da Siena's *Stories from the Life of Christ,* one of the first paintings ever made on canvas (earlier painters used wood panels). Rooms 3 and 4 are dedicated to Duccio, a student of Cimabue (circa 1240–1302) and considered to be the last of the proto-Renaissance painters. Ambrogio Lorenzetti's landscapes in Room 8 are the first truly secular paintings in Western art. Among later works in the rooms on the floor above, keep an eye out for the preparatory sketches used by Domenico Beccafumi (1486–1551) for the 35 etched marble panels he made for the floor of the Duomo. ⊠ *Via San Pietro 29, Città* ☏ *0577/286143* ⊕ *www.pinacotecanazionale.siena.it* ☒ *€4.*

Fodor'sChoice
★
Santa Maria della Scala. For more than 1,000 years, this complex across from the Duomo was home to Siena's hospital, but now it serves as a museum. Restored 15th-century frescoes in the Sala del Pellegrinaio tell the history of the hospital, which was created to give refuge to passing pilgrims and to those in need, and to distribute charity to the poor. Incorporated into the complex is the church of the Santissima Annunziata, with a celebrated *Risen Christ* by Vecchietta (also known as Lorenzo di Pietro, circa 1412–80). Down in the dark, Cappella di Santa Caterina della Notte is where St. Catherine went to pray at night. The subterranean archaeological museum contained within the *ospedale* (hospital) is worth seeing even if you're not particularly taken with Etruscan objects. The displays are clearly marked and can serve as a good introduction to the history of regional excavations. Don't miss della Quercia's stunning original sculpted reliefs from the Fonte Gaia. ⊠ *Piazza del Duomo 1, Città* ☏ *0577/534511* ⊕ *www.santamariadellascala.com* ☒ *€9* ⊘ *Closed Tues.*

WORTH NOTING

Battistero. The Duomo's 14th-century Gothic Baptistery was built to prop up the apse of the cathedral. There are frescoes throughout, but the highlight is a large bronze 15th-century baptismal font designed by Jacopo della Quercia (1374–1438). It's adorned with bas-reliefs by various artists, including two by Renaissance masters: the *Baptism of Christ* by Lorenzo Ghiberti (1378–1455) and the *Feast of Herod* by Donatello. ⊠ *Piazza San Giovanni, Città* ☏ *0577/286300* ⊕ *www.operaduomo.siena.it* ☒ *€4; €13 combined ticket includes the Duomo, Cripta, and Museo dell'Opera.*

San Domenico. Although the Duomo is celebrated as a triumph of 13th-century Gothic architecture, this church, built at about the same time, turned out to be an oversize, hulking brick box that never merited a finishing coat in marble, let alone a graceful facade. Named for the founder of the Dominican order, the church is now more closely associated with St. Catherine of Siena. Just to the right of the entrance is the chapel in which she received the stigmata. On the wall is the only known contemporary portrait of the saint, made in the late 14th century by Andrea Vanni (circa 1332–1414). Farther down is the famous **Cappella delle Santa Testa,** the church's official shrine. Catherine, or bits and pieces of her, was literally spread all over the country—a foot is in Venice, most of her body is in Rome, and only her head (kept in a reliquary on the chapel's altar) and her right thumb are here. She was revered throughout the country long before she was officially named a patron saint of Italy in 1939. On either side of the chapel are well-known frescoes by Sodoma (aka Giovanni Antonio Bazzi, 1477–1549) of *St. Catherine in Ecstasy.* Don't miss the view of the Duomo and town center from the apse-side terrace. ✉ *Piazza San Domenico, Camollìa* ☎ *0577/286848* 🌐 *www.basilicacateriniana.com.*

WHERE TO EAT

$$$ TUSCAN Fodor's Choice ★ 🍴 **Le Logge.** Bright flowers provide a dash of color at this classic Tuscan dining room, and stenciled designs on the ceilings add some whimsy; the wooden cupboards (now filled with wine bottles) lining the walls recall its past as a turn-of-the-19th-century grocery store. The menu, with four or five primi and secondi, changes regularly, but almost always includes their classic *malfatti all'osteria* (ricotta and spinach dumplings in a cream sauce). **Known for:** creative food; fine, affordable wine list; great waitstaff. [$] *Average main: €28* ✉ *Via del Porrione 33, San Martino* ☎ *0577/48013* 🌐 *www.osterialelogge.it* 🕓 *Closed Sun., and 3 wks in Jan.*

$ TUSCAN 🍴 **Osteria Il Grattacielo.** If you're wiped out from too much sightseeing, consider a meal at this hole-in-the-wall restaurant where locals congregate for a simple lunch over a glass of wine. There's a collection of verdure sott'olio, a wide selection of affettati misti, and various types of frittatas, and all of this can be washed down with the cheap, yet eminently drinkable, house red. **Known for:** simple, good-value food; earthy ambience; usually filled with local men arguing about the Palio. [$] *Average main: €10* ✉ *Via Pontani 8, Camollìa* ☎ *0577/289326* 💳 *No credit cards.*

$ TUSCAN Fodor's Choice ★ 🍴 **Trattoria Papei.** The menu hasn't changed for years, and why should it: the pici *al cardinale* (with a duck and bacon sauce) is wonderful, and all the other typically Sienese dishes are equally delicious. Grilled meats are the true specialty; the *bistecca di vitello* (grilled veal steak) is melt-in-your-mouth wonderful. **Known for:** great place to sample local specialties; lively atmosphere; outdoor seating. [$] *Average main: €11* ✉ *Piazza del Mercato 6, Città* ☎ *0577/280894* 🌐 *www.anticatrattoriapapei.com.*

WHERE TO STAY

$ B&B/INN 🏨 **Antica Torre.** The cordial Landolfo family has carefully evoked a private home with their eight guest rooms inside a restored 16th-century tower, and the simple but tastefully furnished rooms have ornate wrought-iron headboards, usually atop twin beds. **Pros:** near the town center; charming atmosphere. **Cons:** narrow stairway up to the rooms; low ceilings. [$] *Rooms from: €110* ✉ *Via Fieravecchia 7, San Martino* ☎ *0577/222255* 🌐 *www.anticatorresiena.it* 🛏 *8 rooms* 🍴 *Free Breakfast.*

$$ B&B/INN 🏨 **Hotel Santa Caterina.** Manager Lorenza Capannelli and her fine staff are welcoming, hospitable, enthusiastic, and go out of their way to ensure a fine stay in rooms where dark, straight-lined wood furniture stands next to beds with floral spreads. **Pros:** friendly staff; a short walk to center of town; breakfast in the garden. **Cons:** on a busy intersection; outside city walls. [$] *Rooms from: €145* ✉ *Via Piccolomini 7, San Martino* ☎ *0577/221105* 🌐 *www.hscsiena.it* 🛏 *22 rooms* 🍴 *Free Breakfast.*

$$ HOTEL Fodor's Choice ★ 🏨 **Palazzo Ravizza.** This romantic palazzo exudes a sense of genteel shabbiness, and lovely guest rooms have high ceilings, antique furnishings, and bathrooms decorated with hand-painted tiles. **Pros:** 10-minute walk to the center of town; pleasant garden with a view beyond the city walls; professional staff. **Cons:** not all rooms have views; some rooms are a little cramped. [$] *Rooms from: €160* ✉ *Pian dei Mantellini 34, Città* ☎ *0577/280462* 🌐 *www.palazzoravizza.it* 🛏 *42 rooms* 🍴 *Free Breakfast.*

SHOPPING

Enoteca Italiana. Italy's only state-sponsored enoteca has a vast selection of wines from all parts of the country. Housed in the fortress that the Florentines built to dominate Siena after they conquered the town in 1555, it's a must for any lover of Italian wines. ✉ *Fortezza Medicea, Piazza Libertà 1, Camollìa* ☎ *0577/228811* 🌐 *www.enoteca-italiana.it* 🕒 *Closed Sun. and Mon.*

AREZZO AND CORTONA

The hill towns of Arezzo and Cortona are the main attractions of eastern Tuscany; despite their appeal, this part of the region gets less tourist traffic than its neighbors to the west. You'll truly escape the crowds if you venture north to the Casentino, which is backwoods Tuscany—tiny towns and abbeys are sprinkled through beautiful forestland, some of which is set aside as a national park.

AREZZO

63 km (39 miles) northeast of Siena, 81 km (50 miles) southeast of Florence.

Arezzo is best known for the magnificent Piero della Francesca frescoes in the church of San Francesco. It's also the birthplace of the poet Petrarch (1304–74), the Renaissance artist and art historian Giorgio

Vasari, and Guido d'Arezzo (aka Guido Monaco), the inventor of contemporary musical notation. Arezzo dates from pre-Etruscan times, when around 1000 BC the first settlers erected a cluster of huts. Arezzo thrived as an Etruscan capital from the 7th to the 4th century BC, and was one of the most important cities in the Etruscans' anti-Roman 12-city federation, resisting Rome's rule to the last.

The city eventually fell and in turn flourished under the Romans. In 1248 Guglielmino degli Ubertini, a member of the powerful Ghibelline family, was elected bishop of Arezzo. This sent the city headlong into the enduring conflict between the Ghibellines (pro-emperor) and the Guelphs (pro-pope). In 1289 Florentine Guelphs defeated Arezzo in a famous battle at Campaldino. Among the Florentine soldiers was Dante Alighieri (1265–1321), who often referred to Arezzo in his *Divine Comedy*. Guelph–Ghibelline wars continued to plague Arezzo until the end of the 14th century, when Arezzo lost its independence to Florence.

GETTING HERE AND AROUND

Arezzo is easily reached by car from the A1, the main highway running between Florence and Rome. Direct trains connect Arezzo with Rome (2½ hours) and Florence (1 hour). Direct bus service is available from Florence, but not from Rome.

VISITOR INFORMATION

Contact Arezzo Tourism Office. ✉ *Emiciclo Giovanni Paolo II* ☎ *0575/1822770* ⊕ *www.arezzoturismo.it.*

EXPLORING

Fodor$Choice ★ **Basilica di San Francesco.** The famous Piero della Francesca frescoes depicting *The Legend of the True Cross* (1452–66) were executed on the three walls of the Capella Bacci, the apse of this 14th-century church. What Sir Kenneth Clark called "the most perfect morning light in all Renaissance painting" may be seen in the lowest section of the right wall, where the troops of Emperor Maxentius flee before the sign of the cross. The rest of the church is decorated with 14th-, 15th-, and 16th-century frescoes of mixed quality. Reservations are recommended June through September. ✉ *Piazza San Francesco 2* ☎ *0575/352727* ⊕ *www. pierodellafrancesca-ticketoffice.it* 🎟 *€8.*

Duomo. Arezzo's medieval cathedral at the top of the hill contains an eye-level fresco of a tender *Maria Maddalena* by Piero della Francesca (1420–92); look for it in the north aisle next to the large marble tomb near the organ. Construction of the Duomo began in 1278 but twice came to a halt, and the church wasn't completed until 1510. The ceiling decorations and the stained-glass windows date from the 16th century. The facade, designed by Arezzo's Dante Viviani, was added later (1901–14). ✉ *Piazza del Duomo 1* ☎.

Piazza Grande. With its irregular shape and sloping brick pavement, framed by buildings of assorted centuries, Arezzo's central piazza echoes Siena's Piazza del Campo. Though not quite so magnificent, it's lively enough during the outdoor antiques fair the first weekend of the month and when the **Giostra del Saracino** (Saracen Joust), featuring medieval costumes and competition, is held here on the third Saturday of June and on the first Sunday of September. ✉ *Piazza Grande.*

Santa Maria della Pieve (*Church of Saint Mary of the Parish*). The curving, tiered apse on Piazza Grande belongs to a fine Romanesque church that was originally an Early Christian structure, which had been constructed over the remains of a Roman temple. The church was rebuilt in Romanesque style in the 12th century. The splendid facade dates from the early 13th century but includes granite Roman columns. A magnificent polyptych, depicting the Madonna and Child with four saints, by Pietro Lorenzetti (circa 1290–1348), embellishes the high altar. ✉ *Corso Italia 7* ☎.

WHERE TO EAT

$$ SEAFOOD Fodor'sChoice ★ 🍴 **I Tre Bicchieri.** Chef Luigi Casotti hails from Amalfi and this shows through in his fine adaptations of dishes, notably seafood, more commonly served near the Bay of Naples. The antipasti include a delicious *tonno scottato ai semi di papavero e agro di cipolla rossa* (lightly brazed tuna in a poppy seed crust with sweet and sour red onions) and an unusual but equally delightful *salmone selvaggio confit con julienne di zucchine, panna acida e polvere di liquirizia* (wild salmon carpaccio with sour cream, zucchini and licorice). **Known for:** creative menu including two tasting menus; superlative wine list; notable chef. [$] *Average main: €18* ✉ *Piazzetta Sopra i Ponti 3–5* ☎ *0575/26557* 🌐 *www.ristoranteitrebicchieri.com* ⏲ *Closed Sun. (except 1st weekend of month).*

$ ITALIAN 🍴 **La Torre di Gnicche.** Wine lovers shouldn't miss this wine bar/eatery, just off Piazza Grande, with more than 700 labels on the list. Seasonal dishes of traditional fare, such as *acquacotta del casentino* (porcini mushroom soup) and *baccalà in umido* (salt-cod stew), are served in the simply decorated, vaulted dining room. **Known for:** the extensive wine list, with many choices by the glass; an ever-changing menu; the location. [$] *Average main: €10* ✉ *Piaggia San Martino 8* ☎ *0575/352035* 🌐 *www.latorredignicche.it* ⏲ *Closed Wed., and Jan.*

WHERE TO STAY

$ B&B/INN FAMILY Fodor'sChoice ★ 🏨 **Calcione.** The elegant Marchesa Olivella Lotteringhi della Stufa has turned her six-century-old family estate (circa 1483) into a top-notch agriturismo. **Pros:** houses sleep up to 10; large swimming pools; quiet, beautiful, remote setting. **Cons:** private transportation is a must—nearest village is 8 km (5 miles) away; no a/c; minimum one-week stay in season. [$] *Rooms from: €100* ✉ *Località Il Calcione 102, 26 km (15 miles) southwest of Arezzo, Lucignano* ☎ *0575/837153* 🌐 *www.calcione.com* ⏲ *Closed Oct.–mid-Mar.* 🛏 *8 rooms* 🍽 *No meals.*

$$ HOTEL FAMILY Fodor'sChoice ★ 🏨 **Castello di Gargonza.** Enchantment reigns at this tiny 13th-century countryside hamlet, part of the fiefdom of the aristocratic Florentine Guicciardini family and reinvented by the modern Count Roberto Guicciardini as an agriturismo. **Pros:** romantic, one-of-a-kind accommodation in a medieval castle; peaceful, isolated setting. **Cons:** standard rooms are extremely basic; a little out of the way for exploring the region; private transportation is a necessity. [$] *Rooms from: €140* ✉ *SR73, Località Gargonza, 32 km (19 miles) southwest of Arezzo, Monte San Savino* ☎ *0575/847021* 🌐 *www.gargonza.it* ⏲ *Closed last 3 wks in Jan., and Feb.* 🛏 *42 rooms* 🍽 *Free Breakfast.*

Arezzo, Cortona, and Southern Tuscany

$$$$
HOTEL
Fodor'sChoice
★

🏨 **Il Borro.** The location has been described as "heaven on earth," and a stay at this elegant Ferragamo estate is sure to bring similar descriptions to mind. **Pros:** superlative service; great location for exploring eastern Tuscany; unique setting and atmosphere. **Cons:** off the beaten track, making private transport a must; not all suites have country views. $ *Rooms from: €480* ⊠ *Località Il Borro 1, outside village of San Giustino Valdarno, 20 km (12 miles) northwest of Arezzo* ☎ *055/977053* ⊕ *www.ilborro.it* ⊘ *Closed Dec.–Mar.* ⇌ *37 rooms* ⑪ *Free Breakfast.*

SHOPPING

Ever since Etruscan goldsmiths set up their shops here more than 2,000 years ago, Arezzo has been famous for its jewelry. Today the town lays claim to being one of the world's capitals of jewelry design and manufacture, and you can find an impressive display of big-time baubles in the town center's shops.

Arezzo is also famous, at least in Italy, for its antiques dealers. The first weekend of every month, between 8:30 and 5:30, a popular and colorful flea market selling antiques and not-so-antique items takes place in the town's main square, **Piazza Grande,** and in the streets and parks nearby.

CORTONA

29 km (18 miles) south of Arezzo, 79 km (44 miles) east of Siena, 117 km (73 miles) southeast of Florence.

Brought into the limelight by Frances Mayes's book *Under the Tuscan Sun* and a subsequent movie, Cortona is no longer the destination of just a few specialist art historians and those seeking reprieve from busier tourist venues. The main street, Via Nazionale, is now lined with souvenir shops and fills with crowds during summer. Although the main sights of Cortona make braving the bustling center worthwhile, much of the town's charm lies in its maze of quiet backstreets. It's here that you will see laundry hanging from windows, find children playing, and catch the smell of simmering pasta sauce. Wander off the beaten track and you won't be disappointed.

GETTING HERE AND AROUND

Cortona is easily reached by car from the A1 autostrada: take the Valdichiana exit toward Perugia, then follow signs for Cortona. Regular bus service, provided by Etruria Mobilità, is available between Arezzo and Cortona (one hour). Train service to Cortona is made inconvenient by the location of the train station, in the valley 3 km (2 miles) steeply below the town itself. From there, you have to rely on bus or taxi service to get up to Cortona.

VISITOR INFORMATION

Contact Cortona Tourism Office. ⊠ *Piazza Signorelli 9* ☎ *0575/637223* ⊕ *www.cortona-italy.com.*

EXPLORING

Museo Diocesano. Housed in part of the original cathedral structure, this nine-room museum houses an impressive number of large, splendid paintings by native son Luca Signorelli (1445–1523), as well as a beautiful *Annunciation* by Fra Angelico (1387/1400–55), which is a delightful surprise in this small town. The former oratory of the Compagnia del Gesù, reached by descending the 1633 staircase opposite the Duomo, is part of the museum. The church was built between 1498 and 1505 and restructured by Giorgio Vasari in 1543. Frescoes depicting sacrifices from the Old Testament by Doceno (1508–56), based on designs by Vasari, line the walls. ✉ *Piazza Duomo 1* ☎ *0575/62830* 🌐 *www.diocesiarezzo.it* 🎟 *€5.*

Santa Maria al Calcinaio. Legend has it that the image of the Madonna appeared on a wall of a medieval *calcinaio* (lime pit used for curing leather), the site on which the church was then built between 1485 and 1513. The linear gray-and-white interior recalls Florence's Duomo. Sienese architect Francesco di Giorgio (1439–1502) most likely designed the sanctuary: the church is a terrific example of Renaissance architectural principles. ✉ *Località Il Calcinaio 227, 3 km (2 miles) southeast of Cortona's center.*

WHERE TO EAT AND STAY

$$ TUSCAN 🍴 **Osteria del Teatro.** Photographs from theatrical productions spanning many years line the walls of this tavern off Cortona's large Piazza del Teatro. The food is simply delicious—try the *filetto al lardo di colonnata e prugne* (beef cooked with bacon and prunes); service is warm and friendly. **Known for:** food that's in season; lively atmosphere; pretty dining room. [$] *Average main: €18* ✉ *Via Maffei 2* ☎ *0575/630556* 🌐 *www.osteria-del-teatro.it* 🕒 *Closed Wed., and 2 wks in Nov.*

$$$$ B&B/INN 🏨 **Il Falconiere.** Accommodation options here include rooms in an 18th-century villa, suites in the *chiesetta* (chapel, or little church), or for more seclusion, Le Vigne del Falco suites at the far end of the property. **Pros:** attractive setting in the valley beneath Cortona; excellent service; elegant, but relaxed; restaurant and cooking school. **Cons:** a car is a must; some find rooms in main villa a little noisy. [$] *Rooms from: €320* ✉ *Località San Martino 370, 3 km (2 miles) north of Cortona* ☎ *0575/612679* 🌐 *www.ilfalconiere.com* 🕒 *Closed last 3 wks in Jan.–mid-Feb.* 🛏 *23 rooms* 🍽 *Free Breakfast.*

SOUTHERN TUSCANY

Southeast of Siena, not far from the Umbrian border, the towns of Montepulciano, Montalcino, and Pienza are Tuscan classics—perched on hills, constructed during the Middle Ages and the Renaissance, and saturated with fine wine. Venture farther south and you encounter Tuscany with a rougher edge: the Maremma region is populated by cowboys, and a good portion of the landscape remains wild. But you won't forget you're in Italy here; the wine is still excellent, and some locals house their wares in Etruscan tombs.

MONTEPULCIANO

65 km (40 miles) southeast of Siena.

Perched on a hilltop, Montepulciano is made up of a pyramid of red-brick buildings set within a circle of cypress trees. At an altitude of almost 2,000 feet, it is cool in summer and chilled in winter by biting winds sweeping down its spiraling streets. The town has an unusually harmonious look, the result of the work of three architects: Antonio da Sangallo "il Vecchio" (circa 1455–1534), Vignola (1507–73), and Michelozzo (1396–1472). The group endowed it with fine palaces and churches in an attempt to impose Renaissance architectural ideals on an ancient Tuscan hill town.

GETTING HERE AND AROUND

From Rome or Florence, take the Chiusi–Chianciano exit from the A1 (Autostrada del Sole). From Siena, take the SR2 south to San Quirico and then the SP146 to Montepulciano. Tra-In offers bus service from Siena to Montepulciano several times a day. Montepulciano's train station is in Montepulciano Stazione, 10 km (6 miles) away.

VISITOR INFORMATION

Contact Montepulciano Tourism Office. ✉ *Piazza Don Minzoni 1* ☎ *0578/757341* 🌐 *www.prolocomontepulciano.it.*

EXPLORING

Duomo. On the Piazza Grande the unfinished facade of Montepulciano's cathedral doesn't measure up to the beauty of its neighboring palaces. On the inside, however, its Renaissance roots shine through. The high altar has a splendid triptych painted in 1401 by Taddeo di Bartolo (circa 1362–1422), and you can see fragments of the tomb of Bartolomeo Aragazzi, secretary to Pope Martin V, which was sculpted by Michelozzo between 1427 and 1436. ✉ *Piazza Grande* ☎ *0578/757341.*

Piazza Grande. Filled with handsome buildings, this large square on the heights of the old historic town is Montepulciano's pièce de résistance. ✉ *Piazza Grande.*

Fodor's Choice ★ **San Biagio.** Designed by Antonio da Sangallo il Vecchio, and considered his masterpiece, this church sits on the hillside below the town walls and is a model of High Renaissance architectural perfection. Inside the church is a painting of the Madonna that, according to legend, was the only thing remaining in an abandoned church that two young girls entered on April 23, 1518. The girls saw the eyes of the Madonna moving, and that same afternoon so did a farmer and a cow, who knelt down in front of the painting. In 1963 the image was proclaimed the Madonna del Buon Viaggio (Madonna of the Good Journey), the protector of tourists in Italy. ✉ *Via di San Biagio* ☎ *0578/757164.*

WHERE TO EAT

$$ TUSCAN Fodor's Choice ★ 🍴 **La Grotta.** You might be tempted to pass right by the innocuous entrance across the street from San Biagio, but you'd miss some fantastic food. Try the *pici fatti a mano con ragù di anatra e lenticchie* (homemade noodles with duck sauce and lentils) or *carrè di agnello alle erbe aromatiche con verdure al forno* (rack of lamb with herbs and baked vegetables). **Known for:** creative menu; the wine list; stellar service. [$] *Average main: €21* ✉ *Via di San Biagio 15* ☎ *0578/757479* 🌐 *www.lagrottamontepulciano.it* ⏲ *Closed Wed., and mid-Jan.–mid-Mar.*

$ TUSCAN Fodor's Choice ★ 🍴 **Osteria del Conte.** As high in Montepulciano as you can get, just behind the Duomo, this small and intimate restaurant is expertly run by the mother-and-son team of Lorena and Paolo Brachi. Passionate about the food they prepare, both have a flair for the region's traditional dishes—the pici *all'aglione* (with garlic sauce) and the *filetto ai funghi porcini* (steak with porcini mushrooms) are mouthwateringly good. **Known for:** fine home cooking; good local wines; attentive service. [$] *Average main: €11* ✉ *Via di San Donato 19* ☎ *0578/756062* 🌐 *www.osteriadelconte.it* 🕒 *Closed Wed.*

WHERE TO STAY

$$$ B&B/INN Fodor's Choice ★ 🏨 **Podere Dionora.** At this secluded and serene country inn, earth-tone fabrics complement antiques in the individually decorated rooms, all of which have functioning fireplaces. **Pros:** secluded setting; great views; attentive service. **Cons:** long walk to the nearest town; need a car to get around. [$] *Rooms from: €280* ✉ *Via Vicinale di Poggiano 9, 3 km (2 miles) east of Montepulciano town center* ☎ *0578/717496* 🌐 *www.dionora.it* 🕒 *Closed mid-Dec.–mid-Mar.* 🔑 *6 rooms* 🍽 *Free Breakfast.*

$ B&B/INN FAMILY 🏨 **San Biagio.** A five-minute walk from the church of the same name, this family-run inn with simply decorated rooms makes a great base for exploring Montepulciano and the surrounding countryside. **Pros:** heated indoor pool; family-friendly atmosphere. **Cons:** some rooms face a busy road; lots of tour groups. [$] *Rooms from: €105* ✉ *Via San Bartolomeo 2* ☎ *0578/717233* 🌐 *www.albergosanbiagio.it* 🔑 *27 rooms* 🍽 *Free Breakfast.*

PIENZA

14 km (9 miles) west of Montepulciano, 52 km (32 miles) southeast of Siena.

Pienza owes its appearance to Pope Pius II (1405–64), who had grand plans to transform his hometown of Corsignano—its former name—into a compact model Renaissance town. The man entrusted with the transformation was Bernardo Rossellino (1409–64), a protégé of the great Renaissance architectural theorist Leon Battista Alberti (1404–72). His mandate was to create a cathedral, a papal palace, and a town hall that adhered to the vainglorious pope's principles. Gothic and Renaissance styles were fused, and the buildings were decorated with Sienese paintings. The net result was a project that expressed Renaissance ideals of art, architecture, and civilized good living in a single scheme: it stands as an exquisite example of the architectural canons that Alberti formulated in the early Renaissance and that were utilized by later architects, including Michelangelo, in designing many of Italy's finest buildings and piazzas. Today the cool nobility of Pienza's center seems almost surreal in this otherwise unpretentious village, renowned for its smooth sheep's-milk pecorino cheese.

GETTING HERE AND AROUND

From Siena, drive south along the SR2 to San Quirico d'Orcia and then take the SP146. The trip should take just over an hour. Tra-In shuttles passengers between Siena and Pienza. There is no train service to Pienza.

VISITOR INFORMATION

Contact Pienza tourism office. ✉ *Piazza Dante 18* ☎ *0578/749071* 🌐 *www.pienza.info.*

EXPLORING

Duomo. This 15th-century cathedral was built by the architect Rossellino under the influence of Alberti. The travertine facade is divided in three parts, with Renaissance arches under the pope's coat of arms encircled by a wreath of fruit. Inside, the cathedral is simple but richly decorated with Sienese paintings. The building's perfection didn't last long—the first cracks appeared immediately after the building was completed, and its foundations have shifted slightly ever since as rain erodes the hillside behind. You can see this effect if you look closely at the base of the first pier as you enter the church and compare it with the last. ✉ *Piazza Pio II* ☎ *0578/749071.*

Palazzo Piccolomini. In 1459 Pius II commissioned Rossellino to design the perfect palazzo for his papal court. The architect took Florence's Palazzo Rucellai by Alberti as a model and designed this 100-room palace. Three sides of the building fit perfectly into the urban plan around it, while the fourth, looking over the valley, has a lovely loggia uniting it with the gardens in back. Guided tours departing every 30 minutes take you to visit the papal apartments, including a beautiful library, the Sala delle Armi (with an impressive weapons collection), and the music room, with its extravagant wooden ceiling forming four letter Ps, for Pope, Pius, Piccolomini, and Pienza. The last tour departs 30 minutes before closing. ✉ *Piazza Pio II* ☎ *0577/286300* 🌐 *www.palazzopiccolominipienza.it* 🎫 *€7* ⏲ *Closed early Jan.–mid-Feb., mid-Nov.–late Nov.*

WHERE TO EAT AND STAY

$$ TUSCAN 🍴 **La Chiocciola.** Take the few minutes to walk from the old town for typical Pienza fare, including homemade pici with hare or wild-boar sauce. The restaurant's version of *formaggio in forno* (baked cheese) with assorted accompaniments such as fresh porcini mushrooms is reason enough to venture here. **Known for:** beloved by locals; simple, well-prepared food; good wine list. [$] *Average main: €15* ✉ *Via Mencatelli 2* ☎ *0578/748683* 🌐 *www.trattorialachiocciola.it* ⏲ *Closed Wed., and 2 wks in Feb.*

$ TUSCAN 🍴 **Osteria Sette di Vino.** Tasty dishes based on the region's cheeses are the specialty at this simple and inexpensive osteria on a quiet, pleasant square in the center of Pienza. Try versions of pici or the starter of radicchio baked quickly to brown the edges. **Known for:** pecorino tasting menu; bean soup; its lively proprietor. [$] *Average main: €10* ✉ *Piazza di Spagna 1* ☎ *0578/749092* 💳 *No credit cards* ⏲ *Closed Wed., July 1–15, and Nov.*

$ B&B/INN FAMILY Fodor's Choice ★ 🏨 **Agriturismo Cerreto.** Built a short distance from Pienza in the 18th and 19th centuries, this grouping of farm buildings is now done in traditional Tuscan decor with terra-cotta flooring, wood beams, wrought-iron beds, and heavy oak furniture in the nine apartments. **Pros:** peaceful country setting; great for families and small groups; good base for exploring the Val d'Orcia. **Cons:** private transportation a must; closest restaurants and town 5 km (3 miles) away. [$] *Rooms from: €110* ✉ *Strada Provinciale per*

Sant'Anna in Camprena, 5 km (3 miles) north of Pienza ☎ 0578/749121
⊕ *www.agriturismocerreto.com ⟳ 9 apartments ⫶⃝ Free Breakfast.*

MONTALCINO

12

23 km (14 miles) west of Pienza, 41 km (25 miles) south of Siena.

Tiny Montalcino, with its commanding view from high on a hill, can claim an Etruscan past. It saw a fair number of travelers, as it was directly on the road from Siena to Rome. During the early Middle Ages it enjoyed a brief period of autonomy before falling under the orbit of Siena in 1201. Now Montalcino's greatest claim to fame is that it produces Brunello di Montalcino, one of Italy's most esteemed reds. Driving to the town, you pass through the brunello vineyards. You can sample the excellent but expensive red in wine cellars in town or visit a nearby winery, such as Fattoria dei Barbi, for a guided tour and tasting; you must call ahead for reservations.

GETTING HERE AND AROUND

By car, follow the SR2 south from Siena, then follow the SP45 to Montalcino. Several Tra-In buses travel between Siena and Montalcino daily, making a tightly scheduled day trip possible. There is no train service available.

VISITOR INFORMATION

Contact Montalcino Tourism Office. ✉ *Costa del Municipio 1* ☎ *0577/849331* ⊕ *www.prolocomontalcino.com.*

EXPLORING

La Fortezza. Providing refuge for the last remnants of the Sienese army during the Florentine conquest of 1555, the battlements of this 14th-century fortress are still in excellent condition. Climb up the narrow, spiral steps for the 360-degree view of most of southern Tuscany. An enoteca for tasting wines is on-site. ✉ *Piazzale Fortezza* ☎ *0577/849211* ▱ *Fortress free, walls €4* ⊘ *Closed Mon. Nov.–Mar.*

Museo Civico e Diocesano d'Arte Sacra. This fine museum is housed in a building that once belonged to 13th-century Augustinian monks. The ticket booth is in the glorious refurbished cloister, and the sacred art collection, gathered from churches throughout the region, is displayed on two floors in former monastic quarters. Although the art here might be called B-list, a fine altarpiece by Bartolo di Fredi (circa 1330–1410), the *Coronation of the Virgin,* makes dazzling use of gold. In addition, there's a striking 12th-century crucifix that originally adorned the high altar of the church of Sant'Antimo. Also on hand are many wood sculptures, a typical medium in these parts during the Renaissance. ✉ *Via Ricasoli 31* ☎ *0577/846014* ⊕ *www.museisenesi.org* ▱ *€4.50* ⊘ *Closed Mon.*

WHERE TO EAT AND STAY

$$
WINE BAR
Fodor's Choice
★

✕ **Enoteca Osteria Osticcio.** Tullio and Francesca Scrivano have beautifully remodeled this restaurant and wineshop, which serves a light menu that pairs nicely with the lovely wines here, the main draw. The *acciughe sotto pesto* (anchovies with pesto) is a particularly fine treat. **Known for:** amazing wine list; gorgeous view of nearby hills; tasty food.

[$] *Average main: €18* ✉ *Via Matteotti 23* ☎ *0577/848056* 🌐 *www.osticcio.it* ⏲ *Closed Wed. No dinner Tues.*

$$$$ RESORT Fodor's Choice ★ 🏨 **Castiglion del Bosco.** This estate, one of the largest still in private hands in Tuscany, was purchased at the beginning of this century and meticulously converted into a second-to-none resort that incorporates a medieval *borgo* (village) and surrounding farmhouses. **Pros:** extremely secluded, in exclusive and tranquil location; includes suites and multi-bedroom villas; top-notch service; breathtaking scenery. **Cons:** well off the beaten track, the nearest town is 12 km (7½ miles) away; private transportation required. [$] *Rooms from: €1392* ✉ *Località Castiglion del Bosco* ☎ *0577/1913111* 🌐 *www.castigliondelbosco.com* 🛏 *33 rooms* 🍴 *Free Breakfast.*

$ B&B/INN 🏨 **La Crociona.** A quiet and serene family-owned farm in the middle of a small vineyard with glorious views houses guests in lovely apartments that can sleep up to five people. **Pros:** peaceful location; great for families or small groups; friendly atmosphere. **Cons:** no a/c; need a car to get around. [$] *Rooms from: €95* ✉ *Località La Croce 15* ☎ *0577/848007* 🌐 *www.lacrociona.com* 🛏 *7 apartments* 🍴 *No meals.*

ABBAZIA DI SANT'ANTIMO

10 km (6 miles) south of Montalcino, 51 km (32 miles) south of Siena.

GETTING HERE AND AROUND

The Abbazia di Sant'Antimo, nestled below the town of Castelnuovo dell'Abate, is a 15-minute drive from Montalcino. Tra-In bus service is extremely limited, and the abbey cannot be reached by train.

EXPLORING

Fodor's Choice ★ **Abbazia di Sant'Antimo.** It's well worth your while to go out of your way to visit this 12th-century Romanesque abbey, as it's a gem of pale stone in the silvery green of an olive grove. The exterior and interior sculpture is outstanding, particularly the nave capitals, a combination of French, Lombard, and even Spanish influences. The sacristy (seldom open) forms part of the primitive Carolingian church (founded in AD 781), its entrance flanked by 9th-century pilasters. The small vaulted crypt dates from the same period. Above the nave runs a *matroneum* (women's gallery), an unusual feature once used to separate the congregation. Equally unusual is the ambulatory, for which the three radiating chapels were almost certainly copied from a French model. Stay to hear the canonical hours celebrated in Gregorian chant. On the road that leads up toward Castelnuovo dell'Abate is a small shop that sells souvenirs and has washrooms. A 2½-hour hiking trail (signed as #2) leads to the abbey from Montalcino. Starting near Montalcino's small cemetery, the trail heads south through woods, along a ridge road to the tiny hamlet of Villa a Tolli, and then downhill to Sant'Antimo. ✉ *Castelnuovo dell'Abate* ☎ *0577/286300* 🌐 *www.antimo.it.*

UMBRIA AND
THE MARCHES

WELCOME TO UMBRIA AND THE MARCHES

TOP REASONS TO GO

★ **Palazzo Ducale, Urbino:** A visit here reveals more about the ideals of the Renaissance than a shelf of history books could.

★ **Assisi, shrine to St. Francis:** Recharge your soul in this rose-color hill town with a visit to the gentle saint's majestic basilica, adorned with great frescoes.

★ **Spoleto, Umbria's musical Mecca:** Crowds may descend and prices ascend here during summer's Festival dei Due Mondi, but Spoleto's hushed charm enchants year-round.

★ **Tantalizing truffles:** Are Umbria's celebrated "black diamonds" coveted for their pungent flavor, their rarity, or their power in the realm of romance?

★ **Orvieto's Duomo:** Arresting visions of heaven and hell on the facade and brilliant frescoes within make this Gothic cathedral a dazzler.

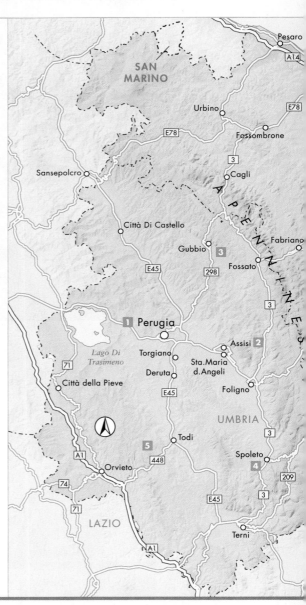

13

1 **Perugia.** Umbria's largest town is home to some of Perugino's great frescoes.

2 **Assisi.** The city of St. Francis is a major pilgrimage site but still maintains its medieval hill-town character.

3 **Northern Umbria.** The quiet towns lying around Perugia include Deruta, which produces exceptional ceramics.

4 **Spoleto.** Don't miss the Piazza del Duomo, the Filippo Lippi frescoes in the cathedral, and the massive castle towering over the town.

5 **Southern Umbria.** Of central Italy's many hill towns, none has a more impressive setting than Orvieto, perched on a plateau 1,000 feet above the surrounding valley.

6 **The Marches.** East of Umbria, the steep, twisting roads of this region lead to well-preserved medieval towns before settling down to the sandy beaches of the Adriatic.

EATING AND DRINKING WELL IN UMBRIA AND THE MARCHES

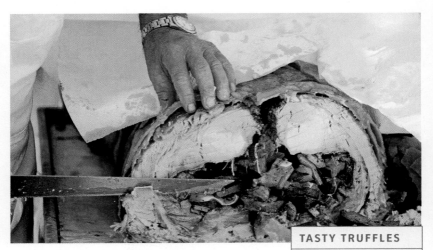

Central Italy is mountainous, and its food is hearty and straightforward, with a stick-to-the-ribs quality that sees hardworking farmers and artisans through a long day's work and helps them make the steep climb home at night.

In restaurants here, as in much of Italy, you're rewarded for seeking out the local cuisines, and you'll often find better and cheaper food if you're willing to stray a few hundred yards from the main sights. Spoleto is noted for its good food and service, probably a result of high expectations from the international arts crowd. For gourmets, however, it's hard to beat Spello, which has both excellent restaurants and first-rate wine merchants.

A rule of thumb for eating well throughout Umbria is to order what's in season; the trick is to stroll through local markets to see what's for sale. A number of restaurants in the region offer *degustazione* (tasting) menus, which give you a chance to try different local specialties without breaking the bank.

TASTY TRUFFLES

More truffles are found in Umbria than anywhere else in Italy. Spoleto and Norcia are prime territory for the *tartufo nero* (reddish-black interior and fine white veins) prized for its extravagant flavor and intense aroma.

The mild summer truffle, *scorzone estivo* (black outside and beige inside), is in season from May through December. The *scorzone autunnale* (burnt brown color and visible veins inside) is found from October through December. Truffles can be shaved into omelets or over pasta, pounded into sauces, or chopped and mixed with oil.

OLIVE OIL

Nearly everywhere you look in Umbria, olive trees grace the hillsides. The soil of the Apennines allows the olives to ripen slowly, guaranteeing low acidity, a cardinal virtue of fine oil. Look for restaurants that proudly display their own oil, often a sign that they care about their food.

Umbria's finest oil is found in Trevi, where the local product is intensely green and fruity. You can sample it in the town's wine bars, which often do double duty, offering olive-oil tastings.

PORK PRODUCTS

Much of traditional Umbrian cuisine revolves around pork. It can be cooked in wood-fire stoves, sometimes basted with a rich sauce made from innards and red wine. The roasted pork known as *porchetta (pictured at left)* is grilled on a spit and flavored with fennel and herbs, leaving a crisp outer sheen.

The art of pork processing has been handed down through generations in Norcia, so much so that charcuterie producers throughout Italy are often known as *norcini.* Don't miss *prosciutto di Norcia,* which is aged for two years.

LENTILS AND SOUPS

The town of Castelluccio di Norcia is particularly known for its lentils and its farro (an ancient grain used by the Romans, similar to wheat), and a variety of beans used in soups. Throughout

Umbria, look for *imbrecciata,* a soup of beans and grains, delicately flavored with local herbs. Other ingredients that find their way into thick Umbrian soups are wild beet, sorrel, mushrooms, spelt, chickpeas, and the elusive, fragrant saffron, grown in nearby Cascia.

WINE

Sagrantino grapes are the star in Umbria's most notable red wines. For centuries they've been used in Sagrantino *passito,* a semisweet wine made by leaving the grapes to dry for a period after picking in order to intensify their sugar content. In recent decades, Montefalco Sagrantino *secco* (dry) has occupied the front stage. Both passito and secco have a deep red-ruby color, with a full body and rich flavor.

In the past few years the phenomenon of the *enoteca* (wineshop and wine bar) has taken off, making it easier to arrange wine tastings. Many also let you sample different olive oils on toasted bread, known as bruschetta. Some wine information centers, such as La Strada del Sagrantino in the town of Montefalco, will help set up appointments for tastings.

Updated by Robert Andrews

Birthplace of saints and home to some of the country's greatest artistic treasures, central Italy is a collection of misty green valleys and picture-perfect hill towns laden with centuries of history.

Umbria and the Marches are the Italian countryside as you've imagined it: verdant farmland, steep hillsides topped with medieval fortresses, and winding country roads. No single town here has the extravagant wealth of art and architecture of Florence, Rome, or Venice, but this works in your favor; small jewels of towns feel knowable, not overwhelming. And the cultural cupboard is far from bare. Orvieto's cathedral and Assisi's basilica are two of the most important sights in Italy, while Perugia, Todi, Gubbio, and Spoleto are rich in art and architecture.

East of Umbria, the Marches (Le Marche to Italians) stretch between the Apennines and the Adriatic Sea. It's a region of great turreted castles on high peaks defending passes and roads—a testament to the centuries of battle that have taken place here. Rising majestically in Urbino is a splendid palace, built by Federico da Montefeltro, where the humanistic ideals of the Renaissance came to their fullest flower, while the town of Ascoli Piceno can lay claim to one of the most beautiful squares in Italy. Virtually every small town in the region has a castle, church, or museum worth a visit—but even without them, you'd still be compelled to stop for the interesting streets, panoramic views, and natural beauty.

UMBRIA AND THE MARCHES PLANNER

MAKING THE MOST OF YOUR TIME

Umbria is a nicely compact collection of character-rich hill towns; you can settle in one, then explore the others, as well as the countryside and forest in between, on day trips.

Perugia, Umbria's largest and liveliest city, is a logical choice for your base, particularly if you're arriving from the north. If you want something a little quieter, virtually any other town in the region will suit your purposes; even Assisi, which overflows with bus tours during the day, is delightfully quiet in the evening and early morning. Spoleto and

Orvieto are the most developed towns to the south, but they're still of modest proportions.

If you have the time to venture farther afield, consider trips to Gubbio, northeast of Perugia, and Urbino, in the Marches. Both are worth the time it takes to reach them, and both make for pleasant overnight stays. In southern Umbria, Valnerina and the Piano Grande are out-of-the-way spots with the region's best hiking.

FESTIVALS

Eurochocolate Festival. If you've got a sweet tooth and are visiting in fall, book early and head to Perugia for the Eurochocolate Festival. This is one of the biggest chocolate festivals in the world, with a million visitors, and is held in the third week of October. ⊕ *www.eurochocolate. com.*

Festival dei Due Mondi. Each summer Umbria hosts one of Italy's biggest arts festivals: Spoleto's Festival of the Two Worlds. Starting out as a classical music festival, it has now evolved into one of Italy's brightest gatherings of arts aficionados. Running from late June through mid-July, it features modern and classical music, theater, dance, and opera. Increasingly there are also a number of small cinema producers and their films. ⊕ *www.festivaldispoleto.com.*

Umbria Jazz Festival. Perugia is hopping for 10 days in July, when more than a million people flock to see famous names in contemporary music perform at the Umbria Jazz Festival. In recent years the stars have included Wynton Marsalis, Sting, Eric Clapton, Lady Gaga, Tony Bennett, and Elton John. ⊕ *www.umbriajazz.com.*

If you want to attend an event, you should make arrangements in advance. And if you don't want to attend, you should plan to avoid the cities during festival time, when hotel rooms and restaurant tables are at a premium. A similar caveat applies for Assisi during religious festivals at Christmas, Easter, the feast of Saint Francis (October 4), and Calendimaggio (May 1), when pilgrims arrive en masse.

GETTING HERE AND AROUND

BUS TRAVEL

Perugia's bus station is in Piazza Partigiani, which you can reach by taking the escalators from the town center.

Local bus services between all the major and minor towns of Umbria are good. Some of the routes in rural areas are designed to serve as many places as possible and are, therefore, quite roundabout and slow. Schedules change often, so consult with local tourist offices before setting out.

Flixbus. Connections between Rome and Perugia, Rome and Urbino, and Perugia and Florence are provided by the bus company Flixbus. ⊕ *www.flixbus.com.*

Sulga Line. Perugia is served by the Sulga Line, which has daily departures to Assisi, Città di Castello, Sansepolcro, Ravenna, Rome's Stazione Tiburtina, and Fiumicino airport in Rome. ☎ *800/099661* ⊕ *www. sulga.eu.*

13

CAR TRAVEL

On the western edge of the region is the Umbrian section of the Autostrada del Sole (A1), Italy's principal north–south highway. It links Florence and Rome with Orvieto and passes near Todi and Terni. The S3 intersects with the A1 and leads on to Assisi and Urbino. The Adriatica superhighway (A14) runs north–south along the coast, linking the Marches to Bologna and Venice.

The steep hills and deep valleys that make Umbria and the Marches so idyllic also make for challenging driving. Fortunately, the area has an excellent, modern road network, but be prepared for tortuous mountain roads if your explorations take you off the beaten track. Central Umbria is served by a major highway, the S75bis, which passes along the shore of Lake Trasimeno and ends in Perugia. Assisi is served by the modern highway S75; the S75 connects to the S3 and S3bis, which cover the heart of the region. Major inland routes connect coastal A14 to large towns in the Marches, but inland secondary roads in mountain areas can be winding and narrow. Always carry a good map, a flashlight, and, if possible, a cell phone in case of a breakdown.

TRAIN TRAVEL

Several direct daily trains run by the Italian state railway, **Trenitalia** (☎ *892021* ⊕ *www.trenitalia.com*), link Florence and Rome with Perugia and Assisi, and local service to the same area is available from Terontola (on the Rome–Florence line) and from Foligno (on the Rome–Ancona line). Intercity trains between Rome and Florence make stops in Orvieto, and the main Rome–Ancona line passes through Narni, Terni, Spoleto, and Foligno.

RESTAURANTS

As befits a landlocked territory, the cuisine of Umbria is firmly based on its fresh agricultural produce. Consequently, most restaurants in the region offer menus that are strictly seasonal, though locals have ensured that the food most associated with Umbria—*tartufi*, or truffles—is available year-round thanks to their mastery of freezing, drying and preserving techniques. Truffles may be added to a variety of dishes, not least the local pastas *stringozzi* (also written *strengozzi* or *strangozzi*) and *ombrichelli*. Lamb, pork, and boar are the most common meats consumed in Umbria, while lentils grown around Castelluccio are also highly prized. Seafood from the Adriatic predominates in the coastal Marches region, often made into *brodetto*, a savory fish soup. Inland, Ascoli Piceno is renowned for its stuffed green olives. *Restaurant reviews have been shortened. For full information, visit Fodors.com.*

HOTELS

Virtually every older town, no matter how small, has some kind of hotel. A trend, particularly around Gubbio, Orvieto, and Todi, is to convert old villas, farms, and monasteries into first-class hotels. The natural splendor of the countryside more than compensates for the distance from town—provided you have a car. Hotels in town tend to be simpler than their country cousins, with a few notable exceptions in Spoleto, Gubbio, and Perugia. *Hotel reviews have been shortened. For full information, visit Fodors.com.*

WHAT IT COSTS (IN EUROS)			
$	$$	$$$	$$$$
Restaurants	under €15	€15–€24	€25–€35	over €35
Hotels	under €125	€125–€200	€201–€300	over €300

13

VISITOR INFORMATION

Umbria regional tourism office. Umbria's regional tourism office is in Perugia. The staff are well informed about the area and can give you a wide selection of leaflets and maps to assist you during your trip. It's open daily 9–6. ⊠ *Piazza Matteotti 18, Perugia* ☎ *075/5736458* ⊕ *www.umbriatourism.it.*

PERUGIA

Perugia is a majestic, handsome, wealthy city, and with its trendy boutiques, refined cafés, and grandiose architecture, it doesn't try to hide its affluence. A student population of more than 30,000 means that the city, with a permanent population of about 170,000, is abuzz with activity throughout the year. Umbria Jazz, one of the region's most important music festivals, attracts music lovers from around the world every July, and Eurochocolate, the international chocolate festival, is an irresistible draw each October for anyone with a sweet tooth.

GETTING HERE AND AROUND

The best approach to the city is by train. The area around the station doesn't attest to the rest of Perugia's elegance, but buses running from the station to Piazza d'Italia, the heart of the old town, are frequent. If you're in a hurry, take the *minimetro,* a one-line subway, to Stazione della Cupa. If you're driving to Perugia and your hotel doesn't have parking facilities, leave your car in one of the lots close to the center. Electronic displays indicate the location of lots and the number of spaces free. If you park in the Piazza Partigiani, take the escalators that pass through the fascinating subterranean excavations of the Roman foundations of the city and lead to the town center.

EXPLORING

TOP ATTRACTIONS

Collegio del Cambio (*Bankers' Guild Hall*). These elaborate rooms, on the ground floor of the **Palazzo dei Priori,** served as the meeting hall and chapel of the guild of bankers and money changers. Most of the frescoes were completed by the most important Perugian painter of the Renaissance, Pietro Vannucci, better known as Perugino. He included a remarkably honest self-portrait on one of the pilasters. The iconography includes common religious themes, such as the Nativity and the Transfiguration seen on the end walls. On the left wall are female figures representing the virtues, and beneath them are the heroes and sages of antiquity. On the right wall are figures presumed to have been painted in part by Perugino's most famous pupil, Raphael. (His hand, experts

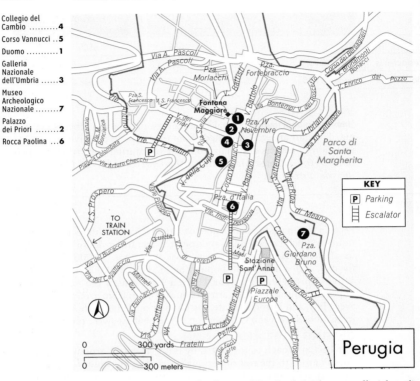

Perugia

say, is most apparent in the figure of Fortitude.) The *cappella* (chapel) of San Giovanni Battista has frescoes painted by Giannicola di Paolo, another student of Perugino's. ⊠ *Corso Vannucci 25* ☏ *075/5728599* ⊕ *www.collegiodelcambio.it* 🎫 *€4.50* ⊗ *Closed Sun. afternoon, also Mon. afternoon Nov.–Mar.*

Corso Vannucci. A string of elegantly connected palazzi expresses the artistic nature of this city center, the heart of which is concentrated along Corso Vannucci. Stately and broad, this pedestrians-only street runs from Piazza Italia to Piazza IV Novembre. Along the way, the entrances to many of Perugia's side streets might tempt you to wander off and explore. But don't stray too far as evening falls, when Corso Vannucci fills with Perugians out for their evening *passeggiata*, a pleasant predinner stroll that may include a pause for an aperitif at one of the many bars that line the street. ⊠ *Perugia.*

Fodor'sChoice **Galleria Nazionale dell'Umbria.** The region's most comprehensive art gal-
★ lery is housed on the fourth floor of the **Palazzo dei Priori.** Enhanced by skillfully lit displays and computers that allow you to focus on the works' details and background information, the collection includes work by native artists—most notably Pintoricchio (1454–1513) and Perugino (circa 1450–1523)—and others of the Umbrian and Tuscan schools, among them Gentile da Fabriano (1370–1427), Duccio (circa

1255–1318), Fra Angelico (1387–1455), Fiorenzo di Lorenzo (1445–1525), and Piero della Francesca (1420–92). In addition to paintings, the gallery has frescoes, sculptures, and some superb examples of crucifixes from the 13th and 14th centuries. Some rooms are dedicated to Perugia itself, showing how the medieval city evolved. ✉ *Corso Vannucci 19, Piazza IV Novembre* ☎ *075/58668415* ⊕ *www.gallerianazionaledellumbria.it* 🎫 *€8* ⊘ *Closed Mon.*

Palazzo dei Priori (*Palace of the Priors*). A series of elegant connected buildings, the palazzo serves as Perugia's city hall and houses three of the city's museums. The buildings string along Corso Vannucci and wrap around the Piazza IV Novembre, where the original entrance is located. The steps here lead to the **Sala dei Notari** (Notaries' Hall). Other entrances lead to the **Galleria Nazionale dell'Umbria,** the **Collegio del Cambio,** and the **Collegio della Mercanzia.** The Sala dei Notari, which dates back to the 13th century and was the original meeting place of the town merchants, had become the seat of the notaries by the second half of the 15th century. Wood beams and an interesting array of frescoes attributed to Maestro di Farneto embellish the room. Coats of arms and crests line the back and right lateral walls; you can spot some famous figures from Aesop's *Fables* on the left wall. The palazzo facade is adorned with symbols of Perugia's pride and past power: the griffin is the city symbol, and the lion denotes Perugia's allegiance to the Guelph (or papal) cause. ✉ *Piazza IV Novembre 25* 🎫 *Free.*

Rocca Paolina. A labyrinth of little streets, alleys, and arches, this underground city was originally part of a fortress built at the behest of Pope Paul III between 1540 and 1543 to confirm papal dominion over the city. Parts of it were destroyed after the end of papal rule, but much still remains. Begin your visit by taking the escalators that descend through the subterranean ruins from Piazza Italia down to Via Masi. In the summer this is the coolest place in the city. ✉ *Piazza Italia* 🎫 *Free.*

WORTH NOTING

Duomo. Severe yet mystical, the Cathedral of San Lorenzo is most famous for being the home of the wedding ring of the Virgin Mary, stolen by the Perugians in 1488 from the nearby town of Chiusi. The ring, kept high up in a red-curtained vault in the chapel immediately to the left of the entrance, is stored under lock—15 locks, to be precise—and key most of the year. It's shown to the public on July 30 (the day it was brought to Perugia) and the second-to-last Sunday in January (Mary's wedding anniversary). The cathedral itself dates from the Middle Ages, and has many additions from the 15th and 16th centuries. The most visually interesting element is the altar to the Madonna of Grace; an elegant fresco on a column at the right of the entrance of the altar depicts *La Madonna delle Grazie* and is surrounded by prayer benches decorated with handwritten notes to the Holy Mother. Around the column are small amulets—symbols of gratitude from those whose prayers were answered. There are also elaborately carved choir stalls, executed by Giovanni Battista Bastone in 1520. The altarpiece (1484), an early masterpiece by Luca Signorelli (circa 1441–1523), shows the Madonna with St. John the Baptist, St. Onophrius, and St. Lawrence. Sections of the church may be closed to visitors during religious services.

UMBRIA THROUGH THE AGES

The earliest inhabitants of Umbria, the Umbri, were thought by the Romans to be the most ancient inhabitants of Italy. Little is known about them; with the coming of Etruscan culture the tribe fled into the mountains in the eastern portion of the region. The Etruscans, who founded some of the great cities of Umbria, were in turn supplanted by the Romans. Unlike Tuscany and other regions of central Italy, Umbria had few powerful medieval families to exert control over the cities in the Middle Ages—its proximity to Rome ensured that it would always be more or less under papal domination.

In the center of the country, Umbria has for much of its history been a battlefield where armies from north and south clashed. Hannibal destroyed a Roman army on the shores of Lake Trasimeno, and the bloody course of the interminable Guelph–Ghibelline conflict of the Middle Ages was played out here. Dante considered Umbria the most violent place in Italy. Trophies of war still decorate the Palazzo dei Priori in Perugia, and the little town of Gubbio continues a warlike rivalry begun in the Middle Ages—every year it challenges the Tuscan town of Sansepolcro to a crossbow tournament. Today the bowmen shoot at targets, but neither side has forgotten that 500 years ago they were shooting at each other.

In spite of—or perhaps because of—this bloodshed, Umbria has produced more than its share of Christian saints. The most famous is St. Francis, the decidedly pacifist saint whose life shaped the Church of his time. His great shrine at Assisi is visited by hundreds of thousands of pilgrims each year. St. Clare, his devoted follower, was Umbria-born, as were St. Benedict, St. Rita of Cascia, and the patron saint of lovers, St. Valentine.

The **Museo Capitolare** displays a large array of precious objects associated with the cathedral, including vestments, vessels, and manuscripts. Outside the Duomo is the elaborate **Fontana Maggiore,** which dates from 1278. It's adorned with zodiac figures and symbols of the seven arts. ✉ *Piazza IV Novembre* ☎ *075/5723832* ⊕ *www.cattedrale.perugia.it* 🎟 *Museum* €6 ⊘ *Museum closed Mon.*

Museo Archeologico Nazionale. An excellent collection of Etruscan artifacts from throughout the region sheds light on Perugia as a flourishing Etruscan city long before it fell under Roman domination in 310 BC. Little else remains of Perugia's mysterious ancestors, although the Arco di Augusto, in Piazza Fortebraccio, the northern entrance to the city, is of Etruscan origin. ✉ *Piazza G. Bruno 10* ☎ *075/5727141* ⊕ *www. polomusealeumbria.beniculturali.it* 🎟 *€5.*

WHERE TO EAT

$$
UMBRIAN
✕ **Antica Trattoria San Lorenzo.** Both the food and the service are outstanding at this popular small, brick-vaulted eatery next to the Duomo. Particular attention is paid to adapting traditional Umbrian cuisine to the modern palate, and there's also a nice variety of seafood dishes on the

menu. **Known for:** impeccable service; quality versions of local recipes; good vegetarian choices. $ *Average main: €22* ⊠ *Piazza Danti 19/a* ☎ *075/5721956* ⊕ *www.anticatrattoriasanlorenzo.com* ☽ *Closed Sun.*

$$ ✕ **Dal Mi' Cocco.** A great favorite with Perugia's university students, it is
UMBRIAN fun, crowded, and inexpensive. You may find yourself seated at a long table with other diners, but some language help from your neighbors could come in handy—the menu is in pure Perugian dialect. **Known for:** authentically casual feel; honest prices; abundant portions. $ *Average main: €15* ⊠ *Corso Garibaldi 12* ☎ *075/5732511* ▭ *No credit cards* ☽ *Closed Mon. and late July–mid-Aug.*

$$ ✕ **La Rosetta.** The dining room of the hotel of the same name is a peace-
ITALIAN ful, elegant spot; in winter you dine inside under medieval vaults, and in summer, in the cool courtyard. The food is simple but reliable, and flawlessly served. **Known for:** elegant, old-fashioned setting; refined versions of local meat dishes; professional service. $ *Average main: €18* ⊠ *Piazza d'Italia 19* ☎ *075/5720841* ⊕ *www.perugiaonline.com/ larosetta/.*

$$ ✕ **La Taverna.** Medieval steps lead to a rustic two-story space where wine
UMBRIAN bottles and artful clutter decorate the walls. Good choices from the regional menu include *caramelle al gorgonzola* (pasta rolls filled with red cabbage and mozzarella and topped with a Gorgonzola sauce) and grilled meat dishes, such as the *medaglioni di vitello al tartufo* (grilled veal with truffles). **Known for:** Umbrian specialties; swift and efficient service; welcoming ambience. $ *Average main: €18* ⊠ *Via delle Streghe 8, off Corso Vannucci* ☎ *075/5724128.*

WHERE TO STAY

$ ⊞ **Alla Posta dei Donini.** Beguilingly comfortable guest rooms are set on
HOTEL lovely grounds, where gardeners go quietly about their business. **Pros:** plush atmosphere; a quiet and private getaway; great restaurant. **Cons:** outside Perugia; uninteresting village; spa sometimes overcrowded. $ *Rooms from: €109* ⊠ *Via Deruta 43, 15 km (9 miles) south of Perugia, San Martino in Campo* ☎ *075/609132* ⊕ *www.postadonini.it* ⌁ *48 rooms* ⦿| *No meals.*

$$ ⊞ **Hotel Fortuna.** The elegant decor in the large rooms, some with bal-
HOTEL conies, complements the frescoes, which date from the 1700s. **Pros:** central but quiet; cozy, friendly atmosphere; elevator. **Cons:** some small rooms; no restaurant; no parking. $ *Rooms from: €128* ⊠ *Via Bonazzi 19* ☎ *075/5722845* ⊕ *www.hotelfortunaperugia.com* ⌁ *52 rooms* ⦿| *Free Breakfast.*

$$ ⊞ **Locanda della Posta.** Renovations have left the lobby and other public
HOTEL areas rather bland, but the rooms in this converted 18th-century palazzo are soothingly decorated in muted colors. **Pros:** some fine views; central location; exudes good taste and refinement. **Cons:** some street noise; some small rooms; no public areas. $ *Rooms from: €139* ⊠ *Corso Vannucci 97* ☎ *075/5728925* ⊕ *www.locandadellapostahotel.it* ⌁ *39 rooms* ⦿| *Free Breakfast.*

$$ ⊞ **Tre Vaselle.** Rooms spread throughout four stone buildings are spa-
HOTEL cious and graced with floors of typical red-clay Tuscan tiles. **Pros:** perfect for visiting the Torgiano wine area and Deruta; friendly staff; nice

pool. **Cons:** somewhat far from Perugia; in center of uninspiring village; service occasionally falters. [$] *Rooms from: €159* ✉ *Via Garibaldi 48, Torgiano* ☎ *075/9880447* 🌐 *www.3vaselle.it* 🛏 *47 rooms* 🍴 *No meals.*

NIGHTLIFE AND PERFORMING ARTS

With its large student population, the city has plenty to offer in the way of bars and clubs. The best ones are around the city center, off Corso Vannucci. *Viva Perugia* is a good source of information about nightlife; the monthly, sold at newsstands, has a section in English.

MUSIC FESTIVALS

Sagra Musicale Umbra. Held mid-September, the Sagra Musicale Umbra celebrates sacred music in Perugia and in several towns throughout the region. ✉ *Perugia* ☎ *338/8668820 information and bookings in Sept., 075/5722271 general information* 🌐 *www.perugiamusicaclassica.com.*

SHOPPING

Take a stroll down any of Perugia's main streets, including Corso Vannucci, Via dei Priori, Via Oberdan, and Via Sant'Ercolano, and you'll see many well-known designer boutiques and specialty shops.

The most typical thing to buy in Perugia is some Perugina chocolate, which you can find almost anywhere. The best-known chocolates made by Perugina (now owned by Nestlé) are the chocolate-and-hazelnut-filled nibbles called Baci (literally, "kisses"). They're wrapped in silver foil that includes a sliver of paper, like the fortune in a fortune cookie, with multilingual romantic sentiments or sayings.

ASSISI

The small town of Assisi is one of the Christian world's most important pilgrimage sites and home of the Basilica di San Francesco—built to honor St. Francis (1182–1226) and erected in swift order after his death. The peace and serenity of the town is a welcome respite after the hustle and bustle of some of Italy's major cities.

Like most other towns in the region, Assisi began as an Umbri settlement in the 7th century BC and was conquered by the Romans 400 years later. The town was Christianized by St. Rufino, its patron saint, in the 3rd century, but it's the spirit of St. Francis, a patron saint of Italy and founder of the Franciscan monastic order, that's felt throughout its narrow medieval streets. The famous 13th-century basilica was decorated by the greatest artists of the period.

GETTING HERE AND AROUND

Assisi lies on the Terontola–Foligno rail line, with almost hourly connections to Perugia and direct trains to Rome and Florence several times a day. The Stazione Centrale is 4 km (2½ miles) from town, with a bus service about every half hour. Assisi is easily reached from the A1 autostrada (Rome–Florence) and the S75b highway. The walled town is closed to traffic, so cars must be left in the parking lots at Porta San

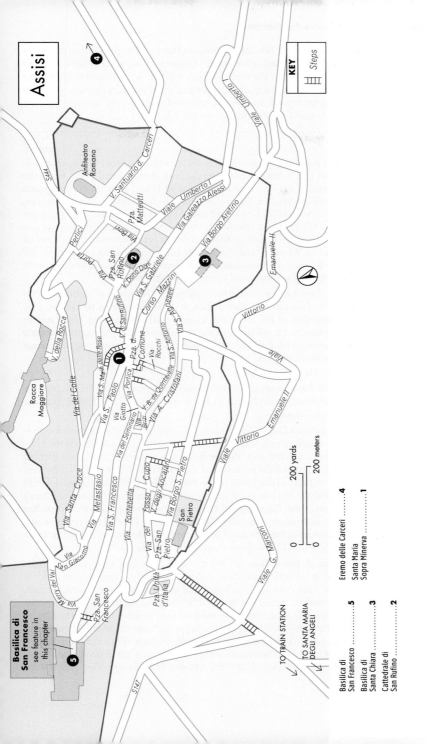

Assisi

Basilica di San Francesco
see feature in this chapter

KEY

| Steps

Rocca Maggiore

Anfiteatro Romano

TO TRAIN STATION

TO SANTA MARIA DEGLI ANGELI

0   200 yards
0   200 meters

San Pietro

Pza. Unità d'Italia

Pza. San Pietro

Pza. San Francesco

Pza. Comune

Pza. Matteotti

Pza. San Rufino

Via Santuario d. Carceri

Viale Umberto I

Via Galeazzo Alessi

Via Borgo Aretino

Via S. Gabriele

Corso Mazzini

Via S. Antonio

Via S. Rocchi

Via A. Cristofani

Via Portica

Via Giotto

Via del Seminario

Via S. Paolo

Via S. Maria delle Rose

Via San Rufino

Via Don Don

Via Bovi

Perlici

Porta Perlici

Via della Rocca

Via del Colle

Via S. Francesco

Via Metastasio

Via Santa Croce

Via San Giacomo

Via Merry del Val

Via Fontebella

Viale Vittorio Emanuele II

Viale G. Marconi

Via Borgo S. Pietro

Via del Fosso

V. degli Ancaiani

Cupo

V. Brizi

V. Brizio Quintavalle

S444

S147

Viale Vittorio Emanuele II

Pietro, near Porta Nuova, or beneath Piazza Matteotti. Pay your parking fee at the *cassa* (ticket booth) before you return to your car to get a ticket to insert in the machine that will allow you to exit. It's a short but sometimes steep walk into the center of town; frequent minibuses (buy tickets from a newsstand or tobacco shop near where you park your car) make the rounds for weary pilgrims.

EXPLORING

Assisi is pristinely medieval in architecture and appearance, owing in large part to relative neglect from the 16th century until 1926, when the celebration of the 700th anniversary of St. Francis's death brought more than 2 million visitors. Since then, pilgrims have flocked here in droves, and today several million arrive each year to pay homage. But not even the constant flood of visitors to this town of just 3,000 residents can spoil the singular beauty of this significant religious center, the home of some of the Western tradition's most important works of art. The hill on which Assisi sits rises dramatically from the flat plain, and the town is dominated by a medieval castle at the very top.

Even though Assisi is sometimes besieged by busloads of sightseers who clamor to visit the famous basilica, it's difficult not to be charmed by the tranquillity of the town and its medieval architecture. Once you've seen the basilica, stroll through the town's narrow winding streets to see beautiful vistas of the nearby hills and valleys peeking through openings between the buildings.

TOP ATTRACTIONS

Basilica di San Francesco. *See the highlighted feature in this chapter for more information.* ⊠ *Piazza di San Francesco* ☎ *075/819001* ⊕ *www.sanfrancescoassisi.org.*

Basilica di Santa Chiara. The lovely, wide piazza in front of this church is reason enough to visit. The red-and-white-striped facade frames the piazza's panoramic view over the Umbrian plains. Santa Chiara is dedicated to St. Clare, one of the earliest and most fervent of St. Francis's followers and the founder of the order of the Poor Ladies—or Poor Clares—which was based on the Franciscan monastic order. The church contains Clare's body, and in the **Cappella del Crocifisso** (on the right) is the cross that spoke to St. Francis. A heavily veiled nun of the Poor Clares order is usually stationed before the cross in adoration of the image. ⊠ *Piazza Santa Chiara* ☎ *075/812216* ⊕ *www.assisisantachiara.it.*

Cattedrale di San Rufino. St. Francis and St. Clare were among those baptized in Assisi's Cattedrale, which was the principal church in town until the 12th century. The baptismal font has since been redecorated, but it's possible to see the crypt of St. Rufino, the bishop who brought Christianity to Assisi and was martyred on August 11, 238 (or 236 by some accounts). Admission to the crypt includes the small **Museo Capitolare,** with its detached frescoes and artifacts. ⊠ *Piazza San Rufino* ☎ *075/812712* ⊕ *www.assisimuseodiocesano.it* ◫ *Church free, Crypt and Museo Capitolare €3.50* ☉ *Crypt and Museo Capitolare closed Wed.*

Continued on page 612

ASSISI'S BASILICA DI SAN FRANCESCO

The legacy of St. Francis, founder of the Franciscan monastic order, pervades Assisi. Each year the town hosts several million pilgrims, but the steady flow of visitors does nothing to diminish the singular beauty of one of Italy's most important religious centers. The pilgrims' ultimate destination is the massive Basilica di San Francesco, which sits halfway up Assisi's hill, supported by graceful arches.

The basilica is not one church but two. The Romanesque **Lower Church** came first; construction began in 1228, just two years after St. Francis's death, and was completed within a few years. The low ceilings and candlelit interior make an appropriately solemn setting for St. Francis's tomb, found in the crypt below the main altar. The Gothic **Upper Church**, built only half a century later, sits on top of the lower one, and is strikingly different, with soaring arches and tall stained-glass windows (the first in Italy). Inside, both churches are covered floor to ceiling with some of Europe's finest frescoes: the Lower Church is dim and full of candlelit shadows, and the Upper Church is bright and airy.

VISITING THE BASILICA

THE LOWER CHURCH

The most evocative way to experience the basilica is to begin with the dark Lower Church. As you enter, give your eyes a moment to adjust. Keep in mind that the artists at work here were conscious of the shadowy environment—they knew this was how their frescoes would be seen.

In the first chapel to the left, a superb fresco cycle by Simone Martini depicts scenes from the life of St. Martin. As you approach the main altar, the vaulting above you is decorated with the *Three Virtues of St. Francis* (poverty, chastity, and obedience) and *St. Francis's Triumph*, frescoes attributed to Giotto's followers. In the transept to your left, Pietro Lorenzetti's *Madonna and Child with St. Francis and St. John* sparkles when the sun hits it. Notice Mary's thumb; legend has it Jesus is asking which saint to bless, and Mary is pointing to Francis. Across the way in the right transept, Cimabue's *Madonna Enthroned Among Angels and St. Francis* is a famous portrait of the saint. Surrounding the portrait are painted scenes from the childhood of Christ, done by the assistants of Giotto.

Nearby is a painting of the crucifixion attributed to Giotto himself.

You reach the crypt via stairs midway along the nave—on the crypt's altar, a stone coffin holds the saint's body. Steps up from the transepts lead to the cloister, where there's a gift shop, and the treasury, which contains holy objects.

THE UPPER CHURCH

The St. Francis fresco cycle is the highlight of the Upper Church. (See facing page.) Also worth special note is the 16th-century choir, with its remarkably delicate inlaid wood. When a 1997 earthquake rocked the basilica, the St. Francis cycle sustained little damage, but portions of the ceiling above the entrance and altar collapsed, reducing their frescoes (attributed to Cimabue and Giotto) to rubble. The painstaking restoration is ongoing. △ **The dress code is strictly enforced—no bare shoulders or bare knees.**

FRANCIS, ITALY'S PATRON SAINT

PREGANDO ASPETTERO' CHE TORNI

St. Francis was born in Assisi in 1181, the son of a noblewoman and a well-to-do merchant. His troubled youth included a year in prison. He planned a military career, but after a long illness Francis heard the voice of God, renounced his father's wealth, and began a life of austerity. His mystical embrace of poverty, asceticism, and the beauty of man and nature struck a responsive chord in the medieval mind; he quickly attracted a vast number of followers. Francis was the first saint to receive the stigmata (wounds in his hands, feet, and side corresponding to those of Christ on the cross). He died on October 4, 1226, in the Porziuncola, the secluded chapel in the woods where he had first preached the virtue of poverty to his disciples. St. Francis was declared patron saint of Italy in 1939, and today the Franciscans make up the largest of the Catholic orders.

THE UPPER CHURCH'S ST. FRANCIS FRESCO CYCLE

The 28 frescoes in the Upper Church depicting the life of St. Francis are the most admired works in the entire basilica. They're also the subject of one of art history's biggest controversies. For centuries they thought to be by Giotto (1267-1337), the great early Renaissance innovator, but inconsistencies in style, both within this series and in comparison to later Giotto works, have thrown their origin into question. Some scholars now say Giotto was the brains behind the cycle, but that assistants helped with the execution; others claim he couldn't have been involved at all.

Two things are certain. First, the style is revolutionary—which

argues for Giotto's involvement. The tangible weight of the figures, the emotion they show, and the use of perspective all look familiar to modern eyes, but in the art of the time there was nothing like it. Second, these images have played a major part in shaping how the world sees St. Francis. In that respect, who painted them hardly matters.

Starting in the transept, the frescoes circle the church, showing events in the saint's life (and afterlife). Some of the best are grouped near the church's entrance—look for the nativity at Greccio, the miracle of the spring, the death of the knight at Celano, and, most famously, the sermon to the birds.

13

IN FOCUS ASSISI'S BASILICA DI SAN FRANCISCO

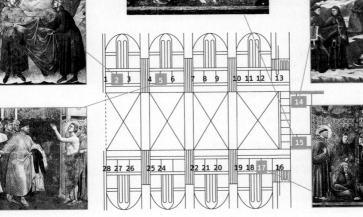

The St. Francis fresco cycle		
1. Homage of a simple man	10. Chasing devils from Arezzo	20. Death of St. Francis
2. Giving cloak to a poor man	11. Before the sultan	21. Apparition before Bishop
3. Dream of the palace	12. Ecstasy of St. Francis	Guido and Fra Agostino
4. Hearing the voice of God	13. Nativity at Greccio	22. Verification of the stigmata
5. Rejection of worldly goods	14. Miracle of the spring	23. Mourning of St. Clare
6. Dream of Innocent III	15. Sermon to the birds	24. Canonization
7. Confirmation of the rules	16. Death of knight at Celano	25. Apparition before Gregory IX
8. Vision of flaming chariot	17. Preaching to Honorius III	26. Healing of a devotee
9. Vision of celestial thrones	18. Apparition at Arles	27. Confession of a woman
	19. Receiving the stigmata	28. Repentant heretic freed

WORTH NOTING

OFF THE BEATEN PATH

Eremo delle Carceri. About 4 km (2½ miles) east of Assisi is a monastery set in a dense wood against Monte Subasio: the Hermitage of Prisons. This was the place where St. Francis and his followers went to "imprison" themselves in prayer. The only site in Assisi that remains essentially unchanged since St. Francis's time, the church and monastery are the kinds of tranquil places that St. Francis would have appreciated. The walk out from town is very pleasant, and many trails lead from here across the wooded hillside of Monte Subasio (now a protected forest), with beautiful vistas across the Umbrian countryside. True to their Franciscan heritage, the friars here are entirely dependent on alms from visitors. ✉ *Via Santuario delle Carceri, 4 km (2½ miles) east of Assisi* ☎ *075/812301* 🎟 *Donations accepted.*

Santa Maria Sopra Minerva. Dating from the time of the Emperor Augustus (27 BC–AD 14), this structure was originally dedicated to the Roman goddess of wisdom, and in later times it was used as a monastery and prison before being converted into a church in the 16th century. The expectations raised by the perfect classical facade are not met by the interior, which was subjected to a thorough Baroque transformation in the 17th century. ✉ *Piazza del Comune* ☎ *075/812361.*

WHERE TO EAT

$ UMBRIAN

🍴 **Buca di San Francesco.** In summer, dine in a cool green garden; in winter, under the low brick arches of the cozy cellars. The unique settings and the first-rate fare make this central restaurant Assisi's busiest. **Known for:** cozy atmosphere; historical surroundings; warm and welcoming service. [$] *Average main: €14* ✉ *Via Eugenio Brizi 1* ☎ *075/812204* ⏲ *Closed Mon., and 10 days in late July.*

$$ UMBRIAN Fodor's Choice ★

🍴 **La Pallotta.** At this homey, family-run trattoria with a crackling fireplace and stone walls, the women do the cooking and the men serve the food. Try the *strangozzi alla pallotta* (thick spaghetti with a pesto of olives and mushrooms). **Known for:** traditional local dishes; fast and courteous service; economical tourist menu. [$] *Average main: €15* ✉ *Vicolo della Volta Pinta 3* ☎ *075/8155273* 🌐 *www.trattoriapallotta.it* ⏲ *Closed Tues.*

$$ UMBRIAN

🍴 **Osteria Piazzetta dell'Erba.** Hip service and sophisticated presentations attract locals, who enjoy a wide selection of appetizers, including smoked goose breast, and four or five types of pasta, plus various salads and a good selection of *torta al testo* (dense flatbread stuffed with vegetables or cheese). For dessert, try the homemade biscuits, which you dunk in sweet wine. **Known for:** friendly staff; well-presented dishes; intimate ambience. [$] *Average main: €16* ✉ *Via San Gabriele dell'Addolorata 15/b* ☎ *075/815352* 🌐 *www.osterialapiazzetta.it* ⏲ *Closed Mon., and a few wks in Jan. or Feb.*

$$ UMBRIAN

🍴 **San Francesco.** An excellent view of the Basilica di San Francesco from the covered terrace is just one reason to enjoy the best restaurant in town, where creative Umbrian dishes are made with aromatic locally grown herbs. The seasonal menu might include gnocchi topped with a sauce of wild herbs and *oca stufata di finocchio selvaggio* (goose stuffed with wild fennel). **Known for:** excellent location; outstanding desserts; pleasant staff. $ *Average main: €20* ⊠ *Via di San Francesco 52* ☎ *075/813302* ⊕ *www.ristorantesanfrancesco.com* ⊘ *Closed Wed. Nov.–Easter, and 1–2 wks early July.*

WHERE TO STAY

Advance reservations are essential at Assisi's hotels between Easter and October and over Christmas. Latecomers are often forced to stay in the modern town of Santa Maria degli Angeli, 8 km (5 miles) away. As a last-minute option, you can always inquire at restaurants to see if they're renting out rooms.

Until the early 1980s, pilgrim hostels outnumbered ordinary hotels in Assisi, and they present an intriguing and economical alternative to conventional lodgings. They're usually called *conventi* or *ostelli* ("convents" or "hostels") because they're run by convents, churches, or other Catholic organizations. Rooms are spartan but peaceful. Check with the tourist office for a list.

$$ **Castello di Petrata.** Wood beams and sections of exposed medieval stonework add a lot of character to this fortress built in the 14th century, while comfortable couches turn each individually decorated room into a delightful retreat. **Pros:** great views of town and countryside; medieval character; pool. **Cons:** slightly isolated; far from Assisi town center; small menu choice in restaurant. $ *Rooms from: €180* ⊠ *Via Petrata 25, Località Petrata* ☎ *075/815451* ⊕ *www.castellopetrata.it* ⊘ *Closed Sun.–Wed. Jan.–mid-Mar.* ⇨ *20 rooms* ○| *Free Breakfast.*

HOTEL
Fodor's Choice
★

$ **Hotel Umbra.** Rooms on the upper floors of this charming 16th-century town house near Piazza del Comune look out over the Assisi rooftops to the valley below, as does the sunny, vine-covered terrace. **Pros:** very central; pleasant small garden; excellent valley views from some rooms. **Cons:** difficult parking; some small rooms; uninspiring breakfasts. $ *Rooms from: €100* ⊠ *Via degli Archi 6* ☎ *075/812240* ⊕ *www.hotelumbra.it* ⊘ *Closed Nov.–late Mar.* ⇨ *24 rooms* ○| *Free Breakfast.*

HOTEL

NORTHERN UMBRIA

To the north of Perugia, placid, walled Gubbio watches over green countryside, true to its nickname, City of Silence—except for its fast and furious festivals in May, as lively today as when they began more than 800 years ago. To the south, along the Tiber River valley, are the towns of Deruta and Torgiano, best known for their hand-painted ceramics and wine—as locals say, go to Deruta to buy a pitcher and to Torgiano to fill it.

GUBBIO

35 km (22 miles) southeast of Città di Castello, 39 km (24 miles) northeast of Perugia, 92 km (57 miles) east of Arezzo.

There's something otherworldly about this jewel of a medieval town tucked away in a mountainous corner of Umbria. Even at the height of

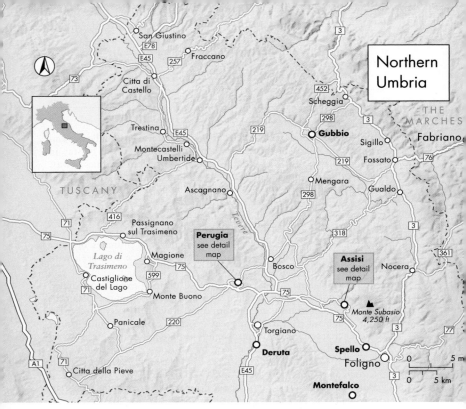

summer, the cool serenity and quiet of Gubbio's streets remain intact. The town is perched on the slopes of Monte Ingino, meaning the streets are dramatically steep. Gubbio's relatively isolated position has kept it free of hordes of high-season visitors, and most of the year the city lives up to its Italian nickname, "La Città del Silenzio" (City of Silence). Parking in the central Piazza dei Quaranta Martiri—named for 40 hostages murdered by the Nazis in 1944—is easy and secure, and it's wise to leave your car in the piazza and explore the narrow streets on foot.

At Christmas, kitsch is king. From December 7 to January 10, colored lights are strung down the mountainside in a shape resembling an evergreen, the world's largest Christmas tree.

GETTING HERE AND AROUND

The closest train station is Fossato di Vico, about 20 km (12 miles) from Gubbio. Twelve daily buses (five on Sunday) connect the train station with the city, a 30-minute trip. If you're driving from Perugia, take the SS298, which rises steeply up toward the Gubbio hills. The trip will take you one hour. There are also 11 buses a day (4 on Sunday) that leave from Perugia's Piazza Partigiani, the main Perugia bus terminal.

VISITOR INFORMATION

Contact **Gubbio Tourism Office.** ⊠ *Via della Repubblica 15* ☎ *075/9220693* ⊕ *www.comune.gubbio.pg.it.*

EXPLORING

Basilica di Sant'Ubaldo. Gubbio's famous *ceri*—three 16-foot-tall pillars crowned with statues of Saints Ubaldo, George, and Anthony—are housed in this basilica atop Monte Ingino. The pillars are transported to the Palazzo dei Consoli on the first Sunday of May, in preparation for the Festa dei Ceri, one of central Italy's most spectacular festivals. ✉ *Monte Ingino* ☎ *075/9273872.*

Duomo. On a narrow street on the highest tier of the town, the Duomo dates from the 13th century, with some Baroque additions—in particular, a lavishly decorated bishop's chapel. ✉ *Via Ducale.*

Funicular. For a bracing ride to the top of Monte Ingino, hop on the funicular that climbs the hillside just outside the city walls at the eastern end of town. It's definitely not for those who suffer from vertigo. Operating hours vary considerably from month to month; check the funicular's website. ✉ *Via San Girolamo* ☎ *075/9277507* 🌐 *www.funiviagubbio.it* 🎫 *€4, €6 round-trip* 🕓 *Closed Wed. Nov.–mid-Mar.*

Palazzo dei Consoli. Gubbio's striking Piazza Grande is dominated by this medieval palazzo, attributed to a local architect known as Gattapone, who is still much admired by today's residents (though some scholars have suggested that the palazzo was in fact the work of another architect, Angelo da Orvieto). In the Middle Ages the Parliament of Gubbio assembled in the palace, which has become a symbol of the town and now houses a museum with a collection famous chiefly for the Tavole Eugubine. These seven bronze tablets are written in the ancient Umbrian language, employing Etruscan and Latin characters, and provide the best key to understanding this obscure tongue. Also in the museum is a fascinating miscellany of rare coins and earthenware pots. A lofty loggia provides exhilarating views over Gubbio's roofscape and beyond. For a few days at the beginning of May, the palace also displays the famous *ceri,* the ceremonial wooden pillars at the center of Gubbio's annual festivities. ✉ *Piazza Grande* ☎ *075/9274298* 🌐 *www.palazzodeiconsoli.it* 🎫 *€7.*

Palazzo Ducale. This scaled-down copy of the Palazzo Ducale in Urbino (Gubbio was once the possession of that city's ruling family, the Montefeltro) contains a small museum and a courtyard. Some of the public rooms offer magnificent views. ✉ *Via Federico da Montefeltro* ☎ *075/9275872* 🌐 *www.comune.gubbio.pg.it* 🎫 *€5* 🕓 *Closed Mon.*

WHERE TO EAT

$$ UMBRIAN 🍴 **Grotta dell'Angelo.** The rustic trattoria sits in the lower part of the old town near the main square. The menu features simple local specialties, including *capocollo* (a type of salami), stringozzi, and lasagna *tartufata* (with truffles). **Known for:** reasonable prices; good antipasti and grilled meats; homey atmosphere. [$] *Average main: €15* ✉ *Via Gioia 47* ☎ *075/9271747* 🌐 *www.grottadellangelo.it* 🕓 *Closed Tues., and Jan. 7–Feb. 7.*

$$ UMBRIAN Fodor's Choice ★ 🍴 **Taverna del Lupo.** One of the city's most famous taverns, this traditional spot has a menu that includes such indulgences as lasagna made in the Gubbian fashion, with ham and truffles, and the *suprema di faraono* (guinea fowl in a delicately spiced sauce) is a specialty. The

restaurant has two fine wine cellars and an extensive wine list. **Known for:** wide menu choice; alluring presentation; good wine list. $ *Average main: €19* ✉ *Via Ansidei 21* ☎ *075/9274368* ⊕ *www.tavernadellupo.it.*

WHERE TO STAY

$

HOTEL

☆ **Hotel Bosone Palace.** A former palace is now home to an elegant hotel, where elaborate frescoes grace the ceilings of the two enormous suites and delightful breakfast room. **Pros:** friendly welcome; excellent location; low rates. **Cons:** some noise in tourist season; dated bathrooms; cheapest rooms are cramped and lack air-conditioning. $ *Rooms from: €67* ✉ *Via XX Settembre 22* ☎ *075/9220688* ⊕ *www.hotelbosone.com* ��� *Closed early Jan.–mid-Feb.* ⤵ *30 rooms* ❍ *Free Breakfast.*

DERUTA

7 km (4½ miles) south of Torgiano, 19 km (11 miles) southeast of Perugia.

This 14th-century medieval hill town is most famous for its ceramics. A drive through the countryside to visit the ceramics workshops is a good way to spend a morning, but be sure to stop in the town itself.

GETTING HERE AND AROUND

From Perugia follow the directions for Rome and the E45 highway; Deruta has its own exits. There are also trains from the smaller St. Anna train station in Perugia. Take the train in the direction of Terni, and get off at Deruta.

VISITOR INFORMATION

Contact Deruta Tourism Office. ✉ *Piazza dei Consoli 4* ☎ *075/9711559* ⊕ *www.turismoderuta.it.*

EXPLORING

Museo Regionale della Ceramica (*Regional Ceramics Museum*). It's only fitting that Deruta is home to an impressive ceramics museum, part of which extends into the adjacent 14th-century former convent of San Francesco. The museum tells the history of ceramics, with panels (in Italian and English) explaining artistic techniques and production processes, and also holds the country's largest collection of Italian ceramics—nearly 8,000 pieces are on display. The most notable are the Renaissance vessels using the *lustro* technique, which originated in Arab and Middle Eastern cultures some 500 years before coming into use in Italy in the late 1400s. Lustro, as the name sounds, gives the ceramics a rich finish, which is accomplished with the use of crushed precious materials such as gold and silver. ✉ *Largo San Francesco* ☎ *075/9711000* ⊕ *www.museoceramicadideruta.it* 🎟 *€7, includes Pinoteca Comunale* ⊘ *Closed Mon. and Tues.*

SHOPPING

Deruta is home to more than 70 ceramics shops. They offer a range of ceramics, including extra pieces from commissions for well-known British and North American tableware manufacturers. If you ask, most owners will take you to see where they actually throw, bake, and paint their wares. A drive along **Via Tiberina Nord** takes you past one shop after another.

13

SPELLO

12 km (7 miles) southeast of Assisi, 33 km (21 miles) north of Spoleto.

Spello is a gastronomic paradise, especially compared with Assisi. Only a few minutes from Assisi by car or train, this hilltop town at the edge of Monte Subasio makes an excellent strategic and culinary base for exploring nearby towns. Its hotels are well appointed and its restaurants serve some of the best cuisine and wines in the region—sophisticated in variety and of excellent quality. Spello's art scene includes first-rate frescoes by Pinturicchio and Perugino, and contemporary artists can be observed at work in studios around town. If antiquity is your passion, the town also has some intriguing Roman ruins. And the warm, rosy-beige tones of the local *pietra rossa* stone on the buildings brighten even cloudy days.

GETTING HERE AND AROUND

Spello is an easy half-hour drive from Perugia. From the E45 highway, take the exit toward Assisi and Foligno. Merge onto the SS75 and take the Spello exit. There are also regular trains on the Perugia–Assisi line. Spello is 1 km (½ mile) from the train station, and buses run every 30 minutes for Porta Consolare. From Porta Consolare, continue up the steep main street that begins as Via Consolare and changes names several times as it crosses the little town, following the original Roman road. As it curves around, notice the winding medieval alleyways to the right and the more uniform Roman-era blocks to the left.

VISITOR INFORMATION

Contact Spello Tourism Office. ⊠ *Piazza Matteotti 3* ☎ *0742/301009* ⊕ *www. prospello.it.*

EXPLORING

Santa Maria Maggiore. The two great Umbrian artists hold sway in this 16th-century basilica. Pinturicchio's vivid frescoes in the Cappella Baglioni (1501) are striking for their rich colors, finely dressed figures, and complex symbolism. Among Pinturicchio's finest works are the *Nativity, Christ Among the Doctors* (on the far left side is a portrait of Troilo Baglioni, the prior who commissioned the work), and the *Annunciation* (look for Pinturicchio's self-portrait in the Virgin's room). The artist painted them after he had already won great acclaim for his work in the Palazzi Vaticani in Rome for Borgia Pope Alexander VI. Two pillars on either side of the apse are decorated with frescoes by Perugino (circa 1450–1523). ⊠ *Piazza Matteotti 18* ☎ *0742/301792* ⊕ *www.smariamaggiore.com.*

WHERE TO STAY

$$
HOTEL

Hotel Palazzo Bocci. Lovely sitting areas, a reading room, bucolic ceiling and wall frescoes, and a garden terrace all add quiet and elegant charm to this 14th-century building, where several rooms have valley views. **Pros:** central location; splendid views of the valley from public areas and some rooms; abundant breakfasts. **Cons:** noisy in summer months; not all rooms have views; needs a brushup. $ *Rooms from: €160* ⊠ *Via Cavour 17* ☎ *0742/301021* ⊕ *www.palazzobocci.com* 🔁 *23 rooms* ⦿ *Free Breakfast.*

$ HOTEL **La Bastiglia.** Polished wood planks and handwoven rugs have replaced the rustic flooring of a former grain mill, and comfortable sitting rooms and cozy bedrooms are filled with a mix of antique and modern pieces. **Pros:** lovely terrace restaurant; leisure and wellness facilities; fine views from top-floor rooms, some with terraces. **Cons:** some shared balconies; no elevator and plenty of steps, so pack light; mix of modern and antique decor not congenial to all. [$] *Rooms from: €100* ✉ *Piazza Vallegloria* ☎ *0742/651277* 🌐 *www.labastiglia.com* 🕒 *Closed 3 wks in Jan.* 🛏 *33 rooms* 🍴 *Free Breakfast.*

MONTEFALCO

6 km (4 miles) southeast of Bevagna, 34 km (21 miles) south of Assisi.

Nicknamed the "balcony over Umbria" for its high vantage point over the valley that runs from Perugia to Spoleto, Montefalco began as an important Roman settlement situated on the Via Flaminia. The town owes its current name ("Falcon's Mount") to Emperor Frederick II (1194–1250). Obviously a greater fan of falconry than Roman architecture, he destroyed the ancient town, which was then called Coccorone, in 1249, and built in its place what would later become Montefalco. Aside from a few fragments incorporated in a private house just off Borgo Garibaldi, no traces remain of the old Roman center. However, Montefalco has more than its fair share of interesting art and architecture and is well worth the drive up the hill.

GETTING HERE AND AROUND

If you're driving from Perugia, take the E45 toward Rome. Take the Foligno exit, then merge onto the SP445 and follow it into Montefalco. The drive takes around 50 minutes. The nearest train station is in Foligno, about 7 km (4½ miles) away. From there you can take a taxi or a bus into Montefalco.

VISITOR INFORMATION

Contact La Strada del Sagrantino. ✉ *Piazza del Comune 17* ☎ *0742/378490* 🌐 *www.stradadelsagrantino.it.*

WHERE TO EAT AND STAY

Montefalco is a good stop for sustenance: here you need go no farther than the main square to find a restaurant or bar with a hot meal, and most establishments—both simple and sophisticated—offer a splendid combination of history and small-town hospitality.

$ UMBRIAN 🍴 **L'Alchimista.** "The Alchemist" is an apt name, as the chef's transformations are magical: Try the *fiore molle della Valnerina,* baked saffron cheese, bacon, and zucchini—served only here. In summer, cold dishes to try are *panzanella* (vegetable salad mixed with bread) or the barley salad tossed with vegetables. **Known for:** extensive wine list; congenial setting and atmosphere; refined but relaxed dining. [$] *Average main: €14* ✉ *Piazza del Comune 14* ☎ *0742/378558* 🌐 *www.ristorantealchimista.it* 🕒 *Closed Tues. and Feb.*

CLOSE UP

The Sagrantino Story

Sagrantino grapes have been used for the production of red wine for centuries. The wine began centuries ago as Sagrantino *passito,* a semisweet version in which the grapes are left to dry for a period after picking to intensify the sugar content. One theory traces the origin of Sagrantino back to ancient Rome in the works of Pliny the Elder, the author of the *Natural History,* who referred to the Itriola grape that some researchers think may be Sagrantino. Others believe that in medieval times Franciscan friars returned from Asia Minor with the grape. ("Sagrantino" perhaps derives from *sacramenti,* the religious ceremony in which the wine was used.)

The passito is still produced today, and is preferred by some. But the big change in Sagrantino wine production came in the past decades, when Montefalco Sagrantino *secco* (dry) came onto the market. Both passito and secco have a deep ruby-red color that tends toward garnet highlights, with a full body and rich flavor.

For the dry wines, producers not to be missed are Terre di Capitani, Antonelli, Perticaia, and Caprai. Try those labels for the passito as well, in addition to Ruggeri and Scacciadiavoli. Terre di Capitani is complex and has vegetable and mineral tones that join tastes of wild berries, cherries, and chocolate—this winemaker pampers his grapes and it shows. Antonelli is elegant, refined, and rich. Perticaia has a full, rounded taste. Caprai is bold and rich in taste, and has the largest market share, including a high percentage exported to the United States. The Ruggeri passito is one of the best, so don't be put off by its homespun label.

At La Strada del Sagrantino in Montefalco's main square, you can pick up a map of the wine route, set up appointments, and book accommodations. Some wineries are small and not equipped to receive visitors. Visit the local enoteche, and ask the sommeliers to guide you to some smaller producers you'll have difficulty finding elsewhere.

13

$$ HOTEL Fodor's Choice ★ 🏨 **Villa Pambuffetti.** If you want to be pampered in the refined atmosphere of a private villa, this is the spot, with the warmth of a fireplace in the winter, a pool to cool you down in summer, and cozy reading nooks and guest rooms year-round. **Pros:** peaceful gardens; refined furnishings; excellent dining room. **Cons:** outside the town center; can get crowded on weekends; slightly dated feel. [$] *Rooms from: €125* ✉ *Viale della Vittoria 20* ☎ *0742/379417* 🌐 *www.villapambuffetti.it* 🛏 *15 rooms* 🍴 *Free Breakfast.*

SPOLETO

For most of the year, Spoleto is one more in a pleasant succession of sleepy hill towns, resting regally atop a mountain. But for three weeks every summer the town shifts into high gear for a turn in the international spotlight during the Festival dei Due Mondi (Festival of Two Worlds), an extravaganza of theater, opera, music, painting, and sculpture. As the world's top artists vie for honors, throngs of art aficionados vie for hotel rooms. If you plan to spend the night in Spoleto during the festival, make sure you have confirmed reservations, or you may find yourself scrambling at sunset.

Spoleto has plenty to lure you during the rest of the year as well: the final frescoes of Filippo Lippi, beautiful piazzas and streets with Roman and medieval attractions, and superb natural surroundings with rolling hills and a dramatic gorge. Spoleto makes a good base for exploring all of southern Umbria, as Assisi, Orvieto, and the towns in between are all within easy reach.

GETTING HERE AND AROUND

Spoleto is an hour's drive from Perugia. From the E45 highway, take the exit toward Assisi and Foligno, then merge onto the SS75 until you reach the Foligno Est exit. Merge onto the SS3, which leads to Spoleto. There are regular trains on the Perugia–Foligno line. From the train station it's a 15-minute uphill walk to the center, so you'll probably want to take a local bus or a taxi.

VISITOR INFORMATION

Contact Spoleto tourism office. ✉ *Largo Ferrer 6, off Corso Mazzini* ☎ *0743/218620* ⊕ *www.comunespoleto.gov.it/turismoecultura.*

EXPLORING

The walled city is set on a slanting hillside, with the most interesting sections clustered toward the upper portion. Parking options inside the walls include Piazza Campello (just below the Rocca) on the southeast end, Via del Trivio to the north, and Piazza San Domenico on the west end. You can also park at Piazza della Vittoria farther north, just outside the walls. There are also several well-marked lots near the train station. If you arrive by train, you can walk 1 km (½ mile) from the station to the entrance to the lower town. Regular bus connections are every 15–30 minutes.

Like most other towns with narrow, winding streets, Spoleto is best explored on foot. Bear in mind that much of the city is on a steep slope, so there are lots of stairs and steep inclines. The well-worn stones can be slippery even when dry; wear rubber-sole shoes for good traction. Several pedestrian walkways cut across Corso Mazzini, which zigzags up the hill, and three escalators connect the main car parks with the upper town. A €9.50 combination ticket purchased at any of the town's museums allows you entry to all the main museums and galleries over seven days.

TOP ATTRACTIONS

Duomo. The 12th-century Romanesque facade received a Renaissance face-lift with the addition of a loggia in a rosy pink stone, creating a stunning contrast in styles. One of the finest cathedrals in the region is lit by eight rose windows that are especially dazzling in the late afternoon sun. The original floor tiles remain from an earlier church destroyed by Frederick I (circa 1123–90).

Above the church's entrance is Bernini's bust of Pope Urban VIII (1568–1644), who had the church redecorated in 17th-century Baroque;

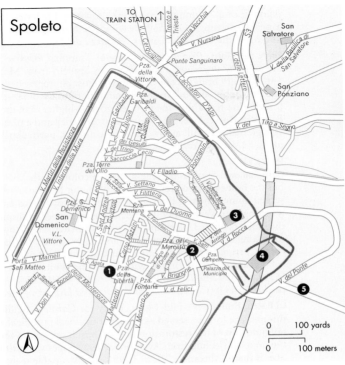

13

fortunately he didn't touch the 15th-century frescoes painted in the apse by Fra Filippo Lippi (circa 1406–69) between 1466 and 1469. These immaculately restored masterpieces—the *Annunciation, Nativity,* and *Dormition*—tell the story of the life of the Virgin. The *Coronation of the Virgin,* adorning the half dome, is the literal and figurative high point. Portraits of Lippi and his assistants are on the right side of the central panel. The Florentine artist-priest, "whose colors expressed God's voice" (the words inscribed on his tomb), died shortly after completing the work. His tomb, which you can see in the right transept (note the artist's brushes and tools), was designed by his son, Filippino Lippi (circa 1457–1504).

Another fresco cycle, including work by Pinturicchio, is in the Cappella Eroli, off the right aisle. Note the grotesques in the ornamentation, then very much in vogue with the rediscovery of ancient Roman paintings. The bounty of Umbria is displayed in vivid colors in the abundance of leaves, fruits, and vegetables that adorn the center seams of the cross vault. In the left nave, not far from the entrance, is the well-restored 12th-century crucifix by Alberto Sozio, the earliest known example of this kind of work, with a painting on parchment attached to a wood cross. To the right of the presbytery is the Cappella della Santissima Icona (Chapel of the Most Holy Icon), which contains a small Byzantine painting of a Madonna given to the town by Frederick Barbarossa as a peace offering in 1185, following his destruction of the cathedral and town three decades earlier. ⊠ *Piazza del Duomo* 🕾 *0743/231063*.

Fodor'sChoice   **Ponte delle Torri** (*Bridge of the Towers*). Standing massive and graceful
★   through the deep gorge that separates Spoleto from Monteluco, this 14th-century bridge is one of Umbria's most photographed monuments, and justifiably so. Built over the foundations of a Roman-era aqueduct, it soars 262 feet above the forested gorge—higher than the dome of St. Peter's in Rome. Sweeping views over the valley and a pleasant sense of vertigo make a walk across the bridge a must, particularly on a starry night. ⊠ *Via del Ponte*.

WORTH NOTING

Casa Romana. Spoleto became a Roman colony in the 3rd century BC, but the best excavated remains date from the 1st century AD. Best preserved among them is the Casa Romana. According to an inscription, it belonged to Vespasia Polla, the mother of Emperor Vespasian (one of the builders of the Colosseum and perhaps better known by the Romans for taxing them to install public toilets, later called "Vespasians"). The rooms, arranged around a large central atrium built over an *impluvium* (rain cistern), are decorated with black-and-white geometric mosaics. ⊠ *Palazzo del Municipio, Via Visiale 9* 🕾 *0743/40255* ⊕ *www.spoletocard.it* 🗟 *€3* 🕙 *Closed Mon. and Tues. and last wk of Dec.*

La Rocca. Built in the mid-14th century for Cardinal Egidio Albornoz, this massive fortress served as a seat for the local pontifical governors, a tangible sign of the restoration of the Church's power in the area when the pope was ruling from Avignon. Several popes spent time here, and one of them, Alexander VI, in 1499 sent his capable teenage daughter Lucrezia Borgia (1480–1519) to serve as governor for three months. The Gubbio-born architect Gattapone (14th century) used the ruins of a Roman acropolis as a foundation and took materials from many Roman-era sites, including the Teatro Romano. La Rocca's plan is long and rectangular, with six towers and two grand courtyards, an upper loggia, and inside some grand reception rooms. In the largest tower, Torre Maestà, you can visit an apartment with some interesting frescoes. The fortress also contains the Museo Nazionale del Ducato, 15 rooms dedicated to the art of the duchy of Spoleto during the Middle Ages. If you phone in advance, you may be able to secure an English-speaking guide. ⊠ *Piazza Campello* 🕾 *0743/224952* ⊕ *www.spoletocard.it* 🗟 *€7.50 including the Museo Nazionale del Ducato* 🕙 *Closed Mon.*

Teatro Romano. The Romans who colonized the city in 241 BC constructed this small theater in the 1st century AD; for centuries afterward it was used as a quarry for building materials. The most intact portion is the hallway that passes under the *cavea* (stands). The rest was heavily restored in the early 1950s and serves as a venue for Spoleto's Festival dei Due Mondi. The theater was the site of a gruesome episode in Spoleto's history: during the medieval struggle between Guelph (papal) and Ghibelline (imperial) forces, Spoleto took the side of the Holy Roman Emperor. Afterward, 400 Guelph supporters were massacred in the theater, their bodies burned in an enormous pyre. In the end, the Guelphs were triumphant, and Spoleto was incorporated into the states of the Church in 1354. Through a door in the west portico of the adjoining building is the **Museo Archeologico,** with assorted artifacts found in excavations primarily around Spoleto and Norcia. The collection contains Bronze Age and Iron Age artifacts from Umbrian and pre-Roman eras. Another section contains black-glaze vases from the Hellenistic period excavated from the necropolis of St. Scolastica in Norcia. The highlight is the stone tablet inscribed on both sides with the Lex Spoletina (Spoleto Law). Dating from 315 BC, this legal document prohibited the desecration of the woods on the slopes of nearby Monteluco. ✉ *Piazza della Libertà* ☎ *0743/223277* 🌐 *www.spoletocard.it* 🎫 *€4.*

WHERE TO EAT

$$ UMBRIAN 🍴 **Apollinare.** Low wooden ceilings and flickering candlelight make this monastery from the 10th and 11th centuries Spoleto's most romantic spot. The kitchen serves sophisticated, innovative variations on local dishes. **Known for:** modern versions of traditional Umbrian dishes; intimate and elegant setting; impeccable service. [$] *Average main: €16* ✉ *Via Sant'Agata 14* ☎ *0743/223256* 🌐 *www.ristoranteapollinare.it* ⏲ *Closed Tues.*

$$ UMBRIAN 🍴 **Il Tartufo.** As the name indicates, dishes prepared with truffles are the specialty here—don't miss the risotto al tartufo. Incorporating the ruins of a Roman villa, the surroundings are rustic on the ground floor and more modern upstairs. **Known for:** recipes incorporating truffles; charming staff; abundant portions, well presented. [$] *Average main: €18* ✉ *Piazza Garibaldi 24* ☎ *0743/40236* 🌐 *www.ristoranteiltartufo.it* ⏲ *Closed Mon., and early Jan.–early Feb. No dinner Sun.*

$ UMBRIAN 🍴 **Osteria del Trivio.** Everything is made on the premises and the seasonal menu changes daily. Dishes might include stuffed artichokes, pasta with local mushrooms, or chicken with artichokes. **Known for:** warm, convivial atmosphere; rustic osteria setting; delicious homemade pasta dishes. [$] *Average main: €14* ✉ *Via del Trivio 16* ☎ *0743/44349* ⏲ *Closed Tues. and 3 wks in Jan.*

$ UMBRIAN 🍴 **Ristorante Il Panciolle.** A small garden filled with lemon trees in the heart of Spoleto's medieval quarter provides one of the most appealing settings you could wish for. Dishes change throughout the year, and may include pastas served with asparagus or mushrooms, as well as grilled meats. **Known for:** authentic local cuisine; affable staff; panoramic terrace. [$] *Average main: €14* ✉ *Via Duomo 3/5* ☎ *0743/45677* 🌐 *www.ilpanciolle.it* ⏲ *Closed Wed. Sept.–Mar.*

WHERE TO STAY

$ HOTEL 🏨 **Hotel Clitunno.** Cozy guest rooms and intimate public rooms, some with timbered ceilings, give the sense of a traditional Umbrian home—albeit one with a good restaurant. **Pros:** friendly staff; good restaurant; convenient central location. **Cons:** difficult to find a parking space; some rooms small and dingy; needs sprucing up. [$] *Rooms from: €66*

✉ *Piazza Sordini 6* ☎ *0743/223340* 🌐 *www.hotelclitunno.com* 🛏 *52 rooms* 🍴 *Free Breakfast.*

$ HOTEL Fodor's Choice ★ 🏨 **Hotel San Luca.** Hand-painted friezes decorate the walls of the spacious guest rooms, and elegant comfort is the grace note throughout—you can sip afternoon tea in oversize armchairs by the fireplace, or take a walk in the sweet-smelling rose garden. **Pros:** very helpful staff; spacious rooms; close to escalators for exploring city. **Cons:** outside the town center; no restaurant; can feel soulless in winter. [$] *Rooms from: €100* ✉ *Via Interna delle Mura 21* ☎ *0743/223399* 🌐 *www.hotelsanluca.com* 🛏 *35 rooms* 🍴 *Free Breakfast.*

PERFORMING ARTS

Fodor's Choice ★ **Festival dei Due Mondi** (*Festival of Two Worlds*). In 1958, composer Gian Carlo Menotti chose Spoleto for the first Festival dei Due Mondi, a gathering of artists, performers, and musicians intending to bring together the "new" and "old" worlds of America and Europe. (The famed, corresponding festival in Charleston, South Carolina is no longer connected to this festival.) The annual event, held in late June and early July, is one of the most important cultural happenings in Europe, attracting big names in all branches of the arts, particularly music, opera, and theater. ✉ *Piazza del Comune 1* ☎ *0743/221689* 🌐 *www.festivaldispoleto.com.*

SOUTHERN UMBRIA

Orvieto, built on a tufa mount, produces one of Italy's favorite white wines and has one of the country's greatest cathedrals and most compelling fresco cycles. Nearby Narni and Todi are pleasant medieval hill towns. The former stands over a steep gorge, its Roman pedigree evident in dark alleyways and winding streets; the latter is a fairy-tale village with incomparable views and one of Italy's most perfect piazzas.

TODI

34 km (22 miles) south of Perugia, 34 km (22 miles) northeast of Orvieto.

As you stand on Piazza del Popolo, looking out onto the Tiber Valley below, it's easy to see why Todi is often described as Umbria's prettiest hill town. Legend has it that the town was founded by the Umbri, who followed an eagle who had stolen a tablecloth. They liked this lofty perch so much that they settled here for good. The eagle is now perched on the insignia of the medieval palaces in the main piazza.

GETTING HERE AND AROUND

Todi is best reached by car, as the town's two train stations are way down the hill and connected to the center by infrequent bus service. From Perugia, follow the E45 toward Rome. Take the Todi/Orvieto exit, then follow the SS79bis into Todi. The drive takes around 40 minutes.

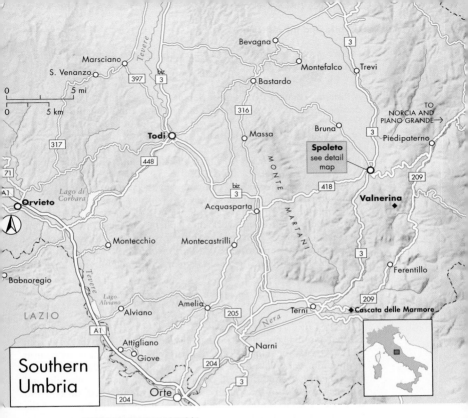

VISITOR INFORMATION

Contact **Todi** tourism office. ✉ *Piazza del Popolo 29–30* ☎ *075/8945416* 🌐 *www.visitodi.eu.*

EXPLORING

Duomo. One end of the Piazza del Popolo is dominated by this 12th-century Romanesque-Gothic masterpiece, built over the site of a Roman temple. The simple facade is enlivened by a finely carved rose window. Look up at that window as you step inside and you'll notice its peculiarity: each "petal" of the rose has a cherub's face in the stained glass. Also take a close look at the capitals of the double columns with pilasters: perched between the acanthus leaves are charming medieval sculptures of saints—Peter with his keys, George and the dragon, and so on. You can see the rich brown tones of the wooden choir near the altar, but unless you have binoculars or request special permission in advance, you can't get close enough to see all the exquisite detail in this Renaissance masterpiece of woodworking (1521–30). The severe, solid mass of the Duomo is mirrored by the Palazzo dei Priori (1595–97) across the way. ✉ *Piazza del Popolo* ☎ *075/8943041.*

Piazza del Popolo. Built above the Roman Forum, Piazza del Popolo is Todi's high point, a model of spatial harmony with stunning views onto the surrounding countryside. In the best medieval tradition, the square was conceived to house both the temporal and the spiritual centers of power. ✉ *Todi.*

WHERE TO EAT AND STAY

$$ UMBRIAN 🍴 **Ristorante Umbria.** Todi's most popular restaurant for more than four decades is reliable for its sturdy country food and the wonderful view from the terrace. Because it has only 16 tables outside, make sure you reserve ahead. **Known for:** traditional Umbrian dishes; terrific vista from terrace; friendly atmosphere. [$] *Average main: €15* ✉ *Via San Bonaventura 13* ☎ *075/8942737* 🌐 *www.ristoranteumbria.it* 🕒 *Closed Tues. and 3–4 wks in Jan. and Feb.*

$ HOTEL 🏨 **Residenza San Lorenzo Tre.** Surrounded by the antique furniture, paintings, and period knickknacks here, you will be as charmed by a sense of being in the 19th century as you are by the magnificent views over valleys and hills. **Pros:** old-world atmosphere; excellent central location; spectacular views. **Cons:** few modern amenities; long flight of steps to enter; small, basic bathrooms. [$] *Rooms from: €95* ✉ *Via San Lorenzo 3* ☎ *075/8944555* 🌐 *www.sanlorenzo3.it* 🕒 *Closed Nov.–mid-Apr.* 🛏 *6 rooms* 🍽 *Free Breakfast.*

ORVIETO

30 km (19 miles) southwest of Todi, 81 km (51 miles) west of Spoleto.

Carved out of an enormous plateau of volcanic rock high above a green valley, Orvieto has natural defenses that made the high walls seen in many Umbrian towns unnecessary. The Etruscans were the first to settle here, digging a honeycombed network of more than 1,200 wells and storage caves out of the soft stone. The Romans attacked, sacked, and destroyed the city in 283 BC; since then, it has grown up out of the rock into an enchanting maze of alleys and squares. Orvieto was solidly Guelph in the Middle Ages, and for several hundred years popes sought refuge in the city, at times needing protection from their enemies, at times seeking respite from the summer heat of Rome.

When painting his frescoes inside the Duomo, Luca Signorelli asked that part of his contract be paid in Orvietan wine, and he was neither the first nor the last to appreciate the region's popular white. In past times the caves carved underneath the town were used to ferment the Trebbiano grapes used in making Orvieto Classico; now local wine production has moved out to more traditional vineyards, but you can still while away the afternoon in tastings at any number of shops in town.

GETTING HERE AND AROUND

Orvieto is well connected by train to Rome, Florence, and Perugia. It's also adjacent to the A1 autostrada that runs between Florence and Rome. Parking areas in the upper town tend to be crowded. A better idea is to follow the signs for the Porta Orvetiana parking lot, then take the funicular that carries people up the hill.

VISITOR INFORMATION

The Carta Orvieto Unica (single ticket) is expensive but a great deal if you want to visit everything. For €20 you get admission to 11 museums and monuments, including the three major sights in town—Cappella di

San Brizio (at the Duomo), Museo Etrusco Claudio Faina, and Orvieto Underground—along with entry to the Torre del Moro, with views of Orvieto, plus a bus and funicular pass.

Contact Orvieto Tourism Office. ⊠ *Piazza del Duomo 24* ☏ *0763/341772.*

EXPLORING

Fodor'sChoice
★

Duomo. Orvieto's stunning cathedral was built to commemorate the Miracle at Bolsena. In 1263 a young priest who questioned the miracle of transubstantiation (in which the Communion bread and wine become the flesh and blood of Christ) was saying Mass at nearby Lago di Bolsena. His doubts were put to rest, however, when a wafer he had just blessed suddenly started to drip blood, staining the linen covering the altar. The cloth and the host were taken to the pope, who proclaimed a miracle and a year later provided for a new religious holiday—the Feast of Corpus Domini. Thirty years later, construction began on a duomo in Orvieto to celebrate the miracle and house the stained altar cloth.

It's thought that Arnolfo di Cambio (circa 1245–1302), the famous builder of the Duomo in Florence, was given the initial commission, but the project was soon taken over by Lorenzo Maitani (circa 1275–1330), who consolidated the structure and designed the monumental facade. Maitani also made the bas-relief panels between the doorways, which graphically tell the story of the Creation (on the left) and the Last Judgment (on the right). The lower registers, now protected by Plexiglas, succeed in conveying the horrors of hell as few other works of art manage to do, an effect made all the more powerful by the worn gray marble. Above, gold mosaics are framed by finely detailed Gothic decoration.

Inside, the cathedral is rather vast and empty; the major works are in the transepts. To the left is the **Cappella del Corporale,** where the square linen cloth (*corporale*) is kept in a golden reliquary that's modeled on the cathedral and inlaid with enamel scenes of the miracle. The cloth is removed for public viewing on Easter and on Corpus Domini (the ninth Sunday after Easter). In the right transept is the **Cappella di San Brizio,** or Cappella Nuova. In this chapel is one of Italy's greatest fresco cycles, notable for its influence on Michelangelo's *Last Judgment,* as well as for the extraordinary beauty of the figuration. In these works, a few by Fra Angelico and the majority by Luca Signorelli, the damned fall to hell, demons breathe fire and blood, and Christians are martyred. Some scenes are heavily influenced by the imagery in Dante's (1265–1321) *Divine Comedy.* ⊠ *Piazza del Duomo* ☏ *0763/342477* ⊕ *www.opsm. it* 🎫 *€4, including Cappella di San Brizio.*

Museo Etrusco Claudio Faina. This superb private collection, beautifully arranged and presented, goes far beyond the usual museum offerings of a scattering of local remains. The collection is particularly rich in Greek- and Etruscan-era pottery, from large Attic amphorae (6th–4th century BC) to Attic black- and red-figure pieces to Etruscan *bucchero* (dark-reddish clay) vases. Other interesting pieces in the collection include a 6th-century sarcophagus and a substantial display of Roman-era coins. ⊠ *Piazza del Duomo 29* ☏ *0763/341216* ⊕ *www.museofaina. it* 🎫 *€4.50* ⊙ *Closed Mon. Nov.–Feb.*

13

Orvieto Underground. More than just about any other town, Orvieto has grown from its own foundations. The Etruscans, the Romans, and those who followed dug into the tufa (the same soft volcanic rock from which catacombs were made) to create more than 1,000 separate cisterns, caves, secret passages, storage areas, and production areas for wine and olive oil. Much of the tufa removed was used as building blocks for the city that exists today, and some was partly ground into *pozzolana,* which was made into mortar. You can see the labyrinth of dugout chambers beneath the city on the **Orvieto Underground tour,** which runs daily at 11, 12:15, 4, and 5:15 (more frequently at busy periods) from Piazza del Duomo 23. ✉ *Orvieto* ☎ *0763/340688* 🌐 *www.orvietounderground.it* 🎟 *Tours €6.*

Pozzo della Cava. If you're short on time but want a quick look at the cisterns and caves beneath the city, head for the Pozzo della Cava, an Etruscan well for spring water. ✉ *Via della Cava 28* ☎ *0763/342373* 🌐 *www.pozzodellacava.it* 🎟 *€4* 🕓 *Closed Mon., and mid-Jan.–early Feb.*

WHERE TO EAT

$ UMBRIAN 🍴 **Le Grotte del Funaro.** Dine inside tufa caves under central Orvieto, where the two windows afford splendid views of the hilly countryside. The traditional Umbrian food is reliably good, with simple grilled meats and vegetables and pizzas. **Known for:** unusual setting; crusty pizzas; good choice of wines. [$] *Average main: €14* ✉ *Via Ripa Serancia 41* ☎ *0763/343276* 🌐 *www.grottedelfunaro.com* 🕓 *Closed Mon., and 10 days in July.*

$$ UMBRIAN 🍴 **Trattoria La Grotta.** The vaulted, plant-filled dining area with white walls adorned with paintings, antique vases, and other knickknacks makes a congenial setting for this small, rustic-style trattoria that is famed for its homemade pasta, perhaps with an artichoke, duck, or wild-boar sauce. Roast lamb, veal, and pork are all good, and the desserts are supplied by Orvieto's most eminent pasticceria. **Known for:** tasty homemade pastas; fresh, local ingredients; warm and welcoming service. [$] *Average main: €16* ✉ *Via Luca Signorelli 5* ☎ *0763/341348* 🕓 *Closed Tues.*

WHERE TO STAY

$$ HOTEL 🏨 **Hotel La Badia.** In a 12th-century monastery, vaulted ceilings and exposed stone walls, along with wood-beam ceilings and polished terracotta floors covered with rugs, establish rustic elegance in guest rooms. **Pros:** elegant atmosphere; fine views; beautiful grounds. **Cons:** slightly overpriced; need a car to get around; sparse breakfasts. [$] *Rooms from: €134* ✉ *Località La Badia, 4 km (2½ miles) south of Orvieto, Orvieto Scalo* ☎ *0763/301959* 🌐 *www.labadiahotel.it* 🕓 *Closed Jan. and Feb.* 🛏 *27 rooms* 🍽 *Free Breakfast.*

$$ HOTEL 🏨 **Hotel Palazzo Piccolomini.** This 16th-century family palazzo has been beautifully restored, with inviting public spaces and handsome guest quarters where contemporary surroundings are accented with old beams, vaulted ceilings, and other distinctive touches. **Pros:** private parking; efficient staff; good location. **Cons:** underwhelming breakfasts; four-star category not completely justified; some rooms and bathrooms

CLOSE UP

Hiking the Umbrian Hills

Magnificent scenery makes the heart of Italy excellent walking, hiking, and mountaineering country. In Umbria, the area around Spoleto is particularly good; several pleasant, easy, and well-signed trails begin at the far end of the Ponte alle Torri bridge over Monteluco. From Cannara, an easy half-hour walk leads to the fields of Pian d'Arca, the site of St. Francis's sermon to the birds. For slightly more arduous walks, you can follow the saint's path, uphill from Assisi to the Eremo delle Carceri, and then continue along the trails that crisscross Monte Subasio. At 4,250 feet, the Subasio's treeless summit affords views of Assisi, Perugia, far-off Gubbio, and the distant mountain ranges of Abruzzo.

For even more challenging hiking, the northern reaches of the Valnerina are exceptional; the mountains around Norcia should not be missed. Throughout Umbria and the Marches, you'll find that most recognized walking and hiking trails are marked with the distinctive red-and-white blazes of the Club Alpino Italiano. Tourist offices are a good source for walking and climbing itineraries to suit all ages and levels of ability, while bookstores, *tabacchi* (tobacconists), and *edicole* (newsstands) often have maps and hiking guides that detail the best routes in their area. Depending on the length and location of your walk, it can be important that you have comfortable walking shoes or boots, appropriate attire, and plenty of water to drink.

13

---

are small. $ *Rooms from: €130* ✉ *Piazza Ranieri 36* ☎ *0763/341743* ⊕ *www.palazzopiccolomini.it* ↪ *33 rooms* ⊙ *Free Breakfast.*

VALNERINA

The Valnerina is 27 km (17 miles) southeast of Spoleto.

The Valnerina (the valley of the River Nera, to the southeast of Spoleto) is the most beautiful of central Italy's many well-kept secrets. The twisting roads that serve the rugged landscape are poor, but the drive is well worth the effort for its forgotten medieval villages and dramatic mountain scenery.

GETTING HERE AND AROUND

You can head into the area from Terni on the S209, or on the SP395bis north of Spoleto, which links the Via Flaminia (S3) with the middle reaches of the Nera Valley through a tunnel.

EXPLORING

Cascata delle Marmore. The road east of Terni (SS Valnerina) leads 10 km (6 miles) to the Cascata delle Marmore (Waterfalls of Marmore), which, at 541 feet, are the highest in Europe. A canal was dug by the Romans in the 3rd century BC to prevent flooding in the nearby agricultural plains. Nowadays the waters are often diverted to provide hydroelectric power for Terni, reducing the roaring falls to an unimpressive trickle, so check with the information office at the falls (there's a timetable on their website in English) or with Terni's tourist office before heading here. On summer evenings, when the falls are in full spate, the cascading water is floodlit to striking effect. The falls are usually at their most energetic at midday and at around 4 pm. This is a good place for hiking, except in December and January, when most trails may be closed. ⊠ *SP79, 10 km (6 miles) east of Terni, Terni* ☎ *0744/62982* ⊕ *www.marmorefalls. it* ⊠ *€10* ⊙ *Closed weekdays in Jan.*

Norcia. The birthplace of St. Benedict, Norcia is best known for its Umbrian pork and truffles. Norcia exports truffles to France and hosts a truffle festival, the Sagra del Tartufo, every February. The surrounding mountains provide spectacular hiking. ⊠ *Terni* ⊕ *42 km (25 miles) east of Spoleto, 67 km (42 miles) northeast of Terni.*

Fodor's Choice **Piano Grande.** A spectacular mountain plain 25 km (15 miles) to the
★ northeast of the valley, Piano Grande is a hang glider's paradise and a wonderful place for a picnic or to fly a kite. It's also nationally famous for the quality of the lentils grown here, which are a traditional part of every Italian New Year's feast. ⊠ *Terni.*

THE MARCHES

An excursion from Umbria into the Marches region allows you to see a part of Italy rarely visited by foreigners. Not as wealthy as Tuscany or Umbria, the Marches has a diverse landscape of mountains and beaches, and marvelous views. Like that of neighbors to the west, the patchwork of rolling hills of Le Marche (as it's known in Italian) is stitched with grapevines and olive trees, bearing luscious wine and olive oil.

Traveling here isn't as easy as in Umbria or Tuscany. Beyond the narrow coastal plain and away from major towns, the roads are steep and twisting. An efficient bus service connects the coastal towns of Pesaro and Urbino. Train travel in the region is slow and stops are limited—although you can reach Ascoli Piceno by rail.

URBINO

75 km (47 miles) north of Gubbio, 116 km (72 miles) northeast of Perugia, 230 km (143 miles) east of Florence.

Majestic Urbino, atop a steep hill with a skyline of towers and domes, is something of a surprise to come upon. Though quite remote, it was once a center of learning and culture almost without rival in Western Europe. The town looks much as it did in the glory days of the 15th century: a cluster of warm brick and pale stone buildings, all topped with russet-color tile roofs. The focal point is the immense and beautiful Palazzo Ducale.

The city is home to the small but prestigious Università di Urbino—one of the oldest in the world—and the streets are usually filled with students. Urbino is very much a college town, with the usual array of bookshops, bars, and coffeehouses. In summer the Italian student population is replaced by foreigners who come to study Italian language and arts at several prestigious private fine-arts academies.

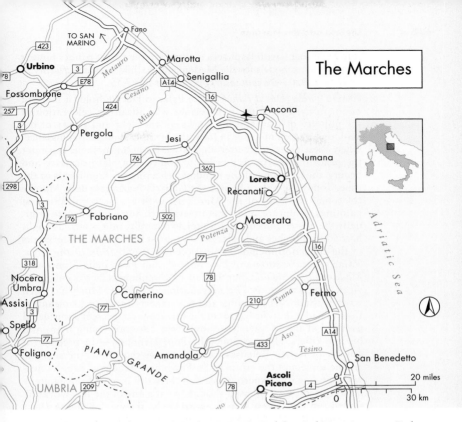

The Marches

Urbino's fame rests on the reputation of three of its native sons: Duke Federico da Montefeltro (1422–82), the enlightened warrior-patron who built the Palazzo Ducale; Raffaello Sanzio (1483–1520), or Raphael, one of the most influential painters in history and an embodiment of the spirit of the Renaissance; and the architect Donato Bramante (1444–1514), who translated the philosophy of the Renaissance into buildings of grace and beauty. Unfortunately there's little work by either Bramante or Raphael in the city, but the duke's influence can still be felt strongly.

GETTING HERE AND AROUND
Take the SS3bis from Perugia, and follow the directions for Gubbio and Cesena. Exit at Umbertide and take the SS219, then the SS452, and at Calmazzo, the SS73bis to Urbino.

VISITOR INFORMATION
Contact Urbino Tourism Office. ✉ *Piazza del Rinascimento 1* ☎ *0722/2613* ⊕ *www.turismo.pesarourbino.it.*

EXPLORING
Casa Natale di Raffaello (*House of Raphael*). This is the house in which the painter was born and where he took his first steps in painting, under the direction of his artist father. There's some debate about the fresco of the Madonna here; some say it's by Raphael, whereas others attribute

it to the father—with Raphael's mother and the young painter himself standing in as models for the Madonna and Child. ✉ *Via Raffaello 57* 🕿 *0722/320105* ⊕ *www.casaraffaello.com* 🎟 *€3.50.*

Fodor'sChoice
★
Palazzo Ducale (*Ducal Palace*). The Palazzo Ducale holds a place of honor in the city. If the Renaissance was, ideally, a celebration of the nobility of man and his works, of the light and purity of the soul, then there's no place in Italy, the birthplace of the Renaissance, where these tenets are better illustrated. From the moment you enter the peaceful courtyard, you know you're in a place of grace and beauty, the harmony of the building reflecting the high ideals of the time. Today the palace houses the **Galleria Nazionale delle Marche** (National Museum of the Marches), with a superb collection of paintings, sculpture, and other objets d'art. Some works were originally the possessions of the Montefeltro family; others were brought here from churches and palaces throughout the region. Masterworks in the collection include Paolo Uccello's *Profanation of the Host,* Titian's *Resurrection* and *Last Supper,* and Piero della Francesca's *Madonna of Senigallia.* But the gallery's highlight is Piero's enigmatic work long known as *The Flagellation of Christ.* Much has been written about this painting, and few experts agree on its meaning. Legend had it that the figures in the foreground represent a murdered member of the Montefeltro family (the barefoot young man) and his two killers. However, Sir John Pope-Hennessy—the preeminent scholar of Italian Renaissance art—argues that they represent the arcane subject of the vision of St. Lawrence. Academic debates notwithstanding, the experts agree that the work is one of the painter's masterpieces. Piero himself thought so: it's one of the few works he signed (on the lowest step supporting the throne). ✉ *Piazza Duca Federico* 🕿 *0722/322625* ⊕ *www.palazzoducaleurbino.it* 🎟 *€6.50.*

WHERE TO EAT AND STAY

$$
ITALIAN
✕ **La Fornarina.** Locals often crowd this small, two-room trattoria near the Piazza della Repubblica. The specialty is meaty country fare, such as *coniglio* (rabbit) and *vitello alle noci* (veal cooked with walnuts) or *ai porcini* (with mushrooms). **Known for:** excellent starters; welcoming atmosphere; hospitable staff. [$] *Average main: €18* ✉ *Via Mazzini 14* 🕿 *0722/320007.*

$$
ITALIAN
✕ **Osteria Angolo Divino.** At this informal restaurant in the center of Urbino, tradition reigns supreme: the menu is written in local dialect, flanked by Italian and English translations. Dishes range from the deliciously simple *spaghetti con pane grattugiato* (spaghetti with bread crumbs) to the temptingly rich *filetto al tartufo* (beef fillet with truffles). **Known for:** calm and pleasant ambience; quality cuisine with experimental elements; traditional osteria-style decor. [$] *Average main: €20* ✉ *Via S. Andrea 14* 🕿 *0722/327559* ⊕ *www.angolodivino.biz* ☾ *Closed Wed. No lunch Tues. and Thurs.*

$$
HOTEL
⛉ **Hotel Bonconte.** Pleasant rooms just inside the city walls and close to the Palazzo Ducale are decorated with a smattering of antiques, and those in front have views of the valley below Urbino. **Pros:** some nice views; central but away from the bustle; good breakfasts. **Cons:** an uphill walk to town center; some rooms are cramped; traffic noise in

some rooms. $ *Rooms from: €132* ✉ *Via delle Mura 28* ☎ *0722/2463* ⊕ *www.viphotels.it* ⇌ *25 rooms* �‖ *Free Breakfast.*

LORETO

31 km (19 miles) south of Ancona, 118 km (73 miles) southeast of Urbino.

There's a strong Renaissance feel about this hilltop town, which is home to one of the most important religious sites in Europe, the Santuario della Santa Casa (House of the Virgin Mary). Bramante and Sansovino gave the church its Renaissance look, although many other artists helped create its special atmosphere. Today the town revolves around the religious calendar; if you can be here on December 10, you will witness the Feast of the Translation of the Holy House, when huge bonfires are lighted to celebrate the miraculous arrival of the house in 1295.

GETTING HERE AND AROUND
If you're driving from Perugia, take the SS318 and then the SS76 highway to Fabriano and then on to Chiaravalle, where it merges with the A14 autostrada. The drive takes around 2½ hours. Trains also go to Loreto, but the station is about a mile outside the town center. Regular buses leave from the station to the center.

VISITOR INFORMATION
Contact Loreto Tourism Office. ✉ *Via Solari 3* ☎ *071/970276* ⊕ *www.turismo. marche.it.*

EXPLORING
Basilica della Santa Casa. Loreto is famous for one of the best-loved shrines in the world, that of the **Santuario della Santa Casa** (House of the Virgin Mary), within the Basilica della Santa Casa. Legend has it that angels moved the house from Nazareth, where the Virgin Mary was living at the time of the Annunciation, to this hilltop in 1295. The reason for this sudden and divinely inspired move was that Nazareth had fallen into the hands of Muslim invaders, whom the angelic hosts viewed as unsuitable keepers of this important shrine. Excavations made at the behest of the Catholic Church have shown that the house did once stand elsewhere and was brought to the hilltop—by either crusaders or a family named Angeli—around the time the angels (*angeli*) are said to have done the job.

The house itself consists of three rough stone walls contained within an elaborate marble tabernacle. Built around this centerpiece is the giant basilica of the Holy House, which dominates the town. Millions of visitors come to the site every year (particularly at Easter and on the December 10 Feast of the Holy House), and the little town of Loreto can become uncomfortably crowded with pilgrims. Many great Italian architects—including Bramante, Antonio da Sangallo the Younger (1483–1546), Giuliano da Sangallo (circa 1445–1516), and Sansovino (1467–1529)—contributed to the design of the basilica. It was begun in the Gothic style in 1468 and continued in Renaissance style through the late Renaissance. The bell tower is by Luigi Vanvitelli (1700–73). Inside the church are a great many mediocre 19th- and 20th-century paintings but also some fine works by Renaissance masters such as Luca Signorelli and Melozzo da Forlì (1438–94).

If you're a nervous air traveler, you can take comfort in the fact that the Holy Virgin of Loreto is the patron saint of air travelers and that Pope John Paul II composed a prayer for a safe flight—available here in a half dozen languages. ✉ *Piazza della Madonna* ☎ *071/9747155* 🌐 *www.santuarioloreto.it.*

ASCOLI PICENO

88 km (55 miles) south of Loreto, 105 km (65 miles) south of Ancona.

Ascoli Piceno sits in a valley ringed by steep hills and cut by the Tronto River. In Roman times it was one of central Italy's best-known market towns, and today, with almost 52,000 residents, it's a major fruit and olive producer, making it one of the most important towns in the region. Despite growth during the Middle Ages and at other times, the streets in the town center continue to reflect the grid pattern of the ancient Roman city. You'll even find the word *rua,* from the Latin *ruga,* used for "street" instead of the Italian *via.* Now largely closed to traffic, the city center is great to explore on foot.

GETTING HERE AND AROUND

From Perugia take the SS75 to Foligno, then merge onto the SS3 to Norcia. From here take the SS4 to Ascoli Piceno. There are also trains, but the journey would be quite long, taking you from Perugia to Ancona before changing for Ascoli Piceno.

VISITOR INFORMATION

Contact Ascoli Piceno Tourism Office. ✉ *Piazza Aringo 7* ☎ *0736/253045* 🌐 *www.turismo.marche.it.*

EXPLORING

Piazza del Popolo. The heart of the town is the majestic Piazza del Popolo, dominated by the Gothic church of **San Francesco** and the **Palazzo del Popolo,** a 13th-century town hall that contains a graceful Renaissance courtyard. The square functions as the living room of the entire city and at dusk each evening is packed with people strolling and exchanging news and gossip—the sweetly antiquated ritual called the *passeggiata,* performed all over the country. ✉ *Ascoli Piceno.*

WHERE TO STAY

$ HOTEL 🏨 **Hotel Pennile.** A modern, family-run hotel in a quiet residential area outside the old city center is pleasantly set amid a grove of olive trees. **Pros:** peaceful; a good budget option; easy parking. **Cons:** distance from town center; no restaurant; basic buffet breakfast. [$] *Rooms from: €99* ✉ *Via G. Spalvieri* ☎ *0736/41645* 🌐 *www.hotelpennile.it* 🛏 *33 rooms* 🍴 *Free Breakfast.*

NAPLES AND CAMPANIA

WELCOME TO NAPLES AND CAMPANIA

TOP REASONS TO GO

★ **Naples, Italy's most operatic city:** Walk through the energy, chaos, and beauty that is Spaccanapoli, the city's historic artery, and you'll create an unforgettable memory.

★ **Pompeii:** The excavated ruins of Pompeii offer a unique, occasionally spooky glimpse into everyday life—and sudden death—in Roman times.

★ **"The Living Room of the World":** Pose oh-so-casually with the beautiful people on La Piazzetta, the central crossroads of the island of Capri—a stage-set square that always seems ready for a gala performance.

★ **Ravello:** High above the famously blue Bay of Salerno, this Amalfi Coast charmer is a contender for the title of "most beautiful village in the world."

★ **Positano, a world made of stairs:** Built like a vertical amphitheater, Positano's only job is to look enchanting on the Amalfi Coast—and it does that very well.

The Golfo di Napoli (Bay of Naples) holds many of Campania's attractions, including Italy's greatest archaeological sites—Pompeii and Herculaneum—and the city of Naples itself. Geological stepping-stones anchored in the bay, the islands of Capri, Ischia, and Procida tip the two points of its watery crescent. Just to the south stands the Sorrento Peninsula, home to the town of Sorrento. Over the Lattari Mountains lies the Amalfi Coast, famed for such beauty spots as Positano, Amalfi, and Ravello.

1 Naples. Italy's third-largest city can seduce you one moment and exasperate you the next: it's lush, chaotic, friendly, amusing, confounding, and very beautiful.

2 Herculaneum, Vesuvius, and Pompeii. Through their excavated ruins, two towns show you how ancient Romans lived the good life—until, one day in AD 79, Mt. Vesuvius buried them in volcanic ash and lava.

3 Ischia and Procida. Although they lack Capri's glitz, these two sister islands in the Bay of Naples share a laid-back charm.

4 Capri. The rocky island mixes natural beauty and *dolce vita* glamour.

5 Sorrento and the Sorrentine Peninsula. Perched over the Bay of Naples with an incomparable view of Mt. Vesuvius, this Belle Époque resort town is sheer delight.

6 The Amalfi Coast. The most shockingly beautiful coastal drive in the world links together Positano, Amalfi, and Ravello, all magically set against a bluer-than-blue sea and sky.

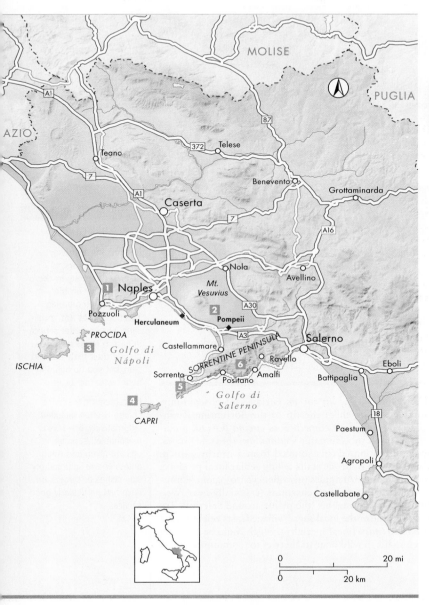

MOLISE

PUGLIA

14

AZIO

A1

Teano

372

Telese

7

A1

Benevento

Grottaminarda

Caserta

7

A16

Nola

Avellino

1 Naples

Mt.
Vesuvius

2

A30

Pozzuoli

Herculaneum

Pompeii

A3

PROCIDA

3

*Golfo di
Nápoli*

Castellammare

SORRENTINE PENINSULA

Salerno

Eboli

ISCHIA

Sorrento

6

Ravello

Amalfi

Battipaglia

5

Positano

4

*Golfo di
Salerno*

CAPRI

Paestum

18

Agropoli

Castellabate

0   20 mi

0   20 km

EATING AND DRINKING WELL IN NAPLES AND CAMPANIA

Think of Neapolitan food and you conjure up images of pasta, pizza, and tomatoes. The stereotype barely scratches the surface of what's available in Naples—to say nothing of the rest of Campania, where the cuisine reflects an enormously diverse landscape.

The region is known for its enclaves of gastronomy, notable among them the tip of the Sorrentine Peninsula. You may well come across *cucina povera*, a cuisine inspired by Campania's *contadino* (peasant) roots, with all the ingredients sourced from a nearby garden. Expect to see roadside stalls selling stellar local produce, including *annurca* apples (near Benevento), giant lemons (Amalfi Coast), roasted chestnuts (especially near Avellino), and watermelons (the plains around Salerno). Try to get to one of the local *sagre*, village feasts celebrating a *prodotto tipico* (local specialty), which could be anything from snails to wild boar to cherries to (commonly) wine.

A TIPPING TIP

Neapolitans are easily recognized in bars elsewhere in Italy by the tip they leave on the counter when ordering. This habit does not necessarily ensure better service in bars in Naples, notorious for their fairly offhand staff, but you do blend in better with the locals.

In restaurants, a service charge is often included (alternatively, 5%–10% is reasonable). In pizzerias, tips are given less often unless you've splurged on side dishes or sweets, or have had particularly good service.

PIZZA

Naples is the undisputed homeland of pizza, and you'll usually encounter it here in two classic forms: *margherita* and *marinara*. Given the larger-than-your-plate portions of standard pizzas, some choose to ask for a *mignon* (kids' portion), or even share, divided between two plates. Take-away outlets in most town centers sell pizza by the slice, along with the usual range of fried *arancini* (rice balls) and *crocchè di patate* (potato fritters).

COFFEE

Given the same basic ingredients—coffee grounds, water, a machine—what makes *caffè* taste so much better in Naples than elsewhere remains a mystery. If you find the end product too strong, ask to have it with a dash of milk (caffè *macchiato*) or a little diluted (caffè *lungo*). Many bars serve with sugar already added, so if you want it without, request *senza zucchero* or *amaro*.

BUFFALO

Long feted for the melt-in-your-mouth mozzarella cheese *(pictured below)* made from its milk, the river buffalo—related to the Asian water buffalo—is also the source of other culinary delights. Throughout the region, look for buffalo ricotta and mascarpone, as well as buffalo *provola* and *scamorza*, which may be lightly smoked (resulting in a golden crust). Caserta has more

mature *nero di bufala* (aged like sheep's cheese), while around Salerno you'll find smoked *caciocavallo* cheese as well as *carne di bufala* (buffalo meat), which can be braised to perfection.

THE ORAL TRADITION

Locals in Campania like to bypass the restaurant menu and ask what the staff recommend. Take this approach and you'll often wind up with a daily special or the house specialty. Although you're unlikely to get multilingual staff outside the larger hotels and main tourist areas, the person you talk to will spare no effort to get the message across.

WINE

Wine in Campania has an ancient pedigree. Some say fancifully that Campania's undisputed king of reds, the *aglianico*, got its name from the word "Hellenic"; and *fiano*, the primary white grape, closely resembles the Roman variety *apianus*. Horace, the Latin poet, extolled the virtues of drinking wine from Campania. A century later, Pliny the Elder was harsher in his judgment: wine from Pompeii would give you a hangover until noon the next day, and Sorrento wine tasted of vinegar.

In recent decades, though, Campania has gained respect for its boutique reds. Due to the rugged landscape, small farms, and limited mechanization, prices can be relatively high, but the quality is high as well.

Updated by
Nick Bruno

A region of evocative names—Capri, Sorrento, Pompeii, Positano, Amalfi—Campania conjures up visions of cliff-shaded, sapphire-hue coves, sun-dappled waters, and mighty ruins. More travelers visit this corner than any other in southern Italy, and it's no wonder.

Home to Vesuvius, the area's unique geology is responsible for Campania's photogenic landscape. A spectacular coastline stretches out along a deep blue sea, punctuated by rocky islands.

Through the ages, the area's temperate climate, warm sea, fertile soil, and natural beauty have attracted Greek colonists, then Roman emperors—who called the region "Campania Felix," or "the happy land"—and later Saracen raiders and Spanish invaders. The result has been a rich and varied history, reflected in everything from architecture to mythology. The highlights span millennia: the near-intact Roman towns of Pompeii and Herculaneum, the Greek temples in Paestum, the Norman and Baroque churches in Naples, the white-dome fisherman's houses of Positano, the *dolce vita* resorts of Capri. Campania piles them all onto one mammoth must-see sandwich.

The region's complex identity is most intensely felt in its major metropolis, Naples. Few who visit remain ambivalent. You needn't participate in the mad whirl of the city, however. The best pastime in Campania is simply finding a spot with a stunning view and indulging in *il dolce far niente* ("the sweetness of doing nothing").

NAPLES AND CAMPANIA PLANNER

MAKING THE MOST OF YOUR TIME

In Campania there are three primary travel experiences: Naples, with its restless exuberance; the resorts (Capri, Sorrento, the Amalfi Coast), dedicated to leisure and indulgence; and the archaeological sites (Pompeii, Herculaneum, Paestum), where the ancient world is frozen in time. Each is wonderful in its own way. If you have a week, you can get a good taste of all three. With less time, you're better off choosing between them rather than stretching yourself thin.

Pompeii, being a day trip, is the simplest to plan for. To get a feel for Naples, you should give it a couple of days at a minimum. The train station makes a harsh first impression (an overhaul has softened the blow), but the city grows on you as you take in the sights and interact with the locals.

That said, many people bypass Naples and head right for the resorts. These places are all about relaxing—you'll miss the point if you're in a rush. Although Sorrento isn't as spectacular as Positano or Capri, it makes a good base because of its central location.

14

DISCOUNTS AND DEALS

Government-run sites are free on the first Sunday of each month—good for those on a budget, but less so for avoiding crowds. The **Campania Artecard** entitles users to free or discounted admission to about four dozen museums and monuments in Naples and beyond. These are the main passes: Naples, three days (€21), has three sights included and a fourth at up to 50% off, plus transportation; Campania region, three days (€32), including Pompeii and other Bay of Naples sights and Ravello and Paestum with two sights included and a third at up to 50% off, plus transportation; Campania region, seven days (€34), with five sights included and a sixth for up to 50% off, but no transportation. Other benefits (which vary depending on the pass) include discounts on audio guides, theater and ferry tickets, city tours, and other activities, and visitors age 18–24 receive generous discounts. For more information, visit the Campania Artecard website (⊕ *www.campaniaartecard. it*) or the tourist office in the Piazza Garibaldi station, which distributes a helpful booklet about the passes.

GETTING HERE AND AROUND

BOAT TRAVEL

Several companies offer a variety of fast craft and passenger and car ferries connecting the islands of Capri, Ischia, and Procida with Naples and Pozzuoli year-round. Hydrofoils and other fast craft leave from Naples's Molo Beverello, adjacent to Piazza Municipio, with some departures in high season also from Mergellina, about 1½ km (1 mile) west of Piazza Municipio. Slower car ferries leave from the berths at Calata Porta di Massa, a 10-minute walk, or 3-minute shuttle bus ride, east of Molo Beverello.

Information on departures is published every day in the local paper, *Il Mattino*. Alternatively, ask at the tourist office or at the port, or contact these companies directly. Always double-check schedules in stormy weather.

Contacts Alilauro. ☏ 081/4972222 ⊕ *www.alilauro.it.* **Caremar.** ☏ 081/18966690 ⊕ *www.caremar.it.* **Gescab** (NLG). ☏ 081/8071812 Sorrento office, 081/4285555 Naples Port office ⊕ *www.gescab.it.* **SNAV.** ☏ 081/4285555 ⊕ *www.snav.it.*

BUS TRAVEL

Within Campania there's an extensive network of local buses, although finding information about it can be trying.

SITA buses. SITA buses bound for Salerno leave every 20 minutes 6 am–9 pm, Monday through Saturday, from its terminal in the port near the Stazione Marittima. There are also four departures from the airport (except Sunday). SITA buses also serve the Amalfi Coast, connecting Sorrento with Salerno. Check the online app moovitapp.com for up-to-the-minute bus updates. ☎ 089/405145 ⊕ www.sitasudtrasporti.it.

CAR TRAVEL

You can get along fine without a car in Campania, and there are plenty of reasons not to have one. Much of Naples is pedestrianized, meaning motorized arteries are often bottlenecked; you can't bring a car to Capri (except in winter, when everything's closed); and parking in the towns of the Amalfi Coast is hard to come by and expensive.

Italy's main north–south route, the A1 (aka the Autostrada del Sole), connects Rome with Naples and Campania. In good traffic the drive to Naples from Rome takes a little more than two hours. The A3 autostrada, a somewhat perilous continuation of the A1, runs south from Naples through Campania and into Calabria. Herculaneum (Ercolano) and Pompeii (Pompei) both have marked exits off the A3. For Vesuvius, take the Portici Ercolano exit. For the Sorrento Peninsula and the Amalfi Coast, exit at Castellammare di Stabia. To get to Paestum, take the A3 to the Battipaglia exit, and follow the road to Capaccio Scalo–Paestum. Roads on the Sorrento Peninsula and Amalfi Coast are narrow and twisting, but they have outstanding views.

If you come to Naples by car, find a garage, agree on the rate, and leave it there for the duration of your stay. (If you park on the street, you run the risk of theft.)

Naples Garage Contacts Garage Cava. ⊠ Via Mergellina 6, Mergellina ☎ 081/660023 ⊕ www.garagecava.it Ⓜ Mergellina. **Grilli.** ⊠ Hotel Ramada, Via Ferraris 40, near Stazione Centrale, Piazza Garibaldi ☎ 081/264344 Ⓜ Garibaldi. **Turistico.** ⊠ Via de Gasperi 14, near port, Toledo ☎ 081/5525442 ⊕ www.garageturistico.it Ⓜ Municipio/Università.

TAXI TRAVEL

You may be able to hail a taxi if you see one driving, but your best bet is to call Radio Taxi or ask someone at your hotel to book one. Taxi ranks can be found outside the central Piazza Garibaldi train station and the port (Molo Beverello), as well as throughout the city. Watch out for overcharging at three locations: the airport, the railway station, and the hydrofoil marina. The fixed rate (be sure to ask for *tariffa predeterminata*!) from the airport to the central station is €18, which covers three people, two large pieces of luggage, and two small pieces. City Airport Taxis offers a private service.

Ask for *il tariffario*, the tariff information sheet of the Comune di Napoli with common fixed rate journeys when taking a taxi, as drivers may invent an exorbitant price, even hiding the tariff sheet—trips around the city should cost €8–€10. You can of course request that the meter is switched on; this often results in your paying less. Taxis charge approximately €3.50 initially (more on Sunday, holidays, and after 10 pm), then €0.05 per 48 meters (or 8 seconds of idling). A copy of the latest tariff sheet can be downloaded at ⊕ *www.comune.napoli.it/taxi*. Other options besides Radio Taxi include Consorttaxi (☎ *081/2222*), La Partenope (☎ *081/0101*), and La 570 (☎ *081/5707070*). In summer, many cabs in Naples have no air-conditioning, so you can bake if caught in a traffic jam.

Contacts City Airport Taxis. ⊕ *www.city-airport-taxis.com/airporttransfers/ city/naples-taxi.* **Radio Taxi Napoli.** ☎ *081/8888* ⊕ *www.taxinapoli.it.*

TRAIN TRAVEL

There are up to five trains every hour between Rome and Naples. Both the Alta Velocità Frecciarossa and Italo trains (the fastest types of train service) make the trip in a little more than an hour, with the Intercity taking two. All trains to Naples stop at the refurbished Stazione Centrale.

The efficient (though run-down) suburban Circumvesuviana runs from Naples's Porta Nolana and stops at Stazione Centrale before continuing to Herculaneum, Pompeii, and Sorrento. Travel time between Naples and Sorrento on the Circumvesuviana line is about 75 minutes.

For ticketing purposes, the region is divided into travel zones by distance from Naples. If you're traveling from Naples to anywhere else in Campania, be sure to ask for a *biglietto integrato*. It's slightly more expensive than the direct ticket (about €1 more), but there will be no need to buy a separate ticket for your subway, tram, or bus ride to the train station as the biglietto integrato covers the whole journey. An *integrato* ticket to Herculaneum costs €2.70, to Pompeii €3.50, and to Sorrento €4.90. Choose a cheaper *corso semplice* direct ticket if no changes required

Contacts Circumvesuviana. ☎ *081/19805000* ⊕ *www.eavsrl.it.* **Stazione Centrale.** ✉ *Piazza Garibaldi, Naples* ☎ *892021 in Italy (fee)* ⊕ *www.trenitalia. com, www.italotreno.it.*

RESTAURANTS

As the birthplace of pizza, Naples prides itself on its vast selection of pizzerias, the most famous of which—Da Michele (where Julia Roberts filmed her pizza scene in *Eat Pray Love*) or Sorbillo—deserve the designation of "incomparable." Many Neapolitans make lunch their big meal of the day, and then have a pizza for supper.

Dining on the Amalfi Coast, Capri, Ischia and Procida revolves largely around seafood. Dishes are prepared using the short, rolled handmade *scialatielli* or large *paccheri* pasta and adorned with local *vongole* (clams) or *cozze* (mussels) and other shellfish. Octopus, squid, and the fresh fish of the season are always on the menu for the second course. Cetara has been famous for its *alici* (anchovies) since Roman times, and even produces alici bread. Eateries range from beachside trattorias to beacons of fine dining with stupendous views. *Restaurant reviews have been shortened. For full information, visit Fodors.com.*

HOTELS

Most parts of Campania have accommodations in all price categories, but they tend to fill up in high season, so reserve well in advance. In summer, on the coast and the islands, hotels that serve meals often require you to take half board. *Hotel reviews have been shortened. For full information, visit Fodors.com.*

WHAT IT COSTS				
	$	$$	$$$	$$$$
Restaurants	under €15	€15–€24	€25–€35	over €35
Hotels	under €125	€125–€200	€201–€300	over €300

Prices in the dining reviews are the average cost of a main course at dinner, or, if dinner is not served, at lunch. Prices in the reviews are the lowest cost of a standard double room in high season.

TOURS

City Sightseeing. Close to the port, beside the main entrance to Castel Nuovo, is the terminal for double-decker buses belonging to City Sightseeing. For €23 you can take up to three different excursions, giving you reasonable coverage of the downtown sights and outlying attractions like the Museo di Capodimonte. ⊠ *Piazza Municipio, Naples* ☎ *081/5517279* ⊕ *www.napoli.city-sightseeing.it.*

Lino Tour. Lino Tour offers tailor-made tours of the attractions in and around Naples. ⊠ *Naples* ☎ *081/8073587* ⊕ *www.linotourcarservice. com.*

NAPLES

Located under the shadow of Vesuvius, Naples is the most vibrant city in Italy—a steaming, bubbling, reverberating minestrone in which each block is a small village and everything seems to be a backdrop for an opera not yet composed.

It's said that northern Italians vacation here to remind themselves of the time when Italy was *molto italiana—really* Italian. In this respect, Naples (Napoli in Italian) doesn't disappoint: Neapolitan rainbows of laundry wave in the wind over alleyways, mothers caress children, men break out into impromptu arias at sidewalk cafés, and street scenes offer Fellini-esque slices of life. Everywhere contrasting elements of faded gilt and romance, grandeur and squalor form a pageant of pure *Italianità*—Italy at its most Italian.

As the historic capital of the region known as Campania, Naples has been perpetually and tumultuously in a state of flux. Neapolitans are instinctively the most hospitable of people, and they've often paid a price for being so, having unwittingly extended a warm welcome to wave after wave of invaders. Lombards, Goths, Normans, Swabians, Spanish viceroys and kings, and Napoleonic generals arrived in turn; most of them proved to be greedy and self-serving. Still, if these foreign

CAMPANIA THROUGH THE AGES

Ancient History. Lying on Mediterranean trade routes plied by several pre-Hellenic civilizations, Campania was settled by the ancient Greeks from approximately 800 BC onward. Here myth and legend blend with historical fact. The town of Herculaneum is said—rather improbably—to have been established by Hercules himself; and Naples in ancient times was called Parthenope, the name attributed to one of the sirens who preyed on hapless sailors in antiquity.

Thanks to archaeological research, some of the layers of myth have been stripped away to reveal a pattern of occupation and settlement well before Rome became established. Greek civilization flourished for hundreds of years all along this coastline, but there was nothing in the way of centralized government until centuries later when the Roman Republic, uniting all Italy for the first time, absorbed the Greek colonies with little opposition. Generally, the peace of Campania was undisturbed during these centuries of Roman rule.

Foreign Influences. Naples and Campania, like Italy in general, decayed along with the Roman Empire and collapsed into the abyss of the Middle Ages. Naples itself regained some importance under the rule of the Angevins in the latter part of the 13th century and continued its progress in the 1440s under Aragonese rule. The nobles who served under the Spanish viceroys in the 16th and 17th centuries enjoyed their pleasures, even as Spain milked the area for taxes.

After a short Austrian occupation, Naples became the capital of the Kingdom of the Two Sicilies, which the Bourbon kings established in 1738. Their rule was generally benevolent as far as Campania was concerned, and their support of papal authority in Rome was important in the development of the country as a whole. Their rule was important artistically, too, contributing to the architecture of the region, and attracting great musicians, artists, and writers who were drawn by the easy life at court. Finally, Giuseppe Garibaldi launched his famous expedition, and in 1860 Naples was united with the rest of Italy.

Modern Times. Things were relatively tranquil through the years that followed—with visitors thronging to Capri, Sorrento, Amalfi, and, of course, Naples—until World War II. Allied bombings did considerable damage in and around Naples. At the fall of the Fascist government, the sorely tried Neapolitans rose up against Nazi occupation troops and in four days of street fighting drove them out of the city. A monument was raised to the *scugnizzo* (the typical Neapolitan street urchin), celebrating the youngsters who participated in the battle. With the end of the war, artists, tourists, writers, and other lovers of beauty returned to the Campania region.

As time passed, some parts of Campania gained increased attention from visitors, while others lost their cachet. Years of misgovernment have left their mark, yet the region's cultural and natural heritage is finally being revalued as local authorities and inhabitants recognize the importance of the area's largest industry—tourism.

14

rulers bled the populace dry with taxes, they left the impoverished city with a rich architectural inheritance.

Much of that inheritance is on display in the Centro Storico neighborhood, where the Piazza del Gesù Nuovo and the surrounding blocks are a showplace for the city's most beloved churches. Compared to most other great metropolises of the world, Naples has little tourist infrastructure, forcing you to become a native very quickly, which you will if you spend enough time wandering through the gridlike narrow streets of the old center.

GETTING HERE AND AROUND

Public transportation in Naples is decent, and includes two subway lines, three funiculars, and a multitude of buses. Tickets cost €1.10 per journey (€1.30 on Metro Linea 2), but a Ticket Integrato Campania costs €1.60 and is valid for 90 minutes on all transport for as far as Pozzuoli to the west and Portici to the east; €4.50 buys a *biglietto giornaliero* (all-day ticket).

Now with a couple of art-decorated stations (Toledo and Università) voted among Europe's most attractive, Naples's Metropolitana provides fairly frequent service and can be the fastest way to get across the traffic-clogged city. Linea 1, Metropolitana Collinare, links the hill area of the Vomero and beyond with the National Archaeological Museum and Piazza Municipio near the port, as well as Stazione Centrale. The older Linea 2 stretches from the train station to Pozzuoli. Trains on both lines run 5:45 am–11 pm.

Bus service is viable, especially with the introduction of larger buses on the regular R1, R2, R3, and R4 routes. Electronic signs display wait times at many stops.

VISITOR INFORMATION

The numerous tourist offices in Naples aren't always open when they claim to be, but most are generally open Monday–Saturday 8:30–8 (Sunday 8:30–2) except where noted. The AACST specializes in information on old Naples but generally just supplies brochures. A second office, which is closed on Sunday, is handily located inside the Palazzo Reale. There's an EPT (Ente Provinciale per il Turismo; open daily 9–6) office in Stazione Centrale staffed by a welcoming team of helpers. Pick up a free map and the latest "Art in Campania" brochure listing key venues and possible savings through the Campania Artecard.

Contacts Azienda Autonoma di Soggiorno Cura e Turismo di Napoli. ⊠ *Via San Carlo 9, Piazza Plebiscito* ☎ *081/402394* ⊕ *www.inaples.it.* **EPT.** ⊠ *Stazione Centrale, Piazza Garibaldi* ☎ *081/268779* ⊕ *www.eptnapoli.info* Ⓜ *Garibaldi.* **I Naples.** ⊠ *Piazza del Gesù Nuovo, Centro Storico* ☎ *081/5512701* ⊕ *www. inaples.it.*

EXPLORING

CENTRO STORICO

To experience the true essence of Naples, you need to explore the Centro Storico, an unforgettable neighborhood that is the heart of old Naples. This is the Naples of peeling building facades and hanging laundry, with small alleyways fragrant with fresh flowers laid at the many shrines to the Blessed Virgin. Here the cheapest pizzerias in town feed the locals like kings, and the raucous street carnival of Neapolitan daily life is punctuated with oases of spiritual calm. All the contradictions of Naples—splendor and squalor, palace and slum, triumph and tragedy—meet here and sing a full-throated chorale. But the Centro Storico is not simply picturesque. It also contains some of Naples's most important sights, including a striking conglomeration of churches—Lombard, Gothic, Renaissance, Baroque, rococo, and Neoclassical. There are the majolica-adorned cloister of Santa Chiara; the sumptuous church of the Gesù Nuovo; two opera-set piazzas; the Duomo, where the Festa di San Gennaro is celebrated every September; the Museo Cappella Sansevero; the greatest painting in Naples—Caravaggio's *Seven Acts of Mercy* altarpiece—on view at the museum complex of Pio Monte; and Via Gregorio Armeno, where shops devoted to *Presepe crèche* (Nativity scene statues) make every day a rehearsal for Christmas. And even though this was the medieval center of the city, the city's flagship museum of modern art, the Madre, is here and night owls will find that many of Naples's most cutting-edge clubs and bars are hidden among its nooks and alleys. For soccer fanatics, there is even a shrine to Diego Maradona.

14

TOP ATTRACTIONS

Duomo. Although the cathedral was established in the 1200s, the current building was erected a century later and has since undergone radical changes—especially during the Baroque period. Inside, the 350-year-old wooden ceiling is supported by 110 ancient columns salvaged from pagan buildings. The 4th-century church of **Santa Restituta**, incorporated into the cathedral, was redecorated in the late 1600s in the Baroque style, though the mosaics in the **Battistero** (Baptistery) are claimed to be the oldest in the Western world. In the **Cappella del Tesoro di San Gennaro**, multicolor marbles and frescoes honor Saint Januarius, the miracle-working patron saint of Naples. Three times a year his dried blood is believed to liquefy during rites in his honor. The most spectacular painting is Ribera's *San Gennaro in the Furnace* (1647), depicting the saint emerging unscathed from the furnace; the **Museo del Tesoro di San Gennaro** houses a rich collection of treasures associated with the saint. ⊠ *Via Duomo 149, Centro Storico* ☎ *081/449097 Duomo, 081/294980* ⊕ *www.museosangennaro.it* ⤴ *Baptistery €1.50; Museo del Tesoro €6; guided visit €8.*

Gesù Nuovo. A stunning architectural contrast to the plain Romanesque frontage of other nearby churches, the oddly faceted stone facade of this elaborate Baroque church dates to the late 16th century. Originally a palace, the building was seized by Pedro of Toledo in 1547 and donated to the Jesuits on the condition the facade remain intact. Recent research has revealed that the symbols on the stones out front are Aramaic musical notes that produce a 45-minute concerto. Behind the entrance is Francesco Solimena's action-packed *Heliodorus' Eviction from the Temple*. The bulk of the interior decoration took more than 40 years and was completed only in the 18th century. You can find the work of familiar Baroque sculptors (Naccherino, Finelli) and painters inside.

The gracious *Visitation* above the altar in the second chapel on the right is by Massimo Stanzione, who also contributed the fine frescoes in the main nave: they're in the presbytery (behind and around the main altar).

Don't miss the votive chapel dedicated to the surgeon and university teacher Saint Giuseppe Moscato, along with a re-creation of his studio. Here hundreds of tiny silver images have been hung on the walls to give thanks to the saint, who was canonized in 1987, for his assistance in medical matters. On the opposite far left corner a smaller chapel similarly gives thanks to San Ciro (Saint Cyrus), also a doctor. Farther down are impressive statues of David and Jeremiah by Fanzago. Left of the altar the wooden heads of various saints are aligned like gods in an antique theater. ⊠ *Piazza Gesù Nuovo, Centro Storico* ☎ *081/5578111.*

Madre (*Museum of Contemporary Art Donnaregina*). With 8,000 square meters (86,111 square feet) of exhibition space, a host of young and helpful attendants, and occasional late-night events, the Madre is one of the most visited museums in Naples. Most of the artworks on the first floor were installed in situ by their creators, but the second-floor gallery exhibits works by international and Italian contemporary artists. The museum also hosts temporary shows by major international artists. ⊠ *Via Settembrini 79, San Lorenzo, Centro Storico* ☎ *081/19737254* ⊕ *www.madrenapoli.it/en* 🎫 *€8 (free Mon.)* ⊘ *Closed Tues.*

Fodor's Choice ★ **Museo Cappella Sansevero** (*Sansevero Chapel Museum*). The dazzling funerary chapel of the Sangro di Sansevero princes combines noble swagger, overwhelming color, and a touch of the macabre—which expresses Naples perfectly. The chapel was begun in 1590 by Prince Giovan Francesco di Sangro to fulfill a vow to the Virgin if he were cured of a dire illness. The seventh Sangro di Sansevero prince, Raimondo, had the building modified in the mid-18th century and is generally credited for its current Baroque styling, the noteworthy elements of which include the splendid marble-inlay floor. A larger-than-life figure, Prince Raimondo was believed to have signed a pact with the devil allowing him to plumb nature's secrets. He commissioned the young sculptor Giuseppe Sammartino to create numerous works, including the chapel's centerpiece, the remarkable *Veiled Christ,* which has a seemingly transparent marble veil some say was produced using a chemical formula provided by the prince. If you have the stomach for it, take a look in the crypt, where some of the anatomical experiments conducted by the prince are gruesomely displayed. ⊠ *Via Francesco de Sanctis 19, off Vicolo Domenico Maggiore, Centro Storico* ☎ *081/5518470* ⊕ *www.museosansevero.it* 🎫 *€7 (€5 with Artecard)* ⊘ *Closed Tues.*

FAMILY Fodor's Choice ★ **Napoli Sotterranea** (*Underground Naples*). Fascinating 90-minute tours of a portion of Naples's fabled underground city provide an initiation into the complex history of the city center. Efforts to dramatize the experience—amphoras lowered on ropes to draw water from cisterns, candles given to navigate narrow passages, objects shifted to reveal secret passages—combine with enthusiastic English-speaking guides to make this particularly exciting for older children.

A short descent delivers you to a section of a 400-km (249-mile) system of quarries and aqueducts used from Greek times until the 1845

14

cholera epidemic, including a highly claustrophobic 1-km (½-mile) walk with only a candle to light your way. At the end of the aqueduct, you come first to a Greek and then a much larger Roman cistern. Near the entrance is the War Museum, which displays uniforms, armed transportation vehicles, and weapons from World War II. Returning aboveground your guide leads you to a small house built above an amphitheater where Nero famously performed three times. During one of his performances an earthquake struck and—so Suetonius relates—the emperor forbade the 6,000 spectators to leave. The rumbling, he insisted, was only the gods applauding his performance. A room at the end of the tour contains examples of that most Neapolitan of art forms, *il presepe* (the crib). Be prepared on the underground tour to go up and down many steps and crouch in very narrow corridors. Temperatures in summer will be much lower below than at street level, so bring a sweater. ⊠ *Piazza San Gaetano 68, along Via dei Tribunali, Centro Storico* ☎ *081/296944* ⊕ *www.napolisotterranea.org* ✆ *€10.*

Fodor's Choice
★

Pio Monte della Misericordia. One of the Centro Storico's defining sites, this octagonal church was built around the corner from the Duomo for a charitable institution seven noblemen founded in 1601. The institution's aim was to carry out acts of Christian charity like feeding the hungry, clothing the poor, nursing the sick, sheltering pilgrims, visiting prisoners, and burying the indigent dead—acts immortalized in the history of art by Caravaggio's famous altarpiece depicting the *Sette Opere della Misericordia* (*Seven Acts of Mercy*). In this haunting work, the artist has brought the Virgin, borne atop the shoulders of two angels, down into the streets of Spaccanapoli, populated by figures in whose spontaneous and passionate movements the people could see themselves. The original church was considered too small and was destroyed in 1658 to make way for a new church that was designed by Antonio Picchiatti and built between 1658 and 1672. Pride of place is given to the great Caravaggio above the altar, but there are other important Baroque paintings on view here. Some hang in the church—among them seven other works of mercy depicted individually by Caravaggio acolytes—while other works, including a wonderful self-portrait by Luca Giordano, are in the adjoining *pinacoteca* (picture gallery). ■TIP➔ **Step into the choral chamber for a bird's-eye view of the Sette Opere della Misericordia.** ⊠ *Via Tribunali 253, Centro Storico* ☎ *081/446973* ⊕ *www.piomontedellamisericordia.it* ✆ *€7, includes audio guide.*

Fodor's Choice
★

San Lorenzo Maggiore. One of the city's unmissable sights has a travel-through-time descent to Roman and Greek times, as well as the grandest medieval church of the Decumano Maggiore. The **Archaeological Area** explores the original streets below the bustling Centro Storico, first with the Roman law courts and then down a level to the streets, markets, and workshops on the *cardo* (north–south road) crossing the *decumani* (east–Wwst road) of the 1st century BC Neapolis.

The church of San Lorenzo features a very unmedieval facade of 18th-century splendor. Due to the effects and threats of earthquakes, the church was reinforced and reshaped along Baroque lines in the 17th and 18th centuries. Begun by Robert d'Anjou in 1270 on the site of a previous 6th-century church, the church has a single, barnlike nave that reflects the Franciscans' desire for simple spaces with enough room to preach to large crowds. A grandiose triumphal arch announces the transept, and the main altar (1530) is the sculptor Giovanni da Nola's masterpiece; this is a copy of the original, now disappeared, pedestal. Also found here is the church's most important monument: the tomb of Catherine of Austria (circa 1323), by Tino da Camaino, among the first sculptors to introduce the Gothic style into Italy.

The apse, designed by an unknown French architect of great caliber, is pure French Angevin in style, complete with an ambulatory of nine chapels covered by a magnificent web of cross arches. The left transept contains the 14th-century funerary monument of Carlo di Durazzo and yet another Cosimo Fanzago masterpiece, the **Cappellone di Sant'Antonio.**

Tickets to the scavi also gives access to the **Museo dell'Opera di San Lorenzo,** installed in the 16th-century palazzo around the *torre campanaria* (bell tower). In Room 1 ancient remains from the Greek agora beneath combine with modern maps to provide a fascinating impression of import and export trends in the 4th century BC. The museum also contains ceramics dug up from the Svevian period, many pieces from the early Middle Ages, large tracts of mosaics from the 6th-century basilica, and helpful models of how the ancient Roman forum and nearby buildings must have looked. An app is available to do further justice to a place that exists in several historical dimensions. ⊠ *Via dei Tribunali 316, Centro Storico* ☎ *081/2110860* ⊕ *www.sanlorenzomaggiore.na.it, www.laneapolissotterrata.it* ⊠ *Excavations and museum €9* Ⓜ *Cavour, Dante.*

Santa Chiara. Offering a stark and telling contrast to the opulence of the nearby Gesù Nuovo, Santa Chiara is the leading Angevin Gothic monument in Naples. The fashionable house of worship for the 14th-century nobility and a favorite Angevin church from the start, the church of St. Clare was intended to be a great dynastic monument by Robert d'Anjou. His second wife, Sancia di Majorca, added the adjoining convent for the Poor Clares to a monastery of the Franciscan Minors; this was the first time the two sexes were combined in a single complex. Built in a Provençal Gothic style between 1310 and 1328 (probably by Gagliardo Primario) and dedicated in 1340, the church had its aspect radically altered in the Baroque period. A six-day fire started by Allied bombs on August 4, 1943, put an end to all that. Around the left side of the church is the **Chiostro delle Clarisse,** the most famous cloister in Naples. ⊠ *Piazza Gesù Nuovo, Centro Storico* ☎ *081/5516673* ⊕ *www.monasterodisantachiara.eu* ⊠ *Museum and cloister €6* Ⓜ *Dante, Università.*

MUSEO ARCHEOLOGICO NAZIONALE

It's only fitting that the Museo Archeologico Nazionale—the single most important and remarkable museum of Greco-Roman antiquities in the world (in spite of itself, some observers say)—sits in the upper *decumanus,* or neighborhood, of ancient Neapolis, the district colonized by the ancient Greeks and Romans. Happily, it's almost always open (its core collection, that is). But if two hours is your limit for gazing at ancient art, nearby you can discover some of the lesser-known delights of medieval and Renaissance Naples, along with the city's lush botanical gardens. Along the way are churches that are repositories for magnificent 15th- and 16th-century art and sculpture.

Fodor's Choice ★ **Museo Archeologico Nazionale** (*National Museum of Archaeology*). Also known as MANN, this legendary museum has experienced something of a rebirth in recent years. Its unrivaled collections include world-renowned archaeological finds that put most other museums to shame, from some of the best mosaics and paintings from Pompeii and Herculaneum to the legendary Farnese collection of ancient sculpture. The core masterpiece collection is almost always open to visitors, while seasonal exhibitions feature intriguing cultural events, collaborations, and contemporary artists. Some of the newer rooms, covering archaeological discoveries in the Greco-Roman settlements and necropolises in and around Naples, have helpful informational panels in English. A fascinating free display of the finds unearthed during digs for the Naples metro has been set up in the Museo station, close to the museum's entrance. ✉ *Piazza Museo 19, Centro Storico* ☎ *848800288, 06/39967050 from overseas and cell phones* ⊕ *www.museoarcheologiconapoli.it* 🎫 *€12* ⊘ *Closed Tues.* Ⓜ *Museo.*

TOLEDO

Naples's setting on what is possibly the most beautiful bay in the world has long been a boon for its inhabitants—the expansive harbor has always brought great mercantile wealth to the city—and, intermittently, a curse. Throughout history, a who's who of Greek, Roman, Norman, Spanish, and French despots has quarreled over this gateway to Campania. Each set of conquerors recognized that the area around the city harbor—today occupied by the Molo Beverello hydrofoil terminal and the 1928 Stazione Marittima—functioned as a veritable welcome mat to the metropolis and consequently should be a fitting showcase of regal authority. This had become imperative because of explosive population growth, which, by the mid-16th century, had made Naples the second-largest city in Europe, after Paris. With the mass migration of the rural population to the city, Naples had grown into a capricious, unplanned, disorderly, and untrammeled capital. Thus, the central aim of the ruling dynasties became the creation of a *Napoli nobilissima*—a "most noble" Naples.

Fodor's Choice ★ **Castel Nuovo.** Known to locals as Maschio Angioino, in reference to its Angevin builders, this imposing castle is now used more for marital than military purposes—a portion of it serves as a government registry office. A white four-tiered triumphal entrance arch, ordered by Alfonso of Aragon after he entered the city in 1443 to seize power from the increasingly beleaguered Angevin Giovanna II, upstages the building's looming Angevin stonework. Across the courtyard within the castle is the Sala Grande, also known as the Sala dei Baroni, which has a stunning vaulted ceiling 92 feet high. You can also visit the Sala dell'Armeria, where a glass floor reveals recent excavations of Roman baths from the Augustan period. The Cappella Palatina features Niccolò di Tommaso's painting of Robert Anjou, one of the first realistic portraits ever. The castle's first floor holds a small gallery that includes a beautiful early Renaissance *Adoration of the Magi* by Marco Cardisco. ✉ *Piazza Municipio, Toledo* ☎ *081/7957722* 🎫 *€6* ⊘ *Closed some Sun.; check in advance.*

14

Galleria Umberto I. The galleria was erected during the "cleanup" of Naples following the devastating cholera epidemic of 1884, part of a massive urban-renewal plan that entailed the destruction of slum areas between the Centro Storico and the Palazzo Reale. With facades on Via Toledo—the most animated street in Naples at the time—the structure, built between 1887 and 1890 according to a design by Emanuele Rocco, had a prestigious and important location. As with its larger predecessor, the Galleria Vittorio Emanuele II in Milan, the Galleria Umberto Primo exalts the taste of the postunification commercial elite in a virtuoso display of late-19th-century technology clothed in traditional style. Here are the iron-ribbed glass barrel vault and 188-feet-high dome by Paolo Boubée, which represented the latest advance in modern form yet was layered over with the reassuring architectural ornament of the 14th century (another era when the bourgeoisie triumphed in Italy). ✉ *Entrances on Via San Carlo, Via Toledo, Via Santa Brigida, and Via Verdi, Toledo* Ⓜ *Toledo.*

Gallerie d'Italia Palazzo Zevallos Stigliano. Tucked inside this beautifully restored 17th-century palazzo, once a bank, is a small museum that's worth seeking out for its outstanding collection of 17th- and 18th-century paintings. Enter through Cosimo Fanzago's gargoyled doorway and take the handsome elevator to the upper floor. The first room to the left holds the star attraction, Caravaggio's last work, *The Martyrdom of Saint Ursula*. The saint here is, for dramatic effect, deprived of her usual retinue of a thousand followers. On the left, a face of pure spite, is the king of the Huns, who has just shot Ursula with an arrow after his proposal of marriage has been rejected. ✉ *Via Toledo 185, Toledo* ☎ *800/454229* ⊕ *www.gallerieditalia.com* ᴇ*€5* Ⓜ *Toledo.*

Palazzo Reale. A leading Naples showpiece created to express Bourbon power and values, the Palazzo Reale dates to 1600. Renovated and redecorated by successive rulers, once lorded over by a dim-witted king who liked to fire his hunting rifles at the birds in his tapestries, it is filled with salons designed in the most lavish 18th-century Neapolitan style. The Spanish viceroys originally commissioned the palace, ordering the Swiss architect Domenico Fontana to build a new residence for King Philip III, should he chance to visit Naples. He died in 1621 before ever doing so. The palace saw its greatest moment of splendor in the 18th century, when Charles III of Bourbon became the first permanent resident; the flamboyant Naples-born architect Luigi Vanvitelli redesigned the facade, and Ferdinando Fuga, under Ferdinand IV, created the **Royal Apartments**, sumptuously furnished and full of precious paintings, tapestries, porcelains, and other objets d'art. To access these 30 rooms, climb the monumental Scalone d'Onore (Staircase). Note that the Palazzo is currently undergoing restoration work, and many rooms and gardens may be inaccessible. Check the website for more information. ✉ *Piazza Plebiscito, Toledo* ☎ *081/400547, 848/082408 schools and guided tours* ⊕ *www.palazzorealenapoli.it* ᴇ*€4, includes audio guide* ⊘ *Closed Wed.*

Gran Caffè Gambrinus. The most famous coffeehouse in town, founded in 1850, sits across from the Palazzo Reale. Although its glory days as an intellectual salon are well in the past, the rooms inside, with mirrored walls and gilded ceilings, make this an essential stop. **Known for: sfogliatelle and rum babà ; terrace overlooking Fontana del Carciofo (Fountain of the Artichoke); dapper baristi ready with a quip.** ✉ *Via Chiaia 1–2, near Piazza Plebiscito, Toledo* ☎ *081/417582* ⊕ *www.grancaffegambrinus.com* Ⓜ *Toledo, Piazza Municipio.*

Piazza Plebiscito (*People's Square*). After spending time as a parking lot, this square was restored in 1994 to one of Napoli Nobilissima's most majestic spaces, with a Doric semicircle of columns resembling Saint Peter's Square in Rome. The piazza was erected in the early 1800s under the Napoleonic regime, but after the regime fell, Ferdinand, the new King of the Two Sicilies, ordered the addition of the Church of San Francesco di Paola. On the left as you approach the church is a statue of Ferdinand and on the right one of his father, Charles III, both of them clad in Roman togas. Around dusk, floodlights come on, creating a magical effect. A delightful sea breeze airs the square, and on Sunday one corner becomes an improvised soccer stadium where local youths emulate their heroes. ✉ *Piazza Plebiscito, Toledo* Ⓜ *Toledo, Piazza Municipio.*

Fodor'sChoice
★
Sant'Anna dei Lombardi (Chiesa di Monteoliveto). Long favored by the Aragonese kings, this church, simple and rather anonymous from the outside, houses some of the most important ensembles of Renaissance sculpture in southern Italy. Begun with the adjacent convent of the Olivetani and its four cloisters in 1411, it was given a Baroque makeover in the mid-17th century by Gennaro Sacco. This, however, is no longer so visible because the bombs of 1943 led to a restoration favoring the original *quattrocento* (15th-century) lines. The wonderful coffered wooden ceiling adds a bit of pomp. Inside the porch is the tomb of Domenico Fontana, one of the major architects of the late 16th century, who died in Naples after beginning the Palazzo Reale.

On either side of the original entrance door are two fine Renaissance tombs. The one on the left as you face the door belongs to the Ligorio family (whose descendant Pirro designed the Villa d'Este in Tivoli) and is a work by Giovanni da Nola (1524). The tomb on the right is a masterpiece by Giuseppe Santacroce (1532) done for the del Pozzo family. To the left of the Ligorio Altar (the corner chapel on the immediate right as you face the altar) is the Mastrogiudice Chapel, whose altar contains precious reliefs of the Annunciation and *Scenes from the Life of Jesus* (1489) by Benedetto da Maiano, a great name in Tuscan sculpture. On the other side of the entrance is the Piccolomini Chapel, with a *Crucifixion* by Giulio Mazzoni (circa 1550), a refined marble altar (circa 1475), a funerary monument to Maria d'Aragona by another prominent Florentine sculptor, Antonello Rossellino (circa 1475), and on the right, a rather sweet fresco of the Annunciation by an anonymous follower of Piero della Francesca.

14

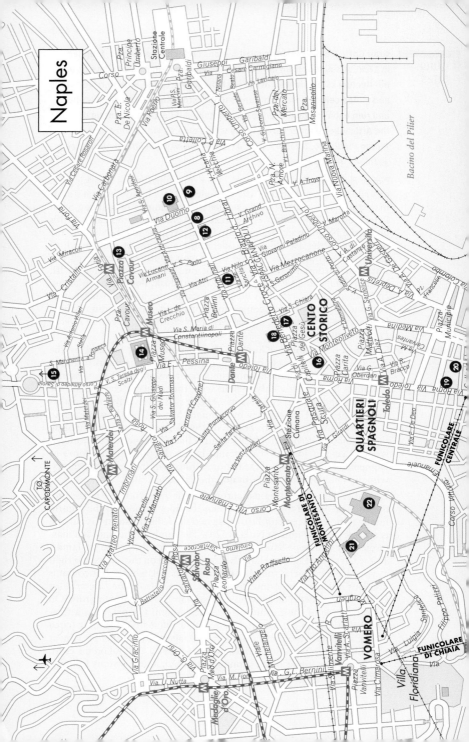

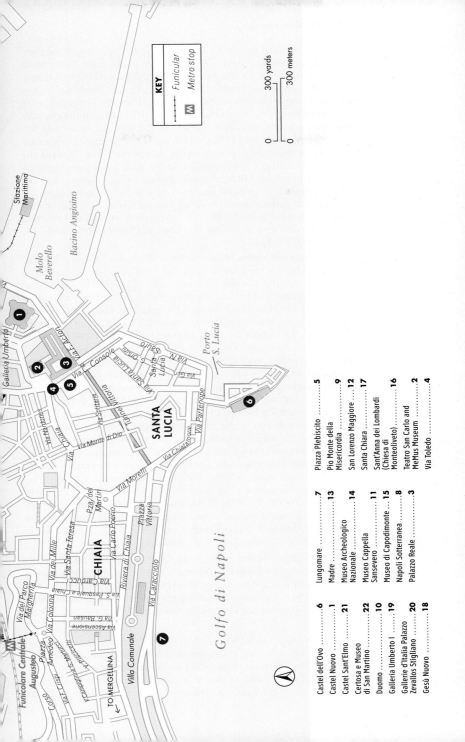

KEY

--- Funicular

Ⓜ Metro stop

0   300 yards

0   300 meters

The true surprises of the church are to the right of the altar, in the presbytery and adjoining rooms. The chapel just to the right of the main altar, belonging to the Orefice family, is richly decorated in pre-Baroque (1596–98) polychrome marbles and frescoes by Luis Rodriguez; from here you continue on through the Oratory of the Holy Sepulchre, with the tomb of Antonio D'Alessandro and his wife, to reach the church's showpiece: a potently realistic life-size group of eight terra-cotta figures by Guido Mazzoni (1492), which make up a Pietà; the faces are said to be modeled from people at the Aragonese court. Toward the rear of the church is Cappella dell'Assunta, with a fun painting in its corner of a monk by Michelangelo's student Giorgio Vasari, and the lovely Sacrestia Vecchia (Old Sacristy), adorned with one of the most successful decorative ensembles Vasari ever painted (1544) and breathtaking wood-inlay stalls by Fra' Giovanni da Verona and assistants (1506–10) with views of famous buildings. ⊠ *Piazza Monteoliveto 15, Toledo* ☎ *081/5513333.*

Teatro San Carlo and MeMus Museum. Out of all the Italian opera houses, La Scala in Milan is the most famous, but San Carlo is more beautiful, and Naples is, after all, the most operatic of cities. The Neoclassical structure, designed by Antonio Niccolini, was built in a mere nine months after an 1816 fire destroyed the original. Many operas were composed for the house, including Donizetti's *Lucia di Lammermoor* and Rossini's *La Donna del Lago.* In the theater, nearly 200 boxes are arranged on six levels, and the 1,115-square-meter (12,000-square-foot) stage permits productions with horses, camels, and elephants, and even has a backdrop that can lift to reveal the Palazzo Reale Gardens. Above the rich red-and-gold auditorium is a ceiling fresco by Giuseppe Cammarano representing Apollo presenting poets to Athena. Performance standards are among Europe's highest—even the great Enrico Caruso was hissed here. If you're not attending an opera, you can still see the splendid theater on a 30-minute guided tour and visit MeMus (Museo Memoria e Musica): San Carlo's theatrically lit museum and archive has props, costumes, stage sets, and multimedia and documents galore. English-language tours, which take place daily except on holidays, can be booked in advance on the theater's website. ⊠ *Via San Carlo 101–103, Toledo* ☎ *848800288 MeMus, 081/7972331 ticket office, 081/7972412 tours* ⊕ *www.teatrosancarlo.it; memus.squarespace.com* 🎫 *Tour €6; MeMus €7; combined ticket €10; €5 for Palazzo Reale ticket holders* ☉ *MeMus closed Wed. and Aug.*

Via Toledo. Sooner or later you'll wind up at one of the busiest commercial arteries, also known as Via Roma, which is thankfully closed to through traffic—at least along the stretch leading from the Palazzo Reale. Don't avoid dipping into this parade of shops and coffee bars where plump pastries are temptingly arranged. ⊠ *Via Toledo, Toledo* Ⓜ *Toledo.*

CHIAIA, SANTA LUCIA, AND NEARBY

The Lungomare is the city's grandest stretch of waterfront. In the 19th century, Naples's waterfront harbored the picturesque quarter that was called Santa Lucia, a district dear to artists and musicians and known for its fishermen's cottages. The fishermen were swept away when an enormous landfill project extended the land out to what is now Via Nazario Sauro and Via Partenope, the address for some of Naples's finest hotels. Huge stretches of the waterfront are blessedly traffic-free, only enhancing their distinctly Neapolitan charm. The area also boasts the chic Chiaia neighborhood surrounding Piazza dei Martiri and the gilded 19th-century Villa Pignatelli.

Castel dell'Ovo (*Castle of the Egg*). The oldest castle in Naples, the 12th-century Castel dell'Ovo dangles over the Porto Santa Lucia on a thin promontory. Built atop the ruins of an ancient Roman villa, the castle these days shares its views with some of the city's top hotels. Its gigantic rooms, rock tunnels, and belvederes over the bay are among Naples's most striking sights. The castle's name comes from the poet Virgil, who is supposed have hidden inside the ancient villa an egg that had protective powers as long as it remained intact. The belief was taken so seriously that to quell the people's panic after Naples suffered an earthquake, an invasion, and a plague in quick succession, its monarch felt compelled to produce an intact egg, solemnly declaring it to be the Virgilian original. ⊠ *Santa Lucia waterfront, Via Eldorado 3, off Via Partenope, Santa Lucia* ☎ *081/7954592* ⌨ *Free.*

Fodor's Choice **Lungomare** (*Seafront*). The first thing mayor Luigi de Magistris did after
★ his 2011 election was to banish traffic from the city's seafront. Strolling, skating, or biking along Via Caracciolo and Via Partenope with Capri, Mt. Vesuvius, and the Castel dell'Ovo in your sights is a favorite Neapolitan pastime. ⊠ *Via Caracciolo, Chiaia* Ⓜ *Mergellina.*

CAPODIMONTE AND VOMERO

The Parco di Capodimonte is the crowning point of the vast mountainous plain that slopes down through the city to the waterfront area. Nearly 5 km (3 miles) removed from the crowds in the Centro Storico, it is enjoyed by locals and visitors alike as a favored escape from the overheated city center. With views over the entire city and bay, the park was first founded in the 18th century as a hunting preserve by Charles of Bourbon. Before long, partly to house the famous Farnese collection that he had inherited from his mother, he commissioned a spectacular Palazzo Reale for the park. Today this palace is the Museo di Capodimonte, which contains among its treasures the city's greatest collection of old master paintings.

To the west is the largely residential Vomero. From the balcony belvedere of the Museo di San Martino, a rich spread of southern Italian amplitude fills the eye: hillsides dripping with luxuriant greenery interspersed with villainously ugly apartment houses, streets short and narrow—leading to an unspeakable as well as unsolvable traffic problem—countless church spires and domes, and far below, the reason it all works, the intensely blue Bay of Naples. To tie together the lower parts with Vomero, everyone uses the *funicolare*—the funicular system that runs on four separate routes up and down the hill.

Castel Sant'Elmo. Perched on the Vomero, this massive castle is almost the size of a small town. Built by the Angevins in the 14th century to dominate the port and the old city, it was remodeled by the Spanish in 1537. The parapets, configured in the form of a six-pointed star, provide fabulous views. The whole bay lies on one side; on another, the city spreads out like a map, its every dome and turret clearly visible; to the east is slumbering Vesuvius. Once a major military outpost, the castle these days hosts occasional cultural events. Its prison, the Carcere alto di Castel Sant'Elmo, is the site of the **Museo del Novecento Napoli,** which traces Naples's 20th-century artistic output, from the Futurist period through the 1980s. ⊠ *Largo San Martino, Vomero* ☎ *848/800288, 081/5587708* ⊕ *www.polomusealecampania.beniculturali.it/index.php/il-castello* 🎫 *€5.*

Fodor's Choice **Certosa e Museo di San Martino.** Atop a rocky promontory with a fabu-
★ lous view of the entire city and majestic salons that would please any monarch, the Certosa di San Martino is a monastery that seems more like a palace. This *certosa,* or charter house, started in 1325, was so sumptuous that by the 18th century Ferdinand IV was threatening to halt the religious order's government subsidy. Although the Angevin heritage can be seen in the pointed arches and cross-vaulted ceiling of the **Certosa Church,** over the years dour Gothic was traded in for varicolored Neapolitan Baroque. Highlights include the **Cappella del Tesoro,** with Luca Giordano's ceiling fresco of Judith holding aloft Holofernes's head and Jusepe de Ribera's masterful *Pietà*; architect and sculptor Cosimo Fanzago's polychrome marble work in the **Chiostro Grande** (Great Cloister); the **Quarto del Priore** (Prior's Quarters), an extravaganza of salons filled with frescoes, majolica-tile floors, and paintings; and the Sezione Presepiale, the world's greatest collection of Christmas cribs. ⊠ *Piazzale San Martino 5, Vomero* ☎ *081/2294589,* ⊕ *www.polomusealecampania.beniculturali.it/index.php/certosa-e-museo* 🎫 *€6* Ⓜ *Vanvitelli.*

Fodor's Choice **Museo di Capodimonte.** The grandiose 18th-century Neoclassical Bour-
★ bon royal palace houses fine and decorative art. Capodimonte's greatest treasure is the excellent collection of paintings displayed in the **Galleria Nazionale,** on the palace's first and second floors. Aside from the artwork, part of the royal apartments still has a collection of beautiful antique furniture (most of it on the splashy scale so dear to the Bourbons) and a staggering range of porcelain and majolica from the various royal residences. Most rooms have fairly comprehensive information cards in English, whereas the audio guide is overly selective and somewhat quirky. The main galleries on the first floor are devoted to work from the 13th to the 18th century, including many pieces by Dutch and Spanish masters. On the second floor look for stunning paintings by Simone Martini (circa 1284–1344), Titian (1488/90–1576), and Caravaggio (1573–1610): for a contrast, don't miss the contemporary art collection including Warhol's iconic version of Vesuvius. The palace is in the vast Bosco di Capodimonte (Capodimonte Park), which served as the royal hunting preserve and later as the site of the Capodimonte porcelain works. ⊠ *Via Miano 2, Capodimonte* ☎ *081/7499111, 081/7499109* ⊕ *www.museocapodimonte.beniculturali.it* 🎫 *€12* ☉ *Closed Wed.*

WHERE TO EAT

CENTRO STORICO

$ ✕**Di Matteo.** Every pizzeria along Via dei Tribunali is worth the long
PIZZA wait—and trust us, all the good ones will be jam-packed—but just
Fodor'sChoice one can claim to have served a U.S. President: Bill Clinton enjoyed a
★ margherita here when the G8 was held in Naples in 1994. **Known for:**
functional decor and pizzaioli working at front; funny pics of Clinton
and the "Pizzaiolo del Presidente" Ernesto Cacialli in 1994; top value,
including filling pizza fritta (fried). $ *Average main: €6 ⊠ Via Tribunali
94, Centro Storico* ☎ *081/455262* ⊕ *www.pizzeriadimatteo.com.*

$ ✕**Gino Sorbillo.** There are three restaurants called Sorbillo along Via
PIZZA dei Tribunali; this is the one with the crowds waiting outside. Order
the same thing the locals come for: a basic Neapolitan pizza (try the
unique pizza al pesto or the stunningly simple marinara—just tomatoes
and oregano). **Known for:** long lines outside; leave your name at the
door and listen to be called; head honcho Gino is a celebrity and pizza
ambassador. $ *Average main: €8 ⊠ Via dei Tribunali 32, Centro Storico*
☎ *081/446643* ⊕ *www.sorbillo.it* ♥ *Closed Sun.*

$ ✕**Palazzo Petrucci Pizzeria.** In a 17th-century mansion facing the grand
NEAPOLITAN Piazza San Domenico Maggiore, Palazzo Petrucci doesn't lack for
dramatic settings for dining—under the vaulted ceiling of the former
stables, near the pizzaiolo and oven action, outside in the piazza, or on
the roof terrace at *giuglia* (obelisk) di San Domenico level. Expect classic *pizze*, *pizze fritte*, and some unusual topping combinations, alongside heaped salads and antipasti. **Known for:** grandest palazzo venue
for a pizza feast; atmospheric views and sounds over the piazza; craft
beer, pizze fritte, and vegan options. $ *Average main: €10 ⊠ Piazza
San Domenico Maggiore 5-7, Centro Storico* ☎ *081/5512460* ⊕ *www.
palazzopetruccipizzeria.it* ♥ *Closed 2 wks in Aug.*

PIAZZA GARIBALDI

$ ✕**Da Michele.** You may recognize Da Michele from the movie *Eat Pray
PIZZA Love,* but for more than 140 years before Julia Roberts arrived this place
was a culinary reference point. Despite offering only two types of pizza—
marinara (with tomato, garlic, and oregano) and margherita (with tomato,
mozzarella, and basil)—plus a small selection of drinks, it still manages
to draw long lines. **Known for:** pizza purists' favorite; marinara and margherita only; long lines outside the humble, historic HQ. $ *Average main:
€6 ⊠ Via Sersale 1/3, off Corso Umberto, between Piazza Garibaldi and
Piazza Nicola Amore, Piazza Garibaldi* ☎ *081/5539204* ⊕ *www.dami-
chele.net* ♥ *Closed Sun., and 2 wks in Aug.* Ⓜ *Garibaldi/Duomo.*

$ ✕**Mimì alla Ferrovia.** Patrons of this Neapolitan institution have included
NEAPOLITAN the filmmaker Federico Fellini and that truly Neapolitan comic genius and
aristocrat, Totò. It's in a fairly seedy area so take a taxi, especially at night,
but it's worth it to sample Mimì's classics such as pasta e fagioli and the sea
bass *al presidente,* baked in a pastry crust and enjoyed by visiting Italian
presidents. **Known for:** crammed with washed-out photos of Italian VIPs;
classic Neapolitan dishes; fresh fish on display from the market. $ *Average
main: €14 ⊠ Via A. D'Aragona 19/21, Piazza Garibaldi* ☎ *081/5538525*
⊕ *www.mimiallaferrovia.com* ♥ *Closed Sun., and last wk in Aug.*

14

TOLEDO

$$
NEAPOLITAN
Fodor's Choice ★

🍴 **Trattoria San Ferdinando.** This cheerful trattoria seems to be run for the sheer pleasure of it, and chatting locals give it a buzzy Neapolitan atmosphere. Try the excellent fish or the traditional (but cooked with a lighter modern touch) pasta dishes, especially those with *verdure* (fresh leafy vegetables) or with *pasta e patate con la provola* (potatoes and smoked mozzarella). **Known for:** excellent, fresh seafood specialties; popular with locals in the evening, so reserve ahead; near Teatro San Carlo. [$] *Average main: €16* ✉ *Via Nardones 117, Toledo* ☎ *081/421964* 🌐 *www.trattoriasanferdinando.com* 🕒 *Closed Sun., and last 3 wks of Aug. No dinner Sat. and Mon.*

CHIAIA, SANTA LUCIA, AND NEARBY

$$
SOUTHERN ITALIAN

🍴 **Amici Miei.** Favored by meat eaters who can't abide another bite of sea bass, this small, dark, and cozy dining den is known for dishes such as tender carpaccio with fresh artichoke hearts. There are also excellent pasta selections, including orecchiette with chickpeas or *alla barese* (with chewy green turnips), and the extravagant *carnevale lasagne,* an especially rich concoction that sustains revelers in the buildup before Lent. **Known for:** a choice of quality meat dishes; Art Nouveau decorative flourishes; superb, friendly service befitting the name. [$] *Average main: €17* ✉ *Via Monte di Dio 78, Chiaia* ☎ *081/7646063* 🌐 *www.ristoranteamicimiei.com* 🕒 *Closed Mon., and late July–early Sept. No dinner Sun.*

$$$
NEAPOLITAN
Fodor's Choice ★

🍴 **Da Dora.** Despite its location up an unpromising-looking *vicolo* (alley) off the Riviera di Chiaia, this small restaurant has achieved cult status for its seafood platters. It's remarkable what owner-chef Giovanni can produce in his tiny kitchen: start with linguine *alla Dora,* laden with local seafood and fresh tomatoes, and perhaps follow up with grilled *pezzogna* (blue-spotted bream). **Known for:** freshest seafood, both raw and cooked; simple, attractive nautical-themed decor; great service. [$] *Average main: €25* ✉ *Via Fernando Palasciano 30, Chiaia* ☎ *081/680519* 🌐 *www.ristorantedora.it* 🕒 *No dinner Sun., no lunch Mon.* [M] *Amedeo.*

$
NEAPOLITAN

🍴 **Gran Caffè Cimmino.** Connoisseurs often say the most refined pastries in town can be found at Gran Caffè Cimmino. Many of the city's lawyers congregate here, to celebrate or commiserate with crisp, light cannoli; airy lemon eclairs; *choux* paste in the form of a mushroom laced with chocolate whipped cream; and delightful wild-strawberry tartlets. **Known for:** Neapolitan breakfast favorite; babà to die for; terrace for watching Chiaia's finest. [$] *Average main: €2* ✉ *Via G. Filangieri 12/13, Chiaia* ☎ *081/418303.*

$
SOUTHERN ITALIAN
Fodor's Choice ★

🍴 **Pescheria Mattiucci.** In the evening, this fourth-generation fish shop becomes a trendy spot to enjoy an aperitif and a light meal. If you want to experience superb Neapolitan sushi and cold wine while sitting on a buoy stool, get here early: service is 7:30–10:30, and a full fish lunch is served Tuesday–Sunday. **Known for:** pescheria counter displaying today's catch; intimate and small place, so get here early or call ahead for dinner; fish lunches. [$] *Average main: €13* ✉ *Vico Belledonne a Chiaia 27, Chiaia* ☎ *081/2512215* 💳 *No credit cards* 🕒 *Closed Mon. No dinner Sun.*

$$ NEAPOLITAN Fodor's Choice ★ 🍴 **Umberto.** Run by the Di Porzio family since 1916, Umberto is one of the city's classic restaurants, combining the classiness of its neighborhood, Chiaia, and the friendliness one finds in other parts of Naples. Try the *tubettoni 'do tre dita* ("three-finger" pasta with octopus, tomato, olives, and capers); it bears the nickname of the original Umberto, who happened to be short a few digits. **Known for:** authentic Pizza DOC (smaller, with chunky cornicione rim); charming host Massimo organizes cultural events here; classic Neapolitan meat sauce alla Genovese. [$] *Average main: €17* ✉ *Via Alabardieri 30–31, Chiaia* ☎ *081/418555* 🌐 *www.umberto.it* 🕒 *No lunch Mon.*

MERGELLINA AND POSILLIPO

$$$ NEAPOLITAN Fodor's Choice ★ 🍴 **Trattoria da Cicciotto.** Chic and charming Da Cicciotto corrals more than a few members of the city's fashionable set—if you dine here, there's a fair chance you'll find a Neapolitan count or off-duty film star enjoying this jewel with a tiny stone terrace (with seats and a canopy) that overlooks a pleasant anchorage. You can appreciate the outdoor setting at either lunch or dinner, and don't even bother with a menu—just start digging into the sublime antipasti and go with the waiter's suggestions. **Known for:** fabulous views over the harbor and bay; freshest seafood; venue for a special occasion; free shuttle from city center. [$] *Average main: €24* ✉ *Calata del Ponticello a Marechiaro 32, Posillipo* ☎ *081/5751165* 🌐 *www.trattoriadacicciotto.it.*

14

WHERE TO STAY

CENTRO STORICO

$$ HOTEL Fodor's Choice ★ 🏨 **Costantinopoli 104.** An oasis of what Italians call *stile liberty* (Art Nouveau style), with impressive stained-glass fittings and striking artwork, this serene, elegant hotel is well placed for touring the Museo Archeologico Nazionale and the Centro Storico. **Pros:** pool (a rarity in Neapolitan hotels) and garden; pleasant service; convenient Centro Storico location. **Cons:** pool is on the small side; hotel can be difficult to find (look for the sign that reads Villa Spinelli, the place's former name); some rooms suffer from nightlife disturbance from Piazza Bellini. [$] *Rooms from: €200* ✉ *Via Costantinopoli 104, Centro Storico* ☎ *081/5571035* 🌐 *www.costantinopoli104.com* 🛏 *19 rooms* 🍴 *Free Breakfast.*

$$ HOTEL Fodor's Choice ★ 🏨 **Hotel Palazzo Decumani.** This contemporary upscale hotel near the Centro Storico's major sights occupies an early-20th-century palazzo, but you won't find heavy, ornate furnishings—the emphasis is on light and space, both in short supply in old Naples. **Pros:** guests-only lounge-bar; large rooms and bathrooms; service on par with fancier hotels. **Cons:** can be hard to find—follow signs from Corso Umberto; some may find decor a tad sparse. [$] *Rooms from: €150* ✉ *Piazzetta Giustino Fortunato 8, Centro Storico* ☎ *081/4201379* 🌐 *www.palazzodecumani.com* 🛏 *28 rooms* 🍴 *Free Breakfast.*

PIAZZA GARIBALDI

$$ HOTEL **Palazzo Caracciolo Napoli MGallery by Sofitel.** Sleek, soigné, and swank, this hotel set in the majestic palace of the very majestic Caracciolos (one of the most gilded names in Neapolitan history) is definitely a diamond in the rough—the rough being its immediate neighborhood, which is a bit far from the tourist or historic quarters. **Pros:** multilingual receptionists; complimentary shuttle to Centro Storico; contemporary room decor. **Cons:** rough neighborhood; a bit far away from sights. [$] *Rooms from: €149* ✉ *Via Carbonara 111, Piazza Garibaldi* ☎ *081/0160111* 🌐 *www.sofitel.com* 🛏 *146 rooms* 🍴 *Free Breakfast.*

TOLEDO

$$ HOTEL **Palazzo Turchini.** Just a few minutes' walk from the Castel Nuovo, Palazzo Turchini is one of the city center's more attractive smaller hotels. **Pros:** good location for the port; more intimate than neighboring business hotels; rooftop terrace. **Cons:** close to a busy traffic hub; rooms a tad business-like; rooms on the small side. [$] *Rooms from: €140* ✉ *Via Medina 21, Toledo* ☎ *081/5510606* 🌐 *www.palazzoturchini.it* 🛏 *27 rooms* 🍴 *Free Breakfast.*

CHIAIA, SANTA LUCIA, AND NEARBY

$$ HOTEL **Chiaja Hotel de Charme.** No views here, but this 18th-century palazzo has a great location and its apartments, all on the first floor, have plenty of atmosphere. **Pros:** good location near Piazza del Plebiscito and the Palazzo Reale; on a bustling pedestrians-only street; some antiques in guest rooms. **Cons:** no views in a town with some great ones; even with a/c, some rooms get hot in summer. [$] *Rooms from: €130* ✉ *Via Chiaia 216, Chiaia* ☎ *081/415555* 🌐 *www.hotelchiaia.it* 🛏 *33 rooms* 🍴 *Free Breakfast.*

$$$$ HOTEL **Grand Hotel Parker's.** A little up the hill from Chiaia, with fine views of the bay and distant Capri, this landmark hotel, first opened in 1870, continues to serve up a supremely elegant dose of old-style atmosphere to visiting VIPs, ranging from rock stars to Russian leaders. **Pros:** excellent restaurant; fabulous views; historic hotel. **Cons:** a very long walk or taxi ride from city center and seafront; not quite as grand as it once was; style is not for minimalists. [$] *Rooms from: €310* ✉ *Corso Vittorio Emanuele 135, Chiaia* ☎ *081/7612474* 🌐 *www.grandhotelparkers.it* 🛏 *82 rooms* 🍴 *Free Breakfast.*

$$$ HOTEL Fodor's Choice ★ **Grand Hotel Vesuvio.** You'd never guess from the modern exterior that this is the oldest of Naples's great seafront hotels—the place where Enrico Caruso died, where Oscar Wilde dallied with lover Lord Alfred Douglas, and where Bill Clinton charmed the waitresses—fortunately, the spacious, soothing interior compensates for what's lacking on the outside. **Pros:** luxurious atmosphere; historic setting and traditionally furnished rooms; directly opposite Borgo Marinaro. **Cons:** spa and pool cost extra; reception staff can be snooty; not all rooms have great views. [$] *Rooms from: €260* ✉ *Via Partenope 45, Santa Lucia* ☎ *081/7640044* 🌐 *www.vesuvio.it* 🛏 *181 rooms* 🍴 *Free Breakfast.*

$$ ⊞ **Hotel Palazzo Alabardieri.** Just off the chic Piazza dei Martiri, this is
HOTEL the most fashionable choice among the city's smaller luxury hotels—for
Fodor's Choice some, there is simply no other hotel in Naples. **Pros:** impressive public
★ salons; central yet quiet location; polite, pleasant staff. **Cons:** no sea
view; difficult to reach by car. Ⓢ *Rooms from: €146* ⊠ *Via Alabardieri
38, Chiaia* ☎ *081/415278* ⊕ *www.palazzoalabardieri.it* ⌿ *44 rooms*
⊺◯⼁ *Free Breakfast.*

$$$ ⊞ **Hotel Santa Lucia.** Neapolitan enchantment can be yours if you stay at
HOTEL this luxurious, quietly understated hotel that overlooks the port immor-
talized in the song "Santa Lucia." Hundreds of boats bob in the water,
seafood restaurants line the harbor, and the medieval Castel dell'Ovo
presides over it all. **Pros:** great views from most rooms; proximity to
the port is convenient for trips to the islands; the bikes for hire are
perfect for the Lungomare. **Cons:** rooms can be small; traditional decor
is a bit boring; not near a metro stop. Ⓢ *Rooms from: €225* ⊠ *Via
Partenope 46, Santa Lucia* ☎ *081/7640666* ⊕ *www.santalucia.it* ⌿ *95
rooms* ⊺◯⼁ *Free Breakfast.*

$$ ⊞ **Il Transatlantico Napoli.** Enjoying perhaps the most enchanting setting
B&B/INN in all of Naples, this modestly priced hotel tops many travelers' dream
Fodor's Choice list of places to stay. **Pros:** fabulous location and views; reasonable
★ prices for maritime-style rooms; boat hire available. **Cons:** dated furni-
ture and fabrics; no elevator; breakfast not included in price. Ⓢ *Rooms
from: €130* ⊠ *Via Luculliana 15, Santa Lucia* ☎ *081/768842* ⊕ *www.
transatlanticonapoli.com* ⌿ *8 rooms* ⊺◯⼁ *No meals.*

$ ⊞ **Pinto-Storey Hotel.** The name juxtaposes a 19th-century Englishman
HOTEL who fell in love with Naples with a certain Signora Pinto; together they
went on to establish this hotel that overflows with warmth, charm, and
late-19th-century (but fully renovated) decor. **Pros:** safe neighborhood;
near public transit; traditional Anglophile atmosphere. **Cons:** not close
to major sights; only a few rooms have views; two-night minimum
in high season. Ⓢ *Rooms from: €88* ⊠ *Via G. Martucci 72, Chiaia*
☎ *081/681260* ⊕ *www.pintostorey.it* ⌿ *16 rooms* ⊺◯⼁ *No meals.*

NIGHTLIFE AND PERFORMING ARTS

NIGHTLIFE

CENTRO STORICO

Caffè Intramoenia. The granddaddy of all the boho bars in Piazza Bellini
was set up as a bookstore in the late 1980s and still has its own small
publishing house with a variety of interesting titles, historic prints, and
photos. Seats in the heated veranda are at a premium in winter, though
many customers sit outside year-round. ⊠ *Piazza Bellini 70, Centro
Storico* ☎ *081/451652* ⊕ *www.intramoenia.it.*

Kestè Art Bar. The cool chrome furnishings at Kestè contrast with the old
arched ceiling inside, but try to get a table out in the beautiful square
in front of the Orientale University. A DJ spins tunes, and there's live
jazz on the tiny stage on weekends. ⊠ *Largo S. Giovanni Maggiore 26,
Centro Storico* ☎ *081/7810034.*

Nea. A beautiful café and contemporary art gallery, Nea is a highly
atmospheric spot to just hang out on student-filled Piazza Bellini,

especially in fine weather at the tables outside or on the steps of the gorgeous music conservatory. ⊠ *Via Costantinopoli 53, Centro Storico* ☎ *081/451358* ⊕ *www.spazionea.it.*

CHIAIA, SANTA LUCIA, AND NEARBY

Fodor'sChoice **Enoteca Belledonne.** Between 8 and 9 in the evening, it seems as though
★ the whole upscale Chiaia neighborhood has descended into this tiny space for an aperitivo. The small tables and low stools are notably uncomfortable, but the cozy atmosphere and the pleasure of being surrounded by glass-front cabinets full of wine bottles with beautiful labels more than makes up for it. Excellent local wines are available by the glass at great prices. ⊠ *Vico Belledonne a Chiaia 18, Chiaia* ☎ *081/403162* ⊕ *www.enotecabelledonne.it.*

CAPODIMONTE AND VOMERO

Fonoteca. By day the city's best independent record store, by night this is *the* place to hear eclectic tunes in Vomero. ⊠ *Via Morghen 31, Vomero* ☎ *081/5560338* ⊕ *www.fonoteca.net.*

SHOPPING

Leather goods, jewelry, and cameos are some of the best items to buy in Campania. In Naples you can generally find good deals on handbags, shoes, and clothing. Most boutiques and department stores are open Monday 4:30–8 and Tuesday–Saturday 9:30–1:30 and 4:30–8. The larger chains now open on Sunday, too.

CENTRO STORICO

Ferrigno. Shops selling Nativity scenes cluster along the Via San Gregorio Armeno off Spaccanapoli, and they're all worth a glance. The most famous is Ferrigno; Maestro Giuseppe Ferrigno died in 2008, but the family business continues, still faithfully using 18th-century techniques. ⊠ *Via San Gregorio Armeno 10, Centro Storico* ☎ *081/5523148* ⊕ *www.arteferrigno.it.*

FAMILY **Ospedale delle Bambole.** This laboratory, with its (usually closed) tiny storefront operation across the street, is a world-famous "hospital" for dolls. In business since 1850, it's a wonderful place to take kids (and their injured toys). It's closed Sunday. ⊠ *Via San Biagio dei Librai 46, Centro Storico* ☎ *081/203067* ⊕ *www.ospedaledellebambole.com.*

TOLEDO

Fodor'sChoice **Ascione.** A family firm established in 1855 and known for its tradition-
★ ally made coral jewelry and artwork, Ascione has a showroom/gallery on the second floor of a wing of the Galleria Umberto. Aficionados should not miss the guided tour (€5) describing the company's rich history, with displays including Egypt's King Farouk's elaborate wedding gift to his bride Farida and what many consider the most beautiful cameo in existence. ⊠ *Piazzetta Matilde Serao 19, Piazza Municipio* ☎ *081/4211111* ⊕ *www.ascione.it.*

CHIAIA, SANTA LUCIA, AND NEARBY

Marinella. Count the British royal family among the customers of this shop that has been selling old-fashioned made-to-measure ties for more than 100 years. ⊠ *Via Riviera di Chiaia 287, Chiaia* ☎ *081/7642365* ⊕ *www.marinellanapoli.it.*

Tramontano. Since 1865, this place has been crafting fine leather luggage, bags, belts, and wallets. ⊠ *Via Chiaia 143, Chiaia* ☎ *081/414837* ⊕ *www.tramontano.it.*

HERCULANEUM, VESUVIUS, AND POMPEII

14

Volcanic ash and mud preserved the Roman towns of Herculaneum and Pompeii almost exactly as they were on the day Mt. Vesuvius erupted in AD 79, leaving them not just archaeological ruins but museums of daily life in the ancient world. The two cities and the volcano that buried them can be visited from either Naples or Sorrento, thanks to the Circumvesuviana, the suburban railroad that provides fast, frequent, and economical service.

HERCULANEUM

10 km (6 miles) southeast of Naples.

A visit to the archaeological site of Herculaneum neatly counterbalances the hustle of its larger neighbor, Pompeii. Although close to the heart of busy Ercolano—indeed, in places right under the town—the ancient site seems worlds apart.

GETTING HERE AND AROUND

To get to Herculaneum by car, take the A3 Naples–Salerno autostrada and exit at Ercolano. Follow signs for the "Scavi" (excavations). The Circumvesuviana railway connects Herculaneum to Naples, Portici, Torre del Greco, Torre Annunziata, Pompeii, and Sorrento.

EXPLORING

Fodor'sChoice ★ **Herculaneum Ruins.** Lying more than 50 feet below the present-day town of Ercolano, the ruins of Herculaneum are set among the acres of greenhouses that make this area an important European flower-growing center. In AD 79, the gigantic eruption of Vesuvius, which also destroyed Pompeii, buried the town under a tide of volcanic mud. The semiliquid mass seeped into the crevices and niches of every building, covering household objects, enveloping textiles and wood, and sealing all in a compact, airtight tomb. Excavation began in 1738 under King Charles of Bourbon, using tunnels. Digging was interrupted but recommenced in 1828, continuing into the following century. Today less than half of Herculaneum has been excavated. With contemporary Ercolano and the unlovely Resina Quarter sitting on top of the site, progress is limited. From the ramp leading down to Herculaneum's well-preserved edifices, you get a good overall view of the site, as well as an idea of the amount of volcanic debris that had to be removed to bring it to light.

About 5,000 people lived in Herculaneum when it was destroyed, many of them fishermen and craftsmen. Although Herculaneum had only one-third the population of Pompeii and has been only partially excavated, what has been found is generally better preserved. In some cases you can even see the original wooden beams, doors, and staircases. Unfortunately, the **Villa dei Papiri** (Villa of Papayri) is currently closed to the public—this excavation outside the main site was built by Julius Caesar's father-in-law (with a replica built by Paul Getty in Malibu almost 2,000 years later). The building is named for almost 2,000 carbonized papyrus scrolls dug up here in the 18th century, leading scholars to believe that this may have been a study center or library. Also worth special attention are the carbonized remains within the **Casa del Tramezzo di Legno** (House of the Wooden Partition).

Be sure to stock up on refreshments beforehand; there is no food at the archaeological site. At the entrance, pick up a free map showing the gridlike layout of the dig, which is divided into numbered blocks, or insulae. Splurge on an audio guide (€8 for one, €13 for two), or join a group with a local guide (€12 per person). Most of the houses are open, and a representative cross section of domestic, commercial, and civic buildings can be seen. ✉ *Corso Resina 6, Ercolano* ☎ *081/7324315* ⊕ *www.pompeiisites.org* 🎫 *€11.*

FAMILY **Museo Archeologico Virtuale (MAV).** With dazzling "virtual" versions of Herculaneum's streets and squares and a multi-D simulation of Vesuvius erupting, Herculaneum's 1st-century-meets-the-21st-century museum is a must for kids and adults alike. After stopping at the ticket office you descend, as in an excavation, to a floor below. You'll experience Herculaneum's Villa dei Papiri before and (even more dramatically) during the eruption, courtesy of special effects; enter "the burning cloud" of AD 79; then emerge, virtually speaking, inside Pompeii's House of the Faun, which can be seen both as it is and as it was for two centuries BC. The next re-creation is again Villa dei Papirii. Then comes a stellar pre- and post-flooding view of Baia's Nymphaeum, the now-displaced statues arrayed as they were in the days of Emperor Claudius, who commissioned them.

Visitors here are invited to take a front-row seat for "Day and Night in the Forum of Pompeii," with soldiers, litter-bearing slaves, and toga-clad figures moving spectrally to complete the spell; or to make a vicarious visit to the Lupanari brothels, their various pleasures illustrated in graphic virtual frescoes along the walls. A wooden model of Herculaneum's theater, its virtual re-creation, reminds us that it was here that a local farmer, while digging a well, first came across what proved to be not merely a single building, but a whole town. Equally fascinating are the virtual baths. For an extra €4, you can see the Sensurround film of Vesuvius erupting. The words of Pliny the Elder provide a timeless commentary while the floor vibrates under your feet. ✉ *Via IV Novembre 44, Ercolano* ☎ *081/7776843, 081/7776784* ⊕ *www.museomav.it* 🎫 *€11.50; €7.50 museum only, €5 eruption simulation only* ⊗ *Closed Mon. Oct.–Feb.*

POMPEII

22 km (14 miles) southeast of Naples, 17 km (10.5 miles) southeast of Herculaneum.

Mention Pompeii and most travelers think of ancient Roman villas, prancing bronze fauns, writhing plaster casts of Vesuvius's victims, and the fabled days of the emperors.

GETTING HERE AND AROUND

To get to Pompeii by car, take the A3 Napoli–Salerno highway to the Pompei exit and follow signs for the nearby "Scavi." There are numerous guarded car parks near the Porta Marina, Piazza Essedra, and Anfiteatro entrances, where you can leave your vehicle for a fee.

Pompeii has two central Circumvesuviana railway stations served by two separate train lines. The Naples–Sorrento train stops at "Pompei Scavi–Villa dei Misteri," 100 yards from the Porta Marina ticket office of the archaeological site, while the Naples–Poggiomarino train stops at Pompei Santuario, more convenient for the Santuario della Madonna del Rosario and the hotels and restaurants in the modern town center. A third Ferrovie della Statale (FS) train station south of the town center is only convenient if arriving from Salerno or Rome.

EXPLORING

Fodor'sChoice **Pompeii.** *See the highlighted feature in this chapter for more information.*
★   ☎ *081/8575347* ⊕ *www.pompeiisites.org €15, tickets are valid for 1 full day; €18 biglietto cumulativo, includes 3 sites (Pompeii, Boscoreale and Oplontis) and valid for 3 days.*

VESUVIUS

8 km (5 miles) northeast of Herculaneum, 16 km (10 miles) east of Naples.

Vesuvius may have lost its plume of smoke, but it has lost none of its fascination—especially for those who live in the towns around the cone.

GETTING HERE AND AROUND

To arrive by car, take the A3 Napoli–Salerno autostrada to the Torre del Greco exit and follow Via E. De Nicola from the tollbooth and follow signs for the Parco Nazionale del Vesuvio.

Vesuvio Express operates a shuttle-bus service (€10) departing every 40 minutes from Ercolano Circumvesuviana station. The vehicles thread their way rapidly up back roads, reaching the top in 20 minutes. Allow at least three hours for the journey, including a 30-minute walk to the crater on a soft cinder track.

Bus Contact Vesuvio Express. ✉ *Piazzale Stazione Circumvesuviano 7, Ercolano* ☎ *081/7393666* ⊕ *www.vesuvioexpress.it.*

EXPLORING

Mt. Vesuvius. Although Vesuvius's destructive powers are on hold, the threat of an eruption remains ever present. Seen from the other side of the Bay of Naples, Vesuvius appears to have two peaks: on the northern side is the steep face of Monte Somma, possibly part of the original

Continued on page 676

ANCIENT POMPEII
TOMB OF A
CIVILIZATION

The site of Pompeii, petrified memorial to Vesuvius's eruption on the morning of August 24, AD 79, is the largest, most accessible, and probably most famous of excavations anywhere.

A busy commercial center with a population of 10,000–20,000, ancient Pompeii covered about 160 acres on the seaward end of the fertile Sarno Plain. Today Pompeii is choked with both the dust of 25 centuries and more than 2 million visitors every year; only by escaping the hordes and lingering along its silent streets can you truly fall under the site's spell. On a quiet backstreet, all you need is a little imagination to sense the shadows palpably filling the dark corners, to hear the ancient pipe's falsetto and the tinny clash of cymbals, to envision a rain of rose petals gently covering a Roman senator's dinner guests. Come in the late afternoon when the site is nearly deserted and you will understand that the true pleasure of Pompeii is not in the seeing but in the feeling.

A FUNNY THING HAPPENS ON THE WAY TO THE FORUM

as you walk through Pompeii. Covered with dust and decay as it is, the city seems to come alive. Perhaps it's the familiar signs of life observed along the ancient streets: bakeries with large ovens just like those for making pizzas, tracks of cart wheels cut into the road surface, graffiti etched onto the plastered surfaces of street walls. Coming upon a *thermopolium* (snack bar), you imagine natives calling out, "Let's move on to the amphitheater." But a glance up at Vesuvius, still brooding over the scene like an enormous headstone, reminds you that these folks—whether

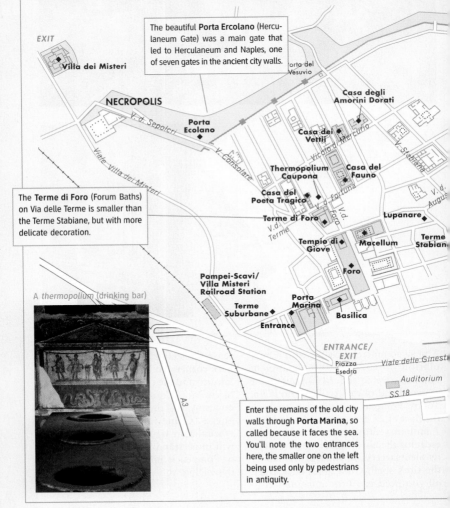

EXIT

Villa dei Misteri

The beautiful **Porta Ercolano** (Herculaneum Gate) was a main gate that led to Herculaneum and Naples, one of seven gates in the ancient city walls.

Porta del Vesuvio

NECROPOLIS

V. d. Sepolcri

Viale Villa dei Misteri

Porta Ecolano

V. Consolare

Casa degli Amorini Dorati

Casa dei Vettii

Vicolo di Mercurio

V. Stabiana

Thermopolium Caupona

Casa del Fauno

The **Terme di Foro** (Forum Baths) on Via delle Terme is smaller than the Terme Stabiane, but with more delicate decoration.

Casa del Poeta Tragico

Terme di Foro

V. d. Terme

V. d. Fortuna

V. d. Foro

Lupanare

V. d. Augus

Tempio di Giove

Macellum

Terme Stabian

Foro

Pompei-Scavi/ Villa Misteri Railroad Station

Porta Marina

A *thermopolium* (drinking bar)

Terme Suburbane

Entrance

Basilica

ENTRANCE/ EXIT

Piazza Esedra

Viale delle Ginest

Auditorium

SS 18

A3

Enter the remains of the old city walls through **Porta Marina**, so called because it faces the sea. You'll note the two entrances here, the smaller one on the left being used only by pedestrians in antiquity.

imagined in your head or actually wearing a mantle of lava dust—have not taken a breath for centuries. The town was laid out in a grid pattern, with two main intersecting streets. The wealthiest took a

Pompeii's cemetery, or Necropolis

whole block for themselves; those less fortunate built a house and rented out the front rooms, facing the street, as shops. There were good numbers of *tabernae* (taverns) and *thermopolia* on almost every corner, and frequent shows at the amphitheater.

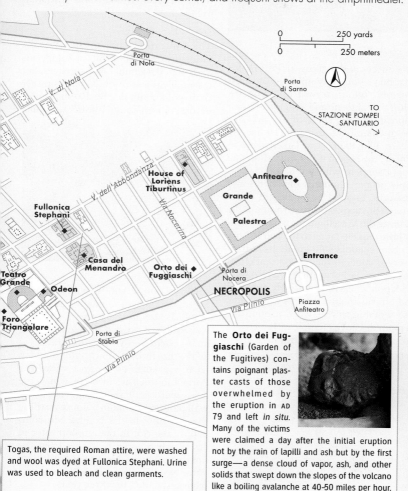

Togas, the required Roman attire, were washed and wool was dyed at Fullonica Stephani. Urine was used to bleach and clean garments.

The **Orto dei Fuggiaschi** (Garden of the Fugitives) contains poignant plaster casts of those overwhelmed by the eruption in AD 79 and left *in situ*. Many of the victims were claimed a day after the initial eruption not by the rain of lapilli and ash but by the first surge—a dense cloud of vapor, ash, and other solids that swept down the slopes of the volcano like a boiling avalanche at 40-50 miles per hour.

PUBLIC LIFE IN ANCIENT POMPEII

Forum

THE CITY CENTER

As you enter the ruins at Porta Marina, make your way uphill to the **Foro** (Forum), which served as Pompeii's cultural, political, and religious center. You can still see some of the two stories of colonnades that used to line the square. Like the ancient Greek *agora* in Athens, the Forum was a busy shopping area, complete with public officials to apply proper standards of weights and measures. Fronted by an elegant three-column portico on the eastern side of the forum is the **Macellum**, the covered meat and fish market dating to the 2nd century BC; here vendors sold goods from their reserved spots in the central market. It was also in the Forum that elections were held, politicians let rhetoric fly, speeches and official announcements were made, and worshippers crowded around the **Tempio di Giove** (Temple of Jupiter), at the northern end of the forum.

Basilica

On the southwestern corner is the **Basilica**, the city's law court and the economic center. These rectangular aisled halls were the model for early Christian churches, which had a nave (central aisle) and two side aisles separated by rows of columns. Standing in the Basilica, you can recognize the continuity between Roman and Christian architecture.

THE GAMES

The **Anfiteatro** (Amphitheater) was the ultimate in entertainment for Pompeians and offered a gamut of experiences, but essentially this was for gladiators rather than wild animals. By Roman standards, Pompeii's amphitheater was quite

Amphitheater

small (seating 20,000). Built in about 80 BC, making it the oldest permanent amphitheater in the Roman world, it was oval and divided into four seating areas. There were two main entrances—at the north and south ends—and a narrow passage on the west called the Porta Libitinensis, through which the dead were probably dragged out. A wall painting found in a house near the theater (now in the Naples Museum) depicts the riot in the amphitheater in AD 59 when several citizens from the nearby town of Nocera were killed. After Nocerian appeals to Nero, shows were suspended for three years.

Fresco of Pyramus and Thisbe in the House of Loreius Tiburtinus

BATHS AND BROTHELS

In its day, Pompeii was celebrated as the Côte d'Azur, the seaside Brighton, the Fire Island of the ancient Roman empire. Evidence of a Sybaritic bent is everywhere—in the town's grandest villas, in its baths, and especially in its rowdiest *lupanaria* (brothels), murals still reveal a worship of hedonism. Satyrs, bacchantes, hermaphrodites, and acrobatic couples are pictured indulging in hanky-panky.

The first buildings to the left past the ticket turnstiles are the **Terme Suburbane** (Suburban Baths), built—by all accounts without permission—right up against the city walls. The baths have eyebrow-raising frescoes in the *apodyterium* (changing room) that strongly suggest that more than just bathing and massaging went on here.

On the walls of **Lupanare** (brothel) are scenes of erotic games in which clients could engage. The **Terme Stabiane** (Stabian Baths) had underground furnaces, the heat from which circulated beneath the floor, rose through flues in the walls, and escaped through chimneys. The water temperature could be set for cold, lukewarm, or hot. Bathers took a lukewarm bath to prepare themselves for the hot room. A tepid bath came next, and then a plunge into cold water to tone up the skin. A vigorous massage with oil was followed by rest, reading, horseplay, and conversation.

Thanks to those deep layers of pyroclastic deposits from Vesuvius that protected the site from natural wear and tear over the centuries, graffiti found in Pompeii provide unique insights into the sort of things that the locals found important 2,000 years ago. A good many were personal and lend a human dimension to the disaster that not even the sights can equal.

At the baths: "What is the use of having a Venus if she's made of marble?"

At the entrance to the front lavatory at a private house: "May I always and everywhere be as potent with women as I was here."

On the Viale ai Teatri: "A copper pot went missing from my shop. Anyone who returns it to me will be given 65 bronze coins."

In the Basilica: "A small problem gets larger if you ignore it."

PRIVATE LIFE IN ANCIENT POMPEII

The facades of houses in Pompeii were relatively plain and seldom hinted at the care and attention lavished on the private rooms within. When visitors arrived they passed the shops and entered an open peristyle, from which the occupants received air, sunlight, and rainwater, the latter caught by the *impluvium*, a rectangular-shaped receptacle under the sloped roof. In the back was a receiving room, the *tablinum*, and behind was another open

House of Paquius Proculus

area, the atrium. Life revolved around this uncovered inner courtyard, with rows of columns and perhaps a garden with a fountain. Only good friends ever saw this part of the house, which was surrounded by *cubicula* (bedrooms) and the *triclinium* (dining area). Interior floors and walls usually were covered with colorful marble tiles, mosaics, and frescoes.

Several homes were captured in various states by the eruption of Vesuvius, each representing a different slice of Pompeiian life. The **Casa del Fauno**

Small Garden
Triclinium
Owner's Quarters
Kitchen
Servant's Quarters
Secondary Atrium
Entrance
Garden
Atrium
Impluvium
Peristyle

(House of the Faun) displayed wonderful mosaics, now at the Museo Archeologico Nazionale in Naples. The **Casa del Poeta Tragico** (House of the Tragic Poet) is a typical middle-class house. On the floor is a mosaic of a chained dog and the inscription *cave canem* ("Beware of the dog"). The **Casa degli Amorini Dorati** (House of the Gilded Cupids) is an elegant, well-preserved home with original marble decorations in the garden. Many paintings and mosaics were executed at **Casa del Menandro** (House of Menander), a patrician's villa named for a fresco of the Greek playwright.

Two blocks beyond the Stabian Baths you'll notice on the left the current digs at the **Casa dei Casti Amanti** (House of the Chaste Lovers). A team of plasterers and painters were at work here when Vesuvius erupted, redecorating one of the rooms and patching up the cracks in the bread oven near the entrance—possibly caused by tremors a matter of days before.

The **House of the Vettii** is the best example of a house owned by wealthy *mercatores* (merchants). It contains vivid murals—a magnificent *pinacoteca* (picture gallery) within the very heart of Pompeii. The scenes here—except for those in the two wings off the atrium—were all painted after the earthquake of AD 62. Once inside, cast an admiring glance at the delicate frieze around the wall of the *triclinium* (on the right of the peristyle garden as you enter from the atrium), depicting cupids engaged in various activities, such as selling oils and perfumes, working as goldsmiths and metalworkers, acting as wine merchants, or performing in chariot races. Another of the main attractions in the Casa dei Vettii is the small cubicle beyond the kitchen area (to the right of the atrium) with its faded erotic frescoes now protected by Perspex screens.

UNLOCKING THE VILLA DEI MISTERI

Villa dei Misteri

There is no more astounding, magnificently memorable evidence of Pompeii's devotion to the pleasures of the flesh than the frescoes on view at the **Villa dei Misteri** (Villa of the Mysteries), a palatial abode 400 yards outside the city gates, northwest of Porta Ercolano. Unearthed in 1909, this villa had more than 60 rooms painted with frescoes; the finest are in the *triclinium*. Painted in the most glowing Pompeiian reds and oranges, the panels relate the saga of a young bride (Ariadne) and her initiation into the mysteries of the cult of Dionysus, who was a god imported to Italy from Greece and then given the Latin name of Bacchus. The god of wine and debauchery also represented the triumph of the irrational—of all those mysterious forces that no official state religion could fully suppress.

Pompeii's best frescoes, painted in glowing reds and oranges, retain an amazing vibrancy.

The Villa of the Mysteries frescoes were painted circa 50 BC, most art historians believe, and represent the peak of the Second Style of Pompeiian wall painting. The triclinium frescoes are thought to have been painted by a local artist, although the theme may well have been copied from an earlier cycle of paintings from the Hellenistic period. In all there are 10 scenes, depicting children and matrons, musicians and satyrs, phalluses and gods. There are no inscriptions (such as are found on Greek vases), and after 2,000 years historians remain puzzled by many aspects of the triclinium cycle. Scholars endlessly debate the meaning of these frescoes, but anyone can tell they are the most beautiful paintings left to us by antiquity. In several ways, the eruption of Vesuvius was a blessing in disguise, for without it, these masterworks of art would have perished long ago.

Planning for Your Day in Pompeii

GETTING THERE

The archaeological site of Pompeii has its own stop (Pompei–Villa dei Misteri) on the Circumvesuviana line to Sorrento, close to the main entrance at the Porta Marina, which is the best place from which to start a tour. If, like many visitors every year, you get the wrong train from Naples (stopping at the other "Pompei" station), all is not lost. There's another entrance to the excavations at the far end of the site, just a seven-minute walk to the Amphitheater.

ADMISSION

Single tickets cost €13 and are valid for one full day. The site is open April–October, weekdays 9–7:30 (last admission at 6), and November–March, weekdays 9–5 (last admission at 3:30). On weekends, the site opens at 8:30 year-round; closing times are the same for each season. For more information, call ☎ 081/8575347 or visit ⊕ www.pompeiisites.org.

WHAT TO BRING

The only restaurant inside the site is both overpriced and busy, so bring along water and snacks. There are some shady, underused picnic tables outside the Porta di Nola, to the northeast of the site. Luggage is not allowed in the site.

TIMING

Visiting Pompeii does have its frustrating aspects: many buildings are blocked off by locked gates, and enormous group tours tend to clog up more popular attractions. But the site is so big that it's easy to lose yourself. To really see the site, you'll need four or five hours, a bit less if you hire a guide.

To get the most out of Pompeii, rent an audio guide and opt for one of the three itineraries (two hours, four hours, or six hours). If hiring a guide, make sure the guide is registered for an English tour and standing inside the gate; agree beforehand on the length of the tour and the price, and prepare yourself for sound bites of English mixed with dollops of hearsay. For a higher-quality (and more expensive) full-day tour, try Context Travel (⊕ www.contexttravel.com).

DISCOUNTS

If you intend to visit other archaeological sites nearby during your trip, you should buy the *biglietto cumulativo* pass, a combination ticket with access to three area sites (Pompeii, Oplontis, Boscoreale); it costs €15 and is valid for three days. The sites around Naples are almost all well served by public transport; ask about transportation options at the helpful information kiosk near the Porta Marina entrance to Pompeii. All sites are free the first Sunday of the month.

crater wall in AD 79; to the south is the present-day cone of Vesuvius, which has actually formed within the ancient crater. The AD 79 cone would have been considerably higher, perhaps peaking at around 9,000 feet. The upper slopes bear the visible scars left by 19th- and 20th-century eruptions, the most striking being the lava flow from 1944 lying to the left (north side) of the approach road from Ercolano on the way up.

As you tour the cities that felt the volcano's wrath, you may be overwhelmed by the urge to explore Vesuvius itself, and it's well worth the trip. The view when the air is clear is magnificent, with the curve of the coast and the tiny white houses among the orange and lemon blossoms. When the summit becomes lost in mist, though, you'll be lucky to see your hand in front of your face. If you notice the summit clearing—it tends to be clearer in the afternoon—head for it. If possible, see Vesuvius after you've toured the ruins of buried Herculaneum to appreciate the magnitude of the volcano's power. Admission to the crater includes a compulsory guide, usually a young geologist who speaks a smattering of English. At the bottom you'll be offered a stout walking stick (a small tip is appreciated when you return it). The climb can be tiring if you're not used to steep hikes. Because of the volcanic stone you should wear athletic or sturdy shoes, not sandals. ☎ *081/7775720* ⊕ *www. parconazionaledelvesuvio.it, www.guidevesuvio.it* ⌹ *€10.*

14

OPLONTIS (TORRE ANNUNZIATA)

20 km (12 miles) southeast of Naples, 5 km (3 miles) west of Pompeii.

Fodor's Choice
★

Surrounded by the fairly drab 1960s urban landscape of Torre Annunziata, Oplontis justifies its reputation as one of the more mysterious archaeological sites to be unearthed in the 20th century. The villa complex has been imaginatively ascribed—from a mere inscription on an amphora—to Nero's second wife, Poppaea Sabina. Her family was well known among the landed gentry of neighboring Pompeii, although, after a kick in the stomach from her emperor husband, she died some 15 years before the villa was overwhelmed by the eruption of 79.

GETTING HERE AND AROUND

By car, take the A3 Napoli–Salerno autostrada to the Torre Annunziata exit. Follow Via Veneto west, then turn left onto Via Sepolcri for the excavations. By train, take the Circumvesuviana railway to Torre Annunziata, the town's modern name (€2.80 from Naples).

EXPLORING

Oplontis. For those overwhelmed by the throngs at Pompeii, a visit to the site of Oplontis offers a chance for contemplation and intellectual stimulation. What has been excavated so far of the Villa of the Empress Poppaea covers more than 7,000 square meters (75,000 square feet), and because the site is bound by a road to the west and a canal to the south, its full extent may never be known.

Complete with porticoes, a large peristyle, a pool, baths, and extensive gardens, the villa is thought by some to have been a school for young philosophers and orators. You have to visit to appreciate the full range of Roman wall paintings; one highlight is found in Room 5, a sitting room that overlooked the sea. ⊠ *Via Sepolcri 1, Torre Annunziata* ☎ *081/8575347* ⊕ *www.pompeiisites.org* ⌹ *€5.50 for Oplontis, Boscoreale, and Stabiae; €15 includes 3-day ticket for Oplontis, Pompeii, and Boscoreale.*

ISCHIA AND PROCIDA

Capri may get star billing among the islands that line the Bay of Naples, but Ischia and Procida also have their own lower-key appeal. Once entirely dependent on its thermal springs, Ischia is now the archaeological front-runner in the bay, thanks to the noted museum in Lacco Ameno. Procida has opened up to tourism, with some newer, smaller hotels remaining open throughout the year, and it has started to capitalize on its chief natural asset, the unspoiled isle of Vivara. Ischia was the setting for much of *The Talented Mr. Ripley* (1999), starring Matt Damon and Gwyneth Paltrow, while Procida's pastel colors will be familiar to anyone who has seen the widely acclaimed Italian film *Il Postino* (1994).

ISCHIA

45 mins by hydrofoil, 90 mins by car ferry from Naples, 60 mins by ferry from Pozzuoli.

Although Capri leaves you breathless with its charm and beauty, Ischia (pronounced "EES-kee-ah"), also called Isola Verde (Green Island)—not, as is often believed, because of its lush vegetation, but for its typical green tuff rock—takes time to cast its spell. In fact, an overnight stay is not long enough; you have to look harder here for the signs of antiquity, the traffic can be reminiscent of Naples, and the island displays all the hallmarks of rapid, uncontrolled urbanization. Ischia does have many jewels, though. There are the wine-growing villages beneath the lush volcanic slopes of Monte Epomeo, and unlike Capri, the island enjoys a life of its own that survives when the tourists head home.

Ischia is volcanic in origin, with thermal springs said to cure whatever ails you. Today the island's main industry, tourism, revolves around the more than 100 thermal baths, most of which are attached to hotels.

Much of the 37 km (23 miles) of coastline are punctuated with a continuum of *stabilimenti balneari* (private bathing establishments) in summer. However, there are also lots of public beaches set against the scenic backdrop of Monte Epomeo and its verdant slopes.

GETTING HERE AND AROUND

Ischia is well connected with the mainland in all seasons. The last boats leave for Naples and Pozzuoli at about 8 pm (though in the very high season there is a midnight sailing), and you should allow plenty of time for getting to the port and buying a ticket. Ischia has three ports—Ischia Porto, Casamicciola, and Forio (hydrofoils only)—so you should choose your ferry or hydrofoil according to your destination. Non-Italians can bring cars to the island relatively freely. Up-to-date schedules are published at ⊕ *www.traghetti-ischia.info*.

Ischia's bus network reaches all the major sites and beaches on one of its 18 lines. The principal lines are CD and CS, circling the island in clockwise and counterclockwise directions—in the summer months runs continue until after midnight. The main bus terminus is in Ischia Porto at the start of Via Cosca, where buses run by the company EAV radiate out around the island. There are also convenient *fermate* (stops) at the two main beaches—Citara and Maronti—with timetables displayed at the terminus. Tickets cost €1.50 per ride, €1.80 for 100 minutes, and €4.50 for a one-day pass; note that conditions can get hot and crowded at peak beach-visiting times.

VISITOR INFORMATION

Contact Azienda Autonoma di Cura, Soggiorno e Turismo. ✉ *Via Iasolino 7, Ischia Porto* ☎ *081/5074231* ⊕ *www.infoischiaprocida.it.*

EXPLORING

Forio. The far-western and southern coasts of Ischia are more rugged and attractive than other areas. Forio, at the extreme west, has a waterfront church and is a good spot for lunch or dinner. ✉ *Forio.*

Giardini Poseidon Terme. The largest spa on the island has the added boon of a natural sauna hollowed out of the rocks. Here you can sit like a Roman senator on stone chairs recessed in the rock and let the hot water cascade over you. With countless thermally regulated pools, promenades, and steam pools, plus lots of kitschy toga-clad statues of the Caesars, Poseidon exerts a special pull on tourists, many of them grandparents shepherding grandchildren. On certain days, the place is overrun with people, so be prepared for crowds and wailing babies. ✉ *Citara Beach, Forio* ☎ *081/9087111* ⊕ *www.giardiniposeidonterme. com* 🎫 *€32 all day, €28 after 1 pm (€5 deposit for keyband); add €3 to prices in Aug. Visitors €6 (6 pm–7 pm, no bathing)* ⊗ *Closed Nov.–mid-Apr.*

Ischia Ponte. Most of the hotels are along the beach in the part of town called Ischia Ponte, which gets its name from the *ponte* (bridge) built by Alfonso of Aragon in 1438 to link the picturesque castle on a small islet offshore with the town and port. For a while the castle was the home of Vittoria Colonna, poetess, granddaughter of Renaissance Duke Federico da Montefeltro (1422–82), and platonic soul mate of Michelangelo, with whom she carried on a lengthy correspondence. You'll find a typical resort atmosphere in this area: countless cafés, shops, and restaurants, and a 1-km (½-mile) fine-sand beach. ✉ *Ischia Ponte.*

Ischia Porto. This is the island's largest town and the usual point of debarkation. It's no workaday port, however, but rather a lively resort with plenty of hotels, the island's best shopping area, and low, flat-roof houses on terraced hillsides overlooking the water. Its narrow streets and villas and gardens are framed by pines. ✉ *Ischia Porto.*

Monte Epomeo. The inland town of Fontana is the base for excursions to the top of this long-dormant volcano that dominates the island landscape. You can reach its 2,589-foot peak in less than 1½ hours of relatively easy walking. ✉ *Ischia.*

Sant'Angelo. On the southern coast, this is a charming village with a narrow path leading to its promontory; the road doesn't reach all the way into town, so it's free of traffic. It's a five-minute boat ride from the beach of Maronti, at the foot of cliffs. ✉ *Sant'Angelo.*

14

WHERE TO EAT

$$
SOUTHERN
ITALIAN

✕ **Da Cocò.** This inviting restaurant with an outside terrace sits on the causeway linking the Aragonese castle to the rest of Ischia. It's renowned for its fresh seafood, which is highly prized by the Ischitani. **Known for:** magical setting near the castello; delicious gelato; good spot to just sit with an aperitivo and nibbles. $ *Average main: €24* ⊠ *Via Aragonese 1, Ischia Ponte* ☏ *081/981823* ⊕ *www.ristorantecocoischia. com* ⊘ *Closed Jan. and Feb.*

$
SOUTHERN
ITALIAN

✕ **O' Padrone Dò Mare.** In a gorgeous seaside location just off the pedestrian stretch, this is the ideal place to enjoy fresh seafood—the name, "owner of the sea," says it all. For more than 70 years, O' Padrone Dò Mare has been an institution on the island, and locals and visitors crowd the terrace. **Known for:** cracking harbor views; spot-on fritto misto di mare seafood medley; local institution. $ *Average main: €13* ⊠ *Corso A. Rizzoli 6, Lacco Ameno* ☏ *081/900244* ⊘ *Closed Nov.–Mar.*

$$$
SOUTHERN
ITALIAN
Fodor's Choice
★

✕ **Umberto a Mare.** This iconic eatery has occupied the space below the Santuario del Soccorso since 1936, when the original Umberto began to grill the local catch on the seafront. Grandson Umberto now presides over the kitchen, conjuring up gourmet dishes such as *crudo di ricciola marinata* (marinated raw Mediterranean amber jack) and *paccheri dolcemare,* a sweet pasta dish with squid, sultanas (golden raisins), pine nuts, and a touch of cinnamon. **Known for:** breathtaking sunset sea views; changing displays of artworks; decades-long reputation for exquisite seafood. $ *Average main: €25* ⊠ *Via Soccorso 8, Forio* ☏ *081/997171* ⊕ *www.umbertoamare.it* ⊘ *Closed Nov.–Mar.*

WHERE TO STAY

$$
HOTEL
Fodor's Choice
★

🏨 **Albergo Il Monastero.** The Castello Aragonese, on its own island, is the unrivaled location for this unique hotel with a peaceful ambience and simple but comfortable rooms overlooking the Mediterranean. **Pros:** stunning views and peaceful garden; hotel is inside the castle; great restaurant on terrace. **Cons:** a long way from the entrance to your room; some consider it too far from the town's action; books up well in advance. $ *Rooms from: €140* ⊠ *Castello Aragonese 3, Ischia Ponte* ☏ *081/992435* ⊕ *www.albergoilmonastero.it* ⊘ *Closed Nov.–late Apr.* ⮑ *23 rooms* ⦿| *Free Breakfast.*

$$$$
HOTEL
Fodor's Choice
★

🏨 **Mezzatorre Resort & Spa.** Far from the madding, sunburned crowds that swamp Ischia, this luxurious getaway in a sleekly renovated former fortress sits in splendid isolation on the extreme promontory of Punta Cornacchia. **Pros:** tranquil retreat with wonderful views; good restaurants and spa; shuttle provided from Lacco Ameno. **Cons:** very isolated; pricey. $ *Rooms from: €399* ⊠ *Via Mezzatorre 23, Forio* ☏ *081/986111* ⊕ *www.mezzatorre.it* ⊘ *Closed Nov.–Apr.* ⮑ *57 rooms* ⦿| *Free Breakfast.*

$$$$
HOTEL
Fodor's Choice
★

🏨 **Terme Manzi.** Dating to the mid-19th century, it was at this hotel that so-called "thermal tourism" began, in one of the largest spas in the south of Italy—the bath where Giuseppe Garibaldi bathed is conserved in a corner. **Pros:** some say five stars are not enough for this glitzy spot; wonderful indoor pool; range of soothing treatments. **Cons:** located in a nondescript square; a bit far from beach; noise may disturb room guests under the terrace restaurant. $ *Rooms from: €355* ⊠ *Piazza*

Bagni 4, Casamicciola Terme ☎ *081/994722* 🌐 *www.termemanzihotel.com* 🛏 *58 rooms* 🍴 *Free Breakfast.*

$$ HOTEL 🏨 **Villa Antonio.** With a superlative panoramic view over the Bay of Cartaromana, Villa Antonio offers a quiet haven close to the action, and direct access to the sea is a few private steps away from the casual whitewashed villa. **Pros:** attractive price; lovely seaside location; beguiling artsy touches. **Cons:** many steps to negotiate before elevator; small windows don't do justice to the view; decor may be a little plain for some. [$] *Rooms from: €125* ✉ *Via S. Giuseppe della Croce, Ischia Ponte* ☎ *081/982660* 🌐 *www.villantonio.it* 🕒 *Closed Nov.–mid-Mar.* 🛏 *18 rooms* 🍴 *Free Breakfast.*

14

PROCIDA

35 mins by hydrofoil, 1 hr by car ferry from Naples.

Lying barely 3 km (2 miles) from the mainland and 10 km (6 miles) from the nearest port (Pozzuoli), Procida is an island of enormous contrasts. It's the most densely populated island in Europe—just more than 10,000 people crammed into less than 3½ square km (2 square miles)—and yet there are oases like Marina Corricella and Vivara, which seem to have been bypassed by modern civilization. The inhabitants of the island—the Procidani—have an almost symbiotic relationship with the Mediterranean: many join the merchant navy, others either fish or ferry vacationers around local waters. And yet land traffic here can be more intense than on any other island in the Bay of Naples.

GETTING HERE AND AROUND

Procida's ferry timetable caters to the many daily commuters who live on the island and work in Naples or Pozzuoli. The most frequent—and cheapest—connections are from the Port of Pozzuoli. After stopping at Procida's main port, Marina Grande (also called Sancio Cattolico), many ferries and hydrofoils continue on to Ischia, for which Procida is considered a halfway house.

EXPLORING

Fodor's Choice ★ **Marina di Corricella.** Perched under the citadel of the Terra Murata, the Marina di Corricella is Procida's most iconic sight. Singled out for the waterfront scenes in *Il Postino* (*The Postman*, the 1995 Oscar winner for Best Foreign Film), this fishermen's cove is one of the most eye-popping villages in Campania—a rainbow-hued, horizontal version of Positano, comprising hundreds of traditional Mediterranean-style stone houses threaded by numerous *scalatinelle* (staircase streets). ✉ *Procida.*

WHERE TO EAT

$$ SOUTHERN ITALIAN 🍴 **La Conchiglia.** A meal here encapsulates the rustic, seaside simplicity of Procida. Picture-postcard views of Corricella and Capri beyond the lapping waves form the backdrop for the fresh seafood and vegetable creations. **Known for:** beachside views and breezes through open windows; freshest ingredients; boat trips and bathing nearby. [$] *Average main: €18* ✉ *Via Pizzaco 10* ☎ *081/8967602* 🌐 *www.laconchigliaristorante.com* 🕒 *Closed mid-Nov.–Mar.*

CAPRI

Fantastic grottoes, soaring conical peaks, caverns great and small, plus villas of the emperors and thousands of legends brush Capri with an air of whispered mystery. Emperor Augustus was the first to tout the island's pleasures by nicknaming it Apragopolis (City of Sweet Idleness) and Capri has drawn escapists of all kinds ever since. Ancient Greek and Roman goddesses were moved aside by the likes of Jacqueline Onassis, Elizabeth Taylor, and Brigitte Bardot, who made the island into a paparazzo's paradise in the 1960s. Today, new generations of glitterati continue to answer the island's call.

Life on Capri gravitates around the two centers of Capri Town (on the saddle between Monte Tiberio and Monte Solaro) and Anacapri, higher up (902 feet). The main road connecting Capri Town with the upper town of Anacapri is well plied by buses. On arriving at the main harbor, the Marina Grande, everyone heads for the famous funicular, which ascends (and descends) several times an hour. Once you're lofted up to Anacapri by bus, you can reach the island heights by taking the spectacular chairlift that ascends to the top of Monte Solaro (1,932 feet) from Anacapri's town center. Within Capri Town and Anacapri foot power is the preferred mode of transportation, as much for convenience as for the sheer delight of walking along these gorgeous street and roads.

GETTING HERE AND AROUND

Capri is well connected with the mainland in all seasons, though there are more sailings April–October. Hydrofoils, Seacats, and similar vessels leave from Molo Beverello (below Piazza Municipio) in Naples, while far less frequent car ferries leave from Calata Porta di Massa, 1,000 yards to the east. There's also service to and from Sorrento's Marina Piccola. Much of Capri is pedestrianized, and a car is a great hindrance, not a help.

Several ferry and hydrofoil companies ply the waters of the Bay of Naples, making frequent trips to Capri. Schedules change from season to season; the tourist office's website (⊕ *www.capritourism.com*) gives updated departure times. However, you can't return to Naples after the last sailing (11 pm in high season, often 8 pm or even earlier in low season). There's little to be gained—sometimes nothing—from buying a round-trip ticket, which will just tie you down to the return schedule of one line. However, book in advance in spring and summer for a Sunday return to the mainland.

VISITOR INFORMATION

Contacts Azienda Autonoma di Cura, Soggiorno e Turismo. ⊠ *Banchina del Porto, Marina Grande* ☎ *081/8370634* ⊕ *www.capritourism.com* ⊠ *Piazza Umberto I* ☎ *081/8370686* ⊕ *www.capritourism.com.*

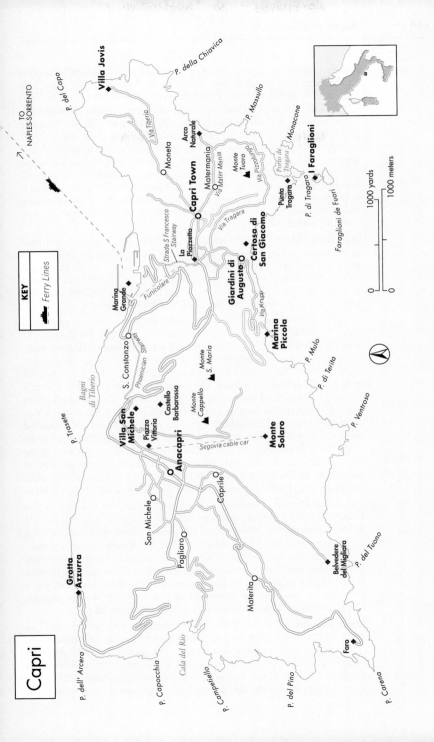

Capri

KEY
— Ferry Lines

TO NAPLES-SORRENTO

Villa Jovis
P. della Chiavica
P. del Capo
Via Tiberia
Moneta
Arco Naturale
Capri Town
Matermania
P. Massullo
Monte Tuoro
Via Mater Mania
Via Pizzolungo
Monacone
Porto de Tragara
Punta Tragara
P. di Tragara
I Faraglioni
Faraglioni de Fuori
Strada S. Francesco Stairway
La Piazzetta
Via Tragara
Certosa di San Giacomo
Marina Grande
Funicolare
Giardini di Augusto
Via Krupp
Marina Piccola
P. Mulo
Bagni di Tiberio
S. Constanzo
Phoenician Stairway
Monte S. Maria
P. di Terita
P. Trasele
Castello Barbarossa
Monte Cappello
Villa San Michele
Piazza Vittoria
Segovia cable car
Monte Solaro
P. Ventroso
Anacapri
San Michele
Caprile
P. dell' Arcera
Pagliaro
Belvedere del Migliara
P. del Tuono
Grotta Azzurra
P. Capocchia
Materita
Cala del Rio
P. Campetiello
P.
P. del Pino
Faro
P. Carena

1000 yards
1000 meters
0
0

EXPLORING

Fodor'sChoice **Anacapri.** A tortuous road leads up to Anacapri, the island's "second
★ city," about 3 km (2 miles) from Capri Town. To get here you can take a
bus either from Via Roma in Capri Town or from Marina Grande (both
€2), or a taxi (about €30 one-way; agree on the fare before starting out).
Crowds are thick down Via Capodimonte leading to Villa San Michele
and around Piazza Vittoria, the square where you catch the chairlift
to the top of Monte Solaro. Via Finestrale leads to the noted **Le Boffe
quarter,** centered on the Piazza Diaz. Le Boffe owes its name to the
distinctive domestic architecture prevalent here, which uses vaults and
sculpted groins instead of crossbeams. Elsewhere, Anacapri is quietly
appealing. It's a good starting point for walks, such as the 80-minute
round-trip journey to the **Migliara Belvedere,** on the island's southern
coast. ⊠ *Anacapri.*

Capri Town. On arrival at the port, pick up the excellent map of the island
at the tourist office. You may have to wait for the funicular railway (€2
one-way) to Capri Town, some 450 feet above the harbor. So this might
be the time to splurge on an open-top taxi—it could save you an hour
in line. From the upper station, walk out into Piazza Umberto I, better
known as the Piazzetta, the island's social hub. ⊠ *Capri.*

Certosa di San Giacomo. An eerie atmosphere hangs around neglected
corners of this once-grand, palatial complex between the Castiglione
and Tuoro hills, which was for centuries a Carthusian monastery dedicated to St. James. It was founded between 1371 and 1374, when Queen
Giovanna I of Naples gave Count Giacomo Arcucci, her secretary, the
land and the means to create it. The count himself then became devoutly
religious and retired here until his death. After the monastery was
sacked by the pirates Dragut and Barbarossa in the 16th century, it was
thoroughly restored and rebuilt—thanks in part to heavy taxes exacted
from the populace. The reopened (2010) Quarto del Priore hosts art
exhibitions from international artists, but the showstopper here is the
Museo Diefenbach, with restored large canvases by influential German
painter K. W. Diefenbach, who visited Capri in 1900 and stayed until
his death in 1913. ⊠ *Via Certosa* ☎ *081/8376218* 🖾 *€4* ⊘ *Closed Mon.*

Fodor'sChoice **Giardini di Augusto** (*Gardens of Augustus*). From the terraces of this
★ beautiful public garden, you can see the village of Marina Piccola
below—restaurants, cabanas, and swimming platforms huddle among
the shoals—and admire the steep, winding Via Krupp, actually a staircase cut into the rock. Friedrich Krupp, the German arms manufacturer,
loved Capri and became one of the island's most generous benefactors.
If you are lucky enough to find this path open (rockfalls often force
closure), do not miss the chance to take it down to Marina Piccola.
⊠ *Via Matteotti, beyond monastery of San Giacomo* 🖾 *€1.*

Grotta Azzurra. Only when the Grotta Azzurra was "discovered" in
1826 by the Polish poet August Kopisch and Swiss artist Ernest Fries,
did Capri become a tourist destination. The watery cave's blue beauty
became a symbol of the return to nature and revolt from reason that
marked the Romantic era, and it soon became a required stop on the
Grand Tour. In reality, the grotto had long been a local landmark.

During the Roman era—as testified by the extensive remains, primarily below sea level, and several large statues now at the Certosa di San Giacomo—it had been the elegant, mosaic-decorated nymphaeum of the adjoining villa of Gradola. Historians can't quite agree if it was simply a lovely little pavilion where rich patricians would cool themselves or truly a religious site where sacred mysteries were practiced. The water's extraordinary sapphire color is caused by a hidden opening in the rock that refracts the light. At highest illumination the very air inside seems tinted blue.

The Grotta Azzurra can be reached from Marina Grande or from the small embarkation point below Anacapri on the northwest side of the island, accessible by bus from Anacapri. If you're pressed for time, however, skip this sometimes frustrating and disappointing excursion. You board one boat to get to the grotto, then transfer to a smaller boat that takes you inside. If there's a backup of boats waiting to get in, you'll be given precious little time to enjoy the gorgeous color of the water and its silvery reflections. ⊠ *Capri* ✆ *€31 from Marina Grande, €14 by rowboat from Grotta Azzurra near Anacapri* ☉ *Excursions don't run if the sea is even minimally rough.*

Fodor's Choice
★
I Faraglioni. Few landscapes set more artists dreaming than that of the famous Faraglioni—three enigmatic, pale-ocher limestone colossi that loom out of the sea just off the Punta Tragara on the southern coast of Capri. Soaring almost 350 feet above the water, the Faraglioni have become for most Italians a beloved symbol of Capri and have been poetically compared to Gothic cathedrals or modern skyscrapers. The first rock is called Faraglione di Terra, since it's attached to the land; at its base is the famous restaurant and bathing lido Da Luigi, where a beach mattress may accompany the luncheon menu. The second is called Faraglione di Mezzo, or Stella, and little boats can often be seen going through its picturesque tunnel, which was caused by sea erosion. The rock farthest out to sea is Faraglione di Scopolo and is inhabited by a wall lizard species with a striking blue belly, considered a local variant by biologists although legend has it that they were originally brought as pets from Greece to delight ancient Roman courtiers. ⊠ *End of Via Tragara.*

Fodor's Choice
★
Marina Piccola. A 10-minute ride from the main bus terminus in Capri (Piazzetta d'Ungheria), Marina Piccola is a delightfully picturesque inlet that provides the Capresi and other sun worshippers with their best access to reasonable beaches and safe swimming. The entire cove is romantically lined with *stabilimenti*—elegant bathing lidos where the striped cabanas are often air-conditioned and the bodies can be Modigliani-sleek. The most famous of these lidos (there's a fee to use the facilities), found closest to the Faraglioni, is **La Canzone del Mare**, once presided over by the noted British music-hall singer Gracie Fields and for decades favored by the smart set, including Noël Coward and Emilio Pucci (who set up his first boutique here). La Canzone del Mare's seaside restaurant offers a dreamy view of the Faraglioni and a luncheon here, although pricey, can serve as an iconic Capri moment. Jutting out into the bay at the center of the marina is the **Scoglio delle Sirene,** or Sirens' Rock—a small natural promontory—which the ancients

believed to be the haunt of the Sirens, the mythical temptresses whose song seduced Odysseus in Homer's *Odyssey*. This rock separates the two small beaches: Pennaulo, to the east, and Marina di Mulo, site of the original Roman harbor, to the west. The small church, **Chiesa di Sant'Andrea,** was built in 1900 to give the local fishermen a place of worship. ⊠ *Via Marina Piccola.*

Fodor'sChoice ★ **Monte Solaro.** An impressive limestone formation and the highest point on Capri (1,932 feet), Monte Solaro affords gasp-inducing views toward the bays of both Naples and Salerno. A 12-minute chairlift ride will take you right to the top (refreshments available at the bar), where you can launch out on a number of scenic trails on the western side of the island. Picnickers should note that even in summer it can get windy at this height, and there are few trees to provide shade or refuge. ⊠ *Piazza Vittoria, Anacapri* ☎ *081/8370420* ⊕ *www.capriseggiovia.it* 🎫 *€8 one-way, €11 round-trip* ☉ *Chairlift closed in adverse weather.*

Fodor'sChoice ★ **Villa Jovis.** In Roman times, Capri was the site of 12 spacious villas, but Villa Jovis is both the best preserved and the largest, occupying nearly 23,000 square feet. Named in honor of the ancient Roman god Jupiter, or Jove, the villa of the emperor Tiberius is riveted to the towering Rocca di Capri like an eagle's nest overlooking the strait separating Capri from Punta Campanella, the tip of the Sorrentine Peninsula. A powerful reminder of the importance of the island in Roman times, the site is even more compelling because of the accounts of the latter years of Tiberius's reign between AD 27 and 37, written by authors and near-contemporaries Suetonius and Tacitus. The Salto di Tiberio (Tiberius's Leap) is where ancient gossips believed Tiberius had enemies (among them his discarded lovers and even unfortunate cooks) hurled over the precipice into the sea some 1,000 feet below. Pick up a site map at the ticket office, which gives a useful breakdown of the various areas of the villa. From La Piazzetta allow 45 minutes each way for the walk to this site. ⊠ *Via A. Maiuri* ☎ *081/8374549* 🎫 *€6* ☉ *Closed Tues. Oct.–Mar.*

Fodor'sChoice ★ **Villa San Michele.** From Anacapri's Piazza Vittoria, picturesque Via Capodimonte leads to Villa San Michele, the charming former home of Swedish doctor and philanthropist Axel Munthe (1857–1949), and which Henry James called "the most fantastic beauty, poetry, and inutility that one had ever seen clustered together." At the ancient entranceway to Anacapri at the top of the Scala Fenicia, the villa is set around Roman-style courtyards, marble walkways, and atria. Rooms display the doctor's varied collections, which range from bric-a-brac to antiquities. Medieval choir stalls, Renaissance lecterns, and gilded statues of saints are all part of the setting, with some rooms preserving the doctor's personal memorabilia. A spectacular pergola path overlooking the entire Bay of Naples leads from the villa to the famous Sphinx Parapet, where an ancient Egyptian sphinx looks out toward Sorrento: you cannot see its face—on purpose. It is said that if you touch the sphinx's hindquarters with your left hand while making a wish, it will come true. The parapet is connected to the little Chapel of San Michele, on the grounds of one of Tiberius's villas.

Besides hosting summer concerts, the Axel Munthe Foundation has an ecomuseum that fittingly reflects Munthe's fondness for animals. Here you can learn about various bird species—accompanied by their songs—found on Capri. Munthe bought up the hillside and made it a sanctuary for birds, and today this little realm is still an Eden. ✉ *Viale Axel Munthe 34, Anacapri* ☎ *081/8371401* 🌐 *www.villasanmichele.eu* 🎟 *€8.*

WHERE TO EAT

$$ SOUTHERN ITALIAN

🍴 **Al Grottino.** This small and friendly family-run restaurant, which is in a 14th-century building handy to the Piazzetta, has arched ceilings and lots of atmosphere; autographed photos of famous customers cover the walls. House specialties are scialatielli *ai fiori di zucchine e gambaretti* (with zucchini flowers and shrimps) and *coccette* (pasta with mussels and clams), but the owner delights in taking his guests through the menu of regional dishes. **Known for:** warm, family-run atmosphere; good value for Capri; Caprese specialties with the freshest ingredients. [$] *Average main: €18* ✉ *Via Longano 27* ☎ *081/8370584* 🌐 *www.ristorantealgrottino.net* 🕓 *Closed Nov.–late Mar.*

$$$ SOUTHERN ITALIAN

🍴 **Aurora.** Though often frequented by celebrities—whose photographs adorn the walls inside and out—this restaurant offers courtesy and *simpatia* irrespective of your star status. The oldest restaurant on the island, now in its third generation, it has a sleekly minimalist interior, but if you want to see and be seen, book a table outside on one of Capri's chicest thoroughfares. **Known for:** historic hangout of the jet set; Papà Gennaro's unusually light pizza all'Acqua; first-rate wine. [$] *Average main: €28* ✉ *Via Fuorlovado 18/22* ☎ *081/8370181* 🌐 *www.auroracapri.com* 🕓 *Closed Nov.–Easter.*

$$ NEAPOLITAN

🍴 **Barbarossa.** Take the staircase behind Piazza Vittoria's bus stop to the covered terrace of this ristorante-pizzeria with panoramic views of the Barbarossa castle and the sea. The no-frills ambience belies the quality of the *cucina*: besides *pizze* they specialize in local dishes—including risotto *con gamberi a limone* (shrimp with lemon). **Known for:** authentic (certified) Vera Pizza Napoletana; lively function room during events; chef's semifreddi and other dessert specials. [$] *Average main: €15* ✉ *Piazza Vittoria 1, Anacapri* ☎ *081/8371483* 🌐 *www.ristorantebarbarossa.com.*

$$$ SOUTHERN ITALIAN
Fodor's Choice ★

🍴 **Da Gelsomina.** Amid its own terraced vineyards with inspiring views to the island of Ischia and beyond, this is much more than just a well-reputed restaurant. The owner's mother was a friend of Axel Munthe, and he encouraged her to open a food kiosk, which evolved into Da Gelsomina; today the specialties include *pollo a mattone,* chicken grilled on bricks, and locally caught rabbit. **Known for:** opened in the 1960s with family links to Axel Munthe; chicken grilled on bricks; fresh produce and wine from their verdant gardens. [$] *Average main: €35* ✉ *Via Migliara 72, Anacapri* ☎ *081/8371499* 🌐 *www.dagelsomina.com* 🕓 *Closed Jan. and Feb., and Tues. in winter. No dinner in winter.*

$$$$ SOUTHERN ITALIAN

🍴 **La Canzone del Mare.** Although it's not primarily a restaurant, luncheon in the covered pavilion of this legendary bathing lido of the Marina Piccola is Capri at its most picture-perfect. The set menus change every year, but a favorite main dish is paccheri *con gamberi e peperoncini verdi* (with shrimp and green peppers). **Known for:** open terrace overlooking Marina Piccola; sunset wine and peaches served with stuzzichini (appetizers); famous haunt of the beautiful people. [$] *Average main: €55* ✉ *Via Marina Piccola 93* ☎ *081/8370104* 🌐 *www.lacanzonedelmare.com* ⏲ *Closed Oct.–Mar. No dinner.*

$$ SOUTHERN ITALIAN Fodor's Choice ★
🍴 **La Capannina.** One of Capri's most celebrity-haunted restaurants for decades, La Capannina is near the busy social hub of the Piazzetta, and the discreet flower-decked veranda is ideal for dining by candlelight. Specialties, aside from an authentic Capri wine with the house label, are ravioli capresi and linguine *con lo scorfano* (with scorpion fish), squid stuffed with caciotta cheese and marjoram, and an exquisite "Pezzogna" (sea bream cooked whole and topped with a layer of potatoes). **Known for:** walls strewn with photos of celebrity clientele; wine bar next door; seafood dishes. [$] *Average main: €23* ✉ *Via Le Botteghe 12b* ☎ *081/8370732* 🌐 *www.capanninacapri.com* ⏲ *Closed Nov.–mid-Mar.*

$$$ SOUTHERN ITALIAN
🍴 **La Fontelina.** Given its position right on the water's edge, seafood is almost de rigueur here, but for a slightly different starter, try the *polpette di melanzane* (eggplant fritters); then dip into the vegetable buffet. The house sangria is a blissful mix of white wine and fresh fruit. **Known for:** lunch stop for beach-club bathers; shuttle boat from Marina Piccola; chef Mario's daily seafood specials. [$] *Average main: €27* ✉ *Via Faraglioni 2* ☎ *081/8370845* 🌐 *www.fontelina-capri.com* ⏲ *Closed mid-Oct.–Easter. No dinner.*

$$$ SOUTHERN ITALIAN
🍴 **Le Grottelle.** This extremely informal trattoria enjoys a distinctive setting: it's built up against limestone rocks not far from the Arco Naturale, with the kitchen in a cave at the back. Whether you stumble over it (and are lucky enough to get a table) or make it your destination after an island hike, Le Grottelle will prove memorable, thanks to that ambience and sea views encompassing the Amalfi Coast's Li Galli islands. **Known for:** breathtaking cliff-clinging location; seafood dishes; cool grotto interiors. [$] *Average main: €25* ✉ *Via Arco Naturale 13* ☎ *081/8375719* ⏲ *Closed Nov.–mid-Mar.*

WHERE TO STAY

$$$$ HOTEL Fodor's Choice ★
🏨 **Caesar Augustus.** A continuing favorite of the Hollywood set, this landmark has long been considered a Caprese paradise thanks to its breathtaking perch atop an Anacapri cliff and the grandeur of its villa, gardens, terraces, and pool. **Pros:** serene terrace views; summer concerts on-site; infinity pool; friendly staff. **Cons:** a bit far from the action for some; no kids under 10 allowed; pricey. [$] *Rooms from: €704* ✉ *Via G. Orlandi 4, Anacapri* ☎ *081/8373395* 🌐 *www.caesar-augustus.com* ⏲ *Closed Nov.–mid-Apr.* 🛏 *55 rooms* 🍽 *Free Breakfast.*

$$$$ RESORT Fodor's Choice ★
🏨 **Capri Palace Hotel & Spa.** This Anacapri icon has grown both physically and conceptually over the years, amassing a noted art collection, launching a fashion and home line (including a line of Capritouch shoes, custom made for each client), and working with some of Italy's top names on unique design touches. **Pros:** noted art collection; stunning (and sometimes surprising) design; postcard views; award-winning spa and dining; five-star service. **Cons:** all that glam comes at a price;

some may find the quiet Anacapri location removed from the action (and water). [$] *Rooms from: €500* ✉ *Via Capodimonte 14, Anacapri* ☎ *081/9780111* 🌐 *www.capripalace.com* 🕓 *Closed mid-Oct.–mid-Apr.* 🛏 *78 rooms* 🍴 *Free Breakfast.*

$$$$ HOTEL Fodor's Choice ★ **Capri Tiberio Palace.** Offering comfort, style, luxury, and sigh-inducing views since the 19th century, this hotel is just a short walk from the Piazzetta—near the action, but not quite in the thick of it. **Pros:** friendly staff; pure luxury; traditional and kosher restaurant. **Cons:** no port-to-door guest shuttle; some rooms are not as large as expected in a five-star. [$] *Rooms from: €500* ✉ *Via Croce 11–15* ☎ *081/9787111* 🌐 *www.capritiberiopalace.com* 🕓 *Closed mid-Oct.–mid-Apr.* 🛏 *77 rooms* 🍴 *Free Breakfast.*

$$$$ HOTEL Fodor's Choice ★ **J. K. Place.** As the most supremely stylish and glamorous hotel in southern Italy, occupying an 1876 villa above Marina Grande harbor, this almost makes other accommodations on Capri seem dowdy and dull. **Pros:** exquisite pool; pleasant walk to the magical Tiberio beach; free shuttle to town. **Cons:** expensive; only for high rollers; pool visible from main road. [$] *Rooms from: €900* ✉ *Via Provinciale Marina Grande 225* ☎ *081/8384001* 🌐 *www.jkcapri.com* 🕓 *Closed mid-Oct.–mid-Apr.* 🛏 *22 rooms* 🍴 *Free Breakfast.*

$$ HOTEL **La Tosca.** It may be hard to find in the warren of side streets in Capri Town, but quiet La Tosca is worth all the trouble, with an unassuming vibe, terrace views, and reasonable rates. **Pros:** simple, unadorned charm; pleasant owner Ettore; quiet spot outside Capri Town. **Cons:** not all rooms have good views; it gets booked up early; rooms may seem to lack panache. [$] *Rooms from: €160* ✉ *Via Birago 5* ☎ *081/8370989* 🌐 *www.latoscahotel.com* 🕓 *Closed Nov.–Feb.* 🛏 *11 rooms* 🍴 *Free Breakfast.*

$$$$ HOTEL Fodor's Choice ★ **Punta Tragara.** Perhaps the most beautiful hotel on Capri—originally a private villa designed by Le Corbusier and the site of a secret wartime meeting between Churchill and Eisenhower—Punta Tragara opened in the 1970s and has a breathtaking location on Punta Tragara over the famed Faraglioni rocks. **Pros:** decadent and luxurious; wonderful views of the Faraglioni; two gorgeous pools. **Cons:** a 10-minute walk from the center; some find the style dated (others find it a plus); small gym. [$] *Rooms from: €800* ✉ *Via Tragara 57* ☎ *081/8370844* 🌐 *www.hoteltragara.com* 🕓 *Closed mid-Oct.–mid-Apr.* 🛏 *44 rooms* 🍴 *Free Breakfast.*

$$$$ HOTEL Fodor's Choice ★ **Quisisana.** Some say there are three villages on Capri: Capri Town, Anacapri, and this celebrated landmark hotel, which looms large in the island's mythology, drawing "didn't I meet you in Saint Tropez?" guests who wouldn't *dream* of staying anywhere else. **Pros:** luxe atmosphere on a large scale; stumbling distance from La Piazzetta; top spa facilities. **Cons:** minimum three-night stay some periods; convention-size and far from cozy; quality of customer service can be patchy. [$] *Rooms from: €450* ✉ *Via Camerelle 2* ☎ *081/8370788* 🌐 *www.quisisana.com* 🕓 *Closed Nov.–mid-Mar.* 🛏 *147 rooms* 🍴 *Free Breakfast.*

$$ B&B/INN **Villa Krupp.** Occupying a beautiful house overlooking the idyllic Gardens of Augustus, this historic hostelry was once the home of Maxim Gorky, whose guests included Lenin. **Pros:** direct access to the Gardens of Augustus; stunning views; much-needed porter service. **Cons:** a lot of steps to be negotiated; rooms are simple; breakfast doesn't match the views. [$] *Rooms*

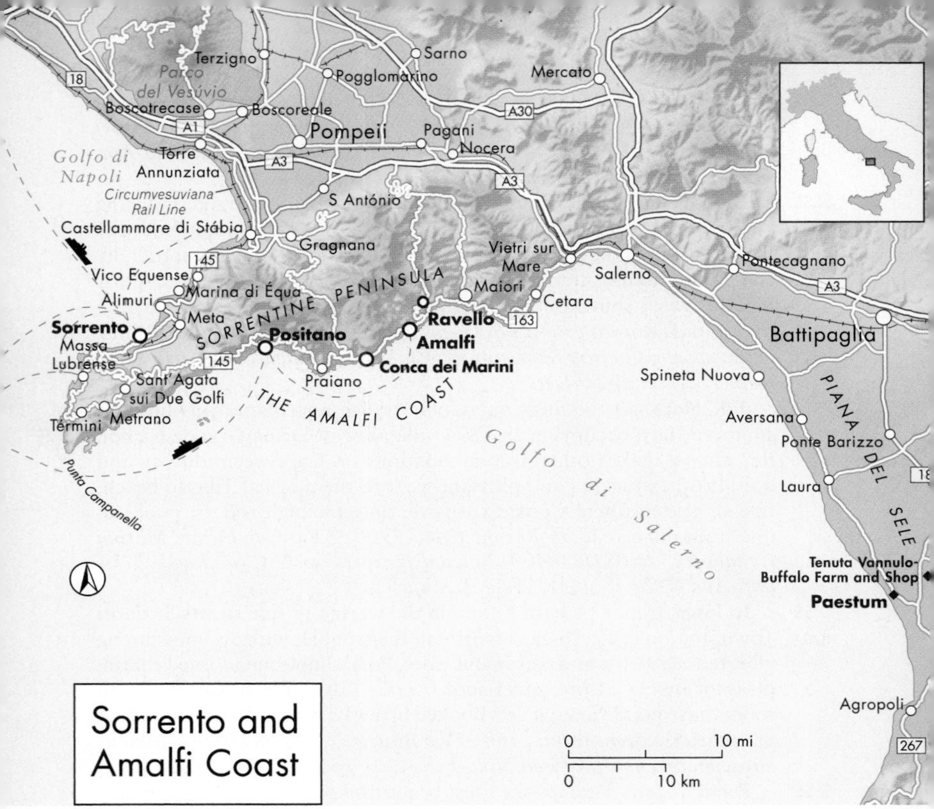

from: €160 ✉ *Viale Matteotti 12* ☎ *081/8370362* 🌐 *www.villakrupp.com* ⏲ *Closed Nov.–Mar.* 🛏 *12 rooms* 🍴 *Free Breakfast.*

$$$ HOTEL 🏨 **Villa Sarah.** Few hotels offer such a quintessentially Caprese spirit as this; located in one of the island's most pleasant residential quarters, you'll feel like a guest in a private villa. **Pros:** gorgeous pool; lush gardens; unfussy decor. **Cons:** a long and steep climb from the Piazzetta; many rooms rather small; pool not large. [$] *Rooms from: €210* ✉ *Via Tiberio 3/a* ☎ *081/8377817* 🌐 *www.villasarah.it* ⏲ *Closed Nov.–Mar.* 🛏 *20 rooms* 🍴 *Free Breakfast.*

SORRENTO AND THE SORRENTINE PENINSULA

As the hub for a whole banquet of must-see sites—Pompeii and Naples to the north, Capri to the west, and the Amalfi Coast to the south—the beautiful, Belle Époque resort town of Sorrento is unequaled. The rest of the Sorrentine Peninsula, with plains and limestone outcroppings, watchtowers and Roman ruins, groves and beaches, monasteries and villages, winding paths leading to isolated coves, and panoramic views of the bays of both Naples and Salerno, remains relatively undiscovered.

SORRENTO

50 km (31 miles) south of Naples.

Winding along a cliff above a small beach and two harbors, the town is split in two by a narrow ravine formed by a former mountain stream. To the east, dozens of hotels line busy Via Correale along the cliff—many have "grand" included in their names, and some indeed are. To the west, however, is the historic sector, which still enchants. It's a relatively flat area, with winding, stone-paved lanes bordered by balconied buildings, some joined by medieval stone arches. The central piazza is named after the poet Torquato Tasso, born here in 1544. This part of town is a delightful place to walk through. Craftspeople are often at work in their stalls and shops and are happy to let you watch; in fact, that's the point. Music spots and bars cluster in the side streets near Piazza Tasso.

GETTING HERE AND AROUND

From downtown Naples, take a Circumvesuviana train from Stazione Centrale (Piazza Garibaldi) or a hydrofoil from Molo Beverello. If you're coming directly from the airport in Naples, pick up a direct bus to Sorrento. By car, take the A3 Naples–Salerno autostrada, exiting at Castellammare, and then following signs for Penisola Sorrentina, then for Sorrento.

VISITOR INFORMATION

Contact Azienda Autonoma di Soggiorno Sorrento-Sant'Agnello. ⊠ *Via L. De Maio 35* ☎ *081/8074033* ⊕ *www.sorrentotourism.com.*

EXPLORING

Convento di San Francesco. Near the Villa Comunale gardens and sharing its view over the Bay of Naples, the convent is celebrated for its 12th-century cloister. Filled with greenery and flowers, the Moorish-style cloister has interlaced pointed arches of tufa rock, alternating with octagonal columns topped by elegant capitals, supporting smaller arches. The combination makes a suitably evocative setting for summer concerts and theatrical presentations. The church portal is particularly impressive, with the 16th-century door (moved from a church across the road in 1947) featuring *intarsia* (inlaid) work. The interior's 17th-century decoration includes an altarpiece, by a student of Francesco Solimena, depicting St. Francis receiving the stigmata. The convent is now an art school, where students' works are often exhibited. ⊠ *Piazza S. Francesco* ☎ *081/8781269* 🎟 *Free.*

Marina Grande. Close to the historic quarter (but not that close—many locals prefer to use the town bus to shuttle up and down the steep hill), the port, or *borgo*, of the Marina Grande is Sorrento's fishing harbor. In recent years it has become unashamedly touristy, with outdoor restaurants and cafés encroaching on what little remains of the original harbor. Most establishments down here are geared to the English-speaking market—expect a "Good evening" rather than a "Buona sera" as you enter. The Marina still remains a magical location for an evening out on the waterfront, but if you're interested in a dip—given the dubious sea-water quality here and the cramped conditions—head out instead toward Massa Lubrense and Nerano. Don't confuse this harbor with Marina Piccola, at the base of the cliff, below Piazza Tasso and the Hotel Excelsior Vittoria; that's the area where ferries and hydrofoils dock. ✉ *Via del Mare.*

Museo Correale di Terranova. In an 18th-century villa with a lovely garden, on land given to the patrician Correale family by Queen Joan of Anjou in 1428, this museum is a highlight of Sorrento and a must for connoisseurs of the *seicento* (17th century). It has an eclectic private collection amassed by the count of Terranova and his brother—one of the finest devoted to Neapolitan paintings, decorative arts, and porcelains. Magnificent 18th- and 19th-century inlaid tables by Giuseppe Gargiulo, Capodimonte porcelains, and rococo portrait miniatures are reminders of the age when pleasure and delight were everything. Also on view are regional Greek and Roman archaeological finds, medieval marble work, glasswork, old master paintings, 17th-century majolicas—even the poet Tasso's death mask. The building itself is fairly charmless, with few period rooms, but the garden offers an allée of palm trees, citrus groves, floral nurseries, and an esplanade with a panoramic view of the Sorrento Coast. ✉ *Via Correale 50* ☎ *081/8781846* 🌐 *www.museocorreale.it* 🎟 *€8* ⏲ *Closed Mon.*

Sedile Dominova. Enchanting showpiece of the Largo Dominova—the little square that is the heart of Sorrento's historic quarter—the Sedile Dominova is a picturesque open loggia with expansive arches, balustrades, and a green-and-yellow-tile cupola, originally constructed in the 16th century. The open-air structure is frescoed with 18th-century trompe-l'oeil columns and the family coats of arms, which once belonged to the *sedile* (seat), the town council where nobles met to discuss civic problems as early as the Angevin period. Today Sorrentines still like to congregate around the umbrella-topped tables near the tiny square. ✉ *Largo Dominova, at Via S. Cesareo and Via P.R. Giuliani* 🎟 *Free.*

Villa Comunale. The largest public park in Sorrento sits on a cliff top overlooking the entire Bay of Naples. It offers benches, flowers, palms, and people-watching, plus a seamless vista that stretches from Capri to Vesuvius. From here steps lead down to Sorrento's main harbor, the Marina Piccola. ✉ *Adjoining church of San Francesco.*

WHERE TO EAT

$$ SOUTHERN ITALIAN

🍴 **Da Emilia.** Near the Marina Grande, and not the most visually prepossessing place in Sorrento, this spot has rickety wooden tables and red-check tablecloths, a refreshing change from the town's (occasionally pretentious) elegance. Go for a plate of honest spaghetti with clams, wash it down with a carafe of the slightly acidic white wine, and watch the fishermen mending their nets. **Known for:** tasty and fresh seafood combos like mussels with Sorrentine lemons; harbor terrace above the rocks; friendly and family-run. [$] *Average main: €20* ✉ *Via Marina Grande 62* ☎ *081/8072720* 🌐 *www.daemilia.it* ⏲ *Closed Nov.–Feb.*

$$$$ SOUTHERN ITALIAN Fodor's Choice ★

🍴 **Don Alfonso 1890.** Don Alfonso has been called the best restaurant in Italy, and it remains a gastronomic giant. The restaurant, a pioneer in upscale farm-to-table cuisine, grows its own produce on a small farm nearby. **Known for:** top-quality dining experience; Slow Food pioneer; Punta Campanella local garden produce. [$] *Average main: €50* ✉ *Corso Sant'Agata 13, Sant'Agata sui Due Golfi* ☎ *081/8780026* 🌐 *www.*

donalfonso.com ⏲ *Closed Mon. and Tues., and Nov.–Mar. No lunch Tues. mid-June–mid-Sept.*

$$ SOUTHERN ITALIAN Fodor's Choice ★ 🍴 **Il Delfino.** Right on the sea, this restaurant is attached to a bathing stabilimento, and you can eat in the sunshine or in a glassed-in nautical-motif dining area. Although you won't see many locals here—they're unlikely to be impressed by the four-language menus—seafood platters are fresh and flavorful, and this informal venue also has a snack bar for light meals. **Known for:** great views over Marina Grande and beyond; bountiful portions; terrace next to the bathing jetty. [$] *Average main: €22* ✉ *Via Marina Grande 216* ☎ *081/8782038* ⏲ *Closed Nov.–Mar.*

$$$$ SOUTHERN ITALIAN Fodor's Choice ★ 🍴 **Ristorante Museo Caruso.** Sorrentine favorites, including *acquerello* (fresh fish appetizer) and ravioli with crab and zucchini sauce, are tweaked creatively here. The staff are warm and helpful, the singer on the sound system is the long-departed "fourth tenor" himself, and the operatic memorabilia (including posters and old photos of Caruso) is viewed in a flattering blush-pink light. **Known for:** Caruso memorabilia aplenty; Turna a Sorriento and the Neapolitan songbook; tasting menus. [$] *Average main: €45* ✉ *Via S. Antonino 12* ☎ *081/8073156* 🌐 *www.ristorantemuseocaruso.com.*

$$ SOUTHERN ITALIAN Fodor's Choice ★ 🍴 **Ristorante 'o Parrucchiano La Favorita.** This restaurant is in a sprawling, multilevel, high-ceiling greenhouse and orchard, with tables and chairs set amid enough tropical greenery to fill a Victorian conservatory; the effect is enchantingly 19th century. Opened in 1868 by an ex-priest (*'o parrucchiano* means "the priest" in the local dialect), La Favorita continues to serve classic Sorrentine cuisine. **Known for:** fecund greenhouse and terrace foliage and fruit; signature cannelloni created in 1870; special occasions and weddings. [$] *Average main: €18* ✉ *Corso Italia 71* ☎ *081/8781321* 🌐 *www.parrucchiano.com* ⏲ *Closed Wed. mid-Nov.–mid-Mar.*

WHERE TO STAY

$$$$ HOTEL Fodor's Choice ★ 🏨 **Bellevue Syrene.** This luxurious retreat, magnificently set on a bluff high over the Bay of Naples, is one of Italy's most legendary hotels, and refurbishment has injected new energy to the property, along with streamlined, Art Deco touches. **Pros:** impeccable design elements; elegant common areas; half board available. **Cons:** very expensive; parking is €25 a day; small pool. [$] *Rooms from: €550* ✉ *Piazza della Vittoria 5* ☎ *081/8781024* 🌐 *www.bellevue.it* ⏲ *Closed Jan.–Mar.* 🛏 *49 rooms* 🍽 *Free Breakfast.*

$$$$ HOTEL Fodor's Choice ★ 🏨 **Excelsior Vittoria.** Overlooking the Bay of Naples, this luxurious Belle Époque dream has been in the same family since 1834; the public salons are virtual museums, with Victorian love seats and *stile liberty* (Art Nouveau) ornamentation. **Pros:** beyond the protected gates you're in the heart of town; gardens buffer city noise; grand spaces and handsome furnishings. **Cons:** not all rooms have sea views; some rooms are rather small; front desk can be cold. [$] *Rooms from: €635* ✉ *Piazza Tasso 34* ☎ *081/8777111* 🌐 *www.exvitt.it* ⏲ *Closed Jan.–Mar.* 🛏 *83 rooms* 🍽 *Free Breakfast.*

$$$$ HOTEL 🏨 **La Favorita.** The glamorous lobby may be a white-on-white extravaganza of Caprese columns, tufted sofas, shimmering crystal chandeliers, ecclesiastical silver objects, and gilded Baroque mirrors, but the

charming staff ensure the vibe is elegantly casual. **Pros:** central location; beautiful terrace; idyllic garden. **Cons:** no views from guest rooms; overpriced in the off-season; rooms near the bar noisy after midnight. [$] *Rooms from: €539* ✉ *Via T. Tasso 61* ☎ *081/8782031* 🌐 *www.hotel-lafavorita.com* ⏲ *Closed Jan.–Mar.* 🛏 *85 rooms* 🍴 *Free Breakfast.*

$$ HOTEL 🏨 **Settimo Cielo.** Even if your wallet won't allow a stay at one of Sorrento's grand hotels, you can still find lodgings overlooking the water, and this hotel on the road to Capo Sorrento is an excellent choice for budget travelers. **Pros:** plenty of parking; excellent views; reasonable prices. **Cons:** 15-minute walk along busy road into Sorrento; no-frills decor; walls not soundproofed. [$] *Rooms from: €140* ✉ *Via Capo 27* ☎ *081/8781012* 🌐 *www.hotelsettimocielo.com* 🛏 *20 rooms* 🍴 *Free Breakfast.*

THE AMALFI COAST

One of the most gorgeous places on Earth, this corner of the Campania region captivates visitors today just as it has for centuries. Poets and millionaires have long journeyed here to see and sense its legendary sights: perfect, precariously perched Positano; Amalfi, a shimmering medieval city; romantic, mountain-high Ravello; and ancient Paestum, with its three legendary Greek temples. Today, the coast's scenic beauty makes it a top destination, drawing visitors from all over the world, who agree with UNESCO's 1997 decision to make this a World Heritage Site. This entire area is also a honeymoon haven—it is arguably the most romantic stretch of coastline in the world.

The justly famed jewels along the water are Positano, Amalfi, and Ravello, but smaller villages—including Conca dei Marini, Furore, Atrani, Scala, and Cetara—offer their own charms. The top towns along the Amalfi Drive may fill up in high season with tour buses, but in the countryside not much seems to have changed since the Middle Ages: mountains are still terraced and farmed for citrus, olives, and wine, and the sea is dotted with fishermen's boats. Vertiginously high villages, dominated by the spires of *chiese* (churches), are crammed with houses spilling down hillsides to the bay and navigated by flights of steps called *scalinatelle* that often lead to outlooks that take your breath away.

Considering the natural splendor of this region, it's no surprise that it has some of the most beautiful beaches in the world. White, sunbaked villages rise above cliffs hollowed out with grottoes and crystal lagoons lapped by emerald green water. Larger beaches, like those in Positano and Amalfi, are easily accessible, but the magic often lies in finding hidden coves and scenic spots, such as the picture-perfect Marina di Praia.

POSITANO

14 km (9 miles) east of Sorrento, 57 km (34 miles) south of Naples.

The most photographed fishing village in the world, this fabled locale is home to some 4,000 *positanesi,* who are joined daily by hordes arriving from Capri, Sorrento, and Amalfi. The town clings to the Monti Lattari with arcaded, cubist buildings, set in tiers up the mountainside, in shades of rose, peach, purple, and ivory.

GETTING HERE AND AROUND

SITA buses leave from the Circumvesuviana train station in Sorrento. Buses also run from Naples and, in summer, Rome. There is a ferry from Sorrento in the summer months.

A word of advice: Wear comfortable walking shoes and be sure your back and legs are strong enough to negotiate those picturesque but daunting and ladderlike scalinatelle. In the center of town, where no buses can go, you're on your own from Piazza dei Mulini. To begin your explorations, make a left turn onto the boutique-flanked Via dei Mulini and head down to the Palazzo Murat, Santa Maria Assunta, and the beach—one of the most charming walks of the coast.

VISITOR INFORMATION

Contact Azienda Autonoma Soggiorno e Turismo. ⊠ *Via Regina Giovanna 13* ☎ *089/875067* ⊕ *www.aziendaturismopositano.it.*

14

EXPLORING

Palazzo Murat. Past a bevy of resort boutiques, head to Via dei Mulini to view the prettiest garden in Positano: the 18th-century courtyard of the Palazzo Murat, named for Joachim Murat, who sensibly chose the palazzo as his summer residence. This was where Murat, designated by his brother-in-law Napoléon as King of Naples in 1808, came to forget the demands of power and lead a simpler life. He built this grand abode (now a hotel) near the church of Santa Maria Assunta, just steps from the main beach. ⊠ *Via dei Mulini 23* ☎ *089/875177* ⊕ *www.palazzomurat.it.*

Santa Maria Assunta. The Chiesa Madre, or parish church of Santa Maria Assunta, lies just south of the Palazzo Murat, its green-and-yellow majolica dome topped by a perky cupola visible from just about anywhere in town. Built on the site of the former Benedictine abbey of Saint Vito, the 13th-century Romanesque structure was almost completely rebuilt in 1700. The last piece of the ancient mosaic floor can be seen under glass behind the altar. Note the carved wooden Christ, a masterpiece of devotional religious art, with its bathetic face and bloodied knees, on view before the altar. At the altar is a Byzantine 13th-century painting on wood of Madonna with Child, known popularly as the Black Virgin. A replica is carried to the beach every August 15 to celebrate the Feast of the Assumption. Legend claims the painting was once stolen by Saracen pirates, who, fleeing in a raging storm, heard from a voice on high saying, "*Posa, posa*" (Put it down, put it down). When they placed the image on the beach near the church, the storm calmed, as did the Saracens. Embedded over the doorway of the church's bell tower, set across the tiny piazza, is a medieval bas-relief of fishes, a fox, and a pistrice (the mythical half-dragon, half-dog sea monster). This is one of the few relics of the medieval abbey of Saint Vito. The Oratorio houses historic statues from the Sacristy; renovations to the Crypt have unearthed part of an extensive Roman villa, buried by the AD 79 eruption and now open for group visits; contact the tourist office for the latest information. Archaeologists have so far brought to light colorful frescoes, ornate bronze works, and an ossuary with a tufo-hewn semicircle of individual seats for skeletons. ⊠ *Piazza Flavio Gioia* ☎ *089/875480* ⊕ *www.chiesapositano.it.*

FAMILY   **Spiaggia Grande.** The walkway from the Piazza Flavio Gioia leads down to the Spiaggia Grande, Positano's main beach, bordered by an esplanade and some of the town's best restaurants. Surrounded by the spectacular amphitheater of houses and villas that leapfrog up the hillsides of Monte Comune and Monte Sant'Angelo, this remains one of the most picturesque beaches in the world. Although it faces stiff competition from Spiaggia di Fornillo beach, which is bigger, the Spiaggia Grande wins the beauty contest hands down. **Amenities:** food and drink; lifeguards; showers; toilets; water sports. **Best for:** snorkeling; swimming. ⊠ *Spiaggia Grande.*

FAMILY   **Via Positanesi d'America.** Just before the ferry ticket booths to the right of
Fodor's Choice   Spiaggia Grande, a tiny road that is the loveliest seaside walkway on the
★   entire coast rises up and borders the cliffs leading to the Fornillo beach. The road is named for the town's large number of 19th-century emigrants to the United States—Positano virtually survived during World War II thanks to the money and packages their descendants sent back home. Halfway up the path lies the Torre Trasìta (Trasìta Tower), the most distinctive of Positano's three coastline defense towers. Now a residence occasionally available for summer rental, the tower was used to spot pirate raids. As you continue along the Via Positanesi d'America, you'll pass a tiny inlet and an emerald cove before Fornillo beach comes into view. ⊠ *Via Positanesi d'America.*

WHERE TO EAT

$$ ✕ **Da Adolfo.** On a little beach where pirates used to build and launch
SOUTHERN   boats, this laid-back trattoria has long been a favorite Positano land-
ITALIAN   mark. The pirates are long gone, but their descendants now operate a free ferry to and from Positano (every half hour in the morning)—look for the boat with the red fish on the mast named for the restaurant—or you can make the steep descent from the main coastal road at Laurito. **Known for:** secluded cove accessed by boat; fresh seafood classics such as seasonal squid; covered terrace overlooking the beach. $ *Average main: €16* ⊠ *Spiaggia di Laurito, Via Laurito 40* ☎ *089/875022* ⊕ *www.daadolfo.com* ☉ *Closed Oct.–Apr.*

$$ ✕ **Lo Guarracino.** In a supremely romantic setting, this partly arbor-
SOUTHERN   covered, poised-on-a-cleft restaurant is about the most idyllic place to
ITALIAN   enjoy lemon pasta and a glass of vino as you watch the yachts come and
Fodor's Choice   go. Set a few steps above Positano's prettiest seaside path, the terrace
★   vista takes in the cliffs, the sea, Li Galli islands, Spiaggia del Fornillo, and Torre Clavel. **Known for:** fabulous views; wood-fired oven for pizze and seafood; romantic Robinson Crusoe–esque terrace. $ *Average main: €22* ⊠ *Via Positanesi d'America 12* ☎ *089/875794* ⊕ *www. loguarracinopositano.it* ☉ *Closed Jan.–Mar.*

$$$ ✕ **Next2.** Wrought-iron gates open from the main thoroughfare of Via
SOUTHERN   Pasitea into Next2's outdoor dining area, which has a stunning view
ITALIAN   over Positano. The two owners are passionate about fine cuisine, particularly seafood—try the pan-seared *bonito* (local tuna) with spinach and sweet-and-sour onions—and they'll walk you through the menu and wine list. **Known for:** exquisitely crafted dishes; excellent wine

selection; cocktails with novel, fresh infusions. $ *Average main: €26* ⊠ *Via Pasitea 242* ☎ *089/8123516* ⊕ *www.next2.it* ⊗ *No lunch.*

$$
SOUTHERN
ITALIAN
Fodor'sChoice
★

✕ **Ristorante il Ritrovo.** Sitting in the tiny town square of Montepertuso, 1,500 feet up the mountainside from Positano, the Ritrovo has been noted for its cucina for more than 20 years. Call for the free shuttle service to and from Positano, and take a seat on the terrace's frescoed wood-paneled dining area. **Known for:** airy, tranquil mountainside location; trademark zuppa saracena seafood soup; amiable padrone Salvatò. $ *Average main: €22* ⊠ *Via Montepertuso 77, Montepertuso* ☎ *089/812005* ⊕ *www.ilritrovo.com* ⊗ *Closed mid-Jan.–mid-Feb.*

WHERE TO STAY

$$$$
HOTEL

🏨 **Hotel Eden Roc.** The closest hotel to the Sponda bus stop, this family-run luxury property provides spectacular views and service. **Pros:** large rooms; magical views over town; electric car rental available. **Cons:** on the main road (take care as you exit the hotel); a bit of a climb from the town center; some rooms are very dated. $ *Rooms from: €360* ⊠ *Via G. Marconi 110* ☎ *089/875844* ⊕ *www.edenroc.it* ⊗ *Closed mid-Nov.–Feb.* ⬳ *25 rooms* ⊙l *Free Breakfast.*

$$$
HOTEL

🏨 **Hotel L'Ancora.** Commanding expansive views of the deep blue and of local Mediterranean color, this hotel is set back a little from the main road and a few-minutes' walk up from the main beach. **Pros:** bright and sunny; all rooms have balconies or terraces and sea views; not far from the Sponda bus stop. **Cons:** a slight climb from the main drag; no on-site pool; below-par breakfast. $ *Rooms from: €290* ⊠ *Via Cristoforo Colombo 36* ☎ *089/875318* ⊕ *www.hotelancorapositano.com* ⊗ *Closed Nov.–Mar.* ⬳ *18 rooms* ⊙l *Free Breakfast.*

$$
HOTEL

🏨 **La Fenice.** This tiny, unpretentious hotel on the outskirts of Positano beckons with bougainvillea-laden views, castaway cottages, and a turquoise seawater pool—all perched over a private beach. **Pros:** small private beach with kayaks; 250 steps to private beach; secluded pool. **Cons:** a 10-minute walk to town; some rooms very small and need a refresh; disappointing breakfasts. $ *Rooms from: €165* ⊠ *Via G. Marconi 4* ☎ *089/875513* ⊕ *www.lafenicepositano.com* ⊗ *Sometimes closed Dec.–Feb.* ⬳ *14 rooms* ⊙l *Free Breakfast.*

$$$$
HOTEL
Fodor'sChoice
★

🏨 **Le Sirenuse.** As legendary as its namesake sirens, this 18th-century palazzo has long set the standard for luxury in Italian hotels: it opened in 1951 with just 12 rooms (John Steinbeck stayed here while writing "Positano," for *Harper's Bazaar* in 1953) and now sprawls over eight floors, where extravagantly stylish guest rooms are accented with antiques and fine linens. **Pros:** unrivaled views, including from poolside terrace; many rooms have whirlpool tubs; close to the bus stop. **Cons:** a bit of a climb from the town center; lower-priced rooms are small; can be noisy. $ *Rooms from: €900* ⊠ *Via Cristoforo Colombo 30* ☎ *089/875066* ⊕ *www.sirenuse.it* ⊗ *Closed Nov.–Mar.* ⬳ *58 rooms* ⊙l *Free Breakfast.*

$$$$
HOTEL

🏨 **Palazzo Murat.** A perfectly central location above the beachside church of Santa Maria Assunta—and an even more perfect entrance through a bougainvillea-draped patio and garden—help make the Murat a top lodging contender. **Pros:** once a regal residence; stunning garden and surroundings; shops and passeggiata on the doorstep. **Cons:** only five rooms have seaside views; constant stream of curious day-trippers; not all balconies secluded.

14

$ *Rooms from: €500* ✉ *Via dei Mulini 23* ☎ *089/875177* 🌐 *www.palazzomurat.it* ⏲ *Closed Nov.–Mar.* 🛏 *31 rooms* 🍴 *Free Breakfast.*

NIGHTLIFE

Fodor's Choice ★ **La Brezza.** A few steps up from (and overlooking) the Spiaggia Grande, popular La Brezza is a fine spot to enjoy a cocktail or one of the bar's signature smoothies. ✉ *Via del Brigantino 1* ☎ *089/875811* 🌐 *www.labrezzapositano.com* ⏲ *Closed Nov.–Mar.*

L'Africana. Off a mile-long footpath from the Marina del Praia—or accessed via an elevator from Statale 163—L'Africana is a golden-oldie classic from the 1960s. With an open-to-the-sea atmosphere, a cave for a dance floor, and wildish shows with partial nudity, you can party the night away here, as Jackie Kennedy once did. The nightclub runs boats from Positano on Saturday—transfer can also be arranged from other points along the coast. Just ring them to get picked up. ✉ *Via Terramare 2, Praiano* ☎ *089/874858, 331/5330612 cell phone* 🌐 *www.africanafamousclub.com.*

CONCA DEI MARINI

13 km (8 miles) east of Positano, 29 km (18 miles) east of Sorrento.

A longtime favorite of the off-duty rich and famous, Conca dei Marini (the name means "seafarers' basin") hides many of its charms, as any sublime hideaway should. On a curve in the road sits the village's most noteworthy attraction, the Emerald Grotto.

EXPLORING

FAMILY **Grotta dello Smeraldo** (*Emerald Grotto*). The tacky road sign and squadron of tour buses may scream tourist trap, and in truth it can be a tad underwhelming. The karstic cave was originally part of the shore, but the lowest end sank into the sea. Intense greenish light filters into the water from an arch below sea level and is reflected off the cavern walls. You visit the Grotta dello Smeraldo, which is filled with huge stalactites and stalagmites, on a large rowboat. Don't let the boatman's constant spiel detract from the experience—just tune out and enjoy the sparkles, shapes, and brilliant colors. The light at the grotto is best from noon to 3 pm. You can take an elevator from the coast road down to the grotto, or in the summer you can drive to Amalfi and arrive by boat (€10, excluding the grotto's €5 admission fee). Companies in Positano, Amalfi, and elsewhere along the coast provide passage to the grotto, but consider one of the longer boat trips that explore Punta Campanella, Li Galli, and the more secluded spots along the coast. ✉ *Via Smeraldo, west of Capo di Conca* ☎ *089/831535* 🎟 *€5* ⏲ *Closed in adverse weather conditions.*

WHERE TO STAY

$$$$ HOTEL Fodor's Choice ★ 🏨 **Monastero Santa Rosa Hotel & Spa.** Set in a 17th-century monastery on the dramatic cliffs above the Amalfi Coast, this boutique resort is destined to become one of Italy's most exclusive retreats. **Pros:** excellent service; meticulously restored property with spa; worth the splurge. **Cons:** out of reach for many budgets; some rooms could be more spacious; a bit remote. $ *Rooms from: €650* ✉ *Via Roma 2* ☎ *089/8321199*

⊕ *www.monasterosantarosa.com* ⊙ *Closed Nov.–mid-Apr.* ⊰ *20 rooms*
†⊙ Free Breakfast.*

AMALFI

18 km (11 miles) east of Positano, 35 km (22 miles) east of Sorrento.
At first glance, it's hard to imagine that this resort destination was one of
the world's great naval powers, and a sturdy rival of Genoa and Pisa for
control of the Mediterranean in the 11th and 12th centuries. Once the
seat of the Amalfi Maritime Republic, the town is set in a verdant valley of
the Lattari Mountains, with cream-color and pastel-hue buildings tightly
packing a gorge on the Bay of Salerno. The harbor, which once launched
the greatest fleet in Italy, now bobs with ferries and blue-and-white fishing
boats. The main street, lined with shops and *pasticcerie,* has replaced a
raging mountain torrent, and terraced hills flaunt the green and gold of
lemon groves. Bearing testimony to its great trade with Tunis, Tripoli, and
Algiers, Amalfi remains honeycombed with Arab-Sicilian cloisters and
covered passages. In a way Amalfi has become great again, showing off
its medieval glory days with sea pageants, convents-turned-hotels, ancient
paper mills, covered streets, and its glimmering cathedral.

GETTING HERE AND AROUND
From April to October the optimal way to get to Amalfi is by ferry from
Salerno. SitaSud buses run from Naples and Sorrento throughout the
year. By car, take the Statale 163 (Amalfitana) from outside Sorrento
or Salerno, or take the Angri exit on the A3 autostrada and cross the
mountainous Valico di Chiunsi.

VISITOR INFORMATION
Contact Amalfi Tourism Office. ⊠ *Via delle Repubbliche Marinare 27*
☏ *089/871107* ⊕ *www.amalfitouristoffice.it.*

EXPLORING
Fodor's Choice **Duomo di Sant' Andrea.** Complicated, grand, delicate, and dominating,
★ the 9th-century Amalfi cathedral has been remodeled over the years
with Romanesque, Byzantine, Gothic, and Baroque elements, but
retains a predominantly Arab-Norman style. Built around 1266 as a
burial ground for Amalfi's elite, the cloister, the first stop on a tour
of the cathedral, is one of southern Italy's architectural treasures. Its
flower-and-palm-filled quadrangle has a series of exceptionally delicate intertwining arches on slender double columns. The chapel at the
back of the cloister leads into the 9th-century basilica, now a museum
housing sarcophagi, sculpture, Neapolitan goldsmiths' artwork, and
other treasures from the cathedral complex. Steps from the **basilica**
lead down into the **Cripta di Sant'Andrea** (Crypt of Saint Andrew). The
cathedral above was built in the 13th century to house the saint's bones,
which came from Constantinople. Following the one-way traffic up to
the cathedral, you can admire the elaborate polychrome marbles and
painted, coffered ceilings from its 18th-century restoration. ⊠ *Piazza*
Duomo ☏ *089/871324* ⊕ *www.parrocchiaamalfi.com* ▦ *€3* ⊙ *Gener-*
ally closed early Jan. and Feb. except for daily services.

FAMILY Fodor's Choice ★ **Museo della Carta** (*Paper Museum*). Uphill from town, the Valle dei Mulini (Valley of the Mills) was for centuries Amalfi's center for papermaking, an ancient trade learned from the Arabs, who learned it from the Chinese. Beginning in the 12th century, former flour mills were converted to produce paper made from cotton and linen. The paper industry was a success, and by 1811 more than a dozen mills here, with more along the coast, were humming. Natural waterpower ensured that the handmade paper was cost-effective. Yet, by the late 1800s the industry had moved to Naples and other more geographically accessible areas. Flooding in 1954 closed most of the mills for good, and many have been converted into private housing. The **Museo della Carta** (Museum of Paper) opened in 1971 in a 15th-century mill: paper samples, tools of the trade, old machinery, and the audiovisual presentation are all enlightening. You can also participate in a paper-making laboratory. ✉ *Via delle Cartiere 23* ☎ *089/8304561* 🌐 *www.museodellacarta.it* 🎫 *€4, includes guided tour* 🕒 *Closed Feb., and Mon. and Thurs. Nov.–Jan.*

WHERE TO EAT

$$ SOUTHERN ITALIAN 🍴 **Al Teatro.** Once a children's theater, this informal and charming white-stucco restaurant in the medieval quarter is 50 steps above the main drag. One house specialty is the grilled squid and calamari with mint sauce, reflecting its position—suspended between sea and mountains. **Known for:** mamma and daughter's warm hospitality; great pizza from wood-fired oven; relaxed gem hidden away. [$] *Average main: €16* ✉ *Via Ercolano Marini 19/21* ☎ *089/872473* 🕒 *Closed Wed., and Jan.–mid-Feb.*

$ SOUTHERN ITALIAN FAMILY 🍴 **Il Tari.** Locals highly recommend this little ristorante a few minutes' walk north of the Duomo. Named after the medieval coin of the Amalfi Republic, the restaurant occupies a former stable whose space has altered little outwardly since those equine days, though the white walls, appealing local art, crisp tablecloths, large panoramic photos, and tile floors make it cozy enough. **Known for:** good-value set-menu options; decent thin-crust pizza; à la carte seafood specials. [$] *Average main: €13* ✉ *Via Pietro Capuano 9–11* ☎ *089/871832* 🌐 *www.amalfiristorantetari.it* 🕒 *Closed Tues.*

$$$$ SOUTHERN ITALIAN 🍴 **La Caravella.** No wonder this is considered the most romantic restaurant in Amalfi, with lace-covered tables, *ciuccio* (donkey) ceramics, tall candles, and fresh floral bouquets in salons graced with frescoes and marble floors. Opened in 1959, it became the first in southern Italy to earn a Michelin star in 1966, and once drew a gilded guest list that included the likes of Andy Warhol and Federico Fellini. **Known for:** the Mezzogiorno's pioneering fine-dining eatery; cheerful dining room full of colorful ceramics; wine dealer expertise. [$] *Average main: €40* ✉ *Via Matteo Camera 12, near Arsenale* ☎ *089/871029* 🌐 *www.ristorantelacaravella.it* 🕒 *Closed Tues., and Nov. and Jan.*

WHERE TO STAY

$ HOTEL 🏨 **Albergo Sant'Andrea.** Occupying one of the best locations in town, this tiny, family-run *pensione* is just across from the magnificent steps leading to Amalfi's cathedral. **Pros:** on the main square; divine views of the Duomo; reliable budget option. **Cons:** steep flight of steps to entrance; very simple rooms (some small); on the piazza, so expect noise. [$] *Rooms from: €90* ✉ *Via Duca Mansone I* ☎ *089/871145*

🌐 *www.albergosantandrea.it* ⏲ *Closed Feb. and Mar.* 🛏 *8 rooms* 🍴 *Free Breakfast.*

$$$$ HOTEL Fodor's Choice ★ 🏨 **Grand Hotel Convento di Amalfi.** This fabled medieval monastery was lauded by such guests as Longfellow and Wagner, and though recent modernization has sacrificed some of its historic charm, it remains an iconic destination. **Pros:** a slice of paradise; iconic Amalfi; sublime terrace and garden walkways. **Cons:** traditionalists will miss its old-world charm; a 10-minute walk to town; limited dining options. [$] *Rooms from: €675* ✉ *Via Annunziatella 46* ☎ *089/8736711* 🌐 *www.ghconventodiamalfi.com* ⏲ *Closed Nov.–Mar.* 🛏 *53 rooms* 🍴 *Free Breakfast.*

RAVELLO

14

5 km (3 miles) northeast of Amalfi, 40 km (25 miles) northeast of Sorrento.

Fodor's Choice ★ Positano may focus on pleasure, and Amalfi on history, but cool, serene Ravello revels in refinement. Thrust over the S163 and the Bay of Salerno on a mountain buttress, below forests of chestnut and ash, above terraced lemon groves and vineyards, it early on beckoned the affluent with its island-in-the-sky views and secluded defensive positioning. Gardens out of the *Arabian Nights,* pastel palazzi, tucked-away piazzas with medieval fountains, architecture ranging from Romano-Byzantine to Norman-Saracen, and those sweeping blue-water, blue-sky vistas have inspired a panoply of large personalities. Today, many visitors flock here to discover this paradisiacal place, some to enjoy the town's celebrated two-month-long summer music festival (the Ravello Festival, 🌐 *www.ravellofestival.com*), others just to stroll through the hillside streets to gape at the bluer-than-blue panoramas of sea and sky.

GETTING HERE AND AROUND

Buses from Amalfi make the 20-minute trip along white-knuckle roads. From Naples, take the A3 Naples–Salerno autostrada; then exit at Angri and follow signs for Ravello. The journey takes about 75 minutes. Save yourself the trouble of driving by hiring a car and driver.

VISITOR INFORMATION

Contact Azienda Autonoma Soggiorno e Turismo. ✉ *Via Roma 18b* ☎ *089/857096* 🌐 *www.ravellotime.it.*

EXPLORING

Auditorium Oscar Niemeyer. Crowning Via della Repubblica and the hillside, which overlooks the spectacular Bay of Salerno, Auditorium Niemeyer is a startling piece of modernist architecture. Designed with a dramatically curved, all-white roof by the Brazilian architect Oscar Niemeyer (designer of Brasília), it was conceived as an alternative indoor venue for concerts, including those of the famed summer Ravello Festival, and is now also used as a cinema. The subject of much controversy since its first conception back in 2000, it raised the wrath of some locals who denounced such an ambitious modernist building in medieval Ravello. They need not have worried. The result, inaugurated in 2010, is a design masterpiece—a huge, overhanging canopied roof suspended over a 400-seat concert area, with a giant eye-shape window allowing spectators to contemplate the extraordinary bay vista during performances. ✉ *Via della Repubblica 12.*

Fodor's Choice
★

Duomo. Ravello's first bishop, Orso Papiciò, founded this cathedral, dedicated to San Pantaleone, in 1086. Rebuilt in the 12th and 17th centuries, it retains traces of medieval frescoes in the transept, an original mullioned window, a marble portal, and a three-story 13th-century bell tower playfully interwoven with mullioned windows and arches. The 12th-century bronze door has 54 embossed panels depicting Christ's life, and saints, prophets, plants, and animals, all narrating biblical lore. Ancient columns divide the nave's three aisles, and treasures include sarcophagi from Roman times and paintings by the southern Renaissance artist Andrea da Salerno. Most impressive are the two medieval pulpits: the earlier one is inset with a mosaic scene of Jonah and the whale, while the more famous one opposite boasts exquisite mosaic work and six twisting columns sitting on lion pedestals. In the crypt is the **Museo del Duomo**, which displays 13th-century treasures from the reign of Frederick II of Sicily. ⊠ *Piazza del Duomo* ☎ *089/858311* ⊕ *www.museoduomoravello.com* 🎫 *€3.*

Fodor's Choice
★

Villa Cimbrone. To the south of Ravello's main square, a somewhat hilly 15-minute walk along Via San Francesco brings you to Ravello's showstopper, the Villa Cimbrone, whose dazzling gardens perch 1,500 feet above the sea. This medieval-style fantasy was created in 1905 by England's Lord Grimthorpe and made world famous in the 1930s when Greta Garbo found sanctuary from the press here. The Gothic *castello-palazzo* sits amid idyllic gardens that are divided by the grand Avenue of Immensity pathway, leading in turn to the literal high point of any trip to the Amalfi Coast—the **Belvedere of Infinity**. This grand stone parapet, adorned with stone busts, overlooks the entire Bay of Salerno and frames a panorama the late writer Gore Vidal, a longtime Ravello resident, described as the most beautiful in the world. The villa itself is now a five-star hotel. ⊠ *Via Santa Chiara 26* ☎ *089/857459* ⊕ *www.villacimbrone.it* 🎫 *€7.*

Fodor's Choice
★

Villa Rufolo. Directly off Ravello's main piazza is the Villa Rufolo, home to some of the most spectacular gardens in Italy, framing a stunning vista of the Bay of Salerno, often called the "bluest view in the world." If one believes the master storyteller Boccaccio, the villa was built in the 13th century by Landolfo Rufolo, whose immense fortune stemmed from trade with the Moors and the Saracens. Norman and Arab architecture mingle in a welter of color-filled gardens so lush the composer Richard Wagner used them as inspiration for Klingsor's Garden, the home of the Flower Maidens, in his opera *Parsifal*. Beyond the Arab-Sicilian cloister and the Norman tower lie the two terrace gardens. The lower one, the "Wagner Terrace," is often the site of Ravello Festival concerts. Highlights of the house are its Moorish cloister—an Arabic-Sicilian delight with interlacing lancet arcs and polychromatic palmette decoration—and the 14th-century Torre Maggiore, or Klingsor's Tower. ⊠ *Piazza del Duomo* ☎ *089/857621* ⊕ *www.villarufolo.it* 🎫 *€7, extra charge for concerts.*

WHERE TO EAT

$
SOUTHERN
ITALIAN
FAMILY

✗ **Cumpa' Cosimo.** More rustic looking than most Ravello spots, Cumpa' Cosimo is run devotedly by Netta Bottone, who both cooks and tours the tables to ensure her clients are content; her family has owned this cantina for more than 75 of its 300-plus years. You can't miss with any of the classic Ravellian dishes, including the favorite (share it—it's huge) *misto* of whatever homemade pasta inspires Netta, served with a fresh, fragrant pesto. **Known for:** fresh produce including catch of the day; warm, family-run hospitality and rustic surroundings; quality meat supplied by nearby butchers. $ *Average main: €14* ⊠ *Via Roma 46* ☎ *089/857156* ⊘ *Sometimes closed Mon. in winter.*

$
PIZZA
FAMILY
Fodor'sChoice
★

✕ **Ristorante Pizzeria Vittoria.** Just south of the Duomo, this is a good place for a return to reality and an informal bite. Vittoria's thin-crust pizza with loads of fresh toppings is the star attraction, and locals praise it *molto*—it was a favorite of Gore Vidal. **Known for:** extensive menu; very popular with locals and tourists; Campanian classics including eggplant parmigiana. $ *Average main: €14* ⊠ *Via dei Rufolo 3* ☎ *089/857947* ⊕ *www.ristorantepizzeriavittoria.it.*

WHERE TO STAY

$$$$
HOTEL

⊞ **Hotel Palumbo.** This is the real deal—the only great hotel left in Ravello that's still a monument to the Grand Tour sensibility that first put the town on the map. **Pros:** impossibly romantic throwback; wonderful coastal retreat; incredible Bay of Salerno views. **Cons:** no on-site pool; breakfast lacks Campanian feeling of abundance; some find style very dated. $ *Rooms from: €581* ⊠ *Via San Giovanni del Toro 16* ☎ *089/857244* ⊕ *www.hotelpalumbo.it* ⇥ *17 rooms* ⦿ *Free Breakfast.*

$$
HOTEL

⊞ **Hotel Parsifal.** In 1288 this diminutive property overlooking the coastline housed an order of Augustinian friars; today the intact cloister hosts travelers intent on enjoying themselves mightily. **Pros:** staying in a former convent in Ravello; charming manager and his family dote on Americans; open year-round. **Cons:** slightly removed from town; tiny rooms; decor and furnishing need a refresh in parts. $ *Rooms from: €160* ⊠ *Viale Gioacchino d'Anna 5* ☎ *089/857144* ⊕ *www.hotelparsifal.com* ⇥ *17 rooms* ⦿ *Free Breakfast.*

$$$$
HOTEL
Fodor'sChoice
★

⊞ **Hotel Villa Cimbrone.** Suspended over the azure sea and set amid legendary rose-filled gardens, this Gothic-style castle was once home to Lord Grimthorpe and a hideaway of Greta Garbo. **Pros:** gorgeous pool and views; surrounded by beautiful gardens; top-rated restaurant. **Cons:** a longish hike from town center (porters can help with luggage); daily arrival of respectful day-trippers; special place comes at a price. $ *Rooms from: €550* ⊠ *Via Santa Chiara 26* ☎ *089/857459* ⊕ *www.villacimbrone.com* ⊘ *Closed Nov.–Mar.* ⇥ *19 rooms* ⦿ *Free Breakfast.*

PAESTUM

99 km (62 miles) southeast of Naples.

For history buffs, a visit to Campania is not complete without seeing the ancient ruins of Paestum. A visit to the ruins to stroll past the incredibly well-preserved temples and see the top-notch collection at the Museo Nazionale is a great day trip from the Amalfi Coast or Naples.

GETTING HERE AND AROUND

By car, take the A3 autostrada south from Salerno, take the Battipaglia exit to SS18. Exit at Capaccio Scala. You can also take a CSTP or SCAT bus (departs hourly) or an FS train from Salerno. The archaeological site is a 10-minute walk from the station.

14

VISITOR INFORMATION

Contact Azienda Autonoma Soggiorno e Turismo di Paestum (*Paestum Tourist Office*). ✉ *Via Magna Grecia 887* ☎ *0828/811016* 🌐 *www.infopaestum.it.*

EXPLORING

Fodor's Choice ★ **Greek Temples.** One of Italy's most majestic sights lies on the edge of a flat coastal plain: the remarkably preserved Greek temples of Paestum. This is the site of the ancient city of Poseidonia, founded by Greek colonists probably in the 6th century BC. When the Romans took it over in 273 BC, they Latinized the name to Paestum and changed the layout of the settlement, adding an amphitheater and a forum. Much of the archaeological material found on the site is displayed in the well-labeled **Museo Nazionale,** and several rooms are devoted to the unique tomb paintings—rare examples of Greek and pre-Roman pictorial art—discovered in the area.

At the northern end of the site opposite the ticket barrier is the **Tempio di Cerere** (Temple of Ceres). Built in about 500 BC, it is thought to have been originally dedicated to the goddess Athena. Follow the road south past the **Foro Romano** (Roman Forum) to the **Tempio di Nettuno** (Temple of Poseidon), a showstopping Doric edifice with 36 fluted columns and an entablature (the area above the capitals) that rivals those of the finest temples in Greece. Beyond is the so-called **Basilica.** It dates from the early 6th century BC. The name is an 18th-century misnomer, though, since it was, in fact, a temple to Hera, the wife of Zeus. Try to see the temples in the late afternoon. ✉ *Via Magna Grecia* ☎ *0828/811023 museum, 081/2395653 ticket office* 🎫 *Site and museum €9, museum only (after site closing time) €4* 🕒 *Museum closed 1st and 3rd Mon. of month.*

FAMILY Fodor's Choice ★ **Tenuta Vannulo—Buffalo Farm and Shop.** Foodies, families, and the curious flock to this novel farm attraction that celebrates humane animal husbandry, organic mozzarella di bufala, and other wonderful products. A tour of the ranch run by the Palmieri family—headed by the serene octogenerian Antonio—brings you nose to glistening snout with probably the most pampered buffalo in the world. Some 600 of them wallow in pools, get a mechanical massage, and flap their ears to classical music. The shop/restaurant is the place to taste and take away cheese, ice cream, yogurt, chocolate, and leather products. ✉ *Contrada Vannulo, Via Galileo Galilei 101, Capaccio* ☎ *0828/727894* 🌐 *www.vannulo.it* 🎫 *€5.*

WHERE TO STAY

$ B&B/INN 🏨 **Azienda Agrituristica Seliano.** This working farm, about 3 km (2 miles) from Paestum's Greek temples, consists of a cluster of 19th-century baronial buildings that have been converted into charming guest rooms. **Pros:** a great taste of a working farm; a banquet every evening; transfers available from the station; cooking courses. **Cons:** confusing to find; not for nondog fans; dated decor. [$] *Rooms from: €90* ✉ *Via Seliano, about 1 km (½ mile) down dirt track west off main road from Capaccio Scalo to Paestum* ☎ *0828/723634* 🌐 *www.agriturismoseliano.it* 🕒 *Closed Nov.–Mar.; will open for bookings* 🛏 *14 rooms* 🍴 *Free Breakfast.*

PUGLIA, BASILICATA, AND CALABRIA

WELCOME TO
PUGLIA, BASILICATA, AND CALABRIA

TOP REASONS TO GO

★ **A wander through Sassi:** The Basilicata town of Matera is endowed with one of the most unusual landscapes in Europe—a complex network of ancient cave dwellings partially hewn from rock, some of which now house chic bars and restaurants.

★ **A trip to peasant-food heaven:** Dine on Puglia's famous puree of fava beans with chicory and olive oil in a humble country restaurant.

★ **Lecce and its Baroque splendors:** The beautiful, friendly city of Lecce might be known for its peculiar brand of fanciful Baroque architecture, but it's not yet famous enough to have lost its Pugliese charm.

★ **The trulli of the Valle d'Itria:** Strange conical houses—many of them still in use—dot the rolling countryside of Puglia, centering around Alberobello, a town still composed almost entirely of these *trulli*. They must be seen to be believed.

The Mezzogiorno ("midday") is the informal name for Italy's languid deep south, known for its sun-drenched olive groves, fertile hills, and time-frozen towns. The area includes the regions of Calabria, the toe of Italy's boot, on the Tyrrhenian and Ionian seas; Puglia, the heel; and between them, Basilicata, the instep. Along both coasts, stretches of dramatic coastline are interspersed with rough-and-tumble fishing and shipping ports. The Mezzogiorno includes Campania and Sicily as well.

1 Bari and the Adriatic Coast. Puglia's biggest city is a lively, quirky, and sometimes seedy port on the Adriatic Coast. It's also home to the region's principal airport.

2 The Gargano Promontory. The spur of Italy's boot has the pretty whitewashed towns of Vieste and Peschici. It's a popular spot for Italian holidaymakers during July and August.

3 The Trulli District. Named for its mysterious conical houses, the Trulli District is centered on the town of Alberobello.

4 The Salento Peninsula. The ports of Puglia include casbah-like fishing villages such as Gallipoli and the gritty shipping centers of Taranto and Brindisi. Italy's heel finally smooths out and terminates in a region of Puglia known as Salento, home to Lecce, famous for its ornate Baroque architecture.

5 Basilicata. One of Italy's least visited and most secluded regions is the place to find Matera, whose cave dwellings make the city feel like a Nativity scene.

6 Calabria. The region that makes up Italy's "toe" is a land of dusty hill towns, rows of olive trees, and spicy food. Cosenza mixes turn-of-the-20th-century cafés with Fascist-era architecture, and Tropea is an enticing seaside getaway.

EATING AND DRINKING WELL IN PUGLIA, BASILICATA, AND CALABRIA

The Mediterranean diet was born here. Southern Italian cuisine is based on seasonal local produce, so don't expect to find, say, grapes in May or watermelon in November, although the mild climate and fertile soil, linked to modern farming methods, means that most vegetable products have a long growing season.

The traditional cuisine reflects its peasant origins, with hearty homemade pasta, thick bean soups, and grilled meat and fish. The emphasis, though, is on vegetables, with zucchini, eggplant, beans, sweet peppers, and at least a dozen varieties of tomatoes transformed into imaginative dishes. Naturally, the local olive oil is never lacking on the table. Dribbled over soup or a thick chunk of bread, it can transform the plainest dish into a gourmet treat. A defining principle of Italian cooking is to take excellent ingredients and prepare them simply. That philosophy reaches its purest expression here.

FABULOUS FAVA

Puré di fave e cicorielle, a puree of fava beans topped with sautéed chicory, is unique to Puglia and Basilicata.

The simple recipe has been prepared here for centuries and continues to be a staple of the local diet. The dried favas are soaked overnight, cooked with potatoes, seasoned with salt and olive oil, and served warm with wild green chicory, often with a sprinkling of ground *peperoncino* (chili pepper). Mix it together before eating, and wash it down with a glass of primitivo or aglianico.

MEAT

As well as for its excellent beef, Basilicata is known for its *salsicce lucane* (sausages), seasoned with salt, cayenne pepper, and fennel seeds. Enormous grills are a feature of many of the region's restaurants, infusing the dining area with the aroma of freshly cooked meat. Adventurous eaters in Puglia should look for *turcinieddhri* (a blend of lamb's innards) and *pezzetti di cavallo* (braised horse meat).

PASTA

Puglia is the home of orecchiette with *cime di rapa* (broccoli rabe) and olive oil, a melodious dish that's wondrous in its simplicity. Try also *cavatelli* (rolled-up orecchiette) and *strascenati* (rectangles of pasta with one rough side and one smooth side).

PEPPERS

If you like it hot, Calabria is the place for you. The region is known for its use of hot little peppers that can range from a mild sprinkling in tomato sauce to the tongue-scorching *'nduja* (spicy pork salami) paste. The local cured meats, such as *soppressata* (dried spicy salami), and *salsiccia piccante* (hot sausage), often sold by street vendors on a roll with peppers, onions, french fries, and mayonnaise, are all spiced with peperoncino. Do try the delicious sweet red onions of Tropea, exclusive to the region.

SEAFOOD

With so much coastline, seafood is an essential element of southern Italian cuisine. Fish can be grilled (*alla griglia*), baked (*al forno*), roasted (*arrosto*), or steamed (*in umido*). Among the highlights are delicate *orata* (sea bream), *branzino* (sea bass), *gamberi rossi* (sweet red shrimp), and calamari. Puglia is the home of *cozze pelose* (a kind of mussel), and Calabria's version of sushi is freshly caught *ricci di mare* (sea urchins), considered a delicacy—and an aphrodisiac!

WINES

Puglia produces around 17% of Italy's wine, more than is produced in the whole of Australia. In the past, most of it was *vino sfuso* (jug wine), but over the past 15 years, producers have been concentrating on quality—with impressive results. The ancient *primitivo* grape (an ancestor of California's *zinfandel*) yields strong, heady wines like Primitivo di Manduria. The *negroamaro* grape is transformed into palatable *rosati* (rosés), as well as the robust Salice Salentino. Pair a dessert with the sweet red Aleatico di Puglia or Moscato di Trani.

In Basilicata, producers use the *aglianico* grape variety to outstanding effect in the prestigious Aglianico del Vulture. In Calabria, they've worked wonders with *gaglioppo*.

15

Updated by
Nick Bruno

Venture off the traffic-filled highways and explore the countryside of Italy's boot, made up of the three separate regions—Puglia, Basilicata, and Calabria—each one with its own character. This is Italy's deep south, where whitewashed buildings stand silently over three turquoise seas, castles guard medieval alleyways, and grandmothers dry their handmade orecchiette, the most Puglian of pastas, in the mid-afternoon heat.

At every turn, these three regions boast dramatic scenery. Geographical divides have preserved an astonishing cultural and linguistic diversity that's unequaled elsewhere on the Italian mainland. Southern Italians are extremely proud of their hometowns and will be glad to direct you to some forgotten local chapel in an olive grove, an unmarked monument, or an obscure work of art. The Greek city-states of Magna Graecia (Greater Greece) once ruled here, and ancient names, such as Lucania, are still commonly used. It's here also that you'll find long-isolated hill communities where Albanian and Greek are still spoken by the descendants of 16th-century refugees from the Balkans.

One of southern Italy's most popular vacation destinations is the Gargano Promontory, where safe, sandy shores and secluded coves are nestled between whitewashed coastal towns and craggy limestone cliffs. You'll also find many beautiful stretches of sandy beaches along the coast of the Salento Peninsula and the Mediterranean shoreline of Calabria and Basilicata. There are cultural gems everywhere, including Valle d'Itria's fairy-tale *trulli* (curious conical structures, some dating from the 15th century), Matera's *Sassi* (a network of ancient dwellings carved out of rock), and the Baroque churches in the town of Lecce, the jewel of the south. Beyond the cities, seaside resorts, and the few major sights, there's a sparsely populated, sunbaked countryside where road signs are rare and expanses of silvery olive trees, vineyards of primitivo and aglianico, and giant prickly pear cacti fight their way through the rocky soil in defiance of the relentless summer heat.

PUGLIA, BASILICATA, AND CALABRIA PLANNER

MAKING THE MOST OF YOUR TIME

If your priority is relaxing on the beach, plan on a few days at a seaside resort in one of the Gargano Promontory's fishing villages, such as Peschici, Rodi Garganico, and Vieste, and perhaps a further stay at one of the Calabrian coastal resorts, such as Diamante or Tropea, or Maratea in Basilicata.

Otherwise, choose a base like Polignano a Mare or Trani, especially if you land or dock in Bari. Take day trips out to the Valle d'Itria, or to the remarkable octagonal Castel del Monte. Then head east along the Adriatic route (SS16), stopping to see the idyllic hilltop Ostuni before continuing on to Lecce, where you'll want to spend at least two to three nights exploring the city's Baroque wonders and taking a day trip down to Otranto and Gallipoli.

Next, take regional roads and Via Appia (SS7) to reach Matera, whose Sassi cave dwellings are a southern Italian highlight; allow at least two nights here. Then it's back out to the SS106 to Calabria, along the coast dotted with ancient Greek settlements, as far as Tropea. At this point, cut inland on the SS107 across the Sila Massif, stopping at the hill resort of Camigliatello or carrying on to the more vibrant lowland Cosenza. Reggio Calabria is worthwhile just to see the celebrated Riace bronzes.

GETTING AROUND

BUS TRAVEL

Direct, if not always frequent, connections operate between most destinations within Calabria, Puglia, and Basilicata. In many cases, bus service is the backup when problems with train service arise. Matera is linked with Bari by frequent Ferrovie Appulo Lucane trains and buses and with Taranto by SITA bus. In Calabria the Romano bus company runs a regular service between various towns. Ferrovie della Calabria operates many of the local routes.

Contacts Bus Romano. ☏ 0962/21709 ⊕ www.autolineeromano.com. **Ferrovie della Calabria.** ☏ 0961/896111, 328/2391123 ⊕ www.ferroviedel-lacalabria.it. **SITA.** ☏ 0835/385007, 080/5790111, 0971/506811 ⊕ www.sitasudtrasporti.it.

CAR TRAVEL

Though roads are generally good in the south, and major cities are linked by fast *autostrade*, or four-lane highways, driving here is a major test of navigation skills. While you can bypass many cities by using the ring roads around them, getting into the center of many cities can be complicated, with mazes of one-way streets, pedestrianized zones, and limited parking facilities. The more upmarket hotels have garage facilities or valet parking at guests' disposal. Phone your hotel for advice and instructions when you are entering city outskirts. The toll-free A3 Napoli–Reggio Calabria autostrada links Naples to the south, with major exits at Sicignano (for the interior of Basilicata and Matera), Cosenza (the Sila Massif and Crotone), and Pizzo (for Tropea). Parts of the A3 in northern Calabria cross uplands more than 3,000 feet high, and snow chains may be required during winter months. In the summer and during holiday weekends this is the main north–south route for Italy's sun seekers, so factor in plenty of time for delays and avoid peak travel times. Take the SS18 for coastal destinations—or for a better view—on the Tyrrhenian side, and likewise the SS106 (which is uncongested and fast) for the Ionian. Given speed detectors and driver-tracking technology, it's best to stick to speed limits and be careful not to enter ZTL (*zona a traffico limitato*) restricted traffic areas (cameras are set up in towns such as Matera and Altamura): you'll be spared an unwelcome ticket when you get home.

If you're squeamish about getting lost, don't plan on night driving in the countryside—roads can be confusing without the aid of landmarks or large towns, and GPS is far from infallible. Bari, Brindisi, and Reggio Calabria are notorious for car thefts and break-ins. In these cities, don't leave valuables in the car, and find a guarded parking space if possible.

TRAIN TRAVEL
Trenitalia trains run to Calabria, either following the Ionian Coast as far as Reggio Calabria or swerving inland to Cosenza and the Tyrrhenian Coast.

Ferrovie Appulo Lucane. This service links Matera to Altamura in Puglia (for connections to Bari) and to Ferrandina (for connections to Potenza). Also offers bus service linking Matera to Altamura in Puglia (for connections to Bari) and to Ferrandina (for connections by bus to Potenza). ☎ *080/5725421, 800/050500 numero verde (freephone)* ⊕ *www.ferrovieappulolucane.it.*

Ferrovie Sud-Est. The private Ferrovie Sud-Est connects Martina Franca with Bari, Lecce and Taranto, and the fishing port of Gallipoli. ☎ *080/5462111 in Bari, 0832/668111 in Lecce, 800/079090 numero verde (freephone)* ⊕ *www.fseonline.it.*

Trenitalia. Within Puglia, the Italian national railroad links Bari to Brindisi, Lecce, and Taranto, but smaller destinations can often be reached only by completing the trip by bus. ☎ *06/3000* ⊕ *www.trenitalia.com.*

RESTAURANTS
Italy's southern region is home to numerous restaurants that feature home cooking or slow-food-inspired menus. That means everything is made with the freshest ingredients, but meals are meant to be enjoyed at leisure and service is not swift. Whether you decide to dine in a well-known restaurant or at a humble country trattoria, plan to give some thought to your menu choices—it's expected—and ask questions—also expected. But most importantly, relax and enjoy. *Restaurant reviews have been shortened. For full information, visit Fodors.com.*

HOTELS
Hotels in the region range from grand, upscale establishments to small and stylish bijou inns to family-run rural *agriturismi* (country hostelries, often part of farms) that compensate for a lack of amenities with their famous southern hospitality. *Fattorie* and *masserie* (small

farms and grander farm estates) offering accommodation are listed at local tourist offices.

In beach areas such as the Gargano Promontory and Salento, campgrounds and bungalow lodgings are ubiquitous and popular with families and budget travelers. Note that many seaside hotels open up just for the summer season, when they often require several-day stays with full or half board. And do remember that in a region like this—blazingly hot in summer and chilly in winter—air-conditioning and central heating can be important. *Hotel reviews have been shortened. For full information, visit Fodors.com.*

WHAT IT COSTS				
	$	$$	$$$	$$$$
Restaurants	under €15	€15–€24	€25–€35	over €35
Hotels	under €125	€125–€200	€201–€300	over €300

Dining prices are the average cost of a main course at dinner, or, if dinner is not served, at lunch. Hotel prices are the lowest cost of a standard double room in high season.

BARI AND THE ADRIATIC COAST

The coast of Puglia has a strong flavor of the Norman presence in the south, embodied in the distinctive Apulian-Romanesque churches, the most atmospheric being in Trani. The busy commercial port of Bari offers architectural nuggets in its compact, labyrinthine old quarter abutting the sea, while Polignano a Mare combines accessibility to the major centers with the charm of a medieval town. For a unique excursion, drive inland to the imposing Castel del Monte, an enigmatic 13th-century octagon.

BARI

260 km (162 miles) southeast of Naples, 450 km (281 miles) southeast of Rome.

The biggest city in the region, Bari is a major port and a transit point for travelers catching ferries across the Adriatic to Greece, Croatia, and Albania. It's also a cosmopolitan city with one of the most interesting historic centers in the region. In recent years, it has become a major center of pilgrimage for Russian Orthodox visitors, due to its connection with St. Nicholas, the patron saint of Russia, as well as of Bari. The old quarter of the city, around the basilica and the harbor castle, is a lively maze of whitewashed alleyways buzzing with bars, cafés, restaurants, and crafts shops. Most of the modern town is set out in a logical 19th-century grid, following the designs of Joachim Murat (1767–1815), Napoléon's brother-in-law and King of the Two Sicilies. The heart is **Piazza della Libertà,** where old and young gather in the evenings to stroll up and down and see and be seen.

PUGLIA, PAST AND PRESENT

Puglia has long been inhabited, conquered, and visited. On sea voyages to their colonies and trading posts in the west, the ancient Greeks invariably headed for Puglia first—it was the shortest crossing—before filtering southward into Sicily and westward to the Tyrrhenian Coast. In turn, the Romans—often bound in the opposite direction—were quick to recognize the strategic importance of the peninsula. Later centuries were to see a procession of other empires raiding or colonizing Puglia: Byzantines, Saracens, Normans, Swabians, Turks, and Spaniards all swept through, each group leaving their mark. Romanesque churches and the powerful castles built by 13th-century Holy Roman Emperor Frederick II (who also served as king of Sicily and Jerusalem) are among the most impressive of the buildings in the region. Frederick II, dubbed "Stupor Mundi" (Wonder of the World) for his wide-ranging interests in literature, science, mathematics, and nature, was one of the foremost personalities of the Middle Ages.

Recent years have brought a huge economic revival after the decades of neglect following World War II. Having benefited from EU funding, state incentive programs, and subsidies for irrigation, Puglia is now Italy's top regional producer of wine, with most of the rest of the land devoted to olives, citrus fruits, and vegetables. The main ports of Bari, Brindisi, and Taranto are thriving centers, though there remain serious problems of unemployment and poverty. However, the much-publicized arrival of thousands of asylum seekers from Eastern Europe and beyond has not significantly destabilized these cities, as had been feared, and the economic and political refugees have dispersed throughout Italy. Today, despite several years of regionwide *recessione*, an air of prosperity still wafts through the streets of Lecce, Trani, and smaller towns like Otranto and Peschici.

GETTING HERE AND AROUND

By car, take the Bari-Nord exit from the A14 autostrada. Bari's train station is a hub for Puglia-bound trains. Alitalia and Ryanair fly to Bari Airport from Rome and Milan.

VISITOR INFORMATION

Contact Bari Tourism Office. ⊠ *Piazza Moro 33/a* ☎ *080/5242361* ⊕ *www. viaggiareinpuglia.it.*

EXPLORING

Fodor'sChoice ★ **Basilica di San Nicola.** The 11th-century Basilica di San Nicola, overlooking the sea in the *città vecchia*, houses the bones of St. Nicholas, the inspiration for Santa Claus. His relics were stolen from Myra, in present-day Turkey, by a band of sailors from Bari and are now buried in the crypt. Because St. Nicholas is also the patron saint of Russia, the church draws both Roman Catholic and Russian Orthodox pilgrims; souvenir shops in the area display miniatures of the Western saint and his Eastern counterpart side by side. ⊠ *Largo Abate Elia 13, Piazza San Nicola* ☎ *080/5737111* ⊕ *www.basilicasannicola.it.*

Castello Svevo. Looming over the cathedral is the huge Castello Svevo, the symbol of Bari. The current building dates from the time of Holy Roman Emperor Frederick II (1194–1250), who rebuilt an existing Norman-Byzantine castle to his own exacting specifications. Designed more for power than beauty, it looks out beyond the cathedral to the small Porto Vecchio (Old Port). Inside, a haphazard collection of medieval Puglian art is frequently enlivened by changing exhibitions featuring local, national, and international artists. ⊠ *Piazza Federico II di Svevia* ☎ *080/5754201* ⊕ *www.musei.puglia.beniculturali.it* 🎫 *€3* 🕙 *Closed Tues.*

Cattedrale di San Sabino. Bari's 12th-century cathedral is the seat of the local bishop and was the scene of many significant political marriages between important families in the Middle Ages. The cathedral is dedicated to San Sabino, a 6th-century bishop who apparently lived to be 105. The architecture reflects the Romanesque style favored by the Normans of that period. Visit the crypt with its ornate columns, polychrome marble altar, and silver-and-gold icon of Maria Santissima di Costantinopoli, also known as the Vergine Odegitria, patron of Bari along with San Nicola. ⊠ *Piazza dell'Odegitria* ☎ *080/5210605* ⊕ *www.arcidiocesibaribitonto.it.*

FAMILY **Via Sparano.** By day, you can lose yourself in the maze of white alleyways in Bari Vecchia, the old town stretching along the harbor, now humming with restaurants, cafés, and crafts shops. Residents leave their doors wide open so you catch a glimpse into the daily routine of southern Italy—matrons hand-rolling pasta with their grandchildren home from school for the midday meal, and workers busy patching up centuries-old arches and doorways. Back in the new town, join the evening *passeggiata* (stroll) on pedestrians-only Via Sparano, then, when night falls, saunter amid the outdoor bars and restaurants in Piazza Mercantile, past Piazza Ferrarese at the end of Corso Vittorio Emanuele. ⊠ *Via Sparano.*

WHERE TO EAT AND STAY

$$$
SEAFOOD
FAMILY
✗ **Ristorante al Pescatore.** In the lively heart of old town, opposite the castle and just around the corner from the cathedral, stands one of Bari's best seafood restaurants with a menu that features a vast variety of fish. Try the house specialty of *crudo di mare,* a platter of mixed local seafood, accompanied by a crisp salad and a carafe of uplifting Pugliese wine. **Known for:** raw seafood antipasto misto crudo; lively atmosphere with tables packed together; taste of the mare Pugliese: ricci di mare. $ *Average main: €30* ⊠ *Piazza Federico II di Svevia 6/8* ☎ *080/5237039* ⊕ *www.alpescatorebari.com.*

$$
HOTEL
🏛 **Palace Hotel.** Conveniently located near the Corso Vittorio Emanuele in the new town as well as the city's medieval center, this downtown landmark has been restored and upgraded with bright color schemes and baroque touches in the decor. **Pros:** convenient location near both the medieval old town and the shops of the new city; comfortable, modern rooms; garage facilities. **Cons:** mainly geared to conferences and business clients; its popularity with conferences and businesspeople means it can get pretty busy; some bathrooms poorly maintained. $ *Rooms from: €134* ⊠ *Via Lombardi 13* ☎ *080/5216551* ⊕ *www. palacehotelbari.com* 🛏 *195 rooms* ⭐ *Free Breakfast.*

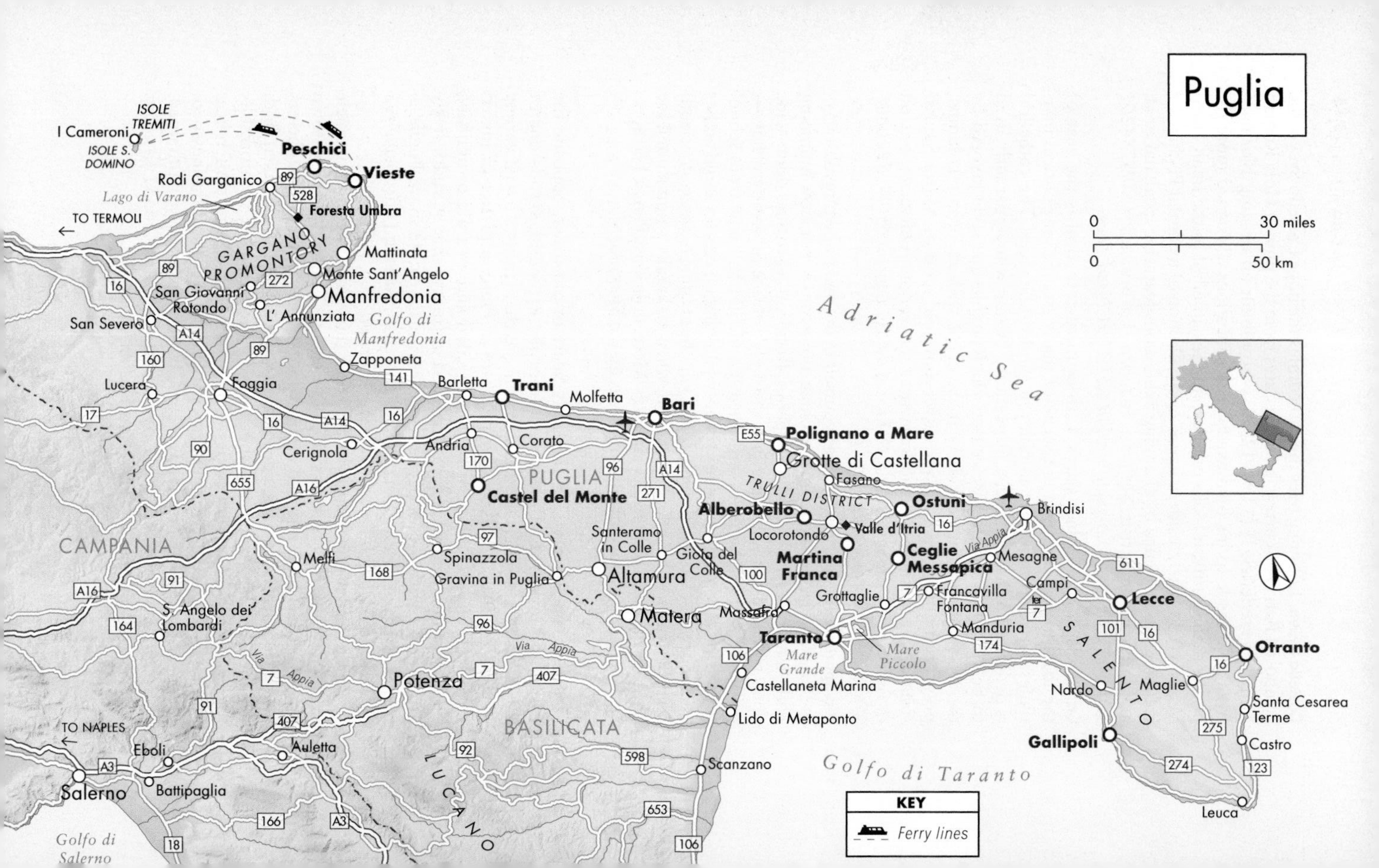

Puglia
0
30 miles
0
50 km
Adriatic Sea
KEY
Ferry lines
ISOLE TREMITI
I Cameroni
ISOLE S. DOMINO
Peschici
Vieste
Rodi Garganico
Lago di Varano
Foresta Umbra
TO TERMOLI
GARGANO PROMONTORY
Mattinata
Monte Sant'Angelo
Manfredonia
San Giovanni Rotondo
L' Annunziata
Golfo di Manfredonia
San Severo
Zapponeta
Lucera
Foggia
Barletta
Trani
Molfetta
Bari
Cerignola
Andria
Corato
Polignano a Mare
Grotte di Castellana
Fasano
TRULLI DISTRICT
PUGLIA
Castel del Monte
CAMPANIA
Alberobello
Ostuni
Brindisi
Valle d'Itria
Locorotondo
Santeramo in Colle
Gioia del Colle
Martina Franca
Ceglie Messapica
Via Appia
Mesagne
Melfi
Spinazzola
Gravina in Puglia
Altamura
Campi
Francavilla Fontana
Grottaglie
Lecce
S. Angelo dei Lombardi
Matera
Massafra
Manduria
Taranto
Mare Grande
Mare Piccolo
SALENTO
Otranto
Potenza
Castellaneta Marina
Nardo
Maglie
Santa Cesarea Terme
TO NAPLES
BASILICATA
Lido di Metaponto
Gallipoli
Castro
Eboli
Auletta
LUCANO
Scanzano
Golfo di Taranto
Salerno
Battipaglia
Leuca
Golfo di Salerno

TRANI

43 km (27 miles) northwest of Bari.

Trani has a harbor filled with fishing boats and a quaint old town with polished cobblestone streets and medieval churches. The town is also justly famous for its sweet dessert wine, Moscato di Trani. It's smaller than the other ports along this coast.

GETTING HERE AND AROUND

By car, take the Trani exit from the A14 autostrada. Frequent trains run from Bari.

VISITOR INFORMATION

Contact Trani Tourism Office. ✉ *Palazzo Palmieri, Piazza Trieste 10* ☎ *0883/588830.*

15

EXPLORING

Castello. One of Federico II's most imposing fortresses, Trani Castle guarded the Adriatic sea route throughout the Middle Ages. It was the scene of several royal weddings of the Swabian and Anjou houses, as well as the place of imprisonment for life of Siffridina, Countess of Caserta, who had supported the losing Swabian dynasty against Charles I of Anjou. In the early 20th century it became a state prison and remained so until 1974. It now contains a museum. ✉ *Piazza Re Manfredi 14* ☎ *0883/506603* 🌐 *www.castelloditrani.beniculturali.it* 🎫 *€10, reduced if no special exhibitions.*

Fodor's Choice ★ **Cattedrale.** The stunning, pinkish-white 11th-century cathedral, considered one of the finest in Puglia, is built on a spit of land jutting into the sea. Dedicated to St. Nicholas the Pilgrim, it was a favorite place of prayer for crusaders embarking for war in the Holy Land. Its lofty bell tower can be visited by request at the nearby Museo Diocesiano. The climb is worth it for the view. ✉ *Piazza Duomo* ☎ *0883/500293* 🌐 *www.cattedraletrani.it* 🎫 *Free, bell tower €5.*

Via Sinagoga and Museo Sant'Anna (*Synagogue Street and Sant'Anna Museum*). In the 12th century one of the largest Jewish communities in southern Italy flourished here, and on Via Sinagoga two of the four synagogues still stand. The 13th-century **Scolanova** has been reconverted to a synagogue after a long period as a Christian church, while the former **Sant'Anna** now houses a museum of Trani's Jewish history. **■ TIP→ Contact Trani Tourism Office to set up tours and visits.** ✉ *Via La Guidea 24, corner of Via San Martino* ☎ *0883/582470* 🌐 *www.fondazioneseca.it* 🎫 *Donations accepted.*

WHERE TO STAY

$ HOTEL FAMILY 🏨 **Hotel Trani.** This centrally located hotel caters mainly to business travelers, but its convenient location near the main sights in Trani's historic center makes it a great option for everyone else. **Pros:** close to the train station and the old town; wheelchair accessible; parking in hotel garage. **Cons:** functional but somewhat basic; often busy with conference delegates; breakfast just adequate. [$] *Rooms from: €90* ✉ *Corso Imbriani 137* ☎ *0883/588010* 🌐 *www.hoteltrani.it* 🛏 *46 rooms* 🍴 *Free Breakfast.*

$$ HOTEL 🏨 **Palazzo Filisio.** This small hotel-restaurant occupies the 17th-century Palazzo Filisio and is superbly positioned in front of the Duomo, in a quiet piazza by the sea. **Pros:** right next to the cathedral; hospitable staff; most rooms have sea views. **Cons:** no parking outside hotel; often occupied by wedding parties; due for refurbishing, so check for disruption. [$] *Rooms from: €140* ✉ *Piazza Mons. Addazzi 2* ☎ *0883/500931* 🌐 *www.palazzofilisio.it* 🕒 *Restaurant closed Mon.* 🛏 *10 rooms* 🍴 *Free Breakfast.*

POLIGNANO A MARE

35 km (22 miles) southeast of Bari, 14 km (9 miles) north of Castellana.

With a well-preserved, whitewashed old town perched on limestone cliffs overlooking the Adriatic, Polignano a Mare makes an atmospheric base for exploring the surrounding area.

It leapt to fame in 2013, when the cast of the popular soap *Beautiful* descended to film some scenes on the Scalinata di Grottone, where there is also a statue of the town's most famous son, Domenico Modugno, author of the song "Volare."

GETTING HERE AND AROUND

From Bari, take the Polignano exit from the SS16. Frequent trains run from Bari.

VISITOR INFORMATION

Contact Polignano Tourism Office. ✉ *Via Martiri Di Dogali 2* ☎ *080/4252336* 🌐 *www.polignanoamare.com.*

WHERE TO STAY

$$ HOTEL 🏨 **Hotel Covo dei Saraceni.** It would be difficult to find a more romantic location than this hotel, perched dramatically on the rocks above the narrow cove of Polignano. **Pros:** magnificent sea views; decent buffet breakfast; spa center in the hotel. **Cons:** popular for wedding receptions so can be busy; some rooms with views of parking lot; many rooms on the small side. [$] *Rooms from: €160* ✉ *Via Conversano 1* ☎ *080/4247010* 🌐 *www.covodeisaraceni.com* 🛏 *32 rooms* 🍴 *Free Breakfast.*

CASTEL DEL MONTE

56 km (35 miles) southwest of Bari.

The isolated Norman Castel del Monte dominates the surrounding countryside from the top of a 1,778-foot-high hill. The nearest town is Andria, 17 km (12 miles) away. Andria is largely modern with chaotic traffic—it's best avoided by taking the ring road around it.

GETTING HERE AND AROUND

Take the Andria-Barletta exit from the A14 autostrada, then follow the SS170d to Castel del Monte. From April through October there's minibus service from Piazza Bersaglieri d'Italia in Andria.

VISITOR INFORMATION

Contact **Castel del Monte Tourism Office.** ⊠ *Via Vespucci 114, Andria* ☎ *0883/592283* ⊕ *www.proloco.andria.ba.it.*

EXPLORING

Fodor's Choice ★ **Castel del Monte.** Crowning an isolated hill 1,778 feet above sea level in the heart of the Alta Murgia national park, this enigmatic octagonal fortress, built by Frederick II in the first half of the 13th century, has puzzled historians and researchers for centuries. The rooms are arranged in a seemingly illogical sequence through eight towers around a central courtyard. Recent interpretations suggest it was an elaborate cultural center conceived by Frederick to study the various scientific disciplines of both the Western and the Arabic worlds. Umberto Eco used it as his inspiration for the riddles in *The Name of the Rose.* It's worth hiring the services of one of the authorized tour guides here to get a deeper insight into the mysteries of this unique monument. Note that if coming by car between April and September, you have to park in designated areas about a mile away and then take a shuttle bus. ⊠ *On signposted minor road, 18 km (11 miles) south of Andria, Andria* ☎ *0883/569997* ⊕ *www.casteldelmonte.beniculturali.it* ⊠ *€10 includes latest exhibition.*

15

THE GARGANO PROMONTORY

Forming the spur of Italy's boot, the Gargano Promontory (Promontorio del Gargano) is a striking contrast to the Adriatic's flatter coastline. This is a land of whitewashed coastal towns, wide sandy beaches interspersed with secluded coves, and craggy limestone cliffs topped by deep-green pine and scrubby Mediterranean *macchia* (underbrush). Not surprisingly, it pulls in the crowds in July and August, driving up the prices considerably. Camping is almost always an option, as plentiful and pretty campgrounds dot the Gargano's curvy, cliff-hugging roads. The beaches and the Foresta Umbra national park are great places for kids to let off steam.

The Gargano Promotory is also known for its excellent gastronomic products, exclusive to the area, such as the Caciocavallo Podolico cheese, Lesina eels, Fave di Carpino beans, and Duretta oranges, first recorded in the year 1000, when the prince of Bari sent the Norman king a basket of them as a gift.

VIESTE

93 km (58 miles) northeast of Foggia, 179 km (111 miles) northwest of Bari.

This large, whitewashed town jutting off the tip of the spur of Italy's boot is an attractive place to wander around. Although curvy mountain roads render it slightly less accessible from the autostrade and mainline rail stations than, say, Peschici and Mattinata, the range of accommodations (including camping) makes it a useful base for exploring Gargano.

The resort attracts legions of tourists in summer, some bound for the Isole Tremiti, a tiny archipelago connected to Vieste by regular ferries.

GETTING HERE AND AROUND

If you're driving from Foggia, take the winding SS89. Regular buses leave from Foggia's train station.

WHERE TO EAT AND STAY

$$

SOUTHERN
ITALIAN
Fodor'sChoice
★

✕ **Al Dragone.** Dine on exquisite Gargano fare at this lauded eatery set in a natural grotto in the heart of the old center, just next to the cathedral. The menu is dominated by locally caught fish, and while dishes draw on traditional recipes, you can expect occasional innovations, such as a cuttlefish, shrimp, and zucchini soufflé. **Known for:** beautifully crafted seafood dishes; atmospheric setting; impressive wine cellar and cigar selection. $ *Average main: €20* ✉ *Via Duomo 8* ☎ *0884/701212* ⊘ *Closed mid-Oct.–Mar. 1.*

$$

SOUTHERN
ITALIAN
FAMILY

✕ **La Teresina.** At this family-run trattoria at the entrance to Viestre's centro storico, Nicola and Libera Palumbo serve homey Pugliese dishes such as bean soup with *cavatelle* (small pasta shells), the classic *orecchiette ai frutti di mare* (seafood pasta), and a substantial fish soup, all made with the best catch of the day. The dining room walls and ceiling are covered with an array of traditional pottery plates, jugs, and amphorae from the nearby ceramic town of Grottaglia. **Known for:** gorgeous, shady terrace; popular with locals; decent if pricey pizza. $ *Average main: €19* ✉ *Via Cesare Battisti 55* ☎ *0884/701773.*

$

HOTEL
FAMILY

⌂ **Palace Hotel Vieste.** Converted from a 17th-century aristocratic residence, the Palace Hotel is next to the Vieste fishing harbor and is a short walk from the historic center. **Pros:** convenient location near harbor; pleasant staff; decent breakfast with lots of fresh fruit. **Cons:** only the suites have balconies; some rooms look onto noisy backstreets; dated decor and small showers. $ *Rooms from: €120* ✉ *Via Santa Maria di Merino* ☎ *0884/701218* ⊕ *www.palacehotelvieste.it* ⇌ *50 rooms* ⊚| *Free Breakfast.*

PESCHICI

22 km (14 miles) northwest of Vieste, 199 km (124 miles) northwest of Bari.

Peschici is a pleasant resort on Gargano's north shore, a cascade of whitewashed houses and streets with a beautiful view over a sweeping cove. Some surrounding areas are particularly popular with campers from northern Europe. Development has not wreaked too much havoc on the town: the mazelike center retains its characteristic low houses topped with little Byzantine cupolas.

GETTING HERE

From Foggia, take the winding S89 road. Regular buses leave from Foggia's train station. Seasonal ferry service leaves from the Trémiti archipelago between June and September.

EXPLORING

Foresta Umbra. In the middle of the Gargano Promontory is the majestic Foresta Umbra (Shady Forest), a dense growth of beech, maple, pine, and oak generally found in more northerly climates, thriving here because of the altitude, reaching 3,200 feet above sea level. Between the trees in this national park are occasional dramatic vistas opening out over the Golfo di Manfredonia. There are nature trails and picnic areas easily reached from Vieste, Peschici, and Mattinata. ⊠ *Centro Visitatori, Laghetto Umbra, Strada Provinciale 52 bis, Monte Sant'Angelo* ☎ *0884/708578 national park* ⊕ *www.forestaumbra.com* ☾ *Visitor center closed Oct.–Easter.*

THE TRULLI DISTRICT

The inland area to the southeast of Bari is one of Italy's oddest enclaves, mostly flat terrain given over to olive cultivation and interspersed with the idiosyncratic habitations that have lent their names to the district. Looking like igloos constructed out of pure stone, the beehive-shape structures have origins that hark to the 15th century and maybe further. The trulli, found nowhere else in the world, are built of local limestone, without mortar, and with a hole in the top for escaping smoke. Some are painted with mystical or religious symbols, some are isolated, and others are joined together with common roofs. Legends of varying credibility surround the trulli—for example, that they were originally built so that residents could quickly take apart their homes when the tax collectors came by. The center of the Trulli District is Alberobello in the enchanting Valle d'Itria: it has the greatest concentration of buildings. You'll spot them all over this region, some in the middle of desolate fields, and many in disrepair, but always adding a quirky charm to the landscape.

15

ALBEROBELLO

59 km (37 miles) southeast of Bari, 45 km (28 miles) north of Taranto.

A well-established international tourist destination, Alberobello's amalgamation of more than 1,000 trulli huddled together along steep, narrow streets is a unique and striking phenomenon that has been designated a UNESCO World Heritage Site. As one of the most popular destinations in Puglia, Alberobello has spawned some excellent restaurants (and some not-so-excellent trinket shops).

GETTING HERE AND AROUND

By car, take the Monopoli exit from the SS16, follow the SP237 to Putignano, then SS172 to Alberobello. Trains run hourly from Bari.

VISITOR INFORMATION

Contact Alberobello Tourism Office. ⊠ *Via Monte Nero 1* ☎ *080/4322822* ⊕ *www.prolocoalberobello.it.*

EXPLORING

Alberobello–Martina Franca road. The trulli in Alberobello itself are impressive, but the most beautiful concentration of conical trulli is along a stretch of about 15 km (9 miles) on the SS172 Alberobello–Martina Franca road that runs through the tranquil Valle D'Itria. Stop to visit some of the wine farms and oil-pressing mills, surrounded by vast groves of ancient gnarled olive trees. Many here operate on an open-door policy and welcome visitors. ✉ *Alberobello.*

Trullo Sovrano. Alberobello's largest trullo, the 18th-century Trullo Sovrano, is up the hill through the trulli zone (head up Corso Vittorio Emanuele past the obelisk and the basilica). Although this house originally belonged to a wealthy family, it has been furnished in the traditional style of the trullo dwellings to give visitors an insight into living conditions in these unique beehive constructions. Guided tours are included in the entrance price. ✉ *Piazza Sacramento 10* 🌐 *www.visitalberobello.it* 🎟 *€1.50.*

WHERE TO EAT AND STAY

$$$ SOUTHERN ITALIAN

🍴 **Il Poeta Contadino.** This is really two establishments under the same management, standing side by side on the main road leading into Alberobello from the SS172. The higher-end, well-regarded Poeta Contadino specializes in regional cooking with a creative twist, while the Osteria del Poeta offers traditional dishes at budget prices. **Known for:** top restaurant for a splurge; great-value osteria food; stunning vaulted ceiling; extensive wine list. [$] *Average main: €27* ✉ *Via Indipendenza 21–27* ☎ *080/4321917* 🌐 *www.ilpoetacontadino.it.*

$$ SOUTHERN ITALIAN Fodor's Choice ★

🍴 **L'Aratro.** This welcoming rustic restaurant set inside adjoining trulli has dark-wood beams, whitewashed walls, and an outdoor patio for summer dining. A certified Slow Food restaurant, the menu includes traditional dishes that use genuine ingredients from the surrounding area like the *antipasti misti,* which could stand as a meal in itself, or seasonal specialties. **Known for:** Slow Food, so local produce abounds; classic regional fare including orrecchiete with cime di rapa greens and anchovies; gorgeous trulli venue. [$] *Average main: €22* ✉ *Via Monte S. Michele 25–29* ☎ *080/4322789* 🌐 *www.ristorantearatro.it.*

$$$ HOTEL

🏨 **Le Alcove.** If you are of a romantic bent, you will welcome this chance to stay in a proper trullo, one of these unusual, conical, whitewashed dwellings for which Alberobello is famous. **Pros:** centrally located near the Trullo Sovrano; quaint, unusual accommodation; heated floors. **Cons:** rooms are rather small and some have narrow metal staircases leading to the upper area; three rooms are not in the main building; sparse furnishings. [$] *Rooms from: €260* ✉ *Piazza Ferdinando IV 7* ☎ *080/4323754* 🌐 *www.lealcove.it* 🛏 *9 rooms* 🍽 *Free Breakfast.*

OSTUNI

50 km (30 miles) west of Brindisi, 85 km (53 miles) southeast of Bari.

This sun-bleached medieval town lies on three hills not far from the coast. From a distance, Ostuni is a jumble of blazingly white houses and churches spilling over a hilltop and overlooking the sea. Don't be surprised if you hear a lot of English and German spoken in the cobbled streets. The White City, as it is called, has cast its spell on a large number of British and German nationals, who have bought second homes here. That doesn't mean that the town has lost its natural native flavor. Religious festivals, fairs, and colorful traditional events are held as always with the same enthusiasm and fervor.

GETTING HERE AND AROUND

By car, take the Ostuni exit from the SS16. Trenitalia runs frequent trains from Bari. The station, however, is 5 km (3 miles) from the town—there is an almost-hourly local bus service.

VISITOR INFORMATION

Contact Ostuni Tourism Office. ✉ *Corso Mazzini 6* ☎ *0831/301268.*

EXPLORING

Ostuni Old Town. Known as "the White City" because of its dazzling white buildings and cobbled streets, Ostuni commands stupendous views out over the coast and the surrounding plain. Its unpolluted sea and clean beaches have earned it international Blue Flag recognition since 2008. The surrounding countryside contains a number of interesting 17th- and 18th-century masserie, many of which are now converted into agriturismi. ✉ *Ostuni* 🌐 *www.viaggiareinpuglia.it.*

Piazza Libertà. The city's main square divides the new town to the west and the old town to the east. The triangular piazza contains the town symbol: the towering Guglia di Sant'Oronzo (the Spire of St. Oronzo), the patron saint of Ostuni, in whose honor an elaborate festival is held every year in late August. ✉ *Ostuni* 🌐 *www.viaggiareinpuglia.it.*

WHERE TO EAT AND STAY

$$ SOUTHERN ITALIAN 🍴 **Osteria del Tempo Perso.** Buried in the side streets of the old town, this laid-back restaurant occupies an actual cave, where ancient rough-hewn stone walls contrast with the elegant table settings; a second room has a plethora of intriguing objects adorning white walls. Service is friendly, and dishes focus on local cuisine, such as delectable eggplant Parmesan, *raganari ai funghi carboncelli* (special local pasta with fresh mushrooms), and fava soup. **Known for:** atmospheric venue; excellent changing menu; superb meat dishes. [$] *Average main: €18* ✉ *Via G. Tanzarella Vitale 47* ☎ *0831/304819* 🌐 *www.osteriadeltempoperso.com* 🕒 *Closed Mon. Sept.–June.*

$$ HOTEL 🏨 **Hotel Relais Sant'Eligio.** Nestled in the valley just below Ostuni and surrounded by venerable olive trees, the Relais Sant'Eligio is a stylish adaptation of a 16th-century posthouse with characteristic stone archways and roughcast plastered walls. **Pros:** pleasant and modern environment with touches of old-world charm; parking at hotel; fab views. **Cons:** outside the city walls and short walk uphill to the old center of Ostuni; limited breakfast choice; showers can lack decent water pressure. [$] *Rooms from: €200* ✉ *Via Giosuè Pinto 50* ☎ *0831/1985171* 🌐 *www.santeligiorelais.it* 🛏 *22 rooms* 🍽 *Free Breakfast.*

$$ B&B/INN 🏨 **La Terra Hotel.** It doesn't get more historic than this 14th-century noble residence situated on one of the narrow streets that wind around the old center of Ostuni. **Pros:** situated inside the walls of the old city near all the sights; great seafood restaurant; some rooms have superb views. **Cons:** car parking ouside the town with shuttle-bus service; street can be noisy

in high season; standard rooms look a bit tired. [$] *Rooms from: €180* ✉ *Via Gaspare Petrarolo 16, near the Cattedrale di Santa Maria Assunta* ☎ *0831/336651* 🌐 *www.laterrahotel.it* 🛏 *17 rooms* 🍴 *Free Breakfast.*

CEGLIE MESSAPICA

11 km (7 miles) southwest of Ostuni, 18 km (11 miles) southeast of Martina Franca.

With its 14th-century Piazza Vecchia, tattered Baroque balconies, and lordly medieval castles, the little whitewashed town of Ceglie Messapica is a jewel and the epitome of everyone's notion of the sleepy southern Italian town. Situated at the center of the triangle formed by Taranto, Brindisi, and Fasano, the town was once the military capital of the region, and often defended itself against invasions from the Taranto city-state, which wanted to clear a route to the Adriatic. Nowadays, Ceglie Messapica is a gourmet capital, with a surprising number of excellent restaurants.

GETTING HERE AND AROUND

By car, take the Ostuni exit from the SS16, and follow SP22 to Ceglie Messapica. Ferrovie del Sud-Est runs frequent trains from Bari.

VISITOR INFORMATION

Contact Ceglie Messapica Tourism Office. ✉ *Via G. Elia 16* ☎ *0831/371003* 🌐 *www.ceglieturismo.it.*

WHERE TO EAT

$$ SOUTHERN ITALIAN

🍴 **Al Fornello Da Ricci.** Any respectable culinary tour of Puglia must pass through this elegant dining room in the whitewashed town of Ceglie Messapica. The distinguished kitchen sends out a long succession of antipasti, all of them inspired by ancient Pugliese traditions—meats, cheeses, perhaps fried zucchini flowers stuffed with fresh goat's-milk ricotta. **Known for:** imaginative dishes; magical outside space; unpretentious. [$] *Average main: €20* ✉ *Via delle Grotte 11* ☎ *0831/377104* 🌐 *www.alfornellodaricci.com* 🕒 *Closed Mon. and Tues. No lunch Wed.–Sat., no dinner Sun.*

$$ SOUTHERN ITALIAN Fodor's Choice ★

🍴 **Cibus.** Amid the vaulted stone archways of this simple but highly acclaimed *osteria* (tavernlike restaurant) in the old city sit rows of bottles and books devoted to the worship of food and wine. It's no wonder, then, that the food is so good: after an *antipasto del territorio* (sampling of local meats, cheeses, and other delights) you could try roasted quail and potatoes baked under red-hot cinders or a selection of roast meats. **Known for:** gorgeous setting; friendly service and Slow Food ethos; noteworthy wine and cheese. [$] *Average main: €16* ✉ *Via Chianche di Scarano* ☎ *0831/388980* 🌐 *www.ristorantecibus.it* 🕒 *Closed Tues.*

MARTINA FRANCA

29 km (18 miles) southwest of Ostuni, 36 km (22 miles) north of Taranto.

Martina Franca is a beguiling town with a dazzling mixture of medieval and Baroque architecture in the light-color local stone. Developed as a military stronghold in the 14th century, all that remains of the defensive walls are the four gates that divide the old part from the modern suburbs. Lose yourselves in the maze of twisting white alleyways, where erstwhile noble palaces jostle with ancient churches and narrow stairways leading up to homes of ordinary citizens. No longer a little-known backwater, the centro storico can be crowded with sightseers on the weekends. The positive side is that this has led to the emergence of top-quality restaurants, and you'll be spoiled for choice. Each July, the town holds the Valle D'Itria music festival (🌐 *www.festivaldellavalleditria.it*).

GETTING HERE AND AROUND

By car, take the Fasano exit from the SS16, then follow the SS172. The Ferrovie Sud-Est runs frequent trains from Bari and Taranto.

VISITOR INFORMATION

Contact Martina Franca Tourism Office. ✉ *Via Dott. Adolfo Ancona 5* ☎ *366/1266045, 333/4378469 English-speaking contact* 🌐 *www.prolocomartinafranca.it.*

15

EXPLORING

Basilica di San Martino. A splendid example of southern Italian Baroque architecture, the Basilica contains rows of lavishly decorated altars in polychrome marbles, as well as treasures like the silver statues of the two patron saints, San Martino and Santa Comasia. To the right of the main altar, you can see the illuminated niche with the sculpture of the Madonna Pastorella as a shepherd girl in a gown of cloth-of-gold, defending Christ's flock from demons. The elaborately sculpted facade is dominated by a dramatic image of St. Martin with his prancing horse in a shell-shaped niche. ✉ *Via Vittorio Emanuele 30* ☎ *080/4306536* 🎟 *Free.*

WHERE TO EAT

$$ MODERN ITALIAN

🍴 **Garibaldi Bistrot.** Enjoy Italian cuisine with an imaginative twist, just around the corner from the Basilica of San Martino. The Garibaldi Bistrot uses the best of local produce to create unusual and delicious combinations such as octopus with puree of fava beans or sausage brushed with primitivo wine and served with cardoncelli mushrooms. **Known for:** excellent pasta dishes; stunning spot on the piazza; generous portions. [$] *Average main: €16* ✉ *Piazza Plebiscito 13* ☎ *080/4837987.*

THE SALENTO PENINSULA

This far south, the mountains run out of steam and the land is uniformly flat. The monotony of endless olive trees is redeemed by the region's most dramatic coastline, with sandstone cliffs falling fast toward the sea. Here you can find a handful of small, alluring fishing towns, such as Otranto and Gallipoli. Taranto and Brindisi don't quite fit this description: both are big ports, where historical importance is obscured by heavy industry. Nonetheless, Taranto has its archaeological museum, and Brindisi, an important ferry jumping-off point, marks the end of the Via Appia (the "Queen of Roads," built by the Romans). Farther south, Salento (the Salentine Peninsula) is the local name for the part of Puglia that forms the end of the heel. Lecce is an unexpected oasis of grace and sophistication, and its swirling architecture will melt even the most uncompromising critic of the Baroque.

TARANTO

100 km (62 miles) southeast of Bari, 40 km (25 miles) south of Martina Franca.

Taranto (stress the first syllable) was an important port even in Greek times, and it's still Italy's largest naval base. It lies toward the back of the instep of the boot on the broad Mare Grande bay, which is connected to a small internal Mare Piccolo basin by two narrow channels, one artificial and one natural. The old town is a series of *palazzi* in varying states of decay and narrow cobblestone streets on an island between the larger and smaller bodies of water, linked by causeways; the modern city stretches inward along the mainland. Circumnavigating the city can be quite tricky, with a confusing series of flyovers and junctions. Take it as slowly as you can and follow the signs for the centro storico where the main sights are situated.

GETTING HERE AND AROUND

By car, the A14 autostrada takes you almost directly to Taranto. Trenitalia runs frequent trains from Bari and Brindisi.

VISITOR INFORMATION

Contact Taranto Tourism Office. ⊠ *Castello Aragonese* ☎ *389/9935679* ⊕ *www.prolocoditaranto.wordpress.com.*

EXPLORING

Castel Sant'Angelo. The monumental Castel San'Angelo, more commonly referred to as the Castello Aragonese, guards the drawbridge leading from the island center of Taranto to the newer city on the mainland. The castle is occupied by the Italian navy, but it's open to the public, and navy personnel conduct regular, free guided tours. The castle, built in its present form by King Ferdinand of Aragon, king of Naples, in the 15th century, contains ruins of older Greek, Byzantine, and Norman constructions as well as the Renaissance Chapel of San Leonardo. ⊠ *Piazza Castello 4* ☎ *099/7753438* ⊕ *www.castelloaragonesetaranto.it* ⊠ *Free.*

Fodor's Choice **MarTA Museo Archeologico Nazionale Taranto.** Taranto's outstanding
★ National Archaeological Museum (the MarTA) occupies the historic premises of the ex-monastery of San Pasquale. The museum dates from 1887, and its collection of Greek and Roman antiquities is considered to be one of the most important in Italy. Many artifacts were discovered in the vicinity, testifying to the city's centuries-old importance as a port. Admire the rich cache of tomb goods, including magnificent gold jewelry, polychrome terra-cottas, objects in ivory and bone, and rare colored glass. A display of Jewish, Christian, and Muslim funeral epitaphs, dating between the 4th and 11th century, demonstrate the peaceful coexistence of the three religions in this multicultural Mediterranean hub from the Byzantine era to the Middle Ages. ⊠ *Via Cavour 10* ☎ *099/4538639* ⊕ *www.museotaranto.beniculturali.it* ⊠ *€8.*

San Domenico. Taranto's most important monument is the ancient church and monastery of San Domenico in the heart of the centro storico. Situated on the narrow strip of land that divides Taranto's two bays, Mare Piccolo and Mare Grande, the present church rises over the ancient Greek acropolis of Taranto where the city is considered to have originated. The statue of Our Lady of Sorrows, much venerated by the local people, stands in the last chapel on the left. Pop into the beautiful 13th-century colonnaded cloister for a quiet moment's respite from sightseeing. ✉ *Via Duomo 33* ☎ *099/4713511* 🎫 *Free* ⏲ *Cloister closed Sun.*

WHERE TO EAT AND STAY

$$ SOUTHERN ITALIAN FAMILY

🍴 **Marco Aurelio.** This pizzeria and restaurant is conveniently located near the entrance to the Archaeological Museum. Bright and cheerful with sunny-colored tablecloths, it offers a menu based on seafood staples like risotto ai frutti di mare and *cozze alla tarantino* (mussels cooked in tomato sauce with garlic, chilies, and parsley). **Known for:** gluten-free options; abundant portions; decent seafood. [$] *Average main: €16* ✉ *Via Cavour 17* ☎ *099/4527893* ⏲ *Closed Tues.*

$ HOTEL

🏨 **Hotel Europa.** Situated on the corner of the point jutting out over Taranto's Mar Piccolo, the Europa has one of the best views in town. **Pros:** great location overlooking the Mar Piccolo bay; 10-minute walk from the Museo Nazionale; courteous staff. **Cons:** rooms a bit old-fashioned; steep stairs to mezzanine areas in some rooms; tricky parking in such a busy area. [$] *Rooms from: €120* ✉ *Via Roma 1* ☎ *099/4525994* 🌐 *www.hoteleuropataranto.it* 🛏 *43 rooms* 🍽 *Free Breakfast.*

LECCE

40 km (25 miles) southeast of Brindisi, 87 km (54 miles) east of Taranto.

Fodor's Choice ★

Lecce is the crown jewel of the Mezzogiorno. The city is called "the Florence of the south," but that term doesn't do justice to Lecce's uniqueness in the Italian landscape. Although its pretty boutiques, lively bars, bustling streets, laid-back student cafés, and evening passeggiata draw comparisons to the cultural capitals of the north, Lecce's impossibly intricate Baroque architecture and its hyperanimated crowds are distinctively southern. The city is a cosmopolitan oasis two steps from the idyllic Otranto–Brindisi coastline and a hop from the olive-grove countryside of Puglia. Relatively undiscovered by foreign tourists, Lecce exudes an optimism and youthful joie de vivre unparalleled in any other Baroque showcase.

Summer is a great time to visit. In July courtyards and piazzas throughout the city are the settings for dramatic productions. Autumn has its charms as well. A Baroque music festival is held in churches throughout the city in September and October.

GETTING HERE AND AROUND

By car from Bari, take the main toll-free coast road via Brindisi and continue along the SS613 to Lecce. Frequent trains run along the coast from Bari and beyond. The closest airport is in Brindisi.

VISITOR INFORMATION

Contact Lecce Tourism Office. ✉ *Corso Vittorio Emanuele II 16* ☎ *0832/682985* 🌐 *www.ilecce.it.*

EXPLORING

Fodor's Choice ★ **Duomo.** Lecce's magnificent Duomo of Santa Maria Assunta never fails to take visitors by surprise. The sheer theatricality of its position, dominating a vast open square concealed in a maze of pedestrianized alleyways, embodies the very spirit of Baroque architecture. The aim was to stun the faithful with a vision of opulence and power; even today it leaves viewers openmouthed, especially at night when the entire piazza is illuminated like a stage set. The 17th-century church, constructed in rose-tinged local stone, is flanked by the ornate Bishops' Palace, the seminary, and the 236-foot-high bell tower, which dominates the centro storico skyline. ✉ *Piazza Duomo, off Corso Vittorio Emanuele II* ☎ *0832/308557* 🌐 *www.cattedraledilecce.it.*

Piazza Sant'Oronzo. This is the hub of Lecce's social life in the heart of the maze of pedestrianized alleyways lined with cafés, little restaurants, and crafts shops. Named after Oronzo, the city's patron saint, who crowns a Roman column that once marked the end of the Old Appian Way, the piazza is also occupied by another city symbol, the somewhat odd-looking 17th-century Sedile, formerly the town hall but now an art and exhibition center. The piazza revolves round the sunken hemicycle of the old **Anfiteatro Romano,** where the rows of seats are clearly visible. ✉ *Piazza Sant'Oronzo.*

Santa Croce. Although Lecce was founded before the time of the ancient Greeks, it's often associated with the term *Barocco leccese,* the result of a citywide impulse in the 17th century to redo the town in an exuberant fashion. But this was Baroque with a difference. Such architecture is often heavy and monumental, but here it took on a lighter, more fanciful air, and the church of Santa Croce is a fine example, along with the adjoining **Palazzo della Prefettura.** The facade is a riot of sculptures of saints, angels, leaves, vines, and columns, all in local, glowing, honey-color stone, creating an overall lighthearted effect. ✉ *Via Umberto I 3* ☎ *0832/6931.*

WHERE TO EAT

$$ SOUTHERN ITALIAN FAMILY 🍴 **Alle Due Corti.** Renowned local culinary experts Rosalba De Carlo and Giorgio Grassi run this traditional trattoria, where the long tradition and culture of Salentine cuisine is treated with both respect and originality. A staple on the menu is *ciciri a tria* (homemade pasta partly boiled and partly fried, with chickpea sauce), rice with potatoes and mussels, or crispy, deep-fried squid. **Known for:** lively locals; hearty, tasty Pugliese food; cookery courses. [$] *Average main: €17* ✉ *Corte dei Giugni 1, corner of Via Prato 42* ☎ *0832/242223* 🌐 *www.alleduecorti.com* ⏲ *Closed Mon. and Jan.*

$$ SOUTHERN ITALIAN 🍴 **Corte dei Pandolfi.** Here you can choose from a vast list of Salento's best wines from the restaurant's ample wine cellar and feast on an unparalleled spread of artisanal *salumi* (cured meats) and local cheeses, accompanied by delicious local honey and *mostarda* (preserved fruit). Traditional primi and secondi include vegetarian specialties, with the menu changing with the season's produce—fresh fish is a staple in the summer months. **Known for:** vegetarian specialists; classic coved ceilings mix with contemporary minimalism; relaxed literary vibe, with books

available. $ *Average main: €16* ✉ *Corte dei Pandolfi 3* ☎ *0832/332309* ⊕ *www.cortedeipandolfi.com.*

$ ✕ **Le Zie.** This tiny, old-fashioned and unpretentious trattoria is a favorite with the local families, and the no-frills charm is matched by the wholesome, unfussy food. Cucina Casareccia Pugliese—home cooking—specialties include *polipo in teglia* (stewed octopus), *baccalà al forno* (baked salt cod), or the ubiquitous rustic *purè di fave e cicoria* (bean puree with wild chicory). **Known for:** warm hospitality; traditional homemade food; best to book ahead. $ *Average main: €14* ✉ *Via Costadura 19* ☎ *0832/245178* ⊘ *Closed Mon. No dinner Sun.*

SOUTHERN
ITALIAN
FAMILY

WHERE TO STAY

$$ 🏨 **Patria Palace.** It's a happy coincidence that the grandest hotel edifice in Lecce happens to be in one of the best possible locations: right in front of the monumental Santa Croce Basilica, the crown jewel of Lecce Baroque. **Pros:** many luxurious, high-ceilinged rooms; ideal location; fabulous roof terrace. **Cons:** a few rooms overlook the noisy backstreets; some rooms outdated and less grand; lobby doesn't match the handsome facade. $ *Rooms from: €136* ✉ *Piazzetta Riccardi 13* ☎ *0832/245111* ⊕ *www.patriapalace.com* ⥱ *67 rooms* ⦿ *Free Breakfast.*

HOTEL
Fodor'sChoice
★

$ 🏨 **President.** Rub elbows with visiting dignitaries at this business hotel and conference center near Piazza Mazzini. **Pros:** comfortable rooms; convenient location; low-season bargains. **Cons:** geared to business over leisure; more international than local flavor; rather somber, functional room decor. $ *Rooms from: €113* ✉ *Via Salandra 6* ☎ *0832/456111* ⊕ *www.hotelpresidentlecce.it* ⥱ *150 rooms* ⦿ *Free Breakfast.*

HOTEL

$$ 🏨 **Risorgimento Resort Lecce.** Despite the fact that this luxury hotel in the heart of the centro storico of Lecce has been a landmark in town since 1880, it is firmly in the 21st century, with a clean, modern decor and vibrant modern color schemes. **Pros:** central location; highly professional staff; spacious rooms. **Cons:** smart, international-style hotel without much local atmosphere; may be noisy in rooms at the front; tiny gym. $ *Rooms from: €166* ✉ *Via Augustus Imperatore 19* ☎ *0832/246311* ⊕ *www.risorgimentoresort.it* ⥱ *47 rooms* ⦿ *Free Breakfast.*

HOTEL

OTRANTO

36 km (22 miles) southeast of Lecce, 188 km (117 miles) southeast of Bari.

In one of the first great Gothic novels, Horace Walpole's 1764 *The Castle of Otranto,* the English writer immortalized this city and its mysterious medieval fortress. Otranto (stress the first syllable) has had more than its share of dark thrills. As the easternmost point in Italy—and therefore closest to the Balkan Peninsula—it's often borne the brunt of foreign invasions, including the massacre of 800 citizens by the Moors in 1480 because they refused to give up their faith. From here, you can see across the sea to Albania on a clear day. If you are a fan of the Neolithic, you will be interested in the **Grotta dei Cervi,** a few miles down the coast. The walls of the cave are covered with hundreds of prehistoric images, painted with red ocher and black bat guano.

GETTING HERE AND AROUND

By car from Lecce, take the southbound SS16 and exit at Maglie. To follow the coast, take the SS53 from Lecce, then follow SS611 south. There's regular train service from Lecce on Ferrovie del Sud-Est.

VISITOR INFORMATION

Contact **Otranto Tourism Office.** ✉ *Piazza Castello* ☎ *0836/801436* 🌐 *www.comune.otranto.le.it.*

EXPLORING

Castello Aragonese. The massive Aragonese Castle is considered a masterpiece of 16th-century military architecture. Rebuilt by the Spanish viceroy Don Pedro di Toledo in 1535 after it was badly damaged in the siege of Otranto (1480) when the invading Turkish armies destroyed the city, its impressive walls and bastions dominate the port and seashore. Various exhibitions are held in the castle during the summer months. ✉ *Piazza Castello* ☎ *0836/801436, 0836/210094* 🌐 *www.comune.otranto.le.it* 🎫 *€7 whole complex; €3 underground vaults only.*

Cattedrale. The best sight in Otranto is the Cattedrale, Santa Maria Annunziata, consecrated in 1088. The 12th-century Pantaleone mosaic, which covers the entire length of the nave, the sanctuary, and apse, depicts scenes from the Old Testament along with traditional medieval chivalric tales and animals, set alongside a Tree of Life. The walls behind the main altar are lined with glass cases containing the skulls and tibias of the 800 martyrs of Otranto, slain by the Ottomans after the seige of 1480 because they refused to renounce their faith. ✉ *Piazza Basilica* ☎ *0836/801436* 🌐 *www.comune.otranto.le.it.*

WHERE TO STAY

$$ HOTEL 🏨 **Corte di Nettuno.** From the wrought-iron gates in the shape of waves, to the statue of the sea god Neptune greeting you at the entrance, a nautical theme prevails throughout the Corte di Nettuno. **Pros:** good location near the marina and sights; quirky decor full of surprises; decent food. **Cons:** some people may find the sea theme overly eccentric; clinical feel in some dated bathrooms; lackadaisical service in low season. [$] *Rooms from: €150* ✉ *Via Madonna del Passo* ☎ *0836/801832* 🌐 *www.cortedinettuno.it* ⏲ *Closed Nov.–Mar.* 🛏 *28 rooms* 🍴 *Free Breakfast.*

$$$ B&B/INN 🏨 **Masseria Montelauro.** Beautifully restored, with stylish designer interiors, this interesting 19th-century former masseria is an oasis of comfort just a short drive from lovely Otranto. **Pros:** interesting building; lovely grounds and pool; friendly, helpful service. **Cons:** car is absolutely necessary; food is pricey; some rooms rather stuffy. [$] *Rooms from: €265* ✉ *SP358, Località Montelauro* ☎ *0836/806203* 🌐 *www.masseriamontelauro.it* ⏲ *Closed Nov.–Apr.* 🛏 *29 rooms* 🍴 *Free Breakfast.*

GALLIPOLI

37 km (23 miles) south of Lecce, 190 km (118 miles) southeast of Bari.

The fishing port of Gallipoli, on the eastern tip of the Golfo di Taranto, is divided between a new town, on the mainland, and the beautiful fortified *borgo antico* (old town), across a 17th-century bridge, crowded onto its own small island in the gulf. The Greeks called it Kallipolis ("the fair city"), the Romans Anxa. Like the infamous Turkish town of the same name on the Dardanelles, the Italian Gallipoli occupies a strategic location and thus was repeatedly attacked through the centuries—by the Normans in 1071, the Venetians in 1484, and the British in 1809. Today life in Gallipoli revolves around its fishing trade. Fishing boats in primary colors breeze in and out of the bay during the day, and Gallipoli's fish market, below the bridge, throbs with activity all morning.

GETTING HERE AND AROUND
From Lecce, take the SS101. From Taranto, follow the coastal SS174. Frequent trains run from Lecce.

VISITOR INFORMATION
Contact Gallipoli Tourism Office. ⊠ *Via Kennedy* ☎ *0833/264283* ⊕ *www.prolocogallipoli.it.*

EXPLORING

FAMILY **Beaches of Gallipoli.** Ample swimming and clean, fine sand make Gallipoli's beaches a good choice for families. The 5-km (3-mile) expanse of sand stretches from Punta Pizzo to Lido San Giovanni and is divided into a series of bathing establishments, which all provide sun beds, umbrellas, showers, changing facilities, and snack bars. Parco Gondar hosts a fun fair and music events. Water-sports equipment can be bought or rented at the waterfront shops in town. **Amenities:** food and drink; lifeguards; parking (fee); showers; toilets; water sports. **Best for:** partiers; snorkeling; sunset; swimming; walking; windsurfing. ⊠ *Gallipoli* ⊕ *www.prolocogallipoli.it.*

Castello Aragonese. The massive bulk of Gallipoli's castle guards the entrance to the island of the borgo antico, which is linked to the new town by a bridge. Rising out of the sea, the present fortress, dating from the 17th to 18th century, is built on the foundations of an earlier Byzantine citadel. It has four towers, and a separate fifth one, known as the Rivellino, where open-air shows are held in summer. ⊠ *Rampa Castello* ☎ *0833/262775* ⊕ *www.castellogallipoli.it* ⊠ *€5* ⊗ *Closed Mon., and Tues. Sun. 1–3.*

Duomo. In the center of the borgo antico, Gallipoli's Duomo is a notable Baroque cathedral from the late 17th century, dedicated to Sant'Agata, patron saint of the city. Built in local limestone, the ornate facade is matched by an equally elaborate interior with columns and altars in fine polychrome marble and paintings by leading local Gallipoli and Neapolitan *maestri* of the time. Particularly interesting are the stone carvings that depict episodes from the city's history. ⊠ *Via Duomo 1* ☎ *0833/261987* ⊕ *www.cattedralegallipoli.it.*

La Purità. A fine example of *gallipolino* Baroque, the 17th-century Church of Santa Maria della Purità stands at the end of the borgo antico overlooking the famed Purità beach. It contains a wealth of works of art, including the painting at the high altar by Luca Giordano, intricately carved wooden choir stalls, and a 19th-century majolica pavement. ⊠ *Riviera Nazario Sauro* ☎ *0833/261699.*

15

WHERE TO EAT AND STAY

$$$ ✕ **Marechiaro.** For more than a century, this historic seafood restaurant
SEAFOOD in the shadow of Gallipoli's Aragonese Castle has been serving diners.
Built on wooden piles, it seems to float like a ship anchored in the bay
by the bridge that connects Gallipoli new town with the island that
contains the old borgo. **Known for:** warm Gallipolino welcome; freshest
raw ricci di mare (sea urchins); jetty terrace over the water. $ *Average
main: €25* ✉ *Lungomare Marconi* ☎ *0833/266143.*

$$ ▥ **Relais Corte Palmieri.** An 18th-century aristocratic house in the center
HOTEL of Gallipoli's borgo antico and a short distance from the Purità beach,
Fodor's Choice the Relais Corte Palmieri has been tastefully renovated to modern stan-
★ dards, while preserving its characteristic frescoes and mosaics. **Pros:**
quiet elegance right in the heart of the historic center; roof garden
with spectacular views; beach nearby. **Cons:** difficult to get to with
own transportation; parking mighty tricky; noisy rooms street side
and near breakfast room. $ *Rooms from: €180* ✉ *Corte Palmieri 3*
☎ *0833/265318* ⊕ *www.relaiscortepalmieri.it* ☾ *Closed late Oct.–late
Mar. or early Apr.* ⇆ *20 rooms* ◎| *Free Breakfast.*

BASILICATA

Occupying the instep of Italy's boot, Basilicata formed part of Magna
Graecia, the loose collection of colonies founded along the coast of
southern Italy whose wealth and military prowess rivaled those of the
city-states of Greece itself. More recently it was made famous by Carlo
Levi (1902–75) in his *Christ Stopped at Eboli*, a book that underscored
the poverty of the region. (The title comes from a local saying that
implied that progress had stopped at Eboli, some 60 miles to the west,
near the coast, and that Basilicata had "been bypassed by Christianity,
by morality, by history itself—that they have somehow been excluded
from the full human experience.")

Basilicata is no longer desolate, as it draws travelers in search of bucolic
settings, great food, and archaeological treasures. The city of Matera,
the region's true highlight, is built on the side of an impressive ravine
that's honeycombed with Sassi, some of them still occupied, forming
a separate enclave that contrasts vividly with the attractive Baroque
town above.

MATERA

62 km (39 miles) south of Bari.

Matera, the town of the unique Sassi, is one of the most intriguing
places in southern Italy. The so-called New Town, full of elegant
Baroque churches, palazzi, and broad piazzas—filled to bursting during the evening passeggiata—is perched on the verge of a steep gully
crowded with the cave dwellings of the past, now converted into hotels,
restaurants, and private homes. Many of the ancient rock churches can
be visited. This is a particularly good time to visit, as Matera has been
elected European Cultural Capital for 2019 and preparations are under
way, with all kinds of initiatives and programs being launched.

GETTING HERE AND AROUND

From Bari, take the SS96 to Altamura, then the SS99 to Matera. Roughly one train per hour (Ferrovie Appulo Lucane) leaves Bari Centrale for Matera.

VISITOR INFORMATION

Contact Proloco Matera Città dei Sassi (Tourism Office). ✉ *Via Lucana 184* ☎ *0835/335508* ⊕ *www.prolocomatera2019.it.*

EXPLORING

Fodor'sChoice ★ **Duomo.** Matera's splendidly restored cathedral, dedicated to the Madonna della Bruna e di Sant'Eustachio, was built in the late 13th century and occupies a prominent position between the two Sassi. Lavishly decorated, it has a typical Apulian-Romanesque flavor; inside, there's a recovered fresco, probably painted in the 14th century, showing scenes from the Last Judgment. On the Duomo's facade the figures of Sts. Peter and Paul stand on either side of a sculpture of Matera's patron, the Madonna della Bruna. ✉ *Piazza Duomo* ☎ *0835/311655* ⊕ *www.prolocomatera2019.it.*

Museo Archaeologico Nazionale Domenico Ridola. Named after local 19th-century medical doctor Domenico Ridola, who investigated archaeological sites in the surrounding area, the museum highlights his excavations of the remains of Paleolithic and Neolithic settlements, as well as a richly endowed 4th-century-BC tomb. Ridola's finds are on view in the museum, which is housed in the former monastery of Santa Chiara. The collection includes an extensive selection of prehistoric and classical finds, notably Bronze Age implements and beautifully decorated red-figure pottery from Magna Graecia. ✉ *Via Ridola 24* ☎ *0835/310058* ⊕ *www.basilicata.beniculturali.it* 🎫 *€2.50* ☾ *Closed Mon. until 2.*

San Giovanni Battista. Considered a jewel of medieval architecture, the 13th-century Romanesque church of San Giovanni Battista was restored to its pre-Baroque simplicity in 1926. The elaborately carved portal is a riot of entwining stone vines, flowers, leaves, human figures, and allegorical creatures. Inside, the three naves are flanked by columns crowned with capitals, each one decorated with symbolic animal forms and other images. No two are alike. ✉ *Via San Biagio* ☎ *0835/334182.*

Fodor'sChoice ★ **Sassi di Matera.** Matera's Sassi are rock-hewn dwellings piled chaotically atop one another, strewn across the sides of a steep ravine. Some date from Paleolithic times, when they were truly just caves. In the years that followed, the grottoes were slowly adapted as houses only slightly more modern, with their exterior walls closed off and canals regulating rainwater and sewage. Until relatively recently, these troglodytic abodes presented a Dante-esque vision of squalor and poverty, which is graphically described in Carlo Levi's 1945 memoir, *Christ Stopped at Eboli.* In the 1960s, however, most of them were emptied of their inhabitants, who were largely consigned to the ugly apartment blocks seen on the way into town. Today, having been designated a UNESCO World Heritage Site, the area has been cleaned up and is gradually being populated once again—and even gentrified, as evidenced by the bars and restaurants that have moved in. The wide Strada Panoramica leads you safely through this desolate region, which still retains its eerie atmosphere and panoramic views.

There are two areas of Sassi, the **Sasso Caveoso** and the **Sasso Barisano,** and both can be seen from vantage points in the upper town. Follow the Strada Panoramica down into the Sassi and feel free to ramble among the strange structures, which, in the words of travel writer H.V. Morton in his *A Traveller in Southern Italy,* "resemble the work of termites rather than of man." There are more than 100 *chiese rupestri,* or rock-hewn churches, some of which have medieval frescoes, three of which are open to the public. The most spectacular is **Santa Maria de Idris,** right on the edge of the Sasso Caveoso, near the ravine. Guided tours of the town and Sassi area are recommended and can be arranged through the tourist office. ⊠ *Sasso Caveoso* ⊕ *www.prolocomatera2019.it.*

WHERE TO EAT

$$
SOUTHERN
ITALIAN
✕ **Il Terrazzino.** Perched on a terrace overlooking the famous Sassi canyon, you can sit outside in summer enjoying the unique view. The restaurant proper, with a menu that is strictly Basilicata, is in a cavern carved out of the cliff side; ask to see the spectacular three-level wine cellar. **Known for:** stupendous views; classic Basilicata meat dishes and fresh pasta; cooling and interesting interiors. $ *Average main: €17* ⊠ *Vico S. Giuseppe 7* ☎ *0835/332503* ⊕ *www.ilterrazzino.org* ⊗ *Closed Tues.*

$$
SOUTHERN
ITALIAN
✕ **Le Botteghe.** A pleasingly restored building down in the depths of the Sassi, with rough white walls and arched ceilings, contains this stylish restaurant. One standout on the menu is the charcoal-grilled steak, specially selected by a local butcher and cooked wonderfully rare—this is one of the finest pieces of meat in the region. **Known for:** heaped pasta portions; relaxed atmosphere; charcoal-barbecued meat. $ *Average main: €15* ⊠ *Piazza San Pietro Barisano 22* ☎ *0835/344072* ⊕ *www.lebotteghematera.it* ⊗ *No lunch Tues.–Fri.*

WHERE TO STAY

$
HOTEL
I Sassi. Opened in 1996, I Sassi claims to be Matera's first "grotto hotel," with rooms inside a succession of caves that overlook the huddle of rooftops, descending flights of stone stairs, and the valley floor of Sasso Barisano. **Pros:** good value; decent breakfast; fabulous views. **Cons:** bathrooms small and basic; rooms are spread out and not connected to each other; tricky access for less fit. $ *Rooms from: €98* ⊠ *Via San Giovanni Vecchio 89* ☎ *0835/331009* ⊕ *www.hotelsassi.it* 🛏 *35 rooms* ⦿⦿ *Free Breakfast.*

$$
HOTEL
Fodor's Choice
★
Locanda di San Martino. Situated at the bottom of the Sassi ravine on the Via Fiorentini (which allows limited car access), the Locanda offers a more upmarket form of cave dwelling, with all modern comforts, including an elevator to whisk you up the cliff side to your room. **Pros:** convenient location if you come by car; comfortable rooms; ancient Roman style spa in the hotel. **Cons:** rooms reached via outdoor walkway; limited parking nearby; spa may be a tad intimate for some. $ *Rooms from: €184* ⊠ *Via Fiorentini 71* ☎ *0835/256600* ⊕ *www. locandadisanmartino.it* 🛏 *38 rooms* ⦿⦿ *Free Breakfast.*

15

$$$$ HOTEL Fodor's Choice ★ **Palazzo Margherita.** This is Francis Ford Coppola's Xanadu—a large and luxurious palazzo in the town of his ancestors and now, thanks to the guiding hand of French designer Jacques Grange, Basilicata's top lodging. **Pros:** professional, courteous staff; a garden pool; spacious rooms with lots of high-tech gadgetry. **Cons:** film star prices; private transport needed; not much to do in Bernalda. *Rooms from: €1200* *Corso Umberto 64* *A 40-min drive south of Matera: take SS7 out of Matera heading for Potenza and then join SS407 for Metaponto and Taranto. Look for turnoff to Bernalda after 25 km (16 miles)* *0835/549060* *www.thefamilycoppolahideaways.com/en/palazzo-margherita* *Closed Jan.–Mar.* *9 rooms* *Free Breakfast.*

$$ HOTEL **Palazzo Viceconte.** If cave dwelling is not your style, an elegant former aristocratic residence in the Duomo piazza will certainly appeal. **Pros:** good location with easy walking to almost all the main sights; on a quiet square; suites are especially spacious. **Cons:** rooms vary considerably in size; parking prices exorbitant; breakfast may disappoint. *Rooms from: €148* *Via San Potito 7* *0835/330699* *www.palazzovice-conte.it* *16 rooms* *Free Breakfast.*

$$$ HOTEL **Sant'Angelo Resort.** What better way to get close to Matera's trogloditic Sassi than to stay in a hotel that actually incorporates some of the caves as highly upgraded guest rooms. **Pros:** unrivaled views; atmospheric rooms with minimalist design; a unique cave-dwelling experience. **Cons:** no elevator and many steps to climb; can feel stuffy and humid at times; lack of natural light. *Rooms from: €290* *Piazza San Pietro Caveoso* *0835/314010* *www.santangeloresort.it* *21 rooms* *Free Breakfast.*

MARATEA

217 km (135 miles) south of Naples.

When encountering Maratea for the first time, you can be forgiven for thinking you've somehow arrived at the French Riviera. The high, twisty road comes complete with glimpses of a turquoise sea below and is divided by the craggy rocks into various separate localities—Maratea, Maratea Porto, Marina di Maratea, Fiumicello, and Cersuta. Maratea is the name given to this cluster of towns, as well as to the main inland village, a tumble of cobblestone streets where the ruins of a much older settlement (Maratea Antica) can be seen. At the summit of the hill stands the gigantic *Cristo Redentore*, a massive statue of Christ reminiscent of the one in Rio de Janeiro. There's no shortage of secluded sandy strips in between the rocky headlands, which can get crowded in August. A summer minibus service connects all the different points once or twice an hour.

GETTING HERE AND AROUND

By car, take the Lagonegro exit from the A3 autostrada and continue along the SS585. Intercity and regional trains from Reggio Calabria and Naples stop at Maratea. In the summer months there's a bus linking the train station to the upper town 4 km (2½ miles) away.

VISITOR INFORMATION

Contact APT Maratea (Azienda di Promozione Turistica). ✉ *Piazza Vitolo* ☎ *0973/030366* ⊕ *www.aptbasilicata.it.*

WHERE TO EAT AND STAY

$$
SOUTHERN
ITALIAN

✕ **Da Cesare.** With an open kitchen so you can watch the chef and a veranda overlooking the azure waters of the Golfo di Policastro, there's always something to see at this family-run seafood restaurant. Even better: it serves some of the freshest catch in town, with specialties of the house that include *linguine con nero di seppia* (flat noodles with cuttlefish ink sauce), grilled squid, and *grigliata mista* (mixed grilled fish and seafood). **Known for:** seafood dishes aplenty; open veranda with views; prominent position on coastal road. $ *Average main: €21* ✉ *Via Nazionale Cersuta 52* ✛ *On main coast road (SS18) in village of Cersuta, about 5 km (3 miles) north of Maratea, 3 km (2 miles) south of Acquafredda* ☎ *0973/871840* ⊗ *Closed Thurs. Nov.–Mar.*

$$$
HOTEL

⬚ **Villa Cheta Elite.** Immersed in Mediterranean greenery and with glorious sea views, this elegant and historic villa is in the seaside village of Acquafredda, just north of Maratea. **Pros:** surrounded by lush vegetation; beautiful views of the coast and mountains; lovely Art Nouveau building. **Cons:** hotel is quite remote, so shops and the town require a car; nearest beach is far away; steps up to entrance. $ *Rooms from: €250* ✉ *Via Timpone 46, Località Acquafredda* ☎ *0973/878134* ⊕ *www.villacheta.it* ⊗ *Closed Oct.–Apr.* ⤸ *23 rooms* ⧼❁⧽ *Free Breakfast.*

CALABRIA

Italy's southernmost mainland region may still be poorer than the rest of the country, but it also claims more than its share of fantastic scenery and great beaches. The accent here is on the landscape, the sea, and the constantly changing dialogue between the two. Don't expect much in the way of big-city sophistication in this least trodden of regions, but instead remain open to the simple pleasures to be found—the country food, the friendliness, the disarming hospitality of the people. Aside from coast and culture, there are also some destinations worth going out of your way for, from the vividly colored murals of Diamante to the hiking trails of the Pollino and Sila national parks.

The drive on the southbound A3 autostrada alone is a breathtaking experience, the more so as you approach Sicily, whose image grows tantalizingly nearer as the road wraps around the coastline once challenged by Odysseus. The road seems to have been under reconstruction since his time, with little sign of completion.

DIAMANTE

51 km (32 miles) south of Maratea, 225 km (140 miles) south of Naples.

A lively and attractive little resort on Calabria's north Tyrrhenian Coast, Diamante styles itself as "the town of murals and peperoncinos." The old town center is accessed over a bridge across the Corvino River, which runs through the town to the sea. The maze of alleyways and whitewashed houses is covered in murals by both local and international artists, many featuring fishers and religious themes, while strings of bright-red chili pods hang from doorways and balconies. The pedestrianized seafront promenade is the town hub, lined with small shops, ice-cream parlors, and bars. Flanking the broad, palm-lined promenade are sparkling beaches to the north and south and interesting archaeological remains in the nearby Cirella district. September's annual Peperoncino Festival is a major event, involving almost the entire town.

GETTING HERE AND AROUND

Driving from Maratea, take the SS18; from Cosenza, take the SS107 to Paola, then the SS18. Regional trains leave from Naples four times a day, with regular service from Paola.

VISITOR INFORMATION

Contact Diamante Tourist Office. ✉ *Via Gullo 1* ☎ *0985/81130* 🌐 *www.prolocodiamante.it.*

WHERE TO EAT AND STAY

$$ SEAFOOD Fodor's Choice ★ 🍴 **'A Cucchiarella.** Situated in the old town center, just off the seafront promenade, this is one of Diamante's most popular restaurants. In the summer, there are tables outside on the pavement where you can enjoy watching the evening passeggiata—and savoring the fish dishes that reign supreme on the menu. **Known for:** exceptional seafood; good vegetarian options; handsome stone-walled dining rooms and a terrace. [$] *Average main: €16* ✉ *Via Cavour 6* ☎ *0985/877287* ⏲ *Closed Mon.*

$$ ITALIAN FAMILY 🍴 **La Guardiola.** With its own private beach on the Diamante Riviera, La Guardiola makes a perfect relaxing lunch stop where you can also enjoy a swim and a siesta under a beach umbrella. The menu centers on the catch of the day and might include spaghetti with sea urchins, fish-stuffed ravioli, and *stuffata di alici alla diamantese* (fresh anchovy stew), plus many pizza options. **Known for:** seafood specialties and pizza on the shore; evenings can be lively, with music and soccer on the TV; beachside views and sunsets. [$] *Average main: €18* ✉ *Lungomare Riviera Bleu* ☎ *0985/876759* 🌐 *www.laguardioladiamante.it.*

$$ HOTEL 🏨 **Grand Hotel San Michele.** A survivor from a vanishing age, the San Michele occupies a Belle Époque–style villa atop a cliff near the village of Cetraro, 20 km (12 miles) south of Diamante on the SS18. **Pros:** beautiful situation; landscaped gardens and 9-hole golf course; pool and private beach. **Cons:** some rooms at garden level with access by steps; breakfast lacks variety; isolated if you lack your own transport. [$] *Rooms from: €180* ✉ *Località Bosco 8/9, Cetraro* ☎ *0982/91012* 🌐 *www.sanmichele.it* 🏌 *9-hole golf course* ⏲ *Closed Nov.–Easter* 🛏 *88 rooms* 🍽 *Free Breakfast.*

$ HOTEL 🏨 **Hotel Ferretti.** The gleaming-white, 1970s wedding cake–like structure stands out on the coastline 1 km (½ mile) out of Diamante's town center. **Pros:** overlooks the sea; beach, pool, and tennis court; quirky 1970s decor. **Cons:** decor not to all tastes; a car is best to get around; limited breakfast options. [$] *Rooms from: €115* ✉ *Via Poseidone 171* ☎ *0985/81428* 🌐 *www.albergoferretti.com* 🛏 *52 rooms* 🍽 *Free Breakfast.*

CASTROVILLARI

68 km (43 miles) northeast of Diamante, 75 km (48 miles) northwest of Cosenza.

Stress the first "i" when you pronounce the name of this provincial Calabrian city, which is nestled in the deep valley under the 7,375-foot-tall Mt. Pollino. The town is notable for its summer jazz festival; many of the festival events are held in the medieval Aragonese castle. You can also visit the historic synagogue, which dates from the early Middle Ages, and 16th-century San Giuliano church.

Castrovillari is also a great jumping-off point for exploring the Albanian-speaking village of Cìvita, as well as Pollino National Park, Italy's biggest national park and a walkers' paradise. Castrovillari's world-class restaurant and inn, La Locanda di Alia, has made the city something of a gastronomic destination.

GETTING HERE AND AROUND

By car, take the A3 autostrada and exit at Frascineto-Castrovillari. Ferrovie della Calabria runs buses from Cosenza, but service is irregular.

WHERE TO EAT AND STAY

$$$

MODERN ITALIAN

Fodor'sChoice

★

✕ **La Locanda di Alia.** Surrounded by a lush garden, with swimming pool, this charming restaurant (and inn) will be a welcome surprise after a drive through the dramatic mountain scenery of Pollino National Park. Gourmet meals cooked by owner-chef Gaetano Alia include the freshest of local produce, prepared with an imaginative twist. **Known for:** award-winning but unpretentious cuisine using Pollino produce; candele pasta with calabrese spicy 'nduja sauce; gorgeous setting and leafy outdoor terrace. $ *Average main: €26* ⊠ *Via Jetticelli 55, off the main street in Castrovillari (look for signs)* ☎ *0981/46370* ⊕ *www.alia. it* ☉ *No dinner Sun.*

$

B&B/INN

🛏 **Alia Jazz Hotel.** You can be assured of a comfortable stay in this hospitable inn adjoining the renowned restaurant, La Locanda di Alia. **Pros:** peaceful situation and informal atmosphere; obliging staff; local art in rooms. **Cons:** rooms in a row all at ground level; gloomy rooms in the winter; some rooms with mezzanine-level bedroom. $ *Rooms from: €90* ⊠ *Via Jetticelle 55, off Castrovillari's main street* ☎ *0981/46370* ⊕ *aliajazzhotel.it/it* 🛏 *14 rooms* ⦿ *Free Breakfast.*

COSENZA

75 km (48 miles) southeast of Diamante, 185 km (115 miles) northeast of Reggio Calabria.

Cosenza has suffered from the chaotic construction boom of the 1950s and '60s, with a sprawling, traffic-clogged modern town that encases the old medieval city, which winds up the hillsides between the Busento and Crati rivers. Its steep, stair-filled centro storico truly hails from another age. Wrought-iron balconies overlook narrow alleyways with old-fashioned storefronts and bars that have barely been touched by centuries of development. Many artists and crafts workers have set up their studios in the abandoned palaces of the former nobility, which line the route to the 12th-century Duomo, a UNESCO World Heritage monument. The medieval castle, open to the public, crowns the Pancrazio Hill, with a magnificent view over the town and the surrounding countryside.

Cosenza is also the gateway to the cool and silent forests of the Sila mountains and villages like Rende (only 13 km [8 miles] away) and the Pollino National Park area (less than 80 km [50 miles]).

GETTING HERE AND AROUND

By car, take the Cosenza exit from the A3 autostrada. By train, change at Paola on the main Rome–Reggio Calabria line. Regional trains run from Naples. Ferrovie della Calabria runs buses from Spezzano della Sila, Castrovillari, and Camigliatello.

VISITOR INFORMATION

Contact Cosenza Tourist Office. ⊠ *Piazza Tommaso Campanella 21* ☎ *328/1754422* ⊕ *www.cosenzaturismo.it.*

EXPLORING

Castello Svevo. Crowning the Pancrazio hill above the old city, with views across to the Sila mountains, Castello Normanno-Svevo is largely in ruins, having suffered successive earthquakes and a lightning strike that ignited gunpowder stored within. The origins are lost to memory. It may have been built by the Byzantines or the Saracens. For a time it was the residence of the Arab Caliph Saati Cayti, before he was ousted by the Normans. The castle takes its name from the great Swabian emperor Frederick II (1194–1250), who added two octagonal towers. The castle is open to the public after extensive restoration. ⊠ *Via del Castello, Colle Pancrazio* ☎ *0984/1811234* ⊕ *www.castellocosenza.it* 🎟 *€4* ⊘ *Closed Mon., and Tues.–Sun. 1–4:30.*

Duomo. Cosenza's original Duomo, probably built in the middle of the 11th century, was destroyed by an earthquake in 1184. A new cathedral was consecrated in the presence of Emperor Frederick II in 1222. After many Baroque additions, later alterations have restored some of the Provençal Gothic style. Inside, on the left of the main altar, you'll see the lovely monument to Isabella of Aragon, who died after falling from her horse en route to France in 1271. ⊠ *Piazza del Duomo 1* ☎ *0984/77864* ⊕ *www.cattedraledicosenza.it* ⊘ *Closed daily noon–4:30 in summer, daily noon–3:30 in winter.*

Museo Diocesano di Cosenza. Situated between the archbishop's palace and the Duomo, the museum contains paintings, silverware, vestments, and other precious objects collected by the archbishops of Cosenza throughout the centuries. Look for the filigree silver cup known as "the Pope," two ivory statuettes attributed to the School of Michaelangelo, the 15th-century "Torquemada" chalice, and paintings by Luca Giordano, Andrea Vaccaro, and Giuseppe Pascaletti. The heart of the museum contains the emblem of Cosenza and the city's greatest treasure: the unique reliquary cross dating back to the 13th century, which was donated by Federico II of Swabia on the occasion of the consecration of the cathedral in 1222. ⊠ *Piazza Aulo Giano Parrasio 16* ☎ *0984/6877171* ⊕ *www.museodiocesanocosenza.it* 🎟 *Free.*

Piazza XV Marzo. Cosenza's noblest square, Piazza XV Marzo (commonly called Piazza della Prefettura), houses government buildings as well as the elegant **Teatro Rendano.** From the square, the **Villa Comunale** (public garden) provides plenty of shaded benches for a rest. ⊠ *Piazza XV Marzo.*

WHERE TO EAT AND STAY

$

SOUTHERN
ITALIAN
FAMILY

✕ **Calabria Bella.** Nestled on the left side of the steps leading up to the Duomo, the family-run Calabria Bella may have a small, unimposing entrance and somewhat rustic decor, but don't let that fool you: its clientele includes everyone from tourists to VIPs from Italian showbiz. Cuisine is typical of the region, with ingredients like porcini mushrooms from the Sila forests and *strigoli,* or bladder campion seedpods, gathered in the nearby fields. **Known for:** excellent, robust cucina calabrese; rustic interior and piazza seating; superb wine cellar. $ *Average main: €14 ⊠ Piazza Duomo 20 ☎ 0984/793531 ⊕ www.ristorantecalabria-bella.it.*

$$$

SEAFOOD
Fodor'sChoice
★

✕ **Hippocampus.** If you are a fish lover, this is the place for you. The Hippocampus is well known in Cosenza for its excellent fresh fish and seafood, with antipasti that are a generous mix of seasonal catches and may include specialties like baby squid steamed in tomato sauce, octopus, and spicy clams. **Known for:** exceptional, super-fresh seafood; chef Rino happy to create vegetarian options; unfussy, welcoming vibe. $ *Average main: €25 ⊠ Via Piave 33 ☎ 0984/22103 ⊗ No lunch Mon., no dinner Sun.*

$

HOTEL

🛏 **Royal Hotel.** This hotel is modern and aims to attract a primarily business clientele. **Pros:** close to pedestrian-only shopping area; free parking; good breakfast array. **Cons:** 20-minute walk from Cosenza's centro storico; bit of a beige '70s decor time capsule in parts; can be busy during business events. $ *Rooms from: €80 ⊠ Via delle Medaglie d'Oro 1 ☎ 0984/412165 ⊕ www.royalhotel.it 🠒 34 rooms ⎮⚬⎮ Free Breakfast.*

RENDE

13 km (8 miles) west of Cosenza.

Rende is a pleasing stop on the way to or from Cosenza. Leave your car in the parking lot at the base of a long and bizarre series of escalators and staircases, which will whisk you off to this pristine hilltop town, whose winding cobblestone streets and turrets preside over idyllic countryside views.

GETTING HERE AND AROUND

By car, take the A3 autostrada and exit at Cosenza-Rende. Local buses make the trip from nearby Cosenza.

WHERE TO EAT

$$

SOUTHERN
ITALIAN
FAMILY

✕ **La Trattoria di Vincenzo.** This cheerful, family-run hostelry a few miles outside Cosenza, in the hamlet of Castiglione Cosentino, offers an authentic Calabrian experience. The dining room is decked with brightly checked tablecloths and curtains and the menu specializes in typical home-cooked dishes using local seasonal ingredients. **Known for:** hunks of local black pork and Podolica beef sizzling at your table;

15

Calabrian cured meats and cheeses; friendly and family run. $ *Average main: €16* ⊠ *Via Ponte Crate 1, between SP229 and SP234, Castiglione Cosentino* ☎ *0984/401828* ⊘ *No dinner Sun.*

CAMIGLIATELLO

30 km (19 miles) east of Cosenza.

Lined with chalets, Camigliatello is one of the Sila Massif's major resort towns. Most of the Sila isn't mountainous at all; it is, rather, an extensive, sparsely populated plateau with areas of thick forest. Unfortunately, there's been considerable deforestation. However, since 1968, when the area was designated a national park called Parco Nazionale della Sila, strict rules have limited the felling of timber, and forests are now regenerating. There are well-marked trails through pine and beech woods, and ample opportunities for horseback riding. Fall and winter see droves of locals hunting mushrooms and gathering chestnuts, while ski slopes near Camigliatello draw crowds.

GETTING HERE AND AROUND

By car, take the Cosenza Nord exit from the A3, then follow the SS107, or, if you are following the 106 highway route on the Ionian coast, branch off at Sibari and follow the signs.

VISITOR INFORMATION

Contact Camigliatello Tourism Office. ⊠ *Via Roma 5* ☎ *0984/578159* ⊕ *www.prolococamigliatello.it.*

EXPLORING

La Fossiata, Ente Parco Nazionale della Sila. A couple of miles east of town, Lago Cecita makes a good starting point for exploring La Fossiata, a lovely wooded conservation area within the park that has many remarkable monumental trees, some centuries old. The forestry commission office in nearby Cupone can provide tourist information, maps, and assistance such as arranging guides. ⊠ *Via Nazionale, Lorica di San Giovanni in Fiore* ☎ *0984/537109 Forestry Commission Office* ⊕ *www.parcosila.it* ⊘ *Closed weekends.*

WHERE TO STAY

$$
HOTEL
FAMILY
Tasso. On the edge of Camigliatello, less than 1 km (½ mile) from the ski slopes, this hotel is in a peaceful, picturesque location. **Pros:** beautiful surroundings; lively evening entertainment; conveniently located near the ski area. **Cons:** nondescript architecture and out-of-date decor; place books up fast, so reserve well in advance; dated bathrooms. $ *Rooms from: €140* ⊠ *Via Torquato Tasso, Spezzano della Sila* ☎ *0984/578113* ⊕ *www.hoteltasso.it* ⟿ *82 rooms* ⏀ *Free Breakfast.*

CROTONE

105 km (65 miles) east of Cosenza, 150 km (94 miles) northeast of Locri.

One of the most important Magna Graecia colonies in Italy, Crotone was a major cultural center in the 5th century BC, when it was the home of thinkers like philosopher and mathematician Pythagoras. Sadly, modern development has eclipsed much of its former beauty, but it preserves something of an old-town feel, with its imposing 16th-century castle and an archaeological museum of some importance. Its coastal waters, stretching to Capo Rizzuto, make up Italy's biggest protected marine area; and the island Castle Le Castella, 15 km (9 miles) from Crotone, is a vision out of a fairy tale.

GETTING HERE AND AROUND

By car, take the Cosenza Nord exit from the A3 autostrada, then follow the SS107. There are regular trains from Sibari.

VISITOR INFORMATION

Contact Crotone Tourism Office. ⊠ *Via Molo Sanità 2* ☎ *0962/955002* ⊕ *www. comune.crotone.it.*

EXPLORING

Museo Archeologico Nazionale. Constructed to house the treasures found at the Sanctuary of Hera Lacinia, as well as many antiquities recovered from the surrounding seabed, the museum is situated in the heart of the old city of Crotone, close to the seafront castle. The most precious part of the collection is the so-called Treasure of Hera, with the goddess's finely wrought gold diadem and belt pendant. You can also see the rare 5th-century-BC bronze *askos* (container for oil) in the form of a mermaid, illegally exported into the United States and subsequently recovered by the Italian government from the Getty Museum in California. ⊠ *Via Risorgimento 121* ☎ *0962/23082* ⊕ *www.beniculturali. it/mibac/opencms/MiBAC* ⌑ *€2* ⊘ *Closed Mon.*

Fodor's Choice **Museo e Parco Archeologico Nazionale di Capo Colonna.** Il Santuario di
★ Hera Lacinia—Sanctuary of Hera Lacinia—was once one of the most important shrines of Magna Graecia. Only one column still remains standing, but the site (known as Capo Colonna because of that single pillar) occupies a stunning position on a promontory 11 km (7 miles) south of the town of Crotone. The ruins are part of a vast park, which also contains a well-appointed museum documenting finds from prehistory to the Roman era. The sanctuary, which dates from the 7th century BC, is fenced off for safety reasons, but a walkway alongside the remains allows viewing. ⊠ *Via Michele Di Donato, Capo Colonna* ☎ *0962/934814* ⊕ *www.archeocalabria.beniculturali.it* ⌑ *Archaeological Park free, museum €2.*

WHERE TO STAY

$$ 🏨 **Hotel Helios.** The Helios is situated on the coastal road running
HOTEL between Crotone and Capo Colonna, a little out of town and just 8 km (5 miles) from the Sanctuary of Hera Lacinia. **Pros:** bright, airy rooms; efficient, courteous staff; on bus route into town. **Cons:** uninspiring architecture; skimpy breakfasts; rooms need a refresh. Ⓢ *Rooms from:*

€128 ⊠ *Viale Magna Grecia at Via Makalla 2* ☎ *0962/901291* ⊕ *www. helioshotels.it* ⟿ *42 rooms* ⊙ *Free Breakfast.*

TROPEA

120 km (75 miles) southwest of Cosenza, 107 km (66 miles) north of Reggio Calabria.

Ringed by cliffs and wonderful sandy beaches, the Tropea Promontory is still just beginning to be discovered by foreign tourists. The main town of Tropea, its old palazzi built in simple golden stone, easily wins the contest for prettiest town on Calabria's Tyrrhenian Coast. On a clear day the seaward views from the waterfront promenade take in Stromboli's cone and at least four of the other Aeolians. You can visit the islands by motorboat, departing daily in summer. Accommodations are good, and beach addicts won't be disappointed by the choice of magnificent sandy bays within easy reach. The beach beside Santa Maria dell'Isola is said to be one of the most beautiful in the Mediterranean, but there are other fine beaches south at Capo Vaticano and north at Briatico.

GETTING HERE AND AROUND
By car, exit the A3 autostrada at Pizzo and follow the southbound SP6/SS522. Eleven trains depart daily from Lamezia Terme.

VISITOR INFORMATION
Contact Tropea Tourism Office. ⊠ *Piazza Ercole 19–23* ☎ *0963/61475* ⊕ *www.prolocotropea.eu.*

EXPLORING
Cattedrale. In Tropea's harmonious warren of lanes, seek out the old Norman Cattedrale, whose main altar contains the locally revered icon of the Madonna di Romania, protectress of the city. Also of interest is the imposing 14th-century "Black Crucifix" in one of the side chapels. It's worth popping into the adjoining **Museo Diocesano,** which contains both an archaeological section and a collection of sacred art, including the life-size statue of Santa Domenica in solid silver, dating from 1738. ■TIP➔ **Cathedral is only open for church services November through March, but if you're quiet and respectful, you can probably sneak a peek.** ⊠ *Largo Duomo* ☎ *0963/61034* ⊡ *Cathedral free, Museo Diocesano €2* ⊙ *Closed Nov.–Mar. except for services.*

Santa Maria dell'Isola. The sanctuary of Santa Maria dell'Isola is the symbol of Tropea, and it is easy to see why. Perched high on a rocky promontory and accessible only by a winding flight of stone steps cut into the cliff side, it dominates the view over the sea from Piazza Ercole, the main town square. Believed to date from the 4th century AD, it has been rebuilt many times and took its present form in the 18th century after it was damaged by an earthquake. The inside of the church is unadorned, but visitors can climb up to the roof to admire the splendid view or wander through the pleasant garden set on the rocks behind the building. The beach below the rock has been classed among the 10 most beautiful beaches in Italy. ⊠ *Largo Marina dell'Isola* ☎ *347/2541232* ⊕ *www.santuariosantamariadellisolatropea.it* ⊡ *Church free, garden €2.*

WHERE TO EAT

$$ ✕ **Pimm's.** Since its glory days in the 1960s, this basement restaurant in
SOUTHERN Tropea's historic center has offered the town's top dining experience for
ITALIAN seafood. The splendid sea views from the rear windows are a surpris-
ing—and substantial—reason to head here. **Known for:** excellent fresh
seafood; perched high above the beach; book a window table for the
azure views. $ *Average main: €22* ✉ *Largo Migliarese 2, at the foot of
Corso Vittorio Emanuele* ☎ *0963/666105.*

REGGIO CALABRIA

115 km (71 miles) south of Tropea, 499 km (311 miles) south of Naples.

Reggio Calabria, on the tip of Italy's toe, was laid low by the same
catastrophic earthquake that struck Messina in 1908. This raw city is
one of Italy's busiest ports, where you can find not only container ships
and cranes but also a wonderful *lungomare* (promenade) made for lazy
passegiatte. Hydrofoils for Sicily depart from here; vehicle-carrying fer-
ries depart from Villa San Giovanni, 13 km (8 miles) north.

GETTING HERE AND AROUND

The A3 autostrada runs directly to Reggio Calabria. A dozen direct
trains depart from Naples and Rome daily. There are daily flights from
Rome, Milan, Turin, and Venice.

VISITOR INFORMATION

Contact I.A.T. Reggio Calabria Tourism Office. ✉ *Stazione Ferroviaria, Via
Barlaam da Seminara 1* ☎ *0965/27120* ⊕ *turismo.reggiocal.it.*

EXPLORING

Fodor'sChoice **Museo Nazionale della Magna Grecia.** Reggio Calabria is home to one
★ of southern Italy's most important archaeological museums. Its prize
exhibit, of course, is the two ancient-Greek statues known as the **Bronzi
di Riace,** which were discovered by an amateur deep-sea diver off Cal-
abria's Ionian Coast in 1972. After a lengthy but necessary conserva-
tion operation, the 5th-century-BC bronzes of two Greek warriors,
thought to be the work of either Pheidias or Polykleitos, now take pride
of place in their special temperature-controlled room, complete with
earthquake-resistant bases. Visitors are allowed to view the bronzes
in groups of 20, every 20 minutes. Make sure you have time to head
upstairs to see the many other antiquities; there are descriptive panels
in English and Italian. ✉ *Piazza De Nava 26* ☎ *0965/812255* ✉ *€8*
⊘ *Closed Mon.*

WHERE TO STAY

$ 🏨 **Excelsior Grand Hotel.** Inviting modern decor coupled with a prime
HOTEL location near the seafront and town's main sights—as well as every
amenity expected from a top international hotel—make this a popular
choice with business travelers as well as tourists. **Pros:** centrally located
near Museo Nazionale della Magna Grecia; rooftop restaurant with
views; near the beach. **Cons:** standard business hotel decor; street noise
in some rooms; some rooms have dated decor and are tiny. $ *Rooms
from: €120* ✉ *Via Vittorio Veneto 64* ☎ *0965/812211* ⊕ *www.grand-
hotelexcelsiorrc.it* ⤳ *84 rooms* ⦿❘ *Free Breakfast.*

15

$ B&B/INN 🏨 **LH Hotel Lido.** This rather quirky art hotel—one of many properties throughout Europe that displays and promotes works of art—near the Museo Nazionale della Magna Grecia and the seafront promenade is perfect for those looking for a more informal lodging experience. **Pros:** near the Museo Nazionale della Magna Grecia; secure parking; pinacoteca art gallery in reception. **Cons:** some rooms are small and oddly shaped; breakfast choice a tad sparse; unreliable Wi-Fi. [$] *Rooms from: €100* ✉ *Via Francesco Cananzi 6* ☎ *0965/25001* 🌐 *www.hotellidoreggiocalabria.it* 🛏 *30 rooms* 🍴 *Free Breakfast.*

STILO

50 km (31 miles) north of Locri, 138 km (86 miles) northeast of Reggio Calabria.

Grandly positioned on the side of the rugged Monte Consolino, the village of Stilo is listed as one of Italy's most beautiful *borghi* (historic villages). It's also known for being the birthplace and home of the philosopher Tommaso Campanella (1568–1639), whose magnum opus was the socialistic *La Città del Sole* (*The City of the Sun,* 1602)—for which he spent 26 years as a prisoner of the Spanish Inquisition.

GETTING HERE AND AROUND

From Reggio Calabria, follow the Ionian coastal SS106 and exit at Stilo. Regular trains run from Lamezia Terme.

16

SICILY

WELCOME TO SICILY

TOP REASONS TO GO

★ **Taormina—Sicily's most beautiful resort:** The view of the sea and Mt. Etna from its jagged cactus-covered cliffs is as close to perfection as a panorama can get.

★ **A walk on Siracusa's Ortygia Island:** Classical ruins rub elbows with faded seaside palaces and fish markets in Sicily's most striking port city, where the Duomo is literally built atop an ancient Greek temple.

★ **Palermo's palaces, churches, and crypts:** Virtually every great European empire ruled Sicily's strategically positioned capital at some point, and it shows most of all in the diverse architecture, from Roman to Byzantine to Arab-Norman.

★ **Valley of the Temples, Agrigento:** This stunning set of ruins is proudly perched above the sea in a grove full of almond trees; not even in Athens will you find Greek temples this finely preserved.

16

1 The Ionian Coast. For many, the Ionian Coast is all about touristy Taormina, spectacularly poised on a cliff near Mt. Etna.

2 Siracusa. Full of fresh fish and remarkable ruins, Siracusa is one of Italy's most charming cities.

3 The Interior. Baroque beauties Ragusa, Modica, and Noto charm visitors with their extraordinary architecture and lively old town centers.

4 Agrigento and Western Sicily. This coast meanders past Monreale and its mosaics, Segesta with its temple, and the fairy-tale town of Erice. Greek ruins stand sentinel in Agrigento at the Valley of the Temples.

5 Palermo. Sicily's capital conceals notes of extraordinary beauty amid the uncontained chaos of fish markets and impossible traffic.

6 The Tyrrhenian Coast. This coast also has several quaint villages, including Cefalù, with its famous cathedral.

7 The Aeolian Islands. You may know these tranquil windswept islands from the *Odyssey*.

EATING AND DRINKING WELL IN SICILY

Sicilian cuisine is one of the oldest in existence, with records of cooking competitions dating to 600 BC. Food in Sicily today reflects the island's unique cultural mix, imaginatively combining fish, fruits, vegetables, and nuts with Italian pastas and Arab and North African elements—couscous is a staple in Palermo.

It's hard to eat badly here. From the lowliest of trattorias to the most highfalutin ristorante, you'll find the classic dishes that have been the staples of the family dinner table for years—basically pasta and seafood. In more formal restaurants, you'll find greater attention to detail and a more sophisticated atmosphere, while less pretentious trattorias tend to be family-run affairs, often without even a menu to guide you. There's also a new wave of creative restaurants that have come up with interesting versions of old standbys, using local and often organic ingredients and changing their menus to reflect the season. No matter where you choose to eat in the most gregarious of regions in the most convivial of countries, you can expect a lively dining experience.

SICILIAN MARKETS

Sicily's natural fecundity is evident wherever you look, from the prickly pears sprouting on roadsides to the slopes of vineyards and citrus groves covering the inland to the ranks of fishing boats moored in every harbor.

You can come face-to-face with this bounty in the clamorous street markets of Palermo and Catania. Here, you'll encounter teetering piles of olives and oranges, enticing displays of cheeses and meats, plus pastries and sweets of every description. The effect is heady and sensuous. Immerse yourself in the hustle and bustle of the Sicilian souk, and you'll emerge enriched.

WINES

The earthy *nero d'avola* grape bolsters many of Sicily's traditionally sunny, expansive reds, and it's often softened with fruity, bright *frappato* to make Sicily's only DOCG wine, Cerasuolo di Vittoria. Red wines from around Mt. Etna that use the grapes *nerello mascalese*- and *nerello cappuccio* have also gained renown; many of the region's best wines are produced organically and sometimes biodynamically. Sicily produces crisp white varieties, too, such as *carricante, catarratto bianco, inzolia,* and *grillo* that marry delightfully with the island's seafood. When it comes to sweet accompaniments, the small island of Pantelleria produces the smooth *passito* dessert wine, made from *zibibbo* grapes, while the Aeolian Islands are known for Malvasia delle Lipari.

DELICIOUS FISH

Pasta *con le sarde,* an emblematic dish that goes back to the Saracen conquerors, with fresh sardines, olive oil, raisins, pine nuts, and wild fennel, gets a different treatment at every restaurant. Grilled *tonno* (tuna) and *orata* (dorado) are coastal staples, while delicate *ricci* (sea urchins) are a specialty. King, however, is *pesce spada* (swordfish), best enjoyed *marinato* (marinated), *affumicato* (smoked), or as the traditional *involtini di pesce spada* (roulades).

LOCAL SPECIALTIES

Many ingredients and recipes are unique to particular Sicilian towns and regions. In Catania, you'll be offered *caserecci alla Norma* (a short pasta with a sauce of tomato, eggplant, ricotta, and basil). The *mandorla* (bitter almond), the pride of Agrigento, plays into everything from risotto *alle mandorle* (with almonds, butter, Grana cheese, and parsley) to incomparable almond *granita*—an absolute must in summer. Pistachios produced around Bronte, on the lower slopes of Etna, go into pasta sauces as well as ice cream and granita, while capers from the Aeolian Islands add zest to salads and fish sauces.

SNACKS

Two favorite Sicilian snacks are *arancini* ("little oranges," rice croquettes with a cheese or meat filling), and *panelle* (seasoned chickpea flour boiled to a paste, cooled, sliced, and fried), normally bought from street vendors or offered as an appetizer at restaurants. Other tidbits to look out for include special foods associated with festivals, such as the ominously named *ossa dei morti* ("dead men's bones," rolled almond cookies). But the most eye-catching of all are the *frutta martorana*: sweet marzipan confections shaped to resemble fruits and temptingly arrayed in bars and *pasticcerie* (pastry shops).

16

Updated by
Liz Humphreys

The island of Sicily has an abundance of history. Some of the world's best-preserved Byzantine mosaics stand adjacent to magnificent Greek temples and Roman amphitheaters, awe-inspiring Romanesque cathedrals, and over-the-top Baroque flights of fancy. Add in the spectacular sight of lava-strewn Mt. Etna plus Sicily's unique cuisine—mingling Arab and Greek spices, Spanish and French techniques, and some of the world's finest seafood, all accompanied by local wines—and you can understand why visitors continue to be drawn here, and often find it hard to leave.

Sicily has beckoned seafaring wanderers since the trials of Odysseus were first sung in Homer's *Odyssey*—an epic that is sometimes called the world's first travel guide. Strategically poised between Europe and Africa, this mystical land of three corners and a fiery volcano once hosted two of the most enlightened capitals of the West—one Greek, in Siracusa, and one Arab-Norman, in Palermo. Sicily has been a melting pot of every great civilization on the Mediterranean: Greek and Roman; then Arab and Norman; and finally French, Spanish, and Italian. The invaders through the ages weren't just attracted by the strategic location, however; they recognized a paradise in Sicily's deep blue skies and temperate climate, its lush vegetation, and rich marine life—all of which prevail to this day.

In modern times, the traditional graciousness and nobility of the Sicilian people have survived side by side with the destructive influences of the Mafia under Sicily's semiautonomous government. In recent years, the island has emerged as something of an international travel hot spot, drawing increasing numbers of visitors. Brits and Germans flock in ever-growing numbers to Agrigento and Siracusa, and in high season Chinese tour groups—as well as Americans—seem to outnumber the locals in

Taormina and the Baroque hill towns. And yet, in Sicily's windswept heartland, vineyards, olive groves, and lovingly kept dirt roads leading to family farmhouses still tie Sicilians to the land and to tradition, forming a happy connectedness that can't be defined by economic measures.

SICILY PLANNER

MAKING THE MOST OF YOUR TIME

You should plan a visit to Sicily around Palermo, Taormina, Siracusa, and Agrigento, four don't-miss destinations. The best way to see them all is to travel in a circle. Start your circuit in the northeast in Taormina, worth at least a night or two. If you have time, stay also in Catania, a lively, fascinating city that's often overlooked. From there, connect to the Catania–Ragusa toll-free *autostrada* (four-lane highway) and head toward the spectacular ancient Greek port of Siracusa, which merits at least two nights. If you have a couple more days, Siracusa makes a good base for visiting the Baroque towns of Noto, Ragusa, and Modica.

Next, backtrack north on the same highway, and take the A19 autostrada toward Palermo. Piazza Armerina's impressive mosaics and Enna, a sleepy mountaintop city, are worthwhile stops in the interior. Take the SS640 to the Greek temples of Agrigento. Stay here for a night before driving west along the coastal SS115, checking out Selinunte's ruins before reaching magical Erice, a good base for one night. You're now near some of Sicily's best beaches at San Vito Lo Capo.

Take the A19 to Palermo, the chaotic and wonderful capital city, to wrap up your Sicilian experience. Give yourself at least two days here—ideally, four or five. Or, if it's the warm season, consider heading east toward Messina and sailing to one of the lovely Aeolian Islands for a few days of leisure.

GETTING HERE AND AROUND

BUS TRAVEL

Air-conditioned coaches connect major and minor cities and are often faster and more convenient than local trains—still single-track on many stretches—but also slightly more expensive. Various companies serve the different routes. SAIS runs frequently between Palermo and Catania, Messina, Siracusa, and other cities, in each case arriving at and departing from near the train stations.

Cuffaro. Services run from outside the Palermo train station to Agrigento. ☎ *091/6161510* ⊕ *www.cuffaro.info.*

Interbus/Etna Trasporti/Segesta/Sicilbus. These companies operate between Acireale, Catania, Caltagirone, Enna, Messina, Noto, Piazza Armerina, Ragusa, Siracusa, and Taormina. ☎ *091/342055, 091/342525, 091/345791* ⊕ *www.interbus.it.*

SAIS. This bus service runs between Catania, Caltagirone, Enna, Messina, Palermo, and Piazza Armerina. ☎ *800/211020 toll-free, 199/244141 from mobile* ⊕ *www.saisautolinee.it.*

CAR TRAVEL

This is the ideal way to explore Sicily. Modern highways circle and bisect the island, making all main cities easily reachable. The A20/E90 autostrada connects Messina and Palermo; Messina, Taormina, and Catania are linked by the A18; running through the interior, from Catania to west of Cefalù, is the A19; threading west from Palermo, the A29/E90 runs to Trapani and the airport, with a leg stretching down to Mazara del Vallo. In general, the south side of the island is less well served, though stretches of the SS115 west of Agrigento are relatively fast and traffic-free.

You'll likely hear stories about the dangers of driving in Sicily. In the big cities—especially Palermo, Catania, and Messina—streets can be a honking mess, with lane markings and stop signs taken as mere suggestions; you can avoid the chaos by driving through at off-peak times or on weekends. However, once outside the urban areas and resort towns, the highways and regional state roads are a driving enthusiast's dream—they're winding, sparsely populated, and well maintained, and around many bends there's a striking new view. Obviously, don't leave valuables in your car, and make sure baggage is stowed out of sight, if possible.

TRAIN TRAVEL

There are direct express trains from Rome to Palermo, Catania, and Siracusa. The Rome–Palermo and Rome–Siracusa trips take at least 10 hours. After Naples, the run is mostly along the coast, so try to book a window seat on the right if you're not on an overnight train. At Villa San Giovanni, in Calabria, the train is separated and loaded onto a ferryboat to cross the strait to Messina—a favorite for kids.

Within Sicily, main lines connect Messina, Taormina, Siracusa, and Palermo. Secondary lines are generally very slow and unreliable. The Messina–Palermo run, along the northern coast, is especially scenic. For schedules, check the website of the Italian state railway.

Contact FS. ☎ *892021 in Italy, 06/68475475 outside Italy* ⊕ *www.trenitalia. com.*

RESTAURANTS

As befitting a major city, Palermo has a huge selection of interesting and varied restaurants, while Catania is best known for its high-quality seafood. In the tourist-heavy coastal towns, dining can be hit or miss, while inland there has been a mini-explosion of new-wave gourmet restaurants in the Baroque towns of Ragusa, Modica, and, especially, Noto, as well as some intriguing options popping up on Mt. Etna. If you're staying in the countryside, country hotels and wineries are your best bets for a good meal. *Restaurant reviews have been shortened. For full information, visit Fodors.com.*

HOTELS

The high-quality hotels tend to be limited to the major cities and resorts of Palermo, Catania, Taormina, Siracusa, Noto, and Agrigento, along with the odd beach resort.

There are also numerous *agriturismo* lodgings (rural bed-and-breakfasts and country inns), some quite basic but others extremely luxe. These country houses usually also offer all-inclusive, full-board plans that can make for some of Sicily's most memorable meals. *Hotel reviews have been shortened. For full information, visit Fodors.com.*

WHAT IT COSTS			
$	$$	$$$	$$$$
Restaurants under €15	€15–€24	€25–€35	over €35
Hotels under €125	€125–€200	€201–€300	over €300

Restaurant reviews are the average cost of a main course at dinner, or, if dinner is not served, at lunch. Hotel reviews are the lowest cost of a standard double room in high season.

THE IONIAN COAST

On the northern stretch of Sicily's eastern coast, lively and chaotic Messina commands an unparalleled position across the Ionian Sea from Calabria, the mountainous tip of mainland Italy's boot. Halfway down the coast, Catania has the vivacity of Palermo, if not the artistic wealth, along with a gritty charm. The city makes a good base for exploring lofty Mt. Etna, as does Taormina, unless you opt to stay at one of the cozy boutique hotels that have sprouted on Etna's slopes.

16

MESSINA

8 km (5 miles) by ferry from Villa San Giovanni, 94 km (59 miles) northeast of Catania, 237 km (149 miles) east of Palermo.

Messina's ancient history lists a series of disasters, but the city nevertheless managed to develop a fine university and a thriving cultural environment. At 5:20 am on December 28, 1908, Messina changed from a flourishing metropolis of 120,000 to a heap of rubble, shaken to pieces by an earthquake that turned into a tidal wave; 80,000 people died as a result and the city was almost completely leveled. As you approach by ferry, you won't notice any outward indication of the disaster, except for the modern countenance of a 3,000-year-old city. The somewhat flat look is a precaution of seismic planning: tall buildings aren't permitted.

GETTING HERE AND AROUND
Frequent hydrofoils and ferries carry passengers and trains across the Straits of Messina from Villa San Giovanni, from just below the train station. There are also regular departures for foot passengers from Reggio Calabria. Cruise ships also stop in Messina's port.

VISITOR INFORMATION
Contact Messina Tourism Office. ✉ *Via dei Mille 270* ☎ *090/2935292* ⊕ *pti. regione.sicilia.it.*

EXPLORING

Duomo. The reconstruction of Messina's Norman and Romanesque Duomo, originally built by the Norman king Roger II and consecrated in 1197, has retained much of the original plan—including a handsome crown of Norman battlements, an enormous apse, and a splendid wood-beam ceiling. The adjoining bell tower contains one of the largest and most complex mechanical clocks in the world: constructed in 1933, it has a host of gilded automatons (a roaring lion among them) that spring into action every day at the stroke of noon. ✉ *Piazza del Duomo* ☎ *090/66841* 🌐 *www.diocesimessina.it* 🕒 *Closed daily 1–4.*

WHERE TO EAT

$ SICILIAN 🍴 **Al Padrino.** The jovial owner of this stripped-down trattoria keeps everything running smoothly. Meat and fish dishes are served with equal verve in the white-wall dining room. **Known for:** home-style Sicilian dishes; pasta alla Norma (with eggplant, tomato, and ricotta); no-frills atmosphere. [$] *Average main: €12* ✉ *Via Santa Cecilia 56* ☎ *090/2921000* 🕒 *Closed Sun., and Aug. No dinner Sat.*

TAORMINA

43 km (27 miles) southwest of Messina.

Fodor's Choice ★ The medieval cliff-side town of Taormina is overrun with tourists, yet its natural beauty is still hard to dispute. The view of the sea and Mt. Etna from its jagged, cactus-covered cliffs is as close to perfection as a panorama can get—especially on clear days, when the snowcapped volcano's white puffs of smoke rise against the blue sky. Writers have extolled Taormina's beauty almost since it was founded in the 6th century BC by Greeks from nearby Naxos; Goethe and D. H. Lawrence were among its well-known enthusiasts. The town's boutique-lined main streets get old pretty quickly, but the many hiking paths that wind through the beautiful hills surrounding Taormina promise a timeless alternative. A trip up to stunning Castelmola (whether on foot or by car) should also be on your itinerary.

GETTING HERE AND AROUND

Buses from Messina or Catania arrive near the center of Taormina, while trains from these towns pull in at the station at the bottom of the hill. Local buses bring you the rest of the way. A cable car takes passengers up the hill from a parking lot about 2 km (1 mile) north of the train station.

FESTIVALS

Taormina Film Festival. This famous festival takes place in June. ✉ *Taormina* ☎ *0942/21142* 🌐 *www.taorminafilmfest.it.*

VISITOR INFORMATION

Contact Taormina Tourism Office. ✉ *Corso Umberto 217* ☎ *0942/610318* 🌐 *www.comune.taormina.me.it.*

EXPLORING

TOP ATTRACTIONS

Fodor's Choice ★ **Villa Comunale.** Stroll down Via Bagnoli Croce from the main Corso Umberto to the Villa Comunale to enjoy the stunning views. Also known as the Parco Duca di Cesarò, the lovely public gardens were designed by Florence Trevelyan Cacciola, a Scottish lady "invited" to leave England following a romantic liaison with the future Edward VII (1841–1910). Arriving in Taormina in 1889, she married a local professor and devoted herself to the gardens, filling them with native Mediterranean and exotic plants, ornamental pavilions, and fountains. ⊠ *Via Bagnoli Croce.*

WORTH NOTING

Castello Saraceno. An unrelenting 20-minute walk up the Via Crucis footpath takes you to the church of the Madonna della Rocca, hollowed out of the limestone rock. Above it towers the medieval Castello Saraceno. Although the gate to the castle has been locked for decades, it's worth the climb just for the panoramic views. ⊠ *Monte Tauro.*

Funivia. Taormina Mare is accessible by a *funivia,* or suspended cable car, that glides past incredible views on its way down. It departs every 15 minutes. In June, July, and August, the normal hours are extended until midnight or later. ⊠ *Via L. Pirandello, downhill from town center toward bus station* ☎ *0942/681493* ☞ *€3 one-way.*

Palazzo Corvaja. Many of Taormina's 14th- and 15th-century palaces have been carefully preserved. Especially beautiful is the Palazzo Corvaja, with characteristic black-lava and white-limestone inlays. Today it houses the tourist office. ⊠ *Largo Santa Caterina* ☎ *0942/620198.*

Taormina Mare. Below the main city of Taormina is Taormina Mare, where summertime beachgoers jostle for space on a pebble beach against the scenic backdrop of the aptly named island of Isolabella. The first section of beach is mainly reserved for expensive resorts, but the far end, next to Isolabella, has a large free area. The "beautiful island" of Isolabella was once a private residence, but is now a nature preserve that can be visited for a small fee. ⊠ *Taormina Mare* ☞ *€4 for Isolabella island visit.*

Teatro Greco. The Greeks put a premium on finding impressive locations to stage their dramas, such as Taormina's hillside Teatro Greco. Beyond the columns you can see the town's rooftops spilling down the hillside, the arc of the coastline, and Mt. Etna in the distance. The theater was built during the 3rd century BC and rebuilt by the Romans during the 2nd century AD. Its acoustics are exceptional: even today a stage whisper can be heard in the last rows. In summer many music and dance performances are held in the Teatro Greco. ⊠ *Via Teatro Greco* ☎ *0942/23220* ⊕ *www.teatrogrecotaormina.com* ☞ *€10.*

WHERE TO EAT

$
SICILIAN
FAMILY
✕ **Bella Blu.** If you fancy a meal with a view but don't want to spend a lot, it would be hard to do much better than to come here for the decent three-course prix-fixe meal. Seafood and pizza are the specialties; try the spaghetti with fresh clams and mussels or the pizza *alla Norma* (with ricotta, eggplant, and tomatoes). **Known for:** lovely views of the

gondola and toward the coast; tasty pizza; gentle prices. $ *Average main: €10 ⊠ Via Pirandello 28 ☎ 0942/24239, 320/8547607 ⊕ www. bellablutaormina.com ⊘ Closed Jan.–Mar.*

$$
SICILIAN

✕**Casa GioLi.** A lot of the food and the atmosphere in touristy Taormina restaurants can be much of the same thing, but Casa GioLi breaks tradition by using only organic products in their reinterpretations of Sicilian dishes. You can enjoy them in a pleasing courtyard or inside surrounded by modern art from young artists. **Known for:** modern takes on traditional Sicilian recipes; lovely courtyard seating; vegetarian options. $ *Average main: €17 ⊠ Via Giordano Bruno 2 ☎ 0942/683017 ⊕ www.casagioli.it ⊘ Closed Tues. Nov.–Mar. No lunch.*

$$
SEAFOOD

✕**La Piazzetta.** Sheltered from the city's hustle and bustle, this elegant little eatery exudes a mood of relaxed sophistication. Classic dishes such as risotto *ai frutti di mare* (with seafood) are competently prepared, the grilled fish is extremely fresh, and the service is informal and friendly. **Known for:** quiet courtyard seating; well-prepared pasta, fish, and seafood dishes; helpful waitstaff. $ *Average main: €19 ⊠ Vico Francesco Paladini, off Corso Umberto ☎ 0942/626317 ⊕ www.ristorantelapiazzettataormina.it ⊘ Closed mid-Nov.–mid-Dec. and mid-Jan.–mid-Feb. No lunch Mon.–Thurs. June–Sept.*

$$$
SICILIAN

✕**Osteria RossoDiVino.** Run by two sisters, this intimate restaurant set in a cobblestone courtyard just before the gate out of Taormina is certainly one of the friendliest in town—and perhaps one of the freshest, too, with daily menus highlighting house-made pastas and freshly caught fish. Although the menu's in Italian only, one of the English-speaking servers (likely a sister) will happily explain all the dishes to non-Italian speakers. **Known for:** daily-changing menus; excellent wine choices; delicious modern Sicilian food. $ *Average main: €26 ⊠ Vico de Spuches 8 ☎ 0942/628653 ⊕ www.osteria-rosso-divino.com ⊘ Closed Jan. and Feb. No dinner Tues.*

$
PIZZA

✕**Vecchia Taormina.** Warm, inviting, and unassuming, one of Taormina's best pizzerias produces deliciously seared crusts topped with fresh, well-balanced ingredients. Try the pizza alla Norma, featuring the classic Sicilian combination of eggplant and ricotta—here, in the province of Messina, it's made with ricotta *al forno* (cooked ricotta), while in the province of Catania, it's made with ricotta *salata* (uncooked, salted ricotta). **Known for:** mouthwatering pizzas; nice outdoor seating; reasonable prices. $ *Average main: €11 ⊠ Vico Ebrei 3 ☎ 0942/625589 ⊕ www.vecchiataormina.it ⊘ Closed Jan. and Feb.*

WHERE TO STAY

$$$$
HOTEL
Fodor's Choice
★

🖵 **Belmond Grand Hotel Timeo.** On a princely perch overlooking the town, the Greek theater, and the bay, this truly grand hotel wears a graceful patina that suggests la dolce vita. **Pros:** feeling of indulgence; amazing location; exemplary service; fantastic views. **Cons:** very expensive; some parts of the hotel look a tad worn; spa on the small side. $ *Rooms from: €720 ⊠ Via Teatro Greco 59 ☎ 0942/6270200 ⊕ www.belmond.com/ grand-hotel-timeo-taormina ⊘ Closed mid-Nov.–late Mar. ⇨ 70 rooms ᵀᴼᴵ Free Breakfast.*

16

$$$$ HOTEL FAMILY Fodor's Choice ★ **Belmond Villa Sant'Andrea.** In a prime location overlooking the beach at Taormina Mare, this elegant hotel in a former late-1800s villa offers phenomenal views of the water, attentive service, and luxurious yet comfortable rooms. **Pros:** beachfront location can't be beat; flawless service; special amenities for kids. **Cons:** limited on-site parking; not so convenient for dining in Taormina town; pricey food and drinks. [$] *Rooms from: €720* ✉ *Via Nazionale 137* ☎ *0942/6271200* 🌐 *www.belmond.com/villa-sant-andrea-taormina-mare* 🕒 *Closed Nov.–mid-Apr.* 🛏 *68 rooms* 🍴 *Free Breakfast.*

$$$$ HOTEL **Hotel Metropole Taormina.** One of the only boutique hotels in Taormina, the trendy Metropole boasts one of the most prime locations in town, with the main shopping street of Corso Umberto on one side and views of the sea on the other. **Pros:** jazz shows a nice touch; lovely spa and public areas; amazing views from restaurant and pool. **Cons:** bathrooms can be small and dark; expensive overall, with high prices particularly in the bar; not all rooms have good views. [$] *Rooms from: €364* ✉ *Corso Umberto 154* ☎ *0942/24013* 🌐 *www.hotelmetropoletaormina.it* 🕒 *Closed Jan.–Mar.* 🛏 *23 rooms* 🍴 *Free Breakfast.*

$$$ HOTEL **Hotel Villa Paradiso.** On the edge of the old quarter, overlooking the lovely public gardens and facing the sea, this family-run hotel is not as well known as some of its neighbors, despite a 100-year history. **Pros:** friendly service; good value; great rooftop views. **Cons:** overall a bit more shabby than chic; not all rooms have views; only three free parking spaces (with paid parking close by). [$] *Rooms from: €259* ✉ *Via Roma 2* ☎ *0942/23921* 🌐 *www.hotelvillaparadisotaormina.com* 🛏 *37 rooms* 🍴 *Free Breakfast.*

$$ HOTEL **Villa Ducale.** The former summer residence of a local aristocrat has been converted into a luxurious hotel where each room has a balcony with a view. **Pros:** away from the hubbub; camera-ready views; personalized service. **Cons:** a 10- to 15-minute walk to the center of Taormina; the restaurant menu can be limited; some rooms a bit dark. [$] *Rooms from: €199* ✉ *Via Leonardo da Vinci 60* ☎ *0942/28153* 🌐 *www.villaducale.com* 🕒 *Closed mid-Nov.–mid-Mar.* 🛏 *17 rooms* 🍴 *Free Breakfast.*

NIGHTLIFE AND PERFORMING ARTS

Taoarte. The Teatro Greco and the Palazzo dei Congressi, near the entrance to the theater, are the main venues for the summer festival dubbed Taoarte, held each year between June and August. Performances encompass classical music, ballet, and theater. ✉ *Taormina* ☎ *391/7462146* 🌐 *www.taoarte.it.*

EN ROUTE The 50-km (30-mile) stretch of road between Taormina and Messina is flanked by lush vegetation and seascapes. Inlets are punctuated by gigantic, oddly shaped rocks.

CASTELMOLA

5 km (3 miles) west of Taormina.

Although many believe that Taormina has the most spectacular views, tiny Castelmola, floating 1,800 feet above sea level, takes the word "scenic" to a whole new level—literally. Along the cobblestone streets within the ancient walls, the 360-degree panoramas of mountain, sea, and sky are so ubiquitous that you almost get used to them (but not quite). Collect yourself with a sip of the sweet almond wine (best served cold) made in the local bars, or with lunch at one of the humble pizzerias or panino shops.

A 10-minute drive on a winding but well-paved road leads from Taormina to Castelmola; you must park in one of the public lots below the village and walk up to the center, only a few minutes away. On a nice day, hikers are in for a treat if they make the trip on foot from Taormina rather than drive. It's a serious uphill climb, but the 1½-km (¾-mile) path offers breathtaking views, which compensate for the somewhat poor maintenance of the path itself. You'll begin at Porta Catania in Taormina, with a walk along Via Apollo Arcageta past the Chiesa di San Francesco di Paola on the left. The Strada Comunale della Chiusa then leads past Piazza Andromaco, revealing good views of the jagged promontory of Cocolanazzo di Mola to the north. Allow around an hour for the ascent, a half hour for the descent. There's another, slightly longer (2-km [1-mile]) path that heads up from Porta Messina past the Roman aqueduct, Convento dei Cappuccini, and the northeastern side of Monte Tauro. You could take one up and the other down. In any case, avoid the midday sun, wear comfortable shoes, and carry plenty of water with you.

GETTING HERE AND AROUND

Regular buses bound for Castelmola leave from Taormina's bus station on Via Pirandello.

EXPLORING

Fodor's Choice ★ **Castello Normanno.** The best place to savor Castelmola's views is from the castle ruins, reached by a set of steep staircases rising out of the town center. In all of Sicily there may be no spot more scenic than atop Castello Normanno: you can gaze upon two coastlines, smoking Mt. Etna, and the town spilling down the mountainside. Come during daylight hours to take full advantage of the vista. ✉ *Castelmola.*

WHERE TO EAT AND STAY

$ SICILIAN 🍴 **Il Vicolo.** Along a side street, this is one of the simpler dining choices in town, and also one of the better ones. It might not have the views you'll find elsewhere, but a pleasant rustic ambience plus a great selection of handmade pasta and, in the evening, *forno a legna* (wood-fired-oven) pizzas make up for that shortcoming. (In winter, pizzas are served weekends only.) Friendly staff serve the food in a pleasing little room. **Known for:** cozy environs; pasta and pizza; signature fish ragù. [$] *Average main: €10* ✉ *Via Pio IX 26* ☎ *0942/28481, 331/9094077* 🕓 *Closed Tues. Sept.–June, and 2 wks late Jan.–early Feb.*

$ HOTEL 🏨 **Villa Sonia.** Many of the rooms at this well-situated hotel in Castelmola have private terraces with gorgeous grab-the-camera views of Etna. **Pros:** free shuttle into Taormina; on-site sauna and pool; friendly service. **Cons:** some rooms are quite small; not much to do in the evening; iffy Wi-Fi. [$] *Rooms from: €99* ✉ *Via Porta Mola 9* ☎ *0942/28082* 🌐 *www.hotelvillasonia.com* 🕓 *Closed Nov.–Dec. 20 and Jan. 8–Mar. 15* 🛏 *35 rooms* 🍽 *Free Breakfast.*

NIGHTLIFE

Bar San Giorgio. This place has lorded over Castelmola's town square since 1907. The interior of the bar is filled with knickknacks that tell a fascinating history of the tiny town. Try the *vino de mandorle* (almond wine) from a recipe produced by the original owner more than a century ago. ⊠ *Piazza Sant'Antonino* ☎ *0942/28228* ⊕ *www.barsangiorgio.com.*

Bar Turrisi. Truly one of the most unusual places to have a drink in all of Italy, this famous bar has cozy nooks and crannies on three levels—all decked out with phallus images of every size, shape, and color imaginable, from bathroom wall murals inspired by the brothels of ancient Greece to giant wooden carvings honoring Dionysus. The roof terrace has extraordinary views of Taormina and the coast, while a limited selection of hearty pasta dishes are served inside. ⊠ *Piazza del Duomo 19* ☎ *0942/28181* ⊕ *www.turrisibar.it.*

MT. ETNA

64 km (40 miles) southwest of Taormina, 30 km (19 miles) north of Catania.

The first time you see Mt. Etna, whether it's trailing clouds of smoke or emitting fiery streaks of lava, is certain to be unforgettable. The best-known symbol of Sicily and one of the world's major active volcanoes, Etna is the largest and highest volcano in Europe—the cone of the crater rises 10,902 feet above sea level. Although you'll get wonderful vantage points of Etna from Taormina, Castelmola, and Catania in particular, it also makes a rewarding day or overnight trip to see the mountain up close with a hike or climb; you can find routes suitable to every fitness level. It's also become a popular destination for wine lovers thanks to the many boutique wineries on its slopes; most accept visitors with an appointment.

GETTING HERE AND AROUND

Reaching the lower slopes of Mt. Etna is easy, either by driving yourself or taking a bus from Catania. Getting to the more interesting higher levels requires taking one of the stout four-wheel-drive minibuses that leave from Piano Provenzana on the north side and Rifugio Sapienza on the south side. A cable car, called the Funivia dell'Etna, from Rifugio Sapienza takes you part of the way.

Cable Car Funivia dell'Etna. ⊠ *Rifugio Sapienza* ☎ *095/914141, 095/914142* ⊕ *www.funiviaetna.com.*

TOURS

Club Alpino Italiano. This is a great resource for Mt. Etna climbing and hiking guides. If you have some experience and don't like a lot of handholding, these are the guides for you. ⊠ *Via Messina 593/a, Catania* ☎ *095/7153515* ⊕ *www.caicatania.it.*

Gruppo Guide Etna Nord. If you're a novice climber, call this company to arrange for a guide. Their service is a little more personalized—and expensive—than others. Reserve ahead. ⊠ *Piazza Attilio Castrogiovanni 19, Linguaglossa* ☎ *095/7774502, 348/0125167* ⊕ *www.guidetnanord.com.*

VISITOR INFORMATION

Contact Nicolosi Tourism Office. ✉ *Via G. Garibaldi 63, Nicolosi* ☎ *095/901505.*

EXPLORING

Fodor's Choice
★

Barone di Villagrande. The oldest winery in Etna offers friendly and informative tours of its stunning property followed by tastings of five wines, accompanied by food pairings; advance reservations are required. Visitors can opt for a more formal lunch as part of the tour. There are also four charming rooms where guests can spend the night. ✉ *Via del Bosco 25* ☎ *095/7082175* ⊕ *www.villagrande.it* 💶 *€20 for tour and tasting.*

Circumetnea. Instead of climbing up Mt. Etna, you can circle it on the Circumetnea, which runs near the volcano's base. The private railroad almost circles the volcano, running 114 km (71 miles) between Catania and Riposto—the towns are just 30 km (19 miles) apart by the coast road. The line is small, slow, and only single-track, but it has some dramatic vistas of the volcano and goes through lava fields. The one-way trip takes about 3½ hours, with departures every 90 minutes or so. After you've made the trip, you can get back to where you started from on the much quicker, but less scenic, conventional state rail service between Riposto and Catania. ✉ *Via Caronda 352, Catania* ☎ *095/541111* ⊕ *www.circumetnea.it* 💶 *€7.90 one-way* ⊘ *Closed Sun.*

Fodor's Choice
★

Mt. Etna. Plato sailed in just to catch a glimpse in 387 BC; in the 9th century AD the oldest gelato of all was shaved off its snowy slopes; and in the 21st century the volcano still claims annual headlines. Etna has erupted a dozen times since 1971, most spectacularly in 1971, 1983, 2001, 2002, 2005, and 2015. There were also a pair of medium-size eruptions in 2008, one in 2009, and fairly constant eruptive activity during the summer of 2011, winter of 2013, and summer of 2014. Travel in the proximity of the crater depends on Mt. Etna's temperament, but you can walk up and down the enormous lava dunes and wander over its moonlike surface of dead craters. The rings of vegetation change markedly as you rise, with vineyards and pine trees gradually giving way to growths of broom and lichen. ✉ *Parco del Etna* ⊕ *www.parcoetna.it.*

OFF THE
BEATEN
PATH

The villages that surround Mt. Etna offer much more than pretty views of the smoldering giant. They're charming and full of character in their own right, and make good bases for visiting nearby cities such as Catania, Acireale, and Taormina. **Zafferana Etnea** is famous for its orange-blossom honey; **Nicolosi,** at nearly 3,000 feet, is known as La Porta dell'Etna (The Door to Etna); **Trecastagni** (The Three Chestnut Trees) has one of Sicily's most beautiful Renaissance churches; **Randazzo,** the largest of the surrounding towns, is the site of a popular Sunday-morning wood, textile, and metalwork market; and **Bronte** is Italy's center of pistachio cultivation. The bars there offer various pistachio delicacies such as nougat, *colomba* (Easter sponge cake), panettone, and ice cream.

16

WHERE TO EAT AND STAY

$
PIZZA
Fodor's Choice
★

✕ **Cave Ox.** You're likely to meet a local winemaker or two at this casual place with a small but amazing cellar focused on local Etna natural wine producers. Dinners are mainly pizza, while lunches offer a selection of rustic antipasti along with daily changing pasta and meat dishes. **Known for:** superlative selection of natural wines from Etna; filling lunches and pizza dinners; local winemaker crowd. $ *Average main: €9* ⊠ *Via Nazionale Solicchiata 159* ☎ *0942/986171, 328/1349683* ⊕ *www.caveox.it* ☾ *Closed Tues.*

$$
MODERN ITALIAN
Fodor's Choice
★

✕ **Shalai.** You might not expect to find a thoroughly contemporary restaurant on the slopes of Mt. Etna, but Shalai, in the boutique hotel of the same name, is a welcome change from the otherwise simple culinary choices in the area. In sleek off-white rooms with a modern vibe, young chef Giovanni Santoro prepares updated and beautifully presented versions of Sicilian classics. **Known for:** innovative modern Sicilian dishes; delicious tasting menus; excellent wine list. $ *Average main: €22* ⊠ *Via Marconi 25, Linguaglossa* ☎ *095/643128* ⊕ *www.shalai.it* ☾ *No lunch weekdays.*

$$$
HOTEL
Fodor's Choice
★

⌂ **Monaci delle Terre Nere.** This cozy boutique hotel on the side of Mt. Etna features spacious, rustic-chic rooms on a real working organic farm with vineyards, along with an elegant Slow Food–inspired restaurant. **Pros:** relaxing and friendly atmosphere; delicious food and wine on offer; black-lava-stone pool with countryside views; eco-conscious ethos. **Cons:** accommodations may be a little quirky for some; not many restaurants in the area; service can be hit or miss. $ *Rooms from: €300* ⊠ *Via Monaci* ☎ *331/1365016* ⊕ *www.monacidelleterrenere.it* ☾ *Closed Jan.–mid-Mar.* ⇥ *23 rooms* ⦿⟟ *Free Breakfast.*

ACIREALE

40 km (25 miles) south of Taormina, 16 km (10 miles) north of Catania.

Acireale sits amid a clutter of rocky pinnacles and lush lemon groves. The craggy coast is known as the Riviera dei Ciclopi, after the legend narrated in the *Odyssey* in which the blinded Cyclops Polyphemus hurled boulders at the retreating Ulysses, thus creating spires of rock, or *faraglioni* (pillars of rock rising dramatically out of the sea). Tourism has barely taken off here, so it's a good destination if you feel the need to put some distance between yourself and the busloads of tourists in Taormina. And though the beaches are rocky, there's good swimming here, too.

The Carnival celebrations, held the two weeks before Lent, are considered the best in Sicily. The streets are jammed with thousands of revelers. Acireale is an easy day trip from Catania.

GETTING HERE AND AROUND

Buses arrive frequently from Taormina and Catania. Acireale is on the main coastal train route, though the station is a long walk south of the center. Local buses pass every 20 minutes or so.

VISITOR INFORMATION

Contact Acireale Tourism Office. ⊠ *Via Oreste Scionti 15* ☎ *095/891999.*

CLOSE UP

Desserts in Sicily

Sicily is famous for its desserts, none more so than the wonderful cannoli (singular *cannolo*), whose delicate pastry shell and just-sweet-enough ricotta filling barely resemble their foreign impostors. They come in all sizes, from pinkie-size bites to holiday cannoli the size of a coffee table. Even your everyday bar will display a window piled high with dozens of varieties of ricotta-based desserts, including delicious fried balls of dough. The traditional cake of Sicily is the *cassata siciliana*, a rich, chilled sponge cake with sheep's-milk ricotta and candied fruit. Often brightly colored, it's the most popular dessert at many Sicilian restaurants, and you shouldn't miss it. From behind bakery windows and glass cases beam tiny marzipan sweets fashioned into brightly colored apples, cherries, and even hamburgers and prosciutto.

If it's summer, do as the locals do and dip your morning brioche—the best in Italy—into a cup of brilliantly refreshing coffee- or almond-flavored granita. The world's first ice cream is said to have been made by the Romans from the snow on the slopes of Mt. Etna. Top-quality gelato is also prevalent throughout the island.

EXPLORING

Belvedere di Santa Caterina. Lord Byron (1788–1824) visited the Belvedere di Santa Caterina to look out over the Ionian Sea during his Italian wanderings. The viewing point is south of the old town, near the Terme di Acireale, off SS114. ✉ *Off SS114.*

Duomo. With its cupola and twin turrets, Acireale's Duomo is an extravagant Baroque construction dating to the 17th century. In the chapel to the right of the altar, look for the 17th-century silver statue of Santa Venera (patron saint of Acireale) made by Mario D'Angelo, and the early-18th-century frescoes by Antonio Filocamo. ✉ *Piazza del Duomo* ☎ *095/601102* 🌐 *www.diocesiacireale.it.*

OFF THE BEATEN PATH

Santa Maria La Scala. A half-hour's walk from Acireale's center, this picturesque harbor is filled with fishers unloading brightly colored boats. Inexpensive lunches are served in the many restaurants along the harbor. Your fresh fish dish is priced by weight. ✉ *Acireale.*

WHERE TO EAT

$$$ SEAFOOD

🍴 **La Grotta.** A dining room within a cave, with part of the cave wall exposed, is a feature of this rustic trattoria above the harbor of Santa Maria La Scala. Try the *insalata di mare* (a selection of delicately boiled fish served with lemon and olive oil), pasta with clams or cuttlefish ink, or fish grilled over charcoal. **Known for:** the catch of the day; superfresh seafood; unique cave setting. [$] *Average main: €30* ✉ *Via Scalo Grande 46* ☎ *095/7648153* 🌐 *www.ristorantelagrotta.info* 🕒 *Closed Tues., and late Oct.*

EN ROUTE

Aci Castello and Aci Trezza. These two gems on the coastline between Acireale and Catania—the Riviera dei Ciclopi (Cyclops Riviera)—fill with city dwellers in the summer months, but even in colder weather their beauty is hard to fault. Heading south from Acireale on the *litoranea* (coastal) road, you'll first reach Aci Trezza, said to be the land of the one-eyed Cyclops in Homer's *Odyssey*. Less developed than Aci Trezza, Aci Castello has its own fish houses plus the imposing Castello Normanno (Norman Castle), which sits right on the water. The castle was built in the 11th century with volcanic rock from Mt. Etna—the same rock that forms the coastal cliffs. ⊠ *Acireale.*

CATANIA

16 km (10 miles) south of Acireale, 94 km (59 miles) south of Messina, 60 km (37 miles) north of Siracusa.

The chief wonder of Catania, Sicily's second city, is that it's there at all. Its successive populations were deported by one Greek tyrant, sold into slavery by another, and driven out by the Carthaginians. Every time the city got back on its feet it was struck by a new calamity: plague decimated the population in the Middle Ages, a mile-wide stream of lava from Mt. Etna swallowed part of it in 1669, and 25 years later a disastrous earthquake forced the Catanesi to begin again.

Today Catania is completing yet another resurrection—this time from crime, filth, and urban decay. Although the city remains loud and full of traffic, signs of gentrification are everywhere. The elimination of vehicles from the Piazza del Duomo and the main artery of Via Etnea, and the cleaning of many of the historic buildings have added to its newfound charm. Home to what is arguably Sicily's best university, Catania is full of exuberant youth, and it shows in the chic *osterie* (taverns) that serve wine, the designer bistros, and the trendy ethnic boutiques that have popped up all over town. Even more impressive is the vibrant cultural life.

GETTING HERE AND AROUND

Catania is well connected by bus and train with Messina, Taormina, Siracusa, Enna, and Palermo. The airport of Fontanarossa serves as a transportation hub for the eastern side of the island. From here you can get buses to most major destinations without going into the city center.

VISITOR INFORMATION

Contact Catania Tourism Office. ⊠ *Via Vittorio Emanuele 172* ☎ *800/841042, 095/7425573* ⊕ *www.comune.catania.it/la-citta/turismo.*

EXPLORING

TOP ATTRACTIONS

Cattedrale di Sant'Agata (Duomo). The Giovanni Vaccarini–designed facade of the cathedral dominates the Piazza del Duomo; composer Vincenzo Bellini is buried inside. Also of note are the three apses of lava that survive from the original Norman structure and a fresco from 1675 in the sacristy that portrays Catania's submission to Etna's attack. Guided tours of the cathedral in English are available with a reservation at least a week in advance. The cathedral's treasures are on view in the **Museo Diocesano Catania** (⊕ *www.museodiocesanocatania. com*), while underneath the Cathedral are the ruins of Greco-Roman baths. ⊠ *Piazza del Duomo, bottom end of Via Etnea* ☎ *095/320044*

⊕ *www.cattedralecatania.it* ✉ *Museum €7, baths €5; combined ticket €10* ⊙ *Museum and baths closed Sun.*

Centro Storico. Black lava stone from Etna, combined with largely Baroque architecture, give Catania's historic center a very distinctive feel. After Catania's destruction by lava and earthquake at the end of the 17th century, the city was rebuilt and "u Liotru" (an elephant carved out of lava) was placed outside the cathedral as a kind of talisman. Also of note in the center are Castello Ursino, which is now a museum, the Greco-Roman theater next to Piazza Duomo, and the Roman amphitheater in Piazza Stesicoro. ✉ *Catania.*

Piazza del Duomo. Shining from a 21st-century renovation, this piazza, which is closed to traffic, has at its heart an elephant carved out of lava, balancing an Egyptian obelisk. This is the city's informal mascot, called "u Liotru" in Sicilian dialect. The square also marks the entrance to Catania's famous *pescheria* (fish market) and is one of the few points in the city where you can see the River Amenano aboveground. Another point of interest is Via Garibaldi, which runs from Piazza del Duomo up toward the impressively huge Porta Garibaldi, a black-and-white triumphal arch built in 1768 to commemorate the marriage of Ferdinando I. ✉ *Piazza del Duomo.*

Via Etnea. Lined with cafés and stores selling high-street jewelry, clothing, and shoes, this street is host to one of Sicily's most enthusiastic *passeggiate* (early-evening strolls), in which Catanese of all ages take part. It is closed to automobile traffic until 10 pm during the week and all day on weekends. ✉ *Via Etnea.*

WORTH NOTING

Agorà Youth Hostel. An underground river, the Amenano, flows through much of Catania. You can glimpse it at the Fontana dell'Amenano, but the best place to experience the river is at the bar-restaurant of the Agorà Youth Hostel. Here you can sit at an underground table as swirls of water rush by. If you're not there when the bar is open, someone at the reception desk can let you in. Apart from the underground river, the bar area aboveground is a lively, fun area to hang out on a Monday evening when many other places are closed. ✉ *Piazza Currò 6* ☎ *095/7233010* ⊕ *www.agorahostel.com.*

Festa di Sant'Agata. Each February 3–5, the Festa di Sant'Agata honors Catania's patron saint with one of Italy's biggest religious festivals. The saint herself was first tortured, then killed, when she spurned a Roman suitor in favor of keeping her religious purity. Since then, the Catanese have honored her memory by pulling her relics through the streets of Catania on an enormous silver-encrusted carriage. The entire festival is highly affecting, even for nonbelievers, and is not to be missed by February visitors. ✉ *Catania* ⊕ *www.festadisantagata.it.*

Museo Belliniano. Catania's greatest native son was the composer Vincenzo Bellini (1801–35), whose operas have thrilled audiences since their premieres in Naples and Milan. His home, now the Museo Belliniano, preserves memorabilia of the man and his work. ✉ *Piazza San Francesco D'Assisi 3* ☎ *095/7150535* ✉ *€5.*

16

QUICK BITES

Pasticceria Savia. The lively Pasticceria Savia makes superlative arancini with *ragù* (a slow-cooked, tomato-based meat sauce). Or you could choose cannoli or other snacks to munch on while you rest. Known for: arancini (rice balls) with ragù (tomato sauce); typical Sicilian pastries like cannoli and paste di mandorla (almond paste); lovely outdoor seating. ✉ *Via Etnea 302–304 and Via Umberto 2, near Villa Bellini* ☎ *095/322335* 🌐 *www.savia.it* 🕓 *Closed Mon.*

WHERE TO EAT

$$$ SEAFOOD 🍴 **Ambasciata del Mare.** When a seafood restaurant sits next door to a fish market, it bodes well for the food's freshness. Choose swordfish or *gamberoni* (large shrimp) from a display case in the front of the restaurant; then enjoy it simply grilled with oil and lemon. **Known for:** ultrafresh fish; delicious seafood; central location. [$] *Average main: €35* ✉ *Piazza del Duomo 6/7* ☎ *095/341003* 🌐 *www.ambasciatadelmare.it* 🕓 *Closed Mon.*

$ CAFÉ 🍴 **Caffè del Duomo.** Sample the hustle and bustle of Catania at Caffè del Duomo, which has handmade cookies and cakes and a great local atmosphere. Take a seat outside in the piazza and order one of the excellent cannoli to eat with your coffee as you watch the world go by. **Known for:** great spot for people-watching; handmade treats. [$] *Average main: €9* ✉ *Piazza Duomo 11–13* ☎ *095/7150556.*

$$$ SICILIAN 🍴 **La Siciliana.** Brothers Salvo and Vito La Rosa serve memorable seafood and meat dishes, exquisite homemade desserts, and a wide choice of wines. The restaurant specializes in the ancient dish *ripiddu nivicatu* (risotto with cuttlefish ink and fresh ricotta cheese), as well as *sarde a beccafico* (stuffed sardines) and calamari *ripieni alla griglia* (stuffed and grilled). **Known for:** black risotto with ricotta; traditional Sicilian dishes; very local atmosphere (little English spoken). [$] *Average main: €30* ✉ *Viale Marco Polo 52a* ☎ *095/376400* 🌐 *www.lasiciliana.it* 🕓 *Closed Mon., and 2 wks in Aug. No dinner Sun.*

$$ SEAFOOD Fodor's Choice ★ 🍴 **Osteria Antica Marina.** Just steps from Catania's famous fish market, this bustling osteria makes a perfect stop for ultrafresh seafood, surrounded by an energetic mix of locals and in-the-know tourists. Antica Marina's famed for its linguine with sea urchin, but you also can't go wrong with spaghetti with mussels and algae or ricotta panzotti in black-squid-ink sauce; just save room for the freshly grilled whole fish. **Known for:** fresh seafood antipasti; scrumptious pastas; straight-from-the-market fish. [$] *Average main: €20* ✉ *Via Pardo 29* ☎ *095/348197* 🌐 *www.anticamarina.it* 🕓 *Closed Wed.*

WHERE TO STAY

$$ HOTEL 🏨 **Romano House.** With a sleek, minimalist design in a 17th-century palace in a convenient location, this boutique hotel caters to design aficionados on a budget. **Pros:** modern design; good-size rooms; in-house restaurant and bar. **Cons:** design sometimes wins over practicality in rooms; neighborhood won't appeal to everyone; street noise can be a problem. [$] *Rooms from: €125* ✉ *Via di Prima 20* ☎ *095/3520611* 🌐 *www.romanohouse.com* 🛏 *47 rooms* 🍽 *No meals.*

$ 🖵 **Una Hotel Palace.** For welcoming service and great views of Etna, this
HOTEL   centrally located hotel overlooking Catania's main shopping street can't
be beat; you can even take your breakfast on the rooftop terrace (for an
extra fee) to enjoy the scenery first thing in the morning. **Pros:** amazing
rooftop views; extremely central location; eager-to-please staff. **Cons:**
bit of a generic feel; some noisy rooms; extra fee for parking. **$** *Rooms
from: €115* ✉ *Via Etnea 218* ☎ *095/2505111 (international number)*
⊕ *www.unahotels.it/en* ⌐ *94 rooms* ⟡ *Free Breakfast.*

NIGHTLIFE AND PERFORMING ARTS

Teatro Massimo Bellini. Opera season (October–June) attracts top sing-
ers and productions to the birthplace of the great composer Vincenzo
Bellini. Guided tours of the theater's lavish interior, built in 1890,
run Tuesday–Saturday 9:30–noon when theater business permits; call
first to ensure you can get a tour. Enter by the box office on Piazza
Bellini. ✉ *Via Perrotta 12* ☎ *095/7306111 info, 095/7306135 box
office, 344/2249701 guided tours* ⊕ *www.teatromassimobellini.it*
🎫 *€6 for guided tours.*

SHOPPING

I Dolci di Nonna Vincenza. The selection of almond-based delights here
may be small, but everything is fresh and phenomenally good. Ask for
boxes of mixed cookies by weight, and enjoy the grab-bag selection at
your leisure later. International shipping is available. Other stores can
be found on Via G. d'Annunzio 216/218, Via San Giuseppe la Rena
30, and at Catania airport. ✉ *Palazzo Biscari, Piazza San Placido 7*
☎ *095/7151844* ⊕ *www.dolcinonnavincenza.it.*

FodorśChoice   **Outdoor Fish and Food Market.** Beginning behind the Fontana Amenano
★   at the corner of Piazza Duomo and spreading westward between Via
Garibaldi and Via Transito, this is one of Italy's most memorable markets. It's a feast for the senses, with thousands of just-caught fish (some
still wriggling), ricotta, fresh produce, endless varieties of meats, plus
a symphony of vendor shouts to fill the ears. The market is at its best
in the early morning and finishes up around 2 pm. ✉ *Corner of Piazza
Duomo* ☉ *Closed Sun.*

SIRACUSA

Siracusa, known to English speakers as Syracuse, is a wonder to behold.
One of the great ancient capitals of Western civilization, the city was
founded in 734 BC by Greek colonists from Corinth and soon grew to
rival—and even surpass—Athens in splendor and power. It became the
largest, wealthiest city-state in the West and a bulwark of Greek civilization. Although Siracusa lived under tyranny, rulers such as Dionysius
filled their courts with Greeks of the highest cultural stature—among
them the playwrights Aeschylus and Euripides, and the philosopher
Plato. The Athenians, who didn't welcome Siracusa's rise, set out to
conquer Sicily, but the natives outsmarted them in what was one of
the greatest military campaigns in ancient history (413 BC). The city
continued to prosper until it was conquered two centuries later by the
Romans.

16

Present-day Siracusa still has some of the finest examples of Baroque art and architecture; dramatic Greek and Roman ruins; and a Duomo that's the stuff of legend—a microcosm of the city's entire history in one building. The modern city also has a wonderful, lively Baroque old town worthy of extensive exploration, as well as pleasant piazzas, outdoor cafés and bars, and a wide assortment of excellent seafood. There are essentially two areas to explore in Siracusa: the Parco Archeologico (Archaeological Zone), on the mainland; and the island of Ortygia, the ancient city first inhabited by the Greeks, which juts out into the Ionian Sea and is connected to the mainland by two small bridges. Ortygia has become increasingly popular with tourists, and although it's filled with lots of modern boutiques (and tourist shops), it still retains its charm despite the crowds.

While Ortygia, a compact area, is a pleasure to amble around without getting unduly tired, in contrast, mainland Siracusa is a grid of wider avenues. At the northern end of Corso Gelone, above Viale Paolo Orsi, the orderly grid gives way to the ancient quarter of Neapolis, where the sprawling Parco Archeologico is accessible from Viale Teracati (an extension of Corso Gelone). East of Viale Teracati, about a 10-minute walk from the Parco Archeologico, the district of Tyche holds the archaeological museum and the church and catacombs of San Giovanni, both off Viale Teocrito (drive or take a taxi or city bus from Ortygia). Coming from the train station, it's a 15-minute trudge to Ortygia along Via Francesco Crispi and Corso Umberto. If you're not up for that, take one of the free electric buses leaving every 10 minutes from the bus station around the corner.

GETTING HERE AND AROUND
On the main train line from Messina and Catania, Siracusa is also linked to Catania by frequent buses.

FESTIVALS
Festa di Santa Lucia. The feast of the city's patron, Santa Lucia, is held on December 13 and 20 at Santa Lucia alla Badia. A splendid silver statue of the saint is carried from the church to the Duomo: a torchlight procession and band music accompany the bearers, while local families watch from their balconies. ⊠ *Piazza del Duomo, near Catacombs of San Giovanni, Ortygia.*

VISITOR INFORMATION
Contact Siracusa Tourism Office. ⊠ *Via Roma 31, Ortygia* ☎ *800/055500* ⊕ *www.siracusaturismo.net.*

EXPLORING

ARCHAEOLOGICAL ZONE
TOP ATTRACTIONS
Fodor'sChoice **Parco Archeologico della Neapolis.** Siracusa is most famous for its dramatic
★ set of Greek and Roman ruins. Although the various ruins can be visited separately, see them all, along with the Museo Archeologico. If the park is closed, go up Viale G. Rizzo from Viale Teracati to the belvedere overlooking the ruins, which are floodlit at night.

Before the park's ticket booth is the gigantic **Ara di Ierone** (Altar of Hieron), which was once used by the Greeks for spectacular sacrifices involving hundreds of animals. The first attraction in the park is the **Latomia del Paradiso** (Quarry of Paradise), a lush tropical garden full of palm and citrus trees. This series of quarries served as prisons for the defeated Athenians, who were enslaved; the quarries once rang with the sound of their chisels and hammers. At one end is the famous **Orecchio di Dionisio** (Ear of Dionysius), with an ear-shape entrance and unusual acoustics inside, as you'll hear if you clap your hands. The legend is that Dionysius used to listen in at the top of the quarry to hear what the slaves were plotting below.

The **Teatro Greco** is the chief monument in the Archaeological Park. Indeed it's one of Sicily's greatest classical sites and the most complete Greek theater surviving from antiquity. Climb to the top of the seating area (which could accommodate 15,000) for a fine view: all the seats converge upon a single point—the stage—which has the natural scenery and the sky as its background. Hewn out of the hillside rock in the 5th century BC, the theater saw the premieres of the plays of Aeschylus. Greek tragedies are still performed here every year in May and June. Above and behind the theater runs the Via dei Sepulcri, in which streams of running water flow through a series of Greek sepulchres.

The well-preserved and striking **Anfiteatro Romano** (Roman Amphitheater) reveals much about the differences between the Greek and Roman personalities. Where drama in the Greek theater was a kind of religious ritual, the Roman amphitheater emphasized the spectacle of combative sports and the circus. This arena is one of the largest of its kind and was built around the 2nd century AD. The corridor where gladiators and beasts entered the ring is still intact, and the seats (some of which still bear the occupants' names) were hauled in and constructed on the site from huge slabs of limestone. ⊠ *Viale Teocrito, entrance on Via Agnello, Archaeological Zone* ☎ *0931/66206* ⊕ *www.regione.sicilia. it/beniculturali/museopaoloorsi* 🎟 *€10, combined ticket with Museo Archeologico €13.50. Free 1st Sun. of month.*

WORTH NOTING

Catacomba di San Giovanni. Not far from the Archaeological Park, off Viale Teocrito, the catacombs below the church of San Giovanni are one of the earliest-known Christian sites in the city. Inside the crypt of San Marciano is an altar where St. Paul preached on his way through Sicily to Rome. The frescoes in this small chapel are mostly bright and fresh, though some dating from the 4th century AD show their age. To visit the catacombs, you must take a 45-minute guided tour (included with the admission price), which leaves about every half hour and is conducted in Italian and English. ⊠ *Piazza San Giovanni, Tyche* ☎ *0931/64694* 🎟 *€8* ⊗ *Closed daily 12:30–2:30, and Mon. in winter.*

Museo Archeologico Regionale Paolo Orsi. The impressive collection of Siracusa's splendid archaeological museum is organized by region and time period around a central atrium and ranges from Neolithic pottery to fine Greek statues and vases. Compare the Landolina Venus—a headless goddess of love who rises out of the sea in measured modesty

16

(a 1st-century-AD Roman copy of the Greek original)—with the much earlier (300 BC) elegant Greek statue of Hercules in Section C. Of a completely different style is a marvelous fanged Gorgon, its tongue sticking out, that once adorned the cornice of the Temple of Athena to ward off evildoers. ⊠ *Viale Teocrito 66, Tyche* ☏ *0931/489511* ⊕ *www. regione.sicilia.it/beniculturali/museopaoloorsi* ⊠ *€8, combined ticket with Parco Archeologico €13.50* ☾ *Closed Mon., and Sun. after 1.*

ORTYGIA

TOP ATTRACTIONS

Fodor's Choice
★ **Duomo.** Siracusa's Duomo is an archive of island history: the bottom-most excavations have unearthed remnants of Sicily's distant past, when the Siculi inhabitants worshipped their deities here. During the 5th century BC (the same time as Agrigento's Temple of Concord was built), the Greeks erected a temple to Athena over it, and in the 7th century Siracusa's first Christian cathedral was built on top of the Greek structure. The massive columns of the original Greek temple were incorporated into the present structure and are clearly visible, embedded in the exterior wall along Via Minerva. The Greek columns were also used to dramatic advantage inside, where on one side they form chapels connected by elegant wrought-iron gates. The Baroque facade, added in the 18th century, displays a harmonious rhythm of concaves and convexes. In front, the piazza is encircled by pink and white oleanders and elegant buildings ornamented with filigree grillwork. ⊠ *Piazza del Duomo, Ortygia* ☏ *0931/65328* ⊠ *€2.*

Fonte Aretusa. A freshwater spring, the Fountain of Arethusa, sits next to the sea, studded with Egyptian papyrus that's reportedly natural. This anomaly is explained by a Greek legend that tells how the nymph Arethusa was changed into a fountain by the goddess Artemis (Diana) when she tried to escape the advances of the river god Alpheus. She fled from Greece, into the sea, with Alpheus in close pursuit, and emerged in Sicily at this spring. It's said if you throw a cup into the Alpheus River in Greece, it will emerge here at this fountain, which is home to a few tired ducks and some faded carp—but no cups. If you want to stand right by the fountain, you need to gain admission through the aquarium; otherwise look down on it from Largo Aretusa. ⊠ *Off promenade along harbor, Ortygia.*

Museo del Papiro. Housed in the 16th-century ex-convent of Sant'Agostino, the small but intriguing Papyrus Museum uses informative exhibits and videos to demonstrate how papyri are prepared from reeds and then painted—an ancient tradition in the city. Siracusa, it seems, has the only climate outside the Nile Valley in which the papyrus plant—from which the word "paper" comes—thrives. ⊠ *Via Nizza 14, Ortygia* ☏ *0931/22100* ⊕ *www.museodelpapiro.it* ⊠ *€5* ☾ *Closed Mon.*

Piazza Archimede. The center of this piazza has a Baroque fountain, the *Fontana di Diana*, festooned with fainting sea nymphs and dancing jets of water. Look for the Chiaramonte-style **Palazzo Montalto,** an arched-window gem just off the piazza on Via Montalto. ⊠ *Piazza Archimede, Ortygia.*

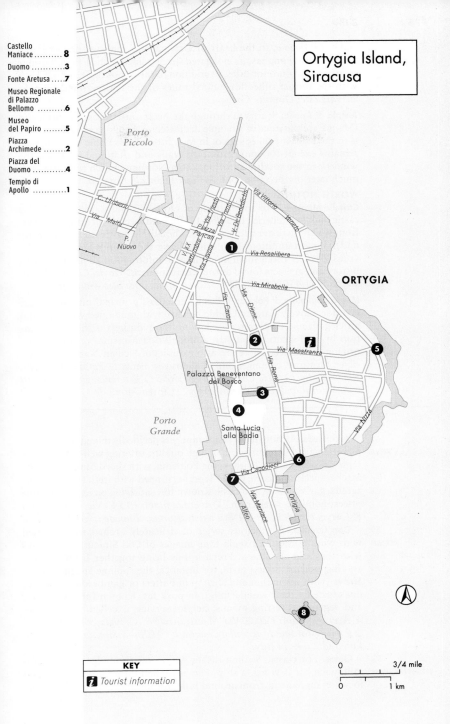

Ortygia Island,
Siracusa

*Porto
Piccolo*

ORTYGIA

C. Umberto

Via Malta

P.
Nuovo

Piazza
Pancali

V. XX Settembre

Via Savoia

Via Trento

Via Trieste

Via Del Benedictis

Via Vittorio Veneto

Via Resalibera

Via Mirabella

Via Cavour

Via Dione

Via Maestranza

Via Roma

Via Nizza

Palazzo Beneventano
del Bosco

*Porto
Grande*

Santa Lucia
alla Badia

Via Capodieci

Via Maniace

L'Alfeo

L. Ortigia

KEY

Tourist information

0   3/4 mile

0   1 km

Fodor's Choice ★ **Piazza del Duomo.** In the heart of Ortygia, this ranks as one of Italy's most beautiful piazzas. Its elongated space is lined with Sicilian Baroque treasures and outdoor cafés, in addition to the imposing Duomo. Check with the tourist office for guided tours of the underground tunnels. ✉ *Piazza del Duomo, Ortygia.*

Tempio di Apollo. Scattered through the piazza just across the bridge to Ortygia are the ruins of a temple dedicated to Apollo, a model of which is in the Museo Archeologico. In fact, little of this noble Doric temple remains except for some crumbled walls and shattered columns; the window in the south wall belongs to a Norman church that was built much later on the same spot. ✉ *Piazza Pancali, Ortygia.*

WORTH NOTING

Castello Maniace. The southern tip of Ortygia island is occupied by this castle built by Frederick II (1194–1250), until recently an army barracks, from which there are fine sea views. Though the castle itself is currently undergoing restorations, you can still visit the grounds and admire the vistas. There's also a small museum with information about the castle's history and artifacts found during excavations. ✉ *Via del Castello Maniace* ☎ *0931/4508211* 🎫 *€2* 🕒 *Closed Mon., and Tues.–Sun. after 1.*

Museo Regionale di Palazzo Bellomo. Siracusa's principal museum of art is inside a lovely Catalan Gothic palazzo with mullioned windows and an elegant exterior staircase. Among the paintings is the *Annunciation* by 15th-century maestro Antonello da Messina, restored to its original brilliance. There are also exhibits of Sicilian Nativity figures, silver, furniture, ceramics, and religious vestments. ✉ *Palazzo Bellomo, Via Capodieci 14/16, Ortygia* ☎ *0931/69511* 🌐 *www.regione.sicilia.it/beniculturali/palazzobellomo* 🎫 *€8* 🕒 *Closed Mon.*

WHERE TO EAT

$$ PIZZA 🍴 **Archimede.** Although the restaurant gets decidedly mixed reviews, the pizzeria part of Archimede is of high quality, offering well-made pizzas with classical names. Witness the Polifema, with sliced tomatoes, mozzarella, speck, and corn; or the Teocrite, topped with fresh tomato, mozzarella, garlic, onion, and basil. **Known for:** satisfying pizzas; reasonable prices; good beer selection. [$] *Average main: €15* ✉ *Via Gemmellaro 8, Ortygia* ☎ *0931/69701* 🌐 *www.trattoriaarchimede.it* 🕒 *Closed Sun.*

$$ SICILIAN Fodor's Choice ★ 🍴 **Don Camillo.** A gracious series of delicately arched rooms, lined with wine bottles and sepia-tone images of Old Siracusa, overflows with locals in the know. Preparations bring together fresh seafood and inspired creativity: taste, for instance, the sublime spaghetti *delle Sirene* (with sea urchin and shrimp in butter) or gamberoni prepared, unexpectedly (and wonderfully), in pork fat. **Known for:** fish, meat, and vegetarian tasting menus; helpful service; excellent wine menu. [$] *Average main: €20* ✉ *Via Maestranza 96, Ortygia* ☎ *0931/67133* 🌐 *www.ristorantedoncamillosiracusa.it* 🕒 *Closed Sun., and 2 wks in Jan. and 2 wks in July.*

$$ MODERN ITALIAN 🍴 **Oinos.** For classic Sicilian dishes with a modern edge, this restaurant–wine bar is worth a stop. Flavor-packed dishes are seasonal and focus on ingredients from around Italy; for instance, in the fall, special

menu items spotlight white truffles from Alba priced by the gram (as is customary) and worth every penny. **Known for:** seasonal dishes; good wine selection; lovely, sophisticated atmosphere. $ *Average main: €20* ✉ *Via della Giudecca 69/75, Ortygia* ☎ *0931/464900* ☉ *Closed Tues.*

$

SICILIAN

✕ **Taberna Sveva.** At this "slow food" tavern conveniently located in the streets right behind the Castello Maniace, you can sit back and enjoy both land-based and seafood dishes. The surroundings are studiously minimalist (no tablecloths, leather mats) and dishes are served on hand-painted ceramic ware. **Known for:** authentic Sicilian dishes; good-value meals; charming setting on a square. $ *Average main: €13* ✉ *Piazza Federico di Svevia 1, Ortygia* ☎ *0931/24663* ☉ *Closed Nov. and Jan., and Wed. Sept. 15–June. No lunch June–Sept.*

WHERE TO STAY

$$

HOTEL

Fodor's Choice

★

Algilà Ortigia Charme Hotel. It's hard to say what's more charming about this boutique hotel: its location overlooking the sea on the edge of the old town, or its delightful interiors, including guest rooms done up in country-chic style, with a mix of modern amenities (Bvlgari toiletries, free minibar) and antique touches (beamed ceilings, hand-painted tiles in the bathroom). **Pros:** wonderfully central location; prime water views; eager-to-please service. **Cons:** no spa, pool, or gym; lots of stairs between floors could be an issue for some; not all rooms have sea views. $ *Rooms from: €150* ✉ *Via Vittorio Veneto 93* ☎ *0931/465186* ⊕ *www.algila.it* ⇒ *54 rooms* ❙⊙❙ *Free Breakfast.*

$

HOTEL

Domus Mariae. On Ortygia's eastern shore, this hotel, in an unusual twist, is owned by Ursuline nuns, who help to make the mood placid and peaceful—but the elegant accommodations are far from monastic. **Pros:** nice breakfast; gorgeous sea views; enthusiastic staff. **Cons:** stairs to climb; not much street parking near the hotel; small rooms. $ *Rooms from: €109* ✉ *Via Vittorio Veneto 76, Ortygia* ☎ *0931/24854* ⊕ *www.domusmariaebenessere.com* ⇒ *12 rooms* ❙⊙❙ *Free Breakfast.*

$$

HOTEL

Grand Hotel Ortigia. An elegant though somewhat old-fashioned design prevails at this venerable institution, which has enjoyed a prime position on the Porto Grande at the base of Ortygia since 1890. **Pros:** wonderful seafront views from the restaurant; attentive service; convenient location. **Cons:** back rooms have no view; small bathrooms; Wi-Fi weak in some rooms. $ *Rooms from: €188* ✉ *Viale Mazzini 12, Ortygia* ☎ *0931/464600* ⊕ *www.grandhotelortigia.it* ⇒ *58 rooms* ❙⊙❙ *Free Breakfast.*

$$

HOTEL

Grand Hotel Villa Politi. European royalty, Winston Churchill, and other VIPs have frequented the grand 18th-century Villa Politi; though now a little faded, it still retains its charm and elegance with rococo furnishings along with modern luxuries like comfy beds. **Pros:** excellent service; free parking in the hotel lot; expansive outdoor pool. **Cons:** a fair distance from the sights of Ortygia; not many restaurants in the neighborhood; not as sparkling and fresh as in the past. $ *Rooms from: €126* ✉ *Via M. Politi 2, Archaeological Zone* ☎ *0931/412121* ⊕ *www. villapoliti.com* ⇒ *100 rooms* ❙⊙❙ *Free Breakfast.*

$

HOTEL

Mercure Siracusa Prometeo. Offering excellent value for money, the Mercure occupies a glass-front building along the busy Viale Teracati

16

and, like most other hotels in the same chain, it's a slick operation with first-rate facilities. **Pros:** a two-minute walk from the archaeological site of Neapolis; swimming pool on the roof; good parking facilities. **Cons:** chain hotel with little character; a long way from the island of Ortygia; €10 charge for breakfast. $ *Rooms from: €91* ⊠ *Viale Teracati 20, Tyche* ☎ *0931/464646* ⊕ *www.hotelmercuresiracusa.com* ⌁ *93 rooms* ⏁⊙⏁ *No meals.*

PERFORMING ARTS

Teatro Greco (*Greek Theater*). From early May to mid-July, Siracusa's ancient Teatro Greco stages performances of classical tragedy and comedy. Tickets run €36–€73, with a small discount if you buy the ticket in person. ⊠ *Teatro Greco, Archaeological Zone* ☎ *0931/487248, 800/542644 toll-free in Italy* ⊕ *www.indafondazione.org.*

THE INTERIOR

Sicily's pretty interior has become more popular with visitors looking for lovely towns with grand architecture and unspoiled vistas—in particular, the UNESCO World Heritage–listed Baroque towns of Ragusa, Modica, Noto, and Caltagirone. It's also great for wine lovers, with many vineyards that can be visited by appointment in and around the Iblea region. The Imperial Roman Villa at Casale, outside Piazza Armerina, gives precious evidence of a bygone epoch. Finally, look out for the sleepy, windy mountaintop city of Enna, dubbed "the Navel of Sicily."

NOTO

36 km (22 miles) southwest of Siracusa.

If Siracusa's Baroque beauties whet your appetite for that over-the-top style, head to Noto, a UNESCO World Heritage Site. Lying about 40 minutes away on the A18/E45, the city is doable as a day trip—though staying overnight lets you see the lovely buildings glow in the setting sun after the tourist hordes have departed. Despite being decimated by an earthquake in 1693 and rebuilt in the prevailing fashion of the day, Noto has remarkable architectural integrity. A prime example of design from the island's Baroque heyday, it presents a pleasing ensemble of honey-color buildings, strikingly uniform in style but never dull. Simply walking Corso Vittorio Emanuele, the pedestrianized main street, qualifies as an aesthetic experience.

GETTING HERE AND AROUND

Trains leave from Siracusa at least 10 times daily (with fewer trains on Sundays); there are also three trains a day from Ragusa. Buses depart numerous times a day from Siracusa, Catania, and Ragusa.

VISITOR INFORMATION

Contact Noto Tourism Office. ⊠ *Corso Vittorio Emanuele 135, Noto* ☎ *339/4816218* ⊕ *www.comune.noto.sr.it.*

EXPLORING

Cattedrale di San Nicolò. Noto's domed cathedral (divine in more ways than one) is an undisputed highlight of the extraordinary Baroque architecture for which the town is world famous. The interior—restored over a 10-year period after the dome collapsed in 1996—is simple compared to the magnificent exterior, but still worth a look. ⊠ *Corso Vittorio Emanuele, Noto.*

Palazzo Nicolaci di Villadorata. For a rare insight into the lifestyle of social climbers in the 18th century, this palace is a must-see. Although it contains about 90 rooms belonging to the noble Nicolaci family, only some are on view to the public. Outside the palace, note the gorgeous balconies featuring mythical creatures. ⊠ *Via Corrado Nicolaci, Noto* ☎ *320/5568038* ⊕ *www.palazzonicolaci.it* ⊠ *€4.*

WHERE TO EAT AND STAY

$$

SICILIAN

Fodor's Choice
★

✕ **Ristorante Crocifisso.** Although getting to Crocifisso is a bit of a hike—it's away from Noto's tourist hub and up a hill only accessible by many steps—intrepid diners will be rewarded with one of the Baroque town's finest restaurants. Traditional dishes are presented in a contemporary style, with the freshest ingredients; if they're on the menu, the *caserecce con le sarde* (homemade pasta with sardines) and *ravioli di ricotta al nero di sepia* (ricotta ravioli with squid ink) are particularly fine. **Known for:** new takes on classic Sicilian dishes; superlative house-made pastas; fantastic wine selection. $ *Average main: €18* ⊠ *Via Principe Umberto 48, Noto* ☎ *0931/571151, 338/8530241* ⊕ *www.ristorantecrocifisso.it* ⊙ *Closed mid-Jan.–late Feb., and Wed. Sept.–June.*

$$

SICILIAN

Fodor's Choice
★

✕ **Ristorante Manna.** The plain exterior here gives no hint of the sleek, cool design inside this welcoming restaurant just off of Noto's main street. Although the small outdoor patio allows for great people-watching, it's inside that the restaurant really shines; the chic multilevel dining area highlights modern art, a stylish complement to the restaurant's thoroughly modern food. **Known for:** modern, creative Sicilian cuisine; delightful staff; cool, contemporary setting. $ *Average main: €18* ⊠ *Via Rocco Pirri 19, Noto* ☎ *0931/836051* ⊕ *www.mannanoto.it* ⊙ *Closed Nov., Jan., and Tues., except for dinner in Aug.*

$

SICILIAN

✕ **Trattoria del Carmine.** Low-key but ever-reliable local dishes are the staples at this affable eatery in the center of town. If you're not tempted by the fish of the day, you can choose between the various land-based dishes on offer, such as ravioli with a pork ragù, roasted veal, and rabbit with olives and mint. **Known for:** traditional Sicilian dishes; generous portions; affordable prices. $ *Average main: €8* ⊠ *Via Ducezio 1/a, Noto* ☎ *0931/838705* ⊕ *www.trattoriadelcarmine.it* ⊙ *Closed Mon., and 3 wks in Jan.*

$$$

HOTEL

🛏 **Gagliardi Boutique Hotel.** For an unbeatable location only a block from the main pedestrian street, visitors to Noto can't do better than this hotel with an industrial vibe in a former 18th-century palace. **Pros:** extremely central location; friendly service; large rooms and good public spaces. **Cons:** only one room has a bathtub; iffy Wi-Fi connection; short on amenities (no restaurant, spa, or pool). $ *Rooms from: €218* ⊠ *Via Silvio Spaventa 41, Noto* ☎ *0931/839730* ⊕ *www.gagliardihotel.com* ⊠ *11 rooms* ¶○¶ *Free Breakfast.*

16

$$ B&B/INN FAMILY 🏨 **Masseria degli Ulivi.** Up on the Hyblean plateau, a good 15-minute drive north of Noto, is this rural *masseria* (farm), surrounded by tastefully designed two-story lodgings and immersed in olive groves. **Pros:** excellent restaurant; airy breakfast room with patio; courteous staff. **Cons:** really need your own transport; Wi-Fi doesn't always work; rooms are sparsely decorated. [$] *Rooms from: €130* ✉ *Contrada Porcari SS287, Villa Vela, Noto* ☎ *0931/813019* 🌐 *www.masseriadegliulivi.com* 🕓 *Closed Nov.–Mar.* 🛏 *34 rooms* 🍴 *Free Breakfast.*

MODICA

37 km (23 miles) west of Noto.

Modica and Ragusa are the two chief cities in Sicily's smallest province, and the centers of a region known as Iblea. The dry, rocky, and gentle countryside filled with canyons and grassy knolls is a unique landscape for Sicily. In Modica, the main artery—Corso Umberto I—is lined with shops and restaurants and is in the valley at the bottom of the town (called Modica Bassa), while the old town of Modica Alta is built atop a ridge. That's part of this UNESCO-listed area's charm; it's a joy to wander its steep 14th-century lanes traversed by endless staircases and lined with Baroque architecture. Modica is also famed for its chocolate—don't miss trying it at one of the many stores on Corso Umberto I.

GETTING HERE AND AROUND

Trains leave from Siracusa about five times a day, while buses from Catania, Siracusa, Ragusa, and Noto also stop in Modica on a regular basis.

VISITOR INFORMATION

Contact **Modica Tourism Office.** ✉ *Corso Umberto I 141* ☎ *0346/6558227* 🌐 *comune.modica.gov.it/site/ufficio-turistico.*

EXPLORING

Cattedrale di San Pietro. Statues of the apostles line the staircase of Modica's main cathedral. It was originally constructed in the 14th century, but following its destruction in the 1693 earthquake, it was rebuilt in an impressive Baroque style. ✉ *Corso Umberto I 120.*

Fodor's Choice ★ **Chiesa di San Giorgio.** This lovely Baroque church in Modica Alta dating from after the 1693 earthquake is reached by climbing 250 steps. It's worth it for the amazing views over the old town. ✉ *Corso San Giorgio* ☎ *0932/941279* 🕓 *Closed daily 12:30–3:30.*

WHERE TO EAT

$$ SICILIAN 🍴 **Locanda del Colonnello.** This Italian neo-bistro uses local ingredients to create deceptively simple dishes with unique combinations and flavors—think sardine-stuffed ravioli and rabbit stew with broccoli. The atmosphere is laid-back and inviting, whether you dine in the casual white interior with old black-and-white photos of Modica lining the walls or on the quiet patio. **Known for:** creative combinations; good Sicilian wine selections; casual yet welcoming vibe. [$] *Average main: €16* ✉ *Vico Biscari 6* ☎ *0932/752423* 🌐 *www.locandadelcolonnello.it* 🕓 *Closed Tues. and Feb.*

SHOPPING

Modica is famous for its chocolate, which uses an ancient technique. Made at a low heat, it has a grainier consistency than most.

Fodor'sChoice ★ **Antica Dolceria Bonajuto.** Bonajuto is the oldest chocolate producer in town, dating from 1880. This busy shop on Modica Bassa's main street lets you sample many varieties of their delightful product before you buy, and also makes renowned cannoli and candied orange peel. ⊠ *Corso Umberto I 159* ☎ *0932/941225* ⊕ *www.bonajuto.it.*

RAGUSA

21 km (13 miles) northwest of Modica.

Ragusa, a modern city with a beautiful historic core, is known for some great local red wines and wonderful cheese—a creamy, doughy, flavorful version of *caciocavallo,* made by hand every step of the way. It also has some wonderful Baroque buildings with fabulous vantage points throughout its narrow, twisty, and steep old town.

GETTING HERE AND AROUND

Trains and buses leave from Siracusa four or five times daily.

VISITOR INFORMATION

Contact Ragusa Tourism Office. ⊠ *Piazza San Giovanni* ☎ *0932/684780* ⊕ *www.comune.ragusa.gov.it.*

EXPLORING

Basilica di San Giorgio. Designed by Rosario Gagliardi in 1738, the duomo is a fine example of Sicilian Baroque. ⊠ *Salita Duomo 15* ☎ *0932/220085* ⊕ *www.diocesidiragusa.it* ☉ *Closed daily noon–4.*

Ibla. The lovely historic center of Ragusa, known as Ibla, was completely rebuilt after the devastating earthquake of 1693. Its tumble of buildings are perched on a hilltop and suspended between a deep ravine and a sloping valley, and the tiny squares and narrow lanes make for pleasant meandering. ⊠ *Ragusa.*

WHERE TO EAT AND STAY

$$$$
SICILIAN
✕ **Duomo.** In an understated palazzo on a cobblestoned street tucked near the Duomo, star chef Ciccio Sultano prepares imaginative and beautifully plated variations on classic Sicilian cuisine. Although dishes can be ordered à la carte, a tasting menu gives diners a fuller experience of the chef's signature style, which uses the finest ingredients from around the island in subtly extravagant combinations. **Known for:** imaginative tasting menus and wine pairings; the freshest Sicilian ingredients; good-value prix-fixe lunch. $ *Average main: €45* ⊠ *Via Capitano Bocchieri 31* ☎ *0932/651265* ⊕ *www.cicciosultano.it* ☉ *Closed early Jan.–late Feb. Closed Sun. and no lunch Mon., except in Aug. and Dec. 26–Jan. 6.*

$$
SICILIAN
✕ **Locanda Gulfi.** On the grounds of the expansive Gulfi winery, which produces well-regarded organic wines, you'll find a unique place for a sophisticated lunch or dinner, with sweeping views of the Chiaramonte hills and vineyards (about a half-hour drive north of Ragusa). The chef skillfully uses local ingredients to prepare Sicilian dishes with a twist; for instance, you might find sardines fried in a cornmeal crust or pumpkin ravioli with

16

Sicilian black truffle. **Known for:** seasonal, local Sicilian dishes; renowned Gulfi wine; vineyard views. [$] *Average main: €18* ✉ *C. da. Patria, Chiaramonte Gulfi* ☎ *0932/928081 reservations, 0932/921654 winery* 🌐 *www.locandagulfi.it* ⏲ *Closed Mon. No dinner Sun.*

$$ B&B/INN Fodor's Choice ★ 🏨 **Eremo della Giubiliana.** Set in the countryside a 20-minute drive from Ragusa, this charming family-run monastery-turned-hotel boasts friendly service and a relaxed but luxurious vibe. **Pros:** peaceful atmosphere; rooms filled with character; top-notch service; five cottages are available. **Cons:** grounds, while lovely, could use better upkeep; restaurant food could be better for the price. [$] *Rooms from: €162* ✉ *Contrada Giubiliana, Marina di Ragusa* ☎ *0932/669119* 🌐 *www.eremodellagiubiliana.it* 🛏 *24 rooms* 🍴 *Free Breakfast.*

$$$ HOTEL 🏨 **La Moresca.** If you plan on visiting Ragusa and Modica but want to stay by the water, you can't do better than this arty boutique hotel on Sicily's southeastern coast; it's two blocks from the beach and a pleasant half-hour drive from either inland town. **Pros:** modern, large bedrooms; arty vibe; friendly and helpful staff. **Cons:** town itself not so charming; no hotel restaurant outside breakfast; car parking can be an issue. [$] *Rooms from: €260* ✉ *Via Dandolo 63, Marina di Ragusa* ☎ *0932/239495* 🌐 *www.lamorescahotel.com* 🛏 *15 rooms* 🍴 *Free Breakfast.*

CALTAGIRONE

66 km (41 miles) northwest of Ragusa.

Built over three hills, this charming Baroque town is a center of Sicily's ceramics industry. Here you can find majolica balustrades, tiled windowsills, and the monumental Scala Santa Maria del Monte.

GETTING HERE AND AROUND

Buses and trains from Catania stop in the lower town, which is a pleasant stroll from the center. Caltagirone is also well connected by local buses and taxis. Connections with Ragusa, Enna, and Piazza Armerina are less frequent.

VISITOR INFORMATION

Contact Caltagirone Tourism Office. ✉ *Via Duomo 15* ☎ *0933/490836* 🌐 *www.comune.caltagirone.ct.it/turismo.*

EXPLORING

Museo della Ceramica. Caltagirone was declared a UNESCO World Heritage Site for its ceramics as well as for its numerous Baroque churches. Although you may find the museum in a state of disarray, you will see one of Sicily's most extensive pottery collections, ranging from Neolithic finds to red-figure ware from 5th-century-BC Athens and 18th-century terra-cotta Nativity figures, on display here. ✉ *Via Roma, inside Giardini Pubblici* ☎ *0933/58418, 0933/58423* 🎟 *€4.*

Scala Santa Maria del Monte. Exactly 142 individually decorated tiled steps lead up to the neglected Santa Maria del Monte church. On July 24 (the feast of San Giacomo, the city's patron saint) and again on August 15 (the feast of the Assumption) this staircase is illuminated with candles that form a tapestry design. Months of work go into preparing the 4,000 *coppi,* or cylinders of colored paper, that hold oil lamps—then, at 9:30 pm on the nights of July 24, July 25, August 14, and August 15, a squad of hundreds of youngsters (tourists are welcome to participate) spring into action to light the lamps, so that the staircase flares up all at once. ✉ *Begins at Piazza Municipio, main town square.*

PIAZZA ARMERINA

30 km (18 miles) northwest of Caltagirone.

A quick look around the fanciful town of Piazza Armerina is rewarding—it has a provincial warmth, and the crumbling yellow-stone architecture with Sicily's trademark bulbous balconies creates quite an effect. The greatest draw, however, lies just down the road: the ancient Roman mosaics at Villa Romana del Casale.

GETTING HERE AND AROUND

Piazza Armerina is linked to Caltagirone, Catania, Enna, and Palermo by regular buses. There's no train station.

VISITOR INFORMATION

Contact **Piazza Armerina Tourism Office.** ✉ *Via Generale Muscará 13* ☎ *0935/680201* 🌐 *www.comune.piazzaarmerina.en.it.*

16

EXPLORING

Fodor's Choice ★ **Villa Romana del Casale (Imperial Roman Villa).** Some of the best mosaics of the Roman world cover more than 12,000 square feet under a shelter that hints at the layout of the original buildings. The exceptionally well-preserved Imperial Roman Villa is thought to have been a hunting lodge of the emperor Maximian (3rd–4th century AD). The excavations were not begun until 1950, and most of the wall decorations and vaulting have been lost. The mosaics were probably made by North African artisans; they're similar to those in the Tunis Bardo Museum, in Tunisia. The entrance was through a triumphal arch that led into an atrium surrounded by a portico of columns, after which the *thermae,* or bathhouse, is reached. It's colorfully decorated with mosaic nymphs, a Neptune, and slaves massaging bathers. The peristyle leads to the main villa, where in the Salone del Circo you look down on mosaics illustrating scenes from the Circus Maximus in Rome. A theme running through many of the mosaics—especially the long hall flanking the whole of one side of the peristyle courtyard—is the capturing and shipping of wild animals, which may have been a major source of the master's wealth. Yet the most famous mosaic is the floor depicting 10 girls wearing the ancient equivalent of bikinis, going through what looks like a fairly rigorous set of training exercises. ✉ *SP15, Contrada Casale, 4 km (2½ miles) southwest of Piazza Armerina* ☎ *0935/680036* 🌐 *www.villaromanadelcasale.it* 🎟 *€10 (free 1st Sun. of month).*

WHERE TO EAT

$$ MODERN ITALIAN Fodor's Choice ★ 🍴 **Al Fogher.** A beacon of culinary light shines in Sicily's interior, a region generally filled with good, but basic, places to eat. Ambitious—and successful—dishes here combine traditional ingredients with the creative flair of chef Angelo Treno. **Known for:** sophisticated preparations; local ingredients; well-thought-out wine list. [$] *Average main:*

€18 ✉ *Contrada Bellia, near SS117bis, Aidone exit* ☎ *0935/684123* ⊕ *alfogher.sicilia.restaurant* ⊗ *Closed Mon. No dinner Sun.*

ENNA

33 km (20 miles) northwest of Piazza Armerina, 136 km (85 miles) southeast of Palermo.

Deep in Sicily's interior, the fortress city of Enna (altitude 2,844 feet) commands exceptional views of the surrounding rolling plains, and, in the distance, Mt. Etna. It's the highest provincial capital in Italy and, thanks to its central location, is nicknamed the "Navel of Sicily." Virtually unknown by tourists and relatively untouched by industrialization, this sleepy town charms and prospers in a distinctly old-fashioned, Sicilian way. Enna makes a good stopover for the night or just for lunch, as it's right along the autostrada between Palermo and Catania (and thus Siracusa).

GETTING HERE AND AROUND

Just off the A19 autostrada, Enna is easily accessible by car. With the train station 5 km (3 miles) below the upper town, the most practical public transportation is by bus from Palermo or Catania.

VISITOR INFORMATION

Contact Enna Tourism Office. ✉ *Via Romo 413* ☎ *0935/502362* ⊕ *www. provincia.enna.it.*

EXPLORING

Castello di Lombardia. The narrow, winding streets are dominated at one end by the impressive, cliff-hanging Castello di Lombardia, built by Frederick II, and easily visible as you approach town. While there is little of note to see inside the castle, climb up the tower for great views from the dead center of the island—on a very clear day, you can see to all three coasts. Immediately to the south you see Lake Pergusa (dried out in late summer), now almost swallowed by Enna's sprawling suburbs and the racetrack around its perimeter. According to Greek mythology, this was where Persephone was abducted by Hades. While a prisoner in his underworld realm she ate six pomegranate seeds, and was therefore doomed to spend half of each year there. For the ancients, she emerged at springtime, triggering a display of wildflowers that can still be admired all over Sicily. ✉ *Piazza di Castello di Lombardia* ▱ *Free.*

Piazza Vittorio Emanuele. In town, head straight for Via Roma, which leads to Piazza Vittorio Emanuele—the center of Enna's shopping scene and evening passeggiata. The attached **Piazza Crispi,** dominated by the shell of the grand old Hotel Belvedere, affords breathtaking panoramas of the hillside and smoking Etna looming in the distance. The bronze fountain in the middle of the piazza is a reproduction of Gian Lorenzo Bernini's famous 17th-century sculpture *The Rape of Persephone,* a depiction of Hades abducting Persephone. ✉ *Piazza Vittorio Emanuele.*

Rocca di Cerere (*Rock of Demeter*). The Greek cult of Demeter, goddess of the harvest, was said to have centered on Enna. It's not hard to see why its adherents would have worshipped at the Rocca di Cerere, protruding out on one end of town next to the Castello di Lombardia. The spot enjoys spectacular views of the expansive countryside and windswept Sicilian interior. ✉ *Enna.*

Torre di Federico II. This mysterious octagonal tower—of unknown purpose—stands above the lower part of town. It has been celebrated for millennia as marking the exact geometric center of the island—thus the tower's, and city's, nickname, Umbilicus Siciliae (Navel of Sicily). The interior is not open to the public, but the surrounding park is. ✉ *Enna.*

WHERE TO EAT AND STAY

$ SICILIAN 🍴 **Centrale.** Housed in an old palazzo, this casual place has served meals since 1889. The seasonal menu includes local preparations such as *maccheroni rossi ai gamberi* (pasta with red shrimp), grilled pork chops, and a 15th-century specialty called *controfiletto alla'Ennese* (a veal fillet with onions, artichokes, pig jowl, and white wine). **Known for:** antipasti buffet; classic Sicilian dishes and local wines; outdoor terrace. [$] *Average main: €13* ✉ *Piazza VI Dicembre 9* ☎ *0935/500963* 🌐 *www.ristorantecentrale.net* 🕒 *No lunch Sat. Sept.–Mar.*

$ HOTEL 🏨 **Hotel Sicilia.** Sicily's interior has few decent accommodations, and of Enna's two hotels, this one has more character. **Pros:** central location; friendly staff; good breakfast. **Cons:** a bit dated; some rooms can be noisy; Wi-Fi not always reliable. [$] *Rooms from: €69* ✉ *Piazza Napoleone Colajanni 7* ☎ *0935/500850* 🌐 *www.hotelsiciliaenna.it* 🛏 *60 rooms* 🍽 *Free Breakfast.*

16

AGRIGENTO AND WESTERN SICILY

The crowning glory of western Sicily is the concentration of Greek temples at Agrigento, on a height between the modern city and the sea. The mark of ancient Greek culture also lingers in the cluster of ruined cliff-side temples at Selinunte and at the splendidly isolated site of Segesta. Traces of the North African culture that for centuries exerted a strong influence on this end of the island are tangible in the coastal town of Marsala. In contrast, the cobblestone streets of hilltop Erice retain a strong medieval complexion, giving the quiet town the air of a last outpost on the edge of the Mediterranean. On the northern coast, not far outside Palermo, Monreale's cathedral glitters with mosaics that are among the finest in Italy.

AGRIGENTO

95 km (59 miles) southwest of Enna.

Agrigento owes its fame almost exclusively to its ancient Greek temples—though it was also the birthplace of playwright Luigi Pirandello (1867–1936). Along the coast, around 12 km (7 miles) to the west of Agrigento near the town of Realmonte, you can view the Scala dei Turchi (Stairs of the Turks), which are natural white cliffs eroded into unusual shapes. By visiting the beaches closest to the temples, near the town of San Leone, you can sunbathe beside the locals.

GETTING HERE AND AROUND

Driving from Enna, take the A19 autostrada 35 km (21 miles) south-west to Caltanissetta; then follow the SS640 to Agrigento. Motorists can also access the town easily via the coastal SS115 and, from Palermo, by the SS189. Buses and trains run from Enna, Palermo, and Catania; both bus and train stations are centrally located.

FESTIVALS

Sagra del Mandorlo in Fiore (*Almond Blossom Festival*). During February and March, when most of the almond trees are in blossom, Agrigento hosts the Sagra del Mandorlo in Fiore, with international folk dances, a costumed parade, and the sale of marzipan and other sweets made from almonds. ⊠ *Agrigento* ⊕ *www.sagradelmandorloinfiore.com.*

VISITOR INFORMATION

Contact Agrigento Tourism Office. ⊠ *Via Empedocle 73* ☎ *0922/20391.*

EXPLORING

Monastero di Santo Spirito. If you head up the hill from the Valle dei Templi to the modern city, you'll have the opportunity to try a local treat or stay at an inexpensive B&B. Just ring the doorbell here and try the *kus-kus* (sweet cake), made of pistachio nuts, almonds, and chocolate, that the nuns prepare. (It's always best to phone ahead to make sure they'll have it.) The cloisters and courtyard of the church are open to the public. ⊠ *Cortile Santo Spirito 9, off Via Porcello* ☎ *0922/20664* ⊕ *www.monasterosantospirito.com.*

Fodor's Choice ★ **Valle dei Templi.** The eight or so monuments within the Valley of the Temples, a UNESCO World Heritage Site, are considered to be, along with the Acropolis in Athens, the finest Greek ruins in the world. Whether you first come upon the valley in the early morning light, bathed by golden floodlights after sunset, or at its very best in February, when the valley is awash in the fragrant blossoms of thousands of almond trees, it's easy to see why Akragas (Agrigento's Greek name) was celebrated by the Greek poet Pindar as "the most beautiful city built by mortals." The temples were originally erected as a showpiece to flaunt the Greek victory over Carthage, and they have withstood a later sack by the Carthaginians, mishandling by the Romans, and neglect by Christians and Muslims.

Although getting to, from, and around the dusty ruins of the Valle dei Templi is pretty easy, this important archaeological zone still deserves several hours. The temples are a bit spread out, but the valley is all completely walkable and usually toured on foot. However, since there's only one hotel (Villa Athena) that's close enough to walk to the ruins, you'll most likely have to drive to reach the site. Parking is at the entrance to the temple area. The site, which opens at 8:30 am, is divided into western and eastern sections. For instant aesthetic gratification, walk through the eastern zone; for a more comprehensive tour, start way out at the western end and work your way back uphill.

You'll want to spend time seeing the eight pillars of the **Tempio di Ercole** (Temple of Hercules) that make up Agrigento's oldest temple complex, dating from the 6th century BC, and the beautiful **Tempio della**

Concordia (Temple of Concord), up the hill from the Temple of Hercules, perhaps the best-preserved Greek temple currently in existence.

Other notable temples are the **Tempio di Giunone** (Temple of Juno), east on the Via Sacra from the Temple of Concord, which commands an exquisite view of the valley (especially at sunset) and the **Tempio di Giove** (Temple of Jupiter); though never completed, it was once considered the eighth wonder of the world.

At the end of Via dei Templi, where it turns left and becomes Via Petrarca, stands the **Museo Archeologico Regionale.** An impressive collection of antiquities from the site includes vases, votives, everyday objects, weapons, statues, and models of the temples. Be sure to visit after you've seen the temples. ⊠ *Zona Archeologica, Via dei Templi* ☎ *0922/621620, 0922/621657* ⊕ *www.parcovalledeitempli.it* 🎫 *€10, €13.50 with museum (free 1st Sun. of month).*

WHERE TO EAT AND STAY

$$
SICILIAN
Fodor'sChoice
★

✕ **Il Re di Girgenti.** You wouldn't expect to find an ultramodern, even hip, place to dine within a few minutes' drive of Agrigento's ancient temples, yet Il Re di Girgenti offers up pleasing versions of Sicilian classics in a trendy, country-chic atmosphere (think funky black-and-white tile floors mixed with shelves lined with old-fashioned crockery) popular with young locals. The thoughtful wine list offers good prices on both local wines and those from throughout Sicily. **Known for:** Sicilian dishes with a twist; contemporary setting; delightful wine selections. $ *Average main: €16* ⊠ *Via Panoramica dei Templi 51* ☎ *0922/401388* ⊕ *www.ilredigirgenti.it* ۞ *Closed Tues.*

$$
SICILIAN

✕ **Trattoria dei Templi.** Along a road on the way up to Agrigento proper from the temple area, this family-run vaulted restaurant serves up some tasty traditional food. The menu includes different homemade pastas each day as well as plenty of fresh fish dishes, all prepared with Sicilian flair. **Known for:** authentic Sicilian dishes; fresh fish; good choice of local wines. $ *Average main: €18* ⊠ *Via Panoramica dei Templi 15* ☎ *0922/403110* ⊕ *www.trattoriadeitempli.com* ۞ *Closed Sun.*

$$
HOTEL

🏨 **Foresteria Baglio della Luna.** Fiery sunsets and moonlight cast a glow over the ancient 12th-century watchtower at the center of this farmhouse-hotel complex in the valley below the temples. **Pros:** quiet setting; pretty gardens; top-notch restaurant. **Cons:** hotel a little dark inside; no pool; location a bit remote. $ *Rooms from: €145* ⊠ *Via Serafino Amabile Guastella 1, Contrada Maddalusa* ☎ *0922/511061* ⊕ *www.bagliodellaluna.com* ۞ *Closed Dec.–Feb.* ⤶ *23 rooms* ⫧ *Free Breakfast.*

$$$$
HOTEL
Fodor'sChoice
★

🏨 **Villa Athena.** The 18th-century Villa Athena, updated into a sleek, luxurious place to stay, complete with gorgeous manicured gardens and swimming pool, holds a privileged position directly overlooking the Temple of Concordia, a 10-minute walk away—an amazing sight both during the day and when it's lit up at night. **Pros:** perfect location to see the Valle dei Templi, with phenomenal temple views; good restaurant and spa; plenty of free parking. **Cons:** expensive; service a bit detached; lack of information on local attractions. $ *Rooms from: €351* ⊠ *Via Passeggiata Archeologica 33* ☎ *0922/596288* ⊕ *www.hotelvillaathena. it* ⤶ *27 rooms* ⫧ *Free Breakfast.*

16

Western Sicily

Tyrrhenian Sea

TO LIVORNO & GENOA

TO NAPLE & ROME

I. DI USTICA

TO SARDINIA

TO SARDINIA

TO TUNIS

Capo San Vito

San Vito lo Capo

Mondello

Palermo see detail map

Golfo di Castellammare

Golfo di Palermo

Golfo di Termini Imerese

I. LEVANZO

Trapani

Erice

Castellammare di Golfo

Monreale

113

A19

Termini Imerese

I. MARÉTTIMO

187

A26

113

118

Cáccamo

Mt. S. Calogero

I. FAVIGNANA

Segesta

119

285

115

Marsala

188

Gibellina

Salaparuta

Corleone

121

624

Prizzi

189

Castelvetrano

Mazara del Vallo

115

Selinunte

115

386

118

Sciacca

Ribera

115

Raffadali

640

Agrigento

Valle dei Templi

TO PANTELLERIA

Mediterranean Sea

PANTELLERIA

KEY

Ferry lines

0   20 mi

0   20 km

TO LINOSA

TO LAMPEDUSA

SELINUNTE

100 km (62 miles) northwest of Agrigento, 114 km (71 miles) southwest of Palermo.

Numerous Greek temple ruins perch on a plateau overlooking an expanse of the Mediterranean at Selinunte (or Selinus). Selinunte is named after a local variety of wild parsley (*Apium graveolens* or *petroselinum*) that in spring grows in profusion among the ruined columns and overturned capitals. Although there are a few places to stay right around Selinunte, many people see it as an easy—and richly rewarding—stopover along the road to or from Agrigento. It takes only an hour or two to see.

GETTING HERE AND AROUND

You can get here by bus or car via the town of Castelvetrano, 11 km (7 miles) north, which is itself accessible from Palermo by car on the A29 autostrada, as well as by bus and train.

VISITOR INFORMATION

Contact Selinunte Tourism Office. ✉ *Via Giovanni Caboto 146, Marinella Selinunte* ☎ *0924/46251, 392/7783067* 🌐 *en.visitselinunte.com.*

16

EXPLORING

Fodor's Choice ★ **Greek Temple Ruins.** Selinunte was one of the most superb colonies of ancient Greece. Founded in the 7th century BC, the city became the rich and prosperous rival of Segesta, which in 409 BC turned to the Carthaginians for help. The Carthaginians, in turn, sent an army to destroy the city. The temples were demolished, the city was razed, and 16,000 of Selinunte's inhabitants were slaughtered. The remains of Selinunte are in many ways unchanged from the day of its sacking—burn marks still scar the Greek columns, and much of the site still lies in rubble at its exact position of collapse. The original complex held seven temples scattered over two sites separated by a harbor. Of the seven, only one—reconstructed in 1958—is whole. ■ TIP→ **This is a large archaeological site, so you might make use of the private navetta (shuttle) to save a bit of walking. Alternatively, if you have a car, you can visit the first temples close to the ticket office on foot and then drive westward to the farther site. Be prepared to show your ticket at various stages.** ✉ *SS115, 13 km (8 miles) southeast of Castelvetrano, Marinella Selinunte* ☎ *0924/46277* 🎫 *€6.*

WHERE TO EAT

$ SICILIAN 🍴 **Lido Zabbara.** Known to the locals as "Da Yoyo"—the owner is constantly getting up and down to attend to his customers—this is really no more than a glorified salad bar right on the beach at Selinunte, although it does also serve a nice selection of grilled fish and seafood (often sardines). Pick up a plate and serve yourself from the various delicacies laid out on the center spread; the lunch buffet is very affordable, while dinner (Friday and Saturday only) doesn't cost very much more. **Known for:** buffet of appetizers and salads; grilled sardines; beachside dining. [$] *Average main: €12* ✉ *Via Pigafetta, Marinella Selinunte* ☎ *0924/46194* 💳 *No credit cards* ⏲ *Closed Nov.–Mar. No dinner Sun.–Thurs.*

MARSALA

88 km (55 miles) northwest of Selinunte.

Marsala is readily associated with the world-famous, richly colored fortified wine named after it, and your main reason for stopping will likely be to visit some of the many wineries in the area. But the quiet seaside town, together with the nearby island of Mozia, were also once the main Carthaginian bases in Sicily: from them, Carthage fought for supremacy over the island against Greece and Rome. In 1773 a British merchant named John Woodhouse happened upon the town and discovered that the wine here was as good as the port the British had long imported from Portugal. Two other wine merchants, Whitaker and Ingram, rushed in, and by 1800 Marsala was exporting its wine all over the British Empire.

GETTING HERE AND AROUND

Buses and trains from Palermo, Trapani, and Castelvetrano stop in Marsala. Drivers can take the coastal SS115.

VISITOR INFORMATION

Contact Marsala Tourism Office. ⊠ *Via XI Maggio 100* ☎ *0923/993338* ⊕ *www.turismocomunemarsala.com.*

EXPLORING

Donnafugata Winery. A respected Sicilian wine producer, the 160-year-old Donnafugata Winery is open for tours of its *cantina* (wine cellar); reservations are required online or by phone. It's an interesting look at the wine-making process in Sicily, and it ends with a tasting of several whites and reds and a chance to buy. Don't miss the delicious, full-bodied red Mille e Una Notte, and the famous Ben Ryè Passito di Pantelleria, a sweet dessert wine made from dried grapes. ⊠ *Via Sebastiano Lipari 18* ☎ *0923/724245, 0923/724263* ⊕ *www.donnafugata.it* 🍷 *Tastings €18–€45* ⊘ *Closed Sun.*

Museo Archeologico Baglio Anselmi. A sense of Marsala's past as a Carthaginian stronghold is captured by the well-preserved Punic warship displayed in the museum, along with some of the amphorae and other artifacts recovered from the wreck. The vessel, which was probably sunk during the great sea battle that ended the First Punic War in 241 BC, was dredged up from the mud near the Egadi Islands in the 1970s. There's also a good display of maritime and archaeological finds. ⊠ *Via Lungomare Boéo 2* ☎ *0923/952535* 🍷 *€4* ⊘ *Closed Mon., and Sun. after 1:30.*

ERICE

45 km (28 miles) northeast of Marsala, 15 km (9 miles) northeast of Trapani.

Perched 2,450 feet above sea level, Erice is an enchanting medieval mountaintop aerie of palaces, fountains, and cobblestone streets. Shaped like an equilateral triangle, the town was the ancient landmark Eryx, dedicated to Aphrodite (Venus). When the Normans arrived, they built a castle on Monte San Giuliano, where today there's a lovely public park with benches and belvederes offering striking views of Trapani, the Egadi Islands offshore, and, on a very clear day, Cape Bon and the Tunisian coast. Because of Erice's elevation, clouds conceal much of the view for most of winter. Sturdy shoes (for the cobblestones) and something warm to wear are recommended.

GETTING HERE AND AROUND
Make your approach via Trapani, which is on the A29 autostrada and well connected by bus and train with Marsala and Palermo. Late March to early January a funivia runs from the outskirts of Trapani to Erice (Monday 1–8, Tuesday to Friday 8:10–8, weekends 9:30–8:30; extended hours from late June to mid-September; see ⊕ *www.funiviaerice.it* for details). Going by car or bus from Trapani takes around 40 minutes.

EXPLORING
Capo San Vito. The cape has a long sandy beach on a promontory overlooking a bay in the Gulf of Castellammare. The town here, San Vito Lo Capo, is famous for its North African couscous, made with fish instead of meat. In late September it hosts the 10-day **Cous Cous Fest** (⊕ *www.couscousfest.it*), a serious international couscous competition and festival with live music and plenty of free tastings. San Vito is also one of the bases for exploring the **Riserva dello Zingaro**; this nature reserve—one of the few stretches of coastline in Sicily which is not built-up—is at its best in late spring, when both wildflowers and birds are plentiful. ⊠ *Capo San Vito, 40 km (25 miles) north of Erice, San Vito Lo Capo.*

16

WHERE TO EAT AND STAY
$ ╳ **Monte San Giuliano.** At this traditional restaurant near the main piazza,
SICILIAN you can sit out on the tree-lined patio or in the white-walled dining room and munch on free *panelle* (chickpea fritters), which are delicate and judiciously seasoned. Follow them up with one of their exemplary pastas, or order the seafood couscous—it's served with a bowl of fish broth on the side so you can add as much as you wish. **Known for:** great pasta and couscous; charming setting; marvelous wine list. $ *Average main: €12* ⊠ *Vicolo San Rocco 7* ☎ *0923/869595* ⊕ *www.montesangiuliano.it* ⊗ *Closed Mon., 2 wks in mid-Jan., and 1st 2 wks of Nov.*

$ ▥ **Hotel Elimo.** Like the town of Erice itself, the Hotel Elimo is old-
HOTEL fashioned and yet full of charm; eccentric knickknacks and artwork fill the lobby, and the 21 homey rooms are all different, many boasting terraces with views of either the cobblestone streets or the valleys below (when they're not shrouded by clouds). **Pros:** convenient location; lots of character; helpful staff; good restaurant. **Cons:** rooms can feel a bit musty; small bathrooms; noise in some rooms. $ *Rooms from: €90* ⊠ *Via Vittorio Emanuele 75* ☎ *0923/869377* ⊕ *www.hotelelimo.it* ⊗ *Closed Jan. and Feb.* ⇥ *21 rooms* ╎⊙╎ *Free Breakfast.*

$ ▥ **Moderno.** This delightful hotel has a creaky old feel to it, but that's
HOTEL part of the charm—the lobby area, scattered with books, magazines, and knickknacks, calls to mind an old relative's living room. **Pros:** central location; great rooftop terrace; well-regarded restaurant. **Cons:** very modest rooms; street-facing rooms can be noisy; old-fashioned feel not for everyone. $ *Rooms from: €100* ⊠ *Via Vittorio Emanuele 67* ☎ *0923/869300* ⊕ *www.hotelmodernoerice.it* ⇥ *40 rooms* ╎⊙╎ *Free Breakfast.*

SHOPPING

Antica Pasticceria del Convento. Here, the sister of the town's most famous baker-nun, Maria Grammatico, sells similar delectable treats. The shop is open March through November. ⊠ *Via Guarnotti 1* ☎ *0923/869777* ⊕ *www.anticapasticceriadelconvento.it.*

Bazar del Miele. One of Sicily's premier food shops is located in Erice. As the name suggests, honey gets the most attention, with more than 15 local varieties for sale, many blended with local fruits like apricots and strawberries. But it's really just scratching the surface in terms of available products, which also include olive oil, grappa, and cheeses. ⊠ *Via Antonio Cordici 16* ☎ *0923/869181* ⊕ *www.bazardelmiele.com.*

Ceramica Ericina. Among Italians, Erice is known for the quality and delicate floral designs of its Majolica ceramics, which are unique to the city. This ceramics store is one of the best in the city. ⊠ *Via Gian Filippa Guarnotti* ☎ *0923/869140.*

Pasticceria Grammatico. Fans of Sicilian sweets make a beeline for this place, run by Maria Grammatico, a former nun who gained international fame with *Bitter Almonds,* her life story cowritten with Mary Taylor Simeti. Her almond-paste creations are works of art, molded into striking shapes, including dolls and animals. There are a few tables and a tiny balcony with wonderful views. ⊠ *Via Vittorio Emanuele 14* ☎ *0923/869390* ⊕ *www.mariagrammatico.it.*

SEGESTA

35 km (22 miles) southeast of Erice, 85 km (53 miles) southwest of Palermo.

Segesta is the site of one of Sicily's most impressive temples, constructed on the side of a windswept, barren hill overlooking a valley of giant fennel. Virtually intact today, the temple is considered by some to be finer in its proportions and setting than any other Doric temple left standing.

GETTING HERE AND AROUND

Three or four daily buses travel from Trapani to Segesta. About as many trains from Palermo and Trapani stop at the Segesta-Tempio station, a 20-minute uphill walk from Segesta. The site is easily reached via the A29 autostrada.

EXPLORING

Fodor's Choice
★ **Tempio Dorico** (*Doric Temple*). Segesta's imposing temple was actually started in the 5th century BC by the Elymian people, who may have been refugees from Troy. At the very least, evidence—they often sided with the Carthaginians, for example—indicates that they were non-Greeks. However, the style is in many ways Greek. The temple was never finished; the walls and roof never materialized, and the columns were never fluted. Wear comfortable shoes, as you need to park your car in the lot at the bottom of the hill and walk about five minutes up to the temple.

If you're up for a longer hike, a little more than 1 km (½ mile) away near the top of the hill are the remains of a fine **theater** with impressive views, especially at sunset, of the plains and the Bay of Castellammare.

(There's also a shuttle bus that leaves every 30 minutes, €1.50 round-trip.) Concerts and plays are staged here in summer. ⊠ *Calatafimi-Segesta* ☎ *0924/952356* 🎫 *€6.*

MONREALE

59 km (37 miles) northeast of Segesta, 10 km (6 miles) southwest of Palermo.

Only a short drive from Palermo, the sleepy town of Monreale is well worth the effort just to see the spectacular gold mosaics inside the Duomo. Try to arrive early in the morning or later in the afternoon to avoid the tour-bus hordes.

GETTING HERE AND AROUND

You can reach Monreale on the frequent buses that depart from Palermo's Piazza dell'Indipendenza. From Palermo, drivers can follow Corso Calatafimi west, though the going can be slow.

EXPLORING

Cloister. The lovely cloister of the abbey adjacent to the Duomo was built at the same time as the church but enlarged in the 14th century. The beautiful enclosure is surrounded by 216 intricately carved double columns, every other one decorated in a unique glass mosaic pattern. Afterward, don't forget to walk behind the cloister to the belvedere, with stunning panoramic views over the Conca d'Oro (Golden Conch) valley toward Palermo. ⊠ *Piazza del Duomo* ☎ *091/6404403* 🎫 *€6* 🕐 *Closed Sun. after 1:30.*

Fodor'sChoice ★ **Duomo.** Monreale's splendid cathedral is lavishly executed with mosaics depicting events from the Old and New Testaments. It's a glorious fusion of Eastern and Western influences, widely regarded as the finest example of Norman architecture in Sicily. After the Norman conquest of Sicily the new princes showcased their ambitions through monumental building projects. William II (1154–89) built the church complex with a cloister and palace between 1174 and 1185, employing Byzantine craftsmen.

The major attraction is the 68,220 square feet of glittering gold mosaics decorating the cathedral interior. *Christ Pantocrator* dominates the apse area; the nave contains narratives of the Creation; and scenes from the life of Christ adorn the walls of the aisles and the transept. The painted wooden ceiling dates from 1816–37. The roof commands a great view (a reward for climbing 172 stairs).

Bonnano Pisano's bronze doors, completed in 1186, depict 42 biblical scenes and are considered among the most important of medieval artifacts. Barisano da Trani's 42 panels on the north door, dating from 1179, present saints and evangelists. ⊠ *Piazza del Duomo* ☎ *091/6404413, 327/3510886* ⊕ *www.monrealeduomo.it* 🎫 *€4* 🕐 *Closed Mon.–Sat. 12:30–2:30.*

WHERE TO EAT

$$
SICILIAN
✕ **La Botte 1962.** It's worth the short drive or inexpensive taxi from Monreale to reach this restaurant, which is famous for well-prepared local specialties (though it's open limited hours, so call before you come). Dine

16

alfresco on seafood dishes such as *bavette don Carmelo,* a narrow version of tagliatelle with a sauce of swordfish, squid, shrimp, and pine nuts. **Known for:** sophisticated cooking; historic setting; hazelnut semifreddo with hot chocolate dessert. [$] *Average main: €16* ✉ *Contrada Lenzitti 20, SS186 Km 10* ☎ *091/414051, 338/4383962* 🌐 *www.mauriziocascino.it* 🕒 *Closed Mon.–Thurs. (except by advance booking of at least 4 days) and Aug.–early Sept. No lunch Fri. and Sat.; no dinner Sun.*

PALERMO

Once the intellectual capital of southern Europe, Palermo has always been at the crossroads of civilization. Favorably situated on a crescent bay at the foot of Monte Pellegrino, it has attracted almost every culture touching the Mediterranean world. To Palermo's credit, it's absorbed these diverse cultures into a unique personality that's at once Arab and Christian, Byzantine and Roman, Norman and Italian. The city's heritage encompasses all of Sicily's varied ages, but its distinctive aspect is its Arab-Norman identity, an improbable marriage that, mixed in with Byzantine and Jewish elements, created some resplendent works of art. These are most notable in the churches, from small jewels such as San Giovanni degli Eremiti to larger-scale works such as the cathedral. No less noteworthy than the architecture is Palermo's chaotic vitality, on display at some of Italy's most vibrant outdoor markets, public squares, street bazaars, and food vendors, and, above all, in its grand, discordant symphony of motorists, motorcyclists, and pedestrians that triumphantly climaxes in the new town center each evening with Italy's most spectacular passeggiata.

GETTING HERE AND AROUND

Palermo is well connected by road and rail; its airport links it to other cities in Italy, as well as around Europe.

VISITOR INFORMATION

Contacts Palermo Tourism Office. ✉ *Piazza Bellini* ☎ *091/7408021* 🌐 *www.cittametropolitana.pa.it/turismo* ✉ *Aeroporto di Palermo* ☎ *091/591698* 🌐 *www.cittametropolitana.pa.it/turismo.*

EXPLORING

Sicily's capital is a multilayered, vigorous metropolis with a strong historical profile; approach it with an open mind. You're likely to encounter some frustrating instances of inefficiency and, depending on the season, stifling heat. If you have a car, park it in a garage as soon as you can, and don't take it out until you're ready to depart.

Palermo is easily explored on foot, but you may choose to spend a morning taking a bus tour to help you get oriented. The Quattro Canti, or Four Corners, is the hub that separates the four sections of the old city: La Kalsa (the old Arab section) to the southeast, Albergheria to the southwest, Capo to the northwest, and Vucciria to the northeast. Each of these is a tumult of activity during the day, though at night the narrow alleys empty out and are best avoided in favor of the more animated avenues of the new city north of Teatro Massimo. Sights to see by day are scattered along three major streets: Corso Vittorio Emanuele, Via Maqueda, and Via Roma. The tourist information office in Piazza Bellini will give you a map and a valuable handout that lists opening and closing times, which sometimes change with the seasons.

TOP ATTRACTIONS

Cattedrale. This church is a lesson in Palermitano eclecticism—originally Norman (1182), then Catalan Gothic (14th to 15th century), then fitted out with a Baroque and Neoclassical interior (18th century). Its turrets, towers, dome, and arches come together in the kind of meeting of diverse elements that King Roger II (1095–1154), whose tomb is inside along with that of Frederick II, fostered during his reign. The back of the apse is gracefully decorated with interlacing Arab arches inlaid with limestone and black volcanic tufa. It's possible to visit the cathedral's roof (€5) for some fabulous city views. ⊠ *Corso Vittorio Emanuele* ☎ *091/334373* ⊕ *www.cattedrale.palermo.it* ☜ *Free. €7 treasury, crypt, royal tombs, and roof visit; €3 treasury, crypt, and tombs; €5 roof visit only* ⊗ *Closed Sun. after 1.*

La Martorana (*Santa Maria dell'Ammiraglio*). Distinguished by an elegant Norman campanile, this church was erected in 1143 but had its interior altered considerably during the Baroque period. High along the western wall, however, is some of the oldest and best-preserved mosaic artwork of the Norman period. Near the entrance is an interesting mosaic of King Roger II being crowned by Christ. In it Roger is dressed in a bejeweled Byzantine stole, reflecting the Norman court's penchant for all things Byzantine. Archangels along the ceiling wear the same stole wrapped around their shoulders and arms. The much plainer San Cataldo is next door. ⊠ *Piazza Bellini 3, Quattro Canti* ☎ *345/8288231* ☜ *€2.*

Museo Archeologico Regionale Salinas (*Salinas Regional Museum of Archaeology*). Several interesting pieces are displayed in this small but excellent collection, including a marvelously reconstructed Doric frieze from the Greek temple at Selinunte, which reveals the high level of artistic culture attained by the Greek colonists in Sicily some 2,500 years ago. There are also lion's head water spouts from 480 BC, as well as other excavated pieces from around Sicily, including Taormina and Agrigento. ⊠ *Piazza Olivella 24, Via Roma, Olivella* ☎ *091/6116807* ⊕ *www.regione.sicilia.it/bbccaa/salinas/index.html* ☜ *€3.*

Palazzo Reale (*Royal Palace*). This historic palace, also called Palazzo dei Normanni (Norman Palace), was the seat of Sicily's semiautonomous rulers for centuries; the building is a fascinating mesh of abutting 10th-century Norman and 17th-century Spanish structures. Because it now houses the Sicilian Parliament, parts of the palace are closed to the public from Tuesday to Thursday when the regional parliament is in session. The must-see **Cappella Palatina** (Palatine Chapel) remains open. Built by Roger II in 1132, it's a dazzling example of the harmony of artistic elements produced under the Normans. Here the skill of French and Sicilian masons was brought to bear on the decorative purity of Arab ornamentation and the splendor of 11th-century Greek Byzantine

16

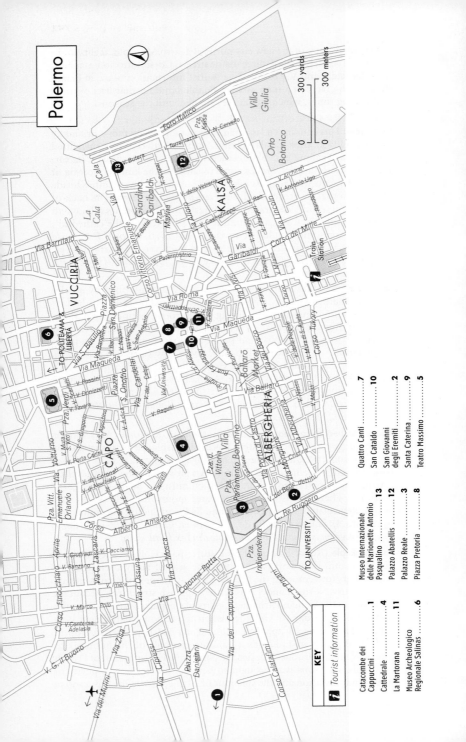

Palermo

KEY

🛈 Tourist information

Catacombe dei Cappuccini	1
Cattedrale	4
La Martorana	11
Museo Archeologico Regionale Salinas	6

Museo Internazionale delle Marionette Antonio Pasqualino	13
Palazzo Abatellis	12
Palazzo Reale	3
Piazza Pretoria	8

Quattro Canti	7
San Cataldo	10
San Giovanni degli Eremiti	2
Santa Caterina	9
Teatro Massimo	5

0   300 yards

0   300 meters

mosaics. The interior is covered with glittering mosaics and capped by a splendid 10th-century Arab honeycomb stalactite wooden ceiling. Biblical stories blend happily with scenes of Arab life—look for one showing a picnic in a harem—and Norman court pageantry.

Upstairs are the royal apartments, including the **Sala di Re Ruggero** (King Roger's Hall), decorated with medieval murals of hunting scenes—an earlier (1120) secular counterpart to the religious themes seen elsewhere. French, Latin, and Arabic were spoken here, and Arab astronomers and poets exchanged ideas with Latin and Greek scholars in one of the most interesting marriages of culture in the Western world. The Sala is always included with entry to the palace or chapel. ⊠ *Piazza Indipendenza, Albergheria* ☏ *091/6262833* ⊕ *www.federicosecondo. org* ✇ *€12 Fri.–Mon., €10 Tues.–Thurs.* ⊘ *Closed Sun. after 1. Royal Apartments closed Tues.–Thurs.*

San Cataldo. Three striking Saracenic scarlet domes mark this church, built in 1154 during the Norman occupation of Palermo. The church now belongs to the Knights of the Holy Sepulchre and has a spare but intense stone interior. If it's closed, inquire next door at La Martorana. ⊠ *Piazza Bellini 3, Kalsa* ☏ *091/6118168* ✇ *€2.50* ⊘ *Closed daily 12:30–3.*

San Giovanni degli Eremiti. Distinguished by its five reddish-orange domes and stripped-clean interior, this 12th-century church was built by the Normans on the site of an earlier mosque—one of 200 that once stood in Palermo. The emirs ruled Palermo for nearly two centuries and brought to it their passion for lush gardens and fountains. One is reminded of this while sitting in San Giovanni's delightful cloister of twin half columns, surrounded by palm trees, jasmine, oleander, and citrus trees. ⊠ *Via dei Benedettini 14–20, Albergheria* ☏ *091/6515019* ✇ *€6.*

Teatro Massimo. Construction of this formidable Neoclassical theater, the largest in Italy, was started in 1875 by Giovanni Battista Basile and completed by his son Ernesto in 1897. A reconstruction project started in 1974 ran into gross delays, and the facility remained closed until just before its centenary in 1997. Its interior is as glorious as ever. *The Godfather: Part III* ended with a famous shooting scene on the theater's steps. Visits, by 30-minute guided tour only, are available in five languages, including English. ⊠ *Piazza Verdi 9, at top of Via Maqueda, Olivella* ☏ *091/6053267* ⊕ *www.teatromassimo.it* ✇ *€8.*

WORTH NOTING

Catacombe dei Cappuccini. The spookiest sight in all of Sicily, this 16th-century catacomb houses nearly 9,000 corpses of men, women, and young children—some in tombs but many mummified and preserved—hanging in rows on the walls, divided by social caste, age, or gender. Most wear signs indicating their names and the years they lived. The Capuchins were founders and proprietors of the bizarre establishment (many of the corpses are Capuchin friars) from 1599 to 1911, and it's still under the auspices of the nearby Capuchin church. It was closed when an adjacent cemetery was opened, making the catacombs redundant. Though memorable, this is not a spot for the faint of heart;

16

PALERMO'S MULTICULTURAL PEDIGREE

Palermo was first colonized by Phoenician traders in the 6th century BC, but it was their descendants, the Carthaginians, who built the important fortress here that caught the covetous eye of the Romans. After the First Punic War, the Romans took control of the city in the 3rd century BC. Following several invasions by the Vandals, Sicily was settled by Arabs, who made the country an emirate and established Palermo as a showpiece capital that rivaled both Córdoba and Cairo in the splendor of its architecture. Nestled in the fertile Conca d'Oro (Golden Conch) plain, full of orange, lemon, and carob groves and enclosed by limestone hills, Palermo became a magical world of palaces, mosques, minarets, and palm trees.

It was so attractive and sophisticated a city that the Norman ruler Roger de Hauteville (1031–1101) decided to conquer it and make it his capital

(1072). The Norman occupation of Sicily resulted in Palermo's golden age (1072–1194), a remarkable period of enlightenment and learning in which the arts flourished. The city of Palermo, which in the 11th century counted more than 300,000 inhabitants, became the European center for the Norman court and one of the most important ports for trade between the East and West.

Eventually the Normans were replaced by the Swabian ruler Frederick II (1194–1250), the Holy Roman Emperor, and incorporated into the Kingdom of the Two Sicilies. You'll also see plenty of evidence in Palermo of the Baroque art and architecture of the long Spanish rule. The Aragonese viceroys also brought the Spanish Inquisition to Palermo, which some historians believe helped foster the protective secret societies that evolved into today's Mafia.

children might be frightened or disturbed. ⊠ *Piazza Cappuccini 1, off Via Cappuccini, Near Palazzo Reale* ☎ *091/6527389* ☒ *€3* ⊘ *Closed daily 1–3, and Sun. after 1 pm late Oct.–late Mar.*

FAMILY **Museo Internazionale delle Marionette Antonio Pasqualino.** With a collection of more than 4,000 pieces showcasing the traditional Sicilian, and farther afield, Opera dei Pupi (puppet show), these masterpieces with their glittering armor and fierce expressions will delight visitors of all ages. There are also regular performances (stop by or call in advance to check times), which center on the chivalric legends of troubadours of bygone times. The museum can be hard to find: look for the small alley just off Piazzetta Antonio Pasqualino 5. ⊠ *Piazzetta Antonio Pasqualino 5, near Via Butera, Kalsa* ☎ *091/328060* ⊕ *www.museomarionettepalermo.it* ☒ *€5* ⊘ *Closed Sun.*

Palazzo Abatellis. Housed in this late-15th-century Catalan Gothic palace with Renaissance elements is the **Galleria Regionale.** Among its treasures are the *Annunciation* (1474), a painting by Sicily's prominent Renaissance master Antonello da Messina (1430–79), and an arresting fresco by an unknown 15th-century painter, titled *The Triumph of Death*, a macabre depiction of the plague years. Call before you visit to make sure that they're open. ⊠ *Via Alloro 4, Kalsa* ☎ *091/6230011, 091/6230006 tickets* ☒ *€8* ⊘ *Closed Mon.*

Piazza Pretoria. The square's centerpiece, a lavishly decorated fountain with 500 separate pieces of sculpture and an abundance of nude figures, so shocked some Palermitans when it was unveiled in 1575 that it got the nickname "Fountain of Shame." It's even more of a sight when illuminated at night. ✉ *Piazza Pretoria, Quattro Canti.*

Quattro Canti. The Four Corners is the intersection of Corso Vittorio Emanuele and Via Maqueda. Four rather exhaust-blackened Baroque palaces from Spanish rule meet at concave corners, each with its own fountain and representations of a Spanish ruler, patron saint, and one of the four seasons. ✉ *Palermo.*

Santa Caterina. The walls of this splendid Baroque church (1596) in Piazza Bellini are covered with extremely impressive decorative 17th-century inlays of precious marble. ✉ *Piazza Bellini, Quattro Canti* ☎ *338/4512011* 🎟 *€2.*

WHERE TO EAT

16

$$ SICILIAN 🍴 **Antica Focacceria San Francesco.** Turn-of-the-20th-century wooden cabinets, marble-top tables, and cast-iron ovens characterize this neighborhood bakery. Come here for the locally beloved snacks that can be combined to make an inexpensive meal. **Known for:** Sicilian street food, like calf's spleen and chickpea fritters; historic atmosphere; meat and pasta specialties. [$] *Average main: €15* ✉ *Via A. Paternostro 58, Kalsa* ☎ *091/320264* 🌐 *www.anticafocacceria.it* 🕓 *Closed 2 wks in mid-Jan.*

$$ SICILIAN 🍴 **Casa del Brodo.** On the edge of the Vucciria is a restaurant that dates to 1890, one of Palermo's oldest. In winter its namesake dish, tortellini *in brodo* (in beef broth), is the specialty of the house. **Known for:** large selection of antipasti; tortellini in brodo; good choice of meat and fish dishes. [$] *Average main: €15* ✉ *Corso Vittorio Emanuele 175, Vucciria* ☎ *091/321655* 🌐 *www.casadelbrodo.it* 🕓 *Closed Tues. Oct.–May, Sun. June–Sept., and Jan.*

$$$$ SICILIAN Fodor's Choice ★ 🍴 **Osteria dei Vespri.** This foodie paradise occupies a cozy-but-elegant space on an unheralded piazza in the historic city center. The winter menu (November–March) is traditional osteria fare with two set menu options, but in the summer months the chef offers a special larger tasting menu built around seasonal ingredients. **Known for:** tasting menus with local ingredients; traditional osteria food in winter; extensive wine cellar. [$] *Average main: €60* ✉ *Piazza Croce dei Vespri 6, Kalsa* ☎ *091/6171631* 🌐 *www.osteriadeivespri.it* 🕓 *No lunch Sun. and Mon. Nov.–Apr.*

$ SICILIAN 🍴 **Pani Ca Meusa.** A civic institution facing Palermo's old fishing port, this joint has been serving its titular calf's spleen sandwich for more than 70 years. The original owner's grandsons produce this local specialty sprinkled with a bit of salt and some lemon and served with or without cheese to a buzzing crowd of Palermo's well-weathered elders. **Known for:** calf's spleen sandwich; a bit of Sicilian history; standing-room-only dining. [$] *Average main: €2* ✉ *Via Cala 62, Porta Carbone, Kalsa* ☎ *091/323433* 💳 *No credit cards* 🕓 *Closed Sun.*

$$ SEAFOOD 🍴 **Piccolo Napoli.** Founded in 1951, this is one of Old Palermo's most esteemed seafood eateries. Locals come at midday to feast on the freshest

of fish; you can begin with a memorable buffet featuring baby octopus, raw *neonata* (tiny fish resembling sardines but with a milder flavor), and chickpea fritters. **Known for:** fresh fish and seafood; local crowds; friendly staff. $ *Average main: €16* ⌧ *Piazzetta Mulino al Vento 4* ☎ *091/320431* ⊕ *www.trattoriapiccolonapoli.it* ☼ *No dinner Sun.*

$ ✕ **Pizzeria I Comparucci.** One of Palermo's best pizzerias serves delicious
PIZZA   Neapolitan pies from a big oven in the open kitchen—the genius is in the crust, which is seared in a matter of seconds. The owners make their money on a quick turnover (so don't expect a long, leisurely meal), but the pizza is delicious, and the place often serves until midnight—later than almost any other restaurant in the neighborhood. **Known for:** pizza, pizza, and more pizza; outdoor seating; late-night dining. $ *Average main: €7* ⌧ *Via Messina 36e, Libertà* ☎ *091/6090467* ☼ *No lunch.*

$$ ✕ **Ristorante Cin Cin.** Though Vincenzo Clemente, the Sicilian-born
SICILIAN   owner of this charming restaurant not far from Palermo's main shopping street, Via Liberta, lived in Louisiana for 20 years, you won't find a trace of the South in his innovative Italian cooking. But you will find lighter and more modern versions of traditional Sicilian dishes, such as exemplary ricotta casserole with pumpkin, mint, and zucchini and ultrafresh *bavettine* pasta with artichoke, leek, speck, dried ricotta, and balsamic vinegar. **Known for:** modernized Sicilian flavors; delicious semifreddo; top-notch cooking classes. $ *Average main: €16* ⌧ *Via Manin 22, Libertà* ☎ *091/6124095* ⊕ *www.ristorantecincin.com* ☼ *Closed Sun. No lunch.*

$ ✕ **Trattoria Altri Tempi.** This small and friendly "retro" restaurant is a
SICILIAN   favorite among locals who pine for the rustic dishes served by their ancestors. A meal begins when the server plunks down a carafe of the house wine and a superb spread of traditional antipasti on your table, and continues with dishes with old-fashioned names: *fave a cunigghiu* is fava beans prepared with olive oil, garlic, and remarkably flavorful oregano; and *pasta al'anciova,* with a concentrated sauce of tomatoes and anchovies. **Known for:** Sicilian grandmothers' food; classic antipasti; complimentary house wine. $ *Average main: €8* ⌧ *Via Sammartino 65/67, Libertà* ☎ *091/323480* ⊕ *www.trattoriaaltritempi.it* ☼ *Closed July, and Sun. in June, Aug., and Sept.*

WHERE TO STAY

$$ ⌂ **Eurostars Centrale Palace.** A stone's throw from Palermo's main historic
HOTEL   sites, the Centrale Palace is the only hotel in the heart of the centro
Fodor's Choice   storico that was once a stately private palace; built in 1717, it weaves
★   old-world charm with modern comfort. **Pros:** sparkling clean; in the center of it all; comfortable rooms. **Cons:** hotel showing its age; traffic noise; some rooms have no view. $ *Rooms from: €130* ⌧ *Corso Vittorio Emanuele 327, Vucciria* ☎ *091/8539* ⊕ *www.eurostarscentralepalace. com* ⇨ *104 rooms* ◯⃘ *Free Breakfast.*

$$ ⌂ **Grand Hotel Piazza Borsa.** Cleverly constructed within Palermo's his-
HOTEL   toric stock exchange, this monastery-turned-hotel is ideally located in the old town, just around the corner from Antica Focacceria San Francesco. **Pros:** very convenient location; interesting architecture; wellness center with fitness equipment, rare for Sicily hotels. **Cons:** somewhat

indifferent staff; some noise issues in rooms; building feels a bit sterile. Ⓢ *Rooms from: €180 ⊠ Via dei Cartari 18, Kalsa ☎ 091/320075 ⊕ www.piazzaborsa.it ⟿ 127 rooms* ⍾ *Free Breakfast.*

$$$
HOTEL
Fodor's Choice
★

☷ Grand Hotel Villa Igiea MGallery by Sofitel. This grande dame set in a private tropical garden at the edge of the bay—a local landmark for a century—still maintains a somewhat faded aura of luxury and comfort. **Pros:** secluded setting; historic building with lots of atmosphere; free shuttle to city center in the summer. **Cons:** could use a refresh; no amenities in the nearby area; a bit far from Palermo attractions. Ⓢ *Rooms from: €217 ⊠ Salita Belmonte 43 ☎ 091/6312111 ⊕ villa-igiea.com ☉ Closed Feb.–mid-Mar. ⟿ 120 rooms* ⍾ *Free Breakfast.*

$$
HOTEL

☷ Hotel Principe di Villafranca. Modern art mixed with antique furnishings, creamy marble floors, and vaulted ceilings evoke a luxurious private home in the heart of Palermo's glitzy shopping district. **Pros:** appealing design; well-maintained building; central location. **Cons:** some rooms on the small side; service can be spotty; some rooms can be noisy. Ⓢ *Rooms from: €156 ⊠ Via G. Turrisi Colonna 4, Libertà ☎ 091/6118523 ⊕ www.principedivillafranca.it ⟿ 32 rooms* ⍾ *Free Breakfast.*

$
B&B/INN

☷ Le Terrazze. Although it's just steps from the bustling streets around the Cattedrale, complete calm envelops this small, beautifully restored B&B, named for its five roof terraces, all with sublime views of Palermo's skyline. **Pros:** convenient location; in summer, breakfast is served on the glorious rooftop; period-style rooms. **Cons:** parking can be difficult; books up quickly. Ⓢ *Rooms from: €110 ⊠ Via Pietro Novelli 14 ☎ 091/6520866, 320/4328567 ⊕ www.leterrazzebb.it ⟿ 2 rooms* ⍾ *Free Breakfast.*

$$
HOTEL

☷ Massimo Plaza Hotel. Small and select, this hotel enjoys one of Palermo's best locations—opposite the Teatro Massimo, on the border of the old and new towns—and has guest rooms that are spacious, comfortably furnished, and, for the most part, well insulated from the noise on Via Maqueda. **Pros:** central location; low-season bargains; tasty breakfast made to order. **Cons:** stairs (no elevator) up to the rooms; plain interiors; some noisy rooms (ask for one in the quieter back). Ⓢ *Rooms from: €154 ⊠ Via Maqueda 437, Vucciria ☎ 091/325657 ⊕ www.massimoplazahotel.com ⟿ 11 rooms* ⍾ *Free Breakfast.*

16

NIGHTLIFE AND PERFORMING ARTS

NIGHTLIFE

Each night between 6 and 9, Palermo's youth gather to shop, socialize, flirt, and plan the evening's affairs in an epic passeggiata along Via Ruggero Settimo (a northern extension of Via Maqueda) and filling Piazza Ruggero Settimo in front of Teatro Politeama. Some trendy bars also line Via Principe del Belmonte, intersecting with Via Roma and Via Ruggero Settimo.

BARS AND CAFÉS

Santa Monica. Immensely popular with the twenty- and thirtysomething crowd, who belly up to the bar for pizza, crepes, and, of course, excellent German-style draft beer, this pub is also a good place to watch televised soccer. It's closed Monday. ✉ *Via E. Parisi 7, Libertà* ☏ *091/324735.*

PERFORMING ARTS

CONCERTS AND OPERA

Teatro Massimo. As the biggest theater in Italy, Teatro Massimo is truly larger than life. Concerts and operas are presented throughout the year, though in summer concerts are usually held outdoors. An opera at the Massimo is an unforgettable Sicilian experience. ✉ *Piazza Verdi, at top of Via Maqueda, Capo* ☏ *091/6053580 tickets, 091/8486000 tickets, 091/6053267 tours* ⊕ *www.teatromassimo.it* ☏ *Tours €8, performances €22–€140.*

Teatro Politeama Garibaldi. The shamelessly grandiose, Neoclassical Teatro Politeama Garibaldi, home of the Orchestra Sinfonica Siciliana, stages a season of opera and orchestral works from October through June. ✉ *Piazza Ruggero Settimo, Libertà* ☏ *091/6072532* ⊕ *www. orchestrasinfonicasiciliana.it.*

PUPPET SHOWS

FAMILY **Figli d'Arte Cuticchio Association.** Palermo's tradition of puppet theater holds an appeal for children and adults alike, and street artists often perform outside the Teatro Massimo in summer. The Figli d'Arte Cuticchio Association hosts performances from September to June. ✉ *Via Bara all'Olivella 95, Kalsa* ☏ *091/323400* ⊕ *www.figlidartecuticchio. com* ☏ *€10.*

SHOPPING

North of Piazza Castelnuovo, Via della Libertà and the surrounding streets represent the luxury end of the shopping scale. A second nerve center for shoppers is the pair of parallel streets connecting modern Palermo with the train station, Via Roma and Via Maqueda, where boutiques and shoe shops become increasingly upscale as you move from the Quattro Canti past Teatro Massimo to Via Ruggero Settimo.

FOOD AND WINE

Enoteca Picone. The best wineshop in town has a fantastic selection of Sicilian and national wines. Although service can be curt, you can taste a selection of wines by the glass in the front of the store. There are tables in the back, where meats and cheeses are also served. ✉ *Via Marconi 36, Libertà* ☏ *091/331300* ⊕ *www.enotecapicone.it.*

I Peccatucci di Mamma Andrea. The charming "Mamma Andrea's Small Sins" sells a plethora of mouthwatering original creations, including jams, preserves, and Sicilian treats like the superb marzipan frutta martorana. ✉ *Via Principe di Scordia 67, near Piazza Florio, Vucciria* ☏ *0392/4907732* ⊕ *www.mammaandrea.it.*

Pasticceria Alba. One of the most famous sweets shops in Italy, this is the place to find favorite pastries such as cannoli and cassata siciliana.

✉ *Piazza Don Bosco 7/C, off Via della Libertà near La Favorita Park, Libertà* ☎ *091/309016* ⊕ *www.pasticceriaalba.it.*

MARKETS

Ballarò Market. Wind your way through the Albergheria district and this historic market, where the Saracens did their shopping in the 11th century—joined by the Normans in the 12th. The market remains faithful to seasonal change as well as the original Arab commerce of fruit, vegetables, and grain; though these days it sees more tourists than locals, it's still fun to experience. Go early; the action dies out by 4 pm most days. ✉ *Ballarò Market, between La Martorana and Quattro Canti, Albergheria.*

Vucciria Market. It's easy to see how this market got its name—*vucciria* translates to "voices" or "hubbub." Though now more for tourists than locals, Palermo's most established outdoor market, in the heart of the centro storico, is a maze of side streets around Piazza San Domenico, where hawkers deliver incessant chants from behind stands brimming with mounds of olives, blood oranges, fennel, and long-stem artichokes. Morning is the best time to see the market in full swing. ✉ *Vucciria Market, Vucciria.*

16

THE TYRRHENIAN COAST

Sicily's northern shore, the Tyrrhenian Coast, is mostly a succession of small holiday towns interspersed with stretches of sand. It's often difficult to find a calm spot among the thousands of tourists and locals in high summer, though the scene quiets down considerably after August. The biggest attraction is the old town of Cefalù, with one of Sicily's most remarkable medieval cathedrals, encrusted with mosaics. The coast on either side is dotted with ancient archaeological remains and Arab-Norman buildings.

Some 48 km (30 miles) south of Cefalù, Pizzo Carbonara (6,500 feet) is the highest peak in Sicily after Mt. Etna. Piano della Battaglia has a fully equipped ski resort with lifts. The area has a very un-Sicilian aspect, with Swiss-type chalets, hiking paths, and even Alpine churches.

CEFALÙ

70 km (43 miles) east of Palermo, 161 km (100 miles) west of Messina.

The coast between Palermo and Messina is dotted with charming villages. Tindari (which dates back to the early-Christian era) and Laghetti di Maranello are two that are worth a stop, but it's Cefalù, a classically appealing old Sicilian town built on a spur jutting out into the sea, that's the jewel of the coast.

GETTING HERE AND AROUND

Trains and buses run between Palermo and Messina. Drivers can take the A20 autostrada.

VISITOR INFORMATION

Contact Cefalù Tourism Office. ✉ *Corso Ruggeri 77* ☎ *0921/421050* ⊕ *cefalu. it.*

EXPLORING

Duomo. Cefalù is dominated by a massive headland—*la rocca*—and a 12th-century Romanesque Duomo, which is one of the finest Norman cathedrals in Italy. Roger II began the church in 1131 as an offering of thanks for having been saved here from a shipwreck. Its mosaics rival those of Monreale. (Whereas Monreale's Byzantine Christ figure is an austere and powerful image, emphasizing Christ's divinity, the Cefalù Christ is softer, more compassionate, and more human.) The traffic going in and out of Cefalù town can be heavy in summer, so you may want to take the 50-minute train ride from Palermo instead of driving. At the Duomo you must be respectfully attired—no shorts or beachwear permitted. ✉ *Piazza del Duomo* ☎ *0921/922021* 🌐 *www.cattedraledicefalu.com.*

WHERE TO EAT AND STAY

$$ SICILIAN 🍴 **Al Porticciolo.** Nicola Mendolia's seaside restaurant is comfortable, casual, and faithfully focused on food. Diners will find a large choice of pizza on offer, plus an extensive selection of seafood, pasta, and meat. **Known for:** high-quality pizza; local seafood; lovely terrace overlooking the water. [$] *Average main: €17* ✉ *Via C. Ortolani di Bordonaro 66* ☎ *0921/921981* 🌐 *www.alporticcioloristorante.com.*

$$ HOTEL 🏨 **Kalura.** This modern hotel is on a small promontory in Caldura, 2 km (1 mile) east of Cefalù, a few minutes away by taxi, and offers bright and cheerful rooms, many with balconies overlooking the sea. **Pros:** beautiful sea views; good swimming; family-friendly environment. **Cons:** outside town; Wi-Fi only in lobby; occasionally indifferent service. [$] *Rooms from: €171* ✉ *Via V. Cavallaro 13* ☎ *0921/421354* 🌐 *www.hotelkalura.com* 🕒 *Closed mid-Nov.–mid-Mar.* 🛏 *84 rooms* 🍽 *Free Breakfast.*

THE AEOLIAN ISLANDS

Off Sicily's northeast coast lies an archipelago of seven spectacular islands of volcanic origin. The Isole Eolie (Aeolian Islands), also known as the Isole Lipari (Lipari Islands), were named after Aeolus, the Greek god of the winds, who is said to keep all the Earth's winds stuffed in a bag in his cave here. The Aeolians are a world of grottoes and clear-water caves carved by waves through the centuries. Superb snorkeling and scuba diving abound in the clearest and cleanest of Italy's waters.

Lipari provides the widest range of accommodations and is a good jumping-off point for day trips to the other islands. Most exclusive are Vulcano and Panarea: the former is noted for its black sands and stupendous sunsets, as well as the acrid smell of its sulfur emissions, whereas the latter is, according to some, the prettiest. Most remarkable is Stromboli (stress the first syllable) with its constant eruptions, while the greenest island—and the one with the best hiking trails—is Salina. The remotest are Filicudi and Alicudi, where electricity was introduced only in the 1980s, and broadband Internet connections are still the stuff of pipe dreams.

The bars in the Aeolian Islands, and especially those on Lipari, are known for their granitas of fresh strawberries, melon, peaches, and other fruits. Many Sicilians on the Aeolians (and in Messina, Taormina, and Catania) begin the hot summer days with a *granita di caffè* (a coffee ice topped with whipped cream), into which they dunk their breakfast rolls. (You can get one any time of day.)

GETTING HERE AND AROUND

Car ferries and much faster hydrofoils carry passengers to and between the islands. They depart from Milazzo and Messina (on Sicily), and from Reggio di Calabria (on the mainland), with the majority stopping at Lipari before continuing on to other islands in the chain. Service is most frequent in summer. May to September, a few car ferries a week also provide overnight service to and from Naples; during that same period hydrofoils run to and from Naples, Cefalù, and Palermo. Operators' websites are the best source of information regarding schedules and fares.

Ferry and Hydrofoil Contacts Liberty Lines. ☎ 0923/873813 ⊕ www.libertylines.it. **N.G.I.** ☎ 090/9283415 Milazzo office, 090/9811955 Lipari office ⊕ www.ngi-spa.it. **Siremar.** ☎ 090/364601, 800/627414 ⊕ www.siremar.it. **SNAV.** ☎ 081/4285555 ⊕ www.snav.it.

LIPARI

16

2 hrs 10 mins from Milazzo by ferry, 1 hr by hydrofoil; 60–75 mins from Reggio di Calabria and Messina by ferry.

The largest and most developed of the Aeolians, Lipari welcomes you with distinctive pastel-color houses. Fields of spiky agaves dot the northernmost tip of the island, Acquacalda, indented with pumice and obsidian quarries. In the west is San Calogero, where you can explore hot springs and mud baths. From the red-lava base of the island rises a plateau crowned with a 16th-century castle and a 17th-century cathedral.

GETTING HERE AND AROUND

Ferries and hydrofoils from Milazzo, which is 41 km (25 miles) west of Messina, stop here. There's also ferry service from Reggio di Calabria and Messina.

EXPLORING

Fodor's Choice
★

Museo Archeologico Eoliano. The vast, multibuilding Museo Archeologico Eoliano is a terrific museum, with an intelligently arranged collection of prehistoric finds—some dating as far back as 4000 BC—from various sites in the archipelago, as well as Greek and Roman artifacts, including an outstanding collection of Greek theatrical masks, and even interesting information on volcanoes. Basic descriptions about the exhibits are provided in English and Italian, though more comprehensive information is only in Italian. That said, there is so much to see, the museum is worth at least a few hours of your time. ⊠ *Via Castello 2* ☎ *090/9880174* ⊕ *www.regione.sicilia.it/beniculturali/museolipari* 🎟 €6.

Fodor's Choice
★

Vulcano. A popular day trip from Lipari is to visit the most notorious of the Aeolian Islands: Vulcano. True to its name—and the origin of the term—Vulcano has a profusion of fumeroles sending up jets of hot vapor, though the volcano here has long been dormant. Travelers visit to soak in the strong-smelling sulfur springs, or to sunbathe or walk on some of the archipelago's best beaches, though the volcanic black sand can be off-putting at first glance. Ascend to the crater (1,266 feet above sea level) on mule back for eye-popping views or take a boat ride into the grottoes around the base. From Capo Grillo you can see all the Aeolians. **Liberty Lines** has high-speed passenger vessels that make the crossing from Lipari in 10 minutes; frequent daily departures are offered year-round. ✉ *Vulcano* ☎ *0923/873813 Liberty Lines* 🌐 *www.libertylines.it.*

WHERE TO EAT AND STAY

$$ SICILIAN Fodor's Choice ★ 🍴 **Filippino.** The views from this upper-town restaurant's outdoor terrace are a fitting complement to the superb fare featured on its menu. Founded in 1910, Filippino is rightly rated as one of the archipelago's best dining venues—you'll understand why when you sample the seafood. *Zuppa di pesce* (fish soup) and the antipasto platter of smoked and marinated fish are absolute musts. Just leave some room for the local version of cassata siciliana, accompanied by sweet Malvasia wine from Salina. **Known for:** pasta, soup, and risotto with fresh seafood; traditional Sicilian recipes; scrumptious local desserts. [$] *Average main: €18* ✉ *Piazza Mazzini Lipari* ☎ *090/9811002* 🌐 *www.filippino.it* 🕘 *Closed Mon. Oct.–Mar.*

$$ HOTEL 🏨 **Les Sables Noirs.** Named for the black sands of the beach in front, this luxury hotel is superbly sited on the beautiful Porto di Ponente, and its cool modern furnishings and inviting pool induce a sybaritic mood. **Pros:** stunning beachfront location; delicious breakfasts; five-minute walk to town. **Cons:** no restaurant; five-night minimum stay in August; iffy Wi-Fi. [$] *Rooms from: €180* ✉ *Porto di Ponente, Vulcano* ☎ *090/9850* 🌐 *www.hotelvulcanosicily.com* 🕘 *Closed mid-Oct.–Apr.* 🛏 *43 rooms* 🍽 *Free Breakfast.*

SALINA

50 mins from Lipari by ferry, 20 mins by hydrofoil.

The second largest of the Aeolians, Salina is also the most fertile—which accounts for its excellent Malvasia dessert wine. Salina is the archipelago's lushest and highest island, too—Mt. Fossa delle Felci rises to more than 3,000 feet—and the vineyards and fishing villages along its slopes add to its allure. Pollara, in the west of the island, has capitalized on its fame as one of the locations in the 1990s cult movie *Il Postino* (*The Postman*) and is an ideal location for an evening passeggiata on well-maintained paths along the volcanic terrain.

GETTING HERE AND AROUND

Ferries and hydrofoils arrive here from Lipari.

WHERE TO STAY

$ HOTEL 🏨 **Hotel Solemar.** In a valley between Salina's two mountains, this hotel has most of the hallmarks of Mediterranean charm—large terraces for contemplation, a location in a sleepy town, and pleasing food served on summer evenings in the restaurant. **Pros:** relaxed atmosphere; helpful staff; terrific views. **Cons:** no pool; hit-or-miss Wi-Fi in public areas; a 15-minute taxi ride from Salina's main port. [$] *Rooms from: €95* ✉ *Via*

Roma 8, Leni ☎ *090/9809445* 🌐 *www.salinasolemarhotel.it* 🕒 *Closed Nov.–Mar.* 🛏 *14 rooms* 🍴 *Free Breakfast.*

PANAREA

2 hrs from Lipari by ferry, 25–50 mins by hydrofoil; 7–9 hrs from Naples by ferry.

Panarea has some of the most dramatic scenery of the islands, including wild caves carved out of the rock and dazzling flora. The exceptionally clear water and the richness of life on the sea floor make Panarea especially suitable for underwater exploration, though there's little in the way of beaches. The outlying rocks and islets make a gorgeous sight, and you can enjoy the panorama on an easy excursion to the small Bronze Age village at Capo Milazzese.

GETTING HERE AND AROUND

Ferries and hydrofoils arrive here from Lipari and Naples.

WHERE TO STAY

$$$$ HOTEL 🏨 **Il Raya.** Although some visitors say it's resting on past laurels, Il Raya is perfectly in keeping with the elite style of Panarea—discreet and expensive, the hotel looks out over the sea toward Stromboli. **Pros:** great views of Stromboli; hippie-chic ambience; lovely pool area. **Cons:** snooty staff; uphill trudge to rooms; in need of renovations. [$] *Rooms from: €500* ✉ *San Pietro* ☎ *090/983013* 🌐 *www.hotelraya.it* 🕒 *Closed mid-Oct.–mid-Apr.* 🛏 *36 rooms* 🍴 *Free Breakfast.*

16

STROMBOLI

3 hrs 45 mins from Lipari by ferry, 65–90 mins by hydrofoil; 9 hrs from Naples by ferry, 5 hrs by hydrofoil.

This northernmost of the Aeolians consists entirely of the cone of an active volcano. The view from the sea—especially at night, as an endless stream of glowing red-hot lava flows into the water—is unforgettable. Stromboli is in a constant state of mild dissatisfaction, and every now and then its anger flares up, so authorities insist that you climb to the top (about 3,031 feet above sea level) only with a guide. The round-trip (climb, pause, and descent), usually starting around 6 pm, takes about six hours; the lava is much more impressive after dark. Some choose to camp overnight atop the volcano—again, a guide is essential. The main town has a small selection of reasonably priced hotels and restaurants, and a choice of lively clubs and cafés. In addition to the island tour, excursions might include boat trips around the naturally battlemented isle of Strombolicchio.

GETTING HERE AND AROUND

Ferries and hydrofoils arrive here from Lipari and Naples.

EXPLORING

Pippo Navigazione. Numerous tour operators have guides that can lead you up Stromboli or take you round in a boat, among them Pippo Navigazione. Boat trips include three-hour day cruises and night tours that explore the area where the lava reaches the sea. ✉ *Stromboli* ☎ *338/9857883, 339/2229714.*

FILICUDI

30–60 mins from Salina and Lipari by hydrofoil; 2 hrs from Cefalù and Palermo, 2 hrs from Milazzo, and 10 hrs from Naples by ferry.

Just a dot in the sea, Filicudi is famous for its unusual volcanic rock formations and the enchanting Grotta del Bue Marino (Grotto of the Sea Ox). The crumbled remains of a prehistoric village are at Capo Graziano. The island, which is spectacular for walking and hiking and is still a truly undiscovered, restful haven, has a handful of hotels and pensioni, and some families put up guests. Car ferries are available only in summer.

GETTING HERE AND AROUND

Ferries and hydrofoils arrive throughout the year from Salina and Lipari, and also in summer from Palermo, Cefalù, Milazzo, and Naples.

WHERE TO STAY

$$ **La Canna.** It's wonderful to wake up to the utter tranquility that
HOTEL characterizes a stay on Filicudi—especially if you happen to be greeting the day at this hotel, set above the tiny port, which commands fabulous views of sea and sky from its flower-filled terrace. **Pros:** relaxed setting; family-friendly atmosphere; great views. **Cons:** an uphill climb from the port; breakfast not included in standard rooms (but half board required in peak season in sea view rooms); no Wi-Fi in guest rooms. $ *Rooms from: €140* ✉ *Via Rosa 43, Filicudi Porto* ☎ *090/9889956* ⊕ *www. lacannahotel.it* ⊗ *Closed mid-Oct.–mid-Apr.* 🛏 *14 rooms* ⦿ *No meals.*

SARDINIA

WELCOME TO SARDINIA

TOP REASONS TO GO

★ **Relax on idyllic beaches:** Covering more than 1,200 miles of coastline, Sardinia's beaches beckon with their turquoise waters, white sand, and rippled dunes.

★ **Discover natural beauty:** A network of trails explores Sardinia's resplendent mountains, deep gorges, lush forests, and cascading waterfalls.

★ **Explore charming towns and villages:** From coastal towns to rural villages, the island is dotted with a variety of settlements that take pride in their history and tradition. Each has its own culture, cuisine, and unique way of life.

★ **Dive or snorkel the outer reefs:** Crystalline waters, warm weather, and outer reefs make Sardinia a paradise for underwater adventurers. Sunken ships and marine reserves provide the ideal place to discover marine life.

★ **Savor Sardinian delicacies:** From pasta and prosciutto to lamb and cheese, the island's cuisine is sure to satisfy any appetite.

The lure of Sardinia lies in its spectacular natural beauty and historical roots, which date back to the Bronze Age. With Europe's highest dunes in the southwest, deepest canyons in the mountainous center, and best beaches on eastern and western coastlines, Sardinia enchants with fortified towns, open-air museums, stunning vistas, and crystalline coastal waters from north to south.

1 Cagliari and the Southern Coast. The gateway to Sardinia's spectacular coastline, Cagliari bustles with modern commercial activity while preserving ancient history as the island's capital. Along the southern coast, rural coastal villages stretch along idyllic waters, and archaeological ruins enrich the breathtaking natural beauty of the dramatic mountain peaks and rugged promontories. Pristine white-sand beaches are set against flawless sapphire seas.

2 Su Nuraxi to the Costa Smeralda. From the UNESCO World Heritage Site of Su Nuraxi—a mysterious complex of beehivelike stone structures near the town of Barumini—to the secluded beaches and coves and the posh towns and resorts along the northern coast, this region is a summer playground for the world's rich and famous. The iconic Porto Cervo serves as its hedonistic heart, where superyachts moor after their owners have spent sun-drenched days in Romazzino, Liscia Ruia, Capriccioli, Rena Bianca, and Del Principe. The Emerald Coast's unparalleled beauty stretches into the archipelago of La Maddalena, the site of one of the world's most important marine wildlife reserves.

FRANCE

La Maddalena

Santa Teresa
Gallura

Palau

Porto Cervo

COSTA SMERALDA

Bassacutena

Arzachena

Punta
Caprara

ISOLA
ASINARA

90   133   427   125

Golfo Aranci

Golfo di Olbia

Olbia

Tempio
Pausania   127

Telti   199

125

Golfo
dell'Asinara   Castelsardo

200

Monti

131

Stintino

Sedini

392

Padru

Porto Torres

Chiaramonti   199

Sorso

Oschiri

389

Sassari

291

Ozieri

Budduso

Siniscola

597

125

Villanova
Monteleone

Bitti

Sas Linnas
Siccas

17

Alghero

Bultei

131

Orosei

105   292

Monte
▲Ortobene

Dorgali

Padria

Orotelli

Nuoro

Cala Gonone

49

129

389   Golfo
di Orosei

Bosa

Macomer

128

Tresnuraghes

Abbasanta   128

Fonni   389

125

292   388

Tortoli

131

Cabras

Asuni

Laconi

198

Bari Sardo

Oristano

Nurallao

Golfo di
Oristano

125

Marrubiu

Su Nuraxi

Porto Palma

Uras   Barumini

126   131   197

COSTA VERDE

Guspini   197   Furtei   128

Piscinas

Samassi

Muravera

Buggerru

Villasor

Monastir

126   Decimomannu   Dolianova

Iglesias   130   131   125

Portoscuso   126

Carloforte

Carbonia   293   Cagliari

ISOLA
SAN PIETRO   195   Golfo di
Cagliari

Sarroch   Villasimius

Sant'Antioco

Giba   Pula

ISOLA
SANT'ANTIOCO   Golfo
di Palmas   195   0   10 mi

Capo Teulada   Chia   0   10 km

Capo Spartivento

EATING AND DRINKING WELL IN SARDINIA

Wining and dining in Sardinia is not just a richly delicious experience, it's also a way to have a close-up encounter with the history, geography, and cultural traditions of the island. Sardinian food has its own culinary identity, a complex and eclectic mix that makes for mouthwatering and often revelatory dishes.

Sardinia's proximity to North Africa and its long Spanish occupation mean that elements of both cultures can be found in the island's kitchens, including couscous and paella. There are also strong regional variations within Sardinia itself, as well as a traditional division between the land-based fare of the interior and the fresh seafood on the coasts. Wherever you go here, you'll find a strong emphasis on seasonal ingredients and ancient cooking techniques.

BREADS, CHEESES, AND SWEET SPECIALTIES

Sardinia has a strong tradition of bread making, and is famous for crispy, paper-thin *pane carasau* flatbread (*carta di musica* in Italian). Famous Sardinian desserts include *sospiri* (morsels of almond dough stuffed with citrus-infused almond paste), *torrone di mandorle* (almond nougat), or *seadas* (cheese-filled pastries topped with honey, also called *sebadas*). The *candelaus*, a fruit-and-almond dessert, and sweet ricotta-stuffed *pardula* cakes are popular in Cagliari. Unmissable is *amaro di corbezzolo*, a honey with a slightly bitter and dazzlingly complex bouquet and taste that's prized around the world. It's made by bees that suck nectar from a plant known as *arbutus,* the tree strawberry.

Ever wondered about all those sheep roaming the rugged slopes of the interior? They're there to produce the raw materials for Italy's original and best pecorino. It's ubiquitous in Sardinia, and comes in various strengths and consistencies.

MEAT

The most popular meat dishes are veal, roast *agnello* (lamb), and *porcheddu* (spit-roasted suckling pig, often requiring a day's notice to be prepared). *Cavallo,* or *carne equino* (horse meat), is also commonly found on restaurant menus, particularly in Sassari, where it's generally served in the form of a *bistecca* (thin steak). Donkey (*asino*) and wild boar (*cinghiale*) are other Sardinian specialties. Sometimes cinghiale is roasted on a spit or prepared using the ancient Sardinian technique of *incarralzadu,* for which it's placed in a large hole lined with fragrant myrtle leaves to extract juicy tenderness. Another option is *suppa quata,* a hearty soup historically cooked by Gallura shepherds that's made from beef broth, bread, and aged pecorino cheese.

SEAFOOD

Whole fish are best eaten roasted or grilled, though you may also find them sautéed in pasta or incorporated into *copaxa de peix,* a fish soup from

Alghero. The most famous—and priciest—Alghero dish is lobster, known as *langouste* or *aragosta.* Lobster doesn't appear on restaurant menus in winter— fortunately, the very time when *riccio di mare* (sea urchin), another local specialty, is best enjoyed. Winter is also the best season for *bottarga,* the dried, cured roe of gray mullet or tuna, often shaved directly onto a pasta dish or just served with crusty bread and olive oil.

STARTERS

Opt for *antipasti di mare* or *di terra* to kick off your meal. Traditional pastas include *malloreddus* (small pasta shells, sometimes flavored with saffron), *culurgiones* (ravioli), and *maccarones de busa* (thick pasta twists). Homemade pastas might be topped with a wild-boar sauce; *fregola,* a semolina pasta, is often served with *arselle* (clams).

WINE

Among the whites, the dry *torbato* of the Alghero Coast and the slightly sparkling *vermentino* from Gallura are standouts. The Oristano region produces the dry, sherrylike *vernaccia* (unrelated to the Tuscan variety), Bosa produces ambertone *Malvasia,* and Barbagia is one of the best sources of *cannonau,* a pleasing red wine with an ancient pedigree. The traditional liqueur *mirto,* which makes a fine after-dinner drink, is made from native wild myrtle berries.

Updated
by Robert
Andrews

The second-largest island in the Mediterranean, Sardinia remains unique and enigmatic with its rugged coastline and white-sand beaches, dramatic granite cliffs, and mountainous inland tracts. Glamorous resorts lie within a short distance of quiet, medieval villages, and ruined castles and ancient churches testify to an eventful history. But although conquerors from all directions—Phoenicians, Carthaginians, Romans, Catalans, Pisans, Piemontese—have left their traces, no outside culture has had a dominant impact. Pockets of foreign influence persist along the coasts, but inland, a proud Sardinian culture flourishes.

As a travel destination, Sardinia's identity is split: the island has some of Europe's most expensive resorts, but it's also home to pristine terrain untouched by commercial development. Fine sand and clean waters draw summer sun worshippers to beaches that rank among the Mediterranean's best. Most famous are those along the Costa Smeralda (Emerald Coast), where the über-rich have anchored their yachts since the 1960s. Less exclusive beach holidays can be had elsewhere on the island at La Maddalena, Villasimius, and Pula, and there are wonderfully intact medieval towns—Cagliari, Oristano, Sassari—on or near the water.

Apart from the glamorous shores and upscale locales found in the east, most of Sardinia's coast is rugged and unreachable, a jagged series of wildly beautiful inlets accessible only by sea. Inland, Sardinia remains shepherd's country, silent and stark. Against this landscape are the striking and mysterious stone *nuraghi* (ancient defensive structures) that provide clues to the island's ancient culture. Found only on Sardinia, these sites have been included on the UNESCO World Heritage List, described as "the finest and most complete example of a remarkable form of prehistoric architecture."

SARDINIA PLANNER

GETTING HERE AND AROUND

AIR TRAVEL

Flying is by far the fastest and easiest way to get to the island. Sardinia's major airport, Aeroporto di Elmas, is in Cagliari, with smaller ones at Alghero (Aeroporto Fertilia) and Olbia (Aeroporto Costa Smeralda).

Airport Contacts Aeroporto di Alghero. ⊠ *Regione Nuraghe Biancu, 9½ km (6 miles) north of Alghero* ☎ *079/935282* ⊕ *www.aeroportodialghero. it.* **Aeroporto di Cagliari.** ⊠ *Via dei Trasvolatori, 8 km (5 miles) northwest of city center, Elmas* ☎ *070/211211* ⊕ *www.cagliariairport.it.* **Aeroporto di Olbia Costa Smeralda.** ⊠ *Strada Statale Orientale Sarda, 4 km (2½ miles) southeast of city center, Olbia* ☎ *0789/563444* ⊕ *www.geasar.it.*

BUS TRAVEL

Cagliari is linked with the other towns of Sardinia by a network of buses. All major cities and most local destinations are served by ARST. City buses in Cagliari, Olbia, Alghero, and Sassari operate on the same system as those on the mainland: buy your ticket first, at a tobacco shop or machine, and punch it in the machine on the bus.

Contacts ARST. ☎ *800/865042 in Italy, daily 7 am–8 pm* ⊕ *www.arst.sardegna. it.* **Cagliari Bus Station.** ⊠ *Piazza Matteotti, Cagliari* ☎ *800/078870* ⊕ *www. ctmcagliari.it.*

CAR TRAVEL

Sardinia is about 270 km (167 miles) long from north to south and takes three to four hours to drive on the main roads; it's roughly 120 km (75 miles) across. Cars may be taken aboard most of the ferry lines connecting Sardinia with the mainland.

Roads are generally in good condition, with clear signposting. *Superstrade* double-lane routes are well developed. Expect winding inland mountain and coastal roads with hairpin turns. Most gas stations are closed in the afternoons, at night, and on Sunday, though at those times you can still use cash to automatically gas up. Try to avoid driving at night, when mountain roads are particularly hazardous and roadside facilities are infrequent, especially in the east. Fog may be an issue in winter.

TRAIN TRAVEL

Ferrovie dello Stato (FS) is the national railway of Italy. You can plan itineraries, purchase tickets, and look for special deals online. The Stazione Centrale in Cagliari is next to the bus station on Piazza Matteotti. There are fairly good connections between Olbia, Cagliari, Sassari, and Oristano. Service on the few other local lines is infrequent and slow. The fastest train between Olbia and Cagliari takes nearly four hours. Local trains connect Sassari with Alghero (one hour). Trenino Verde della Sardegna operates tourist trains on narrow-gauge lines through the island's interior. These high-season-only services are slow but travel through some of Sardinia's most panoramic landscapes.

Contacts **Ferrovie dello Stato.** ☎ *892021 in Italy, 06/68475475 from outside Italy* ⊕ *www.trenitalia.com.* **Trenino Verde della Sardegna.** ☎ *070/26571* ⊕ *www.treninoverde.com.*

WHEN TO GO

The best time to visit Sardinia is May through September. European vacationers flock to the island for sunshine in July and August. Expect to pay the highest rates during these two peak summer months, when roads, tourist sites, and beaches are most crowded. From September to early October, when accommodations start to shut down for the year, you'll find end-of-season deals and fewer tourists. Any other time of year, expect near–ghost towns, with closed restaurants, hotels, and shops.

RESTAURANTS

The full range of eateries can be found in every Sardinian town, from pizzerias to gourmet restaurants, and you'll be especially spoiled for choice in the island's capital, Cagliari, and the resort of Alghero, where good-value fixed-price menus are common. Seafood is ubiquitous, though the most authentic Sard cuisine is based on land products, such as lamb, boar, and suckling pig, not to mention mushrooms, artichokes, and other seasonal produce. Note that, as in other parts of Italy, fish dishes are often priced according to weight (usually by the *etto,* or 100 grams). Many places close in winter; in summer, book ahead to be sure of a table. *Restaurant reviews have been shortened. For full information, visit Fodors.com.*

HOTELS

In Sardinia, there are numerous luxury resorts with stunning beachfront vistas, bed-and-breakfast inns in medieval villages, private villas tucked away on lush hills, modern hotels in the trendy capital, and farmhouses on tranquil mountainsides. During summer months, the most popular destination on the island is the Costa Smeralda in the east. High demand during July and August raises nightly rates to an astronomical range, above €1,500 for the most deluxe accommodations. Find more reasonable hotel rates in other parts of the island, which are equally breathtaking and less crowded. Plan dates well in advance, as many hotels close at the end of September until the following April or May. *Hotel reviews have been shortened. For full information, visit Fodors.com.*

WHAT IT COSTS				
	$	$$	$$$	$$$$
Restaurants	under €15	€15–€24	€25–€35	over €35
Hotels	under €125	€125–€200	€201–€300	over €300

Restaurant reviews are the average cost of a main course at dinner, or, if dinner is not served, at lunch. Hotel reviews are the lowest cost of a standard double room in high season.

TOURS

Horse Country. This resort village in the Oristano region has accommodations, restaurants, an equestrian center, meeting facilities, family activities, and a wellness center. ✉ *Strada a Mare 27, near Oristano, Arborea* ☏ *0783/80500* ⊕ *www.horsecountry.it* ⊘ *Closed mid-Oct.–mid-Mar.*

Visos Viaggi. This travel agent and tour operator specializes in individual tours and villa and hotel accommodations. ✉ *Via Puccini 41, Cagliari* ☏ *070/658772* ⊕ *www.visosviaggi.com.*

CAGLIARI AND THE SOUTHERN COAST

Cagliari (pronounced "*Cahl*-yah-ree") is Sardinia's capital and largest city; it contains the island's principal art and archaeology museums as well as an old cathedral and medieval towers, which have lofty views of the surrounding sea, lagoons, and mountains. East of Cagliari the coast is no less scenic, but it's more developed. Although the coast is uncommercialized for the most part in the old town, up on the hill, the coast, port area, and surrounding regions toward the airport have pockets of development and industrial zones. To the southwest is Pula, an inland town within easy reach of both good beaches and the excavated ruins at Nora.

CAGLIARI

268 km (166 miles) south of Olbia.

Known in Sardinia as Casteddu, the island's capital has steep streets and impressive Italianate architecture, from modern to medieval. This city of nearly 160,000 people is characterized by a busy commercial center and waterfront with broad avenues and arched arcades, as well as by the typically narrow streets of the old hilltop citadel (called, simply, "Castello"). The Museo Archeologico makes a good starting point to a visit. The imposing Bastione di St. Remy and Mercato di San Benedetto (one of the best fish markets in Italy) are both musts.

GETTING HERE AND AROUND

The easiest way to arrive in Cagliari is by plane or boat. From the airport, it's easy to get into the city center by bus or taxi. You can also rent a car at the airport; prebooking before arrival is highly recommended. If you arrive by boat, travel from Palermo (Sicily), Civitavecchia (Rome), or Naples. The port is quite near the city center. Piazza Matteotti is the terminal for Cagliari's city buses, which are operated by Consorzio Trasporti e Mobilità (CTM). Buy tickets at the kiosk here before boarding.

FESTIVALS

FAMILY

Fodor'sChoice

★

Festa di Sant'Efisio. On May 1, thousands of costumed villagers parade through town during Sardinia's greatest annual festival, the Festa di Sant'Efisio, named after the martyred saint who saved the city from the plague in the 17th century. The saint's statue is carried aloft through Cagliari's flower-lined streets, part of a four-day procession from Cagliari to Nora and back again (40 miles round-trip), and is accompanied by colorful costumed groups from throughout the island in an

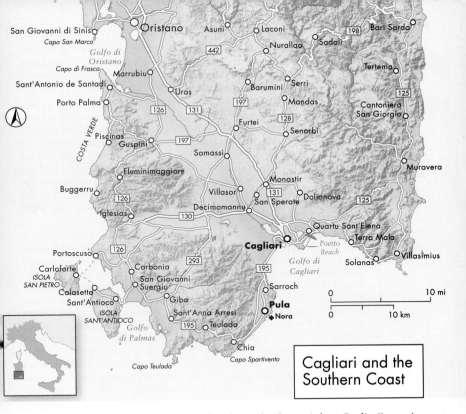

Cagliari and the
Southern Coast

enthusiastic celebration of traditional culture. Ask at Cagliari's tourist office about purchasing tickets for viewing the grand spectacle along the main route in Cagliari. From April on, you can also find tickets at ⊕ *www.boxofficesardegna.it.* ✉ *Cagliari* ⊕ *www.comune.cagliari.it.*

VISITOR INFORMATION

Contact Cagliari Tourism Office. ✉ *Palazzo Civico, Piazza Matteotti* ☎ *070/6777397* ⊕ *www.cagliariturismo.it/en.*

EXPLORING

Anfiteatro Romano. This substantial amphitheater arena dating from the 2nd century AD attests to the importance of this area to the Romans. In summer, the space is used as a concert venue. ■TIP→ **The site is not suitable for the mobility-impaired. If you don't want to enter it, good views can be had from Viale Sant'Ignazio.** ✉ *Viale Sant'Ignazio da Laconi* ☎ *366/256–2826* 🖃 *€3.*

Castello. Perched over the vast expanse of Cagliari and its port, this hillside quarter has narrow streets that hold ancient monuments and piazzas amid apartments with wash hung out to dry on elaborate wrought-iron balconies. The most impressive entrance is through the commanding late-19th-century archway of the Bastione di St. Remy on Piazza Costituzione, though this means climbing numerous steps (walk up Viale Regina Elena to find an elevator). At the top is an impressive panorama of the cityscape and the Gulf of Cagliari. From Piazza Palazzo, holding Cagliari's Cathedral, you can walk to Piazza Indipendenza and the 14th-century limestone St. Pancras Tower, a twin of the nearby Elephant Tower. ⊠ *Castello* ⊕ *www.comune.cagliari.it.*

Duomo. The Cattedrale di Santa Maria, also known as the Duomo, was begun in the 12th century, but major renovation in the 17th century and reconstruction during the mid-1930s have left little of the original medieval church. The tiers of columns on the facade resemble those of medieval Romanesque Pisan churches, but only sections of the central portal, the bell tower, and the two side entrances are from the 13th century. Look for one of the most memorable features inside—the oversize marble pulpit sculpted in the 1300s and divided in half to fit into the church nave; it now lies on either side of the main entrance. ⊠ *Piazza Palazzo* ☎ *070/663837* ⊕ *www.duomodicagliari.it.*

Museo Archeologico. Built within the walls of the Pisan castle erected in the early 1300s, Cagliari's archaeological museum is the world's foremost authority on Sardinia's ancient "nuraghic" civilization, named after the curious stone towers, or *nuraghi,* that are unique to the island. Archaeologists date most of these enigmatic structures to about 1300–1200 BC, the same time the ancient Israelites were establishing themselves in Canaan. Among the highlights on display are bronze statuettes from nuraghic towers and tombs, and the much-celebrated Giganti di Mont'e Prama, giant stone statues representing warriors and boxers, unearthed in the 1970s and only recently restored. Other items worth seeking out in the museum include a pearl-laden Phoenician faience necklace, finds from the Tuvixeddu necropolis, remnants from the archaeological site of Nora, and medieval gold coins. ⊠ *Cittadella dei Musei, Piazza Arsenale* ☎ *070/655911* ⊕ *museoarcheocagliari.beniculturali.it* ⊠ *€7* ☾ *Closed Mon.*

Torre dell'Elefante. This medieval fortified tower was built in 1307 by Giovanni Capula, who also designed the San Pancrazio tower. Standing 100 feet high at the seaward end of Cagliari's bastions, it was used as a prison in the 1800s and is one of the main entrances to the Castello. ⊠ *Via Università* ⊕ *www.beniculturalicagliari.it* ⊠ *€3.*

Torre di San Pancrazio. Marking the edge of the Castello district, the 1305 tower of the imposing medieval Pisan defenses is just outside Cagliari's archaeological museum. You can climb up the limestone tower for a fabulous panorama of the city and its surroundings. As with other defensive structures of this period, the tower's back wall is missing, which allows you to see the series of wooden stairs and landings inside the cross section without climbing a step. ⊠ *Piazza Indipendenza* ⊕ *www.beniculturalicagliari.it* ⊠ *€3.*

OFF THE BEATEN PATH

San Sperate. Considered a *paese museo,* a "museum village," this small town 20 km (12 miles) northwest of Cagliari has houses whose walls have been brightened with murals by local artists and some well-known Italian painters. The murals were begun in the 1960s and continue to be expanded, transforming the entire town into an open-air art gallery with colorful trompe-l'oeils and artistic renderings of daily life. Look for suggestive stone and bronze sculptures by the world-renowned Pinuccio

Sciola that also pay tribute to the region's ancient history. ✉ *Via Sassari, San Sperate* 🌐 *www.sansperate.net.*

WHERE TO EAT

$$ ITALIAN
🍴 **Antico Caffè.** The gilded Antico Caffè once served as an intellectual haunt for famous writers like D. H. Lawrence and Grazia Deledda, who won the Nobel Prize in Literature in 1926. With its street-front terrace and polished-wood-and-brass interior, it has anchored the base of the Bastione di St. Remy since 1855, serving as a social center from breakfast time until well after midnight; the menu features local fish and meat specialties. **Known for:** traditional ambience; convenient location; swift lunches. [$] *Average main: €17* ✉ *Piazza Costituzione 10/11* ☎ *070/658206.*

$$$$ ITALIAN
🍴 **Dal Corsaro.** This highly regarded, elegant but simply furnished restaurant near the port offers modern and creative Italian haute cuisine on three tasting menus (€85, €95, and €105). Simpler and more traditional meals are available at the more casual bistro, Fork, with which it shares a kitchen (and entrance), where the à la carte and fixed-price lunch (€15) menus include such dishes as seafood antipasto, squid tagliatelle, and porcheddu. **Known for:** adventurous and sophisticated cuisine; eclectic taster menus; good-value snack lunches at next-door Fork. [$] *Average main: €85* ✉ *Viale Regina Margherita 28* ☎ *070/664318* 🌐 *www.stefanodeidda.it* 🕒 *Closed Mon. and Dec.–Mar.* 👔 *Jacket required.*

$$ ITALIAN
🍴 **Su Cumbidu.** A meal at this restaurant, which is in Cagliari's lively Marina quarter, near the port, makes for a quick and affordable introduction to Sardinia's rural cuisine. The mainly meat-based dishes can be ordered as part of a fixed-price meal or separately, and portions are large, so go easy on antipasti to leave room for the main courses of lamb, sausage, and the famous Sardinian specialty, porcheddu, or roast suckling pig. **Known for:** traditional meat-based dishes; casual, friendly atmosphere; range of set-price menus. [$] *Average main: €15* ✉ *Via Napoli 13* ☎ *070/670712.*

WHERE TO STAY

$ B&B/INN
🏨 **Hotel BJ Vittoria.** The airy, white rooms, period-style furnishings, and ceramic flooring make this central third-floor pension cozy and characterful. **Pros:** clean rooms; central location near port; air-conditioning. **Cons:** no breakfast; no parking; limited amenities. [$] *Rooms from: €104* ✉ *Via Roma 75* ☎ *070/667970, 349/4473556* 🌐 *www.hotelbjvittoria.it* 💳 *No credit cards* 🛏 *18 rooms* 🍽 *No meals.*

$$ HOTEL
🏨 **Hotel Regina Margherita.** Close to the port and the main sights in downtown Cagliari, this large, modern, four-star hotel has a quiet, calm, and friendly ambience, making it a popular stopover for businesspeople and holidaymakers alike. **Pros:** central position; some rooms have harbor views; free parking. **Cons:** lacks local character; few leisure facilities; breakfast choices sometimes disappoint. [$] *Rooms from: €137* ✉ *Viale Regina Margherita 44* ☎ *070/670342* 🌐 *www.hotelreginamargherita.com* 🛏 *100 rooms* 🍽 *Free Breakfast.*

$ B&B/INN
🏨 **La Ghirlanda.** This elegant apartment with high ceilings and a cool feel makes a quiet haven in the heart of Cagliari's bustling Marina quarter. **Pros:** affable, helpful owners; convenient location near the port and bus

17

and train stations; elegant rooms. **Cons:** no views from the rooms; no parking; breakfast in a bar. Ⓢ *Rooms from: €70* ⊠ *Via Lodovico Baylle 7* ☎ *070/2040610, 339/8892648* ⊕ *www.bnblaghirlanda.com* ⊟ *No credit cards* ⊘ *Closed Nov.–mid-Mar.* ⇗ *3 rooms* ⏉◯⏉ *Free Breakfast.*

$$
HOTEL
Fodor'sChoice
★
T Hotel. In the vicinity of Parco di Monte Claro, about a 15-minute taxi or bus ride from Cagliari's center, this trendy hotel offers contemporary styling and upscale guest rooms in a 15-floor, circular-shape tower with sweeping views of the city. **Pros:** designer rooms and bathrooms; great views from most rooms; free parking and Wi-Fi; outstanding service. **Cons:** 2 km (1¼ miles) from port; extra fee to use spa facilities; constant bustle in public areas. Ⓢ *Rooms from: €140* ⊠ *Via Dei Giudicati 66* ☎ *070/47400* ⊕ *www.thotel.it* ⇗ *207 rooms* ⏉◯⏉ *Free Breakfast.*

NIGHTLIFE AND PERFORMING ARTS

Cagliari's Teatro Lirico stages concerts with local and well-known European artists throughout the year. Contact the tourist office for information.

BARS AND CAFÉS

Caffè de Candia. Relax in the atmospheric interior or casual terrace of this café on the edge of Terrazza Umberto I. It's a great place to enjoy a cappuccino, snack lunch, or glass of vermentino after exploring the Castello quarter. The bar is open daily from 7 am until 9 pm during the week (later in summer) and until 2 am on weekends; DJs occasionally take over in the evenings. ⊠ *Bastione di St. Remy, Via Mario de Candia 3* ☎ *070/6407572.*

Caffè dell'Elfo. The café's central yet secluded location and casual ambience attracts local professionals, who linger in the evening over good wine, Italian snacks, and conversation. It's closed in the daytime and on Sunday, Monday, and Tuesday in winter. ⊠ *Salita Santa Chiara 4–6, off Piazza Yenne* ☎ *070/682399.*

Caffè Libarium Nostrum. A dim bohemian haunt full of wooden beams and brick-lined nooks and crannies, Libarium Nostrum is one of Cagliari's coolest café-bars. It's an occasional venue for live music and DJs, but the real draw is the outdoor terrace high atop Cagliari's medieval ramparts, with lounging sofas for enjoying cocktails and the views. Panini and other snacks are available. ⊠ *Via Santa Croce 33/35* ☎ *346/5220212.*

Caffè Svizzero. Entering this antique, vaulted, and frescoed bar a stone's throw from the port is like stepping back into the 19th century. Order a steaming cappuccino, a glass of the local vermentino, or a freshly squeezed fruit juice, and nibble on a panino, a pizzetta, or a pastry. It's all served with politeness and heaps of old-fashioned charm. ⊠ *Largo Carlo Felice 6–8* ☎ *070/653784* ⊘ *Closed Sun.*

Vinvoglio. In the heart of the old Castello quarter, the two stone-walled rooms of this nocturnal haunt offer an intimate and relaxed setting to enjoy local wines and, on weekends, live jazz. Simple bistro dishes are also available. Arrive early to be sure of a table. Closed daytime and Sunday. ⊠ *Via Lamarmora 45/47* ☎ *328/3592877* ⊕ *www.vinvoglio. wixsite.com/vinvogliojazzclub.*

SHOPPING

Cagliari's best shopping street, full of boutiques and specialty shops for clothes, shoes, bags, and jewelry, is **Via Manno**, just up from the port off Piazza Yenne.

ISOLA. The Istituto Sardo Organizzazione Lavoro Artigiano is a government-sponsored cooperative of artisans. Look for handmade ceramics, woven and wooden goods, baskets, metalwork, and beautiful gold filigree or precious stone jewelry. ☒ *Via Bacaredda 176* ☎ *070/492756* ⊕ *www.isolacagliari.com.*

Sapori di Sardegna. Drop into this shop for Sardinian food products, including local wines, artisanal biscuits, pecorino cheeses, carasau flatbread, honey, and olives. There's a great range of items, and the English-speaking staff are always willing to help you out. ☒ *Vico dei Mille 1* ☎ *070/6848747* ⊕ *www.saborescagliari.com.*

SPORTS AND THE OUTDOORS

BEACHES

FAMILY

Fodor'sChoice

★

Poetto Beach. Only 5 km (3 miles) southeast of the city center and easily accessible by a quick bus ride, Poetto Beach is one of the most enticing spots to relax in summer for both locals and tourists. Its shallow and clean turquoise waters stretch for some 8 km (5 miles), and the beach is lined with cafés, restaurants, snack stands, and parks. Beach lounging chairs and umbrellas are available for rent for €10–€12. From the large, sandy shores, you can admire the pink flamingos that nest in the marshy reeds of the nearby Molentargius lagoon. ■TIP→ **If you're in Cagliari, this postcard setting is a must. Amenities:** food and drink; toilets. **Best for:** swimming; walking. ☒ *Cagliari* ⊕ *Take Viale Diaz from Cagliari to Viale Poetto.*

BOATING AND SAILING

Lega Navale Italiana. This public, state-sponsored organization has information on the island's sailing facilities, as well as everything associated with maritime activity. ☎ *079/9102120, 320/9668519* ⊕ *www.leganavale.it.*

WINDSURFING

FAMILY

Windsurfing Club Cagliari. Sardinia has some of the best windsurfing spots in Europe; Club Cagliari provides advice for beginning to expert surfers. ☒ *Viale Marina Piccola* ☎ *070/372694, 345/2225169* ⊕ *www.windsurfingclubcagliari.it.*

PULA

29 km (18 miles) southwest of Cagliari, 314 km (195 miles) southwest of Olbia.

Resort villages sprawl along the coast southwest of the capital, which has its share of fine scenery and good beaches. On the marshy shoreline between Cagliari's Aeroporto di Elmas and Pula, huge flocks of flamingos are a common sight. Beaches and lodging catering to summer crowds are concentrated 4 km (2½ miles) south of Pula, a little more than 1½ km (1 mile) south of Nora, in a conglomeration that makes up the town of Santa Margherita di Pula. South of here lies one of Sardinia's most magnificent stretches of coastline, with white-sand beaches, turquoise waters, placid coves, and powdery dunes.

GETTING HERE AND AROUND

From Cagliari, drive approximately 40 km (25 miles) on the SS195. Follow directions for Pula/Chia. From Olbia, take SS131 toward Cagliari-Sassari; then, follow SS554 towards Pula/Chia. The journey is approximately 300 km (190 miles).

EXPLORING

Fodor's Choice ★ **Nora.** The narrow promontory outside Pula was the site of a Phoenician, Carthaginian, and then, later, Roman settlement that was first settled some 2,800 years ago. Nora was a prime location as a stronghold and important trading town—Phoenician settlers scouted for good harbors, cliffs to shelter their craft from the wind, and an elevation from which they could defend themselves against attack. An old Roman paved road passes the temple ruins, which include baths, a Roman theater, and an amphitheater now reserved for summer music festivals. Extensive excavations have shed light on life in this ancient city. The channels through which hot air rose to warm the Roman baths can still be made out. Note the difference between the Carthaginians' simple mosaic pavements and the Romans' more elaborate designs in well-preserved multicolor tiles. If the Mediterranean is calm, you can peek under clear waters along the shore for more ruins of the ancient city, which are slowly submerging due to rising seas, earthquakes, and erosion. ■ TIP→ **The archaeological museum at Pula is usually included in admission. The site opens at 9 am for private tours, otherwise at 10 am.** Guided tours usually begin on the hour. ✉ *3 km (2 miles) south of Pula* ☎ *070/9209138* 🎫 *€7.50.*

Sant'Efisio. The simple 11th-century church at the base of the Nora promontory plays a central part in one of the island's most colorful annual events. A four-day procession during the Festa di Sant'Efisio accompanies a statue of the martyred St. Efisius all the way from Cagliari to here and back again, culminating in a huge parade down Cagliari's main avenue—it fills up with costumed Sardinians and decorated *traccas,* or ox-drawn carriages. This is a must-see if you're in southern Sardinia from May 1 to May 4. ✉ *Nora Beach, 3 km (2 miles) south of Pula* 🕐 *Closed weekdays, also Sat. in winter.*

WHERE TO STAY

$$$$ HOTEL Fodor's Choice ★ 🏨 **Faro Capo-Spartivento.** At the end of a rocky track on the southernmost tip of Sardinia, housed within a working cliff-top lighthouse dating from 1856, this unusual hotel self-described as "a door suspended between the sky and the sea" is the ultimate escape, where guests can switch off and tune out in luxurious surroundings. **Pros:** select and secluded; good restaurant; personal attention. **Cons:** remote; difficult to access; extravagant rates. [$] *Rooms from: €600* ✉ *Viale Spartivento ✢ 5 km (3 miles) southwest of Chia* ☎ *333/3129638* 🌐 *www.farocapo-spartivento.com* 🛏 *11 rooms* 🍴 *Free Breakfast.*

$$ HOTEL FAMILY 🏨 **Is Molas Hotel and Golf Course.** If you love golf and stargazing, then the place to stay in southern Sardinia is this peaceful hotel, with 80 Mediterranean-style rooms and an 18-hole golf course. **Pros:** immediate access to golf course; freshwater pool; tranquil setting with rural views.

Cons: poor breakfasts; isolated location; beach shuttle service can be slow. $ *Rooms from: €127* ✉ *SS195, Località Is Molas* ☎ *070/9241006* ⊕ *www.ismolas.it* ⊗ *Closed Nov.–Mar.* ⬎ *80 rooms* ⊚ *Free Breakfast.*

$$$
RESORT
FAMILY
⬚ **Is Morus Relais.** A luxurious enclave hidden in a large palm-filled garden with undulating paths, the Is Morus sits on a sandy cove and has all the amenities of a fine beach resort. **Pros:** lovely grounds; large pool and poolside grill restaurant; good location. **Cons:** restaurant and bar service slow; needs modernizing; poor Wi-Fi. $ *Rooms from: €280* ✉ *SS195, Km 37.4* ☎ *070/921171, 070/921596* ⊕ *www.ismorus.com* ⊗ *Closed mid-Oct.–Mar.* ⬎ *73 rooms* ⊚ *Free Breakfast.*

SU NURAXI TO THE COSTA SMERALDA

A more traditional—and wilder—Sardinia awaits the traveler who ventures into the island's mountainous interior. Inland Sardinians are hardy souls, used to living in a climate that is as unforgiving in winter as it is intolerable in summer. This is, after all, the area that popularized the *vendetta*, a claim to personal revenge against another family or individual that sometimes endured from generation to generation. Old traditions like this are softening with time but are still firmly rooted in the social fabric.

The land is hilly, barren, and beautiful. Here, rare species of wildlife share the rocky uplands with sturdy medieval churches and the mysterious nuraghi left by prehistoric people. The nuraghi were built beginning in the 19th century BC, and they vary from single beehive-shape defensive towers to multitower complexes sheltering whole communities—prehistoric versions of medieval walled towns. As you move northward, the timeless beauty of the landscape begins to show greater signs of modern development. The sunny resort of Alghero, the Spanish-influenced port on the west coast, is one of the island's premier holiday spots. Costa Smeralda, the luxury resort complex on the northeast corner of Sardinia, is considered one of the most prestigious summer destinations for Europeans and continues to attract celebrities and the wealthy.

17

BARUMINI

Barumini is 65 km (40 miles) north of Cagliari.

It's definitely worth a detour to the quiet village of Barumini to visit the extraordinary stone village–fortress of Su Nuraxi.

GETTING HERE AND AROUND

The best way to reach Su Nuraxi is by car. From the capital, follow SS131 to SS197. Direct buses to the site are few and far between.

EXPLORING

FAMILY
Fodor's Choice
★
Su Nuraxi. The most extensive of the island's 7,000 discovered nuraghi, Su Nuraxi is significant enough to merit inclusion on the UNESCO World Heritage List. Concentric rings of thick stone walls conceal dark chambers and narrow passages in a central, beehive-shape tower. The excellent guided tour (which, depending on the nature of the group and language abilities of the guide, may be available in English) allows you

to explore the interior. In the ruins of the surrounding village there are benches, ovens, wells, and other Bronze Age remnants.

The specific functions of individual nuraghi remain a mystery, largely because their construction predates written history. Though this particular type of construction is unique to Sardinia in Italy, similar buildings dating from the same era are found in other parts of the Mediterranean, such as Cyprus and the Balearic islands off Spain. All visits are accompanied by a local guide, start every 30 minutes, and last for approximately 50 minutes. The same ticket also allows entry to a museum and exhibition center in Barumini. ■TIP→ If you're driving from SS131, don't be misled to other, lesser nuraghi—follow the signs all the way to Barumini. ⊠ *SP Barumini–Tuili, 1 km (½ mile) west of Barumini* ☎ *070/9368128* ⊕ *www.fondazionebarumini.it* 🖾 *€12.*

THARROS

16 km (10 miles) west of Oristano, 52 km (32 miles) northwest of Barumini.

Spread across a thin tongue of land that dangles off the Sinis Peninsula, the archaeological site of Tharros ranks as one of Sardinia's most important Phoenician, Carthaginian, and Roman settlements. It's not hard to understand why this evocative site was selected by the ancients, given its sweeping views across the Gulf of Oristano, its defensibility, and the shelter it provides for vessels. Founded around 800 BC, the city was finally abandoned in the 11th century AD, in favor of Oristano.

GETTING HERE AND AROUND

Whether you're heading to Tharros from the north or south, follow the SS131 to Oristano. Drive through Oristano towards Cabras, branching off on SP6 for San Giovanni di Sinis and Tharros.

EXPLORING

Museo Civico di Cabras. This lagoon-side archaeological museum displays many of the better-preserved urns and other artifacts recovered from nearby excavation sites, including Tharros. It is also the main home of the Giganti di Mont'e Prama—unique nuraghic stone statues recovered from the Sinis Peninsula in the 1970s but only recently viewable in their restored state. The visit takes about an hour. Buy a combination ticket to see the Museo Civico and the ruins at Tharros. ⊠ *Via Tharros, off SP6, 10 km (6 miles) northwest of Oristano, Cabras* ☎ *0783/290636* ⊕ *www.museocabras.it* 🖾 *€5, €8 with Tharros* ⊗ *Closed Mon. Nov.–Mar.*

FAMILY **Tharros.** The spectacular site of the Carthaginian and Roman city of Tharros, like Nora to the south, was chosen because it commanded the best views of the gulf and could provide an easy escape route if inland tribes threatened. The Phoenician-Punic city planning here includes sophisticated water channeling and masonry foundations. Two reconstructed Corinthian columns stand as testament to the site's Roman history, and there are baths visible and mosaic fragments from the Roman city. Look for the Cardo Maximus, the main road of the city, built to last for centuries. As at Nora, many more ruins are submerged

17

under water. A climb up the steep hill to a Spanish watchtower affords a scenic view over the Sinis Peninsula. There's a small souvenir shop and attached café for snacks and beverages. You can buy a combined ticket that also allows entry to the **Museo Civico di Cabras,** where some of the finds are displayed, though the best items are in Cagliari's archaeological museum. ⊠ *Off SP6 , 16 km (10 miles) west of Oristano, 113 km (70 miles) northwest of Cagliari, San Giovanni di Sinis* ☎ *0783/370019* ⊕ *www.tharros.sardegna.it* ☞ *€5, €8 with Museo Civico di Cabras* ⊘ *Closed Mon. Nov.–Mar.*

EN ROUTE

On the way to the archaeological ruins in Tharros you pass the ghost town of **San Salvatore,** revived briefly in the 1960s as a locale for spaghetti Westerns and since abandoned, except for a few days every summer, when it is the focus of a religious festival. The saloon from the movie set still stands. Among the dunes past San Salvatore are large rush huts formerly used by fishermen and now much in demand as back-to-nature vacation homes. The 5th-century church of **San Giovanni di Sinis,** on the Sinis Peninsula, is claimed to be the oldest Christian church in Sardinia.

NUORO

107 km (67 miles) northeast of Tharros, 181 km (113 miles) north of Cagliari.

The somewhat shabby provincial capital of Nuoro is on the edge of a gorge in the harsh mountainous area that culminates in Gennargentu, the island's highest massif (6,000 feet). Not much happens here; you can do some (relatively inexpensive) shopping amid strolling locals, or try the local Barbagia sausage, which is great. Just 40 km (25 miles) east of Nuoro is the coastal town of Cala Gonone. Cradled on Orosei Bay, this popular holiday destination has white-sand beaches, mountain views, and the mysterious water caves of Bue Marino.

GETTING HERE AND AROUND

From Cagliari, the drive to Nuoro takes about two hours. Take the SS131 toward Sassari/Oristano/Nuoro, then continue on SS131 DCN toward Nuoro/Olbia. After 55 km (34 miles), turn off, following signs for Nuoro Centro until you reach Nuoro.

FESTIVALS

Nuoro's **Festa del Redentore** (Feast of the Redeemer) is held on the next-to-last Sunday in August. It's the best time to view the various traditional costumes of Sardinia's interior all in one place. The culmination of the feast is the annual pilgrimage of worshippers to the bronze statue of Christ the Redeemer atop Monte Ortobene.

VISITOR INFORMATION

Contact Nuoro Tourism Office. ⊠ *Piazza Italia 8* ☎ *0784/238878.*

EXPLORING

Monte Ortobene. About 7 km (4 miles) northeast of Nuoro is Monte Ortobene, a granite peak at 2,900 feet offering lofty views over the gulch below. Here you can also see up close the imposing bronze statue of the Rendentore, or Christ the Redeemer, overlooking the city. Pilgrimages and mass take place in summer here. Picnic tables make this a favorite spot for an alfresco lunch throughout the year. The mountain is easily reachable via SP45 from Nuoro. ☒ *Nuoro* ⊕ *www.comune.nuoro.it.*

Museo Etnografico Sardo. This ethnographic collection is a must for anyone interested in the cultural context of Sardinia's customs and traditions. Among the 8,000 items in the museum's collection, you can view domestic and agricultural implements, splendid jewelry, traditional musical instruments, and dozens of local costumes. The nearby park on Sant'Onofrio Hill affords magnificent views over Nuoro and the surrounding country. ☒ *Via A. Mereu 56* ☎ *0784/257035* ⊕ *www. isresardegna.it* ☜ *€5* ⊘ *Closed Mon.*

WHERE TO EAT

$$
ITALIAN
FAMILY
Fodor's Choice
★

✕ **Il Portico.** Brotherly love (and ownership) is what makes this old-town restaurant so exceptional, in addition to the quality seafood dishes. Modern artwork, stone pillars, and arched ceilings give way to tables draped in gold linen. **Known for:** innovative takes on traditional cuisine; locals' choice; welcoming atmosphere. $ *Average main: €15* ☒ *Via Mons. Bua 13* ☎ *0784/232909* ⊕ *www.ilporticonuoro.it* ⊘ *Closed Mon., 2 wks in July and Aug., and 2 wks in Jan. and Feb. No dinner Sun.*

$$
ITALIAN
FAMILY

✕ **Il Rifugio.** Family run since 1988, this local spot is packed nearly every night; the dining area is rustic with terra-cotta flooring, brick pillars, straw-base chairs, and a wood-burning stove. The service, presentation, food, and wine list are all exceptional, and only the freshest of local meats and cheeses are served. **Known for:** boisterous and convivial air; unpretentious but well-prepared local dishes; amiable staff. $ *Average main: €16* ☒ *Via A. Mereu 28/36* ☎ *0784/232355* ⊕ *www.trattoriarifugio.com* ⊘ *Closed Wed.*

WHERE TO STAY

$
HOTEL

▦ **Euro Hotel.** Centrally located, this simple, block-style hotel—more or less standard for provincial Nuoro—is ideal for a stopover; rooms are spacious and clean, with parquet flooring and modern amenities. **Pros:** budget rates; ample parking; near train station. **Cons:** not much character; outdated rooms; no restaurant. $ *Rooms from: €90* ☒ *Via Trieste 62* ☎ *0784/34071* ⊕ *www.eurohotelnuoro.it* ⇌ *54 rooms* ⦿ *Free Breakfast.*

$
B&B/INN

▦ **Silvia e Paolo.** Overlooking the cafés and shops of the old town's traffic-free Corso, this quaint bed-and-breakfast has three spacious bedrooms. **Pros:** great location; friendly owners; excellent value. **Cons:** parking may be tricky to find; two rooms share a bathroom; breakfast unavailable after 9:30; checkout at 10. $ *Rooms from: €55* ☒ *Corso Giuseppe Garibaldi 58* ☎ *0784/31280, 328/9212199* ⊕ *www.silviaepaolo.it* ⊘ *Closed mid-Dec.–mid-Jan.* ⇌ *3 rooms* ⦿ *Free Breakfast.*

$$$
HOTEL
Fodor's Choice
★

▦ **Su Gologone.** In the foothills of the Supramonte mountains, you'll find this luxury hotel, where the rooms are country retreats, decked out with traditional Sardinian fabrics, wood chests, paintings, and exposed wood-beam ceilings. **Pros:** locally influenced restaurant; great location for hiking in the Supramonte Valley; museum-like decor. **Cons:** used by groups and wedding parties; some rooms are distant from the

17

main reception area; very remote. $ *Rooms from: €283* ⊠ *Località Su Gologone, Oliena* ☎ *0784/287512* ⊕ *www.sugologone.it* ۞ *Closed early Nov.–late Mar.* ⤲ *70 rooms* ❍❶ *Free Breakfast.*

FONNI

30 km (19 miles) south of Nuoro, 137 km (85 miles) south of Olbia.

In the heart of the Barbagia region, Fonni is the highest town on the island. This mountainous district, including Monte Spada and the Bruncu Spina refuge on the Gennargentu Massif, is Sardinia's most primitive. Life in some villages seems not to have changed much since the Middle Ages. Here a rigidly patriarchal society perpetuates age-old customs and obedience to rural traditions. Although as a tourist you may be looked at with curiosity, a smile can go a long way. High mountain roads wind and loop through the landscape; towns are small and undistinguished, their social fabric formed in complete isolation. On feast days elaborate local costumes are worn as an explicit statement of community identity.

GETTING HERE AND AROUND

To reach Fonni, the highest town in Sardinia, drive (or hire a car and driver) or take a bus from Nuoro. There is no train service.

From Nuoro, take SS389 from the junction of Mamoiada, or take SS128 to the town of Gavoi. From Cagliari, follow SS131, exiting toward the village of Ottana. Continue on SS128, turning at Fonni. From Sassari, follow SS131 south, turning east onto SS129 at Macomer. Continue on SS128, following signs for Fonni.

FESTIVALS

You can see one of the most characteristic of the Barbagia's celebrations in local costume during the **Festa di San Giovanni**, held June 24, in honor of St. John. Events include *palios*, or horse races, live music, and fireworks.

WHERE TO STAY

$ ☷ **Hotel Sa Orte.** Close to the highest peaks of the Gennargentu range
HOTEL   in the center of Sardinia, this hotel, a palazzo in the center of Fonni, provides a warm welcome at any time of the year. **Pros:** generous breakfasts; affable staff; convenient for mountain excursions. **Cons:** some rooms are small and dark; few facilities; no views. $ *Rooms from: €80* ⊠ *Via Roma 14* ☎ *0784/58020* ⊕ *www.hotelsaorte.it* ⤲ *26 rooms* ❍❶ *Free Breakfast.*

ALGHERO

137 km (85 miles) southwest of Olbia.

A tourist-friendly town of about 45,000 inhabitants with a distinctly Spanish flavor, Alghero is also known as "Barcelonetta" (little Barcelona) for its strong Catalan links. Rich wrought-iron scrollwork decorates balconies and screened windows; Spanish motifs appear in stone portals and bell towers. The town was built and inhabited in the 14th century by the Aragonese and Catalans, who constructed seaside ramparts and sturdy towers encompassing an inviting nucleus of narrow, winding streets with honey-color palazzi. The native language spoken here is closer to Catalan than Italian, although you probably have to attend one of the masses conducted in Algherese (or listen in on stories swapped by older fishermen) to hear it.

Besides its historic architectural gems such as the cathedral and Palazzo d'Albis, the fortified city is well worth a visit to simply stroll and discover local culture on narrow cobblestone streets. The city also has a reputation for serving great food at reasonable prices.

GETTING HERE AND AROUND

Alghero International Airport is 15 km (9 miles) from the city center, which you can reach by car, taxi, or public transport. Regional buses connect the town with Sassari and local villages. The closest passenger port to Alghero is Porto Torres, approximately 40 km (25 miles) away.

VISITOR INFORMATION

Contact Alghero Tourism Office. ✉ *Largo Lo Quarter* ☎ *079/979054* 🌐 *www.algheroturismo.eu.*

EXPLORING

Capo Caccia. Head 25 km (16 miles) west of Alghero for the spectacular heights of the imposing limestone headland of Capo Caccia. The rugged promontory, blanketed by thick maquis (brush), forms part of Porto Conte nature reserve and is home to deep caves such as the Grotta di Nettuno. Close by are the beaches of Porto Ferro, Cala Viola and, on the beautiful Porto Conte inlet, Cala Dragunara. ✉ *Alghero* 🌐 *www.parcodiportoconte.it.*

17

FAMILY Fodor's Choice ★

Grotta di Nettuno (*Neptune's Cave*). At the base of a sheer cliff, the pounding sea has carved an entrance to a vast fantastic cavern filled with stunning water pools, stalactites, and stalagmites. The dramatic cave and coves, discovered by fishermen in the 18th century, are popular tourist attractions for their sheer natural beauty. You must visit with a guide; tours start on the hour. It's possible to reach the caves by boat or by land. Between March and October, boat trips depart regularly from the port of Alghero for €16 round-trip (admission to the grotto is extra). To reach the grotto by land, you can descend the 654 dizzying steps of Escala del Cabirol ("Goat Steps"), which are cut into the steep cliff here. ■ TIP→ **By public bus from Alghero's Via Catalogna, the trip to the top of the stairway takes about 50 minutes. Allow 15 minutes for the descent by foot.** ✉ *Off SP55, 13 km (8 miles) west of Alghero* ☎ *079/946540* 🎫 *€13.*

WHERE TO EAT

$$ ITALIAN

🍴 **Il Pavone.** Fresh flowers on white linen tablecloths add color to the bright, glass-encased dining area of this delightful eatery on busy Piazza Sulis; oversize wine bottles capped in wax add Italian charm, and gold-framed paintings cover the back wall. Although the menu changes seasonally, you're likely to find pasta and seafood dishes such as tagliatelle with shrimp, or ravioli au gratin. **Known for:** delicious mains and desserts; impressive wine list; attentive and knowledgeable service. [$] *Average* main: €19 ⊠ *Piazza Sulis 3* ☎ *079/979584* ⊕ *www.ilpavoneristorante. com* ⊗ *Closed 2 wks in Nov. No dinner Sun. late Nov.–Mar.*

$$
SEAFOOD
✕ **La Lepanto.** A covered veranda by the seafront marks out Alghero's top seafood restaurant, an expansive and sunny room complete with crustacean-filled aquarium. It's usually crowded with both locals and tourists in summer. **Known for:** superior seafood in all its forms, including lobster; bright interior with veranda seating; central location. $ *Average main: €19* ⊠ *Via Carlo Alberto 135* ☎ *079/979116* ⊕ *www.lalepanto. com* ⊗ *Closed Jan. and Feb., and Tues. in Mar.*

WHERE TO STAY

$$$
HOTEL
FAMILY
Carlos V. On the shore boulevard opposite the Villa Las Tronas and 15 minutes from the airport, this grand, modern hotel (pronounced "Carlos Quinto") has an array of gardens and terraces, and a huge saltwater pool with sea views. **Pros:** wonderful vistas; good-size pool; a bargain in low season, when rates drop. **Cons:** large-hotel atmosphere; mediocre breakfasts; restricted menu for half- or full-board guests. $ *Rooms from: €244* ⊠ *Lungomare Valencia 24* ☎ *079/9720600* ⊕ *www.hotel-carlosv.it* ⇌ *179 rooms* ⦿⦿ *Free Breakfast.*

$
B&B/INN
San Francesco. The convent that was once attached to the church of San Francesco is a very handy hotel. **Pros:** historic ambience; central location; very tranquil. **Cons:** limited Wi-Fi; somber, sparsely furnished rooms; not a good choice for kids. $ *Rooms from: €95* ⊠ *Via Machin 2* ☎ *079/980330* ⊕ *www.sanfrancescohotel.com* ⊗ *Closed mid-Nov.– Dec.* ⇌ *21 rooms* ⦿⦿ *Free Breakfast.*

$$$$
HOTEL
Fodor's Choice
★
Villa Las Tronas Hotel & Spa. Privacy, elegance, and charm are among the draws of this secluded, stunning mansion estate built more than a century ago. **Pros:** regal setting and exceptional views; incredible service; luxury spa; open year-round, a rarity in these parts. **Cons:** very expensive; rocky beach; usually a three-night minimum stay June–Sept. $ *Rooms from: €331* ⊠ *Lungomare Valencia 1* ☎ *079/981818* ⊕ *www. hotelvillalastronas.it* ⇌ *24 rooms* ⦿⦿ *Free Breakfast.*

SHOPPING

De Filippis. On the so-called Riviera del Corallo, Alghero has long been famed for its coral products, fashioned into elegant jewelry. This shop, with three outlets within a few yards of each other in the old town, has an impressive range of bracelets, brooches, and necklaces. ⊠ *Via Carlo Alberto 23* ☎ *079/979394* ⊕ *www.defilippis.it.*

NIGHTLIFE

Café Latino. In prime position on Alghero's broad city walls, with views down to the yachting marina and across to Capo Caccia, this makes a wonderful place to pause by day or night with a spritz or fruit juice. The menu has a number of food items, too. There's a second entrance, opposite the cathedral on Via Sant'Erasmo. It's closed January to mid-February. ⊠ *Bastioni Magellano 10* ☎ *079/976541* ⊕ *www.cafelatino.it.*

SASSARI

34 km (21 miles) northeast of Alghero, 212 km (132 miles) north of Cagliari.

With a population of about 130,000, Sassari, the island's second-largest city, is an important university town and administrative center, notable for its history of intellectualism and bohemian student culture, an ornate old cathedral, and a good archaeological museum. Look for downtown vendors of *fainè*, a pizzalike chickpea-flour pancake glistening with olive oil, which is a Genoese and Sassarese specialty. The mazelike old town is blissfully isolated from the chaotic traffic swirling though the newer neighborhoods—Sassari is the hub of several highways and secondary roads leading to various coastal resorts, among them Stintino and Castelsardo.

GETTING HERE AND AROUND

Sassari can be reached by plane, ferry, train, bus, or car. The nearest airport is Alghero-Fertilia, about 30 km (19 miles) from Sassari. Inexpensive buses can get you to the center of Sassari. The closest port is Porto Torres, about 20 km (12½ miles) away. Ferries connect Sassari to Genoa and Civitavecchia (Rome). Frequent bus and train services operate between Sassari and Cagliari, Olbia, and Alghero.

VISITOR INFORMATION

Contact Sassari. ⊠ *Via Sebastiano Satta 13* ☎ *079/2008072* ⊕ *www.turismo-sassari.it.*

EXPLORING

Duomo. The elegant stone Duomo is Sassari's must-see sight. The cathedral, dedicated to St. Nicolas, Santa Claus's inspiration, took more than half a millennium to build: the foundations were laid in the 12th century, and the Spanish colonial–style facade was completed in the 18th. Of particular interest in the interior are the ribbed Gothic vaults, the 14th-century painting of the Madonna del Bosco on the high altar, and the early-19th-century tomb of Placido Benedetto di Savoia, the uncle of united Italy's first king. ⊠ *Piazza Duomo 3* ☎ *079/233185* 🎟 *Free.*

FAMILY **Museo Sanna.** Sassari's excellent museum has Sardinia's best archaeological collection outside Cagliari, spanning nuraghic, Carthaginian, and Roman histories, including well-preserved bronze statuettes, household objects from the 2nd millennium BC, and decorated amphorae. ⊠ *Via Roma 64* ☎ *079/272203* ⊕ *www.musei.sardegna.beniculturali.it* 🎟 *€3* ⊗ *Closed Sun. (except 1st Sun. of month) and Mon.*

WHERE TO EAT

$$ ✕ **L'Assassino.** Get a true taste of local Sassarese cooking—and many ITALIAN other Sardinian specialties—at this family-run restaurant in the old town. The menu is not for the squeamish or for vegetarians: horse, donkey, and roast suckling pig (*porcetto,* also spelled *porcheddu*) figure prominently, as do typical Sassarese dishes such as *trippa alla parmigiana* (tripe with Parmesan), *lumaconi in rosso* (snails in a rich tomato sauce), and *cordula con piselli* (sheep's intestines with peas). **Known for:** down-home local cooking; merry atmosphere; pleasant

courtyard seating in summer. [$] *Average main: €16* ✉ *Via Pettenadu 19* ☎ *079/233463* 🌐 *www.trattorialassassino.it* 🕓 *Closed Mon. Oct.–Apr.*

CASTELSARDO

32 km (20 miles) northeast of Sassari.

The walled seaside citadel of Castelsardo holds tiny shops crammed with all kinds of souvenirs, particularly woven baskets, but also rugs and wrought iron. The **Roccia dell'Elefante** (Elephant Rock) on the road into Castelsardo was hollowed out by primitive man to be used as a burial chamber. The local name for one is *domus de janas* (literally, "fairy house").

GETTING HERE AND AROUND

In summer, a daily bus runs between Alghero Airport and Castelsardo. Tickets can be purchased directly from the driver. Check the ARST bus service timetable from Sassari, which operates a route with stops in Castelsardo. The trip takes about an hour. The main bus stop in Castelsardo is located in the central Piazza Pianedda. There is also a stop on the seafront by the beach.

By car, access from Alghero, heading toward Porto Torres. Follow signs for Sassari onto the SS200, merging onto the SS134. Follow signs for Santa Teresa Gallura—the route takes you along the beautiful coastline.

SANTA TERESA GALLURA

100 km (62 miles) northeast of Sassari, 65 km (41 miles) northwest of Olbia.

At the northern tip of Sardinia, Santa Teresa Gallura retains the relaxed, carefree air of a former fishing village. Nearby beaches rival those farther down the coast, but manage not to be as overcrowded with tourists.

GETTING HERE AND AROUND

Ferry crossings from Bonifacio in Corsica operate regularly, up to four times per day. The trip lasts about 50 minutes.

By car, you can drive from Olbia following the SS125 in the direction of Arzachena-Palau. At the fork in Palau, turn left to Santa Teresa Gallura. Continue for 25 km (16 miles). From Cagliari, follow SS131 to Sassari. Before the city center, exit Sassari Latte Dolce, heading in the direction of Platamona-Castesardo, which leads to the scenic coastal road Porto Torres–Santa Teresa.

From Alghero, follow SS291 until Sassari. Continue toward Porto Torres until you reach the northern part of the island.

There is no train station in Santa Teresa Gallura. The nearest main-line train station is in Olbia.

WHERE TO STAY

$ B&B/INN 🏨 **Canne al Vento.** Family-run Canne al Vento has been a quiet, cheerful haven in town since the late 1950s; despite a bland exterior, the place has a defiantly rustic feel, with a bamboo-roof breakfast area and the odd ornamental wagon wheel. **Pros:** abundant and memorable breakfasts; personal, friendly service; clean and orderly rooms. **Cons:** old-fashioned; on a main road; a lengthy walk from the beach. $ *Rooms from: €95* ⊠ *Via Nazionale 23, Santa Teresa Gallura* ☎ *0789/754219* ⊗ *Closed Oct.–Mar.* ⌿ *22 rooms* ⦿⧸ *Breakfast.*

$$ ⊡ **Hotel Corallaro.** A brief walk from the town center, this hotel occupies
HOTEL a panoramic spot right by the beach and has functional, mostly spacious
FAMILY rooms, some with balconies and sea views. **Pros:** welcoming management and staff; steps away from the excellent Rena Bianca beach; airy rooms with plenty of storage space. **Cons:** the few rooms with sea views and balconies fill up early; poor buffet breakfasts; attracts groups. $ *Rooms from: €196* ⊠ *Spiaggia Rena Bianca, Santa Teresa Gallura* ☎ *0789/755475* ⊕ *www.hotelcorallaro.it* ⊗ *Closed early Oct.–mid-May* ⌿ *82 rooms* ⦿⧸ *Free Breakfast.*

LA MADDALENA

45 km (20 miles) northwest of Olbia, 68 km (42 miles) northeast of Castelsardo.

From the port of Palau you can visit the archipelago of La Maddalena, seven granite islands embellished with aromatic scrub and wind-bent pines. The most significant of the handful of sites to see here is Giuseppe Garibaldi's home and tomb. Explore the lively port (also called La Maddalena), then head to one of several picture-postcard coves, the perfect spot for a picnic and to rejuvenate after your journey to the archipelago.

GETTING HERE AND AROUND

The only way to get to this small island is by boat or ferry. From Olbia, take a bus or drive to Palau, then catch the ferry to La Maddalena. During the day, car ferries make the 3-km (2-mile) trip two to four times an hour. The town center is right in front of the dock. Local buses are available for accessing the beaches, although the island is best explored by scooter or bike.

EXPLORING

Fodor'sChoice **Compendio Garibaldino.** Pilgrims from around the world converge on the
★ Compendio Garibaldino, a complex on Isola Caprera that contains the restored home, a museum, and the tomb of Giuseppe Garibaldi (1807–82). The national hero and military leader who laid the groundwork for the first unification of Italy in 1861 lived a simple life as a farmer on the island that he eventually owned. There are guided tours in Italian, and written guides in other languages. You can also buy a combined ticket for the Compendio and the Memoriale Giuseppe Garibaldi, 4 km (2½ miles) away, a multimedia museum that chronicles the swashbuckling career of the Italian hero. For both, take the ferry to Isola Maddalena and then the bridge to Caprera. ⊠ *7 km (4½ miles) east of Isola Maddalena, Caprera* ☎ *0789/727162* ⊕ *www.compendiogaribaldino.it* ⊡ *€7 (free 1st Sun. of month in winter); €11 combined ticket includes Memoriale Giuseppe Garibaldi* ⊗ *Closed Mon. Easter–Oct., and Sun. Nov.–Easter (except 1st Sun. of month).*

17

PORTO CERVO

35 km (22 miles) southeast of La Maddalena, 30 km (19 miles) north of Olbia.

Sardinia's northeastern coast is fringed with low cliffs, inlets, and small bays. This has become an upscale vacationland, with glossy resorts such as Baia Sardinia and Porto Rotondo just outside the confines of the famed Costa Smeralda. Some of Italy's most expensive hotels are here, and magnificent yachts anchor in the waters of Porto Cervo. Golf courses, yacht clubs, and numerous alfresco restaurants and bars cater to those who want to see and be seen.

All along the coast, carefully tended lush vegetation surrounds vacation villages and discreet villas that have sprung up in eclectic architectural styles best described as "bogus Mediterranean." The trend has been to keep this an enclave of the very rich. Outside the peak season, however, prices dip and the majesty of the natural surroundings shines through, justifying all the hype and the Emerald Coast's fame as one of the truly romantic corners of the Mediterranean.

GETTING HERE AND AROUND

Porto Cervo is accessible by boat, car, taxi, and bus. Buses run regularly from Olbia and Palau.

Whichever airport or port of entry into Sardinia you choose, head to Olbia. By car, follow SS125 north towards Arzachena and Costa Smeralda. After 10 km (6 miles), turn right onto SP73 toward Porto Rotondo/Porto Cervo. Continue on SP94 and turn onto SP59 to Porto Cervo. The trip takes about 30 minutes.

WHERE TO STAY

$$$$ RESORT Fodor's Choice ★ **Cala di Volpe.** Long a magnet for the beautiful people, this hyperglamorous five-star Starwood hotel was designed by Jacques Couëlle to resemble an ancient Sardinian fishing village, with its own covered wooden bridge. **Pros:** stunning architecture and grounds; luxurious ambience; professional staff. **Cons:** some rooms disappoint; astronomical rates for room, additional amenities, drinks, and meals; car necessary. [$] *Rooms from: €1,036* ✉ *Cala di Volpe* ☎ *0789/976111* 🌐 *www.caladivolpe.com* 🕓 *Closed early Oct.–late Apr.* 🛏 *121 rooms* 🍴 *Free Breakfast.*

$$$$ HOTEL **Cervo Hotel, Costa Smeralda Resort.** Designed in 1963 by the architect Luigi Vietti, the Cervo Hotel is an integral part of the surrounding resort; low Mediterranean buildings with Spanish tile roofs surround a large pool and garden in the heart of Porto Cervo. **Pros:** open year-round; prime location; superb service. **Cons:** no nearby beach; outdated in places; poor fitness facilities; very expensive rates and extras. [$] *Rooms from: €470* ✉ *Waterfront* ☎ *0789/931111* 🌐 *www.hotelcervocostasmeralda.com* 🛏 *96 rooms* 🍴 *Free Breakfast.*

$$ HOTEL **Nibaru.** Lush gardens and pinkish-red brick buildings with tiled roofs lend this hotel on a secluded inlet the feel of a small resort. **Pros:** courteous staff; nice pool; close to good beaches. **Cons:** no restaurant; no sea view; car necessary to explore the area. [$] *Rooms from: €171* ✉ *Località Cala di Volpe* ☎ *0789/96038* 🌐 *www.hotelnibaru.it* 🕓 *Closed early Oct.–Apr.* 🛏 *58 rooms* 🍴 *Free Breakfast.*

SPORTS AND THE OUTDOORS
BEACHES

The beaches around the Costa Smeralda are some of the most exclusive in Europe, and they don't disappoint, with fine golden sand sheltered by red cliffs and fronting azure waters. Many can only be reached by boat, and there are regular launches from Porto Cervo. Rentals of sun beds and towels are as expensive as you'd expect.

BOATING AND SAILING

Yacht Club Costa Smeralda. The Aga Khan IV and some local associates founded the yacht club in 1967 with a view to promoting nautical activities. The club provides use of its pool, restaurant, bar, and guest rooms to those with memberships at associated yacht clubs. Watch for regattas from June to September, and check out the YCCS Sailing School, which organizes courses on dinghies and cabin cruisers. ✉ *Via della Marina* ☎ *0789/902200* ⊕ *www.yccs.it.*

GOLF

Pevero Golf Course. Designed by Robert Trent Jones Sr. and opened in 1972, Pevero is a world-class course with some of Europe's most beautiful fairways. Stretching nearly 6½ km (4 miles) between the Gulf of Pevero and Cala di Volpe (Bay of Foxes), it provides challenging playing conditions with 70 bunkers, several rocks, and vegetation. The dress code is formal in the upscale Club House. ✉ *Cala di Volpe 20* ☎ *0789/958046* ⊕ *www.peverogolfclub.com* ☑ *€70–€130, depending on season; €50 for golf cart* ⌖ *18 holes, 6700 yards, par 72.*

OLBIA

30 km (19 miles) south of Porto Cervo.

Amid the resorts of Sardinia's northeastern coast, Olbia, a town of about 60,000, is a lively little seaport and port of call for mainland ferries at the head of a long, wide bay.

GETTING HERE AND AROUND

The main airport, Olbia–Costa Smeralda, is only 1½ km (1 mile) from the town center. Inexpensive city buses and taxis are available outside the terminal. Trains operate between Olbia and Cagliari and take about four hours. If you're driving, main roads are clearly marked to reach the city center, outlying areas, and other major towns.

The Olbia–Isola Bianca harbor provides daily connections with the Italian mainland, less than 300 km (186 miles) away. Regular ferries arrive from Genoa, Civitavecchia, and Livorno. Most ferries take between 4 and 10 hours.

VISITOR INFORMATION

Contact Olbia. ✉ *Municipio, Via Dante 1, at Corso Umberto I* ☎ *0789/52206* ⊕ *www.olbiaturismo.it.*

EXPLORING

Basilica San Simplicio. Olbia's little Catholic basilica, a short walk behind the main Corso Umberto I and past the train station, is worth searching out if you have any spare time in Olbia. The simple granite structure dates from the 11th century, part of the great Pisan church-building

17

program, using pillars and columns recycled from Roman buildings. The basilica has a bare, somewhat somber interior, its three naves separated by a series of arches. ⊠ *Via San Simplicio at Via Fausto Noce* ☎ *0789/23542.*

WHERE TO EAT AND STAY

$$
ITALIAN
✕ **Il Gambero.** This backstreet trattoria has a strong rustic flavor, its two rooms ornamented with brass cooking pots, colorful embroideries, old photographs, and agricultural knickknacks. The menu, too, has a local focus, and might include tagliatelle with chestnuts, porcini mushrooms, and smoked ricotta, and tuna with a pistachio crust and balsamic dressing. **Known for:** simple, rustic decor; fresh local meat and seafood dishes; informal but discreet service. $ *Average main: €17* ⊠ *Via Lamarmora 6* ☎ *0789/23874* ⊘ *Closed Mon.*

$$
HOTEL
🏨 **La Locanda del Conte Mameli.** Housed in a remodeled palazzo built at the end of the 19th century for the count after which it is named, this hotel occupies a quiet location on a cobbled backstreet just a few steps from Corso Umberto. **Pros:** small hotel with personal service; antique furnishings; central but quiet location. **Cons:** tricky to access by car; some rooms are slightly cramped and gloomy; breakfast not up to scratch. $ *Rooms from: €141* ⊠ *Via delle Terme 8* ☎ *0789/23008* ⊕ *www.lalocandadelcontemameli.com* ⤳ *8 rooms* ⦿ *Free Breakfast.*

$$$$
HOTEL
🏨 **Petra Segreta Resort and Spa.** Sea and mountain views, top-quality cuisine, and spacious guest rooms that ooze chic, modern charm are the main draws at this romantic boutique hotel outside the picturesque village of San Pantaleo. **Pros:** tranquil mountainside setting with spectacular views; blend of traditional surroundings and modern amenities; two good restaurants. **Cons:** remote and isolated; not suitable for families; three-night minimum stay. $ *Rooms from: €495* ⊠ *Via Buddeu, San Pantaleo* ☎ *0789/1876441* ⊕ *www.petrasegretaresort.com* ⊘ *Closed late Oct.–early Apr.* ⤳ *24 rooms* ⦿ *Free Breakfast.*

TRAVEL SMART
ITALY

GETTING HERE AND AROUND

▌ AIR TRAVEL

Most nonstop flights between North America and Italy serve Rome and Milan, though the airports in Venice, Pisa and Naples also accommodate nonstop flights from the United States. Many travelers find it more convenient to connect via a European hub to Florence, Bologna, or another smaller Italian airport.

Flying time to Milan or Rome is approximately 8–8½ hours from New York, 10–11 hours from Chicago, and 11½ hours from Los Angeles.

Labor strikes are not as frequent in Italy as they were some years ago, but when they do occur they can affect not only air travel, but also local public transit that serves airports. Your airline will usually have details about strikes affecting its flight schedules.

A helpful website for information (location, phone numbers, local transportation, etc.) about all of the airports in Italy is ⊕ *www.italianairportguide.com*.

Airline Security Issues Transportation Security Administration (*TSA*). ☎ 866/289–9673 ⊕ www.tsa.gov.

AIRPORTS

The major gateways to Italy include Rome's Aeroporto Leonardo da Vinci (FCO), better known as Fiumicino, and Milan's Aeroporto Malpensa (MXP). Most flights to Venice, Florence, and Pisa make connections at Fiumicino and Malpensa or another European airport hub. You can take the Ferrovie dello Stato (FS) airport train or bus to Rome's Termini station or to Cadorna or Centrale in Milan; from the latter you can then catch a train to any other location in Italy. It'll take about 40 minutes to get from Fiumicino to Roma Termini, less than an hour to Milano Centrale.

Many carriers fly into the smaller airports. Milan also has Linate (LIN) and

Orio al Serio (BGY) airports and Rome has Ciampino (CIA). Venice is served by Aeroporto di Venezia Marco Polo (VCE), Naples by Aeroporto Internazionale di Napoli Capodichino (NAP), Palermo by Aeroporto di Palermo (PMO) and Cagliari by Aeroporto Elmas (CAG). Florence is serviced by Aeroporto di Firenze (FLR) and by Aeroporto di Pisa (PSA), which is about 2 km (1 mile) outside the center of Pisa and about one hour from Florence. Aeroporto de Bologna (BLQ) is a 20-minute direct Aerobus ride away from Bologna Centrale, which is 35 minutes from Florence by high-speed train.

Many Italian airports have undergone renovations in recent years and have been ramping up security measures, which include random baggage inspection and bomb-detection dogs. All airports have restaurants, snack bars, shopping, and Wi-Fi access. Each also has at least one nearby hotel. In the cases of Milan Linate, Florence, Pisa, Naples, and Bologna, the city centers are less than a 15-minute taxi or bus ride away—so if you encounter a long delay, spend it in town.

When you take a connecting flight from a European airline hub (Frankfurt or Paris, for example) to a local Italian airport (Florence or Venice), be aware that your luggage might not make it onto the second plane with you. The airlines' lost-luggage service is efficient, however, and your delayed luggage is usually delivered to your hotel or holiday rental within 12–24 hours.

Airport Information Aeroporto di Bologna (*BLQ, aka Guglielmo Marconi*). ⊠ 6 km (4 miles) northwest of Bologna ☎ 051/6479615 5 am–midnight ⊕ www.bologna-airport.it. **Aeroporto di Cagliari.** ⊠ 7 km (4½ miles) from Cagliari, Via dei Trasvolatori, Elmas, Cagliari ☎ 070/211211 ⊕ www.cagliari-airport.com. **Aeroporto di Firenze** (*FLR, aka Amerigo Vespucci or Peretola*). ⊠ 6 km (4 miles) northwest of Florence ☎ 055/3061300

⊕ *www.aeroporto.firenze.it.* **Aeroporto di Milan Linate** (*LIN*). ⊠ *8 km (5 miles) southeast of Milan* ☏ *02/232323* ⊕ *www.milanolinate. eu.* **Aeroporto di Palermo** (*PMO, aka Falcone e Borsellino or Punta Raisi*). ⊠ *32 km (19 miles) northwest of Palermo* ☏ *091/7020111, 800/541880 toll-free in Italy* ⊕ *www.gesap.it.* **Aeroporto di Pisa** (*PSA, aka Aeroporto Galileo Galilei*). ⊠ *2 km (1 mile) south of Pisa, 80 km (50 miles) west of Florence* ☏ *050/849300* ⊕ *www.pisa-airport.com.* **Aeroporto di Roma Ciampino** (*CIA*). ⊠ *15 km (9 miles) southwest of Rome* ☏ *06/65951* ⊕ *www.adr.it.* **Aeroporto di Venezia** (*VCE, aka Marco Polo*). ⊠ *6 km (4 miles) north of Venice* ☏ *041/2609260* ⊕ *www. veniceairport.com.* **Aeroporto Fiumicino** (*FCO, aka Leonardo da Vinci*). ⊠ *35 km (20 miles) southwest of Rome* ☏ *06/65951* ⊕ *www.adr. it.* **Aeroporto Internazionale di Napoli** (*NAP, aka Capodichino*). ⊠ *7 km (4 miles) northeast of Naples* ☏ *081/7896111 weekdays 8–4, 848/888777 flight info* ⊕ *www.aeroportodi-napoli.it.* **Aeroporto Malpensa** (*MPX*). ⊠ *45 km (28 miles) north of Milan* ☏ *02/232323* ⊕ *www.airportmalpensa.com.* **Aeroporto Orio al Serio** (*BGY*). ⊠ *Via Orio al Serio 49/51, 24050 Grassobbio (BG)* ☏ *035/326323* ⊕ *www. milanbergamoairport.it.*

FLIGHTS

From the United States, Alitalia and Delta Air Lines serve Rome, Milan, Pisa, and Venice. The major international hubs in Italy (Milan and Rome) are also served by United Airlines and American Airlines. From June through October, the Italy-based Meridiana has nonstop flights from New York to Naples and Palermo.

Alitalia has direct flights from London to Milan and Rome, while British Airways and smaller budget carriers provide services between Great Britain and other locations in Italy. EasyJet connects London's Gatwick and Stansted airports with 19 Italian destinations. Ryanair, departing from Stansted, flies to 28 airports. Meridiana has flights between Gatwick and Olbia on Sardinia in summer. For flights within Italy, check Alitalia and smaller airlines, such as Blue Panorama and Meridiana. Since tickets are frequently sold at discounted prices, it's wise to investigate the cost of flying—even one way—as an alternative to train travel.

Airline Contacts **Aer Lingus.**
☏ *02/43458326 in Italy, 516/6224222 in U.S.* ⊕ *www.aerlingus.com.* **Alitalia.** ☏ *800/223–5730 in U.S., 892/010 in Italy, 06/65640 Rome office* ⊕ *www.alitalia.it.* **American Airlines.** ☏ *800/433–7300, 199/257300 in Italy* ⊕ *www.aa.com.* **British Airways.** ☏ *800/247–9297 in U.S., 02/69633602 in Italy* ⊕ *www.britishairways.com.* **Delta Air Lines.** ☏ *888/750–3284 international reservations, 02/38591451 in Italy* ⊕ *www. delta.com.* **EasyJet.** ☏ *+44330/3655454 from outside U.K., 199/201840 in Italy, 0330/3655000 in U.K.* ⊕ *www.easyjet.com.* **Ryanair.** ☏ *0871/2460000 in U.K., toll number, 895/8958989 in Italy, toll number* ⊕ *www. ryanair.com.* **Transavia.** ☏ *899/009901* ⊕ *www.transavia.com.* **United Airlines.** ☏ *800/864–8331 in U.S., 02/69633256 in Italy* ⊕ *www.united.com.* **Volotea.** ☏ *895/8954404 in Italy, 0034/931220717 outside Italy* ⊕ *www. volotea.com.*

Domestic Carriers **Blue Panorama.**
☏ *06/98956666* ⊕ *www.blue-panorama. com.* **Meridiana.** ☏ *866/387–6359 in U.S., 0789/52682 in Italy, 0844/4822360 U.K. call center.*

▎ BUS TRAVEL

Italy's far-reaching regional bus network, often operated by private companies, is not as attractive an option as in other European countries, partly due to convenient train travel. Schedules are often drawn up with commuters and students in mind and may be sketchy on weekends. But, car travel aside, regional bus companies often provide the only means of getting to out-of-the-way places. Even when this isn't the case, buses can be faster and more direct than local trains, so it's a good idea to compare bus and train schedules. BusItalia–Sita Nord covers Tuscany and Veneto. SitaSud caters to travelers in Puglia, Foggia, Matera, Basilicata, and

Campania. Flix Bus offers a low-cost long-distance service.

All major cities in Italy have urban bus services. It's inexpensive, and tickets should be purchased from newsstands or tobacconists and validated on board (some city buses have ticket machines on the buses themselves). Buses can become jammed during busy travel periods and rush hours.

Smoking is not permitted on Italian buses. All, even those on long-distance routes, offer a single class of service. Cleanliness and comfort levels are high on private motor coaches, which have plenty of legroom, sizable seats, and luggage storage, but often do not have toilets. Private bus lines usually have a ticket office in town or allow you to pay when you board.

Bus Information ACTV. ⊕ actv.avmspa. it. **ANM.** ⊠ Via G. Marino 1, Naples ☎ 800/639525 toll-free in Italy ⊕ www.anm. it. **ATAC.** ☎ 06/46951 ⊕ www.atac.roma. it. **ATAF.** ⊠ Stazione Centrale di Santa Maria Novella, Florence ☎ 800/424500, 199/104245 from mobile phone (toll) ⊕ www.ataf.net. **ATM.** ⊕ www.atm.it. **BusItalia-Sita Nord.** ⊠ Viale dei Cadorna, 105, Florence ☎ 800/373760 toll-free ⊕ www.fsbusitalia.it. **Flix Bus.** ☎ 02/94759208 ⊕ www.flixbus.com. **Marino Bus.** ☎ 080/3112335 ⊕ www.marinobus.it. **SitaSud.** ⊠ Via S. Francesco D'Assisi 1, Putignano ☎ 080/4052245 ⊕ www.sitasudtrasporti. it. **Trasporti Toscani.** ⊠ Via Bellatalla, 1, Pisa ☎ 050/884111 ⊕ www.cttnord.it.

■ CAR TRAVEL

Italy has an extensive network of *autostrade* (toll highways), complemented by equally well-maintained but free *superstrade* (expressways). Save the ticket you're issued at an autostrada entrance, as you'll need it to exit; on some shorter autostrade, you pay the toll when you enter. Tollbooths also accept Visa and MasterCard, allowing you to exit at special lanes where you simply slip the card into a designated slot.

An *uscita* is an exit. A *raccordo annulare* is a ring road surrounding a city; a *tangenziale* generally bypasses a city entirely. *Strade, strade statale, strade regionale,* and *strade provinciale* (regional and provincial highways, denoted by *S, SS, SR,* or *SP* numbers) may be two lanes, as are all secondary roads; directions and turnoffs aren't always clearly marked.

GASOLINE

You'll find gas stations on most main highways. Those on autostrade are open 24 hours. Otherwise, gas stations are generally open Monday through Saturday 7–7, with a break at lunchtime. At self-service stations the pumps are operated by a central machine for payment, which often doesn't take credit cards: it accepts bills in denominations of €5, €10, €20, and €50, and doesn't give change. Stations with attendants accept cash and credit cards. It's not customary to tip the attendant.

At this writing, gasoline (*benzina*) costs about €1.60 per liter and is available in unleaded (*verde*) and superunleaded (*super*). Many rental cars in Italy use diesel (*gasolio*), which costs about €1.47 per liter (remember to confirm the fuel type your car requires before leaving the agency).

DRIVING IN CENTRI STORICI (HISTORIC CENTERS)

To avoid hefty fines (which you may not be notified of until months after your departure from Italy), make sure you know the rules governing where you can and can't drive in historic city centers. You must have a permit to enter many towns, and this rule is very strictly enforced. Check with your lodging or car-rental company to find out about acquiring permits for access.

PARKING

Parking is at a premium in most towns, especially in historic centers. Fines for parking violations are high, and towing is common. Don't think about tearing up a ticket, as car-rental companies can use your credit card to be reimbursed for any fines incurred. It's a good idea to park in a designated (and preferably attended) lot; even small towns often have a large lot at the edge of historic centers.

In congested cities, indoor parking costs €25–€30 for 12–24 hours; outdoor parking costs about €10–€20. Parking in an area signposted *zona disco* (disk zone) is allowed for short periods (from 30 minutes to two hours or more—the time is posted); if you don't have an appropriate cardboard disk (check in the glove box of your rental car) to show what time you parked, you can write your arrival time on a piece of paper. In most metropolitan areas you can find curbside parking spaces, marked by blue lines; once you insert coins into the nearby *parcometro* machine, it prints a ticket that you then leave on your dashboard.

RENTALS

Fiats, Fords, and Alfa Romeos in a variety of sizes are the most typical rental cars. Note that most Italian cars have standard transmission—if you need an automatic, specify one when you make your reservation. This may incur significantly higher rates.

Most American chains have affiliates in Italy, but costs are usually lower if you book a car before leaving home. Rentals at airports usually cost less than city pickups (and airport offices are open later). An auto broker such as ⊕ *www.rent.it* lets you compare rates among companies while guaranteeing the lowest price.

Most rental companies won't rent to someone under age 21. Most also refuse to rent any model larger than an economy or subcompact to anyone under 23, and, further, require customers under that age to pay by credit card. There are no special restrictions on senior citizen drivers. Any additional drivers must be identified in the contract and qualify with the age limits. There's also a supplementary daily fee for additional drivers. Expect to pay extra for add-on features, too. A car seat

(required for children under age three) will cost about €36 for the duration of the rental and should be booked in advance. In some areas, snow chains are compulsory in winter months and can be rented for €30–€60—it may be cheaper to buy your own at the first open garage. Upon rental, all companies require credit cards as a warranty; to rent bigger cars (2,000cc or more), you may be required to show two credit cards.

Hiring a car with a driver can simplify matters, particularly if you plan to indulge in wine tastings or explore the distractingly scenic Amalfi Coast. Search online (the travel forums at ⊕ *Fodors.com* are a good resource) or ask at your hotel for recommendations. Drivers are paid by the day, and are usually rewarded with a tip of about 15% upon completion of the journey.

All rental agencies operating in Italy require you to buy a collision-damage waiver (CDW) and a theft-protection policy, but those costs should already be included in the rates you're quoted. Verify this, along with any deductible, which can vary greatly depending on the company and type of car. Be aware that coverage may be denied if the named driver on the rental contract isn't the driver at the time of an accident. Ask your rental company about other included coverage when you reserve the car or pick it up. Finally, try not to leave valuables in your car, because thieves often target rental vehicles. If you can't avoid doing so—for instance, if you want to stop to see a sight while traveling between cities—park in an attended lot.

ROAD CONDITIONS

Autostrade are well maintained, as are most interregional highways. Typically, autostrade have two or three lanes in both directions; the left lane should be used only for passing. Italians drive fast and are impatient with those who don't. Tailgating (and flashing with bright beams to signal intent to pass) is the norm if you dawdle in the left lane—the only way to avoid it is to stay to the right.

The condition of provincial (county) roads varies, but road maintenance at this level is generally good in Italy. In many small hill towns the streets are winding and extremely narrow, so try to park at the edge of town and explore on foot.

Driving on back roads isn't difficult as long as you're on the alert for bicycles and passing cars. In addition, street and road signs are often missing or placed in awkward spots; a good map or GPS is essential. If you feel pressure from a string of cars in your rearview mirror but don't feel comfortable speeding up, pull off to the right, and let them pass.

Be aware that some maps may not use the SR or SP (strade regionale and strade provinciale) highway designations, which took the place of the old SS designations in 2004. They may use the old SS designation or no numbering at all.

ROADSIDE EMERGENCIES

Automobile Club Italiano offers 24-hour road service; English-speaking operators are available. Your rental-car company may also have an emergency tow service with a toll-free phone number: keep it handy. Be prepared to report which road you're on, the *verso* (direction) you're headed, and your *targa* (license plate number). Also, in an emergency, call the police (☎ 113).

When you're on the road, always carry a good road map and a flashlight—a reflective vest should be provided with the car. A mobile phone is highly recommended, though there are emergency phones on the autostrade and superstrade. To locate them, look on the pavement for painted arrows and the term "SOS."

Emergency Services American Automobile Association (*AAA*). ☎ *800/222–4357* ⊕ *www. aaa.com.* **Automobile Club Italiano** (*ACI*). ☎ *803/116 for emergency service* ⊕ *www. aci.it.*

Rentals Sicily By Car. ☎ *091/6390111, 800/334440 toll-free in Italy* ⊕ *www.autoeuropa.it.*

RULES OF THE ROAD

Driving is on the right. Speed limits are 130 kph (80 mph) on autostrade, reduced to 110 kph (70 mph) when it rains, and 90 kph (55 mph) on state and provincial roads, unless otherwise marked. In towns, the speed limit is 50 kph (30 mph), which may drop as low as 10 kph (6 mph) near schools, hospitals, and other designated areas. Note that right turns on red lights are forbidden. Headlights are required to be on while driving on all roads (large or small) outside municipalities. You must wear seat belts and strap young children under 4 feet 11 inches into car seats at all times. Using handheld mobile phones while driving is illegal—and fines can exceed €1,000. In most Italian towns the use of the horn is forbidden in many areas. A large sign, *"zona di silenzio,"* indicates a "no honking" zone.

In Italy you must be 18 years old to drive a car. A U.S. driver's license is acceptable to rent a car, but by law Italy also requires non-Europeans to carry an International Driver's Permit (IDP), which essentially translates your license into Italian (and a dozen other languages). In practice, it depends on the police officer who pulls you over whether you'll be penalized for not carrying it. The IDP costs only $15, and obtaining one is easy: see the AAA website (⊕ *www.aaa.com*) for more information.

The blood-alcohol content limit for driving is 0.05% (stricter than in the United States). Surpass it and you'll face fines up to €6,000 and the possibility of one year's imprisonment. Enforcement of speeding laws varies depending on the region, but 30 kph (18.5 mph) over the speed limit warrants a fine of €41, 20 kph (12 mph) is €169; greater than 60 kph (37 mph), and your license could be taken away. The police have the power to levy on-the-spot fines.

▌ TRAIN TRAVEL

Traveling by train in Italy is simple and efficient. Service between major cities is frequent, and trains usually arrive on schedule. The fastest trains on the Trenitalia Ferrovie dello Stato (FS)—the Italian State Railways—are Freccie Rosse Alta Velocità. Ferrari mogul Montezemolo launched the competing NTV Italo high-speed service in 2012. Bullet trains on both services run between all major cities from Venice, Milan, and Turin down through Florence and Rome to Naples and Salerno. Seat reservations are mandatory, and you'll be assigned a specific seat; to avoid having to squeeze through narrow aisles, board only at your designated coach (the number on your ticket matches the one near the door of each coach). Reservations are also required for Eurostar and the slower Intercity (IC) trains; tickets for the latter are about half the price they are for the faster trains. If you miss your reserved train, go to the ticket counter within the hour and you may be able to move your reservation to a later one (this depends on the type of reservation, so check the rules when booking). Note that you'll still need to reserve seats in advance if you're using a rail pass.

There are often significant discounts when you book well in advance. On websites, you'll be presented with available promotional fares, such as Trenitalia's "Super Economy" (up to 60% off), "Famiglia" (a 20% discount for one adult and at least one child), and "A/R" (same-day round trip). Italo offers "Low Cost" and "Economy." The caveat is that the discounts come with restrictions on changes and cancellations; make sure you understand them before booking.

Reservations are not available on Interregionale trains, which are slower, make more stops, and are less expensive than high-speed and Intercity trains. Regionale and Espresso trains stop most frequently and are the most economical (many serve commuters). There are refreshments on long-distance trains, purchased from a mobile cart or a dining car, but not on the commuter trains.

All but commuter trains have first and second classes. On local trains, first-class fare ensures you a little more space; on long-distance trains, you also get wider seats (three across as opposed to four) and a bit more legroom, but the difference is minimal. At peak travel times a first-class fare may be worth the additional cost, as the coaches may be less crowded. In Italian, *prima classe* is first class; second is *seconda classe*.

Many cities—Milan, Turin, Genoa, Naples, Florence, Rome, and even Verona included—have more than one train station, so be sure you get off at the right station. When buying tickets, be particularly aware that in Rome and Florence some trains don't stop at all of the cities' stations and may not stop at the main, central station. When scheduling train travel online or through a travel agent, request to arrive at the station closest to your destination in Rome and Florence.

Except for Pisa, Milan, and Rome, none of the major cities have trains that go directly to the airports, but airport shuttle buses connect train stations and airports.

You can purchase train tickets and review schedules online, at travel agencies, at train station ticket counters, and at automatic ticketing machines located in all but the smallest stations. If you'd like to board a train and don't have a ticket, seek out the conductor prior to getting on; he or she will tell you whether you may buy a ticket on board and what the surcharge will be (usually €5). Fines for attempting to ride a train without a ticket are €100 (€50 if paid on the spot) plus the price of the ticket.

For trains without a reservation you must validate your ticket before boarding by punching it at wall- or pillar-mounted yellow or green boxes in train stations or at the track entrances of larger stations. If

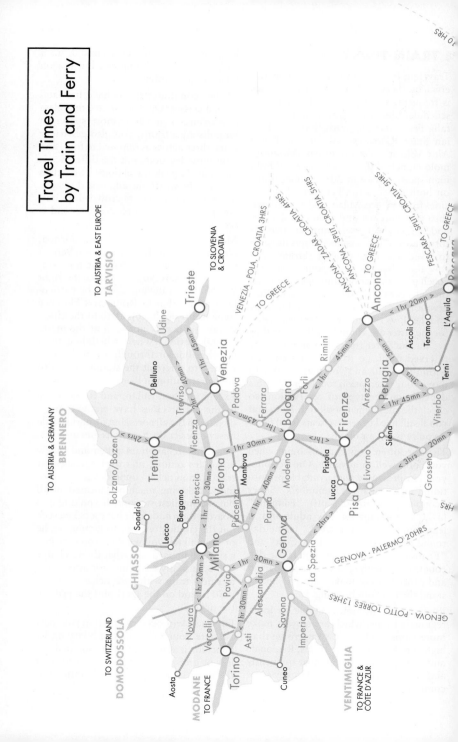

Travel Times by Train and Ferry

TO SWITZERLAND
DOMODOSSOLA

TO AUSTRIA & GERMANY
BRENNERO

TO AUSTRIA & EAST EUROPE
TARVISIO

CHIASSO

Aosta

MODANE
TO FRANCE

Novara

< 1hr 20mn >

Vercelli

< 1hr 30mn >

Asti

Torino

Cuneo

Pavia

Milano

< 1hr 30mn >

Alessandria

Savona

Imperia

VENTIMIGLIA
TO FRANCE &
CÔTE D'AZUR

Lecco

Sondrio

Bergamo

Brescia

< 1hr >

Piacenza

< 1hr 30mn >

Parma

Modena

Genova

La Spezia

< 2hrs >

Bolzano/Bozen

< 2hrs >

Trento

Verona

< 30mn >

Mantova

< 40mn >

Livorno

Pisa

Lucca

Pistoia

Belluno

Udine

Treviso

Vicenza

< 40mn >

< 2hr >

Venezia

< 1hr 45mn >

Padova

Ferrara

< 1hr 45mn >

Bologna

< 1hr >

Firenze

Arezzo

Siena

< 3hrs >

Grosseto

Viterbo

< 20mn >

Forlì

Rimini

< 1hr >

< 45mn >

Ancona

Perugia

15mn >

< 1hr 45mn >

3hrs >

Terni

Ascoli

Teramo

L'Aquila

< 1hr 20mn >

Trieste

TO SLOVENIA
& CROATIA

VENEZIA - POLA, CROATIA 3HRS

TO GREECE

ANCONA - ZADAR, CROATIA 4HRS

ANCONA - SPLIT, CROATIA 5HRS

TO GREECE

PESCARA - SPLIT, CROATIA 3HRS

TO GREECE

10 HRS

HRS

GENOVA - PALERMO 20HRS

GENOVA - PORTO TORRES 13HRS

you forget, find a conductor immediately to avoid a hefty fine.

Train strikes of various kinds are not uncommon, so it's wise to ensure that your train is actually running. During a strike minimum service is guaranteed (especially for distance trains); ask at the station or search online to find out about your particular reservation.

Traveling by night can be a good deal—and somewhat of an adventure—because you'll pass a night without having to have a hotel room. Comfortable trains run on the longer routes (Sicily–Rome, Sicily–Milan, Rome–Turin, Lecce–Milan); request the good-value T3 (three single beds), Intercity Notte, and Carrozza Comfort. The Vagone Letto has private bathrooms and single-, double-, or twin-bed suites. Overnight trains also travel to international destinations like Paris, Vienna, Munich, and other cities.

Information FS-Trenitalia. ☎ *06/68475475 from outside Italy (English), 892021 in Italy* ⊕ *www.trenitalia.com.* **NTV Italo.** ☎ *06/0708* ⊕ *www.italotreno.it.*

TRAIN PASSES

Rail passes promise savings on train travel. But compare prices with actual fares to determine whether a pass will truly pay off. Generally, the more often you plan to travel long distances on high-speed trains, the more sense a rail pass makes.

Italy is one of 28 countries that accept the Eurail Pass, which provides unlimited first- and second-class travel. If you plan to rack up miles across the Continent, get a Global Eurail Pass (covering all participating nations). The Eurail Select Pass allows for travel in two to four contiguous countries. Other options are the Eurail Youth Pass (for those under 27), the Eurail Flexipass (valid for a certain number of travel days within a set period), and the Eurail Saver (aimed at two to five people traveling together).

The Eurail Italy Pass, available for non-European residents, allows up to eight travel days within one month. Three to eight days cost $257–$478 (first class) or $207–$384 (second class). There is a 15% discount if two or more of you are traveling together; family passes offer further discounts, with first-time traveling children under 12 free; kids under four always travel free. Discounts are also given for those under 27.

Passes should be purchased before you leave for Europe, but can be delivered to your hotel for an additional cost. Keep in mind that even with a rail pass you still need to reserve seats on the trains that require them.

Contacts Eurail. ⊕ *www.eurail.com.* **Italia Rail.** ☎ *877/375–7245 in U.S.* ⊕ *www.italiarail. com.* **Rail Europe.** ☎ *800/622–8600 in U.S.* ⊕ *www.raileurope.com.* **RailPass.** ⊕ *www. railpass.com.*

ESSENTIALS

▪ ACCOMMODATIONS

Hotels in Italy are becoming increasingly distinctive. Palazzi, villas, and monasteries have been restored as luxurious lodgings, while retaining their original atmosphere, and small hotels are revamping historic buildings with contemporary decor. Famed Italian wineries are offering rooms and apartments for three-day to weeklong stays.

The lodgings we list are the cream of the crop in each price category. Properties are assigned price categories based on the rate for two people sharing a standard double room in high season, including tax and service.

APARTMENT AND HOUSE RENTALS

Renting a vacation property can be economical depending on your budget and the number of people in your group. Most are owned by individuals and managed by rental agents who advertise online; and because many properties are represented by multiple agents, one may appear on different sites under different names (hence "Chianti Bella Vista," "Tuscan Sun Home," and "Casa Toscana Sole" could all refer to the same villa). In some cases rental agents handle only the online reservation and financial arrangements; in others, the agent or owner may meet you at the property for the initial check-in.

Issues to keep in mind when renting an apartment in a city or town are the neighborhood (street noise and ambience), the availability of an elevator or number of stairs, the furnishings (including pots and linens), what's supplied on arrival (dishwashing liquid, coffee or tea), and the cost of utilities (are all covered by the rental rate?). Inquiries about countryside properties should also include how isolated the property is (do you have to drive 45 minutes to reach the nearest town?). If you're arriving too late in the day to grocery shop, request that provisions for the next day's breakfast be supplied.

Contacts Airbnb. ⊕ *www.aribnb.com.* **Doorways Villa Vacations.** ☎ *610/520–0806, 800/261–4460* ⊕ *www.villavacations.com.* **HomeAway.** ☎ *512/493–0382* ⊕ *www. homeaway.com.* **Hosted Villas.** ☎ *800/374–6637, 416/920–1873* ⊕ *www.hostedvillas. com.* **Interhome.** ☎ *800/882–6864* ⊕ *www. bookinterhome.ca.* **Italy Rents.** ☎ *202/821–4273, 06/99268007 in Italy* ⊕ *www.italyrents. com.* **Parker Villas.** ☎ *800/280–2811* ⊕ *www. parkervillas.com.* **Rent A Villa.** ☎ *877/250–4366, 206/417–3444* ⊕ *www.rentavilla.com.* **Summer In Italy.** ☎ *800/509–8194 in U.S., 089/8426126 in Italy* ⊕ *www.summerini-taly.com.* **Tuscan House.** ☎ *800/844–6939* ⊕ *www.tuscanhouse.com.* **Villas & Apartments Abroad.** ☎ *212/213–6435* ⊕ *www. vaanyc.com.* **Villas of Distinction.** ☎ *800/289–0900* ⊕ *www.villasofdistinction. com.* **WIMCO.** ☎ *888/979–9610, 401/849–8012* ⊕ *www.wimco.com.*

CONVENTS AND MONASTERIES

Throughout Italy tourists can find reasonably priced lodging at convents, monasteries, and religious houses. Religious orders commonly charge about €30–€60 per person per night for rooms that are clean, comfortable, and convenient. Many have private bathrooms; spacious lounge areas and secluded gardens or terraces are standard features. A Continental breakfast ordinarily comes with the room, but be sure to ask. Sometimes, for an extra fee, family-style lunches and dinners are provided, too.

Be aware of three issues when considering a convent or monastery stay: many have a curfew of 11 pm or midnight; you need to book in advance because they fill up quickly; and your best means of booking is usually email or fax—the person answering the phone may not speak English.

Contact Hospites.it. ⊕ *www.hospites.it.*

FARM HOLIDAYS AND AGRITOURISM

Rural accommodations in the *agriturismo* category are growing in popularity among both Italians and visitors; you may have to look a little harder, though, to find an actual working farm or vineyard. Accommodations vary in size and range from luxury apartments, farmhouses, and villas to basic facilities. More than 4,000 farm stays in Italy are listed on the Agriturismo sites below, and local APT tourist offices also have information.

Information Agriturismo.com. ⊕ *www. agriturismo.com.* **Agriturismo.it.** ⊕ *www. agriturismo.it.* **Agriturist-Farm Holidays.** ☎ *0564/417418* ⊕ *www.byfarmholidays. com.* **Turismo Verde.** ☎ *06/3240111* ⊕ *www. turismoverde.it.*

HOME EXCHANGES

With a direct home exchange you stay in someone else's home while they stay in yours. Some outfits also deal with vacation homes, so you're not really occupying someone's full-time residence, just their vacant weekend place.

Italians have historically not been as enthusiastic about home exchanges as others; however, there are many great villas and apartments in Italy owned by foreigners (Americans, English, and others) who use home-exchange services.

Exchange Clubs Home Exchange. com. ☎ *800/877–8723, 310/798–3864, 02/94752664 in Italy* ⊕ *www.homeexchange. com.* **HomeLink International.** ☎ *800/638– 3841, 954/328–1643, 0422/1583934 in Italy* ⊕ *www.homelink.org.* **Intervac Home Exchange.** ☎ *800/756–4663* ⊕ *www.intervac-homeexchange.com.*

∎ COMMUNICATIONS

INTERNET

Getting online in Italian cities isn't difficult: public Internet stations and Internet cafés are fairly common, and Wi-Fi is widely available. Most hotels have Wi-Fi or a computer for guests to use.

Many business-oriented hotels also offer in-room broadband, though some (ironically, often the more expensive ones) charge for broadband and Wi-Fi access. Note that chargers and power supplies may need plug adapters to fit European-style electric sockets (a converter probably won't be necessary).

Italy is also looking to improve city Wi-Fi access; Rome, Venice, and Turin are continuing to develop and expand services, some free for now, some at a daily or weekly rate for temporary access.

Paid and free Wi-Fi hot spots can be found in major airports and train stations, and shopping centers; they're most likely to be free in bars or cafés that want your business.

Contact Provincia Wi-Fi. ☎ *06/40409434* ⊕ *www.freeitaliawifi.it.*

PHONES

With the advent of mobile phones, public pay phones are becoming increasingly scarce in Italy, but they can be found at train and subway stations, main post offices, and in some bars. In rural areas, town squares usually have a pay phone. These require a *scheda telefonica* (prepaid phone card).

CALLING ITALY FROM ABROAD

When telephoning Italy from North America, dial 011 (to get an international line), followed by Italy's country code, 39, and the phone number, including any leading 0. Note that Italian mobile numbers have 10 digits and always begin with a 3; Italian landline numbers will contain from 4 to 10 digits and always begin with a 0. So, for example, when calling Rome, where local numbers start with 06, dial 011 + 39 + 06 + phone number; for a mobile phone, dial 011 + 39 + cell number.

CALLING WITHIN ITALY

For all calls within Italy, whether local or long-distance, you'll dial the entire phone number that starts with 0 or 3 for mobile phone numbers. Calling a mobile phone will cost significantly more than calling a landline, depending on the calling plan.

Italy uses the prefix "800" for toll-free or *numero verde* (green) numbers.

MAKING INTERNATIONAL CALLS

The country code for the United States and Canada is 1 (dial 00 + 1 + area code and number).

Because of the high rates charged by most hotels for long-distance and international calls, you're better off making such calls from public phones or your mobile phone or by using an international calling card.

Although not advised because of the exorbitant cost, you can place international calls or collect calls through an operator by dialing 170.

CALLING CARDS

Prepaid *schede telefoniche* (phone cards) are available throughout Italy for use in pay phones. Cards in different denominations are sold at post offices, newsstands, tobacco shops, and some bars. Before the first use, break off the corner of the card; then, to make a call, insert it into the phone's slot and dial. The card's credit will be displayed in the window as you chat. After you hang up, be sure not to walk off without retrieving the card.

International calling cards are different; you call a toll-free number from any phone, entering the access code found on the back of the card followed by the destination number. With calling cards offered by AT&T and MCI instructions and operator assistance are in English, avoiding language difficulties, and the charges appear on your phone bill. A reliable prepaid card for calling North America and elsewhere in Europe is the TIM Welcome card, offering 500 minutes to the United States for €5. A €10 card is also available. Cards can be purchased from TIM stores, tobacconists, and newsagents.

Calling Cards AT&T Direct. ☎ *800/172444* ⊕ *www.att.com.* **TIM Welcome.** ☎ *800/874874 toll-free in Italy* ⊕ *www.tim.it.* **World Access.** ☎ *800/874804* ⊕ *www.worldaccessnumbers. com.*

MOBILE PHONES

Most mobile phones are now multiband (Europe and North America use different calling frequencies), so if your service provider uses the world-standard GSM network (as do T-Mobile, AT&T, and Verizon), you can use your own phone and provider abroad. But roaming fees can be steep—€0.99 per minute is considered quite low—and overseas you'll normally pay toll charges for incoming calls, too.

■ TIP→ If you're carrying a laptop, tablet, or smartphone, investigate apps and services such as Skype, Viber, and Whatsapp, which offer free or low-cost calling and texting services.

To keep calling expenses to a minimum, consider purchasing an Italian SIM card—these can be purchased for as little as €5, depending on the provider (make sure your home service provider first unlocks your phone for use with a different SIM) and choose a prepaid service plan, topping off the credit as you go. You then have a local number and can make calls at local rates (about €0.15 per minute, and only for those made, not received), or send text messages for a reasonable fee (€0.12 per message or less). Have the service provider enable international calling; use an international calling card with your cell for even more savings.

■ TIP→ If you're a frequent international traveler, save your old mobile phone (ask your service provider to unlock it for you) or buy an unlocked, multiband phone online. Use it as a travel phone, buying a new SIM card with pay-as-you-go service in each destination.

The cost of mobile phones is dropping: you can purchase a dual-band (Europe only) phone in Italy with a prepaid calling credit for as little as €20. Alternatively, you can buy a multiband phone that will also function in North America (European phones aren't usually "locked" to their provider's SIM, which is why they cost more). That means you can use it with your own service provider once you return home. You'll find dedicated mobile phone stores in all but the smallest towns. Service providers include TIM, Tre, Vodafone, and Wind; stop by a multivendor shop to compare offers, or check their websites. Note that you'll need to present your passport to purchase any SIM card.

Rental phones are available online prior to departure and in Italy's cities and larger towns. Shop around for the best deal. Most contracts require a refundable deposit that covers the cost of the mobile phone ($75–$300) and then set up a monthly service plan that's automatically charged to your credit card. Frequently, rental phones will be triple band with a plan that allows you to call North America. You should check the rate schedule, however, to avoid a nasty surprise on your credit card bill two or three months later. Often the local purchase with a prepaid plan will be the more cost-effective one.

▪TIP➔ Beware of mobile phone (and PDA) thieves. Use your device's security code option. Keep your phone or PDA in a secure pocket or purse. Don't lay it on the bar when you stop for an espresso. Don't zip it into the outside pocket of your backpack in crowded cities. Don't leave it in your hotel room. Notify your provider immediately if it's lost or stolen; providers can disable your SIM and give you a new one, copying the original's number and contents.

Contacts **Cellular Abroad.** ☎ 800/287–5072 ⊕ www.cellularabroad.com. **Mobal.** ☎ 888/888–9162, 212/785–5800 for support ⊕ www.mobal.com. **Planet Fone.** ☎ 888/988–4777 ⊕ www.planetfone.com. **TIM for Visitors.** ⊕ www.timforvisitors.tim.it.

▪ CUSTOMS AND DUTIES

Travelers from the United States should experience little difficulty clearing customs at any Italian airport. It may be more difficult to clear customs when returning to the United States, where residents are normally entitled to a duty-free exemption of $800 on items accompanying

them. You'll have to pay a tax (most often a flat percentage) on the value of everything beyond that limit. When you shop in Italy, keep all your receipts handy, as customs inspectors may ask to see them as well as the items you purchased.

Although there's no problem with aged cheese (vacuum-sealed works best), you cannot bring back any of that delicious prosciutto, salami, or any other meat product. Fresh mushrooms, truffles, or fresh fruits and vegetables are also forbidden. There are restrictions on the amount of alcohol allowed in duty-free, too. Generally, you can bring in one liter of wine, beer, or other alcohol without paying a customs duty; visit the travel area of the Customs and Border Patrol Travel website for complete information.

Italy requires documentation regarding the background of all antiques and antiquities before these items are taken out of the country. Under Italian law, all antiquities found on Italian soil are considered state property, and there are other restrictions on antique artwork. Even if purchased from a business in Italy, legal ownership of artifacts may be in question if brought into the United States. Therefore, although they don't necessarily confer ownership, documents such as export permits and receipts are required when importing such items into the United States.

Information in Italy **Dogana Sezione Viaggiatori.** ☎ 06/50241, 800/257428 toll-free ⊕ www.agenziadoganemonopoli.gov.it/portale/dogane.

U.S. Information **U.S. Customs and Border Protection.** ☎ 877/227–5511, 202/325–8000 from outside U.S. ⊕ www.cbp.gov.

▪ EATING OUT

Italian cuisine is still largely regional. Ask what the specialties are—and, by all means, try spaghetti *alla carbonara* (with bacon and egg) in Rome, pizza in Naples, *bistecca alla fiorentina* (steak) n Florence, *cinghiale* (wild boar) in Tuscany, truffles in Piedmont, *la frittura* (fish fry) in Venice, and *risotto alla milanese* n Milan. Although most restaurants in taly serve local dishes, you can find Asian and Middle Eastern alternatives in Rome, Venice, and other cities. The restaurants we list are the cream of the crop in each price category.

MEALS AND MEALTIMES

What's the difference between a *ristorante* and a *trattoria*? Can you order food at an *enoteca*? Can you go to a restaurant just for a snack or order only salad at a pizzeria? The following definitions should help.

Not long ago, *ristoranti* tended to be more elegant and expensive than *trattorie*, which serve traditional, home-style fare in an atmosphere to match, or *osterie*, which serve local wines and simple, regional dishes. But the distinction has blurred considerably, and an osteria in the center of town might now be far fancier (and pricier) than a ristorante across the street. n any sit-down establishment, however, you're generally expected to order at least a two-course meal, such as: a *primo* (first course) and a *secondo* (main course) or a *contorno* (vegetable side dish); an *antipasto* (starter) followed by either a primo or secondo; or a secondo and a *dolce* (dessert).

There is no problem if you'd prefer to eat ess, but consider an enoteca or pizzeria as an alternative, where it's more common to order a single dish. An enoteca menu is often limited to a selection of cheese, cured meats, salads, and desserts, but if there's a kitchen you can also find soups, pastas, and main courses. The typical pizzeria serves *affettati misti* (a selection of cured pork), simple salads, various kinds of bruschetta, *crostini* (similar to bruschetta, with a variety of toppings) and, in Rome and Naples, *fritti* (deep-fried finger food) such as *olive ascolane* (green olives with a meat stuffing) and *supplì* or *arancini* (rice balls stuffed with mozzarella or minced meat).

The most convenient and least expensive places for a quick snack between sights are probably bars, cafés, and pizza *al taglio* (by the slice) spots. Pizza al taglio shops are easy to negotiate, but few have seats. They sell pizza by weight: just point out which kind you want and how much. Kebab stores are also omnipresent in every Italian city.

Note that Italians do not usually walk and eat.

Bars in Italy resemble what we think of as cafés, and are primarily places to get a coffee and a bite to eat, rather than drinking establishments. Expect a selection of panini warmed up on the griddle (*piastra*) and *tramezzini* (sandwiches made of untoasted white bread triangles). In larger cities, bars also serve vegetable and fruit salads, cold pasta dishes, and gelato. Most offer beer and a variety of alcohol, as well as wines by the glass (sometimes good but more often mediocre). A café is like a bar but typically has more tables. Pizza at a café should be avoided—it's usually heated in a microwave.

If you place your order at the counter, ask whether you can sit down. Some places charge for table service (especially in tourist centers); others don't. In self-service bars and cafés, it's good manners to clean your table before you leave. Be aware that in certain spots (such as train stations and stops along the highway) you first pay a cashier; then show your *scontrino* (receipt) at the counter to place your order. Menus are posted outside most restaurants (in English in tourist areas). If not, you might step inside and ask to take a look at the menu, but don't ask for a table unless you intend to stay.

Italians take their food as it's listed on the menu, seldom making special requests such as "dressing on the side" or "hold the olive oil." If you have special dietary needs, however, make them known; they can usually be accommodated. Vegetarians should be firm, as bacon and ham can slip into some dishes. Although mineral water makes its way to almost every table, you can order a carafe of tap water (*acqua di rubinetto* or *acqua semplice*) instead— just keep in mind that such water can be highly chlorinated.

An Italian would never ask for olive oil to dip bread in, and don't be surprised if there's no butter to spread on it either. Wiping your bowl clean with a (small) piece of bread, known locally as *la scarpetta*, is usually considered a sign of appreciation, not bad manners. Spaghetti should be eaten with a fork only, although a little help from a spoon won't horrify locals the way cutting spaghetti into little pieces might. Order your caffè (Italians drink cappuccino only in the morning) after dessert, not with it. As for doggy bags, Italians would never ask for one, though eateries popular with tourists are becoming more accustomed to travelers who do.

Breakfast (*la colazione*) is usually served from 7 to 10:30, lunch (*il pranzo*) from 12:30 to 2, and dinner (*la cena*) from 7:30 to 10, later in the south; outside those hours, best head for a bar. Peak times are usually 1:30 for lunch and 9 for dinner. Enoteche and Venetian *bacari* (wine bars) are also open in the morning and late afternoon for *cicheti* (finger foods) at the counter. Bars and cafés are open from 7 am until 8 or 9 pm; a few stay open until midnight.

Unless otherwise noted, the restaurants listed here are open for lunch and dinner, closing one or two days a week.

PAYING

Most restaurants have a cover charge per person, usually listed at the top of the check as *coperto* or *pane e coperto*. It should be modest (€1–€2.50 per person) except at the most expensive restaurants. Whenever in doubt, ask before you order to avoid unpleasant discussions later. It's customary to leave a small cash tip (between 5% and 10%) in appreciation of good service: you will usually see a *servizio* charge included at the bottom of the check, but the server will not likely receive it.

The price of fish dishes is often given by weight (before cooking), so the price quoted on the menu is for 100 grams of fish, not for the whole dish. (An average fish portion is about 350 grams.) In Tuscany, bistecca alla fiorentina is also often priced by weight (about €4 for 100 grams, or $18 per pound).

Major credit cards are widely accepted in Italy; however, cash is always preferred. More restaurants take Visa and Master-Card than American Express or Diners Club.

When you leave a dining establishment, take your meal bill or receipt with you. Although not a common experience, the Italian finance (tax) police can approach you within 100 yards of the establishment at which you've eaten and ask for a receipt; if you don't have one, they can fine you and will fine the business owner for not providing it. The practice is intended to prevent tax evasion; it's not necessary to show receipts when leaving Italy.

RESERVATIONS AND DRESS

It's always safest to make a reservation for dinner. For popular restaurants, book as far ahead as you can (two to three weeks), and reconfirm as soon as you arrive. Large parties should always call ahead to check the reservations policy. If you change your mind, be sure to cancel, even at the last minute.

Unless they're dining outside or at a seafront resort, Italian men never wear shorts or running shoes in a restaurant. The same applies to women: no casual shorts, running shoes, or rubber sandals when going out to dinner. Shorts are acceptable in pizzerias and cafés.

WINES, BEER, AND SPIRITS

The grape has been cultivated in Italy since the time of the Etruscans, and Italians justifiably take pride in their local varieties, which are numerous. Although almost every region produces good-quality wine, Tuscany, Piedmont, the Veneto,

Puglia, Calabria, and Sicily are some of the more renowned areas, with Le Marche and Umbria being well reputed, too. Italian wine is less expensive in Italy than almost anywhere else, so it's often affordable to order a bottle of wine at a restaurant rather than sticking with the house wine (which is usually good but quite simple). Many bars have their own *aperitivo della casa* (house aperitif); Italians are imaginative with their mixed drinks, so you may want to try one.

You can purchase beer, wine, and spirits in any bar, grocery store, or enoteca, any day of the week, any time of the day. Italian and German beer is readily available, but it can be more expensive than wine. Some excellent microbreweries are beginning to dot the Italian beer horizon, so ask if there's a local brew available to sample.

There's no minimum drinking age in Italy. Italian children begin drinking wine mixed with water at mealtimes when they're teens (or thereabouts). Italians are rarely seen drunk in public, and public drinking, except in a bar or eating establishment, isn't considered acceptable behavior. Bars usually close by 9 pm; hotel and restaurant bars stay open until midnight. Pubs and discos serve until about 2 am.

ELECTRICITY

The electrical current in Italy is 220 volts, 50 cycles alternating current (AC); wall outlets accept Continental-type plugs, with two or three round prongs.

You may purchase a universal adapter, which has several types of plugs in one lightweight, compact unit, at travel specialty stores, electronics stores, and online. You can also pick up plug adapters in Italy in any electric supply store for about €2 each. You'll likely not need a voltage converter, though. Most portable devices are dual voltage (i.e., they operate equally well on 110 and 220 volts)—just check label specifications and manufacturer instructions to be sure. Don't use 110-volt outlets marked "for shavers only" for high-wattage appliances such as hair dryers.

Contacts Walkabout Travel Gear.
☎ 877/2189729 ⊕ www.walkabouttravelgear. com.

■ EMERGENCIES

No matter where you are in the European Union, you can dial ☎ 112 in case of an emergency: the call will be directed to the local police. Not all 112 operators speak English, so you may want to ask a local person to place the call. Asking the operator for "*pronto soccorso*" (first aid and also the emergency room of a hospital) should get you an *ambulanza* (ambulance). If you just need a doctor, ask for "*un medico.*"

Italy has the *carabinieri* (national police force; their emergency number is ☎ 113 from anywhere in Italy) as well as the *polizia* (local police force). Both are armed and have the power to arrest and investigate crimes. Always report the loss of your passport to the carabinieri as well as to your embassy. When reporting a crime, you'll be asked to fill out *una denuncia* (official report)—keep a copy for your insurance company. You should also contact the police any time you have a car accident of any sort.

Local traffic officers, known as *vigili,* are responsible for, among other things, giving out parking tickets. They wear white (in summer), navy, or black uniforms. Should you find yourself involved in a minor car accident in town, contact the vigili.

Pharmacies are generally open weekdays 8:30–1 and 4–8, and Saturday 9–1. Local pharmacies rotate covering the off-hours in shifts: on the door of every pharmacy is a list of which pharmacies in the vicinity will be open late.

Foreign Embassies U.S. Consulate Florence. ⊠ *Lungarno Vespucci 38, Florence* ☎ *055/266951* ⊕ *www.usembassy.gov/italy.* **U.S. Consulate Milan.** ⊠ *Via Principe Amedeo*

2/10, Milan ☎ 02/290351 ⊕ www.usembassy.
gov/italy. **U.S. Consulate Naples.** ✉ Piazza
della Repubblica, Naples ☎ 081/5838111
⊕ www.usembassy.gov/italy. **U.S. Embassy.**
✉ Via Vittorio Veneto 121, Rome ☎ 06/46741
⊕ www.usembassy.gov/italy.

General Emergency Contacts Emergencies.
☎ 115 for fire, 118 for ambulance ⊕ www.vigil-
fuoco.it. **National and State Police.** ☎ 112
for Polizia (National Police), 113 for Carabinieri
(State Police) ⊕ www.poliziadistato.it ⊕ www.
carabinieri.it.

▌ HOURS OF OPERATION

Religious and civic holidays are frequent
in Italy. Depending on the holiday's local
importance, businesses may close for
the day. Businesses don't close Friday or
Monday when the holiday falls on the
weekend, though the Monday following
Easter is a holiday.

Banks are open weekdays 8:30–1:30 and
for one or two hours in the afternoon,
depending on the bank. Most post offices
are open Monday–Saturday 8–1:30, some
until 2; central post offices are open weekdays 8–6:30, Saturday 8–12:30 or 9–6:30.

Most churches are open from early morning until noon or 12:30, when they close
for three hours or more; they open again
in the afternoon, closing at about 6. A
few major churches, such as St. Peter's in
Rome and San Marco in Venice, remain
open all day. Walking around during services is discouraged. Many museums are
closed one day a week, often Monday or
Tuesday. During low season museums
often close early; during high season many
stay open until late at night.

Most shops are open Monday through
Saturday 9–1 and 3:30 or 4–7:30. Clothing shops are generally closed Monday
mornings. Barbers and hairdressers, with
certain exceptions, are closed Sunday and
Monday. Some bookstores and fashion-
or tourist-oriented shops in places such as
Rome and Venice are open all day, as well
as Sunday. Many branches of large chain

supermarkets such as Standa, COOP, and
Esselunga don't close for lunch and are
usually open Sunday; smaller *alimentari*
(delicatessens) and other food shops are
usually closed one evening during the
week (it varies according to the town) and
are almost always closed Sunday.

HOLIDAYS

Traveling through Italy in July and August
can be an odd experience. Although there
are some deals to be had, the heat can
be oppressive, and in August much of the
population is on vacation. Most cities are
deserted (except for foreign tourists) and
privately run restaurants and shops are
closed. National holidays in 2019 include
January 1 (New Year's Day); January 6
(Epiphany); April 21 and 22 (Easter Sunday and Monday); April 25 (Liberation
Day); May 1 (Labor Day or May Day);
June 2 (Festival of the Republic); August
15 (Ferragosto); November 1 (All Saints'
Day); December 8 (Immaculate Conception); and December 25 and 26 (Christmas Day and the Feast of St. Stephen).

In addition, feast days of patron saints
are observed locally. Many businesses
and shops may be closed in Florence,
Genoa, and Turin on June 24 (St. John the
Baptist); in Rome on June 29 (Sts. Peter
and Paul); in Palermo on July 15 (Santa
Rosalia); in Naples on September 19 (San
Gennaro); in Bologna on October 4 (San
Petronio); in Trieste on November 3 (San
Giusto); and in Milan on December 7 (St.
Ambrose). Venice's feast of St. Mark is
April 25, the same as Liberation Day, so
the Madonna della Salute on November
21 makes up for the lost holiday.

▌ MAIL

The Italian mail system has a bad reputation but has become noticeably more
efficient in recent times with some privati-
zation. Allow 7–15 days for mail to get to
the United States. Receiving mail in Italy,
especially packages, can take weeks, usually due to customs (not postal) delays.

You can buy stamps at tobacco shops as well as post offices.

"Posta Prioritaria" (for regular letters and packages) is the name for standard postage. It guarantees delivery within Italy in three to five business days and abroad in five to six working days. A more expensive express delivery is also available, guaranteeing one-day delivery to most places in Italy and three- to five-day delivery abroad. Note that the postal service has no control over customs, however, which makes international delivery estimates meaningless. Mail sent as "Postamail Internazionale" to the United States costs €2.20 for up to 20 grams, €3.70 for 21–50 grams, and €4.60 for 51–100 grams. Mail sent as "Paccocelere" to the United States costs €40 for up to 1 kilogram.

Reliable two-day international mail is generally available during the week in all major cities and at popular resorts via UPS and Federal Express—but again, customs delays can slow down "express" service.

SHIPPING SERVICES

Sending a letter or small package to the United States via Federal Express takes at least two days and costs about €45. Other package services to check are Quick Pack Europe (for delivery within Europe) and Express Mail Service (a global three- to five-day service for letters and packages). Compare prices with those of Paccocelere to determine the cheapest option.

If your hotel can't assist you with shipping, try an Internet café; many offer two-day mail services using major carriers.

If you've purchased antiques, ceramics, or other fragile objects, ask if the vendor will do the shipping for you. In most cases this is possible, and preferable, because many merchants have experience with these kinds of shipments. If so, ask whether the article will be insured against breakage.

MONEY

Prices vary from region to region and are substantially lower in the country than in urban centers. Of Italy's major cities, Milan is by far the most expensive. Resort areas such as Capri, Portofino, and Cortina d'Ampezzo cater to wealthy vacationers and charge top prices. Good value can be had in the scenic Trentino–Alto Adige region of the Dolomites and in Umbria and Le Marche. With a few exceptions, southern Italy and Sicily also offer bargains for those who do their homework before they leave home.

ITEM	AVERAGE COST
Cup of Coffee	€0.80–€1.50
Soft Drink (glass/can/bottle)	€2–€3
Glass of Beer	€2–€5
Sandwich	€3–€4.50
2-km (1-mile) Taxi Ride in Rome	€8.50

Prices here are given for adults. Substantially reduced fees are almost always available for children, students, and senior citizens from the EU; citizens of non-EU countries rarely get discounts, but inquire before you purchase tickets, as this situation is constantly changing.

■TIP→ U.S. banks do not keep every foreign currency on hand, and it may take as long as a week to order. If you're planning to exchange funds before leaving home, don't wait until the last minute.

ATMS AND BANKS

An ATM (*bancomat* in Italian) is the easiest way to get euros in Italy. There are numerous ATMs in large cities and small towns, as well as in airports and train stations. Be sure to memorize your PIN in numbers, as ATM keypads in Italy won't always display letters. Check with your bank to confirm that you have an international PIN (*codice segreto*) that will be recognized in the countries you're visiting; to raise your maximum daily withdrawal allowance; and to learn what your bank's fee is for withdrawing money (Italian banks don't charge withdrawal fees). ■TIP➔ **Be aware that PINs beginning with a 0 (zero) tend to be rejected in Italy.**

Your own bank may charge a fee for using ATMs abroad and for the cost of conversion from euros to dollars. Nevertheless, you can usually get a better rate of exchange at an ATM than you will at a currency-exchange office or even when changing money inside a bank with a teller, the next-best option. Whatever the method, extracting funds as you need them is safer than carrying around a large amount of cash. Finally, it's advisable to carry more than one card that can be used for cash withdrawal, in case something happens to your main one.

CREDIT CARDS

It's a good idea to inform your credit card company before you travel, especially if you're going abroad and don't travel internationally often. Otherwise, the credit card company might put a hold on your card owing to unusual activity—not a welcome occurrence halfway through your trip. Record all your credit card numbers—as well as the phone numbers to call if your cards are lost or stolen. Keep these in a safe place, so you're prepared should something go wrong. MasterCard and Visa have general numbers you can call (collect if you're abroad) if your card is lost. But you're better off calling the number of your issuing bank, because MasterCard and Visa generally just transfer you there; your bank's number is usually printed on your card.

■TIP➔ **North American toll-free numbers aren't available from abroad, so be sure to obtain a local number with area code for any business you may need to contact.**

Although it's usually cheaper (and safer) to use a credit card abroad for large purchases (so you can cancel payments or be reimbursed if there's a problem), note that some credit card companies *and* the banks that issue them add substantial percentages to all foreign transactions, whether they're in a foreign currency or not. Check on these fees before leaving home, so there won't be any surprises when you get the bill. Because of these fees, avoid using your credit card for ATM withdrawals or cash advances (use a debit or cash card instead).

■TIP➔ **Before you charge something, ask the merchant whether he or she plans to do a dynamic currency conversion (DCC). In such a transaction the credit card processor (shop, restaurant, or hotel, not Visa or MasterCard) converts the currency and charges you in dollars. In most cases you'll pay the merchant a 3% fee for this service in addition to any credit card company and issuing-bank foreign-transaction surcharges.**

Merchants who participate in dynamic currency conversion programs are supposed to ask whether you want to be charged in dollars or the local currency, but they don't always do so. And even if they do offer you a choice, they may well avoid mentioning the additional surcharges. The good news is that you *do* have a choice—you can simply say no. If this practice really gets your goat, you can avoid it entirely by using American Express; with its cards, DCC simply isn't an option.

Italian merchants prefer MasterCard and Visa (look for the CartaSi sign), but American Express is usually accepted in popular tourist destinations. Credit cards aren't accepted everywhere, though; if you want to pay with a credit card in a small shop, hotel, or restaurant, it's a good idea to make your intentions known early on.

Reporting Lost Cards American Express. ☏ *800/528–4800 in U.S., 06/72280-735* ⊕ *www.americanexpress.com.* **Diners Club.** ☏ *800/234–6377 in U.S., 514/877–1577 collect from abroad, 800/393939 in Italy* ⊕ *www.dinersclub.com.* **MasterCard.** ☏ *800/307–7309 in U.S., 636/722–7111 collect from abroad, 800/870866 in Italy* ⊕ *www. mastercard.us.* **Visa.** ☏ *800/847–2911 in U.S., 303/967–1096 from abroad, 800/819014 in Italy* ⊕ *usa.visa.com.*

CURRENCY AND EXCHANGE

The euro is the main unit of currency in Italy. Under the euro system there are 100 *centesimi* (cents) to the euro. There are coins valued at 1, 2, 5, 10, 20, and 50 centesimi as well as 1 and 2 euros. There are seven notes: 5, 10, 20, 50, 100, 200, and 500 euros. At this writing, €1 was worth was about $1.23.

Post offices exchange currency at good rates, but employees speak limited English, so be prepared. (Writing your request can help in these cases.)

■TIP➔ **Even if a currency-exchange booth has a sign promising no commission, rest assured that there's some kind of huge, hidden fee. You're almost always better off getting foreign currency at an ATM or exchanging money at a bank or post office.**

▌ PASSPORTS AND VISAS

PASSPORTS

Although somewhat costly, a U.S. passport is relatively simple to obtain and is valid for 10 years. You must apply in person if you're getting a passport for the first time; if your previous passport was lost, stolen, or damaged; or if it has expired and was issued more than 15 years ago or when you were under 16. All children under 18 must appear in person to apply for or renew a passport. Both parents must accompany any child under 14 (or send a notarized statement with their permission) and provide proof of their relationship to the child.

There are 26 regional passport offices as well as more than 7,200 passport acceptance facilities in post offices, public libraries, and other governmental offices. If you're renewing a passport, you may do so by mail; forms are available at passport acceptance facilities and online, where you trace the application's progress.

The cost of a new passport is $135 for adults, $105 for children under 16; renewals are $110 for adults, $105 for children under 16. Allow four to six weeks for processing, both for first-time passports and renewals. For an expediting fee of $60 you can reduce this time to two to three weeks. If your trip is less than two weeks away, you can get a passport even more rapidly by going to a passport office with the necessary documentation. Private expediters can get things done in as little as 48 hours, but charge hefty fees for their services.

■TIP➔ **Before your trip, make two copies of your passport's data page (one for someone at home and another for you to carry separately). Or scan the page and email it to someone at home and/or yourself.**

GENERAL REQUIREMENTS FOR ITALY	
Passport	Must be valid for 6 months after date of arrival
Visa	Tourist visas aren't needed for stays of 90 days or less by U.S. citizens.
Vaccinations	None
Driving	International driver's license required. CDW is compulsory on car rentals and will be included in the quoted price.

VISAS

When staying for 90 days or less, U.S. citizens aren't required to obtain a visa prior to traveling to Italy. A recent law requires that you fill in a declaration of presence within eight days of your arrival—the stamp on your passport at airport arrivals substitutes for this. If you plan to travel or live in Italy or the European Union for longer than 90 days, you must acquire a valid visa from the Italian consulate serving your state *before you leave the United States*. Plan ahead, because the process of obtaining a visa will take at least 30 days, and the Italian government doesn't accept visa applications submitted by visa expediters.

U.S. Passport Information U.S. Department of State. ☎ 877/487–2778 ⊕ *travel.state.gov.*

U.S. Passport Expediters American Passport Express. ☎ *800/455–5166* ⊕ *www. americanpassport.com.* **Travel Document Systems.** ☎ *800/874–5100* ⊕ *www.traveldocs. com.* **Travel the World Visas.** ☎ *202/223– 8822* ⊕ *www.world-visa.com.*

▍ TAXES

A 11.5% V.A.T. (value-added tax) (13% from 2020) is included in the rate at all hotels except those at the upper end of the range. You'll often have to pay a supplementary City Tax (in cash) at your hotel, varying from €1 per night to Rome's exorbitant €5 per night, as well.

No tax is added to the bill in restaurants. A service charge of approximately 10%–15% is often added to your check; in some cases a service charge is included in the prices.

The V.A.T. is 25% on clothing, wine, and luxury goods. On consumer goods it's already included in the amount shown on the price tag (look for the phrase *"IVA inclusa"*), whereas on services it may not be. If you're not a European citizen and if your purchases in a single day total more than €155, you may be entitled to a refund of the V.A.T.

When making a purchase, ask whether the merchant gives refunds—not all do, nor are they required to. If they do, they'll help you fill out the V.A.T. refund form, which you then submit to a company that will issue you the refund in the form of cash, check, or credit card adjustment.

Alternatively, as you leave the country (or, if you're visiting several European Union countries, on leaving the EU), present your merchandise and the form to customs officials, who will stamp it. Once through passport control, take the stamped form to a refund-service counter for an on-the-spot refund (the quickest and easiest option). You may also mail it to the address on the form (or on the envelope with it) after you arrive home, but processing time can be long, especially if you request a credit card adjustment.

Note that in larger cities the cash refund can be obtained at in-town offices prior to departure; just ask the merchant or check the envelope for local office addresses.

Global Blue is the largest V.A.T.-refund service with 270,000 affiliated stores and more than 700 refund counters at major airports and border crossings. Premier Tax Free is another company that represents more than 150,000 merchants worldwide; look for their logos in store windows.

V.A.T. Refunds Global Blue. ☎ *866/706– 6090 in North America, 421232/111111 from outside North America, 00800/32111111 in Italy* ⊕ *www.global-blue.com.* **Premier Tax Free.** ☎ *905/542–1710 in U.S., 06/69923383 in Italy* ⊕ *www.premiertaxfree.com.*

▍ TIME

Italy is in the Central European Time Zone (CET). From March to October it institutes daylight saving time. Italy is 6 hours ahead of U.S. Eastern Standard Time, 1 hour ahead of Great Britain, 10 hours behind Sydney, and 12 hours behind Auckland. Like the rest of Europe, Italy uses the 24-hour (or "military") clock, which means that after noon you continue counting forward: 13:00 is 1 pm, 23:30 is 11:30 pm.

▍ TIPPING

In restaurants a service charge of 10%– 15% may appear on your check, but it's not a given that your server will receive this; so you may want to consider leaving a tip of 5%–10% (in cash) for good service. Tip checkroom attendants €1 per person and restroom attendants €0.50 (more in expensive hotels and restaurants). In major cities, tip €0.50 or more for table service in cafés. At a hotel bar, tip €1 and up for a round or two of drinks.

Italians rarely tip taxi drivers, which isn't to say that you shouldn't. A euro or two is appreciated, particularly if the driver helps with luggage. Service-station attendants are tipped only for special services; give them €1 for checking your tires. Railway and airport porters charge a fixed rate per bag. Tip an additional €0.50 per person, more if the porter is helpful. Give a barber €1–€1.50 and a hairdresser's assistant €1.50–€4 for a shampoo or cut, depending on the type of establishment.

On sightseeing tours, tip guides about €1.50 per person for a half-day group tour, more if they're especially knowledgeable. In monasteries and other sights where admission is free, a contribution (€0.50–€1) is expected.

In hotels, give the *portiere* (concierge) about 10% of the bill for services, or €2.50–€5 for help with dinner reservations and such. Leave the chambermaid about €1 per day, or about €4.50–€5 a week in a moderately priced hotel; tip a minimum of €1 for valet or room service. In an expensive hotel, double these amounts; tip doormen €0.50 for calling a cab and €1.50 for carrying bags to the check-in desk, and tip bellhops €1.50–€2.50 for carrying your bags to the room.

▌ TOURS

Guided tours are a good option when you don't want to do it all yourself. You travel along with a group (sometimes large, sometimes small), stay in pre-booked hotels, often eat with your fellow travelers (the cost of meals may or may not be included in the price of your tour), and follow a set schedule. Not all guided tours are an "if it's Tuesday this must be Belgium" experience, however. A knowledgeable guide can take you places that you might never discover on your own, give you a richer context, and lead you to a more in-depth experience than you would have otherwise. They may be just the thing if you don't have the time or inclination to make travel arrangements on your own.

Whenever you book a guided tour, find out what's included and what isn't. A "land-only" tour includes all your travel (by bus, in most cases) in the destination, but not necessarily your flights to and from or even within it. Also, in most cases prices in tour promotions don't include fees and taxes. You'll also want to review how much free time you'll have, and see if that meets with your personal preferences. Remember, too, that you'll be expected to tip your guide (in cash) at the end of the tour.

Even when planning independent travel, keep in mind that every province and city in Italy has tour guides licensed by the government. Some are eminently qualified in relevant fields such as architecture and art history and are a pleasure to spend time with. Lots of private guides have websites, and you can check the travel forums at ⊕ *Fodors.com* for recommendations (it's best to book before you leave home, especially for major destinations, as popular guides and tours are in demand). Once in Italy, tourist offices and hotel concierges can also provide the names of knowledgeable local guides and the rates for certain services. When hiring on the spot, ask about their background and qualifications—and make sure you can understand each other. Tipping is always appreciated, but never obligatory, for local guides.

Recommended Generalists Abercrombie & Kent. ☎ *800/554–7016, 630/725–3400* ⊕ *www.abercrombiekent.com.* **Andante.** ☎ *888/331–3476* ⊕ *www.andantetravels.com.* **Maupin Tour.** ☎ *800/255–4266, 800/255–4266* ⊕ *www.maupintour.com.* **Perillo Tours.** ☎ *800/431–1515* ⊕ *www.perillotours.com.* **Tauck.** ☎ *800/788–7885* ⊕ *www.tauck.com.* **Travcoa.** ☎ *888/979–2806, 844/840–1149* ⊕ *www.travcoa.com.*

Biking and Hiking Tour Contacts Backroads. ☎ *800/462–2848, 510/527–1555* ⊕ *www.backroads.com.* **Butterfield & Robinson.** ☎ *866/551–9090, 416/864–1354* ⊕ *www.butterfield.com.* **Genius Loci Travel.** ☎ *089/791896* ⊕ *www.genius-loci.it.* **Italian Connection.** ☎ *0932/231816 in Italy,*

335/8016115 Italy mobile ⊕ www.italian-connection.com.

Educational Programs **Road Scholar.**
☎ *800/454–5768, 877/426–8056 ⊕ www.roadscholar.org.*

Golf Tour Contact **Italy Vacations.**
☎ *800/482–5925 ⊕ www.italyvacations.com/vacation-packages/special-interests.*

Wine Tour Contacts **Cellar Tours.**
☎ *310/496–8061, 030/8370783 in Italy*
⊕ *www.cellartours.com.* **Food & Wine Trails.**
☎ *800/367–5348 ⊕ www.foodandwinetrails.com.*

▌ TRIP INSURANCE

Comprehensive trip insurance is valuable if you're booking an expensive or complicated trip (particularly to an isolated region) or if you're booking far in advance. Comprehensive policies typically cover trip cancellation and interruption, letting you cancel or cut your trip short because of illness (yours or that of someone back home), or, in some cases, acts of terrorism in your destination. Such policies usually also cover evacuation and medical care. (For trips abroad you should have at least medical and medical evacuation coverage. With a few exceptions, Medicare doesn't provide coverage abroad, nor does regular health insurance.) Some also cover you for trip delays because of bad weather or mechanical problems as well as for lost or delayed luggage.

Another type of coverage to consider is financial default—that is, when your trip is disrupted because a tour operator, airline, or cruise line goes out of business. Generally you must buy this when you book your trip or shortly thereafter, and it's available to you only if your operator isn't on a list of excluded companies.

Many travel insurance policies have exclusions for preexisting conditions as a cause for cancellation. Most companies waive those exclusions, however, if you take out your policy within a short period

(which varies by company) after the first payment toward your trip.

Always read the fine print of your policy to make sure that you're covered for the risks that most concern you. Compare several policies to be sure you're getting the best price and range of coverage available.

Comprehensive Insurers **Allianz.**
☎ *866/884–3556 ⊕ www.allianztravelinsurance.com.* **CSA Travel Protection.**
☎ *877/243–4135, 240/330–1529 collect*
⊕ *www.csatravelprotection.com.* **HTH Worldwide.** ☎ *610/254–8700, 888/243–2358 toll-free ⊕ www.hthworldwide.com.* **Travel Guard.**
☎ *800/826–5248, 800/3450505 toll-free in Italy ⊕ www.travelguard.com.* **Travelex Insurance.** ☎ *800/228–9792, 603/328–1739 collect*
⊕ *www.travelexinsurance.com.*

Insurance Comparison Info **Insure My Trip.**
☎ *800/487–4722, 401/773–9300 ⊕ www.insuremytrip.com.* **Square Mouth.** ☎ *800/240–0369, 727/564–9203 ⊕ www.squaremouth.com.*

INDEX

PHOTO CREDITS

NOTES

NOTES

NOTES

NOTES

ABOUT OUR WRITERS

 Born of Sicilian stock, Robert Andrews has been living and working in various parts of Italy for most of his adult life. He has written articles and guidebooks on this multi-faceted peninsula, and provides travel consultancy services as well as leading individual and small-group tours in Sicily and Sardinia.

 Nick Bruno is an Italy specialist and a frequent Fodor's contributor. He has authored and updated many books and features. A lifelong interest in history and the Italian language has led to a project researching the lives of his paternal family in Italy before, during and since Il Ventennio Fascista period. For this edition, he updated the Veneto and Friuli-Venezia Giulia, Naples and Campania, and Puglia, Basilicata, and Calabria chapters.

For this edition, Agnes Crawford updated Rome and Side Trips from Rome.

 Liz Humphreys is a transplant to Europe from New York City, where she spent more than a decade in editorial positions for media companies including Condé Nast and Time Inc. Since then she's written and edited for publications including Time Out International, Forbes Travel Guide, and Rough Guides. Liz has an advanced certificate in wine studies from WSET (Wine & Spirit Education Trust), which comes in handy when exploring her beloved Italian wine regions. Liz updated the Venice, Milan, Lombardy, and the Lakes, and Sicily chapters for this edition.

 Fergal Kavanagh travels extensively throughout Italy with his Tune Into English Roadshow, where he teaches English through pop music (www.tuneintoenglish.com). In his twenty five years in the country there is hardly a town square he has not passed through. He updated the Dolomites chapter as well as Travel Smart.

Florence resident Patricia Rucidlo holds master's degrees in Italian Renaissance history and art history. When she's not extolling the virtues of a Pontormo masterpiece or angrily defending the Medici, she's leading wine tours in Chianti and catering private dinner parties. For this edition she updated the Experience Italy and Emilia-Romagna chapters, and contributed to the Tuscany chapter.

 Liz Shemaria is a Florence, Italy-based writer who has contributed to more than a dozen travel and news publications. A third-generation Northern Californian, Liz fell in love with Italy as a University of California, Berkeley art history major, studying the Italian Renaissance. She now aspires to visit every region in Italy.